SECOND EDITION

EDUCATIONAL PSYCHOLOGY
DEVELOPING LEARNERS

Jeanne Ellis Ormrod

UNIVERSITY OF NORTHERN COLORADO

Merrill, an imprint of Prentice Hall
Upper Saddle River, New Jersey   *Columbus, Ohio*

Library of Congress Cataloging-in-Publication Data

Ormrod, Jeanne Ellis.
 Educational psychology: developing learners/ by Jeanne
Ellis Ormrod.—2nd ed.
  p.   cm.
 Includes bibliographical references and index.
 ISBN 0-13-525718-2
  1. Educational psychology.   2. Teaching.   3. Learning.
 4. Classroom management.   I. Title.
 LB1051.066   1998
 370.15—dc21   96-51908
                                                     CIP

Cover photo: © Arthur Tilley/FPG, International
Editor: Kevin M. Davis
Developmental Editor: Linda Kauffman Peterson
Developmental Editor, Ancillaries: Linda Montgomery
Production Editor: Julie Peters
Photo Researcher: Dawn Garrott
Cover Designer: Brian Deep
Production Manager: Deidra M. Schwartz
Design Coordinator: Julia Zonneveld Van Hook
Illustrations: Rolin Graphics
Director of Marketing: Kevin Flanagan
Marketing Manager: Suzanne Stanton
Marketing/Advertising Coordinator: Julie Shough

This book was set in Garamond by The Clarinda Company
and was printed and bound by R.R. Donnelley & Sons
Company. The cover was printed by Phoenix Color Corp.

© 1998 by Prentice-Hall, Inc.
Simon & Schuster/A Viacom Company
Upper Saddle River, New Jersey 07458

Earlier edition, entitled *Educational Psychology: Principles
and Applications,* © 1995 by Prentice-Hall, Inc.

Photo credits: Susan Burger/Lasting Impressions
Photography, pp. 9, 15, 41, 45, 68, 106, 111, 129, 167, 174,
175, 189, 212, 240, 254, 293, 313, 327, 380, 390, 391, 393,
410, 470, 484, 495, 501, 519, 553, 577, 607, 625, 636, 646,
716; Paul Conklin, p. 79; Scott Cunningham/Merrill, pp. xxii,
3, 18, 32, 36, 51, 59, 77, 78, 92, 100, 109, 115 (both), 138,
142, 155, 160, 173, 198, 204, 206, 216, 222, 260, 270, 289,
306, 370, 389, 426, 431, 459, 473, 492, 513, 544, 552, 560,
582, 595, 602, 611, 617, 654, 661, 669, 688, 691, 694, 699;
Mary Kate Denny/Photo Edit, p. 436; Larry Hamill/Merrill,
p. 257, 276, 489, 571, 700; KS Studios/Merrill, p. 447; Linda
Peterson/Merrill, p. 46; Barbara Schwartz, p. 107, 277, 632;
Elliott Smaith/International Stock Photo, p. 264; Tom
Watson/Merrill, pp. 12, 65, 352, 405, 437, 528; Timothy
White, Superstock, p. 442; David Young-Wolff/Photo Edit,
p. 535.

Printed in the United States of America

10 9 8 7 6 5 4 3 2

ISBN 0-13-525718-2

Prentice-Hall International (UK) Limited, *London*
Prentice-Hall of Australia Pty. Limited, *Sydney*
Prentice-Hall Canada Inc., *Toronto*
Prentice-Hall Hispanoamericana, S. A., *Mexico*
Prentice-Hall of India Private Limited, *New Delhi*
Prentice-Hall of Japan, Inc., *Tokyo*
Simon & Schuster Asia Pte. Ltd., *Singapore*
Editora Prentice-Hall do Brasil, Ltda., *Rio de Janeiro*

Soon after I wrote the first edition of *Educational Psychology,* I had the good fortune to return to a middle school classroom, teaching geography to two sections of sixth, seventh, and eighth graders in the fall of 1995. (I must express my gratitude to my dean, Gary Galluzzo, who both allowed and encouraged me to do it as a part of my teaching load that semester.) On my first day back in a K–12 setting, I was quickly reminded of how exciting and energizing the process of teaching growing children can be. And I confirmed once again what I have always known—that principles of educational psychology have clear relevance to the decisions that a classroom teacher must make on an ongoing basis.

I have been teaching educational psychology since 1974, and I've loved every minute of it. How children and adolescents learn and think, how they change as they grow and develop, why they do the things they do, how they are often very different from one another—our understanding of all these things has innumerable implications for classroom practice and, ultimately, for the lives of the next generation.

I have written this textbook in much the same way that I teach my college classes. I want the field of educational psychology to captivate you the way that it has captivated me. So I have tried to make the book interesting and meaningful—perhaps even exciting—as well as informative. I have a definite philosophy about how future teachers can best come to understand and apply educational psychology—a philosophy that has guided me as I have written both the first and second editions of this book. More specifically, I believe that my readers can construct a more accurate and useful understanding of the principles of educational when they:

- Focus on core principles of the discipline
- Relate those principles to their own learning and behavior
- Mentally "process" those principles in an effective manner
- Consider numerous classroom applications of those principles

As I will show you in a moment, I have incorporated a number of features into the book that will encourage you to do all these things. I hope that you will learn a great deal from what educational psychology has to offer, not only about the students you will be teaching, but also about yourself—a human being who continues to learn and develop even now.

FEATURES OF THE BOOK
Focusing on Core Principles

Rather than superficially explore every aspect of educational psychology, I have chosen to offer in-depth treatment of the fundamental principles and concepts that have broad applicability to classroom practice. If I myself couldn't imagine how a principle or concept could possibly be of use to a teacher, I left it out. I highlight many of the key principles in the *Principles/Assumptions* that appear throughout the book.

▲ FOCUSING ON PRINCIPLES

Throughout the text, principles and core concepts are identified, discussed in depth, and summarized in *Principles/Assumptions* tables with concrete examples and educational implications.

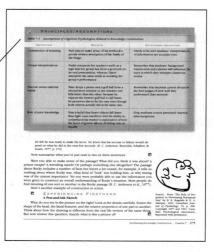

Relating Principles to Your Own Learning and Behavior

A central goal of this text is to help you discover more about yourself as a thinker and learner. If you can understand how you *yourself* learn, you will be in a better position to understand how your students learn and, as a result, to help them learn more effectively. Throughout the book, I've provided many exercises to help you discover important points firsthand and thereby construct a more complete, meaningful understanding of psychological principles of learning, development, motivation, and human behavior. These *Experiencing Firsthand* exercises are in some ways similar to the "hands-on" activities that I often recommend for helping students learn in elementary and secondary classrooms. But because I ask you to use your mind rather than your hands, you might more accurately think of them as "head-on" experiences.

■ EXPERIENCING FIRSTHAND

Numerous exercises embedded in the text allow you to experience firsthand some of the concepts and principles we examine. The understanding you gain from these experiences will enable you not only to see more vividly how psychology principles operate, but also to use these principles more effectively in your own classroom teaching.

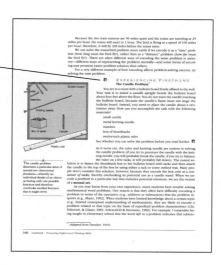

"Processing" Principles Effectively

Research tells us that many students, including many at the college level, use relatively ineffective strategies for reading, studying, and learning. But research also tells us that students *can* acquire effective strategies and that when they begin to use such strategies, they find themselves successfully learning and remembering the things that they read and hear.

One important principle of learning that we will consider in Chapter 6 is that people learn and remember new information more effectively when they relate it to the things that they already know—a process often called *meaningful learning.* I will ask you to reflect on your own knowledge and experiences in *Thinking About What You Know* features at the beginning of each chapter and at various other spots throughout the book. In addition, some of the margin notes designated with a ■ symbol will ask you to consider personal experiences or to recall ideas that we've discussed in previous chapters.

Another effective strategy is *organization*—making connections among the various pieces of information that you're learning; the *Compare/Contrast* tables that appear throughout the book will help you organize some of the key ideas in each chapter. Still another effective strategy is *elaboration*—expanding on information as you study it, drawing inferences, thinking of new examples, making predictions, and so on. Many of the ■ questions in the margin will encourage you to elaborate on the concepts and principles that I describe. The ▲ notes in the margin can help you with *both* organization and elaboration: They will either show you how you can connect the ideas you are reading about with ideas presented in later chapters, or they may provide additional, "elaborative" information about those ideas.

Taking Principles Into the Classroom

Throughout the text, I consistently apply psychological concepts and principles to classroom practice. Some classroom applications are summarized and illustrated in *Into the Classroom* features; many others are highlighted with a 🍎 in the margin. Furthermore, the ■ questions will sometimes ask you to consider possible applications in your own specific circumstances as a teacher.

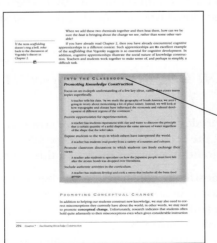

 **INTO THE CLASSROOM**

At least twice in every chapter, some of the teaching strategies are collected and presented together in the *Into the Classroom* features. These not only provide practical strategies for applying the textbook's content to teaching, but also contain concrete examples from a variety of subject areas and grade levels to illustrate those strategies.

In addition, every chapter begins and ends with *case studies*. The case study at the beginning of each chapter presents an example of one or more students dealing with a particular classroom learning task. As we proceed through the chapter, we will continually relate our discussion back to this case, helping you relate chapter content to a classroom context. The case study at the end of each chapter focuses on teachers and teaching. Here I will ask you questions about the case that will help you apply the ideas you have read in the chapter and make instructional decisions based on what you have learned.

CASE STUDIES

Each chapter opens with a case that is referred to throughout the chapter, helping you tie psychological principles to the authentic context of the classroom. Chapters also end with case studies that give you an opportunity to apply what you have learned to teaching decisions. Additional cases are available on the Ormrod Web Site at www.merrilleducation.com

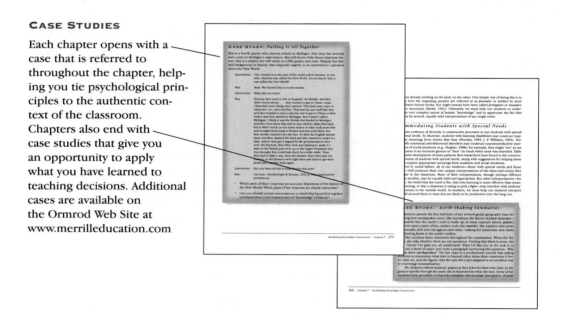

CHANGES IN THE SECOND EDITION

Although most of the content from the first edition remains in the second edition, I have modified and added to the first edition in ways that reflect current trends in educational psychology and educational practice. Among the most significant revisions are the ones that follow.

Expanded Focus on Cognitive Perspectives of Learning

This second edition, like its predecessor, contains more coverage of learning than other books for this course. In fact, the second edition has expanded its coverage of cognitive learning theory. The most significant changes reflecting this expansion are:

- A new chapter on knowledge construction has been added. Chapter 7, "Facilitating Knowledge Construction," includes a discussion of constructivist perspectives of learning and their implications for classroom practice.
- The chapters on learning have been reorganized. After an initial introduction to the various perspectives of learning (Chapter 5), principles of cognitive

psychology—the dominant theoretical orientation at the present time—are presented first and in depth, with emphasis on information processing, knowledge construction, and higher-level thinking skills (Chapters 6–8). Principles from behaviorism and social cognitive theory are presented as well (Chapters 9 and 10), with a particular focus on how these principles can help teachers promote behavior change and enhance students' self-efficacy and self-regulation.

Integrated Coverage of Diversity and Inclusion

Discussions of student diversity and students with special needs have been integrated into every chapter. Cultural diversity and special needs are discussed relative to the topics examined in each chapter, and specific strategies for facilitating the achievement of diverse learners are presented. You will also find a *Students in Inclusive Settings* table at the end of almost every chapter.

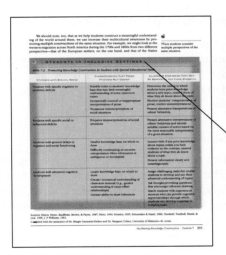

DIVERSITY AND INCLUSION

Each chapter contains a section that examines pertinent issues of diversity and exceptionality. Information in each of these sections is practical and applied, with a *Students in Inclusive Settings* table, and sometimes with an *Into the Classroom* feature as well.

Integration of Planning, Instruction, and Assessment

The processes of planning, instructional strategies, and assessment (Chapters 12–14) are discussed in a more integrated fashion, so that it becomes clear how each of these aspects of teaching is inextricably interwoven with the others and with student characteristics. The two "testing" chapters of the first edition have been consolidated into a single "assessment" chapter, with a focus on classroom assessment practices and a broad view of the forms that assessment can take. Coverage of learner-centered instructional strategies, authentic tasks, and performance and product assessment have been expanded.

New and Expanded Topics

There is expanded discussion of topics such as these: Fostering social skills, Learning as a process of construction, Strategies for promoting knowledge construction, Strategies for promoting conceptual change, Self-regulation, Intrinsic motivation, Authentic activities, Computer-based instruction, Performance assessment, and Communicating with parents.

There are new sections on: Cognitive apprenticeships, Fostering social interaction among diverse groups, The role of emotions in moral development, Distributed intelligence, Homelessness and resiliency, A "mental theories" view of concept learning, The role of standards in planning and assessment, Peer tutoring, Class discussions, In-class and homework activities, Creating a community of learners, and Informal assessment.

SUPPLEMENTARY MATERIALS

Several supplements to the textbook are available to enhance your learning and development as a teacher. Among other things, these include a student study guide, videotapes, a video guide, transparencies, a test bank, a text-specific Web Site at www.merrilleducation.com, an instructor's manual, and a CD-ROM.

Student Study Guide

A student study guide has been designed to supplement this textbook. It provides a number of support mechanisms to help you learn and study more effectively, including:

- Focus questions to consider as you read the text
- Application exercises to give you practice in applying concepts and principles of educational psychology to classroom settings
- Answers to selected margin notes
- Sample test questions

Videotapes and Video Guide

Videos can be a highly effective means of visually enhancing the concepts and principles of educational psychology. The five videotapes that accompany this textbook portray a wide variety of teachers, students, and classrooms in action. In addition to video case studies are "A Private Universe," which examines learner misconceptions in science, and a video by Constance Kamii on a *constructivist* approach to teaching mathematics. Opportunities to react to these videos in class discussions will further develop your ability to think analytically and identify good teaching practices. Your instructor will also have a video guide to help guide and enrich your interpretation and understanding of what you see in these videos.

Transparencies and Electronic Transparencies

The transparencies that your instructor will use in class will include tables and classroom exercises similar to those found in your textbook. These transparencies are designed to help you understand, organize, and remember the concepts and principles that you are studying. The transparencies are also available on CD-ROM.

Test Bank

Many instructors use the test questions that accompany this textbook. Some items (lower-level questions) will simply ask you to identify or explain the concepts and principles you have learned. But many others (higher-level questions) will ask you to apply those same concepts and principles to specific classroom situations—that is, to actual student behaviors and teaching strategies. The lower-level questions may be the kind that you have seen more frequently in your other courses, and they are indeed important for assessing your knowledge of educational psychology. But ultimately, it is the higher-level questions that assess your ability to use principles of educational psychology in your own teaching practice.

Merrill/Prentice Hall Web Site

You can find our web site at www.merrilleducation.com. Here you will find, among other things, additional case studies, tips for teaching, an electronic guide to education on the Internet, and additional exercises.

Instructor's Manual

Available to your instructor are suggestions for learning activities, additional "head-on" exercises, supplemental lectures, case study analyses, group activities, and a list of additional media resources. These have been carefully selected to provide opportunities to support, enrich, and expand upon what you read in the text.

CD-ROM

Available for assistance in lesson planning, this tool includes activities and hand-outs from the instructor's manual; transparencies; supplemental readings and application activities from the study guide; the video guide; and a Test Bank Answer Key (not available elsewhere).

ACKNOWLEDGMENTS

Although I am listed as the sole author of this textbook, I have been fortunate to have had a great deal of assistance in writing it. First and foremost, I must thank my administrative editor, Kevin Davis, whose ideas, insights, and clear commitment to the field of educational psychology have provided much of the driving force behind my writing and productivity. Kevin is a task master, make no mistake about it, and he always insists that I stretch my talents to the limit. Yet he also provides the guidance and support that I need to achieve the things that initially seem so impossible. After spending countless hours working with Kevin in Columbus, in Greeley, at AERA, and on the phone, I can say that he is not only my editor, but also my friend.

I must also thank Linda Peterson, who, as developmental editor for both the first and second editions, has used her boundless creativity to shape much of the pedagogy of the book. Her continuing insistence on *application, application, application!* has kept my focus on the things that future teachers really need to know. Among other things, Linda has been the impetus for the tables and *Into the Classroom* boxes scattered throughout the book—features that were very well received by users of the first edition.

Others at Merrill/Prentice Hall have also contributed in important ways to the product you see before you now. As developmental editor for the ancillary package that accompanies the book, Linda Montgomery has been a constant source of ideas and support. Copy editor Linda Poderski, who has a fine eye for detail, has kept me honest with respect to sentence structure, spelling, and the "new" APA style. Photography editor Dawn Garrott has located many photographs that have given life to the words on the page. And Julie Peters, as production editor, has seemed to have a limitless supply of energy as she's coordinated the many different efforts involved in transforming a manuscript into a book—an incredibly complicated task that, in my mind, should far exceed any normal human being's working memory capacity.

Colleagues Across the Country

As two individuals who have successfully combined educational psychology and special education into a single course at the University of Missouri—St. Louis, Margie Garanzini-Daiber and Peggy Cohen provided some of the ideas for the *Students in Inclusive Settings* tables that you will find near the end of most chapters. Furthermore, many of my professional colleagues nationwide have strengthened the final product considerably by reviewing one or more drafts of either the first or second edition. These reviewers have given the book a balance of perspectives that no single author could possibly do on her own.

Reviewers for the first edition were Timothy A. Bender, Southwest Missouri State University; Stephen L. Benton, Kansas State University; Karen L. Block, University of Pittsburgh; Kathryn J. Biacindo, California State University—Fresno; Barbara Bishop, Eastern New Mexico University; Robert Braswell, Winthrop College; Kay S.Bull, Oklahoma State University; Margaret W. Cohen, University of Missouri—St. Louis; Richard D. Craig, Towson State University; Jose Cruz, Jr., The Ohio State University; Peggy Dettmer, Kansas State University; Joan Dixon, Gonzaga University; Leland K. Doebler, University of Montevallo; Joanne B. Engel, Oregon State University; Kathy Farber, Bowling Green State University; William R. Fisk, Clemson University; Roberta J. Garza, Pan American University—Brownsville; Cheryl Greenberg, University of North Carolina—Greensboro; Richard Hamilton, University of Houston; Frederick C. Howe, Buffalo State College; Janina M. Jolley, Clarion University of Pennsylvania; Caroline Kaczala, Cleveland State University; CarolAnne M. Kardash, University of Missouri—Columbia; Randy Lennon, University of Northern Colorado; Pamela Manners, Troy State University; Teresa McDevitt, University of Northern Colorado; Sharon McNeely, Northeastern Illinois University; Janet Moursund, University of Oregon; Gary A. Negin, California State University; James R. Pullen, Central Missouri State University; Gary F. Render, University of Wyoming; Robert S. Ristow, Western Illinois University; Dale H. Schunk, Purdue University; Mark Seng, University of Texas; Johnna Shapiro, University of California—Davis; Harry L. Steger, Boise State University; Alice A. Walker, SUNY—Cortland; and Jane A. Wolfle, Bowling Green State University.

Reviewers for the second edition were Margaret D. Anderson, SUNY—Cortland; Randy L. Brown, University of Central Oklahoma; Margaret W. Cohen, University of Missouri—St. Louis; Roberta Corrigan, University of Wisconsin—Milwaukee; Leland K. Doebler, University of Montevallo; Arthur Hernandez, University of Texas—San Antonio; Dinah Jackson, University of Northern Colorado; Nancy F. Knapp, University of Georgia; Mary Lou Koran, University of Florida; Pamela Manners, Troy State University; Hermine H. Marshall, San Francisco State University; Michael Meloth, University of Colorado—Boulder; Judy Pierce, Western Kentucky University; Gregg Schraw, University of Nebraska—Lincoln; Julianne C. Turner, University of Notre Dame; and Mary Wellman, Rhode Island College.

Colleagues and Family on the Home Front

In addition to the reviewers I've just listed, my colleagues at the University of Northern Colorado have given me ongoing feedback about the things that do and don't work in the first edition, as well as suggestions for improving the second edition. I am especially grateful to my fellow faculty members in the educational psychology program—Susan Burger (who took many of the photos for the book), Kathy Cochran, John Cooney, Randy Lennon, Teresa McDevitt, and Steven Pulos—and to two of my students—Dinah Jackson and Nancy Thrailkill.

Last but certainly not least, my family has been ever so patient with me as I continue to stare at my computer screen night after night. To my husband Richard, and to my three children—Christina, Alex, and Jeffrey—I will love you always.

J. E. O.
Greeley, Colorado

Contents

Chapter 3
Adapting to Differences in Personal, Social, and Moral Development   93

Chapter 4
Adapting to Individual and Group Differences   143

PART 2

UNDERSTANDING HOW STUDENTS LEARN   197

Chapter 5
Using Multiple Perspectives of Learning   199

Chapter 6
Promoting Effective Cognitive Processing   217

Chapter 7
Facilitating Knowledge Construction   271

Chapter 8
Promoting Higher-Level Thinking Skills   307

Chapter 11
Motivating Students to Learn and Achieve *471*

Chapter 12
Planning for a Productive Classroom *529*

Chapter 15
Developing as a Teacher   695

EDUCATIONAL PSYCHOLOGY

Using Educational Psychology in Teacher Decision Making

THINKING ABOUT WHAT YOU KNOW

At some point in your life, you have undoubtedly tried to teach something to someone else. Perhaps you have had some teaching experience in the public schools. Perhaps you have given an oral presentation in one of your college classes. Perhaps you have helped a friend learn how to shoot a basketball, use a computer, or study for an exam. Perhaps you have taught a small child how to wash dishes, tie shoelaces, or ride a bicycle. Reflect for a moment on the kinds of teaching experiences you have had.

- What strategies did you use in your attempts to help others learn? For example, did you give them verbal explanations? Did you demonstrate certain actions for them? Did you give your "students" feedback about their performance?

- What assumptions about human learning influenced the way that you chose to teach? For example, did you assume that your students could learn from a verbal explanation, or did you think that demonstrating an action would be more effective? Did you think that feedback was important for their learning and motivation?

1

- What assumptions about human development influenced the way that you chose to teach those younger than yourself? For example, did you assume that your "students" needed the task simplified for them? Did you assume they would have more difficulty remembering what you said and did than an adult might? Did you provide more praise than you might have given someone your own age?

- How did you know whether your teaching efforts were successful? For example, did you ask questions to make sure your students understood your explanations? Did you ask them to demonstrate certain actions for you to make sure they could execute them correctly? Did you "test" your students in any way?

HELPING STUDENTS LEARN is what our job as teachers is all about. And as we help them learn, we find ourselves taking on a variety of roles in the classroom. At different times, we may be subject matter experts, tutors, consultants, motivators, behavior managers, confidantes, or evaluators. But above all, we are *decision makers:* We must continually choose among many possible strategies for helping students learn, develop, and achieve. In fact, two researchers (C. M. Clark & Peterson, 1986) have estimated that teachers must make a nontrivial instructional decision approximately once every two minutes! (For example, do my students understand this concept, or should I give them a few more examples? Should I reprimand Bobby and Sharon for whispering or just ignore them?) Yet wise educational decisions are not made in a vacuum; they are made on the basis of a genuine understanding of how students learn and develop and on the basis of solid data about which classroom techniques are effective and which are not.

My purpose in writing this book is to show you how educational psychology can help you in your all-important role as educational decision maker. Together we will explore different perspectives and research findings on how students develop through the school years, how they differ from one another in ways that affect their classroom performance, how they learn most effectively, what things motivate them, and how their learning and achievement can best be measured and evaluated. We will also identify principles and theories of human learning, development, and behavior that can help us make informed, professional decisions in the classroom.

In this first chapter, we will get a taste of what educational psychology is all about. We will sample research findings in a variety of areas—for example, in cognitive development, intelligence testing, thinking processes, motivation, and instructional techniques—and then see how such research leads to the principles and theories that will guide our own behaviors as teachers. In addition, we will look at some common features and themes that appear throughout the book and at the directions in which various parts of the book will lead us.

As with all good teaching and successful learning, we should start by identifying our objectives. By the end of this chapter, you should be able to:

1. Identify some misconceptions you may have about how students learn and develop.

2. Describe differences among three types of research studies—descriptive, correlational, and experimental—and determine the kinds of conclusions that can be drawn from each type.

As teachers, we will continually be making decisions about how best to help students learn, develop, and achieve.

3. Distinguish between principles and theories, and describe how both of these help us in making sound educational decisions.

4. Predict some of the topics you will encounter in future chapters.

5. List three principles that can guide more effective reading and studying of this book.

6. Identify several common themes that underlie effective teaching practice.

7. Describe the diversity you are likely to see among your own students.

CASE STUDY: *More Than Meets the Eye*

Rosa is a personable, outgoing twelve-year-old. Born in South America, she has lived in this country only three years, but she seems to have adjusted well to her new home. She now converses in English with only the slightest hint of an accent. She has made many friends and has an active after-school social life. She has blossomed into a talented athlete, seemingly a natural in almost any sport she tries, and is becoming especially proficient in volleyball and basketball. She also does well in art class and in the school choir, although she sometimes has trouble learning the lyrics.

But after three years in her new homeland, Rosa is still having difficulty in language arts, social studies, science, and mathematics. She often seems distracted in class and sometimes has trouble answering even the simplest questions her teachers ask her. Her test scores are inconsistent—sometimes quite high, but more frequently near the bottom of the class.

Rosa's teachers see occasional indicators that she is a bright and talented girl. For example, she is a skillful "peacemaker," frequently stepping in to help resolve interpersonal conflicts among her classmates. Her short stories, though often filled with grammatical and spelling errors, are imaginative and well developed. And of course there are the occasional high test scores. Rosa's teachers are convinced that Rosa is capable of achieving at a much higher level, but they are puzzled about just how to help her be more successful in her classroom activities.

- What are some possible explanations for Rosa's poor academic performance? Could the source of difficulty lie in her limited experience with English? In her cultural background? In her motivation? In her study skills? In the ways in which her knowledge is assessed? Or perhaps in some combination of these things?

OOPS—A PRETEST

You probably have some good hypotheses about why Rosa is having difficulty. You've been a student for many years now, and in the process you've certainly learned a great deal about how students learn and develop and how teachers can best help them achieve. But exactly how much *do* you know? To find out, I've developed a short pretest, *Ormrod's Own Psychological Survey* (the OOPS test).

EXPERIENCING FIRSTHAND
Ormrod's Own Psychological Survey (OOPS)

Decide whether each of the following statements is *true* or *false*.

1. Most children five years of age and older are natural learners; they know the best way to learn something without having to be taught how to learn it.	T	F
2. By the time they reach second grade, most children believe that rules should be obeyed even when there are no consequences for breaking them.	T	F
3. Scores on intelligence (IQ) tests usually give us some idea about how well students are likely to achieve academically.	T	F
4. When we compare boys and girls, we find that both groups are, on the average, very similar in their mathematical and verbal aptitudes.	T	F

5. The best way to learn and remember a new fact is to repeat it over and over again.   T   F

6. When a student makes comments that contain erroneous beliefs about classroom subject matter, it is best for a teacher to ignore those comments and call on someone else.   T   F

7. Such activities as memorizing poems and solving logic problems are helpful because they provide general exercise for students' minds and help students learn better over the long run.   T   F

8. Taking notes during a lecture usually interferes with students' learning more than it helps.   T   F

9. Students often misjudge how much they know about a topic.   T   F

10. Teachers can reduce inappropriate student behaviors without necessarily having to deal with the underlying causes of those behaviors.   T   F

11. When teachers reward an individual student for appropriate behavior, the behavior of other students may also improve.   T   F

12. Even small amounts of anxiety interfere with students' ability to learn and perform effectively in the classroom.   T   F

13. A well-designed lecture can be an effective way to promote student learning.   T   F

14. A disadvantage of even the best cooperative learning activity is that only a few students do most or all of the work.   T   F

15. The nature of the tests that teachers give affects the ways in which students study and learn classroom material.   T   F ■

Answer Key for the OOPS

Now let's see how well you did on the OOPS. The answers, along with an explanation for each one, are as follows:

1. **Most children five years of age and older are natural learners; they know the best way to learn something without having to be taught how to learn it.**

FALSE—Many students of all ages are relatively naive about how they can best learn something, and they frequently use inefficient strategies when they try to learn something new. For example, most elementary school students and a substantial number of high school students don't **elaborate** on classroom material; they don't analyze, interpret, or otherwise add their own ideas to the things they need to learn (Pressley, 1982; Schommer, 1994a; Siegler, 1986). (To illustrate, many students are likely to take the information presented in a history textbook strictly at face value; they rarely take time to consider why historical figures made the decisions they did or how some events may have led inevitably to others.) Yet elaboration is one of the most effective ways of learning new information—students learn information more quickly and remember it better. We will look at developmental trends in elaboration as we discuss cognitive development in Chapter 2. We'll also explore the very important role that elaboration plays in long-term memory as we discuss information processing in Chapter 6.

How often do you elaborate when you read your textbooks? ■

2. **By the time they reach second grade, most children believe that rules should be obeyed even when there are no consequences for breaking them.**

FALSE—Most elementary school students are in what Lawrence Kohlberg has called the preconventional level of moral reasoning; they define "good" and "bad" in terms of the behaviors for which they are rewarded and punished. According to the research of Kohlberg and others, most students don't recognize the importance of following rules and regulations, even when there are no rewards for doing so, until junior high school at the earliest (Colby & Kohlberg, 1984; Reimer, Paolitto, & Hersh, 1983). We will look at Kohlberg's theory and research when we discuss moral development in Chapter 3.

3. **Scores on intelligence (IQ) tests usually give us some idea about how well students are likely to achieve academically.**

TRUE—Generally speaking, students who get high scores on intelligence tests perform at higher levels on classroom tasks than students with low scores (N. Brody, 1985; Gardner & Hatch, 1990; Perkins, 1995; Sattler, 1988). We should note, however, that a few students in any given classroom are likely to be exceptions to this rule: some students who get high IQ scores may demonstrate low scholastic achievement, and some with low scores may achieve at high levels. We will discuss intelligence tests and IQ scores as we look at individual differences in Chapter 4.

4. **When we compare boys and girls, we find that both groups are, on the average, very similar in their mathematical and verbal aptitudes.**

TRUE—Despite commonly held beliefs to the contrary, boys and girls tend to be similar in their ability to perform both mathematical and verbal academic tasks (Durkin, 1995; Hyde & Linn, 1988; Jacklin, 1989; M. C. Linn & Hyde, 1989). Any differences in the average performance of boys and girls in these areas are usually too small to worry about. We will look at how boys and girls are different—and also at how they are often more similar than we might think—as we explore gender differences in Chapter 4.

5. **The best way to learn and remember a new fact is to repeat it over and over again.**

FALSE—Although repeating information over and over again is better than doing nothing at all with it, repetition is a relatively ineffective way to learn. Students learn information more easily and remember it longer when they connect it with the things they already know and when they elaborate on it (Craik & Watkins, 1973; Klatzky, 1975; Watkins & Watkins, 1974). In Chapter 6, we will look in greater depth at how to promote students' long-term memory for information.

6. **When a student makes comments that contain erroneous beliefs about classroom subject matter, it is best for a teacher to ignore those comments and call on someone else.**

FALSE—As you will discover in Chapter 7, students' misconceptions about the world—for example, beliefs that rivers always run south, rather than north, or that the earth is round only in the sense that a pancake is round—are often strongly held and quite resistant to change (Chinn & Brewer, 1993; Pintrich, Marx, & Boyle, 1993). Ultimately, students need to develop an accurate knowledge base about their world, and

Can you recall times when your own teachers may have treated boys and girls differently because of an erroneous belief about gender differences?

they can only do so if they get corrective feedback about their erroneous beliefs (e.g., Sosniak & Stodolsky, 1994).

7. **Such activities as memorizing poems and solving logic problems are helpful because they provide general exercise for students' minds and help students learn better over the long run.**

FALSE—Research has refuted the idea that the mind is a "muscle" that can be strengthened through general exercise (James, 1890; Perkins & Salomon, 1989; Thorndike 1924). As we will discover in our discussion of transfer and problem solving in Chapter 8, performing one activity typically helps a student perform a second activity only to the extent that the two activities are in some way similar to each other.

Have you ever been required to memorize a poem? Did learning that poem help you learn anything else?

8. **Taking notes during a lecture usually interferes with students' learning more than it helps.**

FALSE—Generally speaking, students who take notes learn more material from a lecture than students who don't take notes (Hale, 1983; Kiewra, 1989). Note taking appears to facilitate learning in at least two ways: It helps students put, or *store,* information into memory more effectively, and it allows them to review that information again at a later time (Di Vesta & Gray, 1972). In Chapter 8, we will look at research concerning the effectiveness of various study strategies.

9. **Students often misjudge how much they know about a topic.**

TRUE—Contrary to popular opinion, students usually are *not* the best judges of what they do and do not know. For example, many students think that if they've spent a long time studying a textbook chapter, they must know the content of that chapter very well. Yet if they have spent most of their study time inefficiently (perhaps by "reading" without paying attention to the meaning or by mindlessly copying definitions into a notebook), they may know far less than they think they do (L. Baker, 1989; Schommer, 1994a). We will consider this *illusion of knowing* further in our discussion of study strategies in Chapter 8.

10. **Teachers can reduce inappropriate student behaviors without necessarily having to deal with the underlying causes of those behaviors.**

TRUE—The term *applied behavior analysis* (sometimes called *behavior modification*) refers to a group of educational and therapeutic techniques through which students' behaviors are changed by the use of reinforcement and other environmental manipulations. These techniques often do not deal with any underlying causes of behavior. (For example, when dealing with a chronically disruptive student, a teacher might make certain classroom privileges contingent on appropriate classroom behavior without regard to the reasons *why* the student is misbehaving.) As we will discover in Chapter 9, applied behavior analysis has often been shown to produce lasting changes in behavior even in situations where other approaches have been unsuccessful (S. N. Elliott & Busse, 1991; Iwata, 1987; K. D. O'Leary & O'Leary, 1972; Piersel, 1987).

11. **When teachers reward an individual student for appropriate behavior, the behavior of other students may also improve.**

TRUE—When teachers reward one student for behaving in a particular way, other students who have observed that student being rewarded sometimes begin to behave in a similar way (Bandura, 1977, 1986). We will identify numerous roles that observation plays in learning as we explore social cognitive theory in Chapter 10.

12. **Even small amounts of anxiety interfere with students' ability to learn and perform effectively in the classroom.**

FALSE—For some classroom tasks, and especially for relatively easy tasks, a moderate level of anxiety *improves* students' learning and performance (Kirkland, 1971; Shipman & Shipman, 1985). We will consider the effects of anxiety on learning and performance in more detail when we discuss motivation in Chapter 11.

13. **A well-designed lecture can be an effective way to promote student learning.**

TRUE—Many students can learn a great deal from a lecture if it is organized and presented in particular ways (Ausubel, Novak, & Hanesian, 1978; Ormrod, 1995b; R. D. Tennyson & Cocchiarella, 1986). We will look at several techniques for facilitating learning through lectures when we consider instructional strategies in Chapter 13.

14. **A disadvantage of even the best cooperative learning activity is that only a few students do most or all of the work.**

FALSE—A well-designed cooperative learning activity includes *individual accountability:* All group members must independently demonstrate what they have learned from the activity. As we will discover in Chapter 13, students often show impressive achievement gains from cooperative learning when they must be individually accountable for what they have learned (Slavin, 1983b; Stevens & Slavin, 1995).

15. **The nature of the tests that teachers give affects the ways in which students study and learn classroom material.**

TRUE—What and how students learn is, in part, a function of the kind of test they expect to take (Corbett & Wilson, 1988; Darling-Hammond, 1991; N. Frederiksen, 1984b; J. R. Frederiksen & Collins, 1989; Poole, 1994). For example, students typically spend more time studying the things they think will be on a test than the things they think the test won't cover. And they are more likely to organize and integrate class material as they study if they expect test questions to require such organization and integration. We will learn about these and several other effects of tests on learning when we consider classroom assessment in Chapter 14.

How many of the fifteen OOPS items did you answer correctly? Did some of the false items seem convincing enough that you marked them true? Did some of the true items contradict certain beliefs that you had? If either of these was the case, you are hardly alone; I myself probably would not have done very well on the OOPS test when I was an undergraduate student. College students often agree with statements that seem obvious but that are, in fact, completely wrong (Gage, 1991; Lennon, Ormrod, Burger, & Warren, 1990). And many students in teacher education classes reject research findings when those findings appear to contradict their own personal experiences (Holt-Reynolds, 1992).

I hope you have learned one important point from taking the OOPS test: Not everything that seems logical is necessarily correct. One of our tasks as we explore the field of educational psychology will be to separate fact from fiction. And as you will discover, our major source of information will be psychological and educational research.

Think of instructors who are particularly good lecturers. Which aspects of their lectures are most effective?

Keep an open mind as you read this book. When you encounter ideas that at first glance strike you as being incorrect, try to think of experiences you have had and observations you have made that are actually consistent with those ideas.

Anyone who lives on the plains of eastern Colorado "knows" that the world must be flat—an obvious but incorrect conclusion. In much the same way, "obvious" beliefs about how human beings learn and develop are often partly or completely inaccurate.

DRAWING CONCLUSIONS FROM PSYCHOLOGICAL AND EDUCATIONAL RESEARCH

It's easy to be persuaded by "common sense" and become convinced that what seems "logical" must be reality. Yet common sense and logic do not always tell us the true story about how people actually learn and develop, nor do they always give us accurate information about how we can best help students be successful in the classroom. Educational psychologists believe that knowledge about teaching and learning should be derived from a more objective source of information—that is, from psychological and educational research.

Most of the ideas presented in this book are based either directly or indirectly on the results of research studies. So let's take a look at three major types of research—descriptive, correlational, and experimental—and at the kinds of conclusions that we can draw from each one.

Interpreting Descriptive Studies

A **descriptive study** does exactly what its name implies—it *describes* a situation. Descriptive studies might give us information about the characteristics of students, teachers, or schools; they might also provide information about the frequency with which certain events or behaviors occur. Descriptive studies allow us to draw conclusions about the way things are—the current state of affairs. The left column of Table 1–1 lists some examples of questions that we could answer with descriptive studies.

Interpreting Correlational Studies

A **correlational study** explores relationships among different things. For instance, it might tell us about the extent to which two human characteristics are associated with one another, or it might give us information about the degree to which certain human behaviors occur in conjunction with certain environmental conditions. In general, correlational studies enable us to draw conclusions about **correlation**—that is, about the extent to which two variables are interrelated.

Table 1–1   Questions We Might Answer with Descriptive, Correlational, and Experimental Studies

DESCRIPTIVE STUDIES	CORRELATIONAL STUDIES	EXPERIMENTAL STUDIES
What percentage of high school students can think abstractly?	Are older students more capable of abstract thought than younger students?	Can abstract thinking skills be improved through specially designed educational programs?
How well have our nation's students performed on a recent standardized achievement test?	Do students who get the highest scores on multiple-choice tests also get the highest scores on essays dealing with the same material?	Does the use of multiple-choice vs. essay tests in the classroom encourage students to study in different ways and therefore affect what students learn?
What kinds of aggressive behaviors do we see in our schools, and with what frequencies do we see them?	Are students more likely to be aggressive at school if their parents are physically violent at home?	Which method is most effective in reducing aggressive behavior—reinforcing appropriate behavior, punishing aggressive behavior, or a combination of both?
To what extent are gender stereotypes evident in such reading textbooks as the *Reading Is Fun* (RIF) series and the *Reading as a Foundation* (RAF) series?	The third-grade teachers in the Hometown School District have all selected either the RIF series or the RAF series to teach reading. Are students using one series developing better reading comprehension skills than students using the other?	Which reading series actually produces greater gains in reading comprehension—RIF or RAF?

The middle column of Table 1–1 lists some examples of questions we might answer with correlational studies. Notice how each of these questions asks about a relationship between two things—between age and abstract thought, between multiple-choice test and essay performance, between student aggression and parental violence, or between reading series and level of reading comprehension.

Correlations between two variables allow us to make *predictions* about one variable if we know the status of the other. For example, if we find that older students are more capable of abstract thought than younger students, we can predict that tenth graders will benefit more from an abstract discussion of democratic government than fourth graders. If we find a correlation between multiple-choice and essay test scores, we can predict that those students who have done well on essay tests in a biology class will probably also do well on a national test covering the same topics in a multiple-choice format.

▲
Correlations are often described numerically with a statistic known as a *correlation coefficient.* Correlation coefficients are discussed in Appendix A.

Interpreting Experimental Studies

Descriptive and correlational studies describe things as they exist naturally in the environment. In contrast, an **experimental study,** or **experiment,** is a study in which the researcher somehow changes or *manipulates* one or more aspects of the environment (often called *independent variables*) and then measures the effects of such changes on something else. In educational research, the "something else" being affected (often called the *dependent variable*) is usually some aspect of student behavior—perhaps an increase in achievement test scores, skill in executing a complex physical movement, persistence in trying to solve difficult problems, or ability to interact appropriately with classmates. When carefully designed, experimental studies enable us to draw conclusions about *causation*—about *why* behaviors occur.

The right-hand column of Table 1–1 lists examples of questions that might be answered through experimental studies. Notice how each of these questions is concerned with a cause-effect relationship—the effect of educational programs on abstract thinking, the effect of test questions on student learning, the effect of reinforcement and punishment on aggressive behavior, or the effect of a reading series on the development of reading comprehension.

As you can see from the examples in the table, the difference between correlational and experimental research is an important one: Whereas correlational studies let us draw conclusions about relationships, only experimental studies enable us to draw conclusions about cause and effect. In the section that follows, we will look at how one phenomenon—visual-spatial thinking—has been studied with both correlational and experimental research studies and at the kinds of conclusions we can draw from each type of study.

What other questions can you think of that each of the three types of studies might answer?

Why can we not draw conclusions about cause-effect relationships from descriptive or correlational studies? In what critical way are experimental studies different?

An Example: Research on Visual-Spatial Thinking

Visual-spatial thinking is the ability to imagine and mentally manipulate two- and three-dimensional figures in one's mind. The exercise that follows provides three examples.

■ EXPERIENCING FIRSTHAND
Three Examples of Visual-Spatial Thinking*

1. The figure on the left is a flag. Which one or more of the three figures on the right represent(s) the *same* side of the flag? Which one or more of them represent(s) the *flip* side?

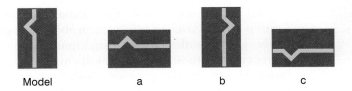

2. When the figure on the left is folded along the dotted lines, it becomes a three-dimensional object. Which one or more of the four figures on the right represent(s) how this object might appear from different perspectives?

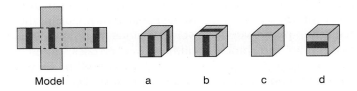

---

* (The three exercises are modeled after Thurstone & Jeffrey [1956], Bennett, Seashore, & Wesman [1982], and Shepard & Metzler [1971], respectively.)

3. When the object on the left is rotated in three-dimensional space, it can look like one or more of the objects on the right. Which one(s)?

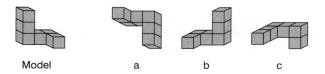

Model   a   b   c

Answer key: (1) Flags *a* and *b* are the flip side; flag *c* is the same side. (2) Depending on the perspective, the object might look like either *a* or *d*. (3) The object can be rotated to look like either *a* or *c*.

Do you think that you have good visual-spatial skills? If so, how did you develop them?

Early exposure to certain types of toys encourages greater visual-spatial thinking ability for both boys and girls.

Here the researchers separated the possible variables affecting visual-spatial thinking and kept all but one of them constant. We will consider this process of **separating and controlling variables** in Chapter 2.

Visual-spatial thinking appears to be related to mathematics achievement, although the nature of this relationship is not totally clear (Fennema & Sherman, 1977; Friedman, 1994, 1995; Threadgill-Sowder, 1985). Many correlational studies have found a relationship between gender and visual-spatial thinking: On the average, boys have slightly better visual-spatial thinking skills than girls (N. S. Anderson, 1987; Fennema, 1980; Halpern, 1992; Law, Pellegrino, & Hunt, 1993; Maccoby & Jacklin, 1974). But such studies do not tell us why this difference occurs. Are males genetically more capable of visual-spatial thought? Do parents encourage their sons to think in "visual-spatial" ways more frequently than they encourage their daughters? Do the typical childhood experiences of boys promote greater development of visual-spatial thinking ability? Unfortunately, correlational studies, though they demonstrate that a relationship exists, do not tell us *why* it exists; they don't tell us whether genetics, parental encouragement, childhood experiences, or perhaps something else is the cause of the difference we see.

An experimental study by Sprafkin, Serbin, Denier, and Connor (1983) gives us information about one probable cause of the gender difference in visual-spatial thinking. These researchers hypothesized that typical "male" toys (e.g., wooden blocks, Legos, trucks) provide greater opportunities for children to explore visual-spatial relationships than do typical "female" toys (e.g., dolls, board games). To test their hypothesis, they randomly selected half of the boys and girls enrolled in a preschool to be members of an experimental, or **treatment,** group, leaving the remaining children as an untrained **control** group. Children in both groups took a test of visual-spatial thinking, revealing that the treatment and control groups were equal (on the average) in visual-spatial ability. During the next six weeks, the experimental group participated in twelve sessions involving instruction and structured play opportunities with blocks, building toys, puzzles, dominoes, and various other materials requiring visual-spatial thought. At the end of the six-week period, these specially trained children obtained higher scores on a test of visual-spatial thinking than the untrained, control group children.

From this study with preschool children, we can draw a conclusion about a cause-effect relationship: We can say that structured exposure to certain types of toys promotes increased visual-spatial thinking ability. Everything else about the two groups of children was the same—for example, both groups began with equivalent visual-spatial thinking ability, and all the children attended the same preschool. Furthermore, because the children were randomly assigned to the training and nontraining conditions, we can assume that both groups were approximately the same (on the average) in terms of such other factors as general intelligence, prior exposure to different types of toys, and home environment. Because the researchers eliminated other possible explanations for the differences they observed in the two groups of preschoolers, they could reasonably draw a conclusion about a cause-effect relationship: that increased exposure to certain types of toys fosters the development of visual-spatial thinking skills.

Drawing Conclusions from Research: A Cautionary Note

Keep in mind that we can only draw conclusions about causal relationships when we have eliminated other possible explanations for the outcomes we observe. As an example, imagine that the Hometown School District wants to find out which of two reading series—*Reading Is Fun* (RIF) and *Reading as a Foundation* (RAF)—leads to better reading in third grade. The district asks each of its third-grade teachers to choose one of these two reading series and use it throughout a particular school year. The district then compares the end-of-year achievement test scores of students in the RIF and RAF classrooms and finds that students who learned reading with the RIF series obtained significantly higher reading comprehension scores than students with the RAF series. We might quickly jump to the conclusion that RIF promotes better reading comprehension than RAF—in other words, that a cause-effect relationship exists between instructional method and reading comprehension. But is this really so?

The fact is, the district hasn't eliminated all other possible explanations for the difference in students' reading comprehension scores. Remember, the third-grade teachers were the ones who selected the instructional series they used. Why did some teachers choose RIF and others choose RAF? Were the teachers who chose RIF different in some way from the teachers who chose RAF? Had RIF teachers taken more graduate courses in reading instruction, did they have higher expectations for their students, or did they devote more class time to reading instruction? If the RIF and RAF teachers were different from each other in any of these ways (or in some other way that we might not happen to think of), then the district hasn't eliminated an alternative explanation: the possibility that the RIF teachers and RAF teachers were somehow different from one another. Probably the best way to study the causal influence of reading series on reading comprehension would be to randomly assign teachers to each reading series, thereby making the two groups of teachers roughly equivalent in such areas as amount of education, expectations for students, and class time devoted to reading instruction.

Draw conclusions about cause-effect relationships only when you have an **experimental study,** a study in which other factors possibly having an effect on behavior have been controlled.

As a general word of caution, be careful that you don't jump to unwarranted conclusions about what actually causes changes in student behavior. Scrutinize descriptions of research carefully, always with a particular question in mind: *Have the researchers ruled out other possible explanations for their results?* Only when the answer to this question is an undeniable yes can you draw a conclusion about a cause-effect relationship.

When experimental studies are sufficiently controlled that they *do* allow us to find causal relationships, then we can begin to develop *principles* and *theories* of human behavior and educational practice. Principles and theories will be extremely helpful to

Can you recall occasions when people have erroneously drawn conclusions about cause-effect relationships from correlational data?

us as we begin to make decisions about how best to help our students learn and achieve in the classroom.

DERIVING PRINCIPLES AND THEORIES

When similar research studies yield similar results time after time, educational psychologists derive **principles** identifying the factors that influence students' learning, development, and behavior. Consider these two principles as examples:

- *When one person's behavior is followed by reinforcement, other people who observe that behavior being reinforced often show an increase in the same behavior.*

- *Taking notes during a lecture leads to better recall of the information presented than does listening to the lecture without taking notes.*

In each case, we see a description of how one thing—the observation of someone else getting reinforcement, or taking notes—causes or influences something else—a higher frequency of a particular behavior, or better memory for information.

Because principles are usually derived from multiple research studies, rather than from just a single study, they can be generalized to a wide variety of situations and to many different types of people. And when principles describe cause-effect relationships, they enable us as teachers to facilitate our students' classroom performance by manipulating the factors that affect learning, development, and behavior.

Yet educational psychologists go a step further: They develop **theories** in an attempt to explain why these principles are true. Theories describe possible underlying, unobservable mechanisms that regulate human learning, development, and behavior. They typically incorporate many principles and encompass a multitude of interrelationships. To illustrate, let's return to the two principles we have just examined and consider a possible theoretical explanation for each one:

Principle:

- *When one person's behavior is followed by reinforcement, other people who observe that behavior being reinforced often show an increase in the same behavior.*

Possible theoretical explanation:

- *People show an increase in a particular behavior when they form an expectation that they will receive reinforcement for the behavior.* When they see someone else being reinforced for behaving in a particular way, they are likely to expect that they themselves will be reinforced for behaving similarly.

Principle:

- *Taking notes during a lecture leads to better recall of the information presented than does listening to the lecture without taking notes.*

Possible theoretical explanation:

- *Information is better remembered when it is mentally processed—that is, when people think about it and do something (mentally) with it.* Taking notes is one way of processing information. At a minimum, note takers must mentally "translate" the spoken word into the written word. Most note takers also interpret and summarize the information they hear.

We can best improve our educational practices when we first identify cause-effect relationships—when we determine the specific factors that affect students' learning, development, and behavior.

Notice how each of these two theoretical explanations proposes an internal mechanism—an "expectation" in the first case, and mental "processing" in the second—to explain human performance.

In general, principles describe the *whats* of human behavior—they describe what things happen under what conditions—whereas theories describe *why* those things happen. Both principles and theories can help us make decisions about how we can best help our students learn and achieve. Several examples of principles, possible theoretical explanations for these principles, and implications for classroom practice are presented in Table 1–2.

Throughout the book, we will examine many principles and theories related to student learning and classroom practice. Yet keep in mind that the principles and theories we study are not necessarily set in stone; they simply represent our best guesses at the present time about human learning, development, and behavior. As future research studies bring us new information, our conceptions of why students behave as they do will continue to evolve into more complete and more accurate explanations. At the present time, no single theory adequately explains everything we know about human learning and development. Nevertheless, each of the theories that we will study provides useful ideas and insights that can guide us as we make decisions about how to help our students learn and achieve.

What principles of child development, human learning, and motivation have you identified from your observations of human behavior? Have you formed any of your own theories to explain these principles?

USING PRINCIPLES AND THEORIES TO MAKE CLASSROOM DECISIONS

THINKING ABOUT WHAT YOU KNOW

Picture yourself standing in front of thirty students. You are trying to teach them something; perhaps you are describing the difference between nouns and pronouns, or explaining how an automobile engine works, or demonstrating the proper position for doing a sit-up, or encouraging them to project their voices when they sing a medley from *Phantom of the Opera* at the school concert next week. Those thirty students are staring back at you with blank faces, and you're certain that they haven't learned a thing.

- Why aren't your students learning? What are some possible reasons related to your students' age level? What are some possible reasons why your students

Table 1–2 *Examples of Principles, Theories, and Their Implications for Teaching Practice*

PRINCIPLE	POSSBILE THEORETICAL EXPLANATION	EDUCATIONAL IMPLICATION
When one person's behavior is followed by reinforcement, other people who observe that behavior being reinforced often show an increase in the same behavior.	People show an increase in behavior when they expect to receive reinforcement for that behavior.	If we want our students to demonstrate appropriate social skills (e.g., sharing, working cooperatively), we should reinforce such behaviors whenever we see them.
Taking notes during a lecture leads to better recall of the information presented than does listening without taking notes.	People remember information better when they mentally process that information in some way.	We should encourage students to do something with the information they hear in a lecture—for example, take notes, put definitions in their own words, or think of applications.
Students perform more poorly on difficult tasks when they are highly anxious.	Excessive levels of anxiety interfere with one's ability to pay attention and process information.	When assigning a challenging task, we should give students plenty of time to complete it. And we should not weigh the importance of any single task too heavily in our overall evaluations of students' performance.
Students remember material better when they are instructed to form mental images of it.	Visual imagery is one effective method by which people can store information in their memories.	When reading a story to students, we should encourage them to imagine the characters and situations.
Older students are more likely than younger students to obey rules in situations where there are no rewards for obedience and no punishment for disobedience.	Moral development is characterized by a series of stages in which people gradually internalize society's rules and conventions.	With younger students especially, we should make sure obedience of school rules is rewarded.

may not *want* to learn whatever it is you are trying to teach them? What are some possible reasons why even the most capable and motivated students may be unable to learn the material?

There are many possible explanations as to why your students aren't learning. Perhaps they don't have enough previous experience with the topic at hand to understand what you are saying to them. Perhaps they are having trouble comprehending something in the abstract manner you have explained it. Perhaps they are distracted by some other event in the classroom and so aren't really paying attention to the lesson. Or perhaps they aren't motivated; they just don't want to learn whatever it is you are trying to teach them.

So what do you do now? Let's consider several principles and theories (listed in bold type) that might relate to your students' difficulty in learning and then identify possible teaching strategies to be derived from each one:

New learning builds on things students have previously learned. Perhaps your students don't have the background knowledge they need in order to understand the material you are presenting. If you think this might be the case, then find out what your students do and don't know about the topic and build instruction on the things they *do* know. (The idea that new learning builds on previous learning underlies many theories of learning but is a particularly prominent feature of cognitive psychology, described in Chapters 6 and 7.)

Children's ability to think about abstract ideas emerges later than their ability to think about concrete objects. Perhaps your students have not yet developed the capacity for abstract thinking. If you think this might be so, then you might make the lesson less abstract—for example, by providing concrete examples or by having students practice the behaviors you want them to learn. (Piaget's theory of cognitive development, described in Chapter 2, proposes that abstract thought emerges in adolescence, in the last of four stages of cognitive development.)

Attention is essential for learning to take place. Perhaps your students were not paying attention. If you think they were not, then you might eliminate any obvious sources of distraction in the classroom so that students can concentrate on the lesson. (Attention plays an important role in both cognitive psychology and social cognitive theory, as we shall discover in Chapters 6 and 10.)

Behaviors increase when they are followed by pleasant consequences (reinforcers). Perhaps your students are not improving their performance because there is no desirable consequence for doing so. If so, then you might tell them that they will have ten minutes of "free time" after they master the lesson. (Reinforcers play a particularly important role in behaviorism, described in Chapter 9.)

Learning increases when learners have a reason for wanting to learn the information or skill being taught. Perhaps your students don't see the relevance of the lesson for their own lives. If so, then you might explain to students how the information or skills you are teaching will be useful to them, either now or in the future. (We will examine the importance of relevance in our discussion of motivation in Chapter 11.)

How can we most effectively help students achieve success in the classroom? There is no easy answer to this question—no recipe for effective teaching. As teachers, we must continually choose from a multitude of possible instructional strategies and approaches. The choices we make should be based on a solid understanding of basic principles and theories of how human beings learn and develop.

Which of these boldfaced statements propose an internal mechanism to explain human performance? In other words, which ones are theories, rather than principles?

Have you ever heard it said that teaching is both a science and an art? How does this description fit with the idea of teachers as decision makers?

LOOKING AHEAD TO THE FOLLOWING CHAPTERS

As teachers, we are decision makers. And we are most likely to make wise decisions when we consider such questions as these in the process:

- What characteristics do our students bring to the classroom?

- What do we know about how students learn?

- How can we convert our knowledge about both diversity and learning into effective teaching practice?

Each of the three major sections of the book addresses one of these questions.

Figure 1–1 provides a graphic overview of the book, with examples of specific questions we will answer in each chapter. Let's look briefly at how each section of the book will help us make decisions in the classroom. As we do so, let's also identify places where we might find possible strategies for helping Rosa, our case study at the beginning of the chapter.

Part 1: Understanding Student Diversity

In Part 1 of the book, we will examine a variety of ways in which our students are likely to be different from one another. In Chapter 2, **"Adapting to Differences in Cognitive and Linguistic Development,"** we will look at developmental differences in children's thinking, learning, and language as they progress through the elementary grades and into high school. One particular topic in the chapter—bilingualism—can give us some ideas about how to help students who, like Rosa, have limited proficiency in English.

As teachers, we will be far more effective if we adapt instruction to the diverse backgrounds and needs of our students.

In Chapter 3, **"Adapting to Differences in Personal, Social, and Moral Development,"** we will look at developmental differences in self-concept and interpersonal relationships. We will also see how children gradually move from a very self-centered and self-serving view of the world during their early years to an increasingly empathic and altruistic one as they grow older.

As we consider **"Adapting to Individual and Group Differences"** in Chapter 4, we will discover several ways in which the students in any single classroom are likely to be a diverse group. As we explore the nature of intelligence and creativity, we will learn how we can foster more intelligent and creative behavior in the classroom. And as we look at a variety of differences among different ethnic groups, between boys and girls, and among children from different socioeconomic backgrounds, we will focus on how we can facilitate the learning and development of all students. In this chapter, we will identify some cultural differences that might affect Rosa's ability to be successful in the classroom.

Part 2: Understanding How Students Learn

In Part 2, we will explore the nature of human learning, thinking, behavior, and motivation. Our task in Chapter 5, **"Using Multiple Perspectives of Learning,"** will be to define what we mean by the term *learning*. We will also look at three perspectives of how people learn: cognitive psychology, behaviorism, and social cognitive theory.

In Chapters 6 and 7, **"Promoting Effective Cognitive Processing"** and **"Facilitating Knowledge Construction,"** we will look more closely at the perspective of learning offered by cognitive psychology, examining the mental processes—the ways of thinking—that affect what and how well people learn and remember. Within this context, we will consider strategies we can use to help our students, including students

Figure 1–1   An Overview of the Book

UNDERSTANDING STUDENT DIVERSITY

- What characteristics do our students bring to the classroom?

Chapter 2   Adapting to Differences in Cognitive and Linguistic Development
- How does logical thinking change with age?
- How do students' learning processes change over time?
- How do language skills develop during the school years?

Chapter 3   Adapting to Differences in Personal, Social, and Moral Development
- What can we do to promote students' self-esteem?
- What roles do students' classmates play in development?
- How do we help students develop a "conscience" about right and wrong?

Chapter 4   Adapting to Individual and Group Differences
- What are intelligence and creativity?
- How do cultural differences affect classroom performance?
- How are boys and girls similar and different?

UNDERSTANDING HOW STUDENTS LEARN

- What do we know about how students learn?

Chapter 5   Using Multiple Perspectives of Learning
- What is learning?
- How can theories of learning help us as teachers?

Chapter 6   Promoting Effective Cognitive Processing
- Why is attention essential before learning can take place?
- How can we help students remember things more effectively?
- Why do students sometimes forget what they've learned?

Chapter 7   Facilitating Knowledge Construction
- What misconceptions are students likely to have about classroom topics?
- How can we correct such misconceptions?
- What happens to students' learning when we try to do too much too fast?

Chapter 8   Promoting Higher-Level Thinking Skills
- How can we teach new concepts?
- How can we help students solve problems?
- How can we help students learn to study effectively?

Chapter 9   Modifying Students' Behavior
- What role does reinforcement play in learning?
- In what situations is reinforcement counterproductive?
- How can we encourage productive classroom behavior?

Chapter 10   Promoting Learning in a Social Context
- What can students learn from watching others?
- How can we enhance students' self-confidence about performing classroom tasks?
- How can we help students develop self-control?

Chapter 11   Motivating Students to Learn and Achieve
- How can we foster intrinsic motivation to learn?
- How does anxiety affect learning and behavior?
- Why do some students have trouble accepting responsibility for their own actions?

BECOMING AN EFFECTIVE TEACHER

- How can we convert our knowledge about both diversity and learning into effective teaching practice?

Chapter 12   Planning for a Productive Classroom
- How can we develop useful classroom objectives?
- How can we get the school year off to a good start?
- How can we keep discipline problems to a minimum?

Chapter 13   Choosing and Implementing Instructional Strategies
- How can we deliver an effective lecture?
- How do class discussions promote students' learning?
- What strategies can we use to help students work cooperatively with one another?

Chapter 14   Assessing What Students Have Learned
- How does classroom assessment affect students' learning?
- In what situations is it inappropriate to assess students' achievement with paper-pencil tests?
- How do we know when the results of our assessments are accurate?

Chapter 15   Developing as a Teacher
- What qualities characterize effective teachers and classrooms?
- How and when do we become expert teachers?

such as Rosa, learn and remember classroom material effectively. In Chapter 8, **"Promoting Higher-Level Thinking Skills,"** we will move to a discussion of more complex cognitive processes, discovering ways to help students learn concepts, apply their knowledge to real-world situations, solve problems, and study effectively.

Chapter 9, **"Modifying Students' Behavior,"** will give us a closer look at behaviorism, a perspective that focuses on how changes in students' behavior are related to specific events within their environments. Here we will consider some ways in which we can structure a classroom environment that will help students acquire more productive behaviors and achieve greater academic success.

In Chapter 10, as we consider **"Promoting Learning in a Social Context,"** we will discover what and how people learn by observing others. When reading about Rosa, you may have noticed that many of her strengths—her ability to interact with other people, her skill in volleyball and basketball, and her ability to perform in the school choir—are things she could learn through watching and modeling the behaviors of others. We will examine various ways that we can facilitate our students' learning through their observations of others. In addition, we will consider how we can help them control their own behavior—a process known as *self-regulation.*

We turn to the topic of **"Motivating Students to Learn and Achieve"** in Chapter 11. Here we will examine a variety of motives that are likely to affect students' behavior in the classroom. We will also discover how students' beliefs about the causes of their successes and failures play a role in the extent to which they either give up easily or "try, try again." Once you have read Chapter 11, you might hypothesize that Rosa has a high need for affiliation—that she has a strong desire for friendly relationships with others.

Part 3: Becoming an Effective Teacher

In Part 3, we will pull together what we have learned about both student diversity and student learning to explore classroom practice in depth. In Chapter 12, **"Planning for a Productive Classroom,"** we will explore strategies for establishing and maintaining a classroom environment conducive to learning and achievement—the aspect of teaching that first-year teachers say is their number one weakness (e.g., Veenman, 1984). Within this context, we will consider how we can best determine appropriate goals and objectives for our classroom curriculum, how we can keep students on-task throughout the school day, and how we can minimize the occurrence of counterproductive classroom behaviors.

In Chapter 13, we will focus on **"Choosing and Implementing Instructional Strategies,"** exploring a variety of approaches to instruction (e.g., lectures, discussions, discovery learning, cooperative learning, reciprocal teaching) that may be effective and appropriate in different situations and for different students. Here we will find some techniques useful in helping students like Rosa—students who have difficulty learning through traditional instructional techniques.

In Chapter 14, **"Assessing What Students Have Learned,"** we will examine many ways that we can measure and evaluate students' classroom achievement, looking at numerous approaches to assessment and considering the qualities of good assessment in general. We will also consider several ways that classroom assessment practices affect student learning and achievement, reminding ourselves that the assessment tools that we use serve an educational purpose, as well as an evaluative one. In this chapter, we will identify some things to consider when we see low test scores in students such as Rosa.

Finally, we will focus on **"Developing as a Teacher"** in Chapter 15. Here we will look at the overall qualities of effective teachers and schools and then identify strategies for promoting our own professional growth.

What specific topics do you hope that this book will cover? In what chapters are you most likely to find them?

TAKING NOTE OF APA STYLE

Throughout the book, you will find references to the various sources from which I am drawing ideas and research findings. As examples, let's look at two sentences that appeared earlier in the chapter:

> Research has refuted the idea that the mind is a "muscle" that can be strengthened through general exercise **(James, 1890; Perkins & Salomon, 1989; Thorndike 1924).**

> An experimental study by **Sprafkin, Serbin, Denier, and Connor (1983)** gives us information about one probable cause of the gender difference in visual-spatial thinking.

Anytime I use ideas from other sources or base my statements on previously reported research, I will indicate the authors' names and the years in which their publications or reports appeared. The years, and sometimes the authors as well, will appear in parentheses, in accordance with the referencing format prescribed by the American Psychological Association (APA). (For more information about APA format, see the *Publication Manual of the American Psychological Association* (4th ed.), 1994, Washington, DC: American Psychological Association.) When you find any of the book's ideas particularly interesting, exciting, or perhaps even disturbing, I urge you to read some of these sources firsthand. You will find all my sources included in the reference list at the back of the book.

STUDYING EDUCATIONAL PSYCHOLOGY MORE EFFECTIVELY

As you read the book, you will gain insights about how you can help your students more effectively learn the things you want to teach them. At the same time, I hope you will also gain insights about how *you yourself* can learn course material. But rather than wait until we get to our discussion of learning in Part 2, let's look briefly at three general principles of effective learning—three principles, also described for you in Table 1–3, that you can apply as you read and study this book:

1. **Students learn more effectively when they relate new information to the things they already know.** Try to connect the ideas you read in the book with things you are already familiar with—for example, with your own past experiences, with your previous coursework, with things you have observed in schools, or with your general knowledge about the world. The "Thinking About What You Know" features in each chapter should give you some ideas about how to apply this strategy.

2. **Students learn more effectively when they elaborate on new information.** As I mentioned earlier in the chapter, elaboration is a process of adding one's own ideas to new information. In most situations, elaboration enables us to learn information with greater understanding, remember it better, and apply it more readily at times when we need it. So try to think *beyond* the information you read. Generate new ex-

Table 1–3   *General Principles to Apply as You Read This Book*

PRINCIPLE	EDUCATIONAL IMPLICATION	EXAMPLE
Students learn more effectively when they relate new information to the things they already know.	As you study new material, think about experiences you have had or things you have previously studied that may help you make sense of what you are trying to learn.	Before you read about Piaget's theory of cognitive development in Chapter 2, try to recall things you may have learned about Piaget in other courses.
Students learn more effectively when they elaborate on new information.	Add your own ideas to the material you are studying; for example, identify logical relationships among ideas, generate your own examples of concepts, and derive your own applications of principles and theories.	As you read about B. F. Skinner's concept of reinforcement in Chapter 9, think about the ways your own behavior is often reinforced.
Students learn more effectively when they periodically check to make sure they have learned.	Stop at the end of each section and subsection and ask yourself questions about what you have just read.	After you read about test reliability in Chapter 14, see whether you can describe reliability in your own words or can explain the concept to another student.

amples of concepts and principles. Draw inferences from factual statements. Identify educational applications of various principles and theories.

How frequently do you apply these principles when you study?

—————■—————

3. **Students learn more effectively when they periodically check to make sure they have learned.** There are times when even the best of us don't concentrate on what we're reading—when we are actually thinking about something else as our eyes go down the page. So stop once in a while (perhaps once every two or three pages) to make sure you have really learned and understood the things that you've been reading. Try to summarize the material. Ask yourself questions about it. Make sure everything makes logical sense to you. Don't become a victim of that *illusion of knowing* I mentioned earlier.

Perhaps you are a student who has been following these principles for years. But in case you are someone for whom such learning strategies are relatively new, I've provided margin notes (designated by a ■) to help you learn and study throughout the book. These notes will give you some suggestions for how you might think about the material you read. With practice, the strategies I recommend will eventually become second nature to you as you read and study in all your classes.

LOOKING AT THE BIG PICTURE: COMMON THEMES THROUGHOUT THE BOOK

In each of the remaining chapters, we will spend a considerable amount of time looking at the implications that various principles and theories have for decision making in the classroom. And so each chapter will include a number of specific recommendations for teaching practice. But as you will discover, certain themes underlying effective educational practice will pop up over and over again. Some particularly prominent ones are these:

Interaction: To learn and develop, students need numerous opportunities to interact both with their physical environments and with other individuals.

Information processing: How effectively students learn and achieve is a function of how they mentally process information. Students need ample time to think about classroom subject matter and to develop appropriate responses to tasks and questions.

Relevance: Students must discover how new information and skills are related both to the things they already know and to their own personal needs.

Classroom climate: Students learn more effectively in a supportive classroom atmosphere—one in which they believe that they are valued as human beings and one in which they feel comfortable taking academic risks.

Challenge: Students are most likely to learn and develop when they encounter challenging tasks—those at which they can succeed only with effort and persistence and those that require them to use newly learned knowledge and procedures. Students should find that they can ultimately be successful at classroom tasks most of the time; however, they must also learn to deal with and benefit from the occasional failures they are likely to encounter along the way.

Expectations: Students achieve at higher levels when their teachers' expectations for their performance are challenging yet attainable. Students exhibit more appropriate and productive classroom behaviors when teachers' expectations for their performance are communicated clearly and concretely.

Diversity: Students will bring a wide variety of backgrounds, skills, perspectives, and needs to any classroom. As a result, some students may benefit more from one instructional strategy, whereas others may benefit more from a very different approach.

Which of these themes have you encountered in other courses in education or psychology?

Table 1–4 presents some examples of where each theme appears throughout the book. (You will eventually see a more detailed version of this table in Chapter 15.) As you will notice in Table 1–4, the last theme I've listed—diversity—appears in *every* chapter. Let's look at this theme more closely.

CONSIDERING STUDENT DIVERSITY

THINKING ABOUT WHAT YOU KNOW

- In what ways are you different from some of your classmates? Are you older or younger than most of them? Have you had experiences that they have not had, or perhaps missed some experiences that they *have* had? Do you have a unique cultural background that affects how you interpret what you hear in class and read in a textbook?

- Can you think of any exceptional strengths that you have? Do you learn more quickly than your classmates? Are you a talented athlete, artist, or musician? Do you think it is important for educational institutions to nurture such talents?

Table 1–4   Finding the Seven Themes Throughout the Book

CHAPTER	INTERACTION	INFORMATION PROCESSING	RELEVANCE
Chapter 2: Adapting to Differences in Cognitive and Linguistic Development	Cognitive development occurs through children's interactions with their physical and social environments.	Theories of cognitive development examine how children's thought processes change over time. Children's language capabilities affect their ability to think about and interpret the world.	Cognitive development involves relating new experiences to existing knowledge.
Chapter 3: Adapting to Differences in Personal, Social, and Moral Development	Social interaction promotes the development of social skills and moral reasoning. Students' self-concepts and self-esteem are influenced by how others behave toward them.		
Chapter 4: Adapting to Individual and Group Differences	Group interaction often leads to more intelligent behavior. Students are more tolerant of cultural differences when they interact in a multicultural social environment.	Numerous cognitive processes are involved in intelligent behavior. Students with culturally diverse backgrounds benefit from being given more time to think about and respond to teacher questions.	Students at risk for failure and dropping out become more involved in school activities when they believe that these activities are relevant to their own needs.
Chapter 5: Using Multiple Perspectives of Learning		Most contemporary theories of learning consider the role that mental processes play in learning.	
Chapter 6: Promoting Effective Cognitive Processing		Cognitive psychologists describe a variety of mental processes, such as attention, meaningful learning, visual imagery, and organization, that promote effective learning.	Effective learning is more likely to occur when students relate new information to the things they already know.
Chapter 7: Facilitating Knowledge Construction	People can sometimes make better sense of a situation when they discuss it as a group and share their ideas.	Students construct their own meanings for the experiences they have and the information they receive.	Students may connect new information to prior misconceptions and misinterpret the information as a result.
Chapter 8: Promoting Higher-Level Thinking Skills		The ways that students mentally process information affect their ability to apply the information to new situations and problems.	Students are most likely to apply what they learn in school to real-world situations when they perceive its relevance to those situations.
Chapter 9: Modifying Students' Behavior	Positive feedback from someone else is frequently an effective reinforcer.	Many early learning theorists refused to consider the role of "thinking" in learning; now, however, such "behaviorists" often incorporate cognitive processes into their explanations of how people learn.	Students are most likely to apply what they've learned in one situation to a second situation if stimuli in the two situations are similar.

CLASSROOM CLIMATE	CHALLENGE	EXPECTATIONS	DIVERSITY
Students are more likely to ask questions about things they don't understand if they believe that such questions will be encouraged, rather than discouraged.	Difficult learning tasks and puzzling phenomena promote cognitive development.	Students may "hear" what they expect their teachers to say, rather than what their teachers actually say.	Students at any particular age and grade level vary in their cognitive and linguistic abilities.
Social, personal, and moral development is most effectively fostered within the context of a warm, supportive, and encouraging environment.	Discussions about controversial moral issues challenge students to think differently about such issues and hence may promote their moral development.	Students' self-concepts are partly the result of expectations that others have for them; their self-concepts, in turn, affect the expectations they have for themselves.	Students differ widely in their social skills, self-concepts, and moral behaviors. Teachers may need to work actively to promote positive relationships among students with diverse backgrounds.
Creativity is more likely to appear when students feel free to take risks. At-risk students are less likely to drop out when teachers have close, trusting relation ships with them.	Students are more likely to think creatively when teachers ask questions that require using information in new ways.	Teachers' expectations influence the way in which they treat students and may ultimately lead to a self-fulfilling prophecy. Boys typically have higher expectations for themselves than girls.	Students vary with respect to intelligence and creativity; both characteristics can be altered by experience. Considerable diversity is found even within a single ethnic group, gender, or socioeconomic group.
			Students have unique backgrounds, experiences, and knowledge that affect their learning.
		When teachers give students more time to respond to questions, their expectations for many students improve.	Different students will process the same information differently. Some students have deficien-cies in one or more specific cognitive processes.
	Teachers can correct students' misconceptions about the world by presenting infor-mation that conflicts with such misconceptions and by asking challenging questions.	Students and teachers alike may sometimes perceive events in a distorted fashion based on what they expected they would see or hear.	Students' different backgrounds and knowledge bases lead them to interpret new experiences in idiosyncratic ways.
	Students are most likely to develop sophisticated study strategies when difficult learning tasks require them to do so.	Students are likely to adopt new study strategies only when they expect such strategies to help them learn and remember more easily.	Some students have more effective study strategies than others; students with special needs often have few if any effective strategies.
Many behaviorists advocate that teachers focus more on reinforcing desirable behaviors than on punishing undesirable ones.		Techniques for changing students' behavior, known collectively as *behavior modification*, are probably effective, in part, because they let students know exactly what is expected of them.	Because students have had unique previous experiences, they often respond to the same environmental stimuli in different ways.

Table 1–4   (continued)

CHAPTER	INTERACTION	INFORMATION PROCESSING	RELEVANCE
Chapter 10: Promoting Learning in a Social Context	Students learn by observing others and modeling their behavior.	Students process information more effectively when they expect to be reinforced for learning it.	Students are most likely to imitate behaviors they believe will help them in their own circumstances.
Chapter 11: Motivating Students to Learn and Achieve	Many students prefer learning activities in which they can actively manipulate and interact with their environment.	Motivation affects what and how information is processed. Too much anxiety interferes with effective information processing.	Students are more motivated to learn school subject matter when they see its relevance for their personal lives and professional aspirations.
Chapter 12: Planning for a Productive Classroom	One strategy for dealing with a student's problem behavior is a private discussion between teacher and student.	One way of analyzing a complex task is to consider the specific cognitive processes necessary for performing it successfully.	Three critical components of teaching—planning, instruction, and assessment—are closely intertwined.
Chapter 13: Choosing and Implementing Instructional Strategies	In discovery learning approaches to instruction, students interact directly with the environment. In class discussions, cooperative learning, and reciprocal teaching activities, students learn through their interactions with one another.	Lectures are effective only to the extent that they help students process information in effective ways. Class discussions and cooperative learning activities help students process information in greater depth. Reciprocal teaching helps students develop better reading comprehension skills.	Students are most likely to benefit from discovery learning activities when they can draw on relevant background knowledge to interpret their observations. Authentic activities are those that closely resemble real-life tasks.
Chapter 14: Assessing What Students Have Learned	Although students often decide which products to include in their portfolios, teacher guidance is essential for ensuring that they make appropriate choices.	The nature of the classroom assessments that students expect influences how students mentally process information as they study.	Authentic assessment involves asking students to perform in situations similar to "real life."

CLASSROOM CLIMATE	CHALLENGE	EXPECTATIONS	DIVERSITY
	Students' self-confidence (their *self-efficacy*) is enhanced when they set and achieve challenging goals.	Students form expectations about the likely consequences of various behaviors, and they behave in ways that bring about the consequences they desire. Students are more likely to engage in certain behaviors when they believe that they can execute those behaviors successfully.	Students differ considerably in their self-confidence about performing school tasks and in their ability to regulate and control their own behaviors. Students benefit from observing a wide variety of models including those of both genders and diverse cultural backgrounds.
Students are more intrinsically motivated when they can control some aspects of classroom life. Many students like to have positive, supportive relationships with their teachers.	In challenging situations, students believe that they have some probability of success; many students find challenges especially motivating.	Students are more motivated when they believe that they are capable of successfully accomplishing a task. Communicating clear expectations for student performance lessens students' anxiety.	Virtually all students are motivated; however, the students in any single classroom are likely to have diverse interests, needs, and goals.
Effective teachers create a classroom climate in which students have a sense of acceptance and belonging.	Some students resist challenging tasks; one effective strategy is to begin the school year with familiar and easily accomplishable tasks and move to more difficult tasks after a supportive classroom climate has been established.	Instructional objectives enable teachers to describe precisely what they expect students to do at the completion of a lesson. Teachers should inform students in advance about behaviors that are unacceptable and the consequences that will follow such behaviors.	Classroom behaviors considered unacceptable in our culture may be quite acceptable in the cultures of some students.
Class discussions are most effective when students believe that they can speak freely.	Reciprocal teaching provides a setting in which students can more effectively read challenging reading materials.	Mastery learning is based on the assumption that all students can eventually master course material.	Different instructional strategies may be appropriate for different students; for example, lectures are most appropriate for students who can think abstractly, and mastery learning is most appropriate for students who need to work on basic skills.
Teachers should portray classroom assessment tasks more as means to facilitate learning than as mechanisms to evaluate performance.	Classroom assessment tasks should be difficult enough that students must expend effort to succeed, but not so difficult that success is beyond reach.	Assessment results should never be used as the sole basis on which to form expectations about students' future achievement. Teachers must take precautions to ensure that their assessments are based on concrete evidence, rather than on subjective impressions.	It may sometimes be necessary and appropriate to tailor assessment methods to accommodate diverse cultural backgrounds or special educational needs.

- What weaknesses do you have in comparison with your fellow students? Do you have trouble performing certain physical activities? Do you have a hard time carrying a tune? Are you too shy to initiate a conversation with your classmates? What things might your instructor do to help you achieve in class despite your weaknesses?

All students are unique individuals, with different strengths they bring to the classroom and different weaknesses that need to be addressed. For example, students have varying physical characteristics: They are different in terms of health, physical strength, muscular coordination, eyesight, and hearing ability. They vary, too, in cognitive abilities; they differ in the speed with which they learn and the extent to which they think abstractly. They show a wide variety of social and emotional characteristics; for example, some may be friendlier and more outgoing than others, and some may appear more self-confident about their own capabilities than their classmates. And they bring diverse cultural backgrounds—different experiences, beliefs, and attitudes—to any classroom of which they become a part.

Accommodating Students with Special Needs

To the extent that our students are different from one another, we will need to tailor instruction for each of them. In many situations, we will be able to accommodate our students' unique needs within the context of regular classroom practices and activities. But occasionally, students will be different enough from their peers that they will require special educational services on our part. We will almost certainly find such **students with special needs** in any classroom of students. Figure 1–2 presents descriptions of some particular special needs that some of our students may have.

In recent years, we have witnessed an increasing tendency to educate students with disabilities and other special educational needs within the regular classroom for most or all of the school day—a practice often called **inclusion.** In the United States, at least, inclusive educational practices are mandated by federal legislation; Figure 1–3 presents relevant legislative acts and amendments.

Inclusion has many benefits: when students with special needs are educated in regular classrooms, they often achieve at higher levels, have greater self-esteem, and behave more appropriately. We are especially likely to see such benefits when regular classroom instruction is tailored to students' specific educational needs and academic levels (Calhoun & Elliott, 1977; Esposito, 1973; Leinhardt, 1980; Lewis & Doorlag, 1991; Madden & Slavin, 1983; S. O'Leary & Schneider, 1977; Semmel, Gottlieb, & Robinson, 1979; Slavin, 1987; Stainback & Stainback, 1992).

With the importance of individualized instruction in mind, we will address the topic of special needs in each of the next thirteen chapters, always drawing from what we have learned about human learning and development, student characteristics, and effective classroom practice. Included in each discussion will be a table with suggestions for accommodating the special needs of students who fall into one of four categories: (1) students with *specific cognitive or academic deficits* (e.g., those with learning disabilities), (2) students with *specific social or behavioral deficits* (e.g., those with emotional and behavioral disorders), (3) students with *general delays in cognitive and social functioning* (e.g., those with mental retardation), and (4) students with *ad-*

Figure 1–2   Students with Special Needs

Mental retardation   Students with mental retardation show developmental delays in most aspects of their academic and social functioning. Intelligence test scores of such students are quite low—usually no higher than 70 (reflecting performance in the bottom 2% of their age-group). These students show other signs of below-average intelligence as well: For example, they learn slowly and perform quite poorly on school tasks in comparison with their age-mates. In addition, students with mental retardation have difficulty functioning in age-appropriate ways in their social environment; they often exhibit social behaviors typical of children much younger than themselves. Mental retardation is described in more depth in Chapter 4.

Learning disabilities   Students with learning disabilities have average or above-average intelligence but demonstrate deficiencies in one or more specific cognitive processes (e.g., in attention, perception, memory, or language-related abilities). Such students typically show an uneven pattern in academic achievement, performing at grade level in some areas of the academic curriculum but exhibiting exceptionally low performance in others. Learning disabilities are described in more depth in Chapter 6.

Speech and communication disorders   Students with speech and communication disorders have abnormalities in spoken language that significantly interfere with classroom performance. Examples include persistent articulation problems (mispronunciations of certain sounds and words), unusually loud or soft speech, stuttering, and immature or abnormal language patterns (e.g., repeating everything another person says). Several strategies for accommodating students with speech and communication disorders are presented within the discussion of linguistic development in Chapter 2.

Emotional and behavioral disorders   Students with emotional and behavioral disorders become identified as students with special needs—and therefore as students who qualify for special services—when their problems have a substantial negative effect on classroom success and achievement. Examples of such emotional and behavioral problems are an inability to establish and maintain satisfactory interpersonal relationships with adults and peers, long-term depression, and exceptionally aggressive or antisocial behavior. Students with emotional and behavioral disorders are discussed in more depth in Chapter 9.

Visual impairments   Students with visual impairments have malfunctions of their eyes or optic nerves that prevent them from seeing normally even with corrective lenses. Some of these students are totally blind. Others have limited sensitivity to light; for example, they see fuzzy patterns of light and dark. Still others have a restricted visual field (sometimes called *tunnel vision*), whereby they can see only a very small area at a given point in time.

Hearing impairments   Students with hearing impairments have a malfunction of the ear or associated nerves that interferes with the perception of sounds within the frequency range of normal human speech. Some hearing-impaired students are completely deaf: They have insufficient sensation to understand any spoken language even with the help of a hearing aid. Others are hard of hearing: They understand some speech but experience exceptional difficulty in doing so.

Physical and health impairments   Students with physical and health impairments have general physical or medical conditions (usually long-term) that interfere with school performance to such an extent that special instruction, curricular materials, equipment, or facilities are necessary. Students in this category may have little or no muscle control, reduced mental alertness, or limited energy and strength. Examples of specific conditions that may qualify students for special services include spinal cord injury, cerebral palsy, multiple sclerosis, muscular dystrophy, epilepsy, cystic fibrosis, asthma, heart problems, arthritis, cancer, and AIDS.

Giftedness   Gifted students (sometimes called "gifted and talented" students) have unusually high ability in one or more areas to the point where they require special educational services to help them meet their full potential. Giftedness is discussed in more detail in Chapter 4.

*Figure 1–3   Key U.S. Federal Legislation Addressing the Education of Students
with Disabilities*

Public Law 93-112, Section 504: Rehabilitation Act (1973)

P.L. 93-112 prohibits the exclusion of individuals with disabilities from federally funded programs and activities when such exclusion would be solely because of their disabilities.

Public Law 94-142: Individuals with Disabilities Education Act, or IDEA (1975)

Originally called the Education for All Handicapped Children Act, P.L. 94-142 has been amended three times: in 1983 (P.L. 98-199), 1986 (P.L. 99-457), and 1990 (P.L. 101-476). The original thrust of the legislation remains the same, however. P.L. 94-142 provides several guarantees for students with disabilities:

A Free and Appropriate Education.   Students with disabilities are entitled to a free educational program designed specifically to meet their unique educational needs. For example, a student with a learning disability who has unusual difficulty with reading is entitled to a special instructional program to promote the development of reading skills. A student with a visual impairment should have access to nonvisual versions of the same school materials that sighted classmates have—perhaps in the form of audiotapes of textbooks or homework assignments printed in braille.

Fair and Nondiscriminatory Evaluation.   When determining that a particular student has a particular disability, school personnel must use tests and other evaluation materials that give an accurate, meaningful, and complete indication of what special educational needs exist. Precautions must be taken to ensure that a student's performance on evaluation instruments is not unduly impaired by any sensory, physical, or communication disabilities or by any language differences that the student may have.

Due Process.   A student can be given special educational services only when due process procedures are followed—that is, only when decisions about the most appropriate education for a student are made on the basis of a fair and impartial hearing and an examination of all available data. Decisions are made by a multidisciplinary team that typically includes the regular classroom teacher, the student's parents, one or more specialists (e.g., reading teacher, psychologist, nurse, speech pathologist), and the school principal.

Individualized Education Program (IEP).   An appropriate instructional program must be developed and described in written form for each student identified as having a disability. This IEP has several components:

- A description of the student's current educational performance

- Short-term and long-term instructional objectives for the student

- Methods to be used in accomplishing the instructional objectives, including the services of any specialists that may be required

- Procedures and criteria to be used in evaluating the success of the prescribed methods

The same multidisciplinary team that evaluated the student typically develops the IEP; this team also reviews the student's progress on a regular basis and revises the IEP when appropriate.

Education in the Least Restrictive Environment (LRE).   The least restrictive environment is the most "normal" educational environment that can reasonably meet a student's needs. To the extent possible, students with disabilities should have the same academic environment, enrichment activities, and opportunities for social interaction that their nondisabled peers have.

Public Law 101-336: Americans with Disabilities Act, or ADA (1990)

P.L. 101-336 prohibits discrimination against individuals with disabilities solely on the basis of their disabilities. Reasonable accommodations must be made to enable people with disabilities to participate in the same daily activities in which other citizens participate; for example, all public services, accommodations, transportation, and telecommunications must be accessible to an individual with a disability.

vanced cognitive development (e.g., those who exhibit giftedness in one or more areas of the curriculum).

We should note here that *all* students stand to gain from being part of a diverse classroom: They develop an increasing awareness of the very heterogeneous nature of the human race and discover that all students, apart from some unique cultural perspectives, language differences, or obvious disabilities, are in many respects very much like themselves (Gearheart, Weishahn, & Gearheart, 1992; Lewis & Doorlag, 1991; J. W. Wood, 1989).

As a teacher, you must ultimately make your own decisions about how best to teach each of your students. Your instructional decisions will be affected not only by the characteristics that your students bring to the classroom but also by your objectives, your resources, and your own personality. Every teacher is likely to develop a unique approach to teaching. As long as your own approach is based on solid research findings about how children and adolescents learn and develop, your students will undoubtedly come out ahead.

CASE STUDY: *More Harm Than Good?*

Mr. Gualtieri, a high school mathematics teacher, begins his class one Monday with an important announcement. "I've just obtained some new instructional software programs for the school's computer laboratory. These programs will give you practice in solving mathematical word problems. I strongly encourage you to stay after school once or twice a week to get extra practice on the computer whenever you're having trouble with the homework assignments I give you."

Mr. Gualtieri is firmly convinced that the new instructional software will help his students perform better in mathematics. To test his hypothesis, he keeps a record of which students report to the computer lab after school and which students do not. He then looks at how well the two groups of students perform on his next classroom test. Much to his surprise, he discovers that, on the average, the students who have stayed after school to use the computer software have gotten *lower* scores than those who did not stay after school. "How can this be?" he puzzles. "Is the computer software actually doing more harm than good?"

- Is the computer software somehow making mathematics *more* difficult for students? Or is there another possible explanation for the result that Mr. Gualtieri has obtained?

- Which kind of study has Mr. Gualtieri conducted—descriptive, correlational, or experimental?

- Is it possible that the two groups of students (those who used the computer lab and those who did not) were different in some way that might affect their performance on Mr. Gualtieri's math test?

- Did Mr. Gualtieri make a good or a bad decision in advising his students to use the computer software? Is there any way to answer this question from the information he has obtained?

Students with disabilities are more successful in the regular classroom when instruction is adapted to their special needs.

SUMMING UP

Importance of Research for Teachers

Many people hold misconceptions about how students learn and develop and about how teachers can most effectively promote classroom achievement. The most accurate information about learning, development, and classroom practice comes from research findings. Different types of research studies—descriptive, correlational, or experimental—answer different questions about education, but all give us information that helps us in making the best choices about how we teach and help students learn.

Principles, Theories, and Decision Making

When research studies yield similar results time after time, educational psychologists derive principles and theories that describe and explain people's learning, development, and behavior. Our job as teachers is to translate these principles and theories into classroom practice. To illustrate, if research consistently tells us that "students learn more effectively when they relate new ideas to their existing knowledge," then we can facilitate our students' learning by helping them connect new material to things they have previously learned or experienced—for example, by pointing out how multiplication is related to addition or how treaties between two countries are similar to the many compromises students make in their daily social interactions.

Overview of the Book

In Parts 1 and 2 of the book, we will examine the diverse characteristics that students bring to the classroom and the nature of human learning and motivation. In Part 3, we will draw on principles from Parts 1 and 2 as we consider effective classroom practice.

Reading About and Studying Educational Psychology

As we examine the ways in which people think and learn, you will discover how people learn most effectively. You can use this information not only to help your students be successful in the classroom but also to help *yourself* learn successfully. For instance, if you relate new information to what you already know, elaborate on that information, and occasionally stop to test yourself on the content you've studied, you are well on your way to making these behaviors an important part of your own success as a student.

Common Themes

Seven themes will underlie many of the recommendations that appear throughout the book: interaction, information processing, relevance, classroom climate, challenge, expectations, and diversity. Diversity is the most prominent theme, appearing in every chapter of the book.

Considering Student Diversity

As teachers, we must remember that all of our students are individuals, with different strengths that they bring to the classroom and different weaknesses that need to be addressed. A few of our students—those with special needs—may be different enough from their peers that they will require special educational services; we will address specific strategies for accommodating the needs of such students in each of the next thirteen chapters. Yet as teachers, we must remember that *all* students stand to benefit from instructional programs tailored to their unique backgrounds and abilities.

KEY CONCEPTS

elaboration (p. 5)
descriptive study (p. 9)
correlational study (p. 9)
correlation (p. 9)
experimental study (p. 10)
visual-spatial thinking (p. 11)
treatment group (p. 12)
control group (p. 12)

principles (p. 14)
theories (p. 14)
students with special needs (p. 28)
inclusion (p. 28)
mental retardation (p. 29)
learning disabilities (p. 29)
speech and communication disorders (p. 29)

emotional and behavioral disorders (p. 29)
physical and health impairments (p. 29)
visual impairments (p. 29)
hearing impairments (p. 29)
giftedness (p. 29)

UNDERSTANDING STUDENT DIVERSITY

WE FIND DIVERSITY in any classroom. Some students are talkative and outgoing; others are more quiet and reserved. Some students learn new material quickly and independently; others need more time and assistance. Some students comply with classroom procedures readily; others need frequent reminders about appropriate behaviors.

Some of the diversity you will see among your students will be the result of developmental differences: Young people change as they grow, and they do so at varying rates. As a result, students at the same grade level will differ considerably in their ability to think logically and abstractly, to use effective study skills, and to express their thoughts clearly. They will also show differences in their views about right and wrong, their ability to see events from someone else's perspective, and their compassion and empathy for the plight of those less fortunate than themselves. As teachers, we must take such developmental differences into account, adapting instruction to the particular developmental level of each student. We will do so in the first two chapters of Part 1 as we consider **"Adapting to Differences in Cognitive and Linguistic Development"** in Chapter 2 and **"Adapting to Differences in Personal, Social, and Moral Development"** in Chapter 3.

Yet we cannot explain all student diversity strictly from a developmental perspective. Even when students are at the same developmental level, they come to us with unique talents, personality characteristics, and behaviors. Some consistently learn more quickly than their classmates; others are especially creative in writing, science, or the arts. We also see diversity between different groups of students; for example, we see more aggression in boys, more close-knit and intimate friendships in girls, more cooperative behavior in students from certain ethnic backgrounds, and higher dropout rates in students from lower-income families. We will explore the nature of such diversity as we consider **"Adapting to Individual and Group Differences"** in Chapter 4.

By understanding the multifaceted nature of student diversity, we will be in a better position to identify appropriate classroom management strategies, instructional methods, and assessment procedures as we move to these topics later in the book. Throughout Part 1, we will focus on how we can help every student learn and achieve success in the classroom. We will continue this focus as we move to Part 2, where we explore how human beings think and learn and how they acquire productive classroom behaviors.

Adapting to Differences in Cognitive and Linguistic Development

- How do school-age children think and learn? Have you ever heard a child say something that seemed illogical and made no sense to you? Have you noticed that many elementary school children often have difficulty with abstract ideas? Have you noticed that adolescents have better study skills than young children? Have *your* study skills improved over the years?

- In what ways is the language of children different from that of adults? Are there differences in vocabulary? In the complexity of sentences? In the ability to read and write? In the ability to learn a second language?

I**N THIS CHAPTER,** we will begin our exploration of how human beings grow and develop. We will first examine several basic principles of development—principles to keep in mind as we consider the many ways in which our students are likely to change during the school years. We then will look at two aspects of development that have major implications for classroom practice: **cognitive development** (changes in thinking processes and capabilities) and **linguistic development** (changes in such language capabilities as reading, listening, and writing). We will consider three perspectives of cognitive development—those of Jean Piaget, information processing theorists, and Lev Vygotsky—and identify a number of principles we can use to adapt instruction for different age groups and for individual students. Later in the chapter, as we turn our attention to linguistic development, we will see how students' language abilities change in many ways during the school years; here we will also identify strategies for promoting greater language proficiency. We will also look at the issue of bilingualism and consider how, when, and why we should teach a second language.

You should find the information described in the following objectives useful as you make decisions about how to help your students learn and achieve within the context of their developmental levels. By the end of the chapter, you should be able to:

1. Identify four general principles of development and their educational implications.

2. Explain basic assumptions and concepts of Piaget's theory of cognitive development, and apply them to classroom practice.

3. Describe the logical reasoning capabilities that children at various ages are likely to demonstrate, and use these capabilities as a basis for making decisions about what and how to teach students at a particular grade level.

4. Describe general trends that information processing theorists have observed in children's knowledge and approaches to learning tasks, and identify ways of helping students learn effectively.

5. Explain the importance of social interaction from Vygotsky's perspective, and identify strategies for helping students master challenging tasks.

6. List several general principles of cognitive development that emerge from the ideas of Piaget, information processing theorists, and Vygotsky.

7. Describe students' language capabilities at the elementary and secondary school levels, and identify ways to promote their listening, reading, speaking, and writing skills.

8. Identify several benefits of learning a second language, and explain the conditions under which each of two forms of bilingual education is more effective.

CASE STUDY: *What If?*

Julie and Joséfa are working together on an assignment on World War II for their high school history class. Julie is puzzled as she reads the assignment:

> Given what you know about the strengths and weaknesses of the Allied Forces and the Axis countries in 1941, how might the war have ended if the Japanese had *not* bombed Pearl Harbor?

"I don't get it," she says.
"What don't you get?" Joséfa asks.
"I don't understand what we're supposed to do."
"Well, we're supposed to speculate on what would have happened if Pearl Harbor hadn't been bombed. For example, maybe the United States wouldn't have joined the Allied Forces. Maybe the Axis powers would have won the war. Maybe all of Europe would be Fascist right now."

Julie just shakes her head. "I still don't understand this assignment. After all, the Japanese *did* bomb Pearl Harbor. And because of that action, the United States joined the Allied Forces. How can we pretend these things didn't happen?"

- Why is Julie having difficulty with her assignment? What can Joséfa do that Julie apparently cannot?

IDENTIFYING BASIC PRINCIPLES OF HUMAN DEVELOPMENT

Julie is having trouble reasoning about a situation that didn't happen—a situation contrary to fact. Yet her classmate Joséfa has no difficulty with the same assignment. As we will discover later in the chapter, the ability to reason logically about contrary-to-fact ideas emerges later in development than the ability to reason about true-to-life information. Joséfa has acquired the ability to reason about contrary-to-fact, but Julie has not. This case study demonstrates the first two of four basic principles of development:

- Development proceeds according to an orderly and predictable pattern.

- Different children develop at different rates.

- Periods of relatively rapid growth (spurts) may appear between periods of slower growth (plateaus).

- Development is affected by both heredity and environment.

Let's look more closely at these four principles because they tend to hold true whether we are talking about the development of thinking, language, personality, or morality. They also have implications for the decisions we make in the classroom (see Table 2–1).

An Orderly and Predictable Pattern of Development

At what age did you first walk? What was your first word? When did you say your first sentence? Do you know when such milestones in your life occurred?

Human development is often characterized by **developmental milestones** that occur in a predictable sequence. For example, children typically learn to walk only after they have already learned to sit up and crawl. They learn the stereotypical behaviors of males and females—for example, that doctors are more likely to be male and that nurses are more likely to be female—only after they have learned to distinguish between men and women. They begin to think logically about contrary-to-fact ideas only after they have learned to think logically about concrete objects and observable events. To some extent, then, we see **universals in development:** We see similar patterns in how children change over time regardless of the specific environment in which they are raised.

PRINCIPLES/ASSUMPTIONS

Table 2–1   General Principles of Human Development

PRINCIPLE	EXAMPLE	EDUCATIONAL IMPLICATION
Development proceeds according to an orderly pattern.	Marsha can think logically about concrete situations but seems incapable of thinking logically when abstract ideas are involved.	Remember that students must acquire certain skills before they can acquire others.
Different students develop at different rates.	In a middle school mathematics classroom, some students readily understand such abstract concepts as infinity and pi (π), but others struggle with the same ideas.	Don't make assumptions about what students can and cannot do on the basis of their age alone.
Periods of relatively rapid growth may occur between periods of slower growth.	Mario grows only an inch a year for several years and then shoots up several inches as he reaches puberty.	Expect that students may demonstrate little progress at some times, yet make dramatic progress at other times.
Development is affected by both heredity and environment.	Monica has difficulty throwing a softball accurately when she is six; however, by age twelve she has the strength and coordination to learn the skill easily.	Remember that the classroom environment has a significant effect on students' development but that the rate of development will also be affected by heredity and maturational processes.

Individual Differences in the Rate of Development

Descriptive research in child and adolescent development tells us the average ages at which various developmental milestones are reached. For example, the average child can hop several times on one foot at age three, starts using repetition as a way of learning information at age seven, and begins puberty at age eleven (for girls) or twelve (for boys) (Berk, 1989; Kail, 1990; G. R. Levin, 1983). But we must remember that not all children reach developmental milestones at the "average" age; some will reach them earlier, and some will reach them later.

By determining the approximate ages at which children can perform certain behaviors and think in certain ways, we can begin to form general expectations about the capabilities of children at a particular age level and to design our educational curriculum and instructional strategies around these expectations. At the same time, we should never jump to conclusions about what any individual student can and cannot do on the basis of age alone.

Spurts and Plateaus in Development

Development does not always proceed at a constant rate. For example, during the early elementary school years, children gain an average of two inches in height per year; during their adolescent growth spurt, they may grow as much as five inches per year (Berk, 1989; A. C. Harris, 1986). Toddlers may speak with a limited vocabulary and one-word "sentences" for several months, yet sometime around their second birthday a virtual explosion in language development occurs, with vocabulary expanding rapidly and sentences becoming longer and longer within the course of a few weeks.

Some theories of how students develop describe **stages** that reflect this pattern of uneven growth and change. In this and the following chapter, we will encounter several theories that describe human development in terms of stages.

Effects of Heredity and Environment

Virtually all aspects of development are affected either directly or indirectly by a child's genetic makeup. Not all inherited characteristics appear at birth; heredity continues to control a child's growth through the process of **maturation**—an unfolding of genetically controlled changes as the child develops. For example, such motor skills as walking, running, and jumping develop primarily as a result of neurological development, increased strength, and increased muscular control—changes that are largely determined by heredity.

Yet the environment plays an equally critical role in most aspects of development. For example, although children's heights and body builds are primarily inherited characteris-

Descriptive research of child development tells us the *average* age at which various developmental milestones are reached. But we must remember that individual children develop at different rates.

This question of *nature vs. nurture* continues to be a source of controversy among developmental theorists. To what extent do *you* believe that various human characteristics are influenced by heredity and environment?

tics, the nutritional value of the food they eat also makes a difference. And self-esteem, though somewhat affected by genetically determined physical features (e.g., height, facial features), is largely the result of such environmental factors as the frequency of one's success experiences and the nature of the interactions one has with others.

As teachers, we should remember that the experiences we provide for our students *will* make a difference in their lives. Yet we should also remember that such experiences can facilitate changes in students only when their maturational levels also allow such changes to occur.

The importance of both environment and maturation has been incorporated into a number of developmental theories. Jean Piaget's theory of cognitive development is a case in point.

LOOKING AT COGNITIVE DEVELOPMENT FROM PIAGET'S PERSPECTIVE

Consider these three students:

Four-year-old Abby is shown a collection of ten wooden beads; eight beads are brown and two are white. Abby is asked, "Are there more *brown* beads or more *wooden* beads?" Abby responds, "More brown beads."

Unlike Abby, ten-year-old Antonio quickly recognizes that if all the beads are wooden and that only some are brown, then there must be more wooden beads than brown ones. Antonio is then given these two logic problems:

If all children are human beings,
And if all human beings are living creatures,
Then must all children be living creatures?

If all children are basketballs,
And if all basketballs are jellybeans,
Then must all children be jellybeans?

Antonio readily agrees with the conclusion that all children must of course be living creatures. But he vehemently denies a conclusion based on exactly the same logic: that all children are jellybeans.

In contrast with Antonio, fifteen-year-old Amanda has no difficulty with either the "living creatures" problem or the "jellybeans" problem. She seems perfectly capable of thinking logically about things that have little basis in reality. Lately, she has been arguing with her high school principal that, because all people are created equal, teachers should not be allowed to evaluate or grade students. From a logical standpoint, her reasoning is as follows:

All people are created equal.
Evaluation of one individual by another implies an unequal relationship.
Therefore, people should not evaluate one another.

These three students show very different logical thinking capabilities—differences that reflect varying levels of cognitive development. Abby has difficulty with a question that to us might seem ridiculously easy. Antonio can draw logical conclusions, but only when those conclusions match reality as he knows it. Amanda, like Joséfa in our opening case study, can think logically about hypothetical and contrary-to-fact ideas as well as real-life situations, an ability that enables her to consider how the world might be different from the way it is now.

One of the best known theories of cognitive development, and of the development of logical thinking in particular, is that of Jean Piaget, a Swiss developmentalist (e.g., Inhelder & Piaget, 1958; Piaget, 1928, 1952, 1959, 1970, 1972, 1980; Piaget & Inhelder, 1967, 1969). In the following pages, we will explore basic assumptions underlying Piaget's theory and look at the four stages of logical thinking that he proposed.

Have you encountered Piaget's theory in other courses? If so, what things do you already know about his theory?

Examining Piaget's Assumptions

Piaget made a number of assumptions about the cognitive development of children. Among the most central ones are these:

- Children are active and motivated learners.

- Children construct knowledge from their experiences.

- Children learn through the two complementary processes of assimilation and accommodation.

- Interaction with one's physical and social environments is essential for cognitive development.

- The process of equilibration promotes progression toward increasingly more complex levels of thought.

- Cognitive development can proceed only after certain genetically controlled neurological changes occur.

Children as Active and Motivated Learners

Piaget believed that children are not just passive receivers of environmental stimulation; he believed that, instead, they are naturally curious about their world and actively seek out information to help them understand and make sense of it. They continually experiment with the objects they encounter, manipulating things and observing the effects of their own actions. For example, my son Alex is always fiddling with and manipulating *something*. Some of his "experiments"—such as setting up a terrarium in which two lizards can survive and grow—make his mother proud. Others—such as sitting on a kitchen barstool and seeing how far he can lean back on two legs without falling over—drive me absolutely crazy.

Capitalize on students' natural curiosity.

Construction of Knowledge

Children's knowledge is not limited to a collection of isolated pieces of information. Instead, children use the information they accumulate to construct an overall view of how the world operates. For example, through his experiences with lizards and a terrarium, my son Alex has developed an understanding of how such aspects of the environment as food, water, and climate interact to sustain life. Through his experiences on the kitchen barstool, he has learned a basic principle of physics: the law of gravity. Because

Provide experiences to help students construct an increasingly more accurate and complete understanding of the world. Help them discover relationships among concepts and ideas.

Piaget proposed that children construct their own body of knowledge from their experiences, his theory is sometimes called a **constructivist** theory.

In Piaget's terminology, the things that children learn and can do are organized as **schemes***—groups of similar thoughts or actions. To illustrate, an infant may have a scheme for putting things in her mouth, a scheme that she will use in dealing with a variety of objects, including her thumb, her toys, and her blanket. A seven-year-old may have a scheme for identifying snakes, one that includes their long, thin bodies, their lack of legs, and their slithery nature. A thirteen-year-old may have a scheme for what constitutes fashion, allowing her to classify her peers as being either "totally radical" or "complete dorks."

Over time, children's schemes are modified with experience and become increasingly better integrated with one another. For instance, children begin to recognize the hierarchical interrelationships of some schemes—the fact that cats and dogs are all animals, for instance. As we will soon see, this progressively more organized body of knowledge allows children to think in increasingly sophisticated and logical ways.

Learning Through Assimilation and Accommodation

Help students assimilate new material into existing schemes by tying it to things they have already learned.

Although children's schemes change over time, the processes by which children develop them remain the same. Piaget proposed that learning and cognitive development occur as the result of two complementary processes—assimilation and accommodation.

Assimilation is a process of dealing with an object or event in a way that is consistent with an existing scheme. For example, the infant may assimilate a new teddy bear into her putting-things-into-the-mouth scheme. The seven-year-old may quickly identify a new slithery object in the backyard as another snake. The thirteen-year-old may readily label a new classmate as being either radical or dorkish.

Encourage accommodation by providing information that students cannot totally assimilate into existing schemes.

But sometimes a new object or event cannot be easily interpreted and assimilated in terms of existing schemes. In these situations, one of two forms of **accommodation** will occur: either an existing scheme will be modified to account for the new object or event, or an entirely new scheme will be formed to deal with it. For example, the infant may have to open her mouth wider than usual to accommodate a teddy bear's fat paw. The thirteen-year-old may have to revise her existing scheme of fashion according to changes in what's hot and what's not. The seven-year-old may find a long, thin, slithery thing that can't possibly be a snake because it has four legs. After some research, the child develops a new scheme—salamander—for this creature.

Assimilation and accommodation typically work hand in hand as children develop their knowledge and understanding of the world. Children interpret each new event within the context of their existing knowledge (assimilation) but at the same time may modify their knowledge as a result of the new event (accommodation). Accommodation rarely happens without assimilation: Our students can only benefit from (accommodate to) new experiences when they can relate those experiences to their current knowledge and beliefs.

Importance of Interaction with the Physical and Social Environments

Provide hands-on experiences with physical objects. Allow and encourage students to explore and manipulate things.

New experiences are essential for learning and cognitive development to occur. For this reason, Piaget stressed the importance of children's interactions with the physical environment. By manipulating the environment—for example, by playing with sand and

---

* Although some writers refer to these as sche*mas*, Piaget himself distinguished between schemes and schemas (e.g., see Piaget, 1970, p. 705). The distinction has apparently been lost in many translations of Piaget's work (S. Pulos, personal communication, 1995).

water, measuring things, practicing with footballs and basketballs, or experimenting in a science lab—a child can develop an understanding of cause-effect relationships, the nature of such physical characteristics as weight and volume, and so on.

Social interaction is equally critical for cognitive development. Through interaction with other people, children begin to realize that different individuals see things differently and that their own view of the world is not necessarily a completely accurate or logical one. To illustrate, a preschool child may have difficulty seeing the world from anyone's perspective but her own. Through social interactions, both pleasant (e.g., a conversation) and unpleasant (e.g., an argument), she begins to realize that her own perspective is a unique one not shared by others. Similarly, an elementary school child may recognize the logical inconsistencies in what he says and does only after someone else points out those inconsistencies. And through discussions with classmates or adults about social and political issues, a high school student may modify her idealistic notions (as an example, remember Amanda's conviction that teachers have no business evaluating students) to reflect the constraints that the real world imposes.

Provide opportunities for children to discuss and exchange ideas and perspectives.

Equilibration

According to Piaget, children are sometimes in a state of **equilibrium;** they can comfortably explain new events in terms of existing schemes. But this equilibrium doesn't continue indefinitely. As children grow, they continue to encounter new events they cannot adequately explain in terms of their current understanding of the world. Such inexplicable events create **disequilibrium,** a sort of mental discomfort. Only through replacing, reorganizing, or better integrating their schemes (in other words, through accommodation) do children become able to understand and explain those previously puzzling

Provide information and experiences that contradict students' existing beliefs.

Students benefit from exploring and manipulating physical objects.

Interactions with other people help children become more aware of the perspectives of others.

events. The movement from equilibrium to disequilibrium and back to equilibrium again is known as **equilibration.** Equilibration and children's need to achieve equilibrium promote the development of more complex levels of thought and knowledge.

To illustrate the process of equilibration, let's return to four-year-old Abby's difficulty with the wooden beads. We show ten wooden beads to Abby—eight brown and two white—and ask her, "Are there more *brown* beads or more *wooden* beads?" Abby tells us that there are more brown beads. She seems quite comfortable with this response; she is in equilibrium. So we ask her to count the *brown* beads (she counts eight of them) and then to count the *wooden* beads (she counts ten). "So then, Abby," we say, "there are *eight* brown beads and *ten* wooden beads. Are there more brown beads or more wooden beads?" If Abby can recognize the inconsistency in her reasoning—that eight cannot possibly be more than ten—she will experience disequilibrium. At this point, she may reorganize her thinking to accommodate the idea that some beads are simultaneously both brown and wooden and so should be included in both categories at the same time.

Importance of Neurological Maturation

According to Piaget, cognitive development can proceed only after certain genetically controlled neurological changes occur—that is, only after the brain matures to a certain extent. Piaget believed that, because of their neurological immaturity, elementary school children cannot think in the same way that adults do, no matter what parents or teachers might do to encourage adultlike thinking. Preschoolers are even less neurologically mature, so they are further limited in their cognitive abilities. Piaget proposed that major physiological changes take place when children are about two years old, again when they are six or seven, and again around puberty, and that these changes allow the development of increasingly more complex thought. We should note that psychologists disagree about the extent to which such neurological changes actually occur (H. Epstein, 1978; Hudspeth, 1985; R. W. Marsh, 1985; Rosser, 1994).

Remember that some students, especially those younger than eleven or twelve, may not yet be capable of understanding certain ideas.

Examining Piaget's Stages of Cognitive Development

A major feature of Piaget's theory is his description of four stages of logical reasoning capabilities:

1. **Sensorimotor stage** (birth until 2 years)

2. **Preoperational stage** (2 years until 6 or 7 years)

3. **Concrete operations stage** (6 or 7 years until 11 or 12 years)

4. **Formal operations stage** (11 or 12 years through adulthood)

These stages are briefly summarized in Figure 2–1. Each stage has its own unique characteristics and capabilities, and each builds upon the accomplishments of former stages, so children must progress through the four stages in the same invariant sequence.

As we will discover later in the chapter, many psychologists (e.g., Rosser, 1994; Siegler, 1994) question Piaget's belief that cognitive development is as stagelike as he proposed. Nevertheless, Piaget's stages do provide insights into the nature of children's thinking at different age levels, and so we will look at them in depth. Before we do so, however, we should note that the ages associated with each stage are *averages;* some children may reach a stage at a slightly younger age than average, and others may reach it at an older age. We should also note that some children may be *transitional* from one stage to the next and so will display characteristics of two adjacent stages during the same time period.

Sensorimotor Stage (birth until 2 years)

Imagine that we show a colorful stuffed clown to six-month-old Karen. Karen reaches for it in much the same way that she reaches for her teddy bear and her stacking blocks; in other words, she has a reaching-and-grasping scheme with which she assimilates this new object. Karen then drops the clown and watches it fall to the floor, applying her letting-go and visually-following-a-moving-object schemes in the process. But now imagine that we put Karen's clown inside a box so that she can no longer see it. Karen seems to forget the clown and turns to play with something else, acting as if she cannot think about a clown that she cannot actually see.

Piaget proposed that children in the sensorimotor stage develop schemes based primarily on behaviors and perceptions. They are not yet capable of *mental* schemes that enable them to think about objects beyond their immediate view, partly because they have few if any words to use to mentally represent the things they cannot see.

Nevertheless, important cognitive capabilities emerge during the sensorimotor stage, especially as children begin to experiment with their environments in a trial-and-error fashion. For example, during the latter part of the stage, children develop **object permanence,** the realization that objects continue to exist even when they are removed from view. And after repeatedly observing that certain actions lead to certain consequences, they begin to develop an understanding of *cause-effect relationships.* Such ideas as object permanence and cause-and-effect are basic building blocks on which later cognitive development will depend.

Preoperational Stage (2 years until 6 or 7 years)

Children who show preoperational thought can form schemes that are relatively independent of immediate perceptions and behaviors. For example, as Karen reaches the preoperational stage, she will be able to think about a clown without having one directly in front of her. This ability to represent external objects and events in one's head **(symbolic thinking)** marks the beginning of true thought as Piaget defined it.

Language skills virtually explode during the early part of the preoperational stage. The words in children's rapidly increasing vocabularies provide labels for newly devel-

SENSORIMOTOR STAGE
(birth until about 2 years old)
Schemes are based on behaviors and perceptions; schemes don't yet represent objects beyond a child's immediate view.

PREOPERATIONAL STAGE
(2 until about 6 or 7 years old)
Schemes now represent objects beyond a child's immediate view, but the child does not yet reason in logical, adultlike ways.

CONCRETE OPERATIONAL STAGE
(6 or 7 until about 11 or 12 years old)
Adultlike logic appears but is limited to reasoning about concrete reality.

FORMAL OPERATIONAL STAGE
(11 or 12 through adulthood)
Logical reasoning processes are applied to abstract ideas as well as to concrete objects.

Figure 2–1 Piaget's Stages of Cognitive Development

To help young students shed their preoperational egocentrism, ask them to present their perspectives to one another and to you, and express your confusion when they do not explain themselves clearly.

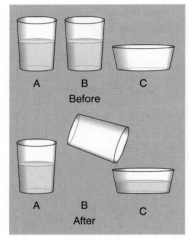

Figure 2–2   Conservation of Liquid: Do Glasses A and C contain the same amount of water?

Ask students to explain their reasoning. Challenge illogical explanations.

oped schemes and serve as symbols that enable them to think about objects and events even when such things are not directly in sight. Language also provides the basis for a new form of social interaction—verbal communication. Children can now express their thoughts and receive information from other people in a way that was previously not possible.

At the same time, preoperational thinking has some definite weaknesses, especially as we compare it with concrete operational thinking (see Table 2–2). For example, children in this stage exhibit **preoperational egocentrism,** an inability to view situations from another person's perspective. They may have trouble understanding why they must share school supplies with a classmate or why they must be careful not to hurt someone else's feelings. They may play games together without ever checking to be sure they are all playing according to the same rules. They may also exhibit **egocentric speech,** saying things without really considering the perspective of the listener; for example, they may leave out critical details as they tell a story, giving a fragmented version that their listener cannot possibly understand.

Preoperational thinking is also illogical (at least from an adult's point of view), especially during the preschool years. As an example, you may recall Abby's insistence that there were more brown beads than wooden beads in a collection of ten wooden beads (her error reflects single classification, described in Table 2–2). Here is another example of the "logic" of children exhibiting preoperational thought:

> We show Nathan the three glasses in Figure 2–2. Glasses A and B are identical in size and shape and contain an equal amount of water. We ask Nathan whether the two glasses of water contain the same amount, and he replies confidently that they do. We then pour the water in Glass B into Glass C. We ask him whether the two glasses of water (A and C) still have the same amount. Nathan replies, "No, that glass [pointing to Glass A] has more because it's taller."

Nathan's response illustrates lack of **conservation:** He does not realize that because no water has been added or taken away, the amount of water in the two glasses must be equivalent. Young children such as Nathan often confuse changes in appearance with changes in amount.

As children approach the later part of the preoperational stage, perhaps at around four or five years of age, they show early signs of being logical. For example, they sometimes draw correct conclusions about conservation problems (e.g., the water glasses) or multiple classification problems (e.g., the wooden beads). They cannot yet explain *why* their conclusions are correct, however; they base their conclusions on "hunches" and "intuition," rather than on any conscious awareness of underlying logical principles. When children move into the concrete operations stage, they become increasingly able both to make logical inferences and to explain the reasoning behind those inferences.

Concrete Operations Stage (6 or 7 years until 11 or 12 years)

Piaget proposed that children's thought processes gradually become organized and integrated with one another into larger systems of mental processes. These systems—known in Piagetian terminology as **operations**—allow children to pull their thoughts together in a way that makes sense and thus to think logically. Such integrated and coordinated thought emerges at the beginning of the concrete operations stage.

Concrete operational thought is different from preoperational thought in a number of ways (see Table 2–2). For example, students now realize that their own thoughts

Table 2–2   Preoperational versus Concrete Operational Thought

PREOPERATIONAL THOUGHT (2 TO 6/7 YRS)	CONCRETE OPERATIONAL THOUGHT (6/7 TO 11/12 YRS)
Preoperational Egocentrism Students do not see things from someone else's perspective; they think their own perspective is the only perspective and must therefore be the correct one. *Example:* A student tells a story without considering what prior knowledge the listener is likely to have.	**Differentiation of One's Own Perspective from the Perspectives of Others** Students recognize that others see things differently than they do; they realize that their own perspective may be an incorrect one. *Example:* A student asks for validation of his or her own thoughts—for example, asking, "Did I get that right?"
Confusion Between Physical and Psychological Events Students confuse external, physical objects with internal thoughts; they think that thoughts have physical reality and that objects think and feel. *Example:* A student is afraid of the "monsters" in a dark closet and worries that a doll will feel lonely if left alone at home.	**Distinction Between Physical and Psychological Events** Students recognize that thoughts do not have physical reality and that physical objects don't have such psychological characteristics as "feelings." *Example:* A student recognizes that imagined monsters don't exist and that dolls have no thoughts or feelings.
Lack of Conservation Students believe that the amount of a substance changes when the substance is reshaped or rearranged, even though nothing has been added or taken away. *Example:* A student asserts that two rows of five pennies similarly spaced have equal amounts; but when one row is spread out so that it is longer than the other row, the student says that the longer row has more pennies. (The student does not yet understand that a number is a constant amount.)	**Conservation** Students recognize that amount stays the same if nothing has been added or taken away, even if the substance is reshaped or rearranged. *Example:* A student asserts that two rows of five pennies are the same number of pennies regardless of their spacing. (The student now has a true understanding of number.)
Irreversibility Students don't recognize that certain processes can be undone, or reversed. *Example:* A student doesn't realize that a row of five pennies made longer can be shortened back to its original length; the student also treats addition and subtraction as two unrelated processes.	**Reversibility** Students understand that certain processes can be reversed. *Example:* A student moves the five pennies in the longer row close together again as a way of demonstrating that both rows have the same amount; the student also recognizes that subtraction is the reverse of addition.
Inability to Reason About Transformations Students focus on static situations; they have difficulty thinking about change processes. *Example:* A student resists the idea that a caterpillar becomes a butterfly through metamorphosis, instead insisting that the caterpillar crawls away and the butterfly comes to replace it (K. R. Harris, 1986).	**Ability to Reason About Transformations** Students can reason about change and its effects. *Example:* A student understands that metamorphosis is the process whereby a caterpillar becomes a butterfly.

Table 2–2   (continued)

PREOPERATIONAL THOUGHT (2 TO 6/7 YRS)	CONCRETE OPERATIONAL THOUGHT (6/7 TO 11/12 YRS)
Single Classification Students are able to classify objects in only one way at any given point in time. *Example:* A student denies that a mother can also be a doctor.	**Multiple Classification** Students recognize that objects may belong to several categories simultaneously. *Example:* A student acknowledges that a mother can also be a doctor, a jogger, and a wife.
Transductive Reasoning Students reason from one specific thing to another, often unrelated, thing. *Example:* A student believes that clouds make the moon grow.	**Deductive Reasoning** Students can draw a logical inference from two or more pieces of information. *Example:* A student deduces that if all children are human beings and if all human beings are living things, then all children must be living things.

Begin to explore hierarchical relationships in the early elementary grades. For example, examine the various levels of classification that biologists use to describe plant and animal life.

and feelings are not necessarily shared by others and may reflect personal opinions rather than reality. As a result, they know that they can sometimes be wrong and begin to seek out external validation for their ideas, asking such questions as "What do you think?" and "Did I get that problem right?"

Students in the concrete operations stage are capable of many forms of logical thought. As an illustration, remember the description of ten-year-old Antonio earlier in the chapter. When given the wooden beads problem, Antonio demonstrated multiple classification: He recognized that some beads were simultaneously both brown and wooden, so there must be more wooden beads than brown beads. Antonio also demonstrated **deductive reasoning:** He recognized that if all children are human beings and all human beings are living creatures, all children must logically be living creatures.

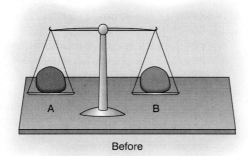
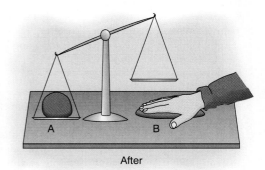

Before   After

Figure 2–3   Conservation of Weight: Two balls of clay—Ball A and Ball B—initially weigh the same amount. When Ball B is flattened into a pancake shape, how does its weight now compare with that of Ball A?

Students show increasingly more complex forms of conservation as they progress through the elementary school years. Some forms of conservation, such as conservation of liquid (illustrated in Figure 2–2) and conservation of number (illustrated by the pennies problem in Table 2–2), appear at six or seven years of age, but other forms of conservation may not appear until several years later. As an example, consider the task involving conservation of weight illustrated in Figure 2–3. Using a balance scale, an adult shows a child that two round balls of clay have the same weight. One ball is removed from the scale and is smashed into a pancake shape. Does the pancake weigh the same as the unsmashed ball, or do the two pieces of clay weigh different amounts? Children typically do not achieve conservation of weight—that is, they do not realize that the flattened pancake weighs the same as the round ball it was earlier—until sometime around nine to twelve years of age (Sund, 1976).

One sign of concrete operational thought is *conservation*—recognition that amount stays the same, despite changes in appearance, if nothing is added or taken away.

Although students displaying concrete operational thought show many signs of logical thinking, their cognitive development is not yet complete (see Table 2–3). For one thing, they may have difficulty thinking about proportions and ratios, formulating and testing hypotheses, and separating and controlling variables—processes central to adult forms of mathematical and scientific reasoning. They also have trouble understanding and reasoning about abstract ideas. In mathematics, this weakness may be reflected in their confusion about such mathematical concepts as *pi (π), infinity,* and *negative numbers.* In social studies, it may limit their comprehension of such abstract notions as democracy, communism, and human rights. Finally, students who show concrete operational thought are likely to have difficulty reasoning about ideas that contradict reality; as an example, you may remember Antonio's denial that if all children are basketballs and all basketballs are jellybeans, then all children must be jellybeans.

Do you now see why the third stage is called "concrete operations"?

Formal Operations Stage (11 or 12 years through adulthood)

Think back once again to our case study at the beginning of the chapter. Julie's thinking was concrete operational: She was unable to speculate about what might have happened if the Japanese had not bombed Pearl Harbor. Yet Joséfa had no difficulty with the same task. Like Joséfa, students who display formal operational thinking are able to think about concepts that have little or no basis in concrete reality—concepts that are abstract, hypothetical, or contrary-to-fact. Furthermore, they begin to recognize that what is logically valid is different from what is true in the real world; for example, *if* all children are basketballs, and *if* all basketballs are jellybeans, then all children *must* be jellybeans. A number of abilities essential for sophisticated mathematical and scientific reasoning also emerge in formal operations (see Table 2–3).

During the elementary years, focus on concrete objects and events. At the secondary level, increase discussion of abstract concepts and hypothetical ideas but avoid strictly abstract methods of presenting information (e.g., entirely verbal lectures) until students show signs of abstract reasoning.

Let's consider how students' capabilities in mathematics are likely to improve once formal operational thinking develops. Abstract verbal problems, such as mathematical word problems, should become easier to solve. Students should become capable of understanding such concepts as *negative numbers* and *infinity;* for example, they should now comprehend how temperature can be below zero and how two parallel lines will

Table 2–3   *Concrete Operational versus Formal Operational Thought*

CONCRETE OPERATIONAL THOUGHT (6/7 TO 11/12 YRS)	FORMAL OPERATIONAL THOUGHT (11/12 YRS THROUGH ADULTHOOD)
Dependence on Concrete Reality Students can reason logically about concrete objects they can observe; they are unable to reason about abstract, hypothetical, or contrary-to-fact ideas. *Example:* A student has difficulty with the concept of *negative numbers,* wondering how something can possibly be less than zero.	**Ability to Reason About Abstract, Hypothetical, and Contrary-to-Fact Ideas** Students can reason about things that are not tied directly to concrete, observable reality. *Example:* A student understands negative numbers and is able to use them effectively in mathematical procedures.
Inability to Formulate and Test Multiple Hypotheses When seeking an explanation for a scientific phenomenon, students identify and test only one hypothesis. *Example:* When asked what makes a pendulum swing more quickly or more slowly, a student says that the weight of the pendulum is the determining factor.	**Formulation and Testing of Multiple Hypotheses** Students seeking an explanation for a scientific phenomenon formulate and test several hypotheses about possible cause-effect relationships. *Example:* When asked what makes a pendulum swing more quickly or more slowly, a student says that weight, length, and strength of the initial push are all possible explanations.
Inability to Separate and Control Variables When attempting to confirm or disconfirm a particular hypothesis about cause-effect relationships, students test (and thereby confound) more than one variable simultaneously. *Example:* In testing possible factors influencing the oscillation rate of a pendulum, a student adds more weight to the pendulum while at the same time also shortening the length of the pendulum.	**Separation and Control of Variables** When attempting to confirm or disconfirm a particular hypothesis, students test one variable at a time while holding all other variables constant. *Example:* In testing factors influencing the rate of oscillation, a student tests the effect of weight while keeping length and strength of push constant; the student then tests the effect of length while keeping weight and push constant.
Lack of Proportional Thought Students cannot reason about proportions. *Example:* A student does not understand the relationship between fractions and decimals.	**Proportional Thought** Students understand proportions and can use them effectively in mathematical problem solving. *Example:* A student works easily with proportions, fractions, decimals, and ratios.
Lack of Combinatorial Thought When asked to generate all possible combinations of several objects, students identify combinations in an unsystematic, random fashion. *Example:* A student who is asked to identify the ways in which four objects (A B C D) might be combined generates five combinations (AB, BC, AD, ABC, BCD) and then cannot think of any more.	**Combinatorial Thought** When asked to generate all possible combinations of several objects, students systematically identify all possible combinations. *Example:* A student who is asked to identify possible combinations of four objects generates all fifteen possibilities (A, B, C, D, AB, AC, AD, BC, BD, CD, ABC, ABD, ACD, BCD, and ABCD).

never touch even if they go on forever. And because they can now use proportions in their reasoning, they can study and understand fractions, ratios, and decimals, and they can use such proportions to solve problems.

Try the following exercise as an illustration of proportional thinking.

■ EXPERIENCING FIRSTHAND
Thinking About Proportions

Mr. Little and Mr. Big are two men from the planet Xeron. People on Xeron don't use centimeters or inches to measure things; they instead use a unit of measurement called a "greenie." Mr. Little is 4 greenies tall. Mr. Big is 7 greenies tall.

One day, the two men travel to the planet Phylus. Phylus has a different unit of measurement—the "reddie." Mr. Little is 10 reddies tall. Figure out how tall Mr. Big is in reddies. (Adapted from Ormrod & Carter, 1985)

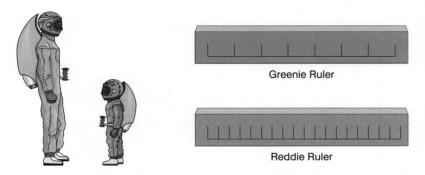

Greenie Ruler

Reddie Ruler

The proportions of the two men's heights in greenies and in reddies should be the same. If we think of Mr. Big's height as *x,* then:

$$\frac{4 \text{ greenies (Mr. Little)}}{7 \text{ greenies (Mr. Big)}} = \frac{10 \text{ reddies (Mr. Little)}}{x \text{ reddies (Mr. Big)}}$$

Solving for *x*, we find that Mr. Big is 17 ½ reddies tall.

Because proportional reasoning typically does not appear until students are eleven or twelve at the earliest (Karplus, Pulos, & Stage, 1983; Schliemann & Carraher, 1993; Tourniaire & Pulos, 1985), extensive work with fractions in elementary school may be premature. For example, my daughter Tina began working with complicated fraction problems, such as adding and subtracting fractions with different denominators, in the fourth grade. She learned the correct procedures for adding and subtracting fractions, but she had absolutely no understanding of what she was doing; in a sense, she was just going through the motions. Before proportional reasoning emerges, individuals may not be cognitively ready to comprehend the reasons underlying the procedures they learn for dealing with fractions and decimals.

Scientific reasoning is also likely to improve once students are capable of formal operational thought. Three formal operational abilities—reasoning logically about hypothetical ideas, formulating and testing hypotheses, and separating and controlling variables—together allow formal operations individuals to use the *scientific method,* in which several possible explanations for an observed phenomenon are proposed and

Hold off on problems involving fractions, ratios, and decimals until students show some capability for proportional reasoning.

As an elementary student, did you have difficulty with fractions or ratios?
■

tested in a systematic manner. As an example, consider the pendulum problem in the exercise that follows.

 EXPERIENCING FIRSTHAND
Pendulum Problem

An object suspended by a rope or string—a pendulum—swings indefinitely at a constant rate (a playground swing and the pendulum of a grandfather clock are two everyday examples). Some pendulums swing back and forth rather slowly, whereas others swing more quickly. What characteristics of a pendulum determine how fast it swings? Write down several possible hypotheses as to what variable or variables might affect a pendulum's rate of swing (its *oscillation rate*).

Once you have generated at least three hypotheses, gather several small, heavy objects (an eraser, a bolt, and a fishing sinker are three possibilities) and a piece of string. Tie one of the objects to one end of the piece of string and set your pendulum in motion. Now conduct one or more experiments to test each of your hypotheses.

What can you conclude? What variable or variables affect the rate at which a pendulum swings?

What hypotheses did you generate? Four possible variables you might have considered are the weight of the object at the bottom, the length of the string, the force with which the pendulum is pushed, and the height from which the object is first dropped; you may have formed additional hypotheses as well.

Did you then test each hypothesis in a systematic fashion? A student capable of formal operational thinking *separates and controls variables,* testing one at a time while holding all others constant. For example, if you were testing the hypothesis that weight makes a difference, you might have tried objects of different weights while keeping constant the length of the string, the force with which you pushed each object, and the height from which you dropped it. Similarly, if you hypothesized that the length of the string was a critical factor, you might have varied the length of the string while continuing to use the same object and starting the pendulum in motion in the same manner. If you carefully separated and controlled the variables that you considered, then you would have come to the correct conclusion: Only length affects a pendulum's oscillation rate.

Because individuals capable of formal operational reasoning can deal with hypothetical and contrary-to-fact ideas, they can envision how the world might be different from—and possibly better than—the way it actually is. As a result, they may exhibit some idealism about social, political, ethical, or religious issues. For example, secondary students may suggest the abolishment of grades (as fifteen-year-old Amanda did earlier in the chapter) or begin to evaluate the legitimacy of their political or religious beliefs and affiliations. Many secondary school students begin to show concern about world problems and to devote some of their energy to such worthy causes as the environment or world hunger (we should note, however, that their devotion is usually evident more in their talk than in their actions; Elkind, 1984).

Idealistic adolescents will often present recommendations for change that seem logical but that may not be practical in today's world. For example, they may argue that racism would disappear overnight if people would only just begin to love one another, or they may propose that a nation should disband its armed forces and eliminate all its weaponry as a way of moving toward world peace. Piaget suggested that adolescent idealism reflects **formal operational egocentrism**—in this case, an inability to separate ab-

Recall how we talked about the importance of separating and controlling variables when we discussed experimental research studies in Chapter 1.

Give students practice in formulating and testing hypotheses and in separating and controlling variables.

Encourage adolescents to discuss "ideal" situations, but point out instances when their ideals are unrealistic.

stract logical thinking from practical considerations and the unpredictability of human behavior. Only through experience do adolescents eventually begin to temper their optimism with some realism about what is possible in a given time frame and with limited resources.

In your own words, can you summarize the characteristics of each of the four stages?

Considering Current Perspectives on Piaget's Theory

Piaget's theory has sparked a great deal of research about children's cognitive development. In general, this research supports Piaget's proposed *sequence* in which different abilities emerge (Driver, 1982; Flavell, 1985; Siegler & Richards, 1982). For example, the ability to reason about abstract ideas emerges only after children are already capable of reasoning about concrete objects and events. And the order in which various conservation tasks are mastered is much as Piaget proposed. Researchers are beginning to question the *ages* at which various abilities actually appear, however. They are also finding that students' logical reasoning capabilities may vary considerably, depending on their previous knowledge and experiences related to the topic at hand.

Capabilities of Preschool Children

Preschool children are apparently more competent than Piaget's description of the preoperational stage would indicate. Children as young as three or four years old are not completely egocentric. In many situations, preschoolers *can* take another individual's perspective (Borke, 1975; Donaldson, 1978; M. E. Ford, 1979; Gelman, 1979); for example, they can often identify such emotions as sadness or anger in others (Lennon, Eisenberg, & Carroll, 1983; Siegel & Hodkin, 1982). Children at this age can also draw logical deductions; for instance, they frequently make inferences when they listen to stories (Donaldson, 1978; Gelman & Baillargeon, 1983). Children as young as four sometimes show conservation; for example, they are more likely to answer a conservation problem correctly if the transformation occurs out of sight, so they are not misled by appearances (Donaldson, 1978; Rosser, 1994; Siegel & Hodkin, 1982). And many supposedly "preoperational" children can correctly solve multiple classification problems if words are used to draw attention to the entire group; for example, many four- and five-year-olds realize that, in a *forest* of eight pine trees and two oak trees, there must of course be more trees than pine trees (Donaldson, 1978; Gelman & Baillargeon, 1983; Resnick, 1989; Rosser, 1994).

Expect some aspects of concrete operational thought in preschool children.

What evidence of logical thinking have you seen in the preschoolers whom you know?

Capabilities of Elementary School Children

Piaget may also have underestimated the capabilities of elementary school students. For example, many students in the elementary grades occasionally show evidence of abstract and hypothetical thought (S. Carey, 1985b; Metz, 1995). As an illustration, consider this hypothetical (and therefore formal operational) situation:

> All of Joan's friends are going to the museum today.
> Pat is a friend of Joan.

Children as young as nine can correctly deduce that "Pat is going to the museum today" even though the situation involves people they don't know and so has no basis in their own concrete reality (Roberge, 1970). And some older elementary school children

Begin to present tasks requiring formal operational thought in the later elementary years.

demonstrate the ability to separate and control variables, especially when they are given hints about the importance of controlling all variables except the one they are testing (Danner & Day, 1977; Metz, 1995).

Capabilities of Adolescents

Formal operational thought processes probably appear later and more gradually than Piaget originally proposed. High school and college students often have difficulty with tasks involving formal operational thinking (Karplus et al., 1983; Neimark, 1979; Siegler & Richards, 1982). Furthermore, students may demonstrate formal operational thought in one content domain while thinking more concretely in another. Evidence of formal operations typically emerges in the physical sciences earlier than in such subjects as history and geography; students often have difficulty thinking about abstract and hypothetical ideas in history and geography until well into the high school years (Lovell, 1979; Tamburrini, 1982).

Effects of Prior Knowledge and Experience

It is becoming increasingly apparent that students' ability to think logically depends to a great extent on the particular knowledge and background experiences they have (S. Carey, 1985a; Gelman & Baillargeon, 1983; Roazzi & Bryant, 1993; Shaffer, 1988; Siegel & Hodkin, 1982; Siegler & Richards, 1982). Preschoolers are less likely to exhibit **transductive reasoning**—for example, saying that clouds make the moon "grow"—when they have accurate information about cause-effect relationships (S. Carey, 1985a). Four-year-olds begin to show conservation after having experience with conservation tasks, especially if they can actively manipulate the materials of the tasks and are asked to discuss their reasoning with someone who already exhibits conservation (Field, 1987; Mayer, 1992; F. B. Murray, 1978). Ten-year-olds can learn to solve logical problems involving hypothetical ideas if they are taught particular strategies to use in solving different kinds of logical problems (Lee, 1985). Junior high and high school students, and adults as well, often apply formal operational thought to topics about which they have a great deal of knowledge, yet think "concretely" about topics with which they are unfamiliar (DeLisi & Staudt, 1980; Girotto & Light, 1993; M. C. Linn, Clement, Pulos, & Sullivan, 1989; Pulos & Linn, 1981; Schliemann & Carraher, 1993).

As an illustration of how knowledge affects formal operational thinking, consider the fishing pond in Figure 2–4. In a study by Pulos and Linn (1981), thirteen-year-old students were shown a similar picture and told, "These four children go fishing every week, and one child, Herb, always catches the most fish. The other children wonder why." If you look at the picture, it is obvious that Herb is different from the three other children in several ways, including the kind of bait he uses, the length of his fishing rod, and the place where he is sitting. Students who were avid fishermen more effectively separated and controlled variables for this situation than they did for the pendulum problem I described earlier, whereas the reverse was true for nonfishermen (Pulos & Linn, 1981).

Piaget Reconsidered

Findings such as those just described indicate that Piaget's stages will not always be accurate descriptions of our own students' logical thinking capabilities. Nevertheless, by presenting a variety of Piagetian tasks involving either concrete or formal operational thinking skills and observing students' responses to such tasks, we can gain valuable insights about how many of our students think and reason. We can then tailor our classroom curriculum and instructional materials accordingly.

Throughout the high school years, continue relating abstract and hypothetical ideas to concrete objects and observable events.

Make sure students have sufficient knowledge about a topic to think logically about it.

Considering the research findings that we have just discussed, which aspects of Piaget's theory are most viable? Which aspects are most in doubt?

Figure 2–4   What are some possible reasons that Herb is catching more fish than the others?
Based on Pulos & Linn, 1981.

Applying Piaget's Theory

Provide hands-on experiences with physical objects, especially when working with elementary school students. Allow and encourage students to explore and manipulate things.

> A kindergarten teacher and his students work with small objects (e.g., blocks, buttons, pennies) to explore such basic elements of arithmetic as conservation of number and the reversibility of addition and subtraction.

Ask students to explain their reasoning, and challenge illogical explanations.

> When learning about pendulums, students in a ninth-grade science class experiment with three variables (weight, length, and height from which the pendulum is

first dropped) to see which variables determine the rate at which a pendulum swings. When a student asserts that weight affects oscillation rate, his teacher points out that he has simultaneously varied both weight and length in his experiment.

When students show signs of egocentric thought, express confusion or explain that others think differently.

A first grader asks, "What's this?" about an object that is out of the teacher's view. The teacher responds, "What's *what?* I can't see the object you're looking at."

Be sure students have certain capabilities for mathematical and scientific reasoning (e.g., conservation of number, reversibility, proportional reasoning, separation and control of variables) before requiring them to perform tasks that depend on these capabilities.

In a unit on fractions in a seventh-grade math class, students express confusion about why ⅔, 4/6, and 8/12 are all equivalent. Before beginning a lesson about how to add and subtract fractions with different denominators—processes that require an understanding of such equivalencies—their teacher uses concrete objects (e.g., sliced pizza pies, plastic rods that can be broken into small segments) to help students understand how two different fractions can be equal.

Relate abstract and hypothetical ideas to concrete objects and observable events.

An eighth-grade science teacher illustrates the idea that heavy and light objects fall at the same speed by having students drop objects of various weights from a second-story window.

Can cognitive development truly be characterized as a series of stages? One contemporary theorist has proposed four stages that may more adequately account for current findings about children's logical thinking (Case, 1985). But many others now believe that cognitive development is more gradual and continuous, so less stagelike, than Piaget suggested. It is to this alternative perspective—to information processing theory that we turn now.

LOOKING AT COGNITIVE DEVELOPMENT FROM AN INFORMATION PROCESSING PERSPECTIVE

THINKING ABOUT WHAT YOU KNOW

Based on your many observations of children over the years, do you think children become better at paying attention as they grow older? Do you think older children remember more than younger children, or vice versa? In what ways do high school students learn and study differently from elementary school students?

Such questions reflect the approach of information processing theorists to cognitive development. Information processing theory emphasizes the development of **cognitive processes**—changes in the way in which children receive, think about, remember, and mentally modify information as they grow older. This perspective of cognitive development has evolved primarily within the last three decades, and its impact is just beginning to be seen in educational settings.

Information processing theorists reject Piaget's notion of discrete developmental stages. Instead, they believe that children's cognitive processes and abilities develop through more steady and gradual *trends;* for example, they propose that children learn faster, remember more, and handle increasingly complex tasks as they grow (Flavell, 1985; Gelman & Baillargeon, 1983; Perlmutter, 1984; Rosser, 1994; Siegler, 1986, 1994). Here are four general trends that we see:

- More focused attention
- More effective learning strategies
- An increasing knowledge base
- Development of metacognition

More Focused Attention

We see two trends in cognitive development related to children's attention and its impact on learning:

- Children become less distractible as they grow older.
- Children's learning becomes increasingly a function of what they actually intend to learn.

Decrease in Distractibility

Young children's attention often moves quickly from one thing to another, and it is easily drawn to objects and events unrelated to whatever they are supposed to be doing. But as they develop, children become better able to focus their attention on a particular task and keep it there, and they are less distracted by irrelevant occurrences (A. T. Higgins & Turnure, 1984; Lane & Pearson, 1982). For example, in one experiment (A. T. Higgins & Turnure, 1984), children at several grade levels were given a difficult learning task. Some children worked on the task in a quiet room, others worked in a room with a little background noise, and still others worked with a great deal of background noise. Preschool and second-grade children learned most quickly under the quiet conditions and most slowly under the very noisy conditions. But sixth graders were able to learn just as easily in the noisy room as in the quiet room. Apparently, the older children could ignore the noise, whereas the younger children could not.

Increasing Influence of the Intention to Learn

Complete the following exercise before you read further.

 EXPERIENCING FIRSTHAND
Six Cards

Look at the six cards below. Try to remember the *colors* of the cards and the order in which each color appears. Study them for about thirty seconds and then cover them with your hand.

 Keep unnecessary distractions to a minimum, especially for young children.

As they grow older, children become better able to focus their attention on a particular task and keep it there.

Now that you have covered the six cards, answer these questions:

- In which spot is the orange card? the green card? the purple card? the blue card?
- Where is the cake? the flowers? the guitar? the pair of scissors?

(Modeled after a task used by Maccoby & Hagen, 1965)

How accurately did you remember the colors of the cards? How accurately did you remember the objects pictured on the cards? If you are like most adults, then you had better success remembering what you intended to learn (the colors) than what you did *not* intend to learn (the objects).

Tell your students what you expect them to learn.

Perhaps because of their distractibility, younger children often remember many things unrelated to the task at hand (J. W. Hagen & Stanovich, 1977). For example, when students in Grades 1 through 7 were asked to perform a series of tasks similar to the one I just described, older students remembered the background colors more accurately than younger students. The older students were no better than younger ones at remembering the objects pictured on the cards, however; in fact, the oldest group in the study remembered the *fewest* number of objects (Maccoby & Hagen, 1965). Older children, then, are better at learning and remembering the things they *intend* to learn; they are not necessarily better at learning irrelevant information.

More Effective Learning Strategies

As they grow, children develop increasingly more effective methods of learning and remembering information. Preschoolers often recognize the need to remember something but seem to have little idea of how to go about learning it, apart from looking or pointing at it (Kail, 1990; Wellman, 1988). But as they progress through the elementary and secondary school grades, children develop a number of **learning strategies**—specific methods of learning information—that help them learn. Let's look at three strategies that appear during the school years:

- Rehearsal
- Organization
- Elaboration

Model rehearsal for elementary students.

Rehearsal

What do you do if you need to remember a telephone number for a few minutes? Do you repeat it to yourself over and over again as a way of keeping it in your memory until you dial it? This process of **rehearsal** is rare in kindergarten children but increases in frequency throughout the elementary school years (Gathercole & Hitch, 1993; Kail, 1990; Longstreth, Madigan, Pan, & Alcorn, 1989; Siegler, 1994; Siegler & Richards, 1982).

Organization

Before you read further, try the short learning exercise below.

■ EXPERIENCING FIRSTHAND
Mental Maneuver

Read the twelve words below *one time only*. Then cover up the page and write the words down in the order that they come to mind.

daisy	apple	dandelion
hammer	pear	wrench
tulip	pliers	peach
banana	rose	saw ■

In what order did you remember the words? Did you recall them in the same order that they appeared, or did you rearrange them somehow? If you are like most people, then you grouped the words into three categories—flowers, tools, and fruit—and remembered one category at a time. In other words, you imposed **organization** on the information.

Research consistently shows that organized information is learned more easily and remembered more completely than unorganized information (e.g., Bower, Clark, Lesgold, & Winzenz, 1969). As children grow older, they are more and more likely to organize the information they receive. This tendency to organize information begins in early childhood and continues to develop well into the high school years (Siegler, 1986; Siegler & Richards, 1982).

Show students how they can organize new material.

Elaboration

If I tell you that I live in Colorado, you will probably conclude that I live in or near the Rocky Mountains. You might also infer that perhaps I do a lot of skiing, hiking, or camping. In this situation, you are learning more than the information I actually gave you; you are also learning some information that you yourself supplied. This process of **elaboration**—adding additional ideas to new information based on what you already know—clearly facilitates learning and memory, sometimes quite dramatically (e.g., B. S. Stein & Bransford, 1979).

As a learning strategy, elaboration appears relatively late in child development (usually around puberty) and gradually increases throughout the teenage years (Siegler, 1986). Even in high school, however, it is primarily high-ability students who use their existing knowledge to help themselves learn new information. Lower-ability high school students are much less likely to use elaboration strategies as an aid to learning (Pressley, 1982).

Earlier, we encountered the process of *construction* in our discussion of Piaget's basic assumptions. We find the same process here as well. Both organization and elaboration are *constructive* in nature: you combine new information with things you've previously learned to construct new knowledge that is uniquely your own.

Encourage students to elaborate on new material—to expand on it using things they already know.

We will look at the processes of rehearsal, organization, and elaboration more closely in Chapter 6.

As children grow older, they show an increasing tendency to rehearse, organize, and elaborate on information.

An Increasing Knowledge Base

Children's knowledge of specific topics and of the world in general—their **knowledge base**—changes in at least two ways as they develop:

- The amount of knowledge they have increases.

- Their knowledge base becomes increasingly integrated.

Increase in the Amount of Knowledge

There is no question that children acquire more and more information as they grow older. This increasing knowledge base is one reason why older children learn new things more easily: They have more existing knowledge to help them understand and elaborate on new events (Flavell, 1985; Halford, 1989; Kail, 1990). Consider the case of an Eskimo man named Tor as an example.

■ **EXPERIENCING FIRSTHAND**
Tor of the Targa

Tor, a young man of the Targa tribe, was out hunting in the ancient hunting territory of his people. He had been away from his village for many days. The weather was bad and he had not yet managed to locate his prey. Because of the extreme temperature he knew he must soon return but it was a matter of honor among his people to track and kill the prey single-handed. Only when this was achieved could a boy be considered a man. Those who failed were made to eat and keep company with the old men and the women until they could accomplish this task.

Suddenly, in the distance, Tor could make out the outline of a possible prey. It was alone and not too much bigger than Tor, who could take him single-handed. But as he drew nearer, a hunter from a neighboring tribe came into view, also stalking the prey. The intruder was older than Tor and had around his neck evidence of his past success at the hunt. "Yes," thought Tor, "he is truly a man." Tor was undecided. Should he challenge the intruder or return home empty handed? To return would mean bitter defeat. The other young men of the tribe would laugh at his failure. He decided to creep up on the intruder and wait his chance. (A. L. Brown, Smiley, Day, Townsend, & Lawton, 1977, p. 1460)

- On what kind of terrain was Tor hunting?

- What was the weather like?

- What kind of prey might Tor have been stalking?

You probably used your knowledge about Eskimos (or Inuits) to speculate that Tor was hunting polar bears or seals on snow and ice, possibly in freezing temperatures or a bad blizzard. But notice that the story itself didn't tell you any of these things; you had to *infer* them. Like you, older children often know a great deal about how Eskimos live and can use that information to help them understand and remember (to elaborate on) this very ambiguous story about Tor. Younger children are less likely to make connections between a new situation and what they already know (A. L. Brown et al., 1977).

The more information children have—the larger their knowledge base—the more easily they can remember new information. This is one reason why adults usually learn information more quickly than children. When the tables are turned—when children have more information than adults—then children are often the more effective learners (Chi, 1978; Rabinowitz & Glaser, 1985). For example, when my son Alex and I used to read books about lizards together, Alex always remembered more than I because he was a self-proclaimed "lizard expert," and I myself knew very little about reptiles of any sort.

Might you see better performance in "low ability" students if you encourage them to work with a topic they know a lot about?

Increasing Integration of the Knowledge Base

Remember, older children are more likely to organize information as they learn it. They are also more likely to make connections between new information and the things they already know. Not surprisingly, then, children's knowledge becomes increasingly better integrated as they grow older. The knowledge base of older children includes many associations and interrelationships among concepts and ideas (Flavell, 1985). In contrast, the knowledge base of younger children includes more separate, isolated facts not connected with one another. This difference may be one reason why older children can think more logically and draw inferences more readily: Their information is better integrated and interconnected.

Show students how various concepts and ideas are related to one another.

Development of Metacognition

As an adult with many years of formal education behind you, you have probably learned a great deal about how you think and learn. For example, you may have learned that you cannot absorb everything in a textbook the first time you read it. You may also have learned that you remember information better when you elaborate on it on the basis of what you already know, rather than when you simply repeat it over and over again in a meaningless fashion.

The term **metacognition** refers both to the knowledge that people have about their own cognitive processes and to their intentional use of certain cognitive processes to facilitate learning and memory. As children develop, their metacognitive knowledge and skills improve in a number of ways, including these:

- Children become increasingly aware of the limitations of their memories.

- Children become more knowledgeable about effective learning strategies.

- Children become increasingly able to identify the things they do and do not know.

Give practice in memory tasks so that students begin to get a sense of how much they can reasonably learn and remember within a certain period of time.

Increasing Awareness of the Limitations of Memory

Young children tend to be overly optimistic about how much they can remember. As they grow older and encounter many new learning tasks, they begin to discover that their memories are not perfect—that they can't remember everything they see or hear.

Let's consider an experiment with elementary school children (Flavell, Friedrichs, & Hoyt, 1970) as an example. Children in four age-groups (ranging from preschool to fourth grade) were shown strips of paper with pictures of one to ten objects. The children were asked to predict how many of the objects they could remember over a short period of time. The average predictions of each age-group and the average number of objects they actually *did* remember were as follows:

Age-Group	Predicted Number	Actual Number
Preschool	7.2	3.5
Kindergarten	8.0	3.6
Grade 2	6.0	4.4
Grade 4	6.1	5.5

Can you recall an occasion when you were overly optimistic about how much you would be able to remember?

Notice how all four age-groups predicted that they would remember more objects than they actually could. But the older children were more realistic about the limitations of their memories than the younger ones. The kindergartners predicted they would remember eight objects, but they actually remembered fewer than four!

Increasing Knowledge About Effective Learning Strategies

As I mentioned earlier, children show greater use of such learning strategies as rehearsal, organization, and elaboration as they develop. With experience, they also become increasingly aware of which strategies are effective in different situations (Flavell, 1985; Siegler, 1986; E. J. Short, Schatschneider, & Friebert, 1993; Wellman, 1985). For example, consider the simple idea that, when you don't learn something the first time you try, you need to study it again. This is a strategy that eight-year-olds use, but six-year-olds do not (Masur, McIntyre, & Flavell, 1973). In a similar way, tenth graders are more aware than eighth graders of the advantages of using elaboration to learn new information (Waters, 1982). Even so, many students of all ages (college students included) seem relatively uninformed about which learning strategies work most effectively in different situations (e.g., Knight, 1988; Ormrod & Jenkins, 1989; Waters, 1982).

Suggest possible strategies that students might use as they study.

As we give our students new learning tasks, we should also give them ideas about possible learning strategies they might use to approach those tasks. It's not enough for us to present new material and hope that our students will know how to study and learn it (e.g., John-Steiner & Souberman, 1978). Many students, even some in the high school grades, are relatively unaware of how best to learn new information and tackle new problems. Rather than leave the development of cognitive and metacognitive skills up to chance, we can provide instruction and guidance in the use of effective strategies. We will consider some specific suggestions for doing so when we discuss metacognition at length in Chapter 8.

Younger students tend to overestimate how much they can remember, whereas older students know the limitations of their memories.

Increasing Awareness of One's Own Knowledge

Children become increasingly more aware of when they actually know something. Young children (e.g., those in the early elementary grades) often think they know or understand something before they actually do. As a result, they don't study classroom material as much as they should, and they often don't ask questions when they receive incomplete or confusing information (Flavell et al., 1970; Markman, 1977).

Even high school and college students sometimes have difficulty assessing their own knowledge accurately. For example, they often think they can spell words they actually cannot spell (P. A. Adams & Adams, 1960; Ormrod & Wagner, 1987). And they often overestimate how well they will perform on an exam (Horgan, 1990). My own students occasionally come to my office expressing frustration about doing poorly on an exam. "I knew the material so well!" they tell me. But when we sit down and begin to talk about the material covered in the exam, it usually becomes clear that although they *thought* they had learned the material well, in fact, they have only a very vague understanding of some ideas and an incorrect understanding of others.

As teachers, we must keep in mind that children of all ages (younger ones especially) are often less efficient learners than adults. A variety of factors that affect children's ability to learn—such factors as attention, intention to learn, prior knowledge, and the awareness and use of effective learning strategies—develop gradually throughout the school years. We cannot expect that school-age children will always learn as quickly as we adults do, or even in the same way that we do.

Exactly how do people become more effective information processors? Lev Vygotsky has proposed that cognitive development (including the development of mental processes) occurs largely as a result of children's interactions with other people; in other words, it occurs within a social, interpersonal context.

Can you remember a time when you performed poorly on a test because you didn't know class material as well as you thought you did?

Provide opportunities for students to test themselves to find out what they do and do not know.

LOOKING AT COGNITIVE DEVELOPMENT FROM VYGOTSKY'S PERSPECTIVE

The Russian psychologist Lev Vygotsky conducted many studies of children's thinking during the 1920s and early 1930s. Yet the significance and usefulness of Vygotsky's work was not fully appreciated by Western psychologists until his writings were translated into English (Vygotsky, 1962, 1978, 1981, 1987).

In the following pages, we will focus on three significant contributions that Vygotsky has made to our understanding of cognitive development:

- The importance of social interaction for cognitive development
- The concept of *scaffolding*
- The interrelationship between language and thought

Social Interaction and the Zone of Proximal Development

Within the past ten years, many prominent psychologists (including many information processing theorists) have rediscovered a principle Vygotsky proposed more than sixty years ago—that children's cognitive development is facilitated and enhanced through their interactions with more advanced and capable individuals such as parents and teachers (A. L. Brown & Reeve, 1987; Davydov, 1995; Diaz, 1990; Feuerstein, 1990; Kozulin & Presseisen, 1995; Rogoff, 1990; Wertsch, 1985; Wozniak, 1987).

According to Vygotsky, we can best understand and describe children's cognitive capabilities when we look at two aspects of their development simultaneously. First, we can determine the extent to which children can perform tasks *independently;* this is their **actual developmental level.** Second, we can determine the extent to which they can perform tasks *with the assistance of a more competent individual;* this is their **level of potential development.**

Children can typically do more difficult things in collaboration with adults than they can do on their own. For example, a child just learning how to use a baseball bat can hit a baseball more successfully when an adult is present to guide her swing. A child can play more difficult piano pieces when an adult helps him locate some of the notes on the keyboard. A student may be able to read more complex prose within a reading group at school than he is likely to read independently at home. And notice how a student who cannot solve division problems with remainders on her own begins to learn the correct procedure through an interaction with her teacher:

Teacher: [*writes 6)44 on the board*] 44 divided by 6. What number times 6 is close to 44?

Child: 6.

Teacher: What's 6 times 6? [*writes 6*]

Child: 36.

Teacher: 36. Can you get one that's any closer? [*erasing the 6*]

Child: 8.

Teacher: What's 6 times 8?

Child: 64 . . . 48.

Teacher: 48. Too big. Can you think of something . . . ?

Child: 6 times 7 is 42. (Pettito, 1985, p. 251)

The range of tasks that children cannot yet perform independently but *can* perform with the help and guidance of others is known as the **zone of proximal development (ZPD).** A child's zone of proximal development includes learning and problem-solving abilities that are just beginning to develop—abilities that are in an immature, embryonic form. Vygotsky proposed that children learn very little from performing tasks they can already do independently. Instead, they develop primarily by attempting tasks within their ZPD—those they can accomplish only in collaboration with a more competent individual.

To promote our students' cognitive development, then, we should present some classroom tasks and assignments they can perform successfully only with assistance—that is, tasks within each student's zone of proximal development. Tasks that students can perform on their own—those within their actual developmental level—may be insufficiently challenging to promote cognitive growth. Students with different zones of proximal development will need different tasks and assignments—a strong case for providing as much individualized instruction as we reasonably can.

Importance of Scaffolding

When adults and other skilled individuals assist children in performing difficult tasks, they often use a technique called **scaffolding** to support the children in their efforts. To understand what we mean here, let's first think about how scaffolding is used in the construction industry. When erecting a new building, a builder will sometimes construct an external structure—a *scaffold*—around the building. This scaffold provides support for the workers (a place where they can stand) until the building itself is strong enough to support them. As the building gains stability, the scaffold becomes less necessary and is gradually removed.

In much the same way, an adult guiding a child through a new task may also provide an initial scaffold to support the child's early efforts in that task. In the teacher-child dialogue about division that we saw earlier, the teacher provided clues about how to proceed, such as searching for the multiple of 6 closest to but still less than 44. Similarly, adults provide scaffolding when they give hints about how to approach a difficult problem, when they physically guide a baseball swing, when they break down a complex task (e.g., driving a car) into smaller, easier steps, and when they show a child how to measure a half cup of margarine as he learns to bake cookies. As children become more adept at performing tasks, adult guidance is gradually phased out, and the children are eventually performing those tasks on their own.

As teachers, we should provide sufficient support (scaffolding) to enable our students to perform challenging tasks successfully; we can then gradually withdraw support as the students become more skilled. Depending on the task and the particular student, we can provide a variety of support mechanisms to help students master tasks within their zone of proximal development. Here are some examples of what we might do in different situations:

- Work with students to develop a plan for dealing with a new task.

- Demonstrate the proper performance of the task in a way that students can easily imitate.

- Divide a complex task into several smaller, simpler tasks.

- Provide structure or guidelines regarding how the task should be accomplished.

- Ask questions that get students thinking in appropriate ways about the task.

- Keep student attention focused on the relevant aspects of the task.

- Keep students motivated to complete the task.

Present some tasks that students can perform successfully only with assistance.

Pair students at different grade levels or classmates with different abilities, letting more advanced students help their partners perform tasks within the ZPD.

What task have you recently performed that was in your zone of proximal development? Who scaffolded your efforts so that you could successfully complete it?

Provide sufficient support (scaffolding) to enable students to perform challenging tasks successfully; gradually withdraw the support as they become more skilled.

Occasionally perform a difficult task in partnership with students. Provide ideas and guidance about how students can learn and think about (how they can mentally process) challenging new tasks.

Teacher scaffolding helps students perform tasks that will maximally promote cognitive development (tasks within their ZPD).

- Remind students what their goal is in performing the task (e.g., what a problem solution should look like). (Diaz, 1990; Gallimore & Tharp, 1990; Rogoff, 1990; Rosenshine & Meister, 1992; D. Wood, Bruner, & Ross, 1976)

As students develop increasing competence, we can gradually withdraw these support mechanisms, eventually allowing students to perform the task independently. In a manner of speaking, when we remove such scaffolding, we allow and encourage students to stand on their own two feet.

Scaffolding in the classroom sometime takes the form of a **cognitive apprenticeship** (J. S. Brown, Collins, & Duguid, 1989; Griffin & Griffin, 1994; Rogoff, 1990): A student and a teacher work together to accomplish a challenging task or solve a difficult problem (perhaps conducting a complex science experiment, solving a "brainteaser" mathematical problem, or translating a difficult passage from German to English). In the process of talking about various aspects of the task or problem, the student and the teacher together analyze the situation and develop the best approach to take, and the teacher models effective ways of thinking about and mentally processing the situation. Once again, we have an instance of *construction:* A cognitive apprenticeship involves two people jointly constructing a means of tackling a task or problem. The idea that two or more people work together to construct meaning and understanding is known as **social constructivism,** a perspective we will explore in more detail in Chapter 7.

With the support and guidance of individuals more competent than themselves, children not only develop increasing skill at various tasks, but they may also develop more sophisticated thought processes (A. L. Brown & Reeve, 1987; Diaz, 1990; Rogoff, 1990; Vygotsky, 1978; Wertsch, 1985). Consider these scenarios as examples of how children might develop new cognitive and metacognitive skills through their interactions with adults:

Meili tells her father, "I need to bring an egg carton to school for an art project." Dad finds an empty one for her and asks, "Hmmm, how are we going to make sure you remember to take it to school tomorrow?" Together, Meili and her father consider various strategies for remembering to take the egg carton in the morning and finally decide that attaching a note to the front of Meili's coat will be a surefire method. Through this discussion, Meili learns that her memory is not always reliable and that external reminders can be helpful.

Mario has been having trouble learning his weekly list of spelling words. "I can spell them all correctly on Thursday night," he tells his teacher, "but I always forget some of them by the test on Friday morning." Together, Mario and his teacher develop a new study strategy: Mario will begin to study and test himself on the words on Monday night, rather than on Thursday, and he will continue to study them every night until he has spelled each word correctly two nights in a row. Using this strategy, Mario improves considerably on his Friday spelling tests, and he has learned a valuable lesson about learning: Studying something once isn't always enough.

Students in a fourth-grade reading group read a short passage about snakes. Their teacher asks, "Who can think of a good title that summarizes what this passage is about?" After hearing

Using Challenging Tasks to Promote Cognitive Development

Model effective learning and study strategies and encourage students to use such strategies themselves.

> A chemistry teacher tells her students, "Learning the symbols for all the elements is going to take some time. Some, like H for hydrogen and O for oxygen, are easy. But others, like K for potassium and Na for sodium, are more challenging. Let's take five new symbols each day and develop a strategy to help ourselves remember each one."

Provide opportunities for students to test their learning efforts—to find out what they do and don't know.

> A social studies teacher has his students read a textbook chapter at home and then gives them a nongraded quiz to help them identify parts of the chapter they may need to read again.

Present some tasks that students can perform successfully only with assistance.

> An elementary teacher assigns students their first research paper, knowing that she will have to give them a great deal of guidance as they work on it.

Provide sufficient support (scaffolding) to enable students to perform challenging tasks successfully; gradually withdraw the support as they become more proficient.

> A physical education teacher begins a lesson on tumbling by demonstrating front and back somersaults in slow motion and physically guiding his students through the correct movements. As the students become more skillful, he stands back from the mat and gives verbal feedback about how to improve.

Encourage students to talk themselves through difficult tasks.

> As her students work on complex mathematical equations such as this one,

$$x = \frac{2(4 \times 9)^2}{6} + 3,$$

> a mathematics teacher gives students a mnemonic (*"Please excuse my dear Aunt Sally"*) they can recite to help them remember the order in which various operations should be performed (*p*arentheses, *e*xponents, *m*ultiplication, *d*ivision, *a*ddition, *s*ubtraction).

several good suggestions, the teacher then asks, "The author says that snakes are helpful to farmers. What evidence does she give to support her statement?" Through such questions as these, the teacher is helping students develop skills essential in reading comprehension—skills such as summarizing and drawing inferences.

One effective method for scaffolding reading comprehension skills can be found in *reciprocal teaching,* an approach that we will consider in Chapter 12.

In all three of these situations, language plays an important role in the development of thinking skills: Children and adults *talk* about ways of thinking. But according to Vygotsky, language plays an even more central role in cognitive development, as we shall see now.

Interdependence of Thought and Language

THINKING ABOUT WHAT YOU KNOW

Can you think of times when you talk to *yourself,* rather than to someone else? For example, do you find it easier to perform a difficult task by talking your way through it—perhaps when you are first learning to use a computer, trying to perform a complicated dance step, or beginning to drive a car with a clutch and a stick shift?

Earlier in the chapter, we considered Piaget's observation that young children often say things without taking into account the perspective of their listeners. Vygotsky proposed that such egocentric speech is better understood as "talking to oneself," rather than as talking to someone else. He pointed out that people are more likely to talk to themselves when they are performing difficult or frustrating tasks. Talking aloud seems to help guide and direct them as they attempt to perform such tasks.

According to Vygotsky, thought and language are separate functions for infants and young toddlers. In these early years, thinking occurs independently of language, and when language appears, it is first used primarily as a means of communication, rather than as a mechanism of thought. But sometime around two years of age, thought and language become intertwined: Children begin to express their thoughts when they speak, and they begin to think in terms of words. At this point, we begin to see **self-talk** (sometimes called **private speech**)—the talking to oneself that Piaget interpreted as egocentric speech. Gradually, this self-talk becomes **inner speech,** wherein children talk to themselves mentally rather than orally. According to Vygotsky, both self-talk and inner speech have a similar purpose: Children guide and direct their own behaviors in much the same way that adults have previously guided them. In a sense, they begin to provide their *own* scaffolding.

Encourage students to talk themselves through new and difficult tasks.

COMPARING PIAGET, INFORMATION PROCESSING, AND VYGOTSKY

Have you already noticed similarities among the three theories of cognitive development?

At first glance, the three views of cognitive development we have examined in this chapter seem very different. For example, Piaget's theory portrays cognitive development as a sequence of relatively discrete stages, each with its own set of abilities and limitations. In contrast, information processing theorists describe cognitive development in terms of gradual changes in cognitive processes and metacognitive awareness. Vygotsky's approach focuses more on the social conditions that facilitate cognitive development than on changes in children's thinking per se.

Despite such differences, several common themes run through at least two of the theories, and sometimes through all three. From these commonalities, we can formulate several general principles of cognitive development:

- Children actively construct their knowledge.

- Cognitive development involves relating new information to prior knowledge.

- Children's knowledge and cognitive processes become increasingly better organized and integrated.

- Social interaction is essential for cognitive development.

- A child's readiness for a particular task determines the extent to which that task promotes cognitive development.

- Children often think in qualitatively different ways at different age levels.

- Cognitive development and linguistic development are closely intertwined.

Table 2–4 presents a summary of these principles and their educational implications. Let's look briefly at each principle.

Active Construction of Knowledge

All three perspectives portray children, not as passive receptacles for incoming information, but as active, constructive processors of that information. Piaget described cognitive development as a process of constructing one's own understanding of the world. Information processing theorists have proposed that children use such processes as organization and elaboration to learn and remember; both of these cognitive processes involve using prior knowledge to construct a meaningful understanding of new information. Vygotsky believed that children actively talk themselves through difficult tasks and that children and adults often work collaboratively to construct a viable approach to a difficult task.

Relating New Information to Prior Knowledge

Piaget proposed that children adapt to their world through the two processes of assimilation and accommodation. Both processes involve relating new experiences to previously learned information—in one case assimilating a new event into an existing scheme, and in the other case either modifying a scheme or developing a new one to accommodate information that doesn't quite "fit" with current understandings of the world. Information processing theorists stress the importance of prior knowledge as well; for example, the more children already know about the world, the greater is their ability to understand, elaborate on, and remember new information. From both perspectives, prior learning provides the foundation upon which new learning builds.

Organization and Integration of Information

Both Piaget and information processing theorists characterize children's knowledge and cognitive processes as becoming increasingly better organized and integrated over time. To illustrate this idea within Piaget's perspective, when children move from the preoperational stage to concrete operations, they become better able to combine two ideas together to help them make logical decisions—for example, to recognize that beads can be both brown and wooden or to realize that one glass contains the same

Table 2–4   *General Principles of Cognitive Development*

PRINCIPLE	EXAMPLE	EDUCATIONAL IMPLICATON
Children actively construct their knowledge.	When Sarah has her first opportunity to use a microscope, she puts many different objects under it to see how they appear.	Provide opportunities for students to experiment with new objects and to experience new events.
Cognitive development involves relating new information to prior knowledge.	When Saori compares the parliamentary system of Great Britain with that of the United States, she realizes that they are alike in some ways but quite different in others.	Make sure students have prior knowledge and experiences to which they can relate new material.
Children's knowledge and cognitive processes become increasingly better organized and integrated.	Samuel learns that dogs, cats, and horses are all mammals and that mammals, birds, and fish are all vertebrates.	Help students discover relationships among concepts and ideas.
Social interaction is essential for cognitive development.	In conversations with her classmates, Shelley is surprised to learn that not all families celebrate Christmas.	Provide opportunities for students to share opinions, perspectives, and beliefs.
A child's readiness for a particular task determines the extent to which that task promotes cognitive development.	Sandy has the highest mathematics achievement in her fifth-grade class, yet even she seems unable to understand her teacher's explanation of the abstract concept π (*pi*).	Remember that some students may not yet be capable of understanding certain ideas or accomplishing certain tasks; gear classroom tasks and assignments to their developmental level.
Children often think in qualitatively different ways at different age levels.	As a third grader, Seth tries to remember ideas presented in class simply by repeating them to himself over and over. But by the time he reaches high school, he learns ideas more easily by interpreting them within the context of things he already knows.	Ask students to describe how they are thinking about information and to explain the logic they are using when drawing conclusions.
Language and cognition are closely intertwined.	Suhila talks to herself the first time she constructs a parallel circuit in physics class; this is a complicated task, and she wants to make sure she remembers all the steps.	Help students increase their vocabulary, and promote reading, writing, and speaking skills.

amount of water as a taller but also narrower glass. Likewise, information processing theorists emphasize the importance of organizing information and have observed that children show a greater tendency to organize information as they grow older.

Importance of Social Interaction

Both Piaget and Vygotsky proposed that social interaction is critical for cognitive development. Piaget suggested that other people, especially peers, help preoperational children to shed their egocentric view of the world and to discover that their own perspectives are not always shared by others. Vygotsky stressed that working cooperatively on tasks and problems with more advanced individuals (e.g, parents, teachers) enables children to develop more sophisticated strategies and thought processes.

Readiness

In all three perspectives, children's readiness for different tasks determines the extent to which those tasks promote learning and cognitive development. Piaget argued that children can benefit from certain experiences only when they begin to make the transition into a stage that allows them to deal with and conceptualize those experiences appropriately (e.g., they benefit from hearing abstract ideas only as they begin to make the transition into formal operations). Vygotsky characterized readiness in terms of the zone of proximal development: Children benefit from tasks they can perform only with the assistance of a more skilled person. From an information processing perspective, students can learn from new experiences only when they have sufficient prior knowledge with which to interpret those experiences.

Qualitative Differences in Thought Processes

Both Piaget and information processing theorists have suggested that children often think differently at different age levels. Piaget portrayed these differences in terms of four different stages of thought and reasoning capabilities. Information processing theorists have instead proposed that young children lack many of the learning strategies (e.g., organization, elaboration) and metacognitive sophistication (e.g., knowing *when* they know something) that adolescents possess. Either way, we must remember that children don't always think the same way that we, as adults, think.

Relationship of Language to Cognitive Development

All three perspectives acknowledge that the development of cognitive abilities and the development of language are closely intertwined. Cognitive development is critical for the development of language: Children can only talk and write about things they can first *think* about. Yet language is equally critical for children's cognitive development: It promotes their social interaction, provides a set of symbols through which they can mentally represent their world, helps them make associations among various pieces of information, and enables them to internalize the problem-solving strategies that adults verbalize. Let's look more closely at the changes in children's language that occur during the school years.

Children begin using recognizable words sometime around their first birthday, and they are putting these words together by their second birthday. During their preschool years, they become capable of forming increasingly longer and more complex sentences. By the time they begin school, at five or six years of age, they use language that seems adultlike in many respects (Dale, 1976). Yet students' language capabilities continue to develop and mature throughout the school years. Numerous changes occur in both **receptive language**—students' ability to understand what they hear and read—and **expressive language**—their ability to communicate effectively through speaking and writing. In the next few pages, we will examine several aspects of linguistic development and their implications for us as teachers:

- Vocabulary
- Syntax
- Listening and reading comprehension
- Oral and written communication skills

We will also look at the issue of learning a second language and consider what happens when children are bilingual—when they know two languages instead of one.

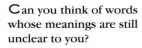

Before you read further, can you predict some of the things that I might say about development in each of these areas?

Development of Vocabulary

One obvious change in students' language during the school years is the increase in their vocabulary. It has been estimated that the average high school graduate knows the meanings of at least 80,000 words (Nippold, 1988). Children learn some words through direct vocabulary instruction at school, but they probably learn many more by inferring meaning from the context in which the words are heard or read (Nippold, 1988).

Can you think of words whose meanings are still unclear to you?

Students' knowledge of word meanings—their knowledge of **semantics**—is not always an all-or-none thing. In many cases, their early understanding of a word's meaning is somewhat vague and "fuzzy"; they have a general idea of what the word means but define it imprecisely and sometimes use it incorrectly. Through repeated encounters with words in different contexts and through direct feedback when they use words incorrectly, students continue to refine their understandings of what different words mean.

One common error that students make in their understanding of words is **undergeneralization:** The meanings they attach to some words are too restricted, leaving out some situations to which those words apply. For example, I once asked my son Jeff, then six years old, to tell me what an *animal* is. He gave me this definition:

> It has a head, tail, feet, paws, eyes, noses, ears, lots of hair.

Like Jeff, young elementary school children often restrict their meaning of *animal* primarily to mammals, such as dogs and horses, and insist that fish, birds, and insects are *not* animals (Saltz, 1971).

Another frequent error is **overgeneralization:** Word meanings are too broad, and so words are applied to situations in which they're not appropriate. For example, when

I asked Jeff to give me some examples of insects, he included black widow spiders in his list. Jeff overgeneralized: All insects have six legs, so spiders, which are eight-legged, do not qualify.

Sometimes even common words have subtleties that children don't master until the upper elementary grades or later. For example, nine-year-old children sometimes confuse situations in which they should use the articles *a* and *the* (Reich, 1986). Children in the upper elementary and junior high grades have trouble with many connectives—such words as *but, although, yet, however,* and *unless* (Nippold, 1988). As an illustration, do the following exercise.

◼ EXPERIENCING FIRSTHAND
Using Connectives

In each of the following pairs of sentences, identify the one that makes more sense:

Jimmie went to school, but he felt sick.
Jimmie went to school, but he felt fine.

The meal was good, although the pie was bad.
The meal was good, although the pie was good.

Even twelve-year-olds have trouble identifying the correct sentence in pairs like these, reflecting only a vague understanding of the connectives *but* and *although* (E. W. Katz & Brent, 1968). (The first sentence is the correct one in both cases.)

Such words as *but* and *although* may be particularly difficult for elementary school children because their meanings are fairly abstract. If we consider Piaget's proposal that abstract thought doesn't emerge until early adolescence, then we realize that students may not fully understand abstract words until the junior high or high school years. Young children in particular are apt to define words (even fairly abstract ones) in terms of the obvious, concrete aspects of their world (Anglin, 1977; Ausubel et al., 1978). For example, when Jeff was four, he defined *summer* as the time of year when school is out and it's hot outside; by the time he was twelve, he knew that adults define summer in terms of the earth's tilt relative to the sun—a much more abstract notion.

We can facilitate our students' semantic development by teaching vocabulary words and their definitions directly and by correcting children's misconceptions of word meanings as those misconceptions reveal themselves in students' speech. We can also encourage our students to *read, read, read:* Avid readers learn many more new words than do students who read infrequently (R. C. Anderson, Wilson, & Fielding, 1988). We will discover additional ways of teaching word meanings when we consider concept learning in Chapter 8.

Teach vocabulary words related to the various topics being studied. Look for and correct students' misconceptions of word meanings.

Development of Syntax

◼ EXPERIENCING FIRSTHAND
Four Sentences

Which of the following sentences are grammatically correct?

The flowers in the garden have grown up straight and tall.
I in garden the pick weeds nasty dare don't.
Why they not does they homework when suppose?
Why aren't you doing your homework? ◼

You undoubtedly recognized that the first and last sentences are grammatically correct and that the two middle ones are not. But *how* were you able to tell the difference? Can you describe the specific grammatical rules you used to make your decision?

The rules that we use to put words together into sentences—those rules of **syntax** that we use to determine which word combinations are grammatically correct and which are not—are incredibly complex (N. Chomsky, 1972). Children have acquired many syntactic rules by the time they enter school; nevertheless, their understanding of correct syntax continues to develop throughout the elementary school years (Reich, 1986).

Although theorists do not yet completely understand the process through which children learn syntactic rules, they are beginning to believe that language learning, including the learning of syntax, is largely a *constructive* process (e.g., Flavell, 1985). Preschool and early elementary school children typically receive little if any direct instruction about how to form sentences. Instead, they apparently construct their own set of rules through their observations of how others form sentences and through the feedback they receive in response to their own speech.

In the process of developing rules of syntax, school-age children sometimes make an error of **overregularization:** They apply syntactical rules in situations in which such rules don't apply (Cazden, 1968; Flavell, 1985; Marcus, 1996; Siegler, 1994). To illustrate, young children might add *-ed* to indicate past tense or *-s* to indicate plural when such suffixes are inappropriate (e.g., "I *goed* to the store," "I have two *feets*"). We see further evidence of incomplete syntactic development in children's responses to the complex sentences they hear. For example, children in one study (C. S. Chomsky, 1969) were shown a doll with a blindfold over its eyes and asked, "Is this doll easy to see or hard to see?" Children as old as eight had trouble interpreting the question. The following conversation with six-year-old Lisa illustrates the problem the children had:

Experimenter:	Is this doll easy to see or hard to see?
Lisa:	Hard to see.
Experimenter:	Will you make her easy to see.
Lisa:	If I can get this untied.
Experimenter:	Will you explain why she was hard to see.
Lisa:	(To doll) Because you had a blindfold over your eyes.
Experimenter:	And what did you do?
Lisa:	I took it off. (from C. S. Chomsky, 1969, p. 30)

R ecognize that some syntax errors may be normal for the age-group.

C ontinue instruction and practice in grammar and composition throughout the high school years.

Young children may also have difficulty interpreting passive sentences (e.g., "The boy is pushed by the girl") and those that contain two or more clauses ("The dog stands on the horse that the giraffe jumps over") (Karmiloff-Smith, 1979; Sheldon, 1974).

Students' knowledge of syntax and grammar continues to develop even at the secondary level (e.g., Perera, 1986). By the time students reach high school, much syntactical development probably occurs as the result of formal language instruction, especially courses in language arts, English composition, and foreign language. Therefore, we should continue instruction and practice in grammar and composition throughout the high school years. Our students are more likely to improve their speech and writing when they have ample opportunities to express their ideas orally and on paper and when they receive direct feedback about ambiguities and grammatical errors in the things they say and write.

Development of Listening and Reading Comprehension

■ EXPERIENCING FIRSTHAND
Ambiguities in Language

Carefully read each of the following statements:

John went to the bank.

Flying planes can be dangerous.

I know more beautiful women than Miss America.

See if you can discover two possible ways of interpreting each one. (from J. R. Anderson, 1990, pp. 376–378) ■

How well do children comprehend the things they hear and read? How accurately do they assess their own comprehension of the spoken and written word? Do they recognize ambiguities and contradictions in the things they hear and read? (For example, was John going to a river bank or to a financial institution? For whom are planes dangerous—those piloting the planes or those located outside the planes? Is Miss America a beautiful woman, or does she *know* beautiful women?) Theorists are just beginning to address such questions about language comprehension, but already they have made some discoveries about how listening and reading comprehension develop over time.

For one thing, it appears that children's conception of what listening comprehension *is* changes throughout the elementary years. Children in the early elementary grades believe that they are good listeners if they simply sit quietly without interrupting the teacher. Older children (e.g., eleven-year-olds) are more likely to recognize that good listening also requires an *understanding* of what is being said (McDevitt, Spivey, Sheehan, Lennon, & Story, 1990). Elementary school children also differ in their beliefs about the course of action they should take when they don't understand something the teacher says. Many children, younger ones especially, apparently believe that it is inappropriate to ask for clarification, perhaps because they have previously been discouraged from asking questions at school or at home (McDevitt, 1990; McDevitt et al., 1990). For example, children growing up in certain cultures, including those in many Asian and Mexican American communities, may believe that initiating a

Describe "good listeners" not only as students who sit quietly and pay attention but also as students who understand and remember the things they hear.

Encourage students to ask questions when they don't understand what they are being told.

Children in the early elementary grades believe that good listening simply means sitting quietly without interrupting.

Be sure students understand the intended meanings of the messages they hear and read—perhaps by asking them to rephrase a message in their own words.

conversation with an adult is disrespectful (Delgado-Gaitan, 1994; C. A. Grant & Gomez, 1996).

Furthermore, children's comprehension of what they hear is influenced by the context in which they hear it. Using various nonverbal contextual clues, they recognize that what is said in a situation is sometimes different from what is actually meant. For example, they may interpret a statement such as "Goodness, this class is noisy today!" to mean "Be quiet" (Flavell, 1985). But unfortunately, younger children are sometimes *too* dependent on the context for determining the meaning of language, to the point where they don't listen carefully enough to understand a spoken message accurately. They may "hear" what they *think* we mean, based on their beliefs about our intentions, rather than hear what we really do mean (Donaldson, 1978). It is important, then, not only to ask students whether they understand what they hear but also to check for that understanding by asking them to rephrase a message in their own words.

In addition to the changes that we see in listening comprehension, children's reading comprehension and their ability to learn from the things they read continue to improve throughout the school years. In the primary grades, reading instruction focuses more on word recognition and basic comprehension skills than on reading as a means of learning new information. Beginning in the later elementary school years, children become increasingly able to learn new information from what they read (Chall, 1979, 1983). Elementary school children tend to take the things they read (as well as the things they hear) at face value, however, with little attempt to evaluate them critically and little sensitivity to obvious contradictions (Chall, 1979, 1983; Markman, 1979; McDevitt & Carroll, 1988). But as they move into the junior high and high school grades, students begin to recognize that different authors sometimes present different viewpoints on a single issue, and they read written material with a critical eye, rather than accept it as absolute truth. At this point, students also become more cognizant of the subtler aspects of fiction—for example, the underlying theme and symbolism of a novel (Chall, 1979, 1983). We will consider ways to promote students' reading comprehension when we explore study skills in Chapter 8 and again when we examine reciprocal teaching in our discussion of instructional methods in Chapter 12.

Students' reading comprehension skills continue to develop throughout the elementary and secondary school years.

Development of Oral and Written Communication Skills

To communicate our ideas effectively to another person, we need to consider the characteristics of the person receiving our message. For example, the person's age will affect the level of vocabulary we use, the person's prior knowledge about the subject matter will affect the starting point of our explanation, and so on. Effective communication, then, requires a speaker or writer to take the other person's perspective into account.

As we considered Piaget's theory earlier in the chapter, we discussed how the egocentrism of preoperational children may hamper their ability to communicate. Preschool children do tailor their speech somewhat to the age of the listener; for example, four-year-olds use simpler language with two-year-olds than they do with their peers (Shatz & Gelman, 1973). These children don't always consider what prior information the listener may or may not have, however. In fact, children continue to show some egocentrism in their speech throughout the elementary school years, particularly when trying to communicate complex information to someone else (Glucksberg & Krauss, 1967).

Students' written work is also plagued by a degree of egocentrism throughout the elementary school years, and sometimes during the high school years as well. As a result, students don't always detect ambiguities in their own writing; thus, they don't understand why others have trouble understanding the things they have written (E. J. Bartlett, 1982). I have found that many students in my college classes have the same difficulty. As an illustration, try this brief exercise:

◼ EXPERIENCING FIRSTHAND
An Example of Student Writing

See whether you can make sense of this paragraph from a research paper I once received from a graduate student:

> It appears to be the case that not only is note taking superior for recall immediately after lecture, but that the entire memory storage and recall process is further strengthened as time goes on when one takes notes on a lecture. And, of course, this is generally how American college students are tested. ◼

Students can develop effective communication skills only when they have opportunities to practice those skills.

Did you have trouble making sense of this paragraph? I certainly did. For example, to what is the author referring when he uses the word *this* in the second sentence? Perhaps *he* knew, but I myself didn't have the foggiest idea.

To help students shed such egocentrism in their speech and writing, we must let them know exactly when we don't understand them. For example, we can ask them to explain who or what they are talking about when they refer to people or things with which we are unfamiliar. We can express our confusion when they describe events and ideas ambiguously. And certainly we must give precise and constructive feedback about how they can communicate their ideas more clearly in their written work.

Learning a Second Language

As the adult workplace becomes increasingly international in scope, the need is greater than ever before for children to learn one or more languages in addition to their native tongue. Although it is a common belief that children lose their ability to learn language as they get older, the evidence regarding the best time to learn a second language is mixed. In general, it appears that people may learn a second language more easily as they grow older, at least in the early stages of learning the language, but that young children are more likely to learn to speak the language as a native speaker would (Carroll, 1985; Durkin, 1995; Long, 1995; Reich, 1986; Snow & Hoefnagel-Höhle, 1978).

In any case, beginning second language instruction in the early years has definite advantages. For one thing, it appears that learning a second language facilitates achievement in such other academic areas as reading, vocabulary, and grammar (Diaz, 1983; Reich, 1986). Instruction in a foreign language also sensitizes young children to the international and multicultural nature of the world in which they live. Students who learn a second language during the elementary school years express more positive attitudes toward people who speak that language, and they are more likely to enroll in foreign language classes in high school (Reich, 1986).

Judging from the data we have at the present time, there is no definitive "best" time for students to learn a second language. Students of all ages can learn a second language; it is never too early or too late to begin to teach them. To the extent that we can, we should teach foreign languages at all grade levels.

Bilingualism

A bilingual student is one who speaks two languages fluently. Some bilingual children have been raised in families in which two languages are spoken regularly. Others have lived for a time in a community where one language is spoken and then moved to a community where a different language is spoken. Still others live in a bilingual society—for example, in Canada (where both English and French are spoken), Wales (where both English and Welsh are spoken), and certain ethnic communities in the United States (where a language such as Spanish or Chinese is spoken along with English).

Research reveals some advantages to being bilingual. For example, bilingual children, when they are truly fluent in both languages, tend to perform better on tasks requiring complex cognitive functioning (e.g., on intelligence tests or on tasks requiring creativity). They also appear to have greater **metalinguistic awareness**—an ability to think about the nature of language itself (Diaz & Klingler, 1991; Garcia, 1992, 1994; Hakuta, 1990; C. E. Moran & Hakuta, 1995).

Why is it often difficult for us to detect ambiguities in our own writing?

Give students lots of practice in both oral and written communication and let them know when you don't understand what they have said or written.

Teach a second language anytime.

Promoting bilingualism. In some situations, learning a second language is essential; this is the case for non-English-speaking students whose families intend to become long-term or permanent residents of an English-speaking country. In other situations, learning a second language, though not essential, is highly desirable; this is the case for English-speaking students who may wish eventually to study or work in societies where a different language is spoken. Bilingualism has social benefits as well: In classrooms in which different students speak only one of two different languages (perhaps some speaking only English and others speaking only Spanish), increased fluency in the second language facilitates interaction among classmates.

How can we help children become fluent in a second language? Unfortunately, research on this topic is often correlational rather than experimental, making it difficult to draw firm conclusions about cause-effect relationships (Lam, 1992; Willig, 1985). Considering the limited research results that we have, it appears that the best approach to teaching a second language depends on the situation. On the one hand, for English-speaking students learning a second language while still living in their native country, it appears that total **immersion** in the second language—hearing and speaking it almost exclusively within the classroom—is the method of choice. Total immersion in a second language helps students become proficient in that language relatively quickly, and any adverse effects of such immersion on students' achievement in other areas of the curriculum appear to be short-lived (Collier, 1992; Genesee, 1985; Lindholm & Fairchild, 1990; W. P. Thomas, Collier, & Abbott, 1993).

On the other hand, for non-English-speaking students who have recently immigrated to an English-speaking country, total immersion in English may actually be detrimental to their academic progress. For these students, **bilingual education**—wherein instruction in academic subject areas is given in students' native language while they are simultaneously taught to speak and write in English—leads to higher academic achievement (e.g., in reading, mathematics, and social studies), greater self-esteem, and a better attitude toward school (García, 1995; Moll & Diaz, 1985; Snow, 1990; Willig, 1985; S. Wright & Taylor, 1995).

Why does immersion work better for some students, whereas bilingual education is more effective for others? As we discovered earlier in the chapter, language is critical for children's cognitive development, promoting social interaction and providing a symbolic means through which they can mentally represent and think about their world. We therefore need a method of teaching a second language without losing the first language in the process. In this country, English-speaking students immersed in a second language at school still have many opportunities—at home, with their friends, and in the local community and culture—to continue using and developing their English. But recent immigrants to this country often have little opportunity outside their immediate families to use their native language. If these students are taught exclusively in English, they may very well lose proficiency in one language (their native tongue) before developing proficiency in another (Willig, 1985).

Given the many advantages of second-language learning and bilingualism that we have seen, perhaps we should begin to think about promoting bilingualism in *all* students (Navarro, 1985; NCSS Task Force on Ethnic Studies Curriculum Guidelines, 1992). By doing so, we would not only promote our students' cognitive and linguistic development but also enhance communication, interaction, and interpersonal understanding among students with diverse linguistic and cultural backgrounds (Minami & Ovando, 1995).

For English-speaking students still living in an English-speaking society, provide total immersion in the second language.

For non-English-speaking students now living in an English-speaking society, teach them to speak and write in English while simultaneously providing other instruction in their native tongue.

INTO THE CLASSROOM

Facilitating Linguistic Development

Teach vocabulary related to topics being studied. Look for and correct students' misconceptions of word meanings.

> A science teacher explains and illustrates the concepts *speed* and *acceleration* and corrects students who erroneously use one term in place of the other.

Give students many opportunities to practice their receptive language skills (listening and reading). Help them learn that being good listeners and readers involves understanding and remembering as well as paying attention.

> A fourth-grade teacher invites a police officer to speak to her class about bicycle safety. Following the officer's departure, she asks her students to summarize the important things to remember when riding a bicycle.

Give students lots of practice in expressive language (speaking and writing). Provide specific and constructive feedback about how well they are communicating.

> A high school history teacher has each student give an oral report on a topic related to early American history. After each report, he speaks with the student individually, identifying parts of the report that were especially effective and providing suggestions for giving a better report the next time.

Teach a second language.

> A second-grade teacher spends a few minutes each day teaching her students some simple French vocabulary and phrases.

CONSIDERING DIVERSITY IN COGNITIVE AND LINGUISTIC DEVELOPMENT

As we noted at the beginning of the chapter, children are often similar in terms of the order in which they acquire specific cognitive and linguistic capabilities. The *rate* at which they acquire these abilities may differ considerably from one child to the next, however; as a result, we are likely to find considerable diversity in the level of development that each student has reached. From the perspective of Piaget's theory, we may see signs of both preoperational and concrete operational thinking in the early elementary grades; for example, some students may demonstrate conservation, whereas others will not. Similarly, we may find evidence of both concrete and formal operational thinking at the middle school and high school levels; for example, some students will think more abstractly than others, and students will differ in such abilities as hypothetical reasoning, separation and control of variables, and proportional thought. From an information processing perspective, we will find diversity in the learning strategies that our students use, as well as in the background knowledge and experiences from which they can draw as they try to understand and elaborate on new information. And from Vygotsky's point of view, we will inevitably have students with different zones of proximal development: The cognitive challenges necessary for optimal cognitive development will vary from one student to the next.

We will find diversity in our students' language capabilities as well. For example, they will vary considerably in the extent of their vocabulary and in their reading and writing skills. Some students may express themselves using **dialects**—forms of English characteristic of particular ethnic groups or regions of the country—other than those that we ourselves use. Differences in both receptive and expressive language will be compounded when we have students with **limited English proficiency (LEP)**. LEP students may have trouble understanding the things they are hearing and reading in the classroom, and as we noted earlier, students from some cultures may be reluctant to ask questions when they don't understand (Delgado-Gaitan, 1994; C. A. Grant & Gomez, 1996). And naturally, these students are likely to have more difficulty expressing themselves both orally and on paper.

As teachers, we must continually be aware of the specific cognitive and linguistic capabilities and weaknesses that individual students possess, and tailor instruction accordingly. For example, as we discovered in our exploration of recent research related to Piaget's theory, our students will display more advanced reasoning skills when dealing with topics with which they are familiar (e.g., avid fishermen will be more likely to separate and control variables in a "fishing" situation than in Piaget's traditional pendulum problem). Students with limited vocabularies or poor reading comprehension skills may benefit from reading simpler textbooks than those we might ordinarily assign to the age-group.

Strategies for teaching students with different dialects are presented in the discussion of ethnic differences in Chapter 4.

Keep individual students' cognitive and linguistic capabilities in mind as you plan and deliver instruction.

STUDENTS IN INCLUSIVE SETTINGS

Table 2–5 Promoting Cognitive and Linguistic Development in Students with Special Educational Needs

STUDENTS WITH SPECIAL NEEDS	CHARACTERISTICS THAT THESE STUDENTS MAY EXHIBIT	CLASSROOM STRATEGIES THAT MAY BE BENEFICIAL FOR THESE STUDENTS
Students with specific cognitive or academic deficits	Distractibility, difficulty paying and maintaining attention	Make sure you have students' attention before giving instructions or presenting information
		Keep distracting stimuli to a minimum
	Few effective learning strategies	Teach learning strategies within the context of classroom lessons
	Difficulties in receptive language (e.g., in word recognition, reading comprehension, listening comprehension)	Assign simpler reading materials Provide extra scaffolding for reading assignments (e.g., shortening assignments, identifying main ideas, having students look for answers to specific questions)
	Difficulties in expressive language (e.g., in syntax, spelling, handwriting)	Provide extra scaffolding for writing activities (e.g., giving students a specific structure to follow as they write, encouraging use of word processing programs with grammar and spelling checkers)

Table 2–5 *(continued)*

Students with Special Needs	Characteristics That These Students May Exhibit	Classroom Strategies That May Be Beneficial For These Students
Students with specific social or behavioral deficits	Lack of attention as a result of off-task behaviors (e.g., acting out, restlessness, daydreaming)	Make sure you have students' attention before giving instructions or presenting information Capture students' attention by gearing instruction toward their personal interests
Students with general delays in cognitive and social functioning	Reasoning abilities characteristic of younger children (e.g., preoperational thought in the upper elementary grades, inability to think abstractly in the secondary grades)	Present new information in a concrete, hands-on fashion
	Absence of learning strategies such as rehearsal or organization	Teach simple learning strategies (e.g., rehearsal) within the context of classroom lessons
	Less developed knowledge base to which new information can be related	Give instructions in concrete and specific terms
	Delayed language development (e.g., in vocabulary, listening comprehension, reading)	Minimize reliance on reading materials as a way of presenting new information
Students with advanced cognitive development	Appearance of formal operational thinking (e.g., abstract thought) at an earlier age	Provide opportunities through which students can explore classroom topics in greater depth or complexity
	Tendency for many regular classroom tasks to be below students' zone of proximal development	Provide opportunities for students to proceed through the curriculum at a more rapid pace
	Greater knowledge base to which new information can be related	Provide challenging tasks (e.g., higher-level reading assignments, more advanced writing assignments)
	Advanced vocabulary	
	Development of reading at an early age	
	Advanced reading comprehension ability	
	More sophisticated expressive language (speaking, writing)	

Sources: Carter & Ormrod, 1982; Cone, Wilson, Bradley, & Reese, 1985; Mercer, 1991; Morgan & Jenson, 1988; Patton, Beirne-Smith, & Payne, 1990; Patton, Payne, Kauffman, Brown, & Payne, 1987; Piirto, 1994; Pressley, 1995; Turnbull, Turnbull, Shank, & Leal, 1995.
Compiled with the assistance of Dr. Margie Garanzini-Daiber and Dr. Margaret Cohen, University of Missouri—St. Louis.

And LEP students will achieve at higher levels in a bilingual education program (García, 1995; Moll & Diaz, 1985; Snow, 1990; Willig, 1985; S. Wright & Taylor, 1995).

Accommodating Students with Special Needs

We are especially likely to see differences in cognitive and linguistic development in our students with special needs. For example, we may have a few students who show especially advanced cognitive development, and perhaps we may have one or two who have not yet acquired the cognitive abilities typical of their age-group; we will consider both of these situations—giftedness and mental retardation—in more detail in Chapter 4. We may also have students with exceptional difficulties in reading or writing despite otherwise normal cognitive development; we will consider such learning disabilities in Chapter 6. Finally, we may have students with speech and communication disorders—abnormalities in spoken language that significantly interfere with their classroom performance.

Table 2–5 presents specific characteristics related to cognitive and linguistic development that we may see in some of our students with special educational needs; it also presents numerous strategies for helping such students achieve academic success. In ad-

INTO THE CLASSROOM

Helping Students with Speech and Communication Disorders

Encourage students to talk, but without forcing them to do so.

A fourth grader has a bad lisp that makes him reluctant to speak in front of many of his classmates. His teacher calls on him only in the context of his advanced reading group, where he feels comfortable expressing his opinions openly with the other group members.

Listen patiently.

A high school sophomore stutters badly and often takes longer than most other students to complete a sentence. Her teacher listens attentively and politely without criticizing or ridiculing her, and he encourages her classmates to do likewise.

Ask students to clarify things they have said when you don't understand.

A seventh grader expresses confusion about an assignment, but his teacher has trouble understanding what he is telling her. The teacher explains the things she *did* understand and asks him to clarify the rest.

Seek the assistance of a specialist when students show chronic speech and language difficulties.

A teacher suspects that a student's continual mispronunciation of the letter *s* may require special remedial services and so seeks the services of the school's speech pathologist.

dition, the final "Into the Classroom" feature of this chapter presents several classroom strategies especially appropriate for students with speech and communication disorders.

LOOKING AT THE BIG PICTURE: RECURRING THEMES IN COGNITIVE AND LINGUISTIC DEVELOPMENT

As you look back on the topics of this chapter, you may notice several themes that appear over and over again in one form or another. Here are five themes that seem to underlie our understanding of cognitive and linguistic development:

- Development of increasingly more complex and abstract capabilities
- Dependence of later knowledge and skills on earlier ones
- Constructive processes
- Importance of challenge
- Development within a social context

Development of Increasingly More Complex and Abstract Capabilities

As we have seen, children become capable of more sophisticated thought processes, learning strategies, and language as they grow older. For example, young children often think illogically and concretely about isolated pieces of information, whereas many adolescents think logically and abstractly about integrated bodies of knowledge. Elementary school students depend primarily on rehearsal to learn new information; secondary school students are better able to organize and elaborate on that information. Students also become increasingly able to use and understand complex syntactical structures and to interpret and analyze the things they read as they progress through the grade levels.

Dependence of Later Knowledge and Skills on Earlier Ones

New knowledge and skills are rarely learned in isolation; instead, children relate their new experiences to things they have already learned. Therefore, early experiences and accomplishments provide an important foundation for later cognitive and linguistic development.

Constructive Processes

We encountered the process of *construction* in all three theories of cognitive development, as well as in our examination of syntactical development. More and more theorists and practitioners are beginning to propose that children do construct their own knowledge, rather than simply learn what someone else tells them. We will explore the process of knowledge construction in greater depth in Chapter 7.

Challenges are critical for cognitive and linguistic development.

Importance of Challenge

Challenge is critical for development. We saw this idea most clearly in Vygotsky's concept of the zone of proximal development. But the importance of challenge appears in other perspectives as well. From Piaget's view, children modify their schemes and develop new ones only when new events cannot easily be interpreted in the light of existing schemes. From an information processing view, children develop more sophisticated learning strategies only when their present ones are not sufficiently effective. And children are likely to develop more sophisticated receptive and expressive language capabilities only if specific tasks require them to do so.

Development Within a Social Context

Both Piaget and Vygotsky have emphasized the importance of social interaction for cognitive development. And of course the development of language also depends heavily on social interaction: Children can only learn to understand speech if they hear others speak, and they can only learn to speak themselves if given an opportunity to do so. In fact, a child's social world has ramifications far beyond cognitive and linguistic development; it has ramifications for personal, social, and moral development as well, as we shall discover in the next chapter.

CASE STUDY: *In the Eye of the Beholder*

Ms. Kontos is teaching a unit on vision to her fifth-grade class. She shows her students a diagram of the various parts of the human eye—lens, cornea, retina, and so on. She then explains that people can see objects because light from the sun or another light source bounces off those objects and into the eye. To illustrate this idea, she shows them this picture:

"Do you all understand how our eyes work?" she asks. Her students nod that they do.

The following day, Ms. Kontos gives her students the following picture:

She asks them to draw how light travels so that the child can see the tree. More than half of the students draw lines something like this:

Obviously, most of Ms. Kontos's students have not really learned what she thought she had taught them.

- What went wrong? Can you explain the students' inability to learn within the context of Piaget's theory of cognitive development? Can you explain it from an information processing perspective? Can you explain it using some of Vygotsky's ideas?

- In what ways might students' language capabilities have been insufficient to enable them to understand?

- What things might Ms. Kontos have done differently?

SUMMING UP

Developmental Principles in the Classroom

Children develop skills and abilities in a somewhat predictable sequence, although not always at the same rate, and their development is a function of environment as well as heredity. As teachers, we need to monitor the growth and development of our students and be sure they acquire the skills necessary for future learning. We must also remember that the things we do in the classroom are likely to affect our students' development over the long run.

Piaget's Theory

Piaget's four stages give us a rough idea of when we can expect to see various logical thinking capabilities emerge, and Piagetian tasks (e.g., conservation problems) can provide valuable insights about how our students are reasoning. Regardless of developmental stage, all learners benefit from building on prior knowledge, discovering relationships among concepts and ideas, and exercising their natural curiosity. As teachers, we

should challenge students' beliefs about the world and expand their experiences to help them progress to more complex levels of thought.

Information Processing Theory

Information processing theorists also believe that cognitive capabilities improve over time, but not necessarily in the discrete stages that Piaget proposed. We must remember that our students will often be less efficient learners than we are; for example, they will have shorter attention spans, less knowledge to which they can relate school subject matter, and less sophisticated learning strategies.

Vygotsky's Theory

Vygotsky's theory encourages us to help students develop by challenging them and stretching the limits of what they know and can do. As we do so, we must give them the guidance and support (the scaffolding) they need to complete difficult tasks successfully.

Linguistic Development

We see continuing improvements in vocabulary, syntax, comprehension, and communication skills throughout the school years. Whether we have English-speaking students, bilingual students, or nonnative speakers of English, we need to be aware of the ways in which language can foster or hinder classroom performance. Checking students' comprehension of the things they read and hear and providing them with ample opportunities for speaking, writing, and interacting with others will allow them to develop increasingly sophisticated language capabilities.

Diversity in Cognitive and Linguistic Development

Our students will vary considerably in the logical thinking skills, learning strategies, and background knowledge they bring to classroom tasks, and different students will find different tasks optimally challenging. Our students will also vary in their vocabulary, reading and writing skills, and general proficiency in English. Some students may be different enough from their classmates in either cognitive or language skills that they will need specially adapted instructional materials and practices.

General Themes

Several themes have appeared throughout our discussion of cognitive and linguistic development. As students develop, more sophisticated thought processes, language capabilities, and understandings of the world emerge from and build upon existing mental capabilities and knowledge; hence, we must remember that the knowledge and skills developed in the early years provide an essential foundation for later development. Students construct their own knowledge, rather than absorb it verbatim from the environment, and misinterpretations are likely to be common, especially in the early years. We should offer ample opportunities for students to acquire new knowledge and skills through challenging academic and social contexts.

KEY CONCEPTS

cognitive development (p. 38)
linguistic development (p. 38)
developmental milestones (p. 40)
universals in development (p. 40)
stages (p. 41)
maturation (p. 41)
constructivism (p. 44)
schemes (p. 44)
assimilation (p. 44)
accommodation (p. 44)
equilibrium (p. 45)
disequilibrium (p. 45)
equilibration (p. 46)
sensorimotor stage (p. 47)
object permanence (p. 47)
preoperational stage (p. 47)
symbolic thinking (p. 47)
preoperational egocentrism (p. 48)
egocentric speech (p. 48)
conservation (p. 48)
operations (p. 48)

concrete operations stage (p. 48)
irreversibility vs. reversibility (p. 49)
single versus multiple classification (p. 50)
transductive versus deductive reasoning (p. 50)
formal operations stage (p. 51)
separation and control of variables (p. 52)
proportional thought (p. 52)
combinatorial thought (p. 52)
formal operational egocentrism (p. 54)
cognitive processes (p. 58)
learning strategies (p. 60)
rehearsal (p. 60)
organization (p. 61)
elaboration (p. 61)
knowledge base (p. 62)
metacognition (p. 63)
actual developmental level (p. 66)
level of potential development (p. 66)

zone of proximal development (ZPD) (p. 66)
scaffolding (p. 67)
cognitive apprenticeship (p. 68)
social constructivism (p. 68)
self-talk (private speech) (p. 69)
inner speech (p. 69)
receptive language (p. 74)
expressive language (p. 74)
semantics (p. 74)
undergeneralization (p. 74)
overgeneralization (p. 74)
syntax (p. 76)
overregularization (p. 76)
metalinguistic awareness (p. 80)
immersion (p. 81)
bilingual education (p. 81)
dialect (p. 83)
limited English proficiency (LEP) (p. 83)

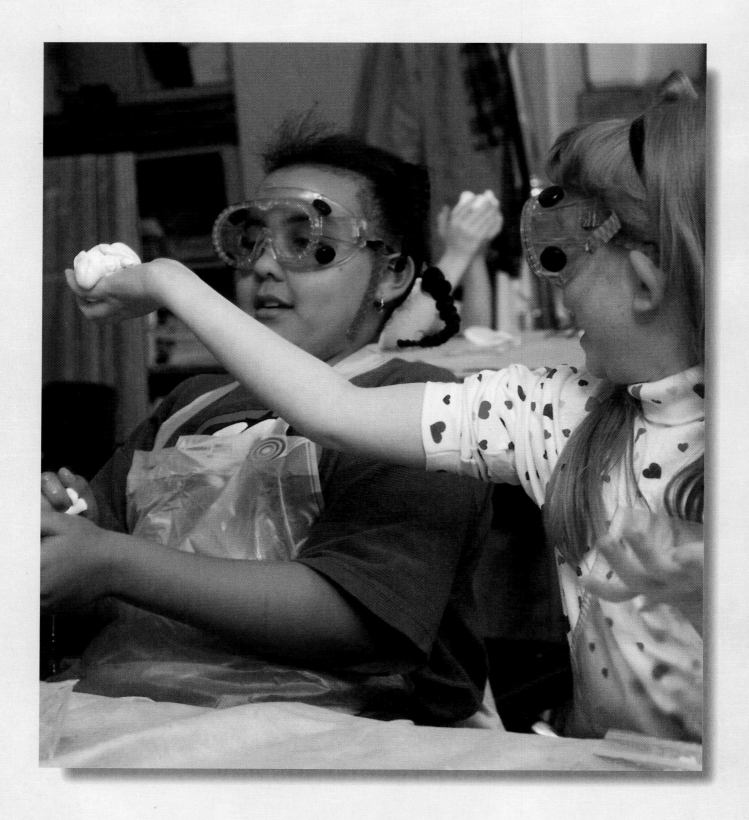

Adapting to Differences in Personal, Social, and Moral Development

THINKING ABOUT WHAT YOU KNOW

What people and events in your life have had a significant impact on the kind of person you are today? Have parents or other family members influenced how you think about yourself or the ways in which you interact with others? Can you think of teachers who've had a major effect on your self-esteem or your behavior? In what ways have your friends and classmates had an effect?

S CHOOL IS NOT JUST A PLACE where students learn reading, writing, and arithmetic. It is also a place where they develop a greater or lesser degree of self-esteem, acquire strategies for getting along with other people, and explore various perspectives on the difference between right and wrong. In other words, school is a place where students grow personally, socially, and morally, as well as academically.

In this chapter, we will consider children's **personal development** (their emerging personalities and self-concepts), **social development** (their increasing ability to interact effectively with other people), and **moral development** (their evolving understanding of right and wrong behavior). We will find that our students will change considerably in all three aspects of development as they progress through the grade levels and also that they are likely to be very different from one another at any single grade level. As we go along, we will identify numerous strategies for helping students develop self-esteem, make friends, cooperate with their classmates, and respect the rights of others.

By the end of the chapter, you should be able to:

1. Describe the multifaceted and hierarchical nature of students' self-concepts, and identify ways to promote greater self-esteem.

2. List typical personality characteristics of different age-groups, and explain how you can adapt instruction to accommodate those characteristics.

3. Describe the role that schools play in the long-term socialization of children and adolescents.

4. Explain how peer relationships promote students' personal and social development, and identify several strategies for helping students develop appropriate social skills.

5. Describe developmental changes in moral reasoning, perspective taking, and prosocial behavior, and explain how you can facilitate growth in all three areas.

6. Describe the diversity you are likely to see among your students with regard to personal, social, and moral development.

CASE STUDY: *The Bad Apple*

Adam seems to cause problems wherever he goes. In the classroom, he is rude and defiant. On a typical school day, he comes to class late, slouches low in his seat, rests his feet on his desk, yells obscenities at classmates and his teacher, and stubbornly refuses to participate in classroom activities.

Away from his teacher's watchful eye, Adam's behavior is even worse. He shoves and pushes students in the hall, steals lunches from smaller boys in the cafeteria, and frequently initiates physical fights on the school grounds.

For obvious reasons, no one at school likes Adam very much. His classmates describe him as a bully, and their parents describe him as a "bad apple," rotten to the core. Even his teacher, who tries to find the best in all her students, has seen few redeeming qualities in Adam and is beginning to write him off as a lost cause.

Adam doesn't seem to be bothered by the hostile feelings he generates. He's counting the days until he can legally drop out of school.

- Why does Adam behave the way he does? What possible factors in his environment—perhaps at home, at school, or among his peers—might have contributed to his aggressiveness, impulsiveness, and apparent self-centeredness?

- What things could a teacher do to help Adam develop more appropriate and productive behavior?

How the Environment Influences Personal, Social, and Moral Development

You might have formed a number of different hypotheses about why Adam behaves as he does. Perhaps a parent encourages aggressive behavior, or at least does nothing to *dis*courage it. Perhaps Adam lives in an inner-city neighborhood in which violence is commonplace and aggression is the best means of self-defense. Perhaps his family can't afford to provide breakfast at home or lunch at school or perhaps has never taught him that stealing infringes on the rights of others. At school, perhaps previous teachers have tolerated Adam's obscene language. Perhaps classmates have learned to stay away from him because of his inappropriate social skills, and he now finds that pushing, shoving, and picking fights are the only ways he can get their attention.

Without a doubt, the most important contributors to children's personal, social, and moral development are *other people,* including parents, teachers, and fellow students. Of these, parents are probably the most influential. They reward their children for some behaviors and punish them for others. They also serve as models for their children—as examples of how one should behave. And they often control the specific activities that their children will engage in, thereby influencing the information that their children encounter and the other people with whom they associate (R. D. Hess & McDevitt, 1989).

But the school environment, including the teachers and peers with whom children interact on a daily basis, also plays a major role in how children develop personally, socially, and morally. For example, teachers are instrumental in helping their students develop a strong sense of self-esteem and in teaching behaviors acceptable both inside and outside the classroom. Students' classmates provide innumerable opportunities to practice social skills and to learn how to look at situations from someone else's point of view. And as we will soon discover, many classroom activities and events provide a context in which students must critically examine their own notions of what actions constitute moral and immoral behavior.

Promoting Personal Development

Psychologists disagree regarding how to define **personality** (Mischel, 1993). For purposes of our discussion, you might think of personality as a set of relatively enduring traits that characterize the way in which a person typically interacts with his or her physical and social environments. When we consider the concept of *personality* in the classroom context, it includes the extent to which our students are outgoing or shy, independent or dependent, energetic or "laid back," self-confident or full of self-doubt.

Research tells us that some aspects of our students' personalities may be, at least in part, because of heredity. For example, we see differences in infants' temperaments—their activity level, adventurousness, shyness, irritability, and distractibility—almost from birth (Bouchard, Lykken, McGue, Segal, & Tellegen, 1990; Clarke-Stewart, 1988; J. Kagan, Snidman, & Arcus, 1992; Plomin, 1989; A. Thomas & Chess, 1977). But contemporary developmentalists believe that environmental factors also play a critical role in determining the kinds of individuals that children become—whether they are friendly and self-confident, or instead unhappy and unsure of their own capabilities, or perhaps even as angry and rebellious as Adam. Parents are among the most important environmental influences on children's personalities, as we shall see now.

How Parents Influence Their Children's Personal Development

Research tells us that parents' behaviors begin to influence their children's personalities even in the first few weeks and months of life. For example, when parents and their infants form a strong, affectionate bond (a process called **attachment**), those infants are likely to develop into amiable, cooperative, and independent children. In contrast, those who do not become closely attached to a parent or some other individual early in life are apt to become immature, unpopular, dependent, and prone to disruptive and aggressive behaviors later on (Hartup, 1989; Jacobson & Wille, 1986; Sroufe, 1983).

Patterns of childrearing, or **parenting,** also appear to play a significant role in children's personal development. Researchers have identified four different styles of parenting that are correlated with children's social behaviors and personalities (Baumrind, 1967, 1971, 1989; Baumrind & Black, 1967; Maccoby & Martin, 1983). These four parenting styles—authoritative, authoritarian, permissive, and uninvolved—are summarized in Table 3–1. Here you will also find suggestions for dealing with children from each type of home.

As you can see from Table 3–1, an authoritative style seems to be most beneficial. Children from authoritative homes are well-adjusted, happy, energetic, self-confident, curious, and independent. They are motivated to do well in school; as a result, they are often high achievers (L. Steinberg, 1993; L. Steinberg, Elmen, & Mounts, 1989). They are likable and cooperative, make friends easily, and show strong leadership skills. They also exhibit self-control and concern for the rights and needs of others.

As you peruse the four parenting styles described in Table 3–1, you may notice that these styles differ from one another in the degree of control that parents exert over their children. At one extreme is the excessively controlling, authoritarian parent; at the other extreme is the noncontrolling (either permissive or uninvolved) parent. It appears that the happy medium of the authoritative home is the optimal situation here—that children thrive when there is some control in their lives (when there are standards for acceptable behavior that are consistently enforced) while at the same time their own individual rights and needs are recognized. Ideally, parents should tailor the degree of control to the developmental level of the child, gradually loosening restrictions as children become capable of greater responsibility and independence (Maccoby & Martin, 1983). Too much control may lead to lack of self-confidence and initiative; too little may

Think about such classic television shows as *Leave It to Beaver* and *The Andy Griffith Show* and such recent programs as *Roseanne* and *Full House*. Which parenting style best characterizes these shows?

Table 3–1 Parenting Styles and Implications for Teachers

WHEN PARENTS EXHIBIT THIS PARENTING STYLE . . .	CHILDREN TEND TO BE . . .	AS TEACHERS WE SHOULD . . .
Authoritative: Provide a loving, supportive, home environment Hold high expectations and standards for their children's behaviors Enforce household rules consistently Explain why some behaviors are acceptable and others are not Include children in family decision making	Happy Self-confident Curious Independent Likable Respectful of others Successful in school	Adopt an authoritative style similar to that of their parents

Authoritarian:
Convey less emotional warmth than authoritative parents
 	
Hold high expectations and standards for their children's behaviors
 	
Establish rules of behavior without regard for the needs of the children
 	
Expect rules to be obeyed without question
 	
Allow little give-and-take in parent-child discussions
	Unhappy
	Anxious
	Low in self-confidence
	Lacking initiative
	Dependent on others
	Lacking in social skills
	Defiant
		Adopt an authoritative style, with particular emphasis on:
		   conveying emotional warmth
		   soliciting students' perspectives on classroom rules and procedures
		   considering students' needs in developing classroom rules

Permissive:
Provide a loving, supportive, home environment
 	
Hold few expectations or standards for their children's behaviors
 	
Rarely punish inappropriate behavior
 	
Allow their children to make many of their own decisions (e.g., about eating, bedtime)
	Selfish
	Unmotivated
	Dependent on others
	Demanding of attention
	Disobedient
	Impulsive
		Adopt an authoritative style, with particular emphasis on:
		   holding high expectations for behavior
		   imposing consequences for inappropriate behavior

Uninvolved:
Provide little if any emotional support for their children
 	
Hold few expectations or standards for their children's behaviors
 	
Have little interest in their children's lives
 	
Seem overwhelmed by their own problems
	Disobedient
	Demanding
	Low in self-control
	Low in tolerance for frustration
	Lacking long-term goals
		Adopt an authoritative style, with particular emphasis on:
		   conveying emotional warmth
		   holding high expectations for behavior
		   imposing consequences for inappropriate behavior

Sources: Baumrind, 1967, 1971, 1989; Baumrind & Black, 1967; Maccoby & Martin, 1983; L. Steinberg, 1993; L. Steinberg, Elmen, & Mounts, 1989.

lead to selfish, impulsive, and possibly delinquent behavior. As we think back to the case of Adam at the beginning of the chapter, we might wonder whether his aggressiveness, impulsiveness, and self-centeredness are the result of having too little control at home.

We should keep in mind here that parent-child interactions are, to some extent, a two-way street. Although children's behaviors are often the result of how their parents treat them, sometimes the reverse is true as well: Parents' behaviors may be the result of how *they are treated by their children* (Clarke-Stewart, 1988; Maccoby & Martin, 1983; Scott-Jones, 1984). Different children have different temperaments that are, to some degree, genetically determined: Some children appear to be naturally quieter and more easygoing, whereas others are more lively or irritable. When children are quick to comply with their parents' wishes, parents may have no reason to be overly controlling. When children are hot-tempered, parents may have to impose more restrictions on behavior and to administer consequences for misbehaviors more frequently. We must be careful that we don't always place total credit or blame on parents for the parenting styles we observe.

As teachers, we can serve as valuable resources to parents about possible strategies for promoting their children's personal development. With newsletters, parent-teacher conferences, and parent discussion groups, we can communicate with parents about ways to help children develop increasingly more appropriate and mature behaviors. The important thing is to communicate information about how to promote children's personal development *without* pointing fingers or being judgmental about the parenting styles we observe.

In our own classrooms, we should probably adopt a style similar to what we see in authoritative parents. For example, we should exert some degree of control in the classroom, holding high expectations for student behavior and enforcing classroom rules consistently. At the same time, we should explain the reasons why some behaviors are acceptable and others are not, provide a supportive environment, and recognize that our students are individuals with their own legitimate needs and points of view. We can include students in classroom decision making, and we can encourage them to be independent and self-reliant. And we should gradually loosen the reins as students demonstrate increasing independence and self-control.

One aspect of personal development in which teachers play an especially important role is the development of students' self-concepts and self-esteem. Let's look at this area of development and find out how, as teachers, we can definitely make a difference.

Offer yourself as a resource to parents about strategies for promoting more appropriate behaviors, but don't pass judgments about the parenting styles you observe.

Adopt an authoritative style in the classroom.

Think of several situations in which it would be appropriate to include your students in classroom decision making.

Enhancing Self-Concept and Self-Esteem

■ EXPERIENCING FIRSTHAND
Describing Yourself

Take out a sheet of paper and a pen or pencil. Now list twenty adjectives or phrases that describe the kind of person you think you are. ■

How did you describe yourself? Are you a good student? Are you physically attractive? Are you friendly? likable? moody? intelligent? test-anxious? strong? uncoordinated?

Your answers to these questions tell you something about your **self-concept**—your beliefs about yourself, your personality, your strengths and weaknesses. They may also tell you something about your **self-esteem**—the extent to which you believe yourself to be a capable and worthy individual.

Students tend to have an overall general feeling of self-worth: They believe either that they are good, capable individuals or that they are somehow inept or unworthy (Harter, 1990). At the same time, they are usually aware that they have both strengths and weaknesses; they realize that they do some things well and other things poorly. For example, students may have somewhat different views about themselves in these three areas (Harter, 1982):

- *Cognitive competence:* Students have general beliefs about their academic ability and performance. For example, they may describe themselves as being smart and performing academic tasks successfully, or perhaps instead as being stupid and doing poorly in school.

- *Social competence:* Students have general beliefs about their ability to relate with other people, especially their peers. For example, they may describe themselves as having many friends and being liked, or instead as having trouble making friends and being unpopular.

- *Physical competence:* Students have general beliefs about their ability to engage in such physical activities as sports and outdoor games. For example, they may describe themseves as doing well at sports and often being selected for athletic teams, or instead as being uncoordinated and frequently excluded from team sports.

In which of these three areas is your own self-esteem highest?

Many students, older ones especially, may make still finer distinctions among the various aspects of themselves, judging some aspects more favorably than others (Durkin, 1995; Harter, 1990; H. W. Marsh, 1990b; Pintrich, Garcia, & De Groot, 1994; Schell, Klein, & Babey, 1996; C. J. Wood, Schau, & Fiedler, 1990). For example, students may define themselves as poor readers but good in mathematics. And they are likely to see a difference between at least two aspects of their physical selves—their athletic capabilities and their physical attractiveness to others. Thus, one's self-concept appears to have several levels of specificity, as Figure 3–1 illustrates.

When we speak of very specific levels of self-esteem, we are talking about **self-efficacy,** a topic that we will consider in our discussion of social cognitive theory in Chapter 10.

Self-concept and self-esteem are important factors influencing behavior and achievement in school: Students tend to behave in ways that are consistent with their beliefs about themselves (Eccles [Parsons], 1984; Fennema & Peterson, 1985; L. H. Fox, 1981; Pintrich & Garcia, 1994; Pintrich et al., 1994; Yu, Elder, & Urdan, 1995). Those who see themselves as "good students" are more likely to pay attention, follow directions in class, use effective learning strategies, work independently and persistently to solve difficult problems, and enroll in challenging courses. In contrast, those who believe that they are "poor students" are likely to misbehave in class, study infrequently or not at all, neglect to turn in homework assignments, and avoid taking difficult subjects. Along a similar vein, students who see themselves as friendly and likable are apt to seek the company of their classmates and to run for student council, whereas those who believe that they are disliked by their classmates may keep to themselves or perhaps even act with hostility and aggression toward their peers. Student with a high sense of physical competence will go out for extracurricular athletics, whereas those who see themselves as total klutzes probably will not.

Clearly, students who have a positive self-concept and high self-esteem are those most likely to succeed academically, socially, and physically (e.g., Cornell et al., 1990). Let's look at the factors that contribute to a positive or negative self-concept and then at several reasons why students' self-concepts become increasingly more stable over time.

Before you read ahead, can you predict what some factors affecting self-concept might be?

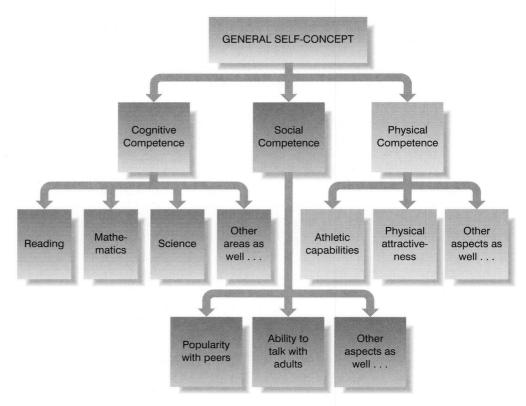

Figure 3–1   Self-concept is multifaceted and hierarchical.

Students who have a positive self-concept and high self-esteem are more likely to succeed academically, socially, and physically.

Factors Influencing the Development of Self-Concept and Self-Esteem

Simply telling our students they are "good" or "smart" or "popular" is unlikely to make much of a dent on low self-esteem (Damon, 1991; L. Katz, 1993). However, at least three factors definitely *do* influence the degree to which students form positive or negative self-concepts:

- Their own prior behaviors and performance

- The behaviors of other individuals toward them

- The expectations that others hold for their future performance

These three factors are summarized in Table 3–2. Each one offers insights as to how, as teachers, we can enhance our students' self-concepts.

Students' prior behaviors and performance.   As we noted earlier, students' self-concepts influence the ways in which they behave. Yet the reverse is true as well: To some extent, stu-

Table 3–2 *Factors Affecting the Development of Self-Concept and Self-Esteem*

FACTOR	EXAMPLE	EDUCATIONAL IMPLICATION
Students' prior behaviors and performance	Arnie thinks of himself as a poor student because an undiagnosed and unremediated learning disability interferes with his ability to read as proficiently as his classmates.	Promote success in academic, social, and physical tasks.
Behaviors of others	Anne has few friends, and she notices that her teacher interacts frequently with the "popular" students in the hallway but rarely if ever speaks to her outside class. She suspects that she must be an unlikable person for some reason.	Communicate overall positive regard for students; for example, seek out their company outside class and express an interest in their well-being.
Expectations for students' future performance	Ashley is pessimistic about her ability to play basketball because her elementary school physical education teacher has often made the comment that boys are naturally better athletes than girls.	Hold high expectations for students' performance.

dents' self-concepts and self-esteem depend on how successfully they have behaved in the past (Damon, 1991; H. W. Marsh, 1990a). Students are more likely to believe that they have an aptitude for mathematics if they have been successful in previous math classes. They are more likely to believe that they are capable athletes if they have mastered physical skills or been victorious in athletic competitions. They are more likely to believe that they are likable, friendly individuals if they have been able to establish and maintain positive relationships with their peers.

The interplay between self-concept and behavior can create a vicious downward cycle: A poor self-concept leads to less productive behavior, which leads to fewer successes, which perpetuates the poor self-concept. To break the cycle, we must make sure our students have numerous opportunities to be successful at academic, social, and physical tasks (Damon, 1991; L. Katz, 1993). For example, we can gear assignments to their developmental levels and cognitive capabilities. We can make sure they have mastered the necessary prerequisite knowledge and skills *before* we assign new tasks. And we can provide scaffolding for difficult tasks, giving students the structure and support they need to accomplish those tasks successfully.

We should note here that how students evaluate their own performance—that is, how they define "success" and "failure"—depends, to some extent, on the students around them (H. W. Marsh, 1990b; H. W. Marsh, Chessor, Craven, & Roche, 1995; H. W. Marsh & Peart, 1988; Nicholls, 1984). Older students in particular are likely to judge themselves in terms of how they compare with their peers. When students see themselves performing better than other students in their class, they are likely to develop a relatively positive self-concept. When their own performance is poorer than that of their classmates, they develop a more negative self-concept. To help our students develop

Promote success in academic, social, and physical tasks as a way of fostering more positive self-concepts.

Minimize competitive and other situations in which students might judge themselves unfavorably in comparison with their classmates.

positive rather than negative self-concepts, then, we probably want to minimize competitive and other situations in which students might judge themselves unfavorably in comparison with their classmates.

Have you ever seen a student's self-esteem destroyed by his or her classmates? How might a teacher intervene in such a situation?

Behaviors of others.   The behaviors of other people, both adults and peers, also play a crucial role in the development of students' self-concepts (Damon, 1991; Durkin, 1995; Griffore, 1981; Harter, 1983; Hartup, 1989; Seltzer, 1982). How these individuals behave toward a child communicates their evaluations of the child and their beliefs about his or her worth as a person. For example, parents who accept their children as they are and who treat their children's interests and problems as important are likely to have children with positive self-concepts and high self-esteem. Parents who punish their children for the things they cannot do, without also praising their children for the things they do well, are likely to have children with low self-esteem (Griffore, 1981; Harter, 1983). Teacher behaviors undoubtedly have a similar effect; for example, the relative proportion of positive and negative feedback from a teacher tells students a great deal about their academic capabilities. And students' classmates communicate information about their social competence through a variety of behaviors—for example, by seeking out their companionship or by ridiculing them in front of others.

Give positive feedback for students' accomplishments, and communicate a genuine interest in students' feelings, opinions, and general well-being.

Obviously, we can't always control how other people treat our students. But we *can* make sure we respond to students in ways that will boost rather than lower their self-esteem. Students who *mis*behave usually capture our attention more readily than those who behave appropriately, so it is often easier to criticize undesirable behavior, rather than praise desirable behavior. As teachers, we must make a concerted effort to catch students in the act of doing something well and praise them accordingly. We must be specific about the things that we are praising, because we will usually be more successful in improving particular aspects of our students' self-concepts than in improving their overall sense of self-worth (H. W. Marsh, 1990b). And more generally, we must treat our students with respect—for example, by asking them about their personal views and opinions about academic subject matter, by seeking their input in important classroom decisions, and by communicating a genuine interest in their well-being (e.g., L. Katz, 1993).

At the same time, our students will only learn what academic responses are incorrect and what classroom behaviors are unacceptable if we let them know when they are doing something wrong. It is inevitable, then, that we occasionally give our students negative feedback. The trick is to give that negative feedback while at the same time also communicating respect and affection for our students as human beings—that is, while communicating **overall positive regard.** For example, when students make mistakes in their academic work, we can point out that errors are a natural part of the learning process and provide valuable information about how to improve in knowledge and skills. When students behave inappropriately in the classroom, we can communicate that although we like them, we disapprove of their present actions—for example, by saying something such as, "You're generally a very kind person, Gail, but you hurt Jenny's feelings just now by making fun of her new sweater."

Provide negative feedback when necessary, but only when communicating overall positive regard as well.

Expectations for students' future performance.   People in a student's life often hold expectations for that student that are communicated in their behaviors. When parents and teachers have high expectations and when they offer support and encouragement for the attainment of challenging goals, students tend to have positive self-concepts (Griffore, 1981; M. J. Harris & Rosenthal, 1985). When parents and teachers expect children to achieve academically, those children are more likely to have confidence in their own academic capabilities (Eccles, Jacobs, Harold-Goldsmith, Jayaratne, & Yee, 1989; Eccles [Parsons] et al., 1983; Parsons, Adler, & Kaczala, 1982).

The result of all the feedback that students receive from those around them is that students' perceptions of themselves are usually similar to how others perceive them (Harter, 1990; Shaffer, 1988). For example, students' beliefs about their academic ability are similar to their classroom teachers' beliefs about their intelligence and aptitude. Their beliefs about their physical ability are correlated with the perceptions of their physical education teachers. And their sense of their own competence in social situations is likely to be a reflection of their actual popularity with peers.

Hold realistically high expectations for students' performance.

Increasing Stability of the Self-Concept

Students' self-concepts become increasingly stable—and therefore increasingly resistant to change—as they grow older (e.g., O'Malley & Bachman, 1983; Savin-Williams & Demo, 1984). Students with the most positive self-concepts in the early years tend to be the ones with the most positive self-concepts in later years as well. Conversely, students who think poorly of themselves in elementary school also have lower self-esteem in high school. Hence, it is especially important to help students develop positive self-concepts during the early elementary school years.

Speculate on possible reasons for this trend before you read further.

There are probably several reasons why students' self-concepts eventually become so resistant to change. First, as I mentioned earlier, people usually behave in ways that are consistent with what they believe about themselves, so their behaviors are likely to produce reactions in others that confirm their self-concepts. To illustrate, a student who thinks of herself as a class clown is likely to continue "entertaining" her class and thus to elicit the continuing laughter of her classmates. Second, people tend to seek out information that confirms what they already believe about themselves: Students with positive self-concepts are more likely to seek out positive feedback, whereas those with negative self-concepts may actually look for information about their weaknesses and limitations (Swann, 1992). Third, people seldom put themselves in situations where they believe that they won't succeed, thereby eliminating any possibility of discovering that they *can* succeed. For example, if a student believes that he is a poor athlete and so refuses to go out for the baseball team, he may never learn that, in fact, he has the potential to become a skillful baseball player. And fourth, many outside factors that contribute to one's self-concept—for example, parental behaviors, socioeconomic circumstances, and one's physical attractiveness—usually remain relatively stable throughout the course of childhood (O'Malley & Bachman, 1983).

Remember that improving a student's self-esteem may take time, especially at the secondary level.

As we have seen, older students have more differentiated self-concepts, as well as more stable ones, than younger students. Let's look at some additional ways in which students at different age levels are likely to exhibit different personality traits.

Considering Developmental Differences in Personality

In the preceding chapter, we discovered some ways in which students' cognitive and linguistic capabilities change as they grow older. In the next few pages, we will consider how students' personal characteristics are also likely to vary, depending on their age level. As we do so, we will draw from a theory of personal development proposed by Erik Erikson (1963, 1972); his eight stages of "psychosocial" development are described

Figure 3–2   Erikson's Eight Stages of Psychosocial Development

Erik Erikson (1963, 1972) has described a series of eight "psychosocial" stages through which people proceed over the course of development. Each stage presents a unique developmental task, and the way in which an individual deals with each task has a particular impact on that individual's personal development.

Trust Versus Mistrust (Infancy)

According to Erikson, the major developmental task of infants is to learn whether or not other people can be trusted to satisfy basic needs. A child's parents and other primary caretakers play a key role here. When caretakers can be depended on to feed a hungry stomach, change an uncomfortable diaper, and provide physical affection at regular intervals, an infant learns *trust*—that others are consistently dependable and reliable. When caretakers ignore the infant's needs, are inconsistent in attending to them, or are even abusive, the infant may instead learn *mistrust*—that the world is an undependable, unpredictable, and possibly dangerous place.

Autonomy Versus Shame and Doubt (Toddler Years)

With the increased muscular coordination that results from physiological maturation and the increased mobility that accompanies learning to crawl and walk, toddlers become capable of satisfying some of their own needs. They are learning to feed themselves, wash and dress themselves, and use the bathroom facilities. When parents and other caretakers encourage the self-sufficient behavior of which toddlers are capable, children develop a sense of *autonomy*—a sense of being able to handle many problems on their own. But when caretakers demand too much too soon, or refuse to let children perform tasks of which they are capable, or ridicule early awkward attempts at self-sufficiency, children may instead develop *shame and doubt* about their ability to handle the problems that the environment presents.

Initiative Versus Guilt (Preschool Years)

During the preschool years, children begin to get their own ideas about the things that they want to do and the activities that they want to pursue; for example, they may undertake simple art projects, make houses and roadways in the sandbox, or play "house" with other children. When parents and preschool teachers encourage and support children in such efforts, children develop *initiative*—independence in planning and undertaking activities. In contrast, when adults instead discourage such activities, children may develop *guilt* about their needs and desires.

Industry Versus Inferiority (Elementary School Years)

When they reach elementary school, children are expected to master many new academic skills, and they soon learn that they can gain the recognition of adults through their written assignments, art projects, dramatic productions, and so on.

Support young children in their efforts to plan and carry out their own activities.

in Figure 3–2. We will also draw from research findings related to child and adolescent development.

Preschool Years

Erikson described the preschool years as a period of *initiative versus guilt.* Preschoolers become increasingly capable of accomplishing tasks on their own, rather than depending on adults to do those tasks for them. With this growing independence, they begin to make their own decisions about the activities they want to pursue. Sometimes they initiate projects that they can readily accomplish, but at other times they may undertake projects that are beyond their limited capabilities or that interfere with the plans and activities of others. Erikson recommended that, as teachers, we can help young children develop *initiative*—independence in planning and undertaking activities—by encouraging and supporting them in their efforts to plan and carry out their own activities, while at the same time helping them recognize that their choices must be

When children are allowed and encouraged to make and do things and when they are praised for their accomplishments, they begin to demonstrate *industry*—a pattern of working hard, persisting at lengthy tasks, and putting work before pleasure. But when children are punished for their efforts or when they find that they can't meet their teachers' and parents' expectations for their performance, they may develop feelings of *inferiority* about their own abilities.

Identity Versus Role Confusion (Adolescence)

As they make the transition from childhood to adulthood, adolescents ponder the roles that they will play in the adult world. Initially, they are likely to experience some *role confusion*—mixed ideas and feelings about the specific ways in which they will fit into society—and may experiment with a variety of behaviors and activities (e.g., tinkering with cars, baby-sitting for neighbors, engaging in extracurricular activities at school, affiliating with particular political or religious groups). Eventually, most adolescents achieve a sense of *identity* regarding who they are and where their lives are headed.

Intimacy Versus Isolation (Young Adulthood)

Once people have established their identities, they are ready to make commitments to one or more other individuals. They become capable of forming *intimate,* reciprocal relationships with others (e.g., through marriage or close friendships) and willingly make the sacrifices and compromises that such relationships require. When people cannot form these intimate relationships (perhaps because of their reluctance or inability to forego the satisfaction of their own needs), then a sense of *isolation* may be the result.

Generativity Versus Stagnation (Middle Age)

During middle age, the primary developmental task is one of contributing to society and helping to guide future generations. When an individual makes a contribution during this period, perhaps by raising a family or by working toward the betterment of the society as a whole, a sense of *generativity*—a sense of productivity and accomplishment—results. In contrast, an individual who is self-centered and unable or unwilling to help society move forward develops a feeling of *stagnation*—a dissatisfaction with the relative lack of production.

Integrity Versus Despair (Retirement Years)

According to Erikson, the final developmental task is a retrospective one. Individuals look back on their lives and accomplishments. They develop feelings of contentment and *integrity* if they believe that they have led a happy, productive life. They may instead develop a sense of *despair* if they look back on a life of disappointments and unachieved goals.

realistic and not conflict with the needs of others. When adults instead discourage the pursuit of these activities or dismiss them as being silly and bothersome, then children may develop *guilt* about their desires to pursue projects independently.

Elementary School Years

Children's self-esteem often drops when they first reach elementary school (Harter, 1990; Stipek, 1981), perhaps because of the many new challenges—both academic and social—that school presents. Describing the elementary school years as a period of *industry versus inferiority,* Erikson proposed that this period is critical for the development of self-confidence. Ideally, elementary school provides many opportunities for children to achieve the recognition of teachers, parents, and peers by producing things (*industry*)—for example, by drawing pictures, solving addition problems, and writing sentences. When children are encouraged to make and do things and are then praised for their accomplishments, they begin to demonstrate industry by being diligent, by

Encourage elementary students to make and do things, and praise them for their accomplishments.

Children in the elementary grades learn that, by producing things, they can achieve the recognition of teachers and parents.

Take special pains to enhance students' self-concepts during early adolescence.

To let students know that you understand their personal concerns, describe instances in your own life in which you felt insecure, embarrassed, confused, or frustrated.

persevering at tasks until they complete them, and by putting work before pleasure. If children are instead ridiculed or punished for their efforts or if they find that they are incapable of meeting their teachers' and parents' expectations, they may develop feelings of *inferiority* and inadequacy about their own capabilities.

Adolescence

We see another drop in self-esteem at about the time that students move from elementary school to junior high school—a drop that is especially pronounced for girls (Eccles & Midgley, 1989; H. W. Marsh, 1990b; Midgley & Eccles, 1990; Sadker & Sadker, 1994; Simmons & Blyth, 1987). The physiological changes that occur with puberty may be a factor here: Boys and girls alike tend to think of themselves as somewhat less attractive when they reach adolescence (Cornell et al., 1990). The changing school environment probably also has a negative impact on self-esteem. Junior high schools are often different from elementary schools in several ways (Eccles & Midgley, 1989). For one thing, students don't have the opportunity to form the close-knit, supportive relationships with teachers they may have had in elementary school. They may also find that their school grades are based more on competitive criteria—that is, on how well they perform in comparison with their classmates. Furthermore, at a time when they probably have an increased need for close friendships, they may find themselves in classes with many people they don't know. Because all these unsettling changes occur simultaneously, it is not surprising that we see a temporary drop in self-esteem. But once they have successfully adjusted to the new junior high school environment, most adolescents enjoy positive self-concepts and general mental health (Durkin, 1995; Nottelmann, 1987; Powers, Hauser, & Kilner, 1989).

We should be aware of two additional aspects of adolescent self-perceptions. First, many adolescents believe that, in any social situation, everyone else's attention is focused squarely on themselves. This self-centered aspect of the adolescent self-concept is sometimes called the **imaginary audience** (Elkind, 1981). Because they believe themselves to be the center of attention, teenagers are often preoccupied with their physical appearance and are otherwise quite critical of themselves, assuming that everyone else is going to be equally observant and critical. Their extreme sensitivity to embarrassment may, in some situations, lead them to respond with undue violence to the insults or verbal attacks of their peers (Lowry, Sleet, Duncan, Powell, & Kolbe, 1995).

A second noteworthy characteristic of adolescent self-concepts is the **personal fable:** Teenagers often believe that they themselves are completely unlike anyone else (Elkind, 1981). For example, they often think that their own feelings are completely unique—that those around them have never experienced such emotions. Hence, they may insist that no one else, least of all their parents and teachers, can possibly know how they feel. They may also have a sense of immortality, believing that they are not susceptible to the normal dangers of life. It is not surprising, then, that many adolescents take seemingly foolish risks, such as driving at high speeds, experimenting with drugs and alcohol, or having unprotected sexual intercourse (Arnett, 1995; DeRidder, 1993; Packard, 1983; S. P. Thomas, Groër, & Droppleman, 1993).

Erikson described adolescence as a period of *identity versus role confusion*. As students make the transition from childhood to adulthood, they begin to wrestle with the question of who they are and how they will eventually fit into the adult world; in other words, they strive to achieve a sense of *identity* regarding the role they will play as adults. In the meantime, they often experience a state of *role confusion*—uncertainty about the direction that their lives will take. In their ongoing search for identity, they may adopt temporary "identities," aligning themselves strongly with a particular peer group, adhering rigidly to a single brand of clothing, or insisting on a certain hairstyle. For example, as a fifteen-year-old, my son Alex described himself as a "skater"—someone for whom skateboarding becomes a way of life as well as a form of transportation—and insisted on wearing the oversized shirts and hip-hugging baggy pants (revealing at least six inches' worth of boxer shorts!) that came with the territory.

Erikson believed that most people achieve a sense of identity by the end of adolescence. But more recent evidence indicates that, even by the high school years, only a small minority of students have begun to think seriously about the eventual role they will play in society and to identify some lifelong goals (Archer, 1982; Durkin, 1995; Marcia, 1980). It appears that adolescents need a period of time in which they are allowed to explore various options for themselves, both in terms of possible careers and in terms of ideological belief systems, before they can achieve a true sense of their adult identity (Marcia, 1980). But once they have done so, they will have a commitment to a particular career, a set of self-chosen social, political, and religious beliefs, and a strong sense of direction about where their own lives are likely to take them (Marcia, 1980).

Adolescents often believe that they are the center of attention—a phenomenon known as the *imaginary audience*.

Provide opportunities for adolescents to explore various career options and to examine a variety of social and political belief systems.

PROMOTING SOCIAL DEVELOPMENT

Let's return for a moment to the case study presented at the beginning of the chapter. Adam engages in several behaviors that most people would consider socially inappropriate: He pushes other students in the corridor, picks fights in the schoolyard, and yells obscenities in class. As a result, his peers want little to do with him, and his teacher has just about given up on him.

As our students grow, they should be learning how society as a whole expects them to behave. They should also be acquiring strategies for getting along with their classmates. In the next few pages, we will identify strategies for promoting such social development as we consider the topics of socialization and peer relationships.

Process of Socialization

Beginning early in their lives, most children learn that there are certain things they can or should do and other things they definitely should *not* do. For example, many parents teach their toddlers not to hit other children, first-grade teachers ask their students to

INTO THE CLASSROOM
Promoting Personal Development

Promote success on classroom tasks.

> A teacher provides a format (scaffolding) for writing an expository paragraph: a sentence expressing the main idea, three sentences that support that idea, and a concluding sentence.

Hold high expectations for students' performance.

> A junior high school swimming coach encourages students to come out for the swim team regardless of prior experience. She works as closely with newcomers as with experienced swimmers so that all team members can improve.

Give positive feedback for students' accomplishments. Provide negative feedback within the context of overall positive regard.

> The same swimming coach tells a student, "Your crawl stroke has really improved. Your timing on the butterfly is a bit off; let's work on that today."

Give students opportunities to examine and try out a variety of adultlike roles.

> A third-grade teacher develops a list of classroom chores, such as getting a hot lunch count, delivering messages to the main office, and feeding the class's goldfish and rabbit. He assigns these chores to students on a rotating basis.

Communicate a genuine interest in students' well-being.

> When a new seventh-grade student is visibly teary-eyed during class, her teacher invites her to take a walk with him during lunchtime. She describes the trouble she is having making friends at her new school, and together they develop some strategies to solve the problem.

In Chapter 4, we will find that boys and girls, as well as children from various cultures, are often socialized quite differently.

sit quietly rather than to interrupt when someone else is speaking, and high school teachers expect their students to turn in homework assignments on time.

The process of shaping behavior so that children fit in with society is called **socialization**. Through socialization, children learn society's **norms**—the rules determining acceptable and unacceptable behavior. They also learn the specific **roles** that different people occupy within their society—the patterns of behavior acceptable for people having various functions within the group. For example, children usually learn that different behaviors are considered appropriate for the teachers and students in a classroom. And many children develop the notion that boys and girls should behave differently and that men and women should do likewise. Norms and roles are, to some extent, culture-specific: Each culture will have its own norms regarding acceptable behavior and will define the roles of various individuals (e.g., teachers vs. students, males vs. females) in a somewhat unique fashion.

Children typically learn their earliest lessons about society's expectations from their parents, who teach them about personal hygiene, table manners, rudimentary interpersonal skills (e.g., saying "please" and "thank you"), and so on. Yet teachers become equally important socialization agents once children reach school age. For example, teachers typically expect and encourage behaviors such as these:

Expect and encourage those behaviors essential for long-term school success.

Obeying school rules

Behaving in an orderly fashion

Showing respect for authority figures

Controlling impulses

Following instructions

Working independently

Completing assigned tasks

Helping and cooperating with classmates

Striving for academic excellence

Delaying the satisfaction of immediate needs and desires in order to attain long-term goals (Helton & Oakland, 1977; R. D. Hess & Holloway, 1984)

To the extent that the behaviors expected of students at school are different from those expected at home, children may become confused, nonproductive, sometimes even resistant (R. D. Hess & Holloway, 1984). In other words, they may experience some **culture shock** when they first enter school.

As teachers, we must especially encourage our students to exhibit those behaviors essential for long-term school success—behaviors such as obeying school rules, following instructions, and working independently. For example, when we expect students to

Remember that some students may experience culture shock when they first enter school; guide them gently and patiently toward the behaviors necessary for success in the classroom.

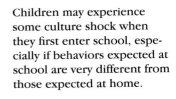

Children may experience some culture shock when they first enter school, especially if behaviors expected at school are very different from those expected at home.

work independently, even those students who have not had this expectation placed on them at home show improved work habits (J. L. Epstein, 1983). At the same time, we must recognize that some students—those whose parents have different expectations for their behavior than we do—will need guidance in meeting our expectations, and they will undoubtedly need our patience and understanding as well.

Importance of Peer Relationships

Students' social development is affected not only by their parents and teachers but also by their **peers**—their friends and classmates. The classroom is very much a "social" place—a place where students interact regularly with one another. In fact, for many students, socializing with their friends is more important than accomplishing classroom assignments (B. B. Brown, 1993; Doyle, 1986a).

A number of years ago, I asked my three children, "What are friends for?" Here are their responses:

Jeff (at age 6):   To play with.

Alex (at age 9):   Friends can help you in life. They can make you do better in school. They can make you feel better.

Tina (at age 12):   To be your friend and help you in good times and bad times. They're there so you can tell secrets. They're people that care. They're there because they like you. They're people you can trust.

Like Jeff, students in the early elementary grades view their age-mates primarily as a source of entertainment; thus, their relationships with peers are relatively superficial. When students reach the later elementary school years, as in the case of Alex, friendships take on an element of trust: Friends begin to believe that they can depend on one another (Damon, 1977). Adolescents like Tina develop increasingly more intimate friendships as they start to share their innermost dreams and secrets with one another (Berndt, 1992; Damon, 1977).

Peers become more influential as children grow and gain greater independence from home and family (R. D. Hess & McDevitt, 1989). In fact, students who have few close friends growing up are those who, later in life, are most likely to drop out of school, have marital problems, and engage in criminal behavior (McCallum & Bracken, 1993). Peer relationships, especially friendships, provide at least three things important for a child's development:

- Emotional support

- Information about acceptable behaviors and values

- An arena for developing social skills

Emotional Support

Students frequently turn to their peers for emotional support in times of trouble or confusion (Asher & Parker, 1989; Buhrmester, 1992; Seltzer, 1982), and as we noted in our discussion of personal development, adolescence is a particularly confusing time. At the secondary school level especially, peers also provide a sense of community for students—a sense that they "belong" to a group (Knapp & Woolverton, 1995). Furthermore, close friendships foster self-esteem and help students develop a better understanding of others (Berndt, 1992).

It's not surprising, then, that friendships become especially important during the adolescent years. Friends often understand a teenager's perspective—the preoccupation with physical appearance, the concerns about the opposite sex, and so on—when no one else seems to. By sharing their thoughts and feelings with one another, students may discover that they aren't as unique as they once thought, thereby breaking holes in the personal fable I spoke of earlier (Elkind, 1981).

Unfortunately, not all students are readily accepted by their peers; some are ignored or even overtly rejected by their classmates. Students with few social skills—for example, those who are overly aggressive and those who are exceptionally fearful or withdrawn—will often experience peer rejection (Cairns, Cairns, Neckerman, Gest, & Gariépy, 1988; Coie & Cillessen, 1993; Juvonen, 1991a; McCallum & Bracken, 1993). And students from minority groups frequently find themselves the targets of derogatory remarks and other forms of racism and discrimination, as do students from low-income families (Knapp & Woolverton, 1995; Nieto, 1995; Olneck, 1995; Pang, 1995; Phelan, Yu, & Davidson, 1994). In the face of widespread rejection by their peers, some students turn to street gangs or deviant subcultures (e.g., Satanism, neo-Nazi groups) to get the emotional support they can find nowhere else (C. C. Clark, 1992).

Peers are a major source of emotional support, especially during the adolescent years.

As a teacher, what might you do to discourage membership in street gangs and deviant subcultures?

Information About Acceptable Behaviors and Values

Most students want to be accepted by their classmates. They look to their friends for approval and may alter their behaviors in order to fit in. So we often see students conforming to the behaviors of the peer group—for example, by wearing clothes with a particular brand name, cheering for a particular athletic team, or avoiding individuals whom the group has identified as a "nerd" or "geek."

Students' peers tend to encourage some behaviors and discourage others, with such **peer pressure** having its strongest effect during the junior high school years (Berndt, 1979; Berndt, Laychak, & Park, 1990; Durkin, 1995; Erwin, 1993). Fortunately, peer groups often encourage such desirable qualities as truthfulness, fairness, cooperation, and a sense of humor (Damon, 1988; McCallum & Bracken, 1993). But they may also encourage students to engage in gender-stereotypical behavior; for example, boys who engage in traditionally "masculine" activities (e.g., playing football) and girls who engage in traditionally "feminine" activities (e.g., putting on makeup) are usually more popular than those who pursue counterstereotypical activities (Huston, 1983). And violent behavior is much more likely when a student's peer group expects or demands it (Lowry et al., 1995).

Sadly, many peer groups convey the message that academic achievement is undesirable, perhaps by making fun of "brainy" students or by encouraging such behaviors as cheating on homework, cutting class, and skipping school (Berndt, 1992; B. B. Brown, 1993; Knapp & Woolverton, 1995; Tomlinson, 1993). In fact, in some ethnic minority groups, a student who achieves good grades is "acting White"—a label some students

Provide opportunities for students associating with the "wrong crowd" to interact with students who have more productive attitudes and values.

want to avoid at all costs (B. B. Brown, 1993; Ogbu, 1992; Tomlinson, 1993). Consider what happened to Kareem Abdul-Jabbar when, as a nine-year-old, he enrolled in a new school:

> I got there and immediately found I could read better than anyone in the school. . . . When the nuns found this out they paid me a lot of attention, once even asking me, a fourth grader, to read to the seventh grade. When the kids found this out I became a target. . . . I got all A's and was hated for it; I spoke correctly and was called a punk. I had to learn a new language simply to be able to deal with the threats. I had good manners and was a good little boy and paid for it with my hide. (Abdul-Jabbar & Knobles, 1983, p. 16)

To cope with such pressure, some students lead "double lives" that enable them to attain academic success while maintaining the acceptance of their peers; for example, although they attend class and do their homework faithfully, they may feign disinterest in certain activities, disrupt class with jokes or goofy behaviors, and express surprise at receiving high grades (B. B. Brown, 1993; Covington, 1992).

An Arena for Developing Social Skills

A child's relationships with parents and teachers are usually lopsided, unequal ones, such that the adults have the upper hand and control the nature of interactions. But in most relationships with peers, each individual is an equal partner. This equality provides a situation in which a child can begin to develop cooperative behaviors, a sense of reciprocity ("You do me a favor, and I'll do you one"), and strategies for resolving conflicts (Asher & Parker, 1989; Erwin, 1993; Hartup, 1989; Salmon, 1979).

As we noted earlier, students with poor social skills (e.g., those such as Adam in the chapter's opening case study) have few friends. But by not interacting frequently with their peers, they rarely get the opportunities they need in order to develop the skills they are lacking (Coie & Cillessen, 1993). And when they do interact with their classmates, their behaviors are often counterproductive, leaving them more isolated than ever. Consider the plight of a seventh-grader named Michelle as an example:

> Michelle is an extremely bright student, and her academic accomplishments have earned her much teacher praise over the years. But despite her many scholastic successes, Michelle has few friends. To draw attention to herself, she talks incessantly about her academic achievements. Her classmates interpret such bragging as a sign of undeserved arrogance, and so they insult her frequently as a way of knocking her down a peg or two. In self-defense, Michelle begins hurling insults at her classmates as soon as she sees them—beating them to the punch, so to speak.

When students routinely offend or alienate others, their peers seldom give them the kind of constructive feedback that allows them to improve their behavior on future occasions. It may be up to us, as teachers, to give them the guidance they so desperately need.

Fostering Social Skills

Social skills are the things that we do to interact effectively with other people—cooperating, sharing, showing courtesy, initiating conversations, and so on. Some social skills are aimed at benefiting someone else more than ourselves; such **prosocial behaviors** include helping, comforting, and showing empathy for another's feelings. Schools and classrooms, as complex social situations, provide the ideal context in

When friends or classmates discourage high academic achievement, ask students to demonstrate what they have learned privately rather than publicly.

Provide opportunities for students to practice cooperation, reciprocity, and conflict-resolution skills.

Think back to our discussion of self-concept. What do Michelle's behaviors tell us about her self-perceptions of social competence?

which social skills and prosocial behaviors can develop (Deutsch, 1993; S. N. Elliott & Busse, 1991).

Students such as Adam and Michelle may be unaware of how socially counterproductive their behaviors really are. As teachers, we can help them develop ways of forming positive and productive interpersonal relationships. Here are some approaches that we can use to promote social skills and prosocial behaviors:

Teach and praise appropriate social behaviors.

Teach specific social skills, provide opportunities for students to practice them, and give feedback. We can teach students appropriate ways of behaving both through explicit verbal instructions and through modeling desired behaviors for them. Such instruction is especially likely to be effective when we also ask students to practice their newly learned social skills (perhaps through role playing) and give them concrete feedback about how they are doing (Baskin & Hess, 1980; S. N. Elliott & Busse, 1991; Hughes, 1988; Vaughn, 1991; Zirpoli & Melloy, 1993).

Label and praise appropriate behaviors when they occur. We should identify and praise the specific social skills that we see our students exhibit (Vorrath, 1985; Wittmer & Honig, 1994). For example, we might say, "Thank you for being so helpful," or, "I'm glad that you two were able to cooperate so well as you worked on your project."

Describe students as being helpful, courteous, or generous.

Describe students as having desirable social behaviors. We can openly describe our students as being helpful, courteous, or generous (Grusec & Redler, 1980; Wittmer & Honig, 1994). For example, eight-year-olds who are told, "You're the kind of person who likes to help others whenever you can," are more likely to share their belongings with others at a later date (Grusec & Redler, 1980).

Teach social problem-solving strategies.

Teach social problem-solving strategies. Some students lack productive strategies for solving social problems; for example, they may barge into a game without asking or respond to any provocation in an aggressive fashion (Hughes, 1988; Neel, Jenkins, & Meadows, 1990; Zirpoli & Melloy, 1993). One strategy that we can teach them is to think carefully about a situation before responding and then talk themselves through the appropriate behaviors for dealing with it (Hughes, 1988). And a strategy that we can use for our classroom as a whole is *mediation training,* teaching students how to mediate conflicts among classmates by asking the opposing sides to express their differing points of view and then working together to devise a reasonable resolution (Deutsch, 1993; Sanchez & Anderson, 1990). We will discuss both of these strategies in more depth when we consider self-regulation in Chapter 10.

Assign cooperative learning activities. Cooperative learning activities, in addition to promoting academic achievement, have social benefits as well. For one thing, they provide an arena in which students can learn and practice help-giving, help-seeking, and conflict-resolution skills. Furthermore, the sharing of materials that such activities require engenders feelings of justice and fairness (Damon, 1988; Lickona, 1991; Webb & Farivar, 1994).

Establish clear guidelines regarding classroom behavior.

Establish and enforce firm rules regarding acceptable classroom behavior. In addition to encouraging appropriate social behaviors, we must actively discourage such inappropriate behaviors as inconsiderateness, aggression, and prejudicial remarks (Bierman, Miller, & Stabb, 1987; Braukmann, Kirigin, & Wolf, 1981; Schofield, 1995). We must have clear guidelines for classroom behavior and impose consequences when such guidelines are not followed. By establishing and enforcing firm rules about aggressive behavior while simultaneously teaching appropriate social skills, we often see noticeable improvements in behavior. We will learn more about establishing rules in our discussion of classroom management in Chapter 12, and we will consider appropriate consequences for undesirable behavior in our discussion of behavior modification in Chapter 9.

But even when our students have the ability to relate effectively with one another, we may find that many of them interact almost exclusively within a small, close-knit group and that a few others remain socially isolated. Yet students have much of value to learn from their classmates, including those very different from themselves. So let's also consider how we can facilitate social interaction among diverse groups of students.

Promoting Social Interaction Among Diverse Groups

Simply putting students in the same school building is rarely sufficient to promote interaction among individual students or among groups of students. For example, students often divide themselves along ethnic lines when they eat lunch and interact in the schoolyard (Schofield, 1995). Immigrant students rarely interact with long-term residents (Olneck, 1995). And students with special needs are often poorly accepted or even rejected by their classmates (Aiello, 1988; Hannah, 1988; Hymel, 1986; Juvonen & Hiner, 1991; Yuker, 1988).

As teachers, we must often take proactive steps to broaden the base of our students' social interactions. Here are some strategies that seem to be effective in doing so:

Set up situations in which students can form new friendships.

Set up situations in which students can form new friendships. We can do many simple things to encourage students to get to know one another. We can set up situations in which they must work or play cooperatively with one another; for example, we can develop structured cooperative learning activities in which all group members must share equal responsibility, or we can provide play equipment that requires the participation of several students (Banks, 1994; Schofield, 1995). We can assign a partner to a student with special needs—a classmate who can provide assistance when needed, perhaps reading to a student with a visual impairment, signing to a student with a hearing impairment, tutoring a student with a learning disability, or taking notes for a student with a physical impairment. We can teach students how to use electronic bulletin boards and other forms of computer-based communication (Spicker, 1992). And the very simple practice of giving students assigned seats in class and then occasionally changing those assignments increases the number of friends they will make (Schofield, 1995).

Minimize or eliminate barriers to social interaction.

Minimize or eliminate barriers to social interaction. Students are less likely to interact with their classmates when there are physical, linguistic, or social barriers to doing so. For example, I am reminded of a junior high girl who could not negotiate the cafeteria steps with her wheelchair and so had to eat lunch alone. Obviously, we must be on the lookout for any physical impediments to the mobility of students with special needs and campaign for the removal of such obstacles. We can teach groups of students who speak different languages (including American Sign Language, with which many students with hearing impairments communicate) some basic vocabulary and simple phrases in one another's native tongues. And we must actively address the prejudices and tensions that sometimes separate diverse ethnic groups (Ulichny, 1994); we will identify specific strategies for doing so in our discussion of multicultural education in Chapter 4.

Assigning partners to students with special needs is one mechanism through which we can facilitate the development of new friendships.

Encourage and facilitate participation in extracurricular activities. Extracurricular activities provide additional opportunities for students to interact and work cooperatively with a wide range of classmates (Genova & Walberg, 1984; Phelan et al., 1994; Schofield, 1995). We must be careful, however, that no single group of students dominates in membership or leadership in any particular activity (Sleeter & Grant, 1994). And schools may need to make special arrangements for after-school transportation for some students (Schofield, 1995).

Encourage and facilitate participation in extracurricular activities.

Develop nondisabled students' understanding of students with special needs. Nondisabled classmates sometimes feel resentment or anger about inappropriate behaviors they believe a classmate with special needs should be able to control (Juvonen, 1991a, 1991b; Juvonen & Hiner, 1991; Juvonen & Weiner, 1993). For example, they are less likely to be tolerant of students with cognitive difficulties or behavioral

Develop nondisabled students' understanding of students with special needs.

One way in which schools can promote positive relationships between students with special needs and other students is by demonstrating that students with special needs are in many ways just ordinary people. This *Kids on the Block* puppet show illustrates how students with disabilities have thoughts and feelings just like everyone else.

(The Kids on the Block is an educational company which uses puppets to teach children about disabilities, differences, and social concerns. Created in 1977, the educational puppet curriculums are in use world-wide by more than 1,700 community based troupes. For information call 1-800-368-KIDS.)

disorders than they are of students with obvious physical disabilities (Madden & Slavin, 1983; Semmel et al., 1979; Ysseldyke & Algozzine, 1984). As teachers, we must help nondisabled students become aware of any difficulties that students with special needs may have as a result of a disability. At the same time, we must also show them the many ways in which such students are normal children with the same thoughts, feelings, and needs as anyone else their age.

Help change the reputations of formerly antisocial students.

Help change the reputations of formerly antisocial students.   Unfortunately, students' bad reputations often live on long after their behavior has changed for the better. Even after students show dramatic improvements in behavior, their classmates may continue to dislike and reject them (Bierman et al., 1987; Juvonen & Hiner, 1991; Juvonen & Weiner, 1993). For example, in the case of formerly aggressive students, the perception of many classmates is "once a bully, always a bully." So when we work to im-

---

INTO THE CLASSROOM
Promoting Social Development

Expect and encourage behaviors essential for students' long-term success.

> On Mondays, a seventh-grade teacher gives homework assignments for the entire week as a way of promoting students' responsibility and independence regarding their schoolwork.

Give students numerous opportunities to interact with one another in pairs or small groups.

> A middle school teacher has students work in groups of three on a complex library research project. She structures the assignment in such a way that each group member has a clearly defined role to perform.

When appropriate to do so, let students work out their own interpersonal difficulties.

> When several students argue about whose turn it is to use the classroom computer, their teacher encourages them to work out a plan that will allow fair and equitable use each week.

Teach and provide practice in ways of interacting effectively with others.

> A teacher notices that one girl in his class rarely speaks to her classmates except to insult them. He schedules several after-school meetings with her, and together they role-play appropriate ways of initiating social interactions. In the weeks that follow, he monitors her interactions with classmates and gives her feedback about her progress.

Promote social interaction among diverse groups.

> A science teacher decides how students will be paired for weekly lab activities. She changes the pairings every month and frequently pairs students from different ethnic backgrounds.

---

prove the behaviors of antisocial students, we must work to improve their reputations as well—for example, by placing them in cooperative learning groups where they can use their newly developed social skills or by encouraging their active involvement in extracurricular activities. In one way or another, we must help them show their peers that they have changed and are worth getting to know better.

Truly productive interpersonal relationships depend on students' ability to respect one another's rights and privileges, to see things from one another's perspective, and to support classmates who are going through hard times. Such capabilities are aspects of students' moral development, a topic we turn to now.

PROMOTING MORAL AND PROSOCIAL BEHAVIOR

In our case study at the beginning of the chapter, we found Adam engaging in immoral behavior: He was routinely stealing lunches in the cafeteria. When we speak of immoral behavior more generally, we are talking about actions that are unfair, cause physical or emotional harm, or violate the rights of others (Smetana, 1983; Turiel, 1983).

Students' beliefs about moral and immoral behavior—their beliefs about what's right and wrong—affect their actions at school and in the classroom. For example, we will have fewer instances of theft or violence when students respect the property and safety of their classmates. We will have fewer infractions of school and classroom rules when students recognize the importance of obeying such rules. We will have fewer cases of cheating when students believe that cheating is morally unacceptable.

Students' beliefs about morality also affect their thinking about the subjects they study in school—such subjects as history, literature, science, and physical education. For example, why do most people believe that the actions of the German Nazis during World War II were morally reprehensible? Was it appropriate for U.S. troops to enter Somalia to bring food and supplies to people who were starving, even though they killed some Somalian citizens in the process? Should laboratory rats be used to study the effects of cancer-producing agents? Why is it important to show good sportsmanship on the athletic field? We simply cannot avoid moral issues as we study school subject matter.

As teachers, we play a significant role in the moral and prosocial development of our students (Pollard, Kurtines, Carlo, Dancs, & Mayock, 1991; Rushton, 1980). Consider the teacher who prepares a class for the arrival of a new student, first by discussing the feelings of uncertainty, apprehension, and loneliness that the student is likely to have, and then by helping the class identify steps it can take to make the student feel at home. This teacher is facilitating perspective taking and setting the stage for students to behave prosocially toward the newcomer. Now consider the teacher who ignores incidents of selfishness and aggression in class and on the playground, perhaps using the rationale that students should always work things out among themselves. This teacher is doing little to promote students' social and moral growth and, in fact, may be inadvertently sending them the message that *anti*social behavior is appropriate.

In the pages that follow, we will look at the multidimensional nature of moral development. We will first consider the emotional underpinnings of moral behavior and then examine the development of moral reasoning, perspective taking, and prosocial behavior. Finally, we will identify a number of things we can do as teachers to promote the moral and prosocial development of our students.

How Emotions Reflect Moral Development

How do you feel when an action on your part inadvertently causes inconvenience for someone else? How do you feel when you hurt someone else's feelings? How do you feel when a friend has a death in the family?

———————————————————————————— ■ ————————————————————————————

Look for signs of shame, guilt, and empathy as indicators that students are developing morally.

Three distinct emotions are associated with moral development. For one thing, by the time children reach the middle elementary grades, most of them will feel **shame;** they will feel embarrassed or humiliated when they fail to meet the standards for moral behavior that parents and teachers have set for them (Damon, 1988). Shortly thereafter, as they begin to develop their own standards for behavior, they will experience **guilt**— a feeling of discomfort when they know that they have caused someone else pain or distress (Damon, 1988; Hoffman, 1991). Both shame and guilt, though unpleasant in nature, are good signs that students are developing a sense of right and wrong and that their future behaviors will improve.

A third emotion involved in moral development is **empathy**—experiencing the same feelings as someone else in unfortunate circumstances (Damon, 1988; Eisenberg, 1982; Hoffman, 1991). Empathy continues to develop throughout the elementary school years, and sometimes into the high school years as well (Eisenberg, 1982). In the primary grade levels, empathy is confined to people that students know—for example, friends and classmates. But by the late elementary school years, students may also begin to feel empathy for people they *don't* know—perhaps for the poor, the homeless, or those living in war-torn nations (Damon, 1988; Hoffman, 1991). Empathy is especially instrumental in the development of prosocial behavior: Students are more likely to act on someone else's behalf if they share that person's feelings of sadness or frustration. As we consider the topics of perspective taking and induction later in the chapter, we will identify teaching strategies that should help students develop empathy for others.

Considering the Development of Moral Reasoning: Kohlberg's Theory

■   EXPERIENCING FIRSTHAND

Heinz's Dilemma

In Europe, a woman was near death from a rare form of cancer. There was one drug that the doctors thought might save her, a form of radium that a druggist in the same town had recently discovered. The druggist was charging $2,000, ten times what the drug cost him to make. The sick woman's husband, Heinz, went to everyone he knew to borrow the money, but he could only get together about half of what the drug cost. He told the druggist that his wife was dying and asked him to sell it cheaper or let him pay later. But the druggist said no. So Heinz got desperate and broke into the man's store to steal the drug for his wife. (Kohlberg, 1984, p. 186)

- Should Heinz have stolen the drug? What would you have done if you were Heinz? Which is worse, stealing something that belongs to someone else or letting another person die a preventable death? Why?

- Do you think that people younger than yourself might answer the same questions differently? How do you think a typical fifth grader might respond? A typical high school student?

The story you just read about Heinz and his dying wife is an example of a **moral dilemma**—a situation to which there is no clear-cut right or wrong response. Lawrence Kohlberg presented moral dilemmas to people of various ages and asked them to propose solutions for each one. Here are three solutions proposed by school-age students. I have given the students fictitious names so that we can refer to them again later.

> *James (a fifth grader):*
> Maybe his wife is an important person and runs a store, and the man buys stuff from her and can't get it any other place. The police would blame the owner that he didn't save the wife. He didn't save an important person, and that's just like killing with a gun or a knife. You can get the electric chair for that. (Kohlberg, 1981, pp. 265–266)

> *Jesse (a high school student):*
> If he cares enough for her to steal for her, he should steal it. If not he should let her die. It's up to him. (Kohlberg, 1981, p. 132)

> *Jules (a high school student):*
> In that particular situation Heinz was right to do it. In the eyes of the law he would not be doing the right thing, but in the eyes of the moral law he would. If he had exhausted every other alternative I think it would be worth it to save a life. (Kohlberg, 1984, pp. 446–447)

These three students present three different reasons to justify why Heinz should steal the lifesaving drug. James bases his decision on the possible advantages and disadvantages of stealing or not stealing the drug for Heinz alone; he does not consider the perspective of the dying woman at all. Likewise, Jesse takes a very self-serving view, proposing that the decision to either steal or not steal the drug depends on how much Heinz loves his wife. Only Jules considers the value of human life in justifying why Heinz should break the law.

After obtaining hundreds of responses to moral dilemmas, Kohlberg proposed that the development of moral reasoning is characterized by a series of stages (e.g., Colby, Kohlberg, Gibbs, & Lieberman, 1983; Kohlberg, 1969, 1976, 1984, 1986; Kohlberg & Turiel, 1971). These stages, as in any stage theory, form an invariant sequence: An individual progresses through them in order, without skipping any. Each stage builds upon the foundation laid by earlier stages but reflects a more integrated and logically consistent set of moral beliefs than those before it.

Kohlberg grouped his stages into three *levels* of morality—the preconventional, conventional, and postconventional levels. These three levels and the two stages within each one are described briefly in Table 3–3. Let's look at each level more closely.

Level I: Preconventional Morality

We see preconventional morality in preschool children, most elementary school students (especially those in the primary grades), some middle and junior high school students, and a few high school students (Colby & Kohlberg, 1984; Reimer et al., 1983). Preconventional morality is the earliest and least mature form of morality, in that the individual has not yet adopted or internalized society's conventions regarding what is morally right or wrong. The preconventional individual's judgments about the morality of behavior are determined primarily by the consequences of those behaviors. Behav-

Why is this level called "preconventional"?

Table 3–3 Kohlberg's Three Levels and Six Stages of Moral Reasoning

STAGE	MORAL REASONING
Level I: Preconventional Morality (seen in preschool children, most elementary school students, some junior high school students, and a few high school students)	
Stage 1: Punishment-avoidance and obedience	Individuals make moral decisions on the basis of what is best for themselves, without regard for the needs or feelings of others. They obey rules only if established by more powerful individuals; they disobey when they can do so without getting caught.
Stage 2: Exchange of favors	Individuals begin to recognize that others also have needs. They may attempt to satisfy the needs of others if their own needs are also met in the process. They continue to define right and wrong primarily in terms of consequences to themselves.
Level II: Conventional Morality (seen in a few older elementary school students, some junior high school students, and many high school students)	
Stage 3: Good boy/good girl	Individuals make moral decisions on the basis of what actions will please others, especially authority figures. They are concerned about maintaining interpersonal relationships through sharing, trust, and loyalty. They now consider someone's intentions in determining innocence or guilt.
Stage 4: Law and order	Individuals look to society as a whole for guidelines concerning what is right or wrong. They perceive rules to be inflexible and believe that it is their "duty" to obey them.
Level III: Postconventional Morality (rarely seen before college)	
Stage 5: Social contract	Individuals recognize that rules represent an agreement among many people about appropriate behavior. They recognize that rules are flexible and can be changed if they no longer meet society's needs.
Stage 6: Universal ethical principle	Individuals adhere to a small number of abstract, universal principles that transcend specific, concrete rules. They answer to an inner conscience and may break rules that violate their own ethical principles.

Sources: Colby & Kohlberg, 1984; Colby, Kohlberg, Gibbs, & Lieberman, 1983; Kohlberg, 1969, 1976, 1984, 1986; Reimer, Paolitto, & Hersh, 1983.

iors that lead to rewards and pleasure are "right"; behaviors that lead to punishment are "wrong." Preconventional individuals will obey people who have control of rewards and punishments; they will not necessarily obey people without such control over consequences. Here we see one reason why, as teachers, we should tell students the consequences for appropriate and inappropriate classroom behavior and apply those consequences consistently.

Stage 1: Punishment-avoidance and obedience. Stage 1 individuals (including our friend James) make moral decisions based on what they think is best for themselves, without regard for the needs or feelings of other people. For these individuals, the only "wrong" behaviors are ones that will be punished. Stage 1 individuals follow rules of behavior that are established by people more powerful than they, whether these people are parents, teachers, or stronger peers. But they may disobey rules if they think they can avoid punishment in doing so. In a nutshell, individuals in Stage 1 will do anything if they can get away with it.

In making moral decisions, Stage 1 individuals seldom consider the intentions or feelings of other people. "Badness" is defined strictly in terms of physical or material consequences. To illustrate, consider the cases of John and Henry:

> John was in his room when his mother called him to dinner. John went down and opened the door to the dining room. But behind the door was a chair, and on the chair was a tray with fifteen cups on it. John did not know the cups were behind the door. He opened the door, the door hit the tray, bang went the fifteen cups, and they all got broken.

> One day when Henry's mother was out, Henry tried to get some cookies out of the cupboard. He climbed up on a chair, but the cookie jar was still too high, and he couldn't reach it. But while he was trying to get the cookie jar, he knocked over a cup. The cup fell and broke. (Based on stories originally used by Piaget, 1932; adapted from Bandura & McDonald, 1963, p. 276)

Even though John's intentions were more honorable than Henry's, the Stage 1 person would declare John to be the naughtier of the two boys because he broke more cups.

Stage 2: Exchange of favors. Individuals in Stage 2, which Kohlberg has often referred to as the *instrumental-relativist* stage, are beginning to recognize that others have needs just as they themselves do. They sometimes address the needs of others by offering to exchange favors ("You scratch my back, and I'll scratch yours"), but they usually try to get the better end of the bargain. To Stage 2 individuals, being "fair" means that everybody gets the same opportunities or the same amount of whatever is being handed out. As teachers, we might hear "That's not fair!" from Stage 2 students who think they're being short-changed.

Like Stage 1 individuals, Stage 2 individuals focus on the physical consequences of behavior, rather than on more abstract, less observable consequences. For example, if a boy at this stage is thinking about insulting a classmate, he may refrain from doing so if he thinks that the classmate will beat him up, but the thought that the insult might hurt the classmate's feelings will not be a deterrent. Similarly, cheating on a test if a student can get away with it is perfectly acceptable; the idea that she would "only be hurting herself" does not yet make sense to her (Reimer et al., 1983).

Kohlberg classified our friend Jesse's response to the Heinz dilemma as a Stage 2 response. Jesse is beginning to recognize the importance of saving someone else's life, but the decision to do so ultimately depends on whether Heinz loves his wife—it depends on *his* feelings alone.

Describe the consequences for appropriate and inappropriate classroom behavior and apply them consistently, especially when dealing with a largely "preconventional" classroom.

Talk about people's well-meaning intentions in situations where their actions have inadvertently led to an undesirable consequence.

Make things as fair as you can, providing the same opportunities to all students.

Level II: Conventional Morality

A few older elementary school students, some middle and junior high school students, and many high school students exhibit conventional morality (Colby & Kohlberg, 1984; Reimer et al., 1983). Conventional morality is characterized by an acceptance of society's conventions concerning right and wrong: The individual obeys rules and follows society's norms even when there is no reward for obedience and no punishment for disobedience. Adherence to rules and conventions is somewhat rigid; a rule's appropriateness or fairness is seldom questioned.

Communicate your approval when students behave in a morally desirable fashion.

Stage 3: Good boy/good girl. Stage 3 individuals look primarily to the people they know, and especially to authority figures (e.g., parents, teachers, popular classmates), for guidance about what is right and wrong. Stage 3 individuals want to please others and gain their approval; they like being told they are a "good boy" or a "good girl." They are also concerned about maintaining interpersonal relationships through sharing, trust, and loyalty. For example, they believe in the Golden Rule—"Do unto others as you would have them do unto you"—and in the importance of keeping promises and commitments.

Stage 3 individuals can put themselves in another person's shoes and consider the perspectives of others in making decisions. They also acknowledge that someone's *intentions* must be considered in determining guilt or innocence. In examining the John and Henry situations I described earlier, the Stage 3 individual would identify Henry as being naughtier than John because of his dishonorable intention: He tried to get cookies behind his mother's back. John, who broke many more cups, would be less naughty because he "meant well."

With Stage 4 students, begin to talk about situations in which breaking laws may be the morally correct thing to do.

Stage 4: Law and order. Stage 4 individuals look to society as a whole, rather than just to the people whom they know, for guidelines (conventions) as to what is right and wrong. They know that rules are necessary for keeping society running smoothly and believe that it is their "duty" to obey them. They see these rules as things that are set in concrete, however; they do not yet recognize that it may occasionally be more "moral" to break laws (perhaps those legitimating racial segregation or interfering with basic human rights) than to follow them. Nor do they recognize that, as the needs of society change, rules should be changed as well.

Level III: Postconventional Morality

Postconventional morality is rarely observed in students before they reach college, and in fact most people never reach this level of moral reasoning at all (Colby & Kohlberg, 1984; Reimer et al., 1983). Postconventional individuals have developed their own set of abstract principles to define what actions are morally right and wrong—principles that typically include such basic human rights as life, liberty, and justice. Postconventional individuals obey rules consistent with their own abstract principles of morality, and they may *dis*obey rules inconsistent with those principles.

At the high school level, begin to talk with students about such abstract principles as justice and human rights.

Stage 5: Social contract. Stage 5 individuals view rules that are determined through a democratic process as a *social contract*—an agreement among many people about how they should all behave. They think of such rules as being useful mechanisms that maintain the general social order and protect individual human rights, rather than as absolute dictates that must be obeyed simply because they are "the law." They also recognize the flexibility of rules; rules that no longer serve the best interests of a society's citizens can and should be changed. An example of Stage 5 thinking can be seen in our friend Jules's response to the Heinz dilemma: Jules proposed that the woman's well-being would be better served by breaking the law than by obeying it.

Stage 6: Universal ethical principle.

Kohlberg described Stage 6 as an "ideal" stage that few people ever reach. This stage represents adherence to a few abstract, universal principles that transcend specific norms and rules for behavior. Such principles typically include respect for human dignity and basic human rights, the belief that all people are truly equal, and a commitment to justice and due process. Stage 6 individuals answer to a strong inner conscience, rather than to authority figures or concrete laws, and they willingly disobey laws that violate their own ethical principles. Martin Luther King Jr.'s "Letter from a Birmingham Jail" illustrates Stage 6 reasoning; here is an excerpt from that letter:

> One may well ask, "How can you advocate breaking some laws and obeying others?" The answer lies in the fact that one has not only a legal but a moral responsibility to obey just laws. One has a moral responsibility to disobey unjust laws, though one must do so openly, lovingly and with a willingness to accept the penalty. An individual who breaks a law that conscience tells him is unjust, and accepts the penalty to arouse the conscience of the community, is expressing in reality the highest respect for law. An unjust law is a human law not rooted in eternal law and natural law. A law that uplifts human personality is just; one which degrades human personality is unjust. (King, 1965, cited in Kohlberg, 1981, pp. 318–319)

Factors Affecting Progression Through Kohlberg's Stages

As you undoubtedly noticed, students at any particular age are not always reasoning at the same level and stage. We see the greatest variability in high school students, some of whom may show Stage 4 reasoning, whereas others are still reasoning at Stage 1. Why is it that different students of the same age sometimes show very different stages of moral reasoning? Kohlberg proposed that two aspects of Piaget's theory of cognitive development—his stages of cognitive development and his concept of *disequilibrium*—affect progression to more advanced stages of moral reasoning.

Stage of cognitive development.

Kohlberg proposed that moral reasoning is somewhat dependent on Piaget's stages of cognitive development. Postconventional morality, because it involves reasoning with abstract principles, cannot occur until an individual has acquired formal operational thought, and even conventional morality probably involves some formal operational thinking capabilities (Kohlberg, 1976). Thus, conventional and postconventional levels of moral reasoning do not usually appear until adolescence. At the same time, progression to an advanced stage of cognitive development does not guarantee equivalent moral development; for example, it is quite possible to be formal operational in logical reasoning but preconventional in moral reasoning. In other words, Kohlberg maintained that cognitive development is a *necessary but insufficient* condition for moral development to occur.

Disequilibrium.

As you should recall from Chapter 2, Piaget proposed that children progress to a higher stage of cognitive development when they experience *disequilibrium*—that is, when they realize that their knowledge and schemes do not adequately explain the events around them. Because disequilibrium is an uncomfortable feeling, children begin to reorganize their thoughts and ideas into a more complex and better integrated system, one that more adequately accounts for their experiences.

In high school social studies classes, identify situations in which the laws or conventions of a particular society might be counterproductive. In physical education classes, explain why the rules of a game sometimes change over time.

Do you know anyone who is very intelligent yet reasons at a preconventional level?

Challenge the moral reasoning of students in a particular stage by presenting reasoning at the next higher stage.

Kohlberg proposed that a similar process promotes moral development. Individuals become increasingly aware of the weaknesses of a particular stage of moral reasoning, especially when their moral judgments are challenged by people reasoning at the next higher stage. By struggling with these challenges and with moral dilemmas such as Heinz's dilemma about whether to steal or let his wife die, individuals begin to restructure their thoughts about morality and so gradually move from one stage to the next.

What Research Tells Us About Kohlberg's Stages

Many research studies of moral development have followed on the heels of Kohlberg's theory. Some research supports Kohlberg's sequence of stages: Generally speaking, people seem to progress through the stages in the order that Kohlberg proposed (e.g., Colby & Kohlberg, 1984; Reimer et al., 1983). At the same time, it appears that people are not always completely in one stage: Their moral thought usually reflects a particular stage, but they also show occasional instances of reasoning in the two surrounding stages. And to some extent, students' levels of moral reasoning may be situation-specific (Durkin, 1995; Hartshorne & May, 1928; Krebs, Vermeulen, Carpendale, & Denton, 1991; Turiel, Smetana, & Killen, 1991). For example, students are more likely to think of lying as immoral if it causes someone else harm than if it has no adverse effect (if it is just a "white lie"). And moral reasoning plays a role in students' decisions about using drugs only when they view drug use as something that may potentially cause harm to others (Berkowitz, Guerra, & Nucci, 1991).

The "fishing" study described in Chapter 2 was an example of how logical reasoning may be somewhat content-specific. Here we find that moral reasoning may be content-specific as well.

Kohlberg's theory has been criticized on the grounds that it focuses on moral *thinking*, rather than on moral *behavior*. Some researchers have found that people at higher stages of moral reasoning do tend to behave more morally as well (Bear & Richards, 1981; Blasi, 1980; Reimer et al., 1983). For example, students at the higher stages are less likely to cheat in the classroom (Kohlberg, 1975). And they are more likely to help people in need and to disobey orders that would cause harm to another individual (Kohlberg & Candee, 1984). We should keep in mind, however, that the relationship between moral reasoning and moral behavior is a weak one at best (Durkin, 1995). Obviously, then, Kohlberg's theory cannot give us the total picture of how morality develops.

Considering Gender Differences in Moral Reasoning: Gilligan's Theory

Kohlberg developed his stages after studying how people solved moral dilemmas, but consider this quirk in his research: Subjects in his studies were almost exclusively males. Carol Gilligan (1977, 1982, 1987; Gilligan & Attanucci, 1988; Gilligan & Wiggins, 1988) believes that Kohlberg's theory does not adequately describe female moral development. Kohlberg's stages emphasize issues of fairness and justice but omit other aspects of morality, especially compassion and caring for those in need, that Gilligan suggests are more characteristic of the moral reasoning and behavior of females. She argues that females are socialized to stress interpersonal relationships and to take responsibility for the well-being of others to a greater extent than males; females therefore develop a morality that emphasizes a greater concern for others' welfare. Consider the dilemma that follows as an illustration of a morality based on compassion.

The Porcupine Dilemma

A group of industrious, prudent moles have spent the summer digging a burrow where they will spend the winter. A lazy, improvident porcupine who has not prepared a winter shelter approaches the moles and pleads to share their burrow. The moles take pity on the porcupine and agree to let him in. Unfortunately, the moles did not antici- pate the problem the porcupine's sharp quills would pose in close quarters. Once the porcupine has moved in, the moles are constantly being stabbed. The question is, what should the moles do? (Meyers, 1987, p. 141, adapted from Gilligan, 1985) ■

According to Gilligan, males are more likely to look at this situation in terms of someone's rights being violated. For example, they might point out that the burrow be- longs to the moles, and so the moles can legitimately throw the porcupine out. If the porcupine refuses to leave, some argue that the moles are well within their rights to kill him. In contrast, females are more likely to show compassion and caring when dealing with the dilemma. For example, they may suggest that the moles simply cover the por- cupine with a blanket; this way, his quills don't annoy anyone and everyone's needs are met (Meyers, 1987).

Gilligan raises a good point: Males and females are often socialized quite differ- ently, as you will discover in Chapter 4. Furthermore, she reminds us that moral rea- soning includes compassion for other human beings, as well as consideration for their rights, thereby broadening our conception of what morality is (Durkin, 1995). Keep in mind, however, that many research studies do *not* find major gender differences in moral reasoning (Durkin, 1995; Nunner-Winkler, 1984; Walker, 1984, 1991).

The theories of Kohlberg and Gilligan both describe the development of moral rea- soning. Let's turn now to recent findings in two other aspects of moral development: perspective taking and prosocial behavior.

Remember that morality includes compassion and caring, as well as respect for the rights of others.

Fostering Perspective Taking: Selman's Theory

To make moral decisions and behave in morally appropriate ways, a child must be able to look at a situation from someone else's perspective—to imagine what someone else may be thinking or feeling. Consider the following situation as an example.

■   EXPERIENCING FIRSTHAND
Holly's Dilemma

Holly is an eight-year-old girl who likes to climb trees. She is the best tree climber in the neighborhood. One day while climbing down from a tall tree she falls off the bottom branch but does not hurt herself. Her father sees her fall. He is upset and asks her to promise not to climb the trees any more. Holly promises.

Later that day, Holly and her friends meet Sean. Sean's kitten is caught up in a tree and cannot get down. Something has to be done right away or the kitten may fall. Holly is the only one who climbs trees well enough to reach the kitten and get it down, but she remembers her promise to her father.

• Does Holly know how Sean feels about the kitten?

• Does Sean know why Holly cannot decide whether to climb the tree?

- What does Holly think her father will think of her if he finds out?

- Does Holly think her father will understand why she climbed the tree? (from Selman & Byrne, 1974, p. 805)

To answer all of these questions, you must look at the situation from the perspectives of three different people: Sean, Holly, and Holly's father.

By presenting situations like the "Holly" story and asking children to view them from various perspectives, Robert Selman (1980) observed that children show an increasing ability to take the perspective of others as they grow older. He described a series of five levels that characterize the development of perspective taking; these levels are summarized in the left-hand column of Table 3–4.

According to Selman, most preschoolers are incapable of taking anyone else's perspective (hence, they are at Level "0"). But by the time children reach the primary grades, most of them have begun to realize that people have different thoughts and feelings, as well as different physical features (Level 1). They view someone else's perspective as a relatively simplistic, one-dimensional entity, however; for example, another person is simply happy, sad, or angry. Furthermore, they tend to equate behavior with feelings: A happy person will smile, a sad person will pout or cry, and so on. Their interpretations of someone else's actions are also overly simplistic, as this scenario illustrates:

> Donald is a new student in a second-grade classroom. A group of boys in the class openly ridicule his unusual hairstyle and shun him at lunch and on the playground. After school, one of the boys makes a cruel remark about Donald's hair, and Donald responds by punching him. The boys decide that Donald is a "mean kid."

The boys at Donald's new school are interpreting his behavior in a simplistic, Level 1 fashion. They do not yet appreciate the many feelings that Donald may be experiencing: anxiety about a new school and community, shame about a hairstyle that was "cool" at his previous school, and frustration at his inability to make new friends.

As they approach the upper elementary grades, students are likely to show signs of Level 2 perspective taking. They now know that other people can have mixed, possibly conflicting feelings about a situation. They also realize that people may feel differently from what their behaviors indicate—that they may try to hide their true feelings. At this point, too, students recognize the importance of intentions: They understand that people may do things they didn't really want or intend to do. For example, Level 2 children would be more likely to appreciate Donald's predicament and to understand that his aggressive behavior may reflect something other than a mean streak. They might also recognize that Donald's punch was an unintended reaction to a thoughtless insult.

At the middle and secondary school grades, most students are at Selman's two highest levels of perspective taking, in which they are able to take an "outsider's" perspective of interpersonal relationships. Students at Levels 3 and 4 appreciate the need to satisfy both oneself and another simultaneously and therefore understand the advantages of cooperation, compromise, and trust. Not surprisingly, then, students' friendships become relationships of mutual sharing and support beginning in the middle and junior high school grades. Additional aspects of perspective taking emerge at Level 4: Students begin to recognize that an individual's behavior is likely to be influenced by many factors—including one's thoughts, feelings, present circumstances, and past

How is Selman's Level 0 similar to Piaget's preoperational stage of cognitive development?

What might you do as a teacher to ease the transition of a new student into your classroom? What might you do to help other students see things from a new student's point of view?

Table 3–4   Development of Perspective Taking and Prosocial Behavior

SELMAN'S LEVELS OF PERSPECTIVE TAKING*	EISENBERG'S LEVELS OF PROSOCIAL BEHAVIOR*
Level 0: Egocentric perspective taking (most preschool and a few early elementary students) Students are incapable of taking anybody else's perspective. They don't realize that others have thoughts and feelings different from their own.	**Level 1: Selfish and self-centered orientation** (most preschool and many early elementary students) Students show little interest in helping others, apart from serving their own interests. They exhibit prosocial behavior primarily to benefit themselves.
Level 1: Subjective perspective taking (most early and middle elementary school students) Students realize that others have thoughts and feelings different from their own but perceive these in a simplistic, one-dimensional fashion.	**Level 2: Superficial "needs of others" orientation** (some preschool and many elementary students) Students show some concern for another's physical and emotional needs, but their concern is simplistic and lacks true understanding of the other's situation.
Level 2: Second-person, reciprocal perspective taking (many upper elementary students) Students realize that others may have mixed and possibly contradictory feelings about a situation. They also understand that people may feel differently from what their behaviors indicate and that they sometimes do things they didn't intend to do.	**Level 3: Approval and stereotypical good boy/girl orientation** (some elementary and secondary students) Students advocate prosocial behavior on the grounds that it's the "right" thing to do and that they will be liked or appreciated if they help. They hold stereotypical views of what "good boys and girls" and "bad boys and girls" do.
Level 3: Third-person, mutual perspective taking (many middle school and junior high school students) Students not only see things from their own and another's perspective but also can take an "outside" perspective of the two-person relationship. They appreciate the need to satisfy both oneself and another simultaneously and therefore understand the advantages of cooperation, compromise, and trust.	**Level 4: Empathic orientation** (a few elementary and many secondary students) Students have true empathy for another's situation and a desire to help a person in need. They seem genuinely concerned with the well-being of others.
Level 4: Societal, symbolic perspective taking (some junior high and many high school students) Students recognize that people are a product of their environment—that past events and present circumstances contribute to personality and behavior. They begin to develop an understanding of the *unconscious*—the idea that people are not always aware of why they act as they do.	**Level 5: Internalized values orientation** (a few high school students) Students have internalized values about helping other people—values that reflect a belief in the dignity, rights, and equality of all human beings. They express a strong desire to help others in need and to improve the conditions of society as a whole.

* The level numbers are those used by Selman and Eisenberg.

Sources: Eisenberg, 1982; Eisenberg, Lennon, & Pasternack, 1986; Eisenberg, Lennon, & Roth, 1983; Selman, 1980.

events—and that other people are not always aware of why they act the way they do. Level 4 perspective taking, then, is based on an understanding of the true complexity of human behaviors, thoughts, and emotions.

How can we promote greater perspective taking in our students? One strategy is to create disequilibrium by presenting perspective taking at one level above that of our students. For example, at the preschool level we can continually point out to students how the feelings of their classmates differ from their own (Level 1). In the early and middle elementary grades, we can begin to discuss situations in which students may

Present perspective taking at one level above that of students.

have mixed feelings or want to hide their feelings—such situations as going to a new school, trying a difficult but enjoyable sport for the first time, or celebrating a holiday without a favorite family member present (Level 2). At the middle and secondary school levels, we can explore aspects of psychology so that students begin to understand the many ways in which people really are a product of their environment (Level 4).

A second strategy is to create opportunities in which students will encounter multiple—and often equally legitimate—perspectives. For example, at the upper elementary grades, we can provide opportunities for students to work more closely with one another on school projects so that they begin to discover the advantages of cooperation, compromise, and trust (Level 3). Students at all grade levels benefit from hearing a variety of perspectives, including those of different genders, races, cultures, religions, and political belief systems.

When children are better able to take the perspective of another individual, they are also more likely to behave in altruistic and socially beneficial ways—that is, to exhibit prosocial behavior in the classroom. It is to the development of such behavior that we turn now.

Create opportunities in which students hear the perspectives of different genders, races, cultures, religions, and political belief systems.

Fostering Prosocial Behavior: Eisenberg's Theory

In most cultures, one intended outcome of children's socialization is the development of such prosocial actions as sharing, helping, cooperating, and comforting—behaviors that promote the well-being of other individuals. People will be more productive adult citizens if, as children, they learn the advantages and good feelings associated with occasionally putting the needs of others before their own. School, because it is often the most social environment in children's lives, provides a perfect medium in which children can learn prosocial behavior.

As a general rule, children act in more prosocial ways as they grow older; for example, they become increasingly generous with age (Eisenberg, 1982; Rushton, 1980). Nancy Eisenberg and her colleagues (Eisenberg, 1982; Eisenberg, Lennon, & Pasternack, 1986; Eisenberg, Lennon, & Roth, 1983) have identified five levels of reasoning about prosocial behavior that can help us predict how children at different ages are likely to behave. Eisenberg's levels of prosocial behavior are summarized in the right-hand column of Table 3–4.

In what ways is Eisenberg's Level 3 similar to Kohlberg's Stage 3?

As you may notice from looking at Table 3–4, there are several parallels between the development of perspective taking and the development of prosocial behavior. When students are incapable of taking someone else's perspective (Selman's Level 0), they are likely to exhibit prosocial behavior only when such behavior simultaneously benefits themselves (Eisenberg's Level 1). When students have a simplistic, one-dimensional view of another person's perspective (Selman's Level 1), they also show an overly simplistic and superficial concern for the needs of others—one without any true empathy for another person's situation (Eisenberg's Level 2). As students increasingly recognize the complexity of human emotions and interpersonal relationships (Selman's Levels 2, 3, and 4), they also begin to show increasing empathy for the situations of others and a greater desire to help their fellow human beings (Eisenberg's Levels 3, 4, and 5).

How can we promote greater empathy and prosocial behavior in our students? Certainly, we can encourage our students to engage in such prosocial behavior as cooperating and sharing with one another and comforting classmates whose feelings have been hurt. We can also acknowledge such behaviors when we see them. And as the cur-

Encourage prosocial behavior and acknowledge and reward it when it occurs.

riculum gives our students an increasingly broader view of the country and world in which they live, we can expose them to situations in which other people's needs may be far greater than their own.

Expose students to situations in which others' needs are far greater than their own.

Integrating the Stages of Moral Reasoning, Perspective Taking, and Prosocial Behavior

Three of the theorists we have just discussed—Kohlberg, Selman, and Eisenberg—portray a particular aspect of moral development in terms of a series of stages or levels. Let's pull together the work of these three theorists to get an overall picture of the moral and prosocial characteristics of children in different grade ranges.

Elementary School Years

In the elementary grades, we can expect most children to be more concerned about the consequences of their behaviors for themselves than for other people. But we should also see evidence they are capable of looking at events from another person's perspective, albeit very simplistically in the early grades. And some elementary school children will behave prosocially toward their classmates, although with some fairly stereotypical notions of what "good boys and girls" should do to help others.

Children tend to act in more prosocial ways as they grow older; for example, they become increasingly empathic with age.

Middle School and Junior High School Years

In the middle and junior high school years, we will see many students in Kohlberg's Stages 2 and 3. Some students (those in Stage 2) will define acceptable behavior as being "anything I can get away with," rather than in terms of an internalized value system; for example, copying another's homework assignment is justifiable if the teacher doesn't find out, even though the assignment might help a student learn valuable new skills. Other students (those in Stage 3) will be operating on the basis of internalized rules or group norms and will follow those rules or norms primarily to attain the approval of teachers, popular and influential classmates, or other real or imagined authority figures. Junior high school students should also be capable of taking an "outside" perspective of a two-person relationship; thus, they appreciate the necessity for cooperation, compromise, and mutual trust. Many of these students still behave prosocially to gain the approval of those around them, but others are now motivated more by true feelings of empathy for a person in need.

High School Years

At the high school level, encourage discussions about human rights issues and get students involved in working toward solutions to human problems.

By high school, most students reason at Kohlberg's conventional level of development; they have internalized society's views (or perhaps the views of a particular subgroup) of what is right and wrong. But they still see rules in a somewhat rigid manner—as absolute and inflexible entities, rather than as socially agreed on and therefore changeable mechanisms for protecting human rights and promoting the advancement of society. In taking the perspective of someone else, many high school students now understand that a person's behaviors, thoughts, and emotions are often the product of a complex interaction among past events and present circumstances. And most students now have a sense of empathy for the needs of other individuals, with a resulting desire to help those people. A few students in this age range (those in Eisenberg's Level 5) are beginning to show a true commitment to preserving and enhancing the dignity, rights, and equality of all human beings.

Summarize what you have just learned about the age-group that you will be teaching.

In all the theories of moral development that we have discussed, we find a common thread: a gradual progression away from self-centeredness toward increased awareness of the needs and perspectives of others and an increased desire to help fellow human beings. What factors in a child's environment affect the development of moral and prosocial behavior? Let's find out.

Promoting Moral Development in the Classroom

It does little good to "lecture" to students about morally appropriate behavior (Damon, 1988). Several other factors, however, *do* seem to make a difference in the development of moral reasoning and behavior. Five important ones are these:

- An authoritative environment
- Reasons why some behaviors are unacceptable
- Practice in recognizing others' emotional states
- Models of moral and prosocial behavior
- Moral issues and dilemmas

These factors are summarized in Table 3–5. Let's look more closely at each one.

Table 3–5   Factors Contributing to Moral Development

FACTOR	EXAMPLE	EDUCATIONAL IMPLICATION
Authoritative environment	As an only child, Louis has never had to share his things with anyone else. His kindergarten teacher firmly requests that he share school supplies with the other children at his table; she also gives the group some guidelines about how to do so in an equitable manner.	Insist that students show consideration and respect for the rights and needs of others; do so within the context of a firm, yet supportive environment.
Reasons why some behaviors are unacceptable	When several middle school girls maliciously ruin Linda's art project, their teacher points out that Linda spent several weeks completing the project and insists that they find a suitable way of making amends.	When students behave in an immoral or antisocial manner, help them recognize that they have caused distress or inconvenience to someone else.
Practice in recognizing others' emotional states	As a high school literature class reads Jane Austen's *Sense and Sensibility,* the teacher asks students to speculate on how Elinor and Marianne might be feeling at various points in the book.	Using both real-life and fictional situations, encourage students to deduce how particular individuals must be feeling.
Models of moral and prosocial behavior	When a fourth-grade class conducts a food drive for homeless families, the students see their teacher bring in three large bags of canned goods he has collected from his neighbors.	Model moral and prosocial behaviors and expose students to other good models as well.
Moral issues and dilemmas	Levi and Logan notice a classmate cheating on an important science test. At lunch, they debate the advantages and disadvantages of telling their teacher what they observed.	Include moral issues and dilemmas in the curriculum.

An Authoritative Environment

Earlier in the chapter, I described an *authoritative* environment—one in which adults hold high expectations and standards for children's behavior within the context of an accepting and supportive environment—as the one most likely to produce happy, well-adjusted, and self-confident children. An authoritative environment has benefits for moral development as well: Children become more sensitive to the needs of others and are more willing to accept responsibility for any wrongdoings they have committed (Damon, 1988; Hoffman, 1970, 1975). As teachers, then, we must hold firm regarding our

Insist that students respect the feelings, rights, and property of others.

expectations that students show consideration for classmates, respect for others' property, and tolerance for diverse cultures, religions, and political views.

Reasons Why Some Behaviors Are Unacceptable

Are you more likely to obey rules when you know the reasons behind them?

Although it is important that we impose consequences for immoral or antisocial behaviors, punishment by itself often focuses children's attention on their own hurt and distress (Hoffman, 1975). Yet to promote students' moral development, we must focus their attention on the hurt and distress that their behaviors have caused *others*. Thus, we should give them reasons why certain behaviors are unacceptable—an approach known as **induction** (Hoffman, 1970, 1975). For example, we might describe how a behavior harms someone else either physically ("Having your hair pulled the way you just pulled Mai's can really be painful") or emotionally ("You probably hurt John's feelings when you call him names like that"). We might also show students how they have caused someone else inconvenience ("Because you ruined Maria's jacket, her parents are making her work around the house to earn the money for a new one"). Still another approach is to explain someone else's perspective, intention, or motive ("This science project you've just ridiculed may not be as fancy as yours, but I know that Michael spent many hours working on it and is quite proud of what he's done").

Induction is victim-centered: It helps students focus on the distress of others and recognize that they themselves have been the cause of it (Hoffman, 1970). The consistent use of induction in disciplining children, particularly when it is accompanied by *mild* punishment for misbehavior, appears to promote cooperation with rules (Baumrind, 1971) and to facilitate the development of such prosocial characteristics as empathy, compassion, and altruism (G. H. Brody & Shaffer, 1982; Hoffman, 1975; Maccoby & Martin, 1983; Rushton, 1980).

Talk about reasons why some behaviors are inappropriate, especially in terms of the harm or inconvenience that those behaviors have caused.

Practice in Recognizing Others' Emotional States

We will have less of a need to explain someone else's feelings if our students are able to recognize those feelings on their own. Yet many students, young ones especially, are poor judges of the emotional states of others. At the preschool level, it may be helpful actually to label a classmate's feelings as "sadness," "disappointment," or "anger " (Chalmers & Townsend, 1990; Wittmer & Honig, 1994). In later years, we might ask students to describe to one another exactly how they feel about particular misbehaviors directed toward them (Doescher & Sugawara, 1989). Or we might ask them how they themselves would feel in the same situation (Hoffman, 1991). And, as teachers, we should describe our own emotional reactions to any inappropriate behaviors (Damon, 1988).

Help students learn to recognize the specific feelings that others are experiencing.

Models of Moral and Prosocial Behavior

On the one hand, children and adolescents are more likely to exhibit moral and prosocial behavior when they see others behaving in morally appropriate ways. For example, when parents are generous and show concern for others, their children tend to do likewise (Rushton, 1980). On the other hand, when children see their peers cheating, they themselves are more likely to cheat (Sherrill, Horowitz, Friedman, & Salisbury, 1970). Television, too, provides both prosocial and antisocial models for children. When children watch television shows that emphasize prosocial behavior (e.g., *Sesame Street* or *Mister Rogers' Neighborhood*), they are more likely to exhibit prosocial behavior themselves; when they see violence on television, they, too, are more likely to be violent (Rushton, 1980).

As teachers, we teach by what we do, as well as by what we say. When we model compassion and consideration of the feelings of others, such behaviors may rub off on our students. When we are instead self-centered and place our own needs before those of others, our students may follow suit.

We can also make use of the models of moral behavior that we find in literature (Ellenwood & Ryan, 1991). For example, in Harper Lee's *To Kill a Mockingbird,* set in the highly segregated and racially charged Alabama of the 1930s, a lawyer defends an obviously innocent African American man who is charged with murder; in doing so, he exemplifies a willingness to fight for high moral principles in the face of strong social pressure to let the man hang for the crime. In John Gunther's *Death Be Not Proud,* we find a young boy who is generous and considerate despite his impending death from cancer (Ellenwood & Ryan, 1991).

Model moral and prosocial behavior, and present additional models through literature.

We will consider modeling in more detail in Chapter 10.

Moral Issues and Dilemmas

Kohlberg proposed that children develop morally when they are challenged by moral dilemmas they cannot adequately deal with at their current stage of moral reasoning. Research confirms his belief: Classroom discussions of controversial topics and moral issues appear to promote the transition to more advanced moral reasoning and increased perspective taking (Blatt & Kohlberg, 1973; D. W. Johnson & Johnson, 1988; Schlaefli, Rest, & Thoma, 1985).

Social and moral issues often arise at school. Sometimes these issues relate to specific student behaviors that appear in the classroom setting. For example, cheating, plagiarism, theft, and interpersonal conflicts are likely to occur in most classrooms at one time or another. And sometimes moral issues are intrinsic in course content. Consider the kinds of questions that might emerge in a study of history, science, or literature—such questions as these:

Incorporate moral issues and dilemmas into classroom discussions.

Is it appropriate to engage in armed conflict, and hence to kill others, when two groups of people disagree about political or religious issues?

Should scientists use their discoveries to gain control over others (e.g., by developing nuclear weapons or methods of chemical warfare or by promoting genetic engineering)?

How can a capitalistic society encourage free enterprise while at the same time protecting the rights of citizens and the ecology of the environment?

Should psychologists study the effects of pain by inflicting it on such animals as rats and earthworms?

Was Hamlet justified in killing Claudius to avenge the murder of his father?

As teachers, we must remember that social and moral issues will not always have right or wrong answers. Nevertheless, we can facilitate student discussions of such issues in a variety of ways (Reimer et al., 1983). First, we can provide a trusting and nonthreatening classroom atmosphere in which students feel free to express their ideas without censure or embarrassment. Second, we can help students identify all aspects of a dilemma, including the needs and perspectives of the various individuals involved. Third, we can help students explore their reasons for thinking as they do—that is, help them clarify and examine the principles on which their moral judgments are based.

Help students identify all aspects of a dilemma, including the needs and perspectives of the various individuals involved.

CONSIDERING DIVERSITY IN PERSONAL, SOCIAL, AND MORAL DEVELOPMENT

Some of your students may face greater challenges in their personal lives than you did. Be especially supportive of such students.

These are not easy times in which to grow up, and many of our students will have experienced challenges we ourselves may never have imagined as children. More than half of our students are likely to spend at least part of their childhood in a single-parent home; for example, some will have been raised by unwed mothers, and many others will have lived through a divorce (Brough, 1990; Nielsen, 1993). Violence in schools and on the streets is on the rise, especially in low-income areas (Gorski & Pilotto, 1993; Lowry et al., 1995; Parks, 1995). Temptations to experiment with drugs and alcohol are everywhere (G. R. Adams, Gullotta, & Markstrom-Adams, 1994; Durkin, 1995; S. P.

Thomas et al., 1993). For students facing such challenges, we must be especially supportive, acting as willing listeners and communicating regularly how much we value each and every one of them (Ogden & Germinario, 1988).

Yet even when our students haven't experienced such challenges, personality, social skills, and moral beliefs will certainly vary considerably from one student to the next. For example, in our discussion of self-concept, we discovered that students are likely to differ in their self-views of cognitive, social, and physical competence. We may see additional diversity in self-concept related to students' group membership. For example, we may find that, when students come from diverse cultural backgrounds, some may have a strong sense of identity with their cultures, whereas others would prefer just to blend in with mainstream society (Olneck, 1995; Pang, 1995). We may also find that many minority students, while having high self-esteem in general, have little faith in their ability to achieve academic success (Covington, 1992; Elrich, 1994; Garcia, 1994; Graham, 1994). As teachers, we will often need to make a special effort to foster positive self-concepts in students from minority cultures. For example, we can help them explore their cultural backgrounds as a way of fostering an appreciation of their ethnic roots (Phinney, 1989; Phinney & Alipuria, 1990; S. Wright & Taylor, 1995). And we must certainly provide whatever scaffolding they need in order to be successful on academic tasks.

We will see diversity in students' social development as well. For example, some cultures (e.g., those in many groups from Asia and South America) value loyalty and foster prosocial behavior far more than others do (Durkin, 1995; Greenfield, 1994; P. B. Smith & Bond, 1994; Triandis, 1995). And children who have grown up in a rural environment tend to be more cooperative than children from an urban environment (Eisenberg & Mussen, 1989).

Definitions of what is "moral" behavior are also likely to differ. For example, although lying is generally discouraged in our own culture, it is a legitimate way of saving face in many others (Triandis, 1995). Furthermore, some cultures emphasize the importance of being considerate of other people (e.g., "Please be quiet so that your sister can study"), whereas others emphasize the importance of tolerating inconsiderate behavior (e.g., "Please try not to let your brother's radio bother you when you study; C. A. Grant & Gomez, 1996). As teachers, we must remember that our students' notions of moral behavior will not always be identical to our own.

Foster students' understanding and appreciation of their own ethnic backgrounds.

Remember that some students' backgrounds have probably been more conducive to promoting social skills than those of other students.

Remember that your students' notions of moral behavior may differ from your own.

Accommodating Students with Special Needs

Some of our students will undoubtedly have special educational needs related to their personal, social, or moral development. For example, many of our students with special needs will have lower self-esteem than their classmates (e.g., Brown-Mizuno, 1990; T. Bryan, 1991). Students with mental retardation will typically have less understanding of how to behave in social situations than their nondisabled peers (Greenspan & Granfield, 1992). Students with emotional and behavioral disorders—for example, those with a history of aggressive and violent behavior—will frequently have poor perspective-taking and social problem-solving abilities, and they may perceive hostile intentions in the most innocent of their classmates' actions (Hughes, 1988; Lind, 1994). Additional characteristics that you may see in students with special needs, along with strategies for promoting the personal, social, and moral development of such students, are presented in Table 3–6.

Table 3–6 *Promoting Personal, Social, and Moral Development in Students with Special Educational Needs*

STUDENTS WITH SPECIAL NEEDS	CHARACTERISTICS THAT THESE STUDENTS MAY EXHIBIT	CLASSROOM STRATEGIES THAT MAY BE BENEFICIAL FOR THESE STUDENTS
Students with specific cognitive or academic deficits	Low self-esteem regarding academic tasks Greater susceptibility to peer pressure Difficulty in perspective taking	Promote academic success (e.g., by providing extra scaffolding for classroom tasks) Use induction to promote perspective taking (e.g., focus students' attention on how their behaviors have caused harm or distress to others)
Students with specific social or behavioral deficits	Poor social skills Difficulties in social problem solving Rejection by peers; few friendships Misinterpretation of social cues (e.g., perceiving hostile intent in innocent interactions) Less empathy for others Difficulty in perspective taking	Teach social skills, provide opportunities to practice them, and give feedback Establish and enforce firm rules regarding acceptable classroom behavior Label and praise appropriate behaviors when they occur Teach social problem-solving strategies (e.g., through mediation training) Provide opportunities for students to make new friends (e.g., through cooperative learning activities) Help change the reputations of formerly antisocial students Use induction to promote empathy and perspective taking
Students with general delays in cognitive and social functioning	Generally low self-esteem Social skills typical of younger children Difficulty identifying and interpreting social cues Concrete, often preconventional, ideas of right and wrong	Promote academic and social success Teach social skills, provide opportunities to practice them, and give feedback Specify rules for classroom behavior in specific, concrete terms Label and praise appropriate behaviors when they occur
Students with advanced cognitive development	Above-average social development and emotional adjustment (although some extremely gifted students may have difficulty because they are so very different from their peers) High self-esteem with regard to academic tasks (more typical of males than females) Conflicts (especially for females) between the need to develop and display abilities, on the one hand, and to gain peer acceptance, on the other For some students, more advanced moral reasoning Concerns about moral and ethical issues at a younger age than peers Greater perspective taking	Talk with students regarding their concerns about their exceptional abilities Engage students in conversations about ethical issues and moral dilemmas Involve students in projects that address social problems at a community, national, or international level

Sources: Asher & Coie, 1990; Bierman, Miller, & Stabb, 1987; Brown-Mizuno, 1990; T. Bryan, 1991; Cartledge & Milburn, 1995; Coie & Cillessen, 1993; Coleman & Minnett, 1992; E. S. Ellis & Friend, 1991; Genshaft, Greenbaum, & Borovosky, 1995; Greenspan & Granfield, 1992; Heward, 1996; Hughes, 1988; Juvonen & Hiner, 1991; Juvonen & Weiner, 1993; Licht, 1992; Lind, 1994; Maker & Schiever, 1989; McCormick & Wolf, 1993; C. D. Mercer, 1991; Neel, Jenkins, & Meadows, 1990; Ormrod, 1995a; Patton, Beirne-Smith, & Payne, 1990; Piirto, 1994; Schonert-Reichl, 1993; Schumaker & Hazel, 1984; Turnbull, Turnbull, Shank, & Leal, 1995; Zeaman & House, 1979; Zirpoli & Melloy, 1993.
Compiled with the assistance of Dr. Margie Garanzini-Daiber and Dr. Margaret Cohen, University of Missouri—St. Louis.

LOOKING AT THE BIG PICTURE: RECURRING THEMES IN PERSONAL, SOCIAL, AND MORAL DEVELOPMENT

Three themes have appeared repeatedly in our discussion of personal, social, and moral development:

- Standards for acceptable behavior and the reasons behind them
- Social interaction
- A warm, supportive environment

These three themes are summarized in Table 3–7. Let's look more closely at each one.

Standards for Acceptable Behavior and the Reasons Behind Them

Standards for acceptable behavior, along with reasons why these standards must be upheld, are essential for promoting children's development. Well-adjusted children are typically those who grow up in an authoritative environment—one in which rules are set for appropriate behavior, reasons are provided regarding *why* the rules are necessary, and infractions of the rules are punished. And moral development is promoted

Communicate clearly what behaviors are and are not acceptable at school and explain why certain behaviors cannot be tolerated.

PRINCIPLES/ASSUMPTIONS

Table 3–7   General Principles of Personal, Social, and Moral Development

PRINCIPLE	EDUCATIONAL IMPLICATION	EXAMPLE
Reasonable standards for behavior, accompanied by reasons why these standards must be adhered to, promote more moral and prosocial behavior.	When imposing rules and restrictions in the classroom, we should show students how such rules and restrictions enhance learning and achievement.	When insisting that students not ask one another about the quiz scores each has received, we can explain that everyone is entitled to privacy about such matters and that someone's low score, if revealed to classmates, might create unnecessary embarrassment.
Social interactions with both adults and peers promote social skills, moral reasoning, perspective taking, and the development of students' self-concepts.	Our classroom schedules should include group-based as well as individual learning activities.	When a topic is controversial (perhaps from a social, political, ethical, or theoretical standpoint), we can have students meet in small groups to exchange ideas, identify various viewpoints, and develop a compromise that takes all perspectives into account.
A warm, supportive environment enhances self-esteem and fosters open, honest classroom interaction.	We must communicate to students that, regardless of their occasional failings or misbehaviors, we like and respect them as people and that we will continue to support them in their efforts to succeed.	When a student shows a pattern of inappropriate and counterproductive classroom behavior (e.g., resistance, hostility), we can find a time to meet privately with the student to find out how we can work together more effectively.

when punishment for rule infractions is accompanied by induction—by descriptions of how one's misbehavior has caused physical or emotional harm to someone else. As teachers, we must communicate clearly to students what behaviors are and are not acceptable at school and explain why some behaviors will not be tolerated.

Provide numerous opportunities for social interaction.

Social Interaction

As we discovered in Chapter 2, social interaction is critical for children's cognitive and linguistic development. In this chapter, we have found that it is equally critical for personal, social, and moral development. For example, students' self-concepts are affected to a considerable extent by the way that others behave toward them. Social skills develop within the context of interactions with others, and especially with peers. Conversations about controversial topics and moral issues help students see things from other viewpoints and create disequilibrium for students at lower stages of moral reasoning; thus, such conversations are critical for the development of perspective taking and moral reasoning. Classroom discussions and other opportunities for social interaction must therefore be an important and frequent component of classroom life.

Provide a warm, supportive classroom environment.

A Warm, Supportive Environment

Development is most effectively fostered within the context of a generally warm and supportive environment. We first saw the importance of a loving yet firm environment in our discussion of authoritative parenting. We also discovered the very critical role

Social interaction is critical for many aspects of students' personal, social, and moral development.

that positive feedback plays in the development of students' self-concepts and self-esteem. And we learned that students are more likely to express their ideas about moral issues in a classroom in which they feel free to express their ideas openly and honestly.

It would be naive for us to think of schools only as places where students learn academic skills. Whether we like it or not, our schools—teachers, administrators, and classmates included—play an important and influential role in children's personal, social, and moral development as well. It is critical that we not leave these important aspects of children's development to chance.

CASE STUDY: *A Discussion of Runaway Slaves*

Mr. Dawson's eighth-grade American history class is learning about the large cotton plantations prevalent in the Southern states before the Civil War. Mr. Dawson explains that such plantations probably would not have been possible without the thousands of slaves who picked the cotton.

"Sometimes the slaves would run away," he says. "And when they did, White people who believed that slavery was wrong would hide them or help them escape to the North. But helping runaway slaves was against the law; a person could be put in jail for doing so. Was it right for these people to help the slaves? Would *you* have helped a slave run away?"

"I don't think I would," says Mark. "Some of the plantation owners might have been my friends, and I wouldn't want them to get angry at me."

"I don't think I would either," says Lacy. "After all, it was against the law. I'd get punished if I broke the law. I wouldn't want to end up in jail."

"I think I might do it," says Kevin, "but only if I was sure I wouldn't get caught."

"I agree with Kevin," says Pam. "Besides, if I were really nice to the slave, he might help me around the house or in my garden."

Mr. Dawson is appalled at what his students are telling him. Where is their sense of injustice about the enslavement of human beings? Isn't the very notion of slavery inconsistent with the idea that all people are created equal?

- Are you as surprised as Mr. Dawson is? What stages of moral reasoning are evident in the opinions of these four students? Are these stages typical or atypical for eighth graders?

SUMMING UP

Personal Development

Some aspects of students' personalities are inherited; others will have been formed early in life. Yet the school environment, including teachers and classmates, also influences students' personal development; for example, students' self-concepts and self-esteem are affected by the expectations that teachers hold for their behavior and by the ways that teachers and classmates treat them. We can promote students' personal development by holding high yet realistic expectations for performance, helping them be successful in classroom tasks, providing positive feedback for things well done, and giving negative feedback within the context of overall positive regard. We must also consider the age range of our students; for example, we can (1) support preschoolers in their efforts to initiate activities, (2) encourage elementary school students to produce things and praise them for their accomplishments, and (3) provide opportunities for secondary school students to explore various career options and a variety of social and political belief systems.

Social Development

Schools are important socialization agents; for example, teachers teach students to control impulses, follow directions, work independently, cooperate with classmates, and delay gratification. As teachers, we must expect and encourage those behaviors essential for students' long-term life success.

Classmates are equally important in students' social development; peer relationships provide emotional support, information about acceptable behaviors and values, and an arena for developing social skills. We can help students develop supportive peer relationships by teaching productive interpersonal skills and by encouraging interaction among diverse groups.

Moral Development

As they move through the grade levels, most students become less self-centered in their solutions to moral problems, gain an increasing ability to see situations from someone else's point of view, and demonstrate prosocial behavior more frequently. As teachers, we can promote the development of more advanced moral reasoning, perspective taking, and prosocial be-

havior by providing an authoritative classroom environment, giving students reasons why certain behaviors are unacceptable, encouraging them to recognize how others feel in various situations, challenging their thinking with moral issues and dilemmas, and modeling moral behavior ourselves.

Diversity in Personal, Social, and Moral Development

Some of our students will face extra challenges in their lives (e.g., family problems, violence, drug addiction), and such challenges will invariably affect their personal, social, and moral development. We will also see differences among our students because of the cultural contexts in which they have been raised; for example, some students' sense of identity may include pride in their ethnic heritage, and their sense of morality is likely to reflect the values of their local community. Students with special needs may, in some instances, need additional support to enhance their self-esteem, social skills, and moral development.

General Themes

Three themes appeared repeatedly in our discussion of personal, social, and moral development. First, students need standards for acceptable behavior, as well as reasons why some behaviors are unacceptable. Second, social interaction plays a critical role in students' lives; among other things, it affects students' self-concepts and promotes the development of social skills, moral reasoning, and perspective taking. Third, students need a warm, supportive environment—one in which they feel comfortable expressing their views openly and honestly, and one in which they get positive feedback for their successes.

KEY CONCEPTS

personal development (p. 94)
social development (p. 94)
moral development (p. 94)
personality (p. 95)
attachment (p. 96)
parenting (p. 96)
authoritative parenting style (p. 97)
authoritarian parenting style (p. 97)
permissive parenting style (p. 97)
uninvolved parenting style (p. 97)

self-concept (p. 98)
self-esteem (p. 98)
overall positive regard (p. 102)
imaginary audience (p. 106)
personal fable (p. 106)
socialization (p. 108)
norms (p. 108)
roles (p. 108)
culture shock (p. 109)

peers (p. 110)
peer pressure (p. 111)
social skills (p. 112)
prosocial behaviors (p. 112)
shame (p. 118)
guilt (p. 118)
empathy (p. 118)
moral dilemma (p. 119)
induction (p. 132)

Adapting to Individual and Group Differences

THINKING ABOUT WHAT YOU KNOW

- Think of people you know who seem to be especially intelligent or creative. What kinds of behaviors indicate that they might have unusual talents? How do you think those individuals might have acquired their talent?

- Have you observed any consistent behavioral differences among people from diverse ethnic backgrounds? Might some of these behaviors affect students' performance in the classroom?

• What consistent differences have you noticed in the behaviors of males and females? To what extent might these behavioral differences be related to school achievement?

———————————————————————————————◧———————————————————————————————

A S WE HAVE ALREADY SEEN, students change in many ways as they grow, and so students of different ages are often very different from one another. Yet we also find differences among students of the *same* age—differences that we can't always explain from a developmental perspective alone. Some students seem to learn faster than others. Some seem to solve problems more easily. Some devise innovative, creative approaches to their classroom assignments. When we talk about ways in which students of the same age are different from one another, we are talking about **individual differences.**

In addition, we often find consistent differences between certain groups of students. For example, we might notice that students from diverse ethnic backgrounds have different ways of showing respect for their teachers. We might see our female students forming closer, more intimate friendships than the males. And we are likely to find that students from lower-income families have lower educational and career aspirations than their classmates from middle-income families. When we talk about how students of one group typically differ from those of another group, we are talking about **group differences.**

In this chapter, we will consider how we can adapt our classroom practices to accommodate the diversity that we are likely to see at any single age level. We will first examine two individual difference variables—intelligence and creativity—related to students' classroom learning and achievement. Later, we will consider how we can adapt instruction for students of different ethnic backgrounds, genders, and income levels. We will also look at the characteristics of students who are at risk of long-term school failure and identify strategies for helping such students achieve academic and social success. But we must be careful not to form unwarranted expectations about our students; at the end of the chapter, we will identify the negative repercussions that such expectations can have.

By the end of the chapter, you should be able to:

1. Explain what "intelligence" is from several different theoretical perspectives, and express optimism that you can promote intelligent behavior in your classroom.

2. Describe ways of adapting instruction for students whose IQ scores make them eligible for special educational services.

3. Explain what creativity is and how it can be fostered in the classroom.

4. List several ways in which students of different ethnic backgrounds may behave differently, and describe how you can meet the diverse needs of a multicultural population.

5. Describe how males and females are likely to be similar and different, and identify strategies for promoting equally high achievement in both girls and boys.

6. List unique needs that students from low-income families often have, and explain how to help such students attain success in the classroom.

7. Describe common characteristics of students who are at risk of failing to acquire basic academic skills, and identify strategies for helping these students learn successfully.

8. Describe the effects that teacher expectations have on students' self-concepts and behaviors, and take precautions against jumping to premature and unwarranted conclusions.

CASE STUDY: *Hidden Treasure*

A six-year-old girl named Lupita has just enrolled in Ms. Padilla's kindergarten classroom. The daughter of migrant workers, Lupita has been raised by her grandmother in Mexico, where she has had little experience with toys, puzzles, paper, crayons, or scissors, and few opportunities to interact with other children. Ms. Padilla rarely calls on Lupita in class because of her apparent lack of academic skills; she is afraid of embarrassing Lupita in front of her classmates. By midyear, Ms. Padilla is thinking about holding Lupita back for a second year of kindergarten.

Lupita is always quiet and well behaved in class; in fact, she's so quiet that Ms. Padilla sometimes forgets she's even there. Yet a researcher's video camera captures a different side to Lupita. On one occasion, Lupita is quick to finish her Spanish assignment and so begins to work on a puzzle during her free time. A classmate approaches, and he and Lupita begin playing with a box of toys. A teacher aide asks the boy whether he has finished his Spanish assignment, implying that he should return to complete it, but the boy does not understand the aide's subtle message. Lupita gently persuades the boy to go back and finish his assignment. She then returns to her puzzle and successfully fits most of it together. Two classmates having difficulty with their own puzzles request Lupita's assistance, and she competently and patiently shows them how to assemble puzzles and how to help each other.

Ms. Padilla is amazed when she views the videotape, which shows Lupita to be a competent girl with strong teaching and leadership skills. Ms. Padilla readily admits, "I had written her off. Her and three others . . . they had met my expectations and I just wasn't looking for anything else." Ms. Padilla and her aides begin working closely with Lupita on academic skills, and they often allow her to take a leadership role in group activities. At the end of the school year, Lupita obtains achievement test scores indicating exceptional competence in language skills and mathematics, and she is promoted to first grade. (Based on a case study in Carrasco, 1981)

- Why might one jump to the conclusion that Lupita has poor academic skills? Might Lupita's background be a reason? Might her classroom behavior be a reason?

- How might teachers' expectations for their students affect the way they behave toward students? How might teachers' expectations affect students' academic achievement?

- What might have happened to Lupita if there had been no researcher to record her behavior with classmates? How might her academic life have been different?

We will inevitably find that some students learn more easily than others. For example, Lupita finishes assignments and completes puzzles more quickly than some of her classmates. We will also find differences in how accurately our students remember information, how readily they connect ideas with one another, and how easily and creatively they apply the things they learn to new situations and problems.

Some of the behaviors that Lupita exhibits may be partly because of either her Mexican heritage or her gender. For example, she is proficient in Spanish and displays the cooperative attitude encouraged in many Hispanic cultures. She is so quiet in class that her teacher often forgets she's there; as we will discover later, girls are typically less assertive in whole-class situations than boys.

In observing our students day after day, we are likely to draw inferences about their academic capabilities, just as Ms. Padilla did for Lupita. Yet we must be careful that such inferences are never set in stone—that we keep an open mind about how each student is likely to perform in future situations. For example, we will soon discover that creativity is domain-specific: Some students may be creative in science, whereas others are more creative in fine arts. We will find, too, that intelligence can change over time, especially during the early years, and that students often behave more intelligently in some contexts than in others.

Be careful not to make predictions about individual students on the basis of group differences alone.

Remember that average group differences are often quite small, with a great deal of overlap between any two groups.

As we consider group differences, such as those among diverse ethnic groups and those between males and females, we need to keep two very important points in mind. First, *there is a great deal of individual variability within any group* (N. S. Anderson, 1987; Garcia, 1994). I will be describing how students of different groups behave *on the average,* yet some students may be very different from that "average" description. Second, *there is almost always a great deal of overlap between two groups* (e.g., Deaux, 1984). Consider gender differences in verbal ability as an example. Research studies often find that girls demonstrate slightly higher verbal performance than boys (Halpern, 1992; Lueptow, 1984; Maccoby & Jacklin, 1974). This difference is sometimes statistically significant; in other words, we cannot explain it as something that happens just by chance in one particular study. Yet the average difference between girls and boys in verbal ability is quite small, with a great deal of overlap between the two groups. Figure 4–1 shows the typical overlap between boys and girls in verbal ability. Notice how

Figure 4–1 Typical "Difference" Between Boys and Girls in Verbal Ability

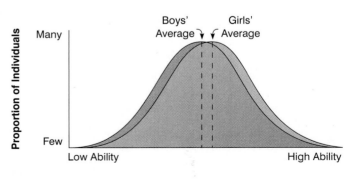

many of the boys are *better* than some of the girls despite the average advantage for girls.

As we shall discover near the end of the chapter, teachers' preconceived notions about how students will behave may actually *increase* the differences among those students. At the same time, if the goal of our educational system is to maximize the learning and development of all students, then there are important individual and group differences of which we should be aware. Several general principles that can guide us as we address student diversity in the classroom are presented in Table 4–1.

In the pages that follow, we will identify many differences that are likely to affect our students' academic achievement; we will also identify numerous simple things that we can do to accommodate those differences. We should never ask ourselves whether particular students can learn. We should instead ask ourselves how we can most effectively help each student master the knowledge and skills essential for school and lifelong success.

⚠ PRINCIPLES/ASSUMPTIONS

Table 4–1 General Principles Regarding Student Diversity

GENERAL PRINCIPLE	EDUCATIONAL IMPLICATION	EXAMPLE
Differences among students are subject to change over time; they are not necessarily *permanent* differences.	We must never make long-range predictions about our students' future success or failure on the basis of their present behaviors.	Although we may see little creativity in a student's performance right now, we should expect that creative behavior is possible in the future if we plan instructional activities that promote such creativity.
There is a great deal of variability within any group of seemingly similar students.	We must be careful not to draw conclusions about students' characteristics and abilities simply on the basis of their gender, ethnic background, or other group membership.	Although few adults in a particular low-income neighborhood have a college degree, we can nevertheless encourage students from this neighborhood to strive for a college education, and we should also support them in their efforts to achieve one.
When two groups differ *on the average* in terms of a particular characteristic, there is usually considerable overlap between the two groups with respect to that characteristic.	We must remember that average differences between groups don't necessarily apply to individual members of those groups.	Although boys, on the average, develop their athletic abilities more than girls, we should provide equal opportunities for both genders to achieve athletic success.
Students achieve at higher levels when instruction takes individual and group differences into account.	We must consider students' unique backgrounds and abilities when planning instructional activities.	We should use cooperative learning activities more frequently when students' cultural backgrounds emphasize the value of cooperation and group achievement.

—————————— **THINKING ABOUT WHAT YOU KNOW** ——————————

What kinds of behaviors make you think that someone is "intelligent"? Do you believe that intelligence is a general ability that contributes to success in many different areas? Or is it possible for an individual to be intelligent in one area yet not in another?

—————————————————— ■ ——————————————————

What exactly is **intelligence**? Unfortunately, psychologists have not yet reached consensus on the answer to this question. But here are several components of what many theorists construe to be intelligent behavior:

- It is *adaptive.* It involves modifying and adjusting one's behaviors in order to accomplish new tasks successfully.

- It is related to *learning ability.* Intelligent people learn information more quickly and easily than less intelligent people.

- It involves the *use of prior knowledge* to analyze and understand new situations effectively.

- It involves the complex interaction and coordination of *many different mental processes.*

- It may be seen in *different arenas*—for example, on academic tasks or in social situations.

Think of someone who you think is intelligent. Does that individual's behavior fit these criteria?

- It is *culture-specific.* What is "intelligent" behavior in one culture is not necessarily intelligent behavior in another culture. (Laboratory of Human Cognition, 1982; Sternberg & Detterman, 1986.)

For most theorists, intelligence is somewhat distinct from what an individual has actually learned (e.g., as reflected in school achievement). At the same time, intelligent thinking and intelligent behavior are, to some extent, *dependent* on prior learning. The more students know about their environment and about the tasks they need to perform, the more intelligently they can behave. Intelligence, then, is not necessarily a permanent, unchanging characteristic. As you will soon discover, it can definitely be modified through experience and learning.

Measuring Intelligence

Curiously, although psychologists cannot pin down exactly what intelligence actually is, they have been trying to measure it for almost a century. In the early 1900s, school officials in France asked Alfred Binet to develop a method of identifying those students unlikely to benefit from regular school instruction and therefore in need of special educational services. To accomplish the task, Binet devised a test that measured general knowledge, vocabulary, perception, memory, and abstract thought. In doing so, he designed the earliest version of what we now call an **intelligence test.**

To get a flavor for what intelligence tests are like, try the following exercise.

A Mock Intelligence Test

See whether you can answer each of these questions:

1. What does the word *quarrel* mean?

2. How are a goat and a beetle alike?

3. What should you do if you get separated from your family in a large department store?

4. Three kinds of people live on the planet Zircox: bims, gubs, and lops. All bims are lops. Some gubs are lops. Which one of the following must also be true?

    a. All bims are gubs.

    b. All lops are bims.

    c. Some gubs are bims.

    d. Some lops are bims.

5. Complete the following analogy:

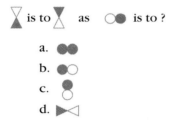

■

The questions I just gave you are modeled after those that appear on many modern-day intelligence tests. What capabilities do you need to answer them successfully? Does general knowledge about the world play a role? Is knowledge of vocabulary important? Is abstract thought involved? The answer to all three questions is yes. Although intelligence tests have evolved considerably since Binet's time, they continue to measure many of the same things that Binet's original test did.

IQ Scores

Scores on intelligence tests were originally calculated by using a formula involving division; hence, they were called "intelligence quotient," or **IQ,** scores. Even though we still use the term *IQ,* intelligence test scores are no longer based on the old formula. Instead, they are determined by comparing a student's performance on the test with the performance of others in the same age-group. A score of 100 indicates average performance: Students with this score have performed better than half of their age-mates on the test and not as well as the other half. Scores below 100 indicate below-average performance on the test; scores above 100 indicate above-average performance.

Figure 4–2 shows the percentage of students getting scores at different points along the scale (e.g., 12.9% get scores between 100 and 105). Notice how the curve is high in the middle and low at both ends. This tells us that we have many more students

Is this description consistent with your previous beliefs about IQ scores?

■

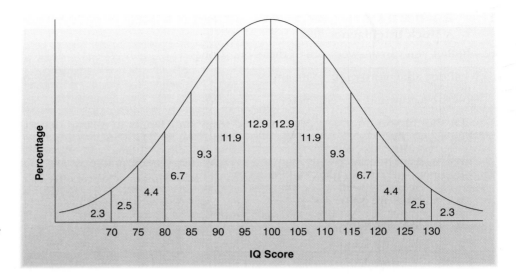

Figure 4–2   Percentage of IQ Scores in Different Ranges

getting scores close to 100 than students getting scores very much higher or lower than 100. For example, if we add up the percentages in the different parts of Figure 4–2, we find that approximately two-thirds (68%) of students get scores within 15 points of 100 (between 85 and 115). In contrast, only 2% of students get scores as low as 70, and only 2% get scores as high as 130. (You can find a more detailed explanation of IQ scores in the discussion of *standard scores* in Appendix B.)

IQ and School Achievement

Modern intelligence tests have been designed with Binet's original purpose in mind: to predict how well individual students are likely to perform in the classroom. Studies repeatedly show that performance on intelligence tests is correlated with school achievement (N. Brody, 1985; Gardner & Hatch, 1990; Neisser et al., 1996; Perkins, 1995; Sattler, 1988). Children with higher IQ scores typically do better on standardized achievement tests, have higher school grades, and complete more years of education. In other words, IQ scores do predict school achievement to some extent. As a result, intelligence tests are often used by school psychologists and other specialists to identify those students who may have special educational needs.

While recognizing the relationship between intelligence test scores and school achievement, we must also keep three points in mind about this relationship. First, intelligence does not necessarily *cause* achievement; it is simply correlated with it. Even though students with high IQs typically perform well in school, we cannot say conclusively that their high achievement is actually the result of their intelligence. Intelligence probably does play an important role in school achievement, but many other factors are also involved—such factors as motivation, quality of instruction, family economics, parental support, and peer group norms.

Second, the relationship between IQ scores and achievement is not a perfect one; there are exceptions to the rule. For a variety of reasons, some students with high IQ scores do not perform well in the classroom. And other students achieve at higher levels than we would predict on the basis of their IQ scores alone. Therefore, we should never base our expectations for students' achievement solely on intelligence test scores.

Under what circumstances might it be appropriate for a teacher to use intelligence test results? What potential dangers are there in relying solely on IQ scores as a measure of students' abilities?

Remember that IQ scores are imprecise predictors of school achievement; some students will achieve at higher or lower levels than we would predict on the basis of IQ scores alone.

Third and most important of all, we must remember that IQ scores simply reflect a student's performance on a particular test at a particular point in time and that some change is to be expected over the years. In fact, the longer the time interval between two measures of intelligence, the greater the change in IQ we are likely to see, especially when young children are involved (Bloom, 1964; Humphreys, 1992; Siegler & Richards, 1982).

How Theorists Conceptualize Intelligence

Up to this point, we have been talking about intelligence in terms of a single IQ score. Yet some theorists do not believe that intelligence is a single entity that people "have" in varying degrees; instead, they propose that people may behave more or less intelligently in different situations and on different kinds of tasks. Let's look at how two contemporary theories of intelligence—Robert Sternberg's triarchic theory and Howard Gardner's theory of multiple intelligences—portray intelligence as a multidimensional and context-dependent entity. We will then look further at the role of context as we consider the notion of "distributed" intelligence.

Sternberg's Triarchic Theory

Robert Sternberg of Yale University (Sternberg, 1984, 1985) has proposed that intelligent behavior involves an interplay of three factors: (1) the environmental *context* in which the behavior occurs, (2) the way in which one's prior *experiences* are brought to bear on a particular task, and (3) the *cognitive processes* required by that task. These three components are summarized in Figure 4–3. Let's look at each one in more detail.

Role of environmental context. Earlier in the chapter, we noted that intelligence is both *adaptive* and *culture-specific*. Sternberg proposes that intelligent behavior involves adaptation: Individuals must adapt their behaviors to deal successfully with specific environmental conditions, modify the environment to better fit their own needs, or select an alternative environment more conducive to success. He also proposes that behavior may be more or less intelligent in different cultural contexts. For example, learning to read is an adaptive response in some cultures yet may be an irrelevant skill in others.

Sternberg has identified three general skills that may be particularly adaptive in Western culture. One such skill is *practical problem-solving ability*—for example, one's ability to identify exactly what the problem *is* in a particular situation, to reason logically (both deductively and inductively), and to generate a multitude of possible problem solutions. A second skill is *verbal ability*—for example, one's ability to speak and write clearly, to develop and use a large vocabulary, and to understand and learn from what one reads. A third skill is *social competence*—for example, one's ability to relate effectively with other human beings, to be sensitive to others' needs and wishes, and to provide leadership.

Role of prior experiences. Sternberg proposes that intelligent behavior sometimes reflects one's ability to deal successfully with a brand new task or situation. At other times, it reflects one's ability to deal with more familiar tasks and situations in a rapid and efficient manner. In both situations, one's prior experiences play a critical role.

When dealing with a new task or situation, people must make some sort of new response. But to do so, they must draw on their past experiences, considering the kinds

Remember that IQ scores are never "permanent"; they simply reflect a student's performance on a particular test at a particular time.

Do you have any prior beliefs about intelligence tests that are inconsistent with the things you've just read? If so, can you resolve the inconsistencies?

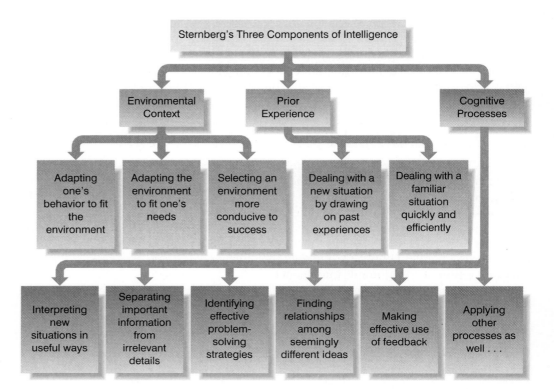

Sternberg's Three Components of Intelligence

- **Environmental Context**
  - Adapting one's behavior to fit the environment
  - Adapting the environment to fit one's needs
  - Selecting an environment more conducive to success

- **Prior Experience**
  - Dealing with a new situation by drawing on past experiences
  - Dealing with a familiar situation quickly and efficiently

- **Cognitive Processes**

- Interpreting new situations in useful ways
- Separating important information from irrelevant details
- Identifying effective problem-solving strategies
- Finding relationships among seemingly different ideas
- Making effective use of feedback
- Applying other processes as well . . .

Figure 4–3 Sternberg's Triarchic Theory of Intelligence

of responses that have been effective in similar situations. Try the following exercise as an illustration.

■ **EXPERIENCING FIRSTHAND**
Finding the Bus Station

You and two friends, Bonnie and Clyde, drive to a small city about two or three hours away to do some sight-seeing. Once you are there, Bonnie and Clyde decide to spend the night so that they can attend a concert scheduled for the following day. You, however, want to return home the same day. Because the car in which you've been traveling belongs to Bonnie, rather than to you, the only way that you can get back home is to take a bus. How might you find your way to the bus station? What strategies have you used in other situations that might help you in your efforts? ■

One strategy is to find a telephone book and look up *bus lines.* Another is to ask directions of a police officer, hotel clerk, or other seemingly knowledgeable person. Still another is to find the city's central business district and wander around; bus stations in most cities are located somewhere in the downtown area. In desperation, you might look for a bus stop, wait for the next bus, get on board, and hope that its last stop is the station. Each of these strategies may be similar to an approach you've used in the past—perhaps to find a friend's home, a suitable place to eat, or a pharmacy open on Saturday nights.

Sternberg further proposes that when people deal with more familiar situations, intelligent behavior involves developing **automaticity**—an ability to respond quickly and efficiently—in the way a task is mentally processed or physically performed. As an example, try the following exercise.

Solving for x

How quickly can you solve for x in this problem?

$$\frac{4}{5} = \frac{x}{30}$$ ■

If you were able to identify the correct answer (24) very quickly and without a great deal of thought and effort, then you show some automaticity (and hence some intelligence) in your ability to solve mathematical problems involving proportions. Automaticity results from experience—from performing certain tasks over and over and over again.

W e will encounter this concept of *automaticity* once again when we explore information processing in Chapter 6.

Role of cognitive processes.   In addition to considering the context in which behavior occurs and the way in which prior experience affects that behavior, we must also consider the way in which an individual thinks about a particular task—in other words, the way in which the task is mentally *processed.* Sternberg proposes that numerous cognitive processes are involved in intelligent behavior: interpreting new situations in ways that promote successful adaptation, separating important and relevant information from unimportant and irrelevant details, identifying possible strategies for solving a problem, finding relationships among seemingly different ideas, making effective use of external feedback about one's performance, and so on. Different cognitive processes are likely to be involved to a greater or lesser degree in different behaviors, and an individual may behave more or less "intelligently" on a task, depending on the specific cognitive abilities and processes needed in that situation.

From Sternberg's perspective, then, intelligence is not a single, general trait. Rather, intelligent behavior is a function of cultural context, experience, and task-specific cognitive processes. Another theorist—Howard Gardner of Harvard University—proposes that there are a number of distinctly different "intelligences," as we shall see now.

Gardner's Theory of Multiple Intelligences

Gardner (1983, 1993; Gardner & Hatch, 1990) believes there are seven different kinds of intelligence that are relatively independent of one another; these intelligences are listed in Table 4–2. As is true for Sternberg's triarchic theory, Gardner's theory of multiple intelligences tells us that we may find different forms of intelligence in different students. For example, some students may show exceptional promise in language, others may be talented in music, and still others may be able to learn mathematics more easily than their classmates.

In which of Gardner's seven kinds of intelligence are you most "intelligent"?

■

Gardner, like Sternberg, believes that intelligence is reflected somewhat differently in different cultures. For example, in our culture, spatial intelligence might be reflected in painting, sculpture, or geometry. But among the Kikuyu people in Kenya, it might be reflected in one's ability to recognize every animal within one's own herd of livestock and to distinguish one's own animals from those of other families. And among the Gikwe bushmen of the Kalahari Desert, it might be reflected in one's ability to recognize and remember many specific locations over a large area (perhaps over several hundred square miles), identifying each location in terms of the rocks, bushes, and other landmarks found there (Gardner, 1983).

Table 4–2   Gardner's Seven Intelligences

TYPE OF INTELLIGENCE	EXAMPLES OF RELEVANT BEHAVIORS
Linguistic Intelligence The ability to use language effectively	Making persuasive arguments Writing poetry Being sensitive to subtle nuances in word meanings
Musical Intelligence The ability to create, comprehend, and appreciate music	Playing a musical instrument Composing a musical work Having a keen awareness of the underlying structure of music
Logical-Mathematical Intelligence The ability to reason logically, especially in mathematics and science	Solving mathematical problems quickly Generating mathematical proofs Formulating and testing hypotheses about observed phenomena*
Spatial Intelligence: The ability to notice details of what one sees and to imagine and "manipulate" visual objects in one's mind	Conjuring up mental images in one's mind Drawing a visual likeness of an object Making fine discriminations among very similar objects
Bodily-Kinesthetic Intelligence The ability to use one's body skillfully	Dancing Playing basketball Performing pantomime
Intrapersonal Intelligence Awareness of one's own feelings, motives, and desires	Discriminating among such similar emotions as sadness and regret Identifying the motives guiding one's own behavior Using self-knowledge to relate more effectively with others
Interpersonal Intelligence The ability to notice subtle aspects of other people's behaviors	Reading another's mood Detecting another's underlying intentions and desires Using knowledge of others to influence their thoughts and behaviors

* This example may remind you of Piaget's theory of cognitive development. Many of the stage-relevant characteristics that Piaget describes fall within the realm of logical-mathematical intelligence.

Concept of Distributed Intelligence

Implicit in our discussion so far is the assumption that intelligent behavior is something that people engage in with little if any help from the objects or people around them. But some theorists point out that people are far more likely to behave intelligently when they have the support of their physical and social environments (Pea, 1993; Perkins, 1995; Sternberg & Wagner, 1994). For example, it's easier for many people to solve for x in $4/5 = x/30$ if they have pencil and paper, or perhaps even a calculator, with which to work the problem out. It should be easier to find the local bus station if one can debate the pros and cons of various strategies with a few friends. As we noted in our

Some theorists, such as Howard Gardner, believe that there are a number of distinctly different "intelligences," such that a person may be more intelligent in one area than in another.

discussion of Vygotsky's theory of cognitive development in Chapter 2, virtually anyone can perform more difficult tasks when he or she has the support structure, or *scaffolding,* to do so. This idea that intelligent behavior depends on people's physical and social support systems (e.g., that two heads are usually better than one) is sometimes referred to as **distributed intelligence** (Pea, 1993).

Being Optimistic About Students' Potential

Contemporary views of intelligence give us reason to be optimistic about our own students' abilities. If intelligence is as multifaceted as theorists such as Sternberg and Gardner believe, then scores from any single IQ test can't possibly give us the complete picture regarding how "intelligent" our students are (Neisser et al., 1996). In fact, we are likely to see intelligent behavior in many of our students—perhaps in *all* of them—in one way or another (e.g., Gardner, 1995). One student may show promise in mathematics, another may be an exceptionally creative writer, a third may be skillful in interpersonal relationships, and a fourth may show talent in art, music, or physical education.

Remember that different students may be intelligent in different ways.

The notion of distributed intelligence tells us that intelligent behavior should be relatively commonplace when students have the right tools or the right group of classmates with which to work. In fact, we find that environmental support systems, including schools and teachers, do influence students' intelligence (Lazar & Darlington, 1982; Lewontin, Rose, & Kamin, 1984; Neisser et al., 1996; Perkins, 1995; Seitz, Rosenbaum, & Apfel, 1985; Zigler & Finn-Stevenson, 1987). For example, permanently changing a child's environment from an impoverished one to an enriched, stimulating one can lead to increases in intelligence of up to 20 or 25 points in measured IQ score (Bloom, 1964; Capron & Duyme, 1989; Scarr & Weinberg, 1976; Skeels, 1966; Zigler & Seitz, 1982).

For optimal intellectual development, children need a variety of stimulating experiences throughout the childhood years, including age-appropriate toys and books, frequent verbal interactions with adults and other children, and numerous opportunities to practice important behavioral and cognitive skills (Bradley & Caldwell, 1984; Brooks-Gunn, Klebanov, & Duncan, 1996; Ericsson & Chalmers, 1994; Ericsson, Krampe, & Tesch-Römer, 1993; R. D. Hess & Holloway, 1984; Honzik, 1967; McGowan & Johnson, 1984). When parents and other primary caretakers cannot provide such experiences for their children, most welcome the availability of enriched preschool and after-school programs. To the extent that schools and society can provide such programs on an ongoing basis, the cognitive development of children and the extent to which those children can go on to lead productive adult lives are greatly enhanced.

Be on the lookout for behaviors that are "intelligent" within the context of students' cultural backgrounds.

We must remember, too, that to the extent that intelligence is culture-dependent, intelligent behavior is likely to take different forms in children from different ethnic backgrounds (Gardner, 1995; Neisser et al., 1996; Perkins, 1995; Sternberg, 1985). For example, in our case study of Lupita, we saw a kindergarten girl with an exceptional ability to work cooperatively with others; cooperation is a valued skill among many Mexican Americans. As another example, the intelligence of Navajo students may be reflected in their ability to help their family and tribe, to perform cultural rituals, or to demonstrate expert craftsmanship (Kirschenbaum, 1989). We must be careful not to limit our conception of intelligence only to students' ability to succeed at traditional academic tasks.

Accommodating Diversity in Intelligence

Don't try to predict academic success during the school years from students' preschool behavior.

Measures of cognitive growth in the first few years of life often have little or no relationship to intelligence in later years: "Bright" babies do not necessarily become the brightest fourth graders, and "slow" toddlers do not always become unintelligent adolescents (Bee et al., 1982; N. Brody, 1985; Siegler & Richards, 1982). But as students progress through the school years, their IQ scores become increasingly more stable: Although they continue to develop cognitively, each one's *relative* intelligence in comparison with that of peers (which is what an IQ score reflects) changes less over time (Bloom, 1964; N. Brody, 1985; Siegler & Richards, 1982).

As teachers, we may have a few students different enough from their classmates on general measures of intelligence that they require special educational services. Such special educational needs will fall into one of two categories: giftedness and mental retardation.

Giftedness

Which one of Gardner's seven intelligences is related to high ability in science? in writing? in art? in leadership?

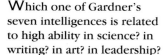

Some students identified as **gifted** have unusually high general intelligence (typically with IQs of 130 or higher); others may have high ability in such specific areas as science, writing, art, or leadership. Although these students are often very different from one another in terms of their unique strengths and talents, they tend to learn more quickly and easily, exhibit greater flexibility in ideas and approaches to tasks, and engage in abstract thinking at an earlier age than is true for their classmates (Carter & Ormrod, 1982; Piirto, 1994; Rabinowitz & Glaser, 1985).

Many gifted students become frustrated when their school experiences don't provide tasks and assignments that challenge them and help them develop their unique talents. Recalling Vygotsky's view of cognitive development from Chapter 2, we could say that gifted students are unlikely to be working within their zone of proximal development if we limit them to the tasks that we assign to other students; thus, they are unlikely to develop new cognitive skills. Many gifted students report being bored by normal classroom activities: They find instruction too slow and often repetitive of things they already know (Feldhusen & Kroll, 1985). As a result, they may lose interest in schoolwork and put in only the minimum effort they need to get by in the classroom (Feldhusen, 1989). In fact, gifted students are among our schools' greatest underachievers; when required to progress at the same rate as their nongifted peers, they achieve at levels far short of their capabilities (Carter, 1991; Gallagher, 1991; Marland, 1972; Reis, 1989). In some situations, then, gifted students will be among those most in need of individualized instruction.

Mental Retardation

Students with **mental retardation** have *significantly below-average general intelligence:* Their IQ scores are usually no higher than 70, and they exhibit consistently poor achievement across virtually all academic subject areas. In addition, they show *deficits in adaptive behavior:* They have difficulty functioning in age-appropriate ways in their social environment and often display social behaviors typical of children much younger than themselves.

Some cases of mental retardation are associated with genetic conditions; for example, most children with Down syndrome have some degree of mental retardation. Other cases are the result of environmental factors, such as an extremely impoverished and unstimulating home environment. Mental retardation, though usually a long-term condition, is not necessarily a lifelong disability, especially in cases where the presumed cause is environmental, rather than genetic (Landesman & Ramey, 1989; Patton, Beirne-Smith, & Payne, 1990). In either situation, students with mental retardation will also be among those most in need of individualized instruction.

As we work with students with special needs, including those who exhibit either giftedness or mental retardation, we must remember that students' IQ scores are not set in stone. Students' environmental experiences—including their school experiences—can and do make a significant difference in how "intelligent" they eventually become. Not only does the environment affect intelligence, but it also affects creativity, as we shall see now.

> What percentage of children get IQ scores of 70 or below? Refer back to Figure 4–2 for the answer.

EXAMINING THE NATURE OF CREATIVITY

Bugs are big,
Bugs are small.
Bugs are black,
Bugs are all . . .
  NEAT!

INTO THE CLASSROOM

Accommodating Diversity in Intelligence

For Gifted Students

Individualize instruction in accordance with students' specific talents.

> A mathematically gifted junior high school student studies calculus via computer-assisted instruction, whereas a classmate with exceptional reading skills is assigned novels appropriate to his reading level.

Form study groups of gifted students with similar abilities and interests.

> A music teacher forms and provides weekly instruction to a quartet of exceptionally talented music students.

Encourage gifted students to set high goals for themselves.

> A teacher encourages a student from a lower socioeconomic background to consider going to college and describes possible sources of financial assistance for higher education.

Seek outside resources to help gifted students develop their exceptional talents.

> A student with a high aptitude for learning foreign languages studies Russian at a local university.

For Students with Mental Retardation

Pace instruction slowly enough to ensure a high rate of success.

> A fifth-grade teacher asks three students with mental retardation to learn two new addition facts a week, while also reviewing previously learned facts each week.

Explain tasks concretely, specifically, and completely.

> A teacher tells a student, "Before we begin today's spelling test, you must do two things. First, write your name at the top of the page." She waits until students have done so and then says, "Second, put the numbers one through six on the first six lines."

Give feedback about specific behaviors, rather than about general areas of performance.

> A teacher tells a student, "You did a good job in science lab this week. You followed my instructions correctly, and you put away the equipment when I asked you to do so."

Consult with specialists in the school district regarding appropriate curricular materials and instructional methods.

> A teacher seeks the advice of the school's special education consultant regarding effective materials for teaching prereading skills to a nonreader.

My critter-happy son Alex wrote the poem about bugs as a second grader. His teacher thought that the poem reflected a certain degree of creativity; so did his not-so-objective mother. What do *you* think?

What exactly do we mean when we use the term **creativity**? Like intelligence, creativity is often defined differently by different people. But most definitions of creativity (e.g., Ripple, 1989) usually include two components:

1. *New and original behavior:* behavior that has not specifically been learned from someone else

2. *An appropriate and productive result:* a useful product or effective problem solution

Can you recall a situation in which you met both criteria for creativity?

Both criteria must be met before we identify behavior as creative.

To illustrate these two criteria, let's say that I am giving a lecture on creativity and want a creative way of keeping my students' attention in class. One possible solution would be to come to class stark naked. This solution certainly meets the first criterion for creativity: It is new and original behavior, and I did not learn it from any other teacher. It does not, however, meet the second criterion: It isn't appropriate or productive (not if I want to maintain my tenured university position, anyway). A second possible solution to the same problem might be to have my students try solving several problems involving creative thinking. This approach is more likely to meet both criteria. Not only is it a relatively original way of teaching, but it is also appropriate and productive in the sense that my students should learn more about creativity through exploring the process firsthand.

Although a certain degree of intelligence is probably necessary for creative thinking, intelligence and creativity are somewhat independent abilities (Sternberg, 1985; I. A. Taylor, 1976; Torrance, 1976). In other words, highly intelligent students are not always the most creative ones. Many theorists believe that the cognitive processes involved in intelligence and creativity may be somewhat different (e.g., see Kogan, 1983). Tasks on intelligence tests often involve **convergent thinking**—pulling several pieces of information together to draw a conclusion or to solve a problem. In contrast, creativity often involves **divergent thinking**—starting with one idea and taking it in many different directions. To see the difference firsthand, try the following exercise.

■ EXPERIENCING FIRSTHAND
Convergent and Divergent Thinking

As examples of convergent and divergent thinking, consider these three questions:

• Why are houses more often built with bricks than with stones?

• What are some possible uses of a brick? Try to think of as many different and unusual uses as you can.

• Add improvements to the wagon drawing so that the object will be more fun to play with. (Modeled after Torrance, 1970) ■

To answer the first question, you pull together the things that you know about several different objects—bricks, stones, and houses—in a convergent fashion. But the other two questions require divergent thinking about a single object: You consider how a brick might be used in many different contexts and how a child's wagon might be embellished in a wide variety of ways.

Look for signs of creativity in a variety of situations and within many different content areas.

Creativity is probably *not* a single entity that people either have or don't have (e.g., Hocevar & Bachelor, 1989). Rather, it is probably a combination of many specific characteristics, thinking processes, and behaviors; among other things, creative individuals are apt to interpret problems and situations in a flexible manner, to possess a great deal of information relevant to a task, to combine existing information and ideas in new ways, and to evaluate their accomplishments in accordance with high standards (Armbruster, 1989; J. R. Hayes, 1989; B. S. Stein, 1989). Furthermore, creativity is probably somewhat specific to different situations and different content areas (R. T. Brown, 1989; Feldhusen & Treffinger, 1980; Ripple, 1989). Students may show creativity in art, writing, or science, but they aren't necessarily creative in all those areas. As teachers, then, we must be careful not to label particular students as "creative" or "not creative." Instead, we should keep our eyes and minds open for instances of creative thinking or behavior in many (perhaps *all*) of our students.

Fostering Creativity in the Classroom

Environmental factors play an important role in the development of creativity (e.g., Esquivel, 1995; Ripple, 1989; Torrance, 1976). Research studies reveal several important characteristics of environments conducive to creativity. Among other things, such environments:

Can you think of teachers who helped you be more creative? What in particular did these teachers do?

- Value creativity

- Focus on internal rather than external rewards

- Promote mastery of a subject area

- Provide thought-provoking questions

- Allow freedom to take risks

- Give the time that creativity requires

Creativity is specific to different content domains. Some students may be creative artists, others may be creative writers, and still others may be creative scientists.

Valuing Creativity

One thing that seems to make a difference is to show students that we value creative thoughts and behaviors. One way in which we can do this is to encourage and reward unusual ideas and responses. For example, we can show our excitement when students complete a project in a unique and unusual manner. And, as we grade assignments and test papers, we should look for responses that, though not what we were looking for, are legitimately correct. Another approach that shows that we value creativity is to engage in creative activities ourselves (Feldhusen & Treffinger, 1980; Hennessey & Amabile, 1987; Parnes, 1967; Torrance & Myers, 1970).

Show students that you value creativity.

Focusing on Internal Rewards

Students are more creative when they engage in activities because they enjoy them and take pride in what they have done; they are less creative when they work for external rewards such as grades (Hennessey, 1995). Therefore, we can foster creativity by giving students opportunities to explore their own special interests—interests they will gladly pursue without having to be prodded. For example, we might tell students in a science class something along this line:

Focus students' attention on the internal rewards that creative activities bring.

> As you plan and develop your research projects for the science fair, choose a topic about which you are genuinely curious. Identify a question that you have about that topic—perhaps a question that no one else has ever asked before! Then design an experiment that can help you answer your question.

We can also foster creativity by downplaying the importance of grades, instead focusing students' attention on the internal satisfaction that their creative efforts bring (Hennessey, 1995; Hennessey & Amabile, 1987; Perkins, 1990; Pruitt, 1989). For example, we might say something like this to students in an art class:

> Please don't worry too much about grades. As long as you show me that you can use the materials as they are meant to be used and as long as you give your best shot on all your assignments, you will do well in this class. The important thing is to find a type of art form that you enjoy and through which you can express yourself.

Promoting Mastery of a Subject Area

Creativity in a particular subject area is more likely to occur when students have considerable mastery of that subject; it is unlikely to occur when students have little or no understanding of the topic. One important way of fostering creativity, then, is to help students master course content (Amabile & Hennessey, 1992; Perkins, 1990; Sternberg, 1985). For example, if we want our students to apply scientific principles in a creative manner—perhaps as they conduct a science fair experiment or develop a solution to an environmental problem—we should make sure they first have those principles down pat.

Help students master the subject area in which you want them to think creatively.

Asking Thought-Provoking Questions

Students are more likely to think creatively when we ask them questions that require them to use previously learned information in a new way (these are frequently called **higher-level questions**). Questions that ask students to engage in divergent thinking may be particularly helpful (Feldhusen & Treffinger, 1980; Feldhusen, Treffinger, &

Ask questions that require students to use information in new ways.

Bahlke, 1970; Perkins, 1990; Torrance & Myers, 1970). For example, here are some questions that a teacher might ask during a unit on the Pony Express:

- What are all the ways mail might have been transported across the United States at that time?
- Most of the time we think of the horse as a means of transportation for the rider and mail. Can you think of other ways a horse could have been used to communicate information from one place to another?
- Can you think of some very unusual way that no one else has thought of to transport mail today? (Feldhusen & Treffinger, 1980, p. 36)

Create an environment in which students feel comfortable taking risks.

Allowing Freedom to Take Risks

Creativity is more likely to appear when students feel free to take risks; it is unlikely to appear when they are afraid of failing (Houtz, 1990). To encourage risk taking, we can allow students to engage in certain activities without evaluating their performance. We can also urge them to think of their mistakes and failures as an inevitable—but usually temporary—aspect of the creative process (Feldhusen & Treffinger, 1980; Hennessey & Amabile, 1987; Parnes, 1967; Pruitt, 1989). For example, when asking students to develop a creative short story, we might give them several opportunities to get our feedback and perhaps the feedback of their peers as well before they turn in a final product.

Give students time to experiment, to think in divergent directions, and to make mistakes.

Giving Time

Students need time to experiment with new materials and ideas, to think in divergent directions, and occasionally to make mistakes. A critical aspect of promoting creativity, then, is to give them that time (Feldhusen & Treffinger, 1980; Pruitt, 1989). For example, when teaching a foreign language, we might ask small groups of students to create and videotape a television commercial spoken entirely in that language. This is hardly a project that students can do in a day; they may need several weeks to brainstorm various ideas, write and revise a script, find or develop the props they need, and rehearse their lines. Creative ideas and projects seldom emerge overnight.

When we discussed intelligence earlier in the chapter, we noted how different behaviors may be "intelligent" in different cultures. We could say the same for creativity as well: What constitutes a work of art or "good music" might vary from one cultural perspective to another. But as we will see now, the diverse ethnic backgrounds among our students will manifest themselves in numerous other ways as well.

EXPLORING ETHNIC DIFFERENCES

■ EXPERIENCING FIRSTHAND
Ruckus in the Lunchroom

In the following passage, a young teenager named Sam is describing an incident at school to his friend Joe:

I got in some trouble at lunch today. Classes went at their usual slow pace through the morning, so at noon I was really ready for lunch. I got in line behind Bubba. As usual the line was moving pretty slow and we were all getting pretty restless.

For a little action Bubba turned around and said, "Hey Sam! What you doin,' man? You so ugly that when the doctor delivered you he slapped your face!"

Everyone laughed, but they laughed even harder when I shot back, "Oh yeah? Well, you so ugly the doctor turned around and slapped your momma!"

It got even wilder when Bubba said, "Well, man, at least my daddy ain't no girl scout!"

We really got into it then. After a while more people got involved—four, five, then six. It was a riot! People helping out anyone who seemed to be getting the worst of the deal.

All of a sudden Mr. Reynolds, the gym teacher, came over to try to quiet things down. The next thing we knew we were all in the office. The principal made us stay after school for a week; he's so straight! On top of that, he sent word home that he wanted to talk to our folks in his office Monday afternoon. Boy! Did I get it when I got home. That's the third notice I've gotten this semester.

As we were leaving the principal's office, I ran into Bubba again. We decided we'd finish where we left off, but this time we would wait until we were off the school grounds. (Adapted from R. E. Reynolds, Taylor, Steffensen, Shirey, & Anderson, 1982, p. 358)

- Exactly what happened in the school cafeteria? Were the boys fighting? Or were they simply having a good time?

The story you just read is actually about "sounding," a friendly exchange of insults that occurs frequently among male youth in some African American communities (e.g., DeLain, Pearson, & Anderson, 1985; R. E. Reynolds et al., 1982). Some boys engage in sounding to achieve status among their peers—those throwing out the greatest insults are the winners—whereas others do it simply for amusement. If you interpreted the cafeteria incident as a knock-down-drag-out fight, you're hardly alone; many eighth graders in a research study did likewise (R. E. Reynolds et al., 1982). When we don't understand the culture in which our students have been raised, we will inevitably misinterpret some of their behaviors.

An **ethnic group** is a group of individuals with the following characteristics:

- Its roots either precede the creation of or are external to the country in which it resides; for example, it may be comprised of people of the same race, national origin, or religious background.

- It has a common set of values, beliefs, and behaviors that influence the lives of its members.

- Its members share a sense of interdependence—a sense that their lives are intertwined. (NCSS Task Force on Ethnic Studies Curriculum Guidelines, 1992)

It is becoming more and more apparent that our schools are not adequately meeting the needs of the diverse ethnic groups they serve. As a result, students from ethnic minorities are often *at risk:* They achieve at levels far below their actual capabilities, and an alarming number of them never graduate from high school (e.g., Garcia, 1992; Santiago, 1986). One likely reason for the low success rates of students from ethnic minority groups is the problem of cultural mismatch, as we shall see now.

The Problem of Cultural Mismatch

As we discovered in Chapter 3, many children entering school for the first time experience some degree of culture shock. This culture shock is more severe for some groups of students than for others (Casanova, 1987; Ramsey, 1987). Most schools in North

Can you think of any ways in which your own school environment was mismatched with the culture in which you were raised?

America and western Europe are based largely on White, middle-class, "mainstream" culture, so students from White, middle-class homes often adjust quickly to the classroom environment. But students who come from other cultural backgrounds, with very different norms regarding acceptable behavior, may find school a confusing and incomprehensible place. For example, recent immigrants to this country may not know what to expect from others or what behaviors others expect of them (C. R. Harris, 1991). Children raised in a society where gender roles are clearly differentiated—where males and females are expected to behave very differently—may have difficulty adjusting to a school in which similar expectations are held for boys and girls (Kirschenbaum; 1989; Vasquez, 1988). Any such **cultural mismatch** between home and school cultures can interfere with students' adjustment to the school setting, and ultimately with their academic achievement as well (Au & Jordan, 1981; García, 1995; Gilliland, 1988; C. R. Harris, 1991; C. D. Lee & Slaughter-Defoe, 1995; Muscella, 1987; Ogbu, 1992; Phelan et al., 1994).

What further compounds cultural mismatch is the fact that teachers may often misinterpret the behaviors of students from ethnic minority groups. For example, we may misinterpret the nature of students' verbal exchanges, just as you might have misinterpreted Sam's behavior in the cafeteria. Certain Native American communities believe that it is unnecessary to say hello or good-bye (Sisk, 1989), yet from our own cultural perspective, we may misunderstand when a student fails to greet us in the morning. In other Native American communities, people rarely express their feelings through facial expressions (Montgomery, 1989); we might easily misinterpret a student's lack of facial expression as an indicator of boredom or disinterest. When students' behaviors are different enough from our own and when we misinterpret those behaviors as being inappropriate, unacceptable, or just plain "odd," we may jump too quickly to the conclusion that these students are unable or unwilling to be successful in the classroom (Bowman, 1989; Hilliard & Vaughn-Scott, 1982). Perhaps this was the case for Ms. Padilla, Lupita's teacher in our case study at the beginning of the chapter.

As teachers, we will rarely, if ever, have a classroom in which all students share our own cultural heritage (e.g., Banks, 1987). Clearly, then, we must educate ourselves about the ways in which students from various ethnic backgrounds are likely to be different from one another and from ourselves.

Examples of Ethnic Diversity

We must keep in mind that we cannot draw conclusions about cultural background on the basis of race alone. For example, African Americans, Asian Americans, Hispanics, and Native Americans are all culturally very heterogeneous populations (Irvine & York, 1995; Maker & Schiever, 1989; Santiago, 1986; A. H. Yee, 1992). We must be careful not to form hard and fast stereotypes about *any* group. At the same time, we must be aware of differences that may exist so that we can better understand why our students sometimes behave as they do.

Researchers have identified a variety of ways in which the cultures of some ethnic minority students may be different from the culture of a typical classroom. Table 4–3 presents a summary of potential differences in eight areas:

- Language and dialect
- Cooperation versus competition

- Private versus public performance

- Eye contact

- Conceptions of time

- Wait time

- Types of questions

- Family relationships and expectations

Let's look more closely at each of these.

Before you read further, can you predict what some of these cultural differences might be?

Language and Dialect

An obvious cultural difference is in language. For example, in the United States, more than six million students speak a language other than English at home (McKeon, 1994; National Association of Bilingual Education, 1993). To the extent that children have not encountered English prior to the school years, they will naturally have difficulty with schoolwork in an English-based classroom (McKeon, 1994; Olneck, 1995; Pang, 1995).

Even when English is spoken at home, it may be a dialect other than the **Standard English** that is typically considered acceptable in school. For example, some African American children learn a different version of English (a different **dialect**) and come to school speaking in ways that their Anglo teachers find unacceptable—for example, by using sentences like these:

- He going home.

- She have a bike.

- He be workin'.

- Ask Albert do he know how to play basketball. (Dale, 1976, pp. 274–275)

At one time, researchers believed that such dialects represented an erroneous and less complex form of speech than Standard English and urged educators to teach students to speak "properly" as quickly as possible. But we now realize that African American dialects are, in fact, very complex language systems with their own predictable grammatical rules and their own unique idioms and proverbs; furthermore, these dialects promote communication and complex thought as readily as Standard English (Dale, 1976; DeLain et al., 1985; Durkin, 1995; Fairchild & Edwards-Evans, 1990).

For many students, their native language is part of their cultural identity (McAlpine, 1992; Ulichny, 1994). The following incident among rural Native American students at a boarding school in Alaska is an example:

Many of the students at the school spoke English with a native dialect and seemed unable to utter certain essential sounds in the English language. A new group of speech teachers was sent in to correct the problem. The teachers worked consistently with the students in an attempt to improve speech patterns and intonation, but found that their efforts were in vain.

One night, the boys in the dormitory were seeming to have too much fun, and peals of laughter were rolling out from under the door. An investigating counselor approached cautiously, and listened quietly outside the door to see if he could discover the source of the laughter. From behind the door he heard a voice, speaking in perfect English, giving instructions to the rest of the crowd. The others were finding the situation very

Table 4–3 *Cultural Differences Found in the Classroom*

CULTURAL DIFFERENCE	EXAMPLE	EDUCATIONAL IMPLICATION
Language or dialect	Terence says, "He be doin' his homework," rather than, "He is doing his homework."	Help students improve their Standard English in some situations (e.g., in their writing) but allow other languages and dialects in less formal situations.
Cooperation versus competition	Despite her exceptional talent in mathematics, Talia does not want to enter the state mathematics competition.	Minimize competition among students in the class and provide opportunities for cooperative learning.
Private versus public performance	Tomas never says a word when his teacher asks him to answer a question in class.	Interact with students individually and in small groups.
Eye contact	Teresa always looks at her feet when her teacher speaks to her.	Don't assume that students aren't paying attention just because they don't look you in the eye.
Conception of time	Timid Wolf is often late to school.	Teach the importance of clock time at school but be patient when some students are not immediately punctual.
Wait time	Tori seems unable to respond to questions as quickly as other students.	Give students time to think after asking a question or posing a problem.
Types of questions	Timothy never responds to "What is this?" questions even when he knows the answers.	Be aware that some students are not used to answering the types of questions that teachers frequently ask.
Family relationships and expectations	Toni sometimes stays home from school to take care of her two younger brothers.	Establish and maintain communication with parents and identify ways in which home and school can work together to help students be successful in the classroom.

amusing. When the counselor entered the room he found that one of the students was speaking. "Joseph," he said, "You've been cured! Your English is perfect." "No," said Joseph returning to his familiar dialect, "I was just doing an imitation of you." "But if you can speak in standard English, why don't you do it all of the time?" the counselor queried. "I can," responded Joseph, "but it sounds funny, and I feel dumb doing it." (Garrison, 1989, p. 121)

Work toward improving Standard English in some situations but allow other dialects in other, less formal ones.

Most educators recommend that all students develop proficiency in Standard English because success in mainstream adult society will be difficult to achieve without such proficiency (e.g., Casanova, 1987; Craft, 1984). At the same time, we should also recognize that other languages and dialects are very appropriate means of communication in many situations (Fairchild & Edwards-Evans, 1990; García, 1995; C. K. Howe, 1994; C. D. Lee & Slaughter-Defoe, 1995; Ulichny, 1994; Vasquez, 1990). For example, although we may wish to encourage Standard English in most written work or in formal oral presentations, we might find other dialects quite appropriate in creative writing or informal classroom discussions.

Cooperation Versus Competition

School achievement in a traditional classroom is often a solitary, individual endeavor: Students receive praise, stickers, and good grades when they themselves perform at a high level, regardless of how their classmates are performing. Sometimes, though, school achievement is quite competitive: A student's performance is evaluated in terms of how it compares with the performance of classmates. For example, some teachers may identify the "best" papers or drawings in the class; others may grade "on a curve," with some students doing very well and others inevitably failing.

Yet in some cultures, it is neither individual achievement nor competitive achievement that is recognized, but rather *group* achievement: The success of the village or community is valued over individual success. Students from such cultures—for example, many Native American, Mexican American, Southeast Asian, and Pacific Islander students—are more accustomed to working cooperatively than competitively, and for the benefit of the community, rather than for themselves (Garcia, 1992; C. A. Grant & Gomez, 1996; Greenfield, 1994; S. Kagan & Knight, 1984; Lomawaima, 1995; Muscella, 1987; Suina & Smolkin, 1994; Tharp, 1994; Triandis, 1995; Vasquez, 1990). They may therefore resist when asked to compete against their classmates. They may also be confused when teachers scold them for helping one another on assignments or for "sharing" answers. And they may feel uncomfortable when their individual achievements are publicly acknowledged. Group work, with an emphasis on cooperation rather than competition, often facilitates the school achievement of such ethnic minority students (Boykin, 1983; Casanova, 1987; Garcia, 1994, 1995; C. A. Grant & Gomez, 1996; McAlpine & Taylor, 1993; Trueba, 1988).

Use cooperative learning techniques involving group interaction and activities; reward students for helping one another learn and achieve.

Private Versus Public Performance

In many classrooms, learning is a very public enterprise. Individual students are often asked to answer questions or demonstrate skills in full view of their classmates, and they are encouraged to ask questions themselves when they don't understand. Such

How do *you* feel about answering a teacher's questions in front of your classmates?

In some cultures, such as in many Mexican American and Native American communities, group achievement is valued over individual or competitive achievement. Children from such cultures are therefore more accustomed to working cooperatively than competitively.

Interact with students frequently in small groups or on a private, one-to-one basis.

Give students the opportunity to practice skills in private until they have mastered them.

practices, which many of us take for granted, may confuse or even alienate the students of some ethnic groups (Au, 1980; Cazden & Leggett, 1981; Crago, Annahatak, & Ningiu-ruvik, 1993; Eriks-Brophy & Crago, 1994; Garcia, 1994; Hidalgo, Siu, Bright, Swap, & Epstein, 1995; Lomawaima, 1995; Vasquez, 1990). For example, children raised in the Yup'ik culture of Alaska are expected to learn by close, quiet observation of adults; they rarely ask questions or otherwise interrupt what the adults are doing (Garcia, 1994). Children from some ethnic backgrounds, including many Puerto Ricans and Native Americans, have been taught that speaking directly and assertively to adults is down-right rude (Hidalgo et al., 1995; Lomawaima, 1995). Many Native American children are also accustomed to practicing a skill privately at first, performing in front of a group only after they have attained a reasonable level of mastery (Garcia, 1994; Sanders, 1987; Suina & Smolkin, 1994). Native Hawaiian students willingly respond as a group when their teacher asks a question, yet often remain silent when called on individually; apparently, these one-on-one interactions with adults remind many students of scoldings they have received from their parents at home (Au, 1980). As you might guess, then, many students from diverse ethnic backgrounds are likely to perform better when they can work one-on-one with the teacher or in a cooperative setting with a small group of classmates (Cazden & Leggett, 1981; Vasquez, 1990). They may also feel more comfortable practicing new skills in privacy until they have sufficiently mastered them (C. A. Grant & Gomez, 1996).

Eye Contact

For many of us, looking someone in the eye is a way of indicating that we are trying to communicate with that individual or that we are listening intently to what the person is saying. But in many Native American cultures, a child who looks an adult in the eye is showing disrespect. Children in such cultures are taught to look down in the presence of adults (Gilliland, 1988). The following anecdote shows how a teacher's recognition of this culturally learned behavior can make a difference:

Don't rely on eye contact as the only indicator that students are paying attention.

> A teacher [described a Native American] student who would never say a word, nor even answer when she greeted him. Then one day when he came in she looked in the other direction and said, "Hello, Jimmy." He answered enthusiastically, "Why hello Miss Jacobs." She found that he would always talk if she looked at a book or at the wall, but when she looked at him, he appeared frightened. (Gilliland, 1988, p. 26)

Conceptions of Time

Many people regulate their lives by the clock: Being on time to appointments, social engagements, and the dinner table is important. This emphasis on punctuality is not characteristic of all cultures, however; for example, many Hispanic and Native American communities don't observe strict schedules and timelines (Burger, 1973; Garrison, 1989; Gilliland, 1988). Not surprisingly, children from these communities may be chronically late for school and have difficulty understanding the need for school tasks to be completed within a certain time frame.

Teach students the importance of clock time at school but be patient when some students are slow to conform.

To succeed in mainstream Western society, students eventually need to learn punctuality. At the same time, we must recognize that not all of our students will be especially concerned about clock time when they first enter our classrooms. Certainly, we should expect students to arrive at class on time and to turn in assignments when they are due. But we must be patient and understanding when, for cultural reasons, students do not develop such habits immediately.

Wait Time

Teachers frequently ask questions of their students and then wait for an answer. But exactly how long *do* they wait? Research indicates that most teachers wait a second or even less for students to reply. Research also indicates that by waiting for longer periods of time—for three seconds or even longer—students are more likely to answer teachers' questions (Rowe, 1987).

This concept **wait time** is an important one to consider when teaching students from different cultural backgrounds. Teachers must remember that many students need time to think their answers through. When students come from non-English-speaking homes, they may also need some mental "translation" time (Gilliland, 1988). And a lengthy pause before responding may also indicate respect; this statement by a Northern Cheyenne illustrates what I mean:

> Even if I had a quick answer to your question, I would never answer immediately. That would be saying that your question was not worth thinking about. (Gilliland, 1988, p. 27)

For many minority groups, students are more likely to participate in class and respond to questions when given several seconds to respond (C. A. Grant & Gomez, 1996; Mohatt & Erickson, 1981; Tharp, 1989).

Yet we should also be aware that some native Hawaiian students, rather than wanting time to think or show respect, may have a preference for **negative wait time:** They often interrupt teachers or classmates who haven't finished speaking. Such interruptions, which would be interpreted as rudeness by many of us, are instead a sign of personal involvement in the community culture of those students (Tharp, 1989).

Types of Questions

Here are some typical questions that elementary school teachers ask beginning students:

What's this a picture of?

What color is this?

What's your sister's name?

These questions seem simple enough to answer. But, in fact, different cultures teach children to answer different kinds of questions. Anglo parents frequently ask their children to identify objects and their characteristics. Yet in certain other cultures, parents rarely ask their children questions that they themselves know the answers to (Crago et al., 1993; Heath, 1980; Rogoff & Morelli, 1989). For example, parents in African American communities in parts of the southeastern United States are more likely to ask questions involving comparisons and analogies; rather than asking, "What's that?" they may instead ask, "What's that like?" (Heath, 1980). And children in these same communities are specifically taught *not* to answer questions that strangers ask about personal and home life—such questions as "What's your name?" and "Where do you live?" The complaints of parents in these communities show you how much of a cultural mismatch there can be between the children and their Anglo teachers:

- "My kid, he too scared to talk, 'cause nobody play by the rules he know. At home I can't shut him up."

- "Miss Davis, she complain 'bout Ned not answerin' back. He says she asks dumb questions she already know about." (Heath, 1980, p. 107)

Increase wait time after asking a question or posing a problem.

We will discover additional advantages of wait time in Chapter 6.

Remember that, in some cultures, interruptions indicate personal involvement, rather than rudeness.

Be aware that some students may not be accustomed to answering the kinds of questions that teachers usually ask.

At the same time, teachers' comments about these children reflect their own lack of understanding about the culture from which the children come:

- "I would almost think some of them have a hearing problem; it is as though they don't hear me ask a question. I get blank stares to my questions. Yet when I am making statements or telling stories which interest them, they always seem to hear me."

- "The simplest questions are the ones they can't answer in the classroom; yet on the playground, they can explain a rule for a ballgame or describe a particular kind of bait with no problem. Therefore, I know they can't be as dumb as they seem in my class." (Heath, 1980, pp. 107 108)

Family Relationships and Expectations

In some cultures—for example, in many Hispanic, Native American, and Asian communities—family bonds and relationships are especially important. Students raised in these cultures are likely to feel responsibility for their family's well-being and a strong sense of loyalty to other family members; they will also go to great efforts to please their parents (Abi-Nader, 1993; Delgado-Gaitan, 1994; Garcia, 1994; C. A. Grant & Gomez, 1996; Hidalgo et al., 1995; Vasquez, 1990).

Relate the school curriculum to students' home environments and cultures.

In many cultures, school achievement is valued highly, and parents encourage their children to do well in school (Delgado-Gaitan, 1992; Duran & Weffer, 1992; Garibaldi, 1992; Hidalgo et al., 1995; Hossler & Stage, 1992; Nieto, 1995; Pang, 1995; H. W. Stevenson, Chen, & Uttal, 1990; A. H. Yee, 1992). But in a few cases, classroom achievement may be less valued than achievement in other areas. For example, in some very traditional Native American communities, children are expected to excel in art, dance, and other aspects of their culture, rather than in more academic pursuits such as reading or mathematics (Kirschenbaum, 1989). We must certainly be sensitive to situations in which the achievements that *we* think are important are not those that are valued by the families of students in our classroom. To the extent that we can do so, we must make an effort to show our students how the school curriculum and classroom activities relate to their own cultural environment and their own life needs.

Establish and maintain open lines of communication with parents and jointly identify ways in which home and school can work together to help students be successful in the classroom.

We must also maintain open lines of communication with our students' parents. Some parents, especially parents of minority children, may be intimidated by school personnel. As teachers, we may often need to take the first step in establishing a productive parent-teacher relationship. By communicating with each other, teachers and parents may soon come to realize that both groups want students to be successful in the classroom, and so they are more likely to work cooperatively together to promote student achievement (Casanova, 1987; García, 1995; Hidalgo et al., 1995; C. K. Howe, 1994; Salend & Taylor, 1993; R. L. Warren, 1988).

Creating a More Multicultural Classroom Environment

Clearly, we must be sensitive to the ways in which students of various ethnic groups are likely to be different from one another. Yet it is just as important that we help our students develop the same sensitivity: As adults, they will inevitably have to work cooperatively with people from a wide variety of backgrounds. It is in our students' best interests, then, that we promote awareness of numerous cultures in every classroom. To promote a truly multicultural classroom environment, we must

- Incorporate the values, beliefs, and traditions of many cultures into the curriculum

- Work to break down ethnic and cultural stereotypes

- Promote social interaction among students from various ethnic groups

- Foster democratic ideals

Incorporating the Values, Beliefs, and Traditions of Many Cultures into the Curriculum

For many educators, the term **multicultural education** does not mean simply cooking ethnic foods, celebrating Cinco de Mayo, or studying famous African Americans during Black History Month. Rather, it means including the perspectives and experiences of numerous cultural groups on a regular basis (Banks, 1994, 1995; Boutte & McCormick, 1992; Cottrol, 1990; García, 1995; Gollnick & Chinn, 1994; C. A. Grant & Gomez, 1996; Ladson-Billings, 1994b; NCSS Task Force on Ethnic Studies Curriculum Guidelines, 1992; Sleeter & Grant, 1994).

As teachers, we can incorporate content from different ethnic groups into many aspects of the school curriculum. Here are some examples of the things we can do:

Incorporate multicultural content into the curriculum.

- In literature, read the work of minority authors and poets.

- In music, learn songs from many cultures and nations.

- In physical education, learn games or folk dances from other countries and cultures.

- In history, look at wars and other major events from diverse perspectives (e.g., the Spanish perspective of the Spanish-American War, the Japanese perspective of World War II, the Native American perspective of the pioneers' westward migration in North America).

- In art, consider the creations and techniques of artists from around the world.

- In current events, consider such issues as discrimination and oppression. (Asai, 1993; Boutte & McCormick, 1992; Casanova, 1987; Cottrol, 1990; Freedman, 1996; Koza, 1996; NCSS Task Force on Ethnic Studies Curriculum Guidelines, 1992; Pang, 1995; Sleeter & Grant, 1994; Ulichny, 1994)

Look for commonalities, as well as differences, among students from different cultural backgrounds.

As we explore various cultures, we should be looking for commonalities as well as differences. For example, we might study how various cultural groups celebrate the beginning of a new year, discovering in the process that "out with the old and in with the new" is a common theme among many such celebrations (Ramsey, 1987). Or we might study the diets of people from different countries, noting how each diet somehow satisfies the four basic food groups. At the secondary level, it can be beneficial to explore the issues that adolescents of all cultures face—such issues as gaining the respect of elders, forming trusting relationships with peers, and finding a meaningful place in society (Ulichny, 1994). One important goal of multicultural education should be to communicate that, underneath it all, people are more alike than different.

Breaking Down Ethnic and Cultural Stereotypes

■ E X P E R I E N C I N G   F I R S T H A N D
Picture This #1

Form a picture in your mind of someone from each of the three places listed below. Use the *first* image that comes to mind in each case.

The Netherlands (Holland)

Mexico

Hawaii

Once you have done so, answer yes or no to each of these questions:

- Was the person from the Netherlands wearing wooden shoes?

- Was the person from Mexico wearing a sombrero?

- Was the person from Hawaii wearing a hula skirt or flowered lei? ■

If you answered yes to any of the three questions, then one or more of your images reflected an ethnic stereotype. Most people in the Netherlands, Mexico, and Hawaii do *not* wear wooden shoes, sombreros, or hula skirts and leis on a regular basis.

Although we and our students should certainly be aware of true differences among various ethnic groups, it is counterproductive for any of us to hold a **stereotype**—a rigid, simplistic, and inevitably erroneous caricature—of any particular group. As teachers, we must make a concerted effort to develop and select curriculum materials that represent all cultural groups in a positive and competent light; for example, we should choose textbooks, works of fiction, and videotapes that portray people of diverse ethnic backgrounds as legitimate participants of mainstream society, rather than as exotic "curiosities" who live in a separate world from the rest of us. And we must definitely avoid or modify curriculum materials that portray members of minority groups in an overly simplistic, romanticized, exaggerated, or otherwise stereotypical fashion (Banks, 1994; Boutte & McCormick, 1992; Drake, 1993; Ladson-Billings, 1994b; Pang, 1995; Rudman, 1993; Russell, 1994; Trueba, 1988).

Yet stereotypes don't exist only in curriculum materials; they also exist in society at large. We can help break down ethnic stereotypes in several simple yet effective ways. For one thing, we can arrange opportunities for students to meet and talk with successful minority models (e.g., Vasquez, 1990). We can also explore the historical roots of stereotypes with our students—for example, by explaining that cultural differences sometimes reflect the various economic and social circumstances in which particular ethnic groups have historically found themselves. And finally, we must emphasize the notion of individual differences—that members of any single ethnic group will often be very different from one another (Garcia, 1994; C. D. Lee & Slaughter-Defoe, 1995; McAlpine & Taylor, 1993; Spencer & Markstrom-Adams, 1990; Trueba, 1988).

Promoting Social Interaction Among Students from Various Ethnic Groups

Students are more likely to be tolerant of one another's differences when they have the opportunity to interact on a regular basis. Such interactions can sometimes occur within the context of planned classroom activities; for example, we can hold classroom discussions in which our students describe the traditions, conventions, and perceptions

Use curriculum materials that represent all cultural groups in a positive and competent light.

Expose students to successful minority models.

Provide opportunities for students to get to know one another better.

of their own ethnic groups. We can also promote friendships among students of diverse ethnic backgrounds by using some of the strategies we identified in Chapter 3—for instance, by using cooperative learning activities, teaching the rudiments of other students' native languages, and encouraging schoolwide participation in extracurricular activities. By learning to appreciate the multicultural differences that exist within a single classroom, our students take an important first step toward appreciating the multicultural nature of the world at large (Casanova, 1987; Craft, 1984; Pettigrew & Pajonas, 1973).

Unfortunately, not all schools have a diverse enough population to foster students' awareness and appreciation of cultural differences on a firsthand basis. In such culturally homogeneous schools, we may have to take our students, either physically or vicariously, beyond school boundaries. For example, we can engage our students in community action projects that provide services to particular ethnic groups—perhaps in preschools, nursing homes, or city cultural centers (e.g., Sleeter & Grant, 1994). Or we can initiate a "Sister Schools Program" in which students from two ethnically different communities regularly communicate through the mail or the Internet, possibly exchanging news, stories, photographs, art projects, and various artifacts from the local environment (Koeppel & Mulrooney, 1992).

By discussing the different traditions, conventions, and perceptions of various cultural groups, students can begin to understand why others sometimes behave differently than they themselves do.

Fostering Democratic Ideals

Ultimately, any multicultural education program must include such democratic ideals as human dignity, equality, justice, and tolerance for diverse points of view (Cottrol, 1990; NCSS Task Force on Ethnic Studies Curriculum Guidelines, 1992; Sleeter & Grant, 1994). We better prepare our students for functioning effectively in a democratic society when we help them understand that virtually any nation includes a diversity of cultures and that such diversity provides a richness of ideas and perspectives that will inevitably yield a more creative, productive society overall.

A democracy includes **equity**—freedom from bias or favoritism—as well as equality. To help our students achieve maximal classroom success, we must be equitable in our treatment of them; in other words, we must tailor instruction to meet the unique characteristics of each and every one. The notion of equitable treatment applies not only to students of diverse ethnic backgrounds but also to both boys and girls. Let's consider how boys and girls are likely to be different and how we can help both genders achieve academic success.

Foster such democratic ideals as human dignity, equality, justice, and tolerance for diverse viewpoints.

EXPLORING GENDER DIFFERENCES

THINKING ABOUT WHAT YOU KNOW

- In what ways do you think males and females are alike and different? Do they have different academic abilities? Different motives? Different interests? Different expectations for themselves?

- How might the environment contribute to gender differences? Do parents treat boys and girls differently? Do classmates? Do teachers?

Are the findings presented in Table 4–4 consistent with your own observations of males' and females' behaviors? If not, can you resolve the discrepancies?

Expect boys and girls to have similar academic aptitudes for different subject areas.

With respect to academic abilities, boys and girls are probably more similar than you think. But in certain other areas, they may be more different than you realize. Researchers have investigated possible differences between males and females in numerous areas; general trends in their findings, along with educational implications, are presented in Table 4–4.

As you can see from Table 4–4, girls and boys are similar in terms of general intellectual ability; any differences in aptitudes for specific academic areas are small, with a great deal of overlap between the two groups (e.g., refer back to the gender differences in verbal ability depicted in Figure 4–1). Girls are generally more concerned about doing well in school, yet boys have greater confidence in their *ability* to succeed. Boys and girls alike tend to be more motivated to achieve in gender-stereotypical areas, and they have greater self-confidence about their chances for success in these areas. As teachers, we should expect our male and female students to have similar academic aptitudes for different subject areas; furthermore, we should encourage both groups to achieve in all areas of the curriculum.

Tracing the Origins of Gender Differences

Obviously, heredity determines the differences in physical characteristics we see in males and females both at birth and when they reach puberty. Heredity accounts for the fact that girls reach puberty earlier than boys; it also accounts for the fact that, after puberty, boys are taller and have more muscle tissue than girls. Adolescent males are better than their female age-mates at tasks involving strength—an advantage that probably results from genetics (J. R. Thomas & French, 1985).

Aside from such physical differences, most theorists believe that biology plays only a minor role in the development of gender differences (Halpern, 1986; Harway & Moss, 1983; Huston, 1983; R. Rosenthal & Rubin, 1982; Ruble, 1988; Schratz, 1978). One likely explanation for many of the gender differences we see is socialization: Boys and girls are taught that some behaviors are more appropriate for males and that others are more appropriate for females. To see what I mean, try the following exercise.

In what ways is the environment different for boys and girls? Can you generate some hypotheses before you read further?

We must convince girls that they have just as much potential for learning such subjects as mathematics and science as boys do.

Picture This #2

Form a picture in your mind of each of the following individuals. Use the *first* image that comes to mind in each case.

A bank president

A kindergarten teacher

A fashion model

A scientist

A building contractor

A secretary

Now answer this question: Which of the following individuals that you pictured were male, and which were female? ■

If you are like most people, your bank president, scientist, and building contractor were males, and your kindergarten teacher, fashion model, and secretary were females. Gender stereotypes—rigid ideas about how males and females "typically" behave—persist throughout our society, and even preschool children are aware of them (Bornholt, Goodnow, & Cooney, 1994; Ruble, 1988). Table 4–5 lists some common components of traditional gender stereotypes.

Many aspects of society conspire to teach growing children to respond to gender stereotypes. For example, parents are more likely to encourage their sons to be independent, athletic, and aggressive, and they tend to have higher career expectations for their sons than for their daughters, especially in stereotypically masculine professions (Block, 1983; Brodzinsky, Messer, & Tew, 1979; Eccles & Jacobs, 1986; Fagot, Hagan, Leinbach, & Kronsberg, 1985; Olneck, 1995; Parsons, Adler, & Kaczala, 1982; Ruble, 1988; Sprafkin et al., 1983; J. R. Thomas & French, 1985). In addition, girls and boys have different toys and play different games (Block, 1983; P. A. Campbell, 1986; Etaugh, 1983). Girls get dolls and stuffed animals, and they play "house" and board games—toys and activities that foster the development of verbal and social skills. Boys get blocks, model airplanes, and science equipment, and they play football, basketball, and video games—toys and activities that foster greater development of visual-spatial skills (Liss, 1983; Sprafkin et al., 1983). Although gender-stereotypical expectations for males and females are evident in virtually any society, they are more pronounced in some cultures than in others (C. A. Grant & Gomez, 1996).

The media promote gender-stereotypical behavior as well. Movies, television programs, and books (including many elementary reading primers) often portray males and females in gender-stereotypical ways: Males are aggressive leaders and successful problem solvers, whereas females are domestic, demure, and obedient followers (Durkin, 1987; Frasher, 1982; Huston, 1983; Ruble & Ruble, 1982; Sadker & Sadker, 1994). Furthermore, males appear far more prominently in history

Traditional "boy" activities give boys many opportunities to manipulate physical objects in space. Such activities also involve more initiative, risk taking, and competition than traditional "girl" activities.

Table 4–4   Gender Differences and Their Educational Implications

CHARACTERISTIC	SIMILARITIES AND DIFFERENCES	EDUCATIONAL IMPLICATION
Scholastic Abilities	Boys and girls are similar in terms of general intellectual ability (e.g., IQ scores). Girls are often slightly better at verbal (language-based) tasks; boys may be somewhat better at tasks involving visual-spatial skills. Boys and girls perform equally well in mathematics, although small gender differences are found in specific aspects of math (e.g., girls are somewhat better at computation; at the high school level, boys are slightly more proficient at problem solving). In recent years, boys and girls are becoming increasingly more *similar* in their academic performance. (N. S. Anderson, 1987; Chipman, Brush, & Wilson, 1985; Durkin, 1995; Fennema, 1980; Halpern, 1992; Hyde & Linn, 1988; Jacklin, 1989; Law, Pellegrino, & Hunt, 1993; M. C. Linn & Hyde, 1989; M. C. Linn & Petersen, 1985; Lueptow, 1984; Maccoby & Jacklin, 1974; Neisser et al., 1996)	Expect boys and girls to have similar aptitudes for all academic subject areas.
Physical and Motor Skills	Prior to puberty, boys and girls have similar physiological capability, but boys tend to develop their physical and motor skills more than girls. After puberty, boys have the advantage in height and muscular strength. (M. C. Linn & Hyde, 1989; J. R. Thomas & French, 1985)	Assume that both genders have similar potential for developing physical and motor skills, especially during the elementary school years.
Motivation	Girls are generally more concerned about doing well in school: they tend to work harder on school assignments, take fewer risks when doing their assignments, get higher grades, and are more likely to graduate from high school. Both genders are more motivated in gender-stereotypical areas: Boys exert more effort in such stereotypically "masculine" area as mathematics, science, and mechanical skills; girls work harder in such stereotypically "feminine" areas as reading, literature, art, and music. (Dwyer, 1974; Eccles [Parsons], 1984; Fennema, 1987; Halpern, 1992; Kelly & Smail, 1986; McCall, 1994; K. Paulson & Johnson, 1983; Sadker & Sadker, 1994; A. H. Stein, 1971; Yu, Elder, & Urdan, 1995)	Encourage both boys and girls to achieve in all areas of the curriculum.
Self-esteem	Boys are more likely to have self-confidence in their ability to control the world and solve problems; girls are more likely to see themselves as competent in interpersonal relationships. Boys and girls also tend to have greater self-esteem in areas consistent with society's stereotypes about what males and females should do.	Show students that they can be successful in counterstereotypical subject areas; for example, show girls that they have just as much potential for learning mathematics and science as boys do.

CHARACTERISTIC	SIMILARITIES AND DIFFERENCES	EDUCATIONAL IMPLICATION
Self-esteem (cont.)	And in general, boys tend to rate their own performance on tasks more positively than girls do; for example, during the elementary school years, both genders perform equally well on mathematics and science achievement tests, yet by high school, boys are more self-confident about their ability to succeed in these subjects. (Block, 1983; Bornholt, Goodnow, & Cooney, 1994; P. A. Campbell, 1986; Eccles, 1989; Fennema, 1987; Fennema & Peterson, 1985; Huston, 1983; Kahle, 1983; H. W. Marsh, 1989; Sadker & Sadker, 1994)	
Explanations for Success and Failure	Boys and girls interpret their successes and failures somewhat differently. Boys tend to attribute their successes to an enduring ability (e.g., they're "smart" or "naturally athletic") and their failures to a lack of effort (they didn't try hard enough). In contrast, girls attribute their successes to effort (they worked very hard) and their failures to a lack of ability (e.g., they "can't do math" or are "not very good at sports"). Boys' beliefs in greater natural ability make them more optimistic about their chances for future success. (Deaux, 1984; Huston, 1983; Stipek, 1984)	Convince girls that their past and present successes indicate an ability to succeed and that they can avoid or overcome failure with sufficient effort.
Expectations and Career Aspirations	Boys have higher expectations for themselves, especially in stereotypically "masculine" areas. Career aspirations tend to be consistent with gender stereotypes; furthermore, girls (but not boys) tend to choose careers that will not interfere with their future roles as wives and mothers. (Deaux, 1984; Durkin, 1987; Eccles [Parsons], 1984; Kelly & Smail, 1986; Lueptow, 1984; Nemerowicz, 1979; J. Smith & Russell, 1984)	Expose students to successful male and female models in a variety of roles and professions. Show students examples of people successfully juggling careers with marriage and parenthood.
Interpersonal Relationships	Boys exhibit more physical aggression, although girls can be just as aggressive as boys in more subtle and less physical ways (e.g., by tattling, gossiping, or snubbing peers). Girls are more affiliative—they form closer and more intimate interpersonal relationships—and they seem to be more sensitive to the subtle, nonverbal messages ("body language") that others give them. (Berndt, 1992; Bjorkqvist, Osterman, & Kaukiainen, 1992; Block, 1983; Brodzinsky, Messer, & Tew, 1979; Deaux, 1984; Durkin, 1995; Eagly, 1987; Jones & Dembo, 1989; M. C. Linn & Hyde, 1989; Lueptow, 1984; Maccoby & Jacklin, 1974; McCallum & Bracken, 1993; Sadker & Sadker, 1994)	Teach both genders less aggressive and more prosocial ways of interacting with one another. To accommodate girls' more affiliative nature, provide opportunities for cooperative group work and interaction with classmates.

Table 4–5   Male and Female Stereotypes

	MALES			FEMALES	
Personality Characteristics					
Aggressive	Self-confident		Affectionate		Gentle
Ambitious	Dominant		Sensitive		Passive
Competitive	Strong		Sympathetic		Submissive
Courageous	Unemotional		Emotional		Weak
Independent			Talkative		
School Subjects					
Mathematics	Mechanics		Art		Reading
Science	Athletics		Music		Literature
Occupations					
Police officer	Repairman		Librarian		Hair stylist
Electrician	Business manager		Fashion model		Nurse
Computer operator	Airline pilot		Child care worker		Ballet dancer
Car mechanic	Scientist		Housekeeper		Seamstress
Engineer			Secretary		

Sources: Kelly & Smail, 1986; Lueptow, 1984; Nash, 1975; Sadker & Sadker, 1994; A. H. Stein, 1971; A. H. Stein & Smithells, 1969.

Use nonsexist curriculum materials that portray both genders in a competent, successful light.

and science textbooks than females do (Sadker & Sadker, 1994; Sadker, Sadker, & Klein, 1991). As teachers, we must make a concerted effort to develop and select curriculum materials that represent both genders in a positive and competent light; nonsexist curriculum materials reduce gender stereotypes when students are exposed to them on a continual and consistent basis (Fennema, 1987; Horgan, 1995; Sadker & Miller, 1982).

As we noted in Chapter 3, schools are important socialization agents for children, and such socialization often includes further encouragement of gender-stereotypical behaviors. Let's look at how the behaviors of two particularly influential groups of people—peers and teachers—promote the development of gender differences.

Peer Behaviors

When students think that they have reasons to "hide" their achievements, keep those achievements private and confidential.

Playmates and classmates do many things to ensure that children adhere to traditional gender stereotypes. Peers often respond more positively to children who play in "gender appropriate" ways and more negatively to those who do not (Fagot & Leinbach, 1983; Huston, 1983). They may also ridicule or avoid students who enroll and excel in "gender inappropriate" subjects—for example, high school girls who excel in science and mathematics (Casserly, 1980; E. H. Luchins & Luchins, 1980; Sadker & Sadker, 1994; Schubert, 1986). As a result, many students will engage in counterstereotypical activities only when their successes in such activities can be hidden from their peers (Eccles, 1989; Huston, 1983; Ruble, 1988). As teachers, we can do a great deal to keep student achievement out of the public eye—for example, by keeping grades confidential* and perhaps by allowing students to demonstrate their achievement through written assignments, rather than through responses to in-class questions.

Remember how quiet and passive Lupita was in our case study at the beginning of the chapter? Boys often take a more active role in class than girls, especially in situations where the two are asked to work together; for example, when paired in a science lab, boys perform experiments while girls take notes (Arenz & Lee, 1990; Eccles, 1989; Kahle & Lakes, 1983; Schubert, 1986; Théberge, 1994). For this reason, it may sometimes be beneficial to group girls with girls, and boys with boys, to ensure that girls become more active participants in classroom activities (Kahle & Lakes, 1983; MacLean, Sasse, Keating, Stewart, & Miller, 1995). Girls are also more likely to assume the role of leader in same-sex groups, thus developing valuable leadership skills (Fennema, 1987).

Occasionally form same-sex groups for cooperative classroom activities.

Teacher Behaviors

During the past twenty years, there has been an increasing tendency for schools to attempt to treat boys and girls similarly (Eccles, 1989). For example, girls' sports are enjoying more publicity and financial support than ever before. Nevertheless, differences in the treatment of boys and girls continue to exist. For example, many elementary physical education teachers, believing that boys are naturally more athletic than girls, may foster the physical development of boys more than that of girls (J. R. Thomas & French, 1985). And teachers and guidance counselors more frequently encourage boys to pursue such subjects as science and mathematics; they are more likely to give girls mixed messages about these subjects or even to discourage girls from pursuing them (Casserly, 1980; L. H. Fox, 1981; Ware & Lee, 1988).

Give equal attention to males and females.

Teachers also tend to give more attention to boys than to girls. This difference occurs partly because, on the average, boys ask more questions and also present more discipline problems (Brophy, 1985; Dweck, 1986; Lindow, Marrett, & Wilkinson, 1985; Morse & Handley, 1985; Sadker & Sadker, 1994). Teachers interact more with high-achieving boys than with high-achieving girls, perhaps because boys seek out more interaction (Fennema, 1987; Sadker & Sadker, 1994). And teachers more frequently discourage girls from speaking without first raising their hands (Sadker & Sadker, 1985). When girls cannot answer a question, their teachers tend to tell them the correct answer; but when boys have equal difficulty, their teachers usually help them think through the correct answer on their own (Sadker & Sadker, 1985). Boys are told to try harder when they fail; girls are simply praised for trying (P. A. Campbell, 1986; Eccles & Jacobs, 1986; L. H. Fox, 1981).

Equally encourage both males and females to think through questions and problems on their own.

In most cases, teachers are probably unaware that they discriminate between boys and girls the way they do. The first step toward ensuring more equitable treatment of males and females is to become aware of existing inequities. Then we can try to correct those inequities—for example, by interacting frequently with *all* of our students, by helping them think through correct answers, by encouraging them to try harder when they experience difficulty, and by holding high expectations for everyone.

---

* In the United States, there are legal as well as pedagogical reasons for keeping grades confidential. The Family Educational Rights and Privacy Act (1974) mandates that a student's records, including grades, be shared only with the student, his or her parents or legal guardians, and school personnel directly involved in the student's education and well-being.

In the last few pages, we have considered numerous strategies for how, as teachers, we can treat male and female students, as well as students from diverse ethnic backgrounds, in an equitable fashion. Yet equity must be extended to students of different socioeconomic circumstances as well. Let's look at some of the specific characteristics that students from lower-income families, including those growing up in true poverty, are likely to have, as well as at some strategies for helping these students achieve classroom success.

EXPLORING SOCIOECONOMIC DIFFERENCES

The concept **socioeconomic status** (often abbreviated as **SES**) encompasses a number of variables, including family income, parents' occupations, and the degree to which parents have received a formal education. Students' school performance is correlated with socioeconomic status: Higher-SES students tend to have higher academic achievement, and lower-SES students tend to be at greater risk for dropping out of school (Frazer & Wilkinson, 1990; R. D. Hess & Holloway, 1984; National Center for Education Statistics, 1989; Scott-Jones, 1984).

Factors Interfering with School Success

Several factors may contribute to the generally lower school achievement of low-SES students:

Connect students with free or reduced-cost meal programs.

Poor nutrition. To the extent that lower-SES families cannot afford nutritional meals for their children, the school performance of these children may be adversely affected. When students are chronically hungry, they may have little interest in school learning (Maslow, 1987). Those who have experienced severe malnutrition either prenatally or in the early years of life tend to have lower IQ scores, poorer attention and memory, and lower school achievement (D'Amato, Chitooran, & Whitten, 1992; Galler, 1984; Lozoff, 1989; Neisser et al., 1996; Ricciuti, 1993; Scott-Jones, 1984).

Provide emotional support for students under stress.

Emotional stress. Students function less effectively when they are under stress, and many low-SES families live in chronically stressful conditions (Conger et al., 1992; Maccoby & Martin, 1983; Seitz et al., 1985; Trueba, 1988). Obviously, the economic problems of the poor family are a source of anxiety; children may wonder where their next meal is coming from or how long it will be before their landlord evicts them for not paying the rent. The preponderance of single-parent homes among low-SES families is another source of stress; a single parent may be overwhelmed with worries about supporting the family (Scott-Jones, 1984).

Facilitate peer acceptance.

Peer rejection. Students from lower-income families are often rejected by their more economically fortunate classmates; as a result, they may have fewer opportunities to become actively involved in school activities (Knapp & Woolverton, 1995).

Hold high expectations for academic and professional achievement.

Lower aspirations. Students from low-SES backgrounds typically have lower aspirations in terms of the educational levels they attain and the career paths they follow; girls are at a particular disadvantage in this regard (Knapp & Woolverton, 1995; S. M. Taylor, 1994). In addition to encouraging our students to aim high in terms of their educational and professional goals, we must also provide the extra support they need to achieve such goals; offering help sessions for challenging classroom material, finding low-cost academic enrichment programs available during the summer, and helping students fill out applications for college scholarships are just a few of the forms that such support might take. (We will consider the importance of goal setting in more detail in our discussion of social cognitive theory in Chapter 10.)

Less parental education. Parents in many lower-SES households have had little education themselves, so they may not be capable of helping their children with schoolwork (Finders & Lewis, 1994). Furthermore, because many low-SES parents have poor reading skills, they may have provided few early reading experiences for their children—experiences so important for later school success (R. D. Hess & Holloway, 1984; Laosa, 1982).

Less parental involvement at school. Economic factors often affect the extent to which parents are able to become involved with their children's schooling. Lower-income parents often have difficulty getting off work, finding suitable child care, and arranging transportation to visit school and meet with teachers (Finders & Lewis, 1994; Salend & Taylor, 1993). In addition, some of these parents may have had bad experiences when they themselves were students and so feel uncomfortable in a school setting (Finders & Lewis, 1994). As teachers, we will have to be especially flexible about when and where we meet with the parents of lower-income students; we will also have to be especially conscientious about establishing comfortable, trusting relationships with them (Finders & Lewis, 1994; Salend & Taylor, 1993).

Remember that students may have few resources at home to help them with their schoolwork.

Be flexible about when and where to meet with parents, and establish comfortable, trusting relationships with them.

Working with Homeless Students

Children of homeless families typically face far greater challenges than other low-SES students. Many of them will have health problems, low self-esteem, a short attention span, poor language skills, and inappropriate behaviors (Coe, Salamon, & Molnar, 1991; Pawlas, 1994). Some may be reluctant to come to school because they lack bathing facilities and appropriate clothing (Gollnick & Chinn, 1994). And some may have moved so frequently from one school to another that there are large gaps in the academic skills they have mastered (Pawlas, 1994).

As teachers, we, too, will face unusual challenges when teaching students living in homeless shelters. Here are several suggestions for giving them the extra support they may need to achieve both academic and social success at school:

- Pair new students with classmates who can "show them the ropes" around school—for example, by explaining school procedures and making introductions to other students.

- Provide a notebook, clipboard, or other portable "desk" on which students can do their homework at the shelter.

- Find adult or teenage volunteers to serve as tutors at the shelter.

- Enlist the help of civic organizations to collect clothing and school supplies for the students.

- Meet with parents at the shelter, rather than at school.

- Share copies of homework assignments, school calendars, and newsletters with shelter officials. (Pawlas, 1994)

Remember that many bright students come from low-income families.

Help low-SES students develop resiliency by being someone whom they know they can trust and depend on in difficult times.

Provide opportunities for lower-SES students to share their life experiences.

Fostering Resilience

As we work with the students of low-income families, we must remember that many of them will succeed in school despite the exceptional hardships they face (Humphreys, 1992; Nieto, 1995; B. Williams & Newcombe, 1994). Some students seem to be **resilient:** They develop characteristics and coping skills that help them rise above their adverse circumstances. As a group, resilient students have likable personalities, positive self-concepts, strong motivation to succeed, and high yet realistic goals. They believe that success comes with hard work, and their bad experiences serve as constant reminders of the importance of getting a good education (McMillan & Reed, 1994; Werner, 1995).

Resilient students usually have one or more individuals in their lives whom they trust and know they can turn to in difficult times (McMillan & Reed, 1994; Werner, 1995). Such individuals may be family members, neighbors, or school personnel; for example, resilient students often mention teachers who have taken a personal interest in them and been instrumental in their school success (McMillan & Reed, 1994). As teachers, we are most likely to promote resiliency in low-SES students when we show them that we like and respect them, are available and willing to listen to their views and concerns, hold high expectations for their performance, and provide the encouragement and support they need to succeed (McMillan & Reed, 1994; Werner, 1995).

When working with students from lower-SES backgrounds, we must remember that many of them may lag behind their peers in such basic academic skills as reading, writing, and computation—skills essential for their academic and lifelong success. Yet we must also remember that they may be exceptionally knowledgeable in other respects. For example, if they work part-time to help their families make ends meet, they may have a good understanding of the working world. If they are children of single, working parents, they may know far more than their classmates about cooking, cleaning house, and taking care of younger siblings. If financial resources have been particularly scarce, they may know firsthand what it is like to go without sufficient food for days at a time or to live in an unheated apartment in the winter; they may therefore have a special appreciation for basic human needs and true empathy for victims of war or poverty around the world.

INTO THE CLASSROOM
Accommodating Group Differences

Be careful not to make predictions about individual students on the basis of group differences alone.

A second-grade teacher reminds herself that even though one of her students is the son of migrant workers, he may nevertheless be as capable of academic success as his wealthier classmates.

Build on students' background experiences.

A teacher asks a classroom of inner-city, African American students to vote on their favorite rap song. She puts the words to the song on an overhead transparency, projects them onto a movie screen, and asks students to translate each line for her. In doing so, she shows students how their local dialect and Standard English are interrelated, and she gives them a sense of pride in the fact that they are bilingual (Ladson-Billings, 1994a).

Use curriculum materials that represent both genders and all cultural groups in a positive and competent light.

A high school history teacher peruses a history textbook for possible gender or ethnic stereotypes; he supplements the textbook with readings that highlight the important roles that certain females and minorities have played in history.

Expose students to successful models of both genders and various ethnic and socioeconomic backgrounds.

A sixth-grade teacher invites a variety of successful professionals, including several females and minorities, to speak with her class about their careers.

Provide opportunities for students of different backgrounds to get to know one another better.

For a cooperative learning activity, a middle school teacher forms cooperative groups that are balanced in terms of both gender and ethnic background.

Use your knowledge of group differences to facilitate the achievement of all students, *not* to form differing expectations for the achievement of different students.

An elementary school physical education teacher realizes that the girls in her class may not have had as much experience throwing overhand as the boys have, so she gives them basic instruction and extra practice in the overhand throw.

IDENTIFYING STUDENTS AT RISK

THINKING ABOUT WHAT YOU KNOW

Do you remember classmates in elementary school who never seemed to complete assignments or get their homework done? Do you remember classmates in high school who did poorly in most of their classes and rarely participated in extracurricular activities? How many of those students eventually graduated from high school? What are they doing now?

Students at risk are students with a high probability of failing to acquire the minimum academic skills necessary for success in the adult world. Many of them drop out before high school graduation; many others graduate without basic skills in reading or mathematics (National Assessment of Educational Progress, 1985; Slavin, 1989). Such individuals are often ill-equipped to make productive contributions to their families, communities, or society at large.

Characteristics of At-Risk Students

Some at-risk students are students with known special needs; for example, they may have learning disabilities or emotional and behavioral problems that interfere with learning and achievement. Others may be students whose cultural backgrounds don't mesh easily with the dominant culture at school. Still others may be students from home environments where academic success is neither supported nor encouraged.

At-risk students come from all socioeconomic levels, but children of poor, single-parent families are especially likely to leave school prior to high school graduation. Boys are more likely to drop out than girls. African Americans, Hispanics, and Native Americans are more likely to drop out than European American and Asian American students. Students at greatest risk for dropping out are those whose families speak little or no English and whose own knowledge of English is also quite limited (Fennema, 1987; Frazer & Wilkinson, 1990; García, 1995; C. K. Howe, 1994; Knapp & Woolverton, 1995; C. D. Lee & Slaughter-Defoe, 1995; National Center for Education Statistics, 1989; Nieto, 1995; Raber, 1990; L. Steinberg, Blinde, & Chan, 1984).

In addition, students at risk, especially those who eventually drop out of school, typically have some or all of the following characteristics:

A history of academic failure. High school dropouts often have a history of poor academic achievement going back as far as third grade (G. A. Hess, Lyons, & Corsino, 1990; Lloyd, 1978). On the average, they have less effective study skills, earn lower grades, obtain lower achievement test scores, and are more likely to repeat a grade level than their classmates who graduate (Jozefowicz, Arbreton, Eccles, Barber, & Colarossi, 1994; Lloyd, 1978; Raber, 1990; L. Steinberg et al., 1984; Wilkinson & Frazer, 1990).

Older age in comparison with classmates. Because low achievers are sometimes retained at the same grade level from one year to the next, they are often older than their classmates (Raber, 1990; Wilkinson & Frazer, 1990). Some (though not all) research studies find that students who are overage in comparison with classmates are those most likely to drop out of school (D. C. Gottfredson, Fink, & Graham, 1994; Roderick, 1994).

Emotional and behavioral problems. Potential dropouts tend to have lower self-esteem than their more successful classmates. And they are more likely to exhibit disruptive behavior, create discipline problems, and engage in criminal activities (Finn, 1991; Jenlink, 1994; Jozefowicz et al., 1994; Raber, 1990; L. Steinberg et al., 1984).

Lack of psychological attachment to school. At-risk students are less likely to identify with their school or to perceive themselves as a vital part of the school community; for example, they engage in fewer extracurricular activities, and they are more likely to express dissatisfaction with school in general (Finn, 1989; Jozefowicz et al., 1994; Raber, 1990; L. Steinberg et al., 1984).

Increasing disinvolvement with school. Dropping out is not really an all-or-none thing. In fact, many high school dropouts show lesser forms of "dropping out" many years before they officially leave school. For example, future dropouts are absent from school more frequently than their peers even in the early elementary grades (Finn, 1989; G. A. Hess et al., 1990; Jozefowicz et al., 1994). They are more likely to have been suspended from school, and they are more likely to show a long-term pattern of drop-

What are possible reasons why some students don't participate in their school's extracurricular activities?

ping out, returning to school, and dropping out again (Raber, 1990). Over time, then, we see decreasing involvement—physical, academic, and social—in school activities.

Why Some Students Drop Out

Students typically drop out for one of three reasons. Some have little family support or encouragement for school success. Others have extenuating life circumstances; for example, they may have medical problems, take an outside job to help support the family, or become pregnant. Still others become dissatisfied with school: They don't do well in their classes, have trouble making and keeping friends, or find the curriculum irrelevant to their own lives and needs (Ekstrom, Goertz, Pollack, & Rock, 1986; Knapp, Turnbull, & Shields, 1990; Parks, 1995; Raber, 1990; L. Steinberg et al., 1984; L. Steinberg, Greenberger, Garduque, & McAuliffe, 1982; Wilkinson & Frazer, 1990).

Helping At-Risk Students Stay in School

At-risk students are a diverse group of individuals with a diverse set of needs, and there is probably no quick fix to keep every student in school until high school graduation (Finn, 1991). Nevertheless, there are several things we can do to help at-risk students succeed and stay in school:

- Identify them as early as possible.

- Make the curriculum relevant.

- Communicate high expectations for academic success.

- Provide extra support for academic success.

- Show students that *they* are the ones who have made success possible.

- Encourage and facilitate identification with school.

Identifying At-Risk Students as Early as Possible

We begin to see indicators of "dropping out"—such indicators as low school achievement and high absenteeism—as early as elementary school. And such other signs as low self-esteem, disruptive behavior, and lack of involvement in school activities often appear years before students officially withdraw from school. So it is quite possible to identify at-risk students early in their school careers and to take steps to prevent or remediate academic difficulties before those difficulties become insurmountable. Research indicates clearly that, for at-risk students, prevention and early intervention are more effective than later intervention efforts (Slavin, Madden, & Karweit, 1989).

Identify at-risk students as early as possible and intervene on their behalf.

Making the Curriculum Relevant

Students are more likely to stay in school if they believe that the curriculum is relevant to their own life experiences and future needs (Knapp et al., 1990). To increase the relevance of school for at-risk students, we should place academic skills within the context of real-world tasks, and particularly within the context of students' local cultural environments. For example, we might teach reading skills by using magazines related to students' interests (e.g., magazines dealing with sports or teen fashions). We might teach writing skills by asking students to write a letter to the editor of a local newspaper. We

Make the curriculum relevant to students' life experiences and future needs.

might teach basic arithmetic by having students calculate the price of soft drinks when purchased individually versus in a six-pack, or the monthly winnings one would receive from an annuitized lottery jackpot.

Communicating High Expectations for Academic Success

Although many at-risk students have a history of failure at academic tasks, under no circumstances should we write these students off. On the contrary, we should communicate to them that school success is both possible and expected (Alderman, 1990; Garcia, 1994; Garibaldi, 1993; C. K. Howe, 1994; Ladson-Billings, 1994a). We can acknowledge to students that we know they have had learning problems in the past, but that there are ways to overcome those problems, and that furthermore we will help them acquire the knowledge and skills they need to succeed in the classroom (Alderman, 1990).

We should note here that it is probably more beneficial to focus students' attention on short-term, specific goals (e.g., learning to do long division or spell a list of one hundred words), rather than on long-term, general ones (e.g., becoming an expert mathematician or a gifted writer). At-risk students will see short-term goals as being more easily accomplishable than long-term goals, and they will achieve success more quickly (Alderman, 1990).

Providing Extra Support for Academic Success

Because at-risk students often have a history of academic failure and because they may have little support for academic achievement on the home front, these students may need more than the usual amount of assistance from teachers and other school personnel in order to succeed. Here are some specific ways in which we can facilitate their academic success:

- Help them develop more effective reading and learning strategies.

- Adapt instruction to their current skills and knowledge.

- Give them relatively structured tasks and tell them exactly what we expect them to do.

- Develop mastery of one skill before moving to a more difficult one.

- Assess their progress frequently and give them specific criteria for measuring their own success.

- Increase one-on-one teacher-student interactions.

- Deliver as much instruction as possible within the regular classroom context; make any necessary instruction in self-contained settings as brief as possible.

- Solicit parent and community cooperation with the school program. (Alderman, 1990; Covington & Beery, 1976; Garibaldi, 1993; Slavin, Karweit, & Madden, 1989)

As you may have noticed, our recommendations for at-risk students are similar to those we might make for *any* student. Research indicates that the most effective programs for at-risk students are those that incorporate normal, educationally sound teaching practices (Slavin, Madden, & Karweit, 1989).

Help students set high yet realistic goals.

Focus on short-term, specific goals.

Provide support for academic success by using educationally sound teaching practices.

Showing Students Their Personal Responsibility for Success

Not only must we help at-risk students achieve academic success, but we must also help them recognize that *they themselves* are the ones responsible for that success (Alderman, 1990). For example, we might give messages such as these:

"Wow, look how much you've improved! That extra practice really helped."

"I can tell by your test score that you have studied hard and learned this material well."

"You really deserved this A. You are writing in complete sentences now, and you are checking your work for spelling and punctuation errors."

Encouraging and Facilitating Identification with School

Students at risk may need extra encouragement to become involved in academic and social school activities. For example, we can help them to become more involved and to feel more psychologically attached to the school community, when we:

- Incorporate students' interests into the school curriculum.

- Show students how academic tasks and assignments are relevant to their own personal needs.

- Include instructional techniques that promote active class involvement (e.g., class discussions, cooperative learning).

- Establish close, trusting relationships with students.

- Encourage participation in athletic programs, extracurricular activities, and student government. (This is especially important when students are having academic difficulties, because it provides an alternative way of experiencing school success.)

- Involve students in school policy and management decisions.

- Give students positions of responsibility in managing school activities. (Finn, 1989; Garibaldi, 1992; Newmann, 1981)

Students are far more likely to stay in school and to try to succeed in school activities when they feel as if they truly belong there.

In the preceding pages I have described a number of ways in which particular groups of students may have characteristics in common. At the same time, we must repeat an important point made earlier in the chapter: *We must never make predictions about individual students on the basis of group differences alone.* A teacher's expectations for a student, either positive or negative, can have a profound impact on how that student ultimately behaves. Let's look at some effects that teacher expectations can have.

AVOIDING UNWARRANTED EXPECTATIONS

Teachers typically draw conclusions about their students relatively early in the school year, forming opinions about each one's strengths, weaknesses, and potential for aca-

Help students recognize their personal responsibility for success.

Here we are talking about increasing students' *self-efficacy* through the *attributions* we give for their success. We will discuss self-efficacy in Chapter 10 and attribution theory in Chapter 11.

Encourage and facilitate identification with school.

Identify at-risk students as early as possible.

> A second-grade teacher speaks with the principal and school counselor about possible ways to help a student who is frequently absent from school and seems to have little interest in her schoolwork.

Use students' strengths to promote high self-esteem.

> A school forms a singing group (the "Jazz Cats") for which students in a low-income, inner-city elementary school must try out. The group performs at a variety of community events, and the students enjoy considerable visibility for their talent. Group members exhibit increased self-esteem, improvement in other school subjects, and greater teamwork and leadership skills (Jenlink, 1994).

Communicate high expectations for students' performance.

> A mathematics teacher tells a group of junior high school students, "Yes, I know that you're finding fractions difficult right now. But I also know that you can learn fractions if you try hard and practice using them. Why don't we try a different approach to learning them today—one that might work a little better for us?"

Provide extra support for academic success.

> A high school English teacher meets with a small group of low-reading-level students to read and discuss reading materials in areas of interest to them.

Show students that they are personally responsible for their successes.

> A teacher tells a student, "Wow, look how much you've improved! That extra practice really helped."

Facilitate students' identification with school.

> A teacher encourages a student with a strong throwing arm to go out for the school baseball team and introduces the student to the baseball coach.

demic success. In many instances, teachers size up their students fairly accurately: they know which ones need help with reading skills, which ones have short attention spans, which ones have trouble working together in the same cooperative group, and so on. But even the best teachers inevitably make errors in their judgments of students; for example, teachers often underestimate the abilities of students who speak in a dialect other than Standard English (Bowie & Bond, 1994; Gollnick & Chinn, 1994; Owens, 1992; J. Taylor, 1983). And such erroneous judgments can have significant effects on how well students perform in the classroom.

Students are more likely to stay in school when they feel as if they truly belong there.

Effects of Teacher Expectations

Teachers' expectations for students have at least three effects:

- They tend to perpetuate themselves.

- They influence how teachers treat students.

- They affect students' self-concepts.

Self-Perpetuating Nature of Expectations

In our case study at the beginning of the chapter, we found Ms. Padilla jumping to the conclusion that Lupita had few academic skills and probably needed a second year of kindergarten. She was quite surprised to see a very different, and very competent, side of Lupita that a researcher's video camera had captured. Ms. Padilla readily admitted that her early expectations had colored her assessment of Lupita: "I had written her off. Her and three others . . . they had met my expectations and I just wasn't looking for anything else."

As we will discover in our discussion of knowledge construction in Chapter 7, people tend to remember things that are consistent with what they already know or believe about the world, and they tend to distort or forget things inconsistent with previously held ideas. Thus, people are likely to confirm and perpetuate their own previously formed beliefs and expectations, just as Ms. Padilla did, and may turn a blind eye and a deaf ear to any evidence to the contrary.

This biasing factor in what people learn and remember is evident in teachers' perceptions of students of different genders and ethnic groups (Halpern, 1986; Martin & Halverson, 1981; C. B. Murray & Jackson, 1982/1983). For example, teachers often underestimate the ability and achievement of minority students and students from low-income families (Commins & Miramontes, 1989; Gaines & Davis, 1990; Garcia, 1994; Graham, 1990; L. P. Jones, 1990; Knapp & Woolverton, 1995). And they may interpret the successful academic performance of both minorities and females as being the result of short-term, unstable factors (e.g., high effort, good luck) while simultaneously attributing poor performance to long-term, stable factors (e.g., low intelligence) (Deaux, 1984; C. B. Murray & Jackson, 1982/1983).

Differential Treatment of Students

Teachers frequently treat their students in ways consistent with their expectations for those students, and such differential treatment is not necessarily a bad thing (Goldenberg, 1992; Good & Brophy, 1994). For example, a teacher who expects a student to have difficulty learning to read, perhaps because that student has illiterate parents or comes from a non-English-speaking home, may spend the extra time that the student needs to develop basic reading skills.

Continually ask yourself whether you are giving inequitable treatment to students for whom you have low expectations.

Yet expectations may lead teachers to behave in ways that create a **self-fulfilling prophecy**; in other words, what they expect students to achieve becomes what students actually *do* achieve. For example, when teachers have high expectations for their students' performance, they create a warmer classroom climate, interact with students more frequently, provide more opportunities for students to respond, and give more positive feedback; they also present more course material and more challenging topics. In contrast, when teachers have low expectations for certain students, they offer fewer opportunities for speaking in class (remember Ms. Padilla's reluctance to call on Lupita for fear of embarrassing her), ask easier questions, give less feedback about students' responses, and present few if any challenging assignments (Babad, 1993; Copeland, 1993; Good & Brophy, 1994; Graham, 1990; M. J. Harris & Rosenthal, 1985; R. Rosenthal, 1994).

Effect on Self-Concept

Can you think of a teacher you've had who did not have as much faith in you as you had in yourself? How did you react to that teacher?

Students are often well aware of the expectations that their teachers have for their performance (Olneck, 1995; R. S. Weinstein, 1993). When they receive the same message over and over again—perhaps that they are incapable of learning difficult materials or perhaps that they can't do *anything* right—they may begin to incorporate that message into their self-concepts and to see themselves as others see them. They will also tend to behave in ways consistent with the self-concepts they form. For example, boys are more likely to hear comments about male-stereotypical characteristics—"My goodness, how strong you're getting!"—whereas girls hear female-stereotypical remarks—"My goodness, you've become such a lady!" When boys think of themselves as strong and girls think of themselves as ladylike, very different behaviors can result (Bem, 1984). Differences among students from different cultural and socioeconomic groups may be partially a result of similar influences. For example, when African American boys are scolded more frequently than Caucasian boys (e.g., L. Grant, 1985), their self-concepts are likely to be adversely affected.

Certainly, teacher expectations don't always affect what students think of themselves. Research indicates that teacher expectation effects are most likely to appear in the early elementary school years (Grades 1 and 2) and again about the time that students first enter junior high school (Grade 7) (Raudenbush, 1984). They are also most likely to appear when false expectations have been formed within the first few weeks of school (Raudenbush, 1984). In general, then, teacher expectations have their strongest effect at transition points in students' academic careers—when they first enter a new school environment.

Reassessing Our Expectations for Students

Sometimes teacher expectations are based on completely erroneous information. More frequently, however, teachers' initial impressions of students are reasonably accurate. In the latter case, a problem emerges when teachers don't *change* their expectations in the light of new data (H. M. Cooper & Good, 1983; Good & Brophy, 1994). As teachers, we must keep in mind what we have learned about intelligence and creativity in this chapter: Ability can and does change over time, especially when environmental conditions are conducive to such change. Accordingly, we must be continually reassessing our expectations for individual students, modifying them as new evidence presents itself. For example, we should be continually on the lookout not only for the weaknesses but also for the strengths that students bring to the classroom (Knapp et al., 1990). We should assess our students' academic progress on a regular basis and with as much objectivity as possible (Goldenberg, 1992). And we must continually remind ourselves that, as teachers, we *can* make a difference in our students' lives (e.g., R. S. Weinstein, Madison, & Kuklinski, 1995).

TAKING INDIVIDUAL AND GROUP DIFFERENCES INTO ACCOUNT

Clearly, different students have different needs. It is often helpful to know how individual differences (e.g., intelligence, creativity) and group differences (e.g., those associated with being female or growing up in a particular ethnic group) potentially affect the behaviors and beliefs that different students bring with them to the classroom. At the same time, we must be careful not to jump to conclusions about our students on the basis of insufficient data. Table 4–6 provides several ideas about how we can take students' individual and group differences into account without simultaneously having those differences bias our judgments, decisions, and actions.

Accommodating Students with Special Needs

We will, of course, see differences among our students with special educational needs, and some of these differences will be related to the individual and group difference variables that we have examined in this chapter. For instance, students from lower socioeconomic backgrounds are more likely to be classified as having mental retardation (Patton et al., 1990). Some cultures discourage females, even those with high IQ scores and considerable academic promise, from pursuing advanced educational opportunities; as a result, we may have some gifted female students who are reluctant to make the most of their advanced cognitive abilities (e.g., Nichols & Ganschow, 1992). There will be other gender differences as well; for example, we will more often see learning disabilities among boys than girls, and we are likely to observe different kinds of problems in boys and girls with emotional and behavioral disorders (Heward, 1996). Table 4–7 presents numerous instances of individual and group differences among students with special needs, along with classroom strategies specifically related to such differences.

Be especially careful not to form unwarranted expectations for students at transition points in their academic careers.

Remember that ability changes over time; don't assume that current deficiencies portend long-term difficulty.

Table 4–6 *Taking Individual and Group Differences into Account*

GENERAL PRINCIPLE	EDUCATIONAL IMPLICATION	EXAMPLE
Intelligence is partly a function of environment and can change over time. In addition, different students are likely to be intelligent in different ways.	We must never jump to conclusions about what our students will or will not be able to do, and we should not assume that a student having difficulty in one area will necessarily have difficulty in another.	We should never use IQ scores as the sole indicator of our students' potential for academic success. Such factors as quality of instruction, student motivation, parental support, and peer group norms will also have a significant effect.
Students tend to be creative in specific content domains, rather than show creativity in every aspect of their behavior. Furthermore, students' level of creativity is influenced by environmental conditions.	We can foster students' creativity in a particular area by valuing creative products, encouraging students to take risks, and giving them the time they need to generate new ideas.	We can form small, cooperative groups that work together over several days or weeks to develop a play, short story, scientific invention, or new team sport.
Each ethnic group has its own norms for appropriate behavior. People from one culture sometimes misinterpret the behaviors of those from a different culture.	As teachers, we must be careful not to interpret students' actions in terms of our own cultural standards for behavior.	When we find students sharing answers, we shouldn't assume they were intentionally cheating; their culture may be one in which group achievement is valued over individual achievement. We should provide opportunities for both group and individual accomplishments and make it clear when each is expected.
On the average, male and female students have similar or equal abilities in all academic areas; however, most have greater self-confidence in areas consistent with traditional gender stereotypes.	We must encourage males and females equally in all areas of the curriculum—in science, mathematics, language arts, art, music, physical education, and so on.	We can expose our students to successful individuals in different professions, making sure they see both men and women in these roles.
Low-income parents sometimes have difficulty giving their children the resources and educational experiences on which successful school learning often builds.	Students from lower-SES homes may need additional support within the school environment to achieve academic success.	We can incorporate enriching outside experiences into the curriculum; for example, we can take students to museums, the zoo, and the city library. At the same time, we must remember that students from low-SES backgrounds have probably had valuable experiences that their wealthier classmates have not.

Table 4–7 *Considering Individual and Group Differences in Students with Special Educational Needs*

STUDENTS WITH SPECIAL NEEDS	CHARACTERISTICS THAT THESE STUDENTS MAY EXHIBIT	CLASSROOM STRATEGIES THAT MAY BE BENEFICIAL FOR THESE STUDENTS
Students with specific cognitive or academic deficits	Average or above-average scores on traditional intelligence tests Gender differences, with learning disabilities being more common in males than females	Remember that students with difficulties in one area (e.g., those with specific learning disabilities) may nevertheless be capable of average or above-average performance in other areas.
Students with specific social or behavioral deficits	Gender differences in the nature of the problems exhibited, with males being more likely to demonstrate overt misbehaviors (e.g., to be aggressive or engage in antisocial behavior) and females being more likely to have internalized problems (e.g., to be socially withdrawn or excessively anxious) Increased probability of being at risk for school failure	Be on the lookout for possible emotional problems when students (especially girls) are exceptionally quiet or withdrawn. Take steps to decrease the likelihood of students dropping out (e.g., by making the curriculum relevant, providing extra support for academic success, facilitating identification with school).
Students with general delays in cognitive and social functioning	Low scores on traditional intelligence tests Gender differences and socioeconomic differences, with general cognitive and social delays (e.g., mental retardation) being more common in males and in students from lower-SES backgrounds	Look for and nurture individual students' strengths in terms of Gardner's multiple intelligences. Remember that the great majority of students from low-SES backgrounds have either average or above-average intelligence.
Students with advanced cognitive development	High scores on traditional intelligence tests (less true for students from culturally diverse backgrounds because of the cultural-specific nature of such tests) For many students, presence of specific areas of giftedness (e.g., in language, mathematics, music), with other areas being less advanced Divergent thinking (e.g., asking unusual questions, giving novel responses) Giftedness manifested in different ways in different cultures (e.g., possible richness of oral language among African American students, possible exceptional sensitivity to the feelings and perspectives of others among Native American students) More self-doubt about one's own abilities among females than males In some cultures, discouragement of females from acting too "intelligently" or pursuing advanced education Little exposure to female and minority role models	Accept and encourage divergent thinking, including responses that you hadn't anticipated. Help students accurately appraise their own abilities. Encourage females as well as males to achieve at high levels, while also identifying avenues whereby students can demonstrate their talents in ways that their families and local cultures value.

Sources: Alderman, 1990; Finn, 1989; Garibaldi, 1993; Heward, 1996; Knapp, Turnbull, & Shields, 1990; Maker & Schiever, 1989; Nichols & Ganschow, 1992; Patton, Beirne-Smith, & Payne, 1990; Piirto, 1994; Pressley, 1995; Sadker & Sadker, 1994; Torrance, 1989; Turnbull, Turnbull, Shank, & Leal, 1995.

Compiled with the assistance of Dr. Margie Garanzini-Daiber and Dr. Margaret Cohen, University of Missouri—St. Louis.

We must remember that *all* students have strengths and talents that we can foster and that *all* students have the potential to develop new skills and abilities. Furthermore, the unique background and qualities that each student brings to class—for example, the realization by many girls that career aspirations must ultimately be balanced against dedication to family, the preference of students from some ethnic backgrounds for cooperative rather than competitive endeavors, and the firsthand awareness of some students from low-income homes regarding such social issues as poverty and homelessness—together create a situation in which we and our students have much to learn from one another.

CASE STUDY: *The Active and the Passive*

Ms. Stewart has noticed that only a few students are active participants in her junior high school science classes. When she asks a question, and especially when she asks one that requires students to draw inferences from the things they are learning in class, the same hands always shoot up. When she gives the matter some thought, she realizes that all of the active participants are White and that most of them are boys.

She sees the same pattern in students' involvement in lab activities. When she puts her classes into small groups for particular lab assignments, the same students (notably the White males) always take charge. The females and minority males take more passive roles, either providing assistance to the group "leaders" or else just sitting back and watching.

Ms. Stewart is a firm believer that students learn much more about science when they participate in class and when they engage in hands-on activities. She is concerned about the lack of involvement of many of her students. She wonders whether they really even care about science.

- What are some possible reasons why the girls and minority students are not participating in classroom activities? What strategies might Ms. Stewart use to increase their participation?

SUMMING UP

Individual and Group Differences

The students in any single classroom will be diverse in terms of both individual differences (e.g., those based on intelligence or creativity) and group differences (e.g., those based on ethnicity, gender, or SES). As teachers, we must remember that there is considerable individual variability within any group and a great deal of overlap between any two groups.

Intelligence

Intelligence involves adaptive behavior and may manifest itself differently in different cultures. Performance on intelligence tests correlates with school achievement; however, two prominent theorists (Sternberg and Gardner) believe that intelligence is comprised of many, somewhat independent abilities and therefore is not accurately reflected in a single IQ score.

Environment has a significant effect on intelligence; as teachers, we must remember that intelligence may change over time, especially during the early years.

Creativity

Creativity is new and original behavior that produces an appropriate and productive result; it is probably a combination of many thinking processes and behaviors that reflect themselves differently in different situations and content areas. We are likely to see more creative behavior when we show students that we value creativity, focus their attention on internal rather than external rewards, promote mastery of the subject matter, and encourage them to take risks.

Ethnic Differences

For students from ethnic minority groups, there is frequently some degree of cultural mismatch between the home and school environments. We may see cultural differences in language, cooperation, private versus public performance, eye contact, conceptions of time, wait time, types of questions asked at home, and family relationships and expectations. All students benefit when we promote increased awareness of cultural differences and foster social interaction among students from diverse ethnic groups.

Gender Differences

Males and females are very similar in terms of academic and physical ability, but they differ somewhat in terms of achievement motivation, self-esteem, explanations for success and failure, and expectations for themselves. Gender differences are probably largely environmental in origin; as teachers, we should hold equally high expectations for both boys and girls and make sure both genders have equal educational opportunities.

Socioeconomic Differences

Such factors as emotional stress, peer rejection, low aspirations, lack of parental education, and homelessness may contribute to the generally lower achievement of students from low-SES families. As teachers, we can help these students be successful in the classroom when we provide the academic and emotional support they need and when we hold high expectations for their performance.

Students at Risk

Students at risk are those with a high probability of failing to acquire the minimum academic skills necessary for success in the adult world; they may graduate from high school without having learned to read or write, or they may drop out prior to graduation. To help such students succeed at school, we should identify them as early as possible, make the curriculum relevant to their needs, provide support for their academic success, and encourage greater involvement in school activities.

Teacher Expectations

Premature and unwarranted expectations for students tend to be self-perpetuating; they influence teachers' behaviors toward students, and ultimately they also influence students' self-concepts and academic achievement. We must remember that students' current deficiencies are not necessarily indicative of long-term difficulty, and we must be careful that we don't give inequitable treatment on the basis of low expectations for performance. As teachers, we must use our knowledge of individual and group differences to help all of our students, including those with special educational needs, to achieve their maximum potential.

KEY CONCEPTS

individual differences (p. 144)
group differences (p. 144)
intelligence (p. 148)
intelligence test (p. 148)
IQ scores (p. 149)
automaticity (p. 152)
distributed intelligence (p. 155)
giftedness (p. 156)
mental retardation (p. 157)

creativity (p. 159)
convergent thinking (p. 159)
divergent thinking (p. 159)
higher-level questions (p. 161)
ethnic group (p. 163)
cultural mismatch (p. 164)
Standard English (p. 165)
dialect (p. 165)
wait time (p. 169)

negative wait time (p. 169)
multicultural education (p. 171)
stereotype (p. 172)
equity in instruction (p. 173)
socioeconomic status (SES) (p. 180)
resilient students (p. 182)
students at risk (p. 183)
self-fulfilling prophecy (p. 190)

UNDERSTANDING HOW STUDENTS LEARN

WHAT THINGS HAVE YOU LEARNED in the past week? Perhaps you have discovered something new about a good friend, read a newspaper article about recent world events, or gained a better understanding of what your role will be as a teacher. Perhaps you have learned how to play racquetball, how to send a message by electronic mail, or how to program your VCR. When you stop to think about it, you are acquiring new knowledge and skills all the time.

As teachers, our primary responsibility is to help students learn the knowledge and skills they will need to become productive adults. In Part 1, we looked at many characteristics that are likely to affect students' ability to learn successfully in the classroom. In Part 2, we will look at the nature of the learning process itself. In Chapter 5, **"Using Multiple Perspectives of Learning,"** we will get an overview of several different learning theories and consider the advantages of using a variety of theories to facilitate students' classroom achievement. In Chapter 6, **"Promoting Effective Cognitive Processing,"** Chapter 7, **"Facilitating Knowledge Construction,"** and Chapter 8, **"Promoting Higher-Level Thinking Skills,"** we will explore principles and theories concerning how students think about and remember information, and how we can help them learn and remember more effectively. In Chapter 9, **"Modifying Students' Behavior,"** we will examine principles related to how people's behavior changes over time and consider how we might apply these principles to encourage more productive behaviors in the classroom. In Chapter 10, **"Promoting Learning in a Social Context,"** we will focus on how students learn from the people around them—not only from their parents and teachers but also from friends and classmates, the media, and society at large. In Chapter 11, **"Motivating Students to Learn and Achieve,"** we will turn our attention to principles and theories of motivation and identify strategies for helping our students *want* to learn the things we are trying to teach them.

When we move on to Part 3 (beginning with Chapter 12), we will continue to apply our knowledge of human learning and motivation in our discussion of such topics as classroom management, instructional strategies, and assessment practices.

Using Multiple Perspectives of Learning

THINKING ABOUT WHAT YOU KNOW

- What do you mean when you say that you have *learned* something? Is your behavior different from what it was before? Is your way of thinking about the world different? What specific change has taken place?

- To what extent does your environment affect your ability to learn? For example, how much do books, films, or classroom materials teach you? How much do other people help you learn—perhaps by demonstrating a new behavior or by telling you how to improve your own performance?

- To what extent do your own thought processes affect your ability to learn? For example, have you discovered that paying attention in class makes a difference? Are there specific things you do when you read a textbook that help you understand it better? Have you developed particular strategies for studying course material that help you remember it more effectively?

WE ARE ALWAYS LEARNING new things. As young children, we learn a variety of motor skills, such as eating with a fork, holding a pencil, and writing the letters of the alphabet. We also learn innumerable pieces of information, such as the spelling of the word *cat,* the concept *molecule,* and the product of $9 \times 8.$ Furthermore, we learn patterns and relationships among pieces of information, such as the "at" pattern found in words like *cat* and *sat,* the relationship of the concept *molecule* to a variety of chemical reactions, and tricks for remembering the nines multiplication table. And we learn that certain situations call for certain behaviors; for example, we raise our hands when we wish to speak in class, turn in an assignment on the day it is due, and apologize when we have hurt someone else's feelings.

In this chapter, we will begin our exploration of human learning. We will first find out what learning is, discovering that some theorists define it in terms of observable behavior changes, whereas others define it in terms of internal mental processes. We will then look at several theoretical perspectives of learning that have evolved over the past one hundred years and consider how each perspective has relevance for our roles as teachers. Finally, we will identify several general principles of learning that have implications for our own classroom practices.

By the end of the chapter, you should be able to:

1. Define *learning* in two different ways and give examples of student learning that reflect each definition.

2. Explain why different perspectives of human learning have emerged over the years and identify key elements and general educational applications of each perspective.

3. List six general principles of learning and their implications for classroom practice.

4. Identify several ways in which students are likely to exhibit diversity in what and how they learn.

CASE STUDY: *Darren's Day at School*

At the dinner table one night, Darren's mother asks him, "How was your day at school?"

Darren shrugs, thinks for a moment, and says, "Okay, I guess."

"What did you learn?" his father asks.

"Nothing much," Darren replies.

Nothing much, indeed! Let's look at several slices of Darren's school day and see how much he actually did learn.

During his daily math lesson, Darren is studying the multiplication tables for the number 9. He finds that some multiplication facts are easy to learn because he can relate them to things he already knows—for example, $9 \times 2 = 18$ is like adding 9 plus 9, and $9 \times 5 = 45$ can be derived from counting by fives. Others, such as $9 \times 4 = 36$ and $9 \times 8 = 72$, are more difficult because he can't connect them to any number facts that he has learned before. When Ms. Caffarella finds Darren and a few of his classmates struggling, she teaches the class two tricks for learning the nines multiplication table:

1. The first digit in the product is one number less than the number by which 9 is being multiplied. For 9×6, the first digit in the product must be $6 - 1$, or 5.

2. The two digits of the product, when added together, equal 9. Because 5 plus *4* equal 9, the product of 9 × 6 must be 54.

With these two tricks, Darren discovers a pattern in the nines table—a pattern that helps him recite the table correctly.

During a geography lesson, Ms. Caffarella describes the trip she took to Greece last summer. She holds up a picture postcard of the Parthenon and explains that the building is made entirely of marble. Darren is sitting near the back of the room and can't see the picture very clearly; he envisions a building made entirely of *marbles* and silently wonders how the ancient Greeks managed to glue them all together so well.

In physical education, Darren's class has begun a unit on soccer. Darren has never played soccer before, and his first attempts to move and control the ball with his feet are clumsy and inept. His teacher watches his footwork closely, praising him when he moves his feet appropriately, and eventually Darren is dribbling and passing the ball successfully to his classmates.

In the afternoon's art lesson, Darren's class is making papier-mâché masks. His friend Carla gives her mask a very large nose by adding a crumpled piece of paper below the eye holes and then covering and shaping it with several pieces of glued paper. Darren watches her closely throughout the process and then makes his own mask's nose in a similar fashion.

- What has Darren learned during his math, geography, physical education, and art lessons? Can you identify one or more principles of learning that might describe what has happened in each situation?

DEFINING LEARNING

Despite his "amnesia" at the dinner table, Darren has clearly learned a number of things at school that day, including the nines table in multiplication, the "fact" that the Parthenon was made with marbles, some rudimentary techniques for moving a soccer ball, and a strategy for making a papier-mâché nose.

But exactly what do we mean when we use the word **learning**? Theorists disagree about how to define the term. Some theorists propose a definition such as this one:

Definition #1: Learning is a relatively permanent change in behavior due to experience.

At the same time, other theorists propose a definition along these lines:

Definition #2: Learning is a relatively permanent change in mental associations due to experience.

How are these two definitions similar? How are they different?

Not all changes reflect learning; some are short-lived and unrelated to specific experiences. For example, feelings of fatigue, stomachaches, and eye blinks are temporary, and students soon return to their original alert, healthy, and open-eyed states.

From a teacher's perspective, what are the potential advantages of defining learning as a change in behavior? What are the potential advantages of defining learning as a change in mental associations?

You may notice two ways in which the definitions are similar. First, when we talk about learning, we are talking about a *relatively permanent change*—something that tends to last for a period of time. Second, the change is *due to experience;* it results from specific experiences that students have had—perhaps a lesson in multiplication, a teacher's description of the Parthenon, soccer instruction, or the opportunity to watch a classmate work with papier-mâché.

But now look at the difference between our two definitions of learning. Notice how the first one describes learning as a change in *behavior,* whereas the second one describes it as a change in *mental associations*. Some learning theories, especially those within the *behaviorist* perspective, focus on how people's behaviors change over time and on the environmental conditions that bring such changes about. Other learning theories, especially those within the *cognitive* perspective, focus more on internal mental processes—on thinking—than on observable behaviors. A synopsis of our two definitions of learning and the theoretical perspectives in which each is used appears in Table 5–1.

In Darren's day at school, we saw several examples of learning as a behavior change: Darren recited the nines tables correctly for the first time, showed improvement in his ability to move a soccer ball with his feet, and tried a new way of shaping papier-mâché. We also saw several examples of learning as a change in mental associations: Darren related $9 \times 2 = 18$ to $9 + 9 = 18$, connected the marble in the Parthenon with the marbles he had at home, and remembered the steps that his friend Carla used to make a nose. Both definitions of learning, then, will be useful to us as we examine the nature of learning itself and as we identify strategies for helping our students learn more effectively.

Why have different theorists proposed different definitions of human learning? And why have different theories gone in different directions to explain the learning process? For the answers to these questions, let's look at the history of how the various theoretical perspectives of learning have evolved.

COMPARE/CONTRAST

Table 5–1   Two Definitions of Learning

DEFINITION	THEORETICAL PERSPECTIVE(S)	EXAMPLES OF LEARNING
Learning is a relatively permanent change in BEHAVIOR due to experience.	Behaviorism	Solving $9 \times 6 = ?$ correctly after previously being unable to do so Exhibiting improvement in soccer skills Working with papier-mâché in a new way
Learning is a relatively permanent change in MENTAL ASSOCIATIONS due to experience.	Cognitive Psychology Social Cognitive Theory	Realizing that 9×2 is the same thing as $9 + 9$ Believing that the columns of the Parthenon are made of marbles Remembering a technique that a classmate has used in making a papier-mâché nose

TRACING THE EVOLUTION OF LEARNING THEORIES

Psychology is a relatively young science, and psychologists did not really begin studying the phenomenon we call *learning* until a little more than one hundred years ago (e.g., James, 1890). Numerous explanations of the learning process have emerged since then; some have come and gone, whereas others have stood the test of time. In the next few pages, we will look briefly at three perspectives of learning: behaviorism, cognitive psychology, and social cognitive theory. Each of these is based on many years of research, and each provides numerous implications for classroom practices; accordingly, we will explore each one in depth in later chapters. The evolution of the three perspectives is depicted graphically in Figure 5–1.

Focusing on Stimuli and Responses: Behaviorism

A problem we encounter when we study "thinking" is that we can never actually *see* thought processes. We cannot directly observe such things as "remembering," "paying attention," or "studying." All we can really observe is people's behaviors: We can see what they do and hear what they say. For example, we can't really observe Karl "remember"; we can only hear him say, "Oh, yes, now I remember . . . the capital of Spain is Madrid." We can't truly determine whether Karen is "paying attention"; we can only

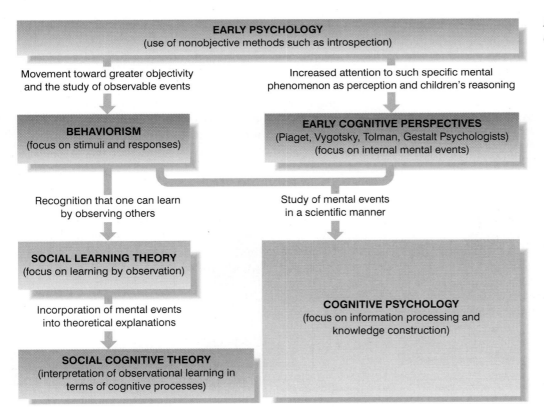

Figure 5–1   The Evolution of Learning Theories

see whether her eyes are directed toward the teacher. And although we don't know whether Keith is actually "studying," we can observe whether his book is lying open on the table in front of him and he is looking at the pages.

At the turn of the century, many psychologists attempted to study thinking and learning through a method known as *introspection:* They asked people to "look" inside their own minds and describe what they were "thinking." But beginning in the early 1900s, some psychologists (e.g., Watson, 1914, 1919, 1925) began to criticize the introspective approach for its lack of objectivity or scientific rigor. They proposed that, to study learning in an objective, scientific manner, theorists must focus on two things that can be observed: people's behaviors (**responses**) and the environmental events (**stimuli**) that precede and follow those responses. Since then, many psychologists have attempted to describe and understand learning and behavior primarily through an analysis of stimulus-response relationships. Such psychologists are called *behaviorists,* and their theories of learning are collectively known as **behaviorism.**

We saw an example of the behaviorist perspective in action in Darren's physical education class. The teacher watched Darren's *footwork* (his responses) very carefully and gave him *praise* (a stimulus) when he made the right moves. Rather than worry about what Darren might be thinking about soccer, the teacher focused exclusively on Darren's behavior and provided a desirable consequence when it showed improvement. The teacher applied a simple behaviorist principle—*a response that is followed by a desired (reinforcing) stimulus is more likely to occur again*—to help Darren develop better soccer skills.

The basic tenets of behaviorism have definite implications for classroom practice. First, the emphasis on *objectivity* in determining whether learning has occurred will minimize the likelihood that we evaluate students' learning and achievement in a biased fashion (perhaps letting our expectations for their performance color our judgments). Second, the focus on stimuli and responses is often useful when students demonstrate inappropriate behaviors—for example, when they talk disrespectfully or get out of their seats so frequently that they distract others. By changing stimuli in the classroom environment—for example, by providing reminders about appropriate responses and by rewarding such responses when they occur—we can often bring about significant improvements in students' behavior. We will discover many other educational applications of behaviorism when we consider this perspective in depth in Chapter 9.

Evaluate students' learning as objectively as you can—for example, by looking at the specific behaviors they exhibit.

Modify the classroom environment so that it brings about the responses that you want students to make.

Behaviorists focus on how students' behaviors change over time and on the environmental conditions that bring about such changes.

Focusing on Mental Processes: Cognitive Psychology

During the first half of the twentieth century, many psychologists adhered to the behaviorist perspective, especially in the United States. Yet as early as the 1920s, some psychologists argued that we cannot completely understand learning unless we consider the thought processes behind it. For example, theorists in Europe—Piaget in Switzerland, Vygotsky in Russia, and a group of German theorists known as *Gestalt* psychologists—focused heavily on the role of thinking processes as they devised their theories of learning and cognitive development. One American psychologist (Tolman, 1932, 1938, 1959) conducted numerous experiments during the 1930s and 1940s to demonstrate that even the behavior of laboratory rats can best be explained by talking about mental processes.

Over the years, it has become increasingly clear that behaviorism alone cannot give us the whole story about learning. During the 1960s, many research studies became increasingly *cognitive* in nature, shifting attention away from a detailed analysis of stimuli and responses and focusing more extensively on the nature of the thought processes that occur as people learn new knowledge and skills; a perspective known as **cognitive psychology** (e.g., Neisser, 1967) soon emerged.

What about behaviorists' concern that thinking cannot be studied objectively? Cognitive psychologists propose that, by observing people's responses to various stimuli, it is possible to draw *inferences*—to make educated guesses—about the internal mental events that logically underlie those responses. As an example of how we might learn about thought processes by observing people's behaviors, try this simple exercise.

Can you think of examples of how scientists in other disciplines have drawn inferences about unobservable phenomena?

■ EXPERIENCING FIRSTHAND
Twenty Words

Read these twenty words silently. Read each word carefully, but read each one *only once*.

goat	car	fork	pig
shirt	plate	pants	cup
plane	cow	bus	hat
knife	shoe	spoon	truck
boat	horse	sock	sheep

Now cover the page and write down as many of the words as you can in whatever order the words come to mind. ■

Did you write the words down in the order in which you read them? Probably not. If you are like most people, then you remembered many of the words in categories. Perhaps you remembered the clothing items, then the vehicles, then the eating utensils, and then the farm animals. From the order in which you wrote down the words (from your *behavior*), we can draw an inference about an internal cognitive process that occurred as you learned the words: You mentally *organized* them into categories.

Learning as Information Processing

Much of cognitive psychology focuses on how people think about and mentally "process" the information they receive; accordingly, it is often referred to as **information processing theory.** For example, consider how Darren remembered some of the nines table by connecting the new facts with things that he already knew (e.g., he re-

Chapter 2 describes cognitive development from the perspective of information processing theory. What concepts and principles can you recall from that discussion?

lated $9 \times 2 = 18$ to $9 + 9 = 18$; he related $9 \times 5 = 45$ to counting by fives). Consider, too, how the teacher's description of a pattern in the nines table enabled Darren to remember more difficult facts such as $9 \times 8 = 72$. One principle from cognitive psychology can help us understand why Darren initially learned some facts more easily than others: *People learn new information more easily when they can relate it to something they already know.* A second principle can help us understand why the teacher's description of a pattern in the nines table helped Darren remember the facts that had previously given him difficulty: *People learn several pieces of new information more easily when they can relate them to an overall organizational structure.*

This focus on the nature of cognitive processes will be extremely helpful to us as teachers. Sometimes our students will have difficulty learning things—perhaps things as simple as $9 \times 8 = 72$ or the fact that the Parthenon was made of marble—even though they are physiologically capable of responding in certain ways and even though the stimuli around them are seemingly conducive to such responses. In such situations, we will need to look closely at how our students are thinking about the things that we want them to learn.

Learning as Constructing Knowledge

Another prominent element of many cognitive learning theories is the notion that learning involves a process of *constructing* knowledge, rather than of simply absorbing it from the outside world (e.g., Bransford & Franks, 1971; Neisser, 1967; Putnam, 1992). We first encountered such **constructivism** in our discussion of cognitive and linguistic development in Chapter 2. For example, Piaget proposed that children construct their own body of knowledge about the world on the basis of the experiences they have with it, and Vygotsky described how a child can work jointly with an adult to devise a means of tackling a difficult task. To experience the process of construction firsthand, try this simple exercise.

◼ EXPERIENCING FIRSTHAND
Three Faces

Figure 5–2 contains three pictures. What do you see in each one? Most people perceive the picture on the left as being that of a woman even though many of her features are missing. Enough features are visible—an eye, parts of the nose, mouth, chin, and hair—that you can construct a meaningful perception from them. Is enough information presented in the other two figures for you to construct two more faces? Construction of a face from the figure on the right may take you a while, but it can be done. ◼

Objectively speaking, the three sets of black splotches in Figure 5–2, and especially the two rightmost sets, leave a lot to the imagination. For example, the woman in the middle is missing half of her face, and the man on the right is missing the top of his head. Yet you know enough about how human faces typically appear that you were probably able to add the missing

When students have difficulty learning new material, consider how they might be thinking about and processing the information.

Cognitive theories of learning can help us understand how students think about and process the information they encounter.

Figure 5–2   Can you construct a person from each of these pictures?
Source: Reprinted from "Age in the Development of Closure Ability in Children" by C. M. Mooney, 1957,
Canadian Journal of Psychology, 11, p. 220. Copyright 1957 by Canadian Psychological Association.
Reprinted with permission.

features yourself (mentally) to perceive a complete picture. Curiously, once you have
constructed faces from the figures, they then seem obvious to you. If you were to close
this book now and not pick it up again for a week or more, you would probably see the
faces almost immediately even if you had had difficulty perceiving them originally.

We saw the process of construction in our case study as well. When Ms. Caffarella
described the Parthenon as being made of marble, Darren envisioned a building made
of marbles similar to the ones that he had at home (such a misconception has been described by Sosniak & Stodolsky, 1994). Just as you did when you were looking at the
black-and-white faces just now, Darren combined new information with things he already knew to construct sense from the information he received.

As teachers, we must always remember that students don't necessarily learn information in the same way that it is presented to them; in some cases, they may even learn
*mis*information. As a result, we should periodically monitor their understanding of
material—by asking questions, encouraging dialogue, and listening carefully to their
ideas and explanations.

Check for students'
understanding of classroom
material and correct any
misconceptions they may
have.

Focusing on the Social Nature of Learning: Social Cognitive Theory

As early as the 1940s, psychologists proposed that people can acquire new ways of behaving simply by watching and imitating the responses that others make (N. E. Miller &
Dollard, 1941). This idea of *modeling* provided the impetus for yet another perspective
of learning—one that considers how people learn from observing those around them.
Originally referred to as *social learning theory,* this perspective has increasingly incorporated cognitive processes into its explanations of learning; it is now most commonly
called **social cognitive theory.**

We saw an example of modeling in Darren's experience with the papier-mâché
masks. Darren watched Carla as she made a nose for her mask; after she finished, he followed the same steps. Notice that Darren imitated what Carla had done only after she
had completed her nose; hence, he made his nose by using his *memory* of what he had

Model desired behaviors for your students and expose them to other appropriate models as well.

previously observed Carla do. According to social cognitive theorists, learning itself occurs at the time that observation takes place; a behavior change as a result of that learning may or may not occur. For example, Darren might possibly have watched Carla and remembered what she had done, yet chosen *not* to make his nose in the same way.

As teachers, we need to keep in mind how influential models can be in our students' learning. For example, students may learn how to solve a long division problem by watching their teacher do the steps on the chalkboard. They may learn how to dribble a soccer ball by observing a classmate demonstrate appropriate technique. They may learn prosocial behavior by seeing a friend be generous, cooperative, or compassionate. But they may learn bad habits—showing poor sportsmanship, cheating on tests, telling offensive jokes—from models as well. We must take care that our students are exposed to as many appropriate models, and as few inappropriate ones, as possible.

INTO THE CLASSROOM
Using Multiple Perspectives of Learning

Consider specific environmental stimuli that may be affecting students' behaviors.

A teacher is concerned that an aspiring comedian in her high school history class is continually distracting other students with his jokes; his humorous remarks often send the entire class into fits of hysterical laughter that make on-task behavior for any length of time almost impossible. She realizes that, by laughing at the student's jokes herself, she is actually perpetuating the problem. Furthermore, the student's joke-telling behavior postpones something that he doesn't want to do—his schoolwork. The teacher decides that the solution to the problem probably lies in changing the environmental consequences of the student's behavior.

Consider how students may be mentally processing (thinking about) the information you present.

When a fourth-grade teacher describes *gravity* as "a force that pulls you down," many of his students confuse "down" with "south" and express their concern that people in Australia are apt to fall into space.

Consider the things that students might learn by observing the behaviors and accomplishments of those around them.

A middle school language arts teacher asks her students to write a humorous limerick about somebody from their hometown of Dover (e.g., "There once was a woman from Dover . . ."). She gives them some ideas about what they might write by showing them several examples of limericks written by last year's class.

Previewing Upcoming Chapters

In terms of the number of articles published in professional journals and the number of presentations given at professional conferences, cognitive psychology's view of learning is the one most in vogue at the present time. Therefore, we will begin our examination of

Table 5–2   How the Three Perspectives of Learning Differ in Terms of Fundamental Issues

ISSUE	BEHAVIORISM	COGNITIVE PSYCHOLOGY	SOCIAL COGNITIVE THEORY
Learning is defined as . . .	a behavior change.	an internal mental phenomenon that may or may not be reflected in behavior.	an internal mental phenomenon that may or may not be reflected in behavior.
The focus of investigation is on . . .	stimuli and responses that can be readily observed.	cognitive processes.	both behavior and cognitive processes.
Principles of learning describe how . . .	people's behaviors are affected by environmental stimuli.	people mentally process the information they receive and construct knowledge from their experiences.	people's observations of those around them affect behavior and cognitive processes.
Educational implications focus on how we can help students . . .	acquire more productive classroom behaviors.	process information in effective ways and construct accurate and complete knowledge about classroom topics.	learn effectively by observing others.

learning theories by looking at specific mental events involved in learning—more specifically, by considering information processing in Chapter 6, knowledge construction in Chapter 7, and complex thinking skills in Chapter 8. We will turn our attention to behaviorist principles in Chapter 9; at that point, we will find that we can better understand how students' behaviors may change over time if we consider the environmental stimuli that bring such changes about. Social cognitive theory integrates elements of both cognitive psychology and behaviorism; hence, I am saving it for last, describing it in Chapter 10.

The three perspectives of learning that we will consider are different in terms of several fundamental issues (see Table 5–2 for a summary). As a result, each perspective will take us in a somewhat different direction as we explore the nature of human learning. Yet keep in mind that no single theoretical orientation can give us a complete picture of how people learn. All three perspectives have valuable lessons to teach us about how we can best help our students achieve in the classroom.

LOOKING AT THE BIG PICTURE: GENERAL PRINCIPLES OF LEARNING

Despite the fundamental differences that we find in various theoretical orientations, several general principles of learning have evolved from the many thousands of research studies conducted over the years:

- The specific *experiences* that people have affect what they know and what they can do.

- People's *interpretations* of their experiences influence the specific things they learn from those experiences.

- New learning builds upon *prior learning*.

- *Motivation* affects what and how much people learn.

- The *consequences* that follow people's behaviors affect their future learning and behavior.

- There is considerable *diversity* in what different people learn from any single experience.

These principles, along with their educational implications, are summarized in Table 5–3. In the pages that follow, we will look at each principle more closely. In our discussion of the final principle—diversity in learning—we will consider some specific implications for students with special educational needs.

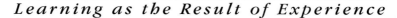

Learning as the Result of Experience

An important part of both definitions of learning presented earlier is that learning is *due to experience.* Students' school experiences will take innumerable forms; reading a chapter in a textbook, observing the correct use of laboratory equipment, receiving praise for an assignment well done, seeing a teacher smoke a cigarette at a basketball game, and hearing one classmate ridicule another for being too "smart" are just a few examples. As teachers, we must create classroom experiences that will maximize students' learning of the skills and information they will need to become productive citizens. We must also take precautions that situations in which counterproductive behavior or incorrect beliefs may be learned are few and far between.

Maximize experiences that promote the acquisition of productive skills and information; minimize situations in which counterproductive behavior or inaccurate knowledge is likely to be learned.

Interpretations of Experience

Thinking processes are key elements of both cognitive psychology and social cognitive theory; they are even beginning to creep into many behaviorist explanations of learning (e.g., Church, 1993; Hulse, 1993; Wasserman, 1993). To put the effects of such cognitive processes in general terms, we can say that people's interpretations of an experience influence the specific knowledge and behaviors they learn from it. For example, consider Ms. Caffarella's description of the Parthenon as being made of marble; some of her students may have understood that the Parthenon was constructed of white stone, but at least one student (Darren) envisioned an edifice built entirely of little glass balls. And consider two students who find a teacher smoking a cigarette at a basketball game; one may conclude that the teacher is unfortunately addicted to nicotine, whereas the other may conclude that smoking is the "cool" thing to do. As teachers, we must remember that, in some situations, students may interpret their experiences in ways that we don't anticipate or intend.

Remember that different students may interpret the same information differently; some may interpret it in ways that are counterproductive for their learning and development.

Effects of Prior Learning

To some extent, the things that people learn from their experiences, as well as the ways in which they interpret those experiences, depend on other things they have *already*

Be sure students have the appropriate prerequisite knowledge and skills for learning new material.

Table 5–3 General Principles of Learning

PRINCIPLE	EDUCATIONAL IMPLICATION	EXAMPLE
The specific *experiences* that people have affect what they know and what they can do.	We should maximize experiences that promote the acquisition of productive skills and information and minimize situations in which counterproductive behaviors or inaccurate knowledge are likely to be learned.	If we want students to take notes during class, we should not assume that effective note-taking skills have developed on their own. Rather, we should specifically teach note-taking skills while we are teaching academic subject matter.
People's *interpretations* of their experiences influence the specific things they learn from those experiences.	We must remember that students may sometimes interpret their experiences in ways that we don't anticipate or intend.	During a lesson on mitosis and meiosis, we should periodically check for students' understanding of these processes— perhaps by asking questions, stimulating classroom discussion, or giving short quizzes—and correct any misconceptions that we observe.
New learning builds upon *prior learning*.	We should be sure students have the appropriate prerequisite knowledge and skills for learning new material.	We should make sure students have mastered basic metric conversions (e.g., converting meters to centimeters) before asking them to make such conversions within the context of more complex tasks.
Motivation affects what and how much people learn.	We should give students reasons for wanting to learn.	We might entice students into learning about the basic food groups by explaining that a balanced diet will give them more strength and energy to do the things they want to do.
The *consequences* that follow people's behaviors affect their future learning and behavior.	We should make sure the consequences of students' behaviors are those that will maximize academic success.	When students write an essay that lacks coherence or has technical errors, we should give specific, concrete feedback about how they can improve next time.
There is considerable *diversity* in what different people learn from any single experience.	We must remember that all students will behave differently in and learn differently from any single classroom event.	When we give a reading assignment, we must realize that different students will remember different things from what they've read.

learned. For example, students will more easily learn the multiplication fact $9 \times 2 = 18$ if they have already learned the addition fact $9 + 9 = 18$. They can learn techniques for keeping a soccer ball away from the opposing team only after they have developed basic dribbling and passing skills. And they will understand that the Parthenon was made of white stone only if they have previously learned what *marble* is. As teachers, we must be sure our students have the prerequisite knowledge and skills for the new things we want to teach them.

Give students reasons for *wanting* to learn.

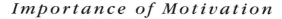

Importance of Motivation

Different learning theorists have different views of what motivation is. For example, many behaviorists talk about the role of *reinforcement* in learning: People are more likely to acquire a new behavior when they are rewarded for doing so. Cognitive psychologists and social cognitive theorists are more likely to describe motivation in terms of internal mental phenomena; for example, they talk about people having an *interest* in a topic, setting *goals* for themselves, or having *expectations* about the consequences that are likely to result from the things they do. Yet virtually all learning theorists, regardless of their particular theoretical orientation, agree that motivation affects what and how much people learn. As teachers, we must give our students reasons for *wanting* to learn the things we need to teach them. In Chapter 11, we will consider various perspectives and principles of human motivation, along with numerous strategies for translating those perspectives and principles into classroom practice.

Make sure the consequences of students' behaviors are those that will maximize academic success; for example, give students feedback that tells them how they can improve their performance.

As teachers, we must remember that different students will learn different things from the same situation.

Effects of Consequences

Another principle on which learning theorists agree is that the consequences of people's behaviors affect their future learning. Behaviorists are most likely to cast such consequences in terms of *reinforcement* and *punishment* for specific responses. Cognitive psychologists and social cognitive theorists are more apt to talk about how people *respond internally* to their own behaviors (e.g., feeling pride regarding their accomplishments), how they process the *feedback* they receive (e.g., using a teacher's suggestions to improve a research paper), and how they *interpret* their success and failure experiences (e.g., attributing a good grade to hard work, but a poor grade to bad luck). Re-

gardless of the theoretical perspective that we are using at any given time, we must be sure the consequences that follow students' behaviors are ones that will ultimately maximize their academic success.

Diversity Among Learners

One final point that emerges from learning research, regardless of its theoretical orientation, is the fact that there is considerable diversity in how different people will behave, as well as in what they will learn, within the context of any single experience. If we look

STUDENTS IN INCLUSIVE SETTINGS

Table 5–4   *Considering General Aspects of Learning in Students with Special Educational Needs*

STUDENTS WITH SPECIAL NEEDS	CHARACTERISTICS THAT THESE STUDENTS MAY EXHIBIT	CLASSROOM STRATEGIES THAT MAY BE BENEFICIAL FOR THESE STUDENTS
Students with specific cognitive or academic deficits	Difficulties in learning in specific areas of the curriculum Difficulties with specific aspects of information processing Difficulty with memory for certain kinds of stimuli (e.g., for visual or auditory stimuli)	Expect average or above-average performance in some subject areas despite poor performance in other areas Identify weaknesses in information processing and provide instruction that enables students to compensate for these weaknesses (e.g., if students have difficulty processing visual material, increase reliance on auditory presentations) Teach specific strategies for remembering information (see Chapter 6 for ideas)
Students with specific social or behavioral deficits	Lower academic achievement than would be predicted on the basis of students' ability, possibly due to classroom misbehavior or poor motivation Emotional or behavioral problems that may have resulted from students' past experiences Inappropriate responses to social stimuli	Make the curriculum relevant to students' needs and interests Provide experiences in which appropriate emotional and behavioral responses can be learned (see Chapter 9 for ideas) Reinforce desired responses
Students with general delays in cognitive and social functioning	Slower learning Slower information processing Inappropriate responses to social stimuli	Pace instruction more slowly and give students numerous opportunities to practice and review the things they learn Teach appropriate responses to specific situations in the classroom, lunchroom, etc.
Students with advanced cognitive development	More rapid learning More rapid and efficient information processing Better memory for information	Provide opportunities for students to study topics in greater depth and to advance through the curriculum more quickly

Sources: Heward, 1996; C. D. Mercer, 1991; Patton, Beirne-Smith, & Payne, 1990; Patton, Payne, Kauffman, Brown, & Payne, 1987; Piirto, 1994; Pressley, 1995; Turnbull, Turnbull, Shank, & Leal, 1995.

Compiled with the assistance of Dr. Margie Garanzini-Daiber and Dr. Margaret Cohen, University of Missouri—St. Louis.

Remember that students will learn somewhat differently in any classroom situation. Look closely at the progress that students are making and tailor subsequent instructional activities to what each of them has and has not learned.

at learning from a behaviorist perspective, we find a great deal of variability in the behaviors that people exhibit and in the ways that those behaviors change over time despite seemingly similar environmental conditions (e.g., Darren and his classmates will improve their soccer skills at different rates and may exhibit different strengths and weaknesses in playing the game). If we look at learning from a cognitive perspective, we find that people often process and interpret information in unique, idiosyncratic ways (consider, once again, Darren's unique interpretation of the marble Parthenon). People bring different backgrounds of knowledge and experience to any new learning situation—backgrounds that inevitably affect the ways in which they will respond to and benefit from that situation.

Students with special educational needs are examples of the great diversity that we are likely to see in student learning. For instance, some students (e.g., students with emotional and behavioral disorders) may have acquired responses that are counterproductive to their own long-term academic and social success. Others (e.g., students with learning disabilities) may have difficulty processing information in particular ways. And still others (e.g., gifted students) may learn more rapidly and efficiently than their classmates. Table 5–4 presents some general characteristics of learning that we are likely to see in students with special needs, along with implications for classroom practice.

In upcoming chapters, we will find innumerable instances of diversity in learning within each perspective of learning that we examine. Yet we must ultimately remember that *all* of our students have the capacity to learn a great deal from their classroom experiences. As teachers, it is paramount that we identify and provide the kinds of experiences that are likely to maximize such learning for every one of them.

CASE STUDY: *What's My Line?*

Mr. Quintero's sixth graders are rehearsing a play called *Wacky Wednesday.* The play is a comedy involving numerous interrelated subplots, and so the course of events sometimes changes in very unpredictable ways. Even though the students have been rehearsing for several weeks, they are still having difficulty remembering many of their lines. Mr. Quintero has been trying all kinds of enticements to improve their memory (e.g., promising candy bars or free time in class), and he has continually praised students when they *did* remember what they were supposed to say. Yet he has seen little improvement over the past two weeks.

Mr. Quintero expresses his concern. "This is getting to be a serious situation, folks. Opening night is only a week and a half away, and most of you still can't remember your lines. I tell you what—during tomorrow's rehearsal, I'll send out for pizza for everyone *if, but only if,* you can all come in here and recite your lines perfectly from beginning to end. Not a single slip-up, okay?"

The students seem excited about the possibility of a pizza party and go home vowing to study their scripts until they know them perfectly. And in fact, they make their way through Act I beautifully. Mr. Quintero praises them profusely for their performance, and they all seem pleased that he approves. But Act II is a different story. Almost every time the story line moves from one subplot to another—in other words, whenever a character's line changes the topic of conversation—the student involved forgets what he or she is supposed to say.

Joanie, the leading lady, sums up the problem nicely. "I have *so* many things to say in this act, Mr. Quintero. Sometimes the things that someone else says or does helps me remember what I need to say next. But at other times, my line just comes out of the blue. How can I remember something like *that*?!"

- Which theoretical perspective(s) would probably be most effective in helping Mr. Quintero's sixth graders remember their lines—behaviorism, cognitive psychology, or social cognitive theory—and why?

- Consider what Mr. Quintero has been doing to encourage his students to improve. Which theoretical perspective do you think he has been using here? Why is this particular perspective probably not working in this situation?

- Notice that the lines most difficult for students to remember are the ones that are least predictable within the context of the play's overall plot. If you were Mr. Quintero, what strategies might you use to help students remember such troublesome lines?

SUMMING UP

Defining Learning

Theorists define learning as a relatively permanent change due to experience. Our students' learning and achievement will include changes both in their behavior and in their ways of thinking.

Overview of Learning Theories

Behaviorists describe learning in terms of the observable responses that people make and the environmental stimuli that influence how those responses change over time. Cognitive psychologists describe learning in terms of such internal mental processes as perception, attention, memory, and study strategies; many cognitive psychologists also portray learning as a process of constructing an understanding of the world that may or may not be accurate. Social cognitive theorists build on elements of both behaviorism and cognitive psychology as they describe what and how people learn by observing and imitating those around them. As teachers, we will find that each of the three perspectives—behaviorism, cognitive psychology, and social cognitive theory—has numerous implications for how we can most effectively help students learn and achieve.

General Principles of Learning

Despite the differences we find among learning theories, these theories also share several general principles of learning—principles related to the effects of experience, interpretation, prior learning, motivation, and consequences. In addition, we must remember that there will be a great deal of diversity in how and what our students will learn from the same classroom learning experience.

KEY CONCEPTS

learning (p. 201)
responses (p. 204)
stimuli (p. 204)

behaviorism (p. 204)
cognitive psychology (p. 205)
information processing theory (p. 205)

constructivism (p. 206)
social cognitive theory (p. 207)

Promoting Effective Cognitive Processing

- What things do you "do" in your mind as you try to learn new information? For example, do you think about the information until it makes sense to you? Do you try to relate it to things that you already know? Do you think of implications that it might have for your own personal situation or perhaps for society in general?

- Of the things that you've learned within the last six months, which ones do you remember most easily? Can you remember places that you visited? People whom you met? Telephone numbers that you dialed? Course material that you memorized verbatim for an exam? Course material that you studied until you understood it? Course material that you *couldn't* understand no matter how hard you tried?

- In general, what factors help you learn and remember information? Does the way that you think about information have an effect? Does the nature of the information itself make a difference? Do the things that you already know play a role?

WE ENCOUNTER A GREAT DEAL of new information in our daily lives. Among other things, we meet new people, look up new telephone numbers, discover new places, and run across new ideas. When we encounter something that we want to remember, we often "do" something mentally with it—perhaps pay extra attention to it, repeat it to ourselves, relate it to things that we already know, or draw inferences from it. The particular ways in which we think about new information affect the ease with which we learn it and the likelihood that we can remember it later on.

In this chapter, we will begin our exploration of **cognitive psychology,** a theoretical perspective that focuses on the mental processes underlying human learning and behavior. Here we will look specifically at **information processing**—in other words, at the cognitive processes that enable human beings to learn and remember information. We will often stop to consider how we can put principles of information processing to work as we make decisions about how best to help our students think and learn most effectively. In the chapter that follows, we will look at a related aspect of human cognition—the construction of knowledge.

By the end of the chapter, you should be able to:

Have you already read the discussion of cognitive development in Chapter 2? If so, what do you recall about information processing theory from that discussion?

1. Identify the basic assumptions underlying cognitive psychology and the implications of these assumptions for classroom practice.

2. Describe a model of human memory and use it to explain how you can design and deliver instruction in ways that facilitate student learning.

3. Describe the conditions under which students are likely either to remember or to forget the things they have learned at an earlier point in time, and identify strategies that you can use to help students remember important information over the long run.

4. Describe the changes in classroom behavior and academic achievement that often occur when students have more time to process information.

5. Explain how cognitive style and learning disabilities reflect diversity in the ways that students process information.

CASE STUDY: *Bones*

Kanesha has been struggling with the latest assignment in her biology class—to learn the names of all the bones in the human body from head (*cranium*) to toe (*metatarsus*). She has learned a few bones quickly and easily; for example, it makes sense that the *nasal bone* is near the nose, and she remembers the *humerus* (upper arm bone) by thinking of it as being just above one's "funny (humorous?) bone." But she is still confused about a few bones; for example, the *tibia* and *fibula* are similar-sounding names and are located in the same place (the lower leg). And she keeps thinking that the *sternum* (at the front of the chest) is in back just like the "stern" of a boat. She has trouble remembering many of the other bones—the coccyx, ulna, sacrum, clavicle, patella—because she's never encountered these words before and can't relate them to anything she knows.

To prepare for her upcoming biology quiz, Kanesha looks at a diagram of the human skeleton and whispers the name of each bone to herself several times. She also writes each name down on a piece of paper. "These terms should certainly sink in if I repeat them enough times," she tells herself.

Kanesha gets a score of only 70% on the biology quiz. As she looks over the questions that she answered incorrectly, she sees that she confused the tibia and the fibula, labeled the ulna as "clavicle," put the sternum in the wrong place, and completely forgot to label the coccyx, sacrum, and patella.

- Why are some of the bones easier for Kanesha to remember than others? Which names would be easiest for *you* to remember?

- Which of Kanesha's strategies for learning the bones do you think are effective? Which ones do you think may *not* be effective?

- How might a teacher help Kanesha and her classmates learn the bones more easily?

IDENTIFYING BASIC ASSUMPTIONS OF COGNITIVE PSYCHOLOGY

Kanesha is thinking about different bones in different ways. She makes some kind of logical "sense" of the nasal bone and humerus; she also tries to make sense of the sternum, but her strategy backfires when she relates this bone to the stern of a boat. Kanesha does little if any thinking about why the other bones have the names they do. The extent to which Kanesha mentally processes the material she needs to learn and the *ways* in which she processes it affect her performance on the biology quiz.

Underlying cognitive psychology are several basic assumptions about how people learn. Our analysis of Kanesha's situation illustrates the first two assumptions in the list below; there are several other assumptions as well:

- Learning is an internal process that may or may not result in a behavior change.

- Cognitive processes influence the nature of what is learned.

- By observing how people respond to particular stimuli, we can draw inferences about their cognitive processes.

- People are selective about the things they process and learn.

- Some learning processes may be unique to human beings.

A summary of these assumptions is presented in Table 6–1; let's examine each one more closely.

Learning as an Internal Process

Give students opportunities to show you what and how they are learning.

As we noted in the preceding chapter, cognitive psychologists view learning as an internal mental phenomenon, rather than as an external behavior change. From this perspective, then, the things that our students learn may or may not be reflected in the behaviors they exhibit. For example, when looking at Kanesha's quiz results, her biology teacher will see no direct evidence of Kanesha's special trick for remembering the

▲ PRINCIPLES/ASSUMPTIONS

Table 6–1   Basic Assumptions of Cognitive Psychology and Their Educational Implications

ASSUMPTION	EXAMPLE	EDUCATIONAL IMPLICATION
Learning as an internal process	Dan learns that Saturn is characterized by rings, but he has no opportunity to demonstrate his knowledge in class.	Give students opportunities to show what they have learned.
Influence of cognitive processes	As Dorothy reads her history textbook, she sees how some historical events are parallel to events in her own life, but she is unable to relate other events to anything with which she is familiar.	Encourage students to think about class material in ways that will help them remember it.
Drawing inferences about cognitive processes by observing behavior	Dana says that 16 + 19 = 25 and that 27 + 27 = 44, indicating that she may be forgetting to "carry" when she does two-digit addition problems.	Look at students' behaviors for indications of possible processing difficulties.
Selectivity about what is learned	Dustin knows that he can't learn everything in his math book, so he decides to memorize the formulas and ignore the rest.	Tell students what things are most important for them to learn.
Uniqueness of some learning processes to humans	Derek learns a great deal about current events by reading a weekly news magazine.	Remember that some principles of learning may be unique to human beings.

humerus, nor will he be aware of Kanesha's association between the sternum and the back end of a boat.

Influence of Cognitive Processes

From the perspective of cognitive psychology, the specific ways in which people think about information are of utmost importance in determining what they learn and how effectively they can remember it. As teachers, we must consider not only *what* students should learn but also *how* they can most effectively learn it. As we proceed through the chapter, we will identify numerous strategies for helping students process classroom material in an effective manner.

Encourage students to think about class material in ways that will help them remember it.

Drawing Inferences from Behavior

Cognitive processes, by their very nature, are phenomena that we cannot directly see. Cognitive psychologists study such processes by observing people's behaviors and then drawing inferences about the mental events that must underlie such behaviors. As teachers, we can do likewise: By observing the things that our students say and write, by asking them to explain their reasoning, by looking closely at the mistakes they make, and so on, we can make some educated guesses about what and how they are thinking about classroom topics.

Look at students' behaviors for indications of possible processing difficulties.

Selectivity About What Is Learned

People are constantly bombarded with information. For example, consider the various stimuli that you are encountering at this very moment. How many separate stimuli appear on these two open pages of your textbook? How many objects do you see right now *in addition to* your textbook? How many sounds are reaching your ears? How many objects do you feel—for example, on your fingertips, on your toes, at your back, and around your waist? I suspect that you have been ignoring most of these stimuli until just now; you were not processing them until I asked you to do so. People can only handle so much information at a given point in time, and so they must be selective about the things they process and learn. They focus on the things they think are important and ignore everything else.

Here it is useful to distinguish between **sensation**—one's ability to sense stimuli in the environment—and **perception**—one's interpretation of stimuli. Things that the body senses are not always perceived (interpreted).

As an analogy, let's consider the kind of mail that a typical household receives. Hundreds of items—packages, letters, bills, brochures, catalogs, fliers, advertisements, requests for donations, and sweepstakes announcements—are delivered to each household every year. Do *you* open, examine, and respond to all the mail that *you* receive? Probably not. If you're like me, then you only "process" a few key items; in particular, you process packages, letters, bills, and a few miscellaneous things that happen to catch your eye. You may inspect other items long enough to know that you don't need them; possibly you even discard some items without opening them at all.

In much the same way, our students will encounter a great deal of information every day—information delivered by way of teacher instruction, textbooks, worksheets, classroom bulletin boards, classmates' behaviors, and so on. They will inevitably make choices as to which pieces of information are most important: They will select a few stimuli to examine and respond to in depth, give other stimuli just a cursory glance, and ignore other stimuli altogether. As teachers, we must help our students make wise decisions about the pieces of information they choose to attend to, process, and save.

Tell students what things are most important for them to learn.

A great deal of human learning occurs through a uniquely human behavior—verbal communication.

Uniqueness of Some Learning Processes to Humans

Some learning theories, especially those within the behaviorist framework, propose that human beings learn in ways similar to those of many other species; for example, the principle that behaviors will increase when followed by certain consequences (the principle of *reinforcement*) can be applied to rats and pigeons, as well as to people. Cognitive psychology, however, deals with aspects of learning that are often uniquely human. For example, a great deal of our learning occurs through verbal communication among individuals, and no other species communicates and learns through such a complex and flexible language. And our extensive use of language in thinking, as well as in communicating, probably helps us relate and associate pieces of information in our minds (e.g., consider Kanesha's association of *humerus* with the "funny bone") in a way that is probably not possible for rats or pigeons.

Remember that some principles of learning may be unique to human beings.

DEFINING KEY CONCEPTS IN COGNITIVE PROCESSING

Before we begin an in-depth look at information processing, we should define some of the basic terminology that we will be using. Let's look at three concepts that will be important in our later discussions:

- Storage
- Encoding
- Retrieval

Storage

The term **storage** refers to the acquisition of information—to the process of putting new information into memory. For example, you have, I hope, been *storing* the ideas that you have been reading in this chapter. And each time you go to class, you undoubtedly store some of the ideas presented in lecture or class discussion. You may store other information from class as well—perhaps the name of the person sitting next to you (George), the size and shape of the classroom (rectangular, about 15 by 30 meters), or the pattern of the instructor's shirt (orange and purple horizontal stripes).

Encoding

We don't always store information exactly as we receive it. We usually change it in some way as we store it; in other words, we **encode** it. For example, when you listen to a story, you may picture some of the story's events in your mind. When you see that orange and purple striped shirt, you may think, "Hmmm, this instructor has really bad taste."

People frequently store information in a different way from how it was presented to them. For example, they may change information from auditory to visual form, as is true when they form a mental picture of a story they are listening to. Or they may change information from visual to auditory form, as is true when they read aloud a passage from a textbook. Furthermore, encoding frequently involves assigning specific *meanings* and *interpretations* to stimuli and events. As an illustration of what I mean, try this exercise.

▣ EXPERIENCING FIRSTHAND
The Old Sea Dog at the Admiral Benbow Inn

Read the following passage *one time only:*

> He was a very silent man by custom. All day he hung round the cove, or upon the cliffs, with a brass telescope; all evening he sat in a corner of the parlour next the fire, and drank rum and water very strong. Mostly he would not speak when spoken to; only look up sudden and fierce, and blow through his nose like a fog-horn; and we and the people who came about our house soon learned to let him be. Every day, when he came back from his stroll, he would ask if any seafaring men had gone by along the road. At first we thought it was the want of company of his own kind that made him ask this question; but at last we began to see he was desirous to avoid them. When a seaman put up at the "Admiral Benbow" (as now and then some did, making by the coast road for Bristol), he would look in at him through the curtained door before he entered the parlour; and he was always sure to be as silent as a mouse when any such was present. For me, at least, there was no secret about the matter; for I was, in a way, a sharer in his alarms. He had taken me aside one day, and promised me a silver fourpenny on the first of every month if I would only keep my "weather-eye open for a seafaring man with one leg," and let him know the moment he appeared. Often enough, when the first of the month came round, and I applied to him for my wage, he would only blow through his nose at me, and stare me down; but before the week was out he was sure to think better of it, bring me my fourpenny piece, and repeat his orders to look out for "the seafaring man with one leg." (from Robert Louis Stevenson's *Treasure Island*)

Now that you have finished the passage, take a few minutes to write down as much of the passage as you can remember. ▣

As you reflected back on the passage you had just read, you probably remembered that the man was afraid of a one-legged seafarer. You may also have recalled that the man paid the story's narrator some money to keep an eye out for such an individual. But could you remember *each and every detail* about the events that took place? Could you recall the *exact words* that the author used to describe the man's behavior? If you are like most people, you stored the gist of the passage (its general meaning) without necessarily storing the specific words that you read (e.g., Brainerd & Reyna, 1992).

Think of an exam that you have taken recently. Which student would have done better on that exam, one who had encoded information verbatim or one who had encoded it in terms of meanings? ▣

Retrieval

Once you have stored information in your memory, you may later discover that you need to use that information. The process of remembering previously stored information—of "finding" that information in memory—is called **retrieval.** Try your hand at retrieval in the following exercise.

EXPERIENCING FIRSTHAND
Retrieval Practice

See how quickly you can answer each of the following questions.

1. What is your name?

2. In what year did World War II end?

3. What is the name of the upper arm bone in the human body?

4. What did you have for dinner three years ago today?

5. When talking about serving appetizers at a party, we sometimes use a French term instead of the word *appetizer.* What is that French term, and how is it spelled? ◼

As you probably just noticed when you tried to answer these questions, retrieving information from memory is sometimes an easy, effortless process; for example, you undoubtedly had little difficulty remembering your name. But other things stored in memory can be retrieved only after some thought and effort; for example, it may have taken you some time to remember that World War II ended in 1945 and that the upper arm bone is the humerus. And still other things, even though they may have been stored in memory at one time, may never be retrieved at all; perhaps a dinner menu three years ago or the correct spelling of *hors d'oeuvre* fall into this category.

How is information stored and encoded in memory? And what factors influence the ease with which we can retrieve it later? Let's take a look at a model of how human memory might work.

USING A MODEL OF HUMAN MEMORY

Please note that, in referring to three components of memory, I am *not* necessarily referring to three separate parts of the brain. The model of memory that I describe here has been derived from studies of human behavior, not from studies of brain physiology.

Information processing theorists do not agree about the exact nature of human memory. But many theorists believe that memory may have three components: a sensory register, a working (or short-term) memory, and a long-term memory. A three-component model of human memory, based loosely on one proposed by Atkinson and Shiffrin in 1968 but modified to reflect more recent research findings, is presented in Figure 6–1. In the pages that follow, we will look at the characteristics of each component of memory and at how information is moved from one component to the next. As we go along, I will often show you our model of memory in a simplified form, each time highlighting the part of the model that we are discussing.

Nature of the Sensory Register

If you have ever played with a lighted sparkler at night, then you've undoubtedly noticed the "tail" of light that followed the sparkler as you waved it about. And if you have ever daydreamed in class, then you may have noticed that when you tuned back in to the lecture, you could still "hear" three or four words spoken just *before* you started paying attention to your instructor, even though you could remember nothing of what was said prior to those few words. The sparkler's tail and the words that you could still "hear" after they had already been spoken were not "out there" in the environment—they were recorded in your sensory register.

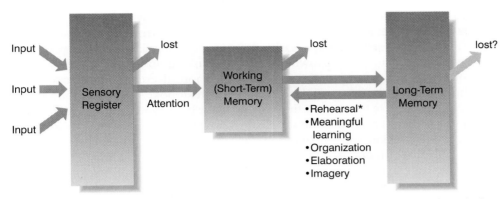

*Rehearsal is probably less effective than the other processes. In fact, theorists disagree as to whether repetition in the absence of connecting new information to existing knowledge promotes long-term memory storage at all.

Figure 6–1   A Model of the Human Memory System

The **sensory register** (see Figure 6–2) is the component of memory that holds the information that you receive—*input*—in more or less its original, *un*encoded form. Probably everything that your body is capable of seeing, hearing, and otherwise sensing is stored in the sensory register. In other words, the sensory register has a *large capacity;* it can hold a great deal of information at one time.

That's the good news. The bad news is that information stored in the sensory register doesn't last very long (e.g., Wingfield & Byrnes, 1981). Visual information—the things that you *see*—probably lasts for less than a second. As a child, I never could spell out my entire name with a sparkler; the *J* had always faded before I got to the final *E*, no matter how quickly I wrote. Auditory information—the things that you *hear*—probably lasts slightly longer, perhaps for two or three seconds. To keep information for any time at all, then, we need to move it on to *working memory.* Whatever information isn't moved is probably lost, or "forgotten."

Moving Information to Working Memory: The Role of Attention

How does information move from the sensory register into working memory? Many theorists believe that **attention** plays a key role here: *Whatever people pay attention to*

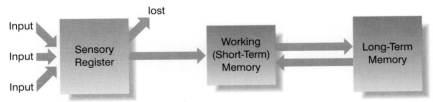

The sensory register holds everything we sense for a very brief period of time.

Figure 6–2   The Sensory Register

Keep in mind that students won't remember the information they receive unless they process it in some way—at a minimum, by paying attention to it.

Remember that students can usually only attend to—and thus learn from—one thing at a time.

(mentally) moves into working memory (see Figure 6–3). Anything in the sensory register that does not get a person's attention disappears from the memory system. For example, imagine yourself reading a textbook for one of your classes. Your eyes are moving down each page, but meanwhile you are thinking about something altogether different—a recent fight with a friend, a high-paying job advertised in the paper, or your growling stomach. What have you learned from the textbook? Absolutely nothing—even though your eyes were focused on the words in your book, you weren't really paying attention to them. And now imagine yourself in class the following day. Your mind is not on the class discussion, but on something else—a fly on the wall, the instructor's orange and purple shirt, or (again) your growling stomach. As a result, you will remember nothing about that class discussion.

Unfortunately, people can only attend to a very small amount of information at any one time. In other words, attention has a *limited capacity*. For example, if you are in a room where several conversations are occurring at once, you can usually only attend to—and therefore can only learn from—*one* of those conversations; this phenomenon is sometimes called the *cocktail party phenomenon* (Cherry, 1953; Norman, 1969). If you are sitting in front of the television set with your textbook open in your lap, you can attend to the *I Love Lucy* rerun *or* to your book, but not to both simultaneously. If you are preoccupied in class with your instructor's ghastly taste in clothing, you are unlikely to be paying attention to the content of the instructor's lecture.

Exactly *how* limited is the limited capacity of human attention? People can often perform two or three well-learned, automatic tasks at once; for example, you can walk and chew gum simultaneously, and you can probably drive a car and drink a Coke at the same time. But when a stimulus or event is detailed and complex (this is the case for both textbooks and *I Love Lucy* reruns) or when a task requires considerable thought (understanding a lecture and driving a car on an icy mountain road are examples of tasks requiring one's utmost concentration), then people can usually attend to only *one* thing at a time (e.g., J. R. Anderson, 1990).

Because of the limited capacity of human attention, only a very small amount of information stored in one's sensory register ever moves on to working memory. The vast majority of information that the body initially receives is quickly lost from the memory system, much as we might quickly discard all that junk mail we receive every day.

Attention in the Classroom

Obviously, it is critical that our students pay attention to the things that we want them to learn. To some extent, we can tell which students are paying attention by their overt behaviors (Grabe, 1986; Piontkowski & Calfee, 1979). But appearances can be deceiving. For example, you can probably think of times when, as a student, you looked at a

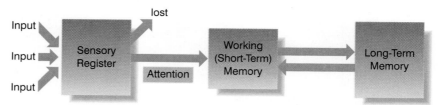

Attention moves information from the sensory register to working memory.

Figure 6–3 The Role of Attention

teacher without really hearing anything that the teacher said. You can probably also think of times when you looked at a textbook without a single word on the page sinking in. Attention is not just a behavior, it is also a mental process. It is not enough that students' eyes and ears are directed toward their classroom material. Their minds must be directed toward it as well.

How can we be sure our students are really paying attention? For one thing, we can ask questions in class that test students' understanding of the things we are presenting; our students are more likely to keep their minds on a lecture or assignment if they know that they will be immediately accountable for it (Grabe, 1986; Piontkowski & Calfee, 1979). We can also ask students to put classroom material to use—for example, by having them draw an inference or solve a problem using new information. A third strategy is to encourage students to take notes; research tells us that note taking usually helps students learn information, partly because it makes them pay attention to what they are hearing or reading (Di Vesta & Gray, 1972; Kiewra, 1989).

Every classroom has students who are easily distracted. Such students are more likely to pay attention when they are seated near their teacher (Schwebel & Cherlin, 1972). We can also help such students by providing a stimulating classroom environment in which everyone *wants* to pay attention. Our students are more likely to pay attention when they find exciting new things to learn every day, when we use a variety of methods to present classroom material, and when we are lively and obviously enthusiastic about our subject matter. They are less likely to keep their minds on their work when they study the same topics and follow the same routine day after day, and when, as teachers, we seem to be as bored with the subject matter as they are (e.g., Berlyne, 1960; Good & Brophy, 1994; Zirin, 1974).

What things do your favorite instructors do to keep your attention?

When we keep our students' attention on the task at hand, we will simultaneously keep misbehaviors to a minimum. We will identify additional strategies for keeping students on task in our discussion of *classroom management* in Chapter 12.

Nature of Working (Short-Term) Memory

Working memory (WM)—sometimes known as **short-term memory (STM)**—is highlighted in Figure 6–4. This is the component of memory where new information is held while it is mentally processed; in other words, it is a temporary "holding bin" for new information. Working memory is also the component where much of our thinking, or information processing, occurs. It is where we try to make sense out of a lecture, understand a textbook passage, or solve a problem.

Generally speaking, working memory is the component that probably does most of the processing, or "work," of the memory system. It has two characteristics that are particularly worth noting: a short duration and a limited capacity.

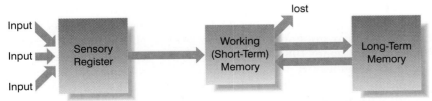

In working memory a limited amount of information is stored for perhaps five to twenty seconds; some of this information is actively "thought about" and processed.

Figure 6–4   Working Memory

A common misconception is that short-term memory lasts much longer than this—perhaps a day, a week, or a month. Did you have a misconception about short-term memory before you read this section?

Do you see why this process is called *maintenance rehearsal?*

Remember that students can process only so much information at a time, and pace instruction accordingly.

Give students guidance about the things on which they should focus their learning efforts.

Short Duration of Working Memory

As its alternative name, "short-term memory," implies, working memory is *short.* Unless information stored in working memory is processed further, it probably lasts only five to twenty seconds at the most (e.g., L. R. Peterson & Peterson, 1959). Working memory is obviously *not* the "place" to leave information that you need to know for an exam next week, or even for information that you'll need for a class later today.

Imagine that you need to make a phone call to a friend, so you look up the friend's number in the telephone book. You have that number in your head (you've paid attention to it, so it's in your working memory) but then discover that someone else is using the telephone. Assuming that you cannot write the number down, what do you do to remember it until the phone is free? You probably repeat the number to yourself over and over again. This process, known as **maintenance rehearsal,** keeps information in working memory for as long as you're willing to continue talking to yourself. But once you stop, the number quickly disappears (e.g., Landauer, 1962; Sperling, 1967).

Limited Capacity of Working Memory

Let's put your working memory to work for a moment.

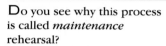

EXPERIENCING FIRSTHAND
A Divisive Situation

Try computing the answer to this division problem in your head:

$$59\overline{)49,383}$$

Did you find yourself having trouble remembering some parts of the problem while you were dealing with other parts? Did you ever arrive at the correct answer of 837? Most people cannot solve a division problem with this many numbers unless they can write the problem down on paper. The fact is, working memory just doesn't have room to hold all that information at once—it has a *limited capacity* (G. A. Miller, 1956; Simon, 1974).

Just like other human beings, our students will have limited space in their working memories. So as we teach them, we must remember that they can only learn so much so fast. A mistake that many new teachers make is to present too much information too quickly, and their students' working memories simply can't keep up. Instead, we should pace our presentation of information in such a way that students have time to process it all. We can accomplish this in numerous ways—for example, by repeating the same idea several times (perhaps rewording it each time), by stopping to write important points on the chalkboard, and by providing numerous examples and illustrations.

We must also remember that our students can probably never learn *everything* presented to them in a lecture or textbook. Most teachers and textbooks present much more information than students can possibly store (Calfee, 1981). For example, one psychologist (E. D. Gagné, 1985) has estimated that students are likely to learn only about one to six new ideas from each minute of a lecture—a small fraction of the ideas that are typically presented during that time! So students are continually making choices about what things to learn and what things *not* to learn. Yet research tells us that students aren't always the best judges as to which things are important and which are not (Garner, Alexander, Gillingham, Kulikowich, & Brown, 1991; Mayer, 1984; R. E. Reynolds & Shirey, 1988). We must help our students make the right choices—perhaps by telling them what information is most important, giving them guidelines on how and what to study, or omitting some of the details that really aren't very important after all.

Moving Information to Long-Term Memory: Connecting New Information with Prior Knowledge

Look at the version of our memory model presented in Figure 6–5. Notice that the arrows between working memory and long-term memory go in both directions. The process of storing new information in long-term memory usually involves drawing on "old" information already stored there; in other words, it necessitates using prior knowledge. Here are four examples:

- When Patrick reads about the feuding between the Montagues and the Capulets in *Romeo and Juliet,* he thinks, "Hmmm . . . sounds a lot like the relationship my family has with our next-door neighbors."

- Pia reads about how Christopher Columbus's first voyage across the Atlantic was financed by Queen Isabella of Spain. "Queen Isabella probably thought that she would make a profit on her investment," Pia thinks.

- Paolo discovers that the initial letters of each of the five great lakes—Huron, Ontario, Michigan, Erie, and Superior—spell the word *HOMES.*

- Like many young children, Priscilla believes that the world is flat. When her teacher tells her that the world is round, Priscilla pictures a flat, circular disk (which is, of course, round *and* flat).

THE FAR SIDE By GARY LARSON

"Mr. Osborne, may I be excused? My brain is full."

Working memory is a bottleneck in the human memory system.

Each student is connecting new information with something that he or she already knows or believes. Patrick finds a similarity between *Romeo and Juliet* and his own neighborhood. Pia interprets Columbus's first voyage in terms of investment and profit. Paolo connects the five Great Lakes with a common, everyday word. And Priscilla relates

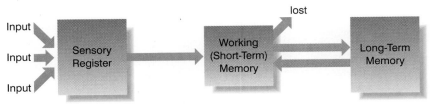

Storage in long-term memory usually involves connecting new information to existing knowledge.

Figure 6–5   Connecting New Information to Existing Knowledge

the idea that the world is round to her previous conception of a flat world and to the many flat, circular objects (e.g., coins, pizzas) that she has encountered over the years.

Later in the chapter, we will look more specifically at the processes through which information is stored in long-term memory. But before we do so, we need to examine the characteristics of long-term memory and the nature of the "old" information stored within it.

Nature of Long-Term Memory

Psychologists sometimes make a distinction between *declarative* knowledge (the facts that you know) and *procedural* knowledge (the skills that you can perform). Both forms of knowledge are stored in long-term memory.

Long-term memory (LTM) is the final component of the human memory system (see Figure 6–6). This component holds information for a relatively long period of time—perhaps a day, a week, a month, a year, or one's entire lifetime. Your own long-term memory is where you've stored such pieces of information as your name, a few frequently used telephone numbers, your general knowledge about the world, and the things that you've learned in school—perhaps the names of the Great Lakes, the year in which World War II ended, or the correct spelling of *hors d'oeuvre*. It is also where you've stored your knowledge about how to perform various behaviors—perhaps how to ride a bicycle, swing a baseball bat, or write a cursive letter *G*.

Long-term memory has three characteristics that are especially worth noting: a long duration, an essentially unlimited capacity, and a rich network of interconnections among the various things stored there.

(Indefinitely) Long Duration of Long-Term Memory

As you might guess, information stored in long-term memory lasts much longer than information stored in working memory. But exactly *how* long is long-term memory? As you well know, people often forget things they have known for a day, a week, or even longer. Some psychologists believe that information may slowly "weaken" and possibly disappear from long-term memory, especially if it is not used on a regular basis (e.g., J. R. Anderson, 1990). Others instead believe that, once information is stored in long-term memory, it remains there permanently but may in some cases be extremely difficult to retrieve (Loftus & Loftus, 1980). The exact duration of long-term memory has never been determined, and perhaps never can be (Eysenck & Keane, 1990).

Unlimited Capacity of Long-Term Memory

Long-term memory seems to be capable of holding as much information as an individual needs to store there—there is probably no such thing as a person "running out of

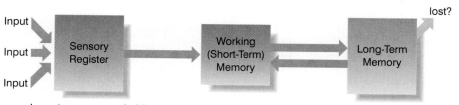

Long-term memory holds a vast amount of information for a long period of time.

Figure 6–6   Long-Term Memory

room." In fact, for reasons that you will discover shortly, the more information already stored in long-term memory, the easier it is to learn new things.

Interconnectedness of Long-Term Memory

Theorists have discovered that the information stored in long-term memory is organized and interconnected to some extent. To see what I mean, try this simple exercise.

◼ EXPERIENCING FIRSTHAND
Horse #1

What is the first word that comes to your mind when you hear the word *horse*? And what word does that second word remind you of? And what does that third word remind you of? Beginning with the word *horse,* follow your train of thought, letting each word remind you of another one, for a sequence of at least eight words. Write down ◼ your sequence of words as each word comes to mind.

You probably found yourself easily following a train of thought from the word *horse,* perhaps something like the route I followed:

horse → cowboy → lasso → rope → knot → Girl Scouts → cookies → chocolate → (salivation response)

The last word in your sequence might be one with little or no obvious relationship to horses. Yet you can probably see a logical connection between each pair of words in the sequence. Information processing theorists believe that related pieces of information in long-term memory are often connected with one another, perhaps in a network similar to the one depicted in Figure 6–7.

◼ EXPERIENCING FIRSTHAND
Horse #2

Now think about a horse once again, this time thinking of all the physical features that horses have. For example, how many legs do horses have? How large are they? What colors do they tend to be? Write down as many things about a horse's appearance as you can think of. ◼

Some theorists propose that much of the information stored in long-term memory is organized as **schemas**—organized bodies of knowledge about specific topics (e.g., Rumelhart & Ortony, 1977). For example, you probably had little difficulty thinking of many characteristics of horses; among other things, you may have thought of four legs, a mane, an elongated head, and a long tail. The various things that you know about horses are closely interrelated in your long-term memory. In other words, we could say that you have a horse schema.

In general, schemas give us an idea of how things "typically" are. They also influence how new information is interpreted and stored in long-term memory, as you will discover in our discussion of knowledge construction in Chapter 7.

Can you summarize the model of memory that I've described in the last few pages? ◼

Critiquing the Three-Component Model

In the last few pages, we have considered the sensory register, working memory, and long-term memory. But are there really three separate components of human memory, and are they as distinctly different from one another as I have portrayed them? Not all cognitive psychologists agree that the model I have just described is an accurate repre-

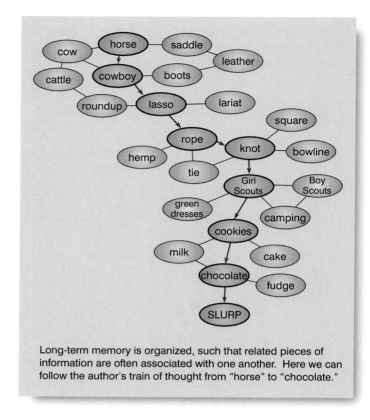

Figure 6–7 Interconnectedness in Long-Term Memory

Long-term memory is organized, such that related pieces of information are often associated with one another. Here we can follow the author's train of thought from "horse" to "chocolate."

Make sure students process important information thoroughly.

sentation of how human memory works (e.g., J. R. Anderson, 1990; Eysenck & Keane, 1990).

As one alternative, some theorists have proposed a **levels of processing** model of memory: They believe that there is really only one "memory" and that our ability to remember information is simply a function of how much we process the information (Cermak & Craik, 1979; Craik & Lockhart, 1972). According to this perspective, we are unlikely to remember things when we pay little or no attention to them, because we hardly process those things at all. When we process information in a superficial way—for example, by observing its general appearance without thinking much about its underlying meaning—we may remember it for a short while (perhaps for a matter of seconds). When we think long and hard about the information that we receive—for example, by trying to understand and make sense of it or by drawing implications from it for our own lives— we are likely to remember that information for a far longer period of time.

Yet the levels of processing perspective probably does not give us a completely accurate picture of human memory either: The "depth" to which information is processed cannot be objectively defined, nor is it always an accurate predictor of how easily that information can be remembered later on (Baddeley, 1978; Eysenck & Keane, 1990; Schwartz & Reisberg, 1991). At the present time, there is probably *no* single theoretical model that explains everything that we know about human memory.

The three-component model of memory that I have presented in this chapter, though perhaps not a perfect one, is similar to how many cognitive psychologists conceptualize human memory. This model also highlights characteristics of memory that

Table 6–2   General Principles of Human Memory

PRINCIPLE	EDUCATIONAL IMPLICATION	EXAMPLE
People are more likely to learn the things that they pay attention to.	We must ensure that students are paying attention to classroom lessons, activities, and materials.	We can ask thought-provoking questions that keep students mentally engaged in the topic at hand.
Information stored in working memory lasts for about five to twenty seconds.	When we want students to remember information for any length of time, we must encourage storage in long-term memory.	We should assess students' knowledge and understanding of material not only immediately after they have learned it but also at later points in time.
Attention and working memory are characterized by a limited capacity.	We must be careful not to present material at such a pace that students experience information overload.	When presenting new ideas in class, we should give students the time they need to attend to and process each idea effectively.
Information stored in long-term memory is interconnected.	We should show students how different aspects of classroom subject matter are related to one another.	We can draw a diagram on the chalkboard that depicts interrelationships among the various concepts that we are teaching.
Long-term memory storage occurs more effectively when new information is related to things already known.	When presenting new information, we should encourage students to make connections to things they have previously learned.	We can ask students to write about material in their textbooks and, specifically, to relate it to their own experiences (Konopak, Martin, & Martin, 1990).

are important for us to keep in mind as we teach; for example, it highlights the importance of *attention* in learning, the *limited capacity* of both attention and working memory, the *interconnectedness* of the knowledge that we acquire, and the importance of *relating* new information with the things that we already know. Several general principles of memory derived from the model are presented in Table 6–2.

Regardless of whether there are three truly distinct components of memory, some aspects of memory are definitely "long-term." Certainly, we remember many things for a considerable length of time, and in this sense, at least, those things are in long-term memory. Let's look more closely at how we store information in long-term memory.

STORING INFORMATION IN LONG-TERM MEMORY

In what ways do we encode information as we store it in long-term memory? How can we think about and process information so that we can remember it easily at a later point in time? How does our prior knowledge affect our ability to learn new information? And how can we learn material successfully when we *don't* have prior knowledge from which to draw? These are issues we turn to now.

How Information Is Encoded in Long-Term Memory

Human memories are undoubtedly stored in some neurological ("brain") form. The forms of encoding I describe are how memories *appear* to us, rather than how they are in a physiological sense.

Information is probably encoded in long-term memory in a number of different forms (e.g., J. M. Clark & Paivio, 1991; E. D. Gagné, 1985; Paivio, 1971, 1986). For example, some information is stored in a *verbal* form, in terms of actual words. Things that you remember word for word—for example, your name, your address, the nursery rhyme "Jack and Jill," Hamlet's soliloquy ("To be or not to be, that is the question . . .")—are all verbally encoded. Other information is encoded in the form of *imagery*—that is, in terms of how that information appears on the surface. For example, if you can "see" the word *hors d'oeuvre* in your mind, if you can picture the face of a relative or close friend with your eyes closed, or if you can "hear" the voice of that individual in your mind, then you are retrieving images. But probably the bulk of information in long-term memory is encoded *semantically,* in terms of its underlying meanings. For example, when you listen to a lecture or read a textbook, you probably store the "gist" of the words that you hear or read more frequently than you store the words themselves.

In many situations, information may be encoded in more than one form simultaneously. For example, stop and think about your last educational psychology class session. Can you recall some of the ideas (meanings) that were presented at that class? Can you recall what your instructor or any classmates looked like that day (images)? Can you recall some of the specific words that were spoken or written on the chalkboard (verbal encoding)?

Present the same information in more than one form—for example, as both a verbal explanation and a diagram.

Research evidence indicates that information encoded in multiple ways is more easily retrieved from long-term memory than information encoded in just one way. For example, students learn and remember information more readily when they receive that information in both a verbal form (e.g., lecture, textbook passage) and a visual form (e.g., picture, map, diagram) (Denis, 1984; Kulhavy, Lee, & Caterino, 1985; Winn, 1991). To the extent that we present information to our students in multiple modalities, we increase the likelihood that they will encode the information in more than one way, and so we also increase the likelihood that they will be able to remember it over the long run.

Long-Term Memory Storage Processes

As I mentioned earlier, theorists don't know exactly how long information stored in long-term memory actually lasts. They have discovered, however, that the specific cognitive processes used to store information in long-term memory affect an individual's ability to remember and use that information at a later point in time (see Figure 6–8). In the next few pages, we will consider five processes that people may use in storing information in long-term memory:

- Rehearsal

- Meaningful learning

- Organization

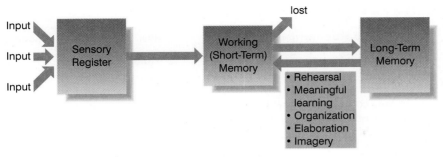

At least five processes may be involved in long-term memory storage: rehearsal (a relatively ineffective process), meaningful learning, organization, elaboration, and visual imagery.

Figure 6–8   Long-Term Memory Storage Processes

- Elaboration

- Visual imagery

These five processes are summarized in Table 6–3. As we discuss each one, we will identify strategies that we can use to help our students store classroom information more effectively.

Rehearsal

Earlier in the chapter, I described how maintenance rehearsal—repeating something over and over again—helps us keep information in working memory indefinitely. Early information processing theorists (e.g., Atkinson & Shiffrin, 1968) believed that **rehearsal** is also a means through which information is stored in long-term memory. In other words, if we repeat something often enough, it might eventually sink in.

The main disadvantage in using rehearsal is that we make few if any connections between new information and the knowledge that we already have in long-term memory. Thus, we are engaging in **rote learning:** We are learning information in a strictly verbatim fashion, without attaching any meaning to it. Contrary to what many students think, rote (meaningless) learning is a slow and relatively ineffective way of storing information in long-term memory (Ausubel, 1968). In fact, some research indicates that information cannot be stored in long-term memory through repetition alone—that *some* associations with existing knowledge must be made (Craik & Watkins, 1973; Klatzky, 1975; Watkins & Watkins, 1974). Another disadvantage of rote learning is that, for reasons you will discover later in the chapter, information stored in a rote fashion—that is, with few connections to other things already learned—is more difficult to retrieve later on.

If you have already read the discussion of cognitive development in Chapter 2, then you may remember that rehearsal is one of the first learning strategies that students develop (usually in the early elementary school years). Rehearsal is probably better than not processing information at all. And in cases where students have little prior knowledge they can draw on to help them understand new material, rehearsal may be one of the few strategies they can use.

If we teach young children, we should expect that rehearsal will be a predominant method through which they will attempt to learn new information. If we observe sec-

Do you recall Kanesha's difficulty remembering the bones that she tried to learn simply by repeating them over and over? Why did she resort to rehearsal for learning some of the bones?

Encourage early elementary students to use rehearsal if they show no evidence of using *any* learning strategy. Encourage older students to use other, more effective storage methods whenever possible.

Table 6–3 *Long-Term Memory Storage Processes*

PROCESS	DEFINITION	HOW INFORMATION IS ENCODED
Rehearsal	Repeating information verbatim, either mentally or aloud	Verbatim (verbal code)
Meaningful Learning	Making connections between new information and prior knowledge	Underlying meaning (semantic code)
Organization	Making connections among various pieces of new information	Underlying meaning (semantic code)
Elaboration	Adding additional ideas to new information based on what one already knows	Underlying meaning (semantic code)
Visual Imagery	Forming a mental "picture" of information	Visual image

ondary students regularly using this strategy to learn their class material, however, we should encourage them to use other, more effective methods of storing information—such methods as meaningful learning, organization, elaboration, and visual imagery.

Meaningful Learning

Meaningful learning is similar to Piaget's concept of *assimilation,* described in Chapter 2.

Meaningful learning is a process of recognizing a relationship between new information and something else already stored in long-term memory. When we use words like *comprehension* or *understanding,* we are talking about meaningful learning. Here are some examples:

- When Juan reads that World War II ended on August 10, 1945, he thinks, "Hey, August tenth is my birthday!"

- Students in a German class notice that the German word *Buch* is pronounced similarly to its English equivalent: *book.*

- Jane encounters a new subtraction fact: 4 − 2 = 2. "That makes sense," she thinks. "After all, two plus two are four, and this is just doing the same thing backward."

- When Julian reads J. D. Salinger's *The Catcher in the Rye,* he sees similarities between Holden Caulfield's emotional struggles and his own adolescent concerns.

Research clearly indicates that meaningful learning is more effective than rote learning (e.g., Ausubel et al., 1978; Bower, Karlin, & Dueck, 1975; Bransford & John-

EXAMPLE	EFFECTIVENESS	EDUCATIONAL IMPLICATION
Repeating a word-for-word definition of *inertia*	Relatively ineffective: Storage is slow, and later retrieval is difficult.	Encourage rehearsal only when more effective strategies are not possible.
Putting a definition of inertia into one's own words or identifying examples of inertia in one's own life experiences	Effective if associations made with prior knowledge are appropriate ones.	Help students understand new information in terms of the things that they already know.
Studying one's lines in a play in terms of how they relate to the overall plot	Effective if organizational structure is legitimate and if it consists of more than a "list" of separate facts.	Present material in an organized fashion and point out the organizational structure and interrelationships in the material.
Thinking about possible reasons why historical figures behaved as they did	Effective if added ideas are appropriate inferences.	Encourage students to go beyond the information itself—for example, to draw inferences and to speculate about possible implications.
Imagining how various characters and events in *Ivanhoe* might have appeared	Individual differences in effectiveness; especially beneficial when used as a supplement to semantic encoding.	Illustrate verbal instruction with visual materials (e.g., pictures, maps, diagrams).

son, 1972). As illustrations of the effectiveness of meaningful learning, try the following two exercises.

■ EXPERIENCING FIRSTHAND
Two Letter Strings, Two Pictures

1. Study each of the following strings of letters until you can remember them perfectly:

    AIIRODFMLAWRS

    FAMILIARWORDS

2. Study each of the two pictures below until you can reproduce them accurately from memory.

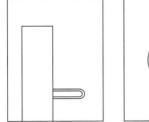 

Source: Figures are from "Comprehension and Memory for Pictures" by G. H. Bower, M. B. Karlin, and A. Dueck, 1975, *Memory and Cognition, 3,* p. 217. Reprinted by permission of Psychonomic Society, Inc. ■

Encourage students to learn information meaningfully, and help them make sense out of new material.

No doubt the second letter string was easier for you to learn because you could relate it to something that you already knew: "familiar words." How easily were you able to learn the two pictures? Do you think that you can remember them well enough to draw them from memory a week from now? Do you think that you would be able to remember them more easily if they had meaningful titles such as "a midget playing a trombone in a telephone booth" and "an early bird who caught a very strong worm"? The answer to the latter question is a very definite yes (Bower et al., 1975).

Meaningful learning in the classroom. Some students approach school assignments with meaningful learning in mind: They try to make sense out of new information in terms of what they already know. These students are likely to be the high achievers in the classroom. Other students instead use such rote learning strategies as repeating something over and over to themselves without really thinking about what they are saying. As you might guess, these students have more difficulty in school (e.g., C. E. Weinstein, 1978).

Yet we cannot always blame students when they take a relatively meaning*less* learning approach to their studies. Inadvertently, many teaching practices encourage students to learn school subjects in a rote fashion. Think back to your own experiences in school. How many times were you allowed to define a word by repeating a dictionary definition, rather than being expected to explain it in your own words? In fact, how many times were you *required* to repeat something back exactly as you heard it? And how many times were you given an exam that tested your knowledge of facts or principles without ever testing your ability to relate those facts and principles to things in your everyday life or to things that you had learned in previous courses? When students expect an upcoming test to focus on the recall of unrelated facts, rather than on the understanding and application of an integrated body of knowledge, many of them will try to learn information at a rote, meaningless level, believing that such an approach will yield a higher test score and that meaningful learning would be counterproductive (Crooks, 1988). It is little wonder that meaningful learning is the exception, rather than the rule, in many classrooms (Cooney, 1991; Novak & Musonda, 1991; Schoenfeld, 1985b).

Why do some students learn things meaningfully, whereas others persist in their attempts at rote memorization? At least three conditions probably facilitate meaningful learning (Ausubel et al., 1978):

- The student has a meaningful learning set.

- The student has previous knowledge to which the new information can be related.

- The student is aware that previously learned information is related to new information.

A meaningful learning set. When students approach a learning task with an attitude that they can make sense out of information—that is, when they have a **meaningful learning set**—they are more likely to learn that information meaningfully. For example, students who recognize that chemical reactions occur in accordance with familiar mathematical principles are more likely to make sense out of those reactions. Students who realize that historical events can often be explained in terms of human personality are more likely to understand why World War II occurred.

My daughter Tina once came home from school with an assignment to learn twelve of the gods and goddesses of ancient Greece (e.g., Zeus was the king of gods, Athena was the goddess of the city and civilization, Apollo was the god of light, Aphrodite was the goddess of love). Unfortunately, there had been little discussion in school of the relevance of these gods and goddesses to anything else Tina knew—for example, to the city of Athens or to the Apollo space flights. And I was reluctant to introduce Tina to the word *aphrodisiac* to help her remember Aphrodite. As a result, Tina had no meaningful learning set for those gods and goddesses, no expectation of connecting them with their domains in any meaningful way. Refusing my motherly offers to help, but determined to do well on an upcoming quiz, she confined herself to her room and repeated those gods and goddesses over and over until she could recite all twelve. A month later, I asked her how many she could still recall. She remembered only Zeus.

Does a teacher present information merely as "something to be learned," or instead as something that can help students better understand their world? Does a teacher ask students to define new terminology by using the exact definitions presented in the textbook, or instead require them to define terms in their own words? When asking students to give examples of a concept, does a teacher expect examples already presented in the textbook, or instead demand that students generate new examples? How we present a learning task clearly affects the extent to which students adopt a meaningful learning set (Ausubel et al., 1978). Ideally, we must communicate our belief that students can and should make sense of the things they study.

Relevant prior knowledge. Meaningful learning can only occur when long-term memory contains information to which a new idea can be related—that is, when long-term memory contains a relevant **knowledge base.** Students will better understand sci-

Find out whether students have sufficient knowledge to understand new topics; for example, give a pretest or ask questions informally in class.

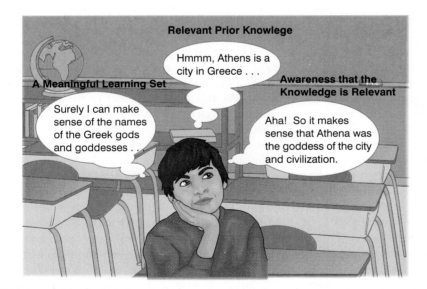

Students are more likely to learn information meaningfully when these three conditions exist.

Meaningful learning is more likely to occur when learners have had experiences to which new information can be related.

What implications does this second condition—relevant prior knowledge—have for teaching students from diverse cultural backgrounds?

Remind students of things they know that have a direct bearing on classroom material.

entific principles if they have already seen those principles in action, either in their own lives or in the laboratory. They will more easily learn the events of an important battle if they have previously visited the battlefield. They will better understand how large the dinosaurs really were if they have seen actual dinosaur skeletons at a museum of natural history. The more information a student has already stored in long-term memory, the easier it is for that student to learn new information, because there are more things with which that new information can be associated.

Awareness of the relevance of prior knowledge. Students often have prior information that relates to something new without ever realizing that this is the case. It may never occur to students that the family feud in *Romeo and Juliet* is similar to neighborhood disputes or, more broadly, to racism. It may never occur to them that a seed is a plant's version of a chicken egg. It may never occur to them that fractions symbolize something they already know—division.

Too often, teachers assume that students make these "obvious" connections. But research tells us that students very frequently *don't* make logical connections between new ideas and their prior knowledge (e.g., Hayes-Roth & Thorndyke, 1979). As a result, they often resort to rote learning strategies unnecessarily. We can facilitate meaningful learning by reminding students of things they know that have a direct bearing on a topic of classroom study (S. Carey, 1986; Machiels-Bongaerts, Schmidt, & Boshuizen, 1991; Resnick, 1989; Spires, Donley, & Penrose, 1990). For example, we can relate works of literature to the thoughts, feelings, and experiences of students themselves. We can explain historical events in terms of the foibles of human personality. We can point out instances when foreign language vocabulary is similar to words in English. We can tie science to students' day-to-day observations and experiences. And we can relate mathematics to such commonplace activities as cooking, building a treehouse, or throwing a ball.

Calvin and Hobbes   by Bill Watterson

Calvin is trying to learn new information meaningfully, but his efforts are in vain because the word feudal *is not in his knowledge base.*

The two storage processes that follow—organization and elaboration—also involve relating new information to prior knowledge; hence, both of these processes incorporate meaningful learning. Yet each one has an additional twist as well.

Organization

Have you ever had an instructor who came to class and spoke aimlessly for an hour, flitting from one idea to another in an unpredictable sequence? Have you ever read a textbook that did the same thing, so that you never knew how ideas related to one another? You undoubtedly found it very difficult to learn in a situation where information was disorganized.

The fact is, we learn and remember a body of new information more easily when we **organize** it (e.g., DuBois, Kiewra, & Fraley, 1988; Mandler & Pearlstone, 1966; Tulving, 1962). By organizing information, we make connections among various pieces of information, rather than learn each piece in isolation; in the process, we often make connections with existing knowledge as well. Consider these examples of how students might organize school learning tasks:

> Giorgio is given a list of eleven events leading up to the American Revolution: the Navigation Acts, the Sugar Act, the Stamp Act, the Tea Act, the Boston Massacre, the Boston Tea Party, the attack of the *Gaspee,* the Battle of Lexington, the Battle of Concord, the Battle of Bunker Hill, and the signing of the Declaration of Independence. He puts them into three groups: British legislation, acts of colonial defiance, and pre-war battles.

> Genevieve has a list of ten spelling words ending with a "long e" sound. She decides to group the words on the basis of their endings. She puts the words ending in *y* in one group, those ending in *ey* in another, and those ending in *ie* in a third, like this:

body	key	movie
family	donkey	cookie
party	monkey	calorie
gravy		

When Greg is trying to learn the components of the human memory system, he makes a chart indicating their capacity and duration, like so:

	Sensory Register	Working Memory	Long-term Memory
Capacity	large	small	large
Duration	very short: <1 second-visual 2-3 sec.-auditory	5-20 seconds	indefinitely long

People are more likely to organize information if the material fits an organizational structure with which they are already familiar—for example, if the material can be placed into discrete categories or into a hierarchical arrangement (Bousfield, 1953; Bransford & Franks, 1971; DuBois et al., 1988; Gauntt, 1991). They are also more likely to learn new material in an organized fashion if that material has been presented to them with its organizational structure laid out for them. As an illustration, let's consider the results of a classic experiment (Bower et al., 1969). College students were given four study trials in which to learn 112 words falling into four categories (e.g., minerals, plants). For some students, the words were arranged in an organized fashion (Figure 6–9 is an example). For other students, the words were arranged randomly—that is, in a mixed-up order. The students with the organized words learned much more quickly. Look at the average number of words that each group remembered after studying them for one study period (about four minutes) and again after three additional study periods:

Number of Study Periods	Organized Words	Unorganized Words
1	73 (65%)	21 (19%)
4	112 (100%)	70 (63%)

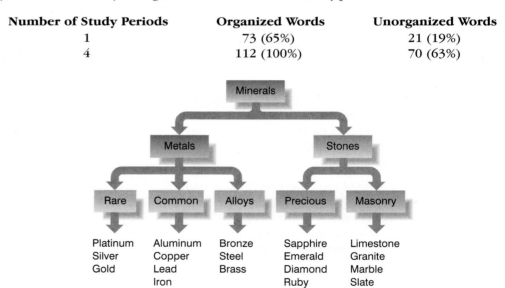

We can remember information more easily when it is organized in some way.

Figure 6–9   Storing Information Through Organization

Source: From "Hierarchical Retrieval Schemes in Recall of Categorized Word Lists" by G. H. Bower, M. C. Clark, A. M. Lesgold, and D. Winzenz, 1969, *Journal of Verbal Learning and Verbal Behavior, 8,* p. 324. Copyright 1969 by Academic Press. Adapted by permission.

Notice that, after studying the words one time, students with organized words remembered more than three times as many words as students who received them in random order. And after four study periods, students with the organized words remembered the entire list of 112!

Unfortunately, many students tend to "organize" the things they study in school merely as a list of separate facts, rather than as a set of interrelated ideas (Kletzien, 1988; Meyer, Brandt, & Bluth, 1980). How can we help our own students organize class material more effectively? Obviously, we should present material in an organized fashion to begin with. For example, we can tell students ahead of time exactly what organizational structure the new material is likely to take—the categories that we will be talking about, the hierarchical nature of certain concepts, and so on. We can also present related pieces of information close together in time; students are more likely to associate related ideas when they encounter those ideas together (Glanzer & Nolan, 1986; Hayes-Roth & Thorndyke, 1979). And we can point out important interrelationships among various concepts and ideas.

Present information in an organized fashion.

We will identify some specific techniques for helping students organize information when we discuss *concept mapping* in Chapter 8 and *advance organizers* in Chapter 13.

Elaboration

As we have already discovered, people often learn by relating a new idea to the things they already know—in other words, by engaging in meaningful learning. In addition, people sometimes use their prior knowledge to expand on a new idea, thereby storing *more* information than was actually presented to them. This process of adding to newly acquired information in some way is called **elaboration.** Here are some examples:

- Marvin reads that Henry VIII divorced his first wife Catherine because, though she delivered a healthy baby daughter, all her sons died within a few days of birth. "Henry apparently wanted a son to succeed him on the throne," Marvin thinks.

- Maria learns that an allosaur had powerful jaws and sharp, pointed teeth. "Allosaurs must have been meat eaters," she deduces.

- Marcus gets a note from a friend who writes, "Meat me by the bak door after skool." Marcus translates his friend's message as, "Meet me by the back door after school."

- When I took a Chinese course in high school, I learned that the Chinese word for "we" is *wŏmen.* "Aha," I thought to myself, "that's the sign on the rest room that *we* girls use."

In most cases, the more students elaborate on new material—the more they use the things they already know to help them understand and interpret it—the more effectively they will store it in long-term memory (e.g., J. R. Anderson, 1990). I remember very little of my two years' Chinese instruction, but the meaning of the word *wŏmen* remains indelibly stored in my long-term memory. Students who elaborate on the things they learn in school are usually better students than those who simply take information at face value (M. A. McDaniel & Einstein, 1989; Pressley, 1982; Waters, 1982).

Can you think of situations in which you learned and remembered something more effectively by elaborating on it?

As teachers, we will often want our students to get in the habit of going beyond the information actually presented to them. We can help them elaborate in numerous ways. For example, we can ask frequent questions along these lines:

Why do you think this happens?

Can you think of some examples of this concept?

Encourage students to elaborate—to use their prior knowledge and experiences to expand on the new things they learn.

Where might this idea be useful? How could we use it in our everyday lives?

What things can you conclude from this information?

We can also encourage elaboration by allowing students to talk about a topic among themselves, asking them to explain an idea on paper, or simply giving them time to think about new information.

Visual Imagery

Earlier in the chapter, we listed imagery as one possible way in which information might be encoded in long-term memory. Numerous research studies indicate that **visual imagery** in particular—in other words, forming mental "pictures" of objects or ideas—can be an effective method of storing information (J. M. Clark & Paivio, 1991; Dewhurst & Conway, 1994; Sadoski, Goetz, & Fritz, 1993). To show you how effective visual imagery can be, let me teach you a few of the Chinese words that I learned in high school.

■ **EXPERIENCING FIRSTHAND**
Five Chinese Words

Try learning these five Chinese words by forming the visual images that I describe:

Chinese Word	English Meaning	Image
fáng	house	Picture a *house* with *fangs* growing on its roof and walls.
mén	door	Picture a rest room *door* with the word *MEN* painted on it.
ké	guest	Picture someone giving someone else (the *guest*) a *key* to the house.
fàn	food	Picture a plate of *food* being cooled by a *fan.*
shū	book	Picture a *shoe* with a *book* sticking out of it.

At this point, find something else to do for a couple of minutes. Stand up and stretch, get a glass of water, or use the bathroom. But be sure to come back to your reading in just a minute or two. . . .

Now that you're back, cover the list of Chinese words, English meanings, and visual images. Can you remember what each of these words means?

ké	fáng
fàn	shū
mén	

■

Did the Chinese words remind you of the visual images that you stored? Did the images help you remember the English meanings of the Chinese words?

You may have remembered all five words easily, or you may have remembered only one or two. People differ in their ability to use visual imagery: Some form visual images quickly and easily, whereas others form them only slowly and with difficulty (J. M. Clark & Paivio, 1991; Kosslyn, 1985; Riding & Calvey, 1981). For those in the former category, imagery can be a powerful means of storing information in long-term memory.

As teachers, we can help many of our students store information more effectively by encouraging them to use visual imagery (J. M. Clark & Paivio, 1991; Cothern, Konopak, & Willis, 1990; West, Farmer, & Wolff, 1991). For example, we can ask them to imagine how certain events in literature or history might have looked. We can demonstrate abstract ideas by using concrete objects—things they can actually see. And we can provide visual materials—pictures, charts, graphs, and so on—that illustrate important ideas.

The last three of our five long-term memory storage processes—organization, elaboration, and visual imagery—are clearly *constructive* in nature: Our encoding of a situation involves putting together several pieces of new information, often in combination with things that we already know. When we organize information, we create a familiar framework (e.g., categories, a hierarchy) into which we can place the specific items that we need to learn. When we elaborate, we create an understanding of new information that clearly goes beyond the information itself. When we use visual imagery, we construct mental "pictures" (perhaps a house with fangs, or a rest room door with *MEN* painted on it) based on how we know certain objects typically look. In Chapter 7, we will examine the constructive nature of long-term memory storage more closely.

Encourage students to form visual images that capture the things they are studying.

Present ideas in a visual manner—for example, with pictures, charts, or graphs.

How Prior Knowledge and Working Memory Affect Long-Term Memory Storage

Occasionally, students' prior knowledge will interfere with something they need to learn; as an example, consider Kanesha's difficulty learning where the sternum is located. But in general, students will store classroom subject matter much more effectively when they have a sufficient knowledge base from which to draw (Alexander, 1996; Alexander, Kulikowich, & Schulze, 1994; Hamman et al., 1995; Schneider, 1993). For example, their ability to form visual images depends to some extent on things they have already learned about the world; they can only picture a house with fangs growing out of it if they already know what houses and fangs look like. Students' prior knowledge facilitates their learning in other ways as well:

- It gives them an idea as to which things are most important to learn; thus, it helps them direct their *attention* appropriately.

- It enables them to understand something—that is, to engage in *meaningful learning*—rather than to learn it at a rote level.

- It provides a framework for *organizing* new information.

- It helps them *elaborate* on the information they receive—for example, by filling in missing details, clarifying ambiguities, or drawing inferences. (Ausubel et al., 1978; P. A. Carpenter & Just, 1986; Rumelhart & Ortony, 1977; West et al., 1991; P. T. Wilson & Anderson, 1986)

Students are most likely to engage in rehearsal—the *least* effective of the storage processes we've examined—when they have little prior knowledge on which to draw (E. Wood, Willoughby, Reilley, Elliott, & DuCharme, 1994).

Yet it is not enough that our students have the knowledge they need to interpret new material. In our discussion of the three conditions that facilitate meaningful learning earlier in the chapter, we noted the importance of *awareness* of the relevance of

Do you now see why Kanesha had such difficulty remembering the coccyx, ulna, sacrum, clavicle, and patella?

prior knowledge to new information. In organization, elaboration, and visual imagery, as well as in meaningful learning, students must be aware of how the things they already know relate to the things they need to learn. To put this idea in information processing terms, students must retrieve relevant information from their long-term memories at the same time they are thinking about new information, such that both the "old" and the "new" are in working memory simultaneously (e.g., Bellezza, 1986; Glanzer & Nolan, 1986).

As teachers, we must keep students' existing knowledge in mind and use it as a starting point whenever we introduce a new topic. For example, we might begin a first-grade unit on plants by asking students to describe what their parents do to keep flowers or vegetable gardens growing. Or, in a secondary English literature class, we might introduce Sir Walter Scott's *Ivanhoe* by asking students to tell the tale of Robin Hood as they know it. We must also remember that students from diverse cultural backgrounds are likely to have different knowledge bases; hence, our starting points for any given lesson must invariably be somewhat culture-specific.

Using Mnemonics When Prior Knowledge Doesn't Help

THINKING ABOUT WHAT YOU KNOW

Can you think of things you had to learn in school that would have been difficult to learn meaningfully no matter how much prior knowledge you had? Can you think of examples in science? mathematics? history? geography? music? a foreign language?

When you were in elementary and secondary school, there were probably numerous times when you had difficulty making sense of material that you needed to learn. Perhaps you had trouble learning the chemical symbols for some of the elements because those symbols seemed unrelated to the elements' names (why is Au the symbol for gold? why is Na the symbol for sodium?). Perhaps you couldn't remember words in a foreign language because those words were very different from their English meanings. Or perhaps you couldn't remember lists of things (e.g., four things that you should do when treating a victim of shock, eleven events leading up to the American Revolution) because they always contained several seemingly unrelated items, and one item didn't help you remember any of the others.

In much the same way, some of the things that we will need to teach our own students may be difficult for them to connect to prior knowledge, organize logically, elaborate on, or visually imagine. If the school district's curriculum requires us to teach the capitals of foreign countries, how do we do this when most of our students have never been to those places? If our students' ability to understand chemistry depends on their knowledge of chemical symbols, how do we help them learn such apparently "meaningless" information? If the foreign language that we are teaching is one whose words are very different from their English equivalents (e.g., as is true for Chinese), how can we help students make these seemingly arbitrary connections? When students are likely to have difficulty finding relationships between new information and their prior knowledge or when a body of information has an organizational structure with no apparent

Introduce a new topic by asking students to retrieve things they already know about the topic.

logic behind it (e.g., as is true for many lists), special memory "tricks" known as **mnemonics** can help them learn classroom material more effectively. Three commonly used mnemonics are these:

- Verbal mediation
- Keyword method
- Superimposed meaningful structures

Give students mnemonics they can use when new information is difficult to learn meaningfully.

Verbal Mediation

A **verbal mediator** is a word or phrase that forms a logical connection or "bridge" between two things. Verbal mediators can be used for such "paired" pieces of information as foreign language words and their English meanings, countries and their capitals, chemical symbols for the elements, and words and their spellings. Here are some examples:

Information to Be Learned	Verbal Mediator
Handschuh is German for "glove ."	A glove is a *shoe* for the *hand.*
Quito is the capital of Ecuador.	Mos*quito*s at the equator.
Au is the symbol for gold.	*'Ay, you* stole my gold watch!
The word *principal* ends in *pal* (not *ple*).	The principal is my *pal.*

What verbal mediator did Kanesha use that helped her remember one bone's location?

Keyword Method

Like verbal mediation, the keyword method is a technique for learning paired information. This method is especially helpful when there is no logical verbal mediator to connect two pieces of information—for example, when there is no obvious sentence or phrase to relate a foreign language word to its English meaning. The keyword method involves two steps, which I will illustrate using the Spanish word *amor* and its English meaning *love:*

1. Identify a concrete object to represent each piece of information. The object may be either a commonly used symbol (e.g., let's use a heart to symbolize *love*) or a "sound alike" word (e.g., let's use a suit of armor to represent *amor*). Such objects are **keywords.**

2. Form a visual image (a "picture" in your mind) of the two objects together. To remember that *amor* means *love,* you might picture a knight in a suit of armor with a huge red heart painted on his chest (see Figure 6–10).

Here are some other examples of the keyword method:

Information to Be Learned	Visual Image
Das Pferd is German for "horse ."	A *horse* driving a *Ford.*
Augusta is the capital of the state of Maine.	A *gust of* wind blowing through a horse's *mane.*
Tchaikovsky composed "Swan Lake."	A *swan* swimming on a *lake,* wearing a *tie* and *cough*ing.

Superimposed Meaningful Structure

A larger body of information (e.g., a list of items) can often be learned by superimposing a meaningful structure on that information—that is, by imposing a familiar shape,

Figure 6–10   Using the keyword method can help you remember that amor *means "love."*

word, sentence, poem, or story on it. Here are some examples of such **superimposed meaningful structures:**

Information to Be Learned	Superimposed Meaningful Structure
The shape of Italy	A "boot"
The shape of France	A "bearskin rug"
The Great Lakes (Huron, Ontario, Michigan, Erie, Superior)	HOMES
Lines on the treble clef (EGBDF)	Elvis's guitar broke down Friday, *or* Every good boy does fine.
The distinction between stalagmites and stalactites	When the "mites" go up, the "tites" come down.
The number of days in each month	Thirty days has September, April, June, and November. . . .

Effectiveness of Mnemonics

Can you think of mnemonics that might be useful for the subject matter that you will be teaching?

Research consistently supports the effectiveness of mnemonics in student learning (Bower & Clark, 1969; Bulgren, Schumaker, & Deshler, 1994; Higbee, 1977; Pressley, Levin, & Delaney, 1982; Scruggs & Mastropieri, 1989; C. E. Weinstein, 1978). Mnemonics help long-term memory storage by providing connections between new information and old, and often by imposing a familiar organizational structure on what are otherwise unrelated pieces of information. Mnemonics also appear to help students retrieve information they have stored at an earlier time. It is to the topic of retrieval from long-term memory that we turn now.

INTO THE CLASSROOM
Helping Students Learn Information

Make sure students are paying attention.

A teacher asks students to take notes during a lecture. He then has students work in pairs to compare notes and identify any important information that someone may have omitted.

Remember that students can process only so much information at a time.

A science teacher paces a lecture so that she presents no more than one important idea every three minutes. She presents each idea two or three times (varying her wording each time) and illustrates it with several examples.

Let students know what material is most important to learn.

When a history teacher prepares his students for an upcoming exam on World War I, he reminds them, "When you study for the test, you should try to understand how the specific events that we discussed contributed to the progress and eventual outcome of the war. Know when each event occurred in relation to other events, but don't try to learn each and every date."

Present the same information in more than one form.

A biology teacher shows her class a diagram of the human heart. She traces the flow of blood with her finger as she describes how the heart pumps blood through the body.

Show students how new material relates to things they already know.

When describing the law of gravity, a teacher asks, "What happens when you let go of something? Which way does it fall? Have you ever seen anything fall *up*?"

Present information in an organized fashion.

A teacher presents spelling lists in terms of the letter patterns within those words. For example, she gives students a list of *uff* words (e.g., *buff, muff, stuff*) and *ough* words (e.g., *rough, tough, enough*).

Encourage students to elaborate on class material.

As a teacher demonstrates the correct way to swing a tennis racket, she asks her students, "Why is it important to have your feet apart rather than together? Why is it important to hold your arm straight as you swing?"

Encourage students to form visual images that capture the things they are studying.

An elementary teacher is reading a short story to his class. After reading a description of the story's main character, he stops and asks his class to imagine the person just as the author has described her—a woman with tousled gray hair, twinkling brown eyes, and a warm, welcoming smile.

Begin at a level consistent with students' existing knowledge base.

At the beginning of the school year, a mathematics teacher gives her students a pretest covering the mathematical concepts and operations they studied the year before. She finds that many students still have difficulty computing the perimeter and area of a rectangle. She reviews these procedures and gives students additional practice with them before beginning a unit on computing the volume of objects with rectangular sides.

Give students mnemonics they can use when new information is difficult to learn meaningfully.

A French teacher suggests that her students can remember the French word for dog (le *chien*) by remembering "dog *chain*."

RETRIEVING INFORMATION FROM LONG-TERM MEMORY

As you learned earlier in the chapter, some information is easily retrieved from long-term memory. No doubt you can quickly retrieve your birthday, the name of your college or university, or a close friend's telephone number. But it may take you longer to "find" some of the other pieces of information stored in your long-term memory. Try the following exercise as an example.

More Retrieval Practice

The answer to each of the following questions has appeared earlier in this chapter. See how many answers you can retrieve from your long-term memory and how quickly you can retrieve each one.

1. What are the five Great Lakes?

2. What is the German word for "book"?

3. In what year did World War II end?

4. Who wrote *The Catcher in the Rye*?

5. About how long does information remain in working memory before it disappears?

6. How do you spell the French term for "appetizer"?   ■

Did you find yourself unable to remember one or more of the answers even though you know you "processed" the information at the time that you read it? If so, then you have just discovered firsthand that, in some cases, information is retrieved from long-term memory only with great difficulty, or perhaps not at all.

Can you still remember what the Chinese words *ké, fàn, mén, fáng,* and *shū* mean? Can you retrieve the visual images that you stored to help you remember these words?

■

Nature of Long-Term Memory Retrieval

Retrieving information from long-term memory appears to be a process of following a "pathway" of associations. One idea reminds us of another idea, which reminds us of still another, and so on, just as we saw in the "Horse #1" exercise earlier in the chapter. Retrieval is successful only when we eventually stumble on the information we are looking for. Therefore, we are most likely to find the desired information if we have connected it to something else—presumably something that is logically related—in long-term memory.

To illustrate this idea, I return once again to all those packages, letters, bills, brochures, catalogs, fliers, advertisements, requests for donations, and sweepstakes announcements that arrive in your mailbox every year. Imagine that, on the average, you receive ten important items—things that you really need to save—every day. At six postal deliveries a week and fifty-two weeks a year, you have been saving 3,120 pieces of mail each year. If you have been saving your mail for the last fifteen years, then you have 46,800 really important things stashed somewhere in your home.

One day you hear that stock in a clothing company (Mod Bod Jeans, Inc.) has tripled in value. You remember that your wealthy Aunt Agnes sent you some Mod Bod stock certificates for your birthday several years ago and that you decided they were important enough to save. But where in the world did you put them? How long will it take you to find them among all those important letters, bills, brochures, catalogs, fliers, and sweepstakes announcements?

How easily you find the certificates and, in fact, whether you find them at all depends on how you have been storing all your mail as you've accumulated it over the years. If you've stored your mail in a logical, organized fashion—for example, by putting all paid bills on a shelf in your closet, all mail order catalogs on the floor under the window, and all items from relatives in a file cabinet (in alphabetical order by last name)—then you should quickly retrieve Aunt Agnes's gift. But if you simply tossed each day's mail randomly around the house, you will be searching your home for a long, long time, possibly without ever finding any evidence that you own Mod Bod stock.

Like a home with fifteen years' worth of mail, long-term memory also contains a great deal of information. And like finding the Mod Bod certificates, the ease with which information is retrieved from long-term memory depends to some extent on whether that information is stored in a logical "place"—that is, whether it is connected with related pieces of information. By making those important connections with existing knowledge, we will know where to "find" the information we store when we need it later on. In contrast, learning something at a rote level is like throwing Aunt Agnes's gift randomly among thousands of pieces of unorganized mail: We may never retrieve it again.

Factors Affecting Retrieval

Even when we connect new information with our existing knowledge base, we can't always find it when we need it. At least four factors promote our ability to retrieve information from long-term memory:

- Making multiple connections with existing knowledge

- Learning information to mastery and "beyond"

- Using information frequently

- Having a relevant retrieval cue

We will discover additional advantages of doing these things when we discuss transfer and problem solving in Chapter 8.

Making Multiple Connections with Existing Knowledge

If retrieving information from long-term memory is a process of following a pathway of associations, what happens if we take the wrong "route" and go in an inappropriate "direction"? In such a situation, we may never find what we are looking for.

We are more likely to retrieve information when we have many possible pathways through which we might get to it—in other words, when we have associated it with many other things in our existing knowledge base. Making multiple connections is like having a cross-referencing system in the way that you store your mail. You may have filed the Mod Bod stock in the "items from relatives" file cabinet, but you've also left numerous notes to yourself in other places about where that stock is—perhaps with your birth certificate (after all, you received the stock on your birthday), with your income tax receipts, or in your safe-deposit box. By looking in any one of these logical places, you will discover the location of your valuable stock.

As teachers, we can help students more effectively remember classroom subject matter over the long run if we help them connect it to numerous pieces of information in their existing knowledge base. For example, we can show them how new material relates to:

- Concepts and ideas within the same subject area (e.g., showing them how multiplication is related to addition)

- Concepts and ideas in other subject areas (e.g., talking about how scientific discoveries have affected historical events)

- Students' general knowledge of the world (e.g., drawing parallels between the "Black Death" of the fourteenth century and the current AIDS epidemic)

Help students relate new information to as many other things as they can.

- Students' personal experiences (e.g., finding similarities between the family feud in *Romeo and Juliet* and students' own interpersonal conflicts)

The more interrelationships our students form among pieces of information in long-term memory, the more easily they can retrieve those pieces later on.

Learning Information to Mastery and Beyond

Is it enough for students to demonstrate mastery of a body of information—for example, to recite all their addition facts or write all their spelling words correctly—on just one occasion? Probably not. Research tells us that people are far more likely to retrieve material if, once they have learned it to a level of mastery, they continue to study it (Krueger, 1929; Semb & Ellis, 1994; Underwood, 1954).

If you have already read Chapter 4, then you may recall that automaticity plays a role in Robert Sternberg's theory of intelligence.

When students continue to practice skills and information they have already mastered, they eventually acquire the skills and information at a level of **automaticity** (Cheng, 1985; Fisk, 1986; Schneider & Shiffrin, 1977; Shiffrin & Schneider, 1977). In other words, when students know something very, very well, they can retrieve it quickly and effortlessly and can use it almost without thinking. As an example, think of a complicated skill that you can perform easily—perhaps driving a car, sewing a hem, or dribbling a basketball. Your first attempts at this activity many years ago probably required a great deal of mental effort: You really had to think about what you were doing. But now you can execute the skill without having to pay much attention to what you are doing—you do it automatically.

Certainly, education must be more than the drill and practice of isolated facts. But some things need to be retrieved quickly and automatically, especially if students need to use that information for complicated tasks (e.g., R. M. Gagné, 1983; LaBerge & Samuels, 1974; Resnick, 1989). For example, second graders reading a story can better focus their efforts on understanding it if they don't have to stop and sound out words like *cat* and *dog*. Fourth graders faced with a multiplication problem such as this one

$$\begin{array}{r} 87 \\ \times\ 59 \\ \hline \end{array}$$

When information must be retrieved rapidly, provide drill and practice exercises that enable students to learn the information to automaticity.

can solve it more easily if they can quickly retrieve such basic multiplication facts as $9 \times 8 = 72$ and $5 \times 7 = 35$. High school chemistry students can more easily interpret Na_2CO_3 (sodium carbonate) if they don't have to stop to think about what the symbols Na, C, and O represent. Remember, working memory has a very limited capacity: It can only do so much at one time. When much of its capacity must be used for retrieving simple facts from long-term memory, there is little room left for understanding more complex situations or solving more difficult problems. Basic information—especially information required in complex tasks—should be practiced frequently until students can retrieve it quickly and effortlessly.

Using Information Frequently

Frequently used information is retrieved more easily than information used rarely or not at all (e.g., R. Brown & McNeill, 1966; Yarmey, 1973). It is easier to remember your own birthday than the birthday of a friend or relative. It is easier to remember the current year than the year in which World War II ended. And it is definitely easier to remember the spelling of *information* than the spelling of *hors d'oeuvre* even though both terms have the same number of letters.

As teachers, we should occasionally have classroom activities that require students to review the things they have learned earlier in the year or in previous years. For example, we might have occasional "refresher" discussions of "old" material, or we might ask students to use the material to understand new topics or to solve new problems. Research is clear on this point: Occasional review enhances students' memory for information over the long run, especially when review sessions are spaced out over several months or years (Bahrick, Bahrick, Bahrick, & Bahrick, 1993; Dempster, 1991; Di Vesta & Smith, 1979; M. A. McDaniel & Masson, 1985).

Periodically review important information; for example, incorporate it into later lessons.

Having a Relevant Retrieval Cue

If you were educated in North America, then you probably learned the names of the five Great Lakes at one time or another. Yet you may have trouble retrieving all five names even though they are all still stored in your long-term memory. Perhaps Lake Michigan doesn't come to mind when you retrieve the other four. The *HOMES* mnemonic provides a **retrieval cue**—a hint about where to "look" in long-term memory. The mnemonic tells you that one lake begins with the letter M, and so you search among the "M" words in your long-term memory until you (we hope) find "Michigan." We are more likely to retrieve information when relevant retrieval cues are present to start our search of long-term memory in the right direction (e.g., Tulving, 1983; Tulving & Thomson, 1973).

For another example of how retrieval cues can facilitate retrieval, try the following exercise.

EXPERIENCING FIRSTHAND
Recall Versus Recognition

Earlier in the chapter, I described a process that keeps information in working memory for longer than the usual five to twenty seconds. Can you retrieve the name of that process from your long-term memory? See if you can before you read any further.

If you can't remember the term to which I am referring, then try answering the same question posed in a multiple-choice format:

What do we call the process that keeps information in working memory for longer than the usual five to twenty seconds?
    a. facilitative construction
    b. internal organization
    c. short-term memorization
    d. maintenance rehearsal

Did you experience an "Aha, now I remember" feeling? The correct answer is d. Perhaps the multiple-choice format of the question provided a retrieval cue for you, directing you to a part of your long-term memory where the correct answer was stored. Generally speaking, it is easier to remember something in a **recognition task** (in which you simply need to recognize correct information among irrelevant information or incorrect statements) than in a **recall task** (in which the correct information is not in front of you but must be retrieved in its entirety from long-term memory) (Semb, Ellis, & Araujo, 1993). A recognition task is easier because it provides more retrieval cues to aid you in your search of long-term memory.

Students should learn to develop their own retrieval cues.

Provide retrieval cues when appropriate.

Teach students to develop their own retrieval cues for things they need to remember.

As teachers, we won't always want to help students retrieve information by putting that information right in front of them. Nevertheless, there will be occasions when providing hints is certainly appropriate. For example, when Sheri asks how the word *liquidation* is spelled, we might respond by saying, "*Liquidation* means to make something liquid. How do you spell *liquid*?" When Shawn wants to know what the chemical symbol Au stands for, we might help him retrieve the answer for himself by a hint like this one: "In class, we talked about how Au comes from the Latin word *aurum.* Can you remember what aurum means?"

In the early grades, teachers typically provide many retrieval cues for their students: They remind students about the tasks they need to do and when they need to do them ("I hear the fire alarm. Remember, we all walk quietly during a fire drill"; or "It's time to go home. Do you all have the field trip permission slip you need to take to your parents?"). But as they grow older, students must develop greater independence, relying more on themselves and less on their teachers for the things they need to remember. At this point, we can teach students ways of providing retrieval cues for *themselves.* For example, if we expect first graders to have a permission slip signed by their parents and returned to us, we might ask them to write a reminder on a piece of masking tape they put on their jackets or lunch boxes. If we give junior high school students a major assignment due several weeks later, we might suggest that they help themselves remember the due date by taping a note to the bedside table or by making an entry on the kitchen calendar.

When you attempted my multiple-choice question a few minutes ago, did you have trouble remembering "maintenance rehearsal" even though it was staring you in the face? If so, why do you think you had difficulty? Let's look at some possible explanations—some possible reasons why people forget.

EXPLAINING WHY PEOPLE SOMETIMES "FORGET"

Certainly, we don't need to remember *everything.* For example, we probably have no reason to remember the phone number of a florist whom we called yesterday, the plot of an *I Love Lucy* show that we watched last week, or the due date of an assignment that we turned in last semester. Much of the information that we encounter on a daily basis is—like our junk mail—not worth keeping.

But as we have just seen, we sometimes have trouble recalling the things that we *do* need. Psychologists have proposed a number of explanations why people seem to "forget." In the following pages, we will consider five possible reasons why our students may have difficulty correctly remembering the things that we have taught them:

- Failure to retrieve

- Reconstruction error

- Interference

- Decay

- Failure to store

These reasons, along with some suggestions for strategies to prevent forgetting, are summarized in Table 6–4.

Failure to Retrieve

A man at the supermarket looks familiar, but you can't remember who he is or when you met him. He smiles at you and says, "Hello. Nice to see you again." Gulp. You desperately search your long-term memory for his name, but you have clearly forgotten who this man is.

A few days later, you have a bowl of chili for dinner. The chili reminds you of the "Chili for Charity" supper at which you worked a few months back. Of course! You and

Table 6–4   Why Students Forget

POSSIBLE REASON FOR FORGETTING	WHAT THIS MEANS	EXAMPLE	EDUCATIONAL IMPLICATION
Failure to retrieve	They cannot find a mental "pathway" of associations that leads them to the information.	Karen cannot remember the goddess of cities and civilization (although she later recognizes the correct answer on a multiple choice test).	Help students relate new information to many things they already know.
Reconstruction error	They can remember some of the information that they need but are filling in the rest on the basis of what seems "logical."	Kenneth spells *separate* as "seperate."	When important details are difficult to fill in logically, make sure students learn them well.
Interference	Various associations in long-term memory (usually among similar items) are interfering with one another.	Kanesha confuses the locations of the tibia and fibula in the lower leg.	Help students learn information meaningfully, rather than at a rote level.
Decay	The information has weakened over time, perhaps because it was not used on a regular basis.	Kevin forgets most of the Russian words that he learned several years ago but has not used since.	Review important information at regular intervals.
Failure to store	They never processed the information in a way that promoted its storage in long-term memory.	Kathy doesn't "remember" that the Great Lakes have fresh water because she wasn't paying attention when her teacher described the Great Lakes.	Make sure students process the information in a manner that promotes its storage in long-term memory (e.g., by paying attention, learning meaningfully, elaborating).

the man at the supermarket had stood side by side serving chili to hundreds of people that night. Oh yes, you recall, his name is Melville Herman.

One reason why we "forget" is an **inability to retrieve:** We can't locate information stored in long-term memory. Sometimes we stumble on the information at a later time, perhaps by accident when we are "looking" for something else. But sometimes we never do retrieve the information, perhaps because we learned it at a rote level or perhaps because there are insufficient retrieval cues to point our long-term memory search in the right direction.

Reconstruction Error

Retrieval isn't necessarily an all-or-nothing phenomenon. Sometimes we retrieve only part of the information we are seeking from long-term memory. In such situations, we sometimes fill in the gaps by using our general knowledge and assumptions about the world (Kolodner, 1985; Loftus, 1991; Rumelhart & Ortony, 1977; P. T. Wilson & Anderson, 1986). Even though the gaps are filled in "logically," they aren't always filled in correctly—a form of forgetting that we can call **reconstruction error.** We will examine the reconstructive nature of retrieval in greater detail in the next chapter.

Interference

■ EXPERIENCING FIRSTHAND
Seven Chinese Words

Here are seven more Chinese words and their English meanings (for simplicity's sake, I've omitted the "tone" marks on the words). Read them two or three times and try to store them in your long-term memory. But don't do anything special to learn the words; for example, don't intentionally develop mnemonics to help you remember them.

Chinese	English
jung	middle
ting	listen
sung	deliver
peng	friend
ching	please
deng	wait
tsung	from

Now cover up the list of words and test yourself. What was the word for *friend*? *please*? *listen*? *wait*? ■

Remember how Kanesha confused *tibia* and *fibula*—two similar sounding names—when trying to learn the bones located in the lower leg.
— ■ —

Did you find yourself getting confused, perhaps forgetting which English meaning went with each Chinese word? If you did, then you were the victim of **interference.** The various pieces of information that you stored in your long-term memory were interfering with one another; in a sense, the pieces were getting "mixed up." Notice that I told you *not* to use mnemonics to learn the Chinese words. Interference is especially likely to occur when pieces of information are similar to one another and when they are learned at a rote level (e.g., Dempster, 1985; Postman & Underwood, 1973; Underwood, 1948, 1957).

Decay

As we noted earlier, some psychologists believe that once information is stored in long-term memory, it remains there forever. But others propose that information may weaken over time and perhaps disappear altogether, especially if it is not used on a regular basis (e.g., J. R. Anderson, 1990; Schwartz & Reisberg, 1991). Psychologists sometimes use the word **decay** when describing this gradual fading process.

One possible explanation of "forgetting" is that the student doesn't store the information to begin with.

Failure to Store

Last on my list of reasons for "forgetting" is **failure to store:** Information never reached long-term memory to begin with. Perhaps a person receiving a piece of information didn't pay attention to it and so it never went beyond the sensory register. Or perhaps the individual, after attending to it, didn't process it any further and so it went no further in the memory system than working memory. Obviously, failure to store is not an explanation of information loss; however, it is one possible reason why students who *think* they have learned something cannot recall it later on.

When students informally test themselves as they learn and study, such "failure to store" is less likely to occur. We will consider this process of **monitoring comprehension** as we examine study strategies in Chapter 8.

As you've been reading this chapter, you may have noticed that long-term memory storage and retrieval processes don't always happen instantaneously. For example, it may take time for our students to relate new material to their existing knowledge, and at some later date it make take time for them to retrieve all the "pieces" of what they have learned. What happens when teachers give students more time to process and retrieve information? The results can be quite dramatic, as we shall see now.

GIVING STUDENTS TIME TO PROCESS: EFFECTS OF INCREASING WAIT TIME

Mr. Harry Smith likes to ask questions in his classroom. He also likes to keep class going at a rapid pace. A typical day might go something like this:

Mr. Smith: Why is it warmer in summer than in winter?

Amelia: Because the sun is hotter.

Mr. Smith: Well, yes, the sun *feels* hotter. What changes in the earth make it feel hotter?

Arnold: The earth is closer to the sun in the summer.

Mr. Smith: That's a possibility, Arnold. But there's something we need to consider here. When it's summer in the Northern Hemisphere, it's winter in the Southern Hemisphere. When North America is having its warmest days, Australia is having its coldest days. Can we use the earth's distance from the sun to explain that?

Arnold: Uh . . . I guess not.

Mr. Smith: So . . . why is it warmer in summer than in winter? (No one responds.) Do you know, Angela? (She shakes her head.) How about you, Andrew?

Maximizing Retrieval and Minimizing Forgetting

Where important information is concerned, never assume that once is enough.

> A language arts teacher introduces the parts of speech (e.g., nouns, verbs, adjectives) early in the school year. Because these concepts will be important for students to know when they study a foreign language in later grades, he continues to review them throughout the year—for example, by frequently incorporating them into classroom activities.

When information must be retrieved rapidly, provide drill and practice exercises that enable students to learn the information to automaticity.

> An elementary school teacher continues to give practice in the addition and subtraction facts until each student can answer every single-digit addition and subtraction fact quickly and accurately.

Teach students to develop their own retrieval cues for things they need to remember.

> A teacher suggests that students tape a note to their jackets, reminding them to return their permission slips tomorrow.

When important details are difficult to fill in logically, make sure students learn them well.

> A teacher gives students extra practice in "problem" spelling words—words that are spelled differently than they are pronounced (e.g., *people, February*).

Provide retrieval cues when appropriate.

> When a student puzzles over how to compute the area of a circle, her teacher says, "We studied this last week. Do you remember the formula?" When the student shakes her head, the teacher continues, "Because the problem involves a circle, the formula probably includes π, doesn't it?"

Andrew:	Nope.
Mr. Smith:	Can you think of anything we discussed yesterday that might help us with an explanation? (No one responds.) Remember, yesterday we talked about how the earth changes its tilt in relation to the sun throughout the year. We talked about how this change in the earth's tilt explains why the days get longer throughout the winter and spring and why they get shorter during the summer and fall. (Mr. Smith continues with an explanation of how the angle of the sun's rays affects temperature on Earth.)

Mr. Smith is hoping that his students will draw a connection between information they learned yesterday (changes in the earth's tilt) and today's topic (the seasons). Unfortunately, Mr. Smith is moving too quickly from one question to the next and from one student to another. His students don't make the connection he expects because he simply doesn't give them enough time to do so.

The problem with Mr. Smith's lesson is one that we see in many classrooms: too short a **wait time**. When teachers ask students a question, they typically wait one second or less for a response. If students don't respond in that short time interval, teachers tend to speak again—sometimes by asking different students the same question, sometimes by rephrasing the question, sometimes even by answering the question themselves (Rowe, 1974, 1987). Teachers are equally reluctant to let much time lapse after students answer questions or make comments in class; once again, they typically allow *one second or less* of silence before responding to a statement or asking another question (Rowe, 1987).

What kind of wait time do your own instructors exhibit? Is it sufficiently long enough to promote good classroom discussions?

Table 6–5 Effects of Increased Wait Time

CHANGES IN STUDENT BEHAVIOR	
Increased student participation	Students talk more, and they are more likely to answer questions correctly.
	More students participate in class; previously quiet students become active contributors.
	Students are more likely to contribute spontaneously to a class discussion—for example, by asking questions and by presenting their own perspectives.
	Students are more likely to talk with one another, as well as to their teacher, within the context of a classroom discussion.
Better quality of student responses	Students' responses are longer and more sophisticated.
	Students are more likely to support their responses with evidence or logic.
	Students are more likely to give a variety of responses to the same question.
	Students are more likely to speculate when they don't know an answer.
Better classroom performance	Students are less likely to feel confused by course content; they are more likely to feel confident that they can master the material.
	Students' motivation to learn increases.
	Students show higher achievement, especially for complex material.
	Discipline problems decrease.
CHANGES IN TEACHER BEHAVIOR	
Different kinds of questions	Teachers ask fewer "simple" questions (e.g., those requiring recall of facts).
	Teachers ask more complex questions (e.g., those requiring students to elaborate or to develop alternative explanations).
Increased flexibility in teaching	Teachers modify the direction of discussion to accommodate students' comments and questions.
	Teachers allow their classes to pursue a topic in greater depth than they had originally anticipated.
Higher expectations	Teachers' expectations for many students, especially previously low-achieving students, begin to improve.

Sources: Mohatt & Erickson, 1981; Rowe, 1974, 1987; Tharp, 1989; Tobin, 1987.

When teachers increase wait time to three seconds or longer, students participate more actively and give more complex responses to questions.

Incorporate a wait time of at least three seconds into question-answer sessions and classroom discussions.

If we consider basic principles of human information processing—for example, if we consider the importance of relating new information to prior knowledge and the difficulty often associated with retrieving information from long-term memory—then we realize that one second is a very short time indeed for students to develop their responses. When teachers increase their wait time by allowing at least *three seconds* to elapse (instead of just one) after their own questions and after students' comments, we see some dramatic changes in both student and teacher behavior, as shown in Table 6–5.

From an information processing perspective, increasing wait time appears to have two benefits for student learning (Tobin, 1987). First, it allows students more time to process information. Second, it appears to change the very nature of teacher-student discussions: for example, teachers are more likely to ask challenging, thought-provoking questions. In fact, the nature of the questions that teachers ask is probably as important as—and perhaps even more important than—the amount of wait time per se (Giaconia, 1988).

When our objective is recall of facts—when students need to retrieve information very quickly, to "know it cold"—then wait time should be short. As we noted earlier, there is a definite advantage to rapid-fire drill and practice for skills that we want students to learn to a level of automaticity. But when our objectives include more complex processing of ideas and issues, longer wait time may provide both teachers and students the time that they need to think things through.

ACCOMMODATING DIVERSITY IN COGNITIVE PROCESSING

As we have explored principles of information processing, we have considered many factors—attention, working memory capacity, long-term memory storage processes, prior knowledge, retrieval, and so on—that influence what and how well our students are likely to learn and remember classroom material. Naturally, our students will differ considerably with regard to these factors; for example, they will have unique knowledge bases on which to draw, and they will elaborate differently on the ideas we present (e.g., Cothern et al., 1990; C. A. Grant & Gomez, 1996). And as we noted in our discussion of ethnic differences in Chapter 4, some students will benefit from more wait time: Those with certain cultural backgrounds (e.g., many Native Americans) may wait several seconds before responding to our questions as a way of showing respect for an adult, and those with limited proficiency in English may require some "mental translation" time.

To some extent, we will see our students processing information in consistently different ways; in other words, we will see differences in our students' *cognitive styles*. We will also find that a few of our students have difficulty with certain aspects of information processing; such difficulty may reflect *learning disabilities*. In the next few pages, we will consider both forms of diversity in students' information processing. We will also examine the information processing capabilities of other students with special educational needs, along with strategies for helping such students learn and process information more effectively.

Cognitive Style

Students with the same intelligence and creativity often approach tasks and mentally "process" information differently, and such **cognitive styles** may influence how well they perform in the classroom (e.g., Messick, 1994b). Let's look at two dimensions of cognitive style: field independence versus field dependence, and impulsivity versus reflection.

Field Independence Versus Field Dependence

■ **EXPERIENCING FIRSTHAND**
Embedded Figure

Look at the two figures below. Can you find the figure on the left hidden within the figure on the right?

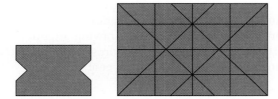

Modeled after the Embedded Figures Test (Witkin, 1969).　■

The exercise I just gave you is an example of a task that reflects the extent to which you perceive things as being either separate from or part of their context; in other words, it reflects an aspect of cognitive style known as field independence versus field dependence. Students who can easily perceive an object separate from its background (its *field*)—those who can essentially ignore an object's surroundings when they need to—are called **field independent.** Students who tend to perceive things primarily within the overall context of surrounding stimuli and who therefore have difficulty separating intermingled items from one another are known as **field dependent.**

Students who are field independent and those who are field dependent bring different strengths to the classroom (J. K. Davis, 1991; Doebler & Eicke, 1979; Kogan, 1983; Kogan & Block, 1991; Shade, 1983; Shipman & Shipman, 1985; Witkin, Moore, Goodenough, & Cox, 1977). Field *in*dependent students are more adept at tasks involving the physical world. They can more easily analyze physical objects and find their component parts—skills that help them in such subjects as mathematics, science, and engineering. And in general, they are more likely to process information effectively; for example, they are more likely to pay attention to relevant stimuli, to relate new ideas to the things they already know, and to impose organization on complex subject matter. In contrast, field *de*pendent students may perform better in situations where context is important, as is often the case in social situations. Some researchers have found field dependent individuals to be more aware of interpersonal issues and more sensitive to the body language and other subtle ways in which people communicate; hence, they may be more likely to learn something from social interactions. Some researchers have proposed that field dependent students have superior interpersonal skills, although the data are clearly mixed on this issue (Kogan & Block, 1991; Messick, 1994b; Witkin et al., 1977).

As teachers, we should keep in mind that field independence and field dependence reflect two ends of a continuum, with many students being somewhere between the two extremes. We should also note that many students are probably able to be *either* field independent or field dependent, depending on the specific skills that a situation calls for (Laboratory of Human Cognition, 1982; Shipman & Shipman, 1985; Witkin & Goodenough, 1981).

When we are sensitive to our students' levels of field dependence or independence, we are likely to have better relationships with them (Doebler & Eicke, 1979). To the extent that we tailor instructional methods to different students' cognitive styles, we are also likely to see higher achievement. Field dependent students may learn better in group situations (e.g., class discussions, study groups) in which they can interact with their classmates. These students are more likely to be motivated when they receive encouragement and praise from teachers and peers. And because they tend not to restructure or reorganize information as they study it, they learn better when curriculum materials are well organized to begin with. In contrast, field independent students may perform better when instruction is individualized. These students tend to be self-motivated and to structure and organize information for themselves. At the same time, these students can probably benefit from our drawing attention to the subtle but important social cues that others give them (Andrews, 1981; Doebler & Eicke, 1979; Shade, 1983; Shipman & Shipman, 1985; Witkin et al., 1977).

Impulsivity Versus Reflection

A second dimension of cognitive style is impulsivity versus reflection. **Impulsivity** is the tendency for some students to do tasks quickly but carelessly, without close attention to detail. **Reflection** is the tendency to approach tasks more slowly and carefully, with greater thought and attention to detail, and to evaluate the quality of one's own work more thoroughly. Impulsive students complete tasks quickly, but often incorrectly. Reflective students complete them more slowly and accurately (Kagan & Kogan, 1970; Kemler Nelson & Smith, 1989; Kogan, 1983; Messick, 1994b; Zelniker & Jeffrey, 1976).

Generally speaking, reflective students perform better on academic tasks than impulsive students, especially when those tasks require close attention to detail (Kogan, 1983; Zelniker & Jeffrey, 1976, 1979). A frequent research finding is that reflective students are better readers; one reason is that they are less likely to confuse letters that look similar to one another, such as *b* and *d* (Shipman & Shipman, 1985; Sunshine & Di Vesta, 1976). Attention to detail is also an important factor in learning to spell (Ormrod, 1985, 1986); thus, we might speculate that a reflective cognitive style leads to better spelling. And, to the extent that multiple-choice tests require students to look closely

Provide group learning opportunities for field dependent students, and provide an organizational structure for their curriculum materials.

Provide opportunities for individualized instruction, especially for field independent students.

Remember that multiple-choice tests may underestimate the achievement of impulsive students.

and carefully at several different alternatives, reflective students are likely to perform better than impulsive students (Shipman & Shipman, 1985).

Impulsivity, along with the potential problems for learning that it creates, is most prevalent in the early school years. As children progress through the elementary grades, they become increasingly reflective. Yet even some high school students may be too impulsive for their own good (Kagan & Kogan, 1970; Kogan, 1983; Shipman & Shipman, 1985).

How can we help students develop greater reflection in their approach to school tasks? Students perform classroom assignments more slowly and carefully when they are concerned about the quality of their performance and want to avoid making mistakes (Kagan & Kogan, 1970; Shipman & Shipman, 1985). Here is a situation in which teacher evaluation is probably beneficial: Our students are more likely to be careful in their work if they know there will be some penalty for errors. We can also encourage students to focus on accuracy, rather than on speed (Kagan & Kogan, 1970), and ask them to talk themselves through tasks that require attention to detail (Messer, 1976). And to the extent that some students are slow to develop reflective work habits, we should make important details *salient*—obvious, distinctive, and virtually impossible to overlook.

When students are overly impulsive, focus their attention on accuracy rather than speed. Ask them to talk themselves through tasks that have lots of detail, and make important details salient.

Changes and Cultural Differences in Students' Cognitive Styles

We must remember that students' cognitive styles are far less stable than intelligence; they can and probably will change over time (Messick, 1994b; Shipman & Shipman, 1985). We must also remember that different styles are useful in different situations; hence, we may want to encourage our students to develop flexibility in the styles they apply to different tasks. For example, we might help field independent students become more aware of the social cues around them, or we might give field dependent students practice in tasks in which they must analyze complex objects in terms of their component parts.

We should also note that various cognitive styles may be partly the result of students' cultural backgrounds (Banks, 1994; Irvine & York, 1995; Shipman & Shipman, 1985). For example, to the extent that certain cultures value and encourage cooperation and group achievement over competition and individual achievement, children of those cultures may be especially tuned in to the social cues around them, hence more field dependent. At the same time, we must keep in mind an important point from our discussion of ethnic differences in Chapter 4: People from any single cultural group are likely to be as different as they are similar. We must be careful not to jump to conclusions about individual students' cognitive styles solely on the basis of their ethnic backgrounds (Banks, 1995; Lomawaima, 1995; O'Neil, 1990).

Learning Disabilities

Students with **learning disabilities** typically have average or above-average scores on intelligence tests, but they experience difficulty with one or more specific aspects of information processing. For example, we might see difficulties such as these (Barkley, 1990; Buchoff, 1990; Conte, 1991; Landau & McAninch, 1993; Lerner, 1985):

- *Attention deficit disorder (ADD):* Students may have trouble attending to and concentrating on a single school task for any length of time. They may be distractible, impulsive, and possibly hyperactive.

- *Perceptual difficulty:* Students may have difficulty understanding or remembering the information they receive through a particular sensory modality. For example, they may have trouble perceiving subtle differences between similar sounds in speech (a difficulty in auditory discrimination) or remembering the correct order of letters in a word (a difficulty in memory for a visual sequence).

- *Difficulty processing oral language:* Students may have trouble understanding spoken language or remembering the things they have been told.

- *Reading difficulty:* Students may have trouble recognizing printed words or comprehending the meaning of the things they read. An extreme form of this condition is known as dyslexia.

- *Written language difficulty:* Students may have problems in handwriting, spelling, or expressing themselves coherently on paper.

- *Mathematical difficulty:* Students may have trouble thinking about or remembering things involving numbers. For example, they may have a poor sense of time or direction, or they may have difficulty learning basic number facts.

- *Difficulty with social perception:* Students may have trouble interpreting the social cues and signals that others give them (e.g., they may have difficulty perceiving another person's feelings or reactions to a situation) and may therefore respond inappropriately in social situations.

Students with learning disabilities invariably show poor performance in one or more specific areas of the academic curriculum; their achievement in those areas is much lower than we would expect on the basis of their overall intelligence level. At the same time, they may exhibit achievement consistent with their intelligence in other subjects.

Some theorists believe that learning disabilities result from specific forms of brain damage (Buchoff, 1990; Conte, 1991; Hammill, Leigh, McNutt, & Larsen, 1981; Landau & McAninch, 1993). But others maintain that some disabilities, especially attention deficit disorder, can also result from environmental factors—perhaps from previously inadequate instruction or from teachers' expectations that students remain quiet and sedentary for much of the school day (Patton, Payne, Kauffman, Brown, & Payne, 1987; Pellegrini & Horvat, 1995).

Compared with their classmates, students with learning disabilities often have difficulty with specific memory-storage processes (Lerner, 1985; C. D. Mercer, 1991; Ormrod & Lewis, 1985; H. L. Swanson & Cooney, 1991; Torgesen, 1977; Wong, 1991a). They often take a "passive" approach to learning, rather than actively involve themselves in a learning task; for example, they may stare at a textbook without thinking about the meaning of the words printed on the page. They may have a smaller working memory capacity and are less likely to use such processes as meaningful learning, organization, and elaboration.

We should note here that learning disabilities may manifest themselves somewhat differently in elementary and secondary school students (Lerner, 1985). At the elementary level, students with learning disabilities are likely to be distractible and to exhibit poor motor coordination, and they often have trouble acquiring one or more basic academic skills. At the secondary level, difficulties with attention and motor skills may diminish. At this level, however, students with learning disabilities may be particularly susceptible to emotional problems that result, at least in part, from frustration about their repeated academic failures. On top of dealing with the usual emotional issues of adolescence (e.g., dating, peer pressure), they must also deal with the more stringent de-

Students with learning disabilities often have less effective learning and memory skills, lower self-esteem, and less motivation to succeed at academic tasks.

mands of the junior high and high school curricula. Learning in secondary schools is highly dependent on reading relatively sophisticated textbooks, yet the reading skills of the average high school student with a learning disability are at only a third- to fifth-grade level (Alley & Deshler, 1979). And secondary school teachers rarely teach reading skills as a part of their course content (Lerner, 1985). For these reasons, students with learning disabilities may be among those most at risk for failure and dropping out.

As teachers, we can do numerous things to help students with learning disabilities achieve academic success. Here are several strategies that should help these students process classroom subject matter more successfully:

- Minimize the presence of other stimuli likely to compete for their attention.

- Give clear yet simple directions about what they should do to complete a task.

- Be explicit about how classroom material is organized.

- Find alternative textbooks that are suitable for their reading levels.

- Provide study guides to help them identify important information as they read.

- Present information through a medium other than written text.

- Provide mnemonics to help them remember specific pieces of information. (Buchoff, 1990; Bulgren et al., 1994; Ellis & Friend, 1991; Landau & McAninch, 1993; Lewis & Doorlag, 1991; Mastropieri & Scruggs, 1992; Semmel et al., 1979)

Furthermore, we should look closely at the errors that students make for clues about the specific processing difficulties they may be having (Lerner, 1985). For example, a student who solves a subtraction problem this way:

$$\begin{array}{r} 65 \\ -28 \\ \hline 43 \end{array}$$

may be applying an inappropriate rule (*always subtract the smaller number from the larger one*) to subtraction. A student who reads the sentence: "I drove the cab" as "I drove the *cat*" may be having trouble using context clues in reading words and sentences. A student who reads the same sentence as "I drove the *car*" may be overly dependent on context and not attending closely enough to the words that actually appear on the page.

Facilitating Cognitive Processing in Students with Special Needs

Students with learning disabilities will certainly not be the only students who have difficulty processing information. For example, students with mental retardation will typically process information more slowly, and students with emotional and behavioral disorders may have difficulty keeping their attention on the task at hand (Turnbull, Turnbull, Shank, & Leal, 1995). In contrast, gifted students are likely to process information more rapidly and in a more complex manner than many of their classmates (B. Clark, 1992; Heward, 1996). Table 6–6 takes a look at students with special educational needs from an information processing point of view.

We must keep in mind that virtually all of our students, including those *without* learning disabilities or other identified special needs, will occasionally have difficulty

Can you imagine what it would be like to be a high school student with third-grade reading skills?

Give students with learning disabilities the extra scaffolding they may need to process information effectively.

Look at the errors that students make for clues about specific processing difficulties.

INTO THE CLASSROOM

Accommodating Diversity in Information Processing

Consider the strengths of both field dependent and field independent students in your instructional planning.

A high school German teacher includes both group learning activities and individualized instruction in each week's lesson plans.

When students are overly impulsive, focus their attention on accuracy, rather than on speed, and teach them to talk themselves through detailed tasks.

To help an impulsive third grader subtract two-digit numbers with regrouping ("borrowing"), his teacher instructs him to say these three phrases to himself as he solves each problem: (1) "Compare top and bottom numbers," (2) "If top number is smaller, borrow," and (3) "Subtract."

Give students with learning disabilities the extra structure they may need to succeed on academic tasks.

A teacher provides a particular format for writing an expository paragraph: one sentence expressing the main idea, followed by three sentences that support that idea and a final, concluding sentence.

When students have exceptional difficulty paying attention, minimize the presence of distracting stimuli.

A teacher has a student with attention deficit disorder sit near her desk, away from distractions that classmates may provide; she also encourages the student to keep his desk clear of all objects and materials except those with which he is presently working (Buchoff, 1990).

When reading difficulties are evident, minimize dependence on reading materials or provide materials written at a lower level.

For two high school students reading at a fifth-grade level, a science teacher assigns fifth-grade reading materials that cover many of the same topics as the regular classroom textbook. The teacher also meets with the students once a week for verbal explanations of class material and a hands-on exploration of scientific principles.

Look at students' errors for clues about possible processing difficulties.

When a student spells *refrigerator* as "refegter" and *hippopotamus* as "hepopoms," her teacher hypothesizes that she has difficulty relating written words to the phonetic sounds they represent.

learning or remembering classroom material. Accordingly, many of the instructional strategies that I've identified in this section—getting students' attention, analyzing their errors, taking their prior knowledge into account, and so on—need not be limited only for use with our students with special needs. *All* of our students stand to benefit from any assistance that we can give them in terms of processing information more effectively.

Table 6–6   Facilitating Information Processing in Students with Special Educational Needs

STUDENTS WITH SPECIAL NEEDS	CHARACTERISTICS THAT THESE STUDENTS MAY EXHIBIT	CLASSROOM STRATEGIES THAT MAY BE BENEFICIAL FOR THESE STUDENTS
Students with specific cognitive or academic deficits	Deficiencies in one or more specific cognitive processes (e.g., perception, encoding) Distractibility, inability to sustain attention in some students Difficulty screening out irrelevant stimuli Less working memory capacity, or less efficient use of working memory Impulsivity in responding	Analyze students' errors as a way of identifying possible processing difficulties. Identify weaknesses in specific aspects of information processing and provide instruction that enables students to compensate for these weaknesses. Present information in an organized fashion and make frequent connections to students' prior knowledge as ways of promoting more effective long-term memory storage. Teach mnemonics to facilitate long-term memory storage and retrieval. Encourage greater reflection before responding (e.g., by reinforcing accuracy rather than speed or by teaching self-instructions [see Chapter 10]).
Students with specific social or behavioral deficits	Lack of attention because of off-task thoughts and behaviors. Possible undiagnosed learning disabilities (e.g., reading disabilities)	Make sure you have students' attention before giving instructions or presenting information. Refer students to a school psychologist for evaluation and diagnosis of possible learning disabilities.
Students with general delays in cognitive and social functioning	Slower information processing Difficulty with attention to task-relevant information Reduced working memory capacity, or less efficient use of working memory Smaller knowledge base on which to build new learning	Keep instructional materials simple, emphasizing relevant stimuli and minimizing irrelevant stimuli. Provide clear instructions that focus students' attention on desired behaviors (e.g., "Listen," "Write," "Stop"). Pace instruction to allow sufficient time for students to think about and process information adequately (e.g., provide ample wait time after questions). Assume little prior knowledge about new topics ("begin at the beginning").
Students with advanced cognitive development	More rapid information processing Larger knowledge base (the nature of which will vary, depending on students' cultural backgrounds) More interconnections among ideas in long-term memory More rapid retrieval of information from long-term memory	Proceed through topics more quickly or in greater depth. Study topics in an interdisciplinary fashion to foster cross-disciplinary integration of material in long-term memory.

Sources: Bulgren, Schumaker, & Deshler, 1994; Heward, 1996; C. D. Mercer, 1991; D. P. Morgan & Jenson, 1988; Patton, Beirne-Smith, & Payne, 1990; Piirto, 1994; Pressley, 1995; H. L. Swanson, 1992; H. L. Swanson & Cooney, 1991; Turnbull, Turnbull, Shank, & Leal, 1995; Zeaman & House, 1979.
Compiled with the assistance of Dr. Margie Garanzini-Daiber and Dr. Margaret Cohen, University of Missouri—St. Louis.

Ms. Llewellyn is a first-year social studies teacher at Madison High School; she recently completed her degree in United States history and knows her subject matter well. Her history classes begin in September with a study of early explorers of the Western Hemisphere. By early October, students are reading about the colonial settlements of the 1600s. By December, they have covered the French and Indian War, the Revolutionary War, and the Declaration of Independence. The winter months are spent studying the nineteenth century (e.g., the Industrial Revolution, the Civil War), and the spring is spent studying the twentieth century (including both world wars, the Korean War, the Vietnam War, and the Persian Gulf crisis).

Ms. Llewellyn has high expectations for her students. In her daily class lectures, she describes historical events in detail, hoping to give her students a sense of how complex many of these events really were. In addition to having students read the usual high school textbook, she also assigns articles in the historical journals that she herself reads.

Occasionally, Ms. Llewellyn stops a lecture a few minutes before the bell rings to ask questions that check her students' recall of the day's topics. Although her students can usually remember the main gist of her lecture, they have difficulty with the details, either mixing them up or forgetting them altogether. A few students remember so little that she can hardly believe they were in class that day, even though she knows for a fact that they were. Her students perform even more poorly on monthly essay exams; it's obvious from their written responses that they can remember little of what Ms. Llewellyn has taught them.

"I explained things so clearly to them," she tells herself. "Perhaps these kids just don't want to learn."

- What are some possible reasons why Ms. Llewellyn's students are having difficulty learning and remembering the things that she teaches them? Can you think of possible reasons related to the class curriculum? to Ms. Llewellyn's style of teaching? to Ms. Llewellyn's reading assignments?

- From an information processing perspective, what things would you do differently than Ms. Llewellyn has?

SUMMING UP

Cognitive Psychology

Cognitive psychology focuses on how people think about and encode new material as they learn it. The things that our students do mentally with the subject matter we present in class will determine how effectively they learn and remember it. As a result, different students are likely to process and learn the same information differently.

Components of Memory

Many theorists propose that human memory has three components. The *sensory register* provides temporary storage for incoming information, holding new input for two or three seconds at most. By paying attention to information, people move it to *working memory,* where they actively think about and make sense of it. Attention and working memory have a limited capacity; hence, our students can pay attention to and think about only a limited amount of information at any one time.

The third component—*long-term memory*—has an extremely large capacity and an indefinitely long duration. Effective long-term memory storage processes include meaningful learning, organization, elaboration, and visual imagery. We can help our students learn information more readily by helping them integrate and make sense of it—for example, by showing them how it relates to the things they already know, by presenting it in an organized fashion, by asking them to draw inferences, and by supplementing verbal instruction with visual materials.

Role of Prior Knowledge

To learn new material meaningfully, our students must have prior knowledge to which they can relate that material. Hence, it is important to assess students' prior knowledge about a topic and to begin instruction at a level suitable for that knowledge base. When important information is difficult for students to connect to prior knowledge, we can provide mnemonic techniques—memory "tricks"—that facilitate long-term memory storage and retrieval.

Retrieval

Retrieving information from long-term memory appears to be a process of following a pathway of associations. Our students' attempts at retrieving information are more likely to be successful if they have learned it to mastery and connected it with numerous other things they know, if they use it frequently, and if relevant retrieval cues are present in their environment. Increasing wait time—in other words, giving students more time to respond to the questions and comments of others—promotes greater retrieval and enhances students' achievement in the classroom.

Diversity in Information Processing

Cognitive styles are the characteristic ways in which individual students are likely to mentally "process" information. Our students will achieve at higher levels when we are aware of their cognitive styles and tailor instruction accordingly—for example, when we provide an organizational structure for the curriculum materials of field dependent students and when we focus the attention of impulsive students on accuracy, rather than on speed.

Students with learning disabilities have average or above-average scores on intelligence tests, but experience difficulty with one or more specific information processing skills. Such students may need extra teacher guidance and support to help them process classroom material effectively.

KEY CONCEPTS

cognitive psychology (p. 218)
information processing (p. 218)
storage (p. 222)
encoding (p. 222)
retrieval (p. 223)
sensory register (p. 225)
attention (p. 225)
working memory (short-term memory)
    (p. 227)
maintenance rehearsal (p. 228)
long-term memory (LTM) (p. 230)
schemas (p. 231)
levels of processing (p. 232)
rehearsal (p. 235)

rote learning (p. 235)
meaningful learning (p. 236)
meaningful learning set (p. 238)
knowledge base (p. 239)
organization (p. 241)
elaboration (p. 243)
visual imagery (p. 244)
mnemonics (p. 247)
verbal mediator (p. 247)
keyword (p. 247)
superimposed meaningful structure
    (p. 248)
automaticity (p. 252)
retrieval cue (p. 253)

recognition task (p. 253)
recall task (p. 253)
inability to retrieve (p. 256)
reconstruction error (p.256)
interference (p. 256)
decay (p. 257)
failure to store (p. 257)
wait time (p. 259)
cognitive style (p. 261)
field independence versus field
    dependence (p. 261)
impulsivity versus reflection (p. 262)
learning disabilities (p. 263)

Facilitating Knowledge Construction

THINKING ABOUT WHAT YOU KNOW

Think back to a time when you and a friend tried to carry on a conversation in a noisy room—perhaps at a party, in a bar where a band was playing, or in a workshop with loud machinery operating nearby. You probably couldn't hear everything your friend was saying to you. Nevertheless, were you able to hear enough to get the gist of what he or she was trying to tell you?

WHEN I WAS A CHILD, my father was the general manager of a textile mill in Lowell, Massachusetts. On Saturday mornings, he would spend a few hours at the mill to touch base with the weekend crew, and occasionally I would tag along. What I remember most vividly about those excursions was our visits to the loom room—a gymnasium-sized room in which dozens of large weaving looms were operating simultaneously. In addition to making fabric, those looms also made a great deal of noise—so much so that I covered my ears tightly with both hands as soon as we entered the room and kept them there until, much to my relief, we eventually exited at the other end. Yet my dad had no difficulty conversing with the loom operators, nor did they with him. To this day, I marvel at the fact that meaningful conversations transpired under such overwhelmingly noisy circumstances.

Clearly, my dad and the loom operators heard only a smattering of the sounds that others were uttering. They combined what they *did* hear with things they could see—perhaps they were reading lips to some extent, and perhaps they were making sense of the speaker's gestures and body language—and constructed some sort of logical meaning from the situation. Like my dad and the loom operators, we, too, must often construct meaning from the stimuli around us—meaning that isn't necessarily obvious from the stimuli themselves.

Many cognitive psychologists portray learning as a process of creating one's own meaning and understanding from one's experiences—a perspective often referred to as **constructivism.** The focus of this chapter is on such constructive processes in learning and memory. After first considering several key assumptions related to knowledge construction, we will revisit long-term memory storage and retrieval processes—topics I introduced in the preceding chapter—this time looking at how such processes are often very constructive in nature. We will discover that students' prior knowledge is likely to influence the specific meanings they store and retrieve in the classroom, and that on some occasions their naive or erroneous beliefs about the world may interfere with their ability to learn new information effectively. We will distinguish between two contrasting views of how we construct meaning—individual constructivism and social constructivism—and then identify specific strategies we can derive from each one to help our students construct an accurate understanding of the world around them.

By the end of the chapter, you should be able to:

1. Describe assumptions related to the perspective that people construct knowledge, rather than absorb it from the environment.

2. Explain how both storage and retrieval are often constructive in nature, and give examples to illustrate your explanation.

3. Explain how students' prior knowledge and beliefs may either help or hinder their ability to learn and remember information.

4. Describe knowledge construction as a process that can occur both within individual students and among groups of students.

5. Describe teaching strategies you can use to support students' efforts to construct a thorough understanding of classroom subject matter.

6. Describe teaching strategies through which you can encourage students to replace current misconceptions they have about the world with more accurate information.

CASE STUDY: *Pulling It All Together*

Rita is a fourth grader who attends school in Michigan. Her class has recently had a unit on Michigan's state history. Rita still knows little about American history; this is a subject she will study as a fifth grader next year. Despite her limited background in history, Rita responds eagerly to an interviewer's question about the New World.

Interviewer: Our country is in the part of the world called America. At one time, America was called the New World. Do you know why it was called the New World?

Rita: Yeah. We learned this in social studies.

Interviewer: What did you learn?

Rita: Because they used to live in England, the British, and they didn't know about . . . they wanted to get to China 'cause China had some things they wanted. They had some cups or whatever—no, they had furs. They had fur and stuff like that and they wanted to have a shorter way to get to China so they took it and they landed in Michigan, but it wasn't called Michigan. I think it was the British that landed in Michigan and they were there first and so they tried to claim that land, but it didn't work out for some reason so they took some furs and brought them back to Britain and they sold them, but they mostly wanted it for the furs. So then the English landed there and they claimed the land and they wanted to make it a state, and so they got it signed by the government or whoever, the big boss, then they were just starting to make it a state so the British just went up to the Upper Peninsula and they thought they could stay there for a little while. Then they had to fight a war, then the farmers, they were just volunteers, so the farmers went right back and tried to get their family put together back again.

Interviewer: Did you learn all this in state history this year?

Rita: Um hum. (VanSledright & Brophy, 1992, p. 849; reprinted by permission)

- Which parts of Rita's response are accurate depictions of the history of the New World? Which parts of her response are clearly *in*accurate?

- Can you identify at least two instances in which Rita has pulled together unrelated ideas in her construction of "knowledge" of history?

CONSIDERING ADDITIONAL ASSUMPTIONS OF COGNITIVE PSYCHOLOGY

Rita has taken bits and pieces of information she has previously learned in school and pulled them into a scenario that makes sense to her. In the process of doing so, she has developed some unique interpretations of historical events. For example, she knows that the British wanted something that could be obtained in the Far East; she also knows that there was once a high demand for animal furs in England. Put them together and *voilà!*—the Chinese had the furs that the British wanted. (In reality, it was the spices of the Far East that the British were after.) Notice, too, how Rita maintains that the British found a shorter way to get to China—one that apparently went right through Michigan. Although Rita's description of historical events has a few elements of truth, these elements have been combined to form an overall "knowledge" of history that should give any historian heart failure.

In the preceding chapter, we identified several key assumptions that underlie cognitive psychology's view of how human beings learn. Many cognitive psychologists share additional assumptions about how knowledge develops—assumptions that can help us better understand Rita's unusual depiction of history:

- Meaning is constructed by the individual, rather than being derived directly from the environment.

- People interpret environmental events in unique, idiosyncratic ways.

- Internal "reality" is not necessarily the same as external "reality."

- Prior knowledge plays a major role in the meanings that people construct.

A summary of these assumptions is presented in Table 7–1; let's examine each one more closely.

Construction of Meaning

If you have read Chapter 2, then you know that this assumption underlies some theories of cognitive and linguistic development as well.

The process of **construction** lies at the core of many cognitive theories of learning: People take many separate pieces of information and use them to create an understanding or interpretation of the world around them (Chan, Burtis, Scardamalia, & Bereiter, 1992; Di Vesta, 1987; Doyle, 1983; Driver, Asoko, Leach, Mortimer, & Scott, 1994; Hegland & Andre, 1992; Marshall, 1988; Prawat, 1992; Schommer, 1994b). As an example, try the following exercise.

■ EXPERIENCING FIRSTHAND
Rocky

Read the following passage *one time only.*

> Rocky slowly got up from the mat, planning his escape. He hesitated a moment and thought. Things were not going well. What bothered him most was being held, especially since the charge against him had been weak. He considered his present situation. The lock that held him was strong but he thought he could break it. He knew, however, that his timing would have to be perfect. Rocky was aware that it was because of his early roughness that he had been penalized so severely—much too severely from his point of view. The situation was becoming frustrating; the pressure had been grinding on him for too long. He was being ridden unmercifully. Rocky was getting angry now.

Table 7–1 **Assumptions of Cognitive Psychologists Related to Knowledge Construction**

ASSUMPTION	EXAMPLE	EDUCATIONAL IMPLICATION
Construction of meaning	Neil tries to make sense of his textbook's poorly written description of the Battle of the Bulge.	Check to be sure students' interpretations of information are accurate ones.
Unique interpretations	Nadia interprets her teacher's smile as a sign that her group has done a good job on its oral presentation, whereas Nancy interprets the same smile as mocking the group's performance.	Remember that students' background experiences and cultures will influence the ways in which they interpret classroom events.
Internal versus external reality	Nate drops a penny and a golf ball from a second-story window to see whether one falls faster than the other. Because he expects the heavier golf ball to fall faster, he perceives this to be the case even though both objects actually fall at the same rate.	Remember that students cannot always be the best judges of how well they understand class material.
Role of prior knowledge	Nate's belief that heavy objects fall faster than light ones interferes with his ability to understand his teacher's explanation of how the force of gravity affects all falling objects equally.	Help students correct previously learned misconceptions.

He felt he was ready to make his move. He knew that his success or failure would depend on what he did in the next few seconds. (R. C. Anderson, Reynolds, Schallert, & Goetz, 1977, p. 372)

Now summarize what you've just read in two or three sentences. ■

Were you able to make sense of the passage? What did you think it was about? A prison escape? A wrestling match? Or perhaps something else altogether? The passage about Rocky includes a number of facts but leaves a lot unsaid; for example, it tells us nothing about where Rocky was, what kind of "lock" was holding him, or why timing was of the utmost importance. Yet you were probably able to use the information you were given to construct an overall understanding of Rocky's situation. Most people do find meaning of one sort or another in the Rocky passage (R. C. Anderson et al., 1977).

Here's another example of construction in action.

■ EXPERIENCING FIRSTHAND
A Pen-and-Ink Sketch

What do you see in the picture on the right? Look at the details carefully. Notice the shape of the head, the facial features, and the relative proportion of one part to another. Think about how the drawing is different from the real life version of the same thing. But now answer this question: Exactly what is this a picture of? ■

Source: From "The Role of Frequency in Developing Perceptual Sets" by B. R. Bugelski & D. A. Alampay, 1961, *Canadian Journal of Psychology, 15,* p. 206. Copyright 1957 and 1961. Canadian Psychological Association. Reprinted with permission.

Did you see a picture of a rat or mouse, or did you see a picture of a bald-headed man? In fact, the drawing isn't a *good* picture of *anything;* too many details have been left out. Despite the missing pieces, you were undoubtedly able to make sense of what you saw (Bugelski & Alampay, 1961).

Just as you constructed meaning from the Rocky passage and from the pen-and-ink sketch, you have undoubtedly constructed a great deal of knowledge about the world from your own personal experiences and from the many subjects you've studied in school. For example, you've constructed some sort of understanding of mathematics from all those mathematical facts and procedures you've learned over the years. You've constructed your own idea of "good sportsmanship" from the games and sporting events in which you have participated. And you've developed some idea of the sequence of historical events in your local area from the bits and pieces of history you've picked up in school, at museums, and in the newspaper. The history you've constructed is, I hope, more accurate than Rita's!

As teachers, we must remember that our students will rarely learn classroom material exactly as it is presented to them. Instead, they will use some of the information they obtain in the classroom—from lectures, from textbooks, from conversations with classmates and teachers, and so on—to construct their own sense of how the world operates. Some of their constructions will be appropriate ones; others, like Rita's, may be a far cry from what we had hoped they would learn.

Remember that students rarely learn something exactly as it is presented to them.

Remember that students' background experiences and cultures will influence the ways in which they construct knowledge from classroom activities.

Unique Interpretations

Different people will often construct different meanings from the same stimuli, perhaps because they each bring their own unique prior experiences and knowledge bases to the same situation. For example, when the Rocky passage was used in an experiment with college students, physical education majors frequently interpreted it as a wrestling match, but music education majors (most of whom had little or no knowledge of wrestling) were more likely to think it was about a prison break (R. C. Anderson et al., 1977). When students in another study looked at the "rat/man" sketch, those who saw the sketch after previously looking at several pictures of animals typically interpreted it as a rat or mouse; in contrast, students who had previously seen pictures of people's faces were more apt to see the bald-headed man (Bugelski & Alampay, 1961).

So, too, are our students likely to have their own idiosyncratic interpretations of the information we present in the classroom. They will bring unique background experiences and cultures to bear on virtually any topic we teach, and these experiences and cultures will provide some of the building blocks from which their own versions of academic "knowledge" are derived.

Different students will inevitably construct somewhat different meanings from the same message.

Internal Versus External Reality

Strictly speaking, the pen-and-ink sketch I showed you earlier is nothing more than a bunch of thick black lines on the page.

Yet most people "see" either a rodent or a man in these lines. Many cognitive psychologists believe that the internal "realities" that people experience—the ways in which they interpret their experiences and the knowledge they construct from those experiences—are not necessarily equivalent to the realities of the physical world (e.g., Bruning, Schraw, & Ronning, 1995; Jonassen, 1991). From this perspective, then, reality is in the eyes of the beholder.

As an example, consider how convinced Rita was that her version of history was exactly what she had learned in her fourth-grade history lessons. So, too, may our own students often have difficulty separating fact from fiction in terms of the knowledge they have constructed. Thus, they may not always be the best judges of how well they understand class material.

Remember that students cannot always be the best judges of how well they understand class material.

Role of Prior Knowledge

In our discussion of information processing in the preceding chapter, we discovered that some prior knowledge about a topic is essential before such long-term memory storage processes as meaningful learning and elaboration can occur. Many cognitive psychologists place considerable importance on the role of prior knowledge, believing that people continually draw on their current understanding of the world to interpret new experiences. When people hold erroneous beliefs about the world—in other words, when they have **misconceptions** about a topic—they will often misinterpret any new information they see or hear related to that topic.

Take students' prior knowledge and beliefs into account.

As teachers, we must remember that our students' misconceptions about the world may have an adverse effect on their ability to learn new material accurately. Our job, then, is twofold: Not only must we help students acquire the information and skills that will enable them to be productive citizens, but we must also help them discard any erroneous beliefs they have constructed over the years. As you will soon discover, the latter task is often easier said than done.

EXAMINING THE CONSTRUCTIVE NATURE OF MEMORY STORAGE AND RETRIEVAL

When you read the Rocky passage, you may have inferred very quickly that the passage was about a particular topic—perhaps about a prison break, a wrestling match, or a caged dog. In other words, you were constructing meaning as you were initially storing the passage in memory. But as we shall see shortly, construction can occur later on, at the time of retrieval, as well. Let's look at some examples of constructive processes in both storage and retrieval. Let's look, too, at how prior knowledge (in the form of *schemas*), expectations, and misconceptions about the world can influence these processes.

Can you make sense of this situation on the basis of your prior knowledge about the world?

Observing Construction in Storage

David

Read the following story *one time only*.

David decided to stop at the dry cleaners on his way to work. He arrived at the dry cleaners shortly before opening time. He waited in his car until he saw the clerk change the sign from "Sorry, We're Closed" to "Open." He gathered his bundle of clothes, then hurried into the store. The clerk at the counter gave him a receipt. The clothes would be ready in a few days.

David arrived at work on time. He went through the revolving doors, then walked swiftly down the crowded corridor. After entering the office he saw that the coffee was made and decided to pour a cup. He sat at his desk and sipped his coffee. David glanced over the pile of paperwork in front of him and noticed that he was getting behind on his work. He looked at the day's schedule and realized that he had better get started.

Instead of going out for lunch David decided to bring a sandwich up from the lobby coffee shop and eat at his desk. Halfway through his lunch, he stopped to make a phone call. He checked the number in his phone book, picked up the receiver and dialed the number. David listened while the phone rang. A man answered the phone. David asked if Chris Miller was there. He was told that he must have the wrong number. He apologized and hung up. David checked the number in his phone book and dialed again. The phone rang. He heard the voice at the other end of the phone say "hello." He realized that he had the right number.

David arrived at the restaurant at 7:30. He walked into the waiting area and looked around. He spotted an empty table in a far corner of the restaurant. He walked to the table and sat down. He checked his watch. When the waiter came he ordered a cup of coffee. Just as he was finishing he spotted his friend. They had dinner together.

(Courtesy of D. Halpern)

Now cover the story with a sheet of paper and answer the following questions from memory.

1. What did David do with his clothes before he went to work?
   a. He took them to the cleaner's and left them there to be cleaned.
   b. He took them into a clothing store for alterations.
   c. He left them in his car.

2. David worked
   a. in an office building
   b. in an automobile factory
   c. at a restaurant

3. David had dinner with
   a. a friend named Chris Miller
   b. a colleague from work
   c. his mother

Chances are you chose alternative *a* in each case. But now look back at the story once again. In fact, it never specifically tells us that David actually *left* his clothes at the cleaners; it only tells us that he gathered his clothes, hurried into the store, got a receipt from the clerk, and heard that the clothes would be ready in a few days. Likewise, the story never specifies exactly where David worked; it only tells us that the building had revolving doors, a crowded corridor, and at least one office. And with whom did David have dinner? We know only he ate with a "friend" of some kind—a friend who could be Chris Miller, a colleague from work, David's mother, or somebody else altogether. If you found yourself answering my three questions with some degree of certainty, then you constructed considerable meaning from the passage—meaning that was not necessarily spelled out for you—based on some of the details you were given.

As teachers, we will find our students constructing their own meanings for virtually all aspects of the classroom curriculum. For example, as the *David* exercise illustrates, the activity of reading is often quite constructive in nature: Students combine the ideas they read with their prior knowledge and then draw logical conclusions about what the text is trying to communicate (Dole, Duffy, Roehler, & Pearson, 1991; Otero & Kintsch, 1992; F. Smith, 1988). So, too, will we find constructive processes in such subject areas as mathematics, science, and social studies (Driver et al., 1994; Resnick, 1989; VanSledright & Brophy, 1992).

Adult readers often skip over letters, and even over entire words, as they read, yet may still understand what they are reading quite accurately (e.g., F. Smith, 1988). Can you explain this phenomenon, using the idea of knowledge construction?

Observing Construction in Retrieval

THINKING ABOUT WHAT YOU KNOW

Have there been times in your life when you remembered an event very differently than someone else did? Were you both equally convinced of the accuracy of your memories?

As we noted in our discussion of forgetting in Chapter 6, retrieval isn't always an all-or-nothing phenomenon. Sometimes we retrieve only bits and pieces of whatever information we are looking for in long-term memory. In such situations, we may construct our "memory" of an event by combining the tidbits we can retrieve with our general knowledge and assumptions about the world (Kolodner, 1985; Loftus, 1991; Rumelhart & Ortony, 1977; P. T. Wilson & Anderson, 1986). As an example of how retrieval of a specific event or idea often involves drawing on our knowledge about other things as well, try the following exercise.

■ EXPERIENCING FIRSTHAND
Missing Letters

Can you fill in the missing letters of these five words?

1. sep-rate

2. exist-nce

3. adole——nce

4. retr—val

5. hors d'o——

Were you able to retrieve the missing letters from your long-term memory—in other words, did you know exactly how each of the words is spelled? If not, then you may have found yourself making reasonable guesses, using either your knowledge of how the words are pronounced or your knowledge of how words in the English language are typically spelled. For example, perhaps you used the *i before e except after c* rule for word 4; if so, then you reconstructed the correct spelling of *retrieval.* Perhaps you used your knowledge that most words ending in *nce* have an *a* before the *n;* in other words, the letters *ance* are a common word ending. Unfortunately, if you used this knowledge for word 2, then you spelled *existence* incorrectly. Neither pronunciation nor typical English spelling patterns would have helped you with *hors d'oeuvre,* a term we've borrowed from the French. (The correct spellings for words 1 and 3 are *separate* and *adolescence.*)

When people fill in the gaps in what they've retrieved on the basis of what seems "logical," they will often make mistakes—a form of forgetting called **reconstruction error.** Rita's version of what she learned in history is a prime example: She retrieved certain facts from her history lessons (e.g., the fact that the British wanted furs, the fact that they eventually settled in what is now Michigan) and constructed a scenario that made some sort of sense to her. So, too, will our own students sometimes fall victim to reconstruction error, pulling together what they can recall in ways we may hardly recognize. If important details are difficult to fill in logically, we must make sure our students learn them well enough that they can retrieve them directly from their long-term memories, rather than have to rely on "logic" as to what those details might be.

When important details are difficult to fill in logically, make sure students learn them well.

What implications does the notion of reconstruction error have for the credibility of eyewitness testimony?

How Schemas Affect the Construction of Meaning

In the preceding chapter, we discovered how cognitive psychologists propose that much of the knowledge stored in long-term memory takes the form of **schemas**—organized bodies of information about specific topics. Such schemas often influence the specific ways in which people construct meanings from their experiences. For example, you were able to see a rodent or a man (or both) in the pen-and-ink sketch because you already knew what rats and men look like: You had schemas for both critters that helped you fill in the missing details. As another example of how schemas influence the meanings we construct, try the following exercise.

EXPERIENCING FIRSTHAND
John

Read the following passage *one time only.*

> John was feeling bad today so he decided to go see the family doctor. He checked in with the doctor's receptionist, and then looked through several medical magazines that were on the table by his chair. Finally the nurse came and asked him to take off his clothes. The doctor was very nice to him. He eventually prescribed some pills for John. Then John left the doctor's office and headed home. (Bower, Black, & Turner, 1979, p. 190)

You probably had no trouble understanding the passage because you have been to a doctor's office yourself and have a schema for how those visits usually go. You can therefore fill in a number of details that the passage doesn't ever tell you. For example, you probably inferred that John must have *gone* to the doctor's office, although the story skips immediately from John's *decision* about going to see the doctor to his checking in with a receptionist. Likewise, you probably concluded that John took his clothes off in the examination room, *not* in the waiting room, even though the story never makes it clear where John did his striptease. When a schema involves a predictable sequence of events related to a particular activity, as is the case in a visit to the doctor's office, it is sometimes called a **script**.

What is the typical script for a trip to the grocery store? to the movies? to a fast-food restaurant?

In some cases, students from diverse cultural backgrounds may come to school with different schemas and scripts and so may interpret the same classroom materials or activities differently (Lipson, 1983; R. E. Reynolds et al., 1982; Steffensen, Joag-Dev, & Anderson, 1979). As an illustration, try the next exercise.

■   E X P E R I E N C I N G   F I R S T H A N D
The War of the Ghosts

Read the following story *one time only*.

One night two young men from Egulac went down to the river to hunt seals, and while they were there it became foggy and calm. Then they heard war-cries, and they thought, "Maybe this is a war-party." They escaped to the shore, and hid behind a log. Now canoes came up, and they heard the noise of paddles, and saw one canoe coming up to them. There were five men in the canoe, and they said:

"What do you think? We wish to take you along. We are going up the river to make war on the people."

One of the young men said: "I have no arrows."

"Arrows are in the canoe," they said.

"I will not go along. I might be killed. My relatives do not know where I have gone. But you," he said, turning to the other, "may go with them."

So one of the young men went, but the other returned home.

And the warriors went on up the river to a town on the other side of Kalama. The people came down to the water, and they began to fight, and many were killed. But presently the young man heard one of the warriors say, "Quick, let us go home: that Indian has been hit." Now he thought: "Oh, they are ghosts." He did not feel sick, but they said he had been shot.

So the canoes went back to Egulac, and the young man went ashore to his house, and made a fire. And he told everybody and said, "Behold I accompanied the ghosts, and we went to fight. Many of our fellows were killed, and many of those who attacked us were killed. They said I was hit, and I did not feel sick."

He told it all, and then he became quiet. When the sun rose he fell down. Something black came out of his mouth. His face became contorted. The people jumped up and cried.

He was dead. (F. C. Bartlett, 1932, p. 65)

Now cover the page and write down as much of the story as you can remember. ■

Compare your own rendition of the story with the original. What differences do you notice? Your version is almost certainly the shorter of the two, and you probably left out a number of details. But did you also find yourself distorting certain parts of the story so that it made more sense to you?

The War of the Ghosts is a Native American ghost story—one that is probably not totally consistent with the schemas and scripts you've learned in your own culture. In an early study of long-term memory (F. C. Bartlett, 1932), students at England's Cambridge

University were asked to read the story twice and then to recall it at various times later on. The students' recollections of the story often included additions and distortions that made the story more consistent with English culture. For example, people rarely go "to the river to hunt seals" because seals are saltwater animals. Students might therefore say that the men went to the river to *fish*. Similarly, the ghostly element of the story did not fit comfortably with the religious beliefs of most Cambridge students and so was often modified. For example, one student was asked to recall the story six months after he had read it; notice how the version he remembers leaves out many of the story's more puzzling aspects (puzzling, at least, from the perspective of mainstream Western culture):

> Four men came down to the water. They were told to get into a boat and to take arms with them. They inquired, "What arms?" and were answered "Arms for battle." When they came to the battle-field they heard a great noise and shouting, and a voice said: "The black man is dead." And he was brought to the place where they were, and laid on the ground. And he foamed at the mouth. (F. C. Bartlett, 1932, pp. 71–72)

As teachers, we need to find out whether students have the appropriate schemas and scripts—the concepts, the knowledge of action sequences, and so on—to understand the subject matter we are teaching. When our students *don't* have such knowledge, we may sometimes need to "back up" and help them develop it before we forge full-steam ahead with new material.

How Expectations Affect the Construction of Meaning

B egin instruction at a level consistent with students' existing knowledge base.

Look back at the case study "Darren's Day at School" at the beginning of Chapter 5. What knowledge did Darren use to interpret Ms. Caffarella's description of the Parthenon? What important knowledge was Darren missing that would have enabled him to interpret her message more accurately?

■ EXPERIENCING FIRSTHAND
Hamlet's Soliloquy

Here is the first part of a well-known soliloquy from William Shakespeare's *Hamlet*. Read it *as quickly as you can* and read it *one time only*.

> To be, or not to be, that is the quastion—
> Whether 'tis nobler in the mind to suffer
> The slings annd arrows of outrageous fortune,
> Or to take arms against a sea of troubles,
> And by opposing end them. To die, to sleep—
> No more; and by a sleep to say we end
> The heart-ache, and the thousand naturel shocks
> That flesh is heir to; 'tis a consummation
> Devoutly to be wished. To die, to sleep—
> To sleep, perchance to dream, ay there's the rubb,
> For in that sleep of death what dreams may come
> When we have shuffled off this mortal coil,
> Must give us pause; there's tha respect
> That makes calamity of so long life.

You may have noticed one or two typographical errors in the passage. But did you catch them all? Altogether, there were five mistakes, as indicated in italicized boldface at the top of the next page.

To be, or not to be, that is the *quastion*—
Whether 'tis nobler in the mind to suffer
The slings *annd* arrows of outrageous fortune,
Or to take arms against a sea of troubles,
And by opposing end them. To die, to sleep—
No more; and by a sleep to say we end
The heart-ache, and the thousand *naturel* shocks
That flesh is heir to; 'tis a consummation
Devoutly to be wished. To die, to sleep—
To sleep, perchance to dream, ay there's the *rubb,*
For in that sleep of death what dreams may come
When we have shuffled off this mortal coil,
Must give us pause; there's *tha* respect
That makes calamity of so long life.

If you didn't notice all the errors—and many people don't—then your perception of the passage was influenced by your expectation of what words *should* have been there on the basis of your general knowledge of how English words are typically spelled and perhaps (if you once memorized Hamlet's soliloquy) on the basis of your recollection of what Hamlet actually said.

Our students will often interpret what they see and hear in the classroom on the basis of what they *expect* the message to be. For example, as we noted in our discussion of listening and reading comprehension in Chapter 2, they might correctly interpret a teacher's statement, "Goodness, this class is noisy today!" to mean "Be quiet" (Flavell, 1985). As another example, imagine you are giving a physics lesson on *force* and *inertia*. The main point you want to make in the lesson is that force is necessary only to get an object in motion; thanks to inertia, force is *not* necessary to keep the object moving. Such an idea contradicts students' everyday experiences; for example, if they want to move a heavy object across the floor, they must continue to push it (Driver et al., 1994). When students are expecting you to say that force is necessary to keep something in motion, this may, in fact, be what they "hear" you telling them.

Expectations are especially likely to influence people's interpretation of events when the information they receive is ambiguous (e.g., Eysenck & Keane, 1990). For example, when I show the rat/man picture to students in my classes, I consistently find that the great majority of students who have been led to expect a nonhuman creature— by previously viewing a picture that is clearly a rodent—*do* in fact see a mouse or rat. Those who are similarly led to expect a person see the baldheaded man.

Expectations and Assessment of Students' Performance

Among the most ambiguous of all the stimuli we encounter are the specific behaviors exhibited by the people around us. Because human behavior does not always communicate a clear message, people often interpret it in accordance with their own expectations (Juvonen, 1991b; Nisbett & Bellows, 1977; Ritts, Patterson, & Tubbs, 1992; Snyder & Swann, 1978). People expect positive behaviors from a person whom they like or admire and so are likely to perceive that person's behaviors in a positive light—a phenomenon referred to as the **halo effect**. In much the same way, they expect inappropriate behaviors from a person whom they dislike, and their perceptions of that

What kinds of expectations do you think your teachers have had for you over the years? Were your teachers accurate in their assessments?

person's behaviors are biased accordingly (we could call this the "horns effect"). For example, imagine that Mr. Alexander, a fifth-grade teacher, has one student, Mary, who consistently performs well in her classwork, and another, Susan, who more typically turns in sloppy, incomplete assignments. Let's say that both girls turn in homework of marginal quality. Mr. Alexander is likely to *over*rate Mary's performance and to *under*rate Susan's.

As we discovered in our discussion of diversity in Chapter 4, teachers' expectations for their students are often influenced by students' ethnicity, gender, and socioeconomic status, and such expectations may unfairly bias teachers' judgments of student performance. Let's look at an experiment by Darley and Gross (1983) as an example: Undergraduate students were told that they were participating in a study on teacher evaluation methods and were asked to view a videotape of a fourth-grade girl named Hannah. There were two versions of the videotape designed to give two different impressions about Hannah's socioeconomic status; Hannah's clothing, the kind of playground on which she played, and information about her parents' occupations indirectly conveyed to some students that she was from a low socioeconomic background and to others that she was from a high socioeconomic background. All students then watched Hannah taking an oral achievement test—one on which she performed at grade level—and were asked to rate Hannah on a number of characteristics. Students who had been led to believe that Hannah came from wealthy surroundings rated her ability well above grade level, whereas students believing that she lived in an impoverished environment evaluated her as being below grade level. The two groups of students also rated Hannah differently in terms of her work habits, motivation, social skills, and general maturity.

Considering Ambiguous Stimuli in the Classroom

Make sure messages to students are clear and unambiguous.

People's interpretations of ambiguous stimuli are particularly susceptible to biases and expectations because some of the information necessary for an "accurate" perception (if such is possible) is simply not available. Yet as we discovered in our discussion of information processing in Chapter 6, even when all the necessary information *is* present, people typically attend only to a small part of that information and ignore the rest. As teachers, we must be careful that the messages we give our students are clear and unambiguous so that there is little room for misinterpretation. And we must continually monitor ourselves regarding the expectations we have for our students' performance, being sure that such expectations are based on objective data, rather than on group membership.

Form expectations for students' performance only on the basis of objective data.

When Meaningful Learning Goes Awry: Effects of Misconceptions

Consider this situation:

This study is depicted in the case study "In the Eye of the Beholder" at the end of Chapter 2.

A class of fifth graders was about to study a unit on light and vision. Based on results of a pretest, it was clear that most students believed incorrectly that vision occurs simply as the result of light shining on an object and making it bright. During the unit, the correct explanation of human vision was presented: light must be reflected off an object *and then travel to the eye* before the object can be seen. Even though students both read and heard the correct explanation of how people see objects, most of them "learned" what they already believed: that an object can be seen as soon as light hits it. Posttest results indicated that only 24% of the class had learned the correct explanation. (Eaton, Anderson, & Smith, 1984)

When previously learned information is incorrect—that is, when it reflects a misconception—new information may be learned incorrectly as well. In fact, students can spend a great deal of time learning the wrong thing!

Many students of all ages have misconceptions about the world—misconceptions they have constructed from the various pieces of information they have received over the years. Figure 7–1 presents some typical examples of misconceptions that students believe to be true. Thanks to the processes of meaningful learning and elaboration—processes that usually facilitate learning—students may change or distort new information to fit their prior misconceptions. And thanks to the fact that students often engage in rote learning—the fact that they often try to learn school material without trying to relate it to anything else they know—they may hold two inconsistent or contradictory ideas in long-term memory at the same time. As a result, students may leave a classroom with their erroneous ideas "confirmed," rather than corrected (Alexander & Judy, 1988; Bishop & Anderson, 1990; S. Carey, 1986; Roth & Anderson, 1988).

Consider the case of Kevin (Roth & Anderson, 1988) as an example. Kevin's fifth-grade class was studying a unit on photosynthesis, the process through which plants produce their own food. On a pretest, Kevin indicated his misconception that plants get food from other sources:

> Food (for plants) can be sun, rain, light, bugs, oxygen, soil and even other dead plants. Also warmth or coldness. All plants need at least three or four of these foods. Plus minerals. (Roth & Anderson, 1988, p. 117)

If you will forgive Kevin's grammar, you should note that his definition of the process of photosynthesis at the end of the instructional unit is fairly accurate:

> Well, in the leaves, in the green plants, they have little chloroplasts which inside that have chlorophyll. When the sun shines on it, it does photosynthesis which changes, well it doesn't really change, but the plant has certain chemicals that change the sunlight . . . well, they have certain chemicals that the sunlight changes into food which is energy for the plant. (Roth & Anderson, 1988, p. 117)

Nevertheless, the unit on photosynthesis didn't put much of a dent in Kevin's original belief about sources of food for plants, as revealed by his response when asked how a plant gets its food:

> Whew, from lots of places. From the soil for one, for the minerals and water, and from the air for oxygen. The sunlight for sun and so it would change chemicals for sugars. It sort of makes its own food and gets food from the ground. And from air. (Roth & Anderson, 1988, p. 118)

Kevin had learned that photosynthesis provides a source of food for plant life. Thanks to his prior misconception, however, Kevin had not learned a critical point of the lesson: Photosynthesis provides the *only* source of food for plants.

As teachers, we must remember that the misconceptions our students have about the world may wreak havoc with the new ideas we present in class. When we consider the topic of *conceptual change* later in the chapter, we will identify some strategies for undoing those misconceptions and helping students construct a more appropriate understanding of the world around them.

Even college students have been known to ignore information presented in class when it is inconsistent with their prior beliefs (Holt-Reynolds, 1992).

Figure 7–1   Common Student Misconceptions

Astronomy

Fact: The earth revolves around the sun.
Misconception: The sun revolves around the earth. It "rises" in the morning and "sets" in the evening, at which point it "goes" to the other side of the earth.

Fact: The earth is shaped more or less like a sphere.
Misconception: The earth is shaped like a round, flat disk.
(Nussbaum, 1985; Sneider & Pulos, 1983; Vosniadou, 1994; Vosniadou & Brewer, 1987)

Biology

Fact: A living thing is something that carries on such life processes as metabolism, growth, and reproduction.
Misconception: A living thing is something that moves and/or grows. The sun, wind, clouds, and fire are living things.

Fact: A plant is a food producer.
Misconception: A plant grows in a garden and is relatively small. Carrots and cabbage are vegetables, not plants. Trees are plants only if they are small.
(Kyle & Shymansky, 1989)

Physics

Fact: An object remains in uniform motion until a force acts on it; a force is needed only to *change* speed or direction.
Misconception: Any moving object has a force acting on it. For example, a ball thrown into the air continues to be pushed upward by the force of the throw until it begins its descent.

Fact: Gravity is the force whereby any two masses are attracted together.
Misconception: Gravity is the "glue" that holds people to the earth. There is no gravity without air.
(S. Carey, 1986; Kyle & Shymansky, 1989)

Geography

Fact: The Great Lakes contain fresh water.
Misconception: The Great Lakes contain salt water.

Fact: Rivers run from higher elevation to lower elevation.
Misconception: Rivers run from north to south. For example, rivers can run from Canada into the United States, but not vice versa.
(Courtesy of R. K. Ormrod)

Educational Psychology

Fact: Meaningful learning is more effective than rote learning.
Misconception: Rote learning is more effective than meaningful learning.

Fact: Negative reinforcement is the removal of a stimulus (usually an aversive, or unpleasant, one). It increases the frequency of the behavior that it follows.
Misconception: Negative reinforcement is the presentation of an aversive stimulus (e.g., a scolding, a spanking). Its effect, if any, is to decrease the frequency of a behavior that it follows.
(Lennon, Ormrod, Burger, & Warren, 1990)

VIEWING KNOWLEDGE CONSTRUCTION AS BOTH AN INDIVIDUAL ACTIVITY AND A SOCIAL PROCESS

Up to this point, we have been talking about the process of construction as something that occurs within a single individual. Theories that focus on how people, as individuals, construct meaning from events are collectively known as **individual constructivism.** Our beginning case study reflects this perspective: Rita took several threads of information she had learned in her fourth-grade history lessons and wove an idiosyncratic picture of how things "must have" happened in the early history of her state. If you have read Chapter 2, then you should note that Piaget's theory of cognitive development has an element of individual constructivism, as do many theorists' perspectives of how children's knowledge of grammar and syntax develops over the years.

Yet people often construct meaning by working together, rather than by working alone, and the knowledge they create is the result of their combined efforts to interpret their experiences. Unlike individually constructed knowledge, which may differ considerably from one individual to another, socially constructed knowledge is typically shared by many people simultaneously. A perspective known as **social constructivism** focuses on such collective efforts to impose meaning on the world (Bruning et al., 1995; Driver et al., 1994; Marshall, 1992; Prawat & Floden, 1994; Rogoff, 1990; Schön, 1987). If you have read Chapter 2, then you have already encountered one social constructivist—Lev Vygotsky.

Think about times when you have been confused about material in one of your classes. In such situations, did you ever work cooperatively with one or more of your classmates—perhaps with students who were equally confused—and make sense of the material *together*?

Sometimes meaning is constructed by a group of people at a single point in time. For example, this would be the case if, by working together, you and a friend make sense of what has previously been confusing course material. But at other times, the social construction of meaning may take weeks, years, or even centuries. We find the latter situation in the development of such academic disciplines as history, social studies, science, and mathematics. Through these disciplines, people have developed such concepts as *revolution, democracy, molecule,* and *square root* and such principles as *supply-and-demand* and the *Pythagorean theorem* to simplify, organize, and explain the very diverse nature of the world in which we live. Literature, music, and fine arts help us impose meaning on the world as well—for example, by trying to describe the thoughts and feelings that characterize human experience. Here we see the very critical role that *culture* plays in knowledge construction: To the extent that different groups of people use different concepts and principles to explain their physical experiences, and to the extent that they have unique bodies of literature, music, and art to capture their psychological experiences, they will inevitably see the world in very diverse ways (e.g., Banks, 1991).

Think of novels that have given you new insights into human nature.

PROMOTING EFFECTIVE KNOWLEDGE CONSTRUCTION

As teachers, we must keep in mind both the individual and social aspects of knowledge construction as we help our students make sense of the world around them. Cognitive psychologists have proposed several strategies we can use to help our students construct an increasingly richer and more sophisticated knowledge base:

- Providing opportunities for experimentation
- Presenting the ideas of others

- Emphasizing conceptual understanding

- Promoting dialogue

- Using authentic activities

- Creating cognitive apprenticeships

Provide opportunities for students to experiment with the physical world.

Unfortunately, the researchers didn't eliminate several other possible explanations for the results they found. Besides the fact that one group used teacher-prescribed procedures and the other group used self-chosen procedures, what other differences between the two groups might account for the results obtained in this study? (You may want to refer back to the discussion regarding "Drawing Conclusions from Research" in Chapter 1.)

Providing Opportunities for Experimentation

By interacting and experimenting with the objects around them, students can discover many characteristics and principles of the world firsthand (e.g., Fosnot, 1996). As teachers, we should provide numerous opportunities for our students to explore concrete objects in a hands-on fashion; we must let them touch, manipulate, modify, combine, and recombine things. For example, at the elementary school level, we might use beads or pennies to help students discover basic addition and subtraction facts, or we might use two balls of clay and a scale to promote the realization that weight remains the same despite changes in an object's shape (Piaget's notion of *conservation*). At the secondary school level, such activities as science labs, in-class demonstrations, and computer simulations should also help our students construct knowledge about the world around them.

Teachers often teach students specific procedures—clearly delineated, step-by-step sequences—for accomplishing certain tasks. Yet on some occasions, it might be more helpful to let students develop such procedures *on their own* through experimentation. For example, when teaching cooking, it may sometimes be more productive to cast aside any cookbook recipes and instead ask students to try different combinations and proportions of ingredients (Hatano & Inagaki, 1993). As another example, let's consider a study in which kindergarten students had one of two different experiences raising animals (Hatano & Inagaki, 1993). Some students had pet rabbits in their classrooms; they took turns feeding and taking care of the rabbits by using procedures their teacher had carefully prescribed for them. Others were raising goldfish at home; these students had to make their own decisions about how best to care for their pets and, in doing so, could experiment with feeding schedules, water purity, and other variables that might affect the fish's welfare. The students who raised the goldfish appeared to develop a more accurate understanding of animals in general—for example, learning that baby animals grow bigger over time—and were able to apply what they learned from their own pets to other species. To illustrate, one goldfish owner, when asked whether we could keep a baby frog the same size forever, said, "No, we can't, because the frog will grow bigger as the goldfish grew bigger. My goldfish were small before, but now they are big" (Hatano & Inagaki, 1993, p. 121).

Hands-on activities similar to the ones I've just described are a key component of an instructional strategy known as *discovery learning*. We will consider this approach in more depth in our discussion of instructional strategies in Chapter 13.

Presenting the Ideas of Others

As we noted earlier, knowledge is constructed not only by people working independently but also by people working together over the course of years or centuries to make sense of the world in which they live. Although it may sometimes be beneficial to have our students discover basic principles for themselves (reinventing the wheel, so to

Students can more effectively construct a meaningful interpretation of the events around them when they examine the ways in which others have interpreted similar events in the past. For example, by reading classic works of literature, they view daily life from the perspectives of numerous authors.

speak), we must also provide opportunities for them to hear and read about the ideas of others—the concepts, principles, theories, and so on, that society has developed to explain both the physical and psychological aspects of human experience (e.g., Driver, 1995). Our students are most likely to construct a productive view of the world when they have the benefit of experiencing the world firsthand *and* the benefit of learning how those before them have interpreted such experience.

Expose students to the ways in which other people interpret physical and social events.

Emphasizing Conceptual Understanding

Let's look back at our beginning case study once again. Rita acquired a few miscellaneous facts in her history lessons, but she clearly had no idea about how those facts were interconnected. Unfortunately, such learning of isolated facts, without any sense of how they fit together, is all too common at both the elementary and secondary grade levels (Brophy & Alleman, 1992; J. Hiebert & Lefevre, 1986; Hollon, Roth, & Anderson, 1991; McRobbie & Tobin, 1995).

Without a doubt, students benefit more from acquiring facts, concepts, and ideas in an integrated, interrelated, and meaningful fashion; in other words, they benefit from developing a **conceptual understanding** of academic subject matter (L. M. Anderson, 1993; Bédard & Chi, 1992; J. J. White & Rumsey, 1994). For example, rather than simply memorize basic mathematical computation procedures, students should also learn that procedures make sense in terms of underlying principles of mathematics (J. Hiebert & Lefevre, 1986). Rather than memorize historical facts as a list of unrelated people, places, and dates, students should place those facts within the context of major social and religious trends, migration patterns, economic considerations, characteristics of human personality, and so on.

Help students learn material in an integrated, interrelated fashion.

Here are several specific strategies through which we can help our students develop a conceptual understanding of classroom subject matter:

- We can organize units around a few core ideas and themes, always relating specific content back to this core.

- We can explore each topic in depth—for example, by considering many examples, examining cause-effect relationships, and discovering how specific details relate to more general principles.

- We can explain how new ideas relate to students' own experiences and to things they have previously learned.

- We can show students—through the things we say, the assignments we give, and the criteria we use to evaluate learning—that conceptual understanding of classroom subject matter is far more important than knowledge of isolated facts.

- We can ask students to teach what they have learned to others—a task that encourages them to focus on main ideas, pulling them together in a way that makes sense. (L. M. Anderson, 1993; Benware & Deci, 1984; Brophy & Alleman, 1992; Hatano & Inagaki, 1993; Prawat, 1993; VanSledright & Brophy, 1992; J. J. White & Rumsey, 1994)

Address fewer topics and spend more time on each one.

We should note here that our students will rarely be able to acquire a conceptual understanding of classroom subject matter overnight. Construction of an integrated understanding of any complex topic will inevitably take time. Accordingly, many educators advocate a *less is more* principle: *Less* material presented more thoroughly is learned *more* completely and with greater understanding (Brophy & Alleman, 1992; Kyle & Shymansky, 1989; Marshall, 1992; Roth & Anderson, 1988; Wiggins, 1989).

Promoting Dialogue

Our students may often be more successful in making sense of the world when they work *together* to construct meaning from the phenomena they observe and the events they experience. Frequent conversations among them are essential for such mutually constructed meanings to develop (Fosnot, 1996; Greeno, Collins, & Resnick, 1996; Hatano & Inagaki, 1993; E. H. Hiebert & Fisher, 1992; Marshall, 1992; Sosniak & Stodolsky, 1994).

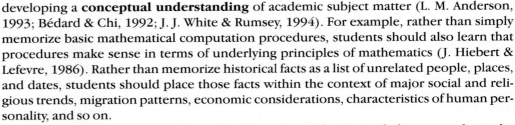

Encourage students to exchange their views through frequent classroom dialogues.

As an example of how members of a classroom might work together to construct meaning, let's consider an interaction in Keisha Coleman's third-grade classroom (P. L. Peterson, 1992). The class has been working with the number line as a way of trying to understand positive and negative numbers, and the students are now specifically addressing how they might solve the problem $-10 + 10 = ?$ by using a number line such as this (on the top of the next page):

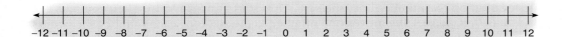

One student, Marta, gives the answer "Zero" and explains herself by saying, "You have to count ten numbers to the right." A second student, Tessa, agrees with Marta's answer of zero but disagrees with her explanation. The following conversation among Ms. Coleman and two of her students, Tessa and Chang, ensues:

Ms. Coleman:	What do you disagree with?
Tessa:	You have to count numbers to the right. If you count numbers to the right, then you couldn't get to zero. You'd have to count to the left.
Ms. Coleman:	Could you explain a little bit more about what you mean by that? I'm not quite sure I follow you. And the rest of *you need to listen very closely so you can make comments about what she's saying* or say whether or not you agree or disagree. Tessa?
Tessa:	Because if you went that way [points to the right] then it would have to be a higher number.
Ms. Coleman:	Any comments about what Tessa's trying to say? Chang?
Chang:	I disagree with what she's trying to say.
Ms. Coleman:	O.K. Your disagreement is?
Chang:	Tessa says if you're counting right, then the number is—I don't really understand. She said, "If you count right, then the number has to go smaller." I don't know what she's talking about. Negative ten plus negative ten is zero.
Ms. Coleman:	You said that you don't understand what she's trying to say?
Chang:	No.
Ms. Coleman:	Do you want to ask her?
Chang:	[Turns to Tessa and asks]: What do you mean by counting to the right?
Tessa:	If you count from ten up, you can't get zero. If you count from ten left, you can get zero.
Chang:	[to Tessa]: Well, negative ten is a negative number—smaller than zero.
Tessa:	I know.
Chang:	Then why do you say you can't get to zero when you're adding to negative ten, which is smaller than zero?
Tessa:	OHHHH! NOW I GET IT! This is positive.
Ms. Coleman:	Excuse me?
Tessa:	You have to count right.
Ms. Coleman:	You're saying in order to get to zero, you have to count to the right? From where, Tessa?
Tessa:	Negative 10. (P. L. Peterson, 1992, pp. 165–166; reprinted by permission)

Ms. Coleman's class continues to struggle with Marta's incomplete explanation of counting "ten numbers to the right" as a way of determining that $-10 + 10 = 0$. Eventually, Tessa offers a revised and more complete explanation. Pointing to the appropriate location on the number line, she says, "You start at negative 10. Then you add 1, 2, 3, 4, 5, 6, 7, 8, 9, 10." She moves one number to the right for each number she counts. She reaches the zero point on the number line when she counts "10" and concludes, "That equals zero."

By asking our students to express their ideas openly with one another and with us—by asking them to explain, discuss, and debate classroom subject matter—we accomplish several things simultaneously:

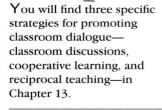

If you have read Chapters 2, 3, and 4, try to recall additional benefits of classroom interaction that those chapters identify.

- We encourage students to clarify and organize their ideas sufficiently so that they can verbalize them to others.

- We provide opportunities for students to *elaborate* on what they have learned—for example, by drawing inferences, generating hypotheses, and asking questions.

- We enable students to discover flaws and inconsistencies in their own thinking, thereby helping them identify gaps in their understanding.

- We expose students to the views of others—views that may reflect a more accurate understanding of the topics under discussion.

- To the extent that we have an ethnically diverse classroom, we can help students discover how different cultures may interpret the world in different, yet perhaps equally valid, ways. (L. M. Anderson, 1993; Banks, 1991; Barnes, 1976; Fosnot, 1996; Hatano & Inagaki, 1993; E. H. Hiebert & Raphael, 1996; Webb & Palincsar, 1996)

You will find three specific strategies for promoting classroom dialogue— classroom discussions, cooperative learning, and reciprocal teaching—in Chapter 13.

Classroom dialogues provide an additional benefit to us as teachers. By listening carefully to students' comments and questions, we can identify and remediate any misconceptions they may have developed—misconceptions that might otherwise interfere with their ability to acquire further knowledge and skills (Presseisen & Beyer, 1994; Sosniak & Stodolsky, 1994).

Using Authentic Activities

Many theorists suggest that students can construct a more useful and productive knowledge base if they learn classroom subject matter within the context of **authentic activities**—activities similar to those they will eventually encounter in the outside world. For example, rather than have students practice writing skills through short, artificial writing exercises, we might ask them to write stories or essays or to send letters to real people. Students' writing improves both in quality and in quantity when they engage in such authentic writing tasks (E. H. Hiebert & Fisher, 1992). Likewise, rather than have students develop map interpretation skills (e.g., interpreting symbols, scale, and latitude and longitude) by answering a series of unrelated questions in a workbook, we might instead have them construct their own maps, asking them to choose appropriate symbols and scale and to integrate information about latitude and longitude. Although students may sometimes feel a bit overwhelmed by the complexity of such map-making activities, they are likely to gain a more complete understanding of how to use and interpret maps effectively than is true for those who simply engage in workbook exercises (Gregg & Leinhardt, 1994).

Incorporate classroom subject matter into "real world" activities.

As teachers, we can identify authentic activities related to virtually any area of the curriculum. For example, we might ask students to:

Give an oral report	Converse in a foreign lanuage
Write an editorial	Play in an athletic event
Participate in a debate	Complete an art project
Find information in the library	Perform in a concert
Conduct an experiment	Tutor a classmate
Graph data	Make a videotape
Construct a chart or model	Perform a workplace routine
Create and distribute a class newsletter	Develop a "home page" for the Internet

By placing classroom activities in such "real world" contexts, we help our students discover the reasons why they are learning academic subject matter; we may also increase the likelihood that, later on, they will actually use the information and skills we have taught them (A. Collins, Brown, & Newman, 1989; De Corte, Greer, & Vershaffel, 1996). We will revisit the importance of authentic activities within the context of our discussion of *situated learning* and *transfer* in Chapter 8, and we will consider a related topic—*authentic assessment*—in Chapter 14.

Many cognitive psychologists advocate authentic activities—activities similar to those that students will eventually encounter in the outside world.

Creating Cognitive Apprenticeships

In **cognitive apprenticeships,** teachers and students work together to accomplish a complex, challenging task—one the students would not be able to accomplish on their own (J. S. Brown et al., 1989; Griffin & Griffin, 1994; Rogoff, 1990). Throughout the task, teachers verbalize their thoughts, making the specific cognitive processes necessary for accomplishing the task easily observable and thereby enabling students to incorporate such cognitive processes into their own thinking.

As an example, imagine that you and your students have certain opinions about issues being addressed in an upcoming election and that you all agree to communicate your opinions by writing a group letter to the editor of the local newspaper. Together you brainstorm about different strategies for expressing your thoughts in a logical and persuasive manner, and then you translate the best strategy into an outline of the major points that you, as a class, want to make in the letter. In doing these things with your students, you demonstrate the value of both brainstorming and outlining as strategies for developing a persuasive essay.

As another example, imagine that you are conducting a science experiment with your students. You might ask yourself and your students, and then jointly answer, questions such as these:

In what ways has the culture in this petri dish changed since yesterday?

How can we measure a motorized vehicle's rate of acceleration in an objective way?

As you work together with students on a difficult task, verbalize your thoughts about how best to accomplish the task, and encourage students to do likewise.

When we add these two chemicals together and then heat them, how can we be sure the *heat* is bringing about the change we see, rather than some other variable?

If the term *scaffolding* doesn't ring a bell, refer back to the discussion of Vygotsky's theory in Chapter 2.

If you have already read Chapter 2, then you have already encountered cognitive apprenticeships in a different context: Such apprenticeships are an excellent example of the *scaffolding* that Vygotsky suggests is so essential for cognitive development. In addition, cognitive apprenticeships illustrate the social nature of knowledge construction: Teachers and students work together to make sense of, and perhaps to simplify, a difficult task.

INTO THE CLASSROOM
Promoting Knowledge Construction

Focus on an in-depth understanding of a few key ideas, rather than cover many topics superficially.

> A teacher tells his class, "As we study the geography of South America, we aren't going to worry about memorizing a lot of place names. Instead, we will look at how topography and climate have influenced the economic and cultural development of different regions of the continent."

Provide opportunities for experimentation.

> A teacher has students experiment with clay and water to discover the principle that a certain quantity of a solid displaces the same amount of water regardless of the shape that the solid takes.

Expose students to the ways in which others have interpreted the world.

> A teacher has students read poetry from a variety of countries and cultures.

Promote classroom discussions in which students can freely exchange their views.

> A teacher asks students to speculate on how the Japanese people must have felt after the atomic bomb was dropped over Hiroshima.

Include authentic activities in the curriculum.

> A teacher has students develop and cook a menu that includes all the basic food groups.

PROMOTING CONCEPTUAL CHANGE

In addition to helping our students construct new knowledge, we may also need to correct misconceptions they currently have about the world; in other words, we may need to promote **conceptual change.** Unfortunately, research indicates that students often hold quite adamantly to their misconceptions even when given considerable instruction that explicitly contradicts those misconceptions (S. Carey, 1986; Chinn & Brewer, 1993; Eaton et al., 1984; Kyle & Shymansky, 1989; Roth & Anderson, 1988).

Psychologists have identified several principles regarding how conceptual change may come about—principles that can guide us as we face the often difficult challenge of helping our students correct those stubborn misconceptions that they hold about the world:

- Conceptual change is more likely to occur when existing misconceptions are identified before instruction begins.

- Students are most likely to revise their current beliefs about the world when they become convinced that these beliefs are incorrect.

- Students must be motivated to learn correct explanations for the phenomena they observe.

- Some misconceptions may persist despite instruction designed to contradict them.

These principles are summarized in Table 7–2. Let's look at the implications of each one.

PRINCIPLES/ASSUMPTIONS

Table 7–2   Principles for Promoting Conceptual Change

PRINCIPLE	EDUCATIONAL IMPLICATION	EXAMPLE
Conceptual change is more likely to occur when existing misconceptions are identified before instruction begins.	We should check for any existing misconceptions that students may have about a topic.	We can probe students' understanding and possible misunderstanding of a topic through a short pretest or a series of discussion questions.
Students are most likely to revise their current beliefs about the world when they become convinced that these beliefs are incorrect.	We can show students how new information contradicts the things they currently believe.	We can ask students to make predictions based on their current beliefs, and then give a demonstration that yields the opposite result.
Students must be motivated to learn correct explanations for the phenomena they observe.	We should give students reasons to *want* to revise their thinking about a topic.	We can show students how a correct understanding has implications for their real-world interests—for example, how the laws of physics relate to auto mechanics.
Some misconceptions may persist despite instruction designed to contradict them.	We should monitor students' understanding both during and after a lesson.	We must carefully scrutinize what students say and write for signs of partial or total misunderstandings.

Identifying Existing Misconceptions Before Instruction Begins

As teachers, we can more easily address students' misconceptions when we know what those misconceptions are (Kyle & Shymansky, 1989; Putnam, 1992; Roth & Anderson, 1988; Vosniadou & Brewer, 1987). Thus, we should probably begin any new topic with some sort of assessment of students' current beliefs about the topic; for example, we might ask them questions, give them a task to perform, or administer a brief pretest. As you gain experience teaching a particular topic year after year, you may eventually find that you can anticipate what your students' prior beliefs and misbeliefs about that topic are likely to be.

Convincing Students That Existing Beliefs Are Inadequate

Show students how new information contradicts the things they currently believe.

As teachers, we can more effectively promote conceptual change when we show our students how new information contradicts things they currently believe and when we explain or demonstrate why their existing conceptions are inadequate for explaining the phenomena they observe. To accomplish these ends, we might use strategies such as these:

- Asking questions that challenge students' current beliefs

- Describing an event or phenomenon that students cannot adequately explain by using their current understanding of the world

- Explaining *why* particular events or phenomena occur (describing cause-effect relationships)

- Showing how the correct explanation of an event or phenomenon is more plausible (how it makes more sense) than anything that students themselves can offer

- Engaging students in discussions of the pros and cons of various explanations of an event or phenomenon

- Pointing out, explicitly, the differences between students' beliefs and "reality" (Brophy, 1992a; Chinn & Brewer, 1993; McKeown & Beck, 1990; Posner, Strike, Hewson, & Gertzog, 1982; Prawat, 1989; Roth, 1990; Roth & Anderson, 1988; Slusher & Anderson, 1996; Vosniadou & Brewer, 1987)

Promote meaningful learning, especially when new material contradicts existing misconceptions.

We should note here that our students will only notice inconsistencies between new information and their previously acquired beliefs if they try to make connections between the "new" and the "old"—in other words, if they engage in meaningful learning (Chinn & Brewer, 1993; O. Lee & Anderson, 1993; Pintrich et al., 1993). In Chapter 6, we found that students who engage in meaningful rather than rote learning acquire new information more quickly and retrieve it more easily. Here we see an additional reason to encourage meaningful learning: It helps "undo" existing misconceptions.

Motivating Students to Learn Correct Explanations

Students are most likely to engage in meaningful learning and to undergo conceptual change regarding their knowledge about classroom subject matter when they are motivated to do so (O. Lee & Anderson, 1993; Pintrich et al., 1993). For example, students should be interested in the subject matter they are studying, set their sights on mastering it, and believe that they are actually *capable* of mastering it (Pintrich et al., 1993). In Chapter 11, we will identify a variety of strategies we can use to encourage such motivation in our students.

Give students reasons to *want* to revise their thinking about a topic.

Monitoring for Persistent Misconceptions

Because of students' natural tendency to reinterpret new information within the context of what they already know and believe about the world, some misconceptions may be especially resistant to change despite our best efforts. These misconceptions are sometimes blatantly incorrect; at other times, they may be sort-of-but-not-quite correct. As an example of the latter situation, students sometimes define the concept *transparent* as "something you can see through" (Roth & Anderson, 1988). Although such a definition is consistent with how we speak about transparency on a day-to-day basis, it may nevertheless reflect the erroneous belief that sight originates with the eye and goes outward to and through the transparent object. *Transparent* is more accurately defined as "something light passes through."

Throughout a lesson, we should continue to check students' beliefs about the topic at hand, looking for subtle signs that their understanding is not quite accurate and giving corrective feedback when necessary. As an example, consider this classroom discussion about vision and opaque objects:

Monitor students' understanding throughout a lesson.

Ms. Ramsey:	[Projects an overhead transparency on the wall] Why can't the girl see around the wall?
Annie:	The girl can't see around the wall because the wall is opaque.
Ms. Ramsey:	What do you mean when you say the wall is opaque?
Annie:	*You can't see through it. It is solid.*
Brian:	(calling out) The rays are what can't go through the wall.
Ms. Ramsey:	I like that answer better. Why is it better?
Brian:	The rays of light bounce off the car and go to the wall. They can't go through the wall.
Ms. Ramsey:	Where are the light rays coming from originally?
Students:	The sun.
Annie:	*The girl can't see the car because she is not far enough out.*
Ms. Ramsey:	So you think her position is what is keeping her from seeing it. (She flips down the overlay with the answer.) Who was better?
Students:	Brian.
Ms. Ramsey:	(to Annie) Would she be able to see if she moved out beyond the wall?
Annie:	Yes.
Ms. Ramsey:	Why?
Annie:	*The wall is blocking her view.*
Ms. Ramsey:	Is it blocking her view? What is it blocking?
Student:	Light rays.
Ms. Ramsey:	Light rays that are doing what?

<table>
<tr><td>Annie:</td><td>If the girl moves out beyond the wall, then the light rays that bounce off the car are not being blocked. (Roth & Anderson, 1988, pp. 129–130)</td></tr>
</table>

Notice how Ms. Ramsey is not satisfied with Annie's original answer that the wall is opaque. With further questioning, it becomes clear that Annie's understanding of opaqueness is off target: She talks about the girl being unable to "see through" the wall, rather than about light's inability to pass through the wall. With Ms. Ramsey's continuing insistence on precise language, Annie eventually begins to bring light rays into her explanation (Roth & Anderson, 1988).

Ask students to apply what they have learned.

Assessment of students' comprehension is important *after* a lesson as well. We are more likely to detect misconceptions when we ask students to *use* and *apply* the things they have learned (as Ms. Ramsey does in the conversation I just described), rather than just to spit back facts, definitions, and formulas memorized in a rote fashion (Roth, 1990; Roth & Anderson, 1988). For example, if we want students in a social studies class to understand that there are usually valid and compelling perspectives on both sides of any controversial issue, rather than to believe that controversy is always a matter of the "good guys" versus the "bad guys," we might ask them to engage in a debate in which they must convincingly present a perspective contrary to their own beliefs. If students in a creative writing class have previously learned that complete sentences are always essential in good writing and we want to convince them otherwise, we might ask them to find examples of how incomplete sentences are sometimes used quite effectively in the short stories and novels they have read.

INTO THE CLASSROOM
Promoting Conceptual Change

Check for prior misconceptions that may lead students to interpret new information incorrectly.

> Before beginning a unit on the seasons and the earth's revolution around the sun, a teacher asks her students, "Why does the sun rise and set each day?" She listens to students' answers for possible indications that some may erroneously believe that the sun revolves around the earth.

Show how new information contradicts the things that students currently believe.

> When several students express their stereotypical beliefs that new immigrants to the country are "lazy," their teacher invites several recent immigrants to visit the class and describe their experiences in adapting to a new culture.

Ask questions that challenge students' misconceptions.

> A physics teacher has just begun a unit on inertia. Several students assert that when a baseball is thrown in the air, some force continues to act on that ball, pushing it upward until the ball begins to drop. The teacher asks, "What force in the air could possibly be pushing that ball upward once it leaves the thrower's hand?"

Show students how the alternative explanation you present is more plausible and useful than their original misconception.

> The same physics teacher points out that the baseball continues to move upward even though no force is pushing it in that direction. He explains the concept *inertia* within this context: The ball only needs a force to get it *started* in a particular direction. Once the force has been exerted, other forces (gravity and air resistance) alter the ball's speed and direction.

Give students corrective feedback about responses that reflect misunderstanding.

> An educational psychology teacher says to an undergraduate student, "Hmmm, you just told me that you could learn a foreign language by playing audiotapes while you sleep. But didn't we just discover last week that attention is essential for effective information processing?"

When pointing out misconceptions that students have, do so in a way that maintains their self-esteem.

> When a student expresses an erroneous belief, her teacher says, "You know, many of my students come to class thinking exactly that. It's a very logical thing to think. But the truth of the matter is . . . ."

CONSIDERING DIVERSITY IN CONSTRUCTIVE PROCESSES

EXPERIENCING FIRSTHAND
Revisiting David

Earlier in the chapter, you read a story about David—a man who went to the cleaners, to work, and eventually to a restaurant. Let's find out how well you can remember parts of that story. *Without looking back at the story,* answer these five multiple-choice questions:

1. At the cleaners, David
   a. tapped on the window glass to get the clerk to open the store.
   b. struggled to get the large bundle of clothing into the store.
   c. waited until the clerk opened the store.

2. When David arrived at the office building where he works, he
   a. walked quietly into his office.
   b. hurried through the crowded corridor.
   c. pushed his way past the other people waiting to go through the revolving door.

3. When David arrived at work, he
   a. poured a cup of coffee.
   b. made a fresh pot of coffee.
   c. checked his calendar for appointments.

4. When David made his first phone call during lunch on Friday, he
   a. was embarrassed because he made a dialing error.
   b. immediately hung up without talking to the man who answered.
   c. apologized for dialing the wrong number.

5. When David arrived at the restaurant Friday evening, he
   a. sat at a corner table because he was uncomfortable about being alone in a restaurant.
   b. found an empty table and drank a cup of coffee.
   c. had to wait for his date, who was late.

(Test items courtesy of D. Halpern)

Could you remember enough details from the story about David to answer the questions correctly? (The correct answers are 1–c, 2–b, 3–a, 4–c, 5–b.)

The story you read about David was part of a longer story used in a research study by Halpern (1985). High school students read a story about two typical days in the life of a character named either "David" or "Linda"; the stories were identical except for the name and gender of the main character. The students later answered multiple-choice and true-false questions about events in the story. When students responded to questions incorrectly, they often chose answers consistent with gender stereotypes about how men and women typically behave. For example, students reading about a male character were likely to indicate that, upon arriving at the cleaners, David "tapped on the window glass to get the clerk to open the store," whereas students reading about a female character were more likely to answer that Linda "struggled to get the large bundle of clothing into the store." (Halpern identified these responses to the questions as male-stereotypical: 1–a, 2–c, 3–c, 4–b, 5–c. She identified these responses to the questions as female-stereotypical: 1–b, 2–a, 3–b, 4–a, 5–a.) In other words, students were filling in gaps in their recall with answers that were the "logical" ways for a character of a particular gender to act. Curiously, students were more likely to make stereotypical reconstruction errors if they read about a main character of the *opposite* gender; they were more apt to remember the story correctly when the story was about someone of the same gender as themselves.

Halpern's results are a good example of one of the assumptions about knowledge construction we considered earlier: *People interpret environmental events in unique, idiosyncratic ways.* Different individuals will have different knowledge bases, including different schemas and scripts, that they will use to make sense of any new situation. For example, as Halpern observed, males and females may construct different meanings regarding people's actions and motives. So, too, may students of diverse cultural backgrounds impose unique meanings on the same event. And in some situations, students from particular backgrounds may have difficulty making any sort of sense of classroom material because their knowledge base lacks the schemas and scripts necessary for understanding it; this is a principle you may have discovered firsthand when you did the *War of the Ghosts* exercise.

Why do you think someone would make more gender-stereotypical reconstruction errors about the *opposite* gender?

Remember that some students, perhaps because of diverse cultural backgrounds, may lack the schemas and scripts necessary for making sense of classroom material.

We should note, too, that as we help students construct a meaningful understanding of the world around them, we can increase their multicultural awareness by promoting *multiple constructions* of the same situation. For example, we might look at the western migration across North America during the 1700s and 1800s from two different perspectives—that of the European settlers, on the one hand, and that of the Native

Have students consider multiple perspectives of the same situation.

STUDENTS IN INCLUSIVE SETTINGS

Table 7–3   Promoting Knowledge Construction in Students with Special Educational Needs

STUDENTS WITH SPECIAL NEEDS	CHARACTERISTICS THAT THESE STUDENTS MAY EXHIBIT	CLASSROOM STRATEGIES THAT MAY BE BENEFICIAL FOR THESE STUDENTS
Students with specific cognitive or academic deficits	Possible holes in students' knowledge base that may limit meaningful understanding of some classroom topics Occasionally unusual or inappropriate interpretations of prose Occasional misinterpretations of social situations	Determine the extent to which students have prior knowledge about a new topic; remind them of what they *do* know about the topic. Monitor students' comprehension of prose; correct misinterpretations. Present alternative interpretations of others' behaviors.
Students with specific social or behavioral deficits	Frequent misinterpretations of social situations	Present alternative interpretations of others' behaviors and identify suitable courses of action based on the most reasonable interpretation of a given situation.
Students with general delays in cognitive and social functioning	Smaller knowledge base on which to draw Difficulty constructing an accurate interpretation when information is ambiguous or incomplete	Assume little if any prior knowledge about topics unless you have evidence to the contrary; remind students of what they *do* know about a topic. Present information clearly and unambiguously.
Students with advanced cognitive development	Larger knowledge base on which to draw Greater conceptual understanding of classroom material (e.g., greater understanding of cause-effect relationships) Greater ability to draw inferences	Assign challenging tasks that enable students to develop and use their advanced understanding of topics. Ask thought-provoking questions that encourage inference drawing. Match students with experienced mentors who can provide cognitive apprenticeships through which students can develop expertise in complex tasks.

Sources: Patton, Payne, Kauffman, Brown, & Payne, 1987; Piirto, 1994; Pressley, 1995; Schumaker & Hazel, 1984; Turnbull, Turnbull, Shank, & Leal, 1995; J. P. Williams, 1991.

Compiled with the assistance of Dr. Margie Garanzini-Daiber and Dr. Margaret Cohen, University of Missouri—St. Louis.

Consider how you might introduce multiple perspectives into the subject matter you will be teaching.

Americans already residing on the land, on the other. One simple way of doing this is to consider how the migrating peoples are referred to as *pioneers* or *settlers* by most United States history books, but might instead have been called *foreigners* or *invaders* by Native Americans (Banks, 1991). Ultimately, we must help our students to understand the very complex nature of human "knowledge" and to appreciate the fact that there may be several, equally valid interpretations of any single event.

Accommodating Students with Special Needs

We will see evidence of diversity in constructive processes in our students with special educational needs. To illustrate, students with learning disabilities may construct inappropriate meanings from stories they hear (Pressley, 1995; J. P. Williams, 1991). Students with emotional and behavioral disorders may construct counterproductive interpretations of social situations (e.g., Hughes, 1988); for example, they might "see" an act of aggression in an innocent gesture or "hear" an insult when none was intended. Table 7–3 contains descriptions of some patterns that researchers have found in the constructive processes of students with special needs, along with suggestions for helping these students acquire appropriate meanings from academic and social situations.

As we've noted before, all of our students—those with special needs and those without—will construct their own unique interpretations of the ideas and events they encounter in the classroom. Many of their interpretations, though perhaps different from one another, may be equally valid and appropriate. But other interpretations—for example, the belief that the earth is flat, that rote learning is more effective than meaningful learning, or that a classmate is trying to pick a fight—may interfere with students' future success in the outside world. As teachers, we must help our students interpret the world around them in ways that are likely to be productive over the long run.

CASE STUDY: *Earth-Shaking Summaries*

Ms. Jackson spends the first half hour of her seventh-grade geography class describing how earthquakes occur. She introduces the theory of *plate tectonics*— the notion that the earth's crust is made up of many separate pieces (*plates*) that rest upon a layer of hot, molten rock (the *mantle*). She explains that plates occasionally shift and rub against each other, making the immediate area shake and leaving *faults* in the earth's surface.

Her students listen attentively throughout her explanation. When she finishes, she asks whether there are any questions. Finding that there is none, she says, "Great! I'm glad you all understand. What I'd like you to do now is to take out a sheet of paper and write a paragraph answering this question: *Why do we have earthquakes?*" She has read in a professional journal that asking students to summarize what they've learned often helps them remember it better later on, and she figures that the task she's just assigned is an excellent way to encourage summarization.

Ms. Jackson collects students' papers as they leave for their next class. As she glances quickly through the stack, she is distressed by what she sees. Some of her students have provided a relatively complete and accurate description of plate

---

tectonics. But the responses of others are vague enough to make her uneasy about how thoroughly they understood her explanation; here are two examples:

Frank: The earth's crust shifts around and shakes us up.

Mitchell: Earthquakes happen when really big plates on the earth move around.

And three of her students clearly have made little sense of the lesson:

Adrienne: Scientists use technology to understand how earthquakes happen. They use computers and stuff.

Tesia: When there are earthquakes, people's plates move around the house.

Jonathan: Earthquakes aren't anybody's fault. They just happen.

Ms. Jackson sighs, clearly discouraged by the feedback she's just gotten about her lesson. "I guess I still have a lot to learn about teaching this stuff," she concludes.

- Why is Ms. Jackson not convinced that Frank and Mitchell have mastered the material? What critical aspects of the lesson did each boy omit in his response?

- What pieces of information from the lesson did Adrienne, Tesia, and Jonathan apparently use when answering Ms. Jackson's question? Can you explain their responses by using the concept of *knowledge construction*?

- What instructional strategies might Ms. Jackson have used to help her students gain a more conceptual understanding of plate tectonics?

SUMMING UP

Knowledge Construction

Many cognitive psychologists believe that individuals *construct* knowledge from their experience, rather than simply absorb it in the form that it is presented to them; the resulting "reality" they perceive is not necessarily identical to the reality of the external world. Some theorists describe the processes by which people construct their own personal understandings of the world; this perspective is sometimes called *individual constructivism*. Other theorists focus more on people's collective efforts to impose meaning on the world around them; this perspective is frequently called *social constructivism*.

Construction in Storage and Retrieval

Constructive processes may occur both when information is being received (during long-term memory storage) and when it is later recalled (during long-term memory retrieval). Students' existing knowledge and beliefs about the world influence the specific meanings they impose on information presented in the classroom.

Promoting Effective Knowledge Construction

As teachers, we can help students construct accurate interpretations of the world around them by (1) providing opportunities for them to experiment with the physical world, (2) presenting the ways that others have interpreted various phenomena over the years (e.g., through the concepts and principles of academic disciplines, through art and literature), (3) emphasizing conceptual understanding, (4) promoting dialogue, (5) using authentic activities, and (6) creating cognitive apprenticeships.

Promoting Conceptual Change

In some situations, erroneous beliefs (misconceptions) will interfere with students' ability to learn classroom subject matter accurately. We are more likely to promote conceptual change when we (1) determine what misconceptions students have prior to instruction, (2) show students that their existing beliefs are inadequate, (3) motivate them to develop a more accurate understanding of the topic in question, and (4) monitor

their written work, as well as their questions and comments in class, for any especially persistent misconceptions.

Diversity in Constructive Processes

Different students are likely to interpret classroom events and subject matter differently, in part, because they each bring diverse experiences and knowledge bases into play when trying to make sense of the things they see and hear. We can increase our students' multicultural awareness by promoting *multiple constructions* of the same situation—by encouraging them to look at events from the perspectives of different groups. At the same time, we must be on the lookout for counterproductive constructions that some of our students (including those with special needs) may derive from their classroom experiences.

KEY CONCEPTS

constructivism (p. 272)
construction (p. 274)
misconceptions (p. 277)
reconstruction error (p. 280)
schema (p. 280)

script (p. 281)
halo effect (p. 283)
individual constructivism (p. 287)
social constructivism (p. 287)
conceptual understanding (p. 290)

authentic activities (p. 292)
cognitive apprenticeship (p. 293)
conceptual change (p. 294)

Promoting Higher-Level Thinking Skills

THINKING ABOUT WHAT YOU KNOW

- How many new concepts (e.g., how much new vocabulary) do you encounter in a typical college course? What things do you do as you try to learn these concepts? Do you figure out their meanings from the contexts in which they appear? Do you look up their meanings in a dictionary or glossary? Do you try to generate your own examples of each concept?

- How often do you use the material that you learn in your college courses? Do you use it to help you learn and understand later material? Can you apply it to situations and problems that your professors give you? Can you apply it to situations and problems in your personal life?

■

IF YOU HAVE READ Chapters 6 and 7, then you have already learned a great deal about learning. For example, from the discussion of information processing in Chapter 6, you've discovered that people store new information more effectively when they relate it to things they have learned previously—that is, when they engage in such cognitive processes as meaningful learning and elaboration. From the discussion of knowledge construction in Chapter 7, you've discovered that learning may be a process of creating one's own idiosyncratic knowledge base by combining both new and old information into something that makes some sort of "sense." Let's now put to work some of the things that you know about learning. Let's see what you can learn about a new topic—the world's diminishing rain forests.

Rain Forests

Read the passage below and then answer the questions that follow it.

Rain forests are home to nearly half of all the plants, animals, and insects in the world. Tropical plants produce chocolate, nuts, tannins, fruits, gums, coffee, waxes, wood and wood products, rubber and petroleum substitutes, and ingredients found in toothpaste, pesticides, fibers, and dyes. In addition, several medical wonders of the twentieth century have come from plants found only in rain forests. These plants have been used to treat high blood pressure, Hodgkin's disease, multiple sclerosis, and Parkinson's disease. A study of the Costa Rican rain forest found that 15 percent of the plants studied had "potential as anticancer agents."

But the rain forests, which provide food and fuel for millions of people in the developing world, are increasingly losing ground. Each year, millions of the developing world's poor head into the rain forest to eke out a subsistence living on plots recently cleared for farming. Rain forest soil is usually too poor to support a farmer's crops for more than a few years, and the land is soon depleted of nutrients. Peasant farmers must then head farther into the rain forest, slashing and burning still more land for farming, and starting the cycle all over. In many cases, cattle ranchers buy up the land abandoned by peasant farmers, but after only a few years, the land is unable to support even herds of cattle.

Every day, nearly seventy-five thousand acres of rain forest disappear from the globe. In a year, twenty-seven million acres of tropical rain forest—a land area the size of Austria or Pennsylvania—vanish. (adapted from Hosmer, 1989, pp. 70–71)

1. What are three illnesses that can be treated by using rain forest plants?

2. How does peasant farming change the nature of rain forest land?

3. Why do peasants continue to farm more and more rain forest land despite the serious environmental consequences of doing so?

4. What things might be done to halt the destruction of rain forests?

5. What are the most useful ideas to be gained from the passage? ■

Which of the five questions were the easiest ones to answer? Which questions were the most *important* ones to answer? You may have found Questions 1 and 2 relatively easy because the answers were clearly stated in the passage. These two questions are **lower-level questions** concerning information actually given to you. You may have found the last three questions more difficult because you had to go beyond the information itself. To answer Question 3, you had to apply something that you know about people in general—the fact that people usually do whatever they need to do to survive—to your understanding of the peasant farmers' plight. To answer Question 4, you had to combine your prior knowledge with information in the passage to generate possible solutions to a difficult problem. And to answer Question 5, you needed to make a judgment about what information was most likely to be useful to you at a later

Unfortunately, many classes devote most of their time to lower-level learning tasks at the expense of higher-level, "thinking" tasks (Blumenfeld, 1992; Freiberg, 1987; Tobin, 1987).

point in time. Such **higher-level questions**—questions that ask us to go beyond the information actually given to us—are usually more difficult than lower-level questions. Yet these higher-level questions are often the most important ones for us to address.

Most theorists and practitioners continue to believe in the importance of having students master basic facts and skills. At the same time, they argue that students must also learn to *use* such facts and skills in a variety of contexts. Thus, the ideal school curriculum should address both lower-level and higher-level objectives (Cole, 1990; Stiggins, 1994).

In the preceding two chapters on information processing and knowledge construction, we focused on how people learn and remember the information they receive. In this chapter, we will focus on some of the complex ways in which people use that information to interpret and respond to the situations and tasks they encounter in their daily lives. We will first look at how people form *concepts*—in other words, at how they categorize objects and events. We will then consider how and under what conditions people are able to apply (*transfer*) their knowledge to new situations and use it in *problem solving*. Finally, we will examine two related topics—people's knowledge and beliefs about their own learning processes and capabilities (*metacognition*) and the ways they translate such knowledge and beliefs into various *study strategies*. Throughout the chapter, we will identify numerous strategies through which we can facilitate such complex cognitive processes in our students.

By the end of the chapter, you should be able to:

1. List several factors influencing students' ability to learn new concepts, explain the process of concept learning from three theoretical perspectives, and identify several ways in which you can promote more effective concept learning in your classroom.

2. List several factors and conditions affecting students' ability to transfer their knowledge to new situations, and explain how you can teach classroom subject matter in such a way that your students will be able to apply it effectively.

3. Use an information processing perspective to describe the conditions under which students are most likely to solve problems successfully, and identify several teaching practices that facilitate successful problem solving.

4. Explain the role that students' metacognitive knowledge plays in their approach to learning tasks and, ultimately, in their academic achievement.

5. Identify a variety of effective study strategies, and describe how you can help students acquire and use such strategies.

CASE STUDY: *A Question of Speed*

Mary is studying for tomorrow's exam in her physics class. As she looks over her class notes, she finds the following statement in her notebook:

Velocity equals acceleration times time.

She also finds a formula expressing the same idea:

$v = a \times t$

Mary dutifully memorizes the statement and formula until she knows both by heart.

The following day, Mary encounters this problem on her physics exam:

An automotive engineer has designed a car that can reach a speed of 50 miles per hour within 5 seconds. What is the car's rate of acceleration?

She puzzles over the problem for several minutes. She thinks about a car reaching 50 miles per hour: Is this the car's acceleration, its velocity, or something else altogether? She realizes that she doesn't know the difference between acceleration and velocity. She finally turns in her exam with this and several similar questions unanswered.

She later confides to a classmate, "I really blew that test today, but I don't know why. I mean, I really studied *hard!*"

- How did Mary study for her physics exam? What things did she *not* do as she studied—things that might have led to better performance?

- If you were Mary's physics teacher, how might you help Mary study more effectively for the next exam?

FACILITATING CONCEPT LEARNING

One critical mistake that Mary made in studying for her exam was not mastering the concepts *velocity* and *acceleration.* Although she memorized "velocity equals acceleration times time," she never really learned what velocity and acceleration *are.* (*Velocity* is the speed at which an object travels in a particular direction. *Acceleration* is the rate with which an object's velocity changes.) As a result, she was unable to apply her knowledge in any meaningful way.

A **concept** is a way of mentally grouping or categorizing objects or events in one's world. Students learn thousands of concepts during their school years. They learn some concepts quickly and easily. They acquire others more gradually, continuing to revise them over time. Like Mary, students often have a "sort-of" knowledge of concepts: They have a rough idea of what a concept is but cannot always identify examples and nonexamples of the concept with complete accuracy. Here are other instances of such "sort-of" knowledge.

- Lisa has recently learned to identify circles, triangles, squares, and rectangles. But she hasn't yet learned that all squares are rectangles as well. Her current conception of *rectangles* is limited to nonsquares—to figures whose widths are unequal to their lengths.

- Lonnigan thinks of an *animal* as something with four legs and fur. He is quite surprised when his teacher says that fish, birds, and insects are also animals.

- Luis learns that a *noun* is "a person, place, or thing." On the basis of this definition, he classifies words like *you* and *me* as nouns because they refer to people. Only later, when Luis learns about other parts of speech, does he realize that *you* and *me* are pronouns, rather than nouns.

- Linda knows that the term *academic freedom* refers to the fact that her professors can present any theory or perspective in class without fear of losing their jobs. But one of her economics professors spends most class sessions talking about football, rather than about supply and demand. Linda is upset at how little she is learning in class but isn't sure whether the concept *academic freedom* means that her professor can legitimately talk about football in an economics class.

In some cases, students **undergeneralize** a concept: They have too narrow a view as to which objects or events are included. Lisa's current conception of a *rectangle* is an undergeneralization because she denies that squares can be rectangles. And Lonnigan undergeneralizes when he excludes fish, birds, and insects from his concept of *animal*. On other occasions, students may **overgeneralize** a concept: They may identify objects and events as examples of a concept when, in fact, they are nonexamples. For example, Luis overgeneralizes when he identifies *you* and *me* as nouns.

How can we help our students acquire an accurate understanding of the concepts they encounter in the classroom? To answer this question, we must consider how students learn concepts in the first place.

If you have read Chapter 7, then you may recall Annie's sort-of-but-not-quite understanding of a *transparent* object: She defined it as "something you can see through," rather than as "something light passes through."

Defining Basic Concepts in Concept Learning

Central to our discussion of concept learning are several key concepts:

- Positive and negative instances
- Defining, correlational, and irrelevant features

These concepts are summarized in Table 8–1.

Positive and Negative Instances

When we talk about specific examples of a concept, we are talking about **positive instances** of that concept. A goldfish is a positive instance of *animal,* a □ is a positive instance of *rectangle,* and *Manitoba* is a positive instance of *noun.*

Those things that are *not* examples of a concept are **negative instances.** A palm tree is a negative instance of *animal,* a △ is a negative instance of *rectangle,* and *you* is a negative instance of *noun.*

In our case study at the beginning of the chapter, Mary failed to recognize that "50 miles per hour" is a positive instance of *velocity.* Students haven't completely learned a concept until they can correctly identify all positive and negative instances—that is, until they can accurately draw the line between what things are examples of the concept and what things are not. Some students may reveal incomplete mastery of a concept by either undergeneralizing or overgeneralizing—by failing to recognize some of its positive instances, on the one hand, or by mistakenly classifying negative instances as being examples of the concept, on the other.

Check students' understanding of a concept by asking them to identify positive and negative instances. Be on the lookout for "sort-of" knowledge of concepts—that is, for instances of undergeneralization or overgeneralization.

Defining, Correlational, and Irrelevant Features

A circle must be round, a square must have four equal sides connected at ninety-degree angles, and an animal must be a consumer of food (rather than produce its own food through photosynthesis). Here we see some **defining features** of the concepts *circle,*

Table 8–1 Basic Concepts in Concept Learning

BASIC CONCEPT	DEFINITION	EXAMPLES		EDUCATIONAL IMPLICATION
Instances				
Positive	Example of the concept	Shark is a positive instance of *fish.*	An oboe is a positive instance of *woodwind.*	Present positive instances of a concept.
Negative	Nonexample of the concept	Porpoise is a negative instance of *fish.*	A trumpet is a negative instance of *woodwind.*	Present negative instances to show what a concept is *not.*
Features				
Defining	Characteristic present in all positive instances	Four lines and four right angles are present in all *rectangles.*	Ice capable of movement is found in all *glaciers.*	Describe a concept in terms of defining features.
Correlational	Characteristic often present but non-essential	A discrepancy between width and length is characteristic of many *rectangles.*	*Glaciers* are usually found closer to the North and South Poles than to the equator.	Point out that certain characteristics, though frequently found, are not always present.
Irrelevant	Characteristic unrelated to concept membership	A *rectangle* can be large or small; size is irrelevant.	*Glaciers* can be found above or below sea level (provided that they are on dry land); elevation is irrelevant.	Point out that some characteristics of the examples given are irrelevant.

square, and *animal.* Defining features are characteristics that must be present in all positive instances of a concept.

Students are most likely to have an accurate understanding of a concept when they know its defining features. As an example, consider this situation:

> A father goes to work. On the way home from work in the evening he stops at a bar to have a drink. His friends there are drunkards and he becomes a drunkard too. Is he still a father? (Saltz, 1971, p. 28)

Most eight-year-old children deny that a drunkard can still be a father (Saltz, 1971). Their response reflects their ignorance about the defining features of the concept *father.* Rather than recognize that fatherhood is defined simply in terms of a biological or adoptive relationship, many young children believe that a defining feature of fatherhood is "goodness," so a "bad" drunkard is automatically disqualified.

"Goodness" is a **correlational feature** of fatherhood—a feature present in many fathers but not essential for concept membership. Similarly, fur and four legs are present on many of the animals that children see at home and in storybooks and so are correlational features of animals. And most rectangles have widths different from their lengths; "nonsquareness" is therefore a correlational feature of rectangles.

Still other characteristics of objects and events—**irrelevant features**—are unrelated to qualifications for concept membership. For example, when we identify an object as being a circle or noncircle, we don't worry about whether the object is red, yellow, or chartreuse. Color is an irrelevant feature for the concept *circle*. And when we decide whether something is an animal, we don't ask how big that thing is. Size is, for the most part, an irrelevant feature for the concept *animal* (although note that we haven't seen one as big as a house since dinosaur days).

When children begin to learn a particular concept, they are often led astray by correlational features, thinking that such features are essential for concept membership (Keil, 1989; Mervis, 1987). Thus, it is not surprising to find Lisa omitting squares from her concept of *rectangles* because most rectangles have widths unequal to their lengths. Nor is it unusual for Lonnigan to exclude fish and birds from his concept of *animals:* Fur and four legs have undoubtedly characterized many of the critters that the people around him have specifically labeled as "animals." The trick in learning a concept is to discover which characteristics *must* be present in positive instances.

Fur and four legs are features of many of the animals that young children encounter and so may be misconstrued as defining features of the concept *animal*.

Examining Factors Affecting Concept Learning

Children seem to learn some concepts—such as *milk, red,* and *circle*—quickly and accurately. They have greater difficulty learning other concepts—such as *plant* and *animal*—to a point where they can readily identify all positive and negative instances. And their difficulties with very abstract concepts—such as *academic freedom* and *intelligence*—may continue well into the adult years.

A number of factors affect the ease or difficulty with which people learn new concepts. Among the most influential ones are these:

- The salience (obviousness) and concreteness of defining features

- The availability of a definition

- The presentation of positive instances

- The presentation of negative instances

- The simultaneous versus sequential presentation of positive and negative instances

Salience and Concreteness of Defining Features

What makes *red* red? What are its defining features? And what are the defining features for the concepts *three, plant,* and *intelligence*? Some concepts have **salient** defining features—features that are obvious and easy to notice. For example, the defining feature of *red*—a particular range of light wavelengths—is easily seen by anyone who isn't color-blind. The defining feature of *three* is almost as obvious: You need one of something, and then another one, and then only one more. But what about the defining feature of *plant*? The process of photosynthesis is not readily observable. Instead, we are more apt to notice other characteristics about plants (e.g., that they have leaves, that they grow in gardens)—characteristics that are correlational rather than defining features. And what about the concept *intelligence*? This concept's defining features are even more difficult to identify; in fact, as you have already learned if you've read the discussion of individual differences in Chapter 4, psychologists don't even agree as to what the defining features of intelligence are!

Concepts are most easily learned when they have defining features that are salient and concrete ones. Concepts are harder to learn when their defining features are nonsalient, abstract, or difficult to pin down. Children, especially younger ones, are often misled by correlational or irrelevant features that are more obvious than the defining features (Anglin, 1977; Ausubel et al., 1978; Keil, 1989). For example, if you have read Chapter 3, then you may remember how my son Jeff, when he was six years old, defined a *friend* as someone "to play with." Jeff focused on something about his friends that he could easily observe. In contrast, my daughter Tina, as a twelve-year-old, more accurately defined a friend as someone "you can trust." Trustworthiness is a far more abstract feature—and therefore a less salient one—than "playing."

As teachers, we can help our students master new concepts by making defining features as salient and concrete as possible. For example, if we want to teach the concept *insect,* we can present a simplified illustration of an insect with its defining features, such as three body parts and three pairs of legs, highlighted in bold black lines. At the same time, we can downplay other, nonessential characteristics that students might see—for example, the color of the insect or the presence of wings.

Availability of a Definition

Not surprisingly, people tend to learn a concept more easily when they are told what its defining features are—in other words, when they are given a definition (e.g., R. M. Gagné, 1985; M. D. Merrill & Tennyson, 1977; R. D. Tennyson & Cocchiarella, 1986). Definitions are particularly valuable when a concept's defining features are nonsalient or abstract. Children can usually learn what a *circle* is and what *red* means even without a definition because roundness and redness are fairly obvious characteristics. But the defining features of *father* and *plant* are far less salient; for concepts like these, a definition can be very helpful.

As teachers, then, we should be sure to give students definitions of the concepts we want them to learn. But we should also remember that a definition is only useful to the extent that students understand it—that is, to the extent that the concept is defined in terms of other concepts that students already know (R. M. Gagné, 1985).

Presentation of Positive Instances

Imagine that a girl who speaks no English has just immigrated to this country. You want to teach this girl the word *red.* What might you do to show her what red means? No

Make defining features salient.

Give definitions that include defining features.

Are definitions likely to be effective when students learn them at a rote level? Why or why not?

doubt you would point to a number of different red objects—perhaps a ball, a pencil, a shirt, a brick—each time saying, "Red." People typically learn a concept more easily when they are shown several positive instances (Barringer & Gholson, 1979; R. D. Tennyson & Cocchiarella, 1986).

Ideally, positive instances should be as different from one another as possible so that they illustrate a concept's entire range. For example, if we limit our examples of *animal* to dogs, cats, cows, and horses, students will understandably draw the conclusion that all animals have four legs and fur (a case of undergeneralization). But if we also present goldfish, robins, beetles, earthworms, and people as positive instances, children are more likely to realize that animals can, in fact, look very different from one another and that not all of them have legs or fur. Thus, we should present as many examples of a concept, including as many *different* examples, as space and time constraints allow (M. D. Merrill & Tennyson, 1978; R. D. Tennyson & Cocchiarella, 1986).

Present a variety of positive instances to illustrate the concept's entire range.

Presentation of Negative Instances

It is certainly more helpful to see what a concept *is* than what it *isn't*. At the same time, students benefit from seeing negative instances of a concept, particularly those instances that are "near misses" (Winston, 1973). To learn what *red* is, the non-English-speaking child can be shown such similar colors as orange and purple and be told that they are "not red." Similarly, when Jeff is playing with someone who continually wants to fight and refuses to share, he can be told, "This boy is not a *friend*." And when student teachers observe a child generate twenty unusual uses for a brick, their educational psychology instructor might tell them that such behavior reflects *creativity,* not intelligence. In the absence of negative instances of a concept, students may overgeneralize a concept—for example, by classifying orange things as "red" or by perceiving creative behavior as "intelligent." By presenting negative instances, including the near misses, we minimize the extent to which such overgeneralization is likely to occur.

Present negative instances to show what a concept is *not*.

Simultaneous Versus Sequential Presentation of Instances

Children learn most concepts through their encounters with a variety of positive and negative instances one by one over a period of weeks, months, or years. In other words, they typically encounter positive and negative instances *sequentially.* Research tells us,

Present positive and negative instances simultaneously.

Mammals

Nonmammals

Students learn concepts more easily when they are shown numerous positive and negative instances simultaneously.

however, that people learn concepts more quickly and easily when they see numerous positive and negative instances all at once, in a *simultaneous* fashion (Bourne, Ekstrand, & Dominowski, 1971; R. M. Gagné, 1985). For example, students will probably learn what *three* means more quickly if they see several sets of three while also seeing sets of two and four. They will learn *noun* more readily when they see both nouns (e.g., *book, girl, Manitoba, freedom*) and non-nouns (e.g., *me, you, pretty, see*) at once. And they will learn what *mammals* are if they consider a variety of mammals (e.g., dogs, squirrels, people, dolphins) along with similar-looking nonmammals (e.g., lizards, frogs, birds, and fish).

Applying Theories of Concept Learning

How do people learn concepts? Over the years, psychologists have proposed a variety of explanations for concept learning. Let's look at theoretical explanations based on each of the following:

- Hypothesis testing

- Prototypes

- Mental "theories"

Hypothesis Testing

■ EXPERIENCING FIRSTHAND
Squerkles

Figure 8–1 shows a bird's-eye view of some positive and negative instances of a lizardlike creature known as a *squerkle.* Before you read any further, look at Figure 8–1 and see whether you can figure out what defines a squerkle. ■

D id you have other hypotheses about squerkles that I haven't mentioned here? If so, what evidence led you to formulate those hypotheses?

When you were trying to learn the concept *squerkle,* you may have noticed yourself forming various hypotheses about its defining features. For example, when you saw four pointy-nosed squerkles and two round-nosed nonsquerkles on the top row, you may have thought that nose shape determines whether a critter is a squerkle. But then you would have found a pointy-nosed nonsquerkle and a round-nosed squerkle, thus squashing that hypothesis. And perhaps you thought that all squerkles had black eyes, or at least you thought so until you reached the bottom row. I hope that you eventually discovered the defining feature of a squerkle: horizontal lines on either the body or the tail. Black eyes and pointy noses are correlational features of squerkles: Most squerkles have them, and only a few nonsquerkles have them. Other characteristics, such as dots, tail length, and number of toes, are features totally irrelevant to squerkleness.

An early theory (Bruner, Goodnow, & Austin, 1956) describes concept learning as a process similar to one that you just went through: People form hypotheses about a concept's defining features and then test them against the positive and negative instances they encounter. As new examples disprove a particular hypothesis, people continue to revise their idea of what a concept is. For example, if Lonnigan encounters only dogs and cats as positive instances of *animal,* he may easily conclude that an animal has fur and four legs. But when he is told that chickens, ants, and snakes are also animals, he will have to form a new hypothesis about what animals are—perhaps that animals are moving things. And when he is told that cars and trains are *not* animals, he will have to revise his thinking once again. By providing a variety of positive and negative in-

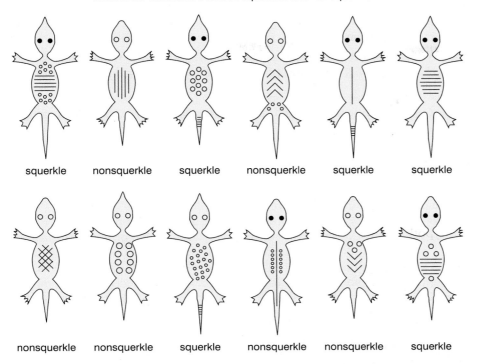

What is the difference between squerkles and nonsquerkles?

squerkle   nonsquerkle   squerkle   nonsquerkle   squerkle   squerkle

nonsquerkle   nonsquerkle   squerkle   nonsquerkle   nonsquerkle   squerkle

Figure 8–1   Learning the Concept Squerkle

stances of concepts, we enable students to refine their hypotheses about—and hence to develop a more accurate understanding of—those concepts.

Knowing that our students' hypotheses will not always be correct ones, we should check their knowledge of a concept by giving them numerous possible examples and asking them to identify the positive instances they see among those examples. For instance, to check students' understanding of *rectangle,* we might show them squares, nonsquare rectangles, triangles, pentagons, and hexagons; those students who have mastered the concept will accurately identify all squares and nonsquare rectangles as positive instances and reject the other shapes.

We can further check students' knowledge of concepts by asking them to generate their own examples. If they have formed an incorrect hypothesis about a particular concept, they may very well give us incorrect examples (e.g., remember Luis's identification of *you* and *me* as *nouns*). By giving feedback as to which examples are correct and which are not and by telling students *why* examples are or are not correct, we can help them develop an increasingly more accurate understanding of the concepts they need to learn.

The hypothesis-testing theory of concept learning is based on the idea that a concept can actually be delineated in terms of specific defining features. But what if the defining features of a particular concept are too subtle or too abstract for children to identify, such as "food production," a defining feature of *plants*? And what if defining features are extremely difficult to pin down, such as those for *intelligence*? In such cases, another theory—one based on *prototypes*—may better help us understand how people learn concepts despite such difficulties.

Ask students to identify positive instances of a concept from among numerous possibilities.

Ask students to generate their own examples of a concept.

Prototypes

■   EXPERIENCING FIRSTHAND
Visual Images

Close your eyes and picture a *bird.* Take a good look at the visual image you create. Now close your eyes again and picture a *vehicle.* Once again, look closely at your image.   ■

What came to mind when I asked you to picture a bird? If you are like most people, then you probably visualized a relatively small bird, perhaps one about the size of a robin or sparrow, rather than a penguin or an ostrich. And what came to mind when I asked you to picture a *vehicle?* You probably thought of a car or truck, rather than a skateboard or an elevator.

For many concepts, people seem to develop a mental **prototype:** They form an idea (perhaps a visual image) of a "typical" example (Rosch, 1973a, 1973b, 1977; R. D. Tennyson & Cocchiarella, 1986). Prototypes are usually based on the positive instances that we encounter most frequently. For example, we see small birds such as robins and sparrows more frequently than we see large birds such as penguins and ostriches. And we see cars and trucks more frequently than we see skateboards and elevators.

Once people have formed a prototype for a particular concept, they compare new objects and events against that prototype. Objects or events similar to the prototype are easily identified as positive instances of the concept. Objects or events very different from the prototype are sometimes mistakenly identified as negative instances of the concept. As an illustration, let's say that your prototype of an *animal* looks something like a small dog (see the prototype on the left-hand side of Figure 8–2 as a possibility). How likely are you to recognize that the following critters are also animals?

horse	whale
grizzly bear	earthworm
frog	sponge
person	

The more different the critter is from your doglike prototype, the less likely you are to identify it as a positive instance.

In some cases, a single "best example" represents a concept fairly accurately. In such situations, it makes sense to present the example to students as a way of helping them develop a mental prototype for the concept. Yet we must make sure our students also know the concept's defining features so that they can correctly recognize any positive instances that *don't* closely resemble the prototype—so that they can identify an ostrich as a bird, a square as a rectangle, and so on.

It may be that people use prototypes to identify positive instances in clear-cut situations (e.g., Is a horse an animal?) but use formal definitions of a concept in more ambiguous situations (e.g., Is a sponge an animal?) (Andre, 1986; Glass, Holyoak, & Santa, 1979). It may also be that young children (children whom Piaget would classify as preoperational or concrete operational) depend more on concrete prototypes, whereas older children (those whom Piaget would classify as formal operational) develop more abstract definitions of concepts. Perhaps for these reasons, prototypical examples presented together with definitions often promote better concept learning than either one of these things alone (Dunn, 1983; R. D. Tennyson, Youngers, & Suebsonthi, 1983).

What is your prototype for the concept *house? chair? plant?* Can you think of positive instances of these concepts that don't resemble your prototypes?

■

Present a "best example" of a concept—one similar to most positive instances—as a prototype.

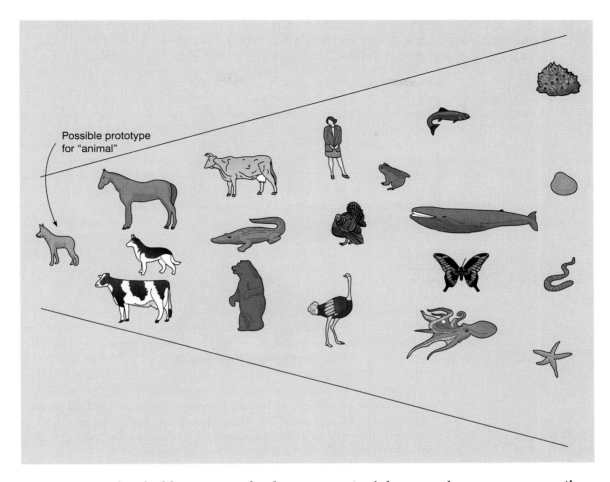

Figure 8–2   *With a doglike prototype for the concept* animal, *horses and cows are more easily recognized as animals than are starfish, earthworms, clams, or sponges.*

Mental "Theories"

■ EXPERIENCING FIRSTHAND
Coffeepots and Raccoons

Consider each of the situations that follow.[*]

1.   Doctors took a coffeepot that looked like this:

[*] (Both scenarios adapted from Keil, 1989, p. 184)

They sawed off the handle, sealed the top, took off the top knob, sealed closed the spout, and sawed it off. They also sawed off the base and attached a flat piece of metal. They attached a little stick, cut a window in it, and filled the metal container with birdseed. When they were done, it looked like this:

After the operation, was this a coffeepot or a bird feeder?

2. Doctors took this raccoon:

and shaved away some of its fur. They dyed what was left all black. Then they bleached a single stripe all white down the center of its back. Then, with surgery, they put in its body a sac of super smelly odor, just as a skunk has. After they were all done, the animal looked like this:

After the operation, was this a skunk or a raccoon?

Chances are, you concluded that the coffeepot had been transformed into a bird feeder but that the raccoon was still a raccoon despite its radical surgery; even fourth graders come to these conclusions (Keil, 1986, 1989). Now how is it possible that the coffeepot could be made into something entirely different, whereas the raccoon could not?

Some psychologists propose that the concepts people form are influenced, in part, by mental "theories" (belief systems) they have about how the world operates (Keil, 1986, 1989; Neisser, 1987). For example, even children as young as eight or nine seem to make a basic distinction between human-made objects (e.g., coffeepots, bird feeders) and biological entities (e.g., raccoons, skunks). Furthermore, they seem to conceptualize the two categories in fundamentally different ways: Human-made objects are defined largely by the *functions* they serve (e.g., keeping coffee warm, feeding birds), whereas biological entities are defined primarily by their origins (e.g., the parents who brought them into being, their DNA). Thus, when a coffeepot begins to hold birdseed, rather than coffee, it becomes a bird feeder by virtue of the fact that its function has changed. But when a raccoon is surgically altered to look like a skunk, it still has raccoon parents and raccoon DNA and so cannot possibly *be* a skunk (Keil, 1987, 1989). Thinking along similar lines, even preschoolers will tell you that you can't change a yellow finch into a bluebird by giving it a coat of blue paint or dressing it in a "bluebird" costume (Keil, 1989).

Our mental theories about the world seem to guide us as we identify potential defining features of the concepts that we are learning (Keil, 1987). For example, if you were trying to learn what a *horse* is, the fact that you know it's an animal would lead you to conclude that its location (in a stable, a pasture, a shopping mall, or whatever) is an irrelevant feature (Keil, 1989). In contrast, if you were trying to learn what the *equator* is, knowing that it's something on a map of the world should lead you to suspect that location is of the utmost importance.

As teachers, we can facilitate students' concept learning by placing concepts in a larger context—by explaining how each one fits into the larger scheme of things. In doing so, we help students make some educated guesses as to what the defining, correlational, and irrelevant features of any given concept are likely to be.

Explain how specific concepts fit into the larger scheme of things.

INTO THE CLASSROOM
Facilitating Concept Learning

Provide a definition of the concept.

> A geometry teacher defines a *sphere* as "the set of points in three dimensional space that are equidistant from a single point."

Present a "best example," or prototype.

> To illustrate the concept *democracy,* a social science teacher describes a hypothetical, "ideal" government.

Present a variety of positive instances.

> A music teacher plays a *primary chord* in several keys.

Present negative instances to show what the concept is not.

> An elementary school teacher shows students why spiders and scorpions are not *insects.*

Ask students to identify positive and negative instances from among numerous possibilities.

> A language arts teacher gives students a list of sentences and asks them to identify the sentences containing a *dangling participle.*

> Ask students to generate their own positive instances of the concept.
>
> > A psychology teacher asks students to think of examples of *reinforcement* in their own lives.
>
> Explain how each concept fits into the larger scheme of things.
>
> > A geography teacher teaches students to use *latitude* and *longitude* to locate various cities on a map.

Ask students to apply concepts to new situations.

We often teach concepts, not for the sake of the concepts themselves, but rather for the usefulness that those concepts have in helping our students better understand and deal with their world. For example, by learning about *nouns* and other parts of speech, students can more easily understand grammatical rules and learn a foreign language. By learning about *rectangles* and other two-dimensional shapes, students can more easily learn how to calculate the area of various surfaces. And by learning about *velocity* and *acceleration,* students can better predict how moving objects are likely to behave. In fact, by asking students to apply concepts—to use them in new situations—we are going to help them remember more about those concepts than they would otherwise (Watts & Anderson, 1971).

Unfortunately, students often have considerable difficulty applying the concepts and ideas they learn in school to other aspects of their lives. How can we help students take the information they learn in one situation and apply it to another situation? Let's find out how we can facilitate such *transfer* of learning.

FACILITATING TRANSFER

Consider these four students:

- Elena is bilingual: She speaks both English and Spanish fluently. She begins a French course in high school and immediately recognizes many similarities between French and Spanish. "Aha," she thinks, "my knowledge of Spanish will help me learn French."

- In his psychology class, Ethan learns the principle of reinforcement: A response followed by a reinforcing stimulus is more likely to occur again. Later that day, he thinks about playing a video game before doing his homework. "Oh, no," he says to himself, "that would be backward. I need to do my homework *first*. Playing the video game can be my reinforcer."

- In her history class, Estelle discovers that she does better on exams when she takes more notes. She decides to take more notes in her geography class as well, and once again the strategy pays off.

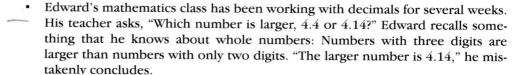
- Edward's mathematics class has been working with decimals for several weeks. His teacher asks, "Which number is larger, 4.4 or 4.14?" Edward recalls something that he knows about whole numbers: Numbers with three digits are larger than numbers with only two digits. "The larger number is 4.14," he mistakenly concludes.

People often use something they have learned in one situation to help them in another situation. Many things that students learn in school and at home are potentially helpful later on—perhaps in more advanced classwork, in their personal lives, or in their later careers. But occasionally students (like Edward) learn something at one time that, rather than helping, actually *interferes* with something they need to learn or do later.

When students learn something at one time that affects how they learn or perform in another situation, **transfer** is occurring. Ideally, transfer of knowledge should be one of the major objectives for classrooms at all grade levels. When people cannot use their basic arithmetic skills to compute correct change or balance a checkbook, when they cannot use their knowledge of English grammar in a job application or business report, and when they cannot apply their knowledge of science to an understanding of personal health or environmental problems, then we have to wonder whether the time spent learning the arithmetic, the grammar, and the science might have been better spent doing something else.

How can we help students successfully apply information from the classroom to new situations and problems, both in class and in the outside world? As we explore the topic of transfer in the pages that follow—as we consider basic concepts, influencing factors, and theoretical perspectives—we will discover numerous answers to this question.

How often do your instructors ask you to apply the things you learn in class to a new situation?

Defining Basic Concepts in Transfer

Let's begin our discussion by looking at different kinds of transfer that may occur:

- Positive versus negative transfer
- Specific versus general transfer

Positive Versus Negative Transfer

When something that a person learns in one situation *helps* that person learn or perform in another situation, we have **positive transfer.** Positive transfer is what we saw in the cases of Elena (whose Spanish facilitated her acquisition of French), Ethan (whose knowledge of reinforcement helped him regulate his own behavior), and Estelle (whose experiences with note taking in history class improved her performance in geography).

In contrast, when something that a person learns at one time *hinders* that person's learning or performance at a later time, we have **negative transfer.** This is the situation we saw for poor Edward: He transferred a principle derived from whole numbers (one number is always larger than another if it has more digits) to a situation where it didn't apply: the comparison of decimals. Another case of negative transfer occurs when students confuse the facts related to the various wars they study in history. For example, some students in the United States believe that the American Revolution was a battle between the English and the French (thus confusing it with the French and Indian War) or between the Northern and Southern states (thus confusing it with the American Civil War; McKeown & Beck, 1990). As still another instance of negative transfer, consider what happens to some students in my undergraduate educational psychology course. After taking other courses where rote learning sufficed or perhaps where verbatim memorization of material was even required, these students transfer the same rote learning strategies to studying educational psychology. As a result, they initially do

Can you think of a recent situation in which you exhibited positive transfer? Can you think of a situation in which you exhibited negative transfer?

poorly on my exams, which focus on meaningful learning and integration of material, rather than on recall of isolated facts.

Obviously, negative transfer is the "bad guy" here. Later in the chapter, as we consider theoretical perspectives of transfer, we will identify a strategy for minimizing the extent to which our students fall victim to negative transfer.

Specific Versus General Transfer

Transfer from one situation to another often occurs when the two situations overlap in content. Consider Elena, the student fluent in Spanish who is now taking French. She already knows how to count to five in Spanish:

uno

dos

tres

cuatro

cinco

She now needs to learn to count in French:

un

deux

trois

quatre

cinq

Elena should have an easy time learning the French numbers because they are very similar to the Spanish that she has already learned. And consider students studying such basic division facts as $6 \div 2 = 3$. If these students transfer something they have learned earlier—their knowledge of such multiplication facts as $2 \times 3 = 6$—their learning task will be easier. When transfer occurs because the original learning task and the transfer task overlap in content, we have **specific transfer.**

But now consider Estelle's strategy of taking more notes in geography because note taking was beneficial in her history class. History and geography don't necessarily overlap in content, but a strategy that she developed in one class has been effectively applied in the other. Here is an instance of **general transfer:** Learning in one situation affects learning and performance in a somewhat dissimilar situation.

Research tells us that specific transfer occurs more frequently than general transfer (Gray & Orasanu, 1987). In fact, the question of whether general transfer occurs at all has been the subject of considerable debate, as you will discover shortly.

What factors affect the likelihood that some form of transfer will occur? Let's see what research tells us.

Examining Factors Affecting Transfer

Research reveals a number of factors influencing the extent to which transfer is likely to occur:

- Amount of instructional time

- Extent to which learning is meaningful, rather than rote

- Extent to which principles, rather than facts, are learned

- Variety of examples and opportunities for practice

- Degree of similarity between two situations

- Length of time between the two situations

- Extent to which information is seen as context-free, rather than context-bound

These factors are summarized as general principles in Table 8–2. Let's look briefly at each one.

Amount of Instructional Time

Instructional time is clearly an important variable affecting transfer: The more time students spend studying a particular topic, the more likely they are to transfer what they learn to a new situation (Cormier & Hagman, 1987; Gick & Holyoak, 1987; Schmidt & Bjork, 1992; Voss, 1987). Conversely, when students study a great many topics without learning very much about any one of them, they are unlikely to apply what they have learned at a later date. Here we see the constructivist principle of *less is more* once again: Our students are more likely to transfer their school learning to new situations, including those beyond the classroom, when we have them study a few things in depth and learn them *well,* rather than study many things superficially (Brophy, 1992b; Porter, 1989).

Examine a few topics in depth, rather than many topics superficially; be sure students learn each topic thoroughly.

Extent to Which Learning Is Meaningful

In our discussion of information processing in Chapter 6, we discovered two advantages of meaningful learning over rote learning: Information is stored more quickly and also is retrieved more easily. Here we find an additional advantage of meaningful learning: Information learned in a meaningful fashion is more likely to be transferred or applied to a new situation (Ausubel et al., 1978; Brooks & Dansereau, 1987; J. Hiebert & Lefevre, 1986; Mayer, 1987).

Remember, meaningful learning involves connecting information with the things that one already knows. The more associations that our students make between new information and the various other things in their long-term memories, the more likely it is that they will "find" (retrieve) that information at a time when it will be useful.

Promote meaningful rather than rote learning of classroom material.

Extent to Which Principles Rather Than Facts Are Learned

EXPERIENCING FIRSTHAND
Central Business Districts

Consider these two ideas from geography:

- Boston's central business district is located near Boston Harbor.

- The central business districts of most older cities, which were settled before the development of modern transportation, are usually found in close proximity to a navigable body of water, such as an ocean or a river.

Which one of these would be more helpful to you if you were trying to find your way around Liverpool, Toronto, or Pittsburgh?

Table 8–2   Basic Principles of Transfer

PRINCIPLE	EDUCATIONAL IMPLICATION	EXAMPLE
As **instructional time** increases, the probability of transfer also increases.	If we want students to transfer what they learn, we should teach a few topics in depth, rather than many topics superficially.	When teaching a unit on the geography of South America, we might decide to focus on cultural similarities and differences across the continent, rather than present a lengthy, encyclopedia-like list of facts about each country.
Meaningful learning leads to greater transfer than rote learning.	We should encourage students to relate new material to the things they already know.	When introducing the concept *gravity* to third graders, we can ask them to think about what happens whenever they throw an object into the air (it comes back down).
Principles transfer more readily than facts.	We should teach general principles (e.g., cause-effect relationships) related to each topic, along with general strategies based on those principles.	When teaching a unit on softball, basketball, soccer, or tennis, we can tell students, "Always keep your eye on the ball," and explain why such vigilance is important.
Numerous and varied **examples** and **opportunities for practice** promote transfer.	We should illustrate new concepts and principles with a variety of examples and engage students in activities that let them practice new skills in different contexts.	After teaching students about what a *complete sentence* is, we can have them practice writing complete sentences in essays, short stories, and class newsletter articles.
As the **similarity** between two situations increases, so does the probability of transfer from one situation to the other.	We should make school tasks as similar as possible to the tasks that students are likely to encounter in the outside world.	When teaching students about the foods that make a balanced diet, we can have them prepare a healthful lunch by using groceries from a local food store.
Transfer is more likely when only a **short amount of time** has elapsed after students have studied a topic.	We should present topics as close in time as possible to the occasions when students will need to use those topics.	After having students learn and play the F Major scale in an instrumental music class, we can have them practice several musical pieces in the key of F Major.
Transfer is more likely when students perceive classroom material to be **context-free,** rather than context-bound.	We should relate topics in one discipline to topics in other disciplines and to tasks in the outside world.	When teaching students how to solve for x in algebra, we can give them word problems in which they must solve for an unknown in such contexts as physics, building construction, and sewing.

Teach general principles.

No doubt the second would prove more useful to you. The first statement is a fact about a particular city, whereas the second statement reflects a general principle applicable to many different cities. People can transfer general (and perhaps somewhat abstract) principles more easily than specific, concrete facts (J. R. Anderson, Reder, & Simon, 1996; P. W. Cheng, Holyoak, Nisbett, & Oliver, 1986; Fong, Krantz, & Nisbett, 1986; Judd, 1932; Perkins & Salomon, 1987).

Specific facts have an important place in the classroom; for example, students should know what two plus three equal, what the Berlin Wall signified, and where to find Africa on a globe. Yet facts themselves have limited utility in new situations. The more we can emphasize general principles instead of specific facts—for example, that two whole numbers added together always equal a larger number, that a country's citizens sometimes revolt when their government officials act unjustly, and that the cultures of various nations are partly a function of their location and climate—the more we facilitate students' ability to transfer the things that we teach them.

Variety of Examples and Opportunities for Practice

Students are more likely to apply something they learn if, within the course of instruction, they are given many examples and have numerous opportunities to practice in different situations (J. R. Anderson et al., 1996; P. W. Cheng et al., 1986; Cormier, 1987; Fong et al., 1986; Perkins & Salomon, 1987; Reimann & Schult, 1996; Ross, 1988; Schmidt & Bjork, 1992; Schmidt & Young, 1987). For example, students will be more apt to use their knowledge of fractions and ratios in the future if they practice using this knowledge in such activities as cooking, converting U.S. dollars to a foreign currency, and drawing things to scale. By using knowledge in many contexts, students store that knowledge in association with all those contexts and so are more likely to retrieve the information on a future occasion (Perkins & Salomon, 1987; Voss, 1987).

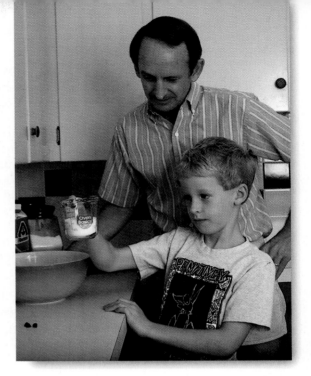

Children are more likely to transfer their knowledge of fractions and ratios to future situations if they have opportunities to practice using fractions and ratios in a variety of contexts.

Provide *many* and *different* examples and opportunities for practice.

Similarity of the Two Situations

Let's return for a minute to the problem that Mary encountered in our case study at the beginning of the chapter:

> An automotive engineer has designed a car that can reach a speed of 50 miles per hour within 5 seconds. What is the car's rate of acceleration?

Let's imagine that Mary eventually learns how to solve this problem by using the $v = a \times t$ principle. Because the velocity (v) is *50* miles per hour and the time (t) is *5* seconds, the rate of acceleration (a) must be *10* miles per hour per second.

Now Mary encounters two additional problems:

> A car salesman tells a customer that a particular model of car can reach a speed of 40 miles per hour within 8 seconds. What is the car's rate of acceleration?

> A biologist reports that a cheetah she has been observing can attain a speed of 60 kilometers per hour within a 10-second period. How quickly is the cheetah able to increase its speed?

Which problem do you think Mary will find easier to solve?

Transfer is more likely to occur when a new situation appears to be similar to a previous situation (Bassok, 1990; Blake & Clark, 1990; Di Vesta & Peverly, 1984; Reed,

Ernst, & Banerji, 1974). Mary will probably have an easier time solving the problem involving the car salesman because it is superficially similar to the problem about the automotive engineer: Both problems involve cars, and both use miles as a unit of measure. The cheetah problem, even though it can be solved by the same approach as the other two, involves a different domain (animals) and a different unit of measure (kilometers).

Make school tasks similar in appearance to the future situations that students are likely to encounter.

Here we see the value of *authentic activities* in the curriculum. Of the many examples and opportunities for practice that we give our students, some should be very similar to the situations that students are likely to encounter in their future studies or in the outside world. The more that school tasks and assignments resemble students' later life experiences, the more likely it is that our students will put their school learning to use.

Yet we should note that the similarity of two situations, while promoting positive transfer, may promote negative transfer as well. Try the following exercise as an example.

■ **E X P E R I E N C I N G   F I R S T H A N D**
A Division Problem

Consider this division problem:

$$20 \div 0.38$$

Is the answer larger or smaller than 20?
■

If you applied your knowledge of division by whole numbers here, you undoubtedly concluded that the answer is smaller than 20. In fact, the answer is 52.63, a number *larger* than 20. And remember Edward's erroneous conclusion—4.14 is larger than 4.4—based on his knowledge of how whole numbers can be compared; many students, even many at the university level, show negative transfer of whole number principles to situations involving decimals (Tirosh & Graeber, 1988). Working with decimals appears, on the surface, to be similar to working with whole numbers; after all, the only difference is a tiny decimal point.

Emphasize differences between topics if negative transfer is likely to occur.

In situations where we don't want our students to transfer something inappropriately, we should make a special effort to point out differences between the two topics being studied. For example, in Edward's situation, it probably would have been helpful for his teacher to identify some of the specific ways in which decimals are *not* like whole numbers. As another example, students studying electronics often confuse series circuits with parallel circuits. Their confusion is not surprising because both circuits involve connecting several resistors to a single battery. In this situation, we might spell out the difference between the two circuits in very specific and concrete terms. As yet another example, I find that my own students in educational psychology often have trouble using the term *maturation* correctly in our discussions of child development because the term has a different meaning in their everyday conversations. Therefore, when I first introduce the concept of *maturation,* I take great pains to show them how psychology's meaning of the word (the unfolding of genetically controlled developmental changes) differs from the meaning they are familiar with (developmental changes in general).

Length of Time Between the Two Situations

People are most likely to apply new information soon after they have learned it. They are less likely to use that information as time goes on (Gick & Holyoak, 1987). To the extent that we can, then, we should try to present topics to students as close in time as possible to the occasions when students will need to use those topics.

To illustrate, let's return once again to the physics principle that Mary learned:

Velocity equals acceleration times time
or
$$v = a \times t$$

Present topics as close in time as possible to the occasions when students will need to use those topics.

The formula tells Mary how to calculate velocity when she knows both the acceleration and the time. But let's say that she instead wants to calculate the rate of acceleration, as she needed to do for the "car" and "cheetah" problems. If Mary is studying algebra concurrently with her physics class or else has studied it very recently, she is more likely to see the usefulness of algebra in rearranging the formula like so:

$$a = \frac{v}{t}$$

Extent to Which Information Is Perceived as Context-Free, Rather Than Context-Bound

In many cases, we would like our students to transfer their knowledge in one content domain to a different domain; for example, we would like them to transfer mathematics to physics, grammar to creative writing, history to current events, and health to personal eating habits. Yet students tend to think of academic subject areas as being separate, unrelated disciplines; they also tend to think of their school learning as being unrelated to real-world concerns (e.g., Perkins & Simmons, 1988; Rakow, 1984). When students see the things they learn in school as being *context-bound*—as being related only to a particular topic or discipline—they are unlikely to transfer it to situations outside that context (Alexander & Judy, 1988; J. R. Anderson et al., 1996; Bassok & Holyoak, 1990; diSessa, 1982; Reed et al., 1974; Voss, 1987).

Relate topics in one academic discipline to other academic disciplines and to the nonacademic world.

When we teach material within a particular academic discipline, then, we should relate that material to other disciplines and to the outside world as frequently as possible (e.g., Blake & Clark, 1990). For example, we might show students how mathematics can be used in physics, how human digestion provides a justification for categorizing food into four basic food groups, or how economic issues affect tropical rain forests. We can also encourage students to brainstorm about specific situations in which they could apply the things they learn in class (J. R. Anderson et al., 1996).

As you can see, then, a variety of factors influence the extent to which transfer is likely to occur. But why do such factors make a difference? Let's turn to several theoretical perspectives as to when and why transfer occurs.

Applying Theories of Transfer

Over the years, educators and psychologists have held differing views as to when and why transfer occurs. In the next few pages, we will consider three perspectives of transfer with a distinctly cognitivist flavor:

- In past years, some theorists have emphasized the value of general *mental "exercise"*: Studying difficult and rigorous subject matter strengthens the mind.

In Chapter 9, we will consider transfer from a behaviorist perspective as well, finding that the occurrence of positive and negative transfer often depends on the similarity of stimuli and responses across situations.

Does this discussion contradict what you previously believed about the value of mental exercise? If so, have you undergone *conceptual change* regarding this issue?

• More recently, cognitive psychologists have stressed the importance of *retrieval:* Transfer occurs only when conditions within a new situation facilitate the retrieval of previously learned information and skills.

• Many theorists now speak of *situated cognition:* Knowledge and thinking skills are typically acquired in specific contexts and are unlikely to be used outside those contexts.

Mental "Exercise"

As a beginning high school sophomore in the fall of 1963, my guidance counselor recommended that I take the two languages that my high school offered: French and Latin. Taking French made a great deal of sense: Growing up in Massachusetts, I was within a day's drive of French-speaking Quebec. "But why should I take Latin," I asked? "I can only use it if I attend Catholic Mass or run across phrases like 'caveat emptor' or 'in Deo speramus.' Hardly anyone speaks the language anymore." My guidance counselor pursed her thin red lips and gave me a look that told me that she knew best. "Latin will discipline your mind, my dear. It will help you learn better."

My guidance counselor's advice reflects an early view of transfer known as **formal discipline.** According to this view, students should study such rigorous subjects as Latin, Greek, mathematics, and logic primarily because such subjects "strengthen" the mind. By undergoing such mental "exercise," the theory proposes, students become capable of learning many other, unrelated things more easily.

But research results have generally discredited this "mind as muscle" notion of transfer (Perkins & Salomon, 1989; Thorndike 1924). For example, practice in memorizing poems does not necessarily make one a faster poem memorizer (James, 1890). And studying computer programming, though often a worthwhile activity in its own right, does not necessarily help a person with dissimilar kinds of logical tasks (Perkins & Salomon, 1989).

Retrieval

Many cognitive psychologists propose that information learned in one situation helps in another situation only if the information is *retrieved* within the context of that second situation (Brooks & Dansereau, 1987; Cormier, 1987; Gick & Holyoak, 1987). For example, Elena's knowledge of Spanish will help her learn French only if she remembers relevant Spanish words while studying her French words. Ethan will apply the principle of reinforcement to his own behavior only if he happens to think of reinforcement while planning the rest of his day.

As you should recall from our discussion of information processing in Chapter 6, information is most easily retrieved when it is associated with many other items in long-term memory. At least four of the factors we have identified as promoting transfer—the amount of instructional time, the extent to which learning is meaningful rather than rote, the extent to which

THE FAR SIDE By GARY LARSON

Brain aerobics

The formal discipline view of transfer portrays the mind as a muscle that benefits from general mental exercise.

general principles rather than facts are learned, and the number of examples and opportunities to practice—should affect our students' ability to make multiple connections between class material and the other things in their world. Students are *un*likely to apply information they have not previously connected to other things (information they have learned at a rote level), partly because they probably won't retrieve it when they need it and partly because they won't see its relevance even if they do retrieve it.

As we noted earlier, people are also more likely to transfer what they've learned in one situation to very *similar* situations. One explanation for this principle is that a similar situation presents helpful *retrieval cues*—reminders of relevant information stored in long-term memory (Gick & Holyoak, 1987; Perkins & Salomon, 1989; Sternberg & Frensch, 1993). A second explanation lies in the concept of *situated cognition*—a concept that we turn to now.

Situated Cognition

Earlier, I mentioned that studying computer programming does not necessarily help a person with other kinds of logical tasks (Perkins & Salomon, 1989). Some theorists propose that knowledge and thinking skills are typically acquired in specific contexts and are unlikely to be used outside those contexts (L. M. Anderson, 1993; Butterworth, 1993; Hirschfeld & Gelman, 1994; Lave, 1993; N. Mercer, 1993; Roazzi & Bryant, 1993; Singley & Anderson, 1989; however, also see J. R. Anderson et al., 1996). This principle is often referred to as **situated cognition**: Knowledge and thinking skills are *situated* within the context in which they develop.

If you have read the discussion of cognitive development in Chapter 2, then you have already seen evidence of situated cognition. As you may recall, Piaget proposed that such thinking abilities as abstract thought, proportional reasoning, and separation and control of variables emerge at about eleven or twelve years of age (at the onset of the formal operations stage) and are then used in a wide variety of tasks. Yet we reviewed evidence in Chapter 2 that this is probably *not* the case: Students are more likely to exhibit formal operational reasoning skills in some domains than in others. They are especially likely to exhibit sophisticated cognitive processes in areas where they have the most experience (DeLisi & Staudt, 1980; Girotto & Light, 1993; M. C. Linn et al., 1989; Pulos & Linn, 1981; Schliemann & Carraher, 1993).

The principle of situated cognition provides additional justification for using authentic activities in the classroom. If we want our students to use the things they learn at school in real-world situations later on, we should teach classroom subject matter within the context of such situations. Furthermore, we may occasionally be able to have students practice their knowledge and skills in so many different contexts that the things they have learned are no longer confined to certain contexts: In other words, those things become context-free (A. Collins et al., 1989).

Researchers have found that learning in one situation can help in a very different situation (e.g., learning history can help one learn geography) if, in the process, one *learns how to learn.* When a student acquires effective learning strategies in one situation—for example, focusing on meaningful rather than rote learning, finding main ideas, or using mnemonics to organize and elaborate on information—those strategies often transfer positively to learning in a very different situation (Brooks & Dansereau, 1987; A. L. Brown, 1978; Perkins, 1995; Pressley, Snyder, & Cariglia-Bull, 1987). Later in the chapter, when we consider metacognition and study strategies, we will examine such potentially transferable strategies in more depth.

Teach class material in a way that promotes multiple connections to other things in your students' world.

When appropriate to do so, provide retrieval cues that remind students of information relevant to the transfer situation.

Is this an instance of specific transfer or general transfer?

It is especially beneficial for students to have opportunities for transferring classroom information to one very important activity: solving problems. It is to this form of transfer—the use of previously learned information to solve new problems—that we turn our attention now.

FACILITATING PROBLEM SOLVING

■ EXPERIENCING FIRSTHAND
Four Problems

How many of these problems can you solve?

1. You buy two apples for 25¢ each and one pear for 40¢. How much change will you get back from a dollar bill?

2. You are building a treehouse with the shape and dimensions illustrated in Figure 8–3. You need to buy planks for a slanted roof. How long must those planks be to reach from one side of the treehouse to the other?

3. You want to demonstrate that metal battleships float even though metal is denser than water. You don't have any toy boats made of metal. What can you use instead to illustrate the principle that a metal object with a hollow interior can float on water?

4. Every day, almost seventy-five thousand acres of tropical rain forest disappear. What steps might be taken to curtail this alarming rate of deforestation? ■

Sometimes problems are straightforward and relatively easy to solve. For example, Problem 1 requires the application of simple addition and subtraction procedures. You have had enough experience with similar problems that you probably had little difficulty finding the correct solution: 10¢. Problem 2, illustrated in Figure 8–3, is more difficult, partly because you don't encounter such problems very often. But if you have studied geometry, then you undoubtedly learned a rule that leads to the correct problem solution. Perhaps you remember the Pythagorean theorem: In any right triangle, the square of the hypotenuse equals the sum of the squares of the other two sides. Looking at the top part of the treehouse (from the dotted line upward) as a triangle, we can find the length for the roof planks (x) this way:

$$x^2 = 3^2 + 4^2$$
$$x^2 = 9 + 16$$
$$x^2 = 25$$
$$x = 5$$

Yet problems don't always have a single correct solution. For example, if you are looking for a metal object with a hollow interior to float on water (Problem 3), you might use a number of different objects to solve your problem—possibly a pie plate, a bucket, or a thimble. And you might identify several possible ways of addressing rain forest deforestation (Problem 4), but you probably wouldn't know which of these (if any) are correct solutions (which ones would successfully help preserve tropical rain forests) until you actually implemented them.

In this section of the chapter, we will explore the multifaceted nature of human problem solving. We will begin by examining several basic concepts that will prove useful in our discussion of this topic. We will then examine several cognitive factors that

How long do the roof planks of
this treehouse need to be?

Figure 8–3   Building a Treehouse

help or hinder successful problem solving. Finally, we will look at the importance of meaningful problem solving—that is, at the importance of having our students understand the steps they take to solve a problem—and at the behaviors that result from learning to solve problems in a rote, meaning*less* fashion. As we go along, you may be able to identify places where you can apply *(transfer!)* your knowledge of transfer.

Defining Basic Concepts in Problem Solving

As the four problems at the beginning of the section illustrate, the problems that human beings need to solve may differ widely in their content and scope; for example, one problem may relate to a backyard treehouse and another may relate to the devastation of tropical rain forests. The four problems also differ widely with respect to the particular strategies that can be used to solve them; for example, one problem might be solved by using the Pythagorean Theorem, whereas another might be solved only by a world summit conference. Yet virtually all problems can be considered to be either *well-*

defined or *ill-defined* (or perhaps somewhere in between), and virtually all problem-solving strategies can be categorized as either *algorithms* or *heuristics*. Let's take a few minutes to consider these two basic distinctions.

Well-Defined and Ill-Defined Problems

Problems differ in the extent to which they are clearly specified and structured (e.g., N. Frederiksen, 1984a). A **well-defined problem** is one in which the goal is clearly stated, all information needed to solve the problem is present, and only one correct answer exists. Calculating the amount of change one gets from a dollar (Problem 1) and determining the length of planks needed for a treehouse roof (Problem 2) are examples of well-defined problems. In both cases, we know exactly what is required to solve the problem.

In contrast, an **ill-defined problem** is one in which the desired goal is unclear, information needed to solve the problem is missing, or several possible solutions to the problem exist. Finding a suitable substitute for a metal ship is, to some extent, an ill-defined problem because there are a number of objects that might serve as a ship substitute, some of which might work better than others. The rain forest deforestation problem (Problem 4) is even less defined. First, the goal—curtailing deforestation—is an ambiguous one. Do we want to stop deforestation altogether or just slow it down a bit? And if we just want to decrease the rate, what rate is acceptable? Second, we undoubtedly need more information before we can solve the problem. For example, it would be helpful to determine whether there are any means of rejuvenating previously cleared and farmed lands, and it would be useful to identify economically reasonable alternatives to slash-and-burn farming practices; some of this needed information may require extensive research. Finally, there is no single "correct" solution for Problem 4: Curtailing deforestation will undoubtedly require a number of steps taken more or less simultaneously. Ill-defined problems, then, are usually more difficult to solve than well-defined ones.

Most problems presented in school are well-defined problems: A question clearly specifies a goal to be reached, all the information needed to solve the problem is present (no more, no less), and there is only one correct answer. Consider this typical mathematics word problem as an example:

> Old MacDonald has planted potatoes in a field 100 meters long and 50 meters wide. If the field yields an average of 5 pounds of potatoes in each square meter, how many pounds of potatoes can MacDonald expect to harvest from his field?

In this problem, the goal is clearly stated: We must determine how many pounds of potatoes the field will yield. We also have all the information that we need to solve the problem, with no irrelevant information to distract us. And there is only one correct answer to the problem, with no room for debate.

But the real world presents ill-defined problems far more often than well-defined ones, and students need practice in dealing with them. Consider this problem as an example:

> Old MacDonald's son wants to go to a small, coeducational college 200 miles away. MacDonald does not know whether he can afford the college tuition; it all depends on how well his potato crop does this summer. What should MacDonald tell his son?

Keep in mind that the distinction between well-defined and ill-defined problems is better conceptualized as a continuum than an "either-or" situation.

Can you think of problems you've encountered recently that were well-defined? Can you think of some that were ill-defined?

Notice how the problem has a rather vaguely stated goal (determining what Mac-Donald should say to his son); it does not identify the specific questions he needs to address before he gives an answer. And we don't have all the information we need to solve the problem: We don't know the size of MacDonald's potato field, the predicted size of his crop, the probable value of the potatoes, the family's day-to-day living expenses, or the cost of college tuition. Finally, there may be no single correct answer here: Whether MacDonald encourages his son to go to college depends not only on finances but also on his beliefs about the value of a college education and on the extent to which the son's contribution to the farm necessitates his staying at home next autumn.

One way of helping our students learn to solve problems is to teach them techniques for better defining ill-defined problems. For example, we can teach them how to break large problems into smaller, well-defined ones (e.g., determining the probable size of the potato crop, calculating the farmer's daily living expenses). We can also teach them how to identify information they need (e.g., the size of the farmer's potato field), as well as information they may *not* need (e.g., the fact that the college is coeducational). And we can teach them techniques for finding necessary information they may not have (e.g., how to measure distance, how to use the library to find the current price of potatoes, how to obtain information about tuition rates at different colleges).

Give students practice in dealing with ill-defined problems.

Show students ways of making ill-defined problems more well-defined.

Problem-Solving Strategies: Algorithms and Heuristics

Some problems can be successfully solved by following specific, step-by-step instructions—that is, by using an **algorithm.** For example, we should be able to put a new bicycle together by reading the "Directions for Assembly" pamphlet that comes with it. We can calculate the length of a slanted roof by using the Pythagorean theorem. When we follow an algorithm faithfully, we invariably arrive at a correct solution.

Yet not all problems come equipped with directions for assembly. There are no rules we can follow to identify a substitute metal ship, no list of instructions we can use to help us solve the deforestation problem. When there is no algorithm for solving a problem, people may instead use a **heuristic**—a general problem-solving strategy that

Calvin and Hobbes   by Bill Watterson

Some problems can be solved by an algorithm—a set of step-by-step instructions that guarantees a correct solution.

may or may not yield a workable solution. For example, one heuristic that we might use in solving the deforestation problem is this: Identify a new behavior that adequately replaces the problem behavior—that is, find something else that peasant farmers can do to meet their survival needs. As another example of a heuristic, consider the addition problem in the exercise that follows.

■ EXPERIENCING FIRSTHAND
Grocery Shopping

Solve this addition problem *as quickly as you possibly can:*
You are purchasing three items at the store, at these prices:

$19.99

$39.98

$29.97

About how much money are you spending? (Don't worry about a possible sales tax.) ■

The fastest way to solve the problem is to round off and approximate. The first item costs about $20, the second about $40, and the third about $30; therefore, you are spending about $90 on your shopping spree. Rounding is often an excellent heuristic for arriving quickly at approximate answers to mathematical problems.

Students in our schools get far more practice solving well-defined problems than ill-defined ones, and they are taught many more algorithms than heuristics. For example, they are likely to spend more school time learning problem-solving strategies useful in determining the length of planks needed for a treehouse roof than strategies applicable to the problem of deforestation. And they are likely to spend more time using laws of physics to make predictions about when battleships will float on water than wrestling with ways of preventing the conflicts that require those battleships in the first place. Yet many real-world problems—problems that our students will encounter after graduation—probably cannot be solved with cut-and-dried algorithms.

Problem-solving strategies—algorithms and heuristics alike—are often specific to a particular content domain. But here are three general problem-solving heuristics that our students may find helpful in a variety of contexts.

- *Identifying subgoals:* Breaking a problem into two or more subproblems that can be better defined and more easily solved

  Example: A group of students wrestling with the problem of diminishing rain forests identifies several smaller problems—poor economic circumstances of local residents, lack of good agricultural land, and lack of government regulation of deforestation practices—and then discusses possible ways to solve each of these problems.

- *Working backward:* Beginning at the *goal* of the problem (at the solution needed) and working backward, one step at a time, toward the initial problem statement

  Example: A student is given this problem:

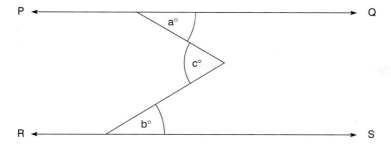

Prove that, if $a + b = c$, then lines PQ and RS must be parallel.

To prove this statement, the student decides to start with the idea that the two lines are, in fact, parallel and then work backward, step by step, to show that $a + b$ must equal c.

- *Drawing an analogy:* Identifying an analogous situation to the problem situation and deriving potential problem solutions from that analogy

  Example: A student attempting to calculate the volume of an irregularly shaped object recognizes that, just as she herself displaces water when she steps into the bathtub, the object will displace its volume when immersed in water. She places the object into a container filled to the brim with water, collects the water that sloshes out, and measures the amount.

Teaching problem-solving strategies. How can we help our students acquire effective problem-solving strategies? Here are a number of possibilities:

For Teaching Algorithms:

- Describe and demonstrate specific algorithms and when they can be used.

- Provide worked-out examples of algorithms being applied.

- Help students understand why particular algorithms are relevant and effective in certain situations.

- When a student's application of an algorithm yields an incorrect answer, look closely at the specific steps that the student has taken until the trouble spot is located.

For Teaching Heuristics:

- Give students practice in defining ill-defined problems.

- Teach heuristics that students can use in situations where no specific algorithms apply; for example, encourage such strategies as rounding, working backward, and drawing analogies.

For Teaching Both Algorithms and Heuristics:

- Teach problem-solving strategies within the context of specific subject areas (*not* as a topic separate from academic content).

Using the subject matter you will be teaching, develop two problems, one that is well-defined and one that is ill-defined. Do your problems require algorithms or heuristics in order to be solved?

You may want to refresh your memory as to what *scaffolding* is by reviewing Vygotsky's theory of cognitive development in Chapter 2. This concept will also be pertinent to our discussion of study strategies later in the chapter.

- Provide scaffolding for difficult problems—for example, by breaking them into smaller and simpler problems, giving hints about possible strategies, or providing partial solutions.

- Have students solve problems in small groups, sharing ideas about problem-solving strategies, modeling various approaches for one another, and discussing the merits of each approach. (Heller & Hungate, 1985; Mayer, 1985, 1992; Noddings, 1985; Resnick, 1983.)

As we have seen, well-defined problems are usually more easily solved than ill-defined problems, and problems that can be solved with algorithms are generally easier than problems that require heuristics. But there are several other factors, cognitive in nature, that affect problem-solving success as well.

Examining Cognitive Factors Affecting Problem Solving

Information processing theorists have identified at least four cognitive factors that affect a person's success in solving a problem:

- Working memory capacity

- Encoding of the problem

- Depth and integration of one's knowledge relevant to the problem

- Retrieval of relevant information from long-term memory

Before you read further, can you guess how each of these factors affects problem solving?

As we consider each of these four factors, we will identify additional ways that we can help our students become more effective problem solvers.

Working Memory Capacity

You may recall from an exercise in Chapter 6 how difficult it is to solve a long division problem in your head. Remember, working memory has a limited capacity: it can only hold a few pieces of information and can only accommodate so much cognitive processing at any one time. If a problem requires an individual to deal with too much information at once or to manipulate that information in a very complex fashion, working memory capacity may be insufficient for effective problem processing. Once working memory capacity is exceeded, the problem cannot be solved (J. R. Anderson, 1987; Johnstone & El-Banna, 1986; Perkins, 1995).

Encourage students to write parts of the problem on paper.

Our students can overcome the limits of their working memories in at least two ways. One obvious way is to create an external record of information relevant to the problem—for example, by writing that information on a piece of paper. (This is typically our strategy when we do long division problems, so that we don't have to hold all the numbers in working memory at once.) Another way to overcome working memory capacity is to learn some skills to a level of automaticity—in other words, to learn them to a point where they can be retrieved quickly, easily, and almost without conscious thought (J. R. Anderson, 1982; N. Frederiksen, 1984a; R. M. Gagné, 1982, 1985; Mayer, 1985; Rabinowitz & Glaser, 1985; Schneider & Shiffrin, 1977).

Teach the information and skills essential in problem solving to a level of automaticity.

As an illustration of the role that automaticity plays in problem solving, try the following exercise.

A Multiplication Problem

See whether you can do this multiplication problem *in your head.* Look at it once, and then close your eyes and try to solve it:

$$\begin{array}{r} 23 \\ \times\ 9 \\ \hline \end{array}$$

■

Were you able to remember the problem at the same time that you were calculating the answer? If so, it was probably because you could remember basic multiplication facts—9×2 and 9×3—without having to think very hard about them. But imagine instead that once you had put the problem in your working memory, you had to stop and think about what 9×3 equals: "Hmm . . . let's see . . . 9 plus 9 is 18 . . . and we need to add 9 more, so that's 19, 20, 21, 22, 23, 24, 25, 26, 27 . . . and now what was the second top number again?" When people must use a significant portion of working memory capacity for retrieving or reconstructing basic skills and information (e.g., for recalling multiplication facts, spelling, or the meaning of *deforestation*), they may not have enough capacity left to solve the problems (e.g., solving complex mathematical equations, writing a persuasive essay, or identifying methods of curtailing deforestation) that require such skills and information. (The answer to the multiplication problem is 207.)

Encoding of the Problem

When we discussed information processing in Chapter 6, we talked about *encoding*—changing the form of new information as we store it in memory. Encoding is clearly a factor affecting our ability to solve problems successfully. Sometimes we encode a problem ineffectively or incorrectly; at other times, we have trouble encoding a problem at all. Let's take a few minutes to consider each of these two circumstances. We will then identify some strategies for helping our students encode problems more effectively.

Encoding a problem ineffectively or incorrectly.

Two Trains and a Bird

Consider the following situation:

> Two train stations are 50 miles apart. At 2 P.M. one Saturday afternoon two trains start toward each other, one from each station. Just as the trains pull out of the stations, a bird springs into the air in front of the first train and flies ahead to the front of the second train. When the bird reaches the second train it turns back and flies toward the first train. The bird continues to do this until the trains meet.
>
> If both trains travel at the rate of 25 miles per hour and the bird flies at 100 miles per hour, how many miles will the bird have flown before the trains meet? (from M. I. Posner, 1973, pp. 150–151)

See whether you can solve the problem. Don't read any further until you have either solved the problem or spent five minutes *trying* to solve it.

If, after five minutes, you are still having trouble solving the problem, try answering this question first:

How long must the bird fly before the trains meet?

Now can you determine how far the bird must fly?

■

Because the two train stations are 50 miles apart and the trains are traveling at 25 miles per hour, the trains will meet in 1 hour. The bird is flying at a speed of 100 miles per hour; therefore, it will fly 100 miles before the trains meet.

We can solve the trains/bird problem more easily if we encode it as a "time" problem (how *long* must the bird fly?), rather than as a "distance" problem (how *far* must the bird fly?). There are often different ways of encoding the same problem in memory—different ways of representing the problem mentally—and some forms of encoding may promote easier problem solution than others.

For a very different example of how encoding affects problem-solving success, try solving the next problem.

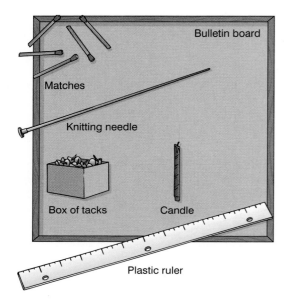

Matches

Knitting needle

Box of tacks

Candle

Bulletin board

Plastic ruler

△

The candle problem illustrates a particular kind of mental set—*functional fixedness*—whereby an individual thinks of an object as having only one possible function and therefore overlooks another function that it might serve.

■ EXPERIENCING FIRSTHAND
The Candle Problem[*]

You are in a room with a bulletin board firmly affixed to the wall. Your task is to *stand a candle upright* beside the bulletin board about four feet above the floor. You do not want the candle touching the bulletin board, because the candle's flame must not singe the bulletin board. Instead, you need to place the candle about a centimeter away. How can you accomplish the task with the following materials?

small candle

metal knitting needle

matches

box of thumbtacks

twelve-inch plastic ruler

See whether you can solve the problem before you read further. ■

As it turns out, the ruler and knitting needle are useless in solving the candle problem (if you try to puncture the candle with the knitting needle, you will probably break the candle; if you try to balance the ruler on a few tacks, it will probably fall down). The easiest solution is to fasten the thumbtack box to the bulletin board with tacks and then attach the candle to the top of the box by using either a tack or some melted wax. Many people don't consider this solution, however, because they encode the box only as a *container of tacks,* thereby overlooking its potential use as a candle stand. When we encode a problem in a particular way that excludes potential solutions, we are the victims of a **mental set.**

As you may know from your own experience, many students have trouble solving mathematical word problems. One reason is that they often have difficulty encoding a problem in terms of the operation (e.g., addition or subtraction) that the problem requires (e.g., Mayer, 1992). When students have limited knowledge about a certain topic (e.g., limited conceptual understanding of mathematics), they are likely to encode a problem related to that topic on the basis of superficial problem characteristics (Chi, Feltovich, & Glaser, 1981; Schoenfeld & Hermann, 1982). For example, I remember being taught in elementary school that the word *left* in a problem indicates that subtrac-

---

[*] (Adapted from Duncker, 1945)

tion is called for. Encoding a "left" problem as a subtraction problem works well in some instances, such as this one:

Tim has 7 apples. He gives 3 apples to Emily. How many apples does he have left?

But it is inappropriate in other instances, such as this one:

Ana went shopping. She spent $3.50 and then counted her money when she got home. She had $2.35 left. How much did Ana have when she started out? (Resnick, 1989, p. 165)

The latter problem requires addition, not subtraction. Obviously, words alone can be deceiving.

When students encode a problem incorrectly, they are less likely to solve it successfully. But sometimes students have difficulty encoding a problem in *any* way, as we shall see now.

Failing to encode a problem.

■   EXPERIENCING FIRSTHAND
Pigs and Chickens

See whether you can solve this problem:

Old MacDonald has a barnyard full of pigs and chickens. Altogether there are 21 heads and 60 legs in the barnyard (not counting MacDonald's own head and legs). How many pigs and how many chickens are running around the barnyard?

Can you figure out the answer? If you are having difficulty, try thinking about the problem this way:

Imagine that the pigs are standing in an upright position on only their two hind legs; their front two legs are raised over their heads. Therefore, all the animals—pigs and chickens alike—are standing on two legs. Can you now figure out how many legs are on the ground and how many must be in the air? From this, can you determine the number of pigs and chickens there must be? ■

In case you are still having difficulty with the problem, follow the logic along with me:

- Obviously, because there are 21 heads, the number of pigs plus the number of chickens must equal 21.

- Because each animal has 2 legs on the ground and because there must be twice as many legs on the ground as there are number of heads, there are 42 (21 × 2) legs on the ground.

- Because there are 42 legs on the ground, there must be 18 (60 − 42) pigs' legs in the air.

- Because each pig has 2 front legs, there must be 9 (18 ÷ 2) pigs.

- Because there are 9 pigs, there must be 12 (21 − 9) chickens.

How could you use algebra to solve this problem? ■

If you initially had trouble solving the Old MacDonald problem, your difficulty may have been the result of your inability to encode the problem in any way that allowed you to solve it. Students often have trouble solving mathematical word problems be-

Some ways of encoding a problem promote more successful problem solving than others.

cause they don't know how to translate those problems into procedures or operations with which they are familiar (Mayer, 1982, 1986; Resnick, 1989; Reusser, 1990). For example, students of all ages tend to have difficulty encoding *relational* problems—problems in which only comparative numbers are given and hence are often unable to solve problems such as these:

> Tim has 7 oranges. Emily has 3 fewer oranges than Tim. How many oranges does Emily have?

> Laura is 3 times as old as Maria was when Laura was as old as Maria is now. In 2 years Laura will be twice as old as Maria was 2 years ago. Find their present ages. (Mayer, 1982, p. 202)

Even college students have trouble encoding and solving the latter problem (Mayer, 1982). (By the way, Laura is 18 and Maria is 12.)

Help students develop useful ways of encoding problems in memory.

Facilitating problem encoding. As you have just seen, encoding a problem appropriately is an essential yet often difficult step in problem solving. How can we help students begin to encode problems more effectively? Here are some things we can do:

- Present the problem in a concrete way; for example, provide real objects that students can manipulate or an illustration of the problem's components (A. S. Luchins & Luchins, 1950; Mayer, 1992).

- Encourage students to make a problem concrete *themselves;* for example, encourage them to draw a picture or diagram of the problem (Anzai, 1991; Lindvall, Tamburino, & Robinson, 1982; Mayer, 1986; Prawat, 1989; K. Schultz & Lochhead, 1991).

- Point out any features of problems students *can* solve that, when those features appear again in a different problem, indicate that the same information can be applied or the same approach to problem solution can be used (Prawat, 1989).

- Mix different kinds of problems together (e.g., problems requiring addition, subtraction, multiplication, or division) so that students get in the habit of encoding different problems differently (Mayer, 1985, 1986).

Depth and Integration of Knowledge Relevant to the Problem

Let's return once again to Mary, our case study at the beginning of the chapter. Mary learned a principle of physics—velocity equals acceleration multiplied by time—at a rote level, without really comprehending what she was studying. As a result, she was unable to use her knowledge to solve a problem about a car's rate of acceleration.

Research consistently indicates that when people have a thorough, conceptual understanding of a topic—when they have stored a great deal of information about that topic, with various pieces of information appropriately organized and interrelated in long-term memory—they can more easily use their knowledge to solve problems (Alexander & Judy, 1988; Chi, Glaser, & Rees, 1982; N. Frederiksen, 1984a; Heller & Hungate, 1985; Reif & Heller, 1982; Voss, Greene, Post, & Penner, 1983). For example, students are more likely to apply a principle of physics to a specific situation if they understand the concepts underlying that principle and the situations to which it relates. They are more likely to apply the Pythagorean theorem to the calculation of a diagonal roof if they have learned that theorem at a meaningful level and have associated it with such ideas as "diagonal" and "measurement." And when proposing possible solutions to the problem of rain forest destruction, they are more likely to draw from their knowledge of several disciplines (e.g., from ecology, economics, and psychology) if they have stored ideas from those disciplines in an interrelated, cross-disciplinary fashion.

Here we see yet another reason for teaching a few topics thoroughly, rather than many topics superficially (the *less is more* notion once again). We also see another reason for providing many and different examples and opportunities for practice. Students can study arithmetic by using such diverse examples as balancing a checkbook, calculating change, or predicting the possible profits and necessary supplies of a lemonade stand (e.g., number of cups, amount of lemonade mix). They can learn basic principles of geography (e.g., that large cities are almost always located near major transportation junctions) by examining maps of different countries, as well as by exploring their own local geographic environment. Only by spending time with a certain topic and studying a variety of examples can our students learn that topic in a meaningful fashion and make multiple connections with situations to which that subject matter applies. All too often, students don't have these critical opportunities (e.g., Porter, 1989).

We should note here that our students are also more likely to make connections between classroom material and its potential applications when they anticipate situations in which they might need to use the material to solve problems (J. R. Anderson et al., 1996). Not only should we focus more of our classroom instruction on the application of information, but we should focus more of our assessment procedures on application as well (e.g., Sternberg & Frensch, 1993). To illustrate, here is an example of how we might ask students to apply their knowledge of geographic principles in an assessment situation:

> A map of a hypothetical country includes information as to where bodies of water (e.g., rivers, lakes) and various forms of vegetation (e.g., grasslands, forests) are located. It also includes information about elevation, rainfall, and temperature ranges. A particular spot on the map is marked X. Students are asked such questions as these:
>
> • If people living at the point marked X on the map began to move elsewhere, where would they go, and what direction might they take?

In what areas do you have the depth of knowledge necessary for solving problems successfully? In what areas has your relative lack of knowledge been a handicap?

Provide many real-world examples of a particular principle or procedure.

Include applications in assessment instruments.

How many examinations have you taken over the years that have tested your ability to remember information, but not your ability to *apply* that information? Did such exams give you the message that knowing something was important but that using it was not?

Facilitate retrieval of information relevant to the problem.

- What would be the distribution of population in country X; that is, where would many people live, and where would very few people live?
- Where would large cities develop in country X?
- How would you judge the country's economic potential; that is, which areas might be best for development, which might be worst, and so on? (adapted from Massialas & Zevin, 1983)

By incorporating the application of classroom material into our classroom assignments and tests, we indirectly teach students that this information can be used in a variety of contexts and furthermore *should* be used in these contexts. We will revisit the importance of assessing higher-level thinking skills in our discussion of classroom assessment in Chapter 14.

Retrieval of Relevant Information from Long-term Memory

Obviously, people cannot solve a problem unless they retrieve from long-term memory the information necessary to solve it. But as we discovered in Chapter 6, long-term memory contains a great deal of information, and people cannot possibly retrieve it all in any given situation. Successful problem solving therefore requires that an individual search among the right pieces of information in long-term memory at the right time.

The parts of long-term memory that an individual searches depends on how that person encoded the problem in the first place. For example, if a student sees the word *left* in a word problem and thinks "subtraction," that student will retrieve rules of subtraction even when addition is required. If a student encodes a box only as a container for tacks, that student will not retrieve other characteristics of boxes (e.g., their flat surfaces, their relative stiffness) that might be useful in solving the candle problem. When people have a mental set about a problem (just as *you* may have had in the pigs/chickens problem or the trains/bird problem), they may unnecessarily restrict their search of long-term memory, overlooking stored information that is critical for problem solution.

Situated cognition influences problem-solving success in much the same way that it affects other forms of transfer: Our students may learn how to solve problems in certain contexts yet *not* solve problems requiring similar algorithms or heuristics once they find themselves in a different context (Carraher, Carraher, & Schliemann, 1985; Gay & Cole, 1967; Lave, 1993; Saljo & Wyndhamn, 1992; Schliemann & Carraher, 1993). As an illustration, let's consider a study with 15- and 16-year-old students (Saljo & Wyndhamn, 1992). The students were asked to figure out how much postage they should put on an envelope that weighed a particular amount, and they were given a table of postage rates that would enable them to determine the correct amount. When students were given the task in a social studies class, most of them used the postage table to find the answer. But when students were given the task in a math class, most of them tried to *calculate* the postage in some manner, sometimes figuring it to several decimal places. Curiously, the students in the social studies class were more likely to solve the problem correctly; as a former social studies teacher myself, I suspect that, in class, they were well accustomed to finding information in tables and charts. In contrast, many of the students in the math class apparently never considered pulling the correct postage directly from the table. Instead, they tried to apply some of the complex mathematical operations that served them so well in their daily assignments—operations that were often counterproductive in this situation.

Retrieval of relevant information is, of course, far more likely when material has been learned at a meaningful level. But the concept of *meaningfulness* has relevance for problem solving as well as for learning. Let's turn to the topic of meaningful problem solving now.

Encouraging Meaningful Problem Solving

■ EXPERIENCING FIRSTHAND
Quarters and Dimes

See whether you can solve this problem before you read further.

> The number of quarters a man has is seven times the number of dimes he has. The value of the dimes exceeds the value of the quarters by two dollars and fifty cents. How many has he of each coin? (Paige & Simon, 1966, p. 79) ■

If you found an answer to the problem—any answer at all—then you overlooked an important point: Quarters are worth more than dimes. If there are more quarters than dimes, the value of the dimes cannot possibly be greater than the value of the quarters. The problem makes no sense, and so it cannot be solved.

Unfortunately, when our schools teach problem solving, they focus on teaching algorithms for well-defined problems while omitting explanations of why the algorithms work (Cooney, 1991; R. B. Davis, 1986; J. Hiebert & Lefevre, 1986; Perkins & Salomon, 1989; Perkins & Simmons, 1988). For example, perhaps you can remember learning how to solve a long division problem, but you probably don't remember learning *why* you multiply the divisor by each digit in your answer and write the product in a particular location below the dividend. Or perhaps you were taught a "key word" method for solving word problems: Words such as *altogether* indicate addition, and words such as *left* mean subtraction. This approach is a meaningless one indeed and, as was true for the "Ana" problem presented earlier, often leads to an erroneous solution.

What algorithms have you learned at a meaningless level? ■

When students learn algorithms at a rote level, without understanding the logic behind them, they may often apply the algorithms "unthinkingly" and inappropriately (Perkins & Simmons, 1988; Prawat, 1989; Resnick, 1989; Schoenfeld, 1982, 1985a; Silver, Shapiro, & Deutsch, 1991). As a result, they may obtain illogical or physically impossible results. Consider these instances of meaningless mathematical problem solving as examples:

- A student is asked to figure out how many chickens and how many pigs a farmer has if the farmer has 21 animals with 60 legs in all. The student adds 21 and 60, reasoning that, because the problem says "how many in all," addition is the logical operation (Lester, 1985).

- A student uses subtraction whenever a word problem contains the word *left*— even when a problem actually requiring addition includes the phrase "John left the room to get more apples" (Schoenfeld, 1982).

- A student learns the process of regrouping ("borrowing") in subtraction. In subtracting a number from 803, the student may "borrow" from the 100s column, but only add 10 to the 1s column (Resnick, 1989). Here is an example:

$$\begin{array}{ccc} {}^{7}\!\!\!\!\not{8} & 0 & {}^{1}3 \\ -5 & 0 & 7 \\ \hline 2 & 0 & 6 \end{array}$$

(The correct answer, of course, is 296.)

How might you teach algorithms in your subject area in a meaningful fashion?

Rather than simply teach algorithms at a rote level, we must instead help students understand *why* they do the things they do to solve problems (T. P. Carpenter, 1985; Greeno, 1991; Heller & Hungate, 1985; J. Hiebert & Lefevre, 1986; J. Hiebert & Wearne, 1993; Resnick, 1983). For example, we might demonstrate the rationale behind "borrowing" in subtraction by using toothpicks, some of which have been bundled into groups of ten or one hundred (see Figure 8–4). By showing our students the logic behind problem-solving procedures, we increase the likelihood that they will apply those procedures at appropriate times and obtain plausible results.

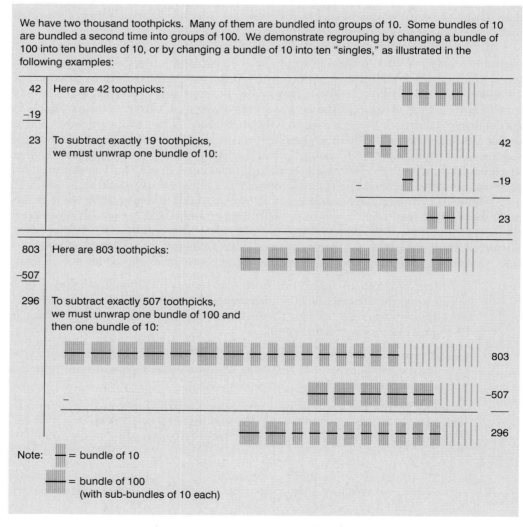

Figure 8–4   Making a Problem-Solving Algorithm Meaningful

Promoting Successful Transfer and Problem Solving

Teach important topics in depth and be sure students learn them thoroughly.

A teacher of a second-year Spanish class teaches only two new verb tenses (preterit and imperfect) during fall semester, saving other tenses (e.g., near past, near future) for later instruction.

Tie class material to things that students already know.

After teaching the fact that water expands when it freezes, a science teacher explains that many of the bumps seen in country roads are frost heaves caused by freezing water.

Give students practice in dealing with ill-defined problems and show them how to make such problems more well-defined.

A teacher asks students in an interdisciplinary class to wrestle with the problem of diminishing rain forests. He starts them off by asking, "What should be the final goal of preservation efforts?" and "What are some of the biological, social, and political factors that you need to consider as you try to solve this problem?"

Teach the information and skills essential in problem solving to a level of automaticity.

An elementary school teacher makes sure that his students have thoroughly mastered the basic multiplication and division facts before teaching them long division.

Provide opportunities for students to apply what they have learned to new situations and problems.

A geography teacher asks students to apply their knowledge of human settlement patterns in explaining why the populations of various countries are distributed as they are.

Ask students to apply what they know in tests and other assessment activities.

A science teacher asks students to use principles of physics to describe how they might move a five-hundred-pound object to a location twenty feet away.

Make school tasks similar to the tasks that students are likely to encounter in the real world.

An English teacher teaches persuasive writing skills by having students write editorials for the school newspaper.

Throughout our discussion of transfer and problem solving, we have repeatedly noted the value of meaningful learning. Do our students realize how important it is to learn class material in a meaningful fashion? Or, like Mary in our case study at the beginning of the chapter, do they believe that rote memorization is a better approach to take? We will answer such questions as these as we discuss the topics of metacognition and study strategies.

Facilitating Metacognition and Study Strategies

- How and when did you learn how to study? Did your teachers give you suggestions as to how you might best learn classroom material? Did your parents provide guidance about your study habits? Did you observe and adapt any of the study strategies that you saw your classmates using? Did you learn how to study mostly through your own trial and error?

- What specific study strategies do you use? For example, do you take notes? Do you outline course material? Do you summarize the things that you read in your textbooks? What does your current grade point average tell you about the effectiveness of your study strategies?

Students vary considerably in the study strategies they use. Consider these three students as examples:

- Nancy is studying for a biology exam. She moves her eyes down each of the assigned pages in the textbook, but all the while she is thinking about the upcoming school dance. Nancy seems to think that as long as her eyes are looking at the page, the information printed on it will somehow sink in.

- Nicola is studying for the same exam. She spends most of her time memorizing terms and definitions in her textbook; eventually, she can recite many of them word for word.

- Norma is also studying for the biology exam. She focuses her efforts on trying to understand basic biological principles and on generating new examples of those principles.

Which student is likely to do best on the biology exam? Considering what we now know about learning and memory, we can predict that Norma will get the highest score of the three girls. Unfortunately, Nicola has not yet discovered that she learns better when she relates new ideas to her prior knowledge than when she memorizes things at a rote level. And poor Nancy knows even less about how to learn effectively: She's not even paying attention to what she thinks she is reading!

When we talk about students' knowledge and beliefs regarding their own cognitive processes and when we talk about students' attempts to regulate their cognitive processes to maximize learning and memory, we are talking about **metacognition** (e.g., A. L. Brown, 1978; Duell, 1986; Flavell, 1979; Flavell & Wellman, 1977; Siegler, 1986). Metacognition includes all of these things:

- Knowing the limits of one's own learning and memory capabilities

- Knowing what learning tasks one can realistically accomplish within a certain amount of time

- Knowing which learning strategies are effective and which are not

- Planning an approach to a learning task that is likely to be successful

- Using effective learning strategies to process and learn new material

- Monitoring one's own knowledge and comprehension—in other words, knowing when information has been successfully learned and when it has not

- Using effective strategies for retrieval of previously stored information

To illustrate, you have undoubtedly learned by now that you can only acquire so much information so fast; you cannot possibly absorb the contents of an entire textbook in one hour. You have also learned that you can store information more quickly and retrieve it more easily if you organize it logically. And perhaps you have also discovered the advantage of checking yourself as you read a textbook, stopping every so often to make sure you've understood what you've just read. In other words, you are metacognitively aware of some things that you need to do (mentally) to learn new information effectively.

The more students know about effective learning strategies—the greater their metacognitive awareness—the higher their classroom achievement is likely to be (L. Baker, 1989; P. L. Peterson, 1988; Perkins, 1995). Unfortunately, many students are unaware of how they can best learn and remember information. Younger children (those in the elementary grades) are especially naive about effective learning strategies (see the discussion of developmental changes in information processing in Chapter 2). But older students are also prone to misconceptions about how they can best learn and remember. For example, many students at all grade levels (even those in college!) erroneously believe that rote learning is an effective study strategy (Dansereau, 1978; Prawat, 1989; Schommer, 1990, 1994a; C. E. Weinstein, 1978).

With each transition to a higher educational level—for example, from elementary school to middle school, from junior high to high school, or from high school to college—teacher expectations for student learning and performance are also higher. At each successive level, students are asked to learn more information and to process it in a more sophisticated fashion. Thus, the simple learning strategies that students develop in grade school (e.g., rehearsal) become less and less effective with each passing year.

Did you have misconceptions about how best to study before you read this book?

Are teachers' expectations for your learning more demanding at the college level than they were at the high school level? If so, have you been able to adapt your study strategies accordingly?

The term metacognition *refers to students' knowledge and beliefs regarding their own cognitive processes, as well as to their attempts to regulate those cognitive processes.*

Yet too often teachers teach content—history, biology, mathematics, and so on—without also teaching students how to *learn* that content (Pressley et al., 1990; J. E. Wilson, 1988). Because students often have little knowledge of how they can best study and learn, they may have difficulty mastering the content that teachers teach. And when they *don't* learn successfully, they may not know why they have failed, nor may they know how to improve their chances of succeeding the next time around (e.g., Horgan, 1990; O'Sullivan & Joy, 1990).

We can better help our students be successful learners if, when teaching specific academic content, we also teach them how to study that content (e.g., Alexander & Judy, 1988; Holt-Reynolds, 1992). But to help students develop and use effective learning and study strategies, we first need to determine which strategies actually work and which do not. Let's see what research tells us about this issue.

Identifying Effective Study Strategies

Research studies point to a number of effective study strategies, including these:

- Identifying important information
- Taking notes
- Retrieving relevant prior knowledge
- Organizing
- Elaborating
- Summarizing
- Monitoring comprehension

As we consider these strategies in the pages that follow, you will undoubtedly find some that you yourself use as you study course material.

Identifying Important Information

THINKING ABOUT WHAT YOU KNOW

What cues do you use to identify important ideas in your textbooks? Are you more likely to believe that something is important if it's printed in *italics* or **boldface**? Do you look for important points in headings, introductions, concluding paragraphs, or summaries? Do you focus on definitions, formulas, or lists of items?

People rarely learn everything they read in a textbook or remember everything they hear in the classroom. Obviously, then, students must be selective in studying course content. The things they choose to study—whether those things are main ideas and critical pieces of information, or isolated facts and trivial details—inevitably affect their learning and school achievement (Dee-Lucas & Larkin, 1991; Dole et al., 1991; R. E. Reynolds & Shirey, 1988).

Students often have difficulty separating central and important information from the trivial and unimportant (Alexander & Jetton, 1996; V. Anderson & Hidi, 1988/1989). Here are some features of books and classroom lectures on which students often focus:

- *The first sentence of a lesson or paragraph:* Many students erroneously believe that the main idea (and perhaps *only* idea) of a paragraph is always found in the first sentence (Mayer, 1984). (We should note here that, in writing instruction, students are often taught to put the main idea first; hence, it is not surprising that they expect to find the same pattern in the writings of others.)

- *Items that look different:* Definitions and formulas often stand out in a textbook—perhaps because they appear in *italics* or **boldface** or perhaps because they are

set apart

- from the rest of the text. As a result, students often focus in on them to the exclusion of other, perhaps more important information (Mayer, 1984). For example, when reading scientific proofs, students often focus their attention on specific equations, rather than on the verbal text that makes those equations meaningful (Dee-Lucas & Larkin, 1991).

- *Items presented in more than one way:* Students are more likely to view material as important when it is presented in several different ways. For example, they are more likely to pay attention to things that teachers describe verbally *and* write on the chalkboard (Kiewra, 1989).

- *Items that are intrinsically interesting:* Students at all levels attend more to interesting statements than to uninteresting ones even if the most interesting statements are relatively unimportant ones (Alexander & Jetton, 1996; V. Anderson & Hidi, 1988/1989; Garner et al., 1991; Garner, Brown, Sanders, & Menke, 1992; R. E. Reynolds & Shirey, 1988).

When important ideas are presented within the middle of a lesson or paragraph, without any obvious cues to make them stand out, and especially when those ideas do not grab students' immediate interest, then students often overlook them.

As teachers, we can facilitate our students' academic success by letting them know what things are most important for them to learn. One obvious thing that we can do is simply tell them exactly what to study. But we can also be more subtle and still get the same message across; here are some examples of things we can do:

- Provide a list of objectives for a lesson.

- Write key concepts and major ideas on the chalkboard.

- Ask questions that focus students' attention toward important points.

Students (especially low-achieving ones) are more likely to learn the important points of a lesson when such "prompts" are provided for them (Kiewra, 1989; R. E. Reynolds & Shirey, 1988; Schraw & Wade, 1991). As students become increasingly able to distinguish important from unimportant information independently of their teacher, these prompts can be gradually phased out.

Taking Notes
No doubt you have at one time or another missed a class and therefore had to rely on a classmate's notes from the class lecture. And no doubt you discovered that the class-

Look through this textbook. Can you find paragraphs in which the main idea is located in the middle or near the end of the paragraph, rather than at the beginning?

Let students know what things are most important to learn.

Do such prompts remind you of Vygotsky's notion of scaffolding?

When teachers write major concepts and ideas on the chalkboard, they provide cues about what things are important for students to learn.

How useful are the notes you take in your classes? Can you think of ways you might improve your notes?

mate's notes were different (perhaps *very* different) from the notes that you yourself usually take. For twenty students in the same classroom, we will find twenty different sets of notes. Each student makes unique assumptions about what is important, what is useful, and what is likely to be on an upcoming exam—assumptions that influence the amount and type of notes that the student takes.

In general, note taking is associated with more successful classroom learning; in fact, when students have *no* opportunity either to take or review notes, they may recall very little of what they hear in a lecture (Hale, 1983; Kiewra, 1989). The process of note taking seems to serve two very important functions—encoding and external storage (Barnett, Di Vesta, & Rogozinski, 1981; Di Vesta & Gray, 1972; Kiewra, 1989):

- *Encoding:* Note taking helps students remember information *even when they have no opportunity to review those notes* (M. J. A. Howe, 1970; Kiewra, 1989). Apparently, the process of taking notes—of writing down things that have been read or heard—helps students encode information in their long-term memories. Furthermore, students who are actively engaged in taking notes are less likely to let their minds wander from what they are reading or listening to in class.

- *External storage:* As we discovered in Chapter 6, retrieval of information from long-term memory is a somewhat undependable process: Even when we have effectively stored information in long-term memory, we can't always find it again. Notes provide an additional means of storing information—in this case, through a mechanism external to the memory system. Whereas memory is often unreliable, notebooks are fairly dependable: The things that we put in them at one time are still present in their original form many days, weeks, or even months later. And reviewing those notes on one or more later occasions does help us remember the information better (Kiewra, 1989).

The extent to which note taking helps students learn and achieve naturally depends on the quantity and quality of the notes taken; the following exercise illustrates this point.

■ **EXPERIENCING FIRSTHAND**
Two Notebooks

Here are two students' notes from the same introductory lesson on dinosaurs.

What differences do you notice in the two sets of notes? From which set could you study more effectively? ■

No doubt you preferred the first set of notes over the second. The first set provides a relatively coherent set of statements about dinosaurs, whereas the second set is too brief and disjointed to make much sense of. In general, quantity of notes is positively correlated with achievement: Students who take more notes do better (Kiewra, 1989). But the quality of notes is equally critical: Notes must reflect the main ideas of a lecture or reading assignment (A. L. Brown, Campione, & Day, 1981; Kiewra, 1985; B. M. Taylor, 1982). Good notes seem to be especially valuable for students who have little prior knowledge about the subject matter they are studying (Shrager & Mayer, 1989).

As teachers, we should encourage students to take notes on their class material. We should also give them suggestions as to what things are most important to include in those notes. And we might occasionally ask to look at students' notebooks, to make sure that the notes students are taking accurately reflect the material they should be emphasizing as they study.

Encourage students to take notes, give suggestions as to what things are most important to include, and occasionally check students' notes for accuracy.

Retrieving Relevant Prior Knowledge

As we discovered in our discussion of information processing in Chapter 6, students can only engage in meaningful learning to the extent that they have previous knowledge to which new information can be related and are also *aware* of the potential relationship. To make multiple connections between new material and their existing knowledge base, students must retrieve the things they already know as they study that new material.

How can we encourage students to think about the things they already know as they encounter new information? One approach that seems to be effective is modeling this strategy for our students. For example, we might read aloud a portion of a textbook, stopping occasionally to tie an idea we read to something we have previously

Model the strategy of making connections to existing knowledge as you read.

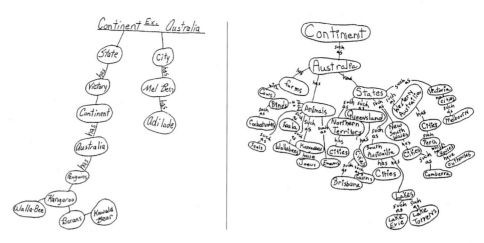

Figure 8–5   Concept maps constructed by two fifth-grade students after watching a slide lecture on Australia.

Source: From *Learning How to Learn* (pp. 100–101) by J. D. Novak and D. B. Gowin, 1984, Cambridge, England: Cambridge University Press. Copyright 1984 by Cambridge University Press. Reprinted with the permission of Cambridge University Press.

Does this approach also remind you of scaffolding?

Encourage students to organize classroom material.

studied in class or to something in our own personal experiences. We can then encourage our students to do likewise, giving suggestions and guiding their efforts as they proceed. Eventually, our students should be able to use the strategy independently, without our assistance (Spires et al., 1990).

Organizing

As we discovered in Chapter 6, organized information is stored and retrieved more easily than unorganized information. When students engage in study activities that help them organize information, they learn more effectively (e.g., DuBois et al., 1988; M. A. McDaniel & Einstein, 1989). For example, one useful way of organizing information is *outlining* the material—a strategy that may be especially helpful to low-achieving students (L. Baker, 1989; M. A. McDaniel & Einstein, 1989; Wade, 1992).

Another strategy that facilitates organization is making a **concept map**—a diagram that depicts the concepts of a unit and their interrelationships (Novak & Gowin, 1984). Figure 8–5 shows concept maps constructed by two fifth-grade students after they watched a slide lecture on Australia. The concepts themselves are in circles; the interrelationships between them are designated by lines and phrases that link pairs of concepts together.

■   EXPERIENCING FIRSTHAND

Mapping Concepts about Concepts

Flip back to the section on concept learning that you read earlier in the chapter. The section contains numerous concepts concerning the topic of concept learning:

undergeneralization	defining features
overgeneralization	correlational features
positive instances	irrelevant features
negative instances	salient

The section also talks about how these concepts are related to one another; for example, *overgeneralization* is a case of incorrectly identifying *negative instances* as examples of a concept, and a concept is easier to learn when its *defining features* are *salient*.

Take out a blank sheet of paper and make a concept map with the ten "concepts about concepts" that I just listed. Write the concepts down in an arrangement that makes sense to you, circle each one, and then add lines and phrases to describe the interrelationships between pairs of concepts. ◼

There is certainly more than one "correct" way to map the ten concepts; the concept map shown in Figure 8–6 is just one of many possibilities. I hope that the exercise helped you organize some of the things that you learned about concepts earlier in the chapter. Furthermore, I hope that it gave you a better understanding of the process of concept mapping itself.

In this map, connections are correctly interpreted by starting at the top and following the lines downward.

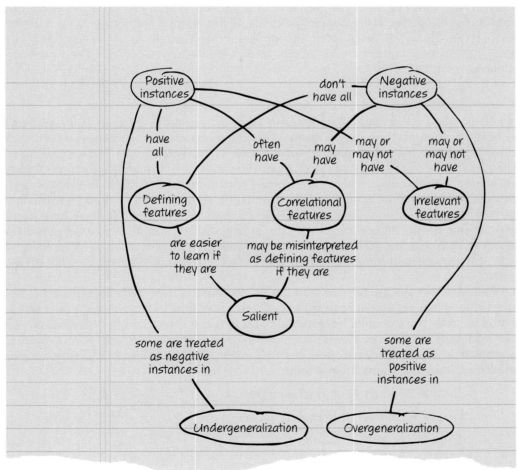

Figure 8–6   One Possible Concept Map for Concepts Related to Concept Learning

Students benefit in numerous ways from constructing their own concept maps for classroom material (Alvermann, 1981; Hawk, 1986; Holley & Dansereau, 1984). By focusing on how concepts relate to one another, students organize material better. They are also more likely to notice how new concepts are related to things they already know; thus, they are more likely to learn the material meaningfully. Furthermore, when students construct a concept map from verbal material (e.g., from a lecture or a textbook), they can encode that material in long-term memory visually, as well as verbally (Novak & Gowin, 1984).

Assign concept-mapping exercises both to help students organize material and to help you assess what they have learned.

Not only do concept maps help students, they may also help us teachers. When we ourselves develop a concept map for a lesson, the organizational scheme of that lesson becomes clearer, and we have a better idea about how to sequence the presentation of ideas. And when we examine the concept maps that our students have constructed, students' understanding of a lesson becomes readily apparent, as do any misconceptions that students may have (Novak & Gowin, 1984; Novak & Musonda, 1991). For example, if you look once again at Figure 8–5, you should notice how very different the two children's knowledge of Australia appears to be even though both children received the same information. And if you look carefully at the concept map on the left, you should detect several misconceptions that the student has. For example, Adelaide is *not* part of Melbourne: It is a different city altogether! If geographic knowledge about Australia is an instructional objective, then this student clearly needs further instruction to correct such misinformation.

Elaborating

Whether they are reading, taking notes in a lecture, or studying for an exam, students typically do better when they elaborate on course material—for example, when they draw inferences from that material or consider its implications. To illustrate, imagine that Pai and Paulo are studying the same reading passage in history. Pai focuses on facts presented in the passage, trying to remember who did what and when. Paulo tries to go beyond the material he actually reads, speculating about possible reasons why people did the things they did, thinking about how a historical event has relevance for current events, and so on. Pai and Paulo may do equally well on simple fact-based questions about the passage. But Paulo will do better on tasks that involve drawing inferences; he will also explain and integrate the material more effectively (Van Rossum & Schenk, 1984).

Model elaboration.

Give students general questions to consider as they read questions that promote elaboration.

How can we encourage our students to elaborate as they study class material? For one thing, when we model retrieval of relevant prior knowledge, we can model elaboration as well—for example, by stopping to identify our own examples of a concept we are reading about, to consider the implications of a new principle, and so on. Another approach is to give students questions to consider as they listen to a lecture or read their textbook—questions such as these:

- Can I think of any additional examples of . . . ?

- What is the difference between . . . and . . . ?

- How are . . . and . . . similar?

- What are the strengths and weaknesses of . . . ?

- What conclusions can I draw about . . . ?

- How might I use . . . ?

- What might happen if . . . ? (adapted from A. King, 1992)

Yet another approach is to teach our students to develop and answer their *own* elaborative questions—a strategy sometimes known as **elaborative interrogation** (Kahl & Woloshyn, 1994; A. King, 1992, 1994; E. Wood et al., 1994). For example, if our students are studying this fact:

The Gulf Stream warms the British Isles.

we might encourage them to ask themselves, "*Why* does the Gulf Stream warm the British Isles?" and then generate a reasonable answer to the question. Or if our students are studying two or more related concepts (e.g., series vs. parallel circuits; monarchies, theocracies, and democracies), we might encourage them to ask questions concerning the similarities and differences among the concepts. Elaborative interrogation is not necessarily an easy strategy for students to develop; accordingly, they may sometimes use it more effectively, at least at first, when they work in pairs or small groups to develop and answer questions (A. King, 1994; E. Wood et al., 1994).

Summarizing

Another important study strategy is summarizing the material being studied (V. Anderson & Hidi, 1988/1989; Dole et al., 1991; Hidi & Anderson, 1986; A. King, 1992). Effective summarizing usually entails at least three processes (Hidi & Anderson, 1986):

- Separating important from unimportant information

- Condensing details into more general ideas

- Identifying important relationships among those general ideas

Many students have trouble summarizing material even at the high school level (V. Anderson & Hidi, 1988/1989). Probably the best way of helping students develop this strategy is to ask them to summarize the things they hear and read on a regular basis. For example, we might occasionally give homework assignments asking them to write a summary of a textbook chapter. Or we might ask them to work in cooperative groups to develop a brief oral presentation that condenses the information they have learned about a particular topic. At the beginning, we should restrict summarizing assignments to short, simple, and well-organized passages involving material with which students are familiar; we can assign more challenging material as students become more proficient summarizers (V. Anderson & Hidi, 1988/1989).

Monitoring Comprehension

■ E X P E R I E N C I N G   F I R S T H A N D
Looking Back

Stop for a minute and ask yourself this question:
What have I learned from the last five pages of this textbook?
Write down your answer on a piece of scrap paper. ■

Now go back and look at the five pages just before this one. Does your answer include all the major points covered in these pages? Is there something that you thought you understood but realize now that you didn't? Is there something that you

Teach students how to generate their own elaborative questions.

When we consider *reciprocal teaching* in Chapter 13, we will discover yet another way of promoting students' elaboration.

Give students practice in summarizing information.

never learned at all—perhaps something that you were "reading" when your mind was someplace altogether different?

Successful students engage in **comprehension monitoring:** They periodically check themselves to make sure they understand the things they are reading or hearing. Furthermore, successful students take steps to correct the situation when they *don't* comprehend—for example, by rereading a section of a textbook or by asking a question in class (L. Baker, 1989; L. Baker & Brown, 1984; Hacker, 1995; Haller, Child, & Walberg, 1988). In contrast, low achievers seldom check themselves or take appropriate action when they don't comprehend. Poor readers, for instance, rarely reread paragraphs they haven't sufficiently understood the first time around (L. Baker & Brown, 1984).

Many students at all grade levels engage in little if any comprehension monitoring (Dole et al., 1991; Markman, 1979; Mayer, 1992; J. W. Thomas, 1993). When students don't monitor their own comprehension, they don't know what they know and what they don't know: They may think they have mastered something when they really haven't (Horgan, 1990; Schraw, Potenza, & Nebelsick-Gullet, 1993; Spires, 1990; Voss & Schauble, 1992). This **illusion of knowing** is seen in students at all levels, even college students (L. Baker, 1989). Perhaps you have a friend who has difficulty on exams despite many hours of reading and studying the textbook. Perhaps you even find yourself in this predicament on occasion. If so, then your friend and you may not be adequately monitoring your comprehension—for example, by asking yourselves questions periodically to make certain that you are learning the things you read. Our case study at the beginning of the chapter provides another example of the illusion of knowing: When Mary studies, she fails to realize that she doesn't understand the difference between *velocity* and *acceleration*, so she is later quite surprised to find herself doing poorly on her test.

To be successful learners—and more specifically, to *know what they know*—students should monitor their comprehension both *while* they study and *after* they study (Horgan, 1990; T. O. Nelson & Dunlosky, 1991; Pressley, Borkowski, & Schneider, 1987; Spires, 1990). As teachers, we can promote better comprehension-monitoring skills in our students by teaching them **self-questioning.** Not only might we provide questions that students can answer as they go along, but we can also encourage students to formulate and ask *themselves* questions; such questions might include both simple, fact-based questions and the elaborative questions that I described earlier. When students "test" themselves about the material they have just studied, they have a better sense of what they do and don't know, and as a result they ultimately learn the material more completely (Dole et al., 1991; Spires, 1990). Because students are often better judges of what they have learned *after* they have studied, rather than during the study session itself (T. O. Nelson & Dunlosky, 1991), we should also suggest that they follow up their studying with a self-test at some later point in time.

■ EXPERIENCING FIRSTHAND
Self-Reflection

Which of the study strategies that I have just described do you use frequently? Which of them do you use seldom or not at all? Take a minute to fill in the empty boxes in Table 8–3. ■

Judging from the entries you have made in Table 8–3, do you think you are using effective study strategies? Do you see areas for improvement? Study strategies are com-

Are some of the questions in the margins of this textbook helping you monitor your comprehension? Do you typically ask similar questions of yourself when you read?

■

Encourage students to "test" themselves by asking themselves questions both as they study and at some later point in time.

As you read a textbook, when is the information in working memory? When is it in long-term memory? With your answers to both questions in mind, explain why students should monitor their comprehension not only as they read but also at a later time.

■

Table 8–3   Which Study Strategies Do You Use, and When?

STUDY STRATEGY	IN WHICH CLASSES OR SUBJECTS DO YOU USE THIS STRATEGY FREQUENTLY?	IN WHICH CLASSES OR SUBJECTS MIGHT YOU BENEFIT FROM USING THIS STRATEGY MORE OFTEN?	WHAT FACTORS AFFECT YOUR ABILITY TO USE THIS STRATEGY SUCCESSFULLY?
Identifying important information			
Taking notes			
Retrieving relevant prior knowledge			
Organizing			
Elaborating			
Summarizing			
Monitoring comprehension			

plex metacognitive skills that are not easily acquired; your own strategies will undoubtedly continue to improve over time as you study increasingly more challenging material in your college courses.

Some of the study strategies that I've just described, such as taking notes and making outlines, are behaviors that we can actually see. Others, such as retrieving relevant prior knowledge and monitoring comprehension, are internal mental processes that we *can't* see. It is probably the latter set of strategies—those internal mental processes— that ultimately affect students' learning (Kardash & Amlund, 1991). As we help students develop study strategies, we must remember that behavioral strategies (e.g., taking notes) are going to be useful only to the extent that they facilitate more effective information processing.

Under what conditions are students most likely to use effective study strategies? It is to this question that we turn now.

Remember that behavioral study strategies are only helpful to the extent that they facilitate more effective information processing.

Examining Factors Affecting Strategy Use

Many students at all grade levels use relatively ineffective study strategies when trying to learn classroom material. Here are three factors that appear to influence their choice and use of strategies:

- Their knowledge base
- Their beliefs about the nature of knowledge and knowledge acquisition
- Training in study strategies

Remember that students are more likely to use effective strategies when they have a knowledge base about the topic from which to draw.

Can you find further justification for the *less is more* principle in the top paragraph?

Knowledge Base

Students are more likely to use effective strategies when they have a fair amount of prior knowledge about a topic (Greene, 1994; Schneider, 1993; E. Wood et al., 1994). Considering what you've learned about long-term memory storage processes in Chapter 6, this principle should hardly surprise you. Such processes as meaningful learning, organization, and elaboration all involve making connections between new material and things already stored in long-term memory—connections that are more likely to be made when long-term memory contains information directly relevant to the topic at hand.

Beliefs About the Nature of Knowledge and Knowledge Acquisition

Different students have different views regarding the nature of knowledge and knowledge acquisition—different **epistemological beliefs**—and such views influence the ways in which they study and learn (Purdie, Hattie, & Douglas, 1996; Schommer, 1994a, 1994b, in press; Schraw & Bruning, 1995). For example, many students believe that knowledge is black-and-white (ideas are indisputably either right or wrong) and that you either have that knowledge or you don't (knowledge is an all-or-nothing proposition). But other students recognize that there may be different, equally valid points of view on the same topic that could all legitimately be called "knowledge" (Schommer, 1994b). The former group of students is more likely to believe that learning should be a relatively rapid process, and so they will give up quickly if they find themselves struggling to understand classroom material (Schommer, 1994b).

As another example of how students' epistemological beliefs may differ, some students believe that when they read a textbook, information is directly transmitted in a relatively unaltered fashion from the page to themselves; they may also believe that studying a textbook simply means learning isolated facts, perhaps in a relatively passive manner. In contrast, other students believe that learning from reading requires them to construct their own meanings from the information presented in the textbook and that they should actively attempt to organize and apply the subject matter about which they are reading. It is the latter students—those who think of reading as a constructive process—who are most likely to process what they read in a meaningful and effective fashion (Purdie et al., 1996; Schommer, 1994a, 1994b; Schraw & Bruning, 1995).

Foster productive epistemological beliefs.

As teachers, we must communicate to our students what we ourselves have already learned about knowledge and knowledge acquisition (Schommer, 1994b):

- That knowledge does not always mean having clear-cut answers to difficult, complex issues

- That knowledge involves knowing the interrelationships among ideas, as well as the ideas themselves

- That learning involves active construction of knowledge, rather than just a passive "reception" of it

- That understanding a body of information and ideas sometimes requires persistence and hard work

In doing so, we increase the likelihood that our students will apply effective study strategies when they study classroom material.

Table 8–4 *Promoting More Effective Study Strategies*

PRINCIPLE	EDUCATIONAL IMPLICATION	EXAMPLE
Study strategies are most effectively learned within the context of particular content domains.	As we present academic content to our students—through lectures, reading assignments, and so on—we should simultaneously teach them how to study that content.	We can give students specific questions to ask themselves (thereby facilitating comprehension monitoring) as they read a chapter in their textbooks.
Students are more likely to acquire sophisticated study strategies when their initial efforts are scaffolded to promote success. Such **metacognitive scaffolding** should be phased out as students become more proficient in strategy use.	We can scaffold students' attempts to use new strategies in a number of ways—for example, by modeling such strategies ourselves, giving clues about when certain strategies are appropriate, providing opportunities for group study (allowing students to observe one another's strategies), requiring mastery of increasingly more complex material, and giving feedback regarding appropriate and inappropriate strategy use.	If we want students to organize material in a particular way, we can provide an organizational chart that cooperative learning groups fill out.
Students learn more effectively when their study strategies are numerous and varied.	As appropriate opportunities arise, we should continue to introduce new strategies—note taking, elaboration, self-questioning, mnemonics, and so on— throughout the school year.	We can suggest that students use such mnemonics as verbal mediation and the keyword method to learn the capitals of South American countries or the meanings of Japanese vocabulary words.
Students are more likely to use effective study strategies when they understand why those strategies are useful.	We should explain the usefulness of various strategies in terms that students understand.	We can show students how note taking helps them keep their minds from wandering during class and how comprehension monitoring enables them to identify weak spots in their knowledge of class material.
Students use strategies more effectively if they know when each one is most appropriate.	We should point out situations in which particular strategies are likely to be helpful.	We can encourage students to elaborate on material—by drawing implications, generating new examples, and so on— when we expect them to apply it to new situations and problems.
Students are most likely to master effective strategies when they can practice them over a long period of time and across a wide variety of tasks.	We should give students numerous and varied opportunities to apply the strategies that we teach them.	We can ask students' previous teachers what strategies they have taught and then explain how such strategies are applicable in our own classrooms as well.
Students are likely to use effective strategies only when they believe that they can ultimately learn classroom material successfully.	As we teach various study strategies, we should make sure each student is eventually able to apply them successfully. We can also expose students to peers who use the strategies effectively.	After a lecture, we can place students into small groups where they look at the notes each group member has taken and then combine everyone's notes into a single, comprehensive set.

Sources: Barnett, Di Vesta, & Rogozinski, 1981; Borkowski, Carr, Rellinger, & Pressley, 1990; A. Collins, Brown, & Newman, 1989; Hattie, Biggs, & Purdie, 1996; Nist, Simpson, Olejnik, & Mealey, 1991; Palincsar & Brown, 1984; Paris, 1988; Paris & Winograd, 1990; Pintrich, Garcia, & De Groot, 1994; Pressley, Borkowski, & Schneider, 1987; Pressley, El-Dinary, Marks, Brown, & Stein, 1992; Pressley, Harris, & Marks, 1992; Rosenshine & Meister, 1992; J. W. Thomas, 1993; Vygotsky, 1978; C. E. Weinstein, Goetz, & Alexander, 1988; West, Farmer, & Wolff, 1991.

Study Strategies Training

Can students be taught to study more effectively? Research studies answer this question with a firm *yes* (DuBois et al., 1988; Kahl & Woloshyn, 1994; C. C. Kulik, Kulik, & Shwalb, 1983; Paris, 1988; Paris, Newman, & McVey, 1982; Pressley, El-Dinary, Marks, Brown, & Stein, 1992; C. E. Weinstein, Goetz, & Alexander, 1988; J. E. Wilson, 1988; E. Wood et al., 1994). Effective study skills training programs often include components such as these:

- Time management (e.g., planning when and how long to study)
- Effective learning and reading strategies
- Note-taking strategies
- Specific memory techniques (e.g., mnemonics)
- Comprehension-monitoring strategies
- Test-taking strategies

Graduates of successful study skills training programs are more confident about their ability to succeed in the classroom and, in fact, do achieve at higher levels (Paris, 1988; Pressley, El-Dinary, et al., 1992; J. E. Wilson, 1988).

How can we help students "learn how to learn"? Researchers have identified principles that describe the conditions under which students are most likely to acquire and use effective study skills. Table 8–4 presents these principles, as well are their implications for classroom practice.

Do you study a little bit each day or procrastinate until the last minute? Why is the former approach more likely to be effective?

INTO THE CLASSROOM
Helping Students Learn to Learn

Teach study skills within the context of academic subject areas.

> When a health teacher tells students to read Chapter 3 of their textbook, he also talks with them about strategies they might use to help them remember the things they read.

Model effective study strategies.

> A student reads aloud a passage describing how, during Columbus's first voyage across the Atlantic, many members of the crew wanted to turn around and return to Spain. The teacher says, "Let's think of some reasons why the crew might have wanted to go home. Do you think some of them might have been homesick? Do you think some of them might have been afraid of what lay ahead in uncharted waters? What other possible reasons can we identify?"

Identify situations in which various strategies are likely to be useful.

> A science teacher says to her class, "We've studied several features of the nine planets in our solar system—size, color, composition, distance from the sun, and duration of revolution around the sun. This sounds like a situation where a two-dimensional chart might help us organize the information better."

Give students opportunities to practice using specific study strategies.

> An elementary school teacher has members of a reading group take turns summarizing the passages that the group reads.

Scaffold students' initial efforts at using various study strategies and gradually remove the scaffolding as they become more proficient.

> A social studies teacher encourages her students to take notes, gives suggestions as to what things are most important to include in those notes, and occasionally checks students' notes for accuracy.

Encourage students to "test" themselves by asking themselves questions both as they study and at some later point in time.

> An elementary school teacher instructs his students to study their spelling words as soon as they get home from school and then to make sure they can still remember how to spell those words after they have eaten dinner. "You might also want to call another student on the telephone and ask that person to test you on the words," he suggests.

CONSIDERING DIVERSITY IN HIGHER-LEVEL THINKING SKILLS

In our discussion of higher-level thinking skills, we have noted the importance of a solid knowledge base for both successful problem solving and effective study strategies. Students with different backgrounds will, of course, have different knowledge about the world, knowing a great deal about some topics yet little if anything about others. Furthermore, students of different cultural backgrounds may come to us with somewhat different concepts and, therefore, with somewhat different ways of categorizing and interpreting their experiences. For example, when giving directions, natives of Hawaii rarely speak in terms of north, south, east, and west; instead, they are more likely to talk about going toward the sea (*makai*) or toward the mountains (*mauka*). Some students may even have concepts that we ourselves don't have; for example, the Mexican Americans in my own community have different names for several varieties of peppers that, for me, all fall into one category—hot peppers.

Furthermore, students' previous experiences may have influenced the particular thinking skills that they have developed. For example, thanks to the phenomenon of situated cognition, some students may have developed effective problem-solving strategies within the contexts of their own home and neighborhood environments (e.g., easily performing complex mathematical calculations while selling gum and candy on the street), yet have difficulty transferring what they've learned to more formal classroom tasks involving similar skills (Carraher et al., 1985; Gay & Cole, 1967). And students whose previous educational experiences have focused on drills and rote memorization (e.g., as is true in some Asian schools) may have little awareness of the value of such learning strategies as meaningful learning and elaboration (e.g., Ho, 1994).

Remember that students from different backgrounds will have different background knowledge; for example, students from different cultures may have somewhat different concepts for categorizing the world.

Remember that students' problem-solving skills may have developed in different contexts and be somewhat context-bound. Remember, too, that some students' educational backgrounds may not have encouraged effective study strategies.

Accommodating Students with Special Needs

We are especially apt to find diversity in the higher-level thinking skills—in concept learning, transfer, problem solving, and study strategies—of our students with special needs. Table 8–5 presents some of the characteristics that we are likely to see in these students.

STUDENTS IN INCLUSIVE SETTINGS

Table 8–5   Promoting Higher-Level Thinking Skills in Students with Special Educational Needs

STUDENTS WITH SPECIAL NEEDS	CHARACTERISTICS THAT THESE STUDENTS MAY EXHIBIT	CLASSROOM STRATEGIES THAT MAY BE BENEFICIAL FOR THESE STUDENTS
Students with specific cognitive or academic deficits	Difficulties in problem solving, perhaps because of limited working memory capacity, inability to identify important aspects of a problem, or inability to retrieve appropriate problem-solving strategies Less metacognitive awareness or control of learning Use of few and relatively inefficient learning strategies Increased strategy use after training	Present simple problems at first and then gradually move to more difficult ones as students gain proficiency and self-confidence. Teach techniques for minimizing the load on working memory during problem solving (e.g., writing the parts of a problem on paper, making a diagram of the problem situation). Teach more effective learning strategies (e.g., taking notes, using mnemonics) and identify occasions when each strategy is likely to be useful. Scaffold students' use of new learning strategies (e.g., provide outlines to guide note taking, ask questions that encourage retrieval of prior knowledge).
Students with specific social or behavioral deficits	Deficiencies in social problem-solving skills Limited learning strategies (for some students)	Teach social problem-solving skills (see Chapter 10 for ideas). Provide guidance in using effective learning and study strategies (e.g., giving outlines that guide note taking, questions that encourage retrieval of prior knowledge).
Students with general delays in cognitive and social functioning	Difficulty in transferring information and skills to new situations Few effective problem-solving strategies Lack of metacognitive awareness or control of learning Lack of learning strategies, especially in the absence of strategies training	Teach new information and skills in the specific contexts and situations in which you want students to be able to use them. Present simple problems and guide students through each step of the solutions. Teach relatively simple learning strategies (e.g., rehearsal, specific mnemonics) and give students ample practice using them.
Students with advanced cognitive development	Rapid concept learning Greater transfer of learning to new situations Greater effectiveness in problem solving; more sophisticated problem-solving strategies; greater flexibility in strategy use; less susceptibility to mental sets Use of relatively sophisticated learning strategies	Place greater emphasis on higher-level thinking skills (e.g., transfer, problem solving) within the curriculum. Teach higher-level thinking skills within the context of specific classroom topics, rather than in isolation from academic content.

Sources: Brownell, Mellard, & Deshler, 1993; Campione, Brown, & Bryant, 1985; Candler-Lotven, Tallent-Runnels, Olivárez, Hildreth, 1994; B. Clark, 1992; E. S. Ellis & Friend, 1991; N. R. Ellis, 1979; Frasier, 1989; K. R. Harris, 1982; Heward, 1996; M. C. Linn, Clement, Pulos, & Sullivan, 1989; Maker, 1993; Maker & Schiever, 1989; Meichenbaum, 1977; C. D. Mercer, 1991; Patton, Beirne-Smith, & Payne, 1990; Piirto, 1994; Porath, 1988; Pressley, 1995; Pulos & Linn, 1981; Scruggs & Mastropieri, 1992; Stanley, 1980; H. L. Swanson, 1993; Torrance, 1989; Turnbull, Turnbull, Shank, & Leal, 1995; Wong, 1991b; Yell, 1993.
Compiled with the assistance of Dr. Margie Garanzini-Daiber and Dr. Margaret Cohen, University of Missouri—St. Louis.

Particularly noteworthy in this context is the diversity that we are apt to find in students' metacognitive awareness and use of study strategies. Many of our students with learning disabilities will demonstrate little knowledge or use of effective strategies (E. S. Ellis & Friend, 1991; H. L. Swanson, 1993; Wong, 1991b). Students with mental retardation are likely to show even greater deficits in metacognitive skills; in addition, they will often have difficulty transferring any strategies they learn to new situations (Campione, Brown, & Bryant, 1985). In contrast, our gifted students will typically have more sophisticated study strategies than their classmates (Candler-Lotven, Tallent-Runnels, Olivárez, & Hildreth, 1994).

For many students with special needs, we may have to teach complex cognitive skills explicitly and with considerable **metacognitive scaffolding**—that is, with close guidance and assistance in the use of specific learning strategies. For example, we might provide partially filled-in outlines to guide students' note taking (Heward, 1996); Figure 8–7

For students with special needs, teach higher-level skills explicitly and with considerable scaffolding.

MUSCLES

A. *Number of Muscles*

    1.   There are approximately _____ muscles in the human body.

B. *How Muscles Work*

    1.   Muscles work in two ways:

        a.   They _____, or shorten.

        b.   They _____, or lengthen.

C. *Kinds of Muscles*

    1.   _____ muscles are attached to the bones by _____.

        a.   These muscles are _____ (voluntary/involuntary).

        b.   The purpose of these muscles is to _____

                _____.

    2.   _____ muscles line some of the body's _____.

        a.   These muscles are _____ (voluntary/involuntary).

        b.   The purpose of these muscles is to _____

                _____.

    3.   The _____ muscle is the only one of its kind; it is also called the _____.

        a.   This muscle is _____ (voluntary/ involuntary).

        The purpose of this muscle is to _____

                _____.

Figure 8–7   An Example of Metacognitive Scaffolding: A Partially Filled-in Outline That Can Guide Students' Note Taking

presents an example of such an outline. We might also indicate when particular strategies (e.g., elaboration, comprehension monitoring) are appropriate and model the use of such strategies with specific classroom subject matter (E. S. Ellis & Friend, 1991). Finally, we must give students opportunities to practice their newly acquired strategies, along with feedback about how effectively they are using each one (E. S. Ellis & Friend, 1991).

LOOKING AT THE BIG PICTURE: PROMOTING HIGHER-LEVEL THINKING SKILLS IN THE CLASSROOM

Teach higher-level thinking skills within the context of specific topics.

As teachers, we will occasionally run across packaged curricular programs designed to teach complex thought processes such as problem solving or study strategies in relative isolation from school subject matter. But our discussion of situated cognition tells us that such programs are likely to have little if any long-term benefit for our students. Instead, we are better advised to teach higher-level thinking skills within the context of specific topics—for example, teaching reasoning and problem-solving skills in science or teaching creativity in writing (M. C. Linn et al., 1989; Porath, 1988; Pulos & Linn, 1981; Stanley, 1980).

If you have already read the discussion of individual differences in Chapter 4, then you are familiar with Robert Sternberg's theory of intelligence. Sternberg proposes that specific cognitive processes are one critical aspect of human intelligence. To the extent that our students are able to process information in sophisticated ways—to separate important information from irrelevant details, find relationships among seemingly different ideas, interpret new situations in useful ways, identify effective problem solving strategies, and so on—they all become more "intelligent" human beings.

Demonstrate both by what you say and by what you do that school is more than just a place for learning isolated facts at a rote level.

If, as teachers, we focus classroom activities on the learning of isolated facts and if we also use assessment techniques that emphasize students' knowledge of those facts, our students will naturally begin to believe that school learning is a process of absorbing information in a rote, meaningless fashion and then regurgitating it later on. In contrast, if we focus class time on *processing* information—on understanding, organizing, elaborating, applying, analyzing, and evaluating it—and if we also assess students' ability to transform classroom material, rather than simply to repeat it in its original form, then our students must begin to develop learning and memory strategies that will serve them well in the world beyond the classroom.

We have spent this chapter, as well as the previous two chapters, emphasizing the cognitive processes that influence students' learning. But learning involves more than just cognition; it involves behavior as well. In the next chapter, we will consider the behavioral side of human learning as we turn our attention to the *behaviorist* perspective.

CASE STUDY: *Checks and Balances*

Mr. Chen has just finished a unit on the three branches of the United States Government—the executive, legislative, and judicial branches. He is appalled at some of his students' responses to the essay question he gives. Here are some examples of things that his students have written in response to this question:

How do the three branches of government provide a system of "checks and balances"? Make up an example to illustrate how one branch might serve as a check and balance for another branch.

Debra: "The judicial branch finds out if people are innocent or guilty. The executive branch executes the sentences that guilty people get."

Mark: "The system of checks and balances is when one branch of government makes sure another branch doesn't do something wrong. I can't think of any examples."

Seth: "I don't have anything about this in my notes. Checks and balances have something to do with the way the government spends money."

Karen: "I did all the reading, honest I did! But now I can't remember anything about this."

- To what extent have Mr. Chen's students learned the concepts that he was trying to teach them (more specifically, the three branches of government and the system of checks and balances)? What strategies might *you* use to teach these concepts?

- What evidence do you see that Mr. Chen's students have poor study skills? If you were teaching Mr. Chen's class, what things might you do to help the students study and learn more effectively?

SUMMING UP

Concept Learning

A concept is a way of mentally grouping or categorizing objects or events. Students truly understand a concept when they know its defining features and can accurately identify both positive and negative instances (examples and nonexamples) of the concept. We can help our students learn concepts more effectively by giving definitions, presenting numerous and varied positive and negative instances (including a prototypical example), and asking students to generate their own examples.

Transfer

Transfer occurs when something learned in one situation either helps (for positive transfer) or hinders (for negative transfer) learning or performance in another situation. Transfer is more likely to occur when relevant information and skills are retrieved in the transfer situa-

tion. Unfortunately, most information and skills are acquired in specific contexts (the phenomenon of situated cognition), decreasing the likelihood that they will be retrieved outside those contexts. We can do many things to help students apply the things they learn in school to new situations; for instance, we can explore topics in depth rather than superficially, show students the many ways in which classroom material can be applied, and give them numerous opportunities to practice using that material, especially in real-world situations.

Problem Solving

Solving problems is one form of transfer. Schools more frequently teach students how to solve well-defined problems, rather than ill-defined ones, yet real-world problems are often quite ill-defined in nature. We can help students become more effective problem solvers in a number of ways—by teaching algorithms and heuristics relevant to various problem situations, helping students understand the meaning and rationale underlying particular problem-solving procedures, providing practice in dealing with and defining ill-defined problems, and promoting automaticity with regard to fundamental knowledge and skills.

Metacognition and Study Strategies

Metacognition includes both the beliefs students have about their own cognitive processes and their attempts to regulate their information processing to maximize learning and memory. Many students of all ages have misconceptions about how they can best learn and remember information; in other words, they are metacognitively naive. In addition to teaching academic content, we should concurrently teach students effective strategies for studying that content (e.g., elaborating, summarizing, monitoring comprehension) and give

them sufficient practice and scaffolding to ensure their success in applying such strategies. Ultimately, we must help our students discover that school is more than just a place for learning isolated facts at a rote level.

Diversity in Higher-Level Thinking Skills

Our students will show considerable diversity in their higher-level thinking skills. For example, students from diverse cultural backgrounds, though they may have developed effective problem-solving strategies within the contexts of their own home and neighborhood environments, may have difficulty transferring what they've learned to more formal classroom tasks involving similar skills. And many of our students with special needs may have acquired few if any effective study strategies and so may need considerable scaffolding in their early attempts at using such strategies.

KEY CONCEPTS

lower-level questions (p. 308)
higher-level questions (p. 309)
concept (p. 310)
undergeneralization (p. 311)
overgeneralization (p. 311)
positive versus negative instances
  (p. 311)
defining features (p. 311)
correlational features (p. 313)
irrelevant features (p. 313)

salience (p. 314)
prototype (p. 318)
transfer (p. 323)
positive versus negative transfer (p. 323)
specific versus general transfer (p. 324)
formal discipline (p. 330)
situated cognition (p. 331)
well-defined versus ill-defined problems
  (p. 334)
algorithm (p. 335)

heuristic (p. 335)
mental set (p. 340)
metacognition (p. 348)
concept map (p. 354)
elaborative interrogation (p. 357)
comprehension monitoring (p. 358)
illusion of knowing (p. 358)
self-questioning (p. 358)
epistemological beliefs (p. 360)
metacognitive scaffolding (p. 365)

Modifying Students' Behavior

- Think about the many new behaviors that you've acquired over the years. For example, what household chores have you learned how to do? What athletic skills have you developed? What behaviors have you acquired in order to interact effectively with other people?

- What stimuli in the environment have encouraged the development of such behaviors? For example, did your mother or father give you an allowance for completing certain household chores? Did friends or coaches praise your athletic achievements? Did you find that others responded more favorably to you when you behaved in certain ways?

AS WE GROW from infants into mature adults, we learn thousands of new behaviors. As toddlers, we learn to walk, feed ourselves, and ask for what we want. As preschoolers, we learn to brush our teeth, ride a tricycle, and use scissors. During the elementary school years, we begin to use a calculator, write in cursive letters, and play team sports. As adolescents, we may learn how to drive a car, ask someone for a date, or perform in an orchestra. In many cases, we develop such behaviors because our environment encourages us, or perhaps even requires us, to do so.

Have you previously studied behaviorism in another class? If so, what behaviorist concepts and principles can you recall?

In our general survey of learning theories in Chapter 5, I described a theoretical perspective known as **behaviorism**—a perspective that focuses on how environmental stimuli bring about changes in the behaviors that people exhibit. In this chapter, we will use behaviorist theories to understand how, as teachers, we can help students acquire behaviors that are perhaps more complex, productive, or prosocial than the ones they exhibit when they first enter our classrooms. After first considering the basic assumptions that underlie the behaviorist perspective, we will examine *classical conditioning,* a form of learning that may explain some of the emotional responses that our students are likely to have to stimuli in their environment. We will then consider *operant conditioning,* a phenomenon whereby students' frequency of making a particular response increases after being followed by reinforcement. Throughout our discussion of behaviorism, we will identify numerous principles we can use to help our students develop productive classroom behaviors and life skills; we will also identify principles through which we can reduce or eliminate any behaviors that are likely to interfere with academic achievement or effective social interaction. At the end of the chapter, we will look at the nature of student diversity from a behaviorist viewpoint; we will also consider how we can facilitate the classroom success of a particular group of students with special needs—those with emotional and behavioral disorders.

By the end of the chapter, you should be able to:

1. Describe the assumptions underlying behaviorism and their implications for classroom practice.

2. Distinguish between classical conditioning and operant conditioning, and use each of these learning theories to explain how a variety of responses may be learned in the classroom.

3. List numerous forms that reinforcement may take in a classroom setting.

4. Explain how you can apply such concepts as shaping, generalization, discrimination, extinction, reinforcement of incompatible behaviors, punishment, and

intermittent reinforcement to help students develop and maintain appropriate and productive classroom behaviors.

5. Use behaviorist principles to explain the diversity that you are likely to see in students' behaviors.

6. Devise strategies for promoting the classroom performance of students with emotional and behavioral disorders.

CASE STUDY: *The Attention Getter*

James is the sixth child in a family of nine children. He likes many things; for example, he likes rock music, comic books, basketball, and strawberry ice cream. But more than anything else, James likes attention.

James is a skillful attention getter. He gets his teacher's attention by blurting answers out in class, throwing paper clips and erasers in the teacher's direction, and refusing to turn in classroom assignments. He gets the attention of classmates by teasing them, poking them, or writing obscenities on the rest room walls. By the middle of the school year, James is getting an extra bonus as well: His antics send him to the main office often enough that he has the school principal's attention at least once a week.

It's true that the attention that James gets is often in the form of a teacher's scolding, a classmate's angry retort, or the principal's admonishment that "We can't have any more of this behavior, young man." But after all—attention is attention.

- Why do you think James chooses such inappropriate behaviors (rather than more appropriate ones) as a way of getting the attention of others? Can you speculate on possible reasons?

- Exactly what has James learned? Can you derive a principle of learning from James's attention-getting behavior?

IDENTIFYING BASIC ASSUMPTIONS OF BEHAVIORISM

When considering James's situation, think back to your own experiences as a student in elementary and secondary school. Which students received the most attention, those who behaved appropriately or those who behaved inappropriately? Chances are that it was the *mis*behaving students to whom your teachers and classmates paid the most attention. James has undoubtedly learned that if he wants to be noticed—if he wants to stand out in a crowd—then he must behave in ways that other students are *not*.

Our case study is a classic example of how students' behaviors are often affected by environmental events—a key assumption of behaviorist views of learning. Let's look at this assumption, as well as several others, that behaviorists share:

- People's behaviors are largely the result of their experiences with environmental stimuli.

- Learning can be described in terms of relationships among observable events—that is, relationships among stimuli and responses.

- Learning involves a change in behavior.

- Learning is most likely to take place when stimuli and responses occur at about the same time—in other words, when there is *contiguity* between them.

- Many species of animals, including humans, learn in similar ways.

These assumptions and their educational implications are summarized in Table 9–1.

Influence of the Environment

Many behaviorists believe that, with the exception of a few simple reflexes, a person is born as a "blank slate" (sometimes referred to by the Latin term *tabula rasa*), with no inherited tendency to behave one way or another. Over the years, the environment "writes" on this slate, slowly molding the individual into an adult with unique characteristics and ways of behaving. In essence, then, behaviorists assume that people are largely the products of their environments, with heredity having little influence on behavior.

Behaviorists often say that individuals are **conditioned** by environmental events. Notice how I just used the verb *condition* in the passive voice: People are being condi-

Is this "blank slate" assumption inconsistent with anything that you've read in earlier chapters?

PRINCIPLES/ASSUMPTIONS

Table 9–1   *Basic Assumptions of Behaviorism and Their Educational Implications*

ASSUMPTION	EXAMPLE	EDUCATIONAL IMPLICATION
Influence of the environment	James misbehaves in class because of the attention he receives for doing so.	Develop a classroom environment that fosters desirable student behaviors.
Focus on observable events (stimuli and responses)	James exhibits certain responses in class (e.g., throwing, teasing, poking); the reactions of his teacher and classmates are stimuli influencing James's behavior.	Think in terms of specific stimuli (including your own behaviors) that may be related to the specific responses that students make.
Learning as a behavior change	James's classroom misbehaviors increase over time.	Don't assume that learning has occurred unless you observe behavior changes in your students.
Contiguity of events	James is most likely to exhibit those misbehaviors that get him attention immediately.	Remember that certain events (e.g., desired responses and reinforcing stimuli) should occur close together in time if you want to promote student learning.
Similarity of learning principles across species	James's misbehaving in order to get attention is similar to a rat's pressing a metal bar in order to get a nugget of food.	Look for applications of animal research to classroom learning situations.

---

tioned by the environment, rather than doing the conditioning themselves. From the behaviorist perspective, people have relatively little control over their own learning.

As teachers, we must keep in mind the very significant effect that students' past and present environments are likely to have on the behaviors they exhibit. We can use this basic principle to our advantage: By changing the environmental events that our students experience, we may also be able to change their behaviors.

Contrast this passive view of learning with the cognitive view presented in Chapters 6 and 7.

Focus on Observable Events

As I mentioned in Chapter 5, behaviorists have traditionally believed that the processes that occur inside a person (e.g., thoughts, beliefs, attitudes) cannot be observed and so cannot be studied scientifically. Many behaviorists describe a person as a "black box"— something that cannot be opened for inspection. Psychological inquiry should instead focus on things that can be observed and studied objectively; more specifically, it should focus on the behaviors that individuals exhibit and the environmental context in which those behaviors occur. Thus, behaviorist principles tend to describe learning in terms of specific responses (symbolized as **R**s) and specific environmental stimuli (symbolized as **S**s).

Yet we should note here that, in recent years, some behaviorists have begun to incorporate cognitive processes into their theoretical explanations. For example, they speak of such animals as rats and pigeons "seeking information," "paying attention to" and "processing" stimuli, "predicting" a future stimulus, and "imagining" future consequences of their behaviors (Rachlin, 1989, 1991; Rescorla, 1967, 1988; Schwartz & Reisberg, 1991; Wagner, 1976, 1978, 1979, 1981). It is becoming increasingly evident, even to behaviorists, just how difficult it is to omit thought from our explanations of learning and behavior.

Learning as Behavior Change

From a behaviorist perspective, not only should scientific inquiry focus on observable events, but learning itself should also be defined in a way that can be observed and documented. For this reason, behaviorists define learning as a change in behavior, rather than as a change in mental associations.

This definition can be an especially useful one for us as teachers. To illustrate, consider this scenario:

> Your students look at you attentively as you explain a difficult concept. When you finish, you ask, "Any questions?" You look around the room, and not a single hand is raised. "Good," you think, "they all understand."

But *do* your students understand? On the basis of what you've just observed, you really have no idea whether they do or not.

THE FAR SIDE By GARY LARSON

"Stimulus, response! Stimulus, response! Don't you ever *think*?"

Don't assume that learning has occurred unless you observe behavior changes in your students.

The only way we can ultimately know that students have learned something is to see learning reflected in their behavior. Many behavior changes tell us that learning has taken place: an improvement in test scores, a greater frequency of independent reading, a reduction in hitting and kicking. But we should never assume that students have learned something simply because they do not tell us otherwise.

Importance of Contiguity

For stimulus-response relationships to develop, certain events must occur in conjunction with other events. When two events occur at more or less the same time, we say that there is **contiguity** between them. Here are two examples to illustrate the concept of contiguity:

- One of your instructors scowls at you as she hands back the exam that she has just corrected. You discover that you have gotten a D− on the exam, and you get an uncomfortable feeling in the pit of your stomach. The next time your instructor scowls at you, that same uncomfortable feeling returns.

- Another instructor smiles and calls on you every time you raise your hand. Although you are fairly quiet in your other classes, you find yourself raising your hand and speaking up more and more frequently in this one.

In the first situation, the instructor's scowl and the D− on your exam are presented more or less simultaneously; here we see contiguity between two stimuli. In the second situation, your response of raising your hand is followed immediately by the instructor's smile and his calling on you; in this case, we see contiguity between a response and two stimuli (although smiling and calling on you are responses that the instructor makes, they are *stimuli* for *you*).

Note that, in both situations, your behavior has changed—in other words, you have learned something. You've learned to respond with an unpleasant feeling in your stomach every time a particular instructor scowls. You've also learned to raise your hand and speak up more frequently in another instructor's class.

Similarity of Learning Principles Across Species

Behaviorists are well known for their experiments with such animals as rats and pigeons. A basic assumption underlying behaviorism is that many species share similar learning processes. Hence, the learning principles we derive from observing one species can be applied to our understanding of other species, including human beings.

What animals have you observed learning something new? For example, have you had a household pet that learned a new trick? Can you think of any similarities in the ways that animals and people learn?

Students in my own educational psychology classes sometimes resent the fact that, in one sense at least, their behavior is being compared to the behavior of rats and pigeons. But the fact is that behaviorist theories developed from the study of nonhuman animals often *do* explain human behavior. In the pages that follow, we will focus on two behaviorist theories—classical conditioning and operant conditioning—that have been derived largely from animal research, yet can nevertheless help us understand many aspects of human learning and behavior.

UNDERSTANDING CLASSICAL CONDITIONING

Consider this situation:

> Alan has always loved baseball. But in a game last year, he was badly hurt by a wild pitch while he was up at bat. Now, although he still plays the game, he gets anxious whenever it is his turn at bat, to the point where he often backs away from the ball, rather than swing at it.

Alan's learning illustrates **classical conditioning,** a theory that explains how we sometimes learn new responses as a result of two stimuli (in this case, the sight of a baseball coming toward him and the pain of the ball's impact) being present at approximately the same time. Alan's current responses to a pitched ball—anxiety and backing away—are ones that he didn't exhibit prior to his painful encounter with a baseball. From a behaviorist perspective, Alan has clearly learned something: His behavior has changed due to experience.

Classical conditioning was first described by Ivan Pavlov (e.g., 1927), a Russian physiologist who was conducting research related to the physiology of salivation. Pavlov often used dogs as his research subjects and presented meat to get them to salivate. He noticed that the dogs frequently began to salivate as soon as they heard the lab assistant coming down the hall, even though the meat that the assistant was carrying was not yet in "smelling" distance. Curious about this phenomenon, Pavlov conducted an experiment to examine more systematically how a dog learns to salivate to a new stimulus. His experiment went something like this:

1. Pavlov flashes a light to see whether the dog will salivate to it. Not surprisingly, the dog does not salivate; in other words, it does not make a response to the light stimulus. Using *S* for stimulus and *R* for response, we can symbolize Pavlov's first observation like so:

$$\textbf{S} \text{ (light)} \rightarrow \textbf{R} \text{ (none)}$$

2. Pavlov flashes the light again and presents meat immediately afterward. He repeats this procedure several times, and the dog salivates every time. The dog is demonstrating something that it already knows how to do—to salivate to meat—so it has not yet learned anything new. We can symbolize Pavlov's second observation like so:

$$\left.\begin{array}{l} \textbf{S} \text{ (light)} \\ \textbf{S} \text{ (meat)} \end{array}\right\} \rightarrow \textbf{R} \text{ (salivation)}$$

3. Pavlov flashes the light once more, but this time without any meat. The dog salivates—it has learned a new response to the light stimulus. We can symbolize Pavlov's third observation this way:

$$\textbf{S} \text{ (light)} \rightarrow \textbf{R} \text{ (salivation)}$$

In more general terms, classical conditioning proceeds as follows:

The word *elicit,* meaning "draw forth or bring out," is frequently used in descriptions of classical conditioning.

1. It begins with a stimulus-response association that already exists—in other words, with an *unconditioned* stimulus-response association. For example, Pavlov's dog salivates automatically whenever it smells meat, and Alan becomes anxious whenever he encounters painful stimuli; no learning is involved in either case. When a stimulus leads to a particular response without prior learning, we say that an **unconditioned stimulus (UCS)** *elicits* an **unconditioned response (UCR)**. The unconditioned response is typically an automatic, involuntary one: The individual has little or no control over it.

2. Conditioning occurs when a **neutral stimulus**—one that doesn't elicit any particular response—is presented immediately before the unconditioned stimulus. For example, in the case of Pavlov's dog, a light is presented immediately before the meat; in the case of Alan, a baseball is pitched immediately before the painful hit. Conditioning is especially likely to occur when both stimuli are presented together on several occasions and when the neutral stimulus occurs *only* when the unconditioned stimulus is about to follow (R. H. Granger & Schlimmer, 1986; R. R. Miller & Barnet, 1993; Rachlin, 1991; Rescorla, 1967, 1988; Schwartz & Reisberg, 1991).

3. Before long, the new stimulus also elicits a response, usually one very similar to the unconditioned response. The neutral stimulus has become a **conditioned stimulus (CS)**, and the response to it is called a **conditioned response (CR)**. For example, Pavlov's dog acquires a conditioned response of salivation to a new, conditioned stimulus—the light. Likewise, Alan acquires conditioned responses of anxiety and backing away to a pitched baseball. Like the unconditioned response, the conditioned response is an involuntary one: It occurs automatically every time the conditioned stimulus is presented.

Explaining Emotional Responses in Terms of Classical Conditioning

◼ EXPERIENCING FIRSTHAND
"Classical" Music

Some songs make people feel certain ways. For example, Handel's "Water Music" always elicits especially "happy" feelings in me, perhaps because it's the music that was played at my wedding. The theme from the television show *Dragnet* still elicits tinges of anxiety for me because the show frightened me when I was a young child. Take a minute and think about particular songs that you might listen to if you wanted to experience each of the feelings listed below.

Feeling	Song
Happiness	_____
Relaxation	_____
Anxiety	_____
Sadness	_____

Why does each of the songs that you've listed make you feel the way you do? Can you trace those feelings to significant occasions in your life when each song was playing? ◼

In some cases, your emotional reactions to a song may be attributable simply to the mood that the song conveys. For example, "Under the Boardwalk," a song released by the Drifters in the 1960s, always cheers me up simply because it's peppy and has a good beat. But in other cases, a song may make you feel the way you do because you associate it with particular events. Consider the case of Brenda as an example:

> At the school dance, Brenda has one dance with Joe, a boy on whom she has a tremendous crush. They dance to "Michelle," an old Beatles song. Later, whenever Brenda hears "Michelle," she feels happy.

In this situation, Joe is initially the source of Brenda's good feelings. A second stimulus—"Michelle"—is associated with Joe, and so the song begins to elicit those same feelings. From a classical conditioning perspective, we can analyze the situation this way:

| UCS: | Joe | → | UCR: | good feelings about Joe |
| CS: | "Michelle" | → | CR: | good feelings about "Michelle" |

Here are some other examples of how emotional responses might be learned through classical conditioning. Notice that, in every case, two stimuli are presented together. One stimulus already elicits a response, and as a result of the pairing, the second stimulus begins to elicit a similar response.

- Bernard falls into a swimming pool and almost drowns. A year later, when his mother enrolls him in swimming lessons at the local recreation center, he cries hysterically as his mother tries to drag him to the side of the pool.

  | UCS: | inability to breathe | → | UCR: | fear of being unable to breathe |
  | CS: | swimming pool | → | CR: | fear of the swimming pool |

- Bobby misses a month of school because of illness. When he returns to school, he does not know how to do his long division assignments. After a number of frustrating experiences in which he fails long division problems, he begins to feel anxious whenever he encounters a division task.

  | UCS: | failure/frustration | → | UCR: | anxiety about failure |
  | CS: | long division | → | CR: | anxiety about long division |

- Beth's teacher catches Beth writing a letter to one of her classmates during class. The teacher reads the note to the entire class, revealing some very personal and private information about Beth. Beth now feels embarrassed whenever she goes into that teacher's classroom.

  | UCS: | humiliation | → | UCR: | embarrassment in response to humiliation |
  | CS: | teacher/classroom | → | CR: | embarrassment in response to teacher/classroom |

Do you remember our earlier example of learning to respond negatively to an instructor's scowl? Can you explain your learning from the perspective of classical conditioning?

Classical conditioning is frequently used to explain why people sometimes respond emotionally to what might otherwise be fairly "neutral" stimuli. When a particu-

Create a pleasant, upbeat classroom atmosphere.

lar stimulus is associated with something that makes us happy or relaxed, it begins to elicit those same feelings of happiness or relaxation. When a stimulus is associated with something that makes us fearful or anxious, it, too, begins to elicit feelings of fear and anxiety.

As teachers, we must be sure the stimuli in our classroom (including our own behaviors toward students) elicit such responses as enjoyment or relaxation and do *not* elicit such responses as fear or anxiety. In general, we should provide a pleasant, upbeat classroom environment for our students. When students first enter school in the primary grades, most of them have little reason to be fearful or anxious. In addition, when they associate school with pleasant stimuli—positive feedback, enjoyable activities, and so on—they soon learn that school is a place where they want to be. But if they instead encounter unpleasant stimuli in school—negative comments, public humiliation, or frustration—they may eventually learn to fear or dislike a particular teacher or perhaps to react negatively to school in general.

We should keep in mind, too, that success usually makes people feel good and that failure often makes them feel bad. To condition positive feelings toward schoolwork, students must associate more success than failure with the various subjects in their school curriculum—with mathematics, science, language arts, social studies, physical education, art, and music. As teachers, we must take care to introduce new ideas and expect new skills only when students are cognitively, socially, and physically ready to learn those ideas and skills.

This is not to say that students should *never* experience failure. We will discover some potential benefits of *occasional* failure in our discussion of social cognitive theory in Chapter 10 and again in our discussion of motivation in Chapter 11.

How Conditioned Responses May Generalize

When people learn a conditioned response to a new stimulus, they may also respond in the same way to similar stimuli—a phenomenon known as **generalization.** For example, a boy who learns to feel anxious about long division tasks may generalize that anx-

When students associate school with pleasant stimuli, they learn that school is a place where they want to be.

iety to other aspects of mathematics. And a girl who experiences humiliation in one classroom may generalize her embarrassment to other classrooms as well. Here we see one more reason why we must be certain to provide a positive classroom atmosphere for our students and to help them associate pleasant feelings with the subject matter and skills we teach them. Students' reactions to school and class activities may generalize to situations far beyond the classroom itself.

Remember that the feelings students develop in response to you, your classroom, and school subject matter may generalize to situations far beyond the classroom itself.

How Conditioned Responses Sometimes Decrease over Time

Pavlov observed that conditioned responses don't necessarily last forever. By pairing a light with meat, he conditioned a dog to salivate to the light alone. When he flashed the light repeatedly without ever again following it with meat, however, the dog salivated less and less. Eventually, the dog no longer salivated at all when it saw the light flash.

After repeated presentations of a conditioned stimulus *in the absence of* the unconditioned stimulus—for example, when a light is never again associated with meat, when mathematics is never again associated with failure, or when a teacher is never again associated with humiliation—the conditioned response may decrease and eventually disappear. This gradual decrease and disappearance of a conditioned response because it no longer occurs in the presence of the unconditioned stimulus is called **extinction.**

Many conditioned responses fade over time. Unfortunately, many others do not; a person's fear of water or anxiety about mathematics may persist for years. One reason that fears or anxieties regarding certain stimuli are likely to persist over time is that people tend to avoid those situations that cause such emotional reactions. If they stay away from a stimulus that makes them fearful, they never have a chance to experience that stimulus in the absence of the unconditioned stimulus with which it was originally paired. As a result, they have no opportunity to learn *not* to be afraid—no opportunity for the response to undergo extinction.

We will consider the nature and effects of anxiety in more detail in our discussion of motivation in Chapter 11.

As teachers, how can we help eliminate the counterproductive conditioned responses that our students may exhibit—for example, their fear of water or their mathematics anxiety? Psychologists have learned that one way to extinguish a negative emotional reaction to a particular conditioned stimulus is to introduce that stimulus *slowly and gradually* while the individual is happy or relaxed (e.g., M. C. Jones, 1924; Wolpe, 1958, 1969). For example, if Bernard is afraid of water, we might begin his swimming lessons someplace where he feels at ease—perhaps on dry land or in the baby pool—and move to deeper water only as he begins to feel more comfortable. If Bernice gets overly anxious every time that she attempts a mathematics problem, we might revert back to easier problems—those that she can readily solve—and gradually increase the difficulty of her assignments only as she demonstrates greater competence and self-confidence.

When a particular subject matter or task is anxiety arousing for students, present it slowly and gradually while they are happy and relaxed.

There is nothing like success to help students feel good about being in the classroom. In this chapter and the ones that follow, we will consider many ways in which we can facilitate student success in classroom learning and achievement. For example, one thing we can do is structure the classroom environment so that appropriate behaviors are reinforced and inappropriate behaviors are not. It is to the role that reinforcement plays in learning—to operant conditioning—that we turn now.

INTO THE CLASSROOM

Applying Principles of Classical Conditioning

Provide a positive classroom environment.

> A third-grade teacher plans many activities that make classroom learning fun. He never ridicules students for mistakes they may make.

Help students be successful.

> A high school mathematics teacher takes a mastery approach to teaching algebra, making sure that her students master each concept and procedure before moving to more advanced material.

When a particular subject or task is anxiety arousing for students, present it slowly and gradually while they are happy and relaxed.

> When teaching a water-phobic child to swim, a swimming instructor begins the first lesson by playing games in the "baby" pool, moving to deeper water very gradually as the child seems comfortable about doing so.

UNDERSTANDING OPERANT CONDITIONING

Mark is a student in Ms. Ferguson's geography class. This is what happens to Mark during the first week in October:

- *Monday:* Ms. Ferguson asks the class to locate Colombia on the globe. Mark knows where Colombia is, and he sits smiling, with his hands in his lap, hoping that Ms. Ferguson will call on him. Instead, Ms. Ferguson calls on another student.

- *Tuesday:* Ms. Ferguson asks the class where Colombia got its name. Mark knows that Colombia is named after Christopher Columbus, so he raises his hand a few inches. Ms. Ferguson calls on another student.

- *Wednesday:* Ms. Ferguson asks the class why people in Colombia speak Spanish, rather than English or French. Mark knows that Colombians speak Spanish because the country's early European settlers came from Spain. He raises his hand high in the air. Ms. Ferguson calls on another student.

- *Thursday:* Ms. Ferguson asks the class why Colombia grows coffee but Canada does not. Mark knows that coffee can only be grown in certain climates. He raises his hand high and waves it wildly back and forth. Ms. Ferguson calls on him.

- *Friday:* Whenever Ms. Ferguson asks a question that Mark can answer, Mark raises his hand high and waves it wildly about.

Notice how several of Mark's behaviors in geography class, such as sitting quietly, smiling, and raising his hand politely, bring no results. But waving his hand wildly does bring Mark the result that he wants: his teacher's attention. The response that has attracted Ms. Ferguson's attention continues. Other responses disappear.

The change that we just saw in Mark's behavior illustrates **operant conditioning,** a form of learning described by many behaviorists, and most notably by B. F. Skinner (e.g., 1938, 1953, 1954, 1968, 1973). The basic principle of operant conditioning is a simple one:

A response that is followed by a reinforcing stimulus (a reinforcer) is more likely to occur again.

When behaviors are followed by desirable consequences, they tend to increase in frequency. When behaviors don't produce results, they typically decrease and may even disappear altogether.

Students often learn and demonstrate new behaviors for the consequences that those behaviors bring. Here are some examples:

- Sergio brings a fancy new bicycle to school and finds himself surrounded by classmates who want to ride it. Suddenly, Sergio has several new "friends."

- Sharon decreases the number of steps that she takes when she bowls. She now gets more strikes and spares than she used to.

- Steven studies hard for his French vocabulary quiz. He gets an A on the quiz.

- Samirah copies her answers to the French quiz from Steven's paper. She gets an A on the quiz.

Many appropriate and productive behaviors—such as studying French or trying a new approach to bowling—are acquired because of the desirable consequences to which they lead. Many inappropriate and undesirable behaviors—such as cheating on a quiz or waving one's hand wildly about—may be acquired for the same reason.

As teachers, we should be sure to reinforce the behaviors we want our students to learn. If we want students to read frequently, to volunteer in class, to demonstrate good form in dribbling and passing a soccer ball, or to work cooperatively with their classmates, we should reinforce such behaviors as they occur. At the same time, we should be careful *not* to reinforce any inappropriate and counterproductive behaviors that students exhibit. If we repeatedly allow Jane to turn in assignments late because she tells us that her dog ate her homework and if we often let Jake get his way by bullying his classmates on the playground, then we are reinforcing (and hence increasing) Jane's excuse making and Jake's aggressiveness. We must keep in mind that operant conditioning principles work whether we are intentionally applying them or not.

In the following pages, we will explore various aspects of the operant conditioning phenomenon. Before we do, however, let's contrast it with classical conditioning.

D o you have any bad habits that the environment has in some way reinforced?

R einforce desirable behaviors; don't inadvertently reinforce *un*desirable ones.

Contrasting Classical and Operant Conditioning

Like classical conditioning, operant conditioning involves both a stimulus and a response. But operant conditioning is different from classical conditioning in two important ways:

- The order of the stimulus and response

- The nature of the response

Let's look briefly at each of these differences.

Order of the Stimulus and Response

In classical conditioning, certain stimuli are followed by certain responses. We can symbolize the relationship like this:

$$S \rightarrow R$$

But in operant conditioning, the response comes first, followed by a reinforcing consequence. The reinforcing consequence is actually a stimulus, so we will use the notation S_{Rf}. We can symbolize the relationship between stimulus and response this way:

$$R \rightarrow S_{Rf}$$

Nature of the Response

In classical conditioning, a response occurs as a result of a particular stimulus; in other words, the stimulus elicits the response. The individual often has little or no control over whether the response occurs. But in operant conditioning, the response is usually a voluntary one: An individual can control whether it occurs. As an example, consider James, the attention getter I described in our case study at the beginning of the chapter. Several of James's responses, such as blurting out answers, throwing erasers across the room, and teasing classmates, increased as a result of the attention (a stimulus) that such responses brought. Yet James willingly made these responses; no particular stimulus forced him to do so.

Identifying Conditions Essential for Operant Conditioning to Occur

Operant conditioning can occur only under three conditions:

- The individual must make a response.

- A reinforcer must follow the response.

- The reinforcer must be presented only when the response has occurred.

Provide opportunities for students to practice correct behaviors.

Making a Response

As we have seen, operant conditioning occurs when a response is followed by a reinforcer. So, to be reinforced—to *learn*—an individual must first make a response.

Operant conditioning theorists believe that little is accomplished by having students sit quietly and listen passively to their teacher. Instead, they propose that students learn only when they are making active, overt responses in the classroom. For example, Pamela will learn her cursive letters most easily by writing them. Peter will learn how to make a good cake only by actually making cakes. Paula will be able to solve mathematical word problems easily only when she works with such problems on a regular basis.

Make sure reinforcers *follow* desired behaviors, rather than vice versa.

Receiving Reinforcement After the Response

Operant conditioning occurs only when a reinforcer comes *after* a response. A teacher who gives students several minutes of free time after they have completed an assignment or who lets students go to lunch only after they have cleaned their desks is following this principle. A teacher who gives students five minutes of free time before they begin working on an assignment or who tells students that they must clean up their mess after they come back from lunch has things in the wrong order.

To be most effective, reinforcement should occur *immediately* after a desired response has occurred; in other words, the response and the reinforcing stimulus should occur in close contiguity. If students find the country of Colombia on a globe, or pronounce *"Comment allez vous?"* like a Frenchman, or execute a good tennis serve, they should receive some form of immediate reinforcement, whether it be a smile, words of praise (*"Très bien!"*), or a tennis opponent's failure to return a serve. The more closely a reinforcer follows a response, the more effective it is likely to be (J. A. Kulik & Kulik, 1988; Rachlin, 1991). Delayed reinforcers sometimes have an effect on behavior, but they are most likely to be effective with older students, and especially with those who immediately realize that a particular behavior will eventually lead to reinforcement (Fowler & Baer, 1981; L. Green, Fry, & Myerson, 1994).

Receiving Reinforcement Only When the Response Has Been Made

For successful operant conditioning, the reinforcer should occur *only* after a particular response has occurred; it should never occur in the absence of that response. In other words, the reinforcer must be **contingent** on the desired response. A teacher who awards an A only to students who have mastered course content or who praises students only when they behave appropriately is making reinforcement contingent on desirable responses. But consider the teacher who laughs at the antics of a chronically misbehaving student and the teacher who gives an A to a student with a hundred excuses for not turning in an assignment. These teachers are giving reinforcement whether acceptable responses occur or not, so their students' behaviors are unlikely to improve.

Specifying the Terminal Behavior in Advance

As teachers, we may often want to use operant conditioning principles to promote desired student behaviors—solving word problems successfully, working cooperatively with classmates, raising one's hand when one has a question, and so on. Operant conditioning theorists recommend that we describe the form and frequency of the behavior that we want a student to demonstrate—the **terminal behavior**—*before* we begin the conditioning process. If we want Danielle to participate in class more frequently, we might describe the terminal behavior this way:

> Danielle will make at least five verbal contributions to the class every day.

If we want Doreen to exhibit better personal hygiene, we might describe the desired terminal behavior like this:

> Doreen will come to school with clean hands and will wash them at least once during the school day.

Operant conditioning theorists urge us to describe terminal behaviors in *specific, concrete, observable terms.* Rather than talk about the need for students to "learn world history," we might instead talk about students being able to describe the antecedents and consequences of World War I. Rather than say that students should "learn responsibility," we might instead talk about their need to follow instructions, bring the necessary books and supplies to class every day, and turn in assignments by the due

Make sure desired behaviors are reinforced immediately in some fashion.

Can you use the concept of *working memory* (Chapter 6) to explain why immediate reinforcement might be better than delayed reinforcement?

Present a reinforcer only when a student has made the desired response.

How is the concept of *contingency* different from the concept of *contiguity*?

Specify desired terminal behaviors in specific, concrete, observable terms.

Have you observed situations in which teachers or schools have specified desired terminal behaviors prior to instruction? What term did they use when referring to these behaviors?

date. An advantage of describing a desired behavior in such concrete terms is that we know exactly when the behavior has been learned and when it has not.

When educators describe desired terminal behaviors in concrete, measurable terms, they are specifying **behavioral objectives** for their students. We will look more closely at behavioral objectives within the context of our discussion of instructional objectives in Chapter 12.

What types of reinforcers are likely to be effective in bringing about desired terminal behaviors? It is to this question that we turn now.

USING REINFORCEMENT IN THE CLASSROOM

EXPERIENCING FIRSTHAND
What Would It Take?

Imagine this scenario:

You are currently enrolled in my educational psychology class. As your instructor, I ask you to spend an hour after class tutoring two classmates who are having difficulty understanding some of the course material. You have no other commitments for that hour; however, you'd really rather spend the time at a nearby coffee shop, where you know several of your friends are having lunch. What would it take for you to spend the hour tutoring your classmates, rather than joining your friends? Would you do it as a way of gaining my approval? Would you do it if I gave you a candy bar? Would you do it if I gave you five dollars? Would you do it simply because it made you feel good inside to be helping someone else? Write down a reward—perhaps one that I have listed or perhaps a different one altogether—that would be sufficient for you to give up meeting your friends in order to help your classmates.

And now imagine this second scenario:

A few weeks later, I ask you to spend the weekend (eight hours a day on both Saturday and Sunday) tutoring the same two struggling classmates. What would it take this time to convince you to do the job? Would my approval do the trick? a candy bar? five dollars? five *hundred* dollars? Or would your internal sense of satisfaction be enough? Once again, write down what it would take for you to agree to help your classmates.

Obviously, there are no "right" answers in the exercise you just completed. Different people would agree to tutor their classmates for different reasons. But you were probably able to identify at least one consequence in each situation that would be sufficiently enticing that you would give up your own personal time to help your classmates.

We often talk about giving students rewards for their academic achievements and for appropriate classroom behaviors. But as you may have noticed, we have not been using the term *reward* in our description of operant conditioning. We have been using the term *reinforcer* instead of reward for a very important reason. The word *reward* brings to mind things we would all agree are pleasant and desirable—things like candy, praise, money, trophies, or special privileges. But some individuals increase their behavior for consequences that others would not find so appealing. A **reinforcer** is *any consequence that increases the frequency of a particular behavior,* whether other people find that consequence pleasant or not. The act of following a particular response with a reinforcer is called **reinforcement.**

Let's return once again to our attention-getting student. James learned that he could get his teacher's attention by blurting out answers in class, throwing objects around the room, and refusing to turn in classroom assignments. We can assume that James's teacher is not smiling or praising him for such behavior. Probably, the teacher is frowning, scolding, or even yelling. We don't usually think of frowning, scolding, and yelling as rewards. Yet those consequences are leading to an increase in James's misbehaviors, so they are apparently reinforcing for James.

Some students may thrive on teacher scoldings even though others dislike them. Some students may respond well to praise, but others (perhaps those who don't want to be labeled "teacher's pet" by their peers) may view a teacher's praise as a fate worse than death (e.g., Pfiffner, Rosen, & O'Leary, 1985). Some students may work at academic tasks simply for the feelings of success and accomplishment that such activities bring, but others may work diligently at the same tasks only if doing so leads to social reinforcers—perhaps the respect of classmates or the opportunity to spend time with friends. Some students like getting As, but others (perhaps those afraid of being labeled a "brain" or "school girl" by their classmates) may actually prefer Cs. An important principle of operant conditioning, then, is that *different stimuli are reinforcing for different individuals.* We must never make assumptions about what specific events are reinforcing for particular students.

How do *you* feel when a teacher praises you in front of your classmates?

Don't make assumptions about what specific events will be reinforcing for particular students.

Reinforcement comes in all shapes and sizes. In the next few pages, we will look at two basic distinctions that operant conditioning theorists make:

- Primary versus secondary reinforcers

- Positive versus negative reinforcement

As we do so, we will identify a number of potentially effective reinforcers we can use in classroom settings.

Primary Versus Secondary Reinforcers

Some reinforcers are stimuli that we just naturally appreciate. Others are an "acquired taste" that we learn to appreciate over time. Here we are talking about the difference between *primary reinforcers* and *secondary reinforcers.*

Primary Reinforcers

A **primary reinforcer** is a reinforcer that satisfies a basic physiological need; hence, we appreciate it without having to learn to do so. Food, water, warmth, and oxygen are all examples of primary reinforcers. To some extent, physical affection and cuddling may address biological needs as well (Harlow & Zimmerman, 1959). And for an adolescent addicted to an illegal substance, the next "fix" is also a primary reinforcer.

Secondary Reinforcers

A **secondary reinforcer** is a stimulus that does not satisfy any physiological need, yet becomes reinforcing over time through its association with another reinforcer. For example, perhaps praise was once associated with a special candy treat from Mother, or a good grade was associated with a hug from Father. Through such associations, consequences such as praise, good grades, money, feelings of success, and perhaps even scolding become reinforcing in their own right: They become secondary reinforcers.

Can you think of other examples of primary and secondary reinforcers?

A primary reinforcer, such as food, is one that satisfies a basic physiological need. A secondary reinforcer, such as praise, is one that we learn to appreciate because of its repeated association with other sources of reinforcement.

Remember that not all students have learned to appreciate such secondary reinforcers as praise and good grades.

Which kind of reinforcer is more common in the classroom? When we think about it, we realize that secondary reinforcers are far more common in classrooms than primary reinforcers. But we must remember that secondary reinforcers are *learned* reinforcers, and not everyone has come to appreciate them. Although most of our students will probably respond positively to such consequences as praise or a good grade, a few students may not.

Positive Versus Negative Reinforcement

Up to this point, we have been speaking of reinforcement as the *presentation* of a particular reinforcing stimulus. But in some cases, we can also reinforce a behavior through the *removal* of a stimulus. Operant conditioning theorists distinguish between these two situations by using the terms *positive reinforcement* and *negative reinforcement.*

Positive Reinforcement

In the last few pages, we have mentioned a variety of reinforcers; for instance, we have talked about the potential reinforcing value of food, praise, good grades, free time, success, and (for some students) even scolding. All of these are examples of **positive reinforcement:** They bring about the increase of a behavior through the *presentation* of a stimulus.

Remember that some consequences that you think of in "negative" terms (e.g., scoldings, bad grades) may nevertheless be *positively* reinforcing for some students.

Whenever a behavior is followed by the presentation of a (reinforcing) stimulus and that behavior increases as a result, we are talking about a positive reinforcer. This is true whether or not the stimulus is one that others would agree is pleasant and desirable. Some students will behave to get a teacher's praise, whereas others (like James in our case study) may behave to get a scolding. Most students will work for As, but a few may actually prefer Cs or even Fs. Depending on the individual, any one of these stimuli—the praise, the scolding, the A, or the F—may be a positive reinforcer.

A variety of positive reinforcers can increase the frequency of desirable student behaviors. Examples include concrete reinforcers, social reinforcers, activity reinforcers, group contingencies, positive feedback, and intrinsic reinforcers. Let's look briefly at each of these.

Concrete reinforcers.   A **concrete reinforcer** is an actual object—something that can be touched. Snacks, stickers, and toys are all examples of concrete reinforcers. Such reinforcers are especially likely to be effective with young children (e.g., Rimm & Masters, 1974).

If necessary, use concrete reinforcers, especially with young children.

Social reinforcers.   A **social reinforcer** is a gesture or sign that one person gives another regarding a recently performed response. A smile, a hug, attention, praise, and "thank you" are all social reinforcers; coming from a teacher, they are often effective reinforcers for students (L. Katz, 1993; Piersel, 1987; Schepis, Reid, & Fitzgerald, 1987). The approval of a student's friends and classmates can also be very reinforcing (G. W. Evans & Oswalt, 1968; Lovitt, Guppy, & Blattner, 1969). As teachers, we can often use simple social gestures—smiles, compliments, nods of approval, and expressions of appreciation—as classroom reinforcers. We can also provide opportunities for students to reinforce one another for desirable academic and social behaviors (T. R. McDaniel, 1987).

Show your approval of appropriate behavior; give students opportunities to reinforce one another as well.

Social reinforcers usually communicate positive regard for a student and approval of his or her behavior. We saw an exception in our case study at the beginning of the chapter, however: James received attention from his teacher and classmates that definitely did *not* communicate either positive regard or approval, but was an effective social reinforcer nonetheless.

Activity reinforcers.   An **activity reinforcer** is an opportunity to engage in a favorite activity. Students will often do one thing—perhaps something they don't like to do—if by doing so they can then do something else—something they *do* like to do. This phenomenon is sometimes called the **Premack principle** (Premack, 1959, 1963). For example, third graders are more likely to sit quietly if being quiet enables them to go to lunch. High school students are more likely to do their homework if their parents make extracurricular activities contingent on getting schoolwork done first.

Follow less enjoyable activities with more enjoyable ones.

Group contingencies.   A **group contingency** is a situation in which students are reinforced only when *everyone* in a particular group (perhaps everyone in the classroom) achieves at a certain level or behaves in an appropriate fashion. Group contingencies are clearly effective in improving academic achievement and classroom behavior, provided that everyone in the group is capable of making the desired response (Lentz, 1988). Consider these two examples as evidence:

- A class of thirty-two fourth graders was not doing very well on weekly spelling tests. On the average, only twelve students (38%) had perfect spelling tests in any given week. Hoping for improvement, their teacher announced that any student with a perfect test score would get free time later in the week. The new reinforcement program had a noticeable effect: The average number of perfect spelling tests rose to twenty-five a week (80%). But then the teacher added a group con-

Some reinforcers, such as praise, are concrete and visible. Others, such as feelings of accomplishment and pride, are less noticeable but equally effective.

Attention can be a very effective reinforcer.

tingency: Whenever the entire class achieved perfect spelling tests by Friday, the class could listen to the radio for fifteen minutes. The group contingency produced an average of thirty perfect spelling tests (94%) a week (Lovitt et al., 1969)!

Make some reinforcers contingent on group performance.

On what occasions have you been reinforced by means of a group contingency?

• Another fourth-grade class was particularly unruly: In any given minute, chances were that one or more students would be talking out of turn or getting out of their seats. In a desperate move, the teacher divided the class into two teams that competed in a "good behavior game." Each time a student was observed talking out of turn or getting out of his or her seat, the student's team received a chalk mark on the chalkboard. The team that received fewer marks during a lesson won special privileges—for example, being first in the lunch line or having free time at the end of the day. When both teams had five marks or fewer, everyone won privileges. Misbehaviors in the class dropped almost immediately to less than 20% of their initial frequency (Barrish, Saunders, & Wolf, 1969).

Why are group contingencies so effective? One reason may be peer pressure: Students encourage their classmates to achieve and to behave themselves, and then reinforce those classmates for doing so (K. D. O'Leary & O'Leary, 1972). Furthermore, students begin to tutor one another in academic subjects, a practice that enhances achievement (e.g., Pigott, Fantuzzo, & Clement, 1986). Group contingencies play an important role in *cooperative learning,* an instructional strategy that we will examine in Chapter 13.

Playing a team sport is an example of a behavior reinforced by a group contingency: The team wins together or loses together.

Positive feedback. Sometimes the simple message that an answer is correct or that a task has been done well—**positive feedback**—is reinforcement enough. For example, you can probably think of times when you were happy about getting an answer right even though knowing the answer did not affect your class grade the tiniest bit. Many students want to do well in school, so feedback that they have been successful may be a sufficient consequence to increase desired classroom behaviors.

Here we see one of the functions that good grades serve—to provide positive feedback about a student's classroom performance. Yet we should note that grades are typically delayed by days or weeks, and they give only vague feedback at best; hence, they are relatively ineffective reinforcers. Researchers have found that feedback is most effective when it tells students exactly what students are doing well and specifically what they can do to improve their performance even further (Bangert-Drowns, Kulik, Kulik, & Morgan, 1991; Brophy, 1981; Clifford, 1990; M. J. Harris & Rosenthal, 1985; Parsons, Kaczala, & Meece, 1982).

Intrinsic reinforcers. Up to this point, we have been talking about **extrinsic reinforcers**—reinforcers provided by the environment (often by other people). In contrast, **intrinsic reinforcers** are reinforcers supplied by people themselves or inherent in the task being performed. Students engage in some activities simply because they like to feel successful or competent. Feeling "proud" after doing a good deed, feeling "successful" after completing a complicated assignment, and feeling "smart" after passing a difficult test are all examples of intrinsic reinforcers. When students show certain be-

Tell students exactly what they have done well and how they can improve their performance further.

Provide opportunities for students to pursue intrinsically reinforcing activities.

We will talk more about such *intrinsic motivation* in Chapter 11.

When students show certain behaviors in the absence of any observable reinforcers, they are probably working for the intrinsic feelings of satisfaction that such activities bring.

haviors in the absence of any observable reinforcers—when they read an entire book without putting it down, when they do extra classwork without being asked, when they practice on their electric guitars into the wee hours of the morning—they are probably working for the intrinsic feelings of satisfaction that such activities bring.

From our perspective as teachers, positive feedback and the intrinsic reinforcement that such feedback brings are probably the most desirable forms of classroom reinforcement. But we must remember that consistent positive feedback and the resulting feelings of success and mastery can occur only when classroom instruction has been carefully tailored to individual skill levels and abilities, and only when students have learned to value academic achievement. When students are not motivated to achieve academic success (for whatever reasons), then social reinforcers, activity reinforcers, group contingencies, and (if necessary) even concrete reinforcers can be used to increase desired classroom behaviors.

Take Two on "What Would It Take?"

In a preceding exercise, I asked you to consider what it would take for you to spend time tutoring two of your classmates when you'd really rather join your friends at the local coffee shop. Classify each one of these consequences of tutoring your classmates in terms of the kind of reinforcer it reflects:

Consequence:	Kind of Reinforcer:
You gain my approval.	_____
You get a candy bar.	_____
You get five dollars.	_____
You feel good about helping somebody else.	_____

You can find the correct answers at the bottom of the page.* But no peeking until you've made your own decisions! ■

Negative Reinforcement

As we have just seen, positive reinforcement involves the presentation of a stimulus. In contrast, **negative reinforcement** brings about the increase of a behavior through the *removal* of a stimulus (typically an unpleasant one). The word *negative* here is not a value judgment; it simply refers to the fact that a stimulus is being taken away. When people behave to get rid of something, they are being negatively reinforced. We saw an example of negative reinforcement in our case study at the beginning of the chapter: When James misbehaved, he was often sent to the principal's office, enabling him to *get out of class* (an environment that may have been aversive for him).

Here are some additional examples of negative reinforcement:

• A rat is getting an electric shock through the floor of its cage. It learns to press a metal bar to terminate the shock.

• Rhonda must read *Ivanhoe* for her English literature class before the end of the month. She doesn't like having this assignment hanging over her head, so she finishes it early. When she's done, she no longer has to worry about it.

_____

*My approval is a social reinforcer, the candy bar and the money are concrete reinforcers, and feeling good about what you have done is an intrinsic reinforcer. Of these, only the candy bar is a primary reinforcer; the other three are secondary reinforcers.

How might you determine which reinforcers are most effective for your students?

An analogy to positive and negative numbers might be helpful here. Positive numbers and positive reinforcement both *add* something to a situation. Negative numbers and negative reinforcement both *subtract* something from a situation.

- Reuben is in the same literature class. Whenever he sits down to read *Ivanhoe,* he finds the novel confusing and difficult to understand. He quickly ends his study sessions by finding other things that he "needs" to do instead—things like playing basketball with his friends, washing his hair, or folding his socks.

- Ms. Randolph yells at her rowdy seventh graders. They quiet down. By yelling, Ms. Randolph has stopped a noisy and unpleasant stimulus (if only temporarily), and so her yelling has been negatively reinforced.

In the examples that I just presented, notice how negative reinforcement sometimes promotes desirable behaviors—such as completing an assignment early—and at other times promotes undesirable behaviors—such as procrastination. And notice, as well, how students are not the only ones who respond to reinforcement in the classroom. After all, teachers are human beings too!

As teachers, we will be using negative reinforcement rarely if at all; ideally, we want to create a classroom environment in which there are few stimuli that students want to be rid of. Nevertheless, we should recognize that negative reinforcement *does* have an effect on behavior. For example, one student may finish an assignment more to "get it out of the way" than for any intrinsic satisfaction the assignment brings. Another may find reasons to leave class early (or perhaps not to come to school at all) if the classroom environment is a stressful, frustrating one. When certain responses enable students to remove unpleasant stimuli—perhaps classroom assignments perhaps even the classroom itself—those responses will increase in frequency.

An example of a response being *negatively reinforced* is completing an assignment early so that you don't have to worry about it anymore.

🍎

When students are consistently behaving in ways that enable them to escape or avoid certain classroom activities, identify and alleviate the reasons that students find those activities unpleasant.

Did you previously think of negative reinforcement as something that leads to a *decrease* in behavior? If so, have you now changed your mental definition of this concept?

Using Reinforcement Effectively

As teachers, we can use reinforcement most effectively in the classroom when we:

- Describe desired behaviors in clear, concrete terms

- Choose an appropriate reinforcer for each student

- Make response-consequence contingencies explicit

- Administer reinforcement consistently

- Monitor students' progress

Describing Desired Behaviors Clearly and Concretely

To increase desirable student behaviors, we need to make sure those behaviors are reinforced. In other words, we need to catch students in the act of being good and give them a reason to be good in the future. Yet what do we mean by "desirable behaviors"?

Specify desired behaviors in clear, concrete terms.

And what do we mean by "being good"? Here are some examples of what we probably *do* mean by such terms:

- Getting classroom tasks done on time
- Working independently when asked to do so
- Cleaning up work materials at the end of class
- Interacting in a prosocial manner with others
- Completing assigned homework

Reinforcement is typically more effective when it follows actual accomplishments such as these, rather than when it follows well-intended but unsuccessful behaviors such as "trying hard" or "meaning well" (e.g., Homme, Csanyi, Gonzales, & Rechs, 1970).

Identify consequences that are truly reinforcing for each student.

Choosing an Appropriate Reinforcer

As we noted earlier, different students will find different consequences reinforcing. How can we determine which reinforcers are likely to be effective with particular students? One approach is to ask students themselves (or perhaps their parents) about the consequences they find especially appealing. Another approach is to observe students' behaviors, keeping a lookout for consequences that students seem to appreciate. The one thing that we don't want to do is *guess* about the reinforcers we should use. Operant conditioning is far more effective when reinforcers are tailored to individual students than when the same consequences are used for everyone (e.g., Pfiffner et al., 1985).

Whenever possible, we should stay away from concrete reinforcers such as toys and candy. Such reinforcers can be expensive, and they also distract students' attention away from the task at hand—their schoolwork. Fortunately, research indicates that many nontangible reinforcers are effective in increasing appropriate student behaviors. Here are some potentially effective reinforcers for school-age children and adolescents:

Rely on social reinforcers, favorite activities, informative feedback, and intrinsic reinforcement (rather than concrete reinforcers) as much as possible.

- Praise
- A special privilege
- A favorite activity
- Feedback that one has been successful
- The internal feeling of satisfaction and accomplishment that success brings
- Parental reinforcement at home for school behaviors (Bates, 1979; Brophy, 1981; Kelley & Carper, 1988; Ormrod, 1995b; Premack, 1959, 1963)

Making Response-Consequence Contingencies Explicit

Reinforcement is more likely to be effective when students know exactly what behaviors are expected of them and what specific consequences will follow those behaviors (e.g., Morris, 1985; Rosswork, 1977). For example, kindergarten students are more likely to respond appropriately when they are told to "sit quietly with your eyes on the teacher" than when they are simply told to "behave yourselves." High school students are more likely to complete their Spanish assignments if they know that by doing so they will be able to take a field trip to a local *Cinco de Mayo* festival than if they are simply told that Spanish will "help you live in a multicultural world."

Describe desirable responses and their consequences in concrete and explicit terms.

One way of communicating our expectations when one or more students fail to exhibit appropriate classroom behaviors is through a **contingency contract.** To develop such a contract, the teacher meets with each student to discuss a problem behavior (e.g., perhaps the student has a tendency to talk to friends when independent seatwork has been assigned, or displays an inability to get along with classmates). The teacher and the student then identify and agree on desired behaviors that the student will demonstrate (e.g., completing seatwork assignments within a certain time frame, or speaking with classmates in a friendly manner and pleasant tone of voice). The two also agree on one or more reinforcers for those behaviors (e.g., a certain amount of free time, or points earned toward a particular privilege or prize) that the student values. Together the teacher and the student write and sign a contract that describes both the behaviors that the student will perform and the reinforcers that will result. Contingency contracts have consistently been shown to be an effective strategy for improving a wide variety of academic and social behaviors (e.g., Brooke & Ruthren, 1984; Rueger & Liberman, 1984; Welch, 1985).

Have you seen a contingency contract being used in the classroom? If so, was it effective in changing a student's behavior?

Administering Reinforcement Consistently

As you might guess, responses increase more quickly when they are reinforced every time they occur—that is, when they are subject to **continuous reinforcement.** As teachers, we will see more rapid improvements in our students' behavior if we reinforce desired responses whenever we observe them.

When trying to increase a desired behavior, reinforce it every time you see it occur.

Monitoring Students' Progress

When we use reinforcement in the classroom, behaviorists urge us to determine, as objectively as possible, whether our efforts are actually bringing about results. More specifically, they urge us to assess the frequency of a desired behavior both before and during our attempts to increase it through operant conditioning.

Determine the baseline level of desired behaviors.

The frequency of a behavior *before* we intentionally use reinforcement to increase it is called the **baseline** level of that behavior. Some behaviors occur frequently even when they are not being explicitly reinforced, whereas other behaviors occur rarely or not at all. For example, Danielle seldom volunteers to speak in class: Her baseline level for classroom speaking is low. She washes her hands several times a day, however; her baseline level for such personal hygiene is relatively high. Baseline levels vary from behavior to behavior and from individual to individual. Whereas Danielle is quiet in class, Donna may talk all the time. And whereas Danielle's hands are always clean, Doreen's hands may look as if they haven't seen a bar of soap in days.

By comparing the baseline frequency of a response with its frequency after we begin reinforcing it, we can determine whether the reinforcer that we are using is actually bringing about a behavior change. As an example, let's reconsider our case study at the beginning of the chapter. James rarely turns in classroom assignments; this is a behavior with a low baseline. An obvious reinforcer to use with James is attention, a consequence that, until now, has effectively reinforced such counterproductive behaviors as blurting out answers in class and throwing objects across the room. When we make our attention contingent on James's turning in assignments, rather than on his refusals to do so, we should see an almost immediate increase in the number of assignments we receive from James. If we see no significant change in James's behavior, we need to consider alternative reinforcers; in other words, we need to find out what it will take for James to work productively in the classroom.

But what if a desired behavior has a baseline level of *zero?* How can we encourage behaviors that students never exhibit at all? Operant conditioning theorists provide a solution to this problem: the process of shaping.

SHAPING NEW BEHAVIORS

Consider this situation:

> Donald seems very shy and withdrawn. He rarely interacts with other students, either in class or on the playground. When he is in a situation where he must interact with a classmate, he doesn't seem to know how to behave.

Donald has apparently not learned how to interact effectively with his classmates. How might we help Donald develop appropriate social behaviors when the baseline level for such behaviors is essentially zero?

When a desired behavior occurs rarely or not at all, we can use a procedure called **shaping.** Shaping is a process of reinforcing a series of responses that increasingly resemble the desired terminal behavior—a process of reinforcing successively closer and closer approximations to that behavior. To shape a new response, we:

1. First reinforce any response that in some way resembles the terminal behavior

2. Then reinforce a response that more closely approximates the terminal behavior (no longer reinforcing the previously reinforced response)

3. Then reinforce a response that resembles the terminal behavior even more closely

4. Continue reinforcing closer and closer approximations to the terminal behavior

5. Finally reinforce only the terminal behavior

Shape a low-frequency response by reinforcing closer and closer approximations over time.

Each response in the sequence is reinforced every time it occurs until we see it regularly. Only at that point do we begin reinforcing a behavior that more closely approaches the terminal behavior.

To illustrate the process of shaping, let's look at how we might shape Donald's social behavior. We might first reinforce him for something that he occasionally does, such as smiling at a classmate. After we begin to see him smiling frequently (perhaps after a few days or weeks), we might reinforce him only when he makes a verbal response to the comments or questions of a classmate. When that behavior occurs frequently, we might reinforce him only when he initiates a conversation. Later steps to take would be reinforcing Donald for approaching a group of peers, for suggesting a group activity, and so on (see Figure 9–1).

As teachers, we must remember that it may often be unreasonable to expect students to make drastic changes in their behavior overnight. When we want them to exhibit responses radically different from the things they are doing now, we may need to shape their behavior by first reinforcing one small step in the right direction, then by reinforcing another small step, and then yet another, until eventually the desired terminal behavior is achieved. If we want rambunctious Bernadette to sit still for twenty-minute periods, we may first have to reinforce her for staying in her seat for just *two* minutes, gradually increasing the "sitting" time required for reinforcement as she makes progress. In much the same way, we can use shaping (and often do) to teach students to

Donald is extremely shy and rarely interacts with his classmates. We can teach him social skills through a process of *shaping*—that is, by reinforcing a series of successively more social behaviors. For example, we can reinforce Donald for: (1) smiling at a classmate, (2) responding appropriately to a classmate's question, (3) initiating a conversation with a single classmate, then (4) initiating interaction with a larger group.

Figure 9–1 *Shaping Donald's Social Behavior*

work independently on classroom assignments. We begin by giving first graders short, structured tasks—tasks that may only take five to ten minutes to complete. As students move through the elementary school years, we expect them to work independently for longer periods of time, and we also give them short assignments to do at home. By the time they reach high school, students have extended study halls (where, with luck, they study independently) and complete lengthy assignments at home. In the college years, student assignments require a great deal of independence and self-direction.

How might you use shaping to teach an eight-year-old to write in cursive? a twelve-year-old to swing a baseball bat? an aggressive high school student to behave prosocially?

CONSIDERING THE EFFECTS OF ANTECEDENT STIMULI

EXPERIENCING FIRSTHAND
Minding Your P's and Q's

Below are a number of examples of the letters *p* and *q*. Read through the examples as quickly as possible, identifying each one as a *p* or a *q*.

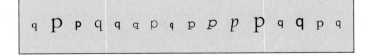

In our discussion of operant conditioning, we have been talking about situations in which a stimulus (a reinforcer, or S_{Rf}) follows a response (R), like so:

$$R \rightarrow S_{Rf}$$

But sometimes we may also have situations in which a stimulus comes *before* a particular response. For example, in the exercise that you just did, you had to make different responses (either "pee" or "cue") to the different stimuli (letters) that you saw on the page. For each letter, a particular stimulus preceded the response that you made, like so:

$$S \rightarrow R$$

When a stimulus increases the likelihood that a particular response will follow, we are talking about an **antecedent stimulus** (we'll refer to it as S_{Ant}).

You have undoubtedly learned that some of your behaviors are more likely to be reinforced in some situations than in others; that is, they are more likely to be reinforced when certain antecedent stimuli are present. For example, the response of talking about how a teacher can apply operant conditioning principles is more likely to be reinforced when you are sitting in your educational psychology class than when you are sitting in an opera house watching *The Barber of Seville.* Similarly, the response of looking up a word in a dictionary to find its correct spelling is more likely to be reinforced when you are writing a research paper than when you are taking a spelling test. When we have an antecedent stimulus that sets the occasion for a particular response, and we then have a reinforcing stimulus that follows that response, we have this situation:

$$S_{Ant} \rightarrow R \rightarrow S_{Rf}$$

In the next few pages, we will examine two phenomena involving antecedent stimuli: generalization and discrimination. We will also consider how we can use discrimination to our advantage as we discuss the process of *cueing.* Finally, we will find that the principles of generalization and discrimination can help us predict the extent to which our students will exhibit positive or negative *transfer* from one situation to another.

How Responses Generalize to New Stimuli

Once people have learned that a response is likely to be reinforced in one set of circumstances (in the presence of one antecedent stimulus), they are likely to make the same response in a similar situation. In other words, they show **generalization** from one stimulus to a similar stimulus. For example, as a young child, after you learned that you should label a **P** as "pee," you undoubtedly generalized that "pee" response to such similar stimuli as *P*, p, and *p*. Similarly, after Lindsey has learned to sit quietly in her kindergarten class, she may generalize that behavior to her first-grade class. After Donald has learned how to make friends at one school, he may generalize his skills to a new town and new school the following year. Our students are likely to generalize frequently from their experiences, exhibiting certain responses in situations similar to ones in which those responses have previously been reinforced.

This process of generalization should remind you of the generalization that occurs in classical conditioning. In fact, the two processes are similar: In both cases, an individual learns a response to one stimulus and then responds in the same way to a similar stimulus. The major difference is one of control: Generalization involves an automatic, involuntary response in classical conditioning, but a voluntary response in operant conditioning.

Expect that students will sometimes generalize responses they have learned in one situation to very similar situations.

Teaching Discrimination Between Stimuli

Sometimes people learn that responses are reinforced only when certain stimuli (certain environmental conditions) are present. For example, you have learned that a response of "pee" is appropriate when you see **p** but not when you see its mirror image (**q**). Similarly, Donald might learn that a classmate who smiles at him is more likely to reinforce his attempts at being friendly than a classmate with a scowl. Lindsey might learn that sitting quietly is reinforced in class, but not on the playground. Martin might learn that he can get up and leave the classroom only after his teacher has given him permission to do so. When people learn that responses are reinforced in the presence of one stimulus but not in the presence of another, perhaps very similar, stimulus, they have learned **discrimination** between the two stimuli.

Occasionally, our students may overgeneralize, exhibiting responses they have learned in situations where such responses are inappropriate. In such cases, we must teach them to discriminate between suitable and unsuitable stimulus conditions. How can we help our students learn to make important discriminations among stimuli? For example, how can we help them learn:

- When they can and cannot talk in class?

- At what points in a lecture they should take notes?

- On what occasions they should carefully check their written work for possible spelling and punctuation errors?

- For what mathematics problems they should use estimation procedures?

- How to recognize and hit a curve ball?

For one thing, we can make sure we reinforce students for exhibiting behaviors *only* in situations where those behaviors are appropriate (only in the presence of the appropriate antecedent stimuli). We can also describe in very concrete terms the conditions under which certain behaviors are and are not acceptable and productive.

Describe the conditions under which certain behaviors are appropriate; reinforce those behaviors only when they *are* appropriate.

Cueing Appropriate Behaviors

As teachers, we may frequently find it useful to use a strategy known as **cueing,** whereby we remind students, either directly or more subtly, about the behaviors we expect of them (G. A. Davis & Thomas, 1989; Emmer, 1987; Krumboltz & Krumboltz, 1972; Zirpoli & Melloy, 1993). For example, we might occasionally say things along these lines:

- "I hear the signal for a fire drill. We need to *line up quietly and then walk in single file to the outside door.*"

- "Students who *have their desks clear* go to lunch first."

- "After you have all *read pages fourteen through nineteen in your textbooks,* I will hand out information about the school ski trip."

- "I see some *art supplies that still need to be put back on the shelves* before we can be dismissed."

Such reminders, often called *cues* or *prompts,* serve as antecedent stimuli that will increase the likelihood that our students will behave in appropriate ways.

Give students occasional verbal cues to remind them of what they are supposed to be doing.

Encouraging Productive Classroom Behaviors Through Operant Conditioning

Reinforce desirable behaviors.

> To a student who has just completed an excellent oral book report, a teacher says, "Nice job, Monica. You made the book sound interesting. I think we *all* want to read it now."

Provide opportunities for students to practice correct behaviors.

> In a unit on basketball, a physical education teacher makes sure that every student has several successful shots at the basket.

Remember that different things are reinforcing to different students.

> A teacher allows students to do the various things they enjoy during the free time they earn that day. For example, some students work on the classroom computer, others work on favorite art projects, and still others converse with friends.

When the baseline level of a desired behavior is low, gradually shape the behavior over time by reinforcing closer and closer approximations.

> A teacher praises a shy and withdrawn boy for smiling or making eye contact with his classmates. After such behaviors become more frequent, the teacher begins praising him when he responds to classmates' questions or comments. As those behaviors also become a frequent occurrence, the teacher praises the boy only when he initiates a conversation with someone else.

When students generalize inappropriately, help them learn to discriminate among stimuli that require different responses.

> When a boy consistently reads one word as another (e.g., reading *cat* as "car"), his teacher points out the differences between the two words and gives the student numerous opportunities to read the words both in isolation and in context.

Cue appropriate behaviors.

> As students are busily working on cooperative group projects, their teacher sees that one group's discussion is being dominated by a single student. He announces to the class, "Please remember a point that I made earlier: You are more likely to create a good product when *all* group members contribute their ideas."

Looking at Transfer from a Behaviorist Perspective

If you have already read Chapter 8, then you are already familiar with the phenomenon of **transfer.** People exhibit transfer when something they learn in one situation affects how they learn or behave in another situation. In some cases, we see **positive transfer,** whereby something that a person has learned at one time *facilitates* learning or behavior later on. In other cases, we see **negative transfer,** whereby something learned at one time actually *interferes* with later learning or performance. Chapter 8 describes several explanations of transfer from a cognitivist perspective.

Behaviorists have offered an alternative explanation of how and when transfer occurs—one based on the extent to which stimuli and responses are similar or different in the learning and transfer situations (e.g., J. F. Hall, 1966; Osgood, 1949). Four principles of transfer can be derived from behaviorist research:

- Maximum positive transfer occurs when stimuli and responses in the two situations are similar.

- Some positive transfer occurs when stimuli are different but responses are similar.

- Negative transfer occurs when stimuli are similar but responses are different.

- No transfer occurs when stimuli and responses are both very different.

These four principles and their implications are presented in Table 9–2. Let's look more closely at each one.

Maximum Positive Transfer: Stimuli Similar/Responses Similar

Consider Elena, a student who first learns Spanish and then learns French. She finds that her knowledge of Spanish often helps her learn French vocabulary more quickly. Let's look at some of her vocabulary words as examples of stimulus-response associations:

English		Spanish	English		French
(*stimulus*)	→	(*response*)	(*stimulus*)	→	(*response*)
one	→	uno	one	→	un
two	→	dos	two	→	deux
three	→	tres	three	→	trois
four	→	cuatro	four	→	quatre
five	→	cinco	five	→	cinq

Notice how the stimuli in the two situations are identical (they are the same English words in both cases) and the responses are very similar. Here is a case where we would expect positive transfer. According to behaviorists, maximum positive transfer occurs when both the stimuli and the responses in two situations are similar. In such a situation, we see the principle of generalization at work: Once people learn how to respond to one stimulus in a particular way, they are likely to respond to similar stimuli in the same way.

From this perspective, we see the advantage of **authentic activities**—classroom activities similar to those that our students will encounter in the outside world. In some instances, we can bring "real world" stimuli into the classroom environment. For example, when we teach students to add and subtract dollars and cents, we might use real money and realistic shopping activities; when we teach students how to fill out job applications, we might use actual application forms from local employers (Schloss & Smith, 1994; Stokes & Baer, 1977). In other instances, we might bring students to real-world contexts to practice skills they have learned in the classroom (Haring & Liberty, 1990; Schloss & Smith, 1994). For example, when my son Jeff was studying map inter-

Expect and encourage transfer when stimuli and responses are similar in two situations.

Use authentic activities to promote positive transfer of school learning to the outside world.

Table 9–2   A Behaviorist Analysis of Transfer

PRINCIPLE	EDUCATIONAL IMPLICATION	EXAMPLE
Maximum positive transfer occurs when stimuli and responses in the two situations are similar.	We should expect and encourage transfer when stimuli and responses are similar in two situations.	We can show students how throwing a discus is in some respects similar to throwing a Frisbee.
Some positive transfer occurs when stimuli are different but responses are similar.	We should expect that students will get some benefit from practicing desired responses in situations dissimilar to the transfer situation.	When a student struggles with the spelling of the word *fluorescent*, we might mention that the ending is spelled in the same way as that of a very different word—*adolescent*.
Negative transfer occurs when stimuli are similar but responses are different.	We should emphasize differences between similar stimuli if the appropriate responses to them are very different.	When introducing beginning French students to the word *bonjour*, we should point out that the word is pronounced very differently in French than what they would predict on the basis of typical English pronunciations.
No transfer occurs when stimuli and responses are both very different.	We should expect little if any transfer when both stimuli and responses are different.	Although students may benefit a great deal from learning a computer programming language, we should not expect this skill to have much effect on their performance in other subject areas.

If you have already read Chapter 7, can you recall why cognitive psychologists also advocate authentic activities?

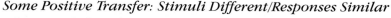

pretation skills in sixth grade, he and his classmates spent a day on a scavenger hunt around the city, traveling from one local merchant to another, using city buses and a map of city bus routes, and collecting a specified item at each stop they made. By using such authentic activities, we increase the number of stimuli that school tasks and real-world tasks share, and so we increase the likelihood that positive transfer from one setting to the other will take place.

Some Positive Transfer: Stimuli Different/Responses Similar

🍎

Expect that students will get some benefit from practicing desired responses in situations dissimilar to the transfer situation.

When people have learned a particular response in one situation, that learning sometimes transfers to another situation requiring a similar response, even though stimuli in the two situations are very different. For example, when a student learns to say "Thank you" after a classmate has offered to share school supplies, he may be more likely to say "Thank you" in a very different context, such as when he receives change for a purchase at the store. When a student learns to spell *pollution* correctly during a spelling lesson, she will be more likely to spell it correctly when writing a letter to the editor of the local newspaper.

Negative Transfer: Stimuli Similar/Responses Different

──────────────── **THINKING ABOUT WHAT YOU KNOW** ────────────────

- Are you someone who plays two different sports that use *rackets*? For example, do you play both tennis and racquetball? If so, do you find that playing one sport interferes with your ability to play the other sport a day or two later?

- Are you someone who has skied in two or more different ways—perhaps trying both waterskiing and downhill snow skiing? If so, did you have some difficulty learning one form of skiing because of habits that you had previously developed when engaging in the other form of skiing?

─────────────────────────── ───────────────────────────

When stimuli in two situations are similar but the desired responses are very different, negative transfer may result because people generalize to a situation in which they *shouldn't* generalize. For example, many people report that they have difficulty playing tennis and racquetball games within a day or so of each other. The two games appear similar—both involve hitting a ball with a racket—but tennis requires a full arm swing, whereas racquetball requires a quick snap of the wrist. So, too, can waterskiing transfer negatively to downhill snow skiing. Both sports involve skis; however, one should lean *back* in waterskiing (leaning forward means falling kerplash) but lean *forward* in downhill skiing (otherwise, one often gets a snowy rear end).

Emphasize differences between similar stimuli if desired responses to each one are very different. Teach two easily confused topics in two different environments.

One way that we can minimize negative transfer in stimuli-similar/responses-different situations is to point out explicitly that two situations are not as similar as they appear; in other words, we can help students *discriminate* between the similar stimuli. For example, we can talk about the many ways in which racquetball is different from tennis, or in which downhill skiing is different from waterskiing. Another strategy is to teach one topic in one environment and the other topic in a completely different environment, thereby minimizing the stimuli that the two topics share (Bilodeau & Schlosberg, 1951; Greenspoon & Ranyard, 1957). For example, students may have an easier time differentiating between the events of World War I and those of World War II if they study the two world wars in different classrooms, with different classmates, or perhaps with a different classroom seating arrangement.

No Transfer: Stimuli Different/Responses Different

From a behaviorist perspective, neither positive nor negative transfer will occur from one situation to another when both stimuli and responses are different in the two situations. To illustrate, the Latin phrase *Veni, vidi, vici* (stimulus) and its English meaning "I came, I saw, I conquered" (response) bear little relationship to anything that a student might learn in a physics class. For the same reason, learning computer programming should not help a student learn psychology, nor should knowledge of algebra transfer to world history.

Expect little if any transfer when both stimuli and responses are different.

REDUCING AND ELIMINATING UNDESIRABLE BEHAVIORS

Up to this point, we have been talking primarily about strategies for promoting desirable behaviors. Yet our students may sometimes exhibit *un*desirable behaviors—

responses that interfere with their own learning and achievement, and possibly with the learning and achievement of others as well. How do we decrease, and in some cases even eliminate, such behaviors? Behaviorists offer several possible strategies:

- Extinction

- Cueing

- Reinforcement of incompatible behaviors

- Punishment

Using Extinction

Extinguish undesirable behaviors by removing reinforcing consequences.

What happens when a response is no longer reinforced? As you might guess, a nonreinforced response decreases in frequency and usually returns to its baseline level—a phenomenon known as **extinction.** For example, the class clown whose jokes are ignored may stop telling jokes. The aggressive child who never gets what she wants by hitting or shoving others may become less aggressive. One way of reducing the frequency of an inappropriate behavior, then, is simply to make sure it is never reinforced.

Unfortunately, teachers and other adults often inadvertently reinforce the very behaviors they want to eliminate. For example, a girl who copies her homework assignment word for word from a classmate and then receives a high grade for that assignment is reinforced for representing someone else's work as her own. A boy whose comments in class are so obnoxious that his teacher has no choice but to give him the attention that he seeks is also being reinforced for inappropriate behavior. As teachers, we must look reflectively at our own behaviors in the classroom, being careful *not* to reinforce, either intentionally or unintentionally, those responses that are not likely to help our students over the long run.

Don't be surprised to see a temporary increase in behaviors that you are no longer reinforcing.

There are several things to keep in mind about extinction, however. First, once reinforcement stops, a previously reinforced response doesn't always decrease immediately. Sometimes there is a temporary *increase* in behavior at the beginning. To illustrate how this might occur, imagine that you have a cantankerous television set, one that gives you a clear picture only when you bang its side once or twice. Eventually, something changes in the inner workings of your set, so that banging is no longer an effective remedy. As you desperately try to get a clear picture, you may bang your television a number of times in succession (more times than you usually do) before giving up that response. In much the same way, the class clown who is now being ignored may increase the frequency of joke telling at first, and the aggressive child may initially become more aggressive, before learning that such behaviors are not producing the desired results.

How is extinction similar in classical and operant conditioning? How is it different?

Second, we may sometimes find situations in which a response does not decrease even when we remove a reinforcer. In such situations—when extinction doesn't occur—chances are that we haven't been able to remove *all* reinforcers of the response. Perhaps the behavior is leading to a naturally reinforcing consequence; for example, a class clown's classmates may continue to snicker even when the teacher ignores his jokes. Or perhaps the response is an intrinsically reinforcing one; for example, a student's physically aggressive behavior may release pent-up energy (and so may "feel good") even if it doesn't otherwise get her what she wants. Only when all reinforcers are removed will extinction occur.

Finally, we must remember that extinction may occur with desirable behaviors as easily as with undesirable ones. The student who is never called on in class may stop raising his hand. The student who never passes a paper-pencil test no matter how hard she studies may eventually stop studying. As teachers, we must be very careful that, while counterproductive classroom behaviors are not being reinforced, productive responses *are* being reinforced, either through such extrinsic reinforcers as attention, praise, or favorite activities or through the intrinsic satisfaction that classroom accomplishments may bring.

Make sure you don't inadvertently extinguish desired behaviors.

Cueing Students About Inappropriate Behaviors

Just as we can use cueing to remind students about what they should be doing, we can also use this strategy to remind them about what they should *not* be doing. Here are three cues that quickly and easily point out inappropriate responses:

- Body language
- Physical proximity
- A brief verbal cue

Body Language

Simple body language can serve as a subtle reminder to students about what they should and should not be doing. Making eye contact with a distracted student is often sufficient to get that student back on task. Such signals as a frown, a raised eyebrow, or a finger to the lips are additional ways of letting students know that we disapprove of their behavior and would like it to cease (Emmer, 1987; Palardy & Mudrey, 1973; Shrigley, 1979; Woolfolk & Brooks, 1985).

Use body language—for example, eye contact, a frown, or a finger to the lips—as a signal that inappropriate behavior is occurring.

Physical Proximity

When the body language doesn't get the attention of a misbehaving student, a more obvious cue is to move closer to the student and stand there until the problem behavior stops (Emmer, 1987; Palardy & Mudrey, 1973; Shrigley, 1979; Woolfolk & Brooks,

Move closer to a misbehaving student and stand there until the problem behavior stops.

Simple body language is often an effective cue. When this teacher is temporarily preoccupied, her hand on a student's shoulder provides a subtle reminder about what he should and should not be doing.

1985). Particularly if we are walking around the room anyway during a classroom activity, this strategy can attract the attention of the guilty party without at the same time drawing undue attention from classmates.

A Brief Verbal Cue

Give a verbal cue that reminds students of what they are supposed to be doing.

Sometimes subtlety just doesn't work, and so we have to be more explicit. In such cases, a brief remark—stating a student's name, reminding a student about correct behavior, or (if necessary) pointing out an inappropriate behavior—may be in order (G. A. Davis & Thomas, 1989; Emmer, 1987). For example, we might say something as simple as, "Please keep your eyes on your own work," or, "Lucy, put the magazine away."

Reinforcing Incompatible Behaviors

EXPERIENCING FIRSTHAND
Asleep on Your Feet

Have you ever tried to sleep while you were standing up? Horses can do it, but most of us humans really can't. In fact, there are many pairs of responses we can't possibly perform simultaneously. Take a minute and identify something that you cannot possibly do when you perform each of these activities:

When You:	You Cannot Simultaneously:
Sit down	_____
Eat crackers	_____
Take a walk	_____

Two behaviors are **incompatible** when they cannot be performed simultaneously; in a sense, the two behaviors are opposites. For example, sitting is incompatible with standing. Eating crackers is incompatible with singing, or at least with singing *well*. Taking a walk is incompatible with taking a nap. In each case, it is physically impossible to perform both activities at exactly the same time.

If you've read the discussion of information processing in Chapter 6, you've also discovered that paying attention to one thing is often incompatible with paying attention to something else.

When our attempts to extinguish an inappropriate behavior are unsuccessful, a second way to reduce that behavior is to reinforce an incompatible (and presumably more desirable) behavior; the inappropriate response must inevitably decrease as the incompatible one increases (e.g., Ayllon & Roberts, 1974; Lentz, 1988; Zirpoli & Melloy, 1993). This is the approach that we are taking when we reinforce a hyperactive student for sitting down: Sitting is incompatible with getting-out-of-seat and roaming-around-the-room behaviors. It is also an approach that we might use to deal with forgetfulness (we reinforce students when they remember to do what they were supposed to do), being off-task (we reinforce on-task behavior), and verbal abusiveness (we reinforce prosocial statements). And consider how we might deal with a chronic litterbug: One student was successfully cured of his littering habit when he was put in charge of his junior high school's "anti-litter" committee and given considerable public recognition for his new position. Not only did the student himself stop dropping banana peels and sunflower seed shells on the floor, but he also launched a massive anti-litter campaign, complete with posters and lunchroom monitors (Krumboltz & Krumboltz, 1972).

Reinforce behaviors that are incompatible with undesirable behaviors.

Administering Punishment

Some misbehaviors require an immediate remedy—not only do they interfere significantly with students' learning, but they may threaten students' physical safety or psychological well-being as well—and so we cannot simply wait for gradual improvements over time. Consider this student as an example:

> Bonnie doesn't handle frustration very well. Whenever she encounters a difficulty or obstacle that she can't immediately overcome, she responds by hitting, kicking, or breaking something. Over the course of the school year, she has knocked over several pieces of furniture, smashed two windows, made several dents in the wall, and broken innumerable pencils. Not only is Bonnie's behavior hindering her academic progress, but it's also getting very expensive.

Bonnie's inappropriate behaviors are difficult to extinguish because they aren't really being reinforced to begin with (not extrinsically, at least). They are also behaviors with no obvious incompatible responses we can reinforce. And we can reasonably assume that Bonnie's teacher has already cued her about her inappropriate behaviors on many occasions. When other strategies are inapplicable or ineffective, punishment may be our only alternative.

Earlier in the chapter, we defined reinforcement as a consequence that increases the frequency of a particular behavior. We will define **punishment** in a similar fashion: It's a consequence that *decreases* the frequency of the response that it follows.

Strictly speaking, punishment is not a part of operant conditioning. B. F. Skinner believed that punishment was a relatively *in*effective means of changing behavior—that it might temporarily suppress a response but could never eliminate it—and suggested that teachers focus their efforts on reinforcing desirable behaviors, rather than on punishing undesirable ones. But despite Skinner's concerns, many behaviorists have found that some forms of punishment can be quite effective in reducing problem behaviors (Frankel & Simmons, 1985; R. V. Hall et al., 1971; Pfiffner & O'Leary, 1987; Rachlin, 1991; G. C. Walters & Grusec, 1977).

Use punishment only when alternative approaches are ineffective.

Different Forms of Punishment

All punishing consequences fall into one of two groups. **Punishment I** involves the presentation of a new stimulus, presumably something that a student finds unpleasant and doesn't want. Spankings, scoldings, and teacher scowls, if they lead to a reduction in the behavior they follow, are all instances of Punishment I. **Punishment II** involves the removal of a previously existing stimulus, presumably one that a student finds desirable and doesn't want to lose. The loss of a privilege, a fine (involving the loss of money or points), and "grounding" (when certain pleasurable outside activities are missed) are all examples of Punishment II.

Over the years, I have observed many occasions when people have used the term *negative reinforcement* when they were really talking about punishment. Remember, negative reinforcement increases a response, whereas punishment has the opposite effect. Table 9–3 should help you understand how negative reinforcement, Punishment I, and Punishment II, are all very different concepts.

Effective forms of punishment in school settings. As a general rule, we will want to use relatively mild forms of punishment in the classroom; severe consequences may lead to such unwanted side effects as resentment, hostility, or perhaps even truancy (Ormrod, 1995b). Researchers and educators have identified sev-

Table 9–3 *Distinguishing Among Positive Reinforcement, Negative Reinforcement, and Punishment*

	EFFECT	EXAMPLES
Positive Reinforcement	Response *increases* when a new stimulus (presumably one that the person finds desirable) is *presented.*	A student *is praised* for writing an assignment in cursive; she begins to write other assignments in cursive as well. A student *gets his lunch money* by bullying a girl into surrendering hers; he begins bullying his classmates more frequently.
Negative Reinforcement	Response *increases* when a previously existing stimulus (presumably one that the person finds undesirable) is *removed.*	A student *no longer has to worry* about a research paper that he has completed several days before the due date; he begins to do his assignments ahead of time whenever possible. A student *escapes the principal's wrath* by lying about her role in a recent incident of school vandalism; she begins lying to school faculty whenever she finds herself in an uncomfortable situation.
Punishment I	Response *decreases* when a new stimulus (presumably one that the person finds undesirable) is *presented.*	A student *is scolded* for taunting other students; she taunts others less frequently after that. A student *is ridiculed by classmates* for asking a "stupid" question in class; he stops asking questions.
Punishment II	Response *decreases* when a previously existing stimulus (presumably one that the person finds desirable) is *removed.*	A student *is removed from the softball team for a week* for showing poor sportsmanship; she rarely shows poor sportsmanship in future games. A student *loses points on a test* for answering a question in a creative but unusual way; he takes fewer risks on future tests.

eral forms of mild punishment that are often effective in reducing classroom misbehaviors:

- *Verbal reprimands (scolding).* Although some students seem to thrive on teacher scolding because of the attention that it brings, most students, particularly if they are scolded relatively infrequently, find verbal reprimands to be unpleasant and punishing (Lentz, 1988; K. D. O'Leary, Kaufman, Kass, & Drabman, 1970; Pfiffner & O'Leary, 1987; Van Houten, Nau, MacKenzie-Keating, Sameoto, & Colavecchia, 1982). Softly spoken reprimands are sometimes more effective than loud ones, possibly because they are less likely to be noticed and so less likely to draw the attention of other students (K. D. O'Leary et al., 1970). Reprimands should be given in private whenever possible: Some students may relish the peer attention they receive when they are scolded in front of their classmates, and others (e.g., many Native American and Hispanic students; C. A. Grant & Gomez, 1996) may feel unnecessarily humiliated.

- *Response cost.* Response cost is the loss either of a previously earned reinforcer or of an opportunity to obtain reinforcement (thus, response cost is an instance of Punishment II). For example, teachers of students with chronic behavior problems sometimes use a point system in their classrooms, awarding points, check marks, or plastic chips for good behavior (reinforcement) and subtracting points for bad behavior (response cost). Students who accumulate a sufficient number of points can use them to "buy" objects, privileges, or enjoyable activities that are otherwise not available. Response cost is especially effective when coupled with reinforcement of appropriate behavior (Iwata & Bailey, 1974; Kazdin, 1972; Lentz, 1988; McLaughlin & Malaby, 1972; E. L. Phillips, Phillips, Fixsen, & Wolf, 1971; Rapport, Murphy, & Bailey, 1982).

- *Time-out.* Time-out is a procedure whereby a misbehaving student is placed in a dull, boring (but not scary) situation—perhaps a separate room designed especially for time-outs, a little-used office, or a remote corner of the classroom. A student undergoing time-out has no opportunity to interact with classmates and no opportunity to obtain reinforcement. The length of the time-out is often quite short (perhaps two to ten minutes, depending on the age of the student), but the student is not released from the time-out situation until inappropriate behavior (e.g., screaming, kicking) has stopped. Time-outs have been used successfully to reduce a variety of disruptive, aggressive, and dangerous behaviors (Alberto & Troutman, 1990; Frankel & Simmons, 1985; Ormrod, 1995b; A. G. White & Bailey, 1990; Zirpoli & Melloy, 1993). (Note: Although some theorists argue that time-out is not really punishment, most students find the boredom of a time-out to be somewhat unpleasant.)

- *Logical consequences.* A logical consequence is a consequence that follows logically from a student's misbehavior; in other words, the punishment fits the crime. For example, if a student destroys a classmate's possession, a reasonable consequence is for the student to replace it or pay for a new one. If two close friends talk so much that they aren't getting their assignments done, a reasonable consequence is for them to be separated. If a student intentionally makes a mess in the cafeteria, a reasonable consequence is to clean it up. The use of logical consequences makes "logical" sense, and numerous research studies and case studies vouch for its effectiveness (Dreikurs & Cassel, 1972; Foxx & Azrin, 1973; Foxx & Bechtel, 1983; R. V. Hall et al., 1971; Lyon, 1984; Schloss & Smith, 1994; L. S. Wright, 1982).

- *In-school suspension.* In-school suspension is similar to time-out in that the student is placed in a quiet, boring room within the school building. In-school suspension often lasts one or more school days, however, and involves close adult supervision. Students receiving in-school suspension spend the day working on the same assignments that their nonsuspended peers do—thus, they are able to keep up with their schoolwork. But they have no opportunity for interaction with classmates and friends—an aspect of school that is reinforcing to most students. Although in-school suspension programs have not been investigated through controlled research studies, many school administrators report that such programs are effective in reducing chronic misbehaviors, particularly when part of the suspension session is devoted to teaching appropriate behav-

Use such mild forms of punishment as reprimands, response cost, time-out, logical consequences, and if necessary, in-school suspension.

iors and (if necessary) tutoring students in areas of academic weakness (DiSciullo, 1984; Huff, 1988; P. M. Short & Noblit, 1985; Sullivan, 1989; Weiss, 1983).

Just as we must use different reinforcers for different students, we must also individualize our use of punishment. For example, some students enjoy the attention that verbal reprimands bring. A few may even appreciate the peace and quiet of an occasional time-out (Solnick, Rincover, & Peterson, 1977). If we find that a particular form of punishment produces no substantial decrease in a student's behavior, we should conclude that it isn't really a punishing consequence for that student and that a different form of punishment for future misbehaviors is called for.

Ineffective forms of punishment. At least four forms of punishment are definitely *not* recommended: physical punishment, psychological punishment, extra classwork, and out-of-school suspension. Each of these produces some undesirable side effects that are counterproductive over the long run (e.g., Ormrod, 1995b; G. C. Walters & Grusec, 1977):

Stay away from physical or psychological punishment, extra classwork, or out-of-school suspension.

- *Physical punishment.* Physical punishment is generally not advised for school-age children (Doyle, 1990a; Zirpoli & Melloy, 1993); furthermore, its use in the classroom is *illegal* in many places. Even mild physical punishment, such as a spank or slap with a ruler, can lead to such undesirable behaviors as resentment of the teacher, inattention to school tasks, lying, aggression, vandalism, avoidance of school tasks, and truancy. And when carried to extreme lengths, physical punishment constitutes child abuse and may cause long-term or possibly even permanent physical damage.

- *Psychological punishment.* Psychological punishment is any consequence that seriously threatens a student's self-esteem. Embarrassing remarks and public humiliation have the potential to inflict long-term psychological harm. Psychological punishment can lead to some of the same side effects as physical punishment: resentment of the teacher, inattention to school tasks, and truancy from school. To the extent that it lowers students' self-esteem, it may also lower students' expectations for future performance and their motivation to learn.

Suspension from school may actually reinforce inappropriate school behavior, rather than punish it.

- *Extra classwork.* Asking a student to complete make-up work for time missed in school is a reasonable and justifiable request. But assigning extra classwork or homework beyond that which is required for other students is inappropriate if it is assigned simply to punish a student's wrongdoing (e.g., H. Cooper, 1989). In this case, we have a very different side effect: We inadvertently communicate the message that "schoolwork is not fun."

- *Out-of-school suspension.* Teachers and administrators are negatively reinforced when they suspend a problem student. After all, they get rid of something they don't want— the student! But out-of-school suspension is usually *not* an effective means of changing a student's behavior (Doyle, 1990a; Moles, 1990). In the first place, being suspended from school may be exactly what the student wants, in which case inappropriate behaviors are being reinforced, rather than punished. And second, because many students with chronic behavior problems also tend to do poorly in their schoolwork, suspension involves a loss of valuable instructional time, thereby decreasing even further their chances for academic success (e.g., Skiba & Raison, 1990).

Using Punishment Humanely

A frequent criticism of using punishment is that it is "inhumane"—that it is somehow cruel and barbaric. And certain forms of punishment, such as physical abuse or public humiliation, do indeed constitute inhumane treatment. We must be *extremely careful* in our use of punishment in the classroom. When administered judiciously, however, some forms of mild punishment can lead to a rapid reduction in misbehavior without causing physical or psychological harm. And when we can decrease counterproductive classroom behaviors quickly and effectively—especially when those behaviors are harmful to self or others—then punishment may, in fact, be one of the most humane approaches we can take. Here are several guidelines for using punishment effectively and humanely:

- Inform students ahead of time that certain behaviors will be punished, and explain how those behaviors will be punished.

- Follow through with specified consequences.

- Administer punishment privately.

- Explain why the punished behavior is unacceptable.

- Emphasize that it is the *behavior* that is undesirable, not the *student*.

- Simultaneously teach and reinforce desirable alternative behaviors.

Let's look at each of these guidelines more closely.

Informing students ahead of time. Students should be informed in advance, explicitly and concretely, about behaviors that are unacceptable and the consequences that will follow such behaviors (e.g., Aronfreed & Reber, 1965). When students are informed of response-punishment contingencies ahead of time, they are less likely to engage in the forbidden behaviors; they are also less likely to be surprised or resentful if punishment must be administered (Aronfreed, 1968; G. D. Gottfredson & Gottfredson, 1985; Moles, 1990).

Too often, the misbehaviors we want to discourage are ambiguous, even to us. For example, when we tell our students that cheating is not allowed or that aggression is unacceptable, what exactly do we mean? Does the term *cheating* include such behaviors as copying someone else's homework? Does it mean that a student cannot seek the assistance of a parent or classmate on an assignment? Does *aggression* include verbal insults? Is poking a classmate during a friendly interaction considered aggressive? We need to tell students exactly what we mean by such terms as *cheating, plagiarism, aggression,* and *disrespect,* and perhaps clarify them even further by describing several concrete examples.

Following through. One mistake that many teachers make is to continue to threaten possible punishment without ever following through. One warning is desirable, but repeated warnings are not. The teacher who says, "If you bring that rubber snake to class one more time, Tommy, I'm going to take it away"—but never does take Tommy's

Ultimately, students should learn that they can control the things that happen to them, and they can only control the events in their lives when they know what responses lead to what outcomes—for example, when they know that certain behaviors will be punished in certain ways. We will consider this idea of control more closely in our discussion of *attribution theory* in Chapter 11.

snake away from him—is giving him the message that no response-punishment contingency really exists.

Administering punishment privately. By administering punishment in private, we protect our students from public embarrassment or humiliation. We also eliminate the possibility that the punishment will draw the attention of classmates—a potential reinforcer for the very behavior that we are trying to eliminate.

Explaining why the punished behavior is unacceptable. We must explain exactly why a certain behavior cannot be tolerated in the classroom—perhaps because it interferes with learning, threatens the safety or self-esteem of other students, or damages school property. Punishment is far more effective when accompanied by one or more reasons why the punished behavior is unacceptable (Baumrind, 1971; Cheyne & Walters, 1970; Griffore, 1981; Harter, 1983; Hoffman, 1970; Parke, 1972, 1974, 1977; Perry & Perry, 1983; G. C. Walters & Grusec, 1977).

Emphasizing that it is the behavior that is undesirable. As teachers, we must emphasize to students that certain behaviors interfere with their success in learning—that they are preventing themselves from becoming the very best they can be.

Simultaneously teaching and reinforcing desirable alternative behaviors. Punishment of misbehavior is almost always more effective when appropriate behaviors are being reinforced at the same time (Rimm & Masters, 1974; G. C. Walters & Grusec, 1977). Furthermore, by reinforcing "good" behavior, as well as punishing the "bad," we give students a far more positive and optimistic message that, yes, behavior can and will improve.

At this point, can you describe positive reinforcement, negative reinforcement, Punishment I, and Punishment II in your own words? Can you think of examples of each of these concepts?

MAINTAINING DESIRABLE BEHAVIORS OVER THE LONG RUN

As we noted in our discussion of extinction, responses that are no longer reinforced decrease in frequency, typically returning to their baseline level; in some cases, this means that the responses disappear altogether. Yet we cannot continue to reinforce every student each time he or she engages in appropriate behavior. And we won't be able to reinforce our students at all after they leave our classrooms at the end of the school year.

So how can we ensure that our students will continue to behave in ways that are in their own best interests over the long run? There are at least two viable strategies: promoting intrinsic reinforcement, and using intermittent reinforcement.

Promoting Intrinsic Reinforcement

The advantage of intrinsic reinforcers is that they come from within individuals themselves, rather than from some outside source. Students will often engage in activities that are enjoyable or satisfy their curiosity. They will also exhibit behaviors that lead to success and to feelings of mastery, accomplishment, and pride. Ideally, it is such internal consequences that will be most effective in sustaining productive behaviors both in the classroom and in the outside world.

Decreasing and Eliminating Undesirable Behaviors

Don't inadvertently reinforce undesirable behaviors.

> A teacher realizes that a particular "problem" student—a girl who makes frequent inappropriate remarks in class—seems to thrive on any kind of attention. He also realizes that the girl's behavior has gotten worse, instead of better. Rather than continue to reinforce the girl by scolding her publicly, he meets with her after school and together they develop a contingency contract designed to improve her behavior.

Cue students when you see them behaving inappropriately.

> As she describes the morning's assignment, a teacher notices that two girls on the other side of the classroom are whispering, giggling, and obviously not paying attention. While continuing her description of the assignment, she walks slowly across the room and stands next to the girls.

Reinforce behaviors that are incompatible with undesirable behaviors.

> A student is out of her seat so frequently that she gets little of her own work done and often distracts her classmates from doing theirs. Her teacher discusses the problem behavior with her, and together they decide that she will earn points for staying in her seat and keeping on task; she may use the points to "buy" time with her friends at the end of the day.

When a misbehavior must be suppressed quickly, choose a mild punishment, yet one that is likely to deter the behavior in the future.

> When members of the school soccer team have an unexcused absence from team practice, they are not allowed to play in that week's soccer game.

Describe both appropriate and inappropriate behaviors, as well as their consequences, in concrete and explicit terms.

> The soccer coach reminds students that, whereas students who miss practice will sit out at the next game, all students who *do* make practice every day will play at least part of the game.

When misbehaviors continue despite all reasonable efforts to correct them, seek the advice of experts.

> A teacher consults with the school psychologist about three students who are often physically aggressive in their interactions with classmates. Together, using applied behavior analysis, they develop a strategy to help these students.

Yet success is not always achieved easily and effortlessly. Many of the tasks that our students will tackle in school—reading, writing, solving mathematical problems, reasoning scientifically, understanding historical and social events, participating skillfully in team sports, learning to play a musical instrument—are complex, challenging, and often frustrating, especially at first. When students struggle with a challenging task and encounter frequent little failures, we should probably provide extrinsic reinforcement

Use extrinsic reinforcers only until students have mastered subject matter sufficiently to find intrinsic reinforcement in what they are doing.

One statement in this paragraph is based on the concept of *shaping*. Another statement reflects the concept of *scaffolding*, described in Chapter 2. Can you identify each of these statements?

for the little improvements they make. And when we find that we must break down a complex task into smaller pieces that, though easier to accomplish, are less rewarding in their own right (e.g., when we assign drill-and-practice exercises related to basic reading or math skills), we will probably need to reinforce students' many seemingly "meaningless" successes. Once our students have mastered tasks and skills to a level that brings them frequent successes and feelings of mastery, however, extrinsic reinforcers should no longer be necessary (Covington, 1992; Lepper, 1981). In fact, for reasons that you will discover when you read about motivation in Chapter 11, it will actually be counterproductive for us to provide extrinsic reinforcers when students are already finding intrinsic reinforcement in the things they are doing.

Using Intermittent Reinforcement

Up to this point, I have been talking about reinforcement as an all-or-nothing occurrence, implying, perhaps, that a response is always reinforced or else never reinforced. But you can probably think of many behaviors that are reinforced inconsistently: Sometimes they are reinforced, and sometimes they are not. Whenever a response is reinforced only occasionally, with some occurrences of the response going unreinforced, we have **intermittent reinforcement.**

Which of your behaviors are reinforced only on an intermittent basis?

Continuous reinforcement and intermittent reinforcement produce somewhat different results. To show you what I mean, let's consider Molly and Maria, two students with low baseline levels for volunteering in class. Their teacher, Mr. Oliver, decides to reinforce the girls for raising their hands. Every time Molly raises her hand, Mr. Oliver calls on her and praises her response; she is receiving continuous reinforcement. But when Maria raises her hand, Mr. Oliver doesn't always notice her. He calls on Maria whenever he sees her hand in the air, but he doesn't often look in her direction; she is therefore receiving intermittent reinforcement. Which girl will more quickly increase her frequency of volunteering?

If you chose Molly, you are correct. One difference that we see between continuous and intermittent reinforcement is in their effect on the *acquisition* of new responses. As we noted earlier in the chapter, responses increase most rapidly when they are continuously reinforced.

But let's move ahead in time a few months. Thanks to Mr. Oliver's attentiveness to Molly and Maria, both girls are now volunteering frequently in class. Mr. Oliver turns his attention to several other students who have been failing to participate. Foolishly, he no longer reinforces either Molly or Maria for raising her hand. As you might expect, the girls' level of class participation goes down: We see signs of extinction. But for which girl will class participation extinguish more rapidly?

If you predicted that Molly's volunteering will decrease more rapidly than Maria's, you are correct. Responses that have previously been reinforced continuously tend to extinguish relatively quickly once reinforcement stops. But because Maria has been receiving intermittent reinforcement, she is accustomed to being occasionally ignored. It may take her longer to realize that she is no longer going to be called on when she raises her hand. Behaviors that have previously been reinforced intermittently decrease slowly (if at all) once reinforcement stops; in other words, they are more *resistant to extinction.*

Once students have acquired desired behaviors, continue reinforcing them on an intermittent basis.

Once students have acquired a desired terminal behavior, we should continue to reinforce that behavior on an intermittent basis, especially if it does not otherwise lead to intrinsic reinforcement. Mr. Oliver doesn't need to call on Molly and Maria every time they raise their hands, but he should certainly call on them once in a while. In a similar manner, we should occasionally reinforce diligent study habits, completed homework assignments, prosocial behaviors, and so on, even for the best of students, as a way of encouraging such responses to continue.

USING APPLIED BEHAVIOR ANALYSIS

Over the past thirty years, behaviorist principles—especially those related to operant conditioning—have had a major impact on educational practice. When we apply behaviorist principles to classroom practice in a systematic way, we have a group of procedures collectively known as **applied behavior analysis** (ABA) or **behavior modification** (the difference between the two terms is a subtle one; see Schloss & Smith, 1994, for more details).

Applied behavior analysis includes such strategies as these:

- Following appropriate behaviors with pleasant consequences (*reinforcement*)

- Reinforcing a sequence of increasingly more productive behaviors (*shaping*)

- Reinforcing "opposite" responses (reinforcement of *incompatible behaviors*)

- Following inappropriate behaviors with unpleasant consequences (*punishment*)

- Making response-consequence contingencies explicit

- Applying consequences consistently

- Maintaining appropriate behaviors over the long run (using *intermittent reinforcement*)

These strategies are summarized in Table 9–4.

Effectiveness of ABA Techniques

How effective are applied behavior analysis techniques in bringing about behavior change? Hundreds of research studies tell us that the systematic use of behaviorist principles can lead to significant improvements in academic performance and classroom behavior. For example, when we reinforce students for successful achievement, we find improvements in such subjects as mathematics, reading, spelling, and creative writing (Piersel, 1987). When we reinforce such appropriate classroom behaviors as paying attention and interacting cooperatively and prosocially with classmates, misbehaviors decrease (S. N. Elliott & Busse, 1991; Iwata, 1987; McNamara, 1987; Ormrod, 1995b). In many situations, behaviorist techniques are effective when others have not been (Emmer & Evertson, 1981; K. D. O'Leary & O'Leary, 1972; Ormrod, 1995b; Piersel, 1987). For this reason, applied behavior analysis will be one of the tools to which I will refer when we discuss classroom management in Chapter 12.

One probable reason that behaviorist techniques often work so well is that students know exactly what is expected of them. Consistent use of reinforcement for appropriate responses informs students in a very concrete way regarding which behaviors are acceptable and which are not. Another likely reason is that, through the gradual process of *shaping*, students attempt to learn new behaviors only when they are truly ready to acquire them. They therefore find that their learning efforts usually lead to success (to reinforcement). And after all, everyone likes to be successful!

Which form of reinforcement—continuous or intermittent—would you use to teach your students to be persistent at difficult tasks?

How might you use some of these principles to deal with James, our case study at the beginning of the chapter?

Can you think of other possible reasons for the success of ABA techniques?

Table 9–4 *Behaviorist Principles and Their Educational Implications*

PRINCIPLE	EDUCATIONAL IMPLICATION	EXAMPLE
A response that is followed by a pleasant consequence is more likely to occur again (*reinforcement*).	We must make sure we reinforce desired classroom behaviors. In other words, we must catch students in the act of being good.	When a student who usually has trouble working independently completes her seatwork without having to be prodded, we might inconspicuously praise her.
A new response can be taught by reinforcing successively closer approximations to it (*shaping*).	When students rarely if ever exhibit a certain desired behavior, we should begin by reinforcing the response that most closely resembles it. Once that response is occurring frequently, we can reinforce increasingly more acceptable responses until students exhibit the desired behavior.	We can reinforce a hyperactive student for sitting quietly for one minute. Once he is able to do so on a regular basis, we can reinforce him for sitting still for two minutes, then for four minutes, and so on.
When a response is reinforced, incompatible responses decrease in frequency (*reinforcement of incompatible behaviors*).	We can reduce inappropriate classroom behaviors by reinforcing opposite behaviors.	When a usually antisocial student works cooperatively and productively with her classmates in a cooperative learning group, we can reinforce her efforts by allowing her to do something she especially enjoys doing.
A response that results in either the presentation of an unpleasant consequence or the removal of a pleasant situation is less likely to occur again (*punishment*).	We can reduce undesirable behaviors (from our point of view) by following them with undesirable consequences (from our students' point of view).	When a member of an athletic team shows unsportsmanlike conduct, we can have her sit out the next game.
A response changes more rapidly when an individual knows that it will be reinforced or punished.	We must make it clear to students what behaviors are and are not acceptable and describe the specific consequences that will follow each one.	When preparing students for an upcoming exam, we can remind them that confirmed cases of cheating will result in a score of zero.
A response changes more rapidly when the same consequence (reinforcement or punishment) is applied consistently.	We must be sure we don't punish an undesirable behavior on some occasions yet inadvertently reinforce it on others.	Whenever a class clown tells racist or sexist jokes in class, we can ask him to write a letter of apology to classmates whom he might have offended. We should also make every effort not to laugh at such jokes.
A response is more resistant to extinction when it is reinforced on some occasions but not others (*intermittent reinforcement*).	Once students are consistently demonstrating appropriate classroom behavior, we should continue to reinforce it on an intermittent basis.	Once a formerly aggressive student has developed appropriate social skills and demonstrates them consistently in the classroom, we should occasionally commend her for her prosocial behavior.

Limitations of Applied Behavior Analysis

But lest you think that behaviorist techniques will always provide the perfect solution to your students' classroom behavior problems, I should point out some potential drawbacks to using these techniques. First, as we will discover in Chapter 11, extrinsic reinforcement for a particular behavior may undermine any intrinsic motivation that a student has for engaging in that behavior. A second potential side effect is that, when students increase the responses that lead to reinforcement, other desirable responses may decrease as a result. Students receiving external reinforcers for their academic work sometimes show less interest in *non*reinforced school activities, less desire to perform beyond minimal standards of performance, and less risk taking and creativity in assignments (Brophy, 1986; Cameron & Pierce, 1994; Clifford, 1990; Kruglanski, Stein, & Riter, 1977; Lepper & Hodell, 1989). For these reasons, before we begin to use external reinforcers to increase certain behaviors, we should be sure such reinforcers are truly necessary—that students show no intrinsic motivation to develop the academic or social skills essential for their school success.

Why do you think external reinforcers might have such effects? Can you form some hypotheses before you read the discussion of this issue in Chapter 11?

Finally, we should note that, particularly when dealing with chronic misbehaviors, ABA may take a fair amount of our instructional time (Hughes, 1988). Ideally, we should *prevent* misbehaviors as often as we can, rather than having to correct them after they have already developed. We will identify numerous preventive strategies in our discussion of classroom management in Chapter 12.

Obviously, we can learn a great deal about human learning and behavior simply by looking at stimulus-response principles, and we can bring about major behavior changes by applying behaviorist principles in a systematic fashion. At the same time, such principles do not by any means give us a complete picture of human learning. For example, although reinforcement may increase the amount of time that students study, it does not necessarily increase the effectiveness of that study time; cognitive psychology provides more guidance as to how we can help students learn information more effectively, remember it longer, and apply it to new situations more readily. Furthermore, it appears that people learn not only the behaviors that they themselves are reinforced for but also the behaviors that they see *others* exhibit. A third perspective of learning—social cognitive theory—provides more guidance about how we can help students learn through their observations of others. We will consider this perspective in the following chapter.

In a number of places throughout the chapter, I have sneaked unobservable phenomena (e.g., thoughts, feelings) into my description of behaviorist principles. Can you find some places where I have done so?

CONSIDERING DIVERSITY IN STUDENT BEHAVIORS

When we take a behaviorist perspective, we realize that our students bring their own unique set of prior experiences to the classroom; such diversity in previous environments is undoubtedly one of the reasons for the different behaviors we see in the classroom. For one thing, our students will have been reinforced and punished—by their parents, siblings, previous teachers, peers, and so on—for different kinds of behaviors. Some students may have been reinforced for completing tasks in a careful and thorough manner, whereas others may have been reinforced for completing tasks quickly and sloppily. Some students may have been reinforced for initiating interactions with agemates; others may have been punished (perhaps in the form of peer rejection) for similar outgoing behavior. Some diversity in students' classroom responses will also be due to the different behaviors that varying cultures encourage (reinforce) and discourage (punish) in their children.

We will also see differences in the secondary reinforcers to which students respond. Remember, secondary reinforcers are those that become reinforcing over time through their association with other reinforcing stimuli; thus, the relative effectiveness of such reinforcers as praise and positive feedback will depend on the extent to which such associations have been made. For example, some Native American students may feel uncomfortable when praised for their work as *individuals* yet feel quite proud when they receive praise for *group* success (C. A. Grant & Gomez, 1996). Such preference for group praise is consistent with the cooperative spirit in which these students have been raised (e.g., see our discussion of ethnic differences in Chapter 4).

Finally, we should note that our students will already have acquired diverse responses to some of the stimuli they will encounter at school. For example, when they have their first experiences throwing a softball, some may be able to generalize from previous experiences throwing a baseball, whereas others may have to start from scratch in developing the skill. When they find themselves in an argument with a classmate, some may try to resolve the conflict through negotiation and compromise, whereas others may decide that the best course of action is a knock-down-drag-out fight.

With such diversity in mind, we must remember that as we use behaviorist principles to bring about behavior change, we will inevitably need to tailor our strategies to the particular students with whom we are working. Effective reinforcers, baseline rates of desired behaviors, and responses to particular antecedent stimuli will all be different for each student.

Accommodating Students with Special Needs

A behaviorist approach allows us to consider characteristics of students with special needs from a somewhat different angle than we have in previous chapters. Table 9–5 presents descriptions of how responses, reinforcement, generalization, and discrimination may be somewhat different in some of our students with special needs. A behaviorist approach may be especially useful for understanding students who must be continually motivated to engage in appropriate academic and social behaviors—for example, students who have been identified as having emotional and behavior disorders.

Emotional and Behavioral Disorders

Let's return one last time to our case study at the beginning of the chapter. James's excessive need for attention, and his consistent disruptive and counterproductive behaviors in the classroom, may indicate that he falls into a particular category of special needs students—those with **emotional and behavioral disorders.** Such students have emotional states or behaviors that have a substantial negative impact on classroom performance; common examples include an inability to establish and maintain satisfactory interpersonal relationships with adults and peers, long-term depression, and exceptionally aggressive or antisocial behavior. These students often qualify for special services designed to enhance their academic success and achievement.

Many emotional and behavioral disorders are believed to be primarily the result of environmental factors, although heredity may make some children more susceptible to these factors than others (Patton et al., 1987). For example, exceptionally aggressive students are apt to come from homes where parents monitor their children's behavior infrequently, use force rather than praise as the primary means of behavior control, punish their children unpredictably, and allow some aggressive behaviors to go unpun-

Table 9–5 Encouraging Appropriate Behaviors in Students with Special Educational Needs

STUDENTS WITH SPECIAL NEEDS	CHARACTERISTICS THAT THESE STUDENTS MAY EXHIBIT	CLASSROOM STRATEGIES THAT MAY BE BENEFICIAL FOR THESE STUDENTS
Students with specific cognitive or academic deficits	Difficulty discriminating among similar stimuli, especially when perceptual deficits exist Difficulty generalizing responses from one situation to another	Emphasize differences among similar stimuli and provide opportunities to practice making subtle discriminations. Promote generalization of new responses (e.g., by pointing out similarities among different situations, by teaching skills in real-world contexts).
Students with specific social or behavioral deficits	Inappropriate responses, especially in social situations; difficulty determining when and where particular responses are appropriate A history of inappropriate behaviors being reinforced (e.g., by previous teachers giving attention for such behaviors) Responsiveness to teacher praise if given in private Occasional difficulty generalizing appropriate responses to new situations	Describe desired behaviors clearly. Give precise feedback regarding students' behavior. Reinforce desired behaviors (e.g., using teacher attention, private praise, activity reinforcers, group contingencies). Shape desired behaviors over time; expect gradual improvement, rather than immediate perfection. Punish inappropriate behaviors (e.g., using time-out or response cost). Promote generalization of new responses to appropriate situations (e.g., by providing opportunities to role-play new responses in a variety of contexts).
Students with general delays in cognitive and social functioning	High reinforcing value of extrinsic reinforcers Behaviors more likely to increase when reinforcement is immediate, rather than delayed. Inappropriate responses in social situations Difficulty discriminating between important and unimportant stimuli Difficulty generalizing responses from one situation to another	Cue students regarding appropriate behaviors. Provide immediate feedback regarding specific behaviors. Reinforce accomplishments immediately (e.g., using concrete reinforcers, activity reinforcers, praise). Use continuous reinforcement during the acquisition of new responses. Shape desired behaviors over time; expect gradual improvement, rather than immediate perfection. Reprimand minor misbehaviors; use time-out or response cost for more serious and chronic misbehaviors. Highlight the stimuli to which you want students to attend. Promote generalization of new responses (e.g., by teaching skills in real-world contexts, by reinforcing generalization).
Students with advanced cognitive development	Unusual and sometimes creative responses to classroom tasks	Keep an open mind regarding acceptable responses to classroom assignments. Encourage and reinforce creative responses.

Sources: Barbetta, 1990; Gearheart, Weishahn, & Gearheart, 1992; Heward, 1996; C. D. Mercer, 1991; D. P. Morgan & Jenson, 1988; Patton, Beirne-Smith, & Payne, 1990; Patton, Payne, Kauffman, Brown, & Payne, 1987; Piirto, 1994; Pressley, 1995; Turnbull, Turnbull, Shank, & Leal, 1995.

Compiled with the assistance of Dr. Margie Garanzini-Daiber and Dr. Margaret Cohen, University of Missouri—St. Louis.

ished (Patterson, 1981, 1982; Patterson, DeBaryshe, & Ramsey, 1989; Patterson & Stouthamer-Loeber, 1984; Shaffer, 1988). Factors at school may exacerbate the problem for these students: Their antisocial behaviors interfere with academic achievement and incur rejection by their classmates, thus leading to both academic and social failure. The students may eventually seek the companionship of the few peers who *will* accept them—peers who typically behave in similarly inappropriate ways. Antisocial students often provide mutual support for one another's antisocial behavior and may introduce one another to drugs, alcohol, or criminal activity (Patterson et al., 1989). Students with a history of aggressive and antisocial behavior are among those who are at high risk for dropping out of school.

Effective educational programs for students with emotional and behavioral disorders are usually individualized and tailored to the unique needs of each student. Nevertheless, there are several things we can do that are likely to benefit many of these students:

- Teach more appropriate interpersonal skills
- Promote success on academic tasks
- Communicate expectations for classroom behavior
- Specify and follow through on consequences for appropriate and inappropriate behaviors
- Look for gradual improvement, rather than immediate perfection
- Show a genuine interest in students' well-being

Teaching Interpersonal Skills

Teach appropriate interpersonal skills.

Many students with emotional and behavioral disorders have never really learned how to behave appropriately; for example, they may lack skills in cooperating, communicating, or resolving interpersonal conflicts (Shaffer, 1988). Research has often shown ABA to be effective in improving the interpersonal skills of students with emotional and behavioral disorders (Heward, 1996; Landau & McAninch, 1993; D. P. Morgan & Jenson, 1988; Turnbull et al., 1995). You can find additional strategies for teaching such skills in the discussion of social development in Chapter 3 and in the discussion of self-regulation in Chapter 10.

Promoting Success on Academic Tasks

Promote success on academic tasks from the very beginning.

Many students with emotional and behavioral disorders show poor performance on academic tasks and assignments. As teachers, we must not delay students' progress on academic skills until after their nonacademic problems have been addressed. Rather, we should begin helping students be successful at classroom tasks beginning with the first day of the school year (Semmel et al., 1979).

Communicating Expectations

Specify exactly what behaviors are acceptable and unacceptable.

With students who have emotional and behavioral disorders, it is especially important to specify exactly which behaviors are acceptable and unacceptable in precise and concrete terms (e.g., Landau & McAninch, 1993). For example, we can provide specific guidelines about when students can speak in class and when they are free to move about the classroom. Students are going to have an easier time meeting our expectations—in terms of both academic performance and classroom behavior—when they know exactly what we expect them to do.

Specifying and Following Through on Consequences

Specify consequences in advance and be consistent in applying them.

When working with students with emotional and behavioral disorders, it is especially important that we describe the consequences—either reinforcing or punishing—to which various behaviors will lead; it is also crucial that we follow through with those consequences (Barkley, 1990; Landau & McAninch, 1993; Lewis & Doorlag, 1991; Patton et al., 1987; J. W. Wood, 1989). At the same time, we should also give students explicit feedback about their behavior (Patton et al., 1987). When praising desirable behavior, rather than saying "Well done" or "Nice job," we should describe exactly what behaviors we are praising. When imposing punishment for inappropriate behavior, we should tell students exactly what they have done wrong. For example, we might say, "You borrowed Austin's book without asking him first. You know that taking other students' possessions without their permission is against class rules."

Give students explicit feedback about their behaviors.

INTO THE CLASSROOM

Helping Students with Emotional and Behavioral Disorders

Make expectations for classroom behavior clear and specific.

A teacher reminds a student, "You cannot borrow Mary's bottle of glue without asking. Check with Mary first to make sure it's all right for you to use her things. If Mary says no, ask another student."

Give feedback about specific behaviors, rather than general areas of performance.

A teacher tells a student, "You did a good job during independent reading today. You focused your attention on your book, and you didn't retaliate when Jerome accidentally brushed past you on his way to my desk."

Specify and follow through on consequences for appropriate and inappropriate behaviors.

A teacher tells a student, "Sam, you know that certain four-letter words, such as the two that you just used, are unacceptable in this classroom. You also know the consequence for such behavior—please go to the time-out corner for ten minutes."

Teach interpersonal skills.

When a student's only comments to classmates are derogatory remarks, her teacher demonstrates more appropriate ways of initiating interaction. Together, they practice the new strategies through various role-playing situations.

Show an interest in students' well-being.

A teacher who sees a girl weeping quietly every day in class takes her aside when the other students have gone to lunch. As the student describes the nasty divorce proceedings in which her parents are involved, the teacher empathizes, explaining that his own parents divorced in an equally unpleasant fashion.

Expect gradual improvement, rather than immediate perfection.

A teacher is pleased that a student who once refused to participate in classroom activities now gets involved in activities two or three days a week, even though that student still has some days when little is accomplished.

Look for gradual improvement, rather than overnight perfection.

Show genuine interest in the student's well-being.

Remember that bringing about behavior change in students with emotional and behavioral disorders may sometimes require persistence and patience on your part.

Looking for Gradual Improvement

Most students with emotional and behavioral disorders are likely to improve slowly and gradually; we will rarely see dramatic changes overnight. As teachers, then, we should look for small, day-to-day improvements, rather than expect immediate perfection. By focusing on small improvements, we and our students alike can be encouraged by the changes we do see, rather than being discouraged by the problems that persist (Gearheart et al., 1992; Patton et al., 1987).

Showing an Interest in Students' Well-Being

My last recommendation—to show a genuine interest in students' well-being—is not necessarily based on behaviorist principles per se. But it is important for us to note that many students with emotional and behavioral disorders have few positive and productive relationships with individuals outside school; we can often help these students simply by showing them that we care about their welfare (Diamond, 1991). For example, we can greet them warmly when we see them in the hallway. We can express concern when they seem upset, worried, or overly stressed. We can lend a ready and supportive ear when they want to share their ideas, opinions, feelings, or frustrations. And we can let them know that such sharing is welcome by sharing aspects of our own personal lives (Diamond, 1991).

You should be aware that the job of helping students with emotional and behavioral disorders is often a challenging one. Many of these students will at first resist any efforts to help them. It may only be when they themselves can observe the natural consequences of their changing behavior—for example, when they start to make new friends or when they get along better with their teachers—that they begin to recognize the value of the assistance that you are giving them (Patton et al., 1987).

CASE STUDY: *Hostile Helen*

Mr. Washington has a close-knit group of friends in one of his high school vocational education classes. He is concerned about one particular student in this group, a girl named Helen. Helen uses obscene language in class. She is rude and disrespectful to Mr. Washington. She taunts and insults classmates outside her own circle of friends. And she is physically aggressive toward classroom facilities—defacing furniture, kicking equipment, punching walls, and so on.

At first, Mr. Washington tries to ignore Helen's hostile and aggressive behaviors, but this strategy doesn't lead to any improvement in her behavior. He then tries praising Helen on those rare occasions when she does behave appropriately, but this strategy doesn't seem to work either.

- In behaviorist terminology, what is Mr. Washington trying to do when he ignores Helen's inappropriate behavior? What are some possible reasons why this approach isn't working?

- In behaviorist terminology, what is Mr. Washington trying to do when he praises Helen's appropriate behavior? What are some possible reasons why this approach isn't working either?

- How might *you* use behaviorist learning principles to bring about a behavior change in Helen?

SUMMING UP

Behaviorism

Behaviorists focus on the role that the environment (stimuli) plays in bringing about changes in behavior (responses). It is clear from behaviorist principles that the classroom environments we create have a significant effect on our students' learning and behavior.

Classical Conditioning

Classical conditioning is one way through which people acquire emotional responses to stimuli in the environment. Classical conditioning occurs when (1) one stimulus (the unconditioned stimulus) already elicits a particular response (the unconditioned response) and (2) that stimulus is presented in conjunction with another stimulus, usually on several occasions. Under these circumstances, the second (conditioned) stimulus begins to elicit a (conditioned) response as well. As teachers, we should create a classroom environment that conditions pleasure and relaxation responses to academic tasks, not an environment that elicits fear and anxiety.

Operant Conditioning

Operant conditioning occurs when a person's response is followed by a reinforcing stimulus, thereby increasing the likelihood that the person will make the same response again. We can increase the frequency of appropriate and productive student behaviors by reinforcing those behaviors whenever they occur or by reinforcing closer and closer approximations to those behaviors (in other words, by shaping them). At the same time, we must also be careful *not* to reinforce undesirable or counterproductive student responses.

Reinforcement takes a variety of forms. Most reinforcers we use in the classroom are likely to be sec-ondary reinforcers, rather than primary reinforcers; in other words, they satisfy no physiological need but have nevertheless become an "acquired taste" for most of our students. Positive reinforcement involves the presentation of a presumably pleasant stimulus, whereas negative reinforcement involves the removal of a presumably *un*pleasant one; both of these consequences will increase the frequency of whatever behaviors they follow. We will use reinforcement most effectively when we describe desired behaviors clearly, individualize reinforcers in accordance with students' preferences, make response-consequence contingencies explicit and consistent, and monitor students' progress.

Effects of Antecedent Stimuli

Once our students have learned a response to a particular stimulus, they will tend to make the same response to similar stimuli (generalization). Seemingly similar situations may sometimes call for very different responses, however; in such situations, it is important that we help students make the necessary discriminations between occasions when particular behaviors are and are not appropriate, perhaps by providing cues regarding the responses we expect them to make. The extent to which antecedent stimuli are similar or different and the extent to which the responses that follow them should be either similar or different will determine the likelihood that students will transfer something they've learned from one situation to another.

Reducing and Eliminating Undesirable Behaviors

Behaviorist principles offer several strategies for reducing and possibly eliminating nonproductive or counterproductive classroom behaviors. As teachers, we might remove the consequences that reinforce an unwanted behavior (resulting in the behavior's extinction), provide cues regarding inappropriate behavior, or reinforce responses incompatible with those that we wish to eliminate. In some situations, we may need to punish inappropriate behaviors, particularly when they interfere significantly with classroom learning or jeopardize students' physical safety or psychological well-being. We should think of punishment as a last resort, however, and abide by strict guidelines in its use, keeping in mind that such consequences as physical punishment, public humiliation, and out-of-school suspension are neither effective nor in our students' long-term best interests.

Maintaining Productive Behaviors

Ideally, desired behaviors are most likely to continue when they lead to such intrinsically reinforcing consequences as feelings of mastery or pride. When intrinsic reinforcement seems unlikely, we can instead maintain productive behaviors over the long run by reinforcing them on an intermittent basis.

Applied Behavior Analysis

Applied behavior analysis encompasses a group of techniques in which behaviorist principles are applied to classroom practice in a systematic fashion. Research indicates that such techniques are often effective in promoting greater academic success and more appropriate classroom behavior. We must be careful that we don't provide extrinsic reinforcement unnecessarily, however; in doing so, we may undermine any intrinsic reinforcers that are currently operating.

Diversity in Student Behaviors

Our students will have different histories of reinforcement and different experiences with the various stimuli in the classroom; hence, they will inevitably display different reactions to the same tasks and situations. Some students with special needs, including those with emotional and behavioral disorders, will exhibit counterproductive classroom behaviors; behaviorist principles may be especially useful in working with such students.

KEY CONCEPTS

behaviorism (p. 372)
conditioning (p. 374)
contiguity (p. 376)
classical conditioning (p. 377)
unconditioned stimulus (UCS) (p. 378)
unconditioned response (UCR) (p. 378)
neutral stimulus (p. 378)
conditioned stimulus (CS) (p. 378)
conditioned response (CR) (p. 378)
generalization in classical conditioning
  (p. 380)
extinction in classical conditioning
  (p. 381)
operant conditioning (p. 383)
contingency (p. 385)
terminal behavior (p. 385)
behavioral objectives (p. 386)
reinforcer (p. 386)
reinforcement (p. 386)

primary versus secondary reinforcers
  (p. 387)
positive reinforcement (p. 388)
concrete reinforcer (p. 389)
social reinforcer (p. 389)
activity reinforcer (p. 389)
Premack principle (p. 389)
group contingency (p. 389)
positive feedback (p. 391)
extrinsic versus intrinsic reinforcers
  (p. 391)
negative reinforcement (p. 392)
contingency contract (p. 395)
continuous reinforcement (p. 395)
baseline (p. 395)
shaping (p. 396)
antecedent stimulus (p. 398)
generalization in operant conditioning
  (p. 398)

discrimination (p. 399)
cueing (p. 399)
transfer (p. 400)
positive versus negative transfer
  (p. 400–401)
authentic activities (p. 401)
extinction in operant conditioning
  (p. 404)
incompatible behaviors (p. 406)
punishment (p. 407)
Punishment I versus Punishment II
  (p. 407)
intermittent reinforcement (p. 414)
applied behavior analysis (behavior
  modification) (p. 415)
emotional and behavioral disorders
  (p. 418)

Promoting Learning in a Social Context

THINKING ABOUT WHAT YOU KNOW

- What behaviors have you learned by watching other people do them first? Can you think of any academic skills you learned by watching someone else— perhaps a mathematical procedure or the correct conjugation of *estudiar*?

What about social skills—perhaps how to answer the telephone or how to apologize to someone whose feelings you've hurt? And what about psychomotor skills—perhaps how to swing a softball bat or write letters in cursive?

- What attitudes and beliefs have you acquired largely through observing the attitudes and beliefs of others? For example, did you adopt your parents' political or religious beliefs? Did you develop attitudes about social issues or the value of literature from any of your teachers? Did you acquire a sense of right and wrong from your parents, your teachers, or your peers?

- What factors affect the likelihood that you will or will not imitate the things you see other people do? Do your own personal characteristics play a role? Do characteristics of the person you're watching play a role? Do aspects of the behavior itself play a role?

WE LEARN MANY BEHAVIORS—academic, social, and motor skills alike—by watching our parents, our teachers, our peers, people we see in the media, and a variety of other individuals we encounter in our daily lives. We also learn which behaviors are likely to get us ahead—and which behaviors are not—by observing the consequences of those behaviors for ourselves and others. Eventually, we develop a sense of what we ourselves are capable of doing, and we begin to direct our behavior toward goals that we value and think we can achieve.

In this chapter, we will explore **social cognitive theory** (also called *social learning theory*), a theory that can help us understand what, when, and how people learn by watching others and how people ultimately begin to assume some control over their own behavior. Social cognitive theory has developed, in large part, through the research efforts of Albert Bandura at Stanford University. You will find references to Bandura and others who build on his ideas (e.g., Dale Schunk, Barry Zimmerman) throughout the chapter.

By the end of the chapter, you should be able to:

1. Identify the basic assumptions and principles of social cognitive theory and their implications for classroom practice.

2. Using the social cognitive perspective, explain how and when reinforcement and punishment influence behavior, and describe the effective use of both types of consequences in the classroom.

3. Identify situations and conditions in which you can use modeling to facilitate your students' learning.

4. Define the concept of *self-efficacy,* explain its effects on students' learning and behavior, and describe ways to enhance it.

5. Describe the development of self-regulation and explain how you can help your students become increasingly self-regulated.

6. Explain the complex interaction of personal variables, environmental variables, and behavior in the learning process.

CASE STUDY: *Parlez-Vous Français?*

Nathan isn't taking French because he wants to; he's enrolled only because of his mother's insistence. Although Nathan does well in his other high school courses, he is convinced that he will be a failure in French. After all, three of his friends took French last year, but they got mostly Ds and Fs on quizzes and homework, and two of them dropped the class after the first semester.

On the first day of French class, Nathan notices that most of his classmates are girls; the few boys in the class are students he doesn't know very well. He sits sullenly in the back row, convinced that he will do no better in French than his friends did. "I do OK in math and science, but I'm just no good at learning languages," he tells himself. "Besides, learning French is a 'girl' thing."

Because Nathan figures he is doomed to failure anyway, he pays little attention to his teacher as she explains simple syntactical structures and demonstrates the correct pronunciation of new vocabulary words. He makes feeble attempts at homework assignments but quickly puts them aside whenever he encounters anything he doesn't immediately understand.

Sure enough, Nathan is right: He can't do French. He gets a D− on his first exam.

- What are some possible reasons why Nathan believes he will do poorly in French class?

- What has Nathan learned by observing those around him?

- Why does Nathan's belief lead to a self-fulfilling prophecy?

IDENTIFYING BASIC ASSUMPTIONS OF SOCIAL COGNITIVE THEORY

When considering Nathan's situation, you might initially think that he has learned nothing from observing someone else. After all, he has apparently not benefited from his teacher's explanations and demonstrations. Yet at second glance, you might realize that Nathan *has* learned something by watching others: He has learned from his three friends that he is unlikely to succeed in French class. As we proceed through the chapter, you will discover some reasons why Nathan apparently learned more from his friends than he did from his teacher.

In our case study of Nathan, we have discovered one critical assumption underlying social cognitive theory: People can learn from observing others. This assumption and several others underlie the social cognitive perspective:

- People can learn from observing others.

- Learning is an internal process that may or may not result in a behavior change.

- Behavior is directed toward particular goals that people have set for themselves.

- Behavior eventually becomes self-regulated.

- Reinforcement and punishment have several indirect effects (rather than a direct effect) on learning and behavior.

Table 10–1 provides a synopsis of these assumptions; let's examine each one in more depth.

Learning by Observation

In our discussion of operant conditioning in the preceding chapter, we found that learning is sometimes a process of trial and error: People try many different responses, increasing the ones that bring about desirable consequences and eliminating the unproductive ones. Social cognitive theorists tell us that people don't always have to "experiment" in this way; they acquire many new responses simply by observing the behaviors of the people around them. For example, a student might learn how to solve a long division problem, spell the word *synonym* correctly, or mouth off at the teacher simply by watching someone else do these things first.

PRINCIPLES/ASSUMPTIONS

Table 10–1   Basic Assumptions of Social Cognitive Theory and Their Educational Implications

ASSUMPTION	EXAMPLE	EDUCATIONAL IMPLICATION
Learning by observation	In his German class, John learns to pronounce *danke schön* by listening carefully to the way his teacher pronounces it.	Demonstrate the behaviors you want students to learn.
Learning as an internal process that may or may not be reflected in behavior	John learns to pronounce *danke schön* correctly in Monday's class but doesn't have an opportunity to use the phrase until Wednesday.	Remember that learning does not always appear immediately, but may instead be reflected in students' later behaviors.
Goal-directed behavior	John hopes to visit Germany someday; he wants to be able to speak German when he gets there.	Help students set appropriate goals for themselves.
Self-regulation of behavior	John practices at home until he is satisfied with his pronunciation.	Encourage students to set high standards for their own performance and to strive to meet those standards.
Indirect effects of reinforcement and punishment	The teacher's praise of his correct pronunciation and her lack of praise for a classmate's mispronunciation tell John that correct pronunciation is important and should be mastered.	Make sure the consequences of students' responses give them the right messages as to which behaviors are acceptable and which are not.

Social cognitive theorists propose that people can sometimes learn more quickly and easily by watching how others behave and noticing which behaviors lead to reinforcement and which lead to punishment.

Learning as an Internal Process

Some of the things people learn appear in their behavior immediately, other things affect their behavior at a later point in time, and still others may never influence their behavior at all. For example, you might attempt to swing a softball bat just as soon as you learn the correct form. But you are not likely to show that you have learned how to apologize tactfully until some later time when an apology is necessary. And you might *never* walk barefoot over hot coals, no matter how many times you see someone else do it.

As we noted in the preceding chapter (and in Chapter 5 as well), behaviorists define learning as a change in behavior; therefore, if a person's behavior hasn't changed, then no learning has occurred. In contrast, the social cognitive perspective, like the cognitive perspective I described in Chapters 6 and 7, separates learning from behavior: It defines learning as an internal mental process that may or may not be reflected in a behavior change.

Goal-Directed Behavior

Because you are reading this book, I am guessing that you want to become a teacher. Do you have other goals as well? Would you like to get your body in better shape? Would you like to find time to read *War and Peace*? Do you want to travel to faraway places? What things are you doing to attain your goals?

Social cognitive theorists propose that people set goals for themselves and direct their behaviors toward the attainment of those goals. Students might set a variety of goals they hope to achieve—perhaps a high grade point average, a college scholarship, popularity with classmates, athletic prowess, or a reputation as the class clown. As we explore social cognitive theory in this chapter, we will frequently encounter the relevance of goal setting for learning and behavior.

Self-Regulation

From a behaviorist perspective, people's behaviors are largely a function of the things that happen *to* them—the stimuli they encounter, the reinforcers that follow their

Do you think your own behaviors are regulated more by the environment or by your own standards regarding what is acceptable and what is not?

behaviors, and so on. In contrast, social cognitive theorists believe that people eventually begin to regulate their *own* learning and behavior. As an example, let's consider Shih-tai, a third grader who is learning to write in cursive. A behaviorist might tell us that Shih-tai can best learn cursive if her teacher reinforces her for increasingly more appropriate responses, thereby shaping skillful penmanship over a period of several weeks or months. But a social cognitive theorist might suggest that Shih-tai can learn to write cursive letters just as easily by looking carefully at the examples her teacher has written on the chalkboard, copying those letters as closely as possible, and then comparing the letters she has written with those on the board. If she is happy with her work, she will give herself a mental pat on the back; if she is not, she may continue to practice until her letters are comparable with those of the teacher. From the social cognitive perspective, people often set their own standards for acceptable and unacceptable behavior and then strive to behave in accordance with those standards.

Indirect Effects of Reinforcement and Punishment

Operant conditioning theorists tell us that reinforcement is necessary for learning, because responses increase only when they are reinforced. Some behaviorists have also argued that punishment is an effective counterpart to reinforcement, decreasing the frequency of a behavior it follows. Implied in the behaviorist perspective is the idea that reinforcement and punishment are directly responsible for the behavior changes we see.

Reinforcement and punishment are less critical in social cognitive theory, but they have several indirect effects on learning and behavior. In the next few pages, we will find out exactly how reinforcement and punishment fit into the social cognitive perspective.

INTERPRETING REINFORCEMENT AND PUNISHMENT FROM A SOCIAL COGNITIVE PERSPECTIVE

According to social cognitive theorists (e.g., Bandura, 1977, 1986; T. L. Rosenthal & Zimmerman, 1978), both reinforcement and punishment influence learning and behavior in a number of ways, including these:

- People form *expectations* about the likely consequences of future responses on the basis of how current responses are reinforced or punished.

- People's expectations are also influenced by their observations of the consequences that befall others—in other words, through *vicarious experiences.*

- Expectations about probable future consequences affect the extent to which people *cognitively process* new information.

- Expectations also affect how people *choose to behave.*

- The *nonoccurrence of an expected consequence* may have a reinforcing or punishing effect in and of itself.

Let's see how each of these factors plays out in social cognitive theory.

Expectations

──────────── **THINKING ABOUT WHAT YOU KNOW** ────────────

- Perhaps you have taken a course in which all the exam questions were based on the textbook, without a single question coming from class lectures. After the first exam, did you find yourself studying the textbook very carefully but skipping class frequently?

- On the other hand, perhaps you have taken a course in which exams were based on the lectures and the assigned textbook readings seemed irrelevant. In that situation, did you go to class regularly but never bother to open your textbook?

According to social cognitive theory, people form expectations about the consequences that are likely to result from various behaviors. When we find that a particular response is reinforced every time we make it, we typically expect to be reinforced for behaving that way in future situations. When we discover that a response frequently leads to punishment, we expect that response to be punished on later occasions as well. For example, you use your own experiences with classroom tests to form expectations as to what specific behaviors (e.g., reading your textbook, going to class) are likely to be reinforced on future tests.

Students sometimes form expectations about what things will be reinforced and punished on the basis of very little hard data. For example, one student might believe (perhaps erroneously) that, by bragging about his high test scores, he will gain the admiration of his classmates (a reinforcer). Another student might believe that her classmates will ridicule and reject (punish) her for being smart, regardless of whether they would actually do so.

From the social cognitive perspective, reinforcement increases the frequency of a behavior only when students know what behavior is actually being reinforced—that is, when they are *aware* of actual response-reinforcement contingencies (Bandura, 1977, 1986; Spielberger & DeNike, 1966). As teachers, then, we should be very clear about what we are reinforcing, so that our students know the real response-reinforcement contingencies operating in the classroom. For example, if Sam gets an A on an essay but we don't let him know *why* he got an A rather than a C or D, he won't necessarily know how to get an A the next time. To improve Sam's performance, we might tell him that the essay earned an A because he supported his opinion with a logical train of thought. Similarly, if we praise Sandra for her "good game" at the basketball tournament even though she only scored one basket, she may understandably be a bit confused. We might instead tell her that we are pleased with her high energy level throughout the game.

> Can you think of an occasion when you chose not to do something because of the ridicule you thought it might bring you?

> Specify response-reinforcement contingencies.

Vicarious Experiences

When I was in third grade, I entered a Halloween costume contest dressed as a tooth. I didn't win the contest; a "witch" won first prize. So the following year, I entered the same contest dressed as a witch, figuring that I was a shoo-in for first place. Our expectations about the consequences of certain responses come not only from making the responses ourselves but also from observing what happens when others make those responses. In other words, we sometimes experience reinforcement and punishment *vicariously.*

When I saw another girl reinforced for dressing as a witch, my own witch-dressing behavior increased as a result. People who observe someone else getting reinforced for a particular behavior tend to exhibit that behavior more frequently themselves—a phenomenon known as **vicarious reinforcement.** For example, by watching the consequences that befall their classmates, students might learn that studying hard leads to good grades, that being elected to class office brings status and popularity, or that neatness counts.

Conversely, when we see someone else get punished for a certain behavior, we are *less* likely to behave that way ourselves—a phenomenon known as **vicarious punishment.** For example, when a coach benches a football player for poor sportsmanlike conduct, other players will be less likely to repeat such behavior. Vicarious punishment may suppress desirable behaviors as well, however. For example, when a teacher belittles a student for asking a seemingly silly question in class, other students will be reluctant to ask questions of their own.

As teachers, we must be extremely careful that we don't vicariously reinforce undesirable behaviors or vicariously punish desirable behaviors. If we give too much attention to a misbehaving student, others who want our attention may misbehave as well. If we ridicule a student who unwittingly volunteers an incorrect answer or erroneous belief, classmates will hardly be eager to respond to our questions or express their ideas and opinions.

How are vicarious reinforcement and punishment different from "ordinary" reinforcement and punishment?

Remember that the consequences you administer to one student may vicariously influence the behavior of many other students as well.

Cognitive Processing

EXPERIENCING FIRSTHAND
Planning Ahead

Quickly skim the contents of Chapter 12 ("Planning for a Productive Classroom") and get a general sense of the topics that it discusses. Once you have done so, imagine yourself in each of these situations:

1. Your educational psychology instructor announces, "Chapter 12 won't be on your test, but please read it anyway." How thoroughly and carefully will you read the chapter? Jot down a brief answer to this question.

2. The following day, your educational psychology instructor announces, "I gave you some incorrect information yesterday. In reality, half of next week's test will be based on the ideas presented in Chapter 12." *Now* how thoroughly and carefully will you read the chapter? Once again, jot down a brief answer.

On the one hand, if you don't expect to be reinforced for reading Chapter 12, you may very well *not* read it very carefully (perhaps you'll read it later, you think to yourself, but you have too many other things to do right now). On the other hand, if you discover that getting an A in your educational psychology course depends on your knowing the material in Chapter 12 like the back of your hand, you are apt to read it slowly and carefully, possibly trying to learn and remember each and every detail.

When we believe that we will be reinforced for learning something, we are more likely to pay attention to it and mentally process it in an effective fashion. When we *don't* expect to be reinforced for learning it, we are far less likely to think about or process it in any significant way. As an example of the latter situation, let's return to

Nathan, our case study at the beginning of the chapter. Nathan is convinced that he can't learn French; as a result, he pays little attention to the things his teacher says in class, and he makes only half-hearted efforts to complete his homework assignments.

Choice of Behavior

If Martha believes that studying for spelling tests will help her do well on those tests, she is likely to study her spelling words faithfully. But if she thinks she will fail her spelling tests whether she studies for them or not, then she may very well find something else to do with her time. Generally speaking, we behave in ways that maximize desirable consequences and minimize undesirable ones. Our expectations for the consequences of different behaviors affect the behaviors that we choose to exhibit.

People learn many things that they never demonstrate because there is no reinforcement for doing so. As an example of what I mean, try this short exercise.

EXPERIENCING FIRSTHAND
Dr. X

How many of the following questions can you answer about your educational psychology instructor? For lack of a better name, I'm going to call your instructor "Dr. X."

1. Is Dr. X right-handed or left-handed?

2. Is Dr. X a flashy dresser or a more conservative one?

3. What kind of shoes does Dr. X wear to class?

4. Does Dr. X wear a wedding ring?

5. Does Dr. X bring a briefcase to class each day?

If you've been going to class regularly, you probably know the answers to at least two of the questions, and possibly you can answer all five, even though you never thought you'd have a reason to know such information. Every time I teach educational psychology, I take a minute sometime during the semester to hide my feet behind the podium; I then ask my students to tell me what my shoes look like. My students first look at me as if I have two heads; information about my shoes is something that many of them have learned, but until now they have had absolutely no reason to demonstrate their knowledge. After a few seconds of awkward silence, at least a half dozen of them (usually the ones sitting in the first two rows) begin to describe my shoes, right down to the rippled soles, scuffed leather, and beige stitching.

Students learn many things in the classroom. They learn facts and figures, they learn ways of getting their teacher's attention, and they may even learn such tiny details as which classmate stores Twinkies in his desk and what kind of shoes the teacher wears to school. Of all the things they learn, students will be most likely to demonstrate the ones they think will bring them reinforcement. The things they think will *not* be reinforced may remain hidden forever. As teachers, we should be sure that our students believe that they will be reinforced for demonstrating their knowledge and skills related to important educational objectives.

Working for Incentives

When you work diligently for a reinforcer that you hope to obtain in the future, you are working for an **incentive.** Incentives are never guaranteed: You never know that

As a teacher, what might you do to help Martha become more optimistic about passing her spelling tests?

Make sure students believe that they will be reinforced for demonstrating what they have learned.

you are going to get an A on a test when you study for it or that you are going to win a Halloween costume contest when you enter it. An incentive is an expected or hoped-for consequence, one that may or may not actually occur. But you probably expect that you have some chance of success, or else you wouldn't put forth the effort in the first place.

People do not work for incentives they don't believe they can achieve. For example, a classroom competition in which one prize will be awarded to the highest test score in a classroom of thirty students provides an incentive to just a handful of top achievers. An incentive is effective only to the extent that it is obtainable and that a student perceives it as such. Therefore, when we provide incentives for student achievement, we should be sure that our students believe they have some probability of achieving those incentives.

Make sure students believe that they can achieve the incentives offered in the classroom.

When a forbidden behavior goes unpunished, it is actually reinforced and so is likely to occur again.

Follow through with the consequences that students expect for certain behaviors.

Some forms of punishment are neither effective nor appropriate for classroom use. See our discussion of this topic in Chapter 9 for guidelines on using punishment judiciously and humanely.

Nonoccurrence of Expected Consequences

When I entered the Halloween costume contest as a witch, I lost once again. (First prize went to a girl with a metal colander over her head. She was dressed as *Sputnik,* the first Soviet satellite launched into space.) That was the last time I entered the contest. I had expected reinforcement and felt cheated when I didn't get it. Social cognitive theorists propose that the nonoccurrence of expected reinforcement is a form of punishment (e.g., Bandura, 1977, 1986). When people think that a certain response is going to be reinforced, yet the response is *not* reinforced, they are less likely to exhibit that behavior in the future.

Perhaps you can think of a time when you broke a rule, expecting to be punished, but got away with your crime. Or perhaps you can remember an occasion when you saw someone else break a rule without being caught. When nothing bad happens after a forbidden behavior, people may actually feel as if they have been reinforced for that behavior. Just as the nonoccurrence of reinforcement is a form of punishment, the nonoccurrence of punishment is a form of reinforcement (Bandura, 1977, 1986).

When students work hard to achieve a desired end result—perhaps a compliment, a certificate, or a special privilege—and the anticipated result doesn't materialize, they will be unlikely to work as hard the next time. And when students break school rules, yet are not punished for doing so, they are more likely to break those rules again. So as teachers, it is important that we follow through with promised reinforcements for desirable student behaviors. It is equally important that we impose the consequences students have come to expect for undesirable behaviors.

As we have seen, students learn many behaviors from observing those around them. But they don't necessarily model everything they see someone else do. When do students imitate the behaviors they see? And what kinds of people are they most likely to imitate? It is to such questions about *modeling* that we turn now.

When a teacher punishes a student, the consequence doesn't just affect the future behavior of that student. It also affects the future behavior of other students who observe the punishment.

MODELING IN THE CLASSROOM

Consider these research findings:

- Students who have difficulty solving subtraction problems that require regrouping ("borrowing") become more successful problem solvers when they see the procedure modeled by someone else. In one experiment, students actually benefited more from watching another student solve subtraction problems than from watching a teacher do it (Schunk & Hanson, 1985).

- In another experiment, young children were taught not to speak to strangers. One group of children heard a lecture about the dangers of following strangers and about the things they should do if a stranger tried to entice them; nevertheless, very few of these children tried to resist a friendly stranger who later appeared on the playground. A second group actually observed another child demonstrate techniques for resisting strangers; most of these children resisted the stranger's advances (Poche, Yoder, & Miltenberger, 1988).

- When a teacher models techniques of learning information from a textbook—such techniques as summarizing information, asking oneself questions about the information, and predicting what a textbook is likely to say next—students begin to demonstrate these same skills, and their reading comprehension improves, in some cases quite dramatically (A. L. Brown & Palincsar, 1987; Palincsar & Brown, 1984).

- When children see aggressive models—whether those models are people the children know, people on television, or cartoon characters—they are more likely to be aggressive themselves. Boys in particular are likely to model the aggressive behaviors they observe (Bandura, 1965; Bandura, Ross, & Ross, 1961, 1963; Friedrich & Stein, 1973; Lowry et al., 1995; Mischel & Grusec, 1966; Steuer, Applefield, & Smith, 1971; R. H. Walters & Thomas, 1963; R. H. Walters, Thomas, & Acker, 1962).

- After watching adults demonstrate such behaviors as cooperation, sympathy, sharing, and generosity, children are more likely to demonstrate similar proso-

Administering Consequences from a Social Cognitive Perspective

Describe the specific behaviors you are reinforcing, so that students are aware of the response-reinforcement contingencies operating in the classroom.

> A teacher tells his class, "Because everyone got at least 80% of the math problems correct this morning, we will have ten minutes of free time at the end of the day."

Make sure students believe that they can achieve the incentives offered in the classroom.

> A teacher realizes that if she were to grade her students' science projects on a curve, only a few students could possibly get As. Instead, she gives her students a checklist of the specific criteria she will use to grade the science projects; she tells her class that any project meeting all criteria will get an A.

Tell students what behaviors are unacceptable in the classroom and describe the consequences that will result when those behaviors occur.

> A teacher reminds students that anyone seen pushing or hitting someone else in the lunch line will go to the end of the line.

Follow through with the reinforcements that you have promised for desirable student behaviors; also follow through with the adverse consequences that students expect for undesirable behaviors.

> When announcing tryouts for an upcoming school play, a teacher tells students that only those who sign up ahead of time may try out. When she holds tryouts the following week, she sticks to her word, turning away any student whose name does not appear on her sign-up sheet.

Remember that the consequences you administer for a particular student's behavior have a potential effect on any students who observe that consequence.

> The student council president—someone who is well liked and highly respected by both students and teachers—is nevertheless punished in accordance with school rules when she is caught cheating on an exam.

cial behaviors (R. Elliott & Vasta, 1970; Friedrich & Stein, 1973; Harter, 1983; Radke-Yarrow, Zahn-Waxler, & Chapman, 1983; Rushton, 1975, 1980).

- When a model preaches one set of moral values and practices another, observers are more likely to do what the model *does* than what the model *says* (J. H. Bryan, 1975).

We learn many different things through modeling. We learn such motor skills as holding a pencil, whittling a piece of wood, and dribbling a basketball by seeing how other people do these things. We also acquire skills in such academic areas as arithmetic and reading more readily by observing others. And we develop interpersonal skills and moral values, at least in part, by watching and imitating the people around us.

Most of the models from which we learn are **live models**—real people that we actually see doing something. We acquire many behaviors by watching family members, neighbors, teachers, and classmates. In a classroom setting, students may learn something by watching their teachers solve an algebraic equation on the chalkboard, observing a visiting police officer demonstrate important rules of bicycle safety, or seeing a classmate perform a perfect hook shot on the basketball court. But we are also influenced by **symbolic models**—by real or fictional characters portrayed in books, in films, on television, and through various other media. For example, students can learn valuable lessons from studying the behaviors of important figures in history or reading stories about people who accomplish great things in the face of adversity.

Think of specific individuals who might serve as positive role models (either real or symbolic) for your own students.

How Modeling Affects Behavior

Social cognitive theorists (e.g., Bandura, 1977, 1986; T. L. Rosenthal & Zimmerman, 1978) propose that modeling has several possible effects on human behavior, including these:

- Observational learning
- Response facilitation
- Response inhibition
- Response *dis*inhibition

Let's examine these four effects and their possible manifestations in classroom situations.

Observational Learning

The observational learning effect is one in which *the observer acquires a new behavior demonstrated by the model.* By seeing and hearing models, students learn how to dissect an earthworm, swim the elementary back stroke, and pronounce *¿Estudia usted español?* correctly. They may also acquire the political and religious beliefs that they hear their parents advocate. And they may adopt the attitudes of their teachers—perhaps enthusiasm about baseball, fear of mathematics, or disdain for the study of history (e.g., Rushton, 1980).

Use modeling as a way of teaching new behaviors.

Response Facilitation

The response facilitation effect is one in which *the observer displays a previously learned behavior more frequently after seeing a model being reinforced for that behavior* (after receiving vicarious reinforcement). As an example, consider this situation:

Use vicarious reinforcement as one way of increasing the desirable behaviors that students have previously learned.

> Billy returns to school in September to discover that his expensive new jeans are no longer in style. All his classmates are now wearing old, well-worn jeans; those with holes in the knees are especially fashionable. When he arrives home after his first day of school, Billy digs through his dresser drawers and the family rag bag, looking for old jeans. The next day, much to his parents' dismay, Billy goes to school wearing a pair of jeans with one large hole in the left knee and a three-inch rip running up the right thigh. Billy's brand new jeans are relegated to the top shelf of his closet, where they remain for the rest of the school year.

Our students are more likely to wear ragged old jeans if their classmates appear to be winning popularity with this attire. Similarly, they are more likely to complete their reading assignments on time and to work cooperatively, rather than competitively, with classmates—behaviors they may have learned long ago—if they see others being reinforced for doing so.

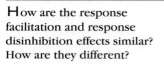

Response Inhibition

Use vicarious punishment as one way of decreasing inappropriate behaviors.

The response inhibition effect is one in which *the observer displays a previously learned behavior less frequently after seeing a model being punished for that behavior* (after receiving vicarious punishment). Students tend to inhibit (*not* engage in) those behaviors that result in adverse consequences for those around them. For example, students are less likely to be aggressive on the playground if they see their friends being punished for aggression. They are less likely to cheat on assignments if their peers are caught in the act. And they are less likely to volunteer to answer questions in class when the incorrect answers of their classmates are ridiculed.

Response Disinhibition

Why is this called the disinhibition effect?

The response disinhibition effect is one in which *the observer displays a previously forbidden or punished behavior more frequently after seeing a model exhibit the behavior without adverse consequences.* Just as students will inhibit behaviors leading to punishment, they will also engage in previously inhibited behaviors *more* frequently if they observe those behaviors going unpunished for other people. For example, students are more likely to chew gum, copy homework from classmates, or fight in the corridors if they see other students getting away with such behaviors. Remember, the nonoccurrence of expected punishment is reinforcing, so naturally any forbidden activities that seem to have no adverse effects for others may easily increase.

How are the response facilitation and response disinhibition effects similar? How are they different?

Yet students don't always model the individuals around them. What factors determine when students are most likely to imitate the behaviors they see? A look at characteristics of effective models will help us with the answer.

Characteristics of Effective Models

EXPERIENCING FIRSTHAND
Five People

Write down the names of five people you admire—five people whose behaviors you would like to imitate in some fashion. Then, beside each name, write down one or more of the reasons *why* you look up to these individuals.

Social cognitive theorists have found some consistency in the types of models that others are most likely to imitate (Bandura, 1977, 1986; T. L. Rosenthal & Bandura, 1978). Effective models typically exhibit one or more of these things:

Do the five people on your list exhibit some or all of these characteristics?

- Competence

- Prestige and power

- "Gender appropriate" behavior

- Behavior relevant to the observer's own situation

Competence

Our students will typically try to imitate people who do something well, not those who do it poorly. They will try to imitate the basketball skills of a professional basketball player, rather than those of the class klutz. They will copy the fashions of a popular classmate, rather than those of a student who is socially isolated. They will adopt the mathematical problem-solving procedures of teachers who clearly know what they are doing, rather than the procedures of teachers who make frequent mistakes at the chalkboard.

Show competence as you model behavior.

Prestige and Power

Children and adolescents often imitate people who are famous or powerful. Some effective models—a world leader, a renowned athlete, a popular rock star—are famous at a national or international level. The prestige and power of other models—a head cheerleader, the captain of the high school hockey team, a gang leader—may be limited to a more local environment.

In addition to modeling desired behaviors ourselves, we can expose our students to a variety of models that they are likely to view as prestigious and powerful. For example, we might invite respected professionals (e.g., police officer, nurse, newspaper reporter) to visit our classroom and talk with students about topics within their areas of expertise. We might also have students read and learn about appropriate models through such media as books and films—for example, by reading Helen Keller's autobiography or watching old news clips of Martin Luther King, Jr.

Have students observe prestigious or powerful models—either live or symbolic—engaging in desirable behaviors.

"Gender Appropriate" Behavior

Remember our friend Nathan's belief that French is a "girl" thing? Students are most likely to model behaviors they believe are appropriate for their gender (with different students sometimes defining *gender appropriate* somewhat differently). For example, many girls and boys limit their academic choices and career aspirations on the basis of the subjects and professions they believe are "for women" and "for men." Some girls may shy away from careers in mathematics as being too "masculine." Some boys may not take typing because they perceive it to be a secretarial skill, and most secretaries are women. Yet mathematics and typing are useful skills for both genders: Mathematics is essential for success in many professions, and facility with typing becomes more and more critical as our society relies increasingly on computers. Exposure to numerous examples of people in "nontraditional careers"—female mathematicians and engineers, male secretaries and nurses—can help broaden students' perceptions as to what behaviors are gender appropriate, hence also broadening their academic choices and possibly enhancing their career aspirations.

Expose students to successful models of both genders.

Behavior Relevant to the Observer's Own Situation

Students are most likely to model the behaviors they believe will help them in their own circumstances. A boy may wear the torn jeans that his popular classmates wear if he thinks he can become popular by doing so; however, he will have less reason to dress this way if he thinks that his thick glasses and adolescent acne will prevent him from ever being popular regardless of his clothing. A teenage girl may be tempted to join her friends in drinking beer if she thinks that doing so helps her become more accepted by them; she is less likely to indulge if she is the "designated driver" and knows that her friends are depending on her to stay sober.

Show students how the behaviors you model are relevant to their own lives.

In the classroom, we are likely to model a variety of behaviors throughout the day. But our students will only adopt these behaviors if they believe that such responses will truly be useful and productive for them. Therefore, we must show them how the problem-solving methods we teach, the writing skills we demonstrate, and the physical fitness regimen we advocate are all applicable to their own situations.

Our students are less likely to perceive the relevance of modeled behaviors when the model is different from them in some obvious way. For example, students from cultures other than our own may think that some of the things we try to teach them don't apply to their own cultural circumstances. Similarly, disabled students may believe that they are incapable of accomplishing the things a nondisabled teacher demonstrates. So it is important that we include individuals from minority cultures and individuals with disabilities in the models we present to our students. Minority students benefit from observing successful minority adults, and students with disabilities become more optimistic about their own futures when they meet adults successfully coping and overcoming their own disabilities (Allen & Seumptewa, 1988; Huston, 1983; E. H. Luchins & Luchins, 1980; Pang, 1995; Vasquez, 1990; Wong-Filmore, 1992).

You can probably think of teachers you've had whom you admired and wanted to be like. Most teachers have one or more characteristics of an effective model; for example, students typically view their teachers as being competent and having power, at least within the school environment. So as teachers, we "teach" not only by what we say but also by what we do. It is critical that we model appropriate behaviors and *not* model inappropriate ones. Do we model fairness to all students, or favoritism to a small few? Do we model enthusiasm and excitement about the subject matter being taught, or merely tolerance for a dreary topic that the class must muddle through as best it can? Do we expound on the virtues of a healthful lifestyle and then step outside the building for a quick cigarette? Our actions often speak louder than our words.

But even when models are competent and prestigious and even when they exhibit behaviors that students think are appropriate for themselves as well, successful modeling does not necessarily occur. What must students do to learn modeled behavior effectively? Let's find out.

Expose students to successful models from diverse cultural backgrounds. Expose them also to models who have become successful despite disabilities.

Avoid modeling undesirable behaviors.

For better or worse, students tend to emulate models who are likely to be attractive and prestigious; they are also likely to behave in traditionally gender-appropriate ways.

Helping Students Learn from Models

According to social cognitive theorists (e.g., Bandura, 1986), four things are necessary before a student can successfully model someone else's behavior:

- Attention

- Retention

- Motor reproduction

- Motivation

These four conditions and their educational implications are summarized in Table 10–2.

Attention

In our case study at the beginning of the chapter, Nathan paid little attention to the things his French teacher said in class. Yet to learn effectively, *a student must pay attention to the model.* Before imitation is possible, our students must observe carefully as we demonstrate proper procedures in the science lab, watch closely as we demonstrate the elementary backstroke, or listen attentively as we pronounce *Comment allez-vous?*

Make sure students are paying attention as you model the behaviors you want them to learn.

Retention

After paying attention, *the student must remember what the model does.* If you have already read the discussion of cognitive processes in Chapter 6, then you know that

---

PRINCIPLES/ASSUMPTIONS

Table 10–2   Four Essential Conditions for Effective Modeling

CONDITION	EDUCATIONAL IMPLICATION	EXAMPLE
Attention	When modeling a new behavior, be sure that students are observing and thinking about what you are doing.	After showing students how to use a microscope, ask them each to demonstrate its correct usage.
Retention	When modeling a complex behavior, provide a mechanism to help students remember the behavior's many facets.	When teaching a basic tennis stroke, provide such words as *ball, bounce, hit,* and *ready* to help students remember what they need to do.
Motor reproduction	Make sure that students are physically capable of performing the behaviors you model.	When teaching cursive writing, remember that fine motor skills develop over time; standards for acceptable performance should take students' current skill levels into account.
Motivation	Make sure that students have a reason to demonstrate the behaviors you model.	After demonstrating appropriate ways to deal with and resolve interpersonal conflicts, ask students to role-play conflict resolution in small groups and commend those who use prosocial strategies.

Describe what you are doing as you model desired behaviors. Provide descriptive labels for complex behaviors.

Have students repeat the descriptive labels as they perform the behavior.

students are more likely to remember information they have encoded in memory in more than one way—perhaps both as a visual image and as a verbal representation. As teachers, then, we may often want to describe what we are doing as we demonstrate the behaviors we want students to learn (Hughes, 1988). We may also want to give descriptive labels to complex behaviors that might otherwise be difficult to remember (Gerst, 1971; T. L. Rosenthal, Alford, & Rasp, 1972). To illustrate, an easy way to help students learn the three arm movements of the elementary back stroke in swimming is to teach them "chicken" (arms bent with hands tucked under armpits), "airplane" (arms straight out to the side), and "soldier" (arms straight and held close to the torso; see Figure 10–1).

It may be especially helpful for students to repeat such labels aloud as they copy a model's actions (R. L. Cohen, 1989; Mace, Belfiore, & Shea, 1989; Schunk, 1989c). As an example, consider this set of self-instructions taught to students who are first learning a basic tennis stroke:

1. Say *ball* to remind yourself to look at the ball.

2. Say *bounce* to remind yourself to follow the ball with your eyes as it approaches you.

3. Say *hit* to remind yourself to focus on contacting the ball with the racket.

4. Say *ready* to get yourself into position for the next ball to come your way. (adapted from Ziegler, 1987)

Tennis students taught to give themselves these simple instructions—*ball, bounce, hit,* and *ready*—improve the accuracy of their returns more quickly than students not taught to do so (Ziegler, 1987).

Motor Reproduction

In addition to attention and retention, *the student must be physically capable of reproducing the modeled behavior.* When a student lacks the ability to reproduce an observed behavior, motor reproduction obviously cannot occur. A girl who is out of shape

Figure 10–1 Students can often more easily remember a complex behavior, such as the elementary backstroke, when those behaviors have verbal labels.

"Chicken" "Airplane" "Soldier"

may not be able to imitate the physical education teacher's chin-ups. For example, first graders who watch a high school student throw a softball do not possess the muscular coordination to mimic that throw. Secondary school students who haven't yet learned to roll their Rs will have trouble repeating the Spanish teacher's tongue twister:

Erre con erre cigarro, erre con erre barril.
Rápido corren los carros del ferrocarril.

As teachers, it will often be useful to have students imitate a desired behavior immediately after they watch us demonstrate it. When they do so, we can give them the feedback they need to improve their performance. Modeling accompanied by verbal guidance and frequent feedback—a technique known as *coaching*—is often more effective than modeling alone (Bandura, 1977; S. N. Elliott & Busse, 1991; Hughes, 1988; Schunk, 1981; Zirpoli & Melloy, 1993). At the same time, we must keep in mind a

As students practice modeled behaviors, give guidance and feedback.

INTO THE CLASSROOM
Making Effective Use of Models

Model desirable behaviors.

> A teacher shows compassion for a student whose pet dog has just died.

Make sure students are paying attention as you model the behaviors you want them to learn.

> A science teacher makes sure all eyes are on her as she demonstrates the proper procedure for lighting a Bunsen burner.

Provide descriptive labels for modeled actions.

> A swimming instructor describes the arm movements of the elementary back stroke as "chicken, airplane, soldier."

Make sure students are physically capable of doing what you ask.

> A Spanish teacher works with students individually on the proper mouth and tongue movements for rolling Rs in the pronunciation of many Spanish words.

Make sure students have a reason to demonstrate the modeled behavior.

> The same Spanish teacher gives students credit in his grade book when they show that they can roll their Rs correctly.

Avoid modeling undesirable behaviors.

> A teacher who has not yet kicked her smoking habit refrains from smoking on school grounds or in public places where she is likely to run into one or more of her students.

Expose students to a variety of exemplary live and symbolic models, including females, minorities, and individuals with disabilities.

> A history teacher has students read *The Diary of Anne Frank.*

Remember that students from some ethnic groups may prefer to practice new skills in private at first.

Make sure students are motivated to demonstrate the modeled behavior.

point I made in the discussion of diversity in Chapter 4: Students from some ethnic groups (e.g., many Native Americans) may prefer to practice new behaviors in private at first, showing us what they have learned only after they have achieved sufficient mastery (Garcia, 1994; C. A. Grant & Gomez, 1996; Sanders, 1987; Suina & Smolkin, 1994).

Motivation

Finally, *the student must be motivated to demonstrate the modeled behavior.* Some students may be eager to show what they have observed and remembered; for example, they may have seen the model reinforced for a certain behavior and so have already been vicariously reinforced. But other students may not have any motivation to demonstrate something they have seen a model do—perhaps because the model was punished or perhaps because they don't see the model's actions as being appropriate for themselves. Increasing students' motivation to engage in classroom activities and strive for important instructional objectives is a topic we will consider at length in Chapter 11.

When all four factors—attention, retention, motor reproduction, and motivation—are present, modeling can be an extremely powerful teaching technique (S. N. Elliott & Busse, 1991; Hughes, 1988; Schloss & Smith, 1994; Zirpoli & Melloy, 1993). Modeling has an additional benefit as well: It frequently boosts students' self-confidence that they themselves can accomplish the things they observe models accomplishing. For example, when a student from an inner-city ghetto meets someone from the same neighborhood who has since grown up to become a doctor, and when a student with a physical disability meets an individual who, despite cerebral palsy, is a top executive at the local bank, these students may begin to believe that they also are capable of such achievements. The development of such beliefs in one's own ability to accomplish high levels of performance—the development of self-efficacy—is the topic we turn to now.

PROMOTING STUDENTS' SELF-EFFICACY

THINKING ABOUT WHAT YOU KNOW

- Do you believe that you'll be able to understand the content of this textbook by reading it and thinking carefully about the ideas I present? Or do you believe that you're going to have trouble with the material regardless of how much you study?

- Do you think you could learn to execute a reasonable swan dive from a high diving board if you were shown how to do it and given time to practice? Or are you such a klutz that no amount of training and practice would help?

- Do you think you could walk barefoot over hot coals unscathed? Or do you think the soles of your feet would be burned to a crisp?

People are more likely to engage in certain behaviors when they believe that they are capable of executing those behaviors successfully—that is, when they have high **self-efficacy** (e.g., Bandura, 1982, 1986). For example, I hope you believe that, with careful thought about what you read, you will be able to understand the ideas I am presenting in this textbook; in other words, I hope you have high self-efficacy for learning educational psychology. You may or may not believe that, with instruction and practice, you will eventually be able to perform a passable swan dive; in other words, you may have high or low self-efficacy about learning to dive. You are probably quite skeptical that you could ever walk barefoot over hot coals, so my guess is that you have low self-efficacy regarding this activity.

The concept of *self-efficacy* is similar to the concept of *self-esteem* that we discussed in Chapter 3, but with an important difference. One's self-esteem tends to pervade a wide variety of activities; for instance, we tend to describe people as having generally high or low self-esteem. Self-efficacy is more situation-specific; for example, people may have high self-efficacy about reading an educational psychology text but not about reading a text on neurosurgery. They may have high self-efficacy about learning to perform a swan dive but not about swimming the entire length of a swimming pool underwater.

How do students' feelings of self-efficacy affect their behavior? And how do feelings of high or low self-efficacy develop? In the next few pages, we will identify several answers to each of these questions.

Can you predict possible answers to these questions before you read on?

How Self-Efficacy Affects Behavior

According to social cognitive theorists (Bandura, 1982, 1986, 1989; Schunk, 1989c; Zimmerman, Bandura, & Martinez-Pons, 1992; Zimmerman & Bandura, 1994), people's sense of self-efficacy affects several aspects of their behavior:

- Their choice of activities
- Their effort and persistence
- Their learning and achievement

Choice of Activities

Imagine yourself on registration day, perusing the hundreds of courses listed in the course bulletin. You fill most of your schedule with required courses, but you have room for an elective. Only two courses are offered at the time slot you have open. Do

A student must believe that she has the ability to make friends before she will actually try to make them.

Interpret reluctance and lack of persistence as possible indicators of low self-efficacy.

you sign up for Advanced Psychoceramics, a challenging seminar taught by the famous Dr. Josiah S. Carberry? Or do you sign up for an English literature course known across campus as being an "easy A"? Perhaps you find the term *psychoceramics* a bit intimidating, and you think that you can't possibly pass such a course, especially if Dr. Carberry is as grouchy a man as everybody claims. So you settle for the literature course, knowing it is one in which you can succeed.

People tend to choose tasks and activities at which they believe they can succeed and to avoid those at which they think they will fail. Students who believe that they can succeed at mathematics are more likely to take math courses than students who believe that they are mathematically incompetent. Students who believe that they can win a role in the school musical are more likely to try out than students with little faith in their acting or singing ability.

Effort and Persistence

Such effort and persistence reflect the fact that students with high self-efficacy are *intrinsically motivated* (more about this in the next chapter).

Think back once again to our case study of Nathan. As you may recall, Nathan was convinced that he couldn't learn French. Because of this low self-efficacy for learning a foreign language, he gave up quickly on his French homework assignments whenever he encountered something he didn't understand.

Students with a high sense of self-efficacy are more likely to exert effort in attempting to accomplish a task. They are also more likely to persist (to "try, try again") when faced with obstacles to their success. In contrast, students with low self-efficacy about a particular task—those who don't believe that they will be successful at the task—will put little effort into it, and they will give up quickly when they encounter obstacles.

Learning and Achievement

If you have already read Chapter 4, then you may recall an advantage that boys often have over girls in this regard: On the average, boys have greater confidence in their ability to accomplish tasks than girls.

Students with high self-efficacy tend to learn and achieve more than students with low self-efficacy even when actual ability levels are the same (Bandura, 1986; J. L. Collins, 1982). In other words, when we have a group of students of equal ability, those students who *believe* that they can do a task are more likely to accomplish it successfully than those who do not believe that they are capable of success. As teachers, then, we should do whatever we can to enhance our students' beliefs that they can be successful at school tasks.

As teachers, what exactly *can* we do to promote greater self-efficacy? We will find several answers to this question as we examine the factors that influence the development of self-efficacy.

Considering Factors in the Development of Self-Efficacy

What factors in Nathan's situation might have contributed to his low self-efficacy to learn French?

Students' feelings of self-efficacy are usually fairly accurate: Students typically have a good sense of what they can and cannot do (Bandura, 1986). But sometimes students underestimate their chances of success, perhaps because of a few bad experiences. For example, a girl who gets a C in science from a teacher with exceptionally strict grading criteria may erroneously believe that she is "no good" in science. A new boy at school whose attempts at being friendly are rejected by two or three thoughtless classmates may erroneously believe that no one likes him.

According to social cognitive theorists (e.g., Bandura, 1986, 1989; Schunk, 1989a; Schunk, Hanson, & Cox, 1987), at least three factors affect the development of self-efficacy:

- One's own previous successes and failures
- Persuasion
- The successes and failures of others

Previous Successes and Failures

Students feel more confident that they can succeed at a task—that is, they have greater self-efficacy—when they have succeeded at that task or at similar ones in the past (Bandura, 1986). For example, Edward is more likely to believe that he can learn to divide fractions if he has already mastered the process of multiplying fractions. Elena will be more confident about her ability to play field hockey if she has already developed skills in soccer.

Once students have developed a high sense of self-efficacy, an occasional failure is unlikely to have much effect on their optimism. When they meet with *consistent* failure in performing an activity, however, they will tend to have little confidence about their ability to succeed at that activity in the future. Each new failure confirms what they already "know" about the task: They can't do it.

It is not surprising, then, that students with a history of academic success have higher self-efficacy for academic tasks than students with lower school performance. For example, students with learning disabilities—students who typically have encountered failure after failure in classroom activities—often have low self-efficacy with regard to the things they study in school (Schunk, 1989c).

Obviously then, it is important for us as teachers to help students succeed at classroom tasks. For example, we can strive to teach important basic skills to mastery. We can also provide the necessary instructional support that enables our students to make noticeable progress on more difficult and complex tasks.

This is not to say that we should *never* allow our students to fail. When students experience a string of successes, particularly when they don't have to work very hard to achieve those successes, they may come to believe that success always comes easily. When they eventually run into an obstacle—as they inevitably will at some point in their academic careers—their high self-efficacy deflates rapidly. Occasional setbacks and difficulties are a valuable part of the learning process: They help students learn that success sometimes comes only through effort and perseverance (Bandura, 1989).

Persuasion

To some extent, we can enhance self-efficacy by assuring students that they can, in fact, be successful. Such statements as "You can do this problem if you work at it" or "I bet Judy will play with you if you just ask her" do give students a slight boost in self-confidence. But we must keep in mind that this boost will be short-lived unless students' efforts at a task ultimately meet with success (Schunk, 1989a).

Successes and Failures of Others

We often form opinions about our own self-efficacy by observing the successes and failures of other individuals, especially those similar to ourselves. For example, you are

Teach basic skills to mastery (see Chapter 13 for ideas). Help students make noticeable progress on difficult tasks (see the discussion of *scaffolding* in Chapter 2 for ideas).

Present some tasks that are challenging yet achievable so that students succeed only with effort and perseverance.

Assure students that they can be successful.

more likely to enroll in Dr. Carberry's Advanced Psychoceramics class if several of your friends have already taken the course and gotten As. After all, if they can do it, so can you. But if your friends in the course have been dropping like flies, then (like Nathan) you may suspect that your own chances of succeeding are pretty slim.

In much the same way, students often consider the successes and failures of their classmates—especially those of similar ability—when appraising their own chances of success. So one thing we can do to enhance our own students' self-efficacy is to tell them that others like themselves have mastered the skills they are learning (assuming, of course, that such is the case). When we tell students that other, similar students have successfully completed a particular academic task, they are likely to complete more of the task themselves and have higher self-efficacy when doing so (Schunk, 1983, 1989c). For example, a class of chemistry students horrified about the number of chemical symbols they must learn can perhaps be reassured with a statement such as this: "I know it seems like a lot to learn in such a short amount of time. My students last year thought so too, but they found that they could learn the symbols within three weeks if they studied a few new symbols each day."

Tell students that others like themselves have succeeded.

When students actually *see* others of similar age and ability successfully reaching a goal, they are especially likely to believe that they, too, can achieve that goal. Hence, students sometimes develop greater self-efficacy when they see a fellow student model a behavior than when they see their teacher model that same behavior. For example, in one study (Schunk & Hanson, 1985), elementary school children having trouble with subtraction were given twenty-five subtraction problems to complete. Those who had seen another student successfully complete the problems got an average of nineteen correct, whereas those who saw a teacher complete the problems got only thirteen correct, and those who saw no model at all only solved eight!

Have students observe successful peer models.

So another thing we can do to enhance our students' self-efficacy regarding academic tasks is to have them observe their peers successfully accomplishing those tasks. It may be especially beneficial for our students to see a peer struggling with a task or problem at first—something they themselves are likely to do—and then eventually mastering it (Hughes, 1988; Schunk et al., 1987).

INTO THE CLASSROOM

Enhancing Self-Efficacy

Teach basic skills to mastery.

> A biology teacher makes sure all students clearly understand the basic structure of DNA before moving to mitosis and meiosis—topics that require a knowledge of DNA's structure.

Help students make noticeable progress on difficult tasks.

> In November, a creative writing teacher shows students samples of their work from September and points out ways in which each student has improved over the two-month period.

> Present some tasks that are challenging but achievable so that students succeed at them only with effort and perseverance.
>
> > A physical education teacher tells her students, "Today we've seen how far each of you can go in the broad jump. We will continue to practice the broad jump a little bit every week. Let's see if each one of you can jump at least two inches farther when I test you again at the end of the month."
>
> Assure students that they can be successful and remind them that others like themselves have succeeded before them.
>
> > Students in beginning band express frustration about learning to play their instruments. Their teacher reminds them that students in last year's beginning band—like themselves—at first had little knowledge about how to play musical instruments but that all of them eventually mastered their instruments.
>
> Have students see successful peer models.
>
> > The students in beginning band class hear the school's advanced band (last year's beginning band class) play a medley from *Phantom of the Opera*.

At the same time, we don't want students to become excessively dependent, either on us or on classmates, as they strive to learn new things. Our students must eventually learn to rely primarily on themselves for their own learning. Social cognitive theorists believe that people can and should ultimately regulate their own behavior. We therefore turn to a topic gaining increasing prominence in psychological and educational literature—the topic of *self-regulation*.

Think of a recent situation in which you had especially high or low self-efficacy. Which of the three factors I've just described affected your self-efficacy in that situation?

PROMOTING SELF-REGULATION

■ EXPERIENCING FIRSTHAND
Self-Reflection About Self-Regulation

In each of the following multiple-choice situations, choose the alternative that most accurately describes your own attitudes and behavior as a college student. No one will see your answers except you, so be honest!

1. In terms of my final course grades, I am trying very hard to:
   a. Earn all As.
   b. Earn all As and Bs.
   c. Earn at least a C in every class.
   d. Keep my overall grade point average above the minimally acceptable level for the program I am in.

2. As I am reading or studying a textbook:
   a. I often notice when my attention is wandering, and I immediately get my mind back on my work.
   b. I sometimes notice when my attention is wandering, but not always.
   c. I often get so lost in my daydreams that I waste a lot of time.

3. Whenever I finish a study session:
    a. I write down how much time I have spent on my schoolwork.
    b. I make a mental note of how much time I have spent on my schoolwork.
    c. I don't really think much about the time I have spent.

4. When I turn in an assignment:
    a. I usually have a very good idea of the grade I will get on it.
    b. I have a rough idea of the grade I will get; I can usually tell when it is either very good or very bad.
    c. I am often surprised by the grade I get.
    d. I don't really think much about the quality of what I have done.

5. When I do exceptionally well on an assignment:
    a. I feel good about my performance and often "treat" myself in some way (e.g., by going shopping, socializing with friends).
    b. I feel good about my performance but don't do anything special for myself afterward.
    c. I don't feel any differently than I had before I received my grade. ◾

The standards we set for ourselves, the extent to which we monitor and evaluate our own behavior, and the consequences we impose on ourselves for our successes and failures are all aspects of **self-regulation.** By observing how our environment reacts when we behave in particular ways—by discovering that some behaviors are reinforced and that others are punished—we begin to distinguish between appropriate and inappropriate responses. Once we have developed an understanding about which responses are appropriate (for ourselves, at least) and which are not, we begin to regulate our own behavior (Bandura, 1986).

Ideally, our students should become increasingly self-regulated as they grow older. For one thing, self-regulated students achieve at higher levels than their classmates (Zimmerman & Bandura, 1994). Furthermore, those students who select appropriate goals and can independently monitor their progress toward such goals will continue to engage in productive behaviors long after they have moved on from a particular school or a particular teacher.

In the next few pages, we will consider six aspects of self-regulation:

- Self-determined standards and goals

- Self-observation

- Self-instructions

- Self-regulatory problem-solving strategies

- Self-evaluation

- Self-imposed contingencies

These six aspects are summarized in Figure 10–2. Each one provides ideas about how we can help our students more successfully regulate and control their own behavior.

Self-Determined Standards and Goals

As human beings, we tend to set standards for our own behavior; in other words, we establish criteria regarding what constitutes acceptable performance. We also establish certain goals that we value and toward which we direct many of our behaviors.

Different individuals often develop different standards and goals for themselves. For example, Robert may be striving for a report card with straight As, whereas Richard is content with Cs. Rebecca may be seeking out many friends of both sexes, whereas Rachel believes that a single, steady boyfriend is the best companion. Yet to some extent, the performance standards and goals that students set for themselves are modeled after those that they see other people adopt (Bandura, 1977, 1986; Bandura & Kupers, 1964). For example, at the high school I attended, many students wanted to go to the best college or university they possibly could; in such an environment, others began to share the same academic aspirations. But at a different high school, getting a job after graduation (or perhaps even *instead* of graduation) might be the aspiration more commonly modeled by a student's classmates.

Students are more likely to be motivated to work toward goals—and thus more likely to accomplish them—when they have set those goals for themselves, rather than when others have imposed goals on them (Schunk, 1985, 1991; Spaulding, 1992). So one way we can help students develop self-regulation is to provide situations in which our students set their own goals. For example, we might ask them to decide how many addition facts they are going to learn by Friday, determine the topic they wish to study for a research project, or identify the particular gymnastic skills they wish to master.

As teachers, we should encourage our students to set goals and standards that are challenging yet realistic. When students' goals and standards are too low—for example,

Students from low-income families typically set low goals for themselves in terms of career aspirations (Durkin, 1995). Can you explain this fact in light of the discussion here?

Have students set some of their own goals for learning and achievement.

Self-selected goals promote a greater sense of *self-determination,* a topic we will consider in Chapter 11.

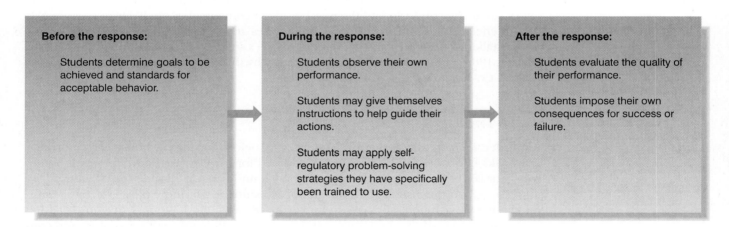

Before the response:	During the response:	After the response:
Students determine goals to be achieved and standards for acceptable behavior.	Students observe their own performance. Students may give themselves instructions to help guide their actions. Students may apply self-regulatory problem-solving strategies they have specifically been trained to use.	Students evaluate the quality of their performance. Students impose their own consequences for success or failure.

Figure 10–2   Aspects of Self-Regulated Behavior

Encourage challenging yet realistic goals and standards.

when intelligent students are content getting Cs on classroom assignments—then they will not achieve at levels at which they are capable of achieving. In such cases, we can show students that more challenging goals are attainable, perhaps by describing individuals of similar ability who have actually attained them with reasonable effort. In contrast, when students' standards are too high—for example, when they are satisfied only if every grade is 100 percent—then they are doomed to frequent failure and equally frequent self-recrimination. Such students may become excessively anxious or depressed when they can't achieve the impossible goals they have set for themselves (Bandura, 1986; Covington, 1992). We can help students understand and accept the fact that no one is perfect and that an occasional failure within an overall pattern of successes is nothing to be ashamed of.

Self-Observation

An important part of self-regulation is to observe oneself in action—a process known as **self-observation.** To make progress toward important goals, we must be aware of how well we are doing at the present time. We must know what aspects of our performance are working well and what aspects need improvement.

Have students observe and record their own behavior.

Yet students are not always accurate observers of their own behavior. They aren't always aware of how frequently they do something wrong or how *in*frequently they do something right. To draw students' attention to the things they do and don't do, we can have students observe and record their own behavior. Is Oliver speaking out of turn too frequently? We can bring the seriousness of the problem to his attention by asking him to make a check mark on a piece of paper every time he catches himself speaking out of turn. Is Olga not paying attention to her assignments during seatwork time? We can ask her to stop and reflect on her behavior every three to five minutes (perhaps with the aid of an egg timer), determining whether she was paying attention to her seatwork assignment during each interval. Figure 10–3 provides an example of the type of form we might give Olga to record her observations.

Research indicates clearly that such self-focused observation and recording can bring about changes (sometimes dramatic ones) in student behavior. For example, self-observation can be used to increase the extent to which students pay attention to their work (their *time on task*) and the number of assignments they are likely to complete. It is also effective in reducing aggressive responses and such disruptive classroom behaviors as talking out of turn and getting out of one's seat (Alberto & Troutman, 1990; K. R. Harris, 1986; Mace et al., 1989; Mace & Kratochwill, 1988; Webber, Scheuermann, McCall, & Coleman, 1993; Yell, 1993).

Self-Instructions

Consider the formerly "forgetful" student who, before leaving the house each morning, now asks herself, "Do I have everything I need for my classes? I have my math homework for Period 1, my history book for Period 2, my change of clothes for P. E. during Period 3 . . ." And consider the once impulsive student who now pauses before beginning a new assignment and says to himself, "OK, what am I supposed to do? Let's see . . . I need to read the directions first. What do the directions tell me to do?" And consider as well the formerly aggressive student who has learned to count to ten every time she gets angry—an action that gives her a chance to cool off.

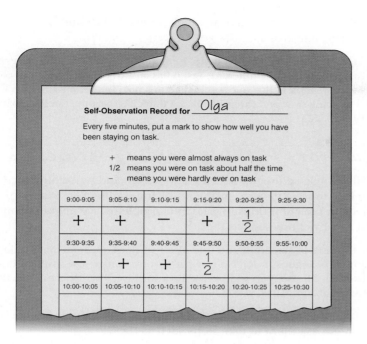

Figure 10–3   *Example of a Self-Observation Sheet That Students Might Use*

Sometimes students simply need a reminder about how to respond in particular situations. By teaching students how to talk themselves through these situations—by teaching them **self-instructions**—we provide them with a means through which *they remind themselves* about appropriate actions, thereby helping them control their own behavior. Such a strategy is often effective in helping students who otherwise seem to behave without thinking (Alberto & Troutman, 1990; Casey & Burton, 1982; Guevremont, Osnes, & Stokes, 1988; Hughes, 1988; Meichenbaum, 1977, 1985; Meichenbaum & Goodman, 1971; Shaffer, 1988; Yell, 1993).

Meichenbaum and Goodman (1971; Meichenbaum, 1977) have successfully taught students to give themselves instructions by using these five steps in sequence:

1. The teacher models self-instruction by repeating instructions aloud while simultaneously performing the activity.

2. The teacher repeats the instructions aloud while the student performs the activity.

3. The student repeats the instructions aloud while performing the activity.

4. The student whispers the instructions while performing the activity.

5. The student simply "thinks" the instructions while performing the activity.

Using these five training steps, Meichenbaum and Goodman were able to teach impulsive elementary school children to slow themselves down and think through what they were doing. For example, notice how one formerly impulsive student was able to

Teach students instructions they can give themselves in troublesome situations.

Can you relate Steps 3, 4, and 5 to Vygotsky's notions of *self-talk* and *inner speech* (Chapter 2)?

Such impulsivity is an aspect of *cognitive style,* a topic discussed in Chapter 6.

How might you use this technique to help a student with sloppy work habits? How might you use it to help a student who responds with uncontrolled anger in frustrating situations?

talk his way through a matching task in which he needed to find two identical pictures among several very similar ones:

> I have to remember to go slowly to get it right. Look carefully at this one, now look at these carefully. Is this one different? Yes, it has an extra leaf. Good, I can eliminate this one. Now, let's look at this one. I think it's this one, but let me first check the others. Good, I'm going slow and carefully. Okay, I think it's this one. (Meichenbaum & Goodman, 1971, p. 121)

Self-Regulatory Problem-Solving Strategies

We can sometimes use self-regulation techniques (including self-instructions) to help students develop more effective problem-solving skills. For example, to promote greater creativity in their solutions to academic problems, we might encourage them to give themselves instructions such as these:

> I want to think of something no one else will think of, something unique. Be free-wheeling, no hangups. I don't care what anyone thinks; just suspend judgment. I'm not sure what I'll come up with; it will be a surprise. The ideas can just flow through me. (Meichenbaum, 1977, p. 62)

Teach students the mental steps they can take to solve problems more effectively.

To help students deal more effectively with social conflicts and other interpersonal problems, we might ask them to take steps such as these:

1. Define the problem.

2. Identify several possible solutions.

3. Predict the likely consequences of each solution.

4. Choose the best solution.

5. Identify the steps required to carry out the solution.

6. Carry the steps out.

7. Evaluate the results. (S. N. Elliott & Busse, 1991; Meichenbaum, 1977; Weissburg, 1985; Yell, 1993)

Such **self-regulatory problem-solving strategies** often help students who have difficulty interacting appropriately with their peers (e.g., students who are either socially withdrawn or overly aggressive) to develop more effective interpersonal skills (K. R. Harris, 1982; Meichenbaum, 1977; Yell, 1993).

Another approach we can take is **mediation training**—a strategy whereby we help students *help one another* solve interpersonal problems. More specifically, we teach students how to mediate conflicts among classmates by asking the opposing sides to express their differing points of view and then working together to devise a reasonable resolution (Deutsch, 1993; D. W. Johnson, Johnson, Dudley, Ward, & Magnuson, 1995; Sanchez & Anderson, 1990). For example, in an experiment involving several classrooms at the second- through fifth-grade levels (D. W. Johnson et al., 1995), students were trained to help their peers resolve interpersonal conflicts by asking the opposing sides to do the following:

1. Define the conflict (the problem)

2. Explain their own perspectives and needs

3. Explain the *other* person's perspectives and needs

4. Identify at least three possible solutions to the conflict

5. Reach an agreement that addressed the needs of both parties

The students took turns serving as mediator for their classmates, such that everyone had experience resolving the conflicts of others. At the end of the training program, the students more frequently resolved their *own* interpersonal conflicts in ways that addressed the needs of both parties, and they were less likely to ask for adult intervention, than students in an untrained control group. Similarly, in a case study involving adolescent gang members (Sanchez & Anderson, 1990), students were given mediation training and were asked to be responsible for mediating gang-related disputes. After only one month of training, rival gang members were exchanging friendly greetings in the corridors, giving one another the "high five" sign, and interacting at lunch; meanwhile, gang-related fights virtually disappeared from the scene.

Teach students strategies for effectively mediating classmates' interpersonal conflicts.

Self-Evaluation

Both at home and in school, students' behaviors are frequently judged by others—by their parents, siblings, teachers, classmates, and so on. But eventually our students should also begin to evaluate their *own* behavior; in other words, they should engage in **self-evaluation.** Once they have developed appropriate standards and goals, and once they have developed some objective techniques for observing their own behavior, there are many ways in which we can allow and encourage them to evaluate their own performance. For example, we can have students:

Once students have set appropriate standards and objective methods of self-observation, encourage them to evaluate their own performance.

- Assemble *portfolios* of what they think is their best work, with self-evaluations of each entry

- Write in daily or weekly *journals,* in which they address the strengths and weaknesses of their performance

- Participate in *peer conferences,* in which several students discuss their reactions to one another's work (Paris & Ayres, 1994)

We will consider *portfolios* in greater depth in our discussion of assessment in Chapter 13.

We might also have students complete self-assessment instruments that show them what to look for as they judge their work (Paris & Ayres, 1994). For example, when asking them to evaluate a project they have just completed, we might ask them to respond to questions such as these:

- What did you like about this project?

- What would have made this project better?

- What grade do you feel you earned on this project? Justify your response. (adapted from Paris & Ayres, 1994, p. 78)

Students who hold different standards for themselves will naturally judge the same behavior in different ways. For example, if Robert and Richard both get all Bs on their report cards, Robert (with the straight-A standard) will judge his performance to be unacceptable, whereas Richard (with acceptability defined as "C") will go home and celebrate. It is essential, then, that we help our students use appropriate criteria for evaluating their performance (L. A. Clark & McKenzie, 1989; Good & Brophy, 1994; Yell,

1993; Zuckerman, 1994). As one example, when asking them to analyze the quality of a summary they have just written, we might ask them to agree or disagree with statements such as these:

- I included a clear main idea statement.

- I included important ideas that support the main idea.

- My summary shows that I understand the relationships between important concepts.

- I used my own words rather than words copied from the text. (Paris & Ayres, 1994, p. 75)

As another example, when asking students to evaluate their on-task behavior in class on a scale of one to five, we might reinforce them when their own self-assessments closely match the ones we ourselves give them (D. J. Smith, Young, West, Morgan, & Rhode, 1988).

Self-Imposed Contingencies

When you accomplish something you've set out to do, especially if the task is a complex and challenging one, you probably feel quite proud of yourself and give yourself a mental pat on the back. In contrast, when you *fail* to accomplish that task, you are probably unhappy with your performance; you may also feel guilty, regretful, or ashamed. Likewise, as our students become increasingly self-regulated, they will begin to reinforce themselves—perhaps by feeling proud or telling themselves they did a good job—when they accomplish their goals. And they will also begin to punish themselves—perhaps by feeling sorry, guilty, or ashamed—when they do something that does not meet their own performance standards.

Yet such **self-imposed contingencies** are not necessarily confined only to the emotional reactions that people have in response to their own behaviors. Many self-regulating individuals reinforce themselves in far more concrete ways when they accomplish something successfully. For example, I spend time doing something I enjoy after every ten pages I write for this textbook. I have a colleague who goes shopping every time she completes a research article or report (she has one of the best wardrobes in town!). Why not teach students to do something similar?

As teachers, we can help students become more self-regulating by teaching them ways in which they can reinforce themselves for their achievements and appropriate behaviors. When students are taught to reinforce themselves for appropriate behavior—perhaps by giving themselves some free time, allowing themselves to engage in a fa-

Do you ever reinforce yourself in some tangible way for your accomplishments? If so, how?

Teach students to reinforce themselves for appropriate behavior.

Once students have developed appropriate standards for behavior, we should encourage them to evaluate their own performance.

vorite activity, or simply praising themselves—their classroom behavior often improves significantly (Bandura & Perloff, 1967; K. R. Harris, 1986; S. C. Hayes et al., 1985; H. C. Stevenson & Fantuzzo, 1986). In fact, self-reinforcement can sometimes be as effective in modifying student behaviors as reinforcement administered by a teacher (Bandura, 1977; Bandura & Perloff, 1967).

As an example, imagine that you are a fifth-grade teacher who has several students performing poorly in arithmetic. How might you teach these students to reinforce themselves for improved performance? In one research study, such students were taught to give themselves points when they did well on their assignments; they could later use these points to "buy" a variety of items and privileges. Within a few weeks, the students were doing as well in arithmetic as their classmates on both in-class assignments and homework (H. C. Stevenson & Fantuzzo, 1986).

■ EXPERIENCING FIRSTHAND
More Self-Reflection

Refer back to the previous self-reflection exercise. Evaluate your responses to each question in terms of what you have just learned about effective self-regulation. ■

When students set challenging goals for themselves and achieve those self-chosen goals through their own efforts, their self-efficacy is enhanced and their motivation to undertake new challenges increases (Bandura, 1989). When students have a high sense of self-efficacy and engage in self-regulatory behaviors, they are more likely to believe that they control their environment, rather than that their environment controls them. In fact, social cognitive theorists assert that people, their behaviors, and the environment all have a somewhat "controlling" influence on one another, as we shall see now.

Fostering Self-Regulated Behavior

Help students set challenging yet realistic goals and standards.

A teacher encourages a pregnant student to stay in school until she graduates. Together they discuss strategies the student can use to juggle motherhood and her studies.

Have students observe and record their own behavior.

A student frequently tips his chair back to the point where he is likely to topple over. Concerned for the student's safety, his teacher asks him to record each instance of such behavior on a sheet of graph paper. Both student and teacher notice how quickly the behavior disappears once the student has become cognizant of his bad habit.

Teach students instructions or reminders to give themselves.

A teacher helps a student control her impulsive behavior on multiple-choice tests by having the student mentally give herself these instructions as she reads each question: "Read the entire question. Then look at each answer carefully and decide whether it is correct or incorrect. Then choose the answer that seems most correct of all."

Provide strategies that students can use to solve interpersonal problems.

A teacher teaches her students a sequence to follow when they find themselves in a conflict with a classmate: *identify* the source of the conflict, *listen* to each other's perspectives, *verbalize* each other's perspectives, and *develop* a solution that provides a reasonable compromise.

Encourage students to evaluate their own performance.

A science teacher asks students to evaluate the lab reports they have written the day before and gives them a list of criteria to use as they do so. She assigns grades on the basis of how accurately students have evaluated their own reports.

Teach students to reinforce themselves for appropriate behavior.

A teacher helps students develop more regular study habits by encouraging them to make a favorite activity—for example, shooting baskets, watching television, or calling a friend on the telephone—contingent on completing their homework first.

UNDERSTANDING RECIPROCAL CAUSATION

Throughout the chapter, we have often referred to aspects of people's environments and to the behaviors that result from various environmental conditions. We have also talked about certain characteristics that people bring with them to a task; for example, we have talked about such personal variables as expectations and self-efficacy. Now which one of these three factors—environment, behavior, or person—lays the foundation for learning? According to social cognitive theorists, all three are essential ingredients, and each one influences the other two. This interdependence among environment, behavior, and person is a phenomenon known as **reciprocal causation** (Bandura, 1989). Some examples of how each factor affects the other two are listed in Table 10–3.

As a concrete illustration of how environment, behavior, and personal factors can mutually influence one another, let's consider "Scene One" in the case of Lorraine:

Scene One

Lorraine, a student in Mr. Broderick's seventh-grade social studies class, often comes to class late and ill-prepared for the day's activities. In class, she spends

△ COMPARE/CONTRAST

Table 10–3   Mutual Influences (Reciprocal Causation) Among Environment, Behavior, and Person

		A GENERAL EXAMPLE	AN EXAMPLE IN LORRAINE'S CASE (SCENE ONE)	AN EXAMPLE IN LORRAINE'S CASE (SCENE TWO)
Effect of Environment	On Behavior	Reinforcement and punishment affect future behavior	Teacher's ignoring Lorraine leads to future classroom failure	New instructional methods lead to improved academic performance
	On Person	Feedback from others affects sense of self-efficacy	Teacher's ignoring Lorraine perpetuates low self-efficacy	New instructional methods capture Lorraine's interest and attention
Effect of Behavior	On Environment	Specific behaviors affect the amount of reinforcement and punishment received	Poor classroom performance leads to the teacher meeting privately with Lorraine and then eventually ignoring her	Better academic performance leads to more reinforcement from the teacher
	On Person	Success and failure affect expectations for future performance	Poor classroom performance leads to low self-efficacy	Better academic performance leads to higher self-efficacy
Effect of Person	On Environment	Self-efficacy affects choices of activities and therefore the specific environment encountered	Attention to classmates rather than to classroom activities affects environment experienced	Attention to classroom activities leads to greater influence of teacher's instruction
	On Behavior	Attention, retention, motor reproduction, and motivation affect degree to which one imitates modeled behavior	Attention to classmates rather than to classroom activities leads to academic failure	Greater self-efficacy and increased motivation lead to more persistent study habits

more time interacting with her friends (e.g., whispering, passing notes) than getting involved in classroom activities. Lorraine's performance on most exams and assignments (when she turns the latter in at all) is unsatisfactory.

One day in mid-October, Mr. Broderick takes Lorraine aside to express his concern about her lack of classroom effort. He suggests that Lorraine could do better if she paid more attention in class; he also offers to work with her after school twice a week to help her understand class material. Lorraine is less optimistic, describing herself as "not smart enough to learn this stuff."

For a week or so after her meeting with Mr. Broderick, Lorraine seems to buckle down and exert more effort, but she never does stay after school for extra help. And before long, Lorraine is back to her old habits. Mr. Broderick eventually concludes that she is a lost cause and decides to devote his time and effort to helping more motivated students.

Can you think of occasions when you, like Lorraine, might have doomed yourself to failure through your own behaviors?

Lorraine's low self-efficacy (a *person* factor) is probably one reason that she spends so much class time engaged in task-irrelevant activities (*behaviors*). The fact that she devotes her attention (another *person* factor) to her classmates, rather than to her teacher, affects the particular stimuli that she experiences (her *environment*). Lorraine's poor performance on assignments and exams (*behaviors*) affects both her self-efficacy (*person*) and Mr. Broderick's treatment of her (*environment*). By eventually concluding that Lorraine is a lost cause, Mr. Broderick begins to ignore Lorraine (*environment*), contributing to her further failure (*behavior*) and even lower self-efficacy (*person*). (See Table 10–3 for a listing of these interactive effects under the column marked "Scene One.") Clearly, Lorraine is showing signs of being at risk for long-term academic failure.

But now imagine that Mr. Broderick learns more about how to deal with students at risk (perhaps he reads research articles on the topic, takes a night course, or reads Chapter 4 of this book). Mr. Broderick develops greater optimism that he can break the vicious cycle of environment/behavior/person for at-risk students such as Lorraine. Midway through the school year, he makes the following changes in his classroom:

- He communicates clearly and consistently that he expects all students to succeed in his classroom.

- He incorporates students' personal experiences and interests into the study of social studies.

- He identifies specific, concrete tasks that students will accomplish each week.

- He provides guidance and structure for how each task should be accomplished.

- After consulting with the school's reading specialist and school psychologist, he helps students develop more effective reading and learning strategies.

- He gives a quiz every Friday so that students can assess their own progress.

- When students perform well on these quizzes, he reminds them that they themselves are responsible for their performance.

Let's see what happens next, as we consider "Scene Two":

Scene Two

By incorporating students' personal experiences and interests into his daily lesson plans, Mr. Broderick begins to capture Lorraine's interest and attention. She begins to realize that social studies has implications for her own life and becomes more involved in classroom activities. With the more structured assignments, better guidance about how to study class material, and frequent quizzes, Lorraine finds herself succeeding in a subject at which she has previously experienced only failure. Mr. Broderick is just as pleased with her performance, something he tells her frequently through his facial expressions, his verbal feedback, and his willingness to provide help whenever she needs it.

By the end of the school year, Lorraine is studying course material more effectively and completing her assignments regularly. She is eagerly looking forward to next year's social studies class, confident that she will continue to do well.

Once again, we see the interplay among environment, behavior, and person. Mr. Broderick's new instructional methods (*environment*) engage Lorraine's attention (*person*) and facilitate her academic performance (*behavior*). Lorraine's improved academic performance, in turn, influences Mr. Broderick's treatment of her (*environment*) and her own self-efficacy (*person*). And her improved self-efficacy, her greater attention to classroom activities, and her increased motivation to succeed (all *person* variables) affect the extent to which she is able to benefit from Mr. Broderick's instruction (*environment*) and her classroom success (*behavior*). (See the column marked "Scene Two" in Table 10–3 for a listing of such interactive effects.)

As you can see, then, the things we do in the classroom—the *environment* we create—affect both the behaviors that students exhibit and the personal factors that influence their learning. Students' behaviors and personal factors, in turn, influence the future classroom environment they experience. As teachers, we must create and maintain a classroom environment that helps students develop the behaviors (e.g., academic and social skills) and personal characteristics (e.g., high self-efficacy and the expectation that their efforts will be rewarded) that are likely to bring them academic and personal success.

Can you explain reciprocal causation in your own words? Can you provide an example from your own experience?

CONSIDERING DIVERSITY FROM A SOCIAL COGNITIVE PERSPECTIVE

As teachers, we will have students from a variety of cultural backgrounds in our classrooms. We may have students from a wide range of socioeconomic levels as well. We will probably have a few students who have special educational needs. And we will almost certainly have both males and females. Social cognitive theory provides several insights regarding how we can adapt our classroom practices to serve students with diverse backgrounds, characteristics, and needs. The concepts of *modeling, self-efficacy,* and *self-regulation* can be especially useful to us here.

Using Diverse Models to Promote Success and Self-Efficacy

Two principles that we considered earlier in the chapter are worth repeating at this point:

- Students are most likely to model the behaviors they believe are relevant to their own situation.

- Students develop greater self-efficacy for a task when they see others like themselves performing the task successfully.

Expose students to successful models who are similar to themselves in terms of cultural background, socioeconomic status, gender, and disability.

Both principles lead us to the same conclusion: *Students need models who are similar to themselves in terms of cultural background, socioeconomic status, gender, and (if applicable) disability.* As teachers, we cannot possibly be all things to all students in this respect. We must therefore expose our students to as wide a variety of successful models—child and adolescent models as well as adults—as we possibly can. In some cases, we may be able to find such models within the school building itself. In other cases, we may be able to invite people from the region or the local community to visit the classroom.

STUDENTS IN INCLUSIVE SETTINGS

Table 10–4 Promoting Social Learning in Students with Special Educational Needs

STUDENTS WITH SPECIAL NEEDS	CHARACTERISTICS THAT THESE STUDENTS MAY EXHIBIT	CLASSROOM STRATEGIES THAT MAY BE BENEFICIAL FOR THESE STUDENTS
Students with specific cognitive or academic deficits	Difficulties predicting the consequences of specific behaviors Low self-efficacy for academic tasks in areas where there has been a history of failure Little self-regulation of learning and behavior	Help students form more realistic expectations regarding the consequences of their behaviors. Scaffold students' efforts on academic tasks to increase the probability of success. Identify students' areas of strength and give them opportunities to tutor other students in those areas. Promote self-regulation (e.g., by teaching self-observation, self-instructions, self-reinforcement). Have students observe classmates who initially have difficulty with a task but eventually master it.
Students with specific social or behavioral deficits	Difficulties predicting the consequences of specific behaviors Friendships with peers who are poor models of effective social skills or prosocial behavior Little self-regulation of behavior Deficits in social problem solving	Discuss possible consequences of various courses of action in social conflict situations. Model appropriate classroom behaviors. Provide opportunities for students to interact with peers who model effective social and prosocial behaviors. Videotape students exhibiting appropriate behaviors and then have them view *themselves* as models for such behavior. Teach self-regulation (e.g., self-observation, self-instructions, self-regulatory problem-solving strategies).
Students with general delays in cognitive and social functioning	Low self-efficacy for academic tasks Tendency to observe others to find guidance about how to behave Low goals for achievement (possibly as a way of minimizing the likelihood of failure) Little if any self-regulation of learning and behavior	Scaffold students' efforts on academic tasks to increase the probability of success. Model desired behaviors and identify peers who can also serve as appropriate models. Encourage students to set high yet realistic goals for their own achievement. Promote self-regulation (e.g., by teaching self-observation, self-instructions, self-reinforcement).
Students with advanced cognitive development	High self-efficacy regarding academic tasks High goals for performance For some students, a history of easy successes and, hence, little experience dealing with failure	Provide the academic support that students need to reach their goals. Provide challenging tasks at which students may sometimes fail; teach constructive strategies for dealing with failure (e.g., persistence, using errors to guide future practice efforts).

Sources: Balla & Zigler, 1979; Bandura, 1989; E. S. Ellis & Friend, 1991; Hughes, 1988; Kehle, Clark, Jenson, & Wampold, 1986; C. D. Mercer, 1991; D. P. Morgan & Jenson, 1988; J. R. Nelson, Smith, Young, & Dodd, 1991; Patton, Beirne-Smith, & Payne, 1990; Piirto, 1994; Schumaker & Hazel, 1984; Schunk, Hanson, & Cox, 1987; Turnbull, Turnbull, Shank, & Leal, 1995; Yell, 1993.

Compiled with the assistance of Dr. Margie Garanzini-Daiber and Dr. Margaret Cohen, University of Missouri—St. Louis.

Yet we need not limit ourselves to live models; students can learn a great deal from symbolic models as well. For example, we might ask our students to read biographies or autobiographies about such successful individuals as Maya Angelou (who, as an African American growing up in Arkansas in the 1930s, was raised in an environment of poverty and racial intolerance), Franklin D. Roosevelt (who had polio and was wheelchair-bound), and Stephen Hawking (who has a degenerative nerve disorder and can communicate only through computer technology). Or we might have them watch the video *Stand and Deliver,* the story of eighteen Mexican American high school students from a lower-income neighborhood in East Los Angeles—students who, through hard work and persistence, earned college credit by passing the National Advanced Placement Calculus Exam.

Model tolerance and respect for diversity.

Although we cannot always be similar to our students in terms of cultural background, socioeconomic status, gender, or disability, we must remember that we are likely to be powerful models for our students nonetheless. Regardless of our own heritage, we must *always* model tolerance and respect for people with diverse backgrounds and characteristics (Boutte & McCormick, 1992).

Promoting Self-Regulation in Students with Special Needs

Most of our students will probably stand to gain from teaching strategies that promote greater self-regulation. But students with special educational needs will often be among those in greatest need of becoming more self-regulated (e.g., E. S. Ellis & Friend, 1991). Such students are especially likely to benefit when we encourage them to set and strive for their own goals, particularly when such goals are concrete, specific, and accomplishable within a reasonable period of time (E. S. Ellis & Friend, 1991; Good & Brophy, 1994). Students with special needs will also be well served when we teach them self-regulatory problem-solving skills and self-reinforcement techniques (E. S. Ellis & Friend, 1991; Yell, 1993).

Teach self-regulatory strategies to students with special needs.

Table 10–4 presents a social cognitive perspective of the characteristics we will often see in our students with special needs; it also presents strategies we can use to promote the academic and social success of these students. As you will undoubtedly notice, such concepts as *modeling, self-efficacy,* and *self-regulation* appear repeatedly in this table.

LOOKING AT THE BIG PICTURE: COMPARING THE THREE PERSPECTIVES OF LEARNING

If you've been reading the chapters of Part II in sequence, then you have now examined three different theoretical perspectives of learning: cognitive psychology, behaviorism, and social cognitive theory. As we noted in Chapter 5, these perspectives share many things in common, including their focus on the effects of experience and prior learning and their acknowledgment that there is considerable diversity in what people will learn in any single situation. The perspectives overlap with one another in other ways as well. For example, social cognitive theory shares behaviorists' belief that the consequences of behavior influence learning, yet it also shares cognitive psychologists' emphasis on the nature of cognitive processes.

In Table 5–2 of Chapter 5, I outlined some of the major similarities and differences among the three perspectives. Now that you have studied each perspective in depth, it

Before you look at Table 10–5, make some comparisons on your own.

should be useful to make additional comparisons as well. Accordingly, you will find the comparisons presented in Table 5–2, along with comparisons related to the issues of *consequences* and *control,* in Table 10–5. (Note that I have reversed the order of the cognitive psychology and behaviorism columns from what they were in Table 5–2 to reflect the order in which we considered these two perspectives.)

It is important to reiterate a point I made in Chapter 5: *No single theoretical orientation can give us a complete picture of how people learn.* All three of the perspectives we have studied have valuable lessons to teach us about how we can best facilitate our students' classroom achievement. For example, principles from cognitive psychology give us ideas about how we can help students learn, remember, and transfer information. Principles from behaviorism yield strategies for helping students develop and

Remember that different theoretical orientations may be useful for facilitating different types of learning.

COMPARE/CONTRAST

Table 10–5   Comparing the Three Perspectives of Learning in More Depth

ISSUE	COGNITIVE PSYCHOLOGY	BEHAVIORISM	SOCIAL COGNITIVE THEORY
Learning is defined as . . .	an internal mental phenomenon that may or may not be reflected in behavior.	a behavior change.	an internal mental phenomenon that may or may not be reflected in behavior.
The focus of investigation is on . . .	cognitive processes.	stimuli and responses that can be readily observed.	both behavior and cognitive processes.
Principles of learning describe how . . .	people mentally process the information they receive and construct knowledge from their experiences.	people's behaviors are affected by environmental stimuli.	people's observations of those around them affect behavior and cognitive processes.
Consequences of behavior . . .	are not a major focus of consideration.	must be experienced directly if they are to affect learning.	can be experienced either directly or vicariously.
Learning and behavior are controlled . . .	primarily by cognitive processes within the individual.	primarily by environmental circumstances.	partly by the environment and partly by cognitive processes; people become increasingly self-regulated (and therefore less controlled by the environment) over time.
Educational implications focus on how we can help students . . .	process information in effective ways and construct accurate and complete knowledge about classroom topics.	acquire more productive classroom behaviors.	learn effectively by observing others.

maintain more productive classroom behaviors. Principles from social cognitive theory show us how we can effectively model the skills we want students to acquire and how we can promote greater self-regulation. And principles from all three perspectives are useful for motivating students to succeed in the classroom, as you will discover in our discussion of motivation in the next chapter.

CASE STUDY: *Teacher's Lament*

Sometimes a teacher just can't win," complains Mr. Adams, a fifth-grade teacher. "At the beginning of the year, I told my students that homework assignments would count for 20 percent of their grades. Yet some students hardly ever turned in any homework even though I continually reminded them about their assignments. After reconsidering the situation, I decided that I probably shouldn't use homework as a criterion for grading. After all, in this poor, inner-city neighborhood, many kids don't have a quiet place to study at home.

"So in November, I told my class that I wouldn't be counting homework assignments when I calculated grades for the first report card. Naturally, some students—the ones who hadn't been doing their homework—seemed relieved. But the students who *had* been doing it were absolutely furious! And now hardly anyone seems to turn in homework anymore."

- Why were the students who had been doing their homework regularly so upset? Can you explain their reaction in terms of social cognitive theory?

- From a social cognitive perspective, Mr. Adams inadvertently punished some students and reinforced others. Which students in the class were reinforced, and how? Which students were punished, and how?

- What might Mr. Adams have done instead of eliminating homework as a criterion for class grades? What things might he do to encourage and help all students complete homework assignments?

SUMMING UP

Social Cognitive Theory

Social cognitive theory focuses on the ways in which people learn by observing others. Social cognitive theorists believe that both environmental conditions (e.g., the consequences of behavior, the presence of models) and personal variables (e.g., goals, expectations, self-efficacy) influence learning. In addition to creating a classroom environment conducive to learning, then, we must also foster those personal characteristics that will enable our students to achieve academic success.

Reinforcement and Punishment

From a social cognitive perspective, reinforcement and punishment affect learning indirectly, rather than directly, and consequences to one student vicariously influence the behaviors of others as well. Students who observe a classmate being reinforced or punished for a particular behavior may conclude that engaging in that behavior will yield similar consequences for themselves. Furthermore, the nonoccurrence of expected reinforcement is punishing, and the nonoccurrence of expected punishment is reinforcing. As teachers, we should recognize that the consequences of students' behaviors are likely to influence the expectations that students form, the ways in which they process information, and the choices they make.

Modeling

Students learn from both live and symbolic models. We should provide numerous opportunities for our students to observe us and others demonstrating important skills. We can also expose our students to exemplary characters portrayed in books, films, and other media.

Four processes are necessary for modeling to occur: *attention* to the model, *retention* (memory) of what the model does, capacity for *motor reproduction* of the modeled behavior, and *motivation* to exhibit the modeled behavior. We should make sure that all four factors are present when we use modeling as an instructional technique.

Self-Efficacy

Students are more likely to engage and persist in certain activities when they believe that they can be successful—when they have high self-efficacy. We can promote greater self-efficacy in our students by having them observe successful peer models, assuring them that they, too, can succeed and making sure that they *do* succeed.

Self-Regulation

As children and adolescents grow and develop, they become increasingly self-regulating; for example, they begin to set standards and goals for themselves, and they observe, guide, and evaluate their own behavior. We can facilitate students' development of self-regulation by letting them set some of their own goals,

by teaching them to guide their own performance through self-instructions and self-regulatory problem-solving strategies, by helping them monitor and evaluate their responses accurately, and by encouraging them to reinforce themselves for good work.

Reciprocal Causation

Environment, behavior, and personal characteristics all interact with one another in their effects on learning—a three-way interdependence known as *reciprocal causation*. As teachers, we must recognize that the environment we create affects both the behaviors that students exhibit and the personal factors that influence their learning. Those behaviors and personal factors will, in turn, influence the future classroom environment that students experience.

Diversity from a Social Cognitive Perspective

As teachers, we must remember that our students need models who are similar to themselves in terms of cultural background, socioeconomic status, gender, and (if applicable) disability. We must remember, too, that students with special needs will often be among those who need the greatest support in developing self-regulatory strategies.

Contrasting the Three Perspectives of Learning

The three theoretical perspectives of learning that we have examined—cognitive psychology, behaviorism, and social cognitive learning—share a focus on the effects of experience and prior learning; all three also acknowledge that different people often learn different things in the same situation. Yet they differ somewhat regarding such issues as reinforcement, cognition, and control. As teachers, we must recognize that all three perspectives have useful applications for classroom practice.

KEY CONCEPTS

social cognitive theory (p. 428)
vicarious reinforcement (p. 434)
vicarious punishment (p. 434)
incentive (p. 435)
live models (p. 439)
symbolic models (p. 439)

self-efficacy (p. 446)
self-regulation (p. 452)
self-observation (p. 454)
self-instructions (p. 455)
self-regulatory problem-solving
    strategies (p. 456)

mediation training (p. 456)
self-evaluation (p. 457)
self-imposed contingencies (p. 458)
reciprocal causation (p. 461)

Motivating Students to Learn and Achieve

- What motivated you to open your textbook and read this chapter today? Do you have an upcoming test on the material the chapter covers? Do you want to appear informed when your instructor calls on you in class? Do you just want to know more about motivation than you know already?

- What motives do we see reflected in the behaviors of a typical classroom of students? Are some students especially interested in certain academic topics? Do some students seem more concerned about socializing with their friends than about accomplishing assigned tasks? Are some students trying hard to *avoid* assigned tasks?

I N ANY SINGLE CLASSROOM, we are likely to find different students motivated in different directions. One student may be keenly interested in the subject matter being taught, seeking out challenging coursework, participating actively in classroom discussions, completing assignments diligently, and getting high marks on classroom assignments. Another may be more concerned about the social side of school, interacting with classmates frequently, attending extracurricular activities almost every day, and perhaps even running for a student government office. Still another may be focused on athletics, excelling in physical education classes, playing or watching sports most afternoons and weekends, and working out daily to make the football team next year. And yet another, perhaps because of an undetected learning disability, poor social skills, or a seemingly uncoordinated body, may be interested only in avoiding academics, social situations, or athletic activities. It's safe to say that virtually all students are motivated in one way or another.

Motivation is something that energizes, directs, and sustains behavior; it gets students moving, points them in a particular direction, and keeps them going. Once students have the ability to perform a particular activity, once they have *learned* something, their level of motivation determines whether they actually engage in the activity and, if so, the length of time and amount of enthusiasm with which they continue to pursue it.

We have already touched on the topic of motivation in previous chapters. In our discussion of knowledge construction in Chapter 7, we learned that students are more likely to revise incorrect beliefs about a topic—to undergo conceptual change—when they are motivated to do so. In our discussion of behaviorism in Chapter 9, we noted that students are more likely to exhibit those behaviors that are followed by reinforcement. In our discussion of social cognitive theory in Chapter 10, we discovered that students more frequently pursue those tasks for which they have high self-efficacy and that they will persist at such tasks even in the face of failure.

In this chapter, we will examine motivation in depth, exploring factors that influence the interest students have in various activities, the choices they make when a number of activities are available to them, and the extent to which they persist with any particular activity. We will consider both academic motives (e.g., learning for learning's sake) and social motives (e.g., doing things to gain the approval of classmates). We will also consider the role of *affect*—people's feelings and emotions—in the learning process. Later, as we explore attribution theory, we will see how students' explanations as to why they have succeeded or failed at a task influence their future choices, behav-

Motivation energizes, directs, and sustains behavior.

iors, and expectations for success. As we go along, we will identify a number of strategies we can use to motivate our students to learn and achieve in the classroom.

By the end of the chapter, you should be able to:

1. Define motivation and describe its effects on students' behavior.

2. Distinguish between extrinsic motivation and intrinsic motivation, and describe a number of strategies for promoting students' intrinsic motivation to achieve classroom success.

3. Contrast learning goals and performance goals in terms of their effects on learning and behavior, and identify several strategies for promoting the motivation to learn.

4. Identify two social needs common among children and adolescents, and describe how such needs can be accommodated in the classroom and used to promote academic achievement.

5. Describe several ways in which emotion (*affect*) influences learning and memory, and identify strategies for keeping students' anxiety at a level that facilitates classroom success.

6. Explain how students' explanations for success and failure (their *attributions*) are likely to influence their thoughts and behaviors, and identify ways to help students make accurate and productive attributions.

7. Describe the nature of the diversity you are likely to see in student motivation.

CASE STUDY: *Quick Draw*

Unlike her more socially oriented classmates, Anya is a quiet student who usually prefers to be alone. Whenever she has free time in class, she grabs a pencil and a piece of paper and begins to sketch something. Her love of drawing appears at other times as well. For example, she decorates her notebooks with elaborate doodles. She embellishes stories and essays with illustrations. She even draws pictures of the words on each week's spelling list.

Not surprisingly, Anya looks forward to her art class, paying particularly close attention on those days when her art teacher describes or demonstrates a new drawing technique. She buries herself in each new drawing assignment, seemingly oblivious to the classroom around her. Anya's art teacher notes with pride how much Anya's skill at drawing has improved over the course of the school year.

Anya makes no bones about her interest. "When I grow up, I want to be a professional artist," she states emphatically. "In the meantime, I'm going to practice, practice, practice."

- Which of Anya's behaviors reflect her interest in art? Are these behaviors likely to facilitate her performance in art class? If so, how?

HOW MOTIVATION AFFECTS BEHAVIOR AND LEARNING

When it comes to art, Anya is highly motivated. We can reasonably form this conclusion on the basis of her close attention in class, her eagerness to draw whenever she can, and her long-term goals. Motivation has several effects on students' behavior and learning, including these:

- It directs behavior toward particular goals.

- It increases effort and energy expended toward those goals.

- It increases initiation of, and persistence in, activities.

- It enhances information processing.

- It determines what consequences are reinforcing.

- It leads to improved performance.

Can you find each of these effects in the case study of Anya?

These effects are summarized in Figure 11–1. Let's look at each one more closely.

Goal-Directed Behavior

As we discovered in Chapter 10, social cognitive theorists propose that individuals set goals for themselves and direct their behaviors toward those goals. Motivation determines the specific goals toward which people strive (Maehr, 1984; Pintrich et al., 1993). Thus, it affects the choices that students make—whether to enroll in trigonometry or home economics, whether to watch the Super Bowl or write an assigned research pa-

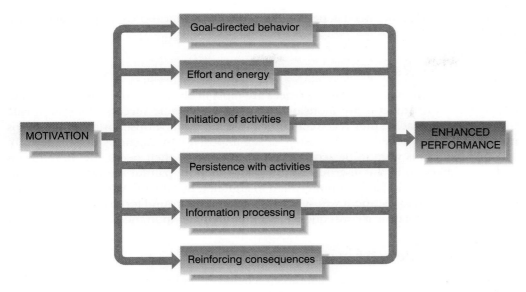

Figure 11–1   *How Motivation Affects Learning and Behavior*

per, whether to try out for the lead in the school play or simply sit in the audience and watch the performance.

Increased Energy and Effort

Motivation increases the amount of effort and energy that students expend in a particular activity (Csikszentmihalyi & Nakamura, 1989; Maehr, 1984; Pintrich et al., 1993). It determines the extent to which students pursue a task enthusiastically and wholeheartedly on the one hand, or apathetically and lackadaisically on the other.

Initiation and Persistence

Motivation determines the degree to which our students will independently initiate and persist at activities (Eccles & Wigfield, 1985; Maehr, 1984; Pintrich et al., 1993; Wigfield, 1994). Students are more likely to begin a task they actually *want* to do. They are also more likely to continue that task until they've completed it, even when they are occasionally interrupted or frustrated in their efforts to do so.

Enhanced Information Processing

From a cognitive perspective, motivation affects what and how information is processed (Eccles & Wigfield, 1985; Lee, 1991; Pintrich et al., 1993; Stipek, 1993; Tobin, 1986; Voss & Schauble, 1992; Wittrock, 1986). For one thing, motivated students are more likely to pay attention, and as we have seen, attention is critical for getting information into both working memory and long-term memory. They also try to understand material—to learn it meaningfully—rather than simply "go through the motions" of learning in a superficial, repetitive, and rote fashion. Furthermore, motivated students are more likely to seek help on a task when they need it, perhaps by asking for clarification or additional practice opportunities.

Nature of Reinforcement

Motivation determines what consequences are most likely to be reinforcing for our students. The more students are motivated to achieve academic success, the more pride they will feel for each A they receive and the more they will be upset by an F or perhaps even by a B (remember our discussion of self-imposed contingencies in Chapter 10). The more students want to be accepted and respected by their peers, the more meaningful membership in the in-group will be, and the more painful the ridicule of classmates will seem. To a student uninterested in athletics, making the school football team is no big deal, but to a student whose life revolves totally around football, making or not making the team may be a consequence of monumental importance.

What consequences are reinforcing to you? What consequences are punishing? Can you tie your preferences to particular motives?

Improved Performance

Because of these other effects—goal-directed behavior, energy and effort, initiation and persistence, information processing, and reinforcement—motivation often leads to improved performance. As you might guess, then, our most motivated students will also tend to be our highest achievers (Gottfried, 1990; Schiefele, 1991a; Schiefele, Krapp, & Winteler, 1992; Walberg & Uguroglu, 1980).

Our work as teachers obviously becomes easier and more productive when our students have the motivation to succeed in the classroom. Yet we must remember that even when *all* of our students are motivated, they won't necessarily be motivated in the same way. Let's distinguish between two major forms that their motivation is likely to take—intrinsic and extrinsic.

DISTINGUISHING BETWEEN INTRINSIC AND EXTRINSIC MOTIVATION

Sometimes students are motivated **intrinsically**—by factors within themselves or inherent in the task they are performing. For example, they may engage in an activity because it gives them pleasure, helps them develop a skill they think is important, or is the ethically and morally right thing to do. At other times, students are motivated **extrinsically**—by factors external to themselves and unrelated to the task they are performing. For example, they may want the good grades, money, or glory that particular activities and accomplishments bring.

Students are most likely to show the beneficial effects of motivation when they are *intrinsically* motivated to engage in classroom activities. Intrinsically motivated students engage in assignments willingly and are eager to learn classroom material. They are also more likely to process information in effective ways—for example, by engaging in meaningful learning, elaboration, and visual imagery (Deci & Ryan, 1985; Entwisle & Ramsden, 1983; Schiefele, 1991a, 1992; Tobias, 1994; Voss & Schauble, 1992). In contrast, extrinsically motivated students may have to be enticed, cajoled, or prodded, are often interested only in performing easy tasks and meeting minimal classroom requirements, and may process information in a rote, superficial manner (Flink, Boggiano, Main, Barrett, & Katz, 1992; O. Lee, 1991; Schiefele, 1991a; Spaulding, 1992).

Under what conditions are students most likely to be intrinsically motivated? One theorist, Abraham Maslow, has proposed that intrinsic motivation emerges only after

Some researchers maintain that our schools foster extrinsic motivation far more frequently than they foster intrinsic motivation (Ryan, Connell, & Grolnick, 1992; Spaulding, 1992). Has this been true in your own experience?

other, more basic human needs have been satisfied. More recently, many theorists have suggested that intrinsic motivation is most likely to be present when two conditions exist: self-efficacy and self-determination. Let's consider how we might promote greater intrinsic motivation in our students by using each of these perspectives.

Applying Maslow's Hierarchy of Needs

Abraham Maslow's work (1959, 1971, 1973a, 1973b, 1976, 1987) has been a central aspect of the *humanist* movement, a perspective especially prominent in psychology during the 1960s and 1970s. Humanism, with roots in clinical and counseling psychology, focuses on how individuals acquire emotions, attitudes, values, and interpersonal skills. Humanist views tend to be grounded more in philosophy than in research, but they provide useful insights into human motivation nevertheless.

Maslow proposed that people have five basic kinds of needs.

1. *Physiological needs:* People are motivated to satisfy needs related to their physical survival (e.g., needs for food, water, oxygen, warmth, exercise, and rest). For example, thirsty students may request a trip to the drinking fountain, students needing to release pent-up energy may become restless and fidgety, and hungry students may be thinking more about their growling stomachs than a teacher's lecture.

2. *Safety needs:* People have a need to feel safe and secure in their environment. For example, students like to know what things are expected of them and are happier when classroom routines are somewhat orderly and predictable.

3. *Love and belonging needs:* People seek affectionate relationships with other people and like to feel that they are accepted as part of a group; in other words, they have a need for affiliation. For example, a fourth grader may place great importance on having a "best" friend. And many adolescents take great pains to fit in with the "cool" crowd—for example, by wearing a certain hairstyle or buying clothes with a certain brand name placed conspicuously upon them.

4. *Esteem needs:* People have a need to feel good about themselves (a *need for self-esteem*) and to believe that other people also feel positively about them (a *need for esteem from others*). To develop positive self-esteem, students will strive for achievement and mastery of their environment. To attain the esteem and respect of others, they will behave in ways that gain them recognition, appreciation, and prestige. For example, a second grader can partially satisfy the need for self-esteem by reading a book "all by myself" or by achieving a special merit badge in Cub Scouts or Campfire Girls. A high school student may try to satisfy the need for esteem from others by running for Student Council treasurer or becoming a star athlete.

5. *Need for self-actualization:* People have a need to **self-actualize**—to grow and become all they are capable of becoming. Individuals striving toward self-actualization seek out new activities as a way of expanding their horizons and strive to learn simply for the sake of learning. For example, one student may be driven by her own curiosity to learn everything she can about dinosaurs; another may pursue an active interest in ballet both as a means of developing her muscle tone and as a way of providing an outlet for creative self-expression.

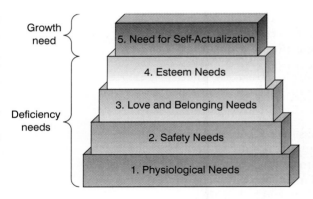

Growth need

Deficiency needs

5. Need for Self-Actualization

4. Esteem Needs

3. Love and Belonging Needs

2. Safety Needs

1. Physiological Needs

Figure 11–2   Maslow's Hierarchy of Needs

How might Maslow's hierarchy come into play in an economically diverse classroom?

Remember that students may be uninterested in learning until deficiency needs—physiological, safety, love and belonging, and esteem needs—have already been addressed.

Maslow further proposed that the five sets of needs form a *hierarchy,* as illustrated in Figure 11–2. When two or more of the needs are unmet, people tend to satisfy them in a particular sequence. They begin with the lowest needs in the hierarchy, satisfying physiological needs first, safety needs next, and so on. They attempt to fulfill higher needs only when lower needs have already been met. For example, a boy with a need for exercise (a physiological need) may become excessively restless in class even though he is scolded by his teacher for his hyperactivity (thereby *not* satisfying his need for esteem from others). A girl with an unfulfilled need for love and belonging may choose not to enroll in intermediate algebra—a class that would satisfy her desire to learn more math—if the peers whose friendships she most values tell her the class is only for nerds. I once knew a boy living in a Philadelphia ghetto who had a strong interest in learning yet often stayed home from school to avoid the violent gangs that hung out on the local street corner. This boy's need for safety took precedence over any need for self-actualization that he might have had.

The first four needs in the hierarchy—physiological, safety, love and belonging, and esteem—result from things that a person *lacks;* hence, Maslow called them **deficiency needs.** Deficiency needs reflect needs that can be met only by external sources—by people and events in one's environment. Furthermore, once these needs are fulfilled, there is no reason to satisfy them further. The last need—self-actualization—is a **growth need:** Rather than simply addressing a deficiency in a person's life, it enhances the person's growth and development. The need for self-actualization is never completely satisfied: People seeking to self-actualize continue to strive for further fulfillment. Self-actualizing activities are intrinsically motivating: People engage in them because doing so gives them pleasure and satisfies their desire to know and grow.

According to Maslow, total self-actualization is rarely if ever achieved, and then typically only by mature adults. Nevertheless, as teachers we can help our students move in this direction by making sure their deficiency needs are at least partially satisfied. Our students may not show much intrinsic motivation to learn classroom material until they are rested and well-fed, feel safe and secure in their classroom, and enjoy the love and respect of their teachers and classmates.

INTO THE CLASSROOM

Attending to Maslow's Deficiency Needs

Make sure students' physiological needs are met.

A teacher who has students for a two-hour block incorporates at least one activity into each class session that allows students to get up, move around, and release any pent-up energy.

A teacher notices that one student comes to school chronically hungry and tired. The student admits that he is rarely given breakfast at home or money for lunch at school. Knowing that the student's mother has limited knowledge of

English, the teacher helps the woman fill out an application for the school's free breakfast and lunch program.

Create a classroom environment in which students feel safe and secure.

A teacher has regular and predictable procedures for how materials are handed out and collected, how assignments are to be completed, and how discipline problems are handled.

When a student is observed threatening his classmates on the playground, his teacher removes him from the situation until it is clear that such behavior will stop.

Attend to students' needs for love and belonging.

During the first month of school, a teacher interviews each student personally to find out what students like and dislike, what their outside interests are, and what they hope to learn in his classroom.

A teacher acknowledges each student's birthday, congratulates students with special personal accomplishments during the year, and sends a card or personal note in times of illness or family tragedy.

Create situations in which students' self-esteem and esteem from others can be enhanced.

A teacher provides a sufficient variety of tasks and activities so that virtually all students can find an area in which they can be exceptional.

A teacher gives awards to recognize special contributions or activities that might otherwise go unnoticed—for example, an award for a student who frequently serves as peacemaker on the playground and an award for a student who has helped her classmates improve skills or grades.

(Some examples presented here are based on recommendations by Wlodkowski, 1978.)

Promoting Self-Efficacy and Self-Determination

■ **EXPERIENCING FIRSTHAND**
Enjoyable Activities

1. Make a list of five different things that you like to do. You might list hobbies, favorite sports, or other activities in which you are intrinsically motivated to engage.

2. Using the scale below, rate each of the activities you've just listed in terms of *how successfully you usually perform it:*

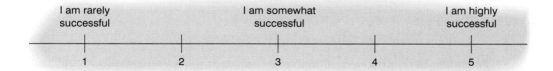

I am rarely successful		I am somewhat successful		I am highly successful
1	2	3	4	5

3. Using the scale below, rate each of the activities you've just listed in terms of *how much choice you have regarding whether or not you engage in the activity:*

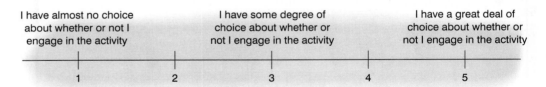

I have almost no choice about whether or not I engage in the activity		I have some degree of choice about whether or not I engage in the activity		I have a great deal of choice about whether or not I engage in the activity
1	2	3	4	5

Take a close look at the numerical ratings you've just assigned to some of your favorite activities. Chances are, your ratings were almost exclusively 3 or higher on both of the scales I asked you to use. A number of theorists have proposed that people are most likely to be intrinsically motivated to perform a certain task when two conditions exist (Boggiano & Pittman, 1992; Corno & Rohrkemper, 1985; Deci, 1992; Deci & Ryan, 1985, 1987, 1992; McCombs, 1988; Spaulding, 1992):

1. They have high *self-efficacy:* They believe that they are capable of successfully accomplishing the task.

2. They have a sense of *self-determination:* They believe that they are in control of their own destinies and can make choices regarding the directions their lives will take.

Self-Efficacy

How is *self-efficacy* similar to Maslow's *need for self-esteem*? How are the two concepts different?

Our students are more likely to be intrinsically motivated to engage in classroom activities when they have high self-efficacy—what some motivation theorists call a *sense of competence*—about their ability to perform those activities successfully (also see Gottfried, 1990; Harter, 1992; Harter, Whitesell, & Kowalski, 1992; MacIver, Stipek, & Daniels, 1991; Schiefele, 1991a; Wigfield, 1994).

In Chapter 10, we identified several strategies for fostering greater self-efficacy in our students:

- Make sure they master basic skills.

- Help them make noticeable progress on difficult tasks.

- Persuade them that they can be successful.

- Expose them to successful peers.

Motivation theorists have offered several additional recommendations for enhancing students' self-efficacy and, indirectly, increasing intrinsic motivation:

- Give them competence-promoting feedback.

- Help them master challenging tasks.

- Promote self-comparison, rather than comparison with others.

- Be sure errors occur within an overall context of success.

Providing competence-promoting feedback.   As we noted in our discussion of behaviorism in Chapter 9, positive feedback is often an effective reinforcer for students. Positive feedback may also promote intrinsic motivation, especially if it conveys the message that students have the ability to perform the task successfully and thereby enhances their self-efficacy (Deci, 1992; Deci & Ryan, 1985). In fact, even negative feedback can be effective in promoting high self-efficacy if it tells students how they can improve their performance and communicates confidence that improvement is likely (Deci & Ryan, 1985). Here are some examples of negative feedback that might have positive outcomes in terms of student motivation:

When giving either positive or negative feedback, communicate the message that students have the ability to be successful.

- "I can see from the past few homework assignments that you're having trouble with long division. I think I know what the problem is. Here, let me show you what you need to do differently."

- "In the first draft of your research paper, many of your paragraphs don't lead logically to the ones that follow. A few headings and transitional sentences would make a world of difference. Let's find a time to discuss how you might use these techniques to improve the flow of your paper."

- "Your time in the 100-meter dash was not as fast as it could be. It's early in the season, though, and if you work on your endurance, I know you'll improve. Also, I think you might get a faster start if you keep low when you come out of the starting blocks."

Promoting mastery of challenging tasks.   You might think of a **challenge** as a situation in which success is neither easy nor guaranteed but can be attained with a significant amount of effort. A challenge encourages people to stretch themselves to their limits—perhaps to experiment with new strategies or to think in new ways.

Encourage students to tackle challenging tasks.

In Chapter 2, we found that challenging activities promote cognitive development. In addition, mastery of such challenges enhances self-efficacy and, as a result, promotes intrinsic motivation. Students who master challenging tasks experience considerable pleasure, satisfaction, and pride in their accomplishments (Clifford, 1990; Cobb, Yackel, & Wood, 1989; Csikszentmihalyi & Nakamura, 1989; Deci & Ryan, 1992; Lan, Repman, Bradley, & Weller, 1994; Malone & Lepper, 1987; Natriello & Dornbusch, 1984; Thompson & Thompson, 1989; Turner, 1995).

Once students are intrinsically motivated, they frequently pursue further challenges of their own accord; they also exhibit considerable persistence in the face of difficulty, and they continue to remain interested in an activity even when they make frequent errors (Covington, 1992; Danner & Lonky, 1981; Deci, 1992; Harter, 1978, 1992). As you can see, then, challenges and intrinsic motivation mutually enhance one another, leading to a "vicious" cycle of the most desirable sort.

Create an environment that encourages students to take risks, and then reinforce them for doing so.

As teachers, there are several things we can do to encourage students to pursue challenging activities. For instance, through the feedback we give and the criteria we use for evaluation, we can create an environment in which students feel free to take risks and make mistakes (Clifford, 1990). We can also provide greater rewards for succeeding at challenging tasks than for achieving an easy success; for example, we might give students a choice between doing an easy task or a more difficult one but give them more points for accomplishing the difficult one (Clifford, 1990; Lan et al., 1994).

Promoting self-comparison, rather than comparison with others.   If we define success in terms of task accomplishment, skill improvement, or academic progress,

Minimize competition.

In competitive situations, some students (e.g., those from some Native American communities) may also be afraid that their own successes may contribute to their classmates' failures (C. A. Grant & Gomez, 1996).

Define success as improvement over time.

Be sure mistakes and errors occur within an overall context of success. Balance challenging tasks with easier ones.

then virtually all of our students can be successful. If we instead define success in terms of how well students perform in comparison with their peers, many will be doomed to failure. Such competition may motivate a few students who believe that they can rise to meet the challenge; however, it will undermine the intrinsic motivation of the majority of their classmates, who will see failure as the most likely outcome (Brophy, 1986; Deci & Ryan, 1985, 1992).

As students progress through the elementary grades, they become increasingly aware of how their performance compares with that of their classmates (Feld, Ruhland, & Gold, 1979; Ruble, 1980). Inevitably, then, some students begin to believe that they simply don't measure up to their peers—in other words, that they are failures. As teachers, we should make an effort not to compound the problem. Most of our students will achieve at higher levels if we encourage them to define success in terms of their own improvement, rather than in terms of how they stack up against others (Covington, 1992; Graham & Golen, 1991).

As teachers, we can do at least two things to encourage self-comparisons, rather than comparisons with others. First, we can minimize the degree to which our students are even aware of the performance levels of their classmates. For example, we should assess their performance independently of how well others are doing, keep their performance on assignments confidential, and give them feedback in private.

In addition, we should encourage students to assess their own performance in much the same way that we, as teachers, are assessing it—that is, in terms of the improvement they are making. We must remember that students are often impatient, expecting success overnight, when in fact the development of knowledge and skills often takes time—perhaps days, months, or even years. Our students may notice their weaknesses—the little failures in their performance—while overlooking the many successful improvements they are making. We can help them focus on their improvement, rather than on their imperfections, if we provide them with concrete mechanisms that highlight improvement—for example, by giving them occasional nongraded quizzes, frequent verbal or written feedback about the "little things" they are doing well, or progress charts they can fill in themselves.

Making sure that errors occur within a context of success. At one time, many educators advocated that students never be allowed to fail at all. But whether we like it or not, occasional failures are a normal, inevitable, and often beneficial part of the learning process, and students need to learn to take such failures in stride. When students never make mistakes, we can reasonably assume that they are not being challenged by the tasks we are assigning. Furthermore, students unaccustomed to failure in their school curriculum have difficulty coping with failure when they eventually do encounter it (Dweck, 1975, 1986).

Yet when students encounter failure *too* frequently, they will develop low self-efficacy, believing that nothing they do will produce positive results. Ideally, then, students should experience occasional failure within the context of overall success. This way, they learn that they *can* succeed if they try, while also developing a realistic attitude about failure—that it at worst is a temporary setback, and at best can give them useful information about how to improve their performance. To keep failure from becoming too frequent an occurrence, we may often want to balance challenging classroom tasks with some that students can accomplish with relative ease (L. Katz & Chard, 1989; Spaulding, 1992).

Self-Determination

Painting Between the Lines

Imagine that I give you a set of watercolor paints, a paintbrush, two sheets of paper, and some paper towels. I ask you to paint a picture of your house, apartment building, or dormitory and then give you these instructions:

> Before you begin, I want to tell you some things that you will have to do. They are rules that I have about painting. You have to keep the paints clean. You can paint only on this small sheet of paper, so don't spill any paint on the big sheet. And you must wash out your brush and wipe it with a paper towel before you switch to a new color of paint, so that you don't get the colors all mixed up. In general, I want you to be a good art student and not make a mess with the paints. (adapted from Koestner, Ryan, Bernieri, & Holt, 1984, p. 239)

How much fun do you think the task will be? After reading my rules about painting, how eager are you to begin painting?   ■

My rules about painting are somewhat restrictive, aren't they? In fact, they are quite *controlling:* They make it clear that I am in charge of the situation and that you, as an art student, have little choice about how you go about your task. Chances are, you have little intrinsic motivation to paint the picture I've asked you to paint (Deci, 1992; Koestner et al., 1984). Furthermore, you would probably be less creative in your painting than if I had not been so controlling (Amabile & Hennessey, 1992).

Students are more likely to be intrinsically motivated when they have a sense of **self-determination**—when they believe that they have some choice and control regarding the things they do and the directions their lives take (Boggiano & Pittman, 1992; Corno & Rohrkemper, 1985; deCharms, 1972; Deci, 1992; Deci & Ryan, 1985, 1987, 1992; Spaulding, 1992; Turner, 1995). Motivation theorists have offered a number of suggestions for enhancing students' sense of self-determination about school activities and assignments:

- Present rules and instructions in an informational, rather than controlling, manner.

- Provide opportunities for students to make choices.

- Evaluate student performance in a noncontrolling fashion.

- Minimize reliance on extrinsic reinforcers.

- Help students keep externally imposed constraints in proper perspective.

Presenting rules and instructions in an informational manner. Virtually any classroom needs a few rules and procedures to ensure that students behave appropriately and that class activities run smoothly. Furthermore, there may be times when we must impose guidelines and restrictions on the ways in which students carry out their assignments. The trick is to present these rules, procedures, guidelines, and restrictions without coming across as controlling students in the way I did in the "Painting Between the Lines" exercise. Instead, we can present them as *information*—for example, as conditions essential to enable the class to accomplish classroom objectives (Deci, 1992; Koestner et al., 1984). Here are three examples of

Present rules and instructions as mechanisms for helping students accomplish classroom objectives.

how we might describe rules or give instructions in an informational, rather than controlling, manner:

- "We can make sure everyone has an equal chance to speak and be heard if we listen without interrupting and if we raise our hands when we want to contribute to the discussion."

- "I'm giving you a particular format to follow when you do your math homework. If you use this format, it will be easier for me to find your answers and, if you answer some problems incorrectly, to figure out how I can help you improve."

- "Let's remember that other students will be using the same paints and brushes later today, so as we work, we need to make sure everything we use now is still in tip-top shape when we're done. It's important, then, that we rinse our brushes in water and wipe them on a paper towel before we switch to a new color. We should also clean our brushes thoroughly when we're done painting."

You can find additional examples of informational instructions in Figure 12–4 of Chapter 12.

Providing opportunities for students to make choices. Sometimes there is only one way to accomplish a particular instructional objective. But more frequently there are a variety of routes to the same destination. In such cases, why not let students choose how they want to get there? For example, we might allow them to make decisions, either individually or as a group, about some or all of the following:

Within reasonable limits, let students make choices.

- Rules and procedures to make the class run more smoothly

- Ways of achieving mastery of a classroom objective (e.g., which of several possible procedures to use, whether to work individually or in small groups)

- Specific topics for research or writing projects

- Specific works of literature to be read

- Due dates for major assignments

- The order in which specific tasks are accomplished during the school day

  - Ways of demonstrating that an objective has been mastered

  - Criteria by which some assignments will be evaluated (Kohn, 1993; Stipek, 1993)

When students can make choices such as these, they are more likely to be interested in what they are doing, to work diligently (even at uninteresting tasks), to complete assignments quickly and efficiently, and to take pride in their work (Brophy, 1987; Condry, 1977; Deci & Ryan, 1985, 1987, 1992; Kohn, 1993; Lepper & Hodell, 1989; M. Morgan, 1984; Ross, 1988; Spaulding, 1992; Stipek, 1993; Turner, 1995; Wang & Stiles, 1976).

In some situations, students' choices can be almost limitless; for example, in a unit on expository writing, a wide variety of student-selected research topics might be equally appropriate. In other situations, we may need to impose certain limits on the choices that students make; for example, if we allow a class to set its own due dates for major assignments, we might insist that the final schedule provide sufficient time for us to grade

Students are more likely to be intrinsically motivated when they have a sense of self-determination about classroom activities.

each assignment. In still other situations, we may want to provide a handful of options from which students can choose; for example, we might allow them to choose from among several works of literature, specialize in one of several art media (e.g., watercolors, pastels, clay), or select a piece of equipment (e.g., parallel bars, rings, floor mats) on which to develop gymnastic skills.

Evaluating student performance in a noncontrolling fashion. As teachers, we will inevitably need to evaluate students' accomplishments. But we must keep in mind that external evaluations may undermine students' intrinsic motivation, especially if those evaluations are communicated in a controlling manner (Benware & Deci, 1984; Deci & Ryan, 1985, 1992; Grolnick & Ryan, 1987; Harter et al., 1992). Ideally, we should present our own evaluations of students' work, not in terms of a "judgment" of some sort (e.g., not in terms of how they *should* perform), but in terms of information that can help them improve their knowledge and skills. Furthermore, we can give students criteria by which they can evaluate *themselves* in the self-comparative manner I described earlier.

Evaluate students in ways that help them improve.

Minimizing reliance on extrinsic reinforcers. In our discussion of behaviorism in Chapter 9, I emphasized the importance of relying on intrinsic reinforcers—for example, on students' own feelings of pride and satisfaction about their accomplishments—as often as possible. A problem with using extrinsic reinforcers—praise, stickers, favorite activities, and so on—is that they may undermine intrinsic motivation, especially when students perceive them as controlling behavior and limiting choices (Bates, 1979; Deci, 1992; Deci & Ryan, 1985, 1987, 1992; Gottfried, Fleming, & Gottfried, 1994; Lepper & Greene, 1978; Lepper & Hodell, 1989; Lepper, Keavney, & Drake, 1996; Ryan & Deci, 1996; however, also see Cameron & Pierce, 1994, 1996). Extrinsic reinforcers may also communicate the message that classroom tasks are unpleasant "chores" to be done (why else would a reinforcer be necessary?), rather than activities to be carried out and enjoyed for their own sake (Hennessey, 1995; Stipek, 1993).

Avoid extrinsic reinforcers when students are intrinsically motivated.

Yet there may be occasions when, despite our efforts, our students will have little interest in acquiring certain knowledge or skills critical for their later success in life. In such situations, we may have to provide extrinsic reinforcers—good grades, free time, special privileges—to encourage their learning. How can we use such reinforcers without diminishing students' sense of self-determination? For one thing, we can use reinforcers such as praise to communicate information, rather than to control behavior (Deci, 1992; Ryan, Mims, & Koestner, 1983); consider these statements as examples:

Use praise to provide information, rather than to control students' behavior.

- "Your description of the main character in your short story makes her come alive."

- "I think you have finally mastered the rolling R sound in Spanish."

- "This poster clearly states the hypothesis, method, results, and conclusions of your science project. Your use of a bar graph makes the differences between your treatment and control groups easy to see and interpret."

Furthermore, as we noted in our discussion of self-regulation in Chapter 10, we may want to encourage *self*-reinforcement—a practice that clearly keeps control in the hands of students.

Encourage self-reinforcement.

Helping students keep externally imposed constraints in perspective. Our students will often encounter circumstances that cast a "controlling" light on school activities; competitions, extrinsic rewards, and external evaluation are frequent events in most schools. For example, students often enter such competitive events as athletic contests, spelling bees, and science fairs. They may make the Honor Roll, win a first-place ribbon at an art exhibit, or receive a free pizza coupon for reading a certain number of books each month. And they will almost inevitably receive grades, in one form or another, that reflect their teachers' evaluations of their achievement.

Encourage students to focus on the intrinsic value of the tasks they perform.

To help our students keep such external constraints in perspective as they engage in a learning task, we should remind them that although competition, extrinsic rewards, or evaluation may be present, the most important thing is for them to focus on the inherent value of the task itself (Amabile & Hennessey, 1992; Hennessey, 1995). For example, we might encourage them to tell themselves something along this line:

> I like to get good grades, and when I bring home a good report card, my parents always give me money. But that's not what's really important. I like to learn a lot. There are a lot of things that interest me, and I want to learn about them, so I work hard because I enjoy it. (Amabile & Hennessey, 1992, p. 68)

As teachers, we would ultimately like our students to be motivated to acquire knowledge and skills simply because they *want* to learn them, rather than because we give them extrinsic reinforcers for doing so. Let's find out more about how we can promote one form of intrinsic motivation—the motivation to learn.

CONSIDERING STUDENTS' MOTIVATION TO LEARN

Consider these two students in a trigonometry class:

- Sheryl detests mathematics and is taking the class for only one reason: A grade of C or better in trigonometry is a requirement for a scholarship at State University, where she desperately wants to go to college.

- Shannon has always liked math. Trigonometry will help her get a scholarship at State University, but in addition, Shannon truly wants to understand how to use trigonometry. She sees its usefulness for her future profession as an architect. Besides, she's discovering that trigonometry is actually a lot of fun.

Which student is going to learn more in class? We can reasonably predict that Shannon will achieve at a higher level than Sheryl. Sheryl is motivated only to get a C or better, not to learn trigonometry. She will do whatever she needs to do to get a passing grade, but she probably won't do much more than that. In contrast, Shannon has the **motivation to learn**—the tendency to find school-related activities meaningful and worthwhile and therefore to attempt to get the maximum benefit from them (Brophy, 1986, 1987; D. W. Johnson & Johnson, 1985b; McCombs, 1988).

Students may have varying degrees of motivation to learn in different aspects of the school curriculum. Some students, like Shannon, may be particularly motivated in mathematics, whereas others may be eager to acquire knowledge or skills in art (remember our case study of Anya), history, athletics, or auto mechanics.

Characteristic of students like Shannon and Anya—students with a motivation to learn—is a focus on learning goals, rather than performance goals. It is to the distinction between these two types of goals and to their implications for us as teachers that we turn now.

Distinguishing Between Learning and Performance Goals

Mr. Wesolowski, the physical education teacher, is teaching a unit on basketball. He asks Tim, Travis, and Tony to get on the court and try dribbling, passing, and shooting baskets. Consider what the three boys are thinking as they begin to practice:

Tim: This is my chance to show all the guys what a great basketball player I am. If I stay near the basket, Travis and Tony will keep passing to me, and I'll score a lot of points. I can really impress Wesolowski and my friends.

Travis: Boy, I hope I don't screw this up. If I shoot at the basket and miss, I'll look like a real jerk. Maybe I should just stay outside the three-point line and keep passing to Tim and Tony.

Tony: I'd really like to become a better basketball player. I can't figure out why I don't get more of my shots into the basket. I'll ask Wesolowski to give me feedback about how I can improve my game. Maybe some of my friends will have suggestions, too.

All three boys want to play basketball well, but for different reasons. Tim is concerned mostly about his performance—about looking good in front of his teacher and classmates—and so he wants to maximize opportunities to demonstrate his skill on the court. Travis is also concerned about the impression he will make, but he just wants to make sure he *doesn't* look *bad.* Unlike Tim and Travis, Tony isn't even thinking about how his performance will appear to others. Instead, he is interested mainly in developing his skill in the game and doesn't expect himself to be an expert on the first day. For Tony, making mistakes is an inevitable part of learning a new skill, not a source of embarrassment or humiliation.

Tony's approach to basketball illustrates a **learning goal**—a desire to acquire additional knowledge or master new skills. In contrast, Tim and Travis are each setting a **performance goal**—a desire to look good and receive favorable judgments from others or else *not* to look bad and receive unfavorable judgments. When we compare students who set learning goals with those who set performance goals, we often find different attitudes and behaviors (e.g., Dweck & Elliott, 1983). Table 11–1 presents some of the differences we are likely to see.

As Table 11–1 illustrates, students with learning goals tend to engage in the very activities that will help them learn: They pay attention in class, process information in ways that promote effective long-term memory storage, and learn from their mistakes. Furthermore, students with learning goals have a healthy perspective about learning, effort, and failure: They realize that learning is a process of trying hard and continuing to persevere even in the face of temporary setbacks. Consequently, it is usually these students who benefit the most from their classroom experiences.

In contrast, students with performance goals—students concerned primarily about how they appear to others—may stay away from some of the very tasks that, because of their challenging nature, would do the most to help them master new skills (Dweck, 1986). Furthermore, because these students may exert only the minimal effort necessary to achieve desired performance outcomes, they may learn only a fraction of what their teachers have to offer them (Brophy, 1986, 1987).

Consider Sheryl and Shannon (our trigonometry students) and Anya from our "Quick Draw" case study. For which girl(s) do we see a learning goal? For which girl(s) do we see a performance goal?

In what areas do you have learning goals? In what areas are you only interested in how you appear to others? How is your learning affected by the particular goals you have?

Table 11–1 Students with Learning Goals Versus Performance Goals

STUDENTS WITH LEARNING GOALS	STUDENTS WITH PERFORMANCE GOALS
Believe that competence develops over time through practice and effort.	Believe that competence is a stable characteristic; people either have talent or they don't.
Choose tasks that maximize opportunities for learning.	Choose tasks that maximize opportunities for demonstrating competence; avoid tasks that make them look incompetent.
React to easy tasks with feelings of boredom or disappointment.	React to easy tasks with feelings of pride or relief.
View effort as something necessary to improve competence.	View effort as a sign of low competence; think that competent people shouldn't have to try very hard.
Are more likely to be intrinsically motivated to learn course material.	Are more likely to be extrinsically motivated—that is, by expectations of external reinforcement and punishment.
Engage in such self-regulatory behaviors as goal setting, self-evaluation, and self-reinforcement.	Exhibit less self-regulation.
Use learning strategies that promote true comprehension of course material (e.g., meaningful learning, elaboration, comprehension monitoring).	Use learning strategies that promote only rote learning (e.g., repetition, copying, word-for-word memorization).
Evaluate their own performance in terms of the progress they make.	Evaluate their own performance in terms of how they compare with others.
View errors as a normal and useful part of the learning process; use errors to help improve performance.	View errors as a sign of failure and incompetence.
Are satisfied with their performance if they try hard, even if their efforts result in failure.	Are satisfied with their performance only if they succeed.
Interpret failure as a sign that they need to exert more effort.	Interpret failure as a sign of low ability and therefore predictive of continuing failure in the future.
View their teacher as a resource and guide to help them learn.	View their teacher as a judge and as a rewarder or punisher.

Sources: C. Ames & Archer, 1988; Anderman & Maehr, 1994; Dweck, 1986; Dweck & Elliott, 1983; Entwisle & Ramsden, 1983; Jagacinski & Nicholls, 1984, 1987; McCombs, 1988; Newman & Schwager, 1995; Nolen, 1988; Powell, 1990; Schiefele, 1991a, 1992; Stipek, 1993.

Fostering the Motivation to Learn

Unfortunately, performance goals are more prevalent than learning goals among today's students. Most students, if they are motivated to succeed in their schoolwork, are primarily concerned about getting good grades, and they prefer short and easy tasks to lengthier, more challenging ones (Blumenfeld, 1992; Doyle, 1983, 1986b).

How can we foster our students' motivation to learn? How can we help them focus more on learning than on simply looking good to others? Among other things, we can:

Students with learning goals recognize that competence comes only from effort and practice.

- Relate subject matter to students' present and future needs

- Capitalize on students' interests

- Model our own interest in the subject matter

- Communicate our belief that students want to learn

- Focus students' attention on learning goals rather than performance goals

Let's look briefly at each of these strategies.

Relating Subject Matter to Students' Present and Future Needs

Relate activities to students' present needs and long-term goals.

Some classroom activities will be naturally fun, interesting, or otherwise intrinsically motivating for students. But others—perhaps the drill and practice so essential for developing automaticity of basic skills, or perhaps complex ideas or procedures with which students must initially struggle—may sometimes be less than exciting. Our students are more apt to be motivated to learn relatively unenticing classroom subject matter, and more likely to use effective information-processing strategies in learning it, when they see its relevance for their personal lives and professional aspirations (C. Ames, 1992; Brophy, 1986, 1987; Brophy & Alleman, 1991; Maehr, 1984; Pintrich et al., 1993). In other words, students learn classroom material more effectively when they have a self-perceived *need to know* that material. Thus, we might illustrate how mathematics plays a role in shopping and budgeting one's allowance, how science facilitates everyday problem solving, and how physical fitness helps one look and feel better. We might show our students how oral and written language skills are critical for making a favorable impression on future employers. We might point out how knowledge of current events and social studies will help them make informed decisions in the voting booth.

Capitalizing on Students' Interests

The Doctor's Office

You have just arrived at the doctor's office for your annual physical checkup. The receptionist tells you that the doctor is running late and that you will probably have to wait an hour before you can be seen. As you sit down in the waiting room, you notice six magazines on the coffee table in front of you: *Better Homes and Gardens, National Geographic, Newsweek, People, Popular Mechanics,* and *Sports Illustrated.*

1. Rate each of these magazines in terms of how *interesting* you think its articles would be to you:

	Not at All Interesting	Somewhat Interesting	Very Interesting
Better Homes and Gardens	_____	_____	_____
National Geographic	_____	_____	_____
Newsweek	_____	_____	_____
People	_____	_____	_____
Popular Mechanics	_____	_____	_____
Sports Illustrated	_____	_____	_____

2. Even though you think that some of the magazines will be more interesting than others, you decide to spend ten minutes reading each one. Estimate how much you think you might *remember* from what you read in each of the six magazines:

	Hardly Anything	A Moderate Amount	Quite a Bit
Better Homes and Gardens	_____	_____	_____
National Geographic	_____	_____	_____
Newsweek	_____	_____	_____
People	_____	_____	_____
Popular Mechanics	_____	_____	_____
Sports Illustrated	_____	_____	_____

Now compare your two sets of ratings. Chances are, the magazines that you rated highest in interest to you are also the magazines from which you will learn and remember the most.

When students are interested in what they are studying, they are more likely to have positive feelings about their schoolwork, to set learning goals rather than performance goals, to engage in such storage processes as meaningful learning and elaboration, and, ultimately, to learn and remember more (Garner et al., 1992; Hidi, 1990; Hidi & Anderson, 1992; Pintrich et al., 1993; Schiefele, 1992; Spaulding, 1992; Tobias, 1994; Wigfield, 1994). In contrast, students who have no interest in their school subjects are apt to approach learning at a rote level—for example, by reading and rereading with little understanding or by memorizing facts in a word-for-word fashion (Schiefele, 1991b).

Sometimes students' interests reflect long-term, fairly stable predispositions toward certain subjects (Alexander & Jetton, 1996); for example, my son Alex was interested in insects, arachnids, and similar creatures from his toddler days until sometime around puberty (at which point, his attention turned to cars and girls). As teachers, we

Relate classroom material to existing student interests.

can certainly capitalize on such interests by giving students some flexibility in the topics about which they read and write. Furthermore, we can tie traditional classroom subjects to things that students are naturally curious about. For example, aspects of ancient history can be related to modern-day events (e.g., the Ark of the Covenant is depicted in the film *Raiders of the Lost Ark*); latitude and longitude might be described within the context of locating the *Titanic* (Brophy, 1986).

Pique students' interest through active involvement, novelty, contradictions, and fantasy.

On other occasions, students' interest can be piqued, at least temporarily, by the activities we develop and the ways we present information. Among other things, we can:

- Provide opportunities for students to get actively involved with the subject matter

- Include variety and novelty in classroom materials or procedures

- Present inconsistent or discrepant information

- Encourage occasional fantasy and make-believe (Brophy, 1986, 1987; Covington, 1992; Deci, 1992; Hidi & Anderson, 1992; Lepper & Hodell, 1989; Palmer, 1965; Paris & Byrnes, 1989; Ross, 1988; Sadker & Sadker, 1985; Schank, 1979; Stipek, 1993; Wade, 1992; Wlodkowski, 1978)

Can you explain the value of inconsistent or discrepant information by using Piaget's concept of *disequilibrium* (see Chapter 2)?

To illustrate, here are some concrete examples of things we might do:

- In a unit on musical instruments, let students experiment with a variety of simple instruments.

- In a lesson about sedimentary, metamorphic, and igneous rocks, give cooperative groups a bag of rocks and have them categorize each one.

- In a lesson about alcoholic beverages, have students role-play being at a party and being tempted to have a beer or wine cooler.

- In a reading group, turn a short story into a play, with each student taking a part.

- In biology, have a classroom debate regarding the ethical implications of conducting medical research on animals.

- In spelling, occasionally depart from the standard word lists, instead asking students to learn how to spell favorite television shows or classmates' surnames.

- In an aerobics workout in physical education, incorporate steps from the jitterbug, twist, or country line dancing.

- In an art class, have students make a mosaic from items they've found on a scavenger hunt around the school building and its grounds.

- In a unit on aerodynamics, have students make paper airplanes and compete to see which design travels farthest.

- In arithmetic, have students play computer games to improve their automaticity for number facts.

- In history, have students read children's perspectives of historical events (e.g., Anne Frank's diary during World War II, Zlata Filipovic's diary during the Bosnian War).

- In health, examine unhealthful eating habits listed in the *Guinness Book of World Records* (e.g., a woman eating 23 hot dogs in three minutes, a man eating 100 yards of spaghetti in 29 seconds).

- In expository writing, let students choose some of the topics they write about.

- In geography, present household objects not found locally and ask students to guess where in the world they might be from.

Modeling Interest in the Subject Matter

Model your own interest in the subject matter.

Our students are more likely to develop an intrinsic motivation to learn classroom material if, as teachers, we model our own interest in the subject matter and our desire to learn more about it (e.g., Deci & Ryan, 1992). For example, we can show students how a topic has enriched our own personal lives. We can let them see how we continue to study that topic ourselves, perhaps by bringing in current magazine articles we have found. We can present our own opinions regarding controversial issues. We can share our curiosity and puzzlement about unresolved questions (Brophy, 1986, 1987; Wlodkowski, 1978). Our students are more likely to become excited about a topic if we ourselves are enthusiastic about it.

Communicating the Belief That Students Want to Learn

Openly make the assumption that students *want* to learn.

Through our statements and actions, we can convey the message that we believe our students are genuinely interested in school subject matter and intrinsically motivated to master it (Brophy, 1986, 1987; Hennessey & Amabile, 1987). To illustrate, here is how one teacher conveyed such a message (Brophy, 1986):

> [She] communicated positive expectations routinely by announcing at the beginning of the year that her class was intended to make the students into "social scientists" and by referring back to this idea frequently throughout the year through such comments as "Since you are social scientists, you will recognize that the description of this area as a tropical rain forest has implications about what kinds of crops will grow there," or "Thinking as social scientists, what conclusions might we draw from this information?" (p. 46)

> We should definitely not communicate the belief that our students will dislike a particular topic or are only working to get good grades (Brophy, 1986).

Focusing Students' Attention on Learning Goals

When we emphasize to students that they need to study to pass tomorrow's exam or that they need to get good grades if they want to go to college, we are encouraging them to focus on performance goals—goals that won't necessarily promote their desire to learn simply for learning's sake. When we instead point out the ways in which school subject matter is going to be useful to them in the future and when we show students that they are actually making progress in their studies, then we are focusing their attention on learning goals—goals that will help them direct their efforts toward true understanding and

Students learn more and are more likely to engage in meaningful learning and elaboration when they are interested in what they are learning.

mastery of subject matter, rather than simply toward "looking good" (C. Ames, 1992; Anderman & Maehr, 1994; Dweck, 1986; Dweck & Elliott, 1983; A. S. Hagen, 1994; Pintrich et al., 1993; Stipek, 1993).

As we focus our students' attention on learning goals, we should also encourage them to set and pursue challenging yet achievable ones. Students benefit little from engaging in tasks easy enough to be mastered quickly, and unless automaticity is important, they benefit even less from repeating tasks they have already mastered. Yet attempting tasks that are *too* difficult may lead more to frustration with the subject matter (and perhaps to a dislike for it as well) than to any real gains. Tasks and assignments that promote the greatest learning and development of skills are those that are difficult but attainable—those at which students may initially fail, but at which they can eventually succeed with effort, practice, and perhaps a little assistance (Brophy, 1986, 1987; Dweck, 1986; Dweck & Elliott, 1983).

Yet despite our efforts to promote learning goals, rather than performance goals, many of our students will continue to be concerned about making mistakes that cause them to look bad in front of their classmates. Students are motivated not only to attain academic goals but to attain social goals as well; for example, most students want to be accepted and respected by their peers. Let's turn our attention now to this very different side of human motivation.

Encourage students to focus on learning goals.

Focusing students' attention on personally relevant learning goals, rather than on performance goals, may be especially beneficial for minority students and students at risk (Alderman, 1990; Garcia, 1992).

Into the Classroom

Promoting Intrinsic Motivation to Learn Classroom Subject Matter

Scaffold student success, especially when students have a history of failure.

Students in a mathematics class have consistently had difficulty with their geometry proofs, so their teacher forms cooperative groups to work together on these tasks. If she observes a group struggling with a particular proof, she provides a hint to steer the group in the right direction.

Define success as eventual, rather than immediate, mastery of class material and acknowledge that occasional mistakes are to be expected.

A middle school teacher consoles a student who is disappointed in her mediocre performance on a difficult assignment. "You're a very talented student, and you're probably used to having your schoolwork come easily. But remember, as students move through the grade levels, assignments become increasingly more challenging. With a little more study and practice, I know you'll improve quite a bit."

Encourage self-comparison, rather than comparison with other students.

In January, an elementary school teacher asks his students to write a short story. After reading the stories that students have written, he hands them back to students; he also returns stories that his students wrote in early September. "Do you see how much your writing has improved over the past four months?" he asks. "The stories that you wrote this week are longer and better developed. Can you find mistakes in spelling, grammar, or punctuation in your September stories that you wouldn't make now?"

Enhance students' sense of self-determination regarding classroom assignments and activities.

A science teacher tells her students, "I know you can't always complete your lab reports the same day that you did the lab in class. Let's see whether we can identify some reasonable due dates for your reports so that *you* have the time you need to write them and *I* have the time I need to read them and give you feedback before the next lab activity."

Help students see the value and importance of school subjects.

The personnel officer of a local business speaks to a high school English class about how correct grammar and spelling affect job success.

Relate classroom material to students' interests.

An elementary school teacher asks students to bring in objects they use to celebrate holidays at home. He incorporates these objects into a lesson on how holiday traditions differ not only from religion to religion but also from family to family.

Model your own interest in the subject matter and your desire to learn more about it.

A student asks a question that her teacher cannot answer. "Interesting question," the teacher replies, "and I don't know the answer myself. Let's see whether we can find an answer when we visit the school library this afternoon. Together we can look for books that can help us learn more."

Communicate your belief that students want to learn.

A junior high school history teacher introduces the next reading assignment this way: "The chapter I've assigned for tonight is an exciting one. As the chapter unfolds, you will see the American colonists become increasingly discontented with British rule. You will also learn how the colonists eventually managed to break free and form the United States of America."

Encourage students to set learning goals.

A Spanish teacher often reminds his students, "The important thing in this class is to learn how to speak Spanish comfortably and with correct pronunciation. We'll all work together until we can communicate easily with one another in Spanish."

Encourage goals that are challenging yet achievable.

On Monday, the coach of a cross-country team tells her students, "Each day this week we'll run the same five-mile course we ran last Friday. Try to cut down your running time a little bit each day. See if you can cut sixty seconds off last Friday's time by the end of the week."

> **Encourage students to use their errors to help themselves learn.**
>
> As a mathematics teacher comes to a student's assistance, she says, "Hmmm, you ended up with zero in the denominator of this fraction. You know that fractions can't have denominators of zero. Let's look at the steps you took as you tried to solve the problem and see if we can find your error."

ATTENDING TO STUDENTS' SOCIAL NEEDS

THINKING ABOUT WHAT YOU KNOW

- How much time do you spend with other people? Are you someone who enjoys being with others a good deal of the time? Or, like Anya, do you prefer to spend much of your time alone?

- How important is it for you to have the recognition and acceptance of your family, teachers, and peers? How often do you do things primarily to win the approval of someone else? How often do you act without regard to what anybody else thinks about your behavior?

To some extent, we are all social creatures: We live, work, and play with our fellow human beings. Yet some people are more socially oriented and more concerned about what others think than other people are. As teachers, we are likely to see a variety of differences among our students in terms of their social needs, including their needs for affiliation and approval.

Satisfying Students' Need for Affiliation

What do all these students have in common?

- Leo and Lamar have declared themselves to be "best friends." They are together most of the time, both in school and out. When one boy gets sick or leaves town for a few days, the other is at a complete loss for something to do.

- Logan goes out for the roller hockey team, not so much because he likes to play roller hockey, but mainly because all his buddies are going out for the team and he doesn't want to be left out.

- Lance is on the telephone almost continually from the minute he arrives home from school until the minute he has to go to bed. He calls one friend to get his history reading assignment, another to set up a double date to the movies, and still another to share the latest gossip about one of their classmates. In between Lance's numerous calls out, others are calling *him*—

Many students have a high need for affiliation: They want and seek out friendly relationships with others.

perhaps to find out whether he is going to tomorrow night's jazz concert or to solicit his advice for the lovelorn.

These students all have a **need for affiliation:** They desire and seek out friendly relationships with others (e.g., C. A. Hill, 1987). Some students have a high need for affiliation: They want to be with other people most of the time, to communicate with one another frequently, and to be accepted by their peers. Other students, such as Anya, have a much lower need for affiliation: They may enjoy the company of others once in a while, but they are not as concerned about being accepted, and they may even prefer to be alone on some occasions.

Students' needs for affiliation will be reflected in the kinds of choices they make at school (Boyatzis, 1973; French, 1956). For example, students with a low need for affiliation may prefer to work alone, whereas students with a high need for affiliation may prefer to work in small groups. When choosing work partners, students with a low affiliation need are apt to choose classmates whom they believe to be competent at the task to be performed; students with a high affiliation need are apt to choose their friends even if such friends are relatively incompetent. Students with a low need for affiliation are likely to choose a class schedule that meets their own interests and ambitions, whereas students with a high need for affiliation are more likely to choose one that enables them to be with their friends.

As teachers, we cannot ignore the high need for affiliation that many students bring to the classroom. On the contrary, as we plan our daily lessons and classroom activities, we must provide some opportunities for students to interact with one another. Although some classroom objectives may be best accomplished when students work independently, others can be accomplished just as easily (perhaps even more so) when students work together. Group-based activities, such as discussions, debates, role playing, cooperative learning tasks, and competitions among two or more teams of equal ability, all provide the means through which students can satisfy their need for affiliation while simultaneously acquiring new knowledge or skills (e.g., Brophy, 1986, 1987). Such activities may also give students a greater sense of "belongingness"; that is, they may help students feel that they are accepted and liked by their classmates and are valued members of the class. Students who have this sense of belongingness within their classroom are likely to exhibit greater interest and self-efficacy with regard to their schoolwork, greater effort in class, and higher academic achievement (Goodenow, 1991).

We must remember, too, that many of our students will want to affiliate not only with their classmates but with us teachers as well. Therefore, we should show our students that we like them, enjoy being with them, and are concerned about their well-being (e.g., McKeachie, Lin, Milholland, & Isaacson, 1966). We can communicate our fondness for students in numerous ways—for example, by expressing an interest in their outside activities and accomplishments, providing extra help or support when it is needed, or lending a sympathetic ear. These "caring" messages may be especially important for students from culturally different backgrounds: Such students are more likely to succeed in our classroom if we show interest in their lives and concern for their individual needs (Phelan, Davidson, & Cao, 1991).

Satisfying Students' Need for Approval

Another social need in which we see differences among students is the **need for approval**—a desire to gain the acceptance and positive judgments of other people (e.g., Igoe & Sulli-

To which one of Maslow's needs is the concept of *need for affiliation* most similar?

Provide opportunities for students to interact with one another.

Show students that you like them, enjoy being with them, and are concerned about their well-being.

Addressing Students' Social Needs

Provide opportunities for students to interact with one another.

> A junior high school science teacher forms two teams of students and asks them to debate the pros and cons of using animals in cancer research.

Show students that you like them, enjoy being with them, and are concerned about their well-being.

> As school lets out, a teacher sees a student who is obviously upset. "I can see that something is troubling you, Frank. I have some time before I have to go home. Would you like to sit down for a bit and talk about what's on your mind?"

Give frequent praise to students with a high need for approval.

> A physical education teacher has one student (Sally) who lacks self-confidence and is continually asking for feedback on her performance. The teacher finds at least one opportunity in each class session to compliment Sally on the things she does well. For example, in a unit on tennis, the teacher tells Sally, "Good, you're keeping your eye on the ball and you're swinging with your entire arm. With some practice, you'll find that you can get the ball over the net more consistently."

Keep students' successes and failures private and confidential unless you have their permission to do otherwise.

> An art teacher would like to use one student's pen-and-ink drawing as an example of good technique, but first checks with the student to make sure it's all right.

van, 1991; Juvonen & Weiner, 1993). Students with a high need for approval are overly concerned with pleasing others and tend to give in easily to group pressure, for fear that they might otherwise be rejected (Crowne & Marlowe, 1964). Whereas other students might engage in a school task for the pleasure that success at the task brings, students with a high need for approval are likely to engage in the task primarily to please their teacher and to persist at it only to the extent that their teacher praises them for doing so (Harter, 1975; S. C. Rose & Thornburg, 1984).

When students have a high need for approval, we can promote their classroom achievement by praising them frequently for the things they do well. At the same time, we must keep in mind that some students (especially at the secondary level) may be more concerned about gaining the approval of their peers than that of their teacher (Juvonen & Weiner, 1993). If being a high achiever is not the socially acceptable thing to do, many students will prefer that their accomplishments be praised privately, rather than publicly. Ultimately, how well our students are accomplishing instructional objectives is no one's business but theirs, their parents', and ours.

Relationships with peers and teachers are, for many students, a source of considerable pleasure and enjoyment. Conversely, difficulties in interpersonal relationships, which may lead to difficulties in satisfying affiliation and approval needs, are often a source of anxiety. Pleasure, enjoyment, anxiety—all of these are examples of feelings, emotions, or what psychologists call *affect,* a topic to which we turn now.

Give frequent praise to students with a high need for approval.

Keep students' successes and failures private and confidential unless you have their permission to do otherwise.

When we speak of motivation, it is difficult not to talk about **affect**—the feelings and emotions that an individual brings to bear on a task—at the same time. As we've just noted, students may have different *affective responses,* depending on whether their needs for affiliation and approval are being satisfied through their relationships with their classmates and teachers. We have seen other instances of how motivation and affect are interrelated as well. For instance, we've discovered that intrinsically motivated individuals find pleasure in what they are doing. We've found that people respond differently to easy tasks—either with feelings of disappointment, on the one hand, or with relief, on the other—depending on whether they have learning goals or performance goals. We've learned that students who master challenging tasks experience considerable pleasure, satisfaction, and pride in their accomplishments. Affect takes other forms as well; love, excitement, anger, sadness, and guilt are all examples of affect.

Defining Hot Cognition

◨ EXPERIENCING FIRSTHAND
Flying High

As you read each of the statements below, decide whether it evokes positive feelings (e.g., happiness, excitement), negative feelings (e.g., sadness, anger), or no feelings whatsoever. Check the appropriate blank in each case.

	Positive Feelings	Negative Feelings	No Feelings
1. The city of Denver opened DIA, its new international airport, in 1995.	_____	_____	_____
2. In a recent commercial airline crash, ninety passengers and eight crew members lost their lives.	_____	_____	_____
3. A dozen people survived that crash, including a three-month-old infant found in the rear of the plane.	_____	_____	_____
4. The area of an airplane in which food is prepared is called the *galley*.	_____	_____	_____
5. Several major airlines are offering $69 round-trip fares to Acapulco, Mexico.	_____	_____	_____
6. Those $69 fares apply only to those flights leaving at 5:30 in the morning.	_____	_____	_____
7. Some flights between North America and Europe now include two full-course meals.	_____	_____	_____

You probably had little if any emotional reaction to statements 1 (the opening of DIA) and 4 (the definition of *galley*). In contrast, you may have had pleasant feelings when you read statements 3 (the surviving infant) and 5 (the low fares to Acapulco), and unpleasant feelings when you read statements 2 (the high number of fatalities) and 6 (the dreadful departure time for those Acapulco flights). Your response to statement 7 (the two full-course meals) may have been positive, negative, or neutral, depending on your previous experiences with airline cuisine.

Sometimes learning and cognitive processing are emotionally charged—a phenomenon known as **hot cognition** (e.g., Hoffman, 1991; P. H. Miller, 1993). For example, students might get excited when they read about advances in science that could lead to effective treatments of spinal cord injuries, cancer, or AIDS. They may feel sad when they read about the living conditions in Third World countries. They will, we hope, get angry when they learn about the atrocities committed against African American slaves in the pre-Civil War days of the United States or against the millions of Jewish people during World War II.

Affect is clearly intertwined with learning and cognition. For one thing, students are more likely to pay attention to things that evoke strong emotions—things that possibly make them excited, sad, or angry (Reisberg & Heuer, 1992). Students who are interested in a topic about which they are reading (perhaps finding it exciting or upsetting) process information more effectively—for example by engaging in more meaningful learning and visual imagery (Hidi & Anderson, 1992; Tobias, 1994). And students can usually retrieve information with high emotional content more easily than they can recall relatively nonemotional information (Baddeley, 1982; Heuer & Reisberg, 1990; Kleinsmith & Kaplan, 1963; Reisberg & Heuer, 1992). In general, then, our students will learn and remember more when they become involved in classroom subject matter not only cognitively but emotionally as well.

Get students emotionally involved with classroom subject matter.

We should note, too, that problem solving is easier when students enjoy what they're doing and that successful problem solutions are often accompanied by feelings of excitement, pleasure, and pride (Bloom & Broder, 1950; Cobb et al., 1989; McLeod & Adams, 1989; M. U. Smith, 1991; Thompson & Thompson, 1989). In contrast, students are likely to feel frustrated and anxious when they fail at a task, especially if it appears to be an easy one, and they are apt to develop a dislike for that task (Eccles & Wigfield, 1985; Harter, 1978; Stodolsky, Salk, & Glaessner, 1991). Let's look more closely at the effects that anxiety has on students' learning and performance.

Exploring the Nature and Effects of Anxiety

You are enrolled in Professor Josiah S. Carberry's course in advanced psychoceramics. Today is your day to give a half hour presentation on the topic of psychoceramic califractions. You have read several books and numerous articles on your topic and undoubtedly know more about psychoceramic califractions than anyone else in the room. And you have prepared the note cards for your presentation carefully and meticulously. As you sit in class waiting for your turn to speak, you should be feeling calm and confident. But instead you're a nervous wreck: Your heart is pounding wildly, your palms are sweaty, and your stomach is in a knot. When Professor Carberry calls you to the front of the classroom and you begin to speak, you have trouble remembering the things you wanted to say, and you can't read your note cards because your hands are shaking so much.

It's not as if you *want* to be nervous about speaking in front of your psychoceramics class. Furthermore, you can't think of a single reason why you *should* be nervous. After all, you are an expert on your topic, you know your underwear isn't showing (you double-checked), and your classmates are not the type to giggle or throw rotten tomatoes if you make a mistake. So what's the big deal? What happened to the self-assured student who stood practicing in front of the mirror last night?

You are a victim of **anxiety:** You have a feeling of uneasiness and apprehension about an event because you're not sure what its outcome will be. This feeling is accompanied by a variety of physiological symptoms, including a rapid heartbeat, increased perspiration, and muscular tension (e.g., a "knot" or "butterflies" in the stomach). Anxiety is similar to fear, but different in one important respect: Although we are usually *afraid* of something in particular (a roaring lion, a lightning storm, or the bogeymen under the bed), we usually don't know exactly why we're *anxious*. And it's difficult to deal with anxiety when we can't pinpoint its cause.

State Anxiety Versus Trait Anxiety

How is the concept of *threat* different from the concept of *challenge*?

Almost everyone is anxious at one time or another. Many students become anxious just before a test they know is going to be difficult, and most get nervous when they have to give a prepared speech in front of their classmates. Such temporary feelings of anxiety are instances of **state anxiety.** State anxiety is often elicited by a **threat** of some sort—by a situation in which students believe that they have little or no chance of succeeding (Combs, Richards, & Richards, 1976; Csikszentmihalyi & Nakamura, 1989; Deci & Ryan, 1992).

But some students are anxious a good part of the time, even when the situation is not a particularly dangerous or threatening one. For example, some students may get excessively nervous even before very easy exams, and others may be so anxious about mathematics that they can't concentrate on the simplest math assignment. When an individual shows a pattern of responding with anxiety even in nonthreatening situations, we have a case of **trait anxiety.** It is our trait-anxious students whose performance is most hampered by anxiety and for whom we may have to take extra steps to convince them that they can succeed at classroom tasks.

How Anxiety Affects Classroom Performance

Imagine, for a moment, that you are not at all anxious—not even the teeniest bit—about your grade in Professor Carberry's psychoceramics class. Without any anxiety at all, will you study for Carberry's tests? Will you turn in the assigned research papers? If you have no anxiety whatsoever, you might not even buy the textbook or go to class. And you probably won't get a very good grade in your psychoceramics class.

Did you previously believe that *any* amount of anxiety is detrimental? If so, have you now revised your thinking about anxiety's effects?

A small amount of anxiety often improves performance: It is **facilitating anxiety.** A little anxiety gets people moving in the directions they need to move to succeed: It makes them go to class, read the textbook, do assignments, and study for exams. It also makes them approach their classwork carefully, thinking about their responses in a thoughtful and reflective fashion, rather than responding too quickly and impulsively (Shipman & Shipman, 1985). Yet too much anxiety often interferes with effective performance: It is **debilitating anxiety.** Excessive anxiety distracts people and interferes with their attention to the task at hand.

At what point does anxiety stop facilitating and begin debilitating performance? In general, very easy tasks—things students can do almost without thinking (e.g., running)—are facilitated by high levels of anxiety. But more difficult tasks—those that require considerable thought and effort—are best performed with only a small or moderate level of anxiety (Bloom & Broder, 1950; Kirkland, 1971; Yerkes & Dodson, 1908). An excessive level of anxiety in difficult situations can interfere with several things critical for successful learning and performance. More specifically, excessively anxious students are likely to have trouble:

- Paying attention to what they need to learn

- Processing information effectively—for example, by engaging in meaningful learning, organization, or elaboration

- Demonstrating the skills and behaviors they have already learned (Covington, 1992; Dusek, 1980; Eysenck, 1992; R. G. Green, 1980; Mueller, 1980; Tobias, 1980; Wine, 1980)

Students are especially likely to have such difficulties when classroom tasks are difficult or complex or when they place heavy demands on either working memory or long-term memory (Eysenck, 1992; Mueller, 1980; Tobias, 1980, 1985).

As you might expect, highly anxious students tend to achieve at levels lower than those at which they are capable of achieving; in other words, they are underachievers (Gaudry & Spielberger, 1971; K. T. Hill, 1984; Tobias, 1980). Excessive anxiety interferes most with such complex classroom activities as learning new concepts, solving problems, and thinking creatively (Levitt, 1967; McLeod & Adams, 1989; Ruebush, 1963; S. B. Sarason, 1972). Highly anxious students are often so preoccupied about doing poorly that they simply can't get their minds on the task they need to accomplish (Eccles & Wigfield, 1985; Wine, 1980).

When asking students to perform difficult tasks, encourage them to do their best, but don't make them unnecessarily anxious about their performance.

Sources of Anxiety

Under what circumstances are our students likely to experience debilitating anxiety? Some common sources of anxiety in school-age children and adolescents are these:

- **Physical appearance**—for example, students may be concerned about being too fat or thin or about reaching puberty either earlier or later than their classmates

- **A new situation**—for example, students may experience uncertainty when moving to a new community or making the transition from elementary school to junior high

- **Academic tasks that have previously been associated with failure**—for example, students may be anxious about studying mathematics because of past difficulties with math

- **Judgment or evaluation by others**—for example, students may be worried about being liked and accepted by classmates or about receiving a low grade from a teacher

- **Classroom tests**—for example, students may panic at the mere thought of having to take an exam

Difficult tasks are best performed with only a small or moderate level of anxiety.

- **The future**—for example, adolescents may worry about how they will make a living after they graduate from high school

- **Any situation in which self-esteem is threatened**—for example, students may feel anxious when they perform a task awkwardly or incorrectly in front of others (Caron, 1963; Covington, 1992; Eccles & Midgley, 1989; Eccles & Wigfield, 1985; Harter, 1992; Harter et al., 1992; N. J. King & Ollendick, 1989; Phelan et al., 1994; B. N. Phillips, Pitcher, Worsham, & Miller, 1980; S. B. Sarason, 1972; Spielberger, 1966; Stipek, 1993; Stodolsky et al., 1991; Vernon, 1969; Wigfield & Meese, 1988; Wine, 1980)

As we discovered in our discussion of behaviorism in Chapter 9, students may sometimes develop feelings of anxiety about particular stimuli through the process of classical conditioning. For example, a student may become especially anxious about mathematics if mathematics has often been associated with failure and frustration. A student may become anxious about taking classroom tests if previous testing situations have been connected with shame and humiliation. As teachers, then, we must make an exceptional effort to ensure that our students do *not* experience important classroom activities under anxiety-arousing circumstances, at least not on a regular basis.

Keeping Students' Anxiety at a Facilitative Level

Reduce the uncertainty of the classroom environment by communicating your expectations for student performance clearly and concretely.

Reduce students' debilitating anxiety by enhancing their self-efficacy.

As teachers, we probably can't eliminate all sources of anxiety for our students; such things as physical appearance, acceptance by peers, and students' future circumstances are often beyond our control. Nevertheless, there are several courses of action we can take to keep students' anxiety about classroom tasks and activities at a productive and facilitative level. For one thing, we can reduce the uncertainty of the classroom environment by communicating our expectations for students' performance clearly and concretely. Highly anxious students, in particular, are likely to perform better in a well-structured classroom, one in which expectations for academic achievement and social behavior are explicitly laid out (Dowaliby & Schumer, 1973; Grimes & Allinsmith, 1970; P. S. Klein, 1975; Stipek, 1993; Tobias, 1977).

In addition, we must make sure our students have a reasonable chance of success and give them reasons to believe that they can succeed with effort; in other words, we must make sure they have high self-efficacy about classroom tasks. With this point in mind, we should:

- Set realistic expectations for performance, taking such factors as students' ability and prior performance level into account

- Match the level of instruction to students' cognitive levels and capabilities—for example, by using concrete materials to teach mathematics to students not yet capable of abstract thought

- Allow students to proceed at their own pace through the curriculum

- Teach strategies (e.g., effective study skills) that enhance learning and performance

- Provide supplementary sources of support for learning subject matter (e.g., additional practice or individual tutoring) until mastery is attained

- Provide feedback about specific behaviors, rather than global evaluations of students' performance

- Allow students to correct errors so that no single mistake is ever a "fatal" one (Brophy, 1986; McCoy, 1990; I. G. Sarason, 1980; Stipek, 1993; Tryon, 1980; Wine, 1980)

Obviously, students' past successes and failures will affect the extent to which they feel anxious about classroom tasks. It appears, however, that the effect of any particular success or failure will depend on how students *interpret* that outcome. Different students often interpret their successes and failures very differently, as we shall see now in our exploration of attribution theory.

INTO THE CLASSROOM

Keeping Students' Anxiety at a Facilitative Level

Be aware of situations in which students are especially likely to be anxious, and take steps to reduce their anxiety on those occasions.

> The day before students are scheduled to take a standardized college aptitude test, their teacher consults the test manual. In accordance with the manual's recommendation, she tells her students, "The best way to prepare for the test is to get a good night's sleep and eat a good breakfast in the morning. As you take the test tomorrow, you certainly want to do the very best that you can do. But keep in mind that you aren't expected to know the answers to *all* of the questions. If you find a question you cannot answer, just skip it and go on to the next one."

Develop classroom routines that help create a comfortable and somewhat predictable work environment.

> An elementary teacher has a list of classroom "chores"—getting a lunch count, feeding the fish, handing out paper, and so on—that are assigned to individual students on a rotating basis.

Communicate expectations for student performance clearly and concretely.

> A high school history teacher begins a unit on World War II this way: "We will focus on the major battles that contributed to the Allied Forces' victory. As you read your textbook, look for reasons why certain battles played a role in the war's final outcome. I will *not* expect you to memorize all the details—dates, generals, numbers of troops, and so on—of every single battle."

Make sure students have a reasonable chance of success and give them reasons to believe that they can succeed with effort.

> A science teacher describes an upcoming test. "On the tests you've taken so far this year, you've only had to describe the basic principles of chemistry we've studied. But on the next test, I'm going to ask you to apply what you know about chemistry to brand new situations and problems. Because this will be something new for you, I'll give you several practice test questions this week. I'll also give you two chances to take the test. If you don't do well the first time, we'll work together on your trouble spots, and then you can take the test again."

■   EXPERIENCING FIRSTHAND
Carberry and Seville #1

1. Professor Carberry has just returned the first set of exams, scored and graded, in your advanced psychoceramics class. You discover that you've gotten one of the few high test scores in the class—an A−. Why did you do so well when most of your classmates did poorly? On a piece of scrap paper, jot down several possible explanations as to why you might have received a high grade in Carberry's class.

2. An hour later, you get the results of the first test in Professor Barbara F. Seville's sociocosmetology class, and you learn that you've *failed* it! Why did you do so poorly? Jot down several possible reasons for your F in Seville's class.

3. You will be taking second exams in both psychoceramics and sociocosmetology in about three weeks' time. How much will you study for each exam?   ■

Here are some possible explanations for your A− in Carberry's class:

*   You studied hard.

*   You're smart.

*   Psychoceramics just comes naturally to you.

*   You were lucky. Carberry asked the right questions; if he'd asked different questions, you might not have done so well.

*   Carberry likes you, so he gave you a good grade even though you didn't know what you were talking about.

*   All those hours you spent in Carberry's office, asking questions about psychoceramics and requesting copies of the articles he's written (which you never actually read), really paid off.

And here are some possibilities as to why you failed the exam in Seville's class:

*   You didn't study enough.

*   You didn't study the right things.

*   You didn't feel well when you took the test.

*   The student next to you was sick, and the constant coughing and wheezing distracted you.

*   You were unlucky. Seville asked the wrong questions; if she'd asked different questions, you would have done better.

*   You're stupid.

*   You've never been very good at sociocosmetology.

*   It was a bad test: The questions were ambiguous and tested knowledge of trivial facts.

*   Seville hates you and so gave you a poor grade out of spite.

The amount of time you spend studying for your upcoming exams will, to some extent, depend on how you've interpreted your earlier performances—your success on Carberry's exam, on the one hand, and your failure on Seville's exam, on the other. For example, let's consider your A− on Professor Carberry's exam. If you think you did well because you studied hard, you will probably spend a lot of time studying for the second test as well. If you think you did well because you're smart or because you're a whiz at psychoceramics, you may not study quite as much. If you believe that your success was a matter of luck, you may not study much at all, but you may consider wearing your lucky sweater on the next exam day. And if you think the A− was a function of how much Carberry likes you, you may decide that time spent flattering him is more important than time spent studying.

Now let's consider your failing grade on Professor Seville's exam. Once again, the reasons you identify for that failure will influence the ways in which you prepare for her second exam—if, in fact, you prepare at all. If you believe that you didn't study enough or didn't study the right things, you may spend more time studying the next time. If you think your poor grade was due to a temporary situation—you were ill, the student sitting next to you distracted you, or Seville asked the wrong questions—then you may study in much the same way as you did before, hoping and praying that you'll do better than before. And if you believe that your failure was due to your stupidity, your ineptitude in sociocosmetology, Seville's dislike of you, or the fact that she writes lousy tests, then you may study even less than you did the first time. After all, what good will it do to study when your poor test performance is beyond your control?

The various causal explanations for success and failure I have just described are called **attributions.** The attributions that people assign to the things that happen to them—their beliefs about *what causes what*—do indeed guide their future behavior. The theoretical examination of these attributions and their influence on behavior is known as **attribution theory** (e.g., Dweck, 1986; Weiner, 1984, 1986, 1994).

Different attributions for failure lead to different behaviors on future occasions.

We should note here that students' attributions are an example of knowledge construction in action. Students use the information they receive to construct their understanding of an event. This understanding will include not only their interpretation of *what* happened but also *why* it happened; thus, it will include their attributions regarding what caused what.

Analyzing Attributions

Our students are apt to form a variety of attributions about the causes of classroom events; they will have beliefs about why they do well or poorly on tests and assignments, why they are popular with their classmates or have trouble making friends, why they are skilled athletes or total klutzes, and so on. They may attribute their school successes and failures to such factors as ability (how smart or proficient they are), effort (how hard they tried), other people (how well the teacher taught or how much their classmates like them), task difficulty (how "easy" or "hard" something is), luck, mood, illness, fatigue, or physical appearance (e.g., Schunk, 1990). These various attributions differ from one another in at least three ways—locus, stability, and controllability (Weiner, 1984, 1986):*

1. *Locus ("place"): Internal versus external.* Students sometimes attribute the causes of events to *internal* things—to factors within themselves. Thinking that a good grade is due to your own hard work and believing that a poor grade is due to your lack of ability are examples of internal attributions. At other times, students attribute events to *external* things—to factors outside themselves. Concluding that you received a scholarship because you "lucked out" and interpreting a classmate's scowl as being due to her bad mood (rather than to anything you yourself might have done to deserve it) are examples of external attributions.

2. *Stability: Stable versus unstable.* Sometimes students believe that events are due to *stable* factors—to things that probably won't change much in the near future. For example, if you believe that you do well in science because of your intelligence or that you have trouble making friends because you're overweight, then you are attributing events to stable, relatively unchangeable causes. But sometimes students instead believe that events are the result of *unstable* factors—to things that can change from one time to the next. Thinking that winning a tennis game was all a matter of luck and believing that you got a bad test grade because you were tired when you took the test are examples of attributions involving unstable factors.

3. *Controllability: Controllable versus uncontrollable.* On some occasions, students attribute events to *controllable* factors—to things they themselves can influence and change. For example, if you believe that a classmate invited you to his birthday party because you always smile and say nice things to him, and if you think that you probably failed a test simply because you didn't study the right things, then you are attributing these events to controllable factors. On other occasions, students attribute events to *uncontrollable* factors—to things over which they themselves have no influence. For example, if you think that you were chosen for the lead in the school play only because the drama teacher likes you or that you played a lousy game of basketball because you were sick, then you are attributing these events to uncontrollable factors.

This dimension is sometimes called *locus of control*.

Intelligence is not necessarily a stable, unchanging characteristic (see Chapter 4), yet many students perceive it to be so (Dweck & Leggett, 1988; Ruble, 1980; Weiner, 1994).

---

* Weiner has actually identified five different dimensions of attributions; see Weiner (1984) for more details.

In Table 11–2, you can find common student attributions analyzed in terms of their locus, stability, and controllability.

You might be thinking to yourself that "ability can change with practice, so is unstable and controllable" or that "teachers' attitudes toward students often depend on how students behave in the classroom and so are really due to internal, unstable, and controllable factors." Perhaps you are right, but keep in mind that students' *beliefs* about the locus, stability, and controllability of their attributions are what affect their future behavior, not the reality of the situation.

Generally speaking, people tend to attribute their successes to internal causes (e.g., high ability, hard work) and their failures to external causes (e.g., luck, the behavior of others) (H. W. Marsh, 1986, 1990a). By patting themselves on the back for the things they do well and putting the blame elsewhere for poor performance, they are

COMPARE/CONTRAST

Table 11–2 Analyzing Various Student Attributions

SUCCESS OR FAILURE ATTRIBUTED TO:	LOCUS	STABILITY	CONTROLLABILITY	EXAMPLES OF ATTRIBUTIONS FOR SUCCESS AND FAILURE
Inherited "ability"	Internal	Stable	Uncontrollable	"I have talent." "I wasn't cut out for this."
Personality	Internal	Stable	Uncontrollable	"I'm naturally outgoing." "I'm a very anxious person."
Effort	Internal	Unstable	Controllable	"I worked really hard to improve my skill." "I didn't study long enough."
Study strategy	Internal	Unstable	Controllable	"The mnemonics I used really helped." "I need to try a different approach."
Health/energy level	Internal	Unstable	Uncontrollable	"I was feeling really good that day." "I had the flu when I tried out."
Task difficulty	External	Stable	Uncontrollable	"Math is easy." "The test was too hard."
Teacher's attitudes	External	Stable	Uncontrollable	"My teacher helps me when I have trouble." "My teacher doesn't like me."
Luck	External	Unstable	Uncontrollable	"This is my lucky day." "You never know when something bad will happen to you."

able to maintain positive self-concepts (Clifford, 1990; Paris & Byrnes, 1989). Attributions don't always reflect the true state of affairs, however; for example, a student may blame a low test grade on a "tricky" test or an "unfair" teacher when that low grade is really due to the student's own lack of effort or poor study skills (e.g., Horgan, 1990).

Be on the lookout for inaccurate attributions.

If students' attributions regarding the reasons for their failures are inaccurate, and especially if students erroneously attribute their failures to stable and uncontrollable causes, they are unlikely to change their future behaviors in ways that will lead to greater success. Let's look more closely at the ways in which students' attributions influence both their thoughts and their behaviors.

How Attributions Influence Cognition and Behavior

Attributions influence several aspects of cognition and behavior:

Before you read ahead, can you make your own predictions about how attributions might affect each of these?

- Emotional reactions to success and failure

- Expectations for future success or failure

- Expenditure of effort

- Help-seeking behavior

- Classroom performance

- Future choices

- Self-efficacy

Emotional Reactions to Success and Failure

Naturally, students will be happy when they succeed. But will they also feel *proud* of their accomplishments? Students will have feelings of pride and satisfaction about their successes only when they attribute those successes to internal causes—that is, to something they themselves have done. When they instead believe that their successes are due to the actions of another person or to some other outside force, they are apt to feel grateful, rather than proud (Weiner, Russell, & Lerman, 1978, 1979).

Along a similar vein, students will usually feel a certain amount of sadness after a failure. They will also feel guilty or ashamed if they believe that their failures are due to internal causes—for example, to their own lack of ability or effort. But when they instead believe that their failures are due to external causes—to events and people outside themselves—they are likely to be angry about those perceived causes (Weiner et al., 1978, 1979).

Expectations for Future Success or Failure

When students attribute their successes and failures to stable factors, they will expect their future performance to be similar to their current performance. In other words, successful students will anticipate that they will continue to succeed, and failing students will believe that they will always be failures. In contrast, when students attribute their successes and failures to *un*stable factors such as effort or luck, then their current success rate will have less influence on their expectation for future success (Dweck, 1978; Fennema, 1987; Schunk, 1990; Weiner, 1986). The most optimistic students—

those who have the highest expectations for future success—are the ones who attribute their successes to stable factors such as innate ability and their failures to unstable factors such as lack of effort or inappropriate strategies (Eccles [Parsons], 1983; Fennema, 1987; Schunk, 1990; Weiner, 1984).

Here we should note a difference between boys and girls that appears consistently in research studies (Deaux, 1984; Durkin, 1987; Dweck, 1978; Fennema, 1987; Huston, 1983; Stipek & Gralinski, 1990). Boys are more likely to attribute their successes to ability and their failures to lack of effort, thus having the attitude that *I know I can do this because I have the ability.* But girls show the reverse pattern: They attribute their successes to effort and their failures to lack of ability, believing that *I don't know whether I can keep on doing it, because I'm not very good at this type of thing.* We see this difference between boys and girls even when their previous levels of achievement are the same, and we are especially likely to see it for such stereotypically "male" domains as mathematics or sports (Eccles & Jacobs, 1986; Eccles et al., 1989; Stipek, 1984). As a result, boys set higher expectations for themselves than girls, particularly in traditionally masculine activities.

Have you observed this difference in the males and females you know? Can you think of individuals who are exceptions to the pattern?

Expenditure of Effort

When students believe that their failures are due to their own lack of effort—that they do have the ability to succeed if they try hard enough—they are likely to try harder in future situations and to persist in the face of difficulty (Dweck, 1975; Feather, 1982; Rowe, 1983; Weiner, 1984). But when students instead attribute failure to lack of innate ability (they couldn't do it even if they tried), they give up easily and sometimes can't even perform tasks they have previously accomplished successfully (Dweck, 1978; Eccles [Parsons], 1983).

Help-Seeking Behavior

Students who believe that success is a result of their own doing—those who attribute success to internal and controllable causes—are more inclined to engage in behaviors that facilitate future learning. These students are more likely to seek their teacher's assistance if they don't understand course material; they are also more likely to attend extra help sessions when they need them (R. Ames, 1983; R. Ames & Lau, 1982). In contrast, students who believe that their learning successes and failures are beyond their own control are unlikely to seek the help they need.

Classroom Performance

We find consistent correlations between students' attributions and their academic achievement. For example, students who expect to succeed get better grades than students of equal ability who expect to fail (Battle, 1966; Eccles [Parsons], 1983). Students who expect to succeed are more likely to approach problem-solving tasks in a logical, systematic manner; students who expect to fail are apt to solve problems through random trial and error or memorize problem solutions at a rote, nonmeaningful level (Tyler, 1958).

Future Choices

As you might expect, students whose attributions lead them to expect success in a particular subject area are more likely to pursue that area—for example, by enrolling in more courses in the same discipline (Eccles [Parsons], 1984; Stipek & Gralinski, 1990;

Weiner, 1986). Students who believe that their chances for future success in an activity are slim will avoid that activity whenever they can. Naturally, when students don't continue to pursue an activity, they can't possibly get better at it.

Self-Efficacy

Young children, especially those in kindergarten and first grade, tend to believe that they have the ability to do well in school if they expend a reasonable amount of effort (Covington, 1992; Dweck & Elliott, 1983; Stipek & Gralinski, 1990). As students get older, many of them begin to attribute their successes and failures to ability—in other words, to something they perceive to be fairly stable and beyond their control (Covington, 1992; Paris & Byrnes, 1989). If these students are usually successful at school tasks, then they will have high self-efficacy about such tasks. But if, instead, they experience frequent failure with their schoolwork, and especially if they attribute this failure to low ability rather than to lack of effort or to poor study strategies, they may develop low self-efficacy concerning their competence in academic subjects (Dweck, 1986; Dweck & Elliott, 1983; Eccles [Parsons], 1983; Schunk, 1990). Secondary students are particularly discouraged by their failure experiences, as are students with a history of learning problems (Eccles & Wigfield, 1985; Pressley, Borkowski, & Schneider, 1987; Stipek & Gralinski, 1990).

Why do different students attribute the same events to different causes? For example, why does one student believe that a failure is merely a temporary setback due to her own lack of effort, whereas another student believes that the failure is due to her lack of ability and so an ominous sign of failures to come, and still another believes that the same failure is the result of the teacher's capricious and unpredictable actions? By looking at factors affecting the development of different attributions, we can identify ways in which to help our students form more productive and optimistic interpretations of their successes and failures.

Older students and those with a history of learning problems are more likely to attribute their failures to lack of innate ability. Why might this be so?

Factors Influencing the Development of Attributions

Researchers have identified at least four factors that seem to influence the attributions that students form:

- The pattern of past successes and failures
- The degree to which successes and failures have been followed by reinforcement or punishment
- Adults' expectations for students' future performance
- Adults' messages regarding their own attributions for students' successes and failures

These factors are reflected in the four conditions for promoting productive attributions that are described in Table 11–3. Let's look more closely at each factor and its implications for the things we do as teachers.

Past Successes and Failures

Students' attributions are partly the result of their previous success and failure experiences (J. D. Klein, 1990; Paris & Byrnes, 1989; Schunk, 1990; Stipek, 1993). Students

Table 11–3   Conditions That Promote Productive Student Attributions

CONDITION	EDUCATIONAL IMPLICATION	EXAMPLE
A history of success on tasks when sufficient effort has been exerted	We should scaffold students' attempts to master classroom subject matter so that they experience success far more often than failure.	When teaching long division, a teacher first gives his students simple problems that enable them to practice the procedure. As they show increasing proficiency, he increases the difficulty of future problems gradually enough that students continue to carry out the division process successfully.
Reinforcement for success, but little if any punishment for failure.	We should provide extrinsic reinforcers for success if students have little intrinsic motivation to learn, and we should encourage students to use their mistakes to help themselves improve.	When high school students use a computer spreadsheet correctly, their teacher shows her pleasure and approval. But when a number of students obtain erroneous results with their spreadsheets, she assigns a cooperative group activity in which each group tries to determine what procedural errors might have led to each set of results.
High expectations for students' performance	We should aim high in terms of what we want to accomplish during the school year, and we should insist that our students do likewise.	When middle school students express their apprehension about a challenging writing assignment they have just been given, their teacher assures them that he will help them develop the skills they need to complete the assignment successfully.
Messages that attribute students' successes and failures to internal and primarily controllable factors	We should interpret students' successes as being partly the result of such controllable factors as effort and effective strategies and partly the result of a relatively long-term and stable ability. We should interpret students' failures as being primarily the result of controllable and changeable factors.	When the girls' soccer team loses its first match of the season by several points, the coach announces that upcoming practices will focus on developing a more aggressive offense. When the team wins its next match two weeks later, she says, "See what a difference good strategies can make? I think you girls have the ability to make the conference playoffs this year. Let's shoot for them, OK?"

who usually succeed when they give a task their best shot are likely to believe that success is due to such internal factors as effort or high ability. Those who frequently fail despite their best efforts are likely to believe that success is due to something beyond their control—perhaps to an ability they don't possess or to such external factors as luck or a teacher's arbitrary judgment. Here we find yet another reason to promote student success on a regular basis: in doing so, we also promote more internal, and thus more productive, attributions.

Facilitate student success as one way of promoting internal attributions.

Reinforcement and Punishment

Generally speaking, children are more likely to attribute events to internal, controllable causes when adults reinforce their successes but don't punish their failures. Conversely, children are more likely to make external attributions when adults punish failures and ignore successes (Katkovsky, Crandall, & Good, 1967). It appears that our students will be more apt to accept responsibility for their failures if, as teachers, we don't make a big deal out of them.

As we noted in our discussion of behaviorism in Chapter 9, however, there may be times when some form of mild punishment may be necessary for discouraging behaviors that seriously interfere with classroom learning. On such occasions, we must make

Reinforce students' successes, but don't make a big deal of their failures.

Make response-consequence contingencies clear.

response-consequence contingencies clear—for example, by describing unacceptable behaviors in advance and by using punishment in a consistent, predictable fashion. In doing so, we can help students learn that their *own behaviors* lead to desirable and undesirable consequences and that they can therefore influence the events that occur by changing the ways they behave. Hence, we help them develop internal attributions regarding the consequences that befall them and a greater sense of control over classroom events.

Adults' Expectations

Parents and teachers communicate their expectations for students' performance—whether high or low—in a variety of subtle ways. For example, teachers who have high expectations for students' performance are likely to:

- Teach more material

- Teach more difficult material

- Insist on high levels of achievement

- Give students more opportunities to respond to questions

- Rephrase questions when students are having trouble answering them

- Give specific feedback about the strengths and weaknesses of students' responses (Brophy & Good, 1970; H. M. Cooper, 1979; M. J. Harris & Rosenthal, 1985)

In contrast, teachers who hold low expectations for their students often:

- Give students more assistance on tasks than they really need

- Accept poor performance

- Criticize incorrect answers to questions

- Overlook good performance when it occurs

- Fail to encourage students to try new and challenging tasks (Brophy & Good, 1970; H. M. Cooper, 1979; Graham, 1991; Graham & Barker, 1990; Schunk, 1989b)

Minority students with a history of academic failure are especially likely to be the recipients of such low-ability signals (Graham, 1990).

Reflect reasonably high expectations for student performance in your behaviors toward students.

To some extent, parents' and teachers' expectations for students are related to students' past performances. Yet even when several students all have the same history of success and failure, adults may hold different expectations for each of these students (perhaps because of differences in students' classroom behavior, socioeconomic status, or gender), and such expectations, in turn, lead to different student attributions and varying levels of achievement (Brophy & Good, 1970; Eccles & Wigfield, 1985; Eccles [Parsons] et al., 1983; C. B. Murray & Jackson, 1982/1983; Palardy, 1969; D. K. Yee & Eccles, 1988). For example, when teachers communicate their belief that students are incapable of mastering subject matter, those students are likely to attribute their failures to low ability and may therefore conclude that there is little to be gained by trying harder. Furthermore, as we discovered in Chapter 4, when teachers expect students *not* to do well, students perform at lower levels than they would otherwise—a self-fulfilling prophecy.

Teachers who hold high expectations for their students are more likely to give specific feedback about the strengths and weaknesses of students' responses.

Adults' Messages Regarding Attributions

Once students have performed—once they've either succeeded or failed in an activity—the adults around them may interpret that performance in a variety of ways. Consider these adult interpretations of a student's success:

- "You did it! You're so smart!"

- "That's wonderful. Your hard work has really paid off, hasn't it?"

- "You've done very well. It's clear that you really know how to study."

- "Terrific! This is certainly your lucky day!"

And now consider these interpretations of a student's failure:

- "Hmmm, maybe this just isn't something you're good at. Perhaps we should try a different activity."

- "Why don't you practice a little more and then try again?"

- "Let's see whether we can come up with some study strategies that might work better for you."

- "Maybe you're just having a bad day."

All of these are well-intended comments, presumably designed to make a student feel good. But notice the different attributions they imply. In some cases, the student's success or failure is attributed to uncontrollable ability—that is, to being smart or not "good at" something. In other cases, success or failure is attributed to controllable (and

How are teacher expectations and teacher attributions likely to be related? For example, if a teacher expects a student to fail, how is he or she likely to interpret a successful performance? Conversely, how is a teacher who expects a student to succeed likely to interpret a failure?

therefore changeable) student behaviors—that is, to hard work or lack of practice, or to the use of effective or ineffective study strategies. In still other cases, the student's success is attributed to external, uncontrollable causes—that is, to a lucky break or a bad day. Students' attributions for their own successes and failures are often similar to the attributions that parents and teachers assign to those successes and failures (Dweck, Davidson, Nelson, & Enna, 1978; Lueptow, 1984; Parsons, Adler, & Kaczala, 1982; Schunk, 1982; D. K. Yee & Eccles, 1988).

Attribute students' successes to a combination of high ability and such controllable factors as effort and learning strategies; attribute their failures solely to factors that are controllable and easily changed.

As teachers, we must be careful about the attributions we assign to student performance. Probably the optimal state of affairs is that we attribute success partly to a relatively stable ability (thus promoting optimism about future success) and partly to such controllable factors as effort and learning strategies (thereby underscoring the fact that continued success will only come as a result of hard work). When considering possible causes for failure, however, we should focus primarily on factors that are internal, unstable, and controllable; thus, attributions for failures should focus on effort and learning strategies, rather than on low ability (which students are likely to believe is stable and uncontrollable) or external factors.

We can communicate appropriate attributions and optimistic expectations for student performance through such statements as these:

- "You've done very well. Obviously you're good at this, and you've been trying very hard to get better."

- "Your project shows a lot of talent and a lot of hard work."

- "The more you practice, the better you will get."

- "Perhaps you need to study a little bit more next time. And let me give you some suggestions on how you might study a little differently, too."

Studies have shown that, when students' failures are consistently attributed to ineffective learning strategies or lack of effort, rather than to low ability or uncontrollable external factors, and when new strategies or increased effort *do* in fact produce success, then students work harder, persist longer in the face of failure, and seek help when they need it (Dweck, 1975; Dweck & Elliott, 1983; Eccles & Wigfield, 1985; Graham, 1991; Schunk, 1990). Yet we must be careful when we attribute either success or failure to a student's effort, as we shall see now.

When attributions to effort can backfire. Although attributions to effort are often beneficial, there are at least two occasions when such attributions can actually be counterproductive. To see what I mean, try the next exercise.

■ EXPERIENCING FIRSTHAND
Carberry and Seville #2

1. Imagine that Professor Carberry wants you to learn to spell the word *psychoceramics* correctly. He gives you ten minutes of intensive training in the spelling of the word. He then praises you profusely when you are able to spell it correctly. In which of the following ways would you be most likely to respond?

    a. You are delighted that he approves of your performance.

  b. You proudly show him that you've also learned how to spell *sociocosmetology*.

  c. You wonder, "Hey, is this all he thinks I can do?"

2. Now imagine that you drop by Professor Seville's office to find out why you did so poorly on her sociocosmetology exam. Professor Seville is warm and supportive, suggesting that you simply try harder next time. But the fact is, you tried as hard as you could the *first* time. Which one of the following conclusions would you be most likely to draw?

  a. You need to try even harder next time.

  b. You need to exert the same amount of effort the next time and just keep your fingers crossed that you'll make some lucky guesses.

  c. Perhaps you just weren't meant to be a sociocosmetologist. ■

Research results tell us that you probably answered *c* to both questions. Let's first consider the situation in which Carberry spent ten minutes teaching you how to spell *psychoceramics*. When students succeed at a very easy task and are then praised for their effort, they may get the unintended message that their teacher doesn't have much confidence in their ability (Barker & Graham, 1987; Graham, 1991; L. Katz, 1993; Schunk, 1989b; Stipek, 1993). Attributing students' successes to effort is likely to be beneficial only when students have, in fact, exerted a great deal of effort.

Attribute students' successes to effort only when they have actually exerted that effort.

And now consider the second scenario, the one in which Seville encouraged you to try harder even though you had already studied as hard as you could for the first exam. When students fail at a task at which they've expended a great deal of effort and are then told that they didn't try hard enough, they are likely to conclude that they simply don't have the ability to perform the task successfully (Alderman, 1990; Curtis & Graham, 1991). Attributing students' failures to lack of effort is likely to be helpful only when they really haven't given classroom tasks their best shot.

Attribute students' failures to *lack* of effort only when they *haven't* exerted sufficient effort.

Rather than attributing the failure of hardworking students to lack of effort, we should probably attribute it to lack of effective strategies (Clifford, 1984; Curtis & Graham, 1991; Pressley, Borkowski, & Schneider, 1987). As we discovered in our discussion of metacognition in Chapter 8, students can and do acquire more effective learning and study strategies over time, especially when they are specifically trained to use these strategies. By teaching effective strategies, not only do we promote our students' academic success, but we also promote their beliefs that they can control that success (Weinstein, Hagen, & Meyer, 1991).

Attribute the failures of hardworking students to lack of effective strategies and then help them acquire such strategies.

For reasons we've just identified, different students may interpret the same events in very different ways. Over time, students gradually develop predictable patterns of attributions and expectations for their future performance. Some remain optimistic, confident that they can master new tasks and succeed in a variety of endeavors. But others, either unsure of their own chances for success or else convinced that they *can't* succeed, begin to display a growing sense of futility. Psychologists have characterized this difference among students as being one of a *mastery orientation* versus *learned helplessness*.

Distinguishing Between a Mastery Orientation and Learned Helplessness

Consider these two students, keeping in mind that *their actual academic ability is the same:*

- Jared is an enthusiastic, energetic learner. He seems to enjoy working hard at school activities and takes obvious pleasure in doing well. He is always looking for a challenge and especially likes to solve the "brain teaser" problems that his teacher assigns as extra credit work each day. He can't always solve the problems, but he takes failure in stride and is eager for more problems the following day.

- Jerry is an anxious, fidgety student. He doesn't seem to have much confidence in his ability to accomplish school tasks successfully. In fact, he is always underestimating what he can do: Even when he has succeeded, he doubts that he can do it again. He seems to prefer filling out drill-and-practice worksheets that help him practice skills he's already mastered, rather than attempting new tasks and problems. As for those daily brain teasers, he sometimes takes a stab at them, but he gives up quickly if the answer isn't obvious.

Attributions play a significant role in the approach that students take toward the activities and challenges they encounter every day in the classroom. Students like Jared attribute their accomplishments to their own abilities and efforts: They have an *I can do it* attitude known as a **mastery orientation.** Students like Jerry instead attribute successes to outside and uncontrollable factors and believe that their failures reflect lack of ability: They have an *I can't do it* attitude known as **learned helplessness** (Dweck, 1986; Dweck & Licht, 1980; Dweck & Reppucci, 1973; Eccles & Wigfield, 1985; C. J. Wood et al., 1990). Obviously, students with a mastery orientation have a higher sense of self-efficacy about classroom tasks than students with learned helplessness.

Even though students with a mastery orientation and those with learned helplessness may have equal ability initially, those with a mastery orientation behave in ways that lead to higher achievement over the long run: They set ambitious goals, seek challenging situations, and persist in the face of failure. Students feeling learned helplessness behave very differently: Because they underestimate their own ability, they set goals they can easily accomplish, avoid the challenges likely to maximize their learning and growth, and respond to failure in counterproductive ways that almost guarantee future failure as well. These and other differences between students with a mastery orientation and those with learned helplessness are presented in Table 11–4.

If you compare Table 11–4 with Table 11–1 (see p. 488), you should notice several parallels between students with a mastery orientation and those with learning goals; for example, both groups prefer challenges rather than easy tasks, persist in the face of difficulty, and have a healthy attitude about mistakes and failure. And in fact, we can reasonably guess that students with a mastery orientation, because they have higher self-efficacy about classroom tasks, will be those most likely to have learning goals rather than performance goals. As we noted earlier in the chapter, high self-efficacy is one of two essential conditions for intrinsic motivation.

Think of this distinction as a continuum of individual differences, rather than as a complete dichotomy. You might also look at it as a difference between *optimists* and *pessimists* (C. Peterson, 1990; Seligman, 1991).

COMPARE/CONTRAST

Table 11–4   Students with a Mastery Orientation Versus Learned Helplessness

STUDENTS WITH A MASTERY ORIENTATION:	STUDENTS WITH LEARNED HELPLESSNESS:
Have self-confidence	Lack self-confidence
Set high goals for themselves	Set low, easy goals for themselves
Prefer new and challenging tasks	Prefer easy tasks and tasks they have already completed successfully
Strive for success	Try to avoid failure
Believe that prior successes are an indication of high ability and future success	Don't see prior successes as indicative of ability and future success; *do* see prior failures as an indication of future failure
Accurately estimate the number of prior successes	Underestimate prior successes, may even *forget* about them
View failure as a challenge to be met	Define themselves as a "failure" when they fail
Persist when facing difficulty; try to determine the source of difficulty; seek assistance if needed	Become anxious and discouraged when facing difficulty; give up quickly
Increase effort and concentration after failure	Decrease effort and concentration after failure; may withdraw from the task
Take pride in their accomplishments	Don't take pride in their accomplishments because they don't believe that they *caused* them
Achieve at higher levels	Achieve at lower levels

Sources: Diener & Dweck, 1978; Dweck, 1975, 1986; Dweck & Licht, 1980; C. Peterson, 1990; C. Peterson & Barrett, 1987; Seligman, 1991; Wood, Schau, & Fiedler, 1990.

Many of the strategies I've suggested for enhancing self-efficacy—giving competence-promoting feedback, encouraging self-comparison rather than comparison with others, providing a realistic perspective as to what constitutes success, and so on—should promote a mastery orientation as well. Yet we must remember that even when students are highly motivated to learn, they cannot always learn on their own. They should have a variety of resources to which they can turn in times of difficulty—their teacher, of course, and possibly such additional resources as supplementary readings, extra practice sheets, self-instructional computer programs, or outside tutoring (perhaps by classmates, older students, or community volunteers). Our students must have sufficient academic support to believe that *I can do this if I really want to.*

Provide the academic support necessary to help students discover that they can learn successfully.

Promoting Productive Attributions

Communicate high expectations for student performance.

> In September, a high school teacher tells his class, "Next spring, I will ask you to write a fifteen-page research paper. Fifteen pages may seem like a lot now, but in the next few months we will work on the various writing skills you will need to research and write your paper. By April, fifteen pages won't seem like a big deal at all!"

Attribute students' successes to a combination of high ability and controllable factors such as effort and learning strategies.

> In a unit on basketball, a physical education teacher tells his class, "From what I've seen so far, you all have the capability to play a good game of basketball. And it appears that many of you have been practicing your basketball regularly after school."

Attribute students' successes specifically to *effort* only when they have actually exerted that effort.

> A teacher observes that his students complete a particular assignment more quickly and easily than he expected. He briefly acknowledges their success and then moves on to a more challenging task.

Attribute students' failures to factors that are controllable and easily changed.

> A high school student seeks his teacher's advice as to how he might do better in her class. She replies, "I think it's great that you are so involved in school activities. After all, you're an active member of the Student Council, first string center for the football team, and president of the Key Club. But I'm wondering whether all these activities are taking away from your study time at home. You might think about some way to cut back just a little on your extracurricular commitments. Let's look at your weekly schedule of activities and see if we can find some times when you might be able to study."

When students fail despite obvious effort, attribute their failures to lack of effective strategies and then help them acquire such strategies.

> A student in an advanced science class is having difficulty on the teacher's challenging weekly quizzes. She works diligently on her science every night and attends the after-school help sessions her teacher offers on Thursdays, yet to no avail. Her teacher observes that the student is trying to learn the material at a rote level—an ineffective strategy for answering the higher-level questions the quizzes typically ask—and helps the student develop strategies that promote more meaningful learning.

CONSIDERING DIVERSITY IN STUDENT MOTIVATION

In our discussion of motivation in this chapter, we have encountered numerous instances of student diversity. As teachers, we are apt to see differences in our students' interests, in their needs for affiliation and approval, and in the degree to which they experience anxiety about classroom tasks. The extent to which our students have high self-efficacy, learning goals, internal attributions, and a mastery orientation will influence the extent to which they prefer challenges, persist at difficult tasks, and take failure in stride. Let's now consider some of the specific ways in which our students' motivation is likely to vary as a function of age, culture, gender, socioeconomic background, and special educational needs.

Whereas young children are likely to attribute their successes to hard work, adolescents are more likely to attribute success to a relatively stable ability over which they have little or no control.

Age Differences

We are likely to see several developmental differences in student motivation. For one thing, whereas young children often want to gain their teachers' approval, older ones are typically more interested in gaining the approval of their peers (Juvonen & Weiner, 1993). As teachers, we must be sensitive to the fact that students' friends and classmates sometimes disapprove of high academic achievement; for example, we must be careful that we don't draw unnecessary public attention to students' classroom successes, especially at the secondary level.

A second noteworthy developmental change is that students often become less intrinsically motivated, and more *extrinsically* motivated, as they progress through the school years (Harter, 1992). Learning goals may go by the wayside as performance goals become more prevalent, and as a result, students will begin to exhibit a preference for easy rather than challenging tasks (Harter, 1992; Igoe & Sullivan, 1991). Increasingly, students will value activities that they believe will have usefulness for them in their personal and professional lives, and subjects that are not directly applicable will decrease in popularity (Wigfield, 1994).

Emphasize the value of the knowledge and skills students are learning, especially at the secondary level.

Finally, as we noted in our discussion of attribution theory, there are developmental changes in the ways that students interpret success. Elementary students tend to attribute their successes to effort and hard work; therefore, they are likely to work harder if they fail. By adolescence, however, students begin to attribute success and failure more to an ability that is fairly stable and uncontrollable. Effort, for them, becomes a sign of low ability; if they have to exert a great deal of effort when playing a musical instrument, running a race, or solving mathematical word problems, they must not have "what it takes" to be successful in these areas. If, as teachers, we praise adolescents for trying hard, we may inadvertently communicate the message that they have little "natural" ability (Nicholls, 1984). As teachers, we can certainly praise elementary students for effort ("You tried really hard!"), but for secondary students, we may want to make reference to ability ("You're really good at this!") as well as to effort.

At the elementary level, attribute success primarily to effort; at the secondary level, attribute it to ability as well as effort.

Keep in mind that students from minority groups may be especially susceptible to debilitating test anxiety.

Point out the value of students' achievement for their families and communities.

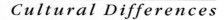

Cultural Differences

We will sometimes see different motivational patterns in students of different cultural backgrounds. For one thing, students from minority groups tend to have more debilitating test anxiety; for example, this is often the case for students of Asian American families (Pang, 1995; B. N. Phillips et al., 1980). With such students, we may need to take extra precautions that classroom tests and other evaluative situations are as relaxed and nonthreatening as we can possibly make them.

We must remember, too, that students from some ethnic groups (e.g., those from many Native American and Hispanic cultures) have especially strong loyalties to their family and may have been raised to achieve for their community, rather than just for themselves as individuals. Motivating statements such as "Think how proud your family will be!" and "If you go to college and get a good education, you can really help your community!" are likely to be especially effective for such students (e.g., Abi-Nader, 1993; Suina & Smolkin, 1994).

Gender Differences

Although in some respects males and females are more similar than they were two or three decades ago (see Chapter 4), we continue to see gender differences in the area of motivation. For example, females are more likely than males to have a high need for affiliation (Block, 1983). Females are also more concerned about doing well in school: They work harder on assignments, earn higher grades, and are more likely to graduate from high school (Halpern, 1992; McCall, 1994). We will typically find more boys than girls among our "underachieving" students—those who are not achieving at levels commensurate with their ability (McCall, 1994).

Despite the fact that females, on the average, have higher school achievement, males have higher long-term aspirations for themselves (e.g., Durkin, 1995). Such high aspirations may be due, in part, to the fact that males interpret their successes and failures in ways that yield greater optimism about what they are ultimately capable of accomplishing. Females are making some headway in this area; for example, girls growing up now are more likely to have career plans than girls who, like me, grew up in the 1950s and 1960s (e.g., A. J. C. King, 1989). Nevertheless, many of the girls in our classrooms—especially those in some ethnic groups—will aspire only to traditional "female" roles (Durkin, 1995; Olneck, 1995; S. M. Taylor, 1994).

Help boys see the relationship between their classroom performance and their long-term goals. Encourage girls to consider a wide range of career options.

As we work to encourage high levels of motivation in all of our students, we may want to focus our efforts in somewhat different directions for males and females. For boys, we may need to stress the relationship of high classroom achievement to their own long-term goals. For girls, we may need to provide extra encouragement to consider a wide variety of career options, including many that they previously have ruled out as being options only for their male counterparts.

Socioeconomic Differences

As we learned in Chapter 4, students from lower-income families are among those most likely to be at risk for failing and dropping out of school. A pattern of failure may start quite early for many lower-income students, especially if they have not had the early experiences (e.g., exposure to children's literature, visits to zoos and museums) upon which school learning often builds.

As teachers, how can we promote the motivation to learn in students from lower socioeconomic groups? One key strategy is to make school activities relevant to their own lives and experiences (Alderman, 1990; Alexander et al., 1994; Hidi & McLaren, 1990; Kintsch, 1980; Knapp et al., 1990; Tobias, 1994). As we present new material, we should draw on the knowledge that students are likely to have, thereby increasing the likelihood of meaningful learning; for instance, we might keep in mind that these students are more likely to have encountered dogs and cats than elephants and zebras, more likely to have seen a grocery store or city park than a dairy farm or airport. We should also relate classroom tasks and activities to the specific, day-to-day needs and interests of our students; for example, we should teach academic subject matter within the context of authentic activities as often as we can.

When working with students from lower socioeconomic backgrounds, we should also remember the two essential conditions for intrinsic motivation—self-efficacy and self-determination. We are most likely to enhance students' self-efficacy if we have high (though realistic) expectations for their performance and if we provide the academic support through which they can meet those expectations (Brophy & Evertson, 1976). And when we give students a sense of self-determination and control over their lives— for example, when we involve them in classroom decision making and when we teach them effective ways of bringing about change in their local communities—they will attend school more regularly and achieve at higher levels (deCharms, 1972; NCSS Task Force on Ethnic Studies Curriculum Guidelines, 1992).

Remember that relevance is especially important for motivating students from lower-income families.

Accommodating Students with Special Needs

Our students with special educational needs will typically be among those who show the greatest diversity in motivation to succeed in the classroom. Some of our gifted students may have high intrinsic motivation to learn classroom subject matter, yet they may become easily bored if class activities don't challenge their abilities (Friedel, 1993; Turnbull et al., 1995). Students with specific or general academic difficulties (e.g., those with learning disabilities, those with mental retardation) may show signs of learned helplessness with regard to classroom tasks, especially if their past efforts have repeatedly met with failure (e.g., Seligman, 1975). Students who have difficulty getting along with their classmates (e.g., those with emotional and behavioral disorders) may inappropriately attribute their social failures to factors beyond their control (Heward, 1996). Table 11–5 presents a summary of these and other motivational patterns in students with special needs.

LOOKING AT THE BIG PICTURE: MOTIVATION AND LEARNING

In this chapter, we've considered many strategies for promoting students' motivation to learn and achieve in the classroom. Table 11–6 presents highlights of our discussion, listing several general principles of human motivation and their implications for classroom practice.

As we've examined the many sides of motivation, we've found that motivation facilitates learning and achievement in a variety of ways; for example, appropriately motivated students pay attention, process information meaningfully, persist in the face of failure, use their errors to help improve skills, and seek out ever more challenging tasks. Yet we have also seen how learning and achievement foster the development of pro-

Table 11–5   Promoting Motivation in Students with Special Educational Needs

STUDENTS WITH SPECIAL NEEDS	CHARACTERISTICS THAT THESE STUDENTS MAY EXHIBIT	CLASSROOM STRATEGIES THAT MAY BE BENEFICIAL FOR THESE STUDENTS
Students with specific cognitive or academic deficits	Less intrinsic motivation to succeed at academic tasks High test anxiety Tendency to attribute poor achievement to low ability, rather than to more controllable factors; tendency to attribute successes to external causes (e.g., luck) Tendency to give up easily; learned helplessness regarding performance on some classroom tasks Reluctance of some students to ask questions or seek assistance, especially at the secondary level	Use extrinsic reinforcers to encourage students' classroom effort and achievement. Establish challenging yet realistic goals for achievement. Minimize anxiety-arousing statements and procedures during testing situations (see Chapter 14 for ideas). Teach effective learning strategies and encourage students to attribute their successes to such strategies. Encourage students to develop more productive attributions regarding their achievement difficulties (e.g., attributing failures to insufficient effort or ineffective strategies). Offer assistance when you think that students may really need it, but refrain from offering help when you know that students are capable of succeeding on their own.
Students with specific social or behavioral deficits	Motivation to succeed in the classroom (although such motivation may be difficult to detect because of students' outward behaviors) Tendency to attribute negative consequences to uncontrollable factors (things just "happen")	Relate the curriculum to specific needs and interests that students may have. Teach behaviors that lead to desired consequences; stress cause-effect relationships between actions and outcomes.
Students with general delays in cognitive and social functioning	Less intrinsic motivation than peers; responsiveness to extrinsic motivators Tendency to attribute poor achievement to low ability or to external sources, rather than to more controllable factors; in some situations, a sense of learned helplessness Tendency to give up easily in the face of difficulty	Set specific and realistic goals for performance. Use extrinsic reinforcers to encourage productive behaviors. Help students see the relationship between their own actions and the consequences that result. Reinforce persistence as well as success.
Students with advanced cognitive development	High intrinsic motivation (e.g., curiosity, motivation to learn) Boredom when classroom tasks don't challenge students' abilities A variety of interests Strong commitment to specific tasks Persistence in the face of failure (although some may give up easily if they aren't accustomed to failure)	Give assignments that students find stimulating and challenging. Provide opportunities for students to pursue complex tasks and activities over an extended period of time. Encourage students to set high goals, but without expecting perfection.

Sources: T. Bryan, 1991; Carr & Borkowski, 1989; B. Clark, 1992; Deshler & Schumaker, 1988; Duchardt, Deshler, & Schumaker, 1995; Dweck, 1986; E. S. Ellis & Friend, 1991; Friedel, 1993; Good & Brophy, 1994; Heward, 1996; Jacobsen, Lowery, & DuCette, 1986; C. D. Mercer, 1991; D. P. Morgan & Jenson, 1988; Patton, Beirne-Smith, & Payne, 1990; Patton, Payne, Kauffman, Brown, & Payne, 1987; B. N. Phillips, Pitcher, Worsham, & Miller, 1980; Piirto, 1994; Pressley, 1995; Renzulli, 1978; Sanborn, 1979; G. F. Schultz & Switzky, 1990; Seligman, 1975; Stipek, 1993; Turnbull, Turnbull, Shank, & Leal, 1995.

Compiled with the assistance of Dr. Margie Garanzini-Daiber and Dr. Margaret Cohen, University of Missouri—St. Louis.

Table 11–6   General Principles of Motivation

PRINCIPLE	EDUCATIONAL IMPLICATION	EXAMPLE
Students are more likely to be intrinsically motivated when they have high self-efficacy and a sense of self-determination.	We should give students the successes they need for high self-efficacy. We should also allow them to make choices regarding certain aspects of classroom tasks and activities.	We can allow students to choose among several ways of accomplishing the same instructional objective, being sure that each choice provides sufficient scaffolding that students are likely to achieve success.
Students with learning goals, rather than performance goals, engage in those behaviors and mental processes most likely to promote effective learning.	We should focus students' attention on the value of acquiring new knowledge and skills, rather than on test scores and classroom grades.	We can model our own enthusiasm for classroom material, showing how it has helped us better understand and deal with the world in which we live.
Students are most likely to succeed at challenging classroom tasks if they are eager to do well but not overly anxious about their performance.	We should keep students' anxiety about classroom activities and assignments at a facilitating (low to moderate) level.	We should hold realistic expectations for student performance and communicate those expectations clearly and concretely.
Students are most likely to put forth effort in the classroom when they attribute their successes and failures to factors over which they have control.	We should foster students' beliefs that classroom success is a function of sufficient effort and appropriate strategies.	When students struggle with classroom material, we can teach them study strategies that will help them process the material more effectively.

ductive motivational patterns: When students discover that they can usually accomplish academic tasks successfully, they bring a sense of self-confidence and a desire to learn when they come to class. So motivation and classroom learning go hand in hand, with each one playing a crucial role in the development of the other.

In our discussion of motivation, we have drawn ideas from each of the perspectives of learning presented in earlier chapters. Here are some examples of how cognitive psychology, behaviorism, and social cognitive theory have each entered into our discussion:

Cognitive Psychology

- We found that students who have learning goals, rather than performance goals, are more likely to engage in *meaningful learning* and *elaboration.*

- We learned that students are more optimistic about the probability of future success when they attribute failure to ineffective *study strategies,* rather than to a general and relatively permanent lack of ability.

- We discussed the idea that students' attributions regarding events—their *constructed interpretations* regarding the causes of successes and failures—influence the ways in which they respond to those events.

Behaviorism

- We learned that motivation determines what particular things are *reinforcing* to different students.

- We found that the degree to which students attribute success to internal factors is affected by the extent to which they are *reinforced* (e.g., praised) for success.

Social Cognitive Theory

- We found that students are more likely to be intrinsically motivated to engage in and persist at classroom tasks when they have high *self-efficacy* about performing those tasks.

- We noted the importance of *modeling* our own interest in school subject matter.

- We talked about how students' *expectations* for future success and failure (based on their attributions regarding previous successes and failures) influence their behaviors.

The principles and theories of learning and motivation that we have examined in Chapters 5 through 11 have yielded innumerable strategies for helping our students learn and achieve more successfully in the classroom. In the chapters to come, we translate these same principles and theories more directly into classroom practice as we consider three critical components of effective teaching—planning, instruction, and assessment.

CASE STUDY: *Writer's Block*

On the first day of school, Mr. Grunwald tells students in his English composition class, "I expect you all to be proficient writers by the end of the school year. In fact, you won't get a passing grade from me unless you can write a decent essay by May."

Mr. Grunwald's statement raises anxious thoughts in many of his students. After all, a passing grade in English composition is a requirement for high school graduation. Furthermore, the colleges and universities to which some students are applying prefer As and Bs in composition. A few students are beginning to worry that their straight A averages will be destroyed.

Mr. Grunwald is far less concerned than his students; he firmly believes that all students should be able to develop writing proficiency before the year is out. He gives his students a new writing assignment each Monday, making each one more challenging than those preceding it. When he finds poorly written work among the papers he grades at the end of the week, he tries to motivate his students to do better with such comments as, "Below average work this time—you can do better," or, "Try harder next week."

The writing skills of some students improve as the year progresses. But those of other students seem almost to be deteriorating. He questions Janis,

---

one of his low-achieving students, about the problem and is startled to hear her response.

"No matter what I do, I seem to get poor grades in your class," she laments. "I've pretty much given up trying. I guess I just wasn't meant to be a writer."

- How is Mr. Grunwald defining success in his English composition class? How are his students defining success? Are they focusing their attention on learning or performance goals?

- To what does Janis attribute her writing failure? What effect has her attribution had on her behavior?

- What strategies might Mr. Grunwald use to help his students become more intrinsically motivated to develop proficient writing skills?

SUMMING UP

Effects of Motivation

Students' motivation affects their learning in a number of ways. It focuses their attention on particular goals and instigates behaviors that help them achieve those goals. It influences what and how information is cognitively processed and determines the specific consequences that are likely to be reinforcing. Ultimately, it leads to higher achievement in the classroom.

Intrinsic and Extrinsic Motivation

Intrinsic motivation arises from conditions within students themselves or from factors inherent in the task being performed. Extrinsic motivation is based on factors external to students and unrelated to the task at hand. We are especially likely to see the positive effects of motivation when our students are intrinsically rather than extrinsically motivated.

Maslow has suggested that students will be intrinsically motivated (in his words, they will strive for self-actualization) only after more basic needs—physiological needs and the needs for safety, love and belonging, and esteem—have already been satisfied. More recently, several theorists have proposed that students are most likely to be intrinsically motivated when two conditions exist: (1) They have high self-efficacy regarding their ability to succeed at classroom tasks, and (2) they have a sense of self-determination—a

sense that they have some control over the course that their lives will take. As teachers, we can promote students' self-efficacy by giving them competence-promoting feedback, helping them master challenging tasks, and defining success in terms of long-term improvement. We can promote a greater sense of self-determination by presenting rules, restrictions, and evaluations in an informational rather than controlling fashion, by minimizing our reliance on extrinsic reinforcers, and by occasionally allowing students to make choices and be involved in classroom decision making.

Motivation to Learn and Learning Goals

One form of intrinsic motivation is the motivation to learn—the tendency to find school-related activities meaningful and therefore worth pursuing for their own sake. Students with learning goals, rather than performance goals, are more likely to recognize that competence comes only through effort and practice, choose activities that maximize their opportunities for learning, and use their errors constructively to improve future performance. We can foster students' motivation to learn and focus their attention on learning goals by relating school subject matter to their personal needs and interests, modeling our own interest in what we teach, and communicating our belief that students genuinely want to learn class material.

Social Needs

Many students come to the classroom with strong social needs, including needs to affiliate with others and to gain their approval. We can accommodate our students' social needs by providing opportunities for group interaction, expressing our concern for students' welfare, and frequently indicating our approval of desirable student behaviors.

Affect and Anxiety

Sometimes learning and information processing are emotionally charged—a phenomenon known as "hot cognition." In general, our students will learn and remember more when they become involved in classroom subject matter emotionally as well as cognitively.

A small amount of anxiety often facilitates performance, but a great deal of anxiety typically debilitates it, especially when difficult tasks are involved. Under most circumstances, we should strive to keep our students' anxiety at a low or moderate level—for example, by clearly communicating our expectations for student performance and by ensuring that students have a good chance of being successful in classroom activities.

Attributions

Attributions are the explanations students give for why they succeed or fail at tasks. Students may attribute events to causes that are (a) internal or external to themselves, (b) stable or unstable, and (c) controllable or uncontrollable. Attributions affect many aspects of behavior and cognition, including students' expecta-tions for future success, expenditure of effort, help-seeking behavior, choice of activities, and, ultimately, classroom performance. As teachers, we can give students reasons for optimism about their future chances of success by attributing both their successes and their failures to factors they can control, including effort (if it has, in fact, influenced the outcome) and cognitive strategies. We should also attribute students' successes (but not failures) to a stable ability on which they can depend. Ultimately, we can promote an *I can do it* attitude (a mastery orientation) by facilitating students' success on classroom tasks, especially challenging ones.

Diversity in Motivation

We will typically see different motives and attributions in different students. The specific patterns we see will depend, in part, on students' age levels, as well as on their gender, their ethnic and socioeconomic backgrounds, and their special educational needs. As teachers, we must remember that different motivational strategies will be more or less effective, depending on the specific students with whom we are working.

Motivation and Learning

Just as motivation affects learning, so, too, does learning play a critical role in motivation—for example, by raising or lowering self-efficacy and by influencing the specific attributions for success and failure that students develop. As teachers, we cannot realistically deal with either students' learning or their motivation in isolation from the other.

KEY CONCEPTS

motivation (p. 472)
intrinsic versus extrinsic motivation
  (p. 476)
self-actualization (p. 477)
deficiency versus growth needs (p. 478)
challenge (p. 481)
self-determination (p. 483)
motivation to learn (p. 486)

learning goals versus performance goals
  (p. 487)
need for affiliation (p. 496)
need for approval (p. 496)
affect (p. 498)
hot cognition (p. 499)
anxiety (p. 500)
state versus trait anxiety (p. 500)

threat (p. 500)
facilitating versus debilitating anxiety
  (p. 500)
attributions (p. 505)
attribution theory (p. 505)
mastery orientation (p. 516)
learned helplessness (p. 516)

BECOMING AN EFFECTIVE TEACHER

IN PART 1, we considered many differences that we are likely to see in our students—differences related to age, ethnicity, gender, socioeconomic status, and so on—and identified numerous implications of such diversity for classroom practice. In Part 2, we looked at the nature of learning and motivation from various theoretical perspectives, deriving additional educational implications from the principles and theories we studied. How do we pull all these things together as we go into the classroom? In other words, what is the overall big picture?

In Part 3, we revisit many of the ideas we considered in Parts 1 and 2 as we explore three closely interwoven components of teaching: planning, instruction, and assessment. In Chapter 12, **"Planning for a Productive Classroom,"** we will identify twelve general principles that underlie effective teaching practice, and we will see many of these principles popping up within our discussion of such topics as instructional objectives, task analysis, and classroom management. We will find that effective teaching and effective classroom management go hand in hand: Many strategies that enhance students' learning—planning classroom activities ahead of time, communicating clear expectations for student performance, providing frequent feedback, and so on—foster appropriate classroom behavior as well.

We will also see our twelve principles in action as we turn our attention to **"Choosing and Implementing Instructional Strategies"** in Chapter 13. Here we will find various theoretical perspectives of learning and motivation translated into such instructional strategies as expository instruction, mastery learning, class discussions, and cooperative learning. We will discover that there is no single "best" instructional method—that using different approaches is one way in which we will be able to accommodate the diversity we are likely to see among our students.

Principles of effective teaching will continue to appear in our discussion of **"Assessing What Students Have Learned"** in Chapter 14. Here we will examine a variety of strategies for determining whether students have achieved our instructional objectives—whether they've acquired the knowledge and skills we've tried to teach them. We'll take a broad view of what it means to assess students' performance; we'll also discover how we can determine whether our methods of assessing students' knowledge and skills are accurate and dependable ones. We will find that classroom assessment practices are teaching tools as well and that they are likely to have a significant impact on how and what our students learn.

Finally, in Chapter 15, as we examine the process of **"Developing as a Teacher,"** we will look at the profession of teaching from a broader perspective, considering the role that, as teachers, we play in students' lives, in schools, and in society as a whole. We will also discover how we ourselves are likely to learn and develop as teachers as we gain experience in the years to come.

Planning for a Productive Classroom

THINKING ABOUT WHAT YOU KNOW

Under what conditions can you most easily study and learn? For example, is it easier to study when you know what your instructors expect you to accomplish? Is it easier to learn when they sequence new information and tasks in a logical order? Do you find that you learn more in class when your instructors have carefully planned their lessons ahead of time?

EFFECTIVE TEACHING BEGINS long before students enter the classroom. Effective teachers engage in a considerable amount of advance planning: They identify the knowledge and skills they want their students to learn, determine the most appropriate sequence in which to teach such knowledge and skills, and develop classroom activities that will promote maximal learning and keep students continually motivated and on-task.

As we begin our examination of effective teaching practice in this chapter, we will first identify twelve principles that emerge from research concerning effective teachers and schools. Drawing on these principles, we will then focus our attention on the *planning* component of teaching, considering how best to determine what the final goals and outcomes (the *objectives*) of our instruction should be and how best to break especially complex objectives into a number of simpler, more manageable ones (*task analysis*). We will also consider how we can plan and create a classroom environment conducive to our students' learning and achievement. As we explore this topic of *classroom management*, we will identify numerous strategies that should keep any nonproductive and counterproductive behaviors to a minimum; nevertheless, we will also consider effective strategies to deal with those misbehaviors that do occur.

Skim the discussion of learning principles in Chapters 6 through 10 and the discussion of human motivation in Chapter 11. Can you find specific principles of learning and motivation that have relevance for planning instructional activities and for creating a classroom environment conducive to learning?

Throughout our discussion, we will revisit principles and concepts that we have encountered in previous chapters. For example, as we consider instructional objectives and task analysis, we will draw from both cognitive and behaviorist views of learning (Chapters 6 and 9, respectively). As we identify classroom management strategies, we will make use of such "old friends" as *scaffolding* (Chapter 2), *socialization* (Chapter 3), and *self-determination* (Chapter 11). And as we consider techniques for reducing students' off-task behaviors, we will rely on principles related to *cueing, applied behavior analysis,* and *self-regulation* (Chapters 9 and 10).

By the end of the chapter, you should be able to:

1. Relate general principles of effective teaching to specific classroom practices.

2. Explain how planning, instruction, assessment, and student characteristics are intertwined.

3. Develop instructional objectives that can facilitate your selection of instructional strategies and assessment procedures.

4. Describe three different ways in which, through task analysis, you can break complex skills and topics into small, manageable components and teach them in an appropriate sequence.

5. Explain how you can establish and maintain a classroom environment conducive to students' learning and achievement.

6. Describe strategies for keeping off-task behaviors to a minimum and for responding effectively to the misbehaviors that do occur.

7. Take student diversity into account when planning for a productive learning environment and when dealing with misbehaviors.

Ms. Corbett received her teaching certificate in May; soon after, she accepted a position as a fifth-grade teacher at Twin Pines Elementary School. She spent the summer planning her classroom curriculum: She identified the objectives she wanted her students to accomplish during the year and developed numerous activities to help them meet those objectives. She now feels well prepared for her first year in the classroom.

After the long, hot summer, most of Ms. Corbett's students seem happy to be back at school. So on the very first day of school, Ms. Corbett jumps head-long into the curriculum she has planned. But three problems quickly present themselves—problems in the form of Eli, Jake, and Vanessa.

These three students seem determined to disrupt the classroom at every possible opportunity. They move about the room without permission, making a point of annoying others as they walk to the pencil sharpener or wastebasket. They talk out of turn, sometimes being rude and disrespectful to their teacher and classmates and at other times belittling the classroom activities that Ms. Corbett has so carefully planned. They rarely complete their in-class assignments, preferring instead to engage in horseplay or practical jokes. They seem particularly prone to misbehavior at "down" times in the class schedule—for example, at the beginning and end of the school day, before and after recess and lunch, and on occasions when Ms. Corbett is preoccupied with other students.

Ms. Corbett continues to follow her daily lesson plans, ignoring her problem students and hoping they will begin to see the error of their ways. Yet, with the three of them egging one another on, the disruptive behavior continues. Furthermore, it begins to spread to other students. By the middle of October, Ms. Corbett's class is a three-ring circus, with general chaos reigning in the classroom and instructional objectives rarely being accomplished. The few students who still seem intent on learning something are having a difficult time doing so.

- In what ways has Ms. Corbett planned for her classroom in advance? In what ways has she *not* planned?

- Why are Eli, Jake, and Vanessa so disruptive right from the start? Can you think of possible reasons related to how Ms. Corbett has begun the school year? Can you think of possible reasons related to our discussion of motivation in the previous chapter? Can you think of possible reasons related to the classroom activities Ms. Corbett has planned?

- Why does the misbehavior of the three problem students continue? Why does it spread to other students in the classroom? Why is it particularly common during "down" times in the school day? Can you answer these questions by using learning principles that you have already studied?

CONSIDERING GENERAL PRINCIPLES OF EFFECTIVE TEACHING

As a first-year teacher, Ms. Corbett is well prepared in some respects but not at all prepared in others. She has carefully thought out the objectives she wishes to accomplish and the activities through which she intends to accomplish those objectives. But she has neglected to think about strategies for keeping her students motivated and on-task or to adapt her instructional strategies on the basis of how her students are progressing. Nor has she considered how she might nip behavior problems in the bud, before such misbehaviors begin to interfere with her students' learning and achievement.

There is probably no single best kind of teacher, no single best type of school (Brophy, 1994; G. A. Davis & Thomas, 1989). Research studies indicate, however, that, in general, effective teachers and effective schools:

1. Have **clear goals** for instruction

2. Ensure the **relevance** of classroom activities to real-world contexts and students' lives

3. Exhibit **adaptation to diversity** by selecting instructional strategies and materials appropriate to the age, backgrounds, cultures, and special needs of individual students

4. Create a classroom **climate** that promotes learning, intrinsic motivation, and achievement

5. Encourage **social interaction** related to classroom subject matter

6. Provide a **structure** that guides students' learning and behavior

7. Facilitate effective **information processing**

8. Support **mastery of fundamentals,** including proficiency in the basic knowledge and skills that provide the foundation for advanced learning

9. Provide the **challenge** so essential for cognitive development

10. Promote **higher-level thinking** skills

11. Communicate **high expectations** (within realistic limits) for students' performance

12. Engage in regular **monitoring** of students' behavior and progress toward classroom goals (Brophy, 1992b; Darling-Hammond, 1995; G. A. Davis & Thomas, 1989; Good & Brophy, 1986; Levine & Lezotte, 1995; Prawat, 1992)

All seven of the major themes listed in Chapter 1 are echoed in these principles. Can you find them?

I must point out that most studies of teacher and school effectiveness are correlational in nature; therefore, we cannot use the results of such studies to draw firm conclusions about cause-effect relationships. But note how several of the principles of effective teaching I've just presented match the seven general themes I listed in Chapter 1; note, too, how virtually all twelve are consistent with principles we've identified throughout the book. No matter how we approach the topic of effective teaching, we seem to draw similar conclusions.

Using the twelve principles of effective teaching, we might form a number of hypotheses as to why Ms. Corbett has gotten off to a bad start in her classroom. For example, perhaps she has neglected to provide a structure—classroom rules, procedures, and so on—to give her students guidance regarding acceptable and unacceptable behavior (Principle 6). Perhaps she is portraying classroom assignments more as "chores to be done," rather than as things relevant to students' own lives (Principle 2). Perhaps Eli, Jake, and Vanessa have not mastered some of the prerequisite skills essential for learning the material Ms. Corbett is presenting (Principle 8); as you will discover later in the chapter, students are more likely to misbehave when they are asked to do things that are probably too difficult for them.

Interplay of Planning, Instruction, Assessment, and Student Characteristics

Each of our dozen principles of effective teaching relates to one or more of three critical components of effective teaching: *planning, instruction,* and *assessment.* Our focus in this chapter will be on planning—on identifying in advance the objectives we want to accomplish and creating a classroom environment that ensures that such objectives *will* be accomplished. Our focus in the following chapter will be on instruction—on the specific strategies we can use to help students learn and achieve most effectively. Then, in Chapter 14, we will address assessment—the various techniques, both formal and informal, that we can use to determine whether our students are achieving the objectives we've established. Yet as we will repeatedly discover in upcoming discussions, each component of effective teaching is invariably influenced by the other two; for example, in this chapter we will find that planning both affects and is affected by the instructional strategies and assessment procedures we choose.

We must keep in mind, too, that at the heart of effective teaching is the *student.* The things we do with regard to planning, instruction, and assessment influence the learning and behaviors that our students exhibit. The characteristics that our students bring to the classroom must also influence the specific approaches to planning, instruction, and assessment that we take. As teachers, we will see a continual interplay among planning, instruction, assessment, and student characteristics. Figure 12–1 graphically depicts this interplay and provides examples of how each component of effective teaching is related to the others.

Let's return once again to our case study. One thing Ms. Corbett *did* do right was to identify the goals that she wanted her students to accomplish and to base her instructional methods on those goals. Let's explore our first principle of effective teaching—having clear goals for instruction—as we consider the topic of instructional objectives.

IDENTIFYING INSTRUCTIONAL OBJECTIVES

THINKING ABOUT WHAT YOU KNOW

As a student, have you ever been in a situation in which you couldn't figure out what your teacher expected you to be able to do? Do you remember feeling confused, frustrated, or otherwise "lost" in that situation?

If we consider the limits of the human information processing system described in Chapter 6, we realize that students are often given far more information in class and in their textbooks than they can possibly remember. They must therefore be selective

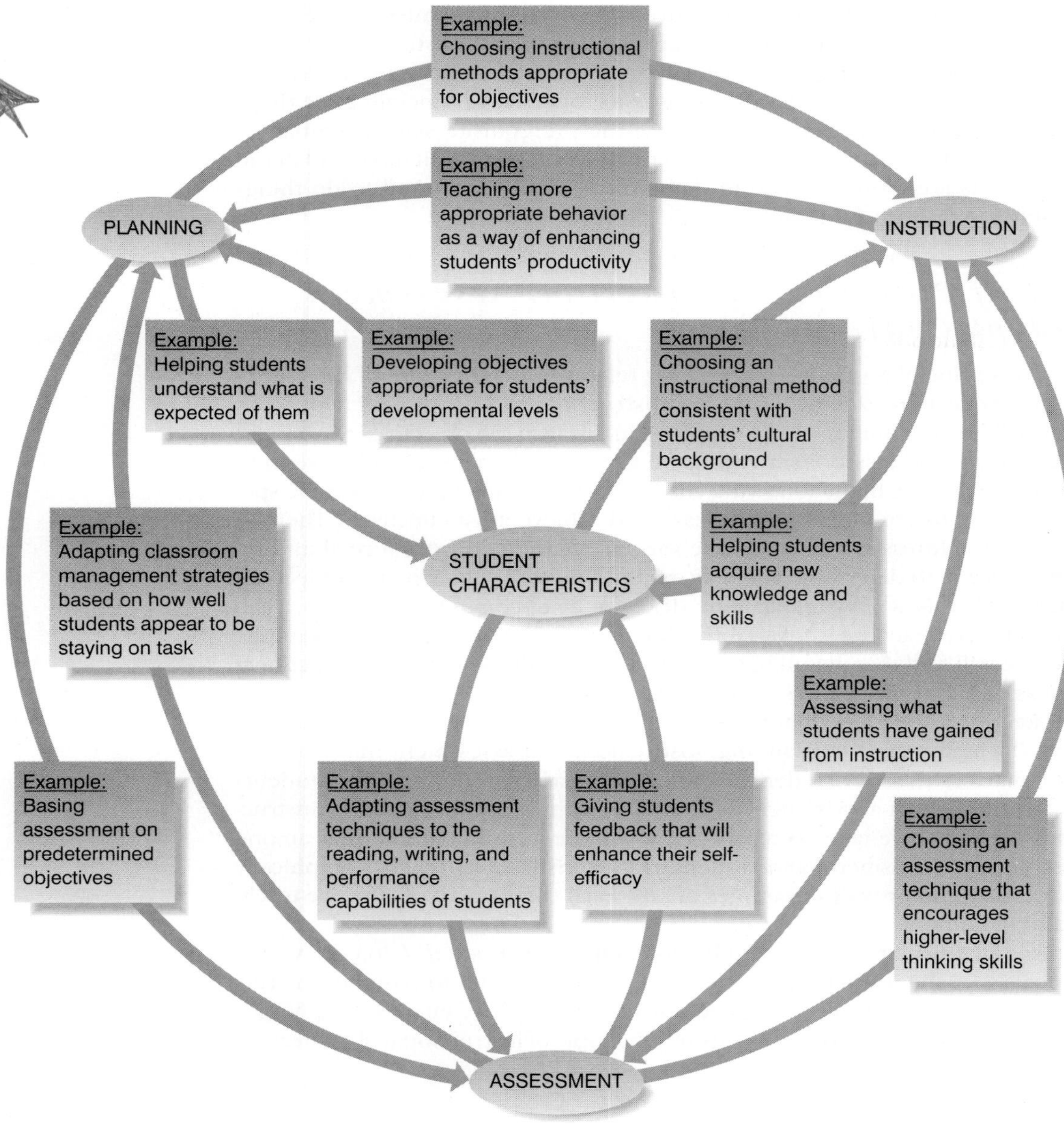

PLANNING
INSTRUCTION
STUDENT CHARACTERISTICS
ASSESSMENT
Example: Choosing instructional methods appropriate for objectives
Example: Teaching more appropriate behavior as a way of enhancing students' productivity
Example: Helping students understand what is expected of them
Example: Developing objectives appropriate for students' developmental levels
Example: Choosing an instructional method consistent with students' cultural background
Example: Helping students acquire new knowledge and skills
Example: Adapting classroom management strategies based on how well students appear to be staying on task
Example: Assessing what students have gained from instruction
Example: Basing assessment on predetermined objectives
Example: Adapting assessment techniques to the reading, writing, and performance capabilities of students
Example: Giving students feedback that will enhance their self-efficacy
Example: Choosing an assessment technique that encourages higher-level thinking skills

Figure 12–1 Interplay of Planning, Instruction, Assessment, and Student Characteristics

when they study: They must choose some things to store in their long-term memories and ignore other things. Yet as we noted in our discussion of metacognition and study strategies in Chapter 8, students are not always the best judges of what is important and what is not. By telling students what we want them to accomplish—in other words, by describing the **instructional objectives** for a particular lesson—we help them make more informed decisions about how best to direct their efforts and allocate their study time. In addition, by describing precisely what we expect our students to be able to do at the completion of a lesson, we enhance their ability to monitor their own comprehension as they study (McAshan, 1979). For example, students who know that they should be able to explain how a plant produces its own food through photosynthesis are more likely to know when they have successfully learned the material than students who are simply told to "read the section on photosynthesis."

Relating Objectives to Instruction and Assessment

As teachers, we, too, benefit from determining the specific objectives of our lessons. Instructional objectives can help us choose the most appropriate method of instruction; they can also help us identify the most appropriate means of evaluating students' achievement. For example, if the objective for a unit on addition is the *knowledge* of number facts, then we may want to use drill and practice (perhaps flash cards) to enhance students' automaticity for these facts, and we may want to use a timed test to measure students' ability to recall these facts quickly and easily. But if the objective is the *application* of number facts, then we may want to focus our instruction and assessment methods on word problems, or perhaps on activities involving real objects, hands-on measurements, and so on. Likewise, if the objective for a course in language arts is for students to know rules of punctuation, then numerous practice exercises in a workbook may be a useful instructional approach, and similar exercises may comprise a reasonable test of students' achievement. But if the objective is for students to use correct punctuation in their own compositions, then the class should spend more time actually writing, and writing samples should be the basis on which students are evaluated.

We find an example of how objectives and instruction closely interconnect in **mastery learning**—an approach to instruction in which students must learn material related to one or more objectives well (they must *master* that material) before proceeding on to additional objectives. Mastery learning is especially suited for objectives that are relatively simple and can be accomplished within a period of a few days or weeks; we will look at this instructional strategy more closely in Chapter 13.

We find objectives and assessment practices coming together most clearly in **outcomes-based education,** or **OBE** (e.g., Boschee & Baron, 1993; Guskey, 1994). In OBE, the *outcomes* of instruction—that is, the objectives that students are expected to achieve—are specified before the school year begins, often at a districtwide level. Classroom assessment is tied directly to these outcomes, and decisions related to students' advancement and graduation are made on the basis of the specific knowledge and skills that each student can demonstrate.

Consider the specific objectives of a lesson or unit as you identify your method of instruction and means of assessment.

If the objective is application, then students should engage in various application activities. For the conclusion of a science activity, this first grader uses his wind finder to determine the direction of the wind.

Choosing Appropriate Objectives

■ EXPERIENCING FIRSTHAND
Looking Ahead "Objectively"

1. At the top of a blank sheet of paper, write down a grade level at which you might eventually teach.

2. Now write down the subject area(s) you are likely to be teaching at that grade level.

3. With both your grade level and subject area(s) in mind, write down at least five *important* objectives you might have for your students. ■

What kinds of objectives did you include in your list? Did you consider both lower-level and higher-level thinking processes? Did you consider improvement of students' classroom behaviors, as well as the improvement of their knowledge and skills? On what basis did you decide that your objectives were important ones for students to achieve?

As teachers, we will often play a significant role in determining the instructional objectives our schools and school districts have for students at different grade levels. And we will undoubtedly add our own objectives to any list that the school district provides for us. The final list of objectives we have for our students is likely to be quite broad in scope. Certainly, it will include the acquisition of certain basic knowledge and skills. But it should also extend well beyond those basics to include such things as the use of higher-level thinking processes, the development of effective interpersonal skills, and the acquisition of positive attitudes toward academic subject matter.

In recent years, various professional groups have begun to provide guidance for us in the form of **standards**—general statements regarding the knowledge and skills that students should achieve and the characteristics that their accomplishments should reflect. As illustrations, here are examples of standards in science and geography:

Find guidance in published *standards* for the discipline.

Example from the *National Science Education Standards* (1996):
As a result of their activities in grades 5–8, all students should develop understanding of

- Structure and function in living systems

- Reproduction and heredity

- Regulation and behavior

- Populations and ecosystems

- Diversity and adaptations of organisms (p. 155)

Example from *Geography for Life: National Geography Standards* (1994):
By the end of the twelfth grade, the student should know and understand how to . . . systematically locate and gather geographic information from a variety of primary and secondary sources, as exemplified by being able to

- Gather data in the field by multiple processes—observing, identifying, naming, describing, organizing, sketching, interviewing, recording, measuring

- Gather data in the classroom and library from maps, photographs, videos, and other media (e.g., CD-ROM), charts, aerial photographs, and other nonbook sources, and then use the data to identify, name, describe, organize, sketch, measure, and evaluate items of geographic interest

- Gather data by spatial sampling in both secondary sources and the field . . .

- Use quantitative measures (e.g., means, medians, and modes) to describe data (p. 53)

As you can see, some sets of standards are more precise than others; in this situation, we find specific, observable behaviors described in the geography standard but not in the science standard.

Yet we must keep in mind that teachers, parents, taxpayers, and even experts cannot always agree on the instructional objectives that students of various age levels should achieve (Sosniak & Stodolsky, 1994; Stiggins, 1994). For example, we hear calls for going "back to the basics" from some constituencies while hearing calls for "creativity" or "critical thinking" from other quarters. As teachers, we must remember that, at least at this point in time, there may be no definitive list of objectives for any age-group. We will ultimately have to tailor our instructional objectives to the particular characteristics that our students bring to the classroom and to the particular expectations of the schools, communities, and larger society in which we teach.

Consider student characteristics and community expectations as you develop objectives.

Developing Useful Objectives

■ EXPERIENCING FIRSTHAND
Being a Good Citizen

Consider this instructional objective:

> *Students will learn and practice principles of good citizenship.*

Write down at least three implications of this objective for your own classroom practice. ■

Certainly, good citizenship is a goal toward which all students should strive. But did you find yourself having trouble translating the objective into specific things you might do in the classroom? Did you also find yourself struggling with what the term *good citizenship* means (honesty? empathy? involvement in school activities? all of the above?)? The "good citizenship" objective is nothing more than *word magic:* It looks great at first glance, but it really doesn't give us specific or useful information about what we want students to achieve (Dyer, 1967).

Some instructional objectives are clearly more useful than others. We can develop instructional objectives that will be helpful both to us and to our students when we:

- Focus on student outcomes

- Consider various domains and levels of objectives

- Identify observable behaviors that reflect desired knowledge and skills

- Consider both short-term and long-term objectives

- Incorporate opportunities for self-regulation and self-determination

Focusing on Student Outcomes

Consider these objectives for a unit on soccer:

- Survey the rules of the game.

- Show students how to kick, dribble, and pass the ball.

- Teach the playing positions (e.g., center forward, goalkeeper) and the roles of players in each position.

The problem with these objectives is that they tell us only what the teacher will do during instruction; they tell us nothing at all about what students should be able to do as a result of that instruction. Useful objectives focus on student behaviors, rather than on teacher behaviors (e.g., Gronlund, 1995). With this point in mind, let's consider some alternative objectives for our soccer unit:

Focus on what students will do, not on what you as the teacher will do.

- Students will describe the basic rules of the game and identify the procedures to be followed in various situations.

- Students will demonstrate appropriate ways of kicking, dribbling, and passing the ball.

- Students will identify the eleven playing positions and describe the roles of players in each position.

Here we have refocused our objectives on student behaviors; in other words, we have described the knowledge and skills we want our students to demonstrate as a result of their unit on soccer.

Objectives are also more useful when they describe learning outcomes, rather than learning processes (Gronlund, 1995). To illustrate, consider these objectives for a French class:

- Students will study the meanings of French words.

- Students will practice pronouncing French words.

- Students will learn how to conjugate French verbs.

Describe learning outcomes, not learning processes.

These objectives describe what students will do during French class; in other words, they describe learning *processes.* But it is usually more important for us to determine what students can do when they complete that class—that is, to describe what the end results or *outcomes* of the class or lesson should be. So let's revise our objectives to reflect student outcomes:

- Students will give the English meanings of French words.

- Students will pronounce French words correctly.

- Students will correctly conjugate common French verbs in the present and past tenses.

Now we know what to expect of students once they finish that French class.

Considering Various Domains and Levels of Objectives

Consider objectives within the psychomotor and affective domains, as well as within the cognitive domain.

What outcomes might result from a soccer lesson or a French class? Might students know the rules of soccer or the correct conjugation of *courir*? Might they be able to dribble a soccer ball down the field or correctly pronounce *beaucoup*? Might they develop greater enthusiasm for soccer or a love of the French language?

As we consider the things we want our students to do as a result of instruction, we must remember that we don't necessarily want to limit our objectives just to the acquisition and use of information (in other words, to the **cognitive domain**). Other important objectives might involve body movements and actions (the **psychomotor domain**). And still others might involve students' feelings, attitudes, and values about the things they learn (the **affective domain**).

What is *affect?* (Chapter 11 has the answer).

When developing instructional objectives, it is often useful to consider *taxonomies* of objectives that enumerate different outcomes of the educational process. Educators have developed taxonomies in the cognitive, psychomotor, and affective domains that identify a variety of student behaviors, listing them in order from the very simple to the more complex; Table 12–1 presents examples of taxonomies in each of the three areas. Although probably not exhaustive lists of all possible student behaviors, such taxonomies nevertheless give us some ideas about the kinds of objectives we may want to consider (e.g., Krathwohl, 1994).

As we develop objectives in each of the three domains, we will often want to include outcomes at varying degrees of complexity and sophistication. As illustrations, consider these objectives for a lesson on the physics of light:

- Students will describe the law of reflection of light.

- Students will describe the law of refraction of light.

Notice how these objectives focus exclusively on knowledge of separate facts—facts that might be learned in isolation from anything else students have already learned. But is this really all we want students to do with the things they learn in school? Don't we also want them to relate new things to the things they already know? And don't we want them to use and apply the things they learn? As we noted in Chapter 8, we may often want students to develop higher-level skills along with the lower-level ones.

What objectives in each domain can you identify for the subject matter you will be teaching?

Write objectives that reflect several levels of knowing and using information and skills.

Consider including objectives in the cognitive, psychomotor, and affective domains and at different levels within each of those domains.

Table 12–1   *Writing Objectives at Different Levels and in Different Domains*

LEVEL AND DEFINITION	EXAMPLES
The Cognitive Domain (Bloom's Taxonomy) (adapted from Bloom, Engelhart, Furst, Hill, & Krathwohl, 1956)	
1. *Knowledge:* Rote memorizing of information in a basically word-for-word fashion	Reciting definitions of terms Remembering lists of items
2. *Comprehension:* Translating information into one's own words	Rewording a definition Paraphrasing a rule
3. *Application:* Using information in a new situation	Applying mathematical principles to the solution of word problems Applying psychological theories of learning to educational practice
4. *Analysis:* Breaking information down into its constituent parts	Discovering the assumptions underlying a philosophical essay Identifying fallacies in a logical argument
5. *Synthesis:* Constructing something new by integrating several pieces of information	Developing a theory Presenting a logical defense of a particular viewpoint within a debate
6. *Evaluation:* Placing a value judgment on data	Critiquing a theory Examining the internal and external validity of an experiment
The Psychomotor Domain (adapted from Harrow, 1972)	
1. *Reflex movements:* Responding to a stimulus involuntarily, without conscious thought	Ducking to avoid being hit by an oncoming object Shifting weight to help maintain one's balance
2. *Basic-fundamental movements:* Making basic voluntary movements directed toward a particular purpose	Walking Holding a pencil
3. *Perceptual abilities:* Responding appropriately to information received through the senses	Following a moving object with one's eyes Maintaining eye-hand coordination

Let's develop some objectives for our lesson on light that reflect higher-level skills:

- Students will identify examples of reflection and refraction in their own lives (e.g., mirrors, eyeglasses).
- Students will use the law of reflection and laws of geometry to determine the actual location of objects viewed in a mirror.
- Students will use the law of refraction to explain how microscopes and telescopes make objects appear larger.

LEVEL AND DEFINITION	EXAMPLES
4. *Physical abilities:* Developing general abilities in the areas of endurance, strength, flexibility, and agility	Running a long distance Exercising with weights Changing direction quickly
5. *Skilled movements:* Performing a complex action with some degree of proficiency or mastery	Swimming Throwing a football Sawing a piece of wood
6. *Nondiscursive communication:* Communicating feelings and emotions through bodily actions	Doing pantomime Dancing to communicate the mood of a musical piece

The Affective Domain
(adapted from Krathwohl, Bloom, & Masia, 1964)

1. *Receiving:* Being aware of, or paying attention to, something	Recognizing that there may be two sides to a story Knowing that there are differences among people of different cultural backgrounds
2. *Responding:* Making an active and willing response to something	Obeying playground rules Reading books for pleasure
3. *Valuing:* Consistently demonstrating interest in a particular activity so that ongoing involvement or commitment in the activity is reflected	Writing a letter to a newspaper regarding an issue one feels strongly about Consistently eating a balanced diet
4. *Organization:* Integrating a new value into one's existing set of values and building a value system	Forming judgments about the directions in which society should move Setting priorities for one's life
5. *Characterization by a value or value complex:* Consistently behaving in accordance with an organized value system and integrating that system into a total philosophy of life	Perceiving situations objectively, realistically, and with tolerance Relying increasingly on the scientific method as a means of answering questions about the world and society

Here we are no longer describing knowledge of facts at a rote level; we are instead focusing on meaningful learning and promoting such complex cognitive processes as concept learning and transfer.

Identifying Observable Behaviors

Consider these objectives for a unit on fractions:

- Students will be aware of how fractions are different from whole numbers.
- Students will know how to reduce fractions to lowest terms.
- Students will understand how improper fractions are converted to mixed numbers.

Here we have described outcomes in terms of knowledge and abilities that we can't see. And if we can't see those outcomes, we really don't know whether they've actually been achieved. So let's rephrase our objectives, this time describing them in terms of observable behaviors that we can see:

- Given pictures of whole and partial objects (e.g., a picture of three whole pizza pies, a picture of a pizza with three of its eight slices missing), students will identify those objects that represent whole numbers and those that represent fractions.

- Students will reduce fractions with numerators and denominators ranging from one to fifty to their lowest terms.

- Students will convert improper fractions with numerators and denominators ranging from one to fifty to mixed numbers.

Do you remember the concept of *terminal behavior* from our discussion of operant conditioning in Chapter 9? Behaviorists argue that, to change students' behavior, we should specify the form and frequency of each desired behavior before we try to teach that behavior. Instructional objectives that describe specific, observable behaviors are sometimes called **behavioral objectives** (e.g., Schloss & Smith, 1994).

Let's stop for a minute to consider the kinds of verbs that indicate specific behaviors and the kinds of verbs that do not. Look at the differences between the words and phrases in each of these two lists:

Nonbehavior Verbs	Behavior Verbs
know	recite
understand	explain
appreciate	choose
remember	write
recognize	identify
be able to	do

We cannot see such things as "knowing" and "understanding," so we really don't know when these things are occurring successfully. But we can readily observe students "reciting" and "explaining" and can easily determine when objectives describing these activities have been accomplished.

Describe outcomes in terms of observable behaviors by using a reasonable level of precision and specificity.

Does this mean that we should identify every single behavior we expect students to exhibit? Probably not. Too much emphasis on describing precise, specific outcomes can lead to very long lists of relatively trivial behaviors (Popham, 1995). Ultimately, we must strike a happy medium for any given lesson or unit: We must describe desired outcomes at a reasonable level of precision and specificity, yet develop a list of objectives short enough (perhaps three to ten items) that we can remember it easily as we develop lesson plans and classroom tests.

In some instances, particularly when we are teaching a complex topic or skill, it may be beneficial to describe a few general and relatively abstract objectives and then to list examples of behaviors that reflect each one (Gronlund & Linn, 1990). To illustrate, here is an example of how we might develop an objective for reading:

Students will demonstrate thinking skills in reading; for example, they will:

1. Distinguish between main ideas and supporting details.

2. Distinguish between facts and opinions.

3. Distinguish between facts and inferences.

4. Identify cause-effect relations.

5. Identify errors in reasoning.

6. Distinguish between valid and invalid conclusions.

7. Identify assumptions underlying conclusions. (adapted from Gronlund, 1995, p. 52)

Obviously, not every facet of critical thinking is included here, but the eight items listed give both us and our students a good idea of the specific kinds of behaviors that reflect achievement of the objective.

When teaching a complex topic or skill, list a few general (and perhaps not directly observable) objectives and then give examples of specific behaviors that reflect each one.

■ EXPERIENCING FIRSTHAND
Looking Back at "Looking Ahead"

Look back at the objectives you developed in the "Looking Ahead 'Objectively'" exercise. Do your objectives reflect:

• A focus on student outcomes?

• Several domains and various levels within those domains?

• Observable behaviors?

If the answer to any of these questions is no, think about how you might revise your objectives to be more useful to both you and your students. ■

Considering Both Short-Term and Long-Term Objectives

Some instructional objectives can easily be accomplished within the course of a single lesson or unit. When we want our students to convert improper fractions to mixed numbers, pronounce certain French words correctly, or pass a soccer ball competently, we are talking about **short-term objectives.** But other objectives may require months or even years of instruction and practice before they are achieved (Brophy & Alleman, 1991; Cole, 1990; Gronlund, 1995). For example, we are talking about such **long-term objectives** when we want our students to use effective learning strategies as they study new subject matter, apply the scientific method as they try to understand and explain the world around them, or read critically rather than take everything at face value.

Consider both short-term and long-term objectives.

Some short-term objectives are "minimum essentials"—things that students *must* be able to do before they proceed to the next unit, course, or grade level (Gronlund, 1995). For example, elementary school students must know addition before they move to multiplication, and high school students must know the symbols for the chemical elements before they learn how chemical reactions are symbolized. In contrast, many long-term objectives can be thought of as "developmental" in nature: They include skills and abilities that continue to evolve and improve throughout the school years and are probably never totally mastered (Gronlund, 1995). Yet even when long-term objectives cannot be completely accomplished within the course of students' formal education, they are often among the most important ones for us to set for our students and must therefore have a prominent place in our list of objectives.

As noted in Chapter 4, you may want to focus the attention of at-risk students more on short-term objectives—objectives they can accomplish in a short amount of time with a reasonable amount of effort—than on long-term, developmental ones toward which they may see little progress over the short run.

Incorporating Opportunities for Self-Regulation and Self-Determination

Up to this point, we have been speaking of instructional objectives as things that we and other school personnel identify. But keep in mind that there may be some occasions in

Long-term objectives, such as those related to writing and written expression, may require months or even years to master.

Occasionally let students identify their *own* objectives.

which it is both appropriate and desirable for our students to identify their *own* objectives. For example, different students might choose different authors to read, different athletic skills to master, or different art media to use. By allowing students to establish some of their own objectives, we are encouraging the *goal setting* that, from the perspective of social cognitive theory, is an important aspect of self-regulation. We are also fostering the sense of *self-determination* that many theorists believe is so critical for intrinsic motivation.

Regardless of whether we or our students are the ones identifying the instructional objectives of a particular lesson or unit, those objectives should be determined before instruction ever begins. But how do we break down a larger instructional task—for example, a course in government, a unit on basketball, or a driver education class—into specific objectives? When we want to analyze the components of a topic or skill, several procedures known collectively as *task analysis* can help us pinpoint what our specific objectives should be.

USING TASK ANALYSIS TO PLAN INSTRUCTION

Consider these five teachers:

- Ms. Begay wants to teach her third-grade class how to learn more from the things they read. She also plans to teach her students how to solve arithmetic word problems.

- Mr. Marzano, a middle school physical education teacher, is beginning a unit on basketball. He wants his students to develop enough proficiency in the sport that they will feel comfortable playing both on organized school basketball teams and in less formal games with friends and neighbors.

- Ms. Flores, an eighth-grade social studies teacher, is going to introduce the intricacies of the federal judicial system to her classes.

- Mr. Wu, a junior high school music teacher, needs to teach his new trumpet students how to play a recognizable version of *Seventy-Six Trombones* in time for the New Year's Day parade.

- Mr. McKenzie must teach the students in his high school driver education class how to drive a car safely through the city streets.

These teachers have something in common: They are all about to teach complex skills or subject matter. And all five could benefit from breaking their skills and topics into smaller, more manageable components; that is, they could benefit from conducting a **task analysis.**

Exactly how do we break a complex task into smaller, simpler components? Figure 12–2 reflects three general approaches (Jonassen, Hannum, & Tessmer, 1989) we might take:

- Behavioral analysis

- Subject matter analysis

- Information processing analysis

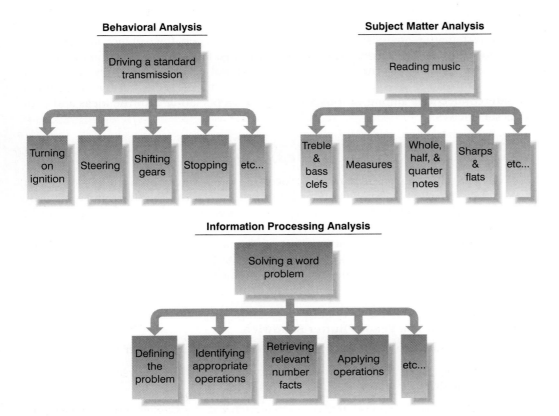

Figure 12–2   Three Ways of Analyzing a Task

Using Behavioral Analysis

Identify the specific behaviors required to perform a task.

One way of analyzing a complex task is to identify the specific behaviors required to perform that task (much as a behaviorist might do). For example, Mr. Marzano can identify the specific physical movements involved in dribbling, passing, and shooting a basketball. Mr. McKenzie can identify the actions required in driving an automobile with a standard transmission—turning on the ignition, steering, accelerating, stepping on the clutch, shifting gears, releasing the clutch, and braking. And Mr. Wu can identify the behaviors that students need to master in order to play a trumpet successfully—holding the instrument with the fingers placed appropriately on the valves, blowing correctly into the mouthpiece, and so on.

Using Subject Matter Analysis

Break down the subject matter in terms of specific topics, ideas, concepts, and so on.

Another approach to task analysis is to break down the subject matter in terms of the specific topics, ideas, concepts, and so on that it includes. To illustrate, Ms. Flores can identify various aspects of the judicial system—for example, such concepts as "innocent until proven guilty" and "reasonable doubt," and the roles that judges and juries play—and their interrelationships. Mr. Wu, who needs to teach his new trumpet students how to read music, as well as how to play the instrument, can consider the basic elements of written music—the difference between the treble and bass clefs, the number of beats associated with different notes, and so on—as well as how those elements are combined into a musical piece.

Subject matter analysis is especially important when the subject matter being taught includes many interrelated ideas and concepts. From an information processing perspective, we can help students learn class material more meaningfully, organize it better in their long-term memories, and remember it more effectively if we teach them the interconnections among various ideas and concepts along with the ideas and concepts themselves.

Using Information Processing Analysis

Break a task down in terms of the specific mental processes it involves.

A third approach, using an information processing perspective once again, is to break a task down in terms of the specific mental processes it involves. To illustrate, Ms. Begay can identify the mental processes involved in successfully solving an arithmetic word problem, such as correct classification (encoding) of the problem in terms of the operation required (e.g., addition, subtraction), and rapid retrieval of basic number facts. Similarly, she can identify some specific cognitive strategies useful in reading comprehension, such as identifying main ideas, learning meaningfully, elaborating, and summarizing.

 EXPERIENCING FIRSTHAND

Making a Peanut Butter Sandwich

Conduct a task analysis for the process of making a peanut butter sandwich.

1. Decide whether your approach should be a behavioral analysis, a subject matter analysis, or an information processing analysis.

2. Now, using the approach you've selected, break the sandwich-making task into a number of small, "teachable" steps.

Conducting task analyses for complex skills and topics has at least two advantages (Desberg & Taylor, 1986; Jonassen et al., 1989). For one thing, when we analyze a task in terms of its specific components—whether those components be behaviors, concepts and ideas, or mental processes—we have a better sense of what things we specifically need to teach our students and the order in which we should teach them. For example, Mr. McKenzie must teach his driver education students how to control the clutch before he can teach them how to shift gears. Mr. Wu must teach his trumpet students how to blow into the mouthpiece before he can teach them how to play different notes. At the same time, we may find that certain skills or topics we thought were important are actually *not* important. For example, a science teacher may realize that learning the history of science, though possibly having value in its own right, has little to do with how well students can apply scientific principles. And a history teacher may quickly discover that learning the names and dates of specific battles is not a prerequisite to students' understanding of how various groups of people have resolved their differences over the years.

Use a task analysis to identify the specific things students need to learn and in what sequence.

A second advantage to conducting a task analysis is that it helps us choose appropriate instructional strategies. Different tasks—and perhaps even different components of a single task—may require different approaches to instruction. For example, if one necessary component of solving arithmetic word problems is the rapid retrieval of math facts from memory, then repeated practice of these facts may be critical for developing automaticity. If another component of solving these problems is identifying the appropriate operation to apply, then an emphasis on meaningful problem solving (as described in Chapter 8) is essential.

Use a task analysis to identify suitable instructional methods.

Developing instructional objectives and conducting task analyses are two important ways in which we can pave the way for more effective instruction. But we must also create a classroom environment in which students are most likely to be productive learners. In the section that follows, we will consider a number of strategies through which we can do exactly that.

INTO THE CLASSROOM
Developing Instructional Objectives and Analyzing Classroom Tasks

Describe objectives in terms of what students will be able to do at the end of instruction—that is, in terms of desired outcomes.

A Spanish teacher knows that students easily confuse the verbs *estar* and *ser* because both are translated in English as *to be*. She identifies this objective for her students: "Students will correctly conjugate *estar* and *ser* in the present tense and use each one in appropriate contexts."

When desired outcomes are limited in scope, describe them in terms of specific, observable behaviors.

An elementary art teacher identifies this objective for his students: "At the end of each session, students will rinse out any paintbrushes and water containers they have used and put all materials away."

When desired outcomes involve a complex topic or skill, list a few general (and perhaps not directly observable) objectives and then give examples of specific behaviors that reflect each one.

> A junior high school principal identifies this objective for students at her school: "Students will demonstrate effective classroom listening skills—for example, by taking complete and accurate notes, answering teacher questions correctly, and seeking clarification when they don't understand."

Consider objectives within the cognitive domain.

> A high school teacher identifies this objective for a unit on English history: "Students will describe what the Magna Carta was and how it laid the groundwork for a more democratic government in England."

Consider objectives within the psychomotor domain.

> A physical education teacher identifies an objective that he wants everyone to accomplish by the end of the school year: "Students will run a mile within eight minutes."

Consider objectives within the affective domain.

> An elementary teacher identifies this objective: "Students will show empathy and compassion for classmates on occasions that call for such prosocial behaviors."

Write objectives that reflect several levels of knowing and using information and skills.

> A high school physics teacher wants students not only to understand the basic kinds of machines (e.g., levers, wedges) but also to recognize examples of these machines in their own lives and use them to solve problems.

Identify both short-term and long-term objectives.

> An elementary school teacher wants students to correctly spell a list of ten new words each week. She also wants them to write a coherent and grammatically correct short story by the end of the school year.

Identify the specific behaviors required to accomplish an objective.

> A gymnastics teacher identifies the specific sequence of movements required to execute a forward roll.

Identify the specific topics, ideas, concepts, and so on that the subject matter includes.

> In a unit on endangered species, a science teacher realizes that he will have to include such topics as habitat destruction, hunting practices, and governmental policies.

Identify the specific mental processes involved in accomplishing an objective.

> A reading teacher recognizes that reading comprehension includes such things as retrieving relevant prior knowledge, drawing inferences, and monitoring comprehension.

In what kind of environment can you most easily study and learn? Can you concentrate on your studies when you work alone somewhere? when you are in the same room with other students who are also working quietly? when those around you are moving about the room or talking about irrelevant topics? when your fellow students are talking with you about the subject matter you are studying?

Just as is true for us, our students are likely to learn more effectively in some classroom environments than in others. Consider these four classrooms as examples:

- Mr. Aragon's classroom is a calm, orderly one. The students are working independently at their seats, and all of them appear to be concentrating on their assigned tasks. Occasionally, students approach Mr. Aragon to seek clarification of an assignment or get feedback about a task they've completed, and he confers quietly with them.

- Mr. Boitano's class is chaotic and noisy. A few students are doing their schoolwork, but most are engaged in very nonacademic activities. One girl is painting her nails behind a large dictionary propped up on her desk, a boy nearby is picking wads of gum off the underside of his desk, several students are exchanging the latest school gossip, and a group of boys is re-creating the Battle of Waterloo with rubber bands and paper clips.

- Mr. Cavalini's classroom is as noisy as Boitano's. But rather than exchanging gossip or waging war, students are debating (often loudly and passionately) about the pros and cons of capital punishment. After twenty minutes of heated discussion, Cavalini stops them, lists their various arguments on the board, and then explains in simple philosophical terms why there is no easy or "correct" resolution of the issue.

- Mr. Durocher believes that students learn most effectively when rules for their behavior are clearly spelled out. So he has rules for almost every conceivable occasion—fifty-three rules in all. Here is a small sample:

  Be in your seat before the bell rings.

  Use a ballpoint pen with blue or black ink for all assignments.

  Use white lined paper with straight edges; do not use paper with loose-leaf holes or spiral notebook "fringe."

  Raise your hand if you wish to speak, and then speak only when called upon.

  Do not ask questions unrelated to the topic being studied.

  Never leave your seat without permission.

  Durocher punishes each infraction severely enough that students follow the rules to the letter. So his students are a quiet and obedient, if somewhat anxious, bunch. Yet they never seem to learn as much as Durocher knows they are capable of learning.

Remember that an effectively managed classroom does not necessarily have to be a quiet one.

Two of these classrooms are quiet and orderly; the other two are active and noisy. Yet as you can see, the activity and noise levels are not good indicators of how much students are learning. Students are learning in Aragon's quiet classroom, but also in Cavalini's rambunctious one. At the same time, neither the students in Boitano's loud, chaotic battlefield nor those in Durocher's peaceful military dictatorship seem to be learning much at all.

Effective **classroom management** has little to do with the noise or activity level of the classroom. But it has everything to do with how effectively students can learn and achieve in that classroom. A well-managed classroom is one in which students are consistently engaged in the learning tasks and classroom activities their teachers have set for them and very few student behaviors interfere with those tasks and activities (Doyle, 1990a, 1990b; Emmer & Evertson, 1981; Munn, Johnstone, & Chalmers, 1990).

Is it possible to *over*manage a classroom? If so, what might be the negative ramifications of doing so?

Establishing and maintaining a classroom environment in which students participate eagerly and actively in classroom activities can be a challenging task indeed. After all, we must tend to the unique needs of many different students, we must often coordinate several activities at the same time, and we must make frequent, quick decisions about how to respond to unanticipated events (Doyle, 1986a). So it is not surprising that beginning teachers usually mention classroom management as their number one concern (Veenman, 1984).

Effective classroom management requires considerable advance planning (Gettinger, 1988). As teachers, we need to think ahead of time about strategies for keeping classroom activities flowing smoothly and for keeping students on task. We must also take steps to minimize the likelihood of disruptive influences and develop procedures for dealing with those disruptions that *do* occur. Here is where Ms. Corbett, in our case study at the beginning of the chapter, went astray: Although she spent a good deal of time planning her curriculum for the upcoming school year, she apparently did not also develop a plan regarding how she might create and maintain a classroom environment in which her students would be productive learners. In the absence of such an environment, no curriculum—not even one grounded firmly in the principles of learning we have studied—is likely to promote student achievement.

Effective teachers establish a classroom environment in which students are focused on learning and achieving instructional objectives, and they take steps to minimize the extent to which nonproductive and counterproductive behaviors are likely to occur (Doyle, 1990b; Kounin, 1970; Munn et al., 1990). More specifically, effective teachers:

Of the classrooms you have observed, which ones were the most effectively managed? What specifically did the teachers of those classrooms do?

- Physically arrange the classroom in a way that facilitates teacher-student interactions and keeps distracting influences to a minimum

- Create a classroom climate in which students have a sense of belonging and an intrinsic motivation to learn

- Set reasonable limits for student behavior

- Plan classroom activities that encourage on-task behavior

- Are continually aware of what all students are doing in the classroom

- Modify instructional strategies when necessary to maintain on-task behavior

In the next few pages, we will consider a number of ways in which we might accomplish these things.

Arranging the Classroom

As we arrange the furniture in the classroom, as we decide where to put various instructional materials and pieces of equipment, and as we determine where each student should be seated, we should consider the effects that various arrangements are likely to have on our students' behaviors. Ultimately, we want a situation in which we can:

- Keep distractions to a minimum

- Interact easily with any student

- Survey the entire classroom at any given point in time

Keeping Distractions to a Minimum

David is more likely to gossip with a friend if that friend is sitting right beside him. Marlene is more likely to play with instructional materials without her teacher's permission if those materials are within easy reach of her desk. Stuart is more likely to poke a classmate with his pencil if he has to brush past that classmate to get to the pencil sharpener. As teachers, we can arrange our classrooms in ways that minimize the extent to which such off-task behaviors are likely to occur (G. A. Davis & Thomas, 1989; Emmer, Evertson, Clements, & Worsham, 1994; Sabers, Cushing, & Berliner, 1991). For example, we can situate overly chatty friends on opposite sides of the room, keep intriguing materials out of sight and reach until it is time to use them, and establish traffic patterns that allow students to move about in the classroom without disturbing one another.

Minimize possible distractions.

Facilitating Teacher-Student Interaction

Ideally, we should arrange desks, tables, and chairs in such a way that we can easily interact and converse with our students (G. A. Davis & Thomas, 1989). Students seated near their teacher are more likely to pay attention, interact with their teacher, and become actively involved in classroom activities; hence, we may want to place chronically misbehaving or uninvolved students close at hand (Doyle, 1986a; Schwebel & Cherlin, 1972; C. S. Weinstein, 1979; Woolfolk & Brooks, 1985).

Arrange your classroom in such a way that you can easily interact with all your students. Place chronically misbehaving or uninvolved students close at hand.

Surveying the Entire Class

As we proceed through the various lessons and activities that we have planned—even when we're working with a single individual or small group—we need to be able to see *all* of our students (Emmer et al., 1994). By occasionally surveying the classroom for possible signs of confusion, frustration, or boredom, we are better able to detect minor student difficulties and misbehaviors before they develop into more serious problems.

Situate yourself such that you can always see all of your students.

Creating an Effective Classroom Climate

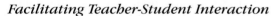

THINKING ABOUT WHAT YOU KNOW

Think back to your many experiences as a student. Can you think of a class in which you were afraid of being ridiculed if you asked a "stupid" question? Can you think of a class in which you and your fellow students spent more time goofing off than getting your work done because no one (not even the instructor!) seemed to take the class seriously? Can

Effective classroom managers situate themselves so that they can see the entire classroom at all times, regardless of what they are doing.

you think of a class in which you never knew what to expect because your instructor was continually changing expectations and giving last-minute assignments without warning?

In addition to the classroom's physical environment, we must also consider the psychological environment, or **classroom climate,** that we create for our students. Ideally, we want a classroom climate in which our students make their own learning a high priority. We also want one in which students feel free to take the risks and make the mistakes so critical for their long-term academic progress. There are several things we can do to create such a classroom climate; more specifically, we can:

- Communicate acceptance of, respect for, and caring about our students as human beings

- Establish a businesslike, yet nonthreatening, atmosphere

- Give students some sense of control with regard to classroom activities

- Create a sense of community among students

Showing Acceptance, Respect, and Caring

As you should recall from our discussion of social needs in Chapter 11, many of the students in our classrooms are likely to have a high need for affiliation: They will want friendly relationships with others and so will seek out such relationships. Many will also have a high need for approval: They will attempt to gain the approval and acceptance of those around them.

Communicate your care and concern through the many "little things" you do each day.

We can help our students meet such needs through our own actions, including the many little things we do on a daily basis. For example, we can give students a smile and warm greeting at the beginning of each class day. We can compliment them when they get a new haircut, excel in an extracurricular activity, or receive recognition in the local newspaper. We can offer our support when they struggle at challenging classroom tasks and let them know we're pleased when they eventually succeed at such tasks. We can be good listeners when they come to school angry or upset. And we can show them how we, too, are fallible human beings by sharing some of our own concerns, problems, and frustrations (Diamond, 1991; Spaulding, 1992). Research is clear on this point: Effective teachers are warm, caring individuals who, through a variety of statements and actions, communicate a respect for students, an acceptance of them as they are, and a genuine concern about their well-being (Charles, 1983; G. A. Davis & Thomas, 1989; Emmer & Evertson, 1981; Emmer et al., 1994; C. B. Hayes, Ryan, & Zseller, 1994; Kim, Solomon, & Roberts, 1995; Palardy & Mudrey, 1973).

Such teacher behaviors may be particularly beneficial for those students who have few caring relationships to draw on at home (Diamond, 1991).

Establishing a Businesslike, Nonthreatening Atmosphere

As we have just seen, an important element of effective classroom management is developing positive relationships with our students. At the same time, we must recognize that we and our students alike are in school to get certain things accomplished. Accordingly, we should maintain a relatively businesslike atmosphere in the classroom most of the time (G. A. Davis & Thomas, 1989). This is not to say that our classroom activities must be boring and tedious; on the contrary, they can often be exciting and engaging. But excitement and entertainment should not be thought of as goals in and of themselves. Rather, they are means to a more important goal: achieving instructional objectives.

Maintain a businesslike atmosphere, focusing on the achievement of instructional objectives. But refrain from behaviors that students will view as threatening.

We should also note that a "businesslike" atmosphere does not mean an uncomfortable or threatening one. As we discovered in our discussion of motivation in Chapter 11, students who are excessively anxious about their class performance are unlikely to give us their best. How can we be businesslike without being threatening? Among other things, we can hold our students accountable for achieving instructional objectives yet not place them under continual surveillance. We can point out their mistakes yet not make them feel like failures (Combs, 1979, 1981; Combs et al., 1976; Rogers, 1969, 1983; Schmuck & Schmuck, 1974). We can admonish them for their misbehaviors yet not hold grudges against them from one day to the next (Spaulding, 1992). And, as we shall see now, we can give them a sense that they themselves have some control over the things that happen to them in the classroom.

Giving Students a Sense of Control

As we discovered in Chapter 11, students who believe that they can control the things that happen to them—those with a sense of self-determination—are more likely to be

The classroom climate should be one in which students believe that they can express their opinions and feelings openly and candidly.

successful in the classroom. For example, such students are more intrinsically motivated, try harder, persist longer, and ultimately achieve at higher levels.

As teachers, we will have specific instructional objectives for our students, and we must control the direction of classroom events to some extent to ensure that those objectives are accomplished. Yet within such constraints we can nevertheless give our students a sense that they, too, control some aspects of classroom life. For example, we can:

Let students control some aspects of classroom life.

- Create regular routines for accomplishing assignments (enabling students to complete them correctly with minimal guidance from us)

- Give students advance notice of upcoming activities and assignments (enabling them to plan ahead)

- Allow students to set some of their own deadlines for completing assignments (enabling them to establish reasonable timelines for themselves)

In what sense do Eli, Jake, and Vanessa have a sense of control in Ms. Corbett's class? What might Ms. Corbett do to help them control their classroom lives in more productive ways?

- Provide opportunities for students to make choices about how to complete assignments or spend their class time (enabling them to set some of their own priorities) (Spaulding, 1992)

By giving students such opportunities to work independently and to choose some of their own means of achieving classroom objectives, we can give them a very real sense of control over certain aspects of their academic lives. We can also promote the self-regulation that, from the perspective of social cognitive theory (Chapter 10), is so essential for self-sustained learning over the long run.

Creating a Sense of Community

Create a sense of shared goals, interpersonal respect, and mutual support.

Ultimately, we want to create a **sense of community** in our classrooms—a sense that both we and our students have shared goals, are mutually respectful and supportive of one another's efforts, and believe that everyone makes an important contribution to classroom learning (Hom & Battistich, 1995; Kim et al., 1995; Lickona, 1991). Theorists have identified several strategies that seem to help create a sense of community in the classroom; more specifically, we can:

- Solicit students' ideas and opinions, and incorporate them into classroom discussions and activities

- Create mechanisms through which students can help make the classroom run more smoothly and efficiently (e.g., by assigning "helper" roles to different students on a rotating basis)

- Emphasize such prosocial values as sharing, cooperation, and helping classmates succeed

- Provide opportunities for students to help one another (e.g., by asking, "Who has a problem that someone else might be able to help you solve?")

- Provide public recognition of students' contributions to the overall success of the classroom (Emmer et al., 1994; Kim et al., 1995; Lickona, 1991; Maskowitz & Hayman, 1976)

When students share a sense of community, they are more likely to stay on-task, to express enthusiasm about classroom activities, and to achieve at high levels (Hom &

Battistich, 1995; Kim et al., 1995). A sense of community in the classroom is also associated with more frequent prosocial behavior and with *less* frequent truancy, disruptive behavior, violence, and drug use (Hom & Battistich, 1995; Kim et al., 1995).

This sense of a community of learners also has implications for instructional practice, as you will discover in Chapter 13.

Setting Limits

Despite students' need for control and self-determination, some degree of order and regularity is essential in any classroom if students are to work productively and consistently toward instructional objectives (Doyle, 1990a; Emmer et al., 1994; Gettinger, 1988). A classroom without any guidelines for appropriate behavior is apt to be chaotic and unproductive. And students must learn that certain behaviors—especially those that cause injury, damage school property, or interfere with classmates' learning and performance—are totally unacceptable and so cannot be tolerated.

As teachers, then, we will need to establish certain limits regarding what constitutes acceptable behavior in the classroom. Not only will such limits promote a more productive learning environment, but they will also contribute to the socialization of students—to the development of those behaviors so essential for successful participation in the adult world.

Experienced educators have offered several suggestions for setting reasonable limits on students' classroom behavior. More specifically, they suggest that we:

- Establish a few rules and procedures at the beginning of the year
- Present rules and procedures in an informational rather than controlling manner
- Periodically review the usefulness of existing rules and procedures
- Acknowledge students' feelings about classroom requirements

As we consider these suggestions, we will also consider how we can preserve students' sense of control and self-determination.

Establishing a Few Rules and Procedures at the Beginning of the Year

The first few days and weeks of the school year are critical ones for establishing classroom procedures and setting expectations for student behavior (Doyle, 1986a; Emmer, Evertson, & Anderson, 1980). Effective classroom managers establish and communicate certain rules and procedures right from the start (Bents & Bents, 1990; G. A. Davis & Thomas, 1989; Doyle, 1986a, 1990a; Emmer & Evertson, 1981; Emmer et al., 1994; Evertson & Emmer, 1982; Gettinger, 1988). They identify acceptable and unacceptable behaviors (see Figure 12–3 for examples). They develop consistent procedures and routines for such things as completing seatwork, asking for help, and turning in assignments. And they have procedures in place for such nonroutine events as school assemblies, field trips, and fire drills.

Establish some rules and procedures at the beginning of the year.

Ideally, our students should understand that rules and procedures are not merely the result of our own personal whims, but are designed to help the classroom run smoothly and efficiently. One way of promoting such understanding is to include students in decision making about the rules and procedures by which the class will operate (G. A. Davis & Thomas, 1989; C. A. Grant & Gomez, 1996; Lickona, 1991; Palardy & Mudrey, 1973). For example, we might solicit students' suggestions for making sure that unnecessary distractions are kept to a minimum and that everyone has a chance to speak during classroom discussion. By incorporating students' ideas and concerns re-

Consider once again our "contagious situation" case study. Did Ms. Corbett get the school year off to a good start in terms of setting limits?

Figure 12–3 Beginning the School Year with a Few Rules

Effective teachers typically begin the school year with a few rules that will help classroom activities run smoothly. Here are several examples of rules you might want to include in your list (adapted from Emmer et al., 1994):

- **Bring all needed materials to class.**

  Students should bring any books, completed homework assignments, permission slips, and so on that will be needed that day.

- **Be in your seat and ready to work when the bell rings.**

  Students should be at their desks, have paper out and pencils sharpened, and be physically and mentally ready to work.

- **Respect and be polite to all people.**

  Students should listen attentively when the teacher or another student is speaking, behave appropriately for a substitute teacher, and refrain from insults, fighting, and other disrespectful or hostile behavior.

- **Respect other people's property.**

  Students should keep the classroom clean and neat, refrain from defacing school property, ask for permission to borrow another's possessions, and return those possessions in a timely fashion.

- **Obey all school rules.**

  Students must obey the rules of the school building as well as the rules of the classroom.

garding the limits we set, we help them understand the purpose of these limits and so to behave in accordance with them (Emmer et al., 1994).

Once rules and procedures have been formulated, we should communicate them clearly and explicitly; we should also describe the consequences of not complying with them. Taking time to clarify rules and procedures seems to be especially important in the early elementary grades, when students may not be as familiar with "how things are done" at school (Evertson & Emmer, 1982; Gettinger, 1988; Shultz & Florio, 1979).

We should keep in mind here that rules and procedures are easier to remember and therefore easier to follow if they are relatively simple and few in number (G. A. Davis & Thomas, 1989). Effective classroom managers tend to stress only the most important rules and procedures at the beginning of the school year, introducing other rules and procedures as they are needed later on (Doyle, 1986a). We should also remember that although a certain degree of order and predictability is essential for student productivity, *too much* order may make our classroom a rather boring, routine place—one without an element of fun and spontaneity. We don't necessarily need rules and procedures for everything!

Presenting Rules and Procedures in an Informational Manner

Describe rules and procedures in an informational rather than controlling manner.

As we have learned, our students are more likely to be intrinsically motivated to follow classroom rules and procedures if we present these things as items of information, rather than as forms of control (Deci & Ryan, 1985, 1987). Some examples of how we might do so are presented in Figure 12–4.

Figure 12–4   Describing Classroom Rules and Procedures

Our students are more likely to be intrinsically motivated to follow classroom rules and procedures if we present them as items of information, rather than as forms of control.

WE MIGHT SAY THIS (INFORMATION):	. . . RATHER THAN THIS (CONTROL):
"You'll get your independent assignments done more quickly if you get right to work."	"Please be quiet and do your own work."
"As we practice for our fire drill, it is important that we line up quickly and be quiet so that we can hear the instructions we are given and will know what to do."	"When the fire alarm sounds, line up quickly and quietly and then wait for further instructions."
"This assignment is designed to help you develop the writing skills you will need in college. College professors do not allow their students to copy word for word from reference materials, so we will practice putting ideas into our own words and giving credit to authors whose ideas we borrow."	"Cheating and plagiarism are not acceptable in this classroom."
"I'm having trouble reading what you've written; some of your words are illegible, and your cross-outs are very confusing. I'm afraid that I may not be giving you as high a grade as you deserve on this assignment.	Use good penmanship on all assignments and erase any errors carefully and completely. Points will be deducted for sloppy writing."

Notice how the informational statements on the left-hand side of Figure 12–4 often include reasons regarding why certain guidelines for student behavior have been set. As we discovered in Chapter 3, our students are more likely to follow rules and procedures when the reasons behind them are explained. For example, we might want to explain how such rules and procedures ensure efficient use of instructional time and maximize the chances of students' success (Gettinger, 1988). Ideally, we want to provide the kind of information that will entice our students to choose voluntarily to obey the limits we set for them (Lepper, 1983).

For more information on the benefits of providing reasons, see our discussion of *induction* in Chapter 3.

Periodically Reviewing the Usefulness of Existing Rules and Procedures

We must keep in mind that the limits we set in the first days or weeks of the school year may be less necessary as the year progresses. For example, we may find that our rules about when students can and cannot move around the room are overly restrictive or that procedures for turning in homework don't adequately accommodate students who must sometimes leave class early to attend athletic events. Accordingly, we should frequently reassess the rules and procedures that we have established and revise them when needed.

Regularly scheduled class meetings provide one mechanism through which we and our students can periodically review classroom rules and procedures (D. E. Campbell,

When it is necessary to change classroom rules and procedures, include students in decision making.

1996; Dreikurs & Cassel, 1972; Glasser, 1969; C. A. Grant & Gomez, 1996). Consider this scenario as an example:

> Every Friday at 2:00, Ms. Ayotte's students move their chairs into one large circle and the weekly class meeting begins. First on the agenda is a review of the past week's successes, including both academic achievements and socially productive events. Next, the group identifies problems that have emerged during the week and brainstorms about possible ways to avert such problems in the future. Finally, the students consider whether existing classroom rules and procedures are serving their purpose. In some cases, they may modify existing rules and procedures; in other cases, they may establish new ones.
>
> During the first few class meetings, Ms. Ayotte leads the group in its discussions. But once students have gotten the hang of things, she begins to relinquish control of the meetings to one or another of her students on a rotating basis.

By providing such opportunities for students to continually revise classroom policies, we find one more way of giving them a sense of ownership in such policies. Furthermore, perhaps because of the authoritative atmosphere and the conversations about moral dilemmas that such student involvement in decision making may entail, more advanced levels of moral reasoning (as described in Chapter 3) may result (A. Higgins, Powers, & Kohlberg, 1984).

Acknowledging Students' Feelings

THINKING ABOUT WHAT YOU KNOW

As a student, have you ever resented the restrictions placed on you? For example, were there times you had to sit quietly in your seat when you would rather have been talking with your classmates or getting up to stretch your legs? Were there times you had to devote an entire evening to a lengthy homework assignment when you would rather have been watching a favorite television show? Were there times you had to stay after school for extra help when you would rather have joined the neighborhood crowd in a game of softball in the park?

There will undoubtedly be times when we must ask our students to do something they would prefer not to do. Rather than pretend that such feelings don't exist, we are better advised to acknowledge them (Deci & Ryan, 1985). For example, we might tell students that we know how difficult it can be to sit quietly during an unexpectedly lengthy school assembly or to spend an entire evening on a particular homework assignment. At the same time, we can explain to them that the behaviors we request of them, though not always intrinsically enjoyable, do, in fact, contribute to the long-term goals they have set for themselves (Deci & Ryan, 1985). By acknowledging students' feelings about tasks they would rather not do and by pointing out the benefits of performing those tasks, we increase the likelihood that they will accept the limitations we impose on their behavior (Deci & Ryan, 1985).

As we discovered in Chapter 3, children who grow up in *authoritative* environments tend to be the most well-adjusted children. Do you see parallels between the authoritative home and the guidelines for setting limits described in this chapter?

Acknowledge students' feelings when you ask them to do something they would rather not do.

Planning Classroom Activities

Plan classroom activities in advance.

As we noted earlier, effective teachers plan each day's activities ahead of time. They think about how to make subject matter interesting and incorporate variety into lessons, perhaps by employing colorful audiovisual aids, using novel activities (e.g., small-group discussions, class debates), or moving to a different location (e.g., to the media center or outside school grounds). And they develop strategies for explaining difficult topics in a way that students can understand (Bents & Bents, 1990; G. A. Davis & Thomas, 1989; Kounin, 1970; Munn et al., 1990). In other words, effective teachers plan activities and strategies designed to keep their students' interest and attention, help them achieve success on school tasks, and minimize the likelihood that they will engage in off-task, nonproductive behaviors.

This is not to say that, as teachers, we must always stick to our carefully laid-out lesson plans. On the contrary, our students' questions and concerns—perhaps about a topic related to the one under study, a controversial current event on the national or international scene, or an exciting or upsetting local news item—may occasionally take priority. When our students' minds are justifiably preoccupied with something other than the topic we had in mind for the day, they will have difficulty paying attention to that preplanned topic and are likely to learn little about it.

In your own classes, how can you tell when your instructors have or have not adequately planned lessons and activities ahead of time?

As we plan our upcoming classroom activities, we should simultaneously plan specific ways of keeping our students on task. Among other things, we can:

- Be sure students will always be busy and engaged

- Choose tasks at an appropriate academic level

- Provide a reasonable amount of structure for activities and assignments

- Make special plans for transition times in the school day

Keeping Students Busy and Engaged

EXPERIENCING FIRSTHAND
Take Five

For the next five minutes, you are going to be a student who has nothing to do. *Remain exactly where you are,* put your book aside, and *do nothing.* Time yourself so that you spend exactly five minutes on this "task." Let's see what happens.

What kinds of responses did you make during your five-minute break? Did you fidget a bit, perhaps wiggling tired body parts, scratching newly detected itches, or picking at your nails? Did you "interact" in some way with something or someone else, perhaps tapping loudly on a table, turning on a radio, or talking with someone else in the room? Did you get out of your seat altogether—something I specifically asked you not to do?

The exercise I just gave you was a somewhat artificial one, to be sure, and the things I am defining as "misbehaviors" in this instance (e.g., wiggling your toes, tapping the table, getting out of your seat) won't necessarily qualify as misbehaviors in your classroom. Yet I hope that the exercise has demonstrated the point I want to make here: It is very difficult for most of us to do *nothing at all* for any length of time. Like us, our students will be most likely to misbehave when they have a lot of free time on their hands.

Effective classroom managers make sure their students are always busy and engaged—that there is little "empty" time in which nothing is going on. As teachers, there are numerous strategies we can use to keep our students busy and engaged; as examples, we can:

- Have something specific for students to do each day, even on the first day of class

- Have materials organized and equipment set up before class

- Have activities that ensure *all* students' involvement and participation

- Maintain a brisk pace throughout each lesson (although not so fast that students can't keep up)

- Ensure that student comments are relevant and helpful but not excessively long-winded

- Spend only short periods of time dealing with individual students during class unless other students are capable of working independently and productively in the meantime

- Have a system in place that ensures that students who finish an assigned task before their classmates have something else to do (Arlin, 1979; G. A. Davis & Thomas, 1989; Doyle, 1986a; Emmer et al., 1980; Emmer et al., 1994; Evertson & Emmer, 1982; Evertson & Harris, 1992; Gettinger, 1988; Kounin, 1970; Kounin & Doyle, 1975; Munn et al., 1990; J. Scott & Bushell, 1974)

Students who are busily engaged in classroom activities rarely exhibit problem behaviors.

Choosing Tasks at an Appropriate Level

Our students are more likely to get involved in their classwork, rather than in off-task behavior, when they have academic tasks and assignments appropriate for their current ability levels (Doyle, 1986a; Emmer et al., 1994; Kounin & Gump, 1974). They are apt to misbehave when they are asked to do things that are probably too difficult for them—in other words, when they are incapable of completing assigned tasks successfully. Thus, classroom misbehaviors are more often observed in lower-ability students—students with a history of struggling in their coursework (Doyle, 1986a).

This is not to say that the classroom activities we plan should be so easy that our students are not challenged by them and learn nothing new in doing them. One workable strategy is to *begin* the school year with relatively easy tasks—more specifically, with tasks that students are familiar with, enjoy, and can successfully complete. Such early tasks and assignments enable students to practice normal classroom routines and procedures; they also give students a sense that they can enjoy and be successful in classroom activities. Once a supportive classroom climate has been established and students are comfortable with classroom procedures, we can gradually introduce more difficult and challenging assignments (Doyle, 1986a, 1990a; Emmer et al., 1980; Emmer et al., 1994; Evertson & Emmer, 1982).

Ensure that tasks and assignments are at an appropriate level for students. Begin the school year with easy and familiar tasks, introducing more difficult tasks once a supportive classroom climate has been established.

With this point in mind, how might Ms. Corbett (in our case study at the beginning of the chapter) have gotten the year off to a better start?

Providing Structure

◼ EXPERIENCING FIRSTHAND
Take Five More

Grab a blank sheet of paper and a pen or pencil, and complete these two tasks:

Task A: Using short phrases, list six characteristics of a good teacher.

Task B: Describe *schooling*.

Don't continue reading until you've spent a total of at least *five minutes* on these tasks.

Once you have completed the two tasks, answer either "Task A" or "Task B" to each of the following questions:

	Task A	Task B
1. For which task did you have a better understanding of what you were being asked to do?	———	———
2. During which task did your mind more frequently wander to irrelevant topics?	———	———
3. During which task did you engage in more off-task behaviors (e.g., looking around the room, doodling on the paper, getting out of your seat)?	———	——— ◼

I am guessing that you found the first task to be a relatively straightforward one, whereas the second wasn't at all clear-cut. Did the ambiguity of what I was asking you to do in Task B lead to a greater number of irrelevant thoughts and more frequent off-task behavior?

Just as may have been the case for you in the preceding exercise, off-task behavior in the classroom occurs more frequently when activities are so loosely structured that students don't have a clear sense of what they are supposed to do. Effective teachers

Structure classroom activities to some extent, explaining the purpose of those activities and the nature of the performance you expect.

tend to give assignments with some degree of structure. They also give clear directions about how to proceed with a task and a great deal of feedback about appropriate responses, especially during the first few weeks of class (Doyle, 1990a; Emmer & Evertson, 1981; Emmer et al., 1980; Evertson & Emmer, 1982; Kounin & Gump, 1974; Munn et al., 1990).

Yet we need to strike a happy medium here. We don't want to structure classroom tasks to the point where students never make their own decisions about how to proceed or to the point where only lower-level thinking skills are required. Ultimately, we want our students to develop and use higher-level processes—for example, to think analytically, critically, and creatively—and we must have classroom assignments and activities that promote such processes (e.g., Doyle, 1986a).

A viable approach can be found in Vygotsky's notion of *scaffolding* (described in Chapter 2): We can provide a great deal of structure for tasks early in the school year, gradually removing that structure as students become better able to structure tasks for themselves. As an example, if we are introducing our students to cooperative learning, we might structure initial group meetings by breaking down each group task into several subtasks, giving clear directions as to how each subtask should be carried out, and assigning every group member a particular role to serve in the group. As the school year progresses and students become more adept at learning cooperatively with their classmates, we can become gradually less directive about how group tasks are accomplished.

Plan for a smooth and rapid transition from one activity to another.

Planning for Transitions

Transition times—as students end one activity and begin a second, or as they move from one classroom to another—are times when misbehaviors are especially likely to occur. Effective classroom managers take steps to ensure that such transitions proceed quickly and without a loss of momentum (Arlin, 1979; Doyle, 1984; Emmer et al., 1994). For example, they establish procedures for moving from one activity to the next. They ensure that there is little slack time in which students have nothing to do. At the secondary level, where students change classes every hour or so, effective classroom managers typically have things for students to do as soon as class begins.

How might we plan for the various transitions that occur throughout the school day? Here are some examples:

Refer once again to our case study at the beginning of the chapter. At what times are Eli, Jake, and Vanessa most likely to engage in misbehavior? Why do you think they are most likely to misbehave at these times?

- A physical education teacher has students begin each class session with five minutes of stretching exercises.

- An elementary school teacher has students follow the same procedure each day as lunchtime approaches. Students must (1) place any assignments they have completed into a basket on the teacher's desk, (2) put any classroom supplies they have used (e.g., pencils, paint, scissors) back where they belong, (3) get their lunch boxes from the coatroom, and (4) line up quietly by the classroom door.

- A middle school mathematics teacher has students copy the new homework assignment as soon as they come to class.

- A junior high school history teacher has formed long-term cooperative learning groups (*base groups*) of three or four students each. The groups are given a few minutes at the end of each class to compare notes on material presented that day and to get a head start on the evening's reading assignment).

- A high school English composition teacher writes a topic or question (e.g., "My biggest pet peeve," "Whatever happened to hula hoops?") on the chalkboard at the beginning of each class period. Students know that when they come to class, they should immediately take out pencil and paper and begin to write on the topic or question of the day.

Notice how all of these strategies, though very different in nature, share a common goal—to keep students focused on their schoolwork.

Monitoring What Students Are Doing

Effective teachers communicate something called **withitness:** They know (and their students *know* that they know) what all students are doing at all times. In a sense, "with-it" teachers act as if they have eyes in the back of their heads. They make it clear that they can see what everyone is doing. They scan the classroom on a regular basis and make frequent eye contact with individual students. They know what misbehaviors are occurring *when* those misbehaviors occur, and they know who the perpetrators are (G. A. Davis & Thomas, 1989; Emmer, 1987; Emmer et al., 1994; Kounin, 1970). Consider this scenario as an example:

Let students know that *you* know what's going on in your classroom.

> An hour and a half of each morning in Mr. Rennaker's elementary school classroom is devoted to reading. Students know that, for part of this time, they will meet with Mr. Rennaker in their small reading groups. They spend the remainder of the time working on independent assignments tailored to the reading skills of individual students. As Mr. Rennaker works with each reading group in one corner of the classroom, he situates himself with his back to the wall so that he can simultaneously keep one eye on students working independently at their seats. He sends a quick and subtle signal—perhaps a stern expression, a finger to the lips, or a call of a student's name—to any student who begins to be disruptive.

When we demonstrate such withitness, especially at the beginning of the school year, our students are more likely to stay on-task and display appropriate classroom behavior (Doyle, 1986a; Woolfolk & Brooks, 1985). And not surprisingly, they are also more likely to achieve at higher levels (Doyle, 1986a).

Modifying Instructional Strategies When Necessary

As we have repeatedly seen, principles of effective classroom management go hand in hand with principles of learning and motivation. When our students are learning and achieving successfully and when they clearly want to pursue the curriculum that the classroom has to offer, they are likely to be busily engaged in productive classroom activities for most of the school day (Doyle, 1986a, 1990a). In contrast, when they have difficulty understanding classroom subject matter or when they have little interest in learning it, they are likely to exhibit the nonproductive or even counterproductive classroom behaviors that result from frustration or boredom.

Research tells us that when students misbehave, beginning teachers often think in terms of what the students are doing wrong. In contrast, experienced, "expert" teachers are more apt to think about what *they themselves* can do differently to keep students on

When students continually misbehave, think about what *you* might do differently in terms of instruction.

task (Sabers et al., 1991). So when behavior problems crop up, we should start thinking as the experts do, by considering such questions as these:

- How can I alter instructional strategies to capture students' interest and excitement?

- Are instructional materials so difficult that students are becoming frustrated? Or are they so easy that students are bored?

- What are students really concerned about? For example, are they more concerned about interacting with their classmates than in gaining new knowledge and skills?

- How can I address students' motives (e.g., their need for affiliation) while simultaneously helping them achieve classroom objectives?

We must always keep in mind our ultimate goal in education: to help students *learn*.

From your own perspective, what are the key ingredients of a successfully managed classroom?

INTO THE CLASSROOM

Establishing and Maintaining a Productive Learning Environment

Physically arrange the classroom in a way that facilitates teacher-student interactions and keeps distracting influences to a minimum.

An elementary school teacher has arranged the twenty-eight student desks in his classroom into seven clusters of four desks each. The students who sit together in clusters form base groups for many of the classroom's cooperative learning activities. The teacher occasionally asks students to move their chairs into a large circle for whole-class discussions.

Show students that you respect them as human beings and are concerned about their well-being.

A high school teacher realizes that she continually admonishes one particular student for his off-task behavior. To establish a more positive relationship with the student, she makes a point to greet him warmly in the hallway before school every day. And at the end of one day in which his behavior has been especially disruptive, she catches him briefly to express her concern, and the two agree to meet the following morning to discuss ways of helping him stay on-task more regularly.

Set reasonable limits for student behavior.

After describing the objectives of an instrumental music class on the first day of school, a junior high school teacher tells his students, "There is one rule for this class to which I will hold firm. You must not engage in any behavior that will interfere with your own learning or with that of your classmates."

Plan classroom activities that encourage on-task behavior.

Before each class, a creative writing teacher writes the day's topic on the chalkboard. Her students know that when they arrive at class, they are to take out a pencil and paper and begin an essay addressing that topic.

> **Show students that you are continually aware of what they are doing.**
>
> While meeting with each reading group in one corner of the classroom, an elementary school teacher sits with his back to the wall so that he can keep an eye on those students who are working in centers or at their desks on independent assignments.
>
> **Modify your plans for instruction when necessary.**
>
> A teacher discovers that students quickly complete the activity she thought would take them an entire class period. She wraps the activity up after fifteen minutes and then begins the lesson she had originally planned for the following day.

Yet despite our best efforts, students may occasionally behave in ways that disrupt classroom activities and interfere with student learning. Effective teachers not only plan and structure a classroom that minimizes potential behavior problems but also deal with the misbehaviors that do occur (Doyle, 1986a, 1990a). What strategies are most effective in dealing with student misbehaviors? It is to this topic that we turn now.

DEALING WITH STUDENT MISBEHAVIORS

THINKING ABOUT WHAT YOU KNOW

Considering your own experiences, what strategies do you think are most effective in dealing with students' misbehaviors? Do these strategies lead to a rapid reduction in inappropriate behavior? Do they lead to long-term improvement? Can you think of strategies that have *neither* of these results?

For purposes of our discussion, we will define a **misbehavior** as any action that can potentially disrupt classroom learning and planned classroom activities (Doyle, 1990a, 1990b). Some classroom misbehaviors are relatively minor ones that have little long-term impact on students' achievement. Such behaviors as talking out of turn, writing notes to classmates during a lecture, and submitting homework assignments after their due date—particularly if such behaviors occur infrequently—generally fall in this category. Other misbehaviors are far more serious, in that they definitely interfere with the learning and achievement of one or more students. For example, when students scream at their teachers, hit their classmates, or habitually refuse to participate in classroom activities, then classroom learning—certainly the learning of the "guilty party," and often the learning of other students as well—may be adversely affected. Furthermore, such behaviors may, in some cases, threaten the physical safety or psychological well-being of others in the classroom.

As teachers, we need to plan ahead regarding how we are going to respond to the variety of misbehaviors that we may see in the classroom. As we do so, we must keep in mind that different strategies may be appropriate under different circumstances. In the following pages, we will consider six general strategies and the situations in which each is likely to be appropriate:

- Ignoring the behavior
- Cueing the student
- Discussing the problem privately with the student
- Promoting self-regulation
- Using applied behavior analysis
- Conferring with parents

These six strategies are summarized in Table 12–2.

Ignoring the Behavior

Consider these misbehaviors:

- Beth rarely breaks classroom rules. But on one occasion, after you have just instructed your students to work quietly and independently at their seats, you see her whisper briefly to the student beside her. None of the other students seems to notice that Beth has disobeyed your instructions.

- Bob is careless in chemistry lab and accidentally knocks over a small container of liquid (a harmless one, fortunately). He quickly apologizes and cleans up the mess with paper towels.

Are these misbehaviors likely to interfere with Beth's or Bob's academic achievement? Are they contagious behaviors that are likely to spread to other students, as the horseplay did in Ms. Corbett's class? The answer to both these questions is "Probably not."

Ignore minor infractions that are unlikely to be repeated or to spread to other students.

There are times when our best course of action is *no* action, at least nothing of a disciplinary nature (e.g., G. A. Davis & Thomas, 1989; Shrigley, 1979; Silberman & Wheelan, 1980). Whenever we stop an instructional activity to deal with a misbehavior, even for a few seconds, we run the danger of disrupting the momentum of that activity and possibly drawing students' attention to their misbehaving classmates (Doyle, 1984, 1986a). If we respond every time a student gets a little bit out of line, our own actions may be more distracting than the student actions we are trying to curtail. Furthermore, by drawing class attention to a particular student's behavior, we may actually be reinforcing that behavior, rather than discouraging it.

Can you relate *ignoring* to a specific concept in operant conditioning?

Beth's misbehavior—whispering briefly to a classmate during independent seatwork—is unlikely to spread to her classmates (they didn't notice her behavior) and is probably not an instance of cheating (it occurred before she began working on the assignment). Bob's misbehavior—knocking over a container of liquid in chemistry lab—has, in and of itself, resulted in an unpleasant consequence for Bob; the natural consequence is that he has to clean up the mess. In both situations, *ignoring* the misbehavior—pretending it didn't happen—is probably the best thing we can do. Generally speaking, here are the circumstances in which ignoring misbehavior may be the wisest course of action:

Table 12–2 Six Strategies for Dealing with Student Misbehavior

STRATEGY	SITUATIONS IN WHICH IT'S APPROPRIATE	POSSIBLE EXAMPLES
Ignoring the behavior	The misbehavior is unlikely to be repeated. The misbehavior is unlikely to spread to other students. Unusual circumstances elicit the misbehavior temporarily. The misbehavior does not seriously interfere with learning.	One student surreptitiously passes a note to another student just before the end of class. A student accidentally drops her books, startling other students and temporarily distracting them from their work. The entire classroom is hyperactive on the last afternoon before spring break.
Cueing the student	The misbehavior is a minor infraction but interferes with student learning. The behavior is likely to change with a subtle reminder.	A student forgets to close his notebook at the beginning of a test. A student taunts a classmate about the outfit she is wearing. Several students are whispering to one another during an independent seatwork assignment.
Discussing the problem privately with the student	Cueing has been ineffective in changing the behavior. The reasons for the misbehavior, if made clear, might suggest possible strategies for reducing it.	A student is frequently late to class. A student refuses to do certain kinds of assignments. A student shows a sudden drop in motivation for no apparent reason.
Promoting self-regulation	The student has a strong desire to improve his or her behavior.	A student doesn't realize how frequently she interrupts her classmates. A student seeks help in learning to control his anger. A student wants to develop more regular study habits.
Using applied behavior analysis	The misbehavior has continued over a period of time and significantly interferes with student learning. The student is unwilling or unable to use self-control techniques.	A student's obscene remarks continue even though her teacher has spoken with her about the behavior on several occasions. A member of the football team displays unsportsmanlike conduct that is potentially dangerous to other players. A student shows a pattern of stealing materials from classmates' tote trays.
Conferring with parents	The source of the problem may lie outside school walls. Parents are likely to work collaboratively with school personnel to bring about a behavior change.	A student does well in class but rarely turns in required homework assignments. A student is caught stealing, vandalizing school property, or engaging in other unethical or illegal behavior. A student falls asleep in class almost every day.

- When the behavior is a rare occurrence and probably won't be repeated
- When the behavior is unlikely to "spread"—that is, to be imitated by other students
- When unusual circumstances (e.g., the last day of school before a holiday, an unsettling event in a student's personal life) elicit inappropriate behaviors only temporarily

- When the behavior is typical for a particular age-group (e.g., when kindergartners become restless after sitting for an extended period of time, when fifth-grade boys and girls resist holding one another's hands during dance instruction)

- When the behavior's result (its natural consequence) is sufficiently unpleasant to deter a student from repeating the behavior

- When the behavior is not seriously affecting students' classroom learning (G. A. Davis & Thomas, 1989; Doyle, 1986a; Dreikurs & Cassel, 1972; Munn et al., 1990; Palardy & Mudrey, 1973; Shrigley, 1979; Silberman & Wheelan, 1980; Wynne, 1990)

Yet in other situations, we definitely need to take steps to stop an inappropriate behavior. One easy and relatively inconspicuous way that we can do so is a strategy known as cueing.

Cueing the Student

Consider these behaviors:

- As you are explaining a difficult concept to your class, Brittany is busily writing. At first, you think she is taking notes, but then you see her pass the paper across the aisle to Brad. A few minutes later, you see the same sheet of paper being passed back to Brittany. Obviously, the two students are spending class time writing notes to each other and probably not hearing a word you are saying.

- You have separated your class into small groups for a cooperative learning exercise. One group seems to be more interested in discussing weekend plans than in accomplishing assigned work. The group is not making the progress that other groups are making and probably won't complete the assignment if its members don't get down to business soon.

In some situations, student misbehaviors, though not serious in nature, *do* interfere with classroom learning and must therefore be discouraged. Effective classroom managers handle such minor behavior problems as unobtrusively as possible: They don't stop the lesson, distract other students, or call unnecessary attention to the behavior they are trying to stop (Doyle, 1990a; Emmer, 1987). An effective strategy in many cases is simply to let a student know, through a signal of one kind or another, that you are aware of the misbehavior and would like it to stop. This process of signaling students is called **cueing**—a strategy we discussed within the context of behaviorism in Chapter 9.

We can cue students about unacceptable behaviors in a variety of ways. One strategy is body language—perhaps frowning, making eye contact, or raising a finger to the lips to indicate "be quiet." A second is to use a physical signal of some kind—perhaps ringing a small bell or flicking the light switch on and off to get students' attention. We might also want to move closer to misbehaving students; such physical proximity communicates our withitness about what they are doing.

In some situations, such subtle cues may not work, and so we will have to be more explicit. When we find that we must use explicit verbal cues, we should try to focus students' attention on what *should* be done, rather than on what *isn't* being done (Emmer

Why is ignoring *not* an effective strategy in Ms. Corbett's classroom?

Cue students by using body language, physical signals, physical proximity, or verbal reminders.

et al., 1994; Good & Brophy, 1994). Here are some examples of simple yet potentially effective verbal cues:

- "Students who are quietest go to lunch first."

- "By now, all groups should have completed the first part of the assignment and be working on the second part."

- "I see some art supplies that still need to be put back on the shelves before we can be dismissed."

Which forms of cueing might Ms. Corbett use with Eli, Jake, and Vanessa?

Discussing the Problem Privately with the Student

Consider these misbehaviors:

- Brandon is almost always several minutes late to your third-period algebra class. When he finally arrives, he takes an additional two or three minutes pulling his textbook and other class materials out of his backpack. On several occasions, you have reminded Brandon about the importance of coming to class on time, yet the tardiness continues.

- Barbara rarely completes classroom assignments; in fact, she often doesn't even *begin* them. On many occasions, you have tried unsuccessfully to get her on-task by explicit verbal cues (e.g., "Your book should be open to page 27," "Your cooperative group is brainstorming about possible solutions to a difficult problem, and they really could use your ideas"). A few times, when you have looked Barbara in the eye and asked her point-blank to get to work, she has defiantly responded, "I'm not going to do it. You can't make me!"

Speak privately with students about chronic misbehaviors.

Sometimes in-class signals are insufficient to change a student's misbehavior. In such situations, talking with the student about the behavior is the next logical step. The discussion should be a *private* one for several reasons. First, as we noted earlier, calling classmates' attention to a problem behavior may actually reinforce that behavior, rather than discourage it. Or instead, the attention of classmates may cause a student to feel excessively embarrassed or humiliated—feelings that may make the student overly anxious about being in the classroom in the future. Finally, when we spend too much class time dealing with a single misbehaving student, other students are more likely to get off-task as well (J. Scott & Bushell, 1974).

Conversations with individual students give us, as teachers, a chance to explain why certain behaviors are unacceptable and must stop. (As we noted earlier, students are more likely to obey rules when they understand the reasons behind those rules.) Furthermore, teacher-student conversations give students a chance to describe possible reasons why their misbehaviors continue despite our requests that they cease. To illustrate, when talking with Brandon, we may discover that his chronic tardiness is due to the fact that, as a diabetic, he must check his blood sugar level between his second- and third-period classes. He can perform the procedure himself, but it takes a few minutes; besides, he would prefer to do it in the privacy of the nurse's office at the other end of the building. When speaking with Barbara about her inability and occasional refusal to do assigned work, she may tell you that she studied the subject matter you are teaching now when she lived in another school district last year, and she is tired of doing the same stuff all over again.

Students' explanations can sometimes provide clues about how best to deal with their behavior over the long run. For example, given Brandon's diabetes, we may not be able to change his ongoing tardiness to class; instead, we might reassign him to a seat by the door so that he can join class unobtrusively each day, and we might ask the student next to him to fill him in quietly on what we have done prior to his arrival. Barbara's expressed boredom with classroom activities suggests that a workable strategy may be to find some enrichment activities for her to do until the rest of the class has completed the topics she has already mastered.

Yet our students won't always provide explanations that lead to such logical solutions. For example, it may be that Brandon is late to class simply because he wants to spend a few extra minutes hanging out with his friends in the hall. Or perhaps Barbara tells you she doesn't want to do her assignments because she's sick and tired of other people telling her what to do all the time. In such circumstances, it is essential that we not get in a power struggle with the student—that we not find ourselves in a situation where one of us must "win" by dominating over the other in some way (e.g., Diamond, 1991). We can use several strategies to avoid such a power struggle:

- Listen empathically to what the student has to say, being openly accepting of the student's feelings and opinions (e.g., "I get the impression that you don't enjoy classroom activities very much; I'd really like to hear what your concerns are").

- Summarize what you believe the student has told you and seek clarification if necessary (e.g., "It sounds as if you'd rather not come across as a know-it-all in front of your friends. Is that the problem you're having, or is it something else?").

- Use **I-messages** that describe the effects of the problem behavior, including our own reactions to it (e.g., "When you come to class late every day, I worry that you are getting farther and farther behind, and sometimes I even feel a little hurt that you don't seem to value your time in my classroom").

- Give the student a choice of some sort (e.g., "Would you rather try to work quietly at your group's table, or would be easier if you sat somewhere by yourself to complete your work?"). (derived from suggestions by Emmer et al., 1994)

Ultimately, we must communicate our interest in the student's long-term school achievement, our concern that the misbehavior is interfering with that achievement, and our commitment to working cooperatively with the student to alleviate the problem.

Yet sometimes, in addition to exploring reasons related to a student's misbehavior and its unacceptability in the classroom, we may also want to develop a long-term plan for changing that student's behavior. In the next section, we explore how we might help students control their own behavior, a strategy that can be very effective when students agree that certain behaviors do, in fact, need to be changed and are willing to cooperate fully with our efforts.

Promoting Self-Regulation

Consider these instances of problem behavior:

- Brian's performance on tests and in-class assignments is usually rather low; he obviously isn't learning much of what he should be learning. As Brian's teacher, you are certain that he is capable of better work, because he occasionally turns in a test or assignment of exceptionally high quality. The root of Brian's prob-

When we confer privately with students about chronic behavior problems, we should communicate our interest in their achievement and welfare over the long run.

lem seems to be that he is off-task most of the time. When he should be paying attention to you, taking notes, or doing an assignment, he is instead sketching pictures of sports cars and airplanes, fiddling with whatever objects he has found on the floor, or simply daydreaming. Brian would really like to improve his academic performance but doesn't seem to know how to go about doing it.

- Bernadette frequently speaks out in class without permission. She blurts out answers to your questions, preventing anyone else from answering them first. She abruptly interrupts other students' comments with her own point of view. And she initiates conversations with one or another of her classmates at the most inopportune times. You have talked with Bernadette several times; she readily agrees that there *is* a problem and vows to restrain herself in the future. After each conversation with you, her behavior improves for a few days, but her mouth is soon off and running once again.

Brian's off-task behavior interferes with his own academic achievement, and Bernadette's excessive chattiness interferes with the learning of her classmates. It is in the best interest of both students to curtail such behaviors. But notice that Brian and Bernadette have something going for them: They both *want* to change their classroom behavior. And when students genuinely want to improve their own behavior, why not teach them ways that they can bring about desired changes *themselves*?

Here we revisit the topic of self-regulation—a topic that we previously addressed in our discussion of social cognitive theory in Chapter 10. Social cognitive theorists offer several strategies for helping students begin to regulate and control their own behavior, including self-observation, self-instructions, self-regulatory problem-solving strategies, self-evaluation, and self-imposed contingencies.

Self-observation is especially valuable when students need a "reality check" about the severity of the problem behavior. Some students may underestimate the frequency with which they exhibit certain misbehaviors or the impact that those behaviors have on classroom learning. Bernadette, for example, seems to blurt things out without even realizing that her actions interfere with her classmates' attempts to participate in classroom discussions. Other students may not be aware of how *in*frequently they exhibit appropriate behaviors. Brian, for instance, may think he is on-task in the classroom far more often than he really is. To draw Bernadette's and Brian's attention to the extent of

Encourage self-regulation by teaching such strategies as self-observation, self-instructions, self-regulatory problem-solving strategies, self-evaluation, and self-imposed contingencies.

their problem, we can ask them simply to record the frequency with which certain behaviors appear. For example, we might ask Bernadette to make a check mark on a piece of paper every time she talks without permission. Or we might equip Brian with a timer that makes a small "beep" once every five minutes and ask him to write down whether or not he was paying attention to his schoolwork each time he hears the beep. Research studies tell us that some behaviors improve significantly when we do nothing more than ask students to record their own behavior. In fact, both Bernadette's and Brian's problems have been successfully dealt with in just this way (Broden, Hall, & Mitts, 1971; K. R. Harris, 1986; Mace et al., 1989; Mace & Kratochwill, 1988).

Self-instructions and *self-regulatory problem-solving strategies* provide students with methods of reminding themselves about appropriate actions. For example, we might provide Bernadette with a simple list of instructions that she can give herself whenever she wants to contribute to a classroom discussion:

1. "Button" my lips (by holding them tightly together)

2. Raise my hand

3. Wait until I'm called on

Likewise, as we noted in Chapter 10, we might help overly aggressive students deal with their interpersonal conflicts more constructively by following a prescribed sequence of steps: defining the problem, identifying several possible solutions, predicting the likely outcome of each approach, choosing and carrying out the best solution, and evaluating the results.

Self-evaluation and *self-imposed contingencies* provide a means through which we can encourage students to evaluate their progress and reinforce themselves for appropriate behavior. For example, we might ask Brian to give himself one point for each five-minute period that he's been on task. We might do something similar with Bernadette, instructing her to give herself one check mark for every fifteen-minute period in which she has spoken only when given permission to do so. After Brian and Bernadette have accumulated a certain number of points or check marks, they might be given permission to engage in a favorite activity.

The self-regulatory strategies I've just described have at least three advantages. For one thing, when we teach our students to monitor and modify their own behavior, rather than to depend on us to do it for them, we as teachers become free to do other things—for example, to *teach*! Second, such strategies are likely to increase students' sense of control and hence their intrinsic motivation to learn in the classroom. Finally, self-regulation techniques benefit students over the long run, promoting productive behaviors that are likely to continue long after students have moved on from a particular school or a particular teacher.

Nevertheless, there may be occasions when our students are either unwilling or unable to change their own behavior. In such situations, we may need to resort to applied behavior analysis.

Self-regulatory strategies provide another means of avoiding power struggles with students: You and they will no longer have to worry about who's in charge.

Using Applied Behavior Analysis

Consider these problem behaviors:

- Burt is out of his chair so often that, at times, you have to wonder whether he even knows where his chair *is*. He finds numerous reasons to roam about the room—he "has to" sharpen a pencil, he "has to" get his homework out of his backpack, he "has to" get a drink of water, and so on. Naturally, Burt gets very little of his work done. Furthermore, his classmates are continually being distracted by his perpetual motion.

• Becky's verbal abusiveness is getting out of hand. She often insults her classmates by using sexually explicit language, and she frequently likens you to a female dog or a certain body part. You have tried praising her on occasions when she is pleasant with others, and she seems to appreciate your doing so, yet her abusive remarks continue unabated.

Imagine that both Burt and Becky are in your class. As a teacher, you have already spoken with each of them about their inappropriate behaviors, yet you've seen no improvement. You have suggested methods of self-regulation, but the two students don't seem interested in changing for the better. So what do you do now?

When a particular misbehavior occurs so frequently that it is clearly interfering with a student's learning and achievement (and possibly with the learning and achievement of classmates as well) and when other interventions such as cueing the student or teaching self-regulatory strategies do not seem to decrease that misbehavior, then a more intensive intervention may be in order. Probably the most widely advocated intervention is *applied behavior analysis,* a group of techniques we examined in Chapter 9. Applied behavior analysis, which is based on such behaviorist concepts as *reinforcement* of appropriate responses, *shaping* of increasingly more complex responses, and *punishment* of inappropriate responses, often leads to substantial improvements in students' classroom behavior (e.g., Ormrod, 1995b).

How might we use behaviorist techniques to bring about an improvement in Burt's classroom behavior? As we noted in Chapter 9, we may often have better luck if we use both reinforcement (for desirable responses) and punishment (for undesirable responses), rather than either of these strategies alone. For example, in Burt's situation, we will probably want to identify an effective reinforcer (given his constant fidgeting, we might suspect that opportunities for physical activity will be reinforcing) and then make that reinforcer contingent on Burt's staying in his seat for a specified length of time. As Burt improves, we may also want to lengthen the interval in which he must stay in his seat before we reinforce him, thereby shaping his behavior to become increasingly more sedentary. At the same time, we should recognize that some out-of-seat behaviors (e.g., getting a reference book from the bookshelf, delivering a completed assignment to the teacher's "In" basket) are quite appropriate; we may therefore want to give Burt a reasonable "allotment" of out-of-seats he can use during the day. Any out-of-seats that exceed this allotment should probably result in a mild yet punishing consequence—perhaps the logical consequence of spending time after school, making up uncompleted work.

We can also combine reinforcement and punishment to curtail Becky's verbal abusiveness. In this case, we might suspect that Becky has learned few social skills with which she can interact effectively with others; we might therefore need to begin by teaching her such skills through modeling, role playing, and so on (see "Fostering Social Skills" in Chapter 3 for additional ideas). Once we know that Becky possesses effective interpersonal skills, we can begin to reinforce her for using those skills (perhaps with praise, as she has responded positively to such feedback in the past). Meanwhile, we should also punish (perhaps by giving her a time-out) any relapses into her old, abusive patterns.

Use behaviorist principles to encourage more productive behavior when other, simpler interventions have been unsuccessful.

If need be, refresh your memory by rereading the section entitled "Using Applied Behavior Analysis" in Chapter 9.

What behaviorist techniques might Ms. Corbett use to help Eli, Jake, and Vanessa become more productive members of her classroom?

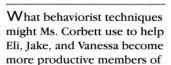

Social cognitive theorists also advocate following through with the consequences students are expecting. Can you recall their rationale?

In our use of both reinforcement and punishment, we must keep in mind two guidelines that we identified in our discussion of behaviorism in Chapter 9. For one thing, we should be very explicit about response-consequence contingencies: We must let our students know ahead of time, in concrete terms, what behaviors will be followed by what consequences (*contingency contracts,* as described in Chapter 9, provide one means through which we might do so). Furthermore, we should follow through with those consequences when the specified behaviors occur; effective classroom managers deal with inappropriate student behaviors quickly and consistently (Doyle, 1986a; Evertson & Emmer, 1982). When we fail to follow through with promised consequences, we communicate the message that we were not really serious about the contingencies we described.

Conferring with Parents

Consider these misbehaviors:

- You assign short homework assignments almost every night; over the past three months, Bobbi has turned in only about a third of them. You're pretty sure that Bobbi's capable of doing the work, and you know from previous teacher conferences that her parents would like her to go on to college. You have spoken with Bobbi about the situation on several occasions, but she shrugs you off as if she doesn't really care whether she does well in your class or not.

- Students have frequently found things missing from their tote trays or desks when Bernie has been in the vicinity. A few students have told you that they've seen Bernie taking things that belong to others. Many of the missing objects have later turned up in Bernie's possession. When you confront him about your belief that he's been stealing from his classmates, Bernie adamantly denies it. He says he has no idea how Cami's gloves or Marvin's baseball trading cards ended up in his desk.

Confer with parents about chronic problems that have serious implications for students' long-term success.

As we deal with classroom misbehaviors, we may sometimes need to involve students' parents, especially when the misbehaviors show a pattern over a period of time and have serious implications for students' long-term success. In some instances, a simple telephone call may be sufficient (Emmer et al., 1994); for example, Bobbi's parents may be unaware that she hasn't been doing her homework (she's been telling them that she doesn't have any) and may be able to take the steps necessary to ensure that it is done from now on. In other cases, a school conference may be more productive; for example, you may want to discuss Bernie's stealing habits with both Bernie and his parent(s) together—something you do more effectively when you all sit face-to-face in the same room.

Speaking with parents about their children's misbehaviors can be a tough situation to handle, especially for beginning teachers. Here are some suggestions for enhancing your chances for a successful outcome:

- *Don't place blame; instead, acknowledge that raising children is rarely easy.* Parents are more apt to respond constructively to your concerns if you don't blame them for their child's misbehavior.

- *Express your desire for whatever support they can give you.* Parents are more likely to be cooperative if you present the problem as one that can be effectively addressed if everyone works together to understand and solve it.

- *Ask for information and be a good listener.* If you show that you truly want to hear their perspective, parents are more likely to share their ideas regarding possible sources of the problem and possible ways of addressing it.

- *Agree on a strategy.* You are more likely to bring about an improvement in behavior if both you and a student's parents have similar expectations for behavior and similar consequences when those expectations are not met. Keep in mind that some parents, if left to their own devices, may administer excessive or ineffective forms of punishment; agreement in your conference as to what an appropriate consequence might be may avert such a situation. (derived from suggestions by Emmer et al., 1994)

As teachers, we must remember that most parents ultimately want what's best for their children (e.g., Hidalgo et al., & Epstein, 1995). It's essential, then, that we not leave them out of the loop when we're concerned about how their children are behaving in school.

INTO THE CLASSROOM
Dealing with Misbehaviors

Ignore minor infractions that are unlikely to be repeated and unlikely to spread to other students.

> A student accidentally knocks over a container of poster paint in art class. The art teacher, while watching to be sure the student cleans up the mess, continues working with other students.

Use physical signals or brief verbal cues to remind students about what they should or should not be doing.

> A teacher looks pointedly at two students who are giggling during a standardized test, and they quickly stop.

Speak privately with students about chronic and clearly inappropriate behaviors.

> A student continually teases a classmate who stutters. The teacher takes the student aside, points out that the classmate is not stuttering by choice, and voices her concern that such teasing may be making the stuttering worse.

Teach self-regulatory strategies when students are motivated to improve their behavior.

> When a student too often speaks without thinking and, in doing so, unintentionally offends or hurts the feelings of classmates, her teacher gives her three mental steps to follow before speaking:
>
> 1. Button my lip.
> 2. Think about what I want to say.
> 3. Think about how to say it nicely.

Use applied behavior analysis when students seem unwilling or unable to control their own behavior.

> When a fourth-grade boy seems unable to stay in his seat for more than five minutes at a time, his teacher sets up a system in which he can earn points toward free time or privileges at the end of the day. For now, he earns one point for every ten minutes he remains seated; she will extend the required time gradually as the school year goes on.

Confer with parents if a collaborative effort might bring about a behavior change.

> At a parent-teacher conference, a teacher expresses his concern that a student is not turning in her homework assignments. Her parents are surprised to hear this, saying that, "Marti usually tells us that she doesn't *have* any homework." Together they work out a strategy for communicating about what assignments have been given and when they are due.

Remember that some behaviors considered unacceptable in your culture may be quite acceptable in the culture in which a student has been raised.

> When two brothers are frequently late for school, their teacher recognizes that the boys are unaccustomed to living by the clock. He explains the importance of getting to school on time and praises them as they become increasingly more punctual in the weeks that follow.

TAKING STUDENT DIVERSITY INTO ACCOUNT

As we plan for a productive classroom, we must always take the diverse characteristics and needs of our students into account. For example, we should make an extra effort to establish a supportive classroom climate, especially for students of ethnic minority groups and for students from lower-income neighborhoods. We may also need to define and respond to misbehaviors in somewhat different ways, depending on the particular ethnic and socioeconomic groups that we have in our classrooms. Finally, we may often have to make special accommodations for students with special educational needs. Let's briefly consider each of these issues.

Taking Special Pains to Create a Supportive Classroom Climate

Earlier in the chapter, we noted the value of creating a warm, supportive classroom atmosphere. Such an atmosphere may be especially important for students from ethnic minority groups (García, 1995; Ladson-Billings, 1994a). For example, African American students in an eighth-grade social studies class were once asked why they liked their teacher so much. Their responses were very revealing:

"She listens to us!"

"She respects us!"

"She lets us express our opinions!"

A warm, supportive classroom climate may be especially important for students from diverse ethnic backgrounds.

"She looks us in the eye when she talks to us!"

"She smiles at us!"

"She speaks to us when she sees us in the hall or in the cafeteria!" (Ladson-Billings, 1994a, p. 68)

Simple gestures such as these go a long way toward establishing the kinds of teacher-student relationships that will lead to a productive learning environment. It's essential, too, that we create a sense of community in the classroom—a sense that we and our students share common goals and are mutually supportive of everyone's reaching those goals. This sense of community is consistent with the cooperative spirit evident in many Hispanic, Native American, and African American groups (e.g., Ladson-Billings, 1994a).

When we find ourselves working with students from lower-socioeconomic backgrounds, not only should we create a classroom climate that is warm and supportive, but we must also take special pains to make sure it feels safe and orderly (Levine & Lezotte, 1995). Many students from low-SES neighborhoods may be exposed to crime and violence on a daily basis; their world may be one in which they can rarely control the course of events. A classroom that is dependable and predictable, as well as supportive, can provide a sense of self-determination they may not be able to find anywhere else; hence, it can be a place to which they look forward to coming each day and a place in which they are most likely to learn and achieve.

Remember that a warm, supportive classroom climate may be especially important for students from diverse ethnic backgrounds.

When working with students from low-SES backgrounds, make an extra effort to create an environment that feels safe and orderly.

Defining and Responding to Misbehaviors

As we determine which behaviors we do not want to allow in our classrooms, we must remember that some behaviors considered unacceptable in our own culture may be quite acceptable in the culture in which a particular student has been raised. Let's consider some examples based on the cultural differences we discussed in Chapter 4:

- *A student is frequently late for school, sometimes arriving more than an hour after the school bell has rung.* A student who is chronically tardy may live in a community that does not observe strict schedules and timelines, a pattern common in some Hispanic and Native American communities.

Table 12–3 *Planning for Students with Special Educational Needs*

STUDENTS WITH SPECIAL NEEDS	CHARACTERISTICS THAT THESE STUDENTS MAY EXHIBIT	CLASSROOM STRATEGIES THAT MAY BE BENEFICIAL FOR THESE STUDENTS
Students with specific cognitive or academic deficits	Uneven patterns of achievement Difficulty with complex cognitive tasks in some content domains Difficulty staying on-task In some students, misbehaviors such as hyperactivity, disruptiveness, inattentiveness In some students, poor time management skills and/or a disorganized approach to accomplishing tasks	Establish challenging yet realistic objectives; modify objectives in accordance with individual students' strengths and weaknesses. Use an information processing analysis to identify the specific cognitive skills involved in a complex task; teach those skills separately to the extent you can do so. Be optimistic in your objectives for students; assume they can succeed, and help them achieve success. Closely monitor students during independent assignments (e.g., remain in close proximity of students who get off-task easily). Make sure students understand their assignments. Make expectations for behavior clear, and enforce classroom rules consistently. Cue students regarding appropriate behavior. For hyperactive students, plan short activities that help them settle down after periods of physical activity (e.g., recess, lunch, physical education). Teach students strategies for organizing their time and work (e.g., tape a schedule of daily activities to their desks, provide folders they can use to carry assignments between school and home).
Student with specific social or behavioral deficits	Frequency of overt misbehaviors (e.g., acting out, aggression, noncompliance, destructiveness, stealing) in some students Difficulty interacting effectively with classmates Difficulty staying on-task Tendency for some students to engage in power struggles with their teacher	Specify in precise terms what behaviors are acceptable and unacceptable in the classroom; establish and enforce rules for behavior. Establish procedures for such routine tasks as sharpening pencils and using the rest room. Use applied behavior analysis and self-regulation techniques to promote more productive classroom behavior. Include the development of social skills in your objectives. Closely monitor students during independent assignments (e.g., remain in close proximity of students who get off-task easily). Give students a sense of self-determination about some aspects of classroom life; minimize the use of coercive techniques. Show students how your expectations for their behavior are in their own best interest. Make a special effort to show students that you care about them as human beings.
Students with general delays in cognitive and social functioning	Difficulty with complex tasks Occasionally disruptive classroom behavior Dependence on others for guidance about how to behave More appropriate classroom behavior when expectations are clear	Establish realistic objectives in both the academic and social arenas. Use task analysis to break complex behaviors into a number of simpler responses that students can more easily learn. Make sure students understand their assignments. Establish clear, concrete rules for classroom behavior. Cue students regarding appropriate behavior. Use applied behavior analysis and self-regulation techniques to promote desired academic and social behaviors.
Students with advanced cognitive development	Greater frequency of responses at higher levels of Bloom's taxonomy (e.g., analysis, synthesis) Off-task behavior in some students, often due to boredom during easy assignments and activities	Identify standards and objectives that challenge students and encourage them to develop their full potential.

Sources: Achenbach & Edelbrock, 1981; Buchoff, 1990; B. Clark, 1992; Diamond, 1991; Friedel, 1993; D. A. Granger, Whalen, Henker, & Cantwell, 1996; Heward, 1996; C. D. Mercer, 1991; D. P. Morgan & Jenson, 1988; Ogden & Germinario, 1988; Patton, Beirne-Smith, & Payne, 1990; Pellegrini & Horvat, 1995; Piirto, 1994; M. C. Reynolds & Birch, 1988; Turnbull, Turnbull, Shank, & Leal, 1995.
Compiled with the assistance of Dr. Margie Garanzini-Daiber and Dr. Margaret Cohen, University of Missouri—St. Louis.

- *Two students are sharing answers as they take a classroom test.* Although this behavior is cheating in your eyes, it may reflect the cooperative spirit and emphasis on group achievement evident in the cultures of many Native American and Mexican American students.

- *Several students are shouting at one another, hurling insults that become increasingly more derogatory and obscene.* Such an interaction might seem to spell trouble, but it may instead be an instance of sounding—a friendly verbal interchange common in some African American communities.

Some of these behaviors are likely to have little if any adverse effect on our students' learning. To the extent that some of them *do* have such an effect, we must be patient and understanding as we begin to shape students' behaviors to be more productive within the school environment.

Furthermore, when we find it necessary to confer with parents about students who exhibit serious behavior problems, we must be aware of the fact that people from different cultural groups sometimes have radically different ideas of how children should be disciplined. For example, many Chinese American parents believe that Western schools are too lenient in the ways they attempt to correct inappropriate behavior (Hidalgo et al., 1995). In some Native American and Asian cultures, a child's misbehaviors may be seen as bringing shame on the family or community; thus, a common disciplinary strategy is to ignore or ostracize the child for an extended period of time (Pang, 1995; Salend & Taylor, 1993). As we confer with parents from cultures different from our own, we must listen with an open mind to the opinions they express and try to find common ground on which to develop strategies for helping their children become more productive students (Salend & Taylor, 1993).

Remember that some behaviors considered unacceptable in your culture may be quite acceptable in the culture in which a student has been raised. When such behaviors interfere with classroom achievement, be patient and understanding as you begin to shape student behavior.

Take parents' opinions about appropriate discipline into account.

Accommodating Students with Special Needs

Throughout the planning process, we must consider the special educational needs that some of our students are likely to have. We may sometimes want to tailor our instructional objectives to students' specific cognitive abilities or disabilities; for example, we may need to modify our expectations for students with learning disabilities in specific areas of weakness, and we may find it beneficial to set more challenging goals for gifted students. We may also need to provide a great deal of guidance and support during our efforts to foster productive classroom behavior in students with emotional and behavioral disorders. Specific suggestions for accommodating students with special needs are presented in Table 12–3.

LOOKING AT THE BIG PICTURE: PLANNING AS AN ONGOING PROCESS

As we plan for each new school year—as we determine our objectives, decide how best to break down and teach the knowledge and skills identified in those objectives, and devise classroom management strategies appropriate for the students we will have in our classroom—we should keep in mind that our plans must invariably change as the year progresses. We may find that our task analyses of desired knowledge and skills were overly simplistic. We may try new instructional strategies that aren't as effective as we had hoped they would be. We may discover that the expectations we have for students' achievement, as reflected in the instructional objectives we've developed, are either unrealistically high or inappropriately low. We may have difficulty striking a reasonable balance between classroom orderliness on the one hand and students' sense of control on the other. As teachers, we must continually revise our plans as instruction proceeds and as classroom assessments reveal the extent to which students are learning and achieving successfully.

CASE STUDY: *Old Friends*

Mr. Schulak has wanted to be a teacher for as long as he can remember. In his numerous volunteer activities over the years—coaching a girls' basketball team, assisting in a Boy Scout troop, teaching Sunday school—he has discovered how much he enjoys working with children. The children obviously enjoy working with him as well: Many of them occasionally call or stop by his home to shoot baskets, talk over old times, or just say hello.

Now that he has completed his college degree and obtained his teaching certificate, Mr. Schulak is a first-year teacher at his hometown's junior high school. He is delighted to find that he already knows many of his students—he has coached them, taught them, or gone to school with their older brothers and sisters—and so he spends the first few days of class renewing his friendships with them. But by the end of the week, he realizes that he and his students have accomplished little of an academic nature.

The following Monday, Mr. Schulak vows to get down to business. He begins each of his six classes that day by describing the objectives for the weeks to come; he then begins the first lesson. He is surprised to discover that many of his students—students with whom he has such a good rapport—are resistant to settling down and getting to work. They want to move from one seat to another, talk with their friends, toss erasers across the room, and, in fact, do anything *except* the academic tasks that Mr. Schulak has in mind. In his second week as a new teacher, Mr. Schulak has already lost total control of his classroom.

- Why is Mr. Schulak having so much difficulty bringing his classroom to order? What critical things has Mr. Schulak not done in his first week of teaching?

- Given that Mr. Schulak has gotten the school year off on the wrong foot, what might he do now to remedy the situation?

SUMMING UP

General Principles of Effective Teaching

Research reveals a number of commonalities that effective teachers share; for example, such teachers typically have clear goals, engage in considerable advance planning to achieve those goals, create a classroom climate that encourages learning and intrinsic motivation, promote higher-level thinking skills as well as mastery of the "basics," adapt instruction to the diverse needs of their students, and monitor students' behavior and progress regularly. Effective teaching involves three critical components of the teaching process—planning, instruction, and assessment—with each of these being inextricably intertwined with one another and with the characteristics of the specific students in the classroom.

Identifying Instructional Objectives

We should describe our instructional objectives in terms of the specific, observable behaviors we want students to demonstrate. As we develop objectives, we should consider both lower-level and higher-level skills. We should also recognize that not all important outcomes lie within the cognitive domain; others may lie in the psychomotor and affective domains.

Using Task Analysis

Task analysis is a means of breaking a complex task into smaller, simpler components that individually lend themselves more readily to instructional planning. Depending on the situation, it may be useful to analyze an instructional objective in terms of the specific behaviors it requires, the specific topics it includes, or the specific mental processes it involves.

Establishing and Maintaining a Productive Learning Environment

Classroom management is a process of establishing and maintaining a classroom environment conducive to students' learning and achievement. As teachers, we want to create a classroom in which students are consistently engaged in classroom tasks and activities and in which few student behaviors interfere with those tasks and activities.

Several strategies are useful for establishing a productive classroom environment. Among other things, we can (a) physically arrange the classroom in a way that facilitates our interactions with students and keeps distracting influences to a minimum, (b) show students that we respect and care about them as human beings and give them a sense that they themselves have some control over their own behavior and learning, (c) set reasonable limits for classroom behavior, (d) plan instructional activities that encourage on-task behavior, (e) demonstrate withitness about what our students are doing in the classroom, and (f) modify our instructional strategies when they are clearly ineffective.

Dealing with Student Misbehaviors

Some minor misbehaviors are probably best ignored: those that probably won't be repeated, those that are unlikely to be imitated by other students, and those that occur only temporarily and within the context of unusual circumstances. Other minor infractions can be dealt with simply and quickly by cueing students about their inappropriate behaviors.

Chronic misbehaviors that significantly interfere with student learning often require greater intervention. In some cases, we may be able to address a problem behavior successfully by having a discussion with the student about the situation. In other circumstances, we may find that self-regulatory strategies or techniques of applied behavior analysis bring about improvement. We may sometimes find it desirable to discuss chronic and serious misbehaviors with a student's parents so that we can coordinate our efforts and work toward a common solution.

Taking Student Diversity into Account

As we plan for a productive classroom, we must consider the characteristics of the students we are likely to have in our classroom. Creating a warm, supportive atmosphere and a sense of community among our students may be especially important for those from diverse cultural backgrounds, those from lower socioeconomic groups, and those with special needs—many of whom are likely to be at risk for failure and dropping out of school. As we deal with classroom misbehavior, we must be especially understanding when students exhibit behaviors that are the product of a particular cultural upbringing or the result of a specific disability.

KEY CONCEPTS

instructional objectives (p. 534)
mastery learning (p. 535)
outcomes-based education (OBE) (p. 535)
standards (p. 536)
cognitive domain (p. 538)
psychomotor domain (p. 538)

affective domain (p. 538)
behavioral objectives (p. 542)
short-term versus long-term objectives (p. 543)
task analysis (p. 545)
classroom management (p. 550)
classroom climate (p. 552)

sense of community (p. 554)
withitness (p. 563)
misbehavior (p. 565)
cueing (p. 568)
I-messages (p. 570)

Choosing and Implementing Instructional Strategies

THINKING ABOUT WHAT YOU KNOW

- What approaches do your instructors use to deliver instruction? For example, do they present lectures or assigned readings on particular topics? Do they ask you to work cooperatively with your classmates to accomplish tasks or master new material? Do they ask you to discover certain ideas by yourself?

- Considering what you have learned about human learning and development, what approaches to instruction might be most appropriate for the students and topics you will be teaching? For example, are there things that your students could learn most easily by hearing or reading about them? Are there tasks that your students could accomplish most effectively by working with others? Are there ideas that your students could be encouraged to discover on their own?

A S WE CONSIDERED PRINCIPLES of human development and learning in earlier chapters, we identified a number of specific instructional strategies that should help our students learn and achieve more successfully. For example, as we looked at

Piaget's theory of cognitive development, we discovered the value of relating abstract ideas to concrete objects and events. In Vygotsky's work, we found how scaffolding can facilitate students' efforts to master new and challenging tasks. As we explored cognitive psychologists' views of learning, we found that, by encouraging students to process information meaningfully, we can help them construct an understanding of the world around them and apply what they've learned more easily to new situations. In our discussions of behaviorism and social cognitive theory, we derived instructional implications from such concepts as reinforcement, shaping, modeling, self-efficacy, and self-regulation.

In this chapter, we will focus our attention more directly on instruction, considering a variety of instructional strategies and identifying specific techniques for using each strategy effectively. As we do so, we will continue to build on principles we've identified in past chapters—principles related to learning, motivation, development, and diversity, as well as the general principles of effective teaching listed in Chapter 12. And we will find further evidence that the three major components of teaching—planning, instruction, and assessment—are almost impossible to separate.

Virtually any instructional strategy can help students achieve numerous instructional objectives, but different strategies lend themselves more readily to different purposes. Some approaches are especially valuable in helping students *learn new material;* expository instruction (e.g., lectures, reading assignments), discovery learning, and mastery learning are among the alternatives we might consider when we want to introduce new information, concepts, and ideas. Other approaches are particularly suitable for helping students *process what they've learned;* for example, teacher questions, classroom discussions, and cooperative learning groups often promote greater elabora-

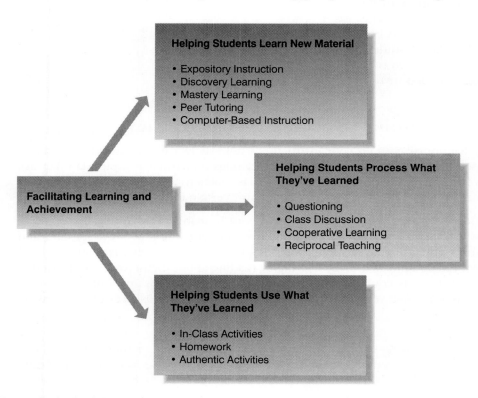

Helping Students Learn New Material

- Expository Instruction
- Discovery Learning
- Mastery Learning
- Peer Tutoring
- Computer-Based Instruction

Facilitating Learning and Achievement

Helping Students Process What They've Learned

- Questioning
- Class Discussion
- Cooperative Learning
- Reciprocal Teaching

Helping Students Use What They've Learned

- In-Class Activities
- Homework
- Authentic Activities

Figure 13–1 Instructional Strategies

tion and conceptual understanding. Still other approaches are designed primarily to help students *use what they've learned in new situations;* in-class activities, homework assignments, and authentic activities provide vehicles for facilitating such transfer of learning. Figure 13–1 identifies the three purposes I've just described, along with strategies especially suitable for accomplishing each one; this figure also presents the organizational scheme I will use in the pages that follow.

Toward the end of the chapter, we will look at some of the broader issues related to instructional practice. We will explore the idea of creating a "community of learners" in our classrooms—an idea that transcends any particular instructional strategy and can promote the all-important sense of community we discussed in Chapter 12. We will also find that, once again, students' characteristics—for example, their gender, cultural background, and special educational needs—are likely to influence the specific instructional strategies that we select.

By the end of the chapter, you should be able to:

1. Describe a variety of instructional strategies for helping students learn new material, process it effectively, and use it in new situations.

2. Describe the conditions under which each instructional strategy is most likely to be effective in promoting students' learning and achievement.

3. Explain what is meant by a "community of learners" and how you might create such a community in your own classroom.

4. Identify instructional strategies that may be especially suited to students of different genders, cultural backgrounds, and special needs.

5. Select instructional strategies appropriate for various instructional objectives.

CASE STUDY: *A Math Problem*

After leaving elementary school behind last year, twelve-year-old Reggie is adjusting easily to middle school. He has made new friends and established good working relationships with his teachers. He has As in almost every subject. But Reggie has a problem—mathematics.

Reggie knows the usual routine in Ms. Keeney's math class. After reviewing the previous night's homework assignment, Ms. Keeney explains a new concept (e.g., *negative number, improper fraction*) or demonstrates a new procedure (e.g., finding prime factors, multiplying fractions) on the chalkboard. She then assigns several in-class exercises through which students can practice the things she has taught them. Finally, she hands out the homework assignment for the following day.

Reggie knows that mathematics is important, so he attends closely to each day's lecture and works diligently at his in-class exercises and homework. Yet despite his efforts, Reggie is feeling completely lost in math class.

"I'm getting farther and farther behind," he complains to his friends. "I'm not sure what I'm supposed to be learning, but whatever it is, I obviously haven't learned it."

- Why is Reggie experiencing difficulty in his mathematics class? Can you think of possible explanations based on what we have learned about cognitive development or human learning?

- What specific things might the teacher do to help students like Reggie experience greater success in mathematics?

HELPING STUDENTS LEARN NEW MATERIAL

Reggie hasn't a clue about what Ms. Keeney's instructional objectives are, perhaps because she's never described them to her students. We might guess from her actions that her major goal is to help students acquire new concepts and procedures. Yet we see little evidence that Ms. Keeney has given much thought to the issue of how best to help her students learn class material effectively: She seems to depend almost exclusively on verbal explanations and chalkboard displays to get her points across.

As teachers, we must keep in mind that there are numerous ways of helping students acquire new knowledge and skills. In the next few pages, we will consider five potentially effective strategies:

- Expository instruction

- Discovery learning

- Mastery learning

- Peer tutoring

- Computer-based instruction

Using Expository Instruction

THINKING ABOUT WHAT YOU KNOW

- How often have your teachers used lectures as a way to teach you something new? Which of your teachers were effective lecturers, and which were not? What specific things did the more effective lecturers do to help you learn and understand classroom material?

- How much have you learned from the textbooks that you have read over the years? Can you think of textbooks that you could easily understand? Can you think of textbooks that were confusing and frustrating to read? What characteristics make for an effective textbook?

Reflecting on your past lectures and textbooks just now, you may have realized that much of your education over the years has taken the form of **expository instruction.** In other words, information was *exposed* to you in essentially the same form you were expected to learn it. Lectures, explanations, textbooks, and educational videos are all examples of expository instruction; in each case, all the information that students need to know is laid out before them.

Some learning theorists, such as B. F. Skinner (e.g., 1968), have criticized expository instruction for putting students in a passive role. As you should recall from our discussion of behaviorism in Chapter 9, operant conditioning occurs when a response is reinforced; hence, students can only learn when they actually *make* a response. Yet students make very few observable responses when they simply sit quietly listening to a lecture, reading a textbook, or watching a video.

Many cognitivists argue, however, that students are often *mentally* active during such seemingly passive activities (e.g., Ausubel et al., 1978). From an information processing perspective, the degree to which students learn from expository instruction is a function of how they process information; in other words, it depends on the particular cognitive responses they make. The more students pay attention, and the more they engage in meaningful learning, organization, elaboration, and so on, the more they are likely to benefit from the lectures they hear and the textbooks they read.

Unfortunately, expository instruction doesn't always present information in ways that facilitate learning. For example, in our "Math Problem" case study, we see no evidence that Ms. Keeney's explanations and chalkboard demonstrations are helping Reggie and his classmates process the new information effectively. We find a similar problem when we look at textbooks: Analyses in such diverse disciplines as history, geography, and science find that the focus of most school textbooks is on teaching specific facts, with little attention to helping students learn these facts in a meaningful fashion (Bochenhauer, 1990; Calfee & Chambliss, 1988; Chambliss, Calfee, & Wong, 1990; McKeown & Beck, 1990).

What specific techniques can we use to help our students learn from expository instruction? The following exercise might give you a few ideas about techniques that work for *you* as a student.

■ EXPERIENCING FIRSTHAND
Finding Pedagogy in the Book

1. Look back at two or three of the chapters you've already read in this book. Find several places where specific things that I've done have helped you learn and remember the material more effectively. What specific techniques did I use to facilitate your information processing?

2. In those same chapters, can you find places where you had difficulty processing the material that I presented? What might I have done differently in these instances?* ■

Have the "Thinking About What You Know" questions and the "Experiencing Firsthand" exercises helped you relate new topics to your own knowledge and experiences? Have you benefited from the chapter overviews and objectives, from the charts and figures, or from the summaries? Researchers have identified a number of factors that facilitate students' learning from expository instruction, including these:

*   Connections to prior knowledge

*   Advance organizers

*   Organization

*   Visual aids

_____

* I'd appreciate your feedback about things that do and don't work. My address is College of Education, University of Northern Colorado, Greeley, CO 80639 USA.

- Pacing

- Summaries

These factors are summarized in Table 13–1. Let's look at each one more closely.

Begin instruction and introduce reading assignments by reminding students about what they already know about a topic.

Connections to Prior Knowledge

As we learned in our discussion of cognitive processes in Chapter 6, long-term memory storage and retrieval are easier when students relate new information to things already

Table 13–1   Principles of Expository Instruction

PRINCIPLE	EDUCATIONAL IMPLICATION	EXAMPLE
Connections to prior knowledge help students learn classroom material meaningfully.	We should remind students of something they already know and point out how a new idea is similar.	When introducing new vocabulary words in a French class, we can identify English words that are spelled similarly and have similar meanings.
An **advance organizer** helps students develop an overall organizational scheme for the material.	We should introduce a new unit by describing the major ideas and concepts to be discussed and showing how they are interrelated.	When beginning a unit on mountains, we can briefly describe the four types that we will be talking about—volcanic, dome, fold, and block mountains.
An **organized presentation** of material helps students make appropriate interconnections among ideas.	We should present related ideas within the same lesson and at the same time.	If we want students to see how two poems have similar symbolism, we can discuss both poems on the same day.
Visual aids help students encode material visually, as well as verbally.	We can illustrate new material through pictures, diagrams, maps, models, and demonstrations.	When describing major battles of the American Civil War, we can present a map illustrating where each battle took place and how some battles were fought in especially strategic locations.
Appropriate **pacing** gives students adequate time to process information.	We must pace our presentation slowly enough that students can engage in meaningful learning, elaboration, and other effective storage processes.	We can intersperse lecture material with hands-on activities illustrating the principles we present.
Summaries help students review and organize material and identify main ideas.	After a lecture or reading assignment, we should summarize the key points of the lesson.	At the end of a unit on clouds, we can summarize the characteristics of the four types we've talked about—cumulus, cirrus, stratus, and cumulonimbus.

stored in long-term memory. Yet unfortunately, students often fail to connect the new things they learn in school with the things they've previously learned (Perkins & Simmons, 1988; Prawat, 1989). When we begin a lesson by reminding students about the relevant information they already have—perhaps acquired from a previous lesson or their own personal experiences—we help them make those critical, meaningful connections.

Analogies provide an additional means of helping students connect new concepts and principles with things they already know. Here are some examples:

- *Radar is like an echo.* In both cases, waves (either radio waves or sound waves) travel from their source, bounce off a distant object, and return to the source. (Mayer, 1984)

- If we think of the *earth's history as a 24-hour day,* then humans have been in existence only for the last minute of that day. (Hartmann, Miller, & Lee, 1984)

- *Peristalsis*—the muscular contractions that push food through the digestive tract—*is like squeezing ketchup out of a single-serving packet.* "You squeeze the packet near one corner and run your fingers along the length of the packet toward an opening at the other corner. When you do this, you push the ketchup through the packet, in one direction, ahead of your fingers, until it comes out of the opening." (Newby, Ertmer, & Stepich, 1994, p. 4)

By using an analogy to compare new material to things with which our students are already familiar, we can help them store that material more meaningfully and retrieve it more easily (Donnelly & McDaniel, 1993; Newby et al., 1994; Simons, 1984; Stepich & Newby, 1988; Zook, 1991). At the same time, we must be careful to point out ways in which the two things are *different;* otherwise, our students may take an analogy too far and draw some incorrect conclusions (Duit, 1990; Zook & Di Vesta, 1991).

Use analogies to compare new ideas and relationships to situations with which students are already familiar.

When we use expository instruction to build on students' existing knowledge base, we must remember that their "knowledge" is not always accurate: They may bring a number of misconceptions to a learning task. As we discovered in our discussion of knowledge construction in Chapter 7, students may impose such erroneous beliefs on the things they are learning and inadvertently distort the new material as a result. Therefore, when using expository instruction, we must be sure to address the typical misconceptions students have when they encounter new topics and to explain why those misconceptions are inaccurate.

Address the typical misconceptions that students have when they encounter new topics.

Advance Organizers

Have you ever had teachers who presented information in such a disorganized and unpredictable manner that you never knew what they were going to say next? Perhaps you learned a few useful tidbits from those teachers, but you may have had little idea about how the tidbits fit together into a meaningful whole.

Unfortunately, many students try to learn a body of information as a list of isolated facts with little or no relationship to one another (Meyer et al., 1980). As teachers, we can help students better organize and interrelate the information in a lesson by providing an **advance organizer**—that is, by giving an introduction that describes an overall organizational scheme for the body of knowledge we are presenting (Ausubel et al., 1978; Corkill, 1992; Mayer, 1979a, 1979b). An advance organizer typically includes the

Provide an advance organizer that gives a general organizational scheme for a lesson.

major concepts and ideas of a lesson and shows how these concepts and ideas are related to one another. Here are some simple examples:

- Today we are going to talk about the two different sounds for the letter *G*. Sometimes *G* is pronounced "guh," and sometimes it is pronounced "juh." Let's look at some examples. . . .

- During the next two weeks, we will be discussing animals known as *vertebrates*. Vertebrates are all similar in one very important respect: They have a backbone. We will be talking about five phyla of vertebrates: mammals, birds, reptiles, amphibians, and fish. And we will see how animals in each of these phyla differ from one another—whether they are warm-blooded or cold-blooded; whether they have hair, scales, or feathers; and whether they lay eggs or bear live young.

- For tonight's homework, please read pages 110 through 124 in your history book. These pages describe Magellan's three-year expedition around the world. As you will discover in your reading, Magellan's ships left Spain in 1519, sailing west and then south to the southernmost tip of South America, then north and west to the Philippines, south around Africa, and finally back up the Atlantic to Spain. As you read, you will learn about why Magellan made the trip, how he dealt with an attempted mutiny, what he called the ocean he found after leaving the Strait of Magellan, and how he died on Mactan Island before his expedition was completed.

In some situations, an advance organizer might take a graphic, rather than strictly verbal, form. For example, Figure 13–2 shows how the overall organizational scheme of a unit on rocks might be presented. But regardless of how we do it, we can help students learn more effectively when we let them know ahead of time how the various concepts and ideas they will be studying are going to fit together.

Organization

Present information in an organized fashion, pointing out the interrelationships you want students to learn.

An advance organizer starts students on the right track in terms of organizing new material. But an equally important strategy is to introduce each new idea within the lesson in such a sequence that the important relationships among the various ideas are crystal clear. In other words, we can help students organize material in a particular way by presenting the information using that same organizational structure (C. L. Tennyson, Tennyson, & Rothen, 1980; R. D. Tennyson & Cocchiarella, 1986). For example, if we want students in an English literature class to discover similarities among various short stories, we should discuss several stories within the same lesson, rather than talk about each one separately. If we want students to use principles from several subject areas simultaneously to analyze new situations or solve large-scale problems (the rain forest problem in Chapter 8 as an example), we should present these subject areas in an interdisciplinary manner, showing students how the ideas of each area tie in with the ideas of others.

Does your instructor's organization of a lecture affect the quality of notes you take?

Visual Aids

In our discussion of information processing in Chapter 6, we noted that visual imagery can be a highly effective way of storing information in long-term memory. We also noted that information encoded in multiple ways is more easily retrieved from long-term

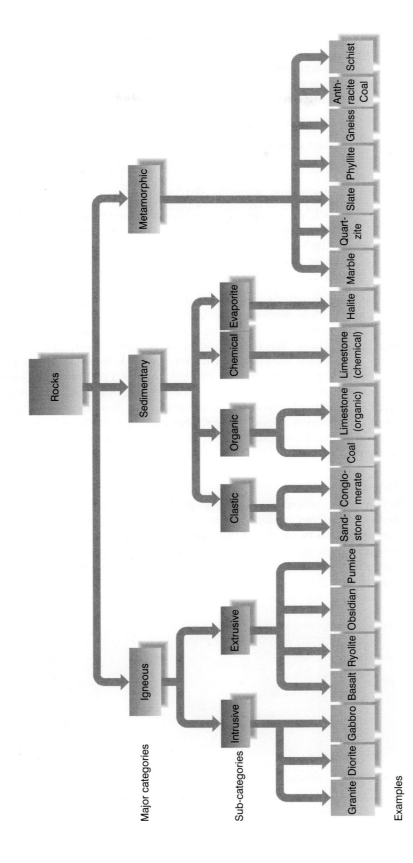

Major categories

Sub-categories

Examples

Figure 13–2   Graphic Advance Organizer for a Unit on Rocks

Source: Adapted from a discussion by R. C. Scott, 1989.

memory than information encoded in just one way. Both principles point to the same conclusion: Supplementing verbal explanations with visual aids should promote more effective long-term memory storage and retrieval.

How might we incorporate a "visual" component into expository instruction? Here are some examples of techniques that research has shown to be effective:

Supplement verbal explanations with visual aids—for instance, with live modeling, physical models, pictures, diagrams, or maps.

- Live modeling (e.g., a demonstration of how to glaze a ceramic pot)

- Physical models (e.g., a concrete model of an atom)

- Pictures (e.g., a photograph of the Allied troops landing on Normandy Beach)

- Diagrams (e.g., a graphic depiction of the human digestive system)

- Maps (e.g., a series of maps showing the acreage of South American rain forest in 1970, 1980, and 1990) (Denis, 1984; Ferguson & Hegarty, 1995; Kulhavy et al., 1985; J. R. Levin & Berry, 1980; Mayer, 1989; Prawat, 1989; Scevak, Moore, & Kirby, 1993; Small, Lovett, & Scher, 1993; Winn, 1991; also see the discussion of modeling in Chapter 10.)

In most situations, visual aids should be simple and concise, and they should include major ideas without overwhelming students with detail (Mayer, 1989). In addition to promoting visual imagery, many visual aids can also show students how major ideas relate to and affect one another; thus, they provide one more way of helping students organize the information they receive (B. F. Jones, Pierce, & Hunter, 1988/1989; J. R. Levin & Mayer, 1993; Mayer, 1989; Winn, 1991). Figures 13–3 and 13–4 provide examples of how visual aids can provide an overall organizational scheme to ideas that students might otherwise fail to integrate. The first shows how a solar eclipse occurs when the moon is aligned directly between the earth and the sun. The second illustrates the typical sequence of events when a group of people work together to solve a problem.

Pacing

Give students time to process information.

As you know, information processing takes time: Due to the limited capacity of working memory, students can only learn so much information so fast. We must therefore pace our presentation of new information to allow our students the time they need to process it—for example, to think about how it relates to things they already know, generate their own examples of new concepts, and draw their own conclusions and implications.

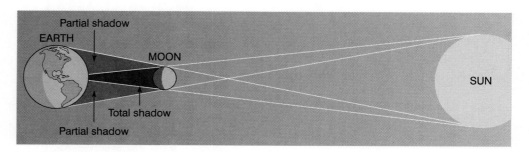

Figure 13–3   Model of a Solar Eclipse

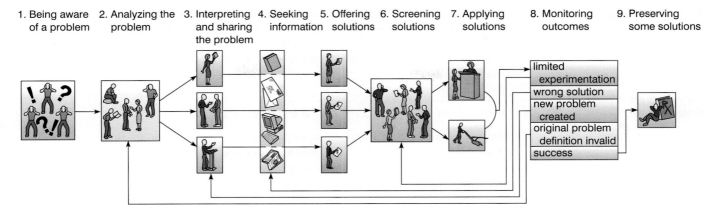

1. Being aware of a problem   2. Analyzing the problem   3. Interpreting and sharing the problem   4. Seeking information   5. Offering solutions   6. Screening solutions   7. Applying solutions   8. Monitoring outcomes   9. Preserving some solutions

limited experimentation
wrong solution
new problem created
original problem definition invalid
success

Figure 13–4   Model Showing How Society Solves a Problem
Source: Adapted from *Adaptation in Cultural Ecosystems: Early 19th Century Jamaica* (p. 231) by R. K. Ormrod, 1974, unpublished doctoral dissertation, The Pennsylvania State University. Adapted by permission of the author.

One strategy for providing this needed processing time is to build redundancy into a lecture—in other words, to present each important idea not just once, but several times, each time using different words to say essentially the same thing. To illustrate, perhaps we might first state the idea, then give an example to illustrate that idea, then state the idea again, and then describe its relevance to students' own lives. If we present the same piece of information several times over, our students are bound to catch it at least one of those times! As an example, notice how redundant my discussion of redundancy is in this paragraph. I used the first three sentences to state and restate a single idea!

Another way of giving students the processing time they need is to stop a lecture at ten-minute intervals and give students a couple of minutes to meet in small groups to compare notes, ask one another questions, and share ideas (R. T. Johnson, 1989; Rowe, 1987). When we give students the opportunity to process lecture information in small groups, they are likely to produce more useful class notes, perform better on complex test questions, and remember information longer (Rowe, 1987).

Do your own instructors give you the time you need during a lecture to process new ideas sufficiently?

Summaries

Earlier, we noted the importance of providing an advance organizer before we begin a lesson: Students tend to learn more effectively when they are given advance notice of the things they will be learning and how those things are interrelated. Students also tend to benefit from summaries presented at the end of a verbal lecture or written passage: They learn more effectively when they hear or read a synopsis of the information they have just studied (Hartley & Trueman, 1982). Summaries are likely to serve multiple functions, helping students (1) review material, (2) determine which of the many ideas they have studied are most important, and (3) pull key ideas into a more cohesive organizational structure.

At the conclusion of a lesson or unit, summarize the material presented.

Perhaps the major advantage of expository instruction is that it enables students to explore a topic in an organized and relatively time-efficient manner. Yet expository instruction has a potential weakness as well: It often occurs in the absence of the actual objects or events under discussion. When students read a textbook passage about amphibians, they probably don't have a frog or toad in front of them to examine firsthand. When students listen to a lecture on the concepts of force and momentum, they may

Consider once again Reggie's "math problem" at the beginning of the chapter. Can you think of some specific things Reggie's teacher might do in terms of expository instruction to help Reggie learn?

have trouble learning such abstract concepts in the absence of actually experiencing or witnessing them in action. Thus, many students—younger ones especially—are apt to have difficulty learning solely from lectures and textbooks. So we may also want to provide opportunities for them to interact directly with the topic at hand, perhaps through discovery learning.

Promoting Discovery Learning

Unlike expository instruction, where information is presented in its final form, **discovery learning** is a process through which students interact with their physical or social environment—for example, by exploring and manipulating objects, performing experiments, or wrestling with questions and controversies—and derive information for themselves. Common examples of discovery learning are laboratory experiments, library research projects, and opportunities for students to learn by trial and error (e.g., as they "fiddle" with computer software, a soccer ball, or watercolor paints). Discovery learning can sometimes be incorporated into other forms of instruction; for example, the "Experiencing Firsthand" exercises in this very "expository" book have, I hope, helped you discover a number of important principles on your own.

We find theoretical justification for discovery learning in the constructivist views of learning that we discussed in Chapter 7: Students are able to construct a more complete understanding of the world when they have opportunities to explore and manipulate their environment. We find further justification in Piaget's theory of cognitive development (Chapter 2): Concrete experiences are critical for cognitive development, especially for children in the sensorimotor, preoperational, and concrete operational stages. From Piaget's perspective, twelve-year-old Reggie (our "math problem" case study) probably has not completely made the transition from concrete operational to formal operational thinking; accordingly, he may need many concrete experiences to help him understand the relatively abstract concepts (e.g., negative numbers, improper fractions) that Ms. Keeney is trying to teach him.

As a teacher, how might you make the concepts of *negative number* and *improper fraction* concrete?

Educators have provided additional arguments for discovery learning that are consistent with principles of information processing (e.g., Bruner, 1960, 1961, 1966; Kuslan & Stone, 1972; Massialas & Zevin, 1983). For one thing, students can better understand and appreciate the ways in which the world is predictable (as reflected in basic principles of science, mathematics, and various other disciplines) when they actually observe such principles in action. In other words, students may learn something more meaningfully when they experience it firsthand. Second, when students *see* something as well as hear or read about it, they can encode that information in long-term memory visually as well as verbally. Finally, because students learn information meaningfully and store it in more than one form, they are more likely to retrieve that information in appropriate situations—for example, when they need it to solve a problem.

How effective is discovery learning? Unfortunately, research does not always give us a clear picture. Ideally, to determine whether discovery learning works better than other approaches, we would need to compare two groups of students who differ on only *one* variable: the extent to which discovery learning is a part of their instructional experience. Yet research studies that make this crucial comparison are few and far between, and the studies that have been conducted give us contradictory results. Nevertheless, here are some general conclusions about discovery learning that we can glean from research findings:

Students may better understand scientific principles when they actually observe those principles in action.

- When we consider *overall academic achievement,* discovery learning is not necessarily better or worse than "traditional" (e.g., more expository) approaches to instruction. Research yields mixed findings on this issue (Giaconia & Hedges, 1982; Horwitz, 1979; Marshall, 1981; Mayer, 1987; P. L. Peterson, 1979).

- When we consider *higher-level thinking skills,* discovery learning is often preferable for fostering transfer, problem solving, creativity, and independent learning (Ferguson & Hegarty, 1995; R. M. Gagné & Brown, 1961; Horwitz, 1979; Mayer, 1974; P. L. Peterson, 1979; Roughead & Scandura, 1968; Shymansky, Hedges, & Woodworth, 1990).

- When we consider *affective objectives,* discovery learning often promotes a more positive attitude toward teachers and schoolwork than does traditional instruction—in other words, students like school better (Giaconia & Hedges, 1982; Horwitz, 1979; P. L. Peterson, 1979; Shymansky et al., 1990).

At least two factors appear to be critical for successful discovery learning:

- Relevant prior knowledge

- Sufficiently structured experiences

Let's look more closely at each of these.

Relevant Prior Knowledge

Students are most likely to benefit from a discovery learning session when they have appropriate and relevant background knowledge they can draw on to interpret their ob-

Make sure students have the necessary prior knowledge for discovering new ideas and principles.

Structure the experience so that students' explorations proceed in fruitful directions.

Decrease the amount of structure as students' reasoning and problem-solving skills develop.

servations (Bruner, 1966; N. Frederiksen, 1984a). For example, having students conduct experiments to determine the influence of gravity on the velocity of a falling object will typically be more beneficial if students are already familiar with the concepts of *gravity* and *velocity*. As cognitive psychologists tell us, meaningful learning can only occur when students have appropriate prior knowledge to which they can relate their new experiences.

Sufficiently Structured Experiences

Young children often learn from random exploration of their environment. For example, preschoolers can discover many properties of sand and water by manipulating dry sand, wet sand, and water in an unstructured setting—perhaps by scooping, pouring, scraping, pushing, digging, dropping, burying, or blowing. Through such play activities, children learn what physical objects do and what people can do *to* those objects (Hutt, Tyler, Hutt, & Christopherson, 1989).

Older students, however, are more likely to benefit from carefully planned and structured activities (Ausubel et al., 1978; Foster, 1972; Kuslan & Stone, 1972; Mayer, 1987; Mayer & Greeno, 1972). For example, high school chemistry students are rarely left to mix their own chemical concoctions; the results of their activities would be uninterpretable, wasteful, or even explosive. Instead, the chemistry teacher prescribes certain actions; students carry out those actions, observe the results, and try to explain them.

One simple way of structuring a discovery session is simply to pose a question and then let students determine their own procedure to answer it. For example, a biology teacher may ask the class, "How can we make a mealworm move backward?" Students can brainstorm a number of approaches to answering the question and then assemble items such as these:

flashlight	turpentine
smoke	burning match
pin	vinegar
hot iron	pencil
noisemaker	straw (for blowing with)
ammonia	wet ink

After watching a mealworm's reaction to each item, students make deductions about its ability to see, hear, and feel (Kuslan & Stone, 1972).

The degree to which a discovery session needs to be structured may depend to some extent on the scientific reasoning and problem-solving skills that students do or do not possess. For example, some students may have difficulty tackling vague, ill-defined problems (as described in Chapter 8). And many other students—particularly those who have not yet acquired formal operational thinking capabilities—may have trouble forming and testing hypotheses, or separating and controlling variables (see Chapter 2). Such students will probably work more effectively when they are given problems and questions that are concrete and well-defined and when they are given specific suggestions regarding how to proceed.

As we have seen, students may benefit little from discovery learning sessions when they do not have the knowledge base they need in order to interpret their observations and discoveries. When students need to learn basic knowledge or skills—knowledge and skills that are essential prerequisites for achieving later instructional objectives—a mastery learning approach is often recommended. We turn to this approach now.

Promoting Discovery Learning

Identify a concept or principle about which students can learn through interaction with their physical or social environment.

> A mathematics teacher realizes that, rather than tell students how to calculate the area of a triangle, she can help them discover the procedure for themselves.

Make sure students have the necessary prior knowledge for discovering new ideas and principles.

> After students in a physics class have studied such concepts as velocity, acceleration, and gravity, their teacher has them measure the speed of a metal ball rolling down ramps of varying degrees of incline.

Structure the experience so that students proceed logically toward any discoveries you want them to make.

> To demonstrate the effects of prejudice, a social studies teacher creates a situation in which each student, because of an arbitrarily chosen physical characteristic that he or she possesses, experiences the prejudice of classmates.

Show puzzling results to arouse curiosity.

> A science teacher shows her class two glasses of water. In one glass, an egg is floating at the water's surface; in the other glass, an egg has sunk to the bottom. The students give a simple and logical explanation for the difference: One egg has more air inside and so is lighter. But then the teacher switches the eggs into opposite glasses. The egg that the students believe to be "heavier" now floats, and the egg they think is "lighter" sinks to the bottom. The students are quite surprised to observe this result and demand to know what is going on. (Ordinarily, water is less dense than an egg, so an egg placed in it will quickly sink. But in this situation, one glass contains salt water—a mixture denser than an egg and therefore capable of keeping it afloat.) (adapted from Palmer, 1965)

Have students record their findings.

> A biology teacher has students make sketches of the specific organs they observe as they dissect an earthworm.

Promoting Mastery Learning

Let's return once again to Ms. Keeney's math class. This class of twenty-seven students is beginning a unit on fractions. It progresses through several lessons as follows:

- The class first studies the basic notion that a fraction represents parts of a whole: The denominator indicates the number of pieces into which the whole has been divided, and the numerator indicates how many of those pieces are present. By the end of the lesson, twenty-three children understand what a fraction is. But Sarah, LaShaun, Jason K., and Jason M. are either partially or totally confused.

- The class then studies the process of reducing fractions to their lowest terms. For example, 2/4 can be reduced to 1/2, and 12/20 can be reduced to 3/5. By the end of the lesson, twenty children understand the process of reducing fractions. But Alison, Reggie, and Jason S. haven't mastered the idea that they need to divide both the numerator and denominator by the same number. And of course, Sarah, LaShaun, and the other two Jasons still don't understand what fractions *are* and so have trouble with this lesson as well.

- Later, the class studies the process of adding two fractions together. At this point, the students only look at situations in which the denominators are the same. For example, 2/5 + 2/5 = 4/5 and 1/20 + 11/20 = 12/20. By the end of the lesson, nineteen children can add fractions with the same denominator. Matt, Charlie, Maria F., and Maria W. keep adding the denominators together, as well as the numerators (thus figuring that 2/5 + 2/5 = 4/10). And Sarah, LaShaun, Jason K., and Jason M. still don't know what fractions actually are.

Can you recall a time when you were unable to master something that was critical for your later classroom success? How did you feel in that situation?

- Finally, the class combines the processes of adding fractions and reducing fractions to their lowest terms. They must first add two fractions together and then, if necessary, reduce the sum to its lowest terms. For example, when they add 1/20 + 11/20 together, they must reduce the sum of 12/20 to 3/5. At this point, we lose Muhammed, Aretha, and Karen because they keep forgetting to reduce the sum to lowest terms. And of course, we've already lost Sarah, LaShaun, Alison, Reggie, Matt, Charlie, the two Marias, and the three Jasons on prerequisite skills. We now have thirteen of our original twenty-seven students understanding what they are doing—less than half the class! (See Figure 13–5.)

When we move through lessons without making sure that all students master the content of each one, then we lose more and more students as we go along. To minimize the likelihood that such a situation will occur, we may want to implement an approach to instruction known as **mastery learning** (Block, 1980; Bloom, 1968, 1974, 1976, 1981, 1984a; Guskey, 1985, 1994; Hunter, 1982; Keller, 1968; J. F. Lee & Pruitt, 1984). In a mastery learning situation, students must learn one lesson well (they must *master* the content) before proceeding to the next lesson. The approach is based on at least three underlying assumptions:

- Almost every student can learn a particular topic to mastery.

- Some students need more time to master a topic than others.

- Some students need more assistance (e.g., individualized tutoring or additional practice exercises) than others.

As you can see, mastery learning represents a very optimistic approach to instruction: It assumes that most children *can* learn school subject matter if they are given sufficient time and instruction to do so.

Mastery learning usually includes the following components:

Use a *task analysis* (see Chapter 12) to identify the content and sequence of each unit.

1. *Small, discrete units.* Course content is broken up into a number of separate units or lessons, with each unit covering a small amount of material.

2. *A logical sequence.* Units are sequenced such that basic concepts and procedures—those that provide the foundation for later units—are learned

Students	Lesson 1: Concept of Fraction	Lesson 2: Reducing to Lowest Terms (Builds on Lesson 1)	Lesson 3: Adding Fractions with Same Denominator (Builds on Lesson 1)	Lesson 4: Adding Fractions with Different Denominators (Builds on Lessons 2 & 3)
Sarah	😟	😟	😟	😟
LaShaun	😟	😟	😟	😟
Jason K.	😟	😟	😟	😟
Jason M.	😟	😟	😟	😟
Alison	🙂	😟	🙂	😟
Reggie	🙂	😟	🙂	😟
Jason S.	🙂	😟	🙂	😟
Matt	🙂	😟	🙂	😟
Charlie	🙂	😟	😟	😟
Maria F.	🙂	🙂	😟	😟
Maria W.	🙂	🙂	😟	😟
Muhammed	🙂	🙂	😟	😟
Aretha	🙂	🙂	🙂	😟
Karen	🙂	🙂	🙂	😟
Kevin	🙂	🙂	🙂	😟
Nori	🙂	🙂	🙂	😟
Marcy	🙂	🙂	🙂	🙂
Janelle	🙂	🙂	🙂	🙂
Joyce	🙂	🙂	🙂	🙂
Ming Tang	🙂	🙂	🙂	🙂
Georgette	🙂	🙂	🙂	🙂
LaVeda	🙂	🙂	🙂	🙂
Mark	🙂	🙂	🙂	🙂
Seth	🙂	🙂	🙂	🙂
Joanne	🙂	🙂	🙂	🙂
Rita	🙂	🙂	🙂	🙂
Shauna	🙂	🙂	🙂	🙂

Students become "lost" when they fail to master important building blocks on which later material will depend. For these students, mastery is indicated by a solid line and nonmastery is indicated by a dotted line. Notice how we have lost 14 of the 27 students by the end of Lesson 4.

Figure 13–5   Sequential Nature of Mastery Learning

first. More complex concepts and procedures, including those that build on basic units, are learned later. For example, a unit in which students learn what a fraction is would obviously come before a unit in which they learn how to add two fractions together.

3. *Demonstration of mastery at the completion of each unit.* Before "graduating" from one unit to the next, students must show that they have mastered the current unit—for example, by taking a test on the content of that unit. (Here is an example of how instruction and assessment often work hand in hand.)

4. *A concrete, observable criterion for mastery of each unit.* Mastery of a topic is defined in specific and concrete terms. For example, to "pass" a unit on adding fractions with the same denominator, students might have to answer at least 90% of test items correctly.

Make sure students demonstrate mastery of one unit before proceeding to the next.

Provide additional instructional activities for students who do not attain mastery on the first attempt.

5. *Additional "remedial" activities for students needing extra help or practice to attain mastery.* Students do not always demonstrate mastery on the first try. Additional support and resources—perhaps alternative approaches to instruction, different materials, workbooks, study groups, and individual tutoring—are provided for students who need them (e.g., Guskey, 1985).

Students engaged in mastery learning often proceed through the various units at their own speed; hence, different students may be studying different units at any given point in time. But it is also possible for an entire class to proceed through a sequence at the same pace: Students who master a unit earlier than their classmates can pursue various enrichment activities, or they can serve as tutors for those still working on the unit (Block, 1980; Guskey, 1985).

We find justification for mastery learning in several theoretical perspectives. For example, operant conditioning theorists tell us that complex behaviors are often more easily learned through *shaping,* whereby a simple response is reinforced until it occurs frequently (until it is mastered), then a slightly more difficult response is reinforced, and so on. We see further justification in cognitive theorists' concept of *automaticity:* Information and skills that need to be retrieved rapidly or used in complex problem-solving situations must be practiced and learned thoroughly. Finally, as social cognitive theorists have noted, the ability to perform a particular task successfully and easily is likely to enhance students' sense of self-efficacy for performing similar tasks.

Research indicates that mastery learning has a number of advantages over nonmastery approaches. In particular, students tend to:

- Learn more and perform better on classroom assessments

- Maintain better study habits, studying regularly rather than procrastinating and cramming

- Enjoy their classes and teachers more

- Have greater interest in the subject

- Have more self-confidence about their ability to learn the subject (Block & Burns, 1976; Born & Davis, 1974; C. C. Kulik, Kulik, & Bangert-Drowns, 1990; J. A. Kulik, Kulik, & Cohen, 1979)

Considering the subject matter you will be teaching, what important information and skills would you want your students to master?

Mastery learning is probably most appropriate when students must learn certain concepts or skills thoroughly (perhaps to a level of automaticity), and especially when, as in Ms. Keeney's math class, those concepts and skills provide the foundation for future educational tasks. When instructional objectives deal with such basics as reading word recognition, addition and subtraction, scientific concepts, or rules of grammar, instruction designed to promote mastery learning may be in order. Nevertheless, the very notion of mastery may be *in*appropriate for many of our long-term objectives. As we noted in the preceding chapter, such skills as critical reading, scientific reasoning, and creative writing may continue to improve over the years without ever really being mastered.

One advantage of a mastery learning approach is that because students must demonstrate mastery at the completion of each unit, they receive frequent feedback about the progress they are making. Two other approaches—peer tutoring and computer-based instruction—may provide even *more* frequent feedback. It is to these approaches that we turn now.

Promoting Mastery Learning

Break course material into small, manageable units of instruction.

> A mathematics teacher breaks instruction on fractions into five units: the basic concept of a fraction, proper versus improper fractions, reducing to lowest terms, adding and subtracting fractions of like denominators, and adding and subtracting fractions of unlike denominators.

Identify the sequence in which these units should logically be arranged.

> An elementary school teacher recognizes that he must be sure students have mastered the four cardinal directions—north, south, east, and west—before he introduces the concepts of *latitude* and *longitude*.

Develop a concrete, observable criterion for mastery of each unit.

> In a German class, students demonstrate mastery of each textbook chapter by getting a score of at least 85% on the chapter quiz and engaging in oral recitations that incorporate the chapter's vocabulary and syntactical structures.

Make sure students demonstrate mastery of one unit before proceeding to the next.

> In the same German class, students must demonstrate mastery of each chapter before proceeding to the next.

Provide additional instructional activities for students who do not attain mastery on the first attempt.

> The teacher of the same German class provides additional exercises plus tutoring from more advanced students for those students unable to attain mastery after two attempts.

Encouraging Peer Tutoring

As we just noted in our discussion of mastery learning, some of our students may need more time to master a topic than others; hence, they may need more instructional time, and perhaps more individualized instruction, than their classmates. As teachers, we can't always devote much time to one-on-one instruction. **Peer tutoring**—students who have mastered a topic teaching those who have not—can provide an effective alternative for teaching fundamental knowledge and skills (A. L. Brown & Palincsar, 1987; Durkin, 1995; Greenwood, Carta, & Hall, 1988; Greenwood et al., 1987; Pigott et al., 1986).

In some cases, peer tutoring leads to greater academic gains than either mastery learning or more traditional whole-class instruction (Greenwood et al., 1988). One possible reason for its effectiveness is that it provides a context in which struggling students may be more comfortable asking questions when they don't understand something. In one study (Graesser & Person, 1994), students asked 240 times as many questions during peer tutoring as they did during whole-class instruction!

In many cases, when one student tutors another, the tutor learns as much from the experience as the student being tutored.

Peer tutoring typically benefits the tutors as well as those being tutored (Durkin, 1995; Greenwood et al., 1988; Semb et al., 1993). When students study material with the expectation that they will be teaching it to someone else, they are more intrinsically motivated to learn it, find it more interesting, process it in a more meaningful fashion, and remember it longer (Benware & Deci, 1984; Semb et al., 1993). Peer tutoring has nonacademic benefits as well: Cooperation and other social skills improve, classroom behavior problems diminish, and friendships develop between students of different ethnic groups and between students with and without disabilities (Greenwood et al., 1988).

As teachers, we must be sure that our tutors have mastered the material they are teaching and that they use sound instructional techniques—asking questions, scaffolding responses when necessary, giving feedback, and so on (Fuchs, Fuchs, Bentz, Phillips, & Hamlett, 1994; Greenwood et al., 1988). We must also be careful that our use of higher-ability students to tutor lower-ability students is not excessive or exploitive. Ultimately, we should use peer tutoring only when we know that *all* students will benefit from it.

Be sure that student tutors know the material sufficiently well to teach it to someone else and that they use appropriate instructional techniques.

Providing Computer-Based Instruction (CBI)

"Tutors" don't necessarily have to be human beings. **Computer-based instruction**—instruction provided via computer technology—provides yet another means through which we can individualize the things our students study, the pace at which they learn it, and the feedback they receive. In the next few pages, we will consider several ways in which computers can be used for instructional purposes:

- Computer-assisted instruction (CAI)
- Games and simulations
- Hypertext and hypermedia
- Computer networks
- Tool applications

Computer-Assisted Instruction (CAI)

■ EXPERIENCING FIRSTHAND
Shocking Lesson

Let's switch gears for a minute. Rather than learn about instruction, take a few minutes to learn a little first aid. What follows is a short lesson on treating victims of traumatic shock. The lesson is presented in a sequence of boxes known as *frames*. Get a sheet of blank paper and cover all but the first frame. Read the information presented in the first frame and then write the answer to the question at the top of your blank paper. Once you have done so, uncover the next frame and check your response against the answer presented in the upper left-hand corner. Read the new information and again respond to the question. Continue in this manner through all the frames, each time getting feedback to the question you just answered, reading the new information, and answering another question.

Frame 1

When the human body is seriously injured, a condition that frequently results is <u>traumatic shock.</u>

? A frequent result of serious injury is traumatic _____.

Frame 2

<u>shock</u>

Burns, wounds, and bone fractures can all lead to traumatic shock.

? Three common types of injuries can lead to traumatic shock:
burns, wounds, and bone _____.

Frame 3

<u>fractures</u>

Traumatic shock is a condition in which many normal bodily functions are depressed.

? When a person is suffering from traumatic shock, normal bodily functions become _____.

Frame 4

<u>depressed</u>

Bodily functions are depressed during shock because not enough blood is circulating through the body.

? The depression of bodily functions during shock is due to an insufficient amount of _____
circulating through the body.

Frame 5

<u>blood</u>

The more blood lost as a result of an injury, the greater the possibility of traumatic shock.

? The probability of shock increases when an injury results in the loss of more _____.

Frame 6

<u>blood</u>

An injured person who may be suffering from shock should be kept lying down and at a comfortable temperature.

? In a cold environment, it is probably best to do which of the following for a person possibly in shock?
    a. Cover the person with a blanket.
    b. Cover the person with cool, damp towels.
    c. Leave the person uncovered.

Frame 7

If you chose *a*, you are correct. Proceed to Frame 9.
If you chose *b* or *c*, you are incorrect. Continue with this frame.

A person who is possibly suffering from traumatic shock should be kept at a comfortable body temperature.

? A possible shock victim should be kept:
   a. as cool as possible
   b. as warm as possible
   c. at a comfortable body temperature

Frame 8

If you chose *c*, you are correct. Continue with this frame.
If you chose *a* or *b*, you are incorrect. Return to Frame 7.

In a cold environment, the person should be covered with a blanket in order to be kept warm. In a warm environment, little or no covering is needed.

? In a cold environment, it is probably best to do which of the following for a person who is possibly suffering from shock?
   a. Cover the person with cool, damp towels.
   b. Leave the person uncovered.
   c. Cover the person with a blanket.

Frame 9

If you chose *c*, you are correct. Continue with this frame.
If you chose *a* or *b*, you are incorrect. Return to Frame 7.

A possible shock victim should be kept lying down. This way, blood will more easily flow to the head and chest, where it is most needed.

? A shock victim should be placed in a _____ position.
   a. sitting
   b. lying down
   c. standing

Frame 10

If you chose *b*, you are correct. Proceed to Frame 11.
If you chose *a* or *c*, you are incorrect. Continue with this frame.

It is best to keep a shock victim lying down. This way, blood circulates more readily to the head and chest.

? A shock victim should be kept _____.
   a. lying down
   b. sitting
   c. standing

Frame 11

If you chose *a*, you are correct. Continue with this frame.
If you chose *b* or *c*, you are incorrect. Return to Frame 4.

. . . the lesson continues . . .

As we noted in our discussion of expository instruction, B. F. Skinner objected to instruction in which students, by making few if any overt responses, played a passive role. In addition, he was concerned that, in most schools, reinforcement (e.g., in the form of positive feedback for assignments completed appropriately or for test questions answered correctly) was intermittent at best, and it was often given days or even weeks after learning had actually occurred. In the "Shocking Lesson" you just studied, you saw an example of **programmed instruction** (Skinner, 1954, 1968)—an approach to instruction that is more consistent with principles of operant conditioning:

1. *Active responding.* By answering questions or filling in blanks, you make an overt, observable response.

2. *Shaping.* Instruction begins with something you already know—the fact that human beings can suffer serious injury. New information is broken into tiny pieces, and instruction proceeds through a gradual presentation of additional pieces in successive *frames* within the lesson. As more information is acquired and questions of increasing difficulty are answered, the terminal behavior is gradually shaped.

3. *Immediate reinforcement.* Because instruction involves a gradual shaping process, there is a high probability of responding correctly to the questions asked. Each answer is reinforced immediately when you receive feedback that the answer is correct.

The first part of the lesson on treating traumatic shock illustrates a **linear program:** All students progress through the same sequence of frames. Beginning with Frame 7, the lesson becomes a **branching program** (e.g., Crowder & Martin, 1961). At this point, instruction progresses more quickly, presenting larger amounts of information in each frame. As a result, questions are more difficult to answer, and students are more likely to make errors. Whenever students respond incorrectly to a question, they proceed to one or more remedial frames for further clarification or practice before continuing on with new information.

Computer-assisted instruction (CAI) is, in a nutshell, programmed instruction via a computer. Most CAI programs are branching programs: They automatically branch to appropriate frames based on the particular responses that students make. Branching programs provide more flexibility than linear programs: Only those students having difficulty with a particular skill or concept proceed to remedial frames. Other students can move on to new information, without having to spend time on practice frames they do not need.

Contemporary CAI programs are likely to incorporate cognitivist principles, as well as those of behaviorists such as Skinner. For example, effective programs often take steps to capture and hold students' *attention,* elicit students' *prior knowledge* about a topic, and encourage long-term retention and transfer (R. M. Gagné, Briggs, & Wager, 1992; P. F. Merrill et al., 1996). Furthermore, some programs provide drill-and-practice of basic knowledge and skills (e.g., math facts, typing, fundamentals of music), helping students develop *automaticity* in these areas (P. F. Merrill et al., 1996).

How might computer-assisted instruction benefit Reggie (our "math problem" case study)?

Choose programs that encourage active responding, promote effective information processing, and provide immediate feedback.

Games and Simulations

Some computer programs instruct students in basic knowledge and skills, whereas others promote higher-level thinking skills (e.g., problem solving) within the context of a gamelike task. One of the best-known examples is *Where in the World is Carmen San Diego?* which teaches geography while the student acts as a detective. Other programs provide simulations of such events as running a lemonade stand, dissecting a frog, or growing plants under varying environmental conditions. Games and simulations are often both motivating and challenging for students, thus keeping them on-task for extended periods of time (P. F. Merrill et al., 1996).

Use games and simulations to motivate and challenge students.

Hypertext and Hypermedia

As a student, have you had experience with computer programs that allowed you to jump around from one topic to other, related topics, thereby enabling you to decide what things to study and in what order to study them? If so, then you've had experience with either hypertext or hypermedia (e.g., Jonassen, 1996; P. F. Merrill et al., 1996). **Hypertext** is a collection of computer-based verbal material that allows students to read about one topic and then proceed to related topics of their own choosing; for example, you might read a short, introductory passage about airplanes and then decide whether to proceed to more specific information about aerodynamics, the history of air travel, or military aircraft. **Hypermedia** includes such other media as pictures, sound, animations, and videos, as well as text; for example, some computer-based encyclopedias enable students to bounce from text to a voice message and then to a video about a particular topic.

Use hypertext and hypermedia when students are capable of making informed choices about what to study and learn.

Hypertext and hypermedia, when used for instructional purposes, are based on the assumption that students benefit from imposing their own organization on a subject area and selecting those topics that are most personally relevant (Jonassen, 1996; Small & Grabowski, 1992). Keep in mind, however, that not all students are capable of making wise choices about what to study and in what sequence to study it. For example, they may be overwhelmed by the large number of choices the computer offers, have trouble identifying important information, or lack sufficient comprehension-monitoring skills to determine when they have sufficiently mastered the material (Garhart & Hannafin, 1986; Lanza & Roselli, 1991; E. R. Steinberg, 1989).

Use computer networks to expand students' access to information located beyond school walls.

Computer Networks

Students' access to new information is not necessarily limited to the computer programs we have in our own schools and classrooms. Through modems and telephone lines, our students can have access to the *Internet*—a worldwide network of computers and computer databases that provide information on virtually any topic in which students are interested. Through such mechanisms as electronic mail ("e-mail") and electronic bulletin boards, computer networks also enable students to communicate directly with those who may have the information they need.

Incorporate computer tools into instruction in various content domains.

Tool Applications

In today's society, students need to know not only about reading, writing, mathematics, science, and so on but also about how to use computers. For example, many professions may require expertise in such *computer tools* as word processing, desktop publishing, databases, and spreadsheets. Hence, our instructional objectives may sometimes include computer skills in addition to skills in more traditional academic areas.

As we teach students to use computer tools, we can simultaneously help them accomplish objectives in more traditional academic areas. Word processing programs can help students revise their short stories, essays, and other written work. Database programs can help students organize information about trees or planets. Spreadsheets enable students to predict changes in weather patterns or trends in the populations of endangered species. Tools known as *music editors* let students create musical compositions and experiment with different notes, keys, instrumental sounds, and time signatures (P. F. Merrill et al., 1996).

Computer programs provide one effective medium for helping students acquire basic information. Some may also promote higher-level thinking processes.

Numerous research studies have documented the effectiveness of computer-based instruction: Students learning through CBI often have higher academic achievement and better attitudes toward their schoolwork than is true for students taught with more traditional methods (J. A. Kulik, Kulik, & Cohen, 1980; Lepper & Gurtner, 1989; P. F. Merrill et al., 1996; Roblyer, Castine, & King, 1988). Furthermore, students involved with CBI may gain an increased sense that they can control their own learning, thereby developing more intrinsic motivation to learn (Swan, Mitrani, Guerrero, Cheung, & Schoener, 1990).

Keep in mind that using a computer *in and of itself* is not necessarily the key to better instruction (R. E. Clark, 1983). A computer can help students achieve at higher levels only when it provides instruction that cannot be offered as easily or effectively through other means. There is little to be gained when a computer merely asks students to read information on a computer screen instead of reading it in a textbook. But there is a great deal to be gained when that same computer asks students to answer questions, solve problems, manipulate data, or experiment with objects or events in ways that are not possible through any other medium.

Many contemporary CBI programs are designed to help students engage in effective information processing of the material they are studying. Some forms of CBI—games, simulations, hypermedia, applications of such tools as databases and spreadsheets—may promote higher-level thinking processes as well (P. F. Merrill et al., 1996). In the pages that follow, we will consider several additional instructional strategies specifically intended to promote such information processing.

In what situations might computer-based instruction be especially relevant to the subject matter you will be teaching?

HELPING STUDENTS PROCESS WHAT THEY'VE LEARNED

Cognitive theories of learning emphasize that it's not enough simply to present the information we want our students to learn. We must also help them process that information in effective ways, by learning it meaningfully, organizing it, elaborating on it, and so on. Some instructional strategies lend themselves especially well to helping students process what they're learning:

- Questioning
- Class discussion

- Cooperative learning

- Reciprocal teaching

Asking Questions

Obviously, part of a teacher's job is to communicate new information to students. Yet unless communication also goes in the opposite direction—from students to teacher—the teacher doesn't really know what, if anything, students have learned. Even very experienced teachers sometimes overestimate what students are actually learning during a classroom lecture (P. W. Fox & LeCount, 1991).

When we ask questions during a group lesson or provide follow-up questions to a reading assignment that students have completed on their own, we can often enhance our students' achievement (Allington & Weber, 1993; Andre, 1987; Armbruster & Ostertag, 1993; Liu, 1990; Redfield & Rousseau, 1981). Questions help us accomplish at least three things. First of all, by asking questions based directly on our instructional material, we can ascertain whether students are learning the material successfully or are confused about particular points. Second, our questions give students the opportunity to monitor their *own* comprehension—to determine whether they understand the information being presented or whether they should ask for help or clarification. And third, when we ask higher-level questions—for example, when we ask them to think of their own examples of a concept or to use a new principle to solve a problem—we are encouraging them to engage in elaboration as they store the information in their long-term memories.

It is important to note here that some students will be less eager to answer our questions than others; for example, many females and ethnic minority students may be reluctant to respond (Kerr, 1991; Sadker & Sadker, 1994; Villegas, 1991). If, in a classroom of thirty students, only a handful are responding to questions regularly, we have no way of knowing whether their answers reflect what the rest of the class does and does not know. As teachers, we must remember to direct our questions to the entire class, not just to the few who raise their hands (Airasian, 1994; G. A. Davis & Thomas, 1989). One approach that solicits *all* students' answers to a question is to conduct a class "vote" regarding several possible answers. Another is to have students write their answers on paper; we can either walk around the room and check individual responses or, if handwriting is large enough, we can ask students to hold their responses up for us to look at from the front of the room (Connolly & Eisenberg, 1990; Fairbairn, 1987).

We must also remember to give students adequate time to respond to the questions we ask. Just as students need time to process the information they are hearing or reading, they also need time to consider the questions we pose and to retrieve any information relevant to possible answers. As we discovered in our discussion of *wait time* in Chapter 6, when teachers allow at least three seconds to elapse after asking questions in class (in comparison with the more typical pause of one second or less), they find that a greater number of students volunteer answers and that those answers are longer, more complex, and more often correct. And as we learned in our exploration of ethnic differences in Chapter 4, some students may require more wait time than others before they are willing to respond to our questions.

Ask questions both to assess students' learning and to encourage effective memory storage and higher-level cognitive processes.

Allow sufficient wait time for students to formulate their answers to questions, especially in a culturally diverse classroom.

Conducting a Class Discussion

As you know from reading Chapter 7, social constructivists propose that people often work together to construct meaningful interpretations of their world. Class discussions in which students feel that they can speak freely, asking questions and presenting their ideas and opinions in either a whole-class or small-group context, obviously provide an important mechanism for promoting such socially constructed understandings (e.g., Bruning et al., 1995; Marshall, 1992).

Use class discussions to promote more complete understanding of complex topics.

In addition, classroom dialogues often facilitate more effective information processing. When students explain their thinking to their classmates, they must organize their thoughts and pull separate ideas into a logical, cohesive whole that makes sense to others (Stevens & Slavin, 1995). Controversial topics may be especially useful for promoting information processing: Students more actively seek out new information, more frequently express their views to their classmates, more readily reevaluate their own positions on the issues, and develop a more conceptual understanding of the subject matter (E. G. Cohen, 1994; D. W. Johnson & Johnson, 1985a; K. Smith, Johnson, & Johnson, 1981).

Class discussions are often more effective when they are structured in some way. For example, we might ask the class to examine a textbook or other source of information with a particular goal in mind (Calfee, Dunlap, & Wat, 1994). Or, when having students wrestle with an especially controversial issue in small groups, we may want to follow a predetermined sequence such as this one (Deutsch, 1993):

1. The classroom is divided into groups of four students apiece. Each group of four subdivides into two pairs.

2. Within a group, each pair of students studies a particular position on the issue and presents its position to the other two students.

3. The group of four has an open discussion of the issue, giving each student an opportunity to argue persuasively for his or her own position.

4. Each pair presents the perspective of the *opposing* side as sincerely and persuasively as possible.

5. The group strives for consensus on a position that incorporates all the evidence presented.

Furthermore, we may find it valuable to provide such guidelines as these for small-group discussions:

- Encourage everyone to participate and listen to everyone's ideas.

- Restate what someone else has said if you don't understand.

- Be critical of ideas rather than people.

- Try to pull ideas from both sides together in a way that makes sense.

- Focus, not on winning, but on resolving the issue in the best possible way.

- Change your mind if the arguments and evidence presented indicate that you should do so. (adapted from Deutsch, 1993)

Class discussions are not necessarily stand-alone instructional strategies. For example, we may often want to incorporate them into expository instruction or discovery learning sessions. Discussions are also an integral part of cooperative learning, a strategy we turn to now.

Facilitating Cooperative Learning

■ **EXPERIENCING FIRSTHAND**
Purple Satin

Imagine yourself as a student in each of the three classrooms described below. Think about how you would behave in each situation.

1. Mr. Alexander tells your class, "Let's find out which students can learn the most in this week's unit on the human digestive system. The three students getting the highest scores on Friday's unit test will get free tickets to the Purple Satin concert." Purple Satin is a popular musical group; you would give your eye teeth to hear them perform, but the concert has been sold out for months.

2. Ms. Bernstein introduces her lesson this way: "Let's see whether each of you can learn all about the digestive system this week. If you can get a score of at least 90% on this Friday's test, then you will get a free ticket to the Purple Satin concert."

3. Mr. Camacho begins the same lesson like this: "Today we begin studying the human digestive system. Let's see how many students can get scores of 90% or better on Friday's test. I want you to work in groups of three to help one another learn the material. If all three members of a group score at least 90% on the test at the end of the week, then that group will get free tickets to the Purple Satin concert."

In which class(es) are you likely to work hard to get free tickets to Purple Satin? How might you work *differently* in the different situations? ■

The first classroom (Mr. Alexander's) is obviously a very competitive one: Only the three best students are getting tickets to the concert. Will you try to earn one of those tickets? It all depends on what you think your chances are of being a top scorer on Friday's test. On the one hand, if you have been doing well on tests all year, then you will undoubtedly study harder than ever for this week's unit. On the other hand, if you have been doing poorly in class despite your best efforts, then you probably won't work for something you are unlikely to get. But in either case, will you help your fellow students learn about the digestive system? If they express confusion about what the pancreas does, will you explain its function? If they forget the reading assignment, will you tell them the pages they need to read? Not if you want to go to the concert yourself!

In Ms. Bernstein's classroom, there's no competition for concert tickets. As long as you get a score of 90% or higher on the test, you get a ticket. Even if you think half the students in class are smarter than you are, you know that you have a good chance of going to the concert, and so you will probably study diligently for Friday's test. But will you help your classmates learn to distinguish between the large and small intestines? Maybe . . . *if* you have the time and are in a good mood.

But now consider Mr. Camacho's classroom. Whether you get a concert ticket depends on how well you *and two other students* score on Friday's test. Are you going to help those two students learn about salivation and digestive enzymes? And can you expect them, in turn, to help you understand where the liver fits into the whole system? Absolutely!

Cooperative learning (e.g., D. W. Johnson & Johnson, 1987; Slavin, 1983a, 1990) is an approach to instruction in which students work in small groups to help one another learn. Unlike an individualistic classroom such as Ms. Bernstein's (where one student's success is unrelated to classmates' achievement) or a competitive classroom such as Mr. Alexander's (where one student's success actually depends on the failure of others), students in a cooperative learning environment such as Mr. Camacho's work together to achieve common successes. In other words, they *sink or swim together* (D. W. Johnson & Johnson, 1987).

Yet cooperative learning is not simply a process of putting students in groups and setting them loose to work on a topic together. Oftentimes, our students will be more accustomed to competitive and individualistic classroom situations than they are to cooperative endeavors with their classmates. For the cooperative learning approach to be successful, we must structure the classroom in such a way that cooperation is not only helpful for academic success but, in fact, even necessary for it (e.g., D. W. Johnson & Johnson, 1987). Table 13–2 presents a number of features that enhance the effectiveness of cooperative groups.

We find justification for cooperative learning in a number of theoretical perspectives. From a cognitivist perspective, group discussions promote more effective information processing and greater conceptual understanding. From a behaviorist point of view, providing rewards for group success is consistent with the operant conditioning notion of a group contingency. From a social cognitive standpoint, we enhance the self-efficacy of our students when we provide an arena in which they can observe the successes of their peers. Considering the work of such developmentalists as Piaget and Kohlberg, we foster both cognitive and moral development when we give students the opportunity to share their ideas and perspectives with one another. And we provide the

How often do adults need to work cooperatively in the workplace? Do you think they might have benefited from cooperative experiences during their school years?

Incorporate the features listed in Table 13–2 into your cooperative learning activities.

In a cooperative learning environment, students sink or swim together.

Table 13–2 Features of Effective Cooperative Learning Sessions

FEATURE	DESCRIPTION	EXAMPLE
Small, heterogeneous groups	Groups are typically comprised of two to six members. They often include a mix of students—boys and girls, high achievers and low achievers, and children of various ethnic backgrounds.	Ms. Edwards doesn't let her students form their own groups, because she knows that most of them would end up working only with classmates similar to themselves.
Varying duration	Some groups are formed on a short-term basis to accomplish specific tasks; others are formed to work toward long-term classroom goals.	Mr. Archibeque assigns his middle school students to **base groups**—cooperative groups that will last the entire school year. The base groups will provide a means through which students can clarify assignments for one another, help one another with class notes, and provide one another with a general sense of support and belonging in the classroom.
Clear goals	Groups have clear, concrete objectives toward which to work.	Ms. Wong asks cooperative groups in her high school Spanish class to write and videotape a television commercial spoken in Spanish.
Guidelines for behavior	Students are trained in the interpersonal skills essential for working cooperatively together—listening attentively, providing encouragement, giving feedback, etc.	When beginning cooperative groups in his junior high school math class, Mr. Palermo gives his students several rules about how to work cooperatively: Make sure everyone has a chance to participate equally, listen attentively to other group members, don't yell or put down others, etc. He also teaches them both how to *get* help (e.g., ask clear, precise questions) and how to *give* help (e.g., give clues, rather than the final answer to a problem) while working together (based on Webb & Farivar, 1994).
Interdependence of group members	Each student's success depends on the help and participation of other group members. In some situations, each student has a unique and essential function within the group (e.g, perhaps serving as group leader, critic, bookkeeper). In other situations, the **jigsaw technique** is useful: New information is divided equally among all group members, and each student must teach his or her portion to the other group members.	Mr. Villanueva uses the jigsaw technique to foster interdependence among group members in his social studies class. He divides a magazine article about the Gulf War into several parts and gives each part to a different group member. Each student is responsible for learning the information contained in his or her part of the article and then teaching it to the rest of the group.

scaffolding that Vygotsky believed was so important when we enable students to support one another's efforts on difficult tasks.

Numerous research studies indicate that cooperative learning activities that include the features listed in Table 13–2—for example, those that involve heterogeneous grouping and provide for both individual accountability and rewards for group success—are effective in many ways. For one thing, students of all ability levels show higher academic achievement; females, members of minority groups, and at-risk students are especially

FEATURE	DESCRIPTION	EXAMPLE
A structure that promotes a particular type of interaction	When students are novices at cooperative learning, it is often helpful to give them a set of steps or "script" that guides their interaction; this strategy is sometimes called **scripted cooperation.**	Mr. McDermott has his fifth graders read their science textbook in pairs. After reading a passage from the book, one member of the pair acts as "recaller," summarizing the contents of the passage. The other student acts as "listener," correcting any errors and recalling additional important information. For the next passage, the two students switch roles. By having his students use this approach, Mr. McDermott helps them improve such study strategies as elaboration, summarizing, and comprehension monitoring (Dansereau, 1988).
Teacher as monitor and resource	The teacher monitors each group to be sure that interactions are productive and socially appropriate. He or she may also provide assistance in situations where group members are unable to provide information or insights critical for accomplishing the group's goal.	Ms. Phansiri monitors her cooperative groups with these questions in mind: • Are students working toward a common goal? • Are they all actively participating? • Are they listening to one another's perspectives? • Are they asking one another questions when they don't understand? • Are they criticizing ideas rather than people?
Individual accountability for achievement	Each student demonstrates individual mastery or accomplishment of the group's goal—for example, by taking a quiz or answering questions in class. This strategy minimizes the likelihood that some students will do most or all of the work while others get a "free ride."	Mr. Villanueva asks his students to write a summary of the magazine article that their cooperative groups have studied about the Gulf War.
Rewards for group success	In addition to being accountable for their own learning and achievement, group members are rewarded for the success of the group as a whole (a **group contingency**).	Ms. James gives her students a quiz over material they have studied in their cooperative groups. She awards bonus points to students in a particular group when all group members perform at or above a certain level on the quiz.
Self-evaluation	Once a group has accomplished its goal, it looks analytically and critically (often with the assistance of the teacher) at the ways in which it has functioned effectively and the ways in which it needs to improve.	At the end of a cooperative group activity, students in Ms. Phansiri's class ask themselves the same questions that Ms. Phansiri had been asking during the activity. For example, did they all participate equally? Did they criticize ideas rather than people?

Sources: Berg, 1994; A. L. Brown & Palincsar, 1989; Casanova, 1987; E. G. Cohen, 1994; Dansereau, 1988; Deutsch, 1993; D. W. Johnson & Johnson, 1987; R. T. Johnson, 1989; Meloth & Deering, 1994; O'Donnell, 1996; O'Donnell & O'Kelly, 1994; Schofield, 1995; Slavin, 1983a, 1983b, 1990; Stevens & Slavin, 1995; Webb & Farivar, 1994.

likely to show increased achievement (Garcia, 1992; D. W. Johnson & Johnson, 1987; Lampe & Rooze, 1994; Larrivee, 1989; Pigott et al., 1986; Qin, Johnson, & Johnson, 1995; Shachar & Sharan, 1994; Sharan & Shachar, 1988; Stevens & Slavin, 1995). The group context promotes such effective storage processes as meaningful learning, organization, and elaboration: By discussing and explaining their ideas with other group members, students must pull their thoughts together in a way that will make sense to someone else (Good, McCaslin, & Reys, 1992; D. W. Johnson & Johnson, 1987; Slavin, 1983a, 1990;

Use cooperative learning to promote higher-level thinking skills, intrinsic motivation, prosocial behavior, and a wider range of friendships.

Might cooperative learning be beneficial for helping struggling students such as Reggie in our case study? Why or why not?

Stevens & Slavin, 1995). Cooperative learning activities may also promote higher-level thinking skills: Students essentially "think aloud," modeling various learning and problem-solving strategies for one another and developing greater metacognitive awareness as a result (A. L. Brown & Palincsar, 1989; Good et al., 1992; Paris & Winograd, 1990).

The benefits of cooperative learning activities are not limited to gains in learning and achievement. Students have higher self-efficacy about their chances of being successful, express more intrinsic motivation to learn school subject matter, and participate more actively in classroom activities. They better understand the perspectives of others and more frequently engage in prosocial behavior—making decisions about how to divide a task fairly and equitably, resolving interpersonal conflicts, and encouraging and supporting one another's learning. Furthermore, they are more likely to believe that they are liked and accepted by their classmates, and increased numbers of friendships across racial and ethnic groups and between students with and without disabilities are likely to form (Deutsch, 1993; Good et al., 1992; D. W. Johnson & Johnson, 1985b, 1987; Larrivee, 1989; Lickona, 1991; H. W. Marsh & Peart, 1988; Slavin, 1983a, 1990; Stevens & Slavin, 1995).

A variation of cooperative learning—one that involves the participation of the teacher, as well as peers—is *reciprocal teaching*. This approach facilitates effective information processing of instructional material; furthermore, it gives students several specific guidelines about how to help one another learn.

INTO THE CLASSROOM
Promoting Cooperative Learning

Form small, heterogeneous groups.

An elementary school teacher divides her class into cooperative groups of four or five students each. He makes sure that each group includes boys and girls, high achievers and low achievers, and students of various ethnic backgrounds.

Provide clear goals toward which groups should work.

In a unit on Shakespeare, an English teacher asks cooperative groups to identify the attitudes toward Jewish people expressed in *The Merchant of Venice*, as reflected in the actions and statements of Shylock and other characters.

Give each group member a different role or task within the group.

A biology teacher asks cooperative groups to prepare for an upcoming classroom debate on the pros and cons of preserving tropical rain forests. She gives each student a unique function. One student acts as *reader* of information about rain forests, another acts as *recorder* of the arguments that group members present, a third acts as *checker* to determine whether all group members agree with each argument, and so on.

Monitor group interactions.

A junior high school social studies teacher asks cooperative groups to identify an effective way of helping the homeless find suitable housing. He observes the groups to be sure interactions within each group are productive and socially appropriate. When he sees a student insulting another because of a difference of opinion, he reminds the group that students should criticize ideas, rather than people.

Provide critical information and insights when (but only when) a group is unlikely or unable to provide such information and insights for itself.

The same middle school teacher tells one group, "The solution you have developed assumes that most taxpayers would be willing to pay much higher taxes than they do now. Is that realistic?"

Make students individually accountable for their achievement.

A mathematics teacher has incorporated cooperative learning into a lesson on calculating the area of a triangle. She gives all students a test to assess their individual mastery of the subject.

Reinforce group success.

The same mathematics teacher awards "bonus" points to students whose entire group performs at or above a certain test score.

Ask students to evaluate their effectiveness in working as a group.

After cooperative groups have completed their assigned tasks, a social studies teacher asks the groups to answer such questions as these: "Did all group members actively participate?" "Did they ask questions when they didn't understand one another?" "Did they criticize ideas rather than people?"

Vary the duration of cooperative groups, depending on the task to be accomplished.

In September, a high school health teacher forms *base groups*—groups of students who will provide support and assistance for one another throughout the school year. As the year progresses, he occasionally forms different, more short-term cooperative groups to accomplish specific tasks—for example, to identify the dangers of alcohol abuse or plan an inexpensive meal encompassing the four food groups.

Encouraging Reciprocal Teaching

As you may recall from our discussion of metacognition in Chapter 8, students typically know very little about how they can best learn information. For example, here are three high school students' descriptions of how they study a textbook (A. L. Brown & Palincsar, 1987, p. 83):

- ". . . I stare real hard at the page, blink my eyes and then open them—and cross my fingers that it will be right here." (Student points at head).

- "It's easy, if [the teacher] says study, I read it twice. If she says read, it's just once through."

- "I just read the first line in each paragraph—it's usually all there."

Obviously, these students have little awareness of how they are processing the information they read. And notice how not one of them mentions any attempt to understand the information, relate it to prior knowledge, or otherwise think about it in any way. These students are probably *not* engaging in meaningful learning, organization, or elaboration; in other words, they are not using cognitive processes that will help them store and retain information in long-term memory.

One obvious objective of our educational system is that students learn to read. But an equally important objective is that students *read to learn*—in other words, that they acquire new information from the things they read. Yet many students apparently are not learning some very important cognitive strategies to use when they read to learn. As a result, they may be getting very little from the reading materials they encounter either in school or in the outside world. In a sense, information in books, magazines, and newspapers may be going "in one ear and out the other."

■ EXPERIENCING FIRSTHAND
Metacogitating

Take a minute to think about what you've been doing in your head as you've been reading this chapter. Decide how frequently you've engaged in the following mental activities:

	Never	Occasionally	Frequently
Identifying and summarizing the main ideas	0	1	2
Asking yourself questions to check your understanding	0	1	2
Trying to clarify what you didn't initially understand	0	1	2
Predicting what you were likely to read next	0	1	2 ■

When we examine the cognitive processes that good readers (successful learners) often use, especially when reading challenging material, we find such strategies as these (A. L. Brown & Palincsar, 1987):

- *Summarizing:* Good readers identify the main ideas—the gist—of what they read.

- *Questioning:* Good readers ask themselves questions to make sure they understand what they are reading; in other words, they monitor their comprehension as they proceed through reading material.

- *Clarifying:* When good readers discover that they don't comprehend something—for example, when a sentence is confusing or ambiguous—they take steps to clarify what they are reading, perhaps by rereading it or making logical inferences.

- *Predicting:* Good readers anticipate what they are likely to read next; they make predictions about the ideas that are likely to follow the ones they are currently reading.

Can you explain the value of these four strategies by relating them to effective memory storage processes? ■

In contrast, poor readers—those who learn little from textbooks and other things they read—rarely summarize, question, clarify, or predict. For example, many students cannot adequately summarize a typical *fifth*-grade textbook until high school or even junior college (A. L. Brown & Palincsar, 1987; Palincsar & Brown, 1984). Clearly, many students do not easily acquire the ability to read for learning.

Reciprocal teaching (A. L. Brown & Palincsar, 1987; Palincsar & Brown, 1984, 1989) is an approach to teaching reading through which students learn effective reading-to-learn strategies by observing and modeling their teacher and fellow students. The teacher and several students meet in a group to read a piece of text, stopping to discuss and process that text aloud as they proceed. Students in the group take turns as "teacher," leading the discussion and asking questions about the text (hence, the term *reciprocal* teaching). The four reading-to-learn strategies that I just listed— summarizing, questioning, clarifying, and predicting—are included in each discussion when appropriate.

To illustrate, here is a reciprocal teaching session for a group of six first graders reading a passage about snowshoe rabbits. In this particular case, the classroom teacher reads the text in small segments (at higher grade levels, the students themselves take turns reading). After each segment, the teacher pauses while students discuss and process that segment. As you read the dialogue, watch for examples of summarizing, questioning, clarifying, and predicting.

> The children were reading about the snowshoe rabbit, and it was the sixteenth day of dialogue. The teacher had just read a segment of text describing the season in which baby rabbits are born and the ways in which the mother rabbit cares for her babies. A student named Kam is the dialogue leader.
>
> Kam: When was the babies born?
> Teacher: That's a good question to ask. Call on someone to answer that question.
> Kam: Robby? Milly?
> Milly: Summer.
> Teacher: What would happen if the babies were born in the winter? Let's think.
>
> Several children make a number of responses, including "The baby would be very cold." "They would need food." "They don't have no fur when they are just born."
>
> Kam: I have another question. How does she get the babies safe?
> Kris: She hides them.

Can you find at least one example each of summarizing, questioning, clarifying, and predicting in this dialogue? What strategies does the teacher use to elicit desired student responses?

Student teachers and students here are engaging in *reciprocal teaching,* an structional strategy that helps students identify and formulate the kinds of questions they should ask one another— questions that mature readers often ask *themselves* as they read.

Kam:	That's right but something else. . . .
Teacher:	There is something very unusual about how she hides them that surprised me. I didn't know this.
Travis:	They are all in a different place.
Teacher:	Why do you think she does this?
Milly:	Probably because I heard another story, and when they're babies they usually eat each other or fight with each other.
Teacher:	That could be! And what about when that lynx comes?

Several children comment that that would be the end of all the babies.

Travis:	If I was the mother, I would hide mine, I would keep them all together.
Kris:	If the babies are hidden and the mom wants to go and look at them, how can she remember where they are?
Teacher:	Good question. Because she does have to find them again. Why? What does she bring them?
Milly:	She needs to bring food. She probably leaves a twig or something.
Teacher:	Do you think she puts out a twig like we mark a trail?

Several children disagree and suggest that she uses her sense of smell. One child, recalling that the snowshoe rabbit is not all white in the winter, suggests that the mother might be able to tell her babies apart by their coloring.

Teacher:	So we agree that the mother rabbit uses her senses to find her babies after she hides them. Kam, can you summarize for us now?
Kam:	The babies are born in the summer. . . .
Teacher:	The mother . . .
Kam:	The mother hides the babies in different places.
Teacher:	And she visits them . . .
Kam:	To bring them food.
Travis:	She keeps them safe.
Teacher:	Any predictions?
Milly:	What she teaches her babies . . . like how to hop.
Kris:	They know how to hop already.
Teacher:	Well, let's read and see. (dialogue courtesy of A. Palincsar)

Model effective learning strategies—for example, summarizing, questioning, clarifying, and predicting—in a group reading situation. Gradually turn the role of "teacher" over to students.

As you can see, students in a reciprocal teaching situation take a much more active role in their own teaching and learning than is true for more traditional reading groups. But students must be taught the skills they eventually use to teach one another. When a reciprocal reading group first begins, the classroom teacher takes a major responsibility for teaching the students (e.g., by summarizing, paraphrasing, and asking questions); in doing so, the teacher models effective ways of processing text. In subsequent sessions, this "teaching" responsibility is gradually turned over to students as they become increasingly capable of using the same processes to help themselves and one another learn. Eventually, students read and discuss a text almost independently of the teacher, working together to construct its meaning and checking one another for comprehension and possible misunderstandings (A. L. Brown & Palincsar, 1987; Palincsar & Brown, 1984, 1989). If you have read Chapter 2, then you may have noticed that reciprocal teaching is an example of Vygotsky's notion of scaffolding: The teacher initially provides a great deal of support, gradually removing the support as students become more proficient in the skills being practiced.

Theoretically, reciprocal teaching provides a means through which effective learning strategies are modeled and eventually used independently by students. It can be employed with an entire classroom of students almost as easily as in a small group. Although teachers are often very skeptical of such a radically different approach to teaching and learning, they become quite enthusiastic once they've tried it themselves (A. L. Brown & Palincsar, 1987; Palincsar & Brown, 1989).

Reciprocal teaching has been used successfully with a wide variety of students, ranging from first graders to college students, to teach effective reading and listening comprehension skills (A. L. Brown & Palincsar, 1987; Palincsar, 1986; Palincsar & Brown, 1984, 1989; Rosenshine & Meister, 1994). For example, in an early study of reciprocal teaching (Palincsar & Brown, 1984), six seventh-grade students with a history of poor reading comprehension participated in twenty reciprocal teaching sessions, each lasting about thirty minutes. Despite this relatively short interven-

INTO THE CLASSROOM
Using Reciprocal Teaching

Model effective learning strategies—in particular, summarizing, questioning, clarifying, and predicting—in a group reading or listening situation.

> As a junior high school teacher assigns a textbook chapter entitled "Exploring Outer Space," she asks students, "What do you think this chapter is about? Can you predict some things that you will probably learn about as you read the chapter?"

Gradually turn the role of "teacher" over to students, scaffolding their initial efforts.

> An elementary school teacher working with a reading group asks one student, "Rachel, can you summarize what we have just read? Remember, the title of this section of the chapter is 'Habits of the Grizzly Bear.'"

Eventually allow students to "teach" without your assistance.

> A middle school teacher working with a group of low-achieving readers has students take turns serving as teacher for the group, addressing questions to other group members about the passage they are reading.

Provide praise and specific feedback about a student's participation.

> A high school teacher commends a student, "That was an excellent question, Raul. You asked the group to clarify an idea that was not clearly explained in the book. Who can answer Raul's question?"

tion, students showed remarkable improvement in their reading comprehension skills. They became increasingly able to process reading material in an effective manner and to do so independently of their classroom teacher. Furthermore, they generalized their new reading strategies to other classes, sometimes even surpassing the achievement of their classmates (A. L. Brown & Palincsar, 1987; Palincsar & Brown, 1984).

Do these findings surprise you? Why or why not?

Not only do we want to encourage our students to engage in effective information processing, but we also want our students to be able to *use* the knowledge and skills they acquire in our classrooms. Let's look at some instructional strategies to help them do exactly that.

HELPING STUDENTS USE WHAT THEY'VE LEARNED

As teachers, how can we best promote transfer? To refresh your memory, skim the section "Examining Factors Affecting Transfer" in Chapter 8.

It's not enough just to present information and have students mentally process it in particular ways. We must also provide opportunities for them to *practice* the things they learn. Such practice should help them develop automaticity for basic information and skills; it can also provide the occasional review so important for long-term retention (see our discussion of "Factors Affecting Retrieval" in Chapter 6). Furthermore, we will often want our students to transfer what they learn in school to real-world tasks and situations.

The nature of the assignments we give will inevitably affect the extent to which long-term retention and transfer are likely to occur. In the next few pages, we will consider how we might encourage students to practice and apply classroom material through three vehicles:

- In-class activities

- Homework

- Authentic activities

Using In-Class Activities

Students are typically asked to accomplish a wide variety of tasks and assignments in class during the school year; for example, they might be asked to read textbooks, complete worksheets, solve problems, write short stories, draw pictures, practice basketball skills, and play musical instruments. Naturally, there are only so many things they can do in any single school year. How do we decide which activities are likely to be most beneficial to their long-term learning and achievement?

Choose activities that facilitate accomplishment of important instructional objectives

As teachers, we should, first and foremost, assign in-class activities that will help students accomplish our instructional objectives (Brophy & Alleman, 1992; Doyle, 1983). In some cases, these objectives may be at a "knowledge" level; for instance, we may want students to conjugate the French verb *être* ("to be"), know members of different biological classes and orders, and be familiar with current events around the globe. But in other cases, we may have higher-level objectives; for instance, we may want our students to write a persuasive essay, use scientific principles to interpret physical phenomena, or use arithmetic operations to solve real-world problems. Particularly when such higher-level objectives are involved, we will want to assign activities that promote conceptual understanding—activities that help students learn classroom material in a meaningful and integrated fashion.

In addition to matching our in-class activities to our objectives, we are more likely to facilitate students' learning and achievement when we assign activities that:

- Accommodate student diversity in abilities and interests

- Clearly define each task and its purpose

- Generate students' interest in accomplishing the task

- Begin at an appropriate difficulty level for students—ideally, presenting a task that challenges students to "stretch" their knowledge and skills (a task within students' zone of proximal development)

- Provide sufficient scaffolding to promote success

- Progress in difficulty and complexity as students become more proficient

- Provide opportunities for frequent teacher monitoring and feedback regarding students' progress

- Encourage students to reflect on and evaluate the work they have completed (Brophy & Alleman, 1991, 1992; Brophy & Good, 1986)

We must remember, too, that the ways in which we assess students' performance will have an impact on what our in-class activities actually accomplish (Doyle, 1983). For example, if we give full credit for completing an assignment without regard to the *quality* of responses, our students may focus more on "getting the work done" than on developing a conceptual understanding of what they are studying. Yet we must be careful that our criteria for acceptable performance are not overly strict: We don't want to discourage students from taking risks and making errors—risks and errors that are inevitable when students are seeking out and pursuing the challenges that are most likely to promote their cognitive growth.

Remember that your assessment criteria will affect what students actually learn and accomplish during classroom activities.

Assigning Homework

There is only so much that our students can accomplish during class time, and homework provides a means through which we can, in essence, extend the school day. Yet we must remember that most students are likely to have little scaffolding at home. Hence, the homework that we assign may often need to focus more on giving students extra practice with familiar information and procedures (perhaps as a way of promoting review and automaticity) or on introducing them to new yet simple material, rather than on having them perform complex tasks they have not yet dealt with in the classroom (H. Cooper, 1989).

Homework is typically more beneficial for older students than for younger ones; research studies tell us that it has a considerable effect on the achievement of high school students but little if any effect on achievement at the elementary level (H. Cooper, 1989). At the same time, we must remember that distractions, responsibilities, and parental involvement at home are likely to influence students' ability to complete the homework we assign.

Assign homework to enhance automaticity of basic knowledge and skills, to encourage review, or to introduce students to new yet relatively simple material.

We can maximize the benefits of homework by following a few simple guidelines (H. Cooper, 1989):

- Use assignments primarily for instructional and diagnostic purposes; minimize the degree to which homework is used to assess learning and determine final class grades.

- Provide the information and structure that students need to complete assignments without assistance from others.

- Give a mixture of required and voluntary assignments (voluntary ones should help give students a sense of self-determination and control, hence enhancing intrinsic motivation).

Communicate your belief that homework will help students learn.

Above all, we should remember *never* to use homework as a form of punishment. Such a practice communicates the wrong message—the message that schoolwork is an unpleasant chore, one to be avoided whenever possible.

Using Authentic Activities

Use authentic activities to promote meaningful connections between classroom subject matter and real-world tasks.

In our discussion of knowledge construction in Chapter 7, and again in our discussion of transfer and situated cognition in Chapter 8, we noted the value of *authentic activities*—activities similar to those that students are likely to encounter in the outside world. When we assign authentic activities, we are more likely to promote meaningful connections between classroom subject matter and real-world contexts and, as a result, more likely to find students applying what they learn in school to their own personal and professional lives.

Effective authentic activities are likely to have these characteristics:

- They require a fair amount of background knowledge about a particular topic; in other words, students must know the subject matter thoroughly and have learned it in a meaningful fashion.

- They promote higher-level thinking skills; for example, they may involve synthesizing information, forming and testing hypotheses, solving problems, and drawing conclusions.

- They convey high expectations for students' performance, yet also encourage students to take risks and experiment with new strategies.

- Their final outcomes are complex and somewhat unpredictable; there is not necessarily a single "right" response or answer. (based on standards proposed by Newmann & Wehlage, 1993)

Remember that some authentic activities are more successfully accomplished when students work in groups, rather than independently.

It may occasionally be possible to assign authentic activities as homework; for example, we might ask students to write an editorial, design an electrical circuit, or plan a family budget while working at home in the evening. But many authentic activities may require considerable classroom dialogue, with students asking questions of one another, sharing their ideas, and offering explanations of their thinking (Newmann & Wehlage, 1993). For example, creating a school newspaper, designing a model city, debating controversial social or political issues, and conversing in a foreign language may be activities that students can perform only as a group. For obvious reasons, such group activities can usually be accomplished more effectively in class than at home, or perhaps through a combination of group work during class and independent work after school hours.

Thinking Authentically

Take a few minutes to think about and answer these questions:

- In what ways will the subject matter that you teach help your students be successful in their personal or professional lives? In other words, how would you like your students to use and apply school subject matter outside the classroom?

- How might you translate those long-term, real-world applications into activities that you can have students do in your classroom?

With your answers in mind, develop several authentic activities appropriate for the subject matter and age range of students that you will be teaching. ◨

By encouraging students to work and learn together through authentic activities, as well as through such other group-based strategies as class discussions, cooperative learning, reciprocal teaching, and peer tutoring, we can ultimately create a *community of learners* in our classrooms. We turn to this concept now.

CREATING A COMMUNITY OF LEARNERS

A competitive classroom environment is often counterproductive when we consider the principles of motivation that we discussed in Chapter 11. For one thing, competitive situations focus students' attention on performance goals, rather than on learning goals (Nicholls, 1984; Spaulding, 1992); hence, students are more likely to worry about how good they appear to their teacher and classmates than about how effectively they are processing classroom material. Second, competition creates a situation in which most students become losers, rather than winners; their self-efficacy decreases as a result, and their intrinsic motivation to learn is undermined (Deci & Ryan, 1985, 1992). Finally, when students consistently see others performing more successfully than themselves, they are more likely to attribute their own failures to lack of ability: They simply don't have what it takes to succeed at classroom tasks (C. Ames, 1984).

In contrast, a cooperative environment enhances students' motivation to learn and achieve in the classroom because it increases the likelihood that students will be successful (C. Ames, 1984; Deci & Ryan, 1985). A cooperative classroom has additional benefits as well. For example, as is true for the other group-based teaching strategies that we've discussed (class discussions, cooperative learning, reciprocal teaching), students who talk with one another about classroom subject matter must pull together and clarify their ideas as they explain themselves to their classmates. Furthermore, students who think and work together can model effective learning and problem-solving strategies for one another and provide mutual scaffolding that enhances success on challenging tasks. Some theorists refer to such "group thinking" as **distributed cognition** (e.g., A. L. Brown et al., 1993; Salomon, 1993).

In our discussion of planning in the preceding chapter, I introduced the idea of creating a *sense of community* in the classroom—a sense that teacher and students have shared goals, respect and support one another's efforts, and believe that everyone makes an important contribution to classroom learning. Some theorists take this idea one step

Create a community of learners—a classroom in which you and your students actively and cooperatively work to help one another learn.

further, proposing that classrooms are most productive when they are **communities of learners** in which teacher and students actively and cooperatively work to help one another learn (A. L. Brown et al., 1993; Prawat, 1992; Rogoff, 1994). A classroom that operates as a community of learners is likely to have characteristics such as these:

- All students are active participants in classroom activities.

- Diversity in students' interests and rates of progress are expected and respected.

- Students and teacher coordinate their efforts at helping one another learn; no one has exclusive responsibility for teaching others.

- Everyone is a potential resource for the others; different individuals are likely to serve as resources on different occasions, depending on the topics and tasks at hand.

- The teacher provides some guidance and direction for classroom activities, but students may also contribute to such guidance and direction.

- The process of learning is emphasized as much as, and sometimes more than, the finished product. (Rogoff, 1994)

A community of learners produces students who are highly motivated to learn—students who insist on going to school even when they are ill and who are disappointed when summer vacation begins (Rogoff, 1994). It also creates an environment in which students' needs for affiliation are met at the very same time that learning goals and an intrinsic motivation to learn classroom subject matter are being encouraged, nurtured, and satisfied. To illustrate, one eighth-grade English teacher described her experiences with a community of learners this way:

> The classroom became . . . like a dining-room table, where people could converse easily about books and poems and ideas. I would watch my students leave the classroom carrying on animated conversations about which book was truly Robert Cormier's best, why sequels are often disappointing, which books they planned to reread or pack into their trunks for summer camp. Books became valuable currency, changing hands after careful negotiation: "Okay, you can borrow Adams's *So Long and Thanks for All the Fish* (Pocket), but you have to lend me the first two books in the Xanth series." The shelves neatly lined with class sets of books gradually gave way to a paperback library, stocked with books donated by students and their families, bonus copies from book clubs, and books I ordered with my budgeted allotment each year. (Moran, 1991, p. 439)

A community of learners may be especially valuable when we have a diverse classroom of students (e.g., Garcia, 1994). Such a community values the contributions of all students, using everyone's diverse backgrounds, cultural perspectives, and unique abilities to enhance the overall performance of the classroom. It also provides a context in which students can more readily form friendships across the lines of ethnicity, gender, socioeconomic status, and disability—friendships that, as we noted in Chapters 3 and 4, are so critical for students' social development and multicultural understanding.

TAKING STUDENT DIVERSITY INTO ACCOUNT

As we consider which instructional strategies are most appropriate for our instructional objectives, we must also consider which strategies are most appropriate for the particular students we will be teaching. Some strategies adapt themselves readily to a wide variety of student abilities and needs. For example, mastery learning provides a means through which students can learn at their own pace. Computer-based instructional programs often tailor instruction to students' prior knowledge and skills. Homework assignments can be easily individualized for the amount and kinds of practice that different students need.

Some strategies may be especially valuable when teaching students from diverse populations. For example, cooperative learning often promotes higher academic achievement for students whose cultural backgrounds are equally cooperative in nature (Boykin, 1983; Casanova, 1987; Garcia, 1994, 1995; McAlpine & Taylor, 1993; Trueba, 1988). Computers can come to our assistance when teaching students with limited ability to read and write in English; English-language tutorials, computer-based "books" that the computer "reads" to a student, and word processing programs with spell checkers and grammar checkers are all useful when working with these students (P. F. Merrill et al., 1996).

Instructional strategies that require student interaction—class discussions, cooperative learning, peer tutoring, and so on—may be our methods of choice when our objectives include promoting social development as well as academic achievement. For example, small-group discussions encourage females to participate more actively than they typically do during whole-class instruction (Théberge, 1994). Peer tutoring encourages friendly relationships across ethnic and racial lines (Greenwood et al., 1988). Cooperative learning groups, especially when students work on tasks involving a number of different skills and abilities, can foster an appreciation for the various strengths that students with diverse backgrounds are likely to contribute (E. G. Cohen, 1994; E. G. Cohen & Lotan, 1995). And virtually any "cooperative" approach to instruction—cooperative learning, peer tutoring, reciprocal teaching—may help students begin to recognize that despite the obvious diversity among them, they are ultimately more similar to one another than they are different (Schofield, 1995).

Remember that different instructional strategies may be more or less effective, depending on students' ability levels, cultural backgrounds, and language skills.

Use cooperative approaches to instruction, such as cooperative learning, peer tutoring, or reciprocal teaching, to promote students' social development.

Accommodating Students with Special Needs

Different instructional strategies may be more or less useful for students with different educational needs. For example, strictly expository instruction (e.g., a lecture) may provide a quick and efficient means of presenting new ideas to students who think abstractly and process information quickly (e.g., gifted students), yet be incomprehensible and overwhelming to students with low cognitive ability (e.g., those with mental retardation). Similarly, discovery learning is often effective in enhancing the academic achievement of students with high ability; however, it may actually be detrimental to the achievement of students with less ability (Corno & Snow, 1986). And mastery learning has been shown to be effective with students who have learning difficulties, including many students with special educational needs (DuNann & Weber, 1976; Leinhardt & Pallay, 1982), yet it may prevent rapid

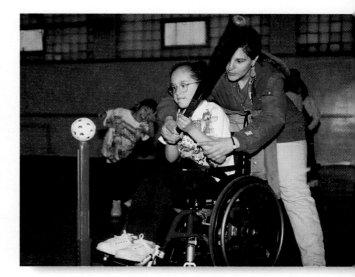

Instructional strategies may sometimes need to be adapted for students with special needs. Here we see a student with a physical disability receive extra scaffolding during physical education.

Table 13–3   *Identifying Instructional Strategies Especially Suitable for Students with Special Educational Needs*

STUDENTS WITH SPECIAL NEEDS	CHARACTERISTICS THAT THESE STUDENTS MAY EXHIBIT	CLASSROOM STRATEGIES THAT MAY BE BENEFICIAL FOR THESE STUDENTS
Students with specific cognitive or academic deficits	Difficulty processing or remembering information presented in particular modalities Poor listening and/or reading skills	During expository instruction (e.g., lectures, reading assignments), provide information through multiple modalities (e.g., with videotapes, audiotapes, graphic materials). Supplement expository instruction with other instructional strategies. Use programmed instruction, computer-assisted instruction, cooperative learning, and peer tutoring as possible means of supplementing instruction in students' areas of weakness. Have students use computer tools (e.g., grammar and spell checkers) that can help them compensate for areas of weakness. Take advantage of hypermedia that present information through multiple modalities. Use reciprocal teaching to promote listening and reading comprehension. Assign homework that provides additional practice in basic skills; individualize assignments for students' unique abilities and needs. Use a mastery learning approach to ensure that students have achieved information and skills essential for later units. Continually monitor students' progress to determine the effectiveness of your instructional strategies.
Students with specific social or behavioral deficits	Frequent off-task behavior Inability to work independently for extended periods of time	Use peer tutoring as a means of providing one-on-one attention and instruction. Use cooperative learning to foster friendships and social skills. Keep unsupervised seatwork assignments to a minimum. Continually monitor students' progress to determine the effectiveness of your instructional strategies.
Students with general delays in cognitive and social functioning	Difficulty thinking abstractly Need for a great deal of repetition and practice of information and skills	Present information in as concrete a manner as possible (e.g., by engaging students in hands-on experiences). Use computer-assisted instruction as a means of providing extended practice in basic skills. Use peer tutoring as a means of promoting friendships with nondisabled classmates. Continually monitor students' progress to determine the effectiveness of instructional strategies.
Students with advanced cognitive development	Rapid learning Greater ability to think abstractly; appearance of abstract thinking at a younger age Greater conceptual understanding of classroom material Ability to learn independently	Use expository instruction (e.g., lectures) as a way of transmitting abstract information about particular topics quickly and efficiently. Ask predominantly higher-level questions. Provide opportunities to pursue topics in greater depth (e.g., through assigned readings, homogeneous cooperative learning or discussion groups, or computer-based instruction). Teach strategies that enable students to learn on their own (e.g., library skills, the scientific method, use of hypermedia and the Internet). Encourage students to communicate via the Internet with others of similar interests and abilities. Use advanced students as peer tutors only to the extent that tutoring sessions help the tutors, as well as those being tutored.

Sources: Carnine, 1989; DuNann & Weber, 1976; Fiedler, Lange, & Winebrenner, 1993; Greenwood, Carta, & Hall, 1988; Heward, 1996; C. C. Kulik, Kulik, & Bangert-Drowns, 1990; C. D. Mercer, 1991; P. F. Merrill et al., 1996; D. P. Morgan & Jenson, 1988; Ormrod, 1995b; Piirto, 1994; Robinson, 1991; Schiffman, Tobin, & Buchanan, 1984; Spicker, 1992; Stevens & Slavin, 1995; Turnbull, Turnbull, Shank, & Leal, 1995; J. W. Wood & Rosbe, 1985.

Compiled with the assistance of Dr. Margie Garanzini-Daiber and Dr. Margaret Cohen, University of Missouri—St. Louis.

learners from progressing at a rate commensurate with their abilities (Arlin, 1984; Nunnally, 1976).

As teachers, we will often need to adapt the instructional strategies we use to the particular strengths and weaknesses that our students with special needs have. For example, when students have difficulty processing information in one modality or another (e.g., when they have certain learning disabilities), it will be especially important to supplement verbal explanations with visual aids during expository instruction. When students have limited social skills (e.g., when they have emotional or behavioral disorders), we may need to teach them appropriate ways of interacting with their classmates prior to such group-based activities as class discussions and cooperative learning. Table 13–3 provides a "memory refresher" about some characteristics of students with special needs that we have considered in previous chapters; it also presents some instructional strategies that we can use to accommodate such characteristics.

LOOKING AT THE BIG PICTURE: CHOOSING INSTRUCTIONAL STRATEGIES

As we consider which instructional strategies to use in our classrooms, we must keep in mind one very important point: *There is no single best approach to classroom instruction.* Each of the strategies that we've examined has its merits, and each is useful in different situations and for different students. Generally speaking, the decision we make regarding an instructional strategy must depend on at least three things: the objective of our lesson, the nature of the subject matter at hand, and the characteristics and abilities of our students. Table 13–4 presents general conditions and specific examples in which each strategy might be most appropriate.

Consider the objective, the topic, and student characteristics when you identify your instructional strategies.

At the same time, we must remember that, in many instances, two or more strategies can often be combined together quite effectively. For example, a mathematics or science class might include discovery learning experiences within an overall mastery learning approach. A social studies class might include expository instruction, class discussions, and reciprocal teaching within the context of a cooperative learning environment. A successful classroom—one in which students are acquiring and using school subject matter in a truly meaningful fashion—is undoubtedly a classroom in which a variety of approaches to instruction can be found.

How might elements of cooperative learning and mastery learning be combined? In what way is CBI also expository instruction?

How will we know when our instructional strategies are effective and when they are not? Effective teachers monitor their students' progress on a regular basis and adapt instruction accordingly. Our classroom assessment practices, both formal and informal, provide the means through which such monitoring takes place. We will consider the multifaceted nature of classroom assessment in the next chapter.

Table 13–4   Choosing an Instructional Strategy

You Might Use . . .	When . . .	For Example, You Might . . .
Expository instruction	The *objective* is to acquire knowledge within the cognitive domain. The *lesson* involves information best learned in terms of a specific organizational structure. *Students* are capable of abstract thought and possess a wealth of knowledge to which they can relate new material.	Enumerate the critical battles of World War I to advanced history students. Describe several defensive strategies to the varsity soccer team.
Discovery learning	The *objective* is to develop firsthand knowledge of physical or social phenomena. The *lesson* involves information that can be correctly deduced from hands-on experimentation with concrete objects or from direct social interaction with others. *Students* have enough knowledge to interpret their findings correctly but sometimes have difficulty learning from strictly abstract material.	Ask students to find out what happens when two primary colors of paint (red and yellow, red and blue, or yellow and blue) are mixed together. Create a classroom situation in which students discover firsthand how it feels to experience "taxation without representation."
Mastery learning	The *objective* is to learn knowledge or skills to a level of mastery (perhaps to automaticity). The *lesson* provides critical information or skills for later instructional units. *Students* vary in the time they need to achieve mastery.	Have each student in band practice the C major scale until he or she can do so perfectly. Have students practice the 100 single-digit addition facts until they can answer all 100 correctly within a five-minute period.
Peer tutoring	The *objective* is to learn basic knowledge or skills. The *lesson* contains material that can effectively be taught by students. *Students* vary in their mastery of the material, yet even the most advanced can gain increased understanding by teaching it to someone else.	Have students work in pairs to practice conjugating irregular French verbs. Have some students help others work through simple mathematical word problems.
Computer-based instruction	The *objective* is to acquire knowledge and skills within the cognitive domain *or* to acquire experience with computer tools. The *lesson* involves information that students can acquire in a piecemeal, step-by-step fashion, and possibly involves the use of a large database. *Students* can learn in the absence of direct interaction with their teacher.	Assign a research project that requires the use of a computer-based encyclopedia. Have students write a composition by using a word processing program.
Questioning	The *objective* is to promote more in-depth cognitive processing of a topic. The *lesson* involves complex material, such that frequent monitoring of students' learning is essential and/or mental elaboration of ideas is beneficial. *Students* are not likely to elaborate spontaneously or to monitor their own comprehension effectively.	Ask questions that promote recall and review of the previous day's lesson. Ask students for examples of how nonrenewable resources are recycled in their own community.

YOU MIGHT USE . . .	WHEN . . .	FOR EXAMPLE, YOU MIGHT . . .
Class discussion	The *objective* is to promote more in-depth processing of a topic. The *lesson* involves complex and possibly controversial issues. *Students* have sufficient knowledge about the topic to voice their ideas and opinions.	Ask students to discuss the ethical implications of the United States' decision to drop an atomic bomb on Hiroshima. Ask groups of four or five students to prepare arguments for an upcoming debate regarding the pros and cons of increasing the minimum wage.
Cooperative learning	The *objective* is to develop the ability to work cooperatively with others on academic tasks. The *lesson* involves tasks that are too large or difficult for a single student to accomplish independently. *Students'* cultural backgrounds emphasize cooperation, rather than competition.	Have groups of two or three students work together on mathematics "brain teasers." Have students in a German class work in small groups to write and videotape a soap opera spoken entirely in German.
Reciprocal teaching	The *objective* is to improve reading comprehension and learning strategies. The *lesson* requires students to cognitively process material in relatively complex ways. *Students* possess poor reading comprehension and learning strategies.	Model four types of questions—summarizing, questioning, clarifying, and predicting—as students read aloud a passage from a textbook. Ask students to take turns being "teacher" and ask similar questions of their classmates.
In-class activities	The *objective* is to have students practice using new information or skills. The *lesson* requires considerable teacher monitoring and scaffolding. *Students* cannot yet work independently on the task.	Have beginning tennis students practice their serves. Have students work in pairs to draw portraits of one another.
Homework	The *objective* is to introduce students to new yet simple material *or* to give students additional practice with familiar information and procedures. The *lesson* is one that students can complete with little if any assistance. *Students* exhibit sufficient self-regulation to perform the task independently.	Have students solve algebra problems similar to ones they've done in class. Have students read the next chapter in their health book.
Authentic activities	The *objective* is to apply classroom material to real-world situations. The *lesson* involves synthesizing and applying a variety of knowledge and skills. *Students* have mastered the knowledge and skills necessary to perform the task.	Have students grow sunflowers by using varying amounts of water, plant food, and sunlight. Have students construct maps of their local community, using appropriate symbols to convey direction, scale, physical features, and so on.

Ms. Mihara is beginning a unit entitled "Customs in Other Lands." Having heard about the benefits of cooperative learning, she asks students to form groups of four that will work together throughout the unit. On Monday, she assigns each group a particular country—Australia, Colombia, Ireland, Israel, Greece, Korea, or Zimbabwe. She then instructs the groups, "Today we will go to the school library, where you can find information on the customs of your country and check out materials you think will be useful. Over the next two weeks, you will have time every day to work as a group. You should learn all you can about the customs of your country. A week from Friday, each group will give an oral report to the rest of the class."

Over the next two weeks, Ms. Mihara runs into more problems than she ever imagined she would. For example, when the students form their groups, she notices that the high achievers have gotten together to form one group and that the socially oriented, "popular" students have flocked to three others. The remaining two groups are comprised of whichever students are left over. Some groups get immediately to work on their task, others spend their group time sharing gossip and planning upcoming social events, and still others flounder aimlessly for days on end.

As the unit progresses, Ms. Mihara hears more and more complaints from students about their task ("Janet and I are doing all the work; Karen and Mary Kay aren't helping at all." "Eugene thinks he can boss the rest of us around because we're studying Ireland and he's Irish." "We're spending all this time together but just can't seem to get anywhere!"). And the group reports at the end of the unit differ markedly in quality: Some are carefully planned and informative, whereas others are disorganized and lack substantive information.

"So much for this cooperative learning stuff," Ms. Mihara mumbles to herself. "If I want students to learn something, I'll just have to teach it to them myself."

- Why have Ms. Mihara's cooperative learning groups not been as productive as she had hoped? Considering the features of cooperative learning that we examined in this chapter, what did Ms. Mihara do wrong?

- How might you orchestrate the cooperative learning unit differently than Ms. Mihara?

Helping Students Learn New Material

Virtually any instructional strategy may be used for multiple purposes simultaneously. Yet some instructional strategies—expository instruction, discovery learning, mastery learning, peer tutoring, and computer-based instruction—are especially suited for helping students learn new material. In expository instruction, information is presented in essentially the same form that students are expected to learn it; lectures, textbooks, and other forms of expository instruction are more effective when we apply principles of information processing—for example, when we help students make meaningful connections between new material and their prior knowledge, and when we give them time to think about the things they are learning. In discovery learning, students develop an understanding of a particular topic by interacting with their physical or social environment; it is more likely to be successful when we provide a structure that nudges students toward desired discoveries and when students have the necessary prior knowledge for appropriately interpreting those discoveries. Mastery learning, peer tutoring, and computer-based instruction all provide a means through which we can easily accommodate individual differences in learning rate as we help students master basic skills.

Helping Students Process What They've Learned

Some strategies, such as questioning, class discussion, cooperative learning, and reciprocal teaching, are especially useful when we want students to go *beyond* the material we've presented—for example, when we want them to elaborate on new ideas, consider multiple perspectives of a single situation, and in general, develop a more conceptual understanding of the topic at hand. All of these approaches involve classroom dialogue; when students must explain their thinking to their classmates, they must organize their thoughts and pull separate ideas into a logical, cohesive whole. Reciprocal teaching has the additional advantage of promoting more sophisticated metacognition and study skills—in particular, by teaching students the four processes of summarizing, questioning, clarifying, and predicting.

Helping Students Use What They've Learned

Still other instructional strategies—in-class assignments, homework, and authentic activities—provide the means through which we can help students use and practice the things they've learned. We must match such assignments and activities to our particular instructional objectives; for example, homework assignments are especially useful for promoting automaticity of well-learned facts and skills, whereas authentic activities may be more appropriate for promoting transfer to real-world contexts.

Accommodating Student Diversity

Different instructional strategies may be appropriate for different students; for example, an abstract lecture is better suited for high achievers, mastery learning may be more effective for students who lack basic skills, and computer-based instruction is especially adaptable to a wide range of ability levels. The notion of a *community of learners*—one in which learning and achievement are a collaborate group effort—provides a context in which we can use the strengths of each member of the classroom to everyone's advantage.

Choosing an Instructional Strategy

Clearly, there is no single "best" instructional strategy. Ultimately, we must match our strategies to our instructional objectives, to the specific topics we are teaching, and to the unique characteristics of the students in our classrooms (see Table 13–3).

KEY CONCEPTS

expository instruction (p. 586)
advance organizer (p. 589)
discovery learning (p. 594)
mastery learning (p. 598)
peer tutoring (p. 601)
computer-based instruction (CBI) (p. 602)
programmed instruction (p. 605)

linear program (p. 605)
branching program (p. 605)
computer-assisted instruction (CAI) (p. 605)
hypertext (p. 606)
hypermedia (p. 606)
cooperative learning (p. 611)
base group (p. 612)

jigsaw technique (p. 612)
scripted cooperation (p. 613)
group contingency (p. 613)
reciprocal teaching (p. 617)
distributed cognition (p. 623)
community of learners (p. 624)

Assessing What Students Have Learned

Think back on your many years as a student. In what different ways have your teachers assessed what you've learned? Have their assessment techniques focused on the important aspects of what you achieved? Can you recall a situation in which a test or other classroom assessment had little relationship to the instructional objectives of the class?

WE WILL OFTEN NEED to assess our students' knowledge and skills in order to make informed decisions in the classroom. For instance, when we begin a new topic, we will want to determine their existing knowledge so that we can gear instruction to an appropriate level. We will also want to monitor their progress as we go along so that we can remediate any difficulties they may be having. And ultimately, we will have to make some determination as to what each student has accomplished during the school year. According to one estimate, we may spend one-third of our time, possibly even more, in assessment-related activities (Stiggins & Conklin, 1992).

It is essential that, as teachers, we use assessment techniques that accurately reflect what our students know and can do; it is equally essential that such techniques promote our students' learning and achievement over the long run. In this chapter, we will examine a variety of potentially effective assessment strategies and learn how to select the strategies most appropriate for different situations. We will identify four characteristics of good assessment—reliability, standardization, validity, and practicality—and then consider how we can incorporate these "RSVP" characteristics into classroom assessment procedures for a diverse population of students. Later in the chapter, we will examine three ways of summarizing students' achievement—test scores, final class grades, and portfolios. Finally, we will look once again at how our assessment techniques are continually interwoven with both our curricular planning and our instructional practices.

By the end of the chapter, you should be able to:

1. Describe a variety of assessment techniques and select techniques appropriate for different situations.

2. Develop assessment techniques that reflect important instructional objectives and promote students' learning and achievement.

3. Define the four "RSVP" characteristics of good assessment—reliability, standardization, validity, and practicality.

4. Describe the advantages and potential weaknesses of informal assessment during classroom instruction.

5. Explain how to design and administer formal paper-pencil and performance instruments in ways that maximize their RSVP characteristics.

6. Accommodate the abilities and needs of a diverse population of students in your classroom assessment practices.

7. Explain how students' achievement can be summarized by means of test scores, final grades, and portfolios.

Ellen and Roz are taking geography this year. Although they have different teachers, they both have the same textbook and often study together. In fact, they are each taking a test on Chapter 6 in their respective classes tomorrow. Here is a snippet of their conversation as they study the night before:

Ellen: Let's see . . . what's the capital of Sweden?

Roz: Stockholm, I think. Why?

Ellen: Because I need to memorize all the capitals of the countries in Europe. I know most of them, I guess. I'd better move on and study the rivers.

Roz: Geez, are you expected to know all those things?

Ellen: Oh, yeah. For our test, Ms. Peterson will give us a map of Europe and ask us to label all the countries, their capitals, and the rivers that run through them.

Roz: Wow! That's not what we're doing in Ms. Montgomery's class at all. We're supposed to learn the topography, climate, and culture of all the European countries. Ms. Montgomery says she'll ask us to use what we know about these things to explain why each country imports and exports the products that it does.

Ellen: That sounds like a really hard test—much harder than mine.

Roz: Oh, I don't know. It all depends on what you're used to. Ms. Montgomery has been giving tests like this all year.

- What instructional objectives does each girl's test reflect? To what extent does it measure lower-level or higher-level skills? Can you classify each test in terms of Bloom's taxonomy (see Chapter 12)?

- Are the two girls likely to study in different ways? If so, how will they study differently? Which girl is likely to remember what she has studied for a longer period of time?

CONSIDERING THE DIFFERENT FORMS THAT ASSESSMENT CAN TAKE

Paper-pencil tests, such as those for which Ellen and Roz are preparing, provide one means through which we can assess our students' achievement. Yet not all classroom assessment involves paper and pencil. The statements our students make in class, the answers they give to our questions, the questions they *themselves* ask—all of these tell us something about what they have learned. Nonverbal behaviors give us information as well: We can observe how well students use a pair of scissors, how carefully they set up

Some tests involve paper and pencil, but others do not. In this industrial arts class, the students have designed and constructed rockets, and their teacher is assessing how well each rocket performs.

laboratory equipment, or what kinds of scores they earn on physical fitness tests. Some forms of assessment take only a few seconds, whereas others may take several hours or even several days. Some are planned and developed in advance, whereas others occur spontaneously during the course of a lesson or classroom activities.

What exactly do we mean when we use the word *assessment?* This definition sums up its major features:

> **Assessment** is a process of observing a sample of students' behavior and drawing inferences about their knowledge and abilities.

Several aspects of our definition are important to note. First of all, we are looking at students' *behavior.* As behaviorists have so clearly told us, it's impossible to look inside students' heads and see what knowledge lurks there; we can only see how students actually respond in the classroom. Second, we typically use just a *sample* of students' classroom behavior; we certainly cannot observe and keep track of every single thing that every single student does during the school day. And finally, we are drawing *inferences* from the specific behaviors we do observe to make judgments about students' overall classroom achievement—a tricky business at best. As we proceed through the chapter, we will discover how to select behaviors that will give us a reasonably accurate estimate of what our students know and can do.

Assessment techniques come in many shapes and sizes:

- Standardized tests versus teacher-developed assessment

- Paper-pencil versus performance assessment

- Traditional versus authentic assessment

- Informal versus formal assessment

Figure 14–1 illustrates these distinctions. Let's look briefly at each one.

Comparing Standardized Tests and Teacher-Developed Assessment Instruments

A few classroom assessments involve tests developed by test construction experts and published for use in many different schools and classrooms. Such assessment instruments are commonly known as **standardized tests.** Many of them are *achievement tests:* They are used to assess students' general academic progress in different areas of the school curriculum (e.g., reading, science, social studies). Other standardized tests, including both *intelligence* and *general scholastic aptitude* tests, are used to assess students' overall ability to learn and perform successfully in normal classroom situations (recall our discussion of intelligence tests in Chapter 4). Still others, known as *specific*

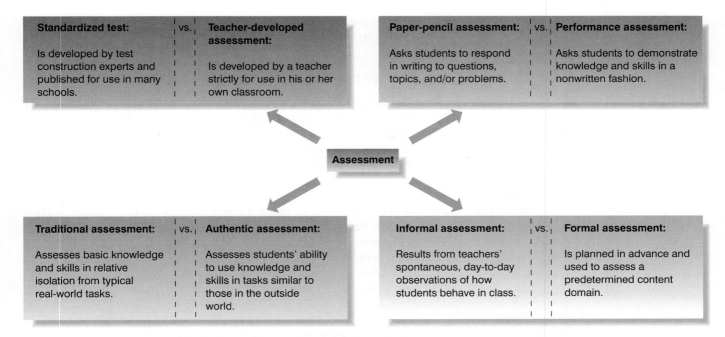

Standardized test:	vs.	Teacher-developed assessment:
Is developed by test construction experts and published for use in many schools.		Is developed by a teacher strictly for use in his or her own classroom.

Paper-pencil assessment:	vs.	Performance assessment:
Asks students to respond in writing to questions, topics, and/or problems.		Asks students to demonstrate knowledge and skills in a nonwritten fashion.

Assessment

Traditional assessment:	vs.	Authentic assessment:
Assesses basic knowledge and skills in relative isolation from typical real-world tasks.		Assesses students' ability to use knowledge and skills in tasks similar to those in the outside world.

Informal assessment:	vs.	Formal assessment:
Results from teachers' spontaneous, day-to-day observations of how students behave in class.		Is planned in advance and used to assess a predetermined content domain.

Figure 14–1   The Many Forms That Classroom Assessment Can Take

aptitude tests, are used to assess students' ability to be successful in particular content domains (e.g., their ability to handle an accelerated mathematics course).

Standardized tests typically come with test manuals that describe the instructions that students should be given and the time limits that should be imposed; they also provide explicit information about how students' responses should be scored. Furthermore, most standardized tests are accompanied by data regarding the typical performance (**norms**) of different groups of students on the test, and these norms are used in calculating students' overall test scores. We will learn more about such *norm-referenced scores* later in the chapter.

Most school districts administer standardized tests at one time or another. But such tests typically assess such broad areas of the curriculum that they yield little information about what students specifically have and have not learned. When we want to assess our students' learning and achievement related to specific instructional objectives—for example, whether students can do long division or whether they've understood what they've just read in Chapter 8 of their social studies book—we will usually want to construct our own **teacher-developed assessment instruments.**

Comparing Paper-Pencil and Performance Assessment

As teachers, we may sometimes choose **paper-pencil assessment,** in which we present questions to answer, topics to address, or problems to solve, and our students must write their responses on paper. Yet we may also find it helpful to use **performance assessment,** in which students directly demonstrate (*perform*) their abilities—for exam-

Some educators use the term *performance assessment* only when referring to complex, real-world tasks. Here we are using the term in a broader sense—to refer to any nonpaper-pencil assessment.

ple, by reciting a poem, jumping hurdles, using a computer spreadsheet, or identifying acids and bases in a chemistry lab.

Comparing Traditional and Authentic Assessment

Historically, teachers' assessment instruments have focused on measuring basic knowledge and skills in relative isolation from tasks more typical of the outside world. Spelling quizzes, mathematics word problems, and physical fitness tests are examples of such **traditional assessment.** Yet ultimately, our students must be able to apply their knowledge and skills to complex tasks outside the classroom. The notion of **authentic assessment**—measuring the actual knowledge and skills we want students to demonstrate in an "authentic," real-life context—is gaining increasing popularity among educators (e.g., Darling-Hammond, 1991; C. Hill & Larsen, 1992; R. L. Linn, Baker, & Dunbar, 1991; Nickerson, 1989; Paris & Ayres, 1994; Valencia, Hiebert, & Afflerbach, 1994).

In some situations, authentic assessment involves paper and pencil. For example, we might ask students to write a letter to a friend or develop a school newspaper. But in many cases, authentic assessment is performance-based and closely integrated with instruction, such as with the *authentic activities* we've discussed in earlier chapters. For example, we might assess students' ability to present a persuasive argument, bake a cake, converse in a foreign language, design and build a bookshelf, or successfully maneuver a car into a parallel parking space. As teachers, we must remember what our students should be able to do when they leave the classroom behind to join the adult world, and our assessment practices must, to some extent, reflect those real-life tasks.

Comparing Informal and Formal Assessment

Informal assessment results from our spontaneous, day-to-day observations of how students behave in class. When we are conducting an informal assessment, we will rarely have a specific agenda as to what we are looking for, and we are likely to learn different things about different students (e.g., Tony is "bright," Jennie is "agile," Marty is "motivated"). In contrast, **formal assessment** is typically planned in advance and used for a specific purpose—perhaps to determine what students have learned about a certain period in history, whether they can solve math problems requiring addition and subtraction, or how they compare with students nationwide in terms of physical fitness. It is "formal" in the sense that a particular time is set aside for it, students often study and prepare for it ahead of time, and we will get information about every student relative to the same instructional objectives. Paper-pencil tests (like those that Ellen and Roz are taking) are examples of formal assessment, as are such structured, performance situations as oral reports and physical fitness tests.

Different kinds of assessment are useful in different situations and for different purposes. Let's look at the various occasions in which assessment is needed and at the kinds of assessment tools suitable on each of these occasions.

USING ASSESSMENT FOR DIFFERENT PURPOSES

There are many possible reasons why we might want to assess our students' learning and performance. For example, a classroom assessment can give students feedback that will help them decide what topics they need to study in more depth and what skills they need to practice further. It can give us diagnostic information that provides clues as to why some students may be having difficulty with a task. It can help us identify the objectives our students have mastered and the objectives they need additional instruction to attain. It can yield data that will enable us to evaluate the overall effectiveness of our instructional strategies and curricular materials.

In some cases, we will engage in **formative evaluation:** We will assess students' learning *before or during instruction* and use the results to make instructional decisions and enhance achievement. Ongoing, formative evaluation enables us to determine how well our students understand the topic at hand, what misconceptions they may have, whether they need further practice on a particular skill, and so on. The continuing feedback that it provides about students' progress then enables us to modify and improve our instructional strategies and thereby enhance our students' learning and achievement.

In other situations, we will engage in **summative evaluation:** We will conduct an assessment *after instruction* to make final decisions about what students have ultimately learned and achieved in a lesson or curricular unit. Summative evaluations are used to determine whether instructional objectives have been mastered, what final grades to assign, which students are eligible for more advanced classes in a particular topic, and so on.

In the next few pages, we will consider the assessment strategies that might be useful in three different situations:

- To facilitate students' learning

- To promote their self-regulation

- To determine whether they have achieved instructional objectives

Then, as we look at the effects of classroom tests, we will find that even the assessment tools we use for summative evaluation are nevertheless likely to influence students' learning as well.

Using Assessment to Facilitate Learning

At what level should instruction begin? What concepts or skills are giving students difficulty and should probably be taught again, perhaps in a different way? What misconceptions have students acquired during the course of instruction that must now be corrected? Either informal assessments (e.g., observing students' performance in class) or formal assessments (e.g., giving brief quizzes) can provide the answers to such questions, and we can tailor further instruction and future lessons accordingly.

Whenever we assess students' performance as a way of facilitating their learning and achievement, our assessment instruments should:

- Assess the specific behaviors and thought processes we want students to acquire

- Be at an appropriate difficulty level

- Encourage risk-taking

- Provide diagnostic information

Assessing the Behaviors and Thought Processes We Want Students to Acquire

It is relatively easy to assess students' knowledge of facts; we can do so simply by asking questions either in class or on paper-pencil tests. In fact, it is fact-based questions that we find most frequently on teacher-developed classroom tests (Bloom, 1984b; J. R. Frederiksen & Collins, 1989; Murnane & Raizen, 1988; Nickerson, 1989; Poole, 1994). Yet we must remember that the specific tasks we assign, including the assessments we give, will lead our students to draw inferences about the instructional objectives we want them to accomplish (Doyle, 1983; Poole, 1994). If our classroom assessments emphasize knowledge of specific, isolated bits of information, then many students will focus on learning at a rote, meaningless level.

Develop assessment techniques that reflect the things you want students to do when they study and learn.

If we want our students to do *more* than memorize facts, we must develop assessment techniques that reflect the things we actually want them to do when they study and learn. For example, we can use paper-pencil instruments that ask students to rephrase ideas in their own words, generate their own examples of concepts, use course material to solve problems, or examine ideas with a critical eye. We can use performance assessments that include complex behaviors and activities. And we can use authentic assessment to encourage students to transfer what they've learned in the classroom to real-life situations.

Assessing at an Appropriate Difficulty Level

How difficult should our assessment instruments be? On the one hand, when they are too easy, our students may not exert much effort (e.g., they may not study very much) and therefore may not learn as much as we would like. Furthermore, high scores based on little achievement may mislead us to believe that our students have learned something they haven't really learned at all. On the other hand, when our assessment instruments are too difficult, students may become discouraged and believe that they are incapable of mastering the subject matter. As you can see, there are dangers in developing measures that are too easy *or* too difficult.

Construct an assessment instrument sufficiently difficult to reflect the level of performance you want students to achieve, but don't make it impossible.

We should keep two things in mind when deciding just how difficult to make our assessment instruments. First, any assessment should reflect the level of performance we actually want our students to achieve. And second, it should be difficult enough that students must expend effort to succeed, but not so difficult that success is beyond reach. In other words, our classroom assessments should be challenging yet accomplishable.

Encouraging Risk Taking

As we noted in our discussion of motivation in Chapter 11, our classroom assessment procedures must create an environment in which students feel free to pursue challenging tasks, take risks, and make mistakes (Clifford, 1990). Without a doubt, our students are more likely to take the risks so essential for maximal learning and cognitive development when our assessment strategies allow room for error—when we give them some leeway to be wrong without penalty.

Give students some leeway to make errors without penalty.

My colleague Dan Wagner, a high school mathematics teacher, uses what he calls a "mastery reform" as a way of allowing students to make occasional mistakes and then learn from them. When it is clear from classroom assessments that students haven't demonstrated mastery of a mathematical procedure, Dan has them complete an assignment that includes the following:

1. *Identification of the error:* Students describe in a short paragraph exactly what it is they do not yet know how to do.

2. *Statement of the process:* Students explain the steps involved in the procedure they are trying to master; in doing so, they must demonstrate their understanding by using words, rather than mathematical symbols.

3. *Practice:* Students show their mastery of the procedure with three new problems similar to the problem(s) they previously solved incorrectly.

4. *Statement of mastery:* Students state in a sentence or two that they have now mastered the procedure.

By completing the four prescribed steps, students can replace a grade on a previous assessment with the higher one that they earn by attaining mastery. Such assignments may have longer-term benefits as well: Dan tells me that many of his students eventually incorporate the four steps into their regular, more internalized learning strategies.

Getting Diagnostic Information

When we assess our students' learning and performance, our assessment procedures should indicate not only where students are going wrong, but also *why* they are going wrong. In other words, we should get sufficient information so that we know how to help our students improve (e.g., Baek, 1994; Baxter, Elder, & Glaser, 1996; Covington, 1992). Furthermore, we should pass such diagnostic information along to students, in the form of specific feedback, so that they know what they need to do differently. Such feedback can also promote greater self-regulation—our second major purpose in assessing students' learning and performance, and the one we turn to next.

Use assessment procedures that provide information about possible sources of learning difficulties.

Using Assessment to Promote Self-Regulation

In our discussion of self-regulation in Chapter 10, we noted the importance of both *self-observation* (students must be aware of how well they are doing at any given time) and *self-evaluation* (students must be able to assess their own performance accurately). An important function of our classroom assessment practices should be to help students engage in such self-regulatory processes (Covington, 1992; Paris & Ayres, 1994; Stiggins, 1994).

Theorists have proposed a number of ways in which we can use classroom assessment procedures to promote greater self-observation and self-evaluation:

Give students the guidance they need to assess their own performance.

*   We can provide students with our criteria for evaluating assignments and ask them to evaluate their own work by using those criteria; for example, when we ask them to write a summary of something they've just read, we might also have them check off the following items as they've completed each one:

    Components of a Good Summary

    _____ I included a clear main idea statement.

    _____ I included important ideas that support the main idea.

    _____ My summary shows that I understand the relationships between important concepts.

    _____ I used my own words, rather than words copied from the text.
    (Adapted from Paris & Ayres, 1994, p. 75)

- We can solicit students' ideas regarding the criteria we should use in assessing their performance.

- We can provide examples of "good" and "poor" products and ask students to compare them with respect to a variety of criteria.

- We can have students reflect on and evaluate their performance by writing in a journal on a daily or weekly basis.

- We can have students write practice test items items similar to those they expect on any tests we ourselves may give them.

- We can have students compare their recent work with their work from the beginning of the school year.

- We can have students create portfolios of their best work, with students making their own decisions about the products that warrant inclusion.

- We can conduct student-teacher conferences (similar to the more traditional parent-teacher conferences) in which our students describe their achievements. (Paris & Ayres, 1994; Stiggins, 1994; Valencia et al., 1994)

Using Assessment to Determine Whether Students Have Achieved Instructional Objectives

Have our students mastered course content? Have they acquired the knowledge and skills they need to move on to more advanced coursework? What kinds of grades should they receive? Should they be promoted? Do they exhibit achievement and skills expected of high school graduates? Such questions can only be answered by determining whether students have achieved our instructional objectives.

Use formal assessment instruments when drawing final conclusions about what students have and have not learned.

We may sometimes find a standardized test that measures the exact knowledge and skills we expect our students to have acquired. But more often than not, we will need to develop our own formal assessment instruments tailored to the particular situation at hand. The specific form that such instruments take—in particular, whether they are paper-pencil or performance in nature—will depend on how we think we can most accurately measure the knowledge or skills in question.

In some situations, the conclusions we draw regarding students' achievement may have long-term implications for their academic careers; for example, the grades on which our conclusions are based affect decisions regarding students' promotion, graduation, and admission to college. So whenever we develop instruments to assess students' final achievement related to a particular topic, unit, or lesson, we must be sure they closely reflect our instructional objectives. We will find guidance about how to maximize the match between our assessments and our objectives in our discussion of formal assessment later in the chapter.

We should note here that when we assess our students' mastery of instructional objectives, we gain information not only about our students but also about the appropriateness of our instructional objectives and the effectiveness of our instructional strategies. For example, if we find that almost all of our students are completing our assignments quickly and easily, we might suspect that we can set our sights higher regarding the things we might reasonably expect them to accomplish. If we discover that many students are struggling with material we have presented through expository instruction, we might wonder whether a different approach to instruction—perhaps a more concrete, hands-on one—would be more effective.

Effects of Classroom Tests on Learning

Let's return to our beginning case study, "Studying Europe." Ellen is studying the names of capitals and rivers of various European countries; unless she can connect these names to something else she knows, she will probably learn them at a rote level. In contrast, Roz is attempting to find relationships among the topography, climate, culture, imports, and exports of those same countries. She must try to make sense of all these relationships; in other words, she must engage in meaningful learning.

Traditionally, teachers have used paper-pencil tests primarily for summative evaluation—to determine what their students have ultimately learned and achieved in the classroom. But a considerable amount of research indicates that classroom testing practices affect the studying and learning processes in which our students engage. More specifically, our tests are likely to affect student learning in these ways:

- They increase students' motivation to learn classroom material.

- They encourage review of previously learned information.

- They influence the cognitive processes that students use when studying.

- They provide learning experiences in and of themselves.

- They provide feedback about what students do and do not know.

These effects are summarized in Table 14–1. Let's look at each one more closely.

Other forms of assessment, such as authentic performance tasks, may have such effects as well; however, we do not yet have enough research data to say so conclusively.

Tests as Motivators

EXPERIENCING FIRSTHAND
Alpha and Omega

Imagine you are a student in two classes, one taught by Mr. Alpha and the other taught by Mr. Omega. Mr. Alpha tells you that you won't be tested on the course material—that you should study it simply because it will help you in your later personal and professional life. Mr. Omega says he will give a test over his course material every three weeks. In which class are you likely to study more?

If you are like most students, you will probably study more in Mr. Omega's class. Most students study class material more and learn it better when they are told they will be tested on it, rather than when they are simply told to learn it (Doyle, 1983; N. Frederiksen, 1984b; Halpin & Halpin, 1982). Tests are especially effective as motivators when students see them as valid measures of class objectives and feel challenged to do their very best (Natriello & Dornbusch, 1984; Paris, Lawton, Turner, & Roth, 1991).

Yet we must remember that a classroom test is an extrinsic motivator; thus, it may undermine any intrinsic motivation our students have to learn (Grolnick & Ryan, 1987). A test is especially likely to have this adverse effect when students perceive it simply as being a teacher's evaluation of their performance, rather than as a mechanism for helping them learn (Spaulding, 1992).

Table 14–1 How Tests Affect Student Learning

PRINCIPLE	EDUCATIONAL IMPLICATION	EXAMPLE
Tests increase students' **motivation** to learn classroom material, especially when students see them as valid measures of class objectives.	We should be sure that our tests are accurate reflections of the things that are most important for students to learn. We can also portray tests as valuable mechanisms for helping students learn.	We can describe how an upcoming quiz will help students determine how well they have mastered the symbols and atomic weights of the chemical elements—knowledge they will need before they can successfully proceed further in chemistry.
Tests encourage **review** of previously learned information.	We can give frequent short tests that encourage students to review material on a regular basis.	As we give students their weekly spelling test, we can also ask them to spell a few words from previous lessons.
Tests influence the **cognitive processes** that students use when they learn.	We should ask questions and present tasks that require meaningful, organized learning, rather than rote memorization of isolated facts.	As we describe an upcoming test on the French and Indian War, we can stress that we will ask students to explain how various battles affected the progress and outcome of the war but will *not* ask students to recall specific dates on which each battle was fought.
Tests provide **learning experiences** in and of themselves.	We should ask questions and present tasks that require students to elaborate—to extend classroom material beyond what they have actually studied.	We can ask students to apply their knowledge of geometry to solve real-world problems they haven't previously encountered.
Tests provide **feedback** about what students do and do not know.	We must give students specific feedback about the strengths and weaknesses of their performance, as well as suggestions for improvement. We can also look at the performance of the class as a whole to determine general areas of weakness we need to address.	As we test our students' physical endurance by asking them to run a mile, we can compare their time with last year's performance and suggest ways to increase speed and endurance. If we find that students are slowing to a walk before they complete the mile, we may want to devote a number of future classes to increasing endurance.

Tests as Mechanisms for Review

As we discovered in our discussion of information processing in Chapter 6, long-term memory is not necessarily "forever": For a variety of reasons, things are more likely to be forgotten as time goes on. Students have a better chance of remembering class material over the long run when they review it at a later time (Dempster, 1991; Kiewra, 1989; M. A. McDaniel & Masson, 1985). Studying for tests provides one way of reviewing material related to important instructional objectives (Dempster, 1991).

Tests as Influences on Information Processing

In our beginning case study, Ellen and Roz are both studying geography, but they are obviously learning different things and in different ways. What and how students learn is, to some extent, a function of the kind of tests they expect to take. Students will typically spend more time studying the things they think will be on a test than the things they think a test won't cover (Corbett & Wilson, 1988; J. R. Frederiksen & Collins, 1989; N. Frederiksen, 1984b). They will also learn information in the way they think it will be tested. For example, the extent to which students focus on memorizing isolated facts at a rote level (as Ellen does) or instead focus on learning an integrated body of information in a meaningful and organized fashion (as Roz does), depends partly on their expectations about the kinds of test questions they will need to answer. Unfortunately, many students believe, incorrectly, that trying to learn information meaningfully—that is, trying to understand and make sense out of the things they study—interferes with their ability to do well on classroom tests that emphasize rote memorization and knowledge of isolated facts (Crooks, 1988).

Students tend to study more for essay tests than for multiple-choice tests (D'Ydewalle, Swerts, & De Corte, 1983; G. Warren, 1979). Why might this be so?

Tests as Learning Experiences

You can probably think of tests you've taken that have actually taught you something. Perhaps an essay question asked you to compare two things you wouldn't have thought to compare and helped you discover similarities you hadn't noticed before. Or perhaps a test problem asked you to apply a concept or idea to a situation you hadn't realized was related to that situation. Such test items not only measured what you learned but also helped you learn *more*.

Generally speaking, the very process of taking a test on classroom material helps students learn that material better; in other words, a test can be a learning experience in and of itself (Foos & Fisher, 1988; N. Frederiksen, 1984b). But we should keep a couple of points in mind here. First of all, a test only helps students learn the material it specifically covers—it doesn't help them learn things not actually on the test (N. Frederiksen, 1984b). And second, there is a potential danger in giving students *incorrect* information on a test (as we often do when we give true-false and multiple-choice questions): Our students may learn and remember that misinformation and have trouble remembering correct information as a result (Voss, 1974).

Tests as Feedback

Tests can provide valuable feedback to our students about what they do and do not know. When students find out how their tests have been scored, they have a better grasp of the knowledge and skills they need to work on. But a test score alone is not very helpful; test results can facilitate student learning only to the extent that these results include concrete information about where students have succeeded and failed. For example, when students can examine the specific items they have answered incorrectly, they may be alerted to "holes" in their knowledge or to misunderstandings and misconceptions they have. And when they get constructive comments on their essay tests—comments that point out the strengths and weaknesses of each response, indicate where answers are ambiguous or imprecise, suggest how an essay might be more complete or better organized, and so on—their understanding of class material and their writing skills are both likely to improve (e.g., Baron, 1987).

Particularly when we use tests and other classroom assessments for summative evaluation purposes—in other words, to make lasting decisions about individual students—we must be sure our assessments are accurate indications of what our students have actually achieved. How do we know when we have assessment instruments and procedures that give us accurate information? We'll answer this question as we consider the characteristics of good assessment.

Classroom assessments provide valuable feedback to students about what they have and have not learned.

INTO THE CLASSROOM

Using Assessment to Promote Students' Learning and Achievement

Give a formal or informal pretest to determine where to begin instruction.

> At the beginning of a new unit on cultural geography, a teacher gives his class a pretest designed to identify misconceptions that students may have about various cultural groups—misconceptions he can then address during instruction.

Emphasize that your classroom assessments are ultimately designed to help students learn.

> A teacher tells her students, "Every Friday we will have a quiz on the things we've covered during the week. Each quiz will tell us whether there are things we still need to work on or whether we can move to new material."

Choose or develop an assessment instrument that reflects the actual knowledge and skills you want students to achieve.

When planning how to assess his students' achievement, a teacher initially decides to use test questions from the test bank that comes with his textbook. When he looks more closely at the test bank, however, he discovers that the items measure only knowledge of isolated facts. Instead, he develops several authentic assessment tasks that better reflect his primary instructional objective—that his students be able to synthesize and apply what they have learned to real-world problems.

Construct assessment instruments that reflect how you want students to process information when they study.

A teacher tells her students, "As you study for next week's vocabulary test, remember that the test questions will ask you to put definitions in your own words and give your own examples to show what each word means."

Consider using quizzes and tests to encourage review of previously studied topics.

Students in one teacher's class know that their tests will sometimes include items from previous units, especially if those topics relate to the new material they are studying.

Use an assessment task as a learning experience in and of itself.

A high school science teacher has students collect samples of the local drinking water and test them for bacterial content. She is evaluating her students on their ability to use correct procedures to test the water, but she also hopes they will learn something about their own drinking water.

Use an assessment to give students specific and concrete feedback about what they have and have not mastered.

As he grades students' persuasive essays, a teacher writes numerous notes in the margins of students' papers to indicate places where they have analyzed a situation correctly or incorrectly, identified a relevant or irrelevant example, proposed an appropriate or inappropriate solution, and so on.

Provide the means through which students can evaluate their *own* performance.

The teacher of a "life skills" class gives her students a checklist of qualities to look for in the pies they have baked.

CONSIDERING FOUR IMPORTANT CHARACTERISTICS OF CLASSROOM ASSESSMENTS

THINKING ABOUT WHAT YOU KNOW

As a student, have you ever been assessed in a way you thought was unfair? If so, *why* was it unfair? For example:

1. Did the teacher judge students' responses inconsistently?

2. Were some students assessed under more favorable conditions than others?

3. Was it a poor measure of what you had learned?

4. Was the assessment so time-consuming that, after a while, you no longer cared how well you performed?

In light of your experiences, what characteristics do *you* think are essential for a good classroom assessment instrument?

---◼---

The four numbered questions I just asked you reflect, respectively, four "RSVP" characteristics of good classroom assessment:

- Reliability

- Standardization

- Validity

- Practicality

A quick review: What do we call a memory aid such as *RSVP*? (You can find the answer in Chapter 6.)
---◼---

These RSVP characteristics are summarized in Table 14–2. Let's look more closely at each one.

Considering Reliability

◼ **EXPERIENCING FIRSTHAND**
Fowl Play

Consider the following sequence of events:

- *Monday:* After a unit on the bone structures of both birds and dinosaurs, Ms. Fowler asks her students to write an essay explaining why many scientists believe that birds are descended from dinosaurs. After school, she tosses the pile of essays in the back seat of her cluttered '57 Chevy.

- *Tuesday:* Ms. Fowler looks high and low for the essays both at home and in her classroom, but she can't find them anywhere.

- *Wednesday:* Because Ms. Fowler wants to use the essay to determine what her students have learned, she asks the class to write the same essay a second time.

- *Thursday:* Ms. Fowler discovers Monday's essays in the back seat of her Chevy.

- *Friday:* Ms. Fowler grades both sets of essays. She is surprised to discover that there is very little consistency between them: Students who wrote the best essays on Monday did not necessarily do well on Wednesday, and some of Monday's poorest performers did quite well on Wednesday.

Which results should Ms. Fowler use—Monday's or Wednesday's? ◼

The **reliability** of an assessment technique is the extent to which it yields consistent information about the knowledge, skills, or abilities we are trying to measure. When we assess our students' learning and achievement, we must be confident that the conclusions we draw don't change much regardless of whether we give the assessment Monday or Wednesday, regardless of whether the weather is sunny or rainy, and regardless of whether we evaluate students' responses while in a good mood or a foul frame

Table 14–2   The RSVP Characteristics of Good Assessment

CHARACTERISTIC	DEFINITION	RELEVANT QUESTIONS TO CONSIDER
Reliability	The extent to which the assessment instrument yields consistent results for each student	How much are students' scores affected by temporary conditions unrelated to the characteristic being measured (*test-retest reliability*)? Do different parts of a single assessment instrument lead to similar conclusions about a student's achievement (*internal consistency reliability*)? Do different people score students' performance similarly (*scorer reliability*)?
Standardization	The extent to which assessment procedures are similar for all students	Are all students assessed on identical or similar content? Do all students have the same types of tasks to perform? Are instructions the same for everyone? Do all students have similar time constraints? Is everyone's performance evaluated using the same criteria?
Validity	The extent to which an assessment instrument measures what it is supposed to measure	Does the assessment tap into a representative sample of the content domain being assessed (*content validity*)? Does the instrument measure a particular psychological or educational characteristic (*construct validity*)? Do students' scores predict their success at a later task (*predictive validity*)?
Practicality	The extent to which an assessment is easy and inexpensive to use	How much class time does the assessment take? How quickly and easily can students' responses be scored? Is special training required to administer or score the assessment? Does the assessment require specialized materials that must be purchased?

of mind. Ms. Fowler's assessment technique has poor reliability: The results are completely different from one day to another. So which day's results should she use? I've asked you a trick question: We have no way of knowing which set is more accurate.

The same assessment instrument will rarely give us *exactly* the same results for the same individual, even if the knowledge or ability we are measuring (e.g., the extent to which a student knows basic addition facts, can execute a swan dive, or can compare the bone structures of birds and dinosaurs) remains the same. Many temporary conditions unrelated to what we are trying to measure—distractions in the classroom, variability in instructions and time limits, inconsistencies in rating students' responses, and so on—are likely to affect our students' performance. Factors such as these almost invariably lead to some degree of fluctuation in our assessment results.

What temporary conditions might have differentially affected students' performance on Ms. Fowler's essay on Monday and Wednesday? Here are a few possibilities:

- *Day-to-day changes in students*—for example, changes in health, motivation, mood, and energy level

  The 24-hour Netherlands Flu was making the rounds in Ms. Fowler's classroom that week.

- *Variations in the physical environment*—for example, variations in room temperature, noise level, and outside distractions

  On Monday, students who sat by the window in Ms. Fowler's classroom enjoyed peace and quiet; on Wednesday, those who sat by the window worked while noisy construction machinery tore up the pavement outside.

- *Variations in administration of the assessment*—for example, variations in instructions, timing, and the teacher's response to student questions

  On Monday, a few students had to write the essay after school because of play rehearsal during class time; Ms. Fowler explained the task more clearly than she had during class that day and gave students as much time as they needed to finish. On Wednesday, a different group of students had to write the essay after school because of a band concert during class time; on this occasion, Ms. Fowler explained the task very hurriedly and collected students' essays before they had finished.

- *Characteristics of the assessment instrument*—for example, the length of the task, and ambiguous or excessively difficult tasks (longer tasks tend to be more reliable ones because small errors have less of an impact on overall results; ambiguous and very difficult tasks increase students' tendency to guess randomly, and often differently, on different occasions)

  The essay topic "Explain why many scientists believe that birds are descended from dinosaurs" was a vague one that students interpreted differently from one day to the next.

- *Subjectivity in scoring*—for example, tasks for which the teacher must make judgments about "rightness" or "wrongness," and situations in which students' responses are scored on the basis of vague, imprecise criteria

  Ms. Fowler graded both sets of essays while she watched "Chainsaw Murders at Central High" on television Friday night; she gave higher scores during kissing scenes, lower scores during stalking scenes.

Whenever we draw conclusions about our students' learning and achievement, we must be confident that the information on which we've based those conclusions is not overly distorted by temporary factors irrelevant to what we are trying to measure. Probably no assessment technique is 100 percent reliable; however, some instruments and procedures provide more reliable results than others, and it is helpful to know how dependable the results of any particular technique are likely to be.

It is often possible to determine a precise *reliability coefficient* that indicates exactly how reliable an assessment technique is (see Appendix A, "Describing Relationships with Correlation Coefficients"). Yet even when we don't calculate the mathematical reliability of an instrument we use, we should take precautions to maximize the extent to which the instrument gives us reliable results. More specially, we should:

- Include several tasks in each instrument and look for consistency in students' performance from one task to another

- Define each task clearly enough that students know exactly what they are being asked to do

- Identify specific, concrete criteria on which we will evaluate students' performance

- Try not to let our expectations for students' performance influence our judgments

- Avoid assessing students' learning when they are obviously ill, tired, or out of sorts

- Administer the assessment in similar ways and under similar conditions for all students

My last recommendation suggests that our assessment procedures be *standardized*—a second important characteristic of good assessment.

Considering Standardization

A second important characteristic of good assessment is **standardization:** It involves similar content and format and is administered and scored in the same way for everyone. In most situations, all students should be given the same instructions, perform identical or similar tasks, have the same time limits, and work under the same constraints (making appropriate adjustments for students with special needs, however). And students' responses should be scored as consistently as possible; for example, we shouldn't use tougher standards for one student than for another.

Perhaps you can now see why the published tests we discussed earlier are called *standardized* tests: They have explicit instructions for administration and scoring. Yet standardization is important in our teacher-developed assessment instruments as well. Standardization reduces some of the error in our assessment results, especially error due to variation in test administration or subjectivity in scoring. So the more assessment is standardized for all students, the higher is its reliability. Equity is an additional consideration: Except in unusual situations, it is only fair to ask all students to be evaluated under similar conditions.

Considering Validity

◾ EXPERIENCING FIRSTHAND
FTOI

Just a few minutes ago, you read my section on *reliability*. Let's see whether you can apply (transfer) your understanding of that concept to this situation:

I have developed a new test called the FTOI: the Fathead Test of Intelligence. It consists of only a tape measure and a table of norms describing how others have performed on the test. Administration of the FTOI is quick and easy: You simply measure a student's head circumference just above the eyebrows (firmly but not too tightly) and compare your measure against the table of norms. Large heads (comparatively speaking) receive high IQ scores. Smaller heads receive low scores.

Does the FTOI have high reliability? Answer the question before you read further. ◾

No matter how often you measure a person's head circumference, you are probably going to get a very similar score: Fatheads will continue to be fatheads, and pinheads will always be pinheads. So the answer to my question is yes: The FTOI has high reliability because it yields consistent results. If you answered no, you were probably thinking that the FTOI isn't a very good measure of intelligence—but that's a problem with the instrument's *validity,* not with its reliability.

The **validity** of an assessment instrument is the extent to which it measures what it is supposed to measure. Does the FTOI measure intelligence? Do scores on a standardized, multiple-choice achievement test actually indicate how much students have learned during the school year? Does students' performance at a school concert reflect what they have achieved in their instrumental music class? To the extent that our assessments don't do these things—to the extent that they are poor measures of students' knowledge and abilities—then we have a problem with validity.

As we noted earlier, numerous irrelevant factors are likely to influence how well our students perform in assessment situations. Some of these—students' health, distractions in the classroom, errors in scoring, and so on—are temporary conditions that lead to fluctuation in our assessment results and thereby lower reliability. But other irrelevant factors—perhaps reading ability, self-efficacy, trait anxiety—are more stable in nature, so their effects on our assessment results will be relatively constant. For example, if Joe has poor reading skills, then he may get consistently low scores on paper-pencil, multiple-choice achievement tests regardless of how much he has actually achieved in science, mathematics, social studies, and so on. If Jane suffers debilitating anxiety whenever she performs in front of an audience, then her performance at a public concert may not be a good reflection of how well she can play the cello. When our assessment results continue to be affected by the same irrelevant variables, then we must call the validity of our instruments into question.

We should note here that reliability is a necessary condition for validity: Assessments can only yield valid results when they also yield reliable results—results that are only minimally affected by variations in administration, subjectivity in scoring, and so on. Reliability does not guarantee validity, however, as the FTOI exercise illustrates.

We should also note that any assessment tool may be valid for some purposes but not for others (e.g., Gronlund & Linn, 1990). A mathematics achievement test may be a valid measure of how well students can add and subtract but a terrible measure of how well they can apply addition and subtraction to real-life situations. A paper-pencil test regarding the rules of tennis may accurately assess students' knowledge regarding how many games in a set, what *deuce* means, and so on, but it probably won't tell us much about how well students can actually play the game.

Psychologists distinguish among different kinds of validity, each of which is important in different situations. In some cases, we might be interested in **construct validity**—the extent to which an assessment accurately measures an underlying, unobservable characteristic such as motivation, self-esteem, or visual-spatial ability.* For example, we might suspect that our observations of students' on-task and off-task behavior in class are indicative of their motivation to learn academic subject matter. In other cases, we might be more interested in **predictive validity**—the extent to which

---

* Psychologists use the term *construct* to refer to a hypothesized internal trait that cannot be directly observed, but must instead be inferred from the consistencies we see in people's behavior. For example, *motivation, self-esteem, intelligence,* and *metacognition* are constructs; none of them can be seen directly.

the results of an assessment predict future behavior. For example, if the school psychologist tells us the IQ score a particular student has obtained on an intelligence test, we may be interested in knowing, as Alfred Binet once was, how well scores from the test predict students' future academic achievement; as we noted in Chapter 4, intelligence tests are often used to make such predictions. But when we are measuring our students' achievement of instructional objectives, we will usually be concerned with **content validity**—the extent to which the tasks we ask students to perform are a representative sample of the knowledge and skills we are trying to assess. Content validity is especially important in our formal assessments; we will discover how to maximize such validity when, later in the chapter, we consider how we can best plan a formal assessment strategy.

Reliability, standardization, validity—all of these are important considerations when we assess our students' learning and achievement. Yet we must also consider the *practicality* of any assessment technique we use.

Considering Practicality

The last of the four RSVP characteristics is **practicality**—the extent to which assessment instruments and procedures are relatively easy to use. Practicality includes such concerns as these:

- How much time will it take to develop the instrument?
- How easily can the assessment be administered to a large group of students?
- Are expensive materials involved?
- How much time will the assessment take away from instructional activities?
- How quickly and easily can students' performance be evaluated?

There is often a trade-off between practicality and such other characteristics as validity and reliability. For example, a true-false test on tennis will be easier to construct and administer, but a performance assessment in which students actually demonstrate their tennis skills—even though it takes more time and energy—is probably a more valid measure of how well students have learned to play the game.

Of our four RSVP characteristics, validity is undoubtedly the most important of all: We *must* have an assessment technique that measures what we want it to measure. Reliability ensures the dependability of our assessment results (in doing so, it indirectly affects their validity), and standardization is necessary to the extent that it enhances the reliability of those results. Practicality should be a consideration only to the extent that validity, reliability, and standardization are not jeopardized.

To what extent do different kinds of assessments meet our RSVP criteria? We will find the answers to these questions as we examine both informal and formal assessment in the pages that follow.

Without looking at Table 14–4, can you now describe each of the four RSVP characteristics of good assessment?

CONDUCTING INFORMAL ASSESSMENTS

As teachers, we need to monitor our students' performance on an ongoing basis. Through informal assessment—through our daily observations of students' verbal and

Informal assessment techniques, such as asking questions in class, provide a means through which we can monitor our students' understanding of classroom material on a daily basis.

nonverbal behaviors—we are likely to draw conclusions about what students have and have not learned, as well as about how future instruction should proceed. Here are just a few of the many forms that informal assessment can take:

Assessment of verbal behaviors:

- Asking questions

- Listening to whole-class and small-group discussions

- Holding brief conferences with individual students

Assessment of nonverbal behaviors:

- Observing how well students perform physical skills

- Looking at the relative frequency of on-task and off-task behaviors

- Identifying the activities in which students engage voluntarily

- Watching the "body language" that may reflect students' feelings about classroom tasks

Informal assessment has a number of advantages (Airasian, 1994; Stiggins, 1994). First and foremost, it provides continuing feedback about the effectiveness of the day's instructional tasks and activities. Second, it is easily adjusted at a moment's notice; for example, when students express misconceptions about a particular topic, we can ask follow-up questions that probe their beliefs and reasoning processes. Third, it provides information that may either support or call into question the data we obtain from more formal assessments such as paper-pencil tests. Finally, informal procedures may often be the only means through which we can assess such affective outcomes as "being interested in" or "valuing" something.

Why do you think affective outcomes are usually assessed informally, rather than formally?

Keeping the RSVP Characteristics in Mind

When we use informal assessment procedures to get information about students' learning and achievement, we must be aware of the strengths and limitations of such procedures in terms of the four RSVP characteristics of good assessment—reliability, standardization, validity, and practicality.

Reliability

Base conclusions on many observations over a long period of time.

Most informal assessments are quite short; for example, we may notice that Naomi is off-task during an activity, hear Manuel's answer to a question we've asked, or have a brief conversation with Jacquie after school. But brief snippets of students' behavior may be unreliable indicators of their overall achievement. Perhaps we happen to look at Naomi during the *only* time she is off-task. Perhaps we ask Manuel one of the few questions to which he *doesn't* know the answer. Perhaps we misinterpret what Jacquie is trying to say during our conversation with her. When we use informal assessment to draw conclusions about what students have learned and achieved, then, we should be sure to base our conclusions on many observations over a long period of time (Airasian, 1994).

Furthermore, it's important to remind ourselves of a principle from our discussion of information processing: Our long-term memories are not completely dependable. We will inevitably remember some instances of students' behaviors but not others. If we are depending heavily on our in-class observations of students, then, we should probably keep ongoing, written records of the things we see and hear (Gronlund, 1993; Stiggins, 1994).

Keep written records of significant observations.

Standardization

Our informal assessments will rarely, if ever, be standardized; for example, we will ask different questions of different students, and we will probably observe each student's behavior in different contexts. Hence, such assessments will definitely *not* be giving us the same information for each student. As teachers, we will rarely be able to make comparisons among our students on the basis of casual observations alone.

Never make comparisons among students solely on the basis of casual observations.

Validity

Even when we see consistency in our students' behavior over time, we are not always getting accurate data about what they know and can do (Airasian, 1994; Stiggins, 1994). For example, Tom may intentionally answer questions incorrectly so that he doesn't look too "smart" in front of his friends. Margot may be reluctant to say anything at all because of a chronic stuttering problem. Jamie may be listening carefully to an expository lesson even though she is doodling in her notebook. As we noted earlier in the chapter, any assessment involves drawing *inferences* about what students have learned, based on the things we observe them do; such inferences will not always be accurate ones, particularly when we are assessing students' performance in an unsystematic and nonstandardized fashion.

Remember that students' behaviors are not always accurate indicators of what they've learned.

Principles from our discussion of knowledge construction (Chapter 7) are also important to keep in mind here: We impose meanings on the things we see and hear, and those meanings are influenced by the things we already know or believe to be true. Our own biases and expectations will affect our interpretations of what particular students are or are not doing, inevitably affecting the accuracy of any conclusions we reach (Airasian, 1994; Stiggins, 1994). As we noted in our discussion of diversity in Chapter 4, inaccurate teacher expectations and interpretations of students' behavior may adversely affect students' learning and performance over the long run.

Remember that your own biases and expectations may distort your interpretations of what you've observed.

Practicality

A definite strength of informal assessment procedures is their practicality: We will typically make our observations spontaneously during the course of instruction. Informal assessment involves little if any of our time either beforehand or after the fact (except for any written records we decide to keep). We have the additional advantage of flexibility: We can adapt our assessment procedures on the spur of the moment, altering them as events in the classroom change.

Despite the practicality of informal assessment techniques, we have noted serious problems regarding their reliability, standardization, and validity. Hence, we should treat any conclusions we draw only as *hypotheses* that we must either confirm or disconfirm through other means (Airasian, 1994). Ultimately, we should rely more heavily on formal assessment techniques to determine whether our students have achieved our instructional objectives.

Treat the conclusions you draw from informal assessment as hypotheses that need confirmation through other means.

A valid and reliable formal assessment is usually one that has been carefully planned and thought out ahead of time. Here are three important questions we should ask ourselves as we plan any formal assessment instrument:

- What content domain are we trying to assess?

- What type of tasks will best measure students' achievement?

- How can we get a representative sample of the domain?

Let's address each question in turn.

Identifying the Domain to Be Assessed

Identify content domains for each assessment small enough to give you specific information about what students have achieved, but not so small that you spend most of your class time in assessment-related activities.

When planning and developing a formal assessment instrument, we first need to identify the specific content domain we want to assess and determine just how broad or narrow that domain is. For example, we may conceivably want to measure something as broad as "what students learned in history class this semester" or as narrow as "what students know about the Russian Revolution." Similarly, we may want to assess something as general as students' overall level of physical fitness or something as specific as their ability to do push-ups. We may be interested in determining whether students have learned enough algebra to move on to a pre-calculus class, or we may instead simply want to find out whether they can solve for x in a quadratic equation.

When we use a single assessment instrument to measure a very broad area of achievement (such as is usually the case when we administer a standardized achievement test), we get relatively little information about the specific things that students have and have not learned. When we devise separate assessments to measure narrower domains, we learn more about what knowledge and skills individual students have acquired, but at the expense of devoting a great deal of classroom time to assessment (Popham, 1990). Somewhere between these two extremes is a happy medium: We need to identify content domains small enough that our assessment instruments give us concrete information about what students have achieved, but not so small that we spend most of our classroom time assessing, rather than teaching.

Selecting Appropriate Tasks

Decide whether paper-pencil or performance tasks better reflect your instructional objectives.

We maximize the content validity of our classroom assessment instruments when the tasks we ask our students to perform are as similar as possible to the things we ultimately want them to be able to do—in other words, when there is a match between assessment tasks and instructional objectives. In some situations, such as when the desired outcome is simple recall of facts, asking students to respond to multiple-choice or short-answer questions on a paper-pencil test may be both valid and practical. In other situations—for instance, when our objective is for students to explain everyday phenomena by using scientific principles or to critique a literary or artistic work—essay questions that require students to follow a logical line of reasoning may be appropriate. *If* we can truly measure the domain we want to measure by having students respond to questions on paper, then a paper-pencil assessment is the method of choice for practicality reasons.

Yet there are many skills—cooking a hard-boiled egg, executing a front dismount from the parallel bars, applying principles of geometry to surveying techniques, identifying specific microorganisms through a microscope—that we cannot easily measure with paper and pencil. For skills such as these, performance assessments are likely to give us greater content validity. Performance assessment may be especially useful when we are concerned about students' ability to apply classroom subject matter to real-world situations.

In the end, we may find that the most valid yet practical approach to assessing our students' achievement is a *combination* of both paper-pencil and performance tasks (Messick, 1994a; D. B. Swanson, Norman, & Linn, 1995). Paper-pencil assessments will allow us to assess students' knowledge in a relatively short and efficient manner; for example, short-answer questions will enable us to sample their knowledge of a broad topic fairly quickly. Performance assessments are far more time-consuming, yet they will often provide information related to our instructional objectives that we cannot gather any other way.

What kinds of performance tasks might be appropriate in the subject area you will be teaching?

Ensuring That the Assessment Provides a Representative Sample

■ EXPERIENCING FIRSTHAND
Ants and Spiders

Consider this situation:

The students in Mr. Tyburczy's biology class are complaining about the quiz they just took. After all, the class spent two weeks studying insects and only one day studying arachnids, yet the quiz was entirely on arachnids. Students who forgot what arachnids were failed the quiz even though some of them knew quite a bit about insects.

Why is Mr. Tyburczy's assessment strategy a poor one? Which aspect of Mr. Tyburczy's quiz are his students complaining about—reliability, standardization, validity, or practicality? ■

Most classroom assessment activities, even paper-pencil ones, can give us only a small sample of what students know and can do. It would be terribly impractical—and in most cases virtually impossible—to assess *everything* that a student has acquired from a unit on insects and arachnids, a chapter in a social studies textbook, or a semester of physical education. Instead, we must typically ask a few questions or present a few tasks to elicit behaviors that we hope are an accurate reflection of students' overall level of knowledge or skill.

Mr. Tyburczy's quiz does elicit a sample of what students may have learned in his unit on insects and arachnids. The problem is that these questions are not representative of the unit as a whole: The focus of the quiz is exclusively on arachnids. The quiz, then, has poor *content validity*. Ideally, Mr. Tyburczy's quiz questions should reflect the various parts of the unit in appropriate proportions. His questions should also ask students to do the kinds of things that his instructional objectives describe—perhaps comparing arachnids to insects, identifying examples of each class, and so on.

How can we ensure that our test is truly a representative sample of what students know and can do? In other words, how can we ensure its content validity? The most widely recommended strategy is to construct a *blueprint* for the content domain we

Can you think of occasions when a test you took covered the entire content domain?

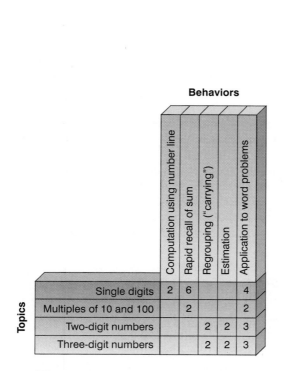

Behaviors

Topics	Computation using number line	Rapid recall of sum	Regrouping ("carrying")	Estimation	Application to word problems
Single digits	2	6			4
Multiples of 10 and 100		2			2
Two-digit numbers			2	2	3
Three-digit numbers			2	2	3

This table provides specifications for a thirty-item paper-pencil test on <u>addition</u>. It assigns different weights (different numbers of items) to different topic-behavior combinations, with some combinations not being measured at all.

Behaviors

Topics	Make simple drawing of machine	Describe work that machine performs	Recognize examples among common objects	Solve problems by using machine
Inclined plane	5%	5%	5%	5%
Wedge	5%	5%	5%	5%
Lever	5%	5%	5%	5%
Wheel and axle	5%	5%	5%	5%
Pulley	5%	5%	5%	5%

This table provides specifications for a combination paper-pencil and performance assessment on <u>simple machines</u>. It assigns equal importance (the same percentage of points) to each topic-behavior combination.

Figure 14–2   Two Examples of a Table of Specifications

Develop a table of specifications for the content domain you want to assess and then develop paper-pencil and/or performance tasks representative of that domain.

Sometimes the behaviors listed in a table of specifications are those in Bloom's taxonomy (see Chapter 12); for example, we might list such behaviors as "knowledge," "comprehension," and "application."

want to assess, whereby we identify the specific things we want to measure and the extent to which each one should be represented on the instrument. This blueprint frequently takes the form of a **table of specifications**—a two-way grid that indicates both the topics to be covered and the behaviors associated with them (the things that students should be able to *do* with each topic). In each cell of the grid, we indicate the relative importance of each topic-behavior combination in terms of a particular number or percentage of tasks or test items to be included in the overall assessment. Figure 14–2 illustrates such tables through two examples—one for a paper-pencil test on addition and a second for a combined paper-pencil and performance assessment on simple machines. Once we have developed a table of specifications, we can develop paper-pencil items or performance tasks that reflect both the topics and the behaviors we want to measure and have some confidence that our assessment instrument has content validity for the domain it is designed to represent.

Once we have planned an assessment strategy—once we have determined the content domain to be measured and the best way to assess it—we can then turn our attention to more specific details, including considerations related to item construction, administration procedures, and criteria for scoring students' responses. We'll address these issues separately for paper-pencil assessment and performance assessment.

USING PAPER-PENCIL ASSESSMENTS

We can often assess students' basic knowledge and skills with paper and pencil; for example, we might give our students a brief quiz to find out whether they can spell *dinosaur,* define *democracy,* or multiply 49 × 56. Written assignments and tests can sometimes help us assess students' higher-level thinking abilities as well; for example, we might ask students to compare the bone structures of birds and dinosaurs, write a persuasive essay about the advantages and disadvantages of a democratic government, or solve a complex mathematical word problem. But regardless of the objectives we use paper and pencil to assess, we must keep our four RSVP characteristics in mind. We'll find out how we can do so as we consider strategies for choosing appropriate tasks and questions, constructing and administering the assessment instrument, and scoring students' responses.

Choosing Appropriate Tasks and Questions

If we believe that a paper-pencil instrument is appropriate for the situation at hand, what specific types of tasks or questions do we give? There are many options from which to choose. We might ask students to write compositions, stories, poems, or research papers. We might ask them to solve well-defined or ill-defined mathematical or scientific word problems. We might ask questions in a variety of formats—perhaps short answer, essay, true-false, matching, or multiple choice. We might even want to use several of these options in combination. We can narrow down the possibilities by addressing several issues:

- Are we trying to assess lower-level or higher-level skills?

- Are recognition tasks or recall tasks more appropriate?

- Should students have access to reference materials?

Assessing Lower-Level or Higher-Level Skills

Questions that require brief responses—short answer, matching, true-false, multiple choice—are often suitable for assessing students' knowledge of single, isolated facts (e.g., Popham, 1995). Questions that require extended responses—essays, for instance—lend themselves more easily to assessing such higher-level skills as problem solving, critical thinking, and the synthesis of ideas (J. R. Frederiksen & Collins, 1989; Murnane & Raizen, 1988; Stiggins, 1994). For example, we might write essay questions that require students to organize information, follow a line of reasoning, design an experiment, or justify their position on a controversial topic. Yet we can also develop multiple-choice items that assess higher-level skills; here are two examples:

Consider using questions that require extended responses for higher-level skills.

1. An inventor has just designed a new device for cutting paper. Without knowing anything else about his invention, we can predict that it is probably which type of machine?

    a. A lever
    b. A movable pulley
    c. An inclined plane
    d. A wedge

Answer: (1) d.

2. Which one of the following French sentences contains a grammatical error?

    a. Je vous aimez.
    b. Le crayon rouge est sur la table verte.
    c. Donnez-moi le crayon rouge, s'il vous plaît.
    d. Avez-vous un billet pour le théâtre ce soir?

Develop written questions that simulate real-world tasks.

With a little ingenuity, we can even develop relatively "authentic" paper-pencil questions—questions that assess students' ability to apply classroom subject matter to real-world tasks (Gronlund, 1993; Gronlund & Linn, 1990; D. B. Swanson et al., 1995). Here are two examples to show you what I mean:

3. You are shopping at your local discount store. You decide to buy a T-shirt that is regularly priced at $11.00, but now is marked 20% off. You also decide to buy two candy bars at 59¢ each. You know that the local sales tax is 6%. How much money will the store clerk ask you for when you get to the checkout counter?

4. Below is a map of a small city named Riverdale. Indicate where in Riverdale you would be most likely to find a *steel mill* and then explain why you chose the location you did.

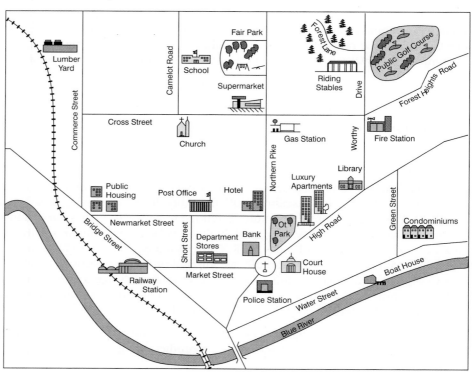

Source: Adapted from "Reconceptualizing Map Learning" by J. E. Ormrod, R. K. Ormrod, E. D. Wagner, & R. C. McCallin, 1988, *American Journal of Psychology, 101,* p. 428. Adapted with permission of the University of Illinois Press.

Answers: (2) a; (3) $10.58; (4) between the river and the railroad tracks, where both water and transportation are easily accessible.

Using Recognition or Recall Tasks

We should also consider whether a particular task assesses recognition or recall. **Recognition tasks** ask students to identify correct answers within the context of incorrect statements or irrelevant information; examples include multiple-choice, true-false, and matching questions. **Recall tasks** require students to generate the correct answers themselves; examples include short-answer questions, essays, and word problems.

Recognition and recall tasks each have their advantages. Students can often answer many recognition questions in a limited period of time; hence, such questions allow us to sample a wide range of knowledge and skills. Furthermore, we can score students' responses quickly and consistently, thus addressing our needs for practicality and reliability. But when we want to assess our students' ability to remember knowledge and skills without the benefit of having the correct answer right in front of them, then recall tasks obviously have greater validity for assessing our instructional objectives.

Giving Students Access to Reference Materials

In some cases, we may want our students to have only one resource—their own long-term memories—as they take a quiz or test. But in other situations, it may be appropriate to let them use reference materials—perhaps a dictionary, an atlas, or a magazine article—as they work. An assessment task in which reference materials are allowed is especially appropriate when our objective is not for students to commit certain things to memory, but rather for them to be able to use and apply these things once they have looked them up. For example, we may not care whether students memorize every principle in a geometry textbook, but we would like them to know how to use geometric principles to predict distances or angles. And we may not necessarily want students to know how to spell every word in the English language, but we would like them to be able to write a composition free of spelling errors if they have a dictionary to assist them.

Use recognition tasks to assess students' ability to recognize facts, particularly when you need to sample from a large content domain. Use recall tasks when it is important to assess students' ability to retrieve information on their own.

Allow students to use reference materials if your objective is application of information that does not necessarily need to be committed to memory.

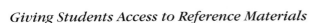

Constructing and Administering the Assessment

Regardless of the kinds of tasks we ask our students to perform, there are several guidelines we should keep in mind as we construct and administer a paper-pencil assessment instrument. More specifically, we should:

- Define tasks clearly and unambiguously
- Specify our scoring criteria in advance

It may often be appropriate to let students use reference materials during a formal assessment when instructional objectives involve finding and applying information, rather than committing information to memory.

- Provide a quiet and comfortable environment

- Try to alleviate students' anxiety about the assessment

- Encourage students to ask questions when tasks are not clear

Defining Tasks Clearly

■   **EXPERIENCING FIRSTHAND**
Assessing Assessment

Your educational psychology instructor gives you a test that includes these questions:

1. List four qualities of a good classroom assessment instrument.

2. Summarize the purposes of classroom assessment.

Take a few minutes to think about how you might answer each of these questions. Jot down your thoughts about what you would include in your responses.   ■

Was your answer to Question 1 as simple as "reliability, standardization, validity, and practicality"? Did you think you would need to explain each of the RSVP character-istics? Did you identify legitimate qualities of "goodness" other than the four RSVP characteristics? And what about Question 2? What purposes would you have focused on, and how long do you think your summary might have been? Words such as *list, qualities,* and *summarize* are difficult to interpret and may even be misleading to students.

Define tasks clearly and unambiguously.

Contrary to what some teachers believe, there is little to be gained from assigning ambiguous tasks when we want to assess our students' learning and achievement (e.g., Sax, 1989). Whether or not students know how to respond to the tasks we present, they should at least understand what we are asking them to do. Therefore, we should define any paper-pencil task as clearly and precisely as we possibly can. As a double-check, we might ask a colleague to read our assignments and questions for clarity; those that seem "obvious" to us may not be obvious at all to someone else.

Specifying Scoring Criteria in Advance

We will typically want to identify correct responses at the same time that we develop our assessment tasks. In situations where there will be more than one correct answer (as may be true for an essay question), we should at least identify the components of a good response. Furthermore, we should describe the scoring criteria to our students long before we give them the assessment; doing so gives them guidance about how they can best prepare for it (e.g., M. Rose, 1991).

Identify general scoring policies to which you will adhere, and describe them to your class.

It is also a good idea to develop policies to guide our scoring when students give answers that are only partially correct, respond correctly to items but include additional *in*correct information, or write responses with numerous grammatical and spelling errors. We must be consistent about how we score students' responses in such situations.

Providing a Quiet and Comfortable Environment

Our students are more likely to perform at their best when they complete a paper-pencil assessment in a comfortable environment—one with acceptable room temperature, adequate lighting, reasonable workspace, and minimal distractions. This comfort

Provide a quiet and comfortable assessment environment.

factor may be especially important for students who are easily distracted, unaccustomed to formal assessments, or relatively uninterested in performing well on them; for example, it may be especially important for our at-risk students (Popham, 1990).

Alleviating Students' Anxiety

 ──────── **THINKING ABOUT WHAT YOU KNOW** ────────

How anxious do you get when you know you will be taking a test in class? For example, do you:

- Worry the night before, wondering whether you've read all the assigned readings?

- Become a little nervous while the test is being handed out, thinking that maybe you don't know everything as well as you should?

- Have a lot of trouble remembering things you knew perfectly well when you studied them?

- Get in such a panic that you can barely read the test items at all?

──────────────── ■ ────────────────

If your answer to any of these questions is yes, then you, like most students, experience **test anxiety.**

Students are typically not anxious about learning new knowledge and skills. But as we discovered in Chapter 11, many of them *are* anxious at the thought that they will be evaluated and judged and perhaps found to be "stupid" or in some other way inadequate. A little bit of test anxiety may actually be a good thing: Students are more likely to prepare for an assessment and to respond to questions carefully and completely if they are concerned about how well they are going to perform on that assessment (Shipman & Shipman, 1985). But their performance is likely to be impaired when they are *very* test anxious, particularly when the tasks we present require them to use what they have learned in a flexible and creative manner (Kirkland, 1971). In cases of extreme test anxiety, students may have difficulty retrieving things from long-term memory and may not even be able to understand what our test questions are asking them to do.

We will see debilitating test anxiety more frequently in older students, minorities, and students from lower-socioeconomic backgrounds (K. T. Hill, 1984; Kirkland, 1971; Pang, 1995; B. N. Phillips et al., 1980). And, as we noted in Chapter 11, students with a history of failure on academic tasks are particularly prone to such anxiety.

As teachers, we can make our students more or less anxious about our classroom assessments simply by how we present them (see Table 14–3). When we describe a classroom assessment as an occasion to "separate the men from the boys" or as "sudden death" for anyone who fails, students' anxiety levels are likely to go sky high. Instead, we should portray such assessments more as opportunities to increase knowledge and improve skills than as occasions for evaluation (Spaulding, 1992). For example, such statements as "We're here to learn, and you can't do that without making mistakes" (Brophy, 1986, p. 47) can help students keep their imperfections in perspective and their anxiety at a facilitating, rather than debilitating, level.

Avoid statements and behaviors that are apt to make students excessively anxious.

Table 14–3 Keeping Students' Test Anxiety at a Facilitative Level

What to Do	What Not to Do
Point out the value of the assessment as a feedback mechanism to improve learning.	Stress the fact that students' competence is being evaluated.
Administer a practice assessment or pretest that gives students an idea of what the final assessment instrument will be like.	Keep the nature of the assessment a secret until the day it is administered.
Encourage students to do their best.	Remind students that failing will have dire consequences.
Provide or allow the use of memory aids (e.g., a list of formulas or a single notecard containing key facts) when instructional objectives do not require students to commit information to memory.	Insist that students commit even trivial facts to memory.
Eliminate time limits unless speed is an important part of the skill being measured.	Give more questions or tasks than students can possibly respond to in the time allotted.
Be available to answer students' questions during the assessment.	Hover over students, watching them closely as they respond.
Use the results of several assessments to make decisions (e.g., to assign grades).	Evaluate students on the basis of a single assessment.

Sources: Blanco, 1972; Brophy, 1986; Gaudry & Bradshaw, 1971; K. T. Hill, 1984; K. T. Hill & Eaton, 1977; Leherissey, O'Neil, & Hansen, 1971; Popham, 1990; Sax, 1989; Sieber, Kameya, & Paulson, 1970.

Encourage students to ask questions when tasks are not clear.

Encouraging Students to Ask Questions

As we noted earlier, even when students don't know the answers to our questions, they should at least know what our questions are asking them to do. Yet despite our best intentions, we may present a task or ask a question that is unclear, ambiguous, or even misleading. (Even after more than twenty years' experience writing exams, I still have students occasionally interpreting my assignments and test questions in ways I didn't anticipate.) To maximize the likelihood that our students will respond in the ways we are seeking, we should encourage them to ask for clarification whenever they are uncertain about the task before them. Such encouragement is especially important for students from minority ethnic populations, many of whom may be reluctant to ask questions during a formal assessment situation (e.g., Cheng, 1987).

Scoring Students' Responses

 EXPERIENCING FIRSTHAND
A Day Like Any Other

Imagine you are a middle school teacher. You have asked your class to write a short story written from the perspective of an animal. Here is a twelve-year-old boy's story:

It was a day like any other, until I heard a strange sound. A sound like no other sound I had heard before. I hurried to my hole hoping nouthing had happened to my babys. They were all right so I gave them the food that was in my mouth.

Then I heard the sound again. I huddled close to my baby rats so they wouldn't be to scared. I wish someone would huddle close to me so I wouldn't be scared.

All of a sudden I started to hear some splashing noises. I looked up and saw that the sky was lite up. I was still standing close to my badys trying to calm them down. I wasn't shure what this was and what would happen to my family and me. And then, as soon as it had started, it stoped. My family and I walked out of the rat hole and discovered that the flowers in the flower box above our hole had bloomed. I knew that all that had scared me before, had happened for a reason.

If you had to give this story a letter grade—A, B, C, D, or F—what grade would you give? On what criteria would you base your decision?

Some paper-pencil tasks can be scored *objectively:* They have definite right and wrong answers, and there is little decision making involved in evaluating students' responses; this is the case for such recognition items as multiple-choice and true-false questions. Yet other paper-pencil tasks, such as short stories and essays, can only be scored *subjectively:* They require teacher judgment about how right or wrong any particular response is. How did you grade the story about the mother rat and her babies? What criteria did you use when you made your decision? To what extent was the student's development of the plot important? To what extent was creativity a factor? To what extent did grammar, spelling, and punctuation errors affect your judgment? Different teachers might weigh each of these criteria differently, and their grades for the same story would differ as a result. In fact, even *you* might grade the story differently next month than you graded it today.

The more variable and complex students' responses on a paper-pencil assessment instrument are, the greater difficulty we will have in scoring those responses objectively and reliably. There are several strategies we can use to maximize the likelihood that we score students' responses in a consistent fashion; more specifically, we should:

- Specify our scoring criteria in concrete terms

- Score grammar and spelling separately from the *content* of students' responses*

- Skim a sample of students' responses ahead of time, looking for responses we didn't anticipate and revising our criteria if necessary

- Score all responses to a single task or question at once (scoring task by task, rather than student by student)

- Score responses on a predefined continuum, rather than on an all-or-none basis if responses are likely to have varying degrees of correctness

- Try not to let our expectations for students' performance influence our judgments of their *actual* performance

- Score some or all responses a second time to check for consistency

Look at our case study of "Studying Europe" once again. Which test can be scored more objectively—Ms. Peterson's or Ms. Montgomery's?

Take steps to score students' responses as objectively as possible.

Can you explain how each of these recommendations affects the reliability of the assessment instrument?

---

* This recommendation is especially important when assessing students with limited English proficiency (Hamp-Lyons, 1992; Scarcella, 1990).

Keeping the RSVP Characteristics in Mind

How do paper-pencil assessments measure up in terms of the RSVP characteristics? Let's consider each one in turn.

Reliability

Remember that subjectively scorable tasks will inevitably have lower reliability than objectively scorable tasks.

As we just noted, when we have tasks and questions with definite right and wrong answers—that is, when we have objectively scorable responses—we can evaluate students' responses with a high degree of consistency and reliability. To the extent that we must make subjective judgments about the relative rightness or wrongness of students' responses, reliability will inevitably decrease to some extent.

Standardization

Standardize your paper-pencil assessments as much as possible, but not at the expense of accommodating student diversity.

As a general rule, paper-pencil instruments are easily standardized: We can present similar tasks and instructions to all students, provide similar time limits and environmental conditions, and score everyone's responses in more or less the same way. At the same time, we probably don't want to go overboard in this respect. For example, we may sometimes allow students to choose the topic about which they want to write, perhaps as a way of increasing their sense of self-determination (I refer you to our discussion of intrinsic motivation in Chapter 11). We may also need to tailor assessment tasks to the particular abilities and disabilities of our students with special needs.

Validity

Consider both the extent to which questions or tasks provide an adequate sample of the content domain *and* the extent to which they reflect your instructional objectives.

When we ask questions that require only short, simple responses—questions such as true-false, multiple choice, and matching—we can sample students' knowledge about many topics within a relatively short period of time. In *this* sense, then, such questions may give us greater content validity. Yet in some situations, such items may *not* be an accurate reflection of our instructional objectives. If we want to assess our students' ability to apply the things they've learned to new situations, or if we want to find out how well students can solve problems (especially the ill-defined ones so common in the adult world), we may need to be satisfied with a few tasks requiring lengthy responses, rather than with many tasks that merely assess what students know at a rote level.

We must remember, too, that recognition tasks will not always reflect the objectives we want our students to achieve. For example, when working adults need to recall certain information in order to perform their jobs, they rarely have the assistance of four multiple-choice alternatives to help them remember. Although recognition items may give us higher reliability, in many cases recall tasks will more closely resemble our instructional objectives.

Practicality

Choose paper-pencil assessment over performance assessment if a paper-pencil instrument can yield a valid measure of your objectives.

Paper-pencil assessment is typically more practical than performance assessment; for instance, we will require no "equipment" other than paper and writing implements, and we can easily assess the knowledge and skills of all of our students at the same time. And some paper-pencil assessments—those that are objectively scorable—have the additional advantage of being relatively quick and easy to score.

Because paper-pencil assessment is so practical, it should generally be our method of choice *if* it can also yield a valid measure of what students know and can do. In situations where paper-pencil tasks are clearly *not* a good reflection of what students have learned, however, we may want to sacrifice such practicality to gain the greater validity that a performance assessment might provide.

USING PERFORMANCE ASSESSMENTS

Performance assessment typically takes one of two forms (Gronlund, 1993; E. H. Hiebert, Valencia, & Afflerbach, 1994; Messick, 1994a). In some cases, we can look at tangible *products* that our students have created—perhaps a pen-and-ink drawing, a scientific invention, or a poster depicting a particular foreign country. In other cases, there is no tangible product per se; in such instances, we must look at the specific *behaviors* that our students perform—perhaps an oral report, a forward roll, or an instrumental solo.

Performance assessment enables us to assess students' mastery of objectives in ways that may simply not be possible in a paper-pencil format. It lends itself especially well to the assessment of complex tasks, such as those that involve coordinating a number of skills simultaneously. It may also be especially useful in assessing such higher-level cognitive skills as problem solving, critical thinking, and creativity.

Choosing Appropriate Performance Tasks

There are probably an infinite number of performance tasks that we could use to assess students' mastery of our instructional objectives. Here are just a few of the many possibilities:

- Playing a musical instrument

- Conversing in a foreign language

- Identifying an unknown chemical substance

- Engaging in a debate about social issues

- Taking dictation in shorthand

- Fixing a malfunctioning machine

- Role-playing a job interview

- Performing a workplace routine

- Performing a computer simulation of a real-world task (some examples are from Gronlund, 1993; C. Hill & Larsen, 1992; D. B. Swanson et al., 1995)

We might even consider placing students' knowledge of traditional academic subject matter in a performance-based context. For example, in a history class, rather than give a paper-pencil test, we might ask students to read old letters, speeches, newspaper articles, and so on and then to draw conclusions about the events going on at the time (E. L. Baker, 1994).

As we select tasks for a performance assessment, we must have a clear purpose in mind; more specifically, we must identify the specific conclusions we wish to draw from our observations of students' performance (Airasian, 1994). We must also consider the extent to which any particular task will enable us to make reasonable inferences and generalizations about what our students know and can do (Popham, 1995; Wiggins, 1992).

Constructing and Administering the Assessment

Many of the guidelines I presented in our discussion of paper-pencil assessment are equally relevant for performance assessment; for example, we should:

- Define tasks clearly and unambiguously

- Specify scoring criteria in advance

- Standardize administration procedures as much as possible

- Encourage students to ask questions

Yet there are additional guidelines to keep in mind as well; among other things, we should:

- Consider incorporating the assessment into normal instructional activities

- Provide an appropriate amount of structure

- Plan classroom management strategies for the assessment activity

Considering Whether to Incorporate Assessment into Normal Instructional Activities

Many theorists and practitioners recommend that we incorporate performance assessments into everyday instructional activities (e.g., Arter & Spandel, 1992; Baxter et al., 1996; Boschee & Baron, 1993; C. Hill & Larsen, 1992; Kennedy, 1992; Stiggins, 1994). There are a couple of advantages in doing so. For one thing, we make more efficient use of the limited time we have with our students if we can combine instruction and assessment into one activity. Second, we will reduce the "evaluative" climate in our classroom; you may recall from our discussion in Chapter 11 that external evaluation lowers students' sense of self-determination and may discourage risk taking.

But we must keep in mind that, by instructing and assessing students in one fell swoop, we may not be able to standardize the conditions under which students are being assessed, and we will not necessarily see students' best work. Furthermore, although it is quite appropriate to give students assistance or feedback during instruction, it may often be *in*appropriate to do so during a summative evaluation of what they have achieved (L. M. Carey, 1994). In some situations, then, and especially in cases of important summative evaluations, we may want to conduct the assessment separately from instructional activities, announce it in advance, and give students some guidance as to how they can maximize their performance (Stiggins, 1994).

Providing an Appropriate Amount of Structure

Provide sufficient structure for a performance task to standardize the assessment, but not so much that you reduce the task's authenticity.

In some cases, we will be able to structure performance tasks to some degree; for example, we can provide detailed directions about what we want students to accomplish, what materials and equipment they should use, and how we will evaluate their performance (Gronlund, 1993; E. H. Hiebert et al., 1994; Stiggins, 1994). Such structure will help standardize our assessment and, hence, enable us to evaluate it more reliably. Yet we must keep in mind that, in some situations, too much structure will reduce the authenticity of a task: It may lessen the extent to which it resembles expectations for performance in the outside world. Ultimately, we must consider both reliability and validity as we determine the appropriate amount of structure to impose in any performance assessment.

In some situations, we can incorporate assessment into everyday instructional activities.

Planning Classroom Management Strategies

As we conduct a performance assessment, we must remember two important principles of classroom management that we identified in Chapter 12: Effective teachers are continually aware of what every student is doing (the notion of *withitness*), and they make sure all students are busy and engaged. Particularly in situations when we must assess only a few students (or perhaps only one) at a time, we must make sure other students are actively involved in a learning activity (L. M. Carey, 1994). For example, in an English class, when one student is giving an oral presentation, we might have the other students jot down notes about the topic being presented, including facts they find interesting, ideas they disagree with, and questions they wonder about. In a unit on soccer, when a few students are demonstrating their ability to dribble and pass the ball as they run down the field, we might have other students work in pairs to practice footwork that keeps the ball away from an opponent.

Even when you can only assess a few students at a time, make sure *all* students are busy and engaged.

Scoring Students' Responses

In a few situations, responses to performance assessment tasks will be objectively scorable; for example, we can easily count the number of errors on a typing test, and we can use a stopwatch to time students' performance in a 100-meter dash. But more often than not, we will find ourselves making somewhat subjective decisions when we use performance assessment. There are no clear-cut right or wrong responses when students give oral reports, create sculptures out of clay, or engage in heated debates on controversial issues. If we aren't careful, our judgments may be unduly influenced by the particular expectations we hold for each student (L. M. Carey, 1994; Stiggins, 1994).

Especially in situations when we are conducting summative rather than formative evaluations, we should carefully consider the criteria we want to use to evaluate students' responses. Our criteria should focus on the most important aspects of the desired performance—those aspects most essential to a "good" response (Wiggins, 1992). They should also be relatively few in number—perhaps no more than five or six—so that we can keep track of them as we observe each student's performance (Airasian, 1994; Gronlund, 1993; Popham, 1995).

Can you explain the value of having only a half dozen criteria using the concept of *working memory* (Chapter 6)?

Develop a checklist or rating scale when you are evaluating students' performance with respect to several different criteria.

In many cases, we will want to have a paper-pencil analysis of how each student has performed with respect to each of our criteria (Airasian, 1994; L. M. Carey, 1994; Gronlund, 1993; Stiggins, 1994). Some tasks lend themselves well to **checklists,** whereby we describe our evaluation criteria in terms of specific qualities that a student's response either does or does not have. Other tasks are more appropriately evaluated with **rating scales,** whereby we describe each criterion as a continuum and determine where the student's response falls along that continuum. Figure 14–3 presents examples of how we can evaluate students' performance in terms of either a checklist or a rating scale. Both types of analyses have instructional benefits as well: They identify any specific areas of difficulty that students are having and so give feedback about how performance can be improved.

Keeping the RSVP Characteristics in Mind

Compared with paper-pencil assessment, performance assessment techniques are relative newcomers on the educational scene; hence, educational psychologists are only beginning to address concerns related to reliability, standardization, validity, and practicality. Let's look at the data that researchers report, as well as at strategies for enhancing each of the four RSVP characteristics.

Reliability

Researchers have reported varying degrees of reliability in performance assessments; in many cases, results are inconsistent over time, and different teachers may rate the same performance very differently (R. L. Linn, 1994; Gronlund, 1993; Kennedy, 1992; Shavelson, Baxter, & Pine, 1992; D. B. Swanson et al., 1995). There are probably a couple of reasons why performance assessments often yield low reliability (L. M. Carey, 1994). For one thing, students don't always behave consistently; even in a task as simple as shooting a basketball, a student is likely to make a basket on some occasions but not on others. Second, we sometimes need to evaluate complex behaviors relatively rapidly; things may happen so quickly that we miss important aspects of a student's performance, and we will often have no tangible product that we can look back on and reevaluate.

Remember that a single performance assessment may not be a reliable indicator of what students have achieved.

We must keep in mind, then, that a single performance assessment may very well *not* be a reliable indicator of what our students have achieved. Accordingly, we should ask students to demonstrate behaviors related to important instructional objectives on more than one occasion (Airasian, 1994; L. M. Carey, 1994). And if possible, we should have more than one rater evaluate each student's performance (C. Hill & Larsen, 1992; Stiggins, 1994).

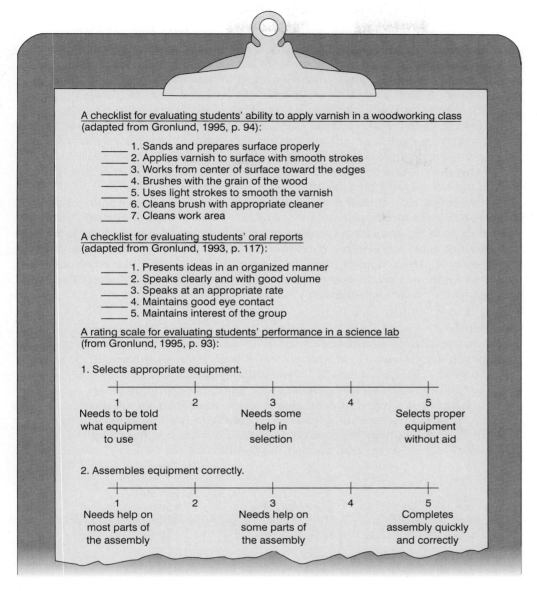

A checklist for evaluating students' ability to apply varnish in a woodworking class
(adapted from Gronlund, 1995, p. 94):

_____ 1. Sands and prepares surface properly
_____ 2. Applies varnish to surface with smooth strokes
_____ 3. Works from center of surface toward the edges
_____ 4. Brushes with the grain of the wood
_____ 5. Uses light strokes to smooth the varnish
_____ 6. Cleans brush with appropriate cleaner
_____ 7. Cleans work area

A checklist for evaluating students' oral reports
(adapted from Gronlund, 1993, p. 117):

_____ 1. Presents ideas in an organized manner
_____ 2. Speaks clearly and with good volume
_____ 3. Speaks at an appropriate rate
_____ 4. Maintains good eye contact
_____ 5. Maintains interest of the group

A rating scale for evaluating students' performance in a science lab
(from Gronlund, 1995, p. 93):

1. Selects appropriate equipment.

1	2	3	4	5
Needs to be told what equipment to use		Needs some help in selection		Selects proper equipment without aid

2. Assembles equipment correctly.

1	2	3	4	5
Needs help on most parts of the assembly		Needs help on some parts of the assembly		Completes assembly quickly and correctly

Figure 14–3   Examples of Checklists and Rating Scales

Standardization

Some performance assessments are easily standardized, but others are not (Airasian, 1994; E. H. Hiebert et al., 1994). For example, if we want to assess typing ability, we can easily make the instructions, time limits, and material to be typed the same for everyone. In contrast, if we want to assess artistic creativity, we may want to give students free rein with regard to the materials they use and the particular products they create. In such nonstandardized situations, it is especially important that we use multiple assessments and look for consistency in students' performance across several occasions.

Refrain from making comparisons among students when a performance assessment isn't standardized for everyone.

Validity

As we have noted, performance assessment tasks are often more valid reflections of what our students have accomplished relative to our instructional objectives. Researchers are finding, however, that students' responses to a *single* performance assessment task are frequently *not* a good indication of their overall achievement (Koretz, Stecher, Klein, & McCaffrey, 1994; R. L. Linn, 1994; Shavelson et al., 1992; D. B. Swanson et al., 1995). *Content validity* is at stake here: If we have time for students to perform only one or two complex tasks, we may not get a sufficiently representative sample of what they have learned and can do. In addition, any biases that affect our judgments—for example, any beliefs that we have about particular students' abilities—may distort the conclusions we draw from their performance, further reducing the validity of our assessments (Airasian, 1994; L. M. Carey, 1994).

As a general rule, then, we will typically want to administer a variety of different performance assessments, or perhaps administer the same task under different conditions, if we want to ensure a reasonable degree of validity in the conclusions we draw from the behaviors we observe (Gronlund, 1993; R. L. Linn, 1994; Messick, 1994a; Shavelson et al., 1992; Stiggins, 1994; D. B. Swanson et al., 1995). For efficiency's sake, we may want to incorporate some of these assessment activities into everyday instructional activities (Shavelson & Baxter, 1992).

Remember that a single performance task may not provide a sufficiently representative sample of the content domain.

Practicality

Unfortunately, performance assessments are often less practical than more traditional paper-pencil assessments (L. M. Carey, 1994; Cizek, 1991; Gronlund, 1993; Kennedy, 1992; Popham, 1995; Shavelson & Baxter, 1992; Worthen & Leopold, 1992). For one thing, administration of an assessment can be quite time-consuming; this is especially true when we must observe students one at a time and when we ask them to perform relatively complex (perhaps authentic) tasks. In addition, we will often need equipment to conduct the assessment, perhaps enough that every student has his or her own set. Clearly, then, we must consider whether the benefits of a performance assessment outweigh any concerns we may have regarding its practicality (Messick, 1994a; Worthen & Leopold, 1992).

Consider whether the benefits of a performance assessment outweigh concerns related to practicality.

> ### INTO THE CLASSROOM
> ### *Using Formal Assessments*
>
> Develop classroom assessments that reflect both the topics you want to assess and the things you expect students to do with those topics.
>
> > A teacher develops a table of specifications for a unit on cooking a balanced meal that his class has just completed, and then he uses it to construct paper-pencil questions and performance tasks that, taken in combination, reflect his instructional objectives.
>
> Let students know what kinds of responses you are expecting.
>
> > When assessing her students' knowledge about color vision, a teacher gives students an essay question that indicates what a good response should include:

"Describe the two major theories of color vision, explain how they are alike and different from a physiological standpoint, and cite evidence that supports each theory."

Maximize the reliability of your results by specifying your scoring criteria in specific, concrete terms.

When evaluating students' progress in their instrumental music class, a music teacher uses several rating scales (e.g., for pitch, tempo) to help him rate their performance consistently.

When holding some or all students to the same standards for achievement, be sure their assessment tasks are identical or equivalent in content, format, administration, and scoring criteria (making appropriate exceptions for students with disabilities).

When three students are absent on the day of a paper-pencil quiz, their teacher writes an alternative set of questions for them based on the same table of specifications he used in constructing the original quiz.

Choose an assessment procedure that will be as practical as possible without sacrificing reliability and validity.

When trying to decide whether to use paper-pencil or performance assessment at the end of a unit on the scientific method, a teacher realizes that a performance test is the only valid way to assess whether students have mastered the ability to separate and control variables. He identifies three performance tasks that he can administer to the class as a whole and believes will adequately reflect their ability to separate and control variables as they test various scientific hypotheses.

Avoid cultural bias in your assessment instruments.

A mathematics teacher creates an assignment in which she asks students to calculate the area of a tennis court. Although she wants to assess her students' ability to calculate area, she realizes that some of her students have probably never played tennis. She rewrites the assignment so that it involves a parking lot instead.

As we've seen, performance assessments are often questionable with regard to reliability and practicality; furthermore, they may give us an insufficient sample of what students have learned. Yet in many situations, they may more closely resemble the long-term objectives we have for our students, and in this sense they may be more valid indicators of students' achievement. As educators gain experience in the use of performance assessment in the years to come, increasingly more valid, reliable, and practical measures of student performance will undoubtedly emerge. In the meantime, the most reliable, valid, and practical assessment strategy overall may be to use *both* paper-pencil and performance assessments when drawing conclusions about what our students have achieved (Gronlund, 1993; R. L. Linn, 1994).

Table 14–4 presents a summary of our RSVP analyses of informal assessment, formal paper-pencil assessment, and formal performance assessment. We turn our attention now to strategies for accommodating student diversity in our assessment practices.

Table 14–4   Evaluating Different Kinds of Assessment in Terms of Their RSVP Characteristics

KIND OF ASSESSMENT	RELIABILITY	STANDARDIZATION	VALIDITY	PRACTICALITY
Informal Assessment	A single, brief assessment is not a reliable indicator of achievement. We must look for consistency in a student's performance across time and in different contexts.	Informal observations are rarely if ever standardized. Thus, we should not compare one student with another on the basis of informal assessment alone.	Students' "public" behavior in the classroom is not always a valid indicator of their achievement; for example, some may try to hide a high level of achievement from their peers.	Informal assessment is definitely practical: It is flexible and can occur spontaneously during classroom instruction.
Formal Paper-Pencil Assessment	Objectively scorable items are highly reliable. We can enhance the reliability of subjectively scorable items by specifying scoring criteria in advance and in concrete terms.	In most instances, paper-pencil instruments are easily standardized for all students. Giving students choices (e.g., about topics to write about or questions to answer), though advantageous from a motivational standpoint, reduces standardization.	Numerous questions and tasks that require only short, simple responses maximize the likelihood that the assessment is a representative sample of the content domain. Questions and tasks requiring lengthier responses, however, may sometimes more closely match our instructional objectives.	Paper-pencil assessment is usually practical: All students can be assessed at once, and no special materials are required.
Formal Performance Assessment	It is often difficult to score performance assessment tasks reliably. We can enhance reliability by specifying scoring criteria in advance and in concrete terms.	Some performance assessment tasks are easily standardized, whereas others may not be.	Performance assessment sometimes provides a more valid measure of what students know and can do than paper-pencil assessment. A single performance task, however, may have low content validity in the sense that it does not provide a representative sample of the content domain. Thus, we should draw conclusions about students' achievement only on the basis of several different performance tasks.	Performance assessment is typically less practical than other approaches: It may involve special materials, and it can take a fair amount of classroom time, especially if students must be assessed one at a time.

TAKING STUDENT DIVERSITY INTO ACCOUNT

As we develop and implement ways to assess our students' learning and achievement, we must remember that students often differ from one another in ways that affect their performance in assessment situations. When two students have *learned equally* yet *per-*

form differently on our assessments, then the information we obtain from those assessments may have questionable validity. In the next few pages, we will look at the effects of student diversity from three angles:

- Cultural bias
- Language differences
- Testwiseness

We will then more specifically consider how we might adapt our classroom assessment procedures to accommodate students with special needs.

Minimizing Cultural Bias

■ EXPERIENCING FIRSTHAND
Predicting the Future

Imagine you are taking a test designed to predict your success in future situations. Here are the first three questions on the test:

1. When you enter a hogan, in which direction should you move around the fire?

2. Why is turquoise often attached to a baby's cradleboard?

3. If you need black wool for weaving a rug, you can obtain the blackest color by (choose one):

    a. dying wool by using a mixture of sumac, ochre, and piñon gum.
    b. dying wool by using a mixture of indigo, lichen, and mesquite.
    c. using the undyed wool of specially bred black sheep.

Try to answer these questions before you read further. ■

Did you have trouble answering some or all of the questions? If so, your difficulty was probably due to the fact that the questions are written from the perspective of a particular culture—that of the Navajos. Unless you have had considerable exposure to Navajo culture, you would probably perform poorly on the test. By the way, the three answers are: (1) clockwise; (2) to ward off evil; and (3) dying wool by using a mixture of sumac, ochre, and piñon gum (Gilpin, 1968).

Is the test culturally biased? That depends. If the test is designed to assess your ability to succeed in a Navajo community, then the questions I just presented may be very appropriate. But if it's designed to assess your ability to succeed in a school system in which knowledge of Navajo culture is totally irrelevant, then such questions are culturally biased.

An assessment instrument has **cultural bias** if any of its items either offend or unfairly penalize some students on the basis of their ethnicity, gender, or socioeconomic status (e.g., Popham, 1995). For example, imagine a test question that implies that boys are more competent than girls, and imagine another that has a picture in which members of a particular ethnic group are engaging in criminal behavior. Such questions have cultural bias because some groups of students (girls, in the first situation, and members of the depicted ethnic group, in the second) may be offended by the questions and

Note that the term *cultural bias* includes biases related to gender and socioeconomic status, as well as to culture.

Scrutinize your assessment instruments carefully for tasks that some students might find offensive or have difficulty answering solely because of their ethnicity, gender, or socioeconomic status.

thus distracted from doing their best on the test. And consider these two assessment tasks:

- Would you rather swim in an ocean, a lake, or a swimming pool? Write a two-page essay defending your choice.

- Mary is making a patchwork quilt from 100 separate squares of fabric, like so:

Each square of fabric has a perimeter of 20 inches. Mary sews the squares together, using a 1/2-inch seam allowance. She then sews the assembled set of squares to a large piece of cotton that will serve as the flip side of the quilt, again using a 1/2-inch seam allowance. What will be the perimeter of the finished quilt?

The first task will obviously be difficult for students who haven't been swimming in all three environments, and even more difficult for those who haven't ever swum at all; students from low-income families might easily fall into one of these two categories. The second task assumes a fair amount of knowledge about sewing (e.g., about what a "seam allowance" is); this is knowledge that some students (especially girls) are more likely to have than others. Such tasks have cultural bias because some students will perform better than others because of differences in their background experiences, *not* because of differences in what they have learned in the classroom.

Look back at the treehouse problem depicted on page 333. Is this problem culturally biased? Why or why not?

Considering Language Differences

When students have little facility with English, minimize your dependence on language to assess knowledge and skills that are not linguistic in nature.

We must remember, too, that students' facility with the English language will often affect their performance on our classroom assessments. Poor reading and writing skills are likely to interfere with success on paper-pencil tasks; poor speaking skills will adversely influence students' ability to accomplish such performance tasks as classroom debates or oral reports. If we are trying to assess students' achievement in areas unrelated to the language arts—perhaps achievement in mathematics, music, or physical education—then we may in some instances want to minimize our dependence on language to assess those areas.

Promoting Testwiseness

■ EXPERIENCING FIRSTHAND
Califractions

Imagine you are enrolled in a course called Califractions. One day, your instructor gives you a surprise quiz before you've had a chance to do the assigned readings. The three quiz questions are presented below; see whether you can figure out the correct answers even though you *haven't* studied any califractions. Choose the single best answer for each item.

1. Because they are furstier than other califractions, califors are most often used to

   a. reassignment of matherugs.
   b. disbobble a fwing.
   c. mangelation.
   d. in the burfews.

2. Calendation is a process of

   a. combining two califors.
   b. adding two califors together.
   c. joining two califors.
   d. taking two califors apart.

3. The furstiest califraction is the

   a. califor.
   b. calderost.
   c. calinga.
   d. calidater.   ■

You may have found that you were able to answer the questions even though you knew nothing whatsoever about califractions. Because the first quiz item says ". . . califors are most often used to . . .," the answer must begin with a verb. Alternatives *a* and *c* apparently begin with nouns ("reassign*ment*" and "mangel*ation*"), and *d* begins with a preposition ("in"), so *b* is the only possible correct answer. Item 2 presents three alternatives (*a, b,* and *c*) that all say the same thing, so because there can only be one right answer, the correct choice must be *d.* And the answer to Item 3 (the "furstiest califraction") must be *a* (a califor) because Item 1 has already stated that califors are furstier than other califractions.

If you did well on the califractions quiz, then you have some degree of **testwiseness;** that is, you use test-taking strategies that enhance your test performance. Testwiseness includes strategies such as these:

- *Using time efficiently:* for example, allocating enough time for each task and saving difficult items for last

- *Avoiding sloppy errors:* for example, checking answers a second time and erasing any stray pencil marks on a computer-scored answer sheet

- *Deductive reasoning:* for example, eliminating two alternatives that say the same thing and using information from one question to answer another

- *Guessing:* for example, eliminating obviously wrong alternatives and then guessing one of the others, and guessing randomly if time runs out and there is no penalty for guessing (Millman, Bishop, & Ebel, 1965; Petersen, Sudweeks, & Baird, 1990)

Even when we can find no culturally biased content in the assessment instruments we use, we must remember that some students may not be familiar with certain types of assessment tasks; for example, students whose prior schooling has occurred within a different culture may be inexperienced in answering true-false, multiple-choice, or essay questions. In some instances, we may be able to make our assessment tasks similar to those with which students have had previous experience. In other situations—perhaps when the school district requests that we give a standardized, multiple-choice achievement test—we should be sure to explain the general nature of the tasks involved (Popham, 1990). For example, we might mention that we don't expect students to know all the answers, and we might point out that many students will not have sufficient time to answer every question. We should also give students ample practice with the forms of any test items or performance tasks we use (Popham, 1990). For example, we might give them some simple multiple-choice tests covering content they know well, and we might give them practice in filling out computer-scored answer forms.

Familiarize students with assessment formats and procedures that are new to them.

Such concerns point to the need for considerable flexibility in our approaches to classroom assessment; they also underscore the importance of assessing students' achievement in a variety of ways, rather than overly depending on a single instrument (Drake, 1993; C. Hill & Larsen, 1992; Sleeter & Grant, 1994). Ultimately, our assessment practices should be fair and equitable to *all* students, regardless of their ethnicity, gender, or socioeconomic status.

Accommodating Students with Special Needs

In some situations, we will have to adapt our classroom assessment instruments to accommodate students with special educational needs. For example, we may need to read paper-pencil test questions to students with limited reading skills (e.g., as is characteristic of some students with learning disabilities). We may need to break a lengthy assessment task into a number of shorter tasks for students with a limited attention span (e.g., for some students with emotional and behavioral disorders). And we may have to devise individualized assessment instruments when we have different instructional objectives for some of our students with special needs (e.g., as may often be the case for students with mental retardation). Additional accommodations for students with special needs are presented in Table 14–5.

Whenever we modify our classroom assessment instruments for students with special needs, we must recognize that there is a trade-off between two of our RSVP characteristics. On the one hand, we are violating the idea that an assessment instrument should be equivalent in content, administration, and so on for everyone—the idea that assessment should be standardized. On the other hand, if we fail to accommodate the particu-

Table 14–5 *Assessing Classroom Achievement in Students with Special Educational Needs*

STUDENTS WITH SPECIAL NEEDS	CHARACTERISTICS THAT THESE STUDENTS MAY EXHIBIT	CLASSROOM STRATEGIES THAT MAY BE BENEFICIAL FOR THESE STUDENTS
Students with specific cognitive or academic deficits	Difficulty processing specific kinds of information Poor listening and/or reading skills Possibly inconsistent performance on classroom assessments due to off-task behaviors (e.g., hyperactivity, inattentiveness)	Look at students' errors for clues about processing difficulties. Make sure that students understand what you want them to do. Minimize reliance on reading skills. Allow extra time for students to process the task before them. Be sure that students are sufficiently motivated to perform well on an assessment. Use performance assessments in cases where students have poor reading and writing skills. Use informal assessments to either confirm or disconfirm results of formal assessments. Monitor students' progress on a regular basis.
Students with specific social or behavioral deficits	Possibly inconsistent performance on classroom assessments due to off-task behaviors or lack of motivation	Be sure that students are sufficiently motivated to perform well on an assessment. Use informal assessments to either confirm or disconfirm results of formal assessments. Monitor students' progress on a regular basis.
Students with general delays in cognitive and social functioning	Slow learning and information processing Limited if any reading skills Poor listening skills	Make sure that students understand what you are asking them to do. Make sure that any reading required on assessment instruments is sufficiently simple that students can understand them. Use performance assessments that require little if any reading or writing. Allow sufficient time for students to complete assigned tasks. Monitor students' progress on a regular basis.
Students with advanced cognitive development	Greater ability to perform exceptionally complex tasks Unusual, sometimes creative, responses to classroom assessment instruments Tendency in some students to hide giftedness to avoid possible ridicule by peers (e.g., African American students may fear that they will be "acting White" if they demonstrate high performance)	Use performance assessments to assess complex activities. Establish criteria for "correct" responses that allow unusual and creative responses. Provide opportunities for students to demonstrate their achievements privately. Keep assessment results confidential.

Sources: DeLisle, 1984; Eccles, 1989; D. Y. Ford & Harris, 1992; Maker & Schiever, 1989; C. D. Mercer, 1991; D. P. Morgan & Jenson, 1988; Patton, Beirne-Smith, & Payne, 1990; B. N. Phillips, Pitcher, Worsham, & Miller, 1980; Piirto, 1994; Scarcella, 1990; Udall, 1989.

Compiled with the assistance of Dr. Margie Garanzini-Daiber and Dr. Margaret Cohen, University of Missouri—St. Louis.

lar disabilities that some of our students may have, we will inevitably obtain results that have little or no meaning—results with little validity regarding the knowledge and skills that our students have acquired. There is no magic formula for determining a reasonable balance between standardization and validity for students with special needs; as teachers, we must use our best professional judgment in each and every case.

SUMMARIZING STUDENTS' ACHIEVEMENT

Many of our assessments will provide a considerable amount of information regarding students' strengths and weaknesses—information that we must eventually boil down into more general indicators of what our students have learned. Initially, we may simply want to determine *test scores* that reflect the overall quality of students' responses on either a paper-pencil or performance assessment. Eventually, we will need to summarize what they have achieved over the course of the semester or school year, perhaps through *final class grades* or *portfolios*. But regardless of how we summarize and report students' achievement, we must maintain *confidentiality* regarding our assessments. We turn to each of these topics now.

Assigning Test Scores

THINKING ABOUT WHAT YOU KNOW

In what different ways has your own performance on classroom assessments been summarized? How often has it been described in terms of the number or percentage of items you answered correctly? How often has it been described in terms of a percentile rank that told you how you compared with your peers? What other kinds of scores have you gotten? Have you ever had trouble figuring out just what a particular test score meant?

Students' performance on a particular assessment is often summarized in terms of a single *test score*. These scores typically take one of three forms: raw scores, criterion-referenced scores, and norm-referenced scores.

Raw Scores

Sometimes a test score is simply the number or percentage of tasks or questions to which a student has responded correctly. Sometimes it is the sum of all the points a student has earned—two points for one task, five for another, and so on. In situations such as these, we have a **raw score**—a score based solely on the number or point value of correct responses.

Use raw scores only when their meaning is easily understood.

Raw scores are easy to calculate, and they appear to be easy to understand. But in fact, we sometimes have trouble knowing what raw scores really mean. For example, is 75% a good score or a bad one? Without knowing what kinds of tasks an assessment instrument includes or how other students have performed on the same assessment, there is no way to determine how good or bad a score of 75% really is. For this reason, raw scores are not always as useful as criterion-referenced or norm-referenced scores.

Criterion-Referenced Scores

A **criterion-referenced score** tells us what students have achieved in relation to specific instructional objectives. Many criterion-referenced scores are "either-or" scores:

They indicate that a student has passed or failed a unit, mastered or not mastered a skill, or met or not met an objective. Others indicate various levels of competence or achievement. For example, a criterion-referenced score on a fifth-grade test of written composition might reflect four levels of writing ability, three of which are acceptable, as follows:

Whenever possible, relate students' test scores to specific instructional objectives.

In progress: Is an underdeveloped and/or unfocused message.

Essential: Is a series of related ideas. The pattern of organization and the descriptive or supporting details are adequate and appropriate.

Proficient: Meets Essential Level criteria and contains a logical progression of ideas. The pattern of organization and the transition of ideas flow. Word choice enhances the writing.

Advanced: Meets Proficient Level criteria and contains examples of one or more of the following: insight, creativity, fluency, critical thinking, or style. (From "District 6 Writing Assessment, Narrative and Persuasive Modes, Scoring Criteria, Intermediate Level" [Working Copy] by School District 6 [Greeley/Evans, CO], 1993. Adapted by permission)

If a particular assessment instrument is designed to assess only one instructional objective, then it may yield a single score. If it is designed to assess several objectives simultaneously, a student's performance may be reported as a checklist of the various objectives passed and not passed. As an example, a student's performance in a swimming class is often reported in a multiple-objective, criterion-referenced fashion (see Figure 14–4).

Figure 14–4   In this swimming class, students' performance is reported in a criterion-referenced fashion.

In most cases, we will probably want to use a criterion-referenced approach to summarize what our students have learned. Only through criterion-referenced assessment can we determine what specific objectives they have attained, what particular skills they have mastered, and where their individual weaknesses lie.

Norm-Referenced Scores

A **norm-referenced score** is derived by comparing a student's performance on an assessment task with the performance of other students (perhaps that of classmates or that of a nationwide *norm group*) on the same task. Rather than tell us specifically what a student has or has not learned, such a score tells us how well the student stacks up against his or her peers.

Norm-referenced scores are frequently used to report the results of standardized tests, and the norm group to which students are compared is often a large, national sample of students who have previously taken the same test. Norm-referenced scores for standardized tests take a number of different forms; some of the most common ones are described in Appendix B ("Interpreting Standardized Test Scores").

When we assign norm-referenced scores on our own teacher-developed assessments, the norm group is likely to be all the students we have in class at the present time: We give high scores to students who exhibit the best performance and low scores to students who, comparatively speaking, perform poorly. To use common lingo, we are "grading on the curve."

For teacher-developed assessments, norm-referenced scores may occasionally be appropriate. For example, such comparative scores may be necessary when designating "first chair" in an instrumental music class or choosing the best entries for a regional science fair. We may also need to resort to a norm-referenced approach when assessing complex skills that are difficult to describe in "mastery" terms (Gronlund & Linn, 1990). Some complex tasks—for example, writing poetry, demonstrating advanced athletic skills, or critically analyzing works of literature—can sometimes be evaluated more easily by comparing students with one another than by specifying an absolute level of accomplishment.

We should probably *not* assign norm-referenced test scores on a regular basis, however. For one thing, such scores tell us little about what we most need to know—whether our students have mastered our instructional objectives. Second, as we discovered in Chapter 11, competitive situations create many more losers than winners; such situations are likely to undermine students' self-efficacy, hence also undermining their intrinsic motivation to learn classroom material. And finally, norm-referenced scores are inconsistent with the *sense of community* that we discussed in Chapter 12.

Whenever we assign scores to students' performance on our classroom assessments, we must also remember the important feedback function that such assessments serve. Accordingly, we should always accompany our test scores with specific, concrete feedback about the strengths and weaknesses of students' responses, as well as with suggestions that can help them improve over the long run (Bangert-Drowns et al., 1991; Deci & Ryan, 1985; Spaulding, 1992).

Determining Final Class Grades

Teachers' grading practices have been a source of considerable controversy among educators. Fueling the controversy are several problems inherent in our attempts to assign

Use norm-referenced scores only when you truly need to compare your students with one another.

Some educators believe that classroom assessment scores should *always* be criterion-referenced, rather than norm-referenced. What do you think?

D: The student has mastered some but not all of the basics in the content do-main. He or she lacks many prerequisites for future learning tasks.

F: The student shows little if any mastery of instructional objectives and cannot demonstrate the most elementary knowledge and skills. He or she lacks most of the prerequisites essential for success in future learning tasks. (based on criteria described by Frisbie & Waltman, 1992)

It can be quite a challenge to summarize students' many achievements in terms of a single class grade, and we inevitably lose a great deal of information in the process. Hence, some educators advocate that we use other techniques for communicating what students have achieved—techniques that reflect the multifaceted nature of students' ac-complishments. One strategy now gaining wide acceptance is the use of *portfolios.*

Using Portfolios

A **portfolio** is a systematic collection of a student's work over a lengthy period of time. For example, students might collect examples of their essays, poems, or artwork. Yet the contents of a portfolio are not always limited to products that can be represented on pa-per; they might also include audiotapes, videotapes, or objects that the student has cre-ated. Some portfolios are "developmental" in nature: Various products are included to show how a student has improved over a period of time. But others may include only the student's best work as a reflection of his or her final achievement (Winograd & Jones, 1992).

Advocates of portfolios offer a number of suggestions for using portfolios effec-tively. More specifically, they recommend that we:

- Consider the specific purpose for which a portfolio will be used

- Involve students in the selection of a portfolio's contents

- Identify the criteria by which products should be selected and evaluated

- Encourage students to reflect on the products they include

- Keep in mind both the strengths and weaknesses of using portfolios for sum-mative evaluation

Considering the Purpose for Which the Portfolio Will Be Used

Different kinds of portfolios are useful for different purposes. Developmental portfolios—those that include products from throughout the school year or perhaps from an even longer period of time—are most useful when we want to see whether our students are making reasonable progress toward long-term instructional objectives. Such portfolios are also invaluable for showing students *themselves* how much they've improved. In contrast, "best work" portfolios are more useful for summarizing stu-dents' final achievement, perhaps as a way of communicating students' accomplish-ments to parents, students' future teachers, or college admissions officers (Airasian, 1994; Arter & Spandel, 1992).

Consider whether a developmental portfolio or a "best work" portfolio is more appropriate.

Involving Students in the Selection of Contents

In most situations, students themselves should decide which products to include in their portfolios (Arter & Spandel, 1992; F. L. Paulson, Paulson, & Meyer, 1991; Popham,

A portfolio of a student's work provides a way of summarizing the student's progress and achievements over a period of time.

Let students choose products to include, but give them the guidance they need to make appropriate choices.

Identify the criteria by which individual products and entire portfolios should be judged. Consider including students in this decision-making process.

Have students explain why they made the choices they did.

1995; Stiggins, 1994). Such practice allows them to feel some "ownership" of their portfolios and, as a result, can enhance their sense of self-determination and their intrinsic motivation to learn.

At the same time, we must give our students the scaffolding they need to make appropriate choices. One effective way of doing so is to schedule periodic conferences with each student in which we jointly discuss the products that best reflect his or her achievements (Popham, 1995). (My son Jeff's teacher also includes parents in such conferences—an excellent strategy for fostering a three-way communication among teacher, student, and parents). We might also want to provide examples of portfolios that other students have created; however, we should do so only if we can keep the identity of those students confidential (F. L. Paulson et al., 1991; Stiggins, 1994).

Identifying Criteria for Selection and Evaluation

As a way of providing additional guidance, it is essential that we identify both the criteria that students should use to make their selections and, if applicable, the criteria by which the entire portfolios will eventually be evaluated (Airasian, 1994; Arter & Spandel, 1992; Popham, 1995; Stiggins, 1994). In some instances, we may want to include our students in the process of identifying these criteria (Popham, 1995). Such a strategy further enhances their sense of self-determination; it can also enhance their understanding of the qualities that are most important in their future projects and assignments.

Encouraging Self-Reflection

In addition to examples of students' work, many portfolios also include documentation that describes each product and the reason why it was included (Arter & Spandel, 1992; L. M. Carey, 1994; F. L. Paulson et al., 1991; Stiggins, 1994). As an example, consider how a student in a creative writing class might explain the selection of two short stories for his portfolio:

> I wrote this first short story last October. It was my first attempt at creative writing. It includes a conflict, a protagonist and antagonist, a climax, and a final resolution. Although the basic elements of a story are there, the main characters aren't developed very much. Also, I don't think the final resolution is likely to happen in real life.

> I wrote this second story in April. It is definitely better than the one I wrote in October. It has more characters, and each one has a personality. The first part of the story foreshadows some of the things that happen later on. The sequence of events is more realistic. It's not a case where everyone lives happily ever after.

Such documentation encourages students to reflect on and judge their own work in ways that we, as teachers, typically do (Airasian, 1994; Arter & Spandel, 1992; Popham, 1995). Thus, it is likely to promote the self-observation and self-evaluation skills that social cognitive theorists advocate; in other words, it will help them develop the self-regulatory capabilities so essential for their long-term success.

Keeping in Mind the Strengths and Weaknesses of Portfolios

Using portfolios has a couple of advantages (Arter & Spandel, 1992; C. Hill & Larsen, 1992; F. L. Paulson et al., 1991; Popham, 1995). First of all, portfolios capture the complex nature of students' achievement, often over a prolonged period of time, in ways that single letter grades can't possibly do. Furthermore, they provide a mechanism through which we can easily intertwine assessment with instruction: Students are likely to include products that we may have assigned primarily for instructional purposes, and they will begin to apply fairly objective criteria when evaluating their own work. In fact, portfolios sometimes influence the very nature of the instruction that takes place; because the focus is on complex skills, teachers may be more likely to *teach* those skills (Koretz et al., 1994).

Use portfolios as a way of capturing the complex nature of students' achievement. Use them also as a means of integrating assessment with instruction.

At the same time, we should note that our RSVP characteristics may be sources of concern. For one thing, when portfolios must be scored in some way, such scoring is often unreliable: There may be little agreement among teachers as to how any particular portfolio should be rated (Koretz et al., 1994; Popham, 1995). Furthermore, we have an obvious standardization problem: Because each portfolio will include a unique set of products, we will be evaluating each student on the basis of different information. We must consider a possible problem with validity as well: A portfolio must include a sufficient number of work samples to provide a representative sample of what our students have accomplished related to our instructional objectives (Arter & Spandel, 1992; Koretz et al., 1994). Last but not least, we must realize that portfolios, if used properly, are likely to take a great deal of a teacher's time, both during class and after hours (Airasian, 1994; Koretz et al., 1994; Popham, 1995); in this sense at least, they are less practical than other methods of summarizing achievement might be. All this is not to say that we should shy away from using portfolios. It *is* to say that we must use them cautiously when they serve as summative evaluations of what our students have accomplished.

Keep in mind the limitations of portfolios with respect to the RSVP characteristics.

Keeping Assessment Results Confidential

Regardless of how we summarize students' achievement—whether it be through test scores, final grades, portfolios, or some other means—we must remember that such summaries must remain *confidential,* known only to ourselves, individual students, their parents, and school officials who reasonably need to be aware of our assessment results. In some countries, such confidentiality is mandated by federal legislation: It is actually illegal to share students' test scores, grades, and school records with other students or with the general public.*

Keeping students' assessment results confidential makes educational as well as legal sense. Students may feel embarrassed or ashamed if their classmates are aware of their low test scores and grades, and they may become even more anxious about their future classroom performance than they would be otherwise. Students with high assessment results may suffer from the revelation of these results as well: In many classrooms, it isn't "cool" to be smart, and high achievers may actually perform at lower levels to avoid risking the rejection of their peers.

INTO THE CLASSROOM

Summarizing Students' Achievement

Base your grades on objective and observable data.

> Carolyn always sits passively at the back of the classroom and never contributes to class discussions. Her teacher is surprised when she earns high scores on his first two classroom tests. He finally realizes that, despite Carolyn's lack of class participation, she is definitely achieving his instructional objectives and so grades her accordingly.

Use as many sources of data as reasonably possible to determine grades.

> When determining semester grades, a teacher considers her students' performance on five paper-pencil tests, three formal performance assessments, a research paper, and numerous smaller assignments.

Don't count everything.

> A teacher frequently assigns homework as a way of encouraging students to practice new skills. He gives students feedback on their work but does not consider these assignments when determining course grades.

Evaluate actual achievement separately from such other factors as effort, improvement, and extra credit projects.

> At a parent-teacher conference, a teacher describes Stan's performance this way: "Stan has gotten all Bs and Cs this term—grades that indicate adequate but not exceptional achievement. I have noticed a great deal of inconsistency in his classroom performance. When he puts forth the effort, he learns class material quite well; otherwise, he does poorly."

Assign criterion-referenced grades unless there is a compelling reason to do otherwise.

---

* In the United States, the relevant legislation is the *Family Educational Rights and Privacy Act* (FERPA). This legislation, also known as the Buckley Amendment, was passed by the United States Congress in 1974.

> A teacher assigns criterion-referenced grades for Algebra I, knowing that those grades will be used by school counselors to determine an appropriate math class for each student next year.

Use portfolios to summarize students' accomplishment of complex, multifaceted tasks.

> A teacher has students develop portfolios of their fiction and nonfiction writing. These portfolios are shared with parents at the end of the school year as a way of documenting the progress that each student has made and the skills that each has mastered.

Keep all assessment results confidential.

> When handing back students' test papers, a teacher hands each test directly to its owner, folding the upper corner of the top sheet so that the test score cannot be seen by classmates.

LOOKING AT THE BIG PICTURE: KEEPING CLASSROOM ASSESSMENT IN PERSPECTIVE

As should be evident by now, there is no way we can reasonably separate assessment from planning and instruction. For example, we have often noted that our assessment tasks must reflect the specific instructional objectives we identified weeks or months earlier when we first planned our course of action in the classroom. We have also noted that our assessment tools are ultimately instructional tools as well. For example, regular assessment provides an opportunity for students to review, practice, and apply the things they have learned in the classroom; it also provides invaluable feedback to both us and our students as to the next best steps to take—whether to spend more time on the same topics or to proceed to new ones, whether to stick with the instructional strategies we've been using or try different approaches, and so on. And the very nature of the assessment tasks we give affects both the things that students believe are most important to learn and the ways in which they study and process information.

As we have seen, the usefulness of various assessment techniques depends on how well matched they are to the situations in which we want to use them and how reliable and valid they are for those situations. Because no assessment instrument ever has perfect reliability or validity, we should never take the results of any single assessment too seriously. Nor should we use our assessment results as an indication that some students are permanently low-achieving or incapable. We must ultimately think of our classroom assessment strategies as tools that will enable us to make more informed decisions about how best to improve classroom instruction and help our students learn and achieve.

Think of classroom assessments primarily as tools that can help you improve classroom instruction and student performance.

Because no assessment instrument has perfect reliability or validity, we should never take the results of any single assessment too seriously.

Knowing that frequent review of class material leads to higher achievement and that a paper-pencil test is one way of providing such review, Mr. Bloskas tells his middle school science students that they will have a quiz every Friday. As a first-year teacher, he has had little experience developing test questions, so he decides to use the questions in the "test bank" that accompanies the class textbook. The night before the first quiz, Mr. Bloskas types thirty multiple-choice and true-false items from the test bank, making sure they cover the specific topics that he has covered in class.

His students complain that the questions are "picky." As he looks carefully at his quiz, he realizes that they are right: The quiz measures nothing more than rote memorization of trivial details. So when he prepares the second quiz, he casts the test bank aside and writes two essay questions asking students to apply scientific principles they have studied to real-life situations. He's proud of his efforts: His quiz clearly measures higher-level thinking skills.

The following Friday, his students complain even more loudly about the second quiz than they had about the first ("This is too hard!" "We never studied this stuff!" "I liked the first quiz better!"). And as Mr. Bloskas scores his students' essays, he is appalled to discover how poorly they have performed. "Back to the test bank," he tell himself.

- What mistakes does Mr. Bloskas make in developing the first quiz? What mistakes does he make in constructing the second quiz? To what extent is each quiz likely to have content validity?

- Why do the students react as negatively as they do to the second test?

SUMMING UP

Assessment and Its Purposes

Assessment is a process of observing a sample of students' behavior and drawing inferences about their knowledge and abilities. In some instances, we will use assessment primarily to facilitate students' future learning and perhaps to promote greater self-regulation; here we are talking about *formative* evaluation. In other situations, we will use assessment to determine whether students have achieved our instructional objectives so that we can make appropriate decisions about the logical next step for students to take; in this case, we are talking about *summative* evaluation. Regardless of our primary purpose in assessing students' achievement, we must remember that the nature of our assessment instruments—for example, whether they measure

lower-level or higher-level skills—will give students messages about what things are most important for them to learn and about how they should study and process information in the future.

Characteristics of Good Assessment

We should keep four "RSVP" characteristics in mind as we develop our classroom assessment strategies. First, an assessment instrument should be *reliable*, yielding consistent results regardless of the circumstances in which we administer and score it. Second, it should be *standardized*, in the sense that it has similar content and is administered and scored in a similar manner for everyone. Third, it should be *valid*, being an accurate reflection of the knowledge or skills we are trying to assess. And finally, it should be *practical,* staying within reasonable costs and time constraints.

Informal Versus Formal Assessment

As teachers, we may sometimes assess students' achievement in relatively informal ways, perhaps simply by observing what they do and listening to what they say. At other times, we will assess achievement more formally, through either paper-pencil or performance-based instruments we have developed ahead of time. Whenever we must draw firm conclusions about what our students have and have not achieved—for example, when we are assigning final grades—we should base those conclusions largely on formal assessments that have some degree of validity and reliability. Especially important in this context is *content validity:* Our assessment tasks should provide a representative sample of what students have accomplished relative to our instructional objectives.

Accommodating Student Diversity

Students often differ from one another in ways that affect their performance on assessment tasks. Two students may have acquired identical knowledge and skills, yet perform differently on a classroom assessment— perhaps because they have difficulties in reading, writing, or processing certain kinds of information (e.g., as might be the case for a student with a learning disability) or perhaps because our assessment instrument is culturally biased. Whenever we suspect that such factors may be impeding students' performance, we should interpret our assessment results cautiously and look for other information that would either confirm or disconfirm those results.

Summarizing Students' Achievement

We will probably need to boil down the results of our assessments into more general indicators of what students have learned. Initially, we will simply want to determine *test scores* that reflect the overall quality of students' responses on either a paper-pencil or performance assessment. Such scores will usually have more meaning when they are either criterion-referenced (when they indicate whether certain objectives have been met) or, in some situations, norm-referenced (when they indicate how each student's performance compares with that of others). Eventually, we will also need to summarize what students have achieved over the course of the semester or school year, perhaps through *final class grades* or *portfolios.* Regardless of how we summarize our students' achievement, we must restrict knowledge of our conclusions to individual students, their parents, and any school personnel involved in making decisions about them.

KEY CONCEPTS

assessment (p. 636)
standardized tests (p. 636)
norms (p. 637)
teacher-developed assessment
  instruments (p. 637)
paper-pencil versus performance
  assessment (p. 637)
traditional versus authentic assessment
  (p. 638)
informal versus formal assessment
  (p. 638)

formative versus summative evaluation
  (p. 639)
reliability (p. 648)
standardization (p. 651)
validity (p. 652)
construct validity (p. 652)
predictive validity (p. 652)
content validity (p. 653)
practicality (p. 653)
table of specifications (p. 658)
recognition task (p. 661)

recall task (p. 661)
test anxiety (p. 663)
checklist (p. 670)
rating scale (p. 670)
cultural bias (p. 675)
testwiseness (p. 677)
raw score (p. 680)
criterion-referenced score (p. 680)
norm-referenced score (p. 682)
portfolio (p. 687)

Developing as a Teacher

THINKING ABOUT WHAT YOU KNOW

- In Parts 1 and 2 of the book, we derived numerous strategies from our understanding of development, individual and group differences, learning, and motivation. Here in Part 3, we've identified additional strategies as we've considered issues in planning, instruction, and assessment. Reflecting back on all the topics we've discussed, which strategies do you think will be especially useful to you in your own classroom teaching?

- Were any of the principles you encountered in this book inconsistent with things you had previously believed? If so, how have you resolved the inconsistencies? Have you revised some of your existing knowledge in light of the new things you've learned? Have you discarded some of your earlier notions altogether? In some cases, have you held fast to the things you believe despite evidence to the contrary, and if so, can you justify your position on the basis of theory and research?

YOU HAVE, I HOPE, LEARNED A GREAT DEAL from reading this book. As a quick measure of how much you've learned, retake the OOPS Test in the exercise that follows.

■ EXPERIENCING FIRSTHAND
OOPS Again

Here is *Ormrod's Own Psychological Survey* (OOPS) once again. Decide whether each of the following statements is *true* or *false*.

1. Most children five years of age and older are natural learners; they know the best way to learn something without having to be taught how to learn it. T F
2. By the time they reach second grade, most children believe that rules should be obeyed even when there are no consequences for breaking them. T F
3. Scores on intelligence (IQ) tests usually give us some idea about how well students are likely to achieve academically. T F
4. When we compare boys and girls, we find that both groups are, on the average, very similar in their mathematical and verbal aptitudes. T F
5. The best way to learn and remember a new fact is to repeat it over and over again. T F
6. When a student makes comments that contain erroneous beliefs about classroom subject matter, it is best for a teacher to ignore those comments and call on someone else. T F
7. Such activities as memorizing poems and solving logic problems are helpful because they provide general exercise for students' minds and help students learn better over the long run. T F
8. Taking notes during a lecture usually interferes with students' learning more than it helps. T F
9. Students often misjudge how much they know about a topic. T F
10. Teachers can reduce inappropriate student behaviors without necessarily having to deal with the underlying causes of those behaviors. T F
11. When teachers reward an individual student for appropriate behavior, the behavior of other students may also improve. T F
12. Even small amounts of anxiety interfere with students' ability to learn and perform effectively in the classroom. T F
13. A well-designed lecture can be an effective way to promote student learning. T F
14. A disadvantage of even the best cooperative learning activity is that only a few students do most or all of the work. T F
15. The nature of the tests that teachers give affects the ways in which students study and learn classroom material. T F
    Now check your answers against the answer key below. ■

Answers: (1) false, (2) false, (3), true, (4) true, (5) false, (6) false, (7) false, (8) false, (9) true, (10) true, (11) true, (12) false, (13) true, (14) false, (15) true.

I hope you did much better on the OOPS test this time; in fact, I hope you got a perfect score of 15! If not, you might seriously consider rereading any sections where you found you had difficulty.

In this chapter, we will look beyond our own, individual classrooms as we consider the larger contexts in which, as teachers, we must work; in particular, we will consider how we are likely to play significant roles in our students' attitudes about schoolwork and in their long-term development while we also operate as an integral part of the school community and society as a whole. We will explore several mechanisms through which we can communicate with students' parents so that, working together, we can more effectively promote students' development, learning, and classroom achievement. Later, we will revisit the seven themes that I presented in Chapter 1, identifying many of the places where they've appeared throughout the book. We will identify issues that are still unresolved—questions that remain unanswered—in education and educational psychology. Finally, we will look ahead to the changes you are likely to see in yourself as you gain experience as a classroom teacher. In essence, this chapter serves as one final "big picture" of classroom teaching.

By the end of the chapter, you should be able to:

1. Describe the larger context of teaching—that is, the role that teachers play in the lives of children while working as an integral part of a school and of society as a whole.

2. Describe several strategies you can use to communicate with parents and thereby work in partnership with them.

3. Identify numerous occasions in which we've seen each of the seven themes identified in Chapter 1, and derive general principles from these themes that can guide your decision making as a classroom teacher.

4. List several unresolved issues in the teaching profession.

5. Predict the ways in which you are likely to change and improve as you gain experience as a teacher.

How valid an assessment instrument is the OOPS as a measure of what you have learned from this book? Especially consider its *content validity* (see Chapter 14) when answering this question.

CASE STUDY: *Going Through the Motions*

"We have great students here," the principal of Bayside High School boasts. "They're bright. They're motivated. Most of our graduates go on to college. Who could ask for anything more?"

Certainly, the students at Bayside High School have the school routine down pat. They come to school every day. They take notes on their teachers' classroom lectures. They do their homework assignments. They study for their tests.

But when you ask the students what they're learning, they have a hard time pinning it down. One student tells you, "Science, history, math, things like that." Another one answers, "Information I'll probably need in college." And a third responds, "Lots of stuff!"

What will they use this "stuff" for, you ask? They look at you blankly. One finally says, "We're not supposed to use it for *anything*. This is just school. We'll worry about real things once we graduate."

- Why do the students at Bayside view their school learning as something separate from the rest of their lives? What might their elementary and secondary teachers have done over the years to help them see the relevance of school for their long-term personal and professional lives?

- Do you think that the students' views about the meaning of school-work are typical of students in this country? Are their views similar to your own?

PLACING TEACHING WITHIN A LARGER CONTEXT

Certainly, we don't want our students to view the things they learn in school as "stuff" unrelated to any other aspect of their lives. The last thing we want to do is portray school as being isolated from, and irrelevant to, the "real" world—the world after graduation.

As teachers, we, too, should avoid the tendency to think of the subject matter we teach in isolation from other things. Instead, we must continually keep in mind how our teaching fits within a larger context. More specifically, we must remember that:

- The specific things that teachers ask students to do give messages about academic work and school in general.

- Schools and teachers have a major impact on students' development over the long run.

- Teachers are more effective when they coordinate their efforts with one another.

- School is only one institution of many that influence students' lives.

Let's consider our role as teachers within each of these contexts.

Giving Messages About Academic Work and School

What activities do we ask students to engage in? What assignments do we give them? Do we require them to spend hours of each day engaged in what seems like meaningless busy work? Do we demonstrate how the things we teach them are related to things they do in their other classes and outside school? Do we give them reasons to pursue school subject matter further once they leave our classrooms behind? What criteria do we use to assess learning and achievement? The answers to such questions are likely to tell us a great deal about the messages we give our students about academic work and school in general (e.g., Doyle, 1983).

All too often, students view school activities and assignments merely as things to "get done" (L. Anderson, 1984; L. M. Anderson, Brubaker, Alleman-Brooks, & Duffy, 1985; Brophy & Alleman, 1991; Doyle, 1986b; Stodolsky et al., 1991). Yet ideally, our students should be well aware of the benefits of the things we ask them to do. We can give students indirect messages about the importance of school and schoolwork in a variety of ways (Brophy & Alleman, 1991; Doyle, 1986b). For example, we can:

- Continually relate material to things beyond our own classrooms

- Develop activities that resemble real-life situations as closely as possible

- Explain the short-term and long-term purposes of the tasks we assign

- Ask students to *do* something with the material they learn—for example, to practice it, apply it, evaluate it, or use it to solve problems

Ultimately, we want to show students that school subject matter isn't just something to be learned for its own sake—that it can in some way enhance the quality of their lives.

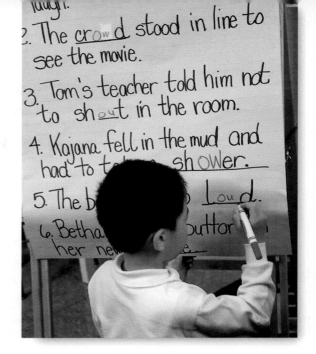

We must help students see their schoolwork as activities that help them achieve important knowledge and skills, rather than just as things to "get done."

Promoting Students' Long-Term Development

School isn't just a place where students learn academics. It is also a place where they develop feelings about the things they study—perhaps a love of physical education, an appreciation for art and music, anxiety about mathematics, or a disdain for writing. And it is a place where students acquire self-esteem, interpersonal skills, and moral values.

Throughout the book, we have identified a number of ways to promote students' long-term personal, social, and moral growth. As examples, we can:

- Help students be successful most of the time—by choosing activities appropriate for their cognitive level and background experiences and by scaffolding their efforts on difficult tasks

- Assign some activities that require cooperation with one or more classmates

- Ask students to wrestle with the moral aspects of academic subject matter

- Acknowledge and reinforce appropriate classroom behaviors

- Take steps to reduce counterproductive behaviors—by giving reasons as to why such behaviors are unacceptable and by applying consequences consistently when the behaviors occur

We must never forget that school is one critical environment in which our students develop the attitudes and skills they need to become productive citizens and work cooperatively with those around them.

Consider the indirect messages you give students about the value of school and schoolwork.

Remember that students' school experiences are likely to have a long-term effect on their self-esteem, interpersonal skills, moral values, and attitudes toward academic subject matter.

Coordinating Efforts with Other Teachers

Although we may spend much of the school day working in our individual classrooms, we must remember that, ultimately, we will be far more effective if we coordinate our efforts with other teachers in our building and school district. Schools are clearly more effective when teachers:

- Communicate regularly with one another

- Have common objectives regarding what students should learn and achieve

- Work together to identify obstacles to students' learning, as well as to develop strategies for overcoming those obstacles

- Are committed, as a group, to promoting equality and multicultural sensitivity throughout the school community (Levine & Lezotte, 1995)

Communicate regularly with your building and district colleagues, and work cooperatively toward common goals.

Our students should get the same message from all of us—that we are working together to help them become successful, productive, and informed citizens.

This "team spirit" has an additional advantage as well: It provides the support structure (the scaffolding) that many beginning teachers may need, especially when working with high-risk students. New teachers report greater confidence in their own ability to help their students learn and achieve—greater self-efficacy about their roles as teachers—when they collaborate regularly with their colleagues (Chester & Beaudin, 1996).

Working Within the Context of Society as a Whole

As teachers, we are important and influential people in our students' lives. At the same time, we are certainly not the *only* people in their lives. Students have parents, siblings, extended families, friends, and acquaintances. They also have contacts with other insti-

We must think of ourselves as team players, rather than as solo artists.

tutions besides school—possibly with youth groups, community organizations, social services, churches, hospitals, mental health clinics, or even parole boards. And many of them are probably growing up in cultural environments very different from our own.

We will be most effective if we understand the environment within which our students live and if we think of ourselves as part of a larger team that promotes their long-term development. For example, we must educate ourselves about students' cultural backgrounds, perhaps by taking coursework or by getting involved in local community events after school hours (Hadaway, Florez, Larke, & Wiseman, 1993; Ladson-Billings, 1994a). We must also keep in contact with other people and institutions who play major roles in students' lives, coordinating our efforts whenever possible. And above all, we must communicate regularly with students' parents or other primary caretakers; we consider several strategies for doing so in the section that follows.

Learn as much as you can about the communities in which your students live, and work cooperatively with individuals who play a key role in students' lives.

COMMUNICATING WITH PARENTS

Effective teachers get parents and other important family members (e.g., grandparents, older siblings) actively involved in school life and in their children's learning (G. A. Davis & Thomas, 1989; Levine & Lezotte, 1995). Perhaps we can best think of our relationship with parents as a *partnership* in which we collaborate to promote students' long-term development and learning (Hidalgo et al., 1995). Such a relationship may be especially important when working with students from diverse cultural backgrounds (García, 1995; Hidalgo et al., 1995; Minami & Ovando, 1995; Salend & Taylor, 1993).

At the very minimum, we must keep in regular contact with parents about the progress that students are making. For one thing, we must keep them informed about their children's progress and accomplishments; we must also alert them to any behaviors that are interfering with their children's learning and achievement. Regular communication also provides a means through which parents can give *us* information— information that might yield ideas about how we can best assist or motivate their children or that will at least help us understand why their children sometimes behave as they do. And finally, we can coordinate our strategies in the classroom with those that parents use at home; our own efforts to help students succeed will almost certainly yield greater returns if expectations for academic performance and social behavior are similar both in and out of school.

Remember that communication with parents should be a two-way street, with information traveling in both directions.

Considering a Variety of Communication Strategies

We can communicate with parents in a number of ways:

- Parental involvement in school activities

- Parent-teacher conferences

- Written communication

- Telephone conversations

- Parent discussion groups

Let's look briefly at how we can use each of these strategies to our own advantage and to the advantage of our students.

Plan activities that entice parents to become involved.

Parental Involvement in School Activities

When we look at effective schools, we are likely to find parents involved in many school activities (Hidalgo et al., 1995; Levine & Lezotte, 1995). For example, we might invite parents to an "open house" or choir performance in the evening, or we might request their help with a fund-raiser on a Saturday afternoon. We might seek volunteers to help with field trips, special projects, or individual tutoring during the school day. And we should certainly use our parents and other family members as resources to give us a multicultural perspective of the community in which we work (Minami & Ovando, 1995).

Take the steps necessary to ensure a productive conference.

Parent-Teacher Conferences

In most school districts, formal parent-teacher conferences are scheduled one or more times a year. Here are several suggestions for conducting smooth, productive conferences with students' parents:

- Schedule each conference at a time that accommodates parents' work schedules and other obligations.

- Prepare for the conference ahead of time; for example, organize your notes, review information you have about the student, plan an agenda for your meeting, and have examples of the student's work at hand.

- Create a warm, nonjudgmental atmosphere. For example, express your appreciation that the parents have come, and give them sufficient time to express their thoughts and perspectives. Remember that your objective is to work cooperatively and constructively together to create the best educational program possible for the student.

- Express your thoughts clearly, concisely, and honestly.

- Avoid educational jargon with which parents may be unfamiliar; describe the student's performance in ways a noneducator can understand.

- After the conference, follow through with anything you have said you will do (Polloway & Patton, 1993; Salend & Taylor, 1993).

Consider including your students in parent-teacher conferences.

In many situations, we may also want to invite students to a parent-teacher conference. By doing so, we increase the likelihood that parents will come to the conference, we encourage our students to reflect on their own academic progress, and *everyone*—including ourselves, our students, and their parents—is likely to leave the conference with a shared understanding of the progress that has been made and the steps that are to be taken next (e.g., Popham, 1995; Stiggins, 1994).

Use informal notes and classroom newsletters in addition to more formal reports.

Written Communication

Written communication can take a variety of forms. For example, it can be a regularly scheduled "report card" documenting a student's academic progress. It can be a quick, informal note acknowledging a significant accomplishment. Or it can be a general newsletter describing noteworthy classroom activities. All of these have something in common: Not only do they let parents know what is happening at school, but they also convey our intention to stay in touch on an ongoing basis.

Telephone Conversations

Telephone calls are useful when issues require immediate attention. We might call a parent to express our concern when a student's behavior deteriorates unexpectedly and without apparent provocation. But we might also call to express our excitement about an important step forward that a student has made. Parents, too, should feel free to call us. Keep in mind that many parents are at work during the school day; hence, it is often helpful to accept and encourage calls at home during the early evening hours.

Parent Discussion Groups

In some instances, we may want to assemble a group of parents to discuss issues of mutual concern. For example, we might want to use such a group as a sounding board when we can pick and choose among topics to include in our classroom curriculum, or perhaps when we are thinking about assigning controversial yet potentially valuable works of literature (e.g., Rudman, 1993). Alternatively, we might want to use a discussion group as a mechanism through which we can all share ideas about how best to promote students' academic, personal, and social development.

Make use of the telephone when issues require immediate attention.

Hold parent discussion groups for issues of general concern.

Setting a Positive Tone

■ EXPERIENCING FIRSTHAND
Putting Yourself in a Parent's Shoes

Imagine that you are the parent of a seventh grader named Tommy. As you and your son are eating dinner one evening, the telephone rings. You get up to answer the phone.

You: Hello?

Ms. J.:   Hi. This is Ms. Johnson, Tommy's teacher. May I talk with you for a few minutes?

You: Of course. What can I do for you?

Ms. J.:   Well, I'm afraid I've been having some trouble with your son, and I thought you ought to know about it.

You: Oh, really? What seems to be the problem?

Ms. J.:   For one thing, Tommy hardly ever gets to class on time. When he does arrive, he spends most of his time talking and laughing with his friends, rather than paying attention to what I'm saying. It seems as if I have to speak to him three or four times every day about his behavior.

You: How long has all this been going on?

Ms. J.:   For several weeks now. And the problem is getting worse, rather than better. I'd really appreciate it if you'd talk with Tommy about the situation.

You: I'll do it right now. And thank you for letting me know about this.

Ms. J.:   You're most welcome. Good night.

You: Good night, Ms. Johnson.

Take a few minutes to jot down some of the things that, as a parent, you might be thinking after this telephone conversation. ■

How might a chronically abusive parent react to the conversation with Ms. Johnson?

Communicate your confidence in each student's ability to succeed, as well as your commitment to working cooperatively with parents.

Identify and address the reasons why some parents may be reluctant to attend school functions or otherwise communicate with you.

You may have had a variety of reactions to your conversation with Ms. Johnson. Here are some of the possibilities:

- Why isn't Tommy taking his schoolwork more seriously?

- Isn't Tommy doing anything *right*?

- Has Ms. Johnson tried anything else besides reprimanding Tommy for his behavior? Or is she laying all of this on *my* shoulders?

Notice how Ms. Johnson focused strictly on the "negatives" of Tommy's classroom performance. As a result, you (as Tommy's parent) may possibly have felt anger at your son or guilt about your ineffective parenting skills. Alternatively, you may instead have maintained your confidence in your son's scholastic abilities and in your own ability to be a parent; if so, you may have begun to wonder about Ms. Johnson's ability to teach and motivate seventh graders.

As teachers, we will be more effective when working with parents if we set a positive, upbeat tone in any communication. For one thing, we will always want to couch any negative aspects of a student's classroom performance within the context of the many things that the student does *well*. (For example, rather than starting out by complaining about Tommy's behavior, Ms. Johnson might have begun by saying that Tommy is a bright and capable young man with many friends and a good sense of humor.) And we must also be clear about our commitment to working *together* with parents to help a student be successful in the classroom.

Encouraging "Reluctant" Parents

Despite our best efforts, we will often find a few parents who are uninvolved in their children's education; for example, some parents may rarely if ever attend scheduled parent-teacher conferences. Before we jump too quickly to the conclusion that these parents are also *uninterested* in their children's education, we must realize that there are several possible reasons why parents might be reluctant to make contact with us. For example, some may have an exhausting work schedule or lack adequate child care. Others may have difficulty communicating in English (Salend & Taylor, 1993). Still others may believe that it's inappropriate to bother teachers with questions about their children's progress or to offer information as to why their children are having difficulty (Hidalgo et al., 1995; Olneck, 1995). And a few may simply have had bad experiences with school when they themselves were children (Salend & Taylor, 1993).

Educators have offered a number of strategies for getting such parents more involved in their children's schooling. In particular, we should:

- Make an extra effort to establish parents' trust and confidence—for example, by demonstrating that we value their input and would never make them appear foolish

- Encourage parents to be assertive when they have questions or concerns

- Find out what different parents do exceptionally well (e.g., carpentry, ethnic cooking) and ask them to share their talents with the class

- Invite other important family members (e.g., grandparents, aunts, uncles) to participate in school activities, especially if a student's cultural background is one that places high value on the extended family

- Identify individuals (e.g., bilingual parents) who can translate for those who speak little or no English

- Conduct parent-teacher conferences or parent discussions at times and locations more convenient for families

- Make use of home visits *provided* that such visits are welcomed (Finders & Lewis, 1994; Hidalgo et al., 1995; C. K. Howe, 1994; Salend & Taylor, 1993)

As we noted in Chapter 4, most parents really *do* want what's best for their children. We will be most successful in communicating and working with parents when we clearly show them that we, too, have their children's best interests at heart.

REVISITING OUR COMMON THEMES

In Chapter 1, I listed seven themes that would underlie much of our discussion in this book:

- Interaction
- Information processing
- Relevance
- Classroom climate
- Challenge
- Expectations
- Diversity

Table 15–1 lists numerous places in which we've seen these themes in one form or another. Let's revisit each theme once again for general guidance about how we can help our students learn, develop, and achieve.

Before you read further, can you recall places in the book where you've encountered each of the seven themes?

Interaction

Throughout the book, we've seen the importance of interacting with the physical environment. For optimal cognitive and intellectual development, students need opportunities to manipulate and experiment with a variety of physical objects (see Piaget's theory in Chapter 2 and the discussions of visual-spatial thinking and intelligence in Chapters 1 and 4, respectively). Furthermore, firsthand experiences with the physical world enable students to encode information visually, as well as verbally, and provide a knowledge base to which more abstract notions can later be connected (see visual imagery in Chapter 6 and discovery learning in Chapter 13). And students are more likely to become interested in classroom activities in which they can become actively and physically involved (see our discussion of fostering interest in classroom subject matter in Chapter 11).

Interaction with other people—for instance, with teachers and classmates—is equally critical. From Piaget's perspective (Chapter 2), social interaction enables developing children to shed their preoperational egocentrism, recognize logical fallacies in their thinking, and temper their adolescent idealism to reflect the constraints that the real world imposes. From Vygotsky's perspective (Chapter 2), interaction with more advanced and capable individuals provides a milieu in which students can accomplish

Give students numerous opportunities to interact with their physical environment.

Give students numerous opportunities for social interaction.

Table 15–1   Reviewing the Seven Themes

CHAPTER	INTERACTION	INFORMATION PROCESSING	RELEVANCE
Chapter 2: Adapting to Differences in Cognitive and Linguistic Development	In Piaget's theory, interaction with the physical and social environments promotes cognitive development. In Vygotsky's theory, children work with more advanced individuals to accomplish tasks within their zone of proximal development.	In Piaget's theory, children construct their own knowledge of the world through processes of assimilation and accommodation. Information processing theorists study changes in the ways that children receive, think about, remember, and mentally change information as they grow older. According to Vygotsky, children guide their own behaviors through self-talk and inner speech. Language provides a mechanism through which students can mentally represent their world and make associations among pieces of information.	According to Piaget, assimilation and accommodation can occur only when children relate new experiences to existing knowledge. Students show more advanced reasoning capabilities when classroom tasks are related to topics with which they are familiar. According to information processing theory, students' prior knowledge influences the degree to which they can understand, elaborate on, and remember new information.
Chapter 3: Adapting to Differences in Personal, Social, and Moral Development	Students' self-concepts and self-esteem are influenced by others' behaviors toward them. Social interaction promotes the development of social skills, moral reasoning, perspective taking, and prosocial behavior.	Some students may have difficulty looking at a situation from someone else's perspective. Some may also have difficulty interpreting others' behaviors accurately.	Students may encounter numerous moral dilemmas relevant to the content domains they study in school—for example, moral dilemmas related to science, history, and literature.
Chapter 4: Adapting to Individual and Group Differences	Students often behave more intelligently when they work with the cooperation and support of others—a phenomenon called distributed intelligence. Teachers interact more frequently and in different ways with boys than with girls. Students are more tolerant of cultural differences when they interact in a multicultural social environment. Students at risk are less likely to drop out when they get involved in extracurricular and other social activities.	According to Sternberg, numerous cognitive processes are involved in intelligent behavior. Increasing teacher wait time often facilitates the classroom performance of students from culturally diverse backgrounds.	Students are more likely to exhibit creativity when they have considerable knowledge related to the task at hand. Students at risk become more psychologically attached to their school when they believe that school activities are relevant to their own needs

CLASSROOM CLIMATE	CHALLENGE	EXPECTATIONS	DIVERSITY
Many students, especially younger ones, think that it is unacceptable to ask their teacher for help, perhaps because they have previously been discouraged from asking questions at school or at home.	Challenge promotes cognitive development, whether the challenge be in the form of disequilibrium (Piaget), a task within the zone of proximal development (Vygotsky), or the increasing need for sophisticated learning strategies (information processing theory). Children are most likely to develop their linguistic capabilities when challenging tasks require them to do so.	Students may "hear" what they expect their teachers to say, rather than what teachers actually do say.	Students at any given age and grade level vary in their cognitive and linguistic abilities. When learning a second language, some students may benefit more from total immersion in that language, whereas others may benefit more from bilingual education. Some students may have special educational needs related to cognitive or linguistic development; for instance, they may be gifted, or they may have learning disabilities, communication disorders, or mental retardation.
Social, personal, and moral development is most effectively fostered within the context of a warm, supportive, and encouraging environment.	Discussions about controversial moral issues challenge students to think differently about such issues and hence may promote their moral development.	Students' self-concepts are partly the result of expectations that others have for them; their self-concepts, in turn, affect the expectations they have for themselves.	Students differ widely in their social skills, self-concepts, and moral behaviors. Teachers can promote friendships among students with diverse backgrounds by setting up situations in which such students must interact and work closely together.
Creativity is more likely to appear when students feel free to take risks. When teachers have high expectations for students' performance, they create a warmer classroom climate, interact with students more frequently, and give more positive feedback. At-risk students are more likely to feel psychologically attached to their school when teachers have close, trusting relationships with them.	Students are more likely to think creatively when teachers ask questions that require using information in new ways.	Teachers' expectations influence the way in which they treat students and may ultimately lead to a self-fulfilling prophecy. IQ scores should not be used as the basis on which teachers develop expectations for students' long-term performance. Boys tend to have higher expectations for themselves than girls. Teachers should notform expectations about individual students based solely on their group membership. Teachers should communicate to at-risk students that school success is both possible and expected.	Considerable diversity is found even within a single ethnic group, gender, or socioeconomic group. Students vary with respect to intelligence and creativity; both characteristics can be enhanced through experience. Students may have trouble adjusting to the school environment when there is a mismatch between home and school cultures. On the average, boys and girls differ with respect to personality, motivation, and career aspirations.

Table 15–1 *(continued)*

CHAPTER	INTERACTION	INFORMATION PROCESSING	RELEVANCE
Chapter 5: Using Multiple Perspectives of Learning		Cognitive and social cognitive theorists consider the role of cognitive processes in learning and behavior.	
Chapter 6: Promoting Effective Cognitive Processing	Increasing teacher wait time can dramatically alter the nature of classroom interactions.	Cognitive psychologists view learning as an internal mental process. Many cognitive psychologists incorporate such concepts as encoding, meaningful learning, elaboration, visual imagery, and retrieval into their explanations of learning and memory. Increasing teacher wait time allows students more time to process information.	Meaningful learning is more likely to occur when students have existing knowledge to which they can relate new information and when they recognize the relevance of that knowledge. Making multiple connections between new information and existing knowledge facilitates later retrieval of the information.
Chapter 7: Facilitating Knowledge Construction	Hands-on experimentation with physical objects helps students construct a more complete understanding of the world. Social constructivism focuses on how people can make more sense of an event or phenomenon when they work together to understand and interpret it.	Students construct their own meanings for the experiences they have and the information they receive.	Students may connect new information to prior misconceptions and misinterpret it as a result. Authentic activities may help students understand the relevance of classroom learning to real-life situations.
Chapter 8: Promoting Higher-Level Thinking Skills	When students study together in small groups, they are exposed to a variety of study strategies, including some that may be more effective than the ones they are currently using.	One theory of concept learning proposes that learners form and test hypotheses. Information learned in one situation is only transferred to another situation when it is retrieved in the second situation. Working memory, encoding, and retrieval affect problem-solving success. Metacognition includes students' knowledge about their own cognitive processes and their attempts to regulate those processes.	Students are most likely to transfer their academic knowledge to real-world situations when they perceive its relevance to those situations. Successful problem solving is more likely to occur when students have thorough and integrated knowledge related to the topic in question. One effective study strategy is retrieving relevant prior knowledge as one studies. Study strategies are most effectively taught within the context of specific content domains.

CLASSROOM CLIMATE	CHALLENGE	EXPECTATIONS	DIVERSITY
			Students have unique backgrounds, experiences, and knowledge that affect their learning.
		When teachers increase their wait time, their expectations for many students, especially previously low-achieving ones, begin to improve.	Different students will encode and store information differently. Cognitive style is the particular way in which a student approaches tasks and mentally processes information. Students with learning disabilities have deficiencies in one or more specific cognitive processes.
A classroom dialogue in which students express their ideas openly with one another promotes a better understanding of the topic at hand.	In a cognitive apprenticeship, teacher and students work together to accomplish a challenging task. Teachers can correct students' misconceptions about the world by presenting information that conflicts with such misconceptions and by asking challenging questions.	Students and teachers alike may sometimes perceive events in a distorted fashion based on what they expected they would see or hear.	Students' different backgrounds and knowledge bases lead them to interpret new experiences in different ways. Students from different cultures may derive different, yet equally valid, meanings from the same event.
	The acquisition of complex study strategies can be facilitated when teachers scaffold students' initial studying efforts.	Students are likely to adopt complex study strategies only when they expect that such strategies will enhance their learning.	Some students have more effective study strategies than others; students with special needs often have few if any effective strategies. Students' differing background knowledge related to the topic at hand will affect their ability to solve problems and use effective study strategies.

709

Table 15–1 *(continued)*

CHAPTER	INTERACTION	INFORMATION PROCESSING	RELEVANCE
Chapter 9: Modifying Students' Behavior	A social reinforcer is a gesture or sign that one person gives another and that communicates positive regard. Positive feedback from someone else is frequently an effective reinforcer. In a group contingency, students are reinforced only when everyone responds appropriately.	Some behaviorists have begun to incorporate cognitive processes into their theoretical explanations of learning.	Students are most likely to transfer what they've learned in one situation to a second situation if stimuli in the two situations are similar.
Chapter 10: Promoting Learning in a Social Context	Students learn by observing others; for example, they may learn through vicarious reinforcement and punishment. Students' self-efficacy is affected by others' successes and failures.	Social cognitive theorists view learning as an internal mental process. Students process information more effectively when they expect to be reinforced for learning it. Attention and retention (memory) are necessary for successful imitation of a model's behavior.	Students are most likely to imitate behaviors they believe will help them in their own circumstances.
Chapter 11: Motivating Students to Learn and Achieve	Most students prefer learning activities in which they can take an active, physical role. Students differ in terms of their needs for affiliation and approval.	Motivation affects what and how information is processed. Students with learning goals and those who are interested in what they are studying are more likely to use effective strategies such as meaningful learning, elaboration, and comprehension monitoring. An excessive level of anxiety interferes with effective information processing. Attributions are students' beliefs about what causes what.	Students are more likely to have intrinsic motivation to learn school subject matter when they see its relevance for their personal lives and professional aspirations; such relevance may be especially important for students from lower socioeconomic backgrounds.
Chapter 12: Planning for a Productive Classroom	One strategy for dealing with a student's problem behavior is a private discussion between teacher and student.	Information processing analysis is one form of task analysis.	Three critical components of teaching—planning, instruction, and assessment—are closely intertwined.

CLASSROOM CLIMATE	CHALLENGE	EXPECTATIONS	DIVERSITY
Skinner recommended that teachers focus their efforts on reinforcing desirable behaviors, rather than on punishing undesirable ones.	Through the process of shaping, students are encouraged to exhibit increasingly more complex behaviors over time.	Cueing is a subtle strategy for reminding students about expectations for their behavior. One probable reason for the success of applied behavior analysis is that such techniques let students know exactly what is expected of them.	Because students have had unique previous experiences, they often respond to the same environmental stimuli in different ways.
	Students' self-efficacy is enhanced when they set and achieve challenging goals.	Students form expectations about the likely consequences of future responses on the basis of how current responses are reinforced and punished. Students are more likely to engage in certain behaviors when they believe that they can execute those behaviors successfully—that is, when they have high self-efficacy.	Students differ considerably in their self-efficacy for performing school tasks and in their ability to regulate their own behaviors. Students benefit from observing a wide variety of models, including those of both genders and diverse cultural backgrounds.
Students are more intrinsically motivated when they can control some aspects of classroom life—for example, when they are involved in classroom decision making. Students are more likely to develop the motivation to learn if their teachers commend successful performance but downplay the importance of mistakes. Many students have a strong need to affiliate with their teachers, as well as with their classmates. Some students become especially anxious when expectations for classroom performance are unclear.	A challenge is a situation in which students believe that there is some probability of success with effort; a threat is one in which students believe that they have little or no chance of success. Students who are intrinsically motivated, and especially those who have a mastery orientation, are more likely to engage in challenging tasks.	Students are more likely to be intrinsically motivated when they expect that they will be able to accomplish a task successfully. Teachers can foster the motivation to learn by communicating the expectation that students will *want* to learn. Communicating clear expectations for student performance lessens students' anxiety. Students' attributions affect their expectations for future success or failure.	Whereas young children often want their teachers' approval, many older ones may be more concerned about gaining the approval of their peers. Students' intrinsic motivation decreases and performance goals become more prevalent as students get older. Students from minority groups may have more test anxiety than their classmates.
Effective teachers create a classroom climate in which students have a sense of acceptance, belonging, and some degree of control. A productive classroom climate is one that is businesslike without being uncomfortable or threatening. Effective teachers set reasonable limits for classroom behavior.	Some students are likely to behave in counterproductive ways when they are given challenging tasks; one workable strategy is to begin the school year with familiar and easily accomplishable tasks, moving to more difficult tasks after a supportive classroom climate has been established.	Instructional objectives enable teachers to describe precisely what they expect students to do at the completion of a lesson. Effective teachers give clear directions about how to proceed with classroom tasks. Teachers should inform students in advance about behaviors that are unacceptable and the consequences that will follow such behaviors.	Classroom behaviors considered unacceptable in our culture may be quite acceptable in the cultures of some students.

Table 15–1   (continued)

CHAPTER	INTERACTION	INFORMATION PROCESSING	RELEVANCE
Chapter 13: Choosing and Implementing Instructional Strategies	In discovery learning, students acquire firsthand knowledge through their self-directed interactions with the environment. In class discussions, cooperative learning, and reciprocal teaching activities, students learn through their interactions with one another. Through reciprocal teaching, students help one another develop more sophisticated metacognitive skills.	Expository instruction is effective to the extent that it facilitates effective cognitive processing of the information presented. Class discussions and cooperative learning activities help students process information meaningfully and with elaboration. Reciprocal teaching promotes development of four metacognitive strategies: summarizing, questioning, clarifying, predicting.	Analogies provide one means of helping students connect new information with their existing knowledge. Students are most likely to benefit from discovery learning when they have relevant background knowledge they can draw on to interpret their observations. Authentic activities are those that closely resemble real-life tasks.
Chapter 14: Assessing What Students Have Learned	Although students often decide which products to include in their portfolios, teacher guidance is essential for ensuring that they make appropriate choices.	The nature of assessments that students expect influences how students mentally process information as they study.	Content validity is maximized when assessment tasks are as similar to instructional objectives as possible. Authentic assessment involves asking students to perform in situations similar to "real life."

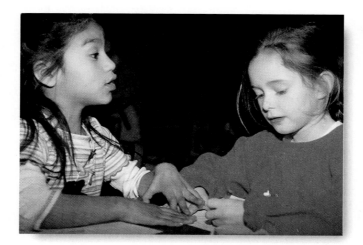

Social interaction promotes cognitive, social, and moral development. It can also help students acquire a better understanding of diverse cultures.

CLASSROOM CLIMATE	CHALLENGE	EXPECTATIONS	DIVERSITY
Class discussions are most effective when students believe that they can speak freely. Some theorists propose that classrooms are most effective when they are seen as a community of learners—that is, when teacher and students actively work to help one another learn.	Reciprocal teaching provides a setting in which students can more effectively read challenging reading materials.	Mastery learning is based on the assumption that all students can eventually master course material. Cooperative learning enhances students' confidence that they can be successful.	Different instructional strategies may be appropriate for different students; for example, lectures are most appropriate for students who can think abstractly, and mastery learning is most appropriate for students who need to work on basic skills.
Teachers should portray classroom assessment tasks more as means to facilitate learning than as mechanisms to evaluate performance. Teachers' evaluation procedures must be consistent with an atmosphere in which students feel free to take risks and make mistakes.	Classroom assessment tasks should be difficult enough that students must expend effort to succeed, but not so difficult that success is beyond reach.	Assessment instruments never have perfect validity; thus, a single assessment should never be used as the sole basis on which to form expectations about students' future performance. Teachers' expectations for student performance may affect their evaluations of subjectively scorable assessment tasks.	It may sometimes be necessary and appropriate to tailor assessment methods to accommodate diverse cultural backgrounds or special educational needs.

tasks they could never accomplish on their own—tasks within their zone of proximal development. Furthermore, through verbal exchanges with others, students gradually develop interpersonal skills, prosocial behavior, internalized moral values, and a sense of who they themselves are (Chapter 3). And by conversing and working with their classmates on a regular basis, students often process information more effectively (Chapter 13), and they become more understanding and accepting of students from other cultures (Chapter 4).

Information Processing

We have found cognitive processes to be important within a variety of contexts. Cognition and information processing figured prominently in theories of cognitive development; for example, Piaget described cognitive development as a process of constructing one's own understanding of the world, information processing theorists consider the development of learning strategies and metacognition, and Vygotsky argued that self-talk and inner speech enable children to guide and direct their own behaviors (Chapter 2). Thinking processes also play an important role in cognitive and social cognitive theories of learning (Chapters 6, 7, 8, and 10) and, more recently, even in behaviorism (Chapter 9). We have seen, too, that the effectiveness of such teaching methods as

Consider how students mentally process and interpret their experiences.

expository instruction, class discussions, cooperative learning, and reciprocal teaching is due, at least in part, to the cognitive processes that these methods promote (Chapter 13). We have found aspects of information processing throughout our discussion of motivation—for example, we found them among the benefits of having learning goals, in the nature of debilitating anxiety, and in the attributions that students make (Chapter 11). Finally, we have noted the influence that classroom assessment instruments are likely to have on how students process information and the extent to which they develop and use higher-level thinking skills (Chapter 14).

Show students how new information and skills are related both to what they already know and to their own personal needs.

What specific ideas do these principles give you for helping students at Bayside High discover the relevance of school?

Relevance

We have noted over and over that students must discover how new information and skills are related both to their existing knowledge of the world and to their own personal needs. From the perspective of Piaget and many contemporary cognitive psychologists, learning and cognitive development occur only to the extent that students can relate their new experiences to the things they already know (Chapters 2, 6, and 7). Furthermore, students are more likely to transfer what they've learned to new situations and problems when they have connected classroom subject matter with the contexts in which they might use it (Chapters 7, 8, and 13). They will be more motivated to learn classroom material when that material relates to their personal interests (Chapter 11). And they are more likely to imitate the behaviors of the models they observe when they believe that such behaviors are applicable to their own situations (Chapter 10).

Create an atmosphere in which students feel comfortable and are willing to take risks.

Classroom Climate

The psychological climate of our classrooms is a critical factor affecting our students' learning, development, and achievement. For example, although a somewhat orderly and businesslike atmosphere is essential if instructional objectives are to be accomplished, students can more effectively focus their attention on those objectives when they feel the affection and positive regard of their teacher and classmates (see Chapters 3, 11, and 12). Furthermore, to maintain intrinsic motivation to learn classroom subject matter, students must have a sense that they have some control over classroom events (Chapters 11 and 12). And certainly students must feel free to take the risks so critical for accomplishing difficult and challenging tasks (see the discussions of creativity, motivation to learn, anxiety, and assessment in Chapters 4, 11, and 14). A warm, accepting, and nonthreatening classroom climate is especially important for our at-risk students (see Chapter 4).

Help students be successful at challenging tasks.

Challenge

Students are most likely to learn and develop when they encounter tasks that challenge their skills and ideas that challenge their ways of thinking. For example, Piaget proposed that children develop increasingly more logical thinking as those around them continue to point out the inconsistencies and logical flaws in the things they say (Chapter 2), and contemporary cognitive psychologists have suggested that students are most likely to correct their misconceptions when such misconceptions are repeatedly challenged (Chapter 7). From Vygotsky's perspective, students enjoy maximum cognitive development when they work within their zone of proximal development—in other words, when they tackle tasks they can only accomplish with the help of other, more experienced individuals (Chapter 2). And when students set challenging goals for themselves and achieve those self-chosen goals through their own efforts, they experience a great deal of self-satisfaction, have higher self-efficacy, and become more motivated to undertake new challenges (Chapters 10 and 11).

We should note here that we must walk a fine line between assigning tasks that are sufficiently challenging and those that are a bit *too* challenging for our students' ability levels. Although occasional errors are inevitable and probably even desirable, we must scaffold our students' efforts sufficiently that they experience those errors within an overall context of success (see the section on fostering a mastery orientation in Chapter 11). A pattern of success experiences is absolutely essential for students' self-esteem, self-efficacy, and motivation to achieve in the classroom (see Chapters 3, 10, and 11).

Expectations

Throughout the book, we have found reasons why students achieve at higher levels when our expectations for their performance are challenging yet attainable, and why they exhibit more productive classroom behaviors when we communicate our expectations for their performance clearly and concretely. As examples, refer back to our discussions of teacher expectations (Chapter 4), students at risk (Chapter 4), attribution theory (Chapter 11), classroom management (Chapter 12), and classroom assessment practices (Chapter 14). When we hold low expectations for our students, we are less likely to give them the support they need to be academically successful and less likely to evaluate their performance in a positive light (Chapters 4 and 14). Yet we must also be sure our expectations are not so unrealistically high that students are bound to fail (see the distinction between threat and challenge in Chapter 11) or so low that our students make little progress and begin to doubt their own capabilities (see the sections on self-concept, self-efficacy, and attribution theory in Chapters 3, 10, and 11, respectively). Above all, we must take every precaution to be sure our assessments of students' achievement are made on the basis of hard data, *not* on the basis of our expectations regarding what they will and will not be able to do (Chapter 14).

Have high yet attainable expectations for students and communicate these expectations clearly.

Diversity

We find diversity among students within the context of virtually every topic we've considered. Not only do we see differences related to students' cultural background, gender, and socioeconomic status (Chapter 4), but we also see more idiosyncratic differences related to students' own unique knowledge and experiences—knowledge and experiences that influence how they think about and interpret new information and how they respond to classroom stimuli (Chapters 5–10). Students have a wide variety of needs and interests as well; when left to their own devices, they are likely to pursue different kinds of activities in the classroom (Chapter 11). Furthermore, even when students are at the same age and grade level, they are often at somewhat different levels of cognitive, social, and moral development (Chapters 2 and 3).

Figure 15–1   General Recommendations for Helping Students with Special Needs

Throughout the book, we've identified specific strategies we can use to help students with a variety of special educational needs. But there are a number of things we can do to help *all* students with special needs learn and achieve in our classrooms. In particular, we should:

- *Obtain as much information as possible about each student.* Even when students have been identified as having a particular special educational need (e.g., when they have been identified as being "gifted" or as having a "learning disability"), we must remember that they are *individuals* first, each with a unique set of strengths and weaknesses. When we know the specific needs that different students have—whether those needs be academic, social, or medical—we are in a much better position to help each and every student be successful at classroom tasks and activities (e.g., Keogh & Becker, 1973; Stephens, Blackhurst, & Magliocca, 1988).

- *Identify any necessary prerequisite knowledge and skills a student may not have acquired.* Some students may lack knowledge and skills essential for their school success, perhaps because of a particular disability or perhaps because of lack of experience. For example, students coming from impoverished home environments have probably seen little of their outside world; for example, if they have never been to a zoo or a farm and if they have never looked at picture books with their parents, then they may never have seen a lion, elephant, cow, or horse. Students with visual impairments often have not been able to observe the cause-effect relationships (e.g., the fact that wood changes its appearance when it is burned) that form a foundation for learning science (Rowe, 1978). Students with reduced physical mobility have probably not had as many opportunities to manipulate objects in their environment. And students with many physically disabling conditions may have had few opportunities to interact with other children and so may not have developed the usual proficiency in interpersonal skills. In some situations, then, we may need to fill in some gaps in the prerequisite knowledge and skills of these students.

- *Hold the same expectations for a student with special needs that we hold for other students whenever such expectations are reasonable.* Students with special needs sometimes have certain disabilities that make it difficult or even impossible to accomplish particular school tasks. Aside from such tasks, we should generally hold the same expectations for our students with special needs as we hold for other students. Rather than thinking of reasons why a student *cannot* do a particular task, we should instead be thinking about how we can help that student *do* it (Kunc, 1984; Lipsky & Gartner, 1987; Stainback & Stainback, 1990).

- *Be flexible in our approach to instruction.* Some instructional methods may work better than others in teaching students with special needs, and we can't always predict which method will be most effective with each student. For example, special educators often try a variety of strategies for helping students with learning disabilities practice and learn their spelling (e.g., having students spell the word aloud, trace the letters with their fingers, type each word on a typewriter). If we don't succeed with a particular approach, we should try again. But each time, we might want to try *differently.*

- *Use technological innovations to facilitate students' learning and performance.* There has been a virtual explosion of technological aids to help students with special needs in their daily school activities. For example, many computers have been adapted for the visually impaired: Some calculators "talk" as buttons are pushed and answers are displayed, some computers "tell" a student what appears on the computer screen, and some computer printers print in braille. Specially adapted joysticks can help students with limited muscle control use a classroom computer. Machines known as augmentative communication devices can provide synthesized speech to facilitate the communication of students incapable of normal speech (Stephens et al., 1988).

- *Maintain an orderly yet accepting classroom.* An orderly classroom—one in which procedures for performing certain tasks are specified, expectations for student behavior are clear, and misbehaviors are treated consistently—makes it easier for students with special needs to adapt comfortably to a regular classroom environment (M. C. Reynolds & Birch, 1988; Scruggs & Mastropieri, 1994). At the same time, we should make these students (and *all* students, for that matter) feel that they are full-fledged members of the classroom community.

- *Promote interaction between students with special needs and their nondisabled classmates.* One feature often found in classrooms where students with special needs function effectively is frequent interaction between these students and their nondisabled classmates (Scruggs & Mastropieri, 1994). Such interaction is likely to enhance the social skills of our nondisabled students as well as those with special needs. Furthermore, it provides a context in which nondisabled students can easily help those with disabilities to learn and achieve; for example, we might ask a hearing student to take notes for a student with a hearing impairment, or we might ask two students to outline a map of Europe with a ridge of clear, dry glue so that a blind student can feel the shapes of the countries. Such "giving," prosocial behaviors are also consistent with the spirit of the *community of learners* I described in Chapter 13.

- *Consult regularly with specialists.* School districts usually employ a variety of educational specialists to help students with special needs; for example, school districts typically have counselors, school psychologists, nurses, speech pathologists, and specialists in such areas as mental retardation and learning disabilities. Although some students with special needs leave the classroom for part of the school day to work with such specialists, in recent years we have seen a trend toward providing more and more special services within the regular classroom context. As classroom teachers, we will need to work closely and cooperatively with educational specialists to develop and deliver an appropriate program for each student (Madden & Slavin, 1983; M. C. Reynolds & Birch, 1988; Scruggs & Mastropieri, 1994).

- *Individualize instruction for* all *students.* Students with special needs blend in better with their classmates when instruction is individualized for everyone. This way, they are not singled out by virtue of any special attention or help they receive. Thus, to the extent that our time and resources allow us to do so, we should try to individualize instruction for *all* students (Madden & Slavin, 1983; M. C. Reynolds & Birch, 1988). When instruction is individually tailored to each and every student's unique needs, everyone benefits.

We will rarely serve our students well if we pretend that they're all alike; for example, we cannot adequately address each student's academic and personal needs if we pretend to be "color-blind" with respect to their race and ethnicity (Boutte & McCormick, 1992; Ladson-Billings, 1994a; Schofield, 1995). We must always remember that each of our students is an individual with unique strengths and weaknesses, and that academic abilities are never fixed in stone (Chapter 4). We must remember, too, that different students are likely to benefit from different instructional methods (Chapter 13) and that some students may need special kinds of assistance in order to be successful (see Figure 15–1 for general recommendations for helping students with special needs). But above all, we must remember that when we apply the twelve principles of effective teaching that we identified in Chapter 12, we can reasonably remain optimistic about the long-term potential of *all* students.

Taken together, the principles and guidelines we've identified throughout our discussions should help us facilitate our students' academic achievement and in other ways make a significant difference in our students' lives. Yet theories and research can't, as yet, tell us everything we would like to know about effective teaching practice. Let's take a minute to consider several unresolved issues.

Tailor classroom tasks and activities to students' unique strengths and weaknesses. Remain optimistic about the long-term potential of *all* students.

IDENTIFYING SEVERAL UNRESOLVED ISSUES

THINKING ABOUT WHAT YOU KNOW

What questions has the book *not* answered for you? Do you think that answers for these questions exist? If so, how might you go about finding them?

Despite the progress that educational researchers and practitioners have made over the years, we don't yet have all the answers about how best to educate growing children and adolescents. For example, here are some issues that I, as a teacher, haven't been able to resolve:

What are some issues that *you* have not yet resolved?

- In a classroom of thirty students, how do we assign tasks maximally challenging for each and every student—tasks within each student's zone of proximal development?

- How can we most effectively integrate students' school experiences with the outside world?

- Where do we draw the line between setting limits for students' behaviors and giving students some sense of control over classroom life?

- As individuals who are ourselves raised in a particular culture, how can we best learn to relate to a classroom of students with diverse cultural backgrounds?

- How do we reconcile the inevitable diversity of our classrooms with the need for consistent standards for assessment and grading?

- How can we maximize the reliability and content validity of our classroom assessment instruments without sacrificing practicality in the process?

As researchers and theorists continue to advance our knowledge of how best to help students learn and develop, and as teachers continue to experiment with new teaching techniques, we may eventually begin to answer questions such as these.

Our beliefs about effective teaching practice will inevitably change over time, just as our theories of human development and learning have evolved over the years. Therefore, it is absolutely essential that we keep ourselves abreast of current research results, theoretical developments, and educational innovations. As teachers, we must not only make decisions about how to help our students in any given year, but we must also make decisions about how best to improve our teaching over the long run.

Keep abreast of current research results, theoretical developments, and educational innovations.

DEVELOPING AS A TEACHER

In earlier chapters, we've talked about how children and adolescents develop as they grow older. Teachers, too, develop over time, particularly as they gain more experience in the classroom. For example, they begin to establish routines to help the classroom function smoothly, learn how to keep class activities moving at a brisk and engaging pace, and become increasingly more flexible in their instruction and classroom management strategies (Berliner, 1988; D. M. Kagan, 1992; H. L. Swanson, O'Connor, & Cooney, 1990).

As a beginning teacher, you may initially find your role a bit overwhelming. After all, you may have twenty-five to thirty-five different students in your classroom at any one time, and they are all likely to have different backgrounds, perspectives, ability levels, and needs. In such a situation, the information that presents itself to you may exceed your working memory capacity! So in the first few weeks or months, you may need to rely heavily on the standard lessons that curriculum development specialists provide (Berliner, 1988). But as time goes on, you will eventually be able to make decisions about routine problems more quickly and efficiently (you will develop automaticity in some of your teaching strategies), allowing you to begin thinking creatively and flexibly about how best to teach your students.

Up to this point, I've been giving you suggestions for how you can best help your students learn and develop. Here are some suggestions for how *you* can learn and develop as a teacher:

- *Continue to take courses in teacher education.* Additional coursework in teaching is one surefire way of keeping up to date on the latest theoretical perspectives and research results related to classroom practice. In general, teacher education definitely *does* enhance teaching effectiveness (Darling-Hammond, 1995).

- *Learn as much as you can about the subject matter you teach.* When we look at effective teachers—for example, those who are flexible in their approaches to instruction, promote conceptual understanding rather than rote memorization, and convey obvious enthusiasm for whatever they are teaching—we typically find teachers who know their subject matter extremely well (Ball, 1991; Brophy, 1991, 1994; Hollon et al., 1991; D. C. Smith & Neale, 1991; Wineburg & Wilson, 1991).

- *Learn as much as you can about specific strategies for teaching your particular subject matter.* In addition to knowing general teaching strategies, it is also helpful to develop strategies specific to the topic you are teaching; a repertoire of such strategies is known as **pedagogical content knowledge.** Effective teachers typically have a great many strategies—activities, mnemonics, analogies, and so on—specific to teaching various topics and skills (Brophy, 1991; Shulman, 1986, 1987). Furthermore, they can usually anticipate—and so can also address—the difficulties students will have, and the kinds of errors they will make, in the process of mastering a skill or body of knowledge (D. C. Smith & Neale, 1991). Some teachers keep journals or other records of the strategies they develop and use in particular situations; they then draw on some of the same strategies again when similar situations present themselves (Berliner, 1988).

- *Believe that you can become an effective teacher.* In our discussion of self-efficacy in Chapter 10, we noted the importance of high self-efficacy for students' classroom success. You, too, must have high self-efficacy if you are going to persist in the face of occasional setbacks and, ultimately, to succeed as a teacher (Ashton, 1985). Students who achieve at the highest levels are most likely to be those whose teachers have confidence in what they *themselves* can achieve in the classroom (Ashton, 1985).

Remember, teaching, like any other complex skill, takes time and practice to master. And you, like any other learner, will inevitably make a few mistakes, particularly at the beginning. But you *will* improve over time. And, particularly if you make classroom decisions on the basis of documented principles and sound educational practice, you *can* make a difference in the lives of your students.

How does automaticity come about? How does it facilitate problem solving? (See Chapters 6 and 8).

Continue taking coursework related to effective teaching practices.

Continue to read and learn about the subject matter you teach.

Acquire strategies specific to teaching your subject matter.

Believe that you *can* be effective.

Becoming a More Effective Teacher

Use some of the standard lessons that curriculum development specialists provide, especially in your first few weeks or months in the classroom.

> A history teacher consults the teaching manual that accompanies her class textbook for ideas about how to make history come alive for her students.

As you gain confidence as a teacher, begin to adapt standard lessons and develop your own lessons.

> A reading teacher notices that the teacher's manual accompanying the school reading series includes mostly knowledge-based, lower-level questions. He develops several higher-level questions he can ask as students read each story.

Keep a journal of the strategies you use and their relative effectiveness.

> As a way of winding down at bedtime, a new teacher reflects back on his day in the classroom. He picks up the notebook and pen on his bedside table and jots down notes about the strategies that did and did not work well in class that day.

Seek the advice and suggestions of your more experienced colleagues.

> A fourth-grade teacher is teaching her students long division, but after a week they still don't understand what they are supposed to do. Over the weekend, she calls two of her fellow teachers for ideas about how she might approach the topic differently.

Continue your education, both formally and informally.

> A middle school science teacher takes advantage of a tour package to Costa Rica designed specifically for teachers. There she will study the plants, animals, and ecology of the rain forest.

Remember that teaching, like any other complex skill, takes time and practice to master.

> A teacher continues to try the new teaching techniques he reads about in professional journals. As he does so, he adds to his repertoire of effective teaching strategies and becomes increasingly able to adjust his methods to the diverse population of students he has in his classroom.

CASE STUDY: *Second Thoughts*

Two brand new teachers have joined the Andover school district. Mr. O'Brien is teaching second grade, and Ms. Koch is teaching high school English. They're old friends from State University, and so they get together to compare notes after their first month of school.

"I'm having a hard time keeping some of my classes under control," Ms. Koch confides. "I'd love to use some of those techniques I learned at State U., but every time I try something new, one student or another does something to distract me, and then I lose the rest of the class. After four weeks, we certainly haven't accomplished as much as I thought we would."

Mr. O'Brien nods sympathetically. "I'm so busy keeping thirty-one second graders in line that, most of the time, I can't even remember the stuff I learned at State. I don't want my principal and the other teachers to think badly of me. After all, I'm a certified teacher now and should know what I'm doing. I worry, too, about what my colleagues must think. I'm beginning to wonder whether I was really cut out to be a teacher."

- Do you think Mr. O'Brien's and Ms. Koch's experiences as beginning teachers are unusual? Why or why not?

- If you were in either teacher's shoes, what strategies might you use to begin moving your class or classes in the right direction? What support might the principal and other classroom teachers provide in the early weeks?

SUMMING UP

Larger Context of Teaching

Our roles as teachers go far beyond teaching specific subject matter. We must consider the messages our classroom activities convey about academic work and school in general and make decisions on the basis of what is in students' best interests over the long run. Ultimately, we must work cooperatively with other teachers and other institutions to promote students' learning, development, and achievement.

Communicating with Parents

We must keep in regular contact with our students' parents, sharing information in both directions about the progress that students are making, and coordinating efforts in school with those on the home front. We can keep the lines of communication open through a variety of mechanisms—for instance, by getting parents involved in school activities, scheduling parent-teacher conferences, sending notes home, and making frequent telephone calls. We may need to make an extra effort to establish productive working relationships with those parents who, on the surface, seem reluctant to become involved in their children's education.

Themes of the Book

Various themes appear and reappear throughout the book. Seven prominent ones are interaction, information processing, relevance, classroom climate, challenge, expectations, and diversity (see Table 15–1). Themes such as these can give us general guidance about effective classroom strategies.

Developing as a Teacher

We don't yet have all the answers about how best to help children learn and develop, so we must continue to keep ourselves current about research results, theoretical developments, and educational innovations. As a beginning teacher, you may initially find your classroom a bit overwhelming, but with experience and continuing education, you can eventually become an expert in the teaching profession.

KEY CONCEPT

pedagogical content knowledge (p. 719)

Describing Relationships with Correlation Coefficients

- Do students with high self-esteem perform better in school than students with low self-esteem?

- Which students are more likely to answer questions correctly—those who answer questions quickly or those who are slower to respond?

- Do two different intelligence tests taken at the same time typically yield similar scores for the same student?

- Are intellectually gifted students more emotionally well-adjusted than their "nongifted" classmates?

Each of these questions asks about a relationship between two variables—whether it be the relationship between self-esteem and school achievement, between speed and accuracy in answering questions, between two sets of intelligence test scores, or between giftedness and emotional adjustment. The nature of such relationships is sometimes expressed in terms of a particular number—a statistic known as a **correlation coefficient.**

A correlation coefficient is a number between -1 and $+1$; most correlation coefficients are decimals (either positive or negative) somewhere between these two extremes. A correlation coefficient for two variables simultaneously tells us two different things about the relationship between those variables:

Direction: The direction of the relationship is indicated by the *sign* of the correlation coefficient—in other words, by whether the number is a positive or negative one. A positive number indicates a *positive correlation:* As one variable increases, the other variable also increases. For example, there is a positive correlation between self-esteem and school achievement: Students with higher self-esteem achieve at higher levels (e.g., H. W. Marsh, 1990a). In contrast, a negative number indicates a *negative correlation:* As one variable increases, the other variable decreases instead. For example, there is a negative correlation between speed and accuracy in answering questions: Students who take longer to answer questions tend to make fewer errors in answering them (e.g., Shipman & Shipman, 1985). Figure A–1 graphically depicts each of these relationships.

Strength: The strength of the relationship is indicated by the *size* of the correlation coefficient. A number close to either $+1$ or -1 (e.g., $+.89$ or $-.76$) indicates a *strong* correlation: The two variables are closely related, so knowing the level of one variable allows us to predict the level of the other variable with some degree of accuracy. For example, we often find a strong relationship between two intelligence tests taken at the same time: Students tend to get similar scores on both tests, especially if both tests cover similar kinds of content (e.g., Anastasi, 1988). In contrast, a number close to 0 (e.g., $+.15$ or $-.22$) indicates a *weak* correlation: Knowing the level of one variable allows us to predict the level of the other vari-

Imagine that each face in these two graphs represents one student in a group of fifty students. Each student is located at a place representing the extent to which the student is high or low on the two characteristics indicated. There is a *positive correlation* between self-esteem and school achievement: students with higher self-esteem tend to achieve at higher levels. There is a *negative correlation* between the length of time it takes for students to respond to questions and the number of errors in their answers: students who take longer to answer questions tend to have fewer errors in their responses.

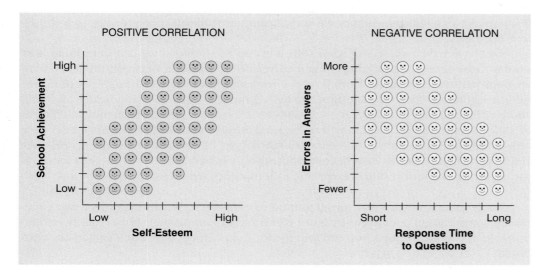

Figure A–1   Positive and Negative Correlations

able, but we cannot predict with much accuracy. For example, there is a weak relationship between intellectual giftedness and emotional adjustment: Generally speaking, students with higher IQ scores show greater emotional maturity than students with lower scores (e.g., Janos & Robinson, 1985), but there are many students who are exceptions to this rule. Correlations in the middle range (e.g., those in the .40s and .50s—whether positive or negative) indicate a *moderate* correlation.

As teachers, we will often find correlation coefficients in the descriptions of research we read in professional books and journals. For example, we might read that students' visual-spatial thinking ability is positively correlated with their success in a mathematics class or that there is a negative correlation between class size and students' achievement test scores. Whenever we see such evidence of correlation, we must remember one very important point: *Correlation does not necessarily indicate causation.* For example, we cannot say that visual-spatial thinking ability specifically *leads to* greater mathematical ability, nor can we say that class size specifically *interferes with* classroom achievement; both of these italicized phrases imply a causal relationship between one variable and another that does not necessarily exist. As we discovered in Chapter 1, only carefully designed experimental studies enable us to draw conclusions about the extent to which one thing causes or influences another.

Using Correlation Coefficients to Determine Reliability

We sometimes use correlation coefficients as an index of the *reliability* of an assessment instrument (see Chapter 14 for an explanation of this concept). In most cases, we begin by getting two scores on the assessment for the same group of students—perhaps by having students perform the same task twice, computing two subscores based on different test questions, or scoring the same test papers at two different times. Each approach gives us a somewhat different angle on reliability; for example, scoring the same test papers twice tells us whether we are scoring our students' performance in a consistent manner.

Once we have two sets of scores for a group of students, we can determine how similar those scores are by computing a correlation coefficient between them. This coefficient will typically range from 0 to +1 (negative coefficients, though possible, are seldom obtained when calculating reliability). A number close to +1 indicates high reliability: The two sets of results are very similar. Although a perfect reliability coefficient of 1.00 is a rare occurrence, many standardized achievement and intelligence tests have reliabilities of .90 or above, reflecting a high degree of consistency in the scores they yield. As reliability coefficients become increasingly lower, they tell us there is more error in our assessment results—error due to temporary, irrelevant factors.

Many calculators are now programmed to compute correlation coefficients. Computing a correlation coefficient by hand is somewhat complicated but certainly not impossible. If you are curious, you can find the formula in most introductory statistics textbooks.

Interpreting Standardized Test Scores

Most scores on published standardized tests are norm-referenced scores. In some cases, these scores are derived by comparing a student's performance with the performance of students at a variety of grade or age levels; such comparisons give us grade- or age-equivalents. In other cases, the scores are based on comparisons only with students of the *same* age or grade; these comparisons give us either percentile scores or standard scores.

Grade- and Age-Equivalents

Imagine that Shantel takes the Mathematical Achievement Test (MAT) and gets 46 of the 60 test items correct (hence, 46 is her raw score). We turn to the norms reported in the test manual and find the average raw scores for students at different grade and age levels:

Normative Data for the MAT

Norms for Grade Levels		Norms for Age Levels	
Grade	*Average* *Raw Score*	Age	*Average* *Raw Score*
5	19	10	18
6	25	11	24
7	30	12	28
8	34	13	33
9	39	14	37
10	43	15	41
11	46	16	44
12	50	17	48

Shantel's raw score of 46 is the same as the average score of eleventh graders in the norm group, so she has a **grade-equivalent score** of 11. Her score is halfway between the average score of sixteen-year-old and seventeen-year-old students, so she has an **age-equivalent score** of about 16½. Shantel is actually only thirteen years old and in eighth grade, so she has obviously done well on the MAT.

In general, grade- and age-equivalents are determined by finding the age or grade level of the norm group whose performance most closely matches our own students. A student who gets the same raw score as the average ten-year-old on a physical fitness test will get an age-equivalent of 10, regardless of whether that student is five, ten, or fifteen years old. A student who performs as well as the average second grader on a reading test will get a grade-equivalent of 2, regardless of what grade level the student is actually in.

Grade- and age-equivalents are frequently used because they seem so simple and straightforward. But they have a serious drawback: They give us no idea of the typical *range* of performance for students at a particular age or grade level. For example, a raw score of 34 on the MAT gives us a grade-equivalent of 8, but obviously not all eighth graders will get raw scores of exactly 34. It is possible, and in fact quite likely, that many

Expect variability in the grade- and age-equivalent scores that students obtain.

"normal" eighth graders will get raw scores several points above or below 34, thus getting grade-equivalents of 9 or 7 (perhaps even 10 or higher, or 6 or lower). Yet grade-equivalents are often used inappropriately as a standard for performance: Parents, school personnel, government officials, and the public at large may believe that *all* students should perform at grade level on an achievement test. Given the normal variability within most classrooms, this goal is probably impossible to meet.

Percentile Ranks

A different approach is to compare our students only with others at the *same* age or grade level. One way of making such a peer-based comparison is by using a **percentile rank:** the percentage of people getting a raw score less than or equal to the student's raw score. To illustrate, let's look once again at Shantel's performance on the MAT. Because Shantel is in eighth grade, we turn to the eighth grade norms and discover that her raw score of 46 is at the 98th percentile. This means that Shantel has done as well as or better than 98% of eighth graders in the norm group on the Mathematics Aptitude Test. Similarly, a student getting a percentile rank of 25 has performed better than 25% of the norm group, and a student getting a score at the 60th percentile has done better than 60%.

Because percentile ranks are relatively simple to understand, they are used frequently in reporting test results. But we need to be aware of a problem with percentiles: They distort actual differences among students. To illustrate, consider the percentile ranks of these four boys on the Basic Skills Test (BST):

Student	Percentile Rank
Ernest	45%ile
Frank	55%ile
Giorgio	89%ile
Nick	99%ile

In terms of the boys' *actual achievement* (as measured by the BST), Ernest and Frank are probably very similar to one another even though their percentile ranks are 10 points apart. Yet 10 points at the upper end of the scale probably reflect a substantial difference in achievement: Giorgio's percentile rank of 89 tells us that he knows quite a bit, but Nick's percentile rank of 99 tells us that he knows an exceptional amount. In general, percentiles tend to *over*estimate differences in the middle range of the characteristic being measured: Scores a few points apart reflect similar achievement or ability. At the same time, percentiles tend to *under*estimate differences at the lower and upper extremes: Scores only a few points apart often reflect significant differences in achievement or ability. We avoid this problem when we use a different type of norm-referenced score—a standard score.

Standard Scores

The school nurse measures the heights of all the students in Ms. Oppenheimer's third-grade class. The heights of Ms. Oppenheimer's twenty-five students are presented on the left side of Figure B–1. The nurse then makes a bar graph of the children's heights, as you can see on the right side of Figure B–1.

Notice the shape of this bar graph: it is high in the middle and low on both ends. This shape tells us that most of Ms. Oppenheimer's students are more or less average in height, with only a handful of very short students (e.g., Pat, Amy, and Wil) and just a few very tall ones (e.g., Hal, Roy, and Jan).

Percentile ranks refer to a percentage of *people*. They do *not* tell us the percentage of items that a student has answered correctly—a common misconception among teacher education students (Lennon et al., 1990).

Remember that percentile ranks overestimate differences between students near the middle of the distribution and underestimate differences between students at the extremes.

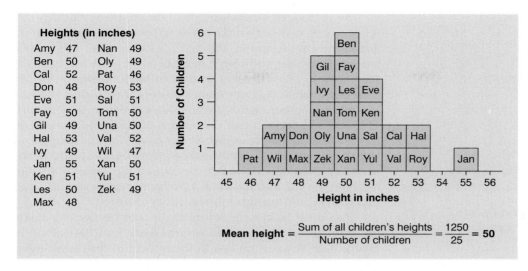

Heights (in inches)			
Amy	47	Nan	49
Ben	50	Oly	49
Cal	52	Pat	46
Don	48	Roy	53
Eve	51	Sal	51
Fay	50	Tom	50
Gil	49	Una	50
Hal	53	Val	52
Ivy	49	Wil	47
Jan	55	Xan	50
Ken	51	Yul	51
Les	50	Zek	49
Max	48		

$$\text{Mean height} = \frac{\text{Sum of all children's heights}}{\text{Number of children}} = \frac{1250}{25} = 50$$

Figure B–1   Heights of Children in Ms. Oppenheimer's Third-Grade Class

Many psychologists believe that educational and psychological characteristics (achievement and aptitude included) typically follow the same pattern we see for height: Most people are close to average, with fewer and fewer people as we move farther from this average. This theoretical pattern of educational and psychological characteristics is called the **normal distribution** (or **normal curve**) and looks like this:

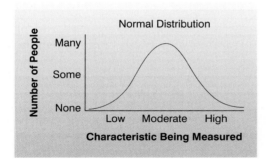

Normal Distribution

Standard scores are test scores that reflect this normal distribution: Many students get scores in the middle range, and only a few get very high or very low scores.

Before we examine standard scores in more detail, we need to understand two numbers we use to derive these scores—the mean and standard deviation. The **mean (M)** is simply the average of a set of scores: We add all the scores together and divide by the number of scores (or people) there are. For example, if we add the heights of all twenty-five students in Ms. Oppenheimer's class and then divide by 25, we get a mean height of 50 (see my calculation at the bottom of Figure B–1). The average student in Ms. Oppenheimer's class, then, is 50 inches tall.

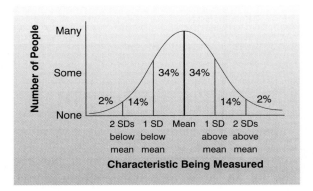

Figure B–2   Normal Distribution Divided by the Mean and Standard Deviation

The **standard deviation (SD)** indicates the *variability* of a set of scores. In other words, it tells us how close together or far apart scores are from one another: A small number tells us they are close together, and a large number tells us they are far apart. For example, third graders tend to be more similar in height than eighth graders (some eighth graders are less than five feet tall, whereas other eighth graders may be almost six feet tall). The standard deviation for the heights of third graders is therefore smaller than the standard deviation for the heights of eighth graders. The procedure for computing a standard deviation is more complex than that for computing a mean. If you are curious, you can find the formula in almost any textbook on either educational testing or introductory statistics.

The mean and standard deviation can be used to divide the normal distribution into several parts, as I have done in Figure B–2. The vertical line in the middle of the curve shows the mean; for a normal distribution, it is at the midpoint and highest point of the curve. The thinner lines to either side reflect the standard deviation: We count out a standard deviation's worth higher than the mean and draw a line and then count another standard deviation and draw another line. We do the same thing below the mean, drawing two lines to tell us the points at which scores are one or two standard deviations below the mean. When we divide the normal distribution in this way, the percentages of students getting scores in each part are always the same. Approximately two-thirds (68%) get scores within one standard deviation of the mean

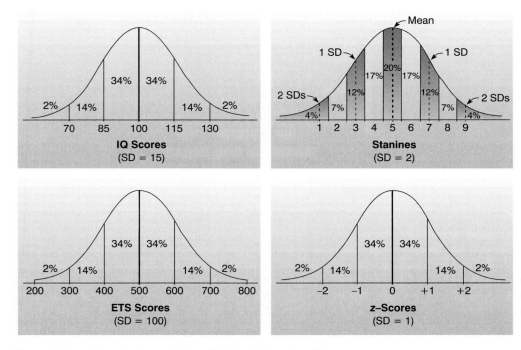

Figure B–3   Distribution of Four Types of Standard Scores

(34% in each direction). As we go farther away from the mean, we find fewer and fewer students, with 28% lying between one and two standard deviations away (14% on each side) and only 4% being more than two standard deviations away (2% at each end).

Now that we better understand the normal distribution and the two numbers that describe it (the mean and standard deviation), let's return to the topic of standard scores. A standard score reflects a student's position in the normal distribution: It tells us how far the student's performance is from the mean in terms of standard deviation units. Unfortunately, not all standard scores use the same scale: Different scores have different means and standard deviations. Four commonly used standard scores, depicted graphically in Figure B–3, are these:

IQ scores. IQ scores are frequently used to report students' performance on intelligence tests. They have a *mean of 100* and, for most tests, a *standard deviation of 15*.

ETS scores. ETS scores are used on tests published by the Educational Testing Service, such as the Scholastic Aptitude Test (SAT) and the Graduate Record Examination (GRE). They have a *mean of 500* and a *standard deviation of 100*; however, no scores fall below 200 or above 800.

Stanines. Stanines (short for *standard nines*) are often used to report standardized achievement test results. They have a *mean of 5* and a *standard deviation of 2*. Because they are always reported as whole numbers, each score reflects a *range* of test performance (reflected by the shaded and nonshaded portions of the third curve in Figure B–3).

***z*-scores.** Standard scores known as *z*-scores are those most frequently used by statisticians. They have a *mean of 0* and a *standard deviation of 1*.

Glossary

Accommodation. Dealing with a new event by either modifying an existing scheme or forming a new one.

Activity reinforcer. An opportunity to engage in a favorite activity.

Actual developmental level. In Vygotsky's theory, the extent to which one can successfully execute a task independently.

Advance organizer. An introduction to a lesson that provides an overall organizational scheme for the lesson.

Affect. The feelings and emotions that an individual brings to bear on a task.

Affective domain. The domain of learning tasks that includes attitudes and values about the things one learns.

Age-equivalent score. A test score that indicates the age level of students to whom a student's test performance is most similar.

Algorithm. A prescribed sequence of steps guaranteeing a correct problem solution.

Antecedent stimulus. A stimulus that increases the likelihood that a particular response will follow.

Anxiety. A feeling of uneasiness and apprehension concerning a situation with an uncertain outcome.

Applied behavior analysis. The systematic application of behaviorist principles in educational and therapeutic settings; sometimes known as *behavior modification*.

Assessment. The process of observing a sample of students' behavior and drawing inferences about their knowledge and abilities.

Assimilation. Dealing with a new event in a way that is consistent with an existing scheme.

Attachment. A strong, affectionate bond formed between a child and another individual (e.g., a parent); usually formed early in the child's life.

Attention. The focusing of mental processes on particular environmental stimuli.

Attribution. A causal explanation for success or failure.

Attribution theory. A theoretical perspective that focuses on (1) people's attributions concerning the causes of events that befall them and (2) the behaviors that result from these attributions.

Authentic activities. Classroom activities similar to those that students are likely to encounter in the outside world.

Authentic assessment. The measurement of students' knowledge and skills in an authentic, "real life" context; in many cases, an integral part of instruction, rather than a separate testing experience.

Authoritarian parenting style. A parenting style characterized by rigid rules and expectations for behavior that children are expected to obey without question.

Authoritative parenting style. A parenting style characterized by emotional warmth, high expectations and standards for behavior, consistent enforcement of rules, explanations regarding the reasons behind these rules, and the inclusion of children in decision making.

Automaticity. The ability to respond quickly and efficiently while mentally processing or physically performing a task.

Base group. A cooperative learning group that lasts an entire semester or school year and provides a means through which students can be mutually supportive of one another's academic efforts and activities.

Baseline. The frequency of a response prior to operant conditioning.

Behavioral objective. An instructional objective that describes a specific, observable behavior.

Behaviorism. A theoretical perspective in which learning and behavior are described and explained in terms of stimulus-response relationships. Adherents to this perspective are called **behaviorists**.

Behavior modification. See *applied behavior analysis*.

Bilingual education. An approach to second-language instruction in which students are instructed in academic subject areas in their native language while simultaneously being taught to speak and write in the second language. The amount of instruction delivered in the native language decreases as students become more proficient in the second language.

Branching program. A form of programmed instruction in which students responding incorrectly to a question proceed to one or more remedial frames for further clarification or practice before continuing on with new information.

Challenge. A situation in which individuals believe that they can succeed with effort.

Checklist. An assessment mechanism that enables one to evaluate students' performance in terms of specific qualities that their performance either does or does not have.

Classical conditioning. The acquisition of a new response as a result of two stimuli being presented at the same time.

Classroom climate. The psychological atmosphere of the classroom.

Classroom management. Establishing and maintaining a classroom environment conducive to learning and achievement.

Cognitive apprenticeship. A mentorship in which teacher and student work together to accomplish a challenging task or solve a difficult problem.

Cognitive development. The development of mental processes and capabilities.

Cognitive domain. The domain of learning tasks that includes knowledge of information, as well as ways of thinking about and using that information.

Cognitive processes. The ways in which one thinks about (processes) information.

Cognitive psychology. A theoretical perspective that focuses on the mental processes underlying human learning and behavior.

Cognitive style. The characteristic way in which a particular individual processes information.

Combinatorial thought. The ability to generate all possible combinations of a group of objects in a systematic fashion.

Community of learners. A classroom in which teacher and students actively and cooperatively work to help one another learn.

Comprehension monitoring. The process of checking oneself to make sure one understands the things being read or heard.

Computer-assisted instruction (CAI). Programmed instruction presented by means of a computer; it is one form of computer-based instruction.

Computer-based instruction (CBI). Instruction provided via computer technology.

Concept. A mental grouping of objects or events that have something in common.

Concept map. A diagram of concepts within an instructional unit and the interrelationships among them.

Conceptual change. Revising one's constructed knowledge in response to contradictory information.

Conceptual understanding. Knowledge acquired in an integrated, interrelated, and meaningful fashion.

Concrete operations stage. Piaget's third stage of cognitive development, in which adultlike logic appears but is limited to concrete reality.

Concrete reinforcer. A reinforcer that can be touched.

Conditioned response (CR). A response that, through classical conditioning, begins to be elicited by a particular stimulus.

Conditioned stimulus (CS). A stimulus that, through classical conditioning, begins to elicit a particular response.

Conditioning. Another word for learning, commonly used by behaviorists.

Conservation. The realization that if nothing is added or taken away, amount stays the same regardless of any alterations in shape or arrangement.

Construction. The process of taking many separate "pieces" of information and using them to build an overall understanding or interpretation of an event.

Constructivism. A theoretical perspective that proposes that learners construct a body of knowledge from their experiences—knowledge that may or may not be an accurate representation of external reality. Adherents to this perspective are called **constructivists.**

Construct validity. The extent to which an assessment accurately measures an unobservable educational or psychological characteristic.

Content validity. The extent to which an assessment includes a representative sample of tasks within the content domain being assessed.

Contiguity. The occurrence of two or more events at the same time. **Contiguous** is the adjective used to refer to events having contiguity.

Contingency. A situation in which one event happens only after another event has already occurred. One event is **contingent** on another's prior occurrence.

Contingency contract. A formal agreement between a teacher and a student regarding behaviors the student will exhibit and reinforcers that will follow those behaviors.

Continuous reinforcement. Reinforcing a response every time it occurs.

Control group. A group of people in a research study who are given either no treatment or a presumably ineffective treatment. The subsequent performance of this group is compared with the performance of one or more treatment groups.

Convergent thinking. Pulling several pieces of information together to draw a conclusion or solve a problem.

Cooperative learning. An approach to instruction whereby students work with their classmates to achieve group goals and help one another learn.

Correlation. The extent to which two variables are related to each other, such that when one variable increases, the other either increases or decreases in a somewhat predictable fashion.

Correlational feature. A characteristic present in many positive instances of a concept but not essential for concept membership.

Correlational study. A research study that explores relationships among variables. Such a study enables researchers to predict one variable on the basis of their knowledge of another.

Correlation coefficient. A statistic that indicates the nature of the relationship between two variables.

Creativity. New and original behavior that yields an appropriate and productive result.

Criterion-referenced score. A test score that specifically indicates what students know and can do.

Cueing. A teacher's signal that a particular behavior is desired or that a particular behavior should stop.

Cultural bias. The extent to which the items or tasks of an assessment instrument either offend or unfairly penalize some students on the basis of their ethnicity, gender, or socioeconomic status.

Cultural mismatch. A situation in which a child's home culture and the school culture hold conflicting expectations for the child's behavior.

Culture shock. A sense of confusion that occurs when students encounter a culture with very different expectations for behavior than the expectations with which they have been raised.

Debilitating anxiety. Anxiety that interferes with performance. A great deal of anxiety is likely to be debilitating.

Decay. A hypothesized weakening over time of information stored in long-term memory, especially if the information is used infrequently or not at all.

Deductive reasoning. Drawing a logical inference about something that must be true, given other information that has already been presented as true.

Deficiency need. In Maslow's hierarchy, a need that results from something a person lacks.

Defining feature. A characteristic that must be present in all positive instances of a concept.

Descriptive study. A research study that describes situations. Such a study enables researchers to draw conclusions about the current state of affairs.

Developmental milestone. The appearance of a new, developmentally more advanced behavior.

Dialect. A form of English characteristic of a particular region or ethnic group.

Discovery learning. An approach to instruction whereby students develop an understanding of a topic in a hands-on fashion through their interaction with the physical or social environment.

Discrimination. Phenomenon in operant conditioning whereby an individual learns that a response is reinforced in the presence of one stimulus but not in the presence of another, similar stimulus.

Disequilibrium. The state of being *un*able to explain new events in terms of existing schemes.

Distributed cognition. A process whereby people think about an issue or problem together, sharing ideas and working to draw conclusions or develop solutions.

Distributed intelligence. The idea that people are more likely to act "intelligently" when they have physical and/or social support systems to assist them.

Divergent thinking. Taking a single idea in many different directions.

Egocentric speech. Speaking without taking the perspective and knowledge of the listener into account.

Elaboration. A cognitive process in which learners expand on new information based on what they already know.

Elaborative interrogation. A study strategy in which students develop and answer elaborative questions about the material they are trying to learn.

Emotional and behavioral disorders. A category of special needs characterized by behaviors or emotional states that have a substantial negative effect on students' classroom performance.

Empathy. Experiencing the same feelings as someone in unfortunate circumstances.

Encoding. Changing the format of new information as it is being stored in memory.

Epistemological beliefs. One's beliefs regarding the nature of knowledge and knowledge acquisition.

Equilibration. The movement from equilibrium to disequilibrium and back to equilibrium. It promotes the development of more complex forms of thought and knowledge.

Equilibrium. A state of being able to explain new events in terms of existing schemes.

Equity in instruction. Instruction without favoritism or bias toward particular individuals or groups of students.

Ethnic group. A group of people with a common set of values, beliefs, and behaviors. Its roots either precede the creation of, or are external to, the country in which it resides.

ETS score. A standard score with a mean of 500 and a standard deviation of 100.

Experimental study (experiment). A research study that involves the manipulation of one variable to determine its possible effect on another variable. It enables researchers to draw conclusions about cause-effect relationships.

Expository instruction. An approach to instruction whereby information is presented in more or less the same form in which students are expected to learn it.

Expressive language. The ability to communicate effectively through speaking and writing.

Extinction. In classical conditioning, the eventual disappearance of a conditioned response as a result of the conditioned stimulus being repeatedly presented alone (in the absence of the unconditioned stimulus); in operant conditioning, the eventual disappearance of a response that is no longer being reinforced.

Extrinsic motivation. Motivation promoted by factors external to the individual and unrelated to the task being performed.

Extrinsic reinforcer. A reinforcer that comes from the outside environment, rather than from within the individual.

Facilitating anxiety. Anxiety that enhances performance. Relatively low levels of anxiety are often facilitating.

Failure to store. One's failure to mentally process information in ways that promote its storage in long-term memory.

Field dependence. The tendency to perceive an object within the context of its surroundings.

Field independence. The tendency to perceive an object separate from its background.

Formal assessment. A systematic attempt to ascertain what students have learned. It is typically planned in advance and used for a specific purpose.

Formal discipline. A view of transfer that postulates that the study of rigorous subjects enhances one's ability to learn other, unrelated things.

Formal operational egocentrism. The inability of individuals in Piaget's formal operations stage to separate abstract logical thinking from practical considerations and the unpredictability of human behavior.

Formal operations stage. Piaget's fourth and final stage of cognitive development, in which logical reasoning processes are applied to abstract ideas, as well as to concrete objects.

Formative evaluation. Evaluation conducted during instruction to facilitate students' learning.

Generalization. A phenomenon in both classical conditioning and operant conditioning whereby an individual learns a response to a particular stimulus and then makes that same response in the presence of similar stimuli.

General transfer. An instance of transfer in which the original learning task and the transfer task do not overlap in content.

Giftedness. A category of special needs characterized by unusually high ability in one or more areas, to the point where students require special educational services to help them meet their full potential.

Grade-equivalent score. A test score that indicates the grade level of students to whom a student's test performance is most similar.

Group contingency. A situation in which an entire group must make a particular response before reinforcement occurs.

Group differences. Consistent differences among certain groups of individuals.

Growth need. In Maslow's hierarchy, a need that serves to enhance a person's growth and development and is never completely satisfied.

Guilt. The feeling of discomfort that individuals experience when they know they have caused someone else pain or distress.

Halo effect. A phenomenon whereby people are more likely to perceive positive behaviors in a person they like or admire.

Hearing impairments. A category of special needs characterized by malfunctions of the ear or associated nerves that interfere with the perception of sounds within the frequency range of normal human speech.

Heuristic. A general problem-solving strategy that may or may not yield a problem solution.

Higher-level questions. Questions that require students to do something new with information they have learned—for example, to apply, analyze, synthesize, or evaluate it.

Hot cognition. Learning or information processing that is emotionally charged.

Hypermedia. A collection of computer-based instructional material, including both verbal text and such other media as pictures, sound, and animations. It is interconnected in such a way that students can learn about one topic and then proceed to related topics of their own choosing.

Hypertext. A collection of computer-based verbal material that allows students to read about one topic and then proceed to related topics of their own choosing.

Ill-defined problem. A problem in which the desired goal is unclear, information needed to solve the problem is missing, or several possible solutions to the problem exist.

Illusion of knowing. Thinking one knows something that one actually does not know.

Imaginary audience. The belief that one is the center of attention in any social situation.

I-message. A message that describes the effects that a student's behavior has (and possibly the feelings that it elicits) for the teacher or for other students.

Immersion. An approach to second-language instruction in which students hear and speak that language almost exclusively within the classroom.

Impulsivity. The tendency to do tasks quickly and carelessly, without close attention to detail.

Inability to retrieve. Failing to locate information that currently exists in long-term memory.

Incentive. A hoped-for, but not certain, consequence of behavior.

Inclusion. The practice of educating all students, even those with severe and multiple disabilities, in neighborhood schools and regular classrooms.

Incompatible behaviors. Two or more behaviors that cannot be performed simultaneously.

Individual constructivism. A theoretical perspective that focuses on the cognitive processes through which people, as individuals, construct meaning from the events around them.

Individual differences. The ways in which individuals of the same age are different from one another.

Induction. Explaining why a certain behavior is unacceptable, often with a focus on the pain or distress that someone has caused another.

Informal assessment. Results from teachers' spontaneous, day-to-day observations of how students behave and perform in class.

Information processing. Mentally manipulating, modifying, and storing the information that one receives.

Information processing theory. A theoretical perspective that focuses on the specific ways in which individuals mentally think about and "process" the information they receive.

Inner speech. "Talking" to oneself mentally, rather than aloud.

In-school suspension. A form of punishment in which a student is placed in a quiet, boring room within the school building. It often lasts one or more school days and involves close adult supervision.

Instructional objective. A statement describing a final goal or outcome of instruction.

Intelligence. The ability to modify and adjust one's behaviors in order to accomplish new tasks successfully. It involves many different mental processes, and its nature may vary, depending on the culture in which one lives.

Intelligence test. A general measure of current cognitive functioning, used primarily to predict academic achievement over the short run.

Interference. A phenomenon whereby something stored in long-term memory inhibits one's ability to remember something else correctly.

Intermittent reinforcement. Reinforcing a response only occasionally, with some occurrences of the response going unreinforced.

Intrinsic motivation. The internal desire to perform a particular task.

Intrinsic reinforcer. A reinforcer supplied by oneself or inherent in the task being performed.

IQ score. A score on an intelligence test. It is determined by comparing one's performance on the test with the performance of others in the same age-group. For most tests, it is a standard score with a mean of 100 and a standard deviation of 15.

Irrelevant feature. A characteristic totally unrelated to qualifications for concept membership.

Irreversibility. An inability to recognize that certain processes can be undone, or reversed.

Jigsaw technique. An instructional technique in which instructional materials are divided among members of a cooperative learning group, with individual students being responsible for learning different material and then teaching that material to other group members.

Keyword method. A mnemonic technique in which an association is made between two ideas by forming a visual image of one or more concrete objects **(keywords)** that either sound similar to, or symbolically represent, those ideas.

Knowledge base. One's knowledge of specific topics and the world in general.

Learned helplessness. A general belief that one is incapable of accomplishing tasks and has little or no control of the environment.

Learning. A relatively permanent change, due to experience, in either behavior or mental associations.

Learning disabilities. A category of special needs characterized by average or above-average intelligence, lower academic achievement than would be predicted from students' IQ scores, and a deficiency in one or more specific cognitive processes.

Learning goal. A desire to acquire additional knowledge or master new skills.

Learning strategy. One or more cognitive processes used intentionally for a particular learning task.

Level of potential development. In Vygotsky's theory, the extent to which one can successfully execute a task with the assistance of a more competent individual.

Levels of processing. A model of memory that focuses on the extent (depth) to which information is processed, rather than on distinct components of memory.

Limited English proficiency (LEP). A limited ability to understand and communicate in oral or written English. For most LEP students, English is not their native language.

Linear program. A form of programmed instruction in which all students proceed through the same sequence of instructional frames.

Linguistic development. The development of language skills and capabilities.

Live model. An individual observed "in the flesh."

Logical consequence. A consequence that follows logically from a student's misbehavior; in other words, the punishment fits the crime.

Long-term memory. The component of memory that holds knowledge and skills for a relatively long period of time.

Long-term objective. An objective that requires months or years of instruction and practice to be accomplished.

Lower-level questions. Questions that require students to express what they have learned in essentially the same way that they learned it—for example, by reciting a textbook's definition of a concept or describing an application that their teacher presented in class.

Maintenance rehearsal. See *rehearsal*.

Mastery learning. An approach to instruction whereby students learn one topic thoroughly before moving to a more difficult one.

Mastery orientation. A general belief that one is capable of accomplishing challenging tasks.

Maturation. The unfolding of genetically controlled changes as a child develops.

Mean. The arithmetic average of a set of scores. It is calculated by adding all the scores and then dividing by the total number of people who have obtained those scores.

Meaningful learning. A cognitive process in which learners relate new information to the things they already know.

Meaningful learning set. An attitude that one can make sense out of the information to be learned.

Mediation training. Training that involves teaching students how to mediate conflicts among classmates by asking the opposing sides to express their differing points of view and then working together to devise a reasonable resolution.

Mental retardation. A category of special needs characterized by significantly below-average general intelligence and deficits in adaptive behavior.

Mental set. Encoding a problem in a way that excludes potential problem solutions.

Metacognition. One's knowledge and beliefs regarding one's own cognitive processes, and resulting attempts to regulate those cognitive processes to maximize learning and memory.

Metacognitive scaffolding. Any technique that guides students in their use of metacognitive strategies.

Metalinguistic awareness. The extent to which one is able to think about the nature of language.

Misbehavior. An action that has the potential to disrupt classroom learning and planned classroom activities.

Misconception. Previously learned but incorrect information.

Mnemonic. A special memory aid or trick designed to help students learn and remember information.

Moral development. The development of one's understanding of right and wrong.

Moral dilemma. A situation in which there is no clear-cut answer regarding the morally correct thing to do.

Motivation. A state that energizes, directs, and sustains behavior.

Motivation to learn. The tendency to find school-related activities meaningful and worthwhile and therefore to try to get the maximum benefit from them.

Multicultural education. Education that includes the perspectives and experiences of numerous cultural groups on a regular basis.

Multiple classification. The recognition that objects may belong to several categories simultaneously.

Need for affiliation. The tendency to seek out friendly relationships with others.

Need for approval. A desire to gain the approval and acceptance of others.

Negative instance. A nonexample of a concept.

Negative reinforcement. A consequence that brings about the increase of a behavior through the removal (rather than the presentation) of a stimulus.

Negative transfer. A phenomenon whereby something learned at one time interferes with learning or performance at a later time.

Negative wait time. The tendency to interrupt someone who has not yet finished speaking.

Neutral stimulus. A stimulus that does not elicit any particular response.

Normal distribution (normal curve). A theoretical pattern of educational and psychological characteristics in which most individuals lie somewhere in the middle range and only a few lie at either extreme.

Norm-referenced score. A score that indicates how a student's performance on an assessment compares with the average performance of other students (with the performance of a norm group).

Norms. As related to socialization, society's rules for acceptable and unacceptable behavior; as related to testing practice, data regarding the typical performance of various groups of students on a standardized test or other norm-referenced assessment.

Object permanence. The realization that objects continue to exist even when removed from view.

Operant conditioning. The increase in frequency of a response after it has been followed by reinforcement.

Operations. In Piaget's theory, organized and integrated systems of thought processes.

Organization. A cognitive process in which learners find connections (e.g., forming categories, identifying hierarchical relationships) among the various pieces of information they need to learn.

Outcomes-based education (OBE). An approach to instruction whereby objectives for students (**outcomes**) are specified before the school year begins and assessment is based on the extent to which such objectives have been achieved.

Overall positive regard. Respect and affection for another individual as a human being despite any shortcomings that the individual may have.

Overgeneralization. Having too broad a meaning for a word, applying the word in situations where it's not appropriate; identifying objects or events as examples of a concept when, in fact, they are not.

Overregularization. Applying syntactical rules in situations where those rules don't apply.

Paper-pencil assessment. Assessment in which students respond to written items in a written fashion.

Parenting. The way in which a parent raises his or her children.

Pedagogical content knowledge. Knowledge about effective methods of teaching a specific content area.

Peer pressure. A phenomenon whereby a student's peers strongly encourage some behaviors and discourage others.

Peers. One's equals or age-mates.

Peer tutoring. An approach to instruction whereby students who have mastered a topic teach those who have not.

Percentile rank (percentile). A test score that indicates the percentage of people in the norm group getting a raw score less than or equal to a particular student's raw score.

Performance assessment. Assessment in which students demonstrate their knowledge and skills in a nonwritten fashion.

Performance goal. A desire either to look good and receive favorable judgments from others or else not to look bad and receive unfavorable judgments.

Permissive parenting style. A parenting style characterized by emotional warmth but few expectations or standards for children's behavior.

Personal development. The development of one's personality and self-concept.

Personal fable. The belief that one is completely unlike anyone else.

Personality. Set of relatively enduring traits that characterize the way in which a person typically interacts with his or her physical and social environments.

Physical and health impairments. A category of special needs characterized by general physical or medical conditions (usually long-term) that interfere with students' school performance to such an extent that special instruction, curricular materials, equipment, or facilities are necessary.

Portfolio. A systematic collection of a student's work over a lengthy period of time.

Positive feedback. A message that an answer is correct or a task has been well done.

Positive instance. A specific example of a concept.

Positive reinforcement. A consequence that brings about the increase of a behavior through the presentation (rather than the removal) of a stimulus.

Positive transfer. A phenomenon whereby something learned at one time facilitates learning or performance at a later time.

Practicality. The extent to which an assessment instrument or procedure is relatively easy to use.

Predictive validity. The extent to which the results of an assessment predict future behavior.

Premack principle. A phenomenon whereby individuals do less preferred activities in order to engage in more preferred activities.

Preoperational egocentrism. The inability of children in Piaget's preoperational stage to view situations from another person's perspective.

Preoperational stage. Piaget's second stage of cognitive development, in which children can think about objects beyond their immediate view but do not yet reason in logical, adultlike ways.

Primary reinforcer. A stimulus that satisfies a basic physiological need.

Principle. A description of how one variable influences another variable. It evolves when similar research studies yield similar results time after time.

Private speech. See *self-talk*.

Programmed instruction (PI). An approach to instruction whereby students independently study a topic that has been broken into small, carefully sequenced segments.

Proportional thought. The ability to understand proportions (e.g., fractions, decimals, ratios) and use them effectively in mathematical problem solving.

Prosocial behavior. Behavior directed toward promoting the well-being of someone else.

Prototype. A mental representation of a "typical" positive instance of a concept.

Psychological punishment. Any consequence that seriously threatens a student's self-concept and self-esteem.

Psychomotor domain. The domain of learning tasks that includes simple and complex physical movements and actions.

Punishment. A consequence that decreases the frequency of the response it follows.

Punishment I. A form of punishment involving the presentation of a new stimulus, presumably one that an individual finds unpleasant.

Punishment II. A form of punishment involving the removal of an existing stimulus, presumably one that an individual views as desirable and doesn't want to lose.

Rating scale. An assessment mechanism that enables one to evaluate students' performance in terms of one or more continua that reflect desired characteristics of that performance.

Raw score. A score based solely on the number or point value of correctly answered items.

Recall task. A memory task in which one must retrieve information in its entirety from long-term memory.

Receptive language. The ability to understand the language one hears and reads.

Reciprocal causation. The interdependence of environment, behavior, and personal variables as these three factors influence learning.

Reciprocal teaching. An approach to teaching reading or listening comprehension whereby students take turns asking teacherlike questions of their classmates.

Recognition task. A memory task in which one must recognize correct information among irrelevant information or incorrect statements.

Reconstruction error. Constructing a logical but incorrect "memory" by using information retrieved from long-term memory plus one's general knowledge of the world.

Reflection. The tendency to approach tasks slowly and with attention to detail, and to evaluate the quality of one's own work carefully.

Rehearsal. A cognitive process in which information is repeated over and over as a possible way of learning and remembering it. When it is used to maintain information in working memory, it is called **maintenance rehearsal.**

Reinforcement. The act of following a particular response with a reinforcer and thereby increasing the frequency of that response.

Reinforcer. A consequence (stimulus) of a response that leads to an increased frequency of that response.

Reliability. The extent to which an assessment instrument yields consistent information about the knowledge, skills, or abilities we are trying to measure.

Resilient students. Students who succeed in school despite exceptional hardships in their home lives.

Response (R). A specific behavior that an individual exhibits.

Response cost. The loss of either a previously earned reinforcer or an opportunity to obtain reinforcement.

Retrieval. The process of "finding" information previously stored in memory.

Retrieval cue. A hint about where to "look" for a piece of information in long-term memory.

Reversibility. The ability to recognize that certain processes can be undone, or reversed.

Roles. Patterns of behavior acceptable for individuals having different functions within a society.

Rote learning. Learning information primarily through verbatim repetition, without understanding it in a meaningful fashion.

Salience. In concept learning, the degree to which a particular feature or characteristic is obvious and easily noticeable.

Scaffolding. A support mechanism, provided by a more competent individual, that helps a learner successfully perform a task within his or her zone of proximal development.

Schema. An organized body of knowledge about a specific topic.

Scheme. In Piaget's theory, an organized group of similar actions or thoughts.

Script. A schema that involves a predictable sequence of events related to some activity.

Scripted cooperation. In cooperative learning, a technique in which cooperative groups follow a set of steps or "script" that guides members' verbal interactions.

Secondary reinforcer. A stimulus that becomes reinforcing over time through its association with another reinforcer; it is sometimes called a **conditioned reinforcer.**

Self-actualization. The tendency for human beings to enhance themselves and fulfill their potential—to strive toward becoming everything they are capable of becoming.

Self-concept. One's beliefs about oneself.

Self-determination. A sense that one has some choice and control regarding the future course of one's life.

Self-efficacy. One's belief that one is capable of executing certain behaviors or reaching certain goals.

Self-esteem. The extent to which one believes oneself to be a capable and worthy individual.

Self-evaluation. The process of evaluating one's own performance or behavior.

Self-fulfilling prophecy. A situation in which one's expectations in and of themselves lead to the expected result.

Self-imposed contingencies. Contingencies that students impose on themselves—the self-reinforcements and self-punishments that follow various behaviors.

Self-instructions. Instructions that students give themselves as they perform a complex behavior.

Self-observation. The process of observing and recording one's own behavior.

Self-questioning. The process of asking oneself questions as a way of checking one's own understanding of a topic.

Self-regulation. The process of setting standards and goals for oneself and engaging in behaviors that lead to the accomplishment of those standards and goals.

Self-regulatory problem-solving strategy. A strategy that helps students solve their own interpersonal problems.

Self-talk. Talking to oneself as a way of guiding oneself through a task; also known as *private speech.*

Semantics. The meanings of words and word combinations.

Sense of community. In the classroom, a widely shared feeling that teacher and students have common goals, are mutually respectful and supportive of one another's efforts, and believe that everyone makes an important contribution to classroom learning.

Sensorimotor stage. Piaget's first stage of cognitive development, in which schemes are based on behaviors and perceptions.

Sensory register. A component of memory that holds incoming information in an unanalyzed form for a very brief period of time (probably less than a second for visual input and two or three seconds for auditory input).

Separation and control of variables. The ability to test one variable at a time while holding all other variables constant.

Shame. A feeling of embarrassment or humiliation that children feel after failing to meet the standards for moral behavior that adults have set.

Shaping. A process of reinforcing successively closer and closer approximations to a desired terminal behavior.

Short-term memory. See *working memory.*

Short-term objective. An objective that can typically be accomplished within the course of a single lesson or unit.

Single classification. The ability to classify objects in only one way at any given point in time.

Situated cognition.   Knowledge and thinking skills that are acquired and used primarily within certain contexts, with limited if any transfer to other contexts.

Social cognitive theory.   A theoretical perspective in which learning by observing others is the focus of study.

Social constructivism.   A theoretical perspective that focuses on people's collective efforts to impose meaning on the world.

Social development.   The development of one's ability to interact effectively with others.

Socialization.   The process of shaping a child's behavior to fit the norms and roles of the child's society.

Social reinforcer.   A gesture or sign that one person gives to another and communicates positive regard.

Social skills.   Behaviors that enable an individual to interact effectively with others.

Socioeconomic status (SES).   One's general social and economic standing in society, encompassing such variables as family income, occupation, and level of education.

Specific transfer.   An instance of transfer in which the original learning task and the transfer task overlap in content.

Speech and communication disorders.   A category of special needs characterized by abnormalities in spoken language that significantly interfere with students' classroom performance.

Stage.   A period in a child's development characterized by certain behaviors and/or reasoning skills. The nature and sequence of different stages of development are believed by stage theorists to be relatively consistent from one child to another.

Stage theory.   A theory that depicts development as a series of stages, with relatively slow growth within each stage and more rapid growth during the transition from one stage to another.

Standard deviation (SD).   A statistic that reflects how close together or far apart a set of scores are and thereby indicates the variability of the scores.

Standard English.   The form of English generally considered acceptable at school, as reflected in textbooks, grammar instruction, and so on.

Standardization.   The extent to which assessment instruments and procedures involve similar content and format and are administered and scored in the same way for everyone.

Standardized test.   A test developed by test construction experts and published for use in many different schools and classrooms.

Standards.   General statements regarding the knowledge and skills that students should achieve and the characteristics that their accomplishments should reflect.

Standard score.   A test score that indicates how far a student's performance is from the mean in terms of standard deviation units.

Stanine.   A standard score with a mean of 5 and a standard deviation of 2; it is always reported as a whole number.

State anxiety.   A temporary feeling of anxiety elicited by a threatening situation.

Stereotype.   A rigid, simplistic, and erroneous caricature of a particular group of people.

Stimulus (S) (pl. stimuli).   A specific object or event that influences an individual's learning or behavior.

Storage.   The process of "putting" new information into memory.

Students at risk.   Students who have a high probability of failing to acquire the minimal academic skills necessary for success in the adult world.

Students with special needs.   Students who are different enough from their peers that they require special educational services.

Summative evaluation.   An evaluation conducted after instruction to assess students' final achievement.

Superimposed meaningful structure.   A mnemonic technique in which a familiar shape, word, sentence, poem, or story is imposed on information and thereby used to remember it.

Symbolic model.   A real or fictional character portrayed in various media.

Symbolic thinking.   The ability to represent and think about external objects and events in one's head.

Syntax.   The set of rules that one uses to put words together into sentences.

Table of specifications.   A two-way grid indicating both the topics to be covered in an assessment and the things that students should be able to do with each topic.

Task analysis.   A process of breaking down a complex objective into a number of simpler, more manageable components.

Teacher-developed assessment instrument.   An assessment tool developed by an individual teacher for use in his or her own classroom.

Terminal behavior.   The form and frequency of a response at the end of operant conditioning.

Test anxiety.   Excessive anxiety about a particular test or about tests in general.

Testwiseness.   Test-taking know-how that enhances test performance.

Theory.   A description of possible underlying mechanisms to explain why certain principles are true.

Threat.   A situation in which individuals believe that they have little or no chance of success.

Time-out.   A procedure whereby a misbehaving student is placed in a dull, boring situation with no opportunity to interact with classmates and no opportunity to obtain reinforcement.

Traditional assessment. Assessment that focuses on measuring basic knowledge and skills in relative isolation from tasks more typical of the outside world.

Trait anxiety. A pattern of responding with anxiety even in nonthreatening situations.

Transductive reasoning. Making a mental leap from one specific thing to another, such as identifying one event as the cause of another simply because the two events occur close together in time.

Transfer. A phenomenon whereby something an individual has learned at one time affects how the individual learns or performs in a later situation.

Treatment group. A group of people in a research study who are given a particular experimental treatment (e.g., a particular method of instruction).

Unconditioned response (UCR). A response that, without prior learning, is elicited by a particular stimulus.

Unconditioned stimulus (UCS). A stimulus that, without prior learning, elicits a particular response.

Undergeneralization. An overly restricted meaning for a word, excluding some situations to which the word does, in fact, apply; an overly narrow view of what objects or events a concept includes.

Uninvolved parenting style. A parenting style characterized by a lack of emotional support and a lack of standards regarding appropriate behavior.

Universals in development. The similar patterns we see in how children change over time regardless of the specific environment in which they are raised.

Validity. The extent to which an assessment instrument measures what it is supposed to measure.

Verbal mediator. A mnemonic technique in which a word or phrase is used to form a logical connection or "bridge" between two pieces of information.

Vicarious punishment. A phenomenon whereby a response decreases in frequency when another (observed) person is punished for that response.

Vicarious reinforcement. A phenomenon whereby a response increases in frequency when another (observed) person is reinforced for that response.

Visual imagery. The process of forming mental "pictures" of objects or ideas.

Visual impairments. A category of special needs characterized by malfunctions of the eyes or optic nerves that prevent students from seeing normally even with corrective lenses.

Visual-spatial thinking. The ability to imagine and mentally manipulate two- and three-dimensional figures in one's mind.

Wait time. The length of time a teacher pauses, either after asking a question or hearing a student's comment, before saying something else.

Well-defined problem. A problem in which the goal is clearly stated, all information needed to solve the problem is present, and only one correct answer exists.

Withitness. A teacher's knowledge of what all students are doing at all times.

Working memory. A component of memory that holds and processes a limited amount of new information; also known as *short-term memory*. The duration of information stored in working memory is believed to be approximately five to twenty seconds.

z-score. A standard score with a mean of 0 and a standard deviation of 1.

Zone of proximal development (ZPD). In Vygotsky's theory, the range of tasks between one's actual developmental level and one's level of potential development—that is, the range of tasks that one cannot yet perform independently, but *can* perform with the help and guidance of others.

References

A bullet (•) indicates a reference new to the 2nd edition.

• Abdul-Jabbar, K., & Knobles, P. (1983). *Giant steps: The autobiography of Kareem Abdul-Jabbar.* New York: Bantam.

• Abi-Nader, J. (1993). Meeting the needs of multicultural classrooms: Family values and the motivation of minority students. In M. J. O'Hair & S. J. Odell (Eds.), *Diversity and teaching: Teacher education yearbook I.* Fort Worth, TX: Harcourt Brace Jovanovich.

• Achenbach, T. M., & Edelbrock, C. S. (1981). Behavioral problems and competencies reported by parents of normal and disturbed children aged four through sixteen. *Monographs of the Society for Research in Child Development, 46*(1, Serial No. 188).

• Adams, G. R., Gullotta, T. P., & Markstrom-Adams, C. (1994). *Adolescent life experiences* (3rd ed.). Pacific Grove, CA: Brooks/Cole.

Adams, P. A., & Adams, J. K. (1960). Confidence in the recognition and reproduction of words difficult to spell. *American Journal of Psychology, 73,* 544–552.

Aiello, B. (1988). The Kids on the Block and attitude change: A 10-year perspective. In H. E. Yuker (Ed.), *Attitudes toward persons with disabilities.* New York: Springer.

• Airasian, P. W. (1994). *Classroom assessment* (2nd ed.). New York: McGraw-Hill.

• Alberto, P. A., & Troutman, A. C. (1990). *Applied behavior analysis for teachers* (3rd ed.). Upper Saddle River, NJ: Merrill/Prentice Hall.

Alderman, M. K. (1990). Motivation for at-risk students. *Educational Leadership, 48*(1), 27–30.

• Alexander, P. A. (1996). The past, present, and future of knowledge research: A reexamination of the role of knowledge in learning and instruction. *Educational Psychologist, 31,* 89–92.

• Alexander, P. A., & Jetton, T. L. (1996). The role of importance and interest in the processing of text. *Educational Psychology Review, 8,* 89–121.

Alexander, P. A., & Judy, J. E. (1988). The interaction of domain-specific and strategic knowledge in academic performance. *Review of Educational Research, 58,* 375–404.

• Alexander, P. A., Kulikowich, J. M., & Schulze, S. K. (1994). How subject-matter knowledge affects recall and interest. *American Educational Research Journal, 31,* 313–337.

Allen, G. G., & Seumptewa, O. (1988). The need for strengthening Native American science and mathematics education. *Journal of College Science Teaching, 17,* 364–369.

Alley, G., & Deshler, D. (1979). *Teaching the learning disabled adolescent: Strategies and methods.* Denver, CO: Love.

• Allington, R. L., & Weber, R. (1993). Questioning questions in teaching and learning from texts. In B. K. Britton, A. Woodward, & M. Binkley (Eds.), *Learning from textbooks: Theory and practice.* Hillsdale, NJ: Erlbaum.

Alvermann, D. E. (1981). The compensatory effect of graphic organizers on descriptive text. *Journal of Educational Research, 75,* 44–48.

• Amabile, T. M., & Hennessey, B. A. (1992). The motivation for creativity in children. In A. K. Boggiano & T. S. Pittman (Eds.), *Achievement and motivation: A social-developmental perspective.* Cambridge, UK: Cambridge University Press.

• Ames, C. (1984). Competitive, cooperative, and individualistic goal structures: A cognitive-motivational analysis. In R. Ames & C. Ames (Eds.), *Research on motivation in education: Vol. 1. Student motivation.* San Diego: Academic Press.

• Ames, C. (1992). Classrooms: Goals, structures, and student motivation. *Journal of Educational Psychology, 84,* 261–271.

• Ames, C., & Archer, J. (1988). Achievement goals in the classroom: Students' learning strategies and motivation processes. *Journal of Educational Psychology, 80,* 260–267.

Ames, R. (1983). Help-seeking and achievement orientation: Perspectives from at-tribution theory. In A. Nadler, J. Fisher, & B. DePaulo (Eds.), *New directions in helping* (Vol. 2). San Diego: Academic Press.

Ames, R., & Lau, S. (1982). An attributional analysis of student help-seeking in academic settings. *Journal of Educational Psychology, 74,* 414–423.

Anastasi, A. (1988). *Psychological testing* (6th ed.). New York: Macmillan.

• Anderman, E. M., & Maehr, M. L. (1994). Motivation and schooling in the middle grades. *Review of Educational Research, 64,* 287–309.

Anderson, J. R. (1982). Acquisition of cognitive skill. *Psychological Review, 89,* 369–406.

• Anderson, J. R. (1987). Skill acquisition: Compilation of weak-method problem solutions. *Psychological Review, 94,* 192–210.

Anderson, J. R. (1990). *Cognitive psychology and its implications* (3rd ed.). New York: W. H. Freeman.

• Anderson, J. R., Reder, L. M., & Simon, H. A. (1996). Situated learning and education. *Educational Researcher, 25*(4), 5–11.

Anderson, L. (1984). The environment of instruction: The function of seatwork in a commercially developed curriculum. In G. Duffy, L. Roehler, & J. Mason (Eds.), *Comprehension instruction: Perspectives and suggestions.* White Plains, NY: Longman.

• Anderson, L. M. (1993). Auxiliary materials that accompany textbook: Can they promote "higher-order" learning? In B. K. Britton, A. Woodward, & M. Binkley (Eds.), *Learning from textbooks: Theory and practice.* Hillsdale, NJ: Erlbaum.

Anderson, L. M., Brubaker, N. L., Alleman-Brooks, J., & Duffy, G. (1985). A qualitative study of seatwork in first-grade classrooms. *Elementary School Journal, 86,* 123–140.

Anderson, N. S. (1987). Cognition, learning, and memory. In M. A. Baker (Ed.), *Sex differences in human performance.* Chichester, UK: John Wiley.

Anderson, R. C., Reynolds, R. E., Schallert, D. L., & Goetz, E. T. (1977). Frameworks for comprehending discourse. *American Educational Research Journal, 14,* 367–381.

• Anderson, R. C., Wilson, P. T., & Fielding, L. G. (1988). Growth in reading and how children spend their time outside of school. *Reading Research Quarterly, 23,* 285–303.

• Anderson, V., & Hidi, S. (1988/1989). Teaching students to summarize. *Educational Leadership, 46*(4), 26–28.

Andre, T. (1986). Problem solving and education. In G. D. Phye & T. Andre (Eds.), *Cognitive classroom learning: Understanding, thinking, and problem solving.* San Diego: Academic Press.

• Andre, T. (1987). Questions and learning from reading. *Questioning Exchange, 1,* 47–86.

Andrews, J. D. (1981). Teaching format and student style: Their interactive effects on the learning of college students. *Research in Higher Education, 14,* 161–178.

Anglin, J. M. (1977). *Word, object, and conceptual development.* New York: Norton.

• Anzai, Y. (1991). Learning and use of representations for physics expertise. In K. A. Ericsson & J. Smith (Eds.), *Toward a general theory of expertise: Prospects and limits.* Cambridge, UK: Cambridge University Press.

Archer, S. L. (1982). The lower age boundaries of identity development. *Child Development, 53,* 1551–1556.

Arenz, B. W., & Lee, M. J. (1990, April). *Gender differences in the attitude, interest, and participation of secondary students in computer use.* Paper presented at the annual meeting of the American Educational Research Association, Boston, MA.

Arlin, M. (1979). Teacher transitions can disrupt time flow in classrooms. *American Educational Research Journal, 16,* 42–56.

Arlin, M. (1984). Time, equality, and mastery learning. *Review of Educational Research, 54,* 65–86.

Armbruster, B. B. (1989). Metacognition in creativity. In J. A. Glover, R. R. Ronning, & C. R. Reynolds (Eds.), *Handbook of creativity.* New York: Plenum Press.

• Armbruster, B., B. & Ostertag, J. (1993). Questions in elementary science and social studies textbooks. In B. K. Britton,

A. Woodward, & M. Binkley (Eds.), *Learning from textbooks: Theory and practice.* Hillsdale, NJ: Erlbaum.

• Arnett, J. (1995). The young and the reckless: Adolescent reckless behavior. *Current Directions in Psychological Science, 4,* 67–71.

Aronfreed, J. (1968). Aversive control of socialization. In W. J. Arnold (Ed.), *Nebraska Symposium on Motivation.* Lincoln: University of Nebraska Press.

Aronfreed, J., & Reber, A. (1965). Internalized behavioral suppression and the timing of social punishment. *Journal of Personality and Social Psychology, 1,* 3–16.

• Arter, J. A., & Spandel, V. (1992). Using portfolios of student work in instruction and assessment. *Educational Measurement: Issues and Practice, 11*(1), 36–44.

• Asai, S. (1993). In search of Asia through music: Guidelines and ideas for teaching Asian music. In T. Perry & J. W. Fraser (Eds.), *Freedom's plow: Teaching in the multicultural classroom.* New York: Routledge.

• Asher, S. R., & Coie, J. D. (Eds.). (1990). *Peer rejection in childhood.* Cambridge, UK: Cambridge University Press.

• Asher, S. R., & Parker, J. G. (1989). Significance of peer relationship problems in childhood. In B. H. Schneider, G. Attili, J. Nadel, & R. P. Weissberg (Eds.), *Social competence in developmental perspective.* Dordrecht, The Netherlands: Kluwer.

• Ashton, P. (1985). Motivation and the teacher's sense of efficacy. In C. Ames & R. Ames (Eds.), *Research on motivation in education: Vol. 2. The classroom milieu.* San Diego: Academic Press.

Atkinson, R. C., & Shiffrin, R. M. (1968). Human memory: A proposed system and its control processes. In K. W. Spence & J. T. Spence (Eds.), *The psychology of learning and motivation: Advances in research and theory* (Vol. 2). San Diego: Academic Press.

Au, K. H. (1980). Participation structures in a reading lesson with Hawaiian children: Analysis of a culturally appropriate instructional event. *Anthropology and Education Quarterly, 11,* 91–115.

Au, K. H., & Jordan, C. (1981). Teaching reading to Hawaiian children: Finding a culturally appropriate solution. In H. T. Trueba, G. P. Guthrie, & K. H. Au (Eds.),

Culture and the bilingual classroom: Studies in classroom ethnography. Rowley, MA: Newbury House.

Ausubel, D. P. (1968). *Educational psychology: A cognitive view.* New York: Holt, Rinehart & Winston.

Ausubel, D. P., Novak, J. D., & Hanesian, H. (1978). *Educational psychology: A cognitive view* (2nd ed.). New York: Holt, Rinehart & Winston.

• Ayllon, T., & Roberts, M. D. (1974). Eliminating discipline problems by strengthening academic performance. *Journal of Applied Behavior Analysis, 7,* 71–76.

• Babad, E. (1993). Teachers' differential behavior. *Educational Psychology Review, 5,* 347–376.

• Baddeley, A. D. (1978). The trouble with levels: A reexamination of Craik and Lockhart's framework for memory research. *Psychological Review, 85,* 139–152.

• Baddeley, A. D. (1982). *Your memory: A user's guide.* New York: Macmillan.

• Baek, S. (1994). Implications of cognitive psychology for educational testing. *Educational Psychology Review, 6,* 373–389.

• Bahrick, H. P., Bahrick, L. E., Bahrick, A. S., & Bahrick, P. E. (1993). Maintenance of foreign language vocabulary and the spacing effect. *Psychological Science, 4,* 316–321.

• Baker, E. L. (1994). Learning-based assessments of history understanding. *Educational Psychologist, 29,* 97–106.

Baker, L. (1989). Metacognition, comprehension monitoring, and the adult reader. *Educational Psychology Review, 1,* 3–38.

Baker, L., & Brown, A. L. (1984). Metacognitive skills of reading. In D. Pearson (Ed.), *Handbook of reading research.* White Plains, NY: Longman.

• Ball, D. L. (1991). Research on teaching mathematics: Making subject-matter knowledge part of the equation. In J. Brophy (Ed.), *Advances in research on teaching: Vol. 2. Teacher's knowledge of subject matter as it relates to their teaching practice.* Greenwich, CT: JAI Press.

• Balla, D. A., & Zigler, E. (1979). Personality development in retarded persons. In N. R. Ellis (Ed.), *Handbook of mental deficiency: Psychological theory and research* (2nd ed.). Hillsdale, NJ: Erlbaum.

Bandura, A. (1965). Influence of models' reinforcement contingencies on the acquisition of imitative responses. *Journal of Personality and Social Psychology, 1,* 589–595.

Bandura, A. (1977). *Social learning theory.* Upper Saddle River, NJ: Prentice Hall.

Bandura, A. (1982). Self-efficacy mechanism in human agency. *American Psychologist, 37,* 122–147.

Bandura, A. (1986). *Social foundations of thought and action: A social cognitive theory.* Upper Saddle River, NJ: Prentice Hall.

Bandura, A. (1989). Human agency in social cognitive theory. *American Psychologist, 44,* 1175–1184.

Bandura, A., & Kupers, C. J. (1964). Transmission of patterns of self-reinforcement through modeling. *Journal of Abnormal & Social Psychology, 69,* 1–9.

Bandura, A., & McDonald, F. J. (1963). Influences of social reinforcement and the behavior of models in shaping children's moral judgments. *Journal of Abnormal and Social Psychology, 67,* 274–281.

Bandura, A., & Perloff, B. (1967). Relative efficacy of self-monitored and externally imposed reinforcement systems. *Journal of Personality and Social Psychology, 7,* 111–116.

Bandura, A., Ross, D., & Ross, S. A. (1961). Transmission of aggression through imitation of aggressive models. *Journal of Abnormal & Social Psychology, 63,* 575–582.

Bandura, A., Ross, D., & Ross, S. A. (1963). Imitation of film-mediated aggressive models. *Journal of Abnormal & Social Psychology, 66,* 3–11.

• Bangert-Drowns, R. L., Kulik, C. C., Kulik, J. A., & Morgan, M. (1991). The instructional effect of feedback in test-like events. *Review of Educational Research, 61,* 213–238.

Banks, J. A. (1987, April). *Ethnicity, class, and cognitive styles: Research and teaching implications.* Paper presented at the annual meeting of the American Educational Research Association, Washington, DC.

• Banks, J. A. (1991). Multicultural literacy and curriculum reform. *Educational Horizons, 69*(3), 135–140.

• Banks, J. A. (1994). *An introduction to multicultural education.* Needham Heights, MA: Allyn & Bacon.

• Banks, J. A. (1995). Multicultural education: Historical development, dimensions, and practice. In J. A. Banks & C. A. M. Banks (Eds.), *Handbook of research on multicultural education.* New York: Macmillan.

• Barbetta, P. M. (1990). GOALS: A group-oriented adapted levels system for children with behavior disorders. *Academic Therapy, 25,* 645–656.

Barker, G., & Graham, S. (1987). Developmental study of praise and blame as attributional cues. *Journal of Educational Psychology, 79,* 62–66.

• Barkley, R. A. (1990). *Attention-deficit hyperactivity disorder: A handbook for diagnosis and treatment.* New York: Guilford.

• Barnes, D. (1976). *From communication to curriculum.* London: Penguin.

Barnett, J. E., Di Vesta, F. J., & Rogozinski, J. T. (1981). What is learned in note taking? *Journal of Educational Psychology, 73,* 181–192.

Baron, J. B. (1987). Evaluating thinking skills in the classroom. In J. B. Baron & R. J. Sternberg (Eds.), *Teaching thinking skills: Theory and practice.* New York: W. H. Freeman.

Barringer, C., & Gholson, B. (1979). Effects of type and combination of feedback upon conceptual learning by children: Implications for research in academic learning. *Review of Educational Research, 49,* 459–478.

Barrish, H. H., Saunders, M., & Wolf, M. M. (1969). Good behavior game: Effects of individual contingencies for group consequences on disruptive behavior in a classroom. *Journal of Applied Behavior Analysis, 2,* 119–124.

Bartlett, E. J. (1982). Learning to revise: Some component processes. In M. Nystrand (Ed.), *What writers know: The language, process, and structure of written discourse.* San Diego: Academic Press.

• Bartlett, F. C. (1932). *Remembering: A study in experimental and social psychology.* Cambridge, UK: Cambridge University Press.

Baskin, E. J., & Hess, R. D. (1980). Does affective education work? A review of seven programs. *Journal of School Psychology, 8,* 40–50.

Bassok, M. (1990). Transfer of domain-specific problem-solving procedures. *Journal of Experimental Psychology: Learning, Memory, and Cognition, 16,* 522–533.

Bassok, M., & Holyoak, K. (1990, April). *Transfer of solution procedures between quantitative domains.* Paper presented at the annual meeting of the American Educational Research Association, Boston, MA.

Bates, J. A. (1979). Extrinsic reward and intrinsic motivation: A review with implications for the classroom. *Review of Educational Research, 49,* 557–576.

Battle, E. (1966). Motivational determinants of academic competence. *Journal of Personality and Social Psychology, 4,* 634–642.

Baumrind, D. (1967). Child care practices anteceding three patterns of preschool behavior. *Genetic Psychological Monographs, 75,* 43–88.

Baumrind, D. (1971). Current patterns of parental authority. *Developmental Psychology Monograph, 4* (No. 1, Part 2).

• Baumrind, D. (1989). Rearing competent children. In W. Damon (Ed.), *Child development today and tomorrow.* San Francisco: Jossey-Bass.

Baumrind, D., & Black, A. E. (1967). Socialization practices associated with dimensions of competence in preschool boys and girls. *Child Development, 38,* 291–327.

• Baxter, G. P., Elder, A. D., & Glaser, R. (1996). Knowledge-based cognition and performance assessment in the science classroom. *Educational Psychologist, 31,* 133–140.

• Bear, G. G., & Richards, H. C. (1981). Moral reasoning and conduct problems in the classroom. *Journal of Educational Psychology, 73,* 644–670.

• Bédard, J., & Chi, M. T. H. (1992). Expertise. *Current Directions in Psychological Science, 1,* 135–139.

Bee, H. L., Barnard, K. E., Eyres, S. J., Gray, C. A., Hammond, M. A., Spietz, A. L., Snyder, C., & Clark, B. (1982). Prediction of IQ and language skill from perinatal status, child performance, family characteristics, and mother-infant interaction. *Child Development, 53,* 1134–1156.

• Bellezza, F. S. (1986). Mental cues and verbal reports in learning. In G. H. Bower (Ed.), *The psychology of learning and motivation: Advances in research and theory* (Vol. 20). San Diego: Academic Press.

Bem, S. L. (1984). Androgyny and gender schema theory: A conceptual and empirical integration. In R. A. Dienstbier & T. B. Sonderegger (Eds.), *Nebraska symposium on motivation* (Vol. 34). Lincoln: University of Nebraska Press.

• Bennett, G. K., Seashore, H. G., & Wesman, A. G. (1982). *Differential Aptitude Tests.* San Antonio, TX: Psychological Corporation.

Bents, M., & Bents, R. (1990, April). *Perceptions of good teaching among novice, advanced beginner, and expert teachers.* Paper presented at the annual meeting of the American Educational Research Association, Boston, MA.

• Benware, C., & Deci, E. L. (1984). Quality of learning with an active versus passive motivational set. *American Educational Research Journal, 21,* 755–765.

• Berg, K. F. (1994, April). Scripted cooperation in high school mathematics: Peer interaction and achievement. Paper presented at the annual meeting of the American Educational Research Association, New Orleans, LA.

Berk, L. E. (1989). *Child development.* Needham Heights, MA: Allyn & Bacon.

• Berkowitz, M. W., Guerra, N., & Nucci, L. (1991). Sociomoral development and drug and alcohol abuse. In W. M. Kurtines & J. L. Gewirtz (Eds.), *Moral behavior and development: Vol. 3. Application.* Hillsdale, NJ: Erlbaum.

Berliner, D. C. (1988, February). *The development of expertise in pedagogy.* Paper presented at the American Association of Colleges for Teacher Education, New Orleans, LA.

Berlyne, D. E. (1960). *Conflict, arousal, and curiosity.* New York: McGraw-Hill.

Berndt, T. J. (1979). Developmental changes in conformity to peers and parents. *Developmental Psychology, 15,* 608–616.

• Berndt, T. J. (1992). Friendship and friends' influence in adolescence. *Current Directions in Psychological Science, 1,* 156–159.

Berndt, T. J., Laychak, A. E., & Park, K. (1990). Friends' influence on adolescents' academic achievement motivation: An experimental study. *Journal of Educational Psychology, 82,* 664–670.

Bierman, K. L., Miller, C. L., & Stabb, S. D. (1987). Improving the social behavior and peer acceptance of rejected boys: Effect of social skill training with instructions and prohibitions. *Journal of Consulting and Clinical Psychology, 55,* 194–200.

Bilodeau, I. M., & Schlosberg, H. (1951). Similarity in stimulating conditions as a variable in retroactive inhibition. *Journal of Experimental Psychology, 41,* 199–204.

Bishop, B. A., & Anderson, C. W. (1990). Student conceptions of natural selection and its role in evolution. *Journal of Research in Science Teaching, 27,* 415–427.

• Bjorkqvist, K., Osterman, K., & Kaukiainen, A. (1992). The development of direct and indirect aggressive strategies in males and females. In K. Bjorkqvist & P. Niemala (Eds.), *Of mice and women: Aspects of female aggression.* San Diego: Academic Press.

Blake, S. B., & Clark, R. E. (1990, April). *The effects of metacognitive selection on far transfer in analogical problem solving tasks.* Paper presented at the annual meeting of the American Educational Research Association, Boston, MA.

Blanco, R. F. (1972). *Prescriptions for children with learning and adjustment problems.* Springfield, IL: Charles C. Thomas.

Blasi, A. (1980). Bridging moral cognition and moral action: A critical review of the literature. *Psychological Bulletin, 88,* 593–637.

Blatt, M. M., & Kohlberg, L. (1973). The effects of classroom moral discussion upon children's level of moral judgment. In L. Kohlberg & E. Turiel (Eds.), *Recent research in moral development.* New York: Holt, Rinehart & Winston.

Block, J. H. (1980). Promoting excellence through mastery learning. *Theory Into Practice, 19*(1), 66–74.

Block, J. H. (1983). Differential premises arising from differential socialization of the sexes: Some conjectures. *Child Development, 54,* 1335–1354.

Block, J. H., & Burns, R. B. (1976). Mastery learning. In L. Shulman (Ed.), *Review of research in education* (Vol. 4). Itasca, IL: Peacock.

Bloom, B. S. (1964). *Stability and change in human characteristics.* New York: Wiley.

Bloom, B. S. (1968). Mastery learning. In *Evaluation comment* (Vol. 1, No. 2). Los Angeles: University of California, Center for the Study of Evaluation of Instructional Programs.

Bloom, B. S. (1974). An introduction to mastery learning theory. In J. H. Block

(Ed.), *Schools, society, and mastery learning.* New York: Holt, Rinehart & Winston.

Bloom, B. S. (1976). *Human characteristics and school learning.* New York: McGraw-Hill.

Bloom, B. S. (1981). *All our children learning.* New York: McGraw-Hill.

Bloom, B. S. (1984a). The search for methods of group instruction as effective as one-to-one tutoring. *Educational Leadership, 41,* 4–17.

Bloom, B. S. (1984b). The 2 sigma problem: The search for methods of group instruction as effective as one-to-one tutoring. *Educational Research, 13,* 4–16.

Bloom, B. S., & Broder, L. J. (1950). *Problem-solving processes of college students.* Chicago: University of Chicago Press.

Bloom, B. S., Englehart, M. D., Furst, E. J., Hill, W. H., & Krathwohl, D. R. (1956). *Taxonomy of educational objectives. The classification of educational goals: Handbook I. Cognitive domain.* New York: David McKay.

• Blumenfeld, P. C. (1992). The task and the teacher: Enhancing student thoughtfulness in science. In J. Brophy (Ed.), *Advances in research on teaching: Vol. 3. Planning and managing learning tasks and activities.* Greenwich, CT: JAI Press.

Bochenhauer, M. H. (1990, April.) *Connections: Geographic education and the National Geographic Society.* Paper presented at the annual meeting of the American Educational Research Association, Boston, MA.

• Boggiano, A. K., & Pittman, T. S. (Eds.). (1992). *Achievement and motivation: A social-developmental perspective.* Cambridge, UK: Cambridge University Press.

Borke, H. (1975). Piaget's mountains revisited: Changes in the egocentric landscape. *Developmental Psychology, 11,* 240–243.

Borkowski, J. G., Carr, M., Rellinger, E., & Pressley, M. (1990). Self-regulated cognition: Interdependence of metacognition, attributions, and self-esteem. In B. F. Jones & L. Idol (Eds.), *Dimensions of thinking and cognitive instruction.* Hillsdale, NJ: Erlbaum.

Born, D. G., & Davis, M. L. (1974). Amount and distribution of study in a personalized instruction course and in a lecture course. *Journal of Applied Behavior Analysis, 7,* 365–375.

- Bornholt, L. J., Goodnow, J. J., & Cooney, G. H. (1994). Influences of gender stereotypes on adolescents' perceptions of their own achievement. *American Educational Research Journal, 31,* 675–692.
- Boschee, F., & Baron, M. A. (1993). *Outcome-based education: Developing programs through strategic planning.* Lancaster, PA: Technomic.
- Bouchard, T. J., Jr., Lykken, D. T., McGue, M., Segal, N. L., & Tellegen, A. (1990, October 12). Sources of human psychological differences: The Minnesota study of twins reared apart. *Science, 250,* 223–228.
- Bourne, L. E., Jr., Ekstrand, D. R., & Dominowski, R. L. (1971). *The psychology of thinking.* Upper Saddle River, NJ: Prentice Hall.
- Bousfield, W. A. (1953). The occurrence of clustering in the recall of randomly arranged associates. *Journal of General Psychology, 49,* 229–240.
- Boutte, G. S., & McCormick, C. B. (1992). Authentic multicultural activities: Avoiding pseudomulticulturalism. *Childhood Education, 68*(3), 140–144.
- Bower, G. H., Black, J. B., & Turner, T. J. (1979). Scripts in memory for text. *Cognitive Psychology, 11,* 177–220.
- Bower, G. H., & Clark, M. C. (1969). Narrative stories as mediators for serial learning. *Psychonomic Science, 14,* 181–182.
- Bower, G. H., Clark, M. C., Lesgold, A. M., & Winzenz, D. (1969). Hierarchical retrieval schemes in recall of categorized word lists. *Journal of Verbal Learning and Verbal Behavior, 8,* 323–343.
- Bower, G. H., Karlin, M. B., & Dueck, A. (1975). Comprehension and memory for pictures. *Memory and Cognition, 3,* 216–220.
- Bowie, R., & Bond, C. (1994). Influencing future teachers' attitudes toward Black English: Are we making a difference? *Journal of Teacher Education, 45*(2), 112–118.
- Bowman, B. T. (1989). Educating language-minority children: Challenges and opportunities. *Phi Delta Kappan, 71,* 118–120.
- Boyatzis, R. E. (1973). Affiliation motivation. In D. C. McClelland & R. S. Steele (Eds.), *Human motivation: A book of readings.* Morristown, NJ: General Learning Press.
- Boykin, A. W. (1983). The academic performance of Afro-American children. In

J. T. Spence (Ed.), *Achievement and achievement motives.* San Francisco: W. H. Freeman.
- Bradley, R. H., & Caldwell, B. M. (1984). The relation of infants' home environments to achievement test performance in first grade: A follow-up study. *Child Development, 55,* 803–809.
- Brainerd, C. J., & Reyna, V. F. (1992). Explaining "memory free" reasoning. *Psychological Science, 3,* 332–339.
- Bransford, J. D., & Franks, J. J. (1971). The abstraction of linguistic ideas. *Cognitive Psychology, 2,* 331–350.
- Bransford, J. D., & Johnson, M. K. (1972). Contextual prerequisites for understanding: Some investigations of comprehension and recall. *Journal of Verbal Learning and Verbal Behavior, 11,* 717–726.
- Braukmann, C. J., Kirigin, K. A., & Wolf, M. M. (1981). Behavioral treatment of juvenile delinquency. In S. W. Bijou & R. Ruiz (Eds.), *Behavior modification: Contributions to education.* Hillsdale, NJ: Erlbaum.
- Broden, M., Hall, R. V., & Mitts, B. (1971). The effect of self-recording on the classroom behavior of two eighth-grade students. *Journal of Applied Behavior Analysis, 4,* 191–199.
- Brody, G. H., & Shaffer, D. R. (1982). Contributions of parents and peers to children's moral socialization. *Developmental Review, 2,* 31–75.
- Brody, N. (1985). The validity of tests of intelligence. In B. B. Wolman (Ed.), *Handbook of intelligence.* New York: Wiley.
- Brodzinsky, D. M., Messer, S. M., & Tew, J. D. (1979). Sex differences in children's expression and control of fantasy and overt aggression. *Child Development, 50,* 372–379.
- Brooke, R. R., & Ruthren, A. J. (1984). The effects of contingency contracting on student performance in a PSI class. *Teaching of Psychology, 11,* 87–89.
- Brooks, L. W., & Dansereau, D. F. (1987). Transfer of information: An instructional perspective. In S. M. Cormier & J. D. Hagman (Eds.), *Transfer of learning: Contemporary research and applications.* San Diego: Academic Press.
- Brooks-Gunn, J., Klebanov, P. K., & Duncan, G. J. (1996). Ethnic differences in children's intelligence test scores: Role of economic deprivation, home environ-

ment, and maternal characteristics. *Child Development, 67,* 396–408.
- Brophy, J. E. (1981). Teacher praise: A functional analysis. *Review of Educational Research, 51,* 5–32.
- Brophy, J. E. (1985). Interactions of male and female students with male and female teachers. In L. C. Wilkinson & C. B. Marrett (Eds.), *Gender influences in classroom interaction.* San Diego: Academic Press.
- Brophy, J. E. (1986). *On motivating students* (Occasional Paper No. 101). East Lansing: Michigan State University, Institute for Research on Teaching.
- Brophy, J. E. (1987). Synthesis of research on strategies for motivating students to learn. *Educational Leadership, 45*(2), 40–48.
- Brophy, J. E. (Ed.). (1991). *Advances in research on teaching: Vol. 2. Teacher's knowledge of subject matter as it relates to their teaching practice.* Greenwich, CT: JAI Press.
- Brophy, J. E. (1992a). Conclusions: Comments on an emerging field. In J. Brophy (Ed.), *Advances in research on teaching: Vol. 3. Planning and managing learning tasks and activities.* Greenwich, CT: JAI Press.
- Brophy, J. E. (1992b). Probing the subtleties of subject-matter teaching. *Educational Leadership, 49*(7), 4–8.
- Brophy, J. E. (Ed.). (1994). *Advances in research on teaching: Vol. 4. Case studies of teaching and learning in social studies.* Greenwich, CT: JAI Press.
- Brophy, J. E., & Alleman, J. (1991). Activities as instructional tools: A framework for analysis and evaluation. *Educational Researcher, 20*(4), 9–23.
- Brophy, J. E., & Alleman, J. (1992). Planning and managing learning activities: Basic principles. In J. Brophy (Ed.), *Advances in research on teaching: Vol. 3. Planning and managing learning tasks and activities.* Greenwich, CT: JAI Press.
- Brophy, J. E., & Evertson, C. (1976). *Learning from teaching: A developmental perspective.* Needham Heights, MA: Allyn & Bacon.
- Brophy, J. E., & Good, T. L. (1970). Teachers' communication of differential expectations for children's classroom performance: Some behavioral data. *Journal of Educational Psychology, 61,* 365–374.
- Brophy, J. E., & Good, T. L. (1986). Teacher effects. In M. C. Wittrock (Ed.), *Hand-*

book of research on teaching (3rd ed.). New York: Macmillan.

• Brough, J. A. (1990). Changing conditions for young adolescents: Reminiscences and realities. *Educational Horizons, 68,* 78–81.

Brown, A. L. (1978). Knowing when, where, and how to remember: A problem of metacognition. In R. Glaser (Ed.), *Advances in instructional psychology*. Hillsdale, NJ: Erlbaum.

• Brown, A. L., Ash, D., Rutherford, M., Nakagawa, K., Gordon, A., & Campione, J. C. (1993). Distributed expertise in the classroom. In G. Salomon (Ed.), *Distributed cognitions: Psychological and educational considerations*. Cambridge, UK: Cambridge University Press.

Brown, A. L., Campione, J., & Day, J. (1981). Learning to learn: On training students to learn from texts. *Educational Researcher, 10*(2), 14–21.

Brown, A. L., & Palincsar, A. S. (1987). Reciprocal teaching of comprehension strategies: A natural history of one program for enhancing learning. In J. Borkowski & J. D. Day (Eds.), *Cognition in special education: Comparative approaches to retardation, learning disabilities, and giftedness*. Norwood, NJ: Ablex.

• Brown, A. L., & Palincsar, A. S. (1989). Guided, cooperative learning and individual knowledge acquisition. In L. B. Resnick (Ed.), *Knowing, learning, and instruction: Essays in honor of Robert Glaser*. Hillsdale, NJ: Erlbaum.

Brown, A. L., & Reeve, R. A. (1987). Bandwidths of competence: The role of supportive contexts in learning and development. In L. S. Liben (Ed.), *Development and learning: Conflict or congruence?* Hillsdale, NJ: Erlbaum.

Brown, A. L., Smiley, S. S., Day, J. D., Townsend, M. A. R., & Lawton, S. C. (1977). Intrusion of a thematic idea in children's comprehension and retention of stories. *Child Development, 48,* 1454–1466.

• Brown, B. B. (1993). School culture, social politics, and the academic motivation of U.S. students. In T. M. Tomlinson (Ed.), *Motivating students to learn: Overcoming barriers to high achievement*. Berkeley, CA: McCutchan.

• Brown, J. S., Collins, A., & Duguid, P. (1989). Situated cognition and the culture of learning. *Educational Researcher, 18*(1), 32–42.

Brown, R., & McNeill, D. (1966). The "tip of the tongue" phenomenon. *Journal of Verbal Learning and Verbal Behavior, 5,* 325–337.

Brown, R. T. (1989). Creativity: What are we to measure? In J. A. Glover, R. R. Ronning, & C. R. Reynolds (Eds.), *Handbook of creativity*. New York: Plenum Press.

• Brownell, M. T., Mellard, D. F., & Deshler, D. D. (1993). Differences in the learning and transfer performance between students with learning disabilities and other low-achieving students on problem-solving tasks. *Learning Disabilities Quarterly, 16,* 138–156.

• Brown-Mizuno, C. (1990). Success strategies for learners who are learning disabled as well as gifted. *Teaching Exceptional Children, 23*(1), 10–12.

Bruner, J. S. (1960). *The process of education*. Cambridge, MA: Harvard University Press.

Bruner, J. S. (1961). The act of discovery. *Harvard Educational Review, 31,* 21–32.

Bruner, J. S. (1966). *Toward a theory of instruction*. Cambridge, MA: Harvard University Press.

Bruner, J. S., Goodnow, J., & Austin, G. (1956). *A study of thinking*. New York: Wiley.

• Bruning, R. H., Schraw, G. J., & Ronning, R. R. (1995). *Cognitive psychology and instruction* (2nd ed.). Upper Saddle River, NJ: Merrill/Prentice Hall.

Bryan, J. H. (1975). Children's cooperation and helping behaviors. In E. M. Hetherington (Ed.), *Review of child development research* (Vol. 5). Chicago: University of Chicago Press.

• Bryan, T. (1991). Social problems and learning disabilities. In B. Y. L. Wong (Ed.), *Learning about learning disabilities*. San Diego: Academic Press.

• Buchoff, T. (1990). Attention deficit disorder: Help for the classroom teacher. *Childhood Education, 67*(2), 86–90.

Bugelski, B. R., & Alampay, D. A. (1961). The role of frequency in developing perceptual sets. *Canadian Journal of Psychology, 15,* 205–211.

• Buhrmester, D. (1992). The developmental courses of sibling and peer relationships. In F. Boer & J. Dunn (Eds.), *Children's sibling relationships: Developmental and clinical issues*. Hillsdale, NJ: Erlbaum.

• Bulgren, J. A., Schumaker, J. B., & Deshler, D. D. (1994). The effects of a recall enhancement routine on the test performance of secondary students with and without learning disabilities. *Learning Disabilities Research and Practice, 9,* 2–11.

Burger, H. G. (1973). Cultural pluralism and the schools. In C. S. Brembeck & W. H. Hill, *Cultural challenges to education: The influence of cultural factors in school learning*. Lexington, MA: Heath.

• Butterworth, G. (1993). Context and cognition in models of cognitive growth. In P. Light & G. Butterworth (Eds.), *Context and cognition: Ways of learning and knowing*. Hillsdale, NJ: Erlbaum.

Cairns, R. B., Cairns, B. D., Neckerman, H. J., Gest, S. D., & Gariépy, J. (1988). Social networks and aggressive behavior: Peer support or peer rejection? *Developmental Psychology, 24,* 815–823.

Calfee, R. (1981). Cognitive psychology and educational practice. In D. C. Berliner (Ed.), *Review of research in education* (Vol. 9). Washington, DC: American Educational Research Association.

Calfee, R., & Chambliss, M. J. (1988, April). *The structure of social studies textbooks: Where is the design?* Paper presented at the annual meeting of the American Educational Research Association, New Orleans, LA.

• Calfee, R., Dunlap, K., & Wat, A. (1994). Authentic discussion of texts in middle grade schooling: An analytic-narrative approach. *Journal of Reading, 37,* 546–556.

Calhoun, G., & Elliott, R. (1977). Self-concept and academic achievement of educable retarded and emotionally disturbed pupils. *Exceptional Children, 44,* 379–380.

• Cameron, J., & Pierce, W. D. (1994). Reinforcement, reward, and intrinsic motivation: A meta-analysis. *Review of Educational Research, 64,* 363–423.

• Cameron, J., & Pierce, W. D. (1996). The debate about rewards and intrinsic motivation: Protests and accusations do not alter the results. *Review of Educational Research, 66,* 39–51.

• Campbell, D. E. (1996). *Choosing democracy: A practical guide to multicultural education*. Upper Saddle River, NJ: Merrill/Prentice Hall.

Campbell, P. A. (1986). What's a nice girl like you doing in a math class? *Phi Delta Kappan, 67,* 516–520.

Campione, J. C., Brown, A. L., & Bryant, N. R. (1985). Individual differences in learning and memory. In R. J. Sternberg (Ed.), *Human abilities: An information-processing approach.* New York: W. H. Freeman.

Canady, R. L., & Hotchkiss, P. R. (1989). It's a good score! Just a bad grade. *Phi Delta Kappan, 71,* 68–71.

Candler-Lotven, A., Tallent-Runnels, M. K., Olivárez, A., & Hildreth, B. (1994, April). *A comparison of learning and study strategies of gifted, average-ability, and learning-disabled ninth-grade students.* Paper presented at the annual meeting of the American Educational Research Association, New Orleans, LA.

Capron, C., & Duyme, M. (1989). Assessment of effects of socioeconomic status on IQ in a full cross-fostering study. *Nature, 340,* 552–554.

Carey, L. M. (1994). *Measuring and evaluating school learning* (2nd ed.). Needham Heights, MA: Allyn & Bacon.

Carey, S. (1985a). Are children fundamentally different kinds of thinkers and learners than adults? In S. F. Chipman, J. W. Segal, & R. Glaser (Eds.), *Learning and thinking skills: Vol. 2. Research and open questions.* Hillsdale, NJ: Erlbaum.

Carey, S. (1985b). *Conceptual change in childhood.* Cambridge: MIT Press.

Carey, S. (1986). Cognitive science and science education. *American Psychologist, 41,* 1123–1130.

Carnine, D. (1989). Teaching complex content to learning disabled students: The role of technology. *Exceptional Children, 55,* 524–533.

Caron, A. J. (1963). Curiosity, achievement, and avoidant motivation as determinants of epistemic behavior. *Journal of Abnormal and Social Psychology, 67,* 535–549.

Carpenter, P. A., & Just, M. A. (1986). Cognitive processes in reading. In J. Orasanu (Ed.), *Reading comprehension: From research to practice.* Hillsdale, NJ: Erlbaum.

Carpenter, T. P. (1985). Learning to add and subtract: An exercise in problem solving. In E. A. Silver (Ed.), *Teaching and learning mathematical problem solving: Multiple research perspectives.* Hillsdale, NJ: Erlbaum.

Carr, M., & Borkowski, J. G. (1989). Attributional training and the generalization of reading strategies with underachieving children. *Learning and Individual Differences, 1,* 327–341.

Carraher, T. N., Carraher, D. W., & Schliemann, A. D. (1985). Mathematics in the streets and in the schools. *British Journal of Developmental Psychology, 3,* 21–29.

Carrasco, R. L. (1981). Expanded awareness of student performance: A case study in applied ethnographic monitoring in a bilingual classroom. In H. T. Trueba, G. P. Guthrie, & K. H. Au (Eds.), *Culture and the bilingual classroom: Studies in classroom ethnography.* Rowley, MA: Newbury House.

Carroll, J. B. (1985). Second-language abilities. In R. J. Sternberg (Ed.), *Human abilities: An information-processing approach.* New York: W. H. Freeman.

Carter, K. R. (1991). Evaluation of gifted programs. In N. Buchanan & J. Feldhusen (Eds.), *Conducting research and evaluation in gifted education: A handbook of methods and applications.* New York: Teachers College Press.

Carter, K. R., & Ormrod, J. E. (1982). Acquisition of formal operations by intellectually gifted children. *Gifted Child Quarterly, 26,* 110–115.

Cartledge, G., & Milburn, J. F. (1995). *Teaching social skills to children and youth: Innovative approaches* (3rd ed.). Needham Heights, MA: Allyn & Bacon.

Casanova, U. (1987). Ethnic and cultural differences. In V. Richardson-Koehler (Ed.), *Educator's handbook: A research perspective.* White Plains, NY: Longman.

Case, R. (1985). *Intellectual development: Birth to adulthood.* San Diego: Academic Press.

Casey, W. M., & Burton, R. V. (1982). Training children to be consistently honest through verbal self-instructions. *Child Development, 53,* 911–919.

Casserly, P. L. (1980). Factors affecting female participation in Advanced Placement programs in mathematics, chemistry, and physics. In L. H. Fox, L. Brody, & D. Tobin (Eds.), *Women and the mathematical mystique.* Baltimore: Johns Hopkins University Press.

Cazden, C. B. (1968). The acquisition of noun and verb inflections. *Child Development, 39,* 433–448.

Cazden, C. B., & Leggett, E. L. (1981). Culturally responsive education: Recommendations for achieving *Lau* Remedies II. In H. T. Trueba, G. P. Guthrie, & K. H. Au (Eds.), *Culture and the bilingual classroom: Studies in classroom ethnography.* Rowley, MA: Newbury House.

Cermak, L. S., & Craik, F. I. M. (Eds.). (1979). *Levels of processing in human memory.* Hillsdale, NJ: Erlbaum.

Chall, J. S. (1979). The great debate: Ten years later, with a modest proposal for reading stages. In L. B. Resnick & P. A. Weaver (Eds.), *Theory and practice of early reading.* Hillsdale, NJ: Erlbaum.

Chall, J. S. (1983). *Stages of reading development.* New York: McGraw-Hill.

Chalmers, J., & Townsend, M. (1990). The effects of training in social perspective taking on socially maladjusted girls. *Child Development, 61,* 178–190.

Chambliss, M. J., Calfee, R. C., & Wong, I. (1990, April). *Structure and content in science textbooks: Where is the design?* Paper presented at the annual meeting of the American Educational Research Association, Boston, MA.

Chan, C. K. K., Burtis, P. J., Scardamalia, M., & Bereiter, C. (1992). Constructive activity in learning from text. *American Educational Research Journal, 29,* 97–118.

Charles, C. M. (1983). *Elementary classroom management.* White Plains, NY: Longman.

Cheng, L. R. (1987). *Assessing Asian language performance.* Rockville, MD: Aspen.

Cheng, P. W. (1985). Restructuring versus automaticity: Alternative accounts of skill acquisition. *Psychological Review, 92,* 414–423.

Cheng, P. W., Holyoak, K. J., Nisbett, R. E., & Oliver, L. M. (1986). Pragmatic versus syntactic approaches to training deductive reasoning. *Cognitive Psychology, 18,* 293–328.

Cherry, E. C. (1953). Some experiments on the recognition of speech, with one and with two ears. *Journal of the Acoustical Society of America, 25,* 975–979.

Chester, M. D., & Beaudin, B. Q. (1996). Efficacy beliefs of newly hired teachers in urban schools. *American Educational Research Journal, 33,* 233–257.

Cheyne, J. A., & Walters, R. H. (1970). Punishment and prohibition: Some origins of self-control. In T. M. Newcomb (Ed.), *New directions in psychology.* New York: Holt, Rinehart & Winston.

Chi, M. T. H. (1978). Knowledge structures and memory development. In R. S. Siegler (Ed.), *Children's thinking: What develops?* Hillsdale, NJ: Erlbaum.

Chi, M. T. H., Feltovich, P., & Glaser, R. (1981). Categorization and representation of physics problems by experts and novices. *Cognitive Science, 5,* 121–152.

Chi, M. T. H., Glaser, R., & Rees, E. (1982). Expertise in problem solving. In R. J. Sternberg (Ed.), *Advances in the psychology of human intelligence.* Hillsdale, NJ: Erlbaum.

• Chinn, C. A., & Brewer, W. F. (1993). The role of anomalous data in knowledge acquisition: A theoretical framework and implications for science instruction. *Review of Educational Research, 63,* 1–49.

Chipman, S. F., Brush, L. R., & Wilson, D. M. (Eds.). (1985). *Women and mathematics: Balancing the equation.* Hillsdale, NJ: Erlbaum.

Chomsky, C. S. (1969). *The acquisition of syntax in children from 5 to 10.* Cambridge: MIT Press.

Chomsky, N. (1972). *Language and mind* (enlarged ed.). San Diego: Harcourt Brace Jovanovich.

• Church, R. M. (1993). Human models of animal behavior. *Psychological Science, 4,* 170–173.

• Cizek, G. J. (1991). Innovation or enervation? Performance assessment in perspective. *Phi Delta Kappan, 72,* 695–699.

Clark, B. (1992). *Growing up gifted: Developing the potential of children at home and at school* (4th ed.). Upper Saddle River, NJ: Merrill/Prentice Hall.

• Clark, C. C. (1992). Deviant adolescent subcultures: Assessment strategies and clinical interventions. *Adolescence, 27*(106), 283–293.

Clark, C. M., & Peterson, P. L. (1986). Teachers' thought processes. In M. C. Wittrock (Ed.), *Handbook on research on teaching* (3rd ed.). New York: Macmillan.

Clark, J. M., & Paivio, A. (1991). Dual coding theory and education. *Educational Psychology Review, 3,* 149–210.

• Clark, L. A., & McKenzie, H. S. (1989). Effects of self-evaluation training of seriously emotionally disturbed children on the generalization of their classroom rule following and work behaviors across settings and teachers. *Behavioral Disorders, 14,* 89–98.

Clark, R. E. (1983). Reconsidering research on learning from media. *Review of Educational Research, 53,* 445–459.

Clarke-Stewart, K. A. (1988). Parents' effects on children's development: A decade of progress? *Journal of Applied Developmental Psychology, 9,* 41–84.

Clifford, M. M. (1984). Thoughts on a theory of constructive failure. *Educational Psychologist, 19,* 108–120.

• Clifford, M. M. (1990). Students need challenge, not easy success. *Educational Leadership, 48*(1), 22–26.

Cobb, P., Yackel, E., & Wood, T. (1989). Young children's emotional acts while engaged in mathematical problem solving. In D. B. McLeod & V. M. Adams (Eds.), *Affect and mathematical problem solving: A new perspective.* New York: Springer-Verlag.

• Coe, J., Salamon, L., & Molnar, J. (1991). *Homeless children and youth.* New Brunswick, NJ: Transaction.

• Cohen, E. G. (1994). Restructuring the classroom: Conditions for productive small groups. *Review of Educational Research, 64,* 1–35.

• Cohen, E. G., & Lotan, R. A. (1995). Producing equal-status interaction in the heterogeneous classroom. *American Educational Research Journal, 32,* 99–120.

Cohen, R. L. (1989). Memory for action events: The power of enactment. *Educational Psychology Review, 1,* 57–80.

• Coie, J. D., & Cillessen, A. H. N. (1993). Peer rejection: Origins and effects on children's development. *Current Directions in Psychological Science, 2,* 89–92.

Colby, A., & Kohlberg, L. (1984). Invariant sequence and internal consistency in moral judgment stages. In W. M. Kurtines & J. L. Gewirtz (Eds.), *Morality, moral behavior, and moral development.* New York: Wiley.

Colby, A., Kohlberg, L., Gibbs, J., & Lieberman, M. (1983). A longitudinal study of moral judgment. *Monographs of the Society for Research in Child Development, 48*(1–2, Serial No. 200).

Cole, N. S. (1990). Conceptions of educational achievement. *Educational Researcher, 19*(3), 2–7.

• Coleman, J. M., & Minnett, A. M. (1992). Learning disabilities and social competence: A social ecological perspective. *Exceptional Children, 59,* 234–246.

• Collier, V. P. (1992). The Canadian bilingual immersion debate: A synthesis of research findings. *Studies in Second Language Acquisition, 14,* 87–97.

• Collins, A., Brown, J. S., & Newman, S. E. (1989). Cognitive apprenticeship: Teaching the crafts of reading, writing, and mathematics. In L. B. Resnick (Ed.), *Knowing, learning, and instruction: Essays in honor of Robert Glaser.* Hillsdale, NJ: Erlbaum.

Collins, J. L. (1982, March). *Self-efficacy and ability in achievement behavior.* Paper presented at the annual meeting of the American Educational Research Association, New York.

Combs, A. W. (1979). *Myths in education: Beliefs that hinder progress and their alternatives.* Needham Heights, MA: Allyn & Bacon.

Combs, A. W. (1981). Humanistic education: Too tender for a tough world? *Phi Delta Kappan, 62,* 446–449.

Combs, A. W., Richards, A. C., & Richards, F. (1976). *Perceptual psychology: A humanistic approach to the study of persons.* New York: Harper & Row.

Commins, N. L., & Miramontes, O. B. (1989). Perceived and actual linguistic competence: A descriptive study of four low-achieving Hispanic bilingual students. *American Educational Research Journal, 26,* 443–472.

• Condry, J. (1977). Enemies of exploration: Self-initiated versus other-initiated learning. *Journal of Personality and Social Psychology, 35,* 466–477.

• Cone, T. E., Wilson, L. R., Bradley, C. M., & Reese, J. H. (1985). Characteristics of LD students in Iowa: An empirical investigation. *Learning Disability Quarterly, 8,* 211–220.

• Conger, R., Conger, K., Elder, G., Lorenz, F., Simons, R., & Whitbeck, L. (1992). A family process model of economic hardship and adjustment of early adolescent boys. *Child Development, 63,* 526–541.

Connolly, F. W., & Eisenberg, T. E. (1990). The feedback classroom: Teaching's silent friend. *T.H.E. Journal, 17*(5), 75–77.

• Conte, R. (1991). Attention disorders. In B. Y. L. Wong (Ed.), *Learning about learning disabilities.* San Diego: Academic Press.

Cooney, J. B. (1991). Reflections on the origin of mathematical intuition and some implications for instruction. *Learning and Individual Differences, 3,* 83–107.

Cooper, H. (1989). Synthesis of research on homework. *Educational Leadership, 47*(3), 85–91.

Cooper, H. M. (1979). Pygmalion grows up: A model for teacher expectation communication and performance influence. *Review of Educational Research, 49,* 389–410.

Cooper, H. M., & Good, T. (1983). *Pygmalion grows up: Studies in the expectation communication process.* White Plains, NY: Longman.

Copeland, J. T. (1993). Motivational approaches to expectancy confirmation. *Current Directions in Psychological Science, 2,* 117–121.

Corbett, H. D., & Wilson, B. (1988). Raising the stakes in statewide mandatory minimum competency testing. *Politics of Education Association Yearbook,* 27–39.

Corkill, A. J. (1992). Advance organizers: Facilitators of recall. *Educational Psychology Review, 4,* 33–67.

Cormier, S. M. (1987). The structural processes underlying transfer of training. In S. M. Cormier & J. D. Hagman (Eds.), *Transfer of learning: Contemporary research and applications.* San Diego: Academic Press.

Cormier, S. M., & Hagman, J. D. (1987). Introduction. In S. M. Cormier & J. D. Hagman (Eds.), *Transfer of learning: Contemporary research and applications.* San Diego: Academic Press.

Cornell, D. G., Pelton, G. M., Bassin, L. E., Landrum, M., Ramsay, S. G., Cooley, M. R., Lynch, K. A., & Hamrick, E. (1990). Self-concept and peer status among gifted program youth. *Journal of Educational Psychology, 82,* 456–463.

Corno, L., & Rohrkemper, M. M. (1985). The intrinsic motivation to learn in classrooms. In C. Ames & R. Ames (Eds.), *Research on motivation in education: Vol. 2. The classroom milieu.* San Diego: Academic Press.

Corno, L., & Snow, R. E. (1986). Adapting teaching to individual differences among learners. In M. C. Wittrock (Ed.), *Handbook of research on teaching* (3rd ed.). New York: Macmillan.

Cothern, N. B., Konopak, B. C., & Willis, E. L. (1990). Using readers' imagery of literary characters to study text meaning construction. *Reading Research and Instruction, 30,* 15–29.

Cottrol, R. J. (1990). America the multicultural. *American Educator, 14*(4), 18–21.

Covington, M. V. (1992). *Making the grade: A self-worth perspective on motivation and school reform.* Cambridge, UK: Cambridge University Press.

Covington, M. V., & Beery, R. M. (1976). *Self-worth and school learning.* New York: Holt, Rinehart & Winston.

Craft, M. (1984). Education for diversity. In M. Craft (Ed.), *Educational and cultural pluralism.* London: Falmer Press.

Crago, M. B., Annahatak, B., & Ningiuruvik, L. (1993). Changing patterns of language socialization in Inuit homes. *Anthropology and Education Quarterly, 24,* 205–223.

Craik, F. I. M., & Lockhart, R. S. (1972). Levels of processing: A framework for memory research. *Journal of Verbal Learning and Verbal Behavior, 11,* 671–684.

Craik, F. I. M., & Watkins, M. J. (1973). The role of rehearsal in short-term memory. *Journal of Verbal Learning and Verbal Behavior, 12,* 598–607.

Crooks, T. J. (1988). The impact of classroom evaluation practices on students. *Review of Educational Research, 58,* 438–481.

Crowder, N. A., & Martin, G. (1961). *Trigonometry.* Garden City, NY: Doubleday.

Crowne, D. P., & Marlowe, D. (1964). *The approval motive: Studies in evaluative dependence.* New York: Wiley.

Csikszentmihalyi, M., & Nakamura, J. (1989). The dynamics of intrinsic motivation: A study of adolescents. In C. Ames & R. Ames (Eds.), *Research on motivation in education: Vol. 3. Goals and cognitions.* San Diego: Academic Press.

Curtis, K. A., & Graham, S. (1991, April). *Altering beliefs about the importance of strategy: An attributional intervention.* Paper presented at the annual meeting of the American Educational Research Association, Chicago.

Dale, P. S. (1976). *Language development: Structure and function* (2nd ed.). New York: Holt, Rinehart & Winston.

D'Amato, R. C., Chitooran, M. M., & Whitten, J. D. (1992). Neuropsychological consequences of malnutrition. In D. I. Templer, L. C. Hartlage, & W. G. Cannon (Eds.), *Preventable brain damage: Brain vulnerability and brain health.* New York: Springer.

Damon, W. (1977). *The social world of the child.* San Francisco: Jossey-Bass.

Damon, W. (1988). *The moral child: Nurturing children's natural moral growth.* New York: Free Press.

Damon, W. (1991). Putting substance into self-esteem: A focus on academic and moral values. *Educational Horizons, 70*(1), 12–18.

Danner, F. W., & Day, M. C. (1977). Eliciting formal operations. *Child Development, 48,* 1600–1606.

Danner, F. W., & Lonky, E. (1981). A cognitive-developmental approach to the effects of rewards on intrinsic motivation. *Child Development, 52,* 1043–1052.

Dansereau, D. F. (1978). The development of a learning strategies curriculum. In H. F. O'Neil, Jr. (Ed.), *Learning strategies.* San Diego: Academic Press.

Dansereau, D. F. (1988). Cooperative learning strategies. In C. E. Weinstein, E. T. Goetz, & P. A. Alexander (Eds.), *Learning and study strategies: Issues in assessment, instruction, and evaluation.* San Diego: Academic Press.

Darley, J. M., & Gross, P. H. (1983). A hypothesis-confirming bias in labeling effects. *Journal of Personality and Social Psychology, 44,* 20–33.

Darling-Hammond, L. (1991). The implications of testing policy for quality and equality. *Phi Delta Kappan, 73,* 220–225.

Darling-Hammond, L. (1995). Inequality and access to knowledge. In J. A. Banks & C. A. M. Banks (Eds.), *Handbook of research on multicultural education.* New York: Macmillan.

Davis, G. A., & Thomas, M. A. (1989). *Effective schools and effective teachers.* Needham Heights, MA: Allyn & Bacon.

Davis, J. K. (1991). Educational implications of field dependence-independence. In S. Wapner & J. Demick (Eds.), *Field dependence-independence: Cognitive style across the life span.* Hillsdale, NJ: Erlbaum.

Davis, R. B. (1986). Conceptual and procedural knowledge in mathematics: A summary analysis. In J. Hiebert (Ed.), *Conceptual and procedural knowledge: The case of mathematics.* Hillsdale, NJ: Erlbaum.

Davydov, V. V. (1995). The influence of L. S. Vygotsky on education theory, research, and practice (S. T. Keer, Trans.). *Educational Researcher, 24*(3), 12–21.

Deaux, K. (1984). From individual differences to social categories: Analysis of a decade's research on gender. *American Psychologist, 39,* 105–116.

• deCharms, R. (1972). Personal causation training in the schools. *Journal of Applied Social Psychology, 2,* 95–113.

• Deci, E. L. (1992). The relation of interest to the motivation of behavior: A self-determination theory perspective. In K. A. Renninger, S. Hidi, & A. Krapp (Eds.), *The role of interest in learning and development.* Hillsdale, NJ: Erlbaum.

Deci, E. L., & Ryan, R. M. (1985). *Intrinsic motivation and self-determination in human behavior.* New York: Plenum Press.

Deci, E. L., & Ryan, R. M. (1987). The support of autonomy and the control of behavior. *Journal of Personality and Social Psychology, 53,* 1024–1037.

• Deci, E. L., & Ryan, R. M. (1992). The initiation and regulation of intrinsically motivated learning and achievement. In A. K. Boggiano & T. S. Pittman (Eds.), *Achievement and motivation: A social-developmental perspective.* Cambridge, UK: Cambridge University Press.

• De Corte, E., Greer, B., & Verschaffel, L. (1996). Mathematics teaching and learning. In D. C. Berliner & R. C. Clafee (Eds.), *Handbook of educational psychology.* New York: Macmillan.

Dee-Lucas, D., & Larkin, J. H. (1991). Equations in scientific proofs: Effects on comprehension. *American Educational Research Journal, 28,* 661–682.

• DeLain, M. T., Pearson, P. D., & Anderson, R. C. (1985). Reading comprehension and creativity in black language use: You stand to gain by playing the sounding game! *American Educational Research Journal, 22,* 155–173.

• Delgado-Gaitan, C. (1992). School matters in the Mexican American home: Socializing children to education. *American Educational Research Journal, 29,* 495–513.

• Delgado-Gaitan, C. (1994). Socializing young children in Mexican American families: An intergenerational perspective. In P. M. Greenfield & R. R. Cocking (Eds.), *Cross-cultural roots of minority child development.* Hillsdale, NJ: Erlbaum.

• DeLisi, R., & Staudt, J. (1980). Individual differences in college students' perfor-

mance on formal operational tasks. *Journal of Applied Developmental Psychology, 1,* 201–208.

DeLisle, J. R. (1984). *Gifted children speak out.* New York: Walker.

Dempster, F. N. (1985). Proactive interference in sentence recall: Topic-similarity effects and individual differences. *Memory and Cognition, 13,* 81–89.

• Dempster, F. N. (1991). Synthesis of research on reviews and tests. *Educational Leadership, 48*(7), 71–76.

Denis, M. (1984). Imagery and prose: A critical review of research on adults and children. *Text, 4,* 381–401.

• DeRidder, L. M. (1993). Teenage pregnancy: Etiology and educational interventions. *Educational Psychology Review, 5,* 87–107.

Desberg, P., & Taylor, J. H. (1986). *Essentials of task analysis.* Lanham, MD: University Press of America.

• Deshler, D. D., & Schumaker, J. B. (1988). An instructional model for teaching students how to learn. In J. L. Graden, J. E. Zins, & M. J. Curtis (Eds.), *Alternative educational delivery systems: Enhancing instructional options for all students.* Washington, DC: National Association of School Psychologists.

• Deutsch, M. (1993). Educating for a peaceful world. *American Psychologist, 48,* 510–517.

• Dewhurst, S. A., & Conway, M. A. (1994). Pictures, images, and recollective experience. *Journal of Experimental Psychology: Learning, Memory, and Cognition, 20,* 1088–1098.

Diamond, S. C. (1991). What to do when you can't do anything: Working with disturbed adolescents. *Clearing House, 64,* 232–234.

Diaz, R. M. (1983). Thought and two languages: The impact of bilingualism on cognitive development. In E. W. Gordon (Ed.), *Review of research in education* (Vol. 10). Washington, DC: American Educational Research Association.

Diaz, R. M. (1990, April). *The social origins of self-regulation: A Vygotskian perspective.* In B. McCombs (Chair), *Theoretical perspectives on socialization and children's development of self-regulated learning.* Symposium conducted at the meeting of the American Educational Research Association, Boston, MA.

Diaz, R. M., & Klingler, C. (1991). Toward an explanatory model of the interaction be-

tween bilingualism and cognitive development. In E. Bialystok (Ed.), *Language processing in bilingual children.* Cambridge, UK: Cambridge University Press.

Diener, C. I., & Dweck, C. S. (1978). An analysis of learned helplessness: Continuous changes in performance, strategy, and achievement cognitions following failure. *Journal of Personality and Social Psychology, 36,* 451–462.

DiSciullo, M. (1984). In-school suspension: An alternative to unsupervised out-of-school. *Clearing House, 57,* 328–330.

diSessa, A. A. (1982). Unlearning Aristotelian physics: A study of knowledge-based learning. *Cognitive Science, 6,* 37–75.

Di Vesta, F. J. (1987). The cognitive movement and education. In J. A. Glover & R. R. Ronning (Eds.), *Historical foundations of educational psychology.* New York: Plenum Press.

Di Vesta, F. J., & Gray, S. G. (1972). Listening and notetaking. *Journal of Educational Psychology, 63,* 8–14.

Di Vesta, F. J., & Peverly, S. T. (1984). The effects of encoding variability, processing activity, and rule example sequences on the transfer of conceptual rules. *Journal of Educational Psychology, 76,* 108–119.

• Di Vesta, F. J., & Smith, D. A. (1979). The pausing principle: Increasing the efficiency of memory for ongoing events. *Contemporary Educational Psychology, 4,* 288–296.

Doebler, L. K., & Eicke, F. J. (1979). Effects of teacher awareness of the educational implications of field-dependent/field-independent cognitive style on selected classroom variables. *Journal of Educational Psychology, 71,* 226–232.

Doescher, S. M., & Sugawara, A. I. (1989). Encouraging prosocial behavior in young children. *Childhood Education, 65,* 213–216.

Dole, J. A., Duffy, G. G., Roehler, L. R., & Pearson, P. D. (1991). Moving from the old to the new: Research on reading comprehension instruction. *Review of Educational Research, 61,* 239–264.

Donaldson, M. (1978). *Children's minds.* New York: Norton.

• Donnelly, C. M., & McDaniel, M. A. (1993). Use of analogy in learning scientific concepts. *Journal of Experimental Psychology: Learning, Memory, and Cognition, 19,* 975–987.

Dowaliby, F. J., & Schumer, H. (1973). Teacher-centered versus student-centered mode of college classroom instruction as related to manifest anxiety. *Journal of Educational Psychology, 64,* 125–132.

Doyle, W. (1983). Academic work. *Review of Educational Research, 53,* 159–199.

Doyle, W. (1984). How order is achieved in classrooms: An interim report. *Journal of Curriculum Studies, 16,* 259–277.

Doyle, W. (1986a). Classroom organization and management. In M. C. Wittrock (Ed.), *Handbook of research on teaching* (3rd ed.). New York: Macmillan.

Doyle, W. (1986b). Content representation in teachers' definitions of academic work. *Journal of Curriculum Studies, 18,* 365–379.

Doyle, W. (1990a). Classroom management techniques. In O. C. Moles (Ed.), *Student discipline strategies: Research and practice.* Albany: State University of New York Press.

Doyle, W. (1990b, April). *Whatever happened to all the research in classroom management?* Paper presented at the annual meeting of the American Educational Research Association, Boston, MA.

• Drake, D. D. (1993). Student diversity: Implications for classroom teachers. *Clearing House, 66,* 264–266.

Dreikurs, R., & Cassel, P. (1972). *Discipline without tears* (2nd ed.). New York: Dutton.

Driver, R. (1982). Piaget and science education: A stage of decision. In S. Modgil & C. Modgil (Eds.), *Jean Piaget: Consensus and controversy.* New York: Praeger.

• Driver, R. (1995). Constructivist approaches to science teaching. In L. P. Steffe & J. Gale (Eds.), *Constructivism in education.* Hillsdale, NJ: Erlbaum.

• Driver, R., Asoko, H., Leach, J., Mortimer, E., & Scott, P. (1994). Constructing scientific knowledge in the classroom. *Educational Researcher, 23*(7), 5–12.

DuBois, N. F., Kiewra, K. A., & Fraley, J. (1988, April). *Differential effects of a learning strategy course.* Paper presented at the annual meeting of the American Educational Research Association, New Orleans, LA.

• Duchardt, B. A., Deshler, D. D., & Schumaker, J. B. (1995). A strategy intervention for enabling students with learning disabilities to identify and change their ineffective beliefs. *Learning Disability Quarterly, 18,* 186–201.

Duell, O. K. (1986). Metacognitive skills. In G. D. Phye & T. Andre (Eds.), *Cognitive classroom learning: Understanding, thinking, and problem solving.* San Diego: Academic Press.

Duit, R. (1990, April). *On the role of analogies, similes, and metaphors in learning science.* Paper presented at the annual meeting of the American Educational Research Association, Boston, MA.

DuNann, D. G., & Weber, S. J. (1976). Short- and long-term effects of contingency managed instruction on low, medium, and high GPA students. *Journal of Applied Behavior Analysis, 9,* 375–376.

Duncker, K. (1945). On problem solving. *Psychological Monographs, 58,* Whole No. 270.

Dunn, C. S. (1983). The influence of instructional methods on concept learning. *Science Education, 67,* 647–656.

• Duran, B. J., & Weffer, R. E. (1992). Immigrants' aspirations, high school process, and academic outcomes. *American Educational Research Journal, 29,* 163–181.

Durkin, K. (1987). Social cognition and social context in the construction of sex differences. In M. A. Baker (Ed.), *Sex differences in human performance.* Chichester, UK: John Wiley.

• Durkin, K. (1995). *Developmental social psychology: From infancy to old age.* Cambridge, MA: Blackwell.

• Dusek, J. B. (1980). The development of test anxiety in children. In I. G. Sarason (Ed.), *Test anxiety: Theory, research, and applications.* Hillsdale, NJ: Erlbaum.

Dweck, C. S. (1975). The role of expectations and attributions in the alleviation of learned helplessness. *Journal of Personality and Social Psychology, 31,* 674–685.

Dweck, C. S. (1978). Achievement. In M. E. Lamb (Ed.), *Social and personality development.* New York: Holt, Rinehart & Winston.

Dweck, C. S. (1986). Motivational processes affecting learning. *American Psychologist, 41,* 1040–1048.

Dweck, C. S., Davidson, W., Nelson, S., & Enna, B. (1978). Sex differences in learned helplessness: II. The contingencies of evaluative feedback in the classroom and III. An experimental analysis. *Developmental Psychology, 14,* 268–276.

Dweck, C. S., & Elliott, E. S. (1983). Achievement motivation. In E. M. Hetherington (Ed.), *Handbook of child psychology: Vol. 4. Socialization, personality, and social development* (4th ed.). New York: Wiley.

• Dweck, C. S., & Leggett, E. L. (1988). A social-cognitive approach to motivation and personality. *Psychological Review, 95,* 256–273.

Dweck, C. S., & Licht, B. (1980). Learned helplessness and intellectual achievement. In J. Garber & M. E. P. Seligman (Eds.), *Human helplessness: Theory and applications.* San Diego: Academic Press.

Dweck, C. S., & Reppucci, N. D. (1973). Learned helplessness and reinforcement responsibility in children. *Journal of Personality and Social Psychology, 25,* 109–116.

Dwyer, C. A. (1974). Influence of children's sex role standards on reading and arithmetic achievement. *Journal of Educational Psychology, 66,* 811–816.

D'Ydewalle, G., Swerts, A., & De Corte, E. (1983). Study time and test performance as a function of test expectations. *Contemporary Educational Psychology, 8*(1), 55–67.

Dyer, H. S. (1967). The discovery and development of educational goals. *Proceedings of the 1966 Invitational Conference on Testing Problems.* Princeton, NJ: Educational Testing Service.

Eagly, A. H. (1987). *Sex differences in social behavior: A social-role interpretation.* Hillsdale, NJ: Erlbaum.

Eaton, J. F., Anderson, C. W., & Smith, E. L. (1984). Students' misconceptions interfere with science learning: Case studies of fifth-grade students. *Elementary School Journal, 84,* 365–379.

Eccles, J. S. (1989). Bringing young women to math and science. In M. Crawford & M. Gentry (Eds.), *Gender and thought: Psychological perspectives.* New York: Springer-Verlag.

Eccles, J. S., & Jacobs, J. E. (1986). Social forces shape math attitudes and performance. *Signs: Journal of Women in Culture and Society, 11,* 367–380.

Eccles, J. S., Jacobs, J., Harold-Goldsmith, R., Jayaratne, T., & Yee, D. (1989, April). *The relations between parents' category-based and target-based beliefs: Gender roles and biological influences.* Paper presented at the Society for Research in Child Development, Kansas City, MO.

Eccles, J. S., & Midgley, C. (1989). Stage-environment fit: Developmentally appropriate classrooms for young adolescents. In C. Ames & R. Ames (Eds.), *Research on motivation in education: Vol. 3. Goals and cognition.* San Diego: Academic Press.

Eccles, J. S., & Wigfield, A. (1985). Teacher expectations and student motivation. In J. B. Dusek (Ed.), *Teacher expectancies.* Hillsdale, NJ: Erlbaum.

Eccles (Parsons), J. S. (1983). Expectancies, values, and academic behaviors. In J. T. Spence (Ed.), *Achievement and achievement motivation.* San Francisco: W. H. Freeman.

Eccles (Parsons), J. S. (1984). Sex differences in mathematics participation. In M. Steinkamp & M. Maehr (Eds.), *Women in science.* Greenwich, CT: JAI Press.

Eccles (Parsons), J. S., Adler, T. F., Futterman, R., Goff, S. B., Kaczala, C. M., Meece, J. L., & Midgley, C. (1983). Expectations, values, and academic behaviors. In J. T. Spence (Ed.), *Achievement and achievement motivation* (pp. 75–146). San Francisco: W. H. Freeman.

Eisenberg, N. (1982). The development of reasoning regarding prosocial behavior. In N. Eisenberg (Ed.), *The development of prosocial behavior.* San Diego: Academic Press.

Eisenberg, N., Lennon, R., & Pasternack, J. F. (1986). Altruistic values and moral judgment. In N. Eisenberg (Ed.), *Altruistic emotion, cognition, and behavior.* Hillsdale, NJ: Erlbaum.

Eisenberg, N., Lennon, R., & Roth, K. (1983). Prosocial development: A longitudinal study. *Developmental Psychology, 19,* 846–855.

• Eisenberg, N., & Mussen, P. H. (1989). *The roots of prosocial behavior in children.* Cambridge, UK: Cambridge University Press.

Ekstrom, R. B., Goertz, M. E., Pollack, J. M., & Rock, D. A. (1986). Who drops out of high school and why? Findings from a national study. *Teachers College Record, 87,* 356–373.

Elkind, D. (1981). *Children and adolescents: Interpretive essays on Jean Piaget* (3rd ed.). New York: Oxford.

Elkind, D. (1984). *All grown up and no place to go.* Reading, MA: Addison-Wesley.

• Ellenwood, S., & Ryan, K. (1991). Literature and morality: An experimental curriculum. In W. M. Kurtines & J. L. Gewirtz (Eds.), *Moral behavior and development: Vol. 3. Application.* Hillsdale, NJ: Erlbaum.

Elliott, R., & Vasta, R. (1970). The modeling of sharing: Effects associated with vicarious reinforcement, symbolization, age, and generalization. *Journal of Experimental Child Psychology, 10,* 8–15.

• Elliott, S. N., & Busse, R. T. (1991). Social skills assessment and intervention with children and adolescents. *School Psychology International, 12,* 63–83.

• Ellis, E. S., & Friend, P. (1991). Adolescents with learning disabilities. In B. Y. L. Wong (Ed.), *Learning about learning disabilities.* San Diego: Academic Press.

• Ellis, N. R. (Ed.). (1979). *Handbook of mental deficiency: Psychological theory and research.* Hillsdale, NJ: Erlbaum.

• Elrich, M. (1994). The stereotype within. *Educational Leadership, 51*(8), 12–15.

Emmer, E. T. (1987). Classroom management and discipline. In V. Richardson-Koehler (Ed.), *Educators' handbook: A research perspective.* White Plains, NY: Longman.

Emmer, E. T., & Evertson, C. M. (1981). Synthesis of research on classroom management. *Educational Leadership, 38,* 342–347.

Emmer, E. T., Evertson, C. M., & Anderson, L. M. (1980). Effective classroom management at the beginning of the school year. *Elementary School Journal, 80,* 219–231.

• Emmer, E. T., Evertson, C. M., Clements, B. S., & Worsham, M. E. (1994). *Classroom management for secondary teachers* (3rd ed.). Needham Heights, MA: Allyn & Bacon.

• Entwisle, N. J., & Ramsden, P. (1983). *Understanding student learning.* London: Croom Helm.

Epstein, H. (1978). Growth spurts during brain development: Implications for educational policy and practice. In J. Chall & A. Mirsky (Eds.), *Education and the brain: The 77th yearbook of the National Society for the Study of Education, Part II.* Chicago: University of Chicago Press.

Epstein, J. L. (1983). Longitudinal effects of family-school-person interactions on student outcomes. *Research in Sociol-ogy of Education and Socialization, 4,* 101–127.

• Ericsson, K. A., & Chalmers, N. (1994). Expert performance: Its structure and acquisition. *American Psychologist, 49,* 725–747.

• Ericsson, K. A., Krampe, R. T., & Tesch-Römer, C. (1993). The role of deliberate practice in the acquisition of expert performance. *Psychological Review, 100,* 363–406.

• Eriks-Brophy, A., & Crago, M. B. (1994). Transforming classroom discourse: An Inuit example. *Language and Education, 8*(3), 105–122.

Erikson, E. H. (1963). *Childhood and society* (2nd ed.). New York: Norton.

Erikson, E. H. (1972). *Eight ages of man.* In C. S. Lavatelli & F. Stendler (Eds.), *Readings in child behavior and child development.* San Diego: Harcourt Brace Jovanovich.

• Erwin, P. (1993). *Friendship and peer relations in children.* Chichester, UK: Wiley.

Esposito, D. (1973). Homogeneous and heterogeneous ability grouping: Principal findings and implications for evaluating and designing more effective educational environments. *Review of Educational Research, 43,* 163–179.

• Esquivel, G. B. (1995). Teacher behaviors that foster creativity. *Educational Psychology Review, 7,* 185–202.

Etaugh, C. (1983). Introduction: The influence of environmental factors on sex differences in children's play. In M. B. Liss (Ed.), *Social and cognitive skills: Sex roles and children's play.* San Diego: Academic Press.

Evans, E. D., & Craig, D. (1990). Teacher and student perceptions of academic cheating in middle and senior high schools. *Journal of Educational Research, 84*(1), 44–52.

Evans, G. W., & Oswalt, G. L. (1968). Acceleration of academic progress through the manipulation of peer influence. *Behaviour Research and Therapy, 6,* 189–195.

Evertson, C. M., & Emmer, E. T. (1982). Effective management at the beginning of the year in junior high classes. *Journal of Educational Psychology, 74,* 485–498.

• Evertson, C. M., & Harris, A. H. (1992). What we know about managing classrooms. *Educational Leadership, 49*(7), 74–78.

• Eysenck, M. W. (1992). *Anxiety: The cognitive perspective.* Hove, UK: Erlbaum.

Eysenck, M. W., & Keane, M. T. (1990). *Cognitive psychology: A student's handbook*. Hove, UK: Erlbaum.

Fagot, B. I., Hagan, R., Leinbach, M. D., & Kronsberg, S. (1985). Differential reactions to assertive and communicative acts of toddler boys and girls. *Child Development, 56,* 1499–1505.

Fagot, B. I., & Leinbach, M. D. (1983). Play styles in early childhood: Social consequences for boys and girls. In M. B. Liss (Ed.), *Social and cognitive skills: Sex roles and children's play*. San Diego: Academic Press.

• Fairbairn, D. M. (1987). The art of questioning your students. *Clearing House, 61,* 19–22.

Fairchild, H. H., & Edwards-Evans, S. (1990). African American dialects and schooling: A review. In A. M. Padilla, H. H. Fairchild, & C. M. Valadez (Eds.), *Bilingual education: Issues and strategies*. Newbury Park, CA: Sage.

Feather, N. T. (1982). *Expectations and actions: Expectancy-value models in psychology*. Hillsdale, NJ: Erlbaum.

Feld, S., Ruhland, D., & Gold, M. (1979). Developmental changes in achievement motivation. *Merrill-Palmer Quarterly, 25,* 43–60.

Feldhusen, J. F. (1989). Synthesis of research on gifted youth. *Educational Leadership, 26*(1), 6–11.

Feldhusen, J. F., & Kroll, M. D. (1985). Parent perceptions of gifted children's educational needs. *Roeper Review, 7,* 249–252.

Feldhusen, J. F., & Treffinger, D. J. (1980). *Creative thinking and problem solving in gifted education*. Dubuque, IA: Kendall/Hunt.

Feldhusen, J. F., Treffinger, D. J., & Bahlke, S. J. (1970). Developing creative thinking: The Purdue Creativity Program. *Journal of Creative Behavior, 4,* 85–90.

Fennema, E. (1980). Sex-related differences in mathematics achievement: Where and why. In L. H. Fox, L. Brody, & D. Tobin (Eds.), *Women and the mathematical mystique*. Baltimore: Johns Hopkins University Press.

Fennema, E. (1987). Sex-related differences in education: Myths, realities, and interventions. In V. Richardson-Koehler (Ed.), *Educators' handbook: A research perspective*. White Plains, NY: Longman.

Fennema, E., & Peterson, P. (1985). Autonomous learning behavior: A possible explanation of gender-related differences in mathematics. In L. C. Wilkinson & C. B. Marrett (Eds.), *Gender influences in classroom interaction*. San Diego: Academic Press.

• Fennema, E., & Sherman, J. (1977). Sex-related differences in mathematics achievement, spatial visualization, and affective factors. *American Educational Research Journal, 14,* 51–71.

• Ferguson, E. L., & Hegarty, M. (1995). Learning with real machines or diagrams: Application of knowledge to real-world problems. *Cognition and Instruction, 13,* 129–160.

• Feuerstein, R. (1990). The theory of structural cognitive modifiability. In B. Z. Presseisen (Ed.), *Learning and thinking styles: Classroom interaction*. Washington, DC: National Education Association.

• Fiedler, E. D., Lange, R. E., & Winebrenner, S. (1993). In search of reality: Unraveling the myths about tracking, ability grouping, and the gifted. *Roeper Review, 16*(1), 4–7.

Field, D. (1987). A review of preschool conservation training: An analysis of analyses. *Developmental Review, 7,* 210–251.

• Finders, M., & Lewis, C. (1994). Why some parents don't come to school. *Educational Leadership, 51*(8), 50–54.

Finn, J. D. (1989). Withdrawing from school. *Review of Educational Research, 59,* 117–142.

Finn, J. D. (1991). How to make the dropout problem go away. *Educational Researcher, 20*(1), 28–30.

Fisk, A. D. (1986). Frequency encoding is not inevitable and is not automatic: A reply to Hasher & Zacks. *American Psychologist, 41,* 215–216.

Flavell, J. H. (1979). Metacognition and cognitive monitoring: A new area of cognitive-developmental inquiry. *American Psychologist, 34,* 906–911.

Flavell, J. H. (1985). *Cognitive development* (2nd ed.). Upper Saddle River, NJ: Prentice Hall.

Flavell, J. H., Friedrichs, A. G., & Hoyt, J. D. (1970). Developmental changes in memorization processes. *Cognitive Psychology, 1,* 324–340.

Flavell, J. H., & Wellman, H. M. (1977). Metamemory. In R. V. Kail, Jr. & J. W. Hagen (Eds.), *Perspectives on the development of memory and cognition*. Hillsdale, NJ: Erlbaum.

• Flink, C., Boggiano, A. K., Main, D. S., Barrett, M., & Katz, P. A. (1992). Children's achievement-related behaviors: The role of extrinsic and intrinsic motivational orientations. In A. K. Boggiano & T. S. Pittman (Eds.), *Achievement and motivation: A social-developmental perspective*. Cambridge, UK: Cambridge University Press.

Fong, G. T., Krantz, D. H., & Nisbett, R. E. (1986). The effects of statistical training on thinking about everyday problems. *Cognitive Psychology, 18,* 253–292.

Foos, P. W., & Fisher, R. P. (1988). Using tests as learning opportunities. *Journal of Educational Psychology, 80,* 179–183.

• Ford, D. Y., & Harris, J. J. (1992). The American achievement ideology and achievement differentials among preadolescent gifted and nongifted African American males and females. *Journal of Negro Education, 61*(1), 45–64.

• Ford, M. E. (1979). The construct validity of egocentrism. *Psychological Bulletin, 86,* 1169–1188.

• Fostnot, C. T. (1996). Constructivism: A psychological theory of learning. In C. T. Fosnot (Ed.), *Constructivism: Theory, perspectives, and practice*. New York: Teachers College Press.

Foster, J. (1972). *Discovery learning in the primary school*. London: Routledge & Kegan Paul.

Fowler, S. A., & Baer, D. M. (1981). "Do I have to be good all day?" The timing of delayed reinforcement as a factor in generalization. *Journal of Applied Behavior Analysis, 14,* 13–24.

Fox, L. H. (1981). *The problem of women and mathematics*. New York: Ford Foundation.

Fox, P. W., & LeCount, J. (1991, April). *When more is less: Faculty misestimation of student learning*. Paper presented at the annual meeting of the American Educational Research Association, Chicago.

• Foxx, R. M., & Azrin, N. H. (1973). The elimination of autistic self-stimulatory behavior by overcorrection. *Journal of Applied Behavior Analysis, 6,* 1–14.

• Foxx, R. M., & Bechtel, D. R. (1983). Overcorrection: A review and analysis. In S. Axelrod & J. Apsche (Eds.), *The effects of punishment on human behavior*. San Diego: Academic Press.

• Frankel, F., & Simmons, J. Q. (1985). Behavioral treatment approaches to pathological unsocialized physical aggression in young children. *Journal of Child Psychiatry, 26,* 525–551.

Frasher, R. S. (1982). A feminist look at literature for children: Ten years later. In E. M. Sheridan (Ed.), *Sex stereotypes and reading: Research and strategies.* Newark, DE: International Reading Association.

Frasier, M. M. (1989). Identification of gifted black students: Developing new perspectives. In C. J. Maker & S. W. Schiever (Eds.), *Critical issues in gifted education: Vol. 2. Defensible programs for cultural and ethnic minorities.* Austin, TX: PRO-ED.

Frazer, L. H., & Wilkinson, L. D. (1990, April). *At-risk students: Do we know which ones will drop out?* Paper presented at the annual meeting of the American Educational Research Association, Boston, MA.

Frederiksen, J. R., & Collins, A. (1989). A systems approach to educational testing. *Educational Researcher, 18*(9), 27–32.

Frederiksen, N. (1984a). Implications of cognitive theory for instruction in problem solving. *Review of Educational Research, 54,* 363–407.

Frederiksen, N. (1984b). The real test bias: Influences of testing on teaching and learning. *American Psychologist, 39,* 193–202.

• Freedman, K. (1996). The social reconstruction of art education: Teaching visual culture. In C. A. Grant & M. L. Gomez, *Making schooling multicultural: Campus and classroom.* Upper Saddle River, NJ: Merrill/Prentice Hall.

Freiberg, H. J. (1987). Teacher self-evaluation and principal supervision. *NASSP Bulletin* (National Association of Secondary School Principals), *71,* 85–92.

French, E. G. (1956). Motivation as a variable in work partner selection. *Journal of Abnormal and Social Psychology, 53,* 96–99.

• Friedel, M. (1993). *Characteristics of gifted/creative children.* Warwick, RI: National Foundation for Gifted and Creative Children.

• Friedman, L. (1994, April). *The role of spatial skill in gender differences in mathematics: Meta-analytic evidence.* Paper presented at the annual meeting of the American Educational Research Association, New Orleans, LA.

• Friedman, L. (1995). The space factor in mathematics: Gender differences. *Review of Educational Research, 65,* 22–50.

Friedrich, L. K., & Stein, A. H. (1973). Aggressive and pro-social television programs and the natural behavior of preschool children. *Society for Research in Child Development Monographs, 38*(Whole No. 151).

• Frisbie, D. A., & Waltman, K. K. (1992). Developing a personal grading plan. *Educational Measurement: Issues and Practices, 11,* 35–42. Reprinted in K. M. Cauley, F. Linder, & J. H. McMillan (Eds.), (1994). *Educational psychology 94/95.* Guilford, CT: Dushkin.

• Fuchs, L. S., Fuchs, D., Bentz, J., Phillips, N. B., & Hamlett, C. L. (1994). The nature of student interactions during peer tutoring with and without prior training and experience. *American Educational Research Journal, 31,* 75–103.

Gage, N. L. (1991). The obviousness of social and educational research results. *Educational Researcher, 20*(1), 10–16.

Gagné, E. D. (1985). *The cognitive psychology of school learning.* Boston: Little, Brown.

Gagné, R. M. (1982). Developments in learning psychology: Implications for instructional design; and effects of computer technology on instructional design and development. *Educational Technology, 22*(6), 11–15.

Gagné, R. M. (1983). Some issues in the psychology of mathematics instruction. *Journal of Research in Mathematics Education, 14*(1), 7–18.

Gagné, R. M. (1985). *The conditions of learning and theory of instruction* (4th ed.). New York: Holt, Rinehart & Winston.

• Gagné, R. M., Briggs, L. J., & Wager, W. W. (1992). *Principles of instructional design* (4th ed.). Fort Worth, TX: Harcourt Brace Jovanovich.

Gagné, R. M., & Brown, L. T. (1961). Some factors in the programming of conceptual learning. *Journal of Experimental Psychology, 62,* 313–321.

Gaines, M. L., & Davis, M. (1990, April). *Accuracy of teacher prediction of elementary student achievement.* Paper presented at the annual meeting of the American Educational Research Association, Boston, MA.

Gallagher, J. J. (1991). Personal patterns of underachievement. *Journal for the Education of the Gifted, 14,* 221–233.

Galler, J. R. (Ed.). (1984). *Human nutrition: A comprehensive treatise: Vol. 5. Nutrition and behavior.* New York: Plenum Press.

• Gallimore, R., & Tharp, R. (1990). Teaching mind in society: Teaching, schooling, and literate discourse. In L. C. Moll (Ed.), *Vygotsky and education: Instructional implications and applications of sociohistorical psychology.* Cambridge, UK: Cambridge University Press.

• Garanzini-Daiber, M., & Cohen, M. (1996). [Unpublished materials prepared for Merrill/Prentice Hall].

Garcia, E. E. (1992). "Hispanic" children: Theoretical, empirical, and related policy issues. *Educational Psychology Review, 4,* 69–93.

• Garcia, E. E. (1994). *Understanding and meeting the challenge of student cultural diversity.* Boston: Houghton Mifflin.

• García, E. E. (1995). Educating Mexican American students: Past treatment and recent developments in theory, research, policy, and practice. In J. A. Banks & C. A. M. Banks (Eds.), *Handbook of research on multicultural education.* New York: Macmillan.

Gardner, H. (1983). *Frames of mind: The theory of multiple intelligences.* New York: Basic Books.

• Gardner, H. (1993). *Multiple intelligences: The theory in practice.* New York: Basic Books.

• Gardner, H. (1995). Reflections on multiple intelligences: Myths and messages. *Phi Delta Kappan, 77,* 200–209.

• Gardner, H., & Hatch, T. (1990). Multiple intelligences go to school: Educational implications of the theory of multiple intelligences. *Educational Researcher, 18*(8), 4–10.

• Garhart, C., & Hannafin, M. J. (1986). The accuracy of cognitive monitoring during computer-based instruction. *Journal of Computer-Based Instruction, 13,* 88–93.

• Garibaldi, A. M. (1992). Educating and motivating African American males to succeed. *Journal of Negro Education, 61*(1), 4–11.

• Garibaldi, A. M. (1993). Creating prescriptions for success in urban schools: Turning the corner on pathological explanations for academic failure. In T. M.

Tomlinson (Ed.), *Motivating students to learn: Overcoming barriers to high achievement*. Berkeley, CA: McCutchan.

Garner, R., Alexander, P. A., Gillingham, M. G., Kulikowich, J. M., & Brown, R. (1991). Interest and learning from text. *American Educational Research Journal, 28*, 643–659.

• Garner, R., Brown, R., Sanders, S., & Menke, D. J. (1992). "Seductive details" and learning from text. In K. A. Renninger, S. Hidi, & A. Krapp (Eds.), *The role of interest in learning and development*. Hillsdale, NJ: Erlbaum.

Garrison, L. (1989). Programming for the gifted American Indian student. In C. J. Maker & S. W. Schiever (Eds.), *Critical issues in gifted education: Vol. 2. Defensible programs for cultural and ethnic minorities*. Austin, TX: PRO-ED.

• Gathercole, S. E., & Hitch, G. J. (1993). Developmental changes in short-term memory: A revised working memory perspective. In A. F. Collins, S. E. Gathercole, M. A. Conway, & P. E. Morris (Eds.), *Theories of memory*. Hove, UK: Erlbaum.

Gaudry, E., & Bradshaw, G. D. (1971). The differential effect of anxiety on performance in progressive and terminal school examinations. In E. Gaudry & C. D. Spielberger (Eds.), *Anxiety and educational achievement*. Sydney, Australia: Wiley.

Gaudry, E., & Spielberger, C. D. (Eds.). (1971). *Anxiety and educational achievement*. Sydney, Australia: Wiley.

Gauntt, H. L. (1991, April). *The roles of prior knowledge of text structure and prior knowledge of content in the comprehension and recall of expository text*. Paper presented at the annual meeting of the American Educational Research Association, Chicago.

• Gay, J., & Cole, M. (1967). *The new mathematics and an old culture*. New York: Holt, Rinehart & Winston.

Gearheart, B. R., Weishahn, M. W., & Gearheart, C. J. (1992). *The exceptional child in the regular classroom* (5th ed.). Upper Saddle River, NJ: Merrill/Prentice Hall.

• Gelman, R. (1979). Preschool thought. *American Psychologist, 34*, 900–905.

Gelman, R., & Baillargeon, R. (1983). A review of some Piagetian concepts. In J. H. Flavell & E. M. Markman (Eds.), *Handbook of child psychology: Vol.*

3. Cognitive development. New York: Wiley.

Genesee, F. (1985). Second language learning through immersion: A review of U.S. programs. *Review of Educational Research, 55*, 541–561.

Genova, W. J., & Walberg, H. J. (1984). Enhancing integration in urban high schools. In D. E. Bartz & M. L. Maehr (Eds.), *Advances in motivation and achievement: Vol 1. The effects of school desegregation on motivation and achievement*. Greenwich, CT: JAI Press.

• Genshaft, J. L., Greenbaum, S., & Borovosky, S. (1995). Stress and the gifted. In J. L. Genshaft, M. Bireley, & C. L. Hollinger (Eds.), *Serving gifted and talented students: A resource for school personnel*. Austin, TX: PRO-ED.

• *Geography for life: National geography standards*. (1994). Washington, DC: National Geographic Research and Exploration.

Gerst, M. S. (1971). Symbolic coding processes in observational learning. *Journal of Personality & Social Psychology, 19*, 7–17.

• Gettinger, M. (1988). Methods of proactive classroom management. *School Psychology Review, 17*, 227–242.

Giaconia, R. M. (1988). Teacher questioning and wait-time (Doctoral dissertation, Stanford University, 1988). *Dissertation Abstracts International, 49*, 462A.

Giaconia, R. M., & Hedges, L. V. (1982). Identifying features of effective open education. *Review of Educational Research, 52*, 579–602.

Gick, M. L., & Holyoak, K. J. (1987). The cognitive basis of knowledge transfer. In S. M. Cormier & J. D. Hagman (Eds.), *Transfer of learning: Contemporary research and applications*. San Diego: Academic Press.

Gilligan, C. F. (1977). In a different voice: Women's conceptions of self and morality. *Harvard Educational Review, 47*, 481–517.

Gilligan, C. F. (1982). *In a different voice*. Cambridge, MA: Harvard University Press.

Gilligan, C. F. (1987). Moral orientation and moral development. In E. F. Kittay & D. T. Meyers (Eds.), *Women and moral theory*. Totowa, NJ: Rowman & Littlefield.

• Gilligan, C. F., & Attanucci, J. (1988). Two moral orientations. In C. F. Gilligan, J. V.

Ward, & J. M. Taylor (Eds.), *Mapping the moral domain: A contribution of women's thinking to psychological theory and education*. Cambridge, MA: Center for the Study of Gender, Education, and Human Development (distributed by Harvard University Press).

• Gilligan, C. F., & Wiggins, G. (1988). The origins of morality in early childhood relationships. In C. F. Gilligan, J. V. Ward, & J. M. Taylor (Eds.), *Mapping the moral domain: A contribution of women's thinking to psychological theory and education*. Cambridge, MA: Center for the Study of Gender, Education, and Human Development (distributed by Harvard University Press).

Gilliland, H. (1988). Discovering and emphasizing the positive aspects of the culture. In H. Gilliland & J. Reyhner (Eds.), *Teaching the Native American*. Dubuque, IA: Kendall/Hunt.

Gilpin, L. (1968). *The enduring Navaho*. Austin: University of Texas Press.

• Girotto, V., & Light, P. (1993). The pragmatic bases of children's reasoning. In P. Light & G. Butterworth (Eds.), *Context and cognition: Ways of learning and knowing*. Hillsdale, NJ: Erlbaum.

• Glanzer, M., & Nolan, S. D. (1986). Memory mechanisms in text comprehension. In G. H. Bower (Ed.), *The psychology of learning and motivation: Advances in research and theory* (Vol. 20). San Diego: Academic Press.

Glass, A. L., Holyoak, K. J., & Santa, J. L. (1979). *Cognition*. Reading, MA: Addison-Wesley.

Glasser, W. (1969). *Schools without failure*. New York: Harper & Row.

Glucksberg, S., & Krauss, R. M. (1967). What do people say after they have learned to talk? Studies of the development of referential communication. *Merrill-Palmer Quarterly, 13*, 309–316.

• Goldenberg, C. (1992). The limits of expectations: A case for case knowledge about teacher expectancy effects. *American Educational Research Journal, 29*, 517–544.

• Gollnick, D. M., & Chinn, P. C. (1994). *Multicultural education in a pluralistic society* (4th ed.). Upper Saddle River, NJ: Merrill/Prentice Hall.

Good, T. L., & Brophy, J. E. (1986). School effects. In M. Wittrock (Ed.), *Handbook of research on teaching* (3rd ed.). New York: Macmillan.

Good, T. L., & Brophy, J. E. (1994). *Looking in classrooms* (6th ed.). New York: HarperCollins.

Good, T. L., McCaslin, M. M., & Reys, B. J. (1992). Investigating work groups to promote problem solving in mathematics. In J. Brophy (Ed.), *Advances in research on teaching: Vol. 3. Planning and managing learning tasks and activities*. Greenwich, CT: JAI Press.

Goodenow, C. (1991, April). *The sense of belonging and its relationship to academic motivation among pre- and early adolescent students*. Paper presented at the annual meeting of the American Educational Research Association, Chicago.

Gorski, J. D., & Pilotto, L. (1993). Interpersonal violence among youth: A challenge for school personnel. *Educational Psychology Review, 5*, 35–61.

Gottfredson, D. C., Fink, C. M., & Graham, N. (1994). Grade retention and problem behavior. *American Educational Research Journal, 31*, 761–784.

Gottfredson, G. D., & Gottfredson, D. C. (1985). *Victimization in schools*. New York: Plenum Press.

Gottfried, A. E. (1990). Academic intrinsic motivation in young elementary school children. *Journal of Educational Psychology, 82*, 525–538.

Gottfried, A. E., Fleming, J. S., & Gottfried, A. W. (1994). Role of parental motivational practices in children's academic intrinsic motivation and achievement. *Journal of Educational Psychology, 86*, 104–113.

Grabe, M. (1986). Attentional processes in education. In G. D. Phye & T. Andre (Eds.), *Cognitive classroom learning: Understanding, thinking, and problem solving*. San Diego: Academic Press.

Graesser, A. C., & Person, N. K. (1994). Question asking during tutoring. *American Educational Research Journal, 31*, 104–137.

Graham, S. (1990). Communicating low ability in the classroom: Bad things good teachers sometimes do. In S. Graham & V. S. Folkes (Eds.), *Attribution theory: Applications to achievement, mental health, and interpersonal conflict*. Hillsdale, NJ: Erlbaum.

Graham, S. (1991). A review of attribution theory in achievement contexts. *Educational Psychology Review, 3*, 5–39.

Graham, S. (1994). Motivation in African Americans. *Review of Educational Research, 64*, 55–117.

Graham, S., & Barker, G. (1990). The downside of help: An attributional-developmental analysis of helping behavior as a low-ability cue. *Journal of Educational Psychology, 82*, 7–14.

Graham, S., & Golen, S. (1991). Motivational influences on cognition: Task involvement, ego involvement, and depth of information processing. *Journal of Educational Psychology, 83*, 187–194.

Granger, D. A., Whalen, C. K., Henker, B., & Cantwell, C. (1996). ADHD boys' behavior during structured classroom social activities: Effects of social demands, teacher proximity, and methylphenidate. *Journal of Attention Disorders, 1*(1), 16–30.

Granger, R. H., Jr., & Schlimmer, J. C. (1986). The computation of contingency in classical conditioning. In G. H. Bower (Ed.), *The psychology of learning and motivation: Advances in research and theory* (Vol. 20). San Diego: Academic Press.

Grant, C. A., & Gomez, M. L. (1996). *Making schooling multicultural: Campus and classroom*. Upper Saddle River, NJ: Merrill/Prentice Hall.

Grant, L. (1985). Race-gender status, classroom interaction, and children's socialization in elementary school. In L. C. Wilkinson & C. B. Marrett (Eds.), *Gender influences in classroom interaction*. San Diego: Academic Press.

Gray, W. D., & Orasanu, J. M. (1987). Transfer of cognitive skills. In S. M. Cormier & J. D. Hagman (Eds.), *Transfer of learning: Contemporary research and applications*. San Diego: Academic Press.

Green, L., Fry, A. F., & Myerson, J. (1994). Discounting of delayed rewards: A life-span comparison. *Psychological Science, 5*, 33–36.

Green, R. G. (1980). Test anxiety and cue utilization. In I. G. Sarason (Ed.), *Test anxiety: Theory, research, and applications*. Hillsdale, NJ: Erlbaum.

Greene, B. A. (1994, April). *Instruction to enhance comprehension of unfamiliar text: Should it focus on domain-specific or strategy knowledge?* Paper presented at the annual meeting of the American Educational Research Association, New Orleans, LA.

Greenfield, P. M. (1994). Independence and interdependence as developmental scripts: Implications for theory, research, and practice. In P. M. Greenfield & R. R. Cocking (Eds.), *Cross-cultural roots of minority child development*. Hillsdale, NJ: Erlbaum.

Greeno, J. G. (1991). A view of mathematical problem solving in school. In M. U. Smith (Ed.), *Toward a unified theory of problem solving: Views from the content domains*. Hillsdale, NJ: Erlbaum.

Greeno, J. G., Collins, A. M., & Resnick, L. B. (1996). Cognition and learning. In D. C. Berliner & R. C. Calfee (Eds.), *Handbook of educational psychology*. New York: Macmillan.

Greenspan, S., & Granfield, J. M. (1992). Reconsidering the construct of mental retardation: Implications of a model of social competence. *American Journal of Mental Retardation, 96*, 442–453.

Greenspoon, J., & Ranyard, R. (1957). Stimulus conditions and retroactive inhibition. *Journal of Experimental Psychology, 53*, 55–59.

Greenwood, C. R., Carta, J. J., & Hall, R. V. (1988). The use of peer tutoring strategies in classroom management and educational instruction. *School Psychology Review, 17*, 258–275.

Greenwood, C. R., Dinwiddie, G., Bailey, V., Carta, J. J., Dorsey, D., Kohler, F. W., Nelson, C., Rotholz, D., & Schulte, D. (1987). Field replication of classwide peer tutoring. *Journal of Applied Behavior Analysis, 20*, 151–160.

Gregg, M., & Leinhardt, G. (1994, April). *Constructing geography*. Paper presented at the annual meeting of the American Educational Research Association, New Orleans, LA.

Griffin, M. M., & Griffin, B. W. (1994, April). *Some can get there from here: Situated learning, cognitive style, and map skills*. Paper presented at the annual meeting of the American Educational Research Association, New Orleans, LA.

Griffore, R. J. (1981). *Child development: An educational perspective*. Springfield, IL: Charles C. Thomas.

Grimes, J. W., & Allinsmith, W. (1970). Compulsivity, anxiety, and school achievement. In P. H. Mussen, J. J. Conger, & J. Kagan (Eds.), *Readings in child development and personality*. New York: Harper & Row.

- Grolnick, W. S., & Ryan, R. M. (1987). Autonomy in children's learning: An experimental and individual difference investigation. *Journal of Personality and Social Psychology, 52,* 890–898.
- Gronlund, N. E. (1993). *How to make achievement tests and assessments* (5th ed.). Needham Heights, MA: Allyn & Bacon.
- Gronlund, N. E. (1995). *How to write and use instructional objectives* (5th ed.). Upper Saddle River, NJ: Merrill/Prentice Hall.
- Gronlund, N. E., & Linn, R. L. (1990). *Measurement and evaluation in teaching* (6th ed.). New York: Macmillan.
- Grusec, J. E., & Redler, E. (1980). Attribution, reinforcement, and altruism. *Developmental Psychology, 16,* 525–534.

Guevremont, D. C., Osnes, P. G., & Stokes, T. F. (1988). The functional role of preschoolers' verbalization in the generalization of self-instructional training. *Journal of Applied Behavior Analysis, 21,* 45–55.

Guskey, T. R. (1985). *Implementing mastery learning.* Belmont, CA: Wadsworth.
- Guskey, T. R. (1994, April). *Outcome-based education and mastery learning: Clarifying the differences.* Paper presented at the annual meeting of the American Educational Research Association, New Orleans, LA.
- Hacker, D. J. (1995, April). *Comprehension monitoring of written discourse across early-to-middle adolescence.* Paper presented at the annual meeting of the American Educational Research Association, San Francisco.
- Hadaway, N. L., Florez, V., Larke, P. J., & Wiseman, D. (1993). Teaching in the midst of diversity: How do we prepare? In M. J. O'Hair & S. J. Odell (Eds.), *Diversity and teaching: Teacher education yearbook I.* Fort Worth, TX: Harcourt Brace Jovanovich.
- Hagen, A. S. (1994, April). *Achievement motivation processes and the role of classroom context.* Paper presented at the annual meeting of the American Educational Research Association, New Orleans, LA.

Hagen, J. W., & Stanovich, K. G. (1977). Memory: Strategies of acquisition. In R. V. Kail, Jr. & J. W. Hagen (Eds.), *Perspectives on the development of memory and cognition.* Hillsdale, NJ: Erlbaum.

Hakuta, K. (1990). Language and cognition in bilingual children. In A. M. Padilla, H. H. Fairchild, & C. M. Valadez (Eds.), *Bilingual education: Issues and strategies.* Newbury Park, CA: Sage.

Hale, G. A. (1983). Students' predictions of prose forgetting and the effects of study strategies. *Journal of Educational Psychology, 75,* 708–715.

Halford, G. S. (1989). Cognitive processing capacity and learning ability: An integration of two areas. *Learning and Individual Differences, 1,* 125–153.

Hall, J. F. (1966). *The psychology of learning.* Philadelphia: J. B. Lippincott.

Hall, R. V., Axelrod, S., Foundopoulos, M., Shellman, J., Campbell, R. A., & Cranston, S. S. (1971). The effective use of punishment to modify behavior in the classroom. *Educational Technology, 11*(4), 24–26. Reprinted in K. D. O'Leary & S. O'Leary (Eds.). (1972). *Classroom management: The successful use of behavior modification.* New York: Pergamon.

Haller, E. P., Child, D. A., & Walberg, H. J. (1988). Can comprehension be taught? A quantitative synthesis of "metacognitive" studies. *Educational Researcher, 17*(9), 5–8.

Halpern, D. F. (1985). The influence of sex-role stereotypes on prose recall. *Sex Roles, 12,* 363–375.

Halpern, D. F. (1986). *Sex differences in cognitive abilities.* Hillsdale, NJ: Erlbaum.
- Halpern, D. F. (1992). *Sex differences in cognitive abilities* (2nd ed.). Hillsdale, NJ: Erlbaum.

Halpin, G., & Halpin, G. (1982). Experimental investigations of the effects of study and testing on student learning, retention, and ratings of instruction. *Journal of Educational Psychology, 74,* 32–38.
- Hamman, D., Shell, D. F., Droesch, D., Husman, J., Handwerk, M., Park, Y., & Oppenheim, N. (1995, April). *Middle school readers' on-line cognitive processes: Influence of subject-matter knowledge and interest during reading.* Paper presented at the annual meeting of the American Educational Research Association, San Francisco.

Hammill, D. D., Leigh, J. E., McNutt, G., & Larsen, S. C. (1981). A new definition of learning disabilities. *Learning Disability Quarterly, 4,* 336–342.
- Hamp-Lyons, L. (1992). Holistic writing assessment for L.E.P. students. In *Focus on evaluation and measurement* (Vol. 2). Washington, DC: U.S. Department of Education.

Hannah, M. E. (1988). Teacher attitudes toward children with disabilities: An ecological analysis. In H. E. Yuker (Ed.), *Attitudes toward persons with disabilities.* New York: Springer.
- Haring, N. G., & Liberty, K. A. (1990). Matching strategies with performance in facilitating generalization. *Focus on Exceptional Children, 22*(8), 1–16.

Harlow, H. F., & Zimmerman, R. R. (1959). Affectional responses in the infant monkey. *Science, 130,* 421–432.

Harris, A. C. (1986). *Child development.* St. Paul, MN: West.

Harris, C. R. (1991). Identifying and serving the gifted new immigrant. *Teaching Exceptional Children, 23*(4), 26–30.
- Harris, K. R. (1982). Cognitive-behavior modification: Application with exceptional students. *Focus on Exceptional Children, 15,* 1–16.

Harris, K. R. (1986). Self-monitoring of attentional behavior versus self-monitoring of productivity: Effects of on-task behavior and academic response rate among learning disabled children. *Journal of Applied Behavior Analysis, 19,* 417–423.

Harris, M. J., & Rosenthal, R. (1985). Mediation of interpersonal expectancy effects: 31 meta-analyses. *Psychological Bulletin, 97,* 363–386.

Harrow, A. J. (1972). *A taxonomy of the psychomotor domain: A guide for developing behavioral objectives.* New York: David McKay.

Harter, S. (1975). Mastery motivation and the need for approval in older children and their relationship to social desirability response tendencies. *Developmental Psychology, 11,* 186–196.
- Harter, S. (1978). Pleasure derived from optimal challenge and the effects of extrinsic rewards on children's difficulty level choices. *Child Development, 49,* 788–799.

Harter, S. (1982). The perceived competence scale for children. *Child Development, 53,* 87–97.

Harter, S. (1983). Developmental perspectives on the self-system. In E. M. Hetherington (Ed.), *Handbook of child psychology: Vol. 4. Socialization, per-*

sonality, and social development (4th ed.). New York: Wiley.

Harter, S. (1990). Causes, correlates, and the functional role of global self-worth: A life-span perspective. In R. J. Sternberg & J. Kolligian, Jr. (Eds.), *Competence considered.* New Haven, CT: Yale University Press.

• Harter, S. (1992). The relationship between perceived competence, affect, and motivational orientation within the classroom: Processes and patterns of change. In A. K. Boggiano & T. S. Pittman (Eds.), *Achievement and motivation: A social-developmental perspective.* Cambridge, UK: Cambridge University Press.

• Harter, S., Whitesell, N. R., & Kowalski, P. (1992). Individual differences in the effects of educational transitions on young adolescents' perceptions of competence and motivational orientation. *American Educational Research Journal, 29,* 777–807.

Hartley, J., & Trueman, M. (1982). The effects of summaries on the recall of information from prose: Five experimental studies. *Human Learning, 1,* 63–82.

Hartmann, W. K., Miller, R., & Lee, P. (1984). *Out of the cradle: Exploring the frontiers beyond earth.* New York: Workman.

• Hartshorne, H., & May, M. A. (1928). *Studies in the nature of character: Vol. 1. Studies in deceit.* New York: Macmillan.

Hartup, W. W. (1989). Social relationships and their developmental significance. *American Psychologist, 44,* 120–126.

Harway, M., & Moss, L. T. (1983). Sex differences: The evidence from biology. In M. B. Liss (Ed.), *Social and cognitive skills: Sex roles and children's play.* San Diego: Academic Press.

• Hatano, G., & Inagaki, K. (1993). Desituating cognition through the construction of conceptual knowledge. In P. Light & G. Butterworth (Eds.), *Context and cognition: Ways of learning and knowing.* Hillsdale, NJ: Erlbaum.

• Hattie, J., Biggs, J., & Purdie, N. (1996). Effects of learning skills interventions on student learning: A meta-analysis. *Review of Educational Research, 66,* 99–136.

Hawk, P. P. (1986). Using graphic organizers to increase achievement in middle school life science. *Science Education, 70,* 81–87.

• Hayes, C. B., Ryan, A. W., & Zseller, E. B. (1994, April). *African American students' perceptions of caring teacher behaviors.* Paper presented at the annual meeting of the American Educational Research Association, New Orleans, LA.

Hayes, J. R. (1989). Cognitive processes in creativity. In J. A. Glover, R. R. Ronning, & C. R. Reynolds (Eds.), *Handbook of creativity.* New York: Plenum Press.

Hayes, S. C., Rosenfarb, I., Wulfert, E., Munt, E. D., Korn, Z., & Zettle, R. D. (1985). Self-reinforcement effects: An artifact of social standard setting? *Journal of Applied Behavior Analysis, 18,* 201–214.

Hayes-Roth, B., & Thorndyke, P. W. (1979). Integration of knowledge from text. *Journal of Verbal Learning and Verbal Behavior, 18,* 91–108.

Heath, S. B. (1980). Questioning at home and at school: A comparative study. In G. Spindler (Ed.), *The ethnography of schooling: Educational anthropology in action.* New York: Holt, Rinehart & Winston.

Hegland, S., & Andre, T. (1992). Helping learners construct knowledge. *Educational Psychology Review, 4,* 223–240.

Heller, J. I., & Hungate, H. N. (1985). Implications for mathematics instruction of research on scientific problem solving. In E. A. Silver (Ed.), *Teaching and learning mathematical problem solving: Multiple research perspectives.* Hillsdale, NJ: Erlbaum.

Helton, G. B., & Oakland, T. D. (1977). Teachers' attitudinal responses to differing characteristics of elementary school students. *Journal of Educational Psychology, 69,* 261–266.

• Hennessey, B. A. (1995). Social, environmental, and developmental issues and creativity. *Educational Psychology Review, 7,* 163–183.

Hennessey, B. A., & Amabile, T. M. (1987). *Creativity and learning.* Washington, DC: National Education Association.

Hess, G. A., Jr., Lyons, A., & Corsino, L. (1990, April). *Against the odds: The early identification of dropouts.* Paper presented at the annual meeting of the American Educational Research Association, Boston, MA.

Hess, R. D., & Holloway, S. D. (1984). Family and school as educational institutions. In R. D. Parke, R. N. Emde, H. P. McAdoo, & G. P. Sackett (Eds.), *Review of child development research* (Vol. 7). Chicago: University of Chicago Press.

Hess, R. D., & McDevitt, T. M. (1989). Family. In E. Barnouw (Ed.), *International encyclopedia of communications.* New York: Oxford University Press.

• Heuer, F., & Reisberg, D. (1990). Vivid memories of emotional events: The accuracy of remembered minutiae. *Memory and Cognition, 18,* 496–506.

• Heward, W. L. (1996). *Exceptional children: An introduction to special education* (5th ed.). Upper Saddle River, NJ: Merrill/Prentice Hall.

• Hidalgo, N. M., Siu, S., Bright, J. A., Swap, S. M., & Epstein, J. L. (1995). Research on families, schools, and communities: A multicultural perspective. In J. A. Banks & C. A. M. Banks (Eds.), *Handbook of research on multicultural education.* New York: Macmillan.

Hidi, S. (1990). Interest and its contribution as a mental resource for learning. *Review of Educational Research, 60,* 549–571.

Hidi, S., & Anderson, V. (1986). Producing written summaries: Task demands, cognitive operations, and implications for instruction. *Review of Educational Research, 86,* 473–493.

• Hidi, S., & Anderson, V. (1992). Situational interest and its impact on reading and expository writing. In K. A. Renninger, S. Hidi, & A. Krapp (Eds.), *The role of interest in learning and development.* Hillsdale, NJ: Erlbaum.

• Hidi, S., & McLaren, J. (1990). The effect of topic and theme interestingness on the production of school expositions. In H. Mandl, E. De Corte, N. Bennett, & H. F. Friedrich (Eds.), *Learning and instruction in an international context.* Oxford, UK: Pergamon.

• Hiebert, E. H., & Fisher, C. W. (1992). The tasks of school literacy: Trends and issues. In J. Brophy (Ed.), *Advances in research on teaching: Vol. 3. Planning and managing learning tasks and activities.* Greenwich, CT: JAI Press.

• Hiebert, E. H., & Raphael, T. E. (1996). Psychological perspectives on literacy and extensions to educational practice. In D. C. Berliner & R. C. Calfee (Eds.), *Handbook of educational psychology.* New York: Macmillan.

• Hiebert, E. H., Valencia, S. W., & Afflerbach, P. P. (1994). Definitions and perspectives.

In S. W. Valencia, E. H. Hiebert, & P. P. Afflerbach (Eds.), *Authentic reading assessment: Practices and possibilities*. Newark, DE: International Reading Association.

• Hiebert, J., & Lefevre, P. (1986). Conceptual and procedural knowledge in mathematics: An introductory analysis. In J. Hiebert (Ed.), *Conceptual and procedural knowledge: The case of mathematics*. Hillsdale, NJ: Erlbaum.

• Hiebert, J., & Wearne, D. (1993). Instructional tasks, classroom discourse, and students' learning in second-grade arithmetic. *American Educational Research Journal, 30,* 393–425.

Higbee, K. L. (1977). *Your memory: How it works and how to improve it*. Upper Saddle River, NJ: Prentice Hall.

• Higgins, A., Powers, C., & Kohlberg, L. (1984). The relationship of moral atmosphere to judgments of responsibility. In W. M. Kurtines & J. L. Gewirtz (Eds.), *Morality, moral behavior, and moral development*. New York: Wiley.

Higgins, A. T., & Turnure, J. E. (1984). Distractibility and concentration of attention in children's development. *Child Development, 55,* 1799–1810.

Hill, C., & Larsen, E. (1992). *Testing and assessment in secondary education: A critical review of emerging practices*. Berkeley: University of California, National Center for Research in Vocational Education.

• Hill, C. A. (1987). Affiliation motivation: People who need people . . . but in different ways. *Journal of Personality and Social Psychology, 52,* 1008–1018.

Hill, K. T. (1984). Debilitating motivation and testing: A major educational problem, possible solutions, and policy applications. In R. Ames & C. Ames (Eds.), *Research on motivation in education: Vol. 1. Student motivation*. San Diego: Academic Press.

Hill, K. T., & Eaton, W. O. (1977). The interaction of test anxiety and success/failure experiences in determining children's arithmetic performance. *Developmental Psychology, 13,* 205–211.

Hilliard, A., & Vaughn-Scott, M. (1982). The quest for the minority child. In S. G. Moore & C. R. Cooper (Eds.), *The young child: Reviews of research* (Vol. 3). Washington, DC: National Association for the Education of Young Children.

• Hirschfeld, L. A., & Gelman, S. A. (Eds.). (1994). *Mapping the mind: Domain specificity in cognition and culture*. Cambridge, UK: Cambridge University Press.

• Ho, D. Y. F. (1994). Cognitive socialization in Confucian heritage cultures. In P. M. Greenfield & R. R. Cocking (Eds.), *Cross-cultural roots of minority child development*. Hillsdale, NJ: Erlbaum.

Hocevar, D., & Bachelor, P. (1989). A taxonomy and critique of measurements used in the study of creativity. In J. A. Glover, R. R. Ronning, & C. R. Reynolds (Eds.), *Handbook of creativity*. New York: Plenum Press.

Hoffman, M. L. (1970). Moral development. In P. H. Mussen (Ed.), *Carmichael's manual of child psychology* (Vol. 2). New York: Wiley.

Hoffman, M. L. (1975). Altruistic behavior and the parent-child relationship. *Journal of Personality and Social Psychology, 31,* 937–943.

• Hoffman, M. L. (1991). Empathy, social cognition, and moral action. In W. M. Kurtines & J. L. Gewirtz (Eds.), *Moral behavior and development: Vol. 1. Theory*. Hillsdale, NJ: Erlbaum.

Hoge, R. D., & Coladarci, T. (1989). Teacher-based judgments of academic achievement: A review of literature. *Review of Educational Research, 59,* 297–313.

Holley, C. D., & Dansereau, D. F. (1984). *Spatial learning strategies: Techniques, applications, and related issues*. San Diego: Academic Press.

• Hollon, R. E., Roth, K. J., & Anderson, C. W. (1991). Science teachers' conceptions of teaching and learning. In J. Brophy (Ed.), *Advances in research on teaching: Vol. 2. Teacher's knowledge of subject matter as it relates to their teaching practice*. Greenwich, CT: JAI Press.

Holt-Reynolds, D. (1992). Personal history-based beliefs as relevant prior knowledge in course work. *American Educational Research Journal, 29,* 325–349.

• Hom, A., & Battistich, V. (1995, April). *Students' sense of school community as a factor in reducing drug use and delinquency*. Paper presented at the annual meeting of the American Educational Research Association, San Francisco.

Homme, L. E., Csanyi, A. P., Gonzales, M. A., & Rechs, J. R. (1970). *How to use contingency contracting in the classroom*. Champaign, IL: Research Press.

Honzik, M. P. (1967). Environmental correlates of mental growth: Prediction from the family setting at 21 months. *Child Development, 38,* 337–364.

Horgan, D. (1990, April). *Students' predictions of test grades: Calibration and metacognition*. Paper presented at the annual meeting of the American Educational Research Association, Boston, MA.

• Horgan, D. D. (1995). *Achieving gender equity: Strategies for the classroom*. Needham Heights, MA: Allyn & Bacon.

Horwitz, R. A. (1979). Psychological effects of the "open classroom." *Review of Educational Research, 49,* 71–85.

Hosmer, E. (1989). Paradise lost: The ravaged rain forest. In G. R. Pitzl (Ed.), *Geography 89/90* (4th ed.). Guilford, CT: Dushkin. (Reprinted from *Multinational Monitor,* 1987 (June), pp. 6–8, 13)

Hossler, D., & Stage, F. K. (1992). Family and high school experience influences on the postsecondary educational plans of ninth-grade students. *American Educational Research Journal, 29,* 425–451.

• Houtz, J. C. (1990). Environments that support creative thinking. In C. Hedley, J. Houtz, & A. Baratta (Eds.), *Cognition, curriculum, and literacy*. Norwood, NJ: Ablex.

• Howe, C. K. (1994). Improving the achievement of Hispanic students. *Educational Leadership, 51*(8), 42–44.

Howe, M. J. A. (1970). Using students' notes to examine the role of the individual learner in acquiring meaningful subject matter. *Journal of Educational Research, 64,* 61–63.

Hudspeth, W. J. (1985). Developmental neuropsychology: Functional implications of quantitative EEG maturation [Abstract]. *Journal of Clinical and Experimental Neuropsychology, 7,* 606.

Huff, J. A. (1988). Personalized behavior modification: An in-school suspension program that teaches students how to change. *School Counselor, 35,* 210–214.

Hughes, J. N. (1988). *Cognitive behavior therapy with children in schools*. New York: Pergamon.

• Hulse, S. H. (1993). The present status of animal cognition: An introduction. *Psychological Science, 4,* 154–155.

Humphreys, L. G. (1992). What both critics and users of ability tests need to know. *Psychological Science, 3,* 271–274.

Hunter, M. (1982). *Mastery teaching*. El Segundo, CA: TIP.

Huston, A. C. (1983). Sex-typing. In E. M. Hetherington (Ed.), *Handbook of child psychology: Vol. 4. Socialization, personality, and social development* (4th ed.). New York: Wiley.

Hutt, S. J., Tyler, S., Hutt, C., & Christopherson, H. (1989). *Play, exploration, and learning: A natural history of the pre-school.* London: Routledge.

Hyde, J. S., & Linn, M. C. (1988). Gender differences in verbal ability: A meta-analysis. *Psychological Bulletin, 104,* 53–69.

Hymel, S. (1986). Interpretations of peer behavior: Affective bias in childhood and adolescence. *Child Development, 57,* 431–445.

Igoe, A. R., & Sullivan, H. (1991, April). *Gender and grade-level differences in student attributes related to school learning and motivation.* Paper presented at the annual meeting of the American Educational Research Association, Chicago.

Inhelder, B., & Piaget, J. (1958). *The growth of logical thinking from childhood to adolescence* (A. Parsons & S. Milgram, Trans.). New York: Basic Books.

• Irvine, J. J., & York, D. E. (1995). Learning styles and culturally diverse students: A literature review. In J. A. Banks & C. A. M. Banks (Eds.), *Handbook of research on multicultural education.* New York: Macmillan.

Iwata, B. A. (1987). Negative reinforcement in applied behavior analysis: An emerging technology. *Journal of Applied Behavior Analysis, 20,* 361–378.

Iwata, B. A., & Bailey, J. S. (1974). Reward versus cost token systems: An analysis of the effects on students and teacher. *Journal of Applied Behavior Analysis, 7,* 567–576.

Jacklin, C. N. (1989). Female and male: Issues of gender. *American Psychologist, 44,* 127–133.

• Jacobsen, B., Lowery, B., & DuCette, J. (1986). Attributions of learning disabled children. *Journal of Educational Psychology, 78,* 59–64.

Jacobson, J. L., & Wille, D. E. (1986). The influence of attachment pattern on developmental changes in peer interaction from the toddler to the preschool period. *Child Development, 57,* 338–347.

Jagacinski, C. M., & Nicholls, J. G. (1984). Conceptions of ability and related affects in task involvement and ego involvement. *Journal of Educational Psychology, 76,* 909–919.

Jagacinski, C. M., & Nicholls, J. G. (1987). Competence and affect in task involvement and ego involvement: The impact of social comparison information. *Journal of Educational Psychology, 79,* 107–114.

James, W. (1890). *Principles of psychology.* New York: Holt.

Janos, P. M., & Robinson, N. M. (1985). Psychosocial development in intellectually gifted children. In F. D. Horowitz & M. O'Brien (Eds.), *The gifted and talented: Developmental perspectives.* Washington, DC: American Psychological Association.

• Jenlink, C. L. (1994, April). *Music: A lifeline for the self-esteem of at-risk students.* Paper presented at the annual meeting of the American Educational Research Association, New Orleans, LA.

• Johnson, D. W., & Johnson, R. T. (1985a). Classroom conflict: Controversy versus debate in learning groups. *American Educational Research Journal, 22,* 237–256.

• Johnson, D. W., & Johnson, R. T. (1985b). Motivational processes in cooperative, competitive, and individualistic learning situations. In C. Ames & R. Ames (Eds.), *Research on motivation in education: Vol. 2. The classroom milieu.* San Diego: Academic Press.

Johnson, D. W., & Johnson, R. T. (1987). *Learning together and alone: Cooperative, competitive, and individualistic learning* (2nd ed.). Upper Saddle River, NJ: Prentice Hall.

Johnson, D. W., & Johnson, R. T. (1988). Critical thinking through structured controversy. *Educational Leadership, 45*(8), 58–64.

• Johnson, D. W., Johnson, R., Dudley, B., Ward, M., & Magnuson, D. (1995). The impact of peer mediation training on the management of school and home conflicts. *American Educational Research Journal, 32,* 829–844.

Johnson, R. T. (1989, October). *Ways to change the way we teach.* Workshop presented at the University of Northern Colorado, Greeley.

John-Steiner, V., & Souberman, E. (1978). Afterword. In L. S. Vygotsky, *Mind in society: The development of higher psychological processes.* Cambridge, MA: Harvard University Press.

Johnstone, A. H., & El-Banna, H. (1986). Capacities, demands, and processes: A predictive model for science education. *Education in Chemistry, 23,* 80–84.

• Jonassen, D. H. (1991). Objectivism versus constructivism: Do we need a new philosophical paradigm? *Educational Technology Research and Development, 39*(3), 5–14.

• Jonassen, D. H. (1996). *Computers in the classroom: Mindtools for critical thinking.* Upper Saddle River, NJ: Merrill/Prentice Hall.

Jonassen, D. H., Hannum, W. H., & Tessmer, M. (1989). *Handbook of task analysis procedures.* New York: Praeger.

Jones, B. F., Pierce, J., & Hunter, B. (1988/1989). Teaching students to construct graphic representations. *Educational Leadership, 46*(4), 20–25.

• Jones, G. P., & Dembo, M. H. (1989). Age and sex role differences in intimate friendships during childhood and adolescence. *Merrill-Palmer Quarterly, 35,* 445–462.

Jones, L. P. (1990, April). *Black and white achievement gap: The role of teacher expectations.* Paper presented at the annual meeting of the American Educational Research Association, Boston, MA.

Jones, M. C. (1924). The elimination of children's fears. *Journal of Experimental Psychology, 7,* 382–390.

• Jozefowicz, D. M., Arbreton, A. J., Eccles, J. S., Barber, B. L., & Colarossi, L. (1994, April). *Seventh-grade student, parent, and teacher factors associated with later school dropout or movement into alternative educational settings.* Paper presented at the annual meeting of the American Educational Research Association, New Orleans, LA.

Judd, C. H. (1932). Autobiography. In C. Murchison (Ed.), *History of psychology in autobiography* (Vol. 2). Worcester, MA: Clark University Press.

Juvonen, J. (1991a). Deviance, perceived responsibility, and negative peer reactions. *Developmental Psychology, 27,* 672–681.

Juvonen, J. (1991b, April). *The effect of attributions and interpersonal attitudes on social emotions and behavior.* Paper presented at the annual meeting of the American Educational Research Association, Chicago.

Juvonen, J., & Hiner, M. (1991, April). *Perceived responsibility and annoyance as* mediators of negative peer reactions. Paper presented at the annual meeting of the American Educational Research Association, Chicago.

- Juvonen, J., & Weiner, B. (1993). An attributional analysis of students' interactions: The social consequences of perceived responsibility. *Educational Psychology Review, 5,* 325–345.

Kagan, D. M. (1992). Professional growth among preservice and beginning teachers. *Review of Educational Research, 62,* 129–169.

Kagan, J., & Kogan, N. (1970). Individual variation in cognitive processes. In P. H. Mussen (Ed.), *Carmichael's manual of child psychology* (Vol. 1, 3rd ed.). New York: Wiley.

- Kagan, J., Snidman, N., & Arcus, D. M. (1992). Initial reactions to unfamiliarity. *Current Directions in Psychological Science, 1,* 171–174.

Kagan, S., & Knight, G. P. (1984). Maternal reinforcement style and cooperation-competition among Anglo-American and Mexican-American children. *Journal of Genetic Psychology, 145,* 37–47.

- Kahl, B., & Woloshyn, V. E. (1994). Using elaborative interrogation to facilitate acquisition of factual information in cooperative learning settings: One good strategy deserves another. *Applied Cognitive Psychology, 8,* 465–478.

Kahle, J. B. (1983). *The disadvantaged majority: Science education for women.* Burlington, NC: Carolina Biological Supply Co.

Kahle, J. B., & Lakes, M. K. (1983). The myth of equality in science classrooms. *Journal of Research in Science Teaching, 20,* 131–140.

Kail, R. (1990). *The development of memory in children* (3rd ed.). New York: W. H. Freeman.

Kane, R. J. (1983). In defense of grade inflation. *Today's Education, 67*(4), 41.

Kardash, C. M., & Amlund, J. T. (1991). Self-reported learning strategies and learning from expository text. *Contemporary Educational Psychology, 16,* 117–138.

Karmiloff-Smith, A. (1979). Language development after five. In P. Fletcher & M. Garman (Eds.), *Language acquisition: Studies in first language development.* Cambridge, UK: Cambridge University Press.

Karplus, R., Pulos, S., & Stage, E. K. (1983). Proportional reasoning of early adoles-

cents. In R. Lesh & M. Landau (Eds.), *Acquisition of mathematics concepts and processes.* San Diego: Academic Press.

Katkovsky, W., Crandall, V. C., & Good, S. (1967). Parental antecedents of children's beliefs in internal-external control of reinforcements in intellectual achievement situations. *Child Development, 38,* 765–776.

Katz, E. W., & Brent, S. B. (1968). Understanding connectives. *Journal of Verbal Learning and Verbal Behavior, 7,* 501–509.

- Katz, L. (1993). All about me: Are we developing our children's self-esteem or their narcissism? *American Educator, 17*(2), 18–23.

Katz, L., & Chard, S. (1989). *Engaging children's minds: The project approach.* Norword, NJ: Ablex.

Kazdin, A. E. (1972). Response cost: The removal of conditional reinforcers for therapeutic change. *Behavior Therapy, 3,* 533–546.

- Kehle, T., Clark, E., Jenson, W. R., & Wampold, B. (1986). Effectiveness of the self-modeling procedure with behaviorally disturbed elementary age children. *School Psychology Review, 15,* 289–295.

- Keil, F. C. (1986). The acquisition of natural kind and artifact terms. In W. Demopolous & A. Marras (Eds.), *Language learning and concept acquisition.* Norwood, NJ: Ablex.

- Keil, F. C. (1987). Conceptual development and category structure. In U. Neisser (Ed.), *Concepts and conceptual development: Ecological and intellectual factors in categorization.* Cambridge, UK: Cambridge University Press.

- Keil, F. C. (1989). *Concepts, kinds, and cognitive development.* Cambridge: MIT Press.

Keller, F. S. (1968). Goodbye teacher. *Journal of Applied Behavior Analysis, 1,* 79–89.

Kelley, M. L., & Carper, L. B. (1988). Home-based reinforcement procedures. In J. C. Witt, S. N. Elliott, & F. M. Gresham (Eds.), *Handbook of behavior therapy in education.* New York: Plenum Press.

Kelly, A., & Smail, B. (1986). Sex stereotypes and attitudes to science among eleven-year-old children. *British Journal of Educational Psychology, 56,* 158–168.

- Kemler Nelson, D. G., & Smith, J. D. (1989). Holistic and analytic process-

ing in reflection-impulsivity and cognitive development. In T. Globerson & T. Zelniker (Eds.), *Cognitive style and cognitive development.* Norwood, NJ: Ablex.

Kennedy, R. (1992). What is performance assessment? *New Directions for Education Reform, 1*(2), 21–27.

Keogh, B. A., & Becker, L. D. (1973). Early detection of learning problems: Questions, cautions, and guidelines. *Exceptional Children, 39,* 5–11.

Kerr, B. (1991). Educating gifted girls. In N. Coangelo & G. A. Davis (Eds.), *Handbook of gifted education.* Needham Heights, MA: Allyn & Bacon.

Kiewra, K. A. (1985). Investigating note taking and review: A depth of processing alternative. *Educational Psychologist, 20,* 23–32.

Kiewra, K. A. (1989). A review of note taking: The encoding-storage paradigm and beyond. *Educational Psychology Review, 1,* 147–172.

- Kim, D., Solomon, D., & Roberts, W. (1995, April). *Classroom practices that enhance students' sense of community.* Paper presented at the annual meeting of the American Educational Research Association, San Francisco.

King, A. (1992). Comparison of self-questioning, summarizing, and notetaking-review as strategies for learning from lectures. *American Educational Research Journal, 29,* 303–323.

- King, A. (1994). Guiding knowledge construction in the classroom: Effects of teaching children how to question and how to explain. *American Educational Research Journal, 31,* 338–368.

- King, A. J. C. (1989). Changing sex roles, lifestyles, and attitudes in an urban society. In K. Hurrelmann & U. Engel (Eds.), *The social world of adolescents: International perspectives.* New York: de Gruyter.

King, N. J., & Ollendick, T. H. (1989). Children's anxiety and phobic disorders in school settings: Classification, assessment, and intervention issues. *Review of Educational Research, 59,* 431–470.

- Kintsch, W. (1980). Learning from text, levels of comprehension, or: Why anyone would read a story anyway. *Poetics, 9,* 87–98.

Kirkland, M. C. (1971). The effect of tests on students and schools. *Review of Educational Research, 41,* 303–350.

Kirschenbaum, R. J. (1989). Identification of the gifted and talented American Indian student. In C. J. Maker & S. W. Schiever (Eds.), *Critical issues in gifted education: Vol. 2. Defensible programs for cultural and ethnic minorities.* Austin, TX: PRO-ED.

Klatzky, R. L. (1975). *Human memory.* San Francisco: W. H. Freeman.

Klein, J. D. (1990, April). *The effect of interest, task performance, and reward contingencies on self-efficacy.* Paper presented at the annual meeting of the American Educational Research Association, Boston, MA.

Klein, P. S. (1975). Effects of open vs. structured teacher-student interaction on creativity of children with different levels of anxiety. *Psychology in the Schools, 12,* 286–288.

• Kleinsmith, L. J., & Kaplan, S. (1963). Paired associate learning as a function of arousal and interpolated interval. *Journal of Experimental Psychology, 65,* 190–193.

Kletzien, S. B. (1988, April). *Achieving and nonachieving high school readers' use of comprehension strategies for reading expository text.* Paper presented at the annual meeting of the American Educational Research Association, New Orleans, LA.

• Knapp, M. S., Turnbull, B. J., & Shields, P. M. (1990). New directions for educating the children of poverty. *Educational Leadership, 48*(1), 4–9.

• Knapp, M. S., & Woolverton, S. (1995). Social class and schooling. In J. A. Banks & C. A. M. Banks (Eds.), *Handbook of research on multicultural education.* New York: Macmillan.

Knight, S. L. (1988, April). *Examining the relationship between teacher behaviors and students' cognitive reading strategies.* Paper presented at the annual meeting of the American Educational Research Association, New Orleans, LA.

• Koeppel, J., & Mulrooney, M. (1992). The Sister Schools Program: A way for children to learn about cultural diversity— when there isn't any in their school. *Young Children, 48*(1), 44–47.

• Koestner, R., Ryan, R. M., Bernieri, F., & Holt, K. (1984). Setting limits in children's behavior: The differential effects of controlling versus informational styles on intrinsic motivation and creativity. *Journal of Personality, 52,* 233–248.

Kogan, N. (1983). Stylistic variation in childhood and adolescence: Creativity, metaphor, and cognitive style. In J. H. Flavell & E. M. Markman (Eds.), *Handbook of child psychology: Vol. 3. Cognitive development.* New York: Wiley.

• Kogan, N., & Block, J. (1991). Field dependence-independence from early childhood through adolescence: Personality and socialization aspects. In S. Wapner & J. Demick (Eds.), *Field dependence-independence: Cognitive style across the life span.* Hillsdale, NJ: Erlbaum.

Kohlberg, L. (1969). Stage and sequence: The cognitive-developmental approach to socialization. In D. A. Goslin (Ed.), *Handbook of socialization theory and research.* Chicago: Rand McNally.

Kohlberg, L. (1975). The cognitive-developmental approach to moral education. *Phi Delta Kappan, 57,* 670–677.

Kohlberg, L. (1976). Moral stages and moralization: The cognitive-developmental approach. In T. Lickona (Ed.), *Moral development and behavior: Theory, research, and social issues.* New York: Holt, Rinehart & Winston.

Kohlberg, L. (1981). *The philosophy of moral development: Moral stages and the idea of justice.* San Francisco: Harper & Row.

Kohlberg, L. (1984). *The psychology of moral development: The nature and validity of moral stages.* San Francisco: Harper & Row.

Kohlberg, L. (1986). A current statement on some theoretical issues. In S. Modgil & C. Modgil (Eds.), *Lawrence Kohlberg: Consensus and controversy.* Philadelphia: Falmer Press.

Kohlberg, L., & Candee, D. (1984). The relationship of moral judgment to moral action. In W. M. Kurtines & J. L. Gewirtz (Eds.), *Morality, moral behavior, and moral development.* New York: Wiley.

Kohlberg, L., & Turiel, E. (1971). Moral development and moral education. In G. Lesser (Ed.), *Psychology and educational practice.* Glenview, IL: Scott, Foresman.

• Kohn, A. (1993). Choices for children: Why and how to let students decide. *Phi Delta Kappan, 75*(1), 8–20.

• Kolodner, J. (1985). Memory for experience. In G. H. Bower (Ed.), *The psychology of learning and motivation: Advances in research and theory* (Vol. 19). San Diego: Academic Press.

• Konopak, B. C., Martin, S. H., & Martin, M. A. (1990). Using a writing strategy to enhance sixth-grade students' comprehension of content material. *Journal of Reading Behavior, 22,* 19–37.

• Koretz, D., Stecher, B., Klein, S., & McCaffrey, D. (1994). The Vermont portfolio assessment program: Findings and implications. *Educational Measurement: Issues and Practices, 13*(3), 5–16.

• Kosslyn, S. M. (1985). Mental imagery ability. In R. J. Sternberg (Ed.), *Human abilities: An information-processing approach.* New York: W. H. Freeman.

Kounin, J. S. (1970). *Discipline and group management in classrooms.* New York: Holt, Rinehart & Winston.

Kounin, J. S., & Doyle, P. H. (1975). Degree of continuity of a lesson's signal system and the task involvement of children. *Journal of Educational Psychology, 67,* 159–164.

Kounin, J. S., & Gump, P. V. (1974). Signal systems of lesson settings and the task-related behavior of preschool children. *Journal of Educational Psychology, 66,* 554–562.

• Koza, J. K. (1996). Multicultural approaches to music education. In C. A. Grant & M. L. Gomez, *Making schooling multicultural: Campus and classroom.* Upper Saddle River, NJ: Merrill/Prentice Hall.

• Kozulin, A., & Presseisen, B. Z. (1995). Mediated learning experience and psychological tools: Vygotsky's and Feuerstein's perspectives in a study of study learning. *Educational Psychologist, 30,* 67–75.

• Krathwohl, D. R. (1994). Reflections on the taxonomy: Its past, present, and future. In L. W. Anderson & L. A. Sosniak (Eds.), *Bloom's taxonomy: A forty-year perspective. Ninety-third yearbook of the National Society for the Study of Education, Part II.* Chicago: National Society for the Study of Education.

Krathwohl, D. R., Bloom, B. S., & Masia, B. B. (1964). *Taxonomy of educational objectives: Handbook II. Affective domain.* New York: David McKay.

• Krebs, D. L., Vermeulen, S. C. A., Carpendale, J. I., & Denton, K. (1991). Structural and situational influences on moral judgment: The interaction between stage and dilemma. In W. M. Kurtines & J. L. Gewirtz (Eds.), *Moral behavior and development: Vol. 2. Research.* Hillsdale, NJ: Erlbaum.

Krueger, W. C. F. (1929). The effect of over-learning on retention. *Journal of Experimental Psychology, 12,* 71–78.

• Kruglanski, A., Stein, C., & Riter, A. (1977). Contingencies of exogenous reward and task performance: On the "minimax" strategy in instrumental behavior. *Journal of Applied Social Psychology, 2,* 141–148.

Krumboltz, J. D., & Krumboltz, H. B. (1972). *Changing children's behavior.* Upper Saddle River, NJ: Prentice Hall.

Kulhavy, R. W., Lee, J. B., & Caterino, L. C. (1985). Conjoint retention of maps and related discourse. *Contemporary Educational Psychology, 10,* 28–37.

Kulik, C. C., Kulik, J. A., & Bangert-Drowns, R. L. (1990). Effectiveness of mastery learning programs: A meta-analysis. *Review of Educational Research, 60,* 265–299.

Kulik, C. C., Kulik, J. A., & Shwalb, B. J. (1983). College programs for high-risk and disadvantaged students: A meta-analysis of findings. *Review of Educational Research, 53,* 397–414.

Kulik, J. A., & Kulik, C. C. (1988). Timing of feedback and verbal learning. *Review of Educational Research, 58,* 79–97.

Kulik, J. A., Kulik, C. C., & Cohen, P. A. (1979). A meta-analysis of outcome studies of Keller's Personalized System of Instruction. *American Psychologist, 34,* 307–318.

Kulik, J. A., Kulik, C. C., & Cohen, P. A. (1980). Effectiveness of computer-based college teaching: A meta-analysis of findings. *Review of Educational Research, 50,* 525–544.

Kunc, N. (1984). Integration: Being realistic isn't realistic. *Canadian Journal for Exceptional Children, 1*(1), 4–8.

Kuslan, L. I., & Stone, A. H. (1972). *Teaching children science: An inquiry approach* (2nd ed.). Belmont, CA: Wadsworth.

Kyle, W. C., & Shymansky, J. A. (1989). Enhancing learning through conceptual change teaching. *NARST News, 31*(April), 7–8.

LaBerge, D., & Samuels, S. J. (1974). Toward a theory of automatic information processing in reading. *Cognitive Psychology, 6,* 293–323.

• Laboratory of Human Cognition. (1982). Culture and intelligence. In R. J. Sternberg (Ed.), *Handbook of human intelligence.* Cambridge, UK: Cambridge University Press.

• Ladson-Billings, G. (1994a). *The dreamkeepers: Successful teachers of African American children.* San Francisco: Jossey-Bass.

• Ladson-Billings, G. (1994b). What we can learn from multicultural education research. *Educational Leadership, 51*(8), 22–26.

Lam, T. C. M. (1992). Review of practices and problems in the evaluation of bilingual education. *Review of Educational Research, 62,* 181–203.

• Lampe, J. R., & Rooze, G. E. (1994, April). *Enhancing social studies achievement among Hispanic students using cooperative learning work groups.* Paper presented at the annual meeting of the American Educational Research Association, New Orleans, LA.

• Lan, W. Y., Repman, J., Bradley, L., & Weller, H. (1994, April). *Immediate and lasting effects of criterion and payoff on academic risk taking.* Paper presented at the annual meeting of the American Educational Research Association, New Orleans, LA.

Landau, S., & McAninch, C. (1993). Young children with attention deficits. *Young Children, 48*(4), 49–58.

Landauer, T. K. (1962). Rate of implicit speech. *Perceptual and Motor Skills, 15,* 646.

Landesman, S., & Ramey, C. (1989). Developmental psychology and mental retardation: Integrating scientific principles with treatment practices. *American Psychologist, 44,* 409–415.

Lane, D. M., & Pearson, D. A. (1982). The development of selective attention. *Merrill-Palmer Quarterly, 28,* 317–337.

• Lanza, A., & Roselli, T. (1991). Effect of the hyper-textual approach versus the structured approach on students' achievement. *Journal of Computer-Based Instruction, 18*(2), 48–50.

Laosa, L. M. (1982). School, occupation, culture, and family: The impact of parental schooling on the parent-child relationship. *Journal of Educational Psychology, 74,* 791–827.

Larrivee, B. (1989). Effective strategies for academically handicapped students in the regular classroom. In R. E. Slavin, N. L. Karweit, & N. A. Madden (Eds.), *Effective programs for students at risk.* Needham Heights, MA: Allyn & Bacon.

• Lave, J. (1993). Word problems: A microcosm of theories of learning. In P. Light & G. Butterworth (Eds.), *Context and cognition: Ways of learning and knowing.* Hillsdale, NJ: Erlbaum.

• Law, D. J., Pellegrino, J. W., & Hunt, E. B. (1993). Comparing the tortoise and the hare: Gender differences and experience in dynamic spatial reasoning tasks. *Psychological Science, 4,* 35–40.

Lazar, I., & Darlington, R. (1982). Lasting effects of early education: A report from the consortium for longitudinal studies. *Monographs of the Society for Research in Child Development, 47*(Serial No. 195, Nos. 2–3).

• Lee, C. D., & Slaughter-Defoe, D. T. (1995). Historical and sociocultural influences on African and American education. In J. A. Banks & C. A. M. Banks (Eds.), *Handbook of research on multicultural education.* New York: Macmillan.

Lee, J. F., Jr., & Pruitt, K. W. (1984). *Providing for individual differences in student learning: A mastery learning approach.* Springfield, IL: Charles C. Thomas.

Lee, O. (1991, April). *Motivation to learn subject matter content: The case of science.* Paper presented at the annual meeting of the American Educational Research Association, Chicago.

• Lee, O., & Anderson, C. W. (1993). Task engagement and conceptual change in middle school science classrooms. *American Educational Research Journal, 30,* 585–610.

• Lee, S. (1985). Children's acquisition of conditional logic structure: Teachable? *Contemporary Educational Psychology, 10,* 14–27.

Leherissey, B. L., O'Neil, H. F., Jr., & Hansen, D. N. (1971). Effects of memory support on state anxiety and performance in computer-assisted learning. *Journal of Educational Psychology, 62,* 413–420.

Leinhardt, G. (1980). Transition rooms: Promoting maturation or reducing education? *Journal of Educational Psychology, 72,* 55–61.

Leinhardt, G., & Pallay, A. (1982). Restrictive educational settings: Exile or haven? *Review of Educational Research, 52,* 557–578.

• Lennon, R., Eisenberg, N., & Carroll, J. L. (1983). The assessment of empathy in early childhood. *Journal of Applied Developmental Psychology, 4,* 295–302.

Lennon, R., Ormrod, J. E., Burger, S. F., & Warren, E. (1990, October). *Belief sys-*

tems of teacher education majors and their possible influences on future classroom performance. Paper presented at the Northern Rocky Mountain Educational Research Association, Greeley, CO.

Lentz, F. E. (1988). Reductive procedures. In J. C. Witt, S. N. Elliott, & F. M. Gresham (Eds.), *Handbook of behavior therapy in education*. New York: Plenum.

• Lepper, M. R. (1981). Intrinsic and extrinsic motivation in children: Detrimental effects of superfluous social controls. In W. A. Collins (Ed.), *Minnesota Symposia on Child Psychology* (Vol. 14). Hillsdale, NJ: Erlbaum.

Lepper, M. R. (1983). Social-control processes and the internalization of social values: An attributional perspective. In E. T. Higgins, D. N. Ruble, & W. W. Hartup (Eds.), *Social cognition and social development*. New York: Cambridge University Press.

Lepper, M. R., & Greene, D. (Eds.). (1978). *The hidden costs of reward*. Hillsdale, NJ: Erlbaum.

Lepper, M. R., & Gurtner, J. (1989). Children and computers: Approaching the twenty-first century. *American Psychologist, 44,* 170–178.

Lepper, M. R., & Hodell, M. (1989). Intrinsic motivation in the classroom. In C. Ames & R. Ames (Eds.), *Research on motivation in education: Vol. 3. Goals and cognitions*. San Diego: Academic Press.

• Lepper, M. R., Keavney, M., & Drake, M. (1996). Intrinsic motivation and extrinsic rewards: A commentary on Cameron and Pierce's meta-analysis. *Review of Educational Research, 66,* 5–32.

Lerner, J. W. (1985). *Learning disabilities: Theories, diagnosis, and teaching strategies* (4th ed.). Boston: Houghton Mifflin.

Lester, F. K. (1985). Methodological considerations in research on mathematical problem-solving instruction. In E. A. Silver (Ed.), *Teaching and learning mathematical problem solving: Multiple research perspectives*. Hillsdale, NJ: Erlbaum.

Levin, G. R. (1983). *Child psychology*. Monterey, CA: Brooks/Cole.

Levin, J. R., & Berry, J. K. (1980). Children's learning of all the news that's fit to picture. *Educational Communications and Technology, 28,* 177–185.

• Levin, J. R., & Mayer, R. E. (1993). Understanding illustrations in text. In B. K. Britton, A. Woodward, & M. Binkley (Eds.), *Learning from textbooks: Theory and practice*. Hillsdale, NJ: Erlbaum.

• Levine, D. U., & Lezotte, L. W. (1995). Effective schools research. In J. A. Banks & C. A. M. Banks (Eds.), *Handbook of research on multicultural education*. New York: Macmillan.

Levitt, E. E. (1967). *The psychology of anxiety*. Indianapolis, IN: Bobbs-Merrill.

Lewis, R. B., & Doorlag, D. H. (1991). *Teaching special students in the mainstream* (3rd ed.). New York: Macmillan.

Lewontin, R. C., Rose, S., & Kamin, L. J. (1984). *Not in our genes*. New York: Pantheon.

• Licht, B. (1992). Achievement-related beliefs in children with learning disabilities. In L. J. Meltzer (Ed.), *Strategy assessment and instruction for students with learning disabilities: From theory to practice*. Austin, TX: PRO-ED.

• Lickona, T. (1991). Moral development in the elementary school classroom. In W. M. Kurtines & J. L. Gewirtz (Eds.), *Moral behavior and development: Vol. 3. Application*. Hillsdale, NJ: Erlbaum.

• Lind, G. (1994, April). *Why do juvenile delinquents gain little from moral discussion programs?* Paper presented at the annual meeting of the American Educational Research Association, New Orleans, LA.

Lindholm, K. J., & Fairchild, H. H. (1990). Evaluation of an elementary school bilingual immersion program. In A. M. Padilla, H. H. Fairchild, & C. M. Valadez (Eds.), *Bilingual education: Issues and strategies*. Newbury Park, CA: Sage.

Lindow, J., Marrett, C. B., & Wilkinson, L. C. (1985). Overview. In L. C. Wilkinson & C. B. Marrett (Eds.), *Gender influences in classroom interaction*. San Diego: Academic Press.

Lindvall, C. M., Tamburino, J. L., & Robinson, L. (1982, March). *An exploratory investigation of the effect of teaching primary grade children to use specific problem-solving strategies in solving simple story problems*. Paper presented at the annual meeting of the American Educational Research Association, New York.

• Linn, M. C., Clement, C., Pulos, S., & Sullivan, P. (1989). Scientific reasoning during adolescence: The influence of instruction in science knowledge and reasoning strategies. *Journal of Research in Science Teaching, 26,* 171–187.

Linn, M. C., & Hyde, J. S. (1989). Gender, mathematics, and science. *Educational Researcher, 18*(8), 17–19, 22–27.

Linn, M. C., & Petersen, A. C. (1985). Emergence and characterization of sex differences in spatial ability: A meta-analysis. *Child Development, 56,* 1479–1498.

• Linn, R. L. (1994). Performance assessment: Policy promises and technical measurement standards. *Educational Researcher, 23*(9), 4–14.

Linn, R. L., Baker, E. L., & Dunbar, S. B. (1991). Complex, performance-based assessment: Expectations and validation criteria. *Educational Researcher, 20*(8), 15–21.

Lipsky, D. K., & Gartner, A. (1987). Capable of achievement and worthy of respect: Education for handicapped students as if they were full-fledged human beings. *Exceptional Children, 54,* 69–74.

Lipson, M. Y. (1983). The influence of religious affiliation on children's memory for text information. *Reading Research Quarterly, 18,* 448–457.

Liss, M. B. (1983). Learning gender-related skills through play. In M. B. Liss (Ed.), *Social and cognitive skills: Sex roles and children's play*. San Diego: Academic Press.

• Liu, L. G. (1990, April). *The use of causal questioning to promote narrative comprehension and memory*. Paper presented at the annual meeting of the American Educational Research Association, Boston, MA.

Lloyd, D. N. (1978). Prediction of school failure from third-grade data. *Educational and Psychological Measurement, 38,* 1193–1200.

• Loftus, E. F. (1991). Made in memory: Distortions in recollection after misleading information. In G. H. Bower (Ed.), *The psychology of learning and motivation: Advances in research and theory* (Vol. 27). San Diego: Academic Press.

Loftus, E. F., & Loftus, G. R. (1980). On the permanence of stored information in the human brain. *American Psychologist, 35,* 409–420.

• Lomawaima, K. T. (1995). Educating Native Americans. In J. A. Banks & C. A. M. Banks (Eds.), *Handbook of research on multicultural education.* New York: Macmillan.

- Long, M. (1995). The role of the linguistic environment in second language acquisition. In W. C. Ritchie & T. K. Bhatia (Eds.), *Handbook of language acquisition: Vol. 2. Second language acquisition.* San Diego: Academic Press.

Longstreth, L. E., Madigan, S. A., Pan, J., & Alcorn, M. B. (1989, June). *The role of rehearsal in the development of digit span.* Paper presented at the annual meeting of the American Psychological Society, Alexandria, VA.

- Lovell, K. (1979). Intellectual growth and the school curriculum. In F. B. Murray (Ed.), *The impact of Piagetian theory: On education, philosophy, psychiatry, and psychology.* Baltimore: University Park Press.

Lovitt, T. C., Guppy, T. E., & Blattner, J. E. (1969). The use of free-time contingency with fourth graders to increase spelling accuracy. *Behaviour Research and Therapy, 7,* 151–156.

- Lowry, R., Sleet, D., Duncan, C., Powell, K., & Kolbe, L. (1995). Adolescents at risk for violence. *Educational Psychology Review, 7,* 7–39.

Lozoff, B. (1989). Nutrition and behavior. *American Psychologist, 44,* 231–236.

Luchins, A. S., & Luchins, E. H. (1950). New experimental attempts at preventing mechanization in problem solving. *Journal of General Psychology, 42,* 279–297.

Luchins, E. H., & Luchins, A. S. (1980). Female mathematicians: A contemporary appraisal. In L. H. Fox, L. Brody, & D. Tobin (Eds.), *Women and the mathematical mystique.* Baltimore: Johns Hopkins University Press.

Lueptow, L. B. (1984). *Adolescent sex roles and social change.* New York: Columbia University Press.

Lyon, M. A. (1984). Positive reinforcement and logical consequences in the treatment of classroom encopresis. *School Psychology Review, 13,* 238–243.

Maccoby, E. E., & Hagen, J. W. (1965). Effects of distraction upon central versus incidental recall: Developmental trends. *Journal of Experimental Child Psychology, 2,* 280–289.

Maccoby, E. E., & Jacklin, C. N. (1974). *The psychology of sex differences.* Stanford, CA: Stanford University Press.

Maccoby, E. E., & Martin, J. A. (1983). Socialization in the context of the family: Parent-child interaction. In E. M. Hetherington (Ed.), *Handbook of child psychology: Vol. 4. Socialization, personality, and social development* (4th ed.). New York: Wiley.

Mace, F. C., Belfiore, P. J., & Shea, M. C. (1989). Operant theory and research on self-regulation. In B. J. Zimmerman & D. H. Schunk (Eds.), *Self-regulated learning and academic achievement: Theory, research, and practice.* New York: Springer-Verlag.

Mace, F. C., & Kratochwill, T. R. (1988). Self-monitoring. In J. C. Witt, S. N. Elliott, & F. M. Gresham (Eds.), *Handbook of behavior therapy in education.* New York: Plenum.

Machiels-Bongaerts, M., Schmidt, H. G., & Boshuizen, H. P. A. (1991, April). *The effects of prior knowledge activation on free recall and study time allocation.* Paper presented at the annual meeting of the American Educational Research Association, Chicago.

- MacIver, D., Stipek, D. J., & Daniels, D. (1991). Explaining within-semester changes in student effort in junior high school and senior high school courses. *Journal of Educational Psychology, 83,* 201–211.

- MacLean, D. J., Sasse, D. K., Keating, D. P., Stewart, B. E., & Miller, F. K. (1995, April). *All-girls' mathematics and science instruction in early adolescence: Longitudinal effects.* Paper presented at the annual meeting of the American Educational Research Association, San Francisco.

Madden, N. A., & Slavin, R. E. (1983). Mainstreaming students with mild handicaps: Academic and social outcomes. *Review of Educational Research, 53,* 519–569.

Maehr, M. L. (1984). Meaning and motivation: Toward a theory of personal investment. In R. Ames & C. Ames (Eds.), *Research on motivation in education: Vol. 1. Student motivation.* San Diego: Academic Press.

- Maker, C. J. (1993). Creativity, intelligence, and problem solving: A definition and design for cross-cultural research and measurement related to giftedness. *Gifted Education International, 9*(2), 68–77.

Maker, C. J., & Schiever, S. W. (Eds.). (1989). *Critical issues in gifted education: Vol. 2. Defensible programs for cultural and ethnic minorities.* Austin, TX: PRO-ED.

- Malone, T., & Lepper, M. (1987). Making learning fun: A taxonomy of intrinsic motivation for learning. In R. Snow & M. Farr (Eds.), *Aptitude, learning, and instruction: III. Cognitive and affective process analyses.* Hillsdale, NJ: Erlbaum.

Mandler, G., & Pearlstone, Z. (1966). Free and constrained concept learning and subsequent recall. *Journal of Verbal Learning and Verbal Behavior, 5,* 126–131.

Marcia, J. E. (1980). Identity in adolescence. In J. Adelson (Ed.), *Handbook of adolescent psychology.* New York: Wiley.

- Marcus, G. F. (1996). Why do children say "breaked"? *Current Directions in Psychological Science, 5,* 81–85.

Markman, E. M. (1977). Realizing that you don't understand: A preliminary investigation. *Child Development, 48,* 986–992.

Markman, E. M. (1979). Realizing that you don't understand: Elementary school children's awareness of inconsistencies. *Child Development, 50,* 643–655.

Marland, S. P. (1972). *Education of the gifted and talented.* Washington, DC: Government Printing Office.

Marsh, H. W. (1986). Verbal and math self-concepts: An internal external frame of reference model. *American Educational Research Journal, 23,* 129–149.

Marsh, H. W. (1989). Age and sex effect in multiple dimensions of self-concept: Preadolescence to early-adulthood. *Journal of Educational Psychology, 81,* 417–430.

Marsh, H. W. (1990a). Causal ordering of academic self-concept and academic achievement: A multiwave, longitudinal panel analysis. *Journal of Educational Psychology, 82,* 646–656.

Marsh, H. W. (1990b). A multidimensional, hierarchical model of self-concept: Theoretical and empirical justification. *Educational Psychology Review, 2,* 77–172.

- Marsh, H. W., Chessor, D., Craven, R., & Roche, L. (1995). The effects of gifted and talented programs on academic self-concept: The big fish strikes again. *American Educational Research Journal, 32,* 285–319.

Marsh, H. W., & Peart, N. (1988). Competitive and cooperative physical fitness training programs for girls: Effects on physical fitness and on multidimensional self-concepts. *Journal of Sport and Exercise Psychology, 10,* 390–407.

Marsh, R. W. (1985). Phrenobylsis: Real or chimera? *Child Development, 56,* 1059–1061.

Marshall, H. H. (1981). Open classrooms: Has the term outlived its usefulness? *Review of Educational Research, 51,* 181–192.

• Marshall, H. H. (1988). Work or learning: Implications of classroom metaphors. *Educational Researcher, 17*(9), 9–16.

• Marshall, H. H. (1992). *Redefining student learning: Roots of educational change.* Norwood, NJ: Ablex.

Martin, C. L., & Halverson, C. F. (1981). A schematic processing model of sex typing and stereotyping in children. *Child Development, 52,* 1119–1134.

• Maskowitz, G., & Hayman, J. L. (1976). Success strategies of inner-city teachers: A year-long study. *Journal of Educational Research, 69,* 283–289.

Maslow, A. H. (1959). *New knowledge in human values.* New York: Harper & Row.

Maslow, A. H. (1971). *The farther reaches of human nature.* New York: Viking.

Maslow, A. H. (1973a). Self-actualizing people: A study of psychological health. In R. J. Lowry (Ed.), *Dominance, self-esteem, self-actualization: Germinal papers of A. H. Maslow.* Monterey, CA: Brooks/Cole.

Maslow, A. H. (1973b). Theory of human motivation. In R. J. Lowry (Ed.), *Dominance, self-esteem, self-actualization: Germinal papers of A. H. Maslow.* Monterey, CA: Brooks/Cole.

Maslow, A. H. (1976). *Religion, values, and peak experiences.* Harmondsworth, UK: Penguin.

Maslow, A. H. (1987). *Motivation and personality* (3rd ed.). New York: Harper & Row.

Massialas, B. G., & Zevin, J. (1983). *Teaching creatively: Learning through discovery.* Malabar, FL: Robert E. Krieger.

• Mastropieri, M. A., & Scruggs, T. E. (1992). Science for students with disabilities. *Review of Educational Research, 62,* 377–411.

Masur, E. F., McIntyre, C. W., & Flavell, J. H. (1973). Developmental changes in apportionment of study time among items in a multitrial free recall task. *Journal of Experimental Child Psychology, 15,* 237–246.

Mayer, R. E. (1974). Acquisition processes and resilience under varying testing conditions for structurally different problem solving procedures. *Journal of Educational Psychology, 66,* 644–656.

Mayer, R. E. (1979a). Can advance organizers influence meaningful learning? *Review of Educational Research, 49,* 371–383.

Mayer, R. E. (1979b). Twenty years of research on advance organizers: Assimilation theory is still the best predictor of results. *Instructional Science, 8,* 133–167.

Mayer, R. E. (1982). Memory for algebra story problems. *Journal of Educational Psychology, 74,* 199–216.

Mayer, R. E. (1984). Aids to text comprehension. *Educational Psychologist, 19,* 30–42.

Mayer, R. E. (1985). Implications of cognitive psychology for instruction in mathematical problem solving. In E. A. Silver (Ed.), *Teaching and learning mathematical problem solving: Multiple research perspectives.* Hillsdale, NJ: Erlbaum.

Mayer, R. E. (1986). Mathematics. In R. F. Dillon & R. J. Sternberg (Eds.), *Cognition and instruction.* San Diego: Academic Press.

Mayer, R. E. (1987). *Educational psychology: A cognitive approach.* Boston: Little, Brown.

Mayer, R. E. (1989). Models for understanding. *Review of Educational Research, 59,* 43–64.

Mayer, R. E. (1992). *Thinking, problem solving, cognition* (2nd ed.). New York: W. H. Freeman.

Mayer, R. E., & Greeno, J. G. (1972). Structural differences between learning outcomes produced by different instructional methods. *Journal of Educational Psychology, 63,* 165–173.

• McAlpine, L. (1992). Language, literacy, and education: Case studies of Cree, Inuit, and Mohawk communities. *Canadian Children, 17*(1), 17–30.

• McAlpine, L., & Taylor, D. M. (1993). Instructional preferences of Cree, Inuit, and Mohawk teachers. *Journal of American Indian Education, 33*(1), 1–20.

McAshan, H. H. (1979). *Competency-based education and behavioral objectives.* Englewood Cliffs, NJ: Educational Technology.

• McCall, R. B. (1994). Academic underachievers. *Current Directions in Psychological Science, 3,* 15–19.

• McCallum, R. S., & Bracken, B. A. (1993). Interpersonal relations between school children and their peers, parents, and teachers. *Educational Psychology Review, 5,* 155–176.

• McCombs, B. L. (1988). Motivational skills training: Combining metacognitive, cognitive, and affective learning strategies. In C. E. Weinstein, E. T. Goetz, & P. A. Alexander (Eds.), *Learning and study strategies: Issues in assessment, instruction, and evaluation.* San Diego: Harcourt Brace Jovanovich.

• McCormick, M. E., & Wolf, J. S. (1993). Intervention programs for gifted girls. *Roeper Review, 16,* 85–88.

McCoy, L. P. (1990, April). *Correlates of mathematics anxiety.* Paper presented at the annual meeting of the American Educational Research Association, Boston, MA.

McDaniel, M. A., & Einstein, G. O. (1989). Material-appropriate processing: A contextualist approach to reading and studying strategies. *Educational Psychology Review, 1,* 113–145.

• McDaniel, M. A., & Masson, M. E. J. (1985). Altering memory representations through retrieval. *Journal of Experimental Psychology: Learning, Memory, and Cognition, 11,* 371–385.

McDaniel, T. R. (1987). Practicing positive reinforcement. *Clearing House, 60,* 389–392.

McDevitt, T. M. (1990). Encouraging young children's listening skills. *Academic Therapy, 25,* 569–577.

McDevitt, T. M., & Carroll, M. (1988). Are you trying to trick me? Some social influences on children's responses to problematic messages. *Merrill-Palmer Quarterly, 34,* 131–145.

McDevitt, T. M., Spivey, N., Sheehan, E. P., Lennon, R., & Story, R. (1990). Children's beliefs about listening: Is it enough to be still and quiet? *Child Development, 61,* 713–721.

McGowan, R. J., & Johnson, D. L. (1984). The mother-child relationship and other antecedents of childhood intelligence: A causal analysis. *Child Development, 55,* 810–820.

McKeachie, W. J., Lin, Y., Milholland, J., & Isaacson, R. (1966). Student affiliation motives, teacher warmth, and academic achievement. *Journal of Personality and Social Psychology, 4,* 457–461.

McKeon, D. (1994). When meeting "common" standards is uncommonly difficult. *Educational Leadership, 51*(8), 45–49.

McKeown, M. G., & Beck, I. L. (1990). The assessment and characterization of young learners' knowledge of a topic in history. *American Educational Research Journal, 27,* 688–726.

McLaughlin, T. F., & Malaby, J. (1972). Intrinsic reinforcers in a classroom token economy. *Journal of Applied Behavior Analysis, 5,* 263–270.

McLeod, D. B., & Adams, V. M. (Eds.). (1989). *Affect and mathematical problem solving: A new perspective.* New York: Springer-Verlag.

McMillan, J. H., & Reed, D. F. (1994). At-risk students and resiliency: Factors contributing to academic success. *Clearing House, 67*(3), 137–140.

McNamara, E. (1987). Behavioural approaches in the secondary school. In K. Wheldall (Ed.), *The behaviourist in the classroom.* London: Allen & Unwin.

McRobbie, C., & Tobin, K. (1995). Restraints to reform: The congruence of teacher and student actions in a chemistry classroom. *Journal of Research in Science Teaching, 32,* 373–385.

Meichenbaum, D. (1977). *Cognitive-behavior modification: An integrative approach.* New York: Plenum Press.

Meichenbaum, D. (1985). Teaching thinking: A cognitive-behavioral perspective. In S. F. Chipman, J. W. Segal, & R. Glaser (Eds.), *Thinking and learning skills: Vol. 2. Research and open questions.* Hillsdale, NJ: Erlbaum.

Meichenbaum, D., & Goodman, J. (1971). Training impulsive children to talk to themselves: A means of developing self-control. *Journal of Abnormal Psychology, 77,* 115–126.

Meloth, M. S., & Deering, P. D. (1994). Task talk and task awareness under different cooperative learning conditions. *American Educational Research Journal, 31,* 138–165.

Mercer, C. D. (1991). *Students with learning disabilities* (4th ed.). New York: Merrill/Macmillan.

Mercer, N. (1993). Culture, context, and the construction of knowledge in the classroom. In P. Light & G. Butterworth (Eds.), *Context and cognition: Ways of learning and knowing.* Hillsdale, NJ: Erlbaum.

Merrill, P. F., Hammons, K., Vincent, B. R., Reynolds, P. L., Christensen, L., & Tolman, M. N. (1996). *Computers in education* (3rd ed.). Needham Heights, MA: Allyn & Bacon.

Merrill, M. D., & Tennyson, R. D. (1977). *Concept teaching: An instructional design guide.* Englewood Cliffs, NJ: Educational Technology.

Merrill, M. D., & Tennyson, R. D. (1978). Concept classification and classification errors as a function of relationships between examples and non-examples. *Improving Human Performance, 7,* 351–364.

Mervis, C. B. (1987). Child-basic object categories and early lexical development. In U. Neisser (Ed.), *Concepts and conceptual development: Ecological and intellectual factors in categorization.* Cambridge, UK: Cambridge University Press.

Messer, S. B. (1976). Reflection-impulsivity: A review. *Psychological Bulletin, 83,* 1026–1052.

Messick, S. (1994a). The interplay of evidence and consequences in the validation of performance assessments. *Educational Researcher, 23*(2), 13–23.

Messick, S. (1994b). The matter of style: Manifestations of personality in cognition, learning, and testing. *Educational Psychologist, 29,* 121–136.

Metz, K. E. (1995). Reassessment of developmental constraints on children's science instruction. *Review of Educational Research, 65,* 93–127.

Meyer, B. J. F., Brandt, D. H., & Bluth, G. J. (1980). Use of top-level structure in text: Key for reading comprehension of ninth-grade students. *Reading Research Quarterly, 16,* 72–103.

Meyers, D. T. (1987). The socialized individual and individual autonomy: An intersection between philosophy and psychology. In E. F. Kittay & D. T. Meyers (Eds.), *Women and moral theory.* Totowa, NJ: Rowman & Littlefield.

Midgley, C., & Eccles, J. S. (1990, April). The classroom environment during math instruction and the transition to junior high school. In D. H. Hecht (Chair), *Current Research in Mathematics Classrooms and Student Characteristics: Implications of Research for Classroom Assessment.* Symposium conducted at the annual meeting of the American Educational Research Association, Boston, MA.

Miller, G. A. (1956). The magical number seven, plus or minus two: Some limits on our capacity for processing information. *Psychological Review, 63,* 81–97.

Miller, N. E., & Dollard, J. C. (1941). *Social learning and imitation.* New Haven, CT: Yale University Press.

Miller, P. H. (1993). Focus on the interface of cognition, social-emotional behavior, and motivation. In P. H. Miller (Ed.), *Theories of developmental psychology* (3rd ed.). New York: W. H. Freeman.

Miller, R. R., & Barnet, R. C. (1993). The role of time in elementary associations. *Current Directions in Psychological Science, 2,* 106–111.

Millman, J., Bishop, C. H., & Ebel, R. (1965). An analysis of test-wiseness. *Educational and Psychological Measurement, 25,* 707–726.

Minami, M., & Ovando, C. J. (1995). Language issues in multicultural contexts. In J. A. Banks & C. A. M. Banks (Eds.), *Handbook of research on multicultural education.* New York: Macmillan.

Mischel, W. (1993). *Introduction to personality* (5th ed.). Fort Worth, TX: Harcourt Brace Jovanovich.

Mischel, W., & Grusec, J. E. (1966). Determinants of the rehearsal and transmission of neutral and aversive behaviors. *Journal of Personality and Social Psychology, 3,* 197–205.

Mohatt, G., & Erickson, F. (1981). Cultural differences in teaching styles in an Odawa school: A sociolinguistic approach. In H. T. Trueba, G. P. Guthrie, & K. H. Au (Eds.), *Culture and the bilingual classroom: Studies in classroom ethnography.* Rowley, MA: Newbury House.

Moles, O. C. (Ed.). (1990). *Student discipline strategies: Research and practice.* Albany: State University of New York Press.

Moll, L. C., & Diaz, S. (1985). Ethnographic pedagogy: Promoting effective bilingual instruction. In E. E. Garcia & R. V. Padilla (Eds.), *Advances in bilingual education research.* Tucson: University of Arizona Press.

Montgomery, D. (1989). Identification of giftedness among American Indian people. In C. J. Maker & S. W. Schiever (Eds.), *Critical issues in gifted education: Vol. 2. Defensible programs for cultural and ethnic minorities.* Austin, TX: PRO-ED.

Mooney, C. M. (1957). Age in the development of closure ability in children. *Canadian Journal of Psychology, 11,* 219–226.

Moran, C. E., & Hakuta, K. (1995). Bilingual education: Broadening research perspectives. In J. A. Banks & C. A. M. Banks (Eds.), *Handbook of research on multicultural education.* New York: Macmillan.

Moran, S. (1991). Creative reading: Young adults and paperback books. *Horn Book Magazine, 67,* 437–441.

Morgan, D. P., & Jenson, W. R. (1988). *Teaching behaviorally disordered students: Preferred practices.* New York: Merrill/Macmillan.

Morgan, M. (1984). Reward-induced decrements and increments in intrinsic motivation. *Review of Educational Research, 54,* 5–30.

Morris, R. J. (1985). *Behavior modification with exceptional children: Principles and practices.* Glenview, IL: Scott, Foresman.

Morse, L. W., & Handley, H. M. (1985). Listening to adolescents: Gender differences in science classroom interaction. In L. C. Wilkinson & C. B. Marrett (Eds.), *Gender influences in classroom interaction.* San Diego: Academic Press.

Mueller, J. H. (1980). Test anxiety and the encoding and retrieval of information. In I. G. Sarason (Ed.), *Test anxiety: Theory, research, and applications.* Hillsdale, NJ: Erlbaum.

Munn, P., Johnstone, M., & Chalmers, V. (1990, April). *How do teachers talk about maintaining effective discipline in their classrooms?* Paper presented at the annual meeting of the American Educational Research Association, Boston.

Murnane, R. J., & Raizen, S. A. (Eds.). (1988). *Improving indicators of the quality of science and mathematics education in grades K–12.* Washington, DC: National Academy Press.

Murray, C. B., & Jackson, J. S. (1982/1983). The conditioned failure model of black educational underachievement. *Humboldt Journal of Social Relations, 10,* 276–300.

Murray, F. B. (1978). Teaching strategies and conservation training. In A. M. Lesgold, J. W. Pellegrino, S. D. Fokkema, & R. Glaser (Eds.), *Cognitive psychology and instruction.* New York: Plenum Press.

Muscella, D. (1987, March). *The construction of a learning environment: A typology of personal constructs.* Paper presented at the annual meeting of the American Educational Research Association, Washington, DC.

Nash, S. C. (1975). The relationship among sex-role stereotyping, sex-role preferences, and the sex difference in spatial visualization. *Sex Roles, 1,* 15–32.

National Assessment of Educational Progress. (1985). *The reading report card: Progress toward excellence in our schools; trends in reading over four national assessments, 1971–1984.* Princeton, NJ: NAEP.

National Association of Bilingual Education. (1993). Census reports sharp increase in number of non-English-speaking Americans. *NABE News, 16*(6), 1, 25.

National Center for Education Statistics. (1989). *Dropout rates in the United States: 1988.* Washington, DC: U.S. Department of Education.

National Science Education Standards. (1996). Washington, DC: National Academy Press.

Natriello, G., & Dornbusch, S. M. (1984). *Teacher evaluative standards and student effort.* White Plains, NY: Longman.

Navarro, R. A. (1985). The problems of language, education, and society: Who decides. In E. E. Garcia & R. V. Padilla (Eds.), *Advances in bilingual education research.* Tucson: University of Arizona Press.

NCSS Task Force on Ethnic Studies Curriculum Guidelines. (1992). Curriculum guidelines for multicultural education. *Social Education, 56,* 274–294.

Neel, R. S., Jenkins, Z. N., & Meadows, N. (1990). Social problem-solving behaviors and aggression in young children: A descriptive observational study. *Behavioral Disorders, 16*(1), 39–51.

Neimark, E. D. (1979). Current status of formal operations research. *Human Development, 22,* 60–67.

Neisser, U. (1967). *Cognitive psychology.* New York: Appleton-Century-Crofts.

Neisser, U. (Ed.). (1987). *Concepts and conceptual development: Ecological and intellectual factors in categorization.* Cambridge, UK: Cambridge University Press.

Neisser, U., Boodoo, G., Bouchard, T. J., Boykin, A. W., Brody, N., Ceci, S. J., Halpern, D. F., Loehlen, J. C., Perloff, R., Sternberg, R. J., & Urbina, S. (1996). Intelligence: Knowns and unknowns. *American Psychologist, 51,* 77–101.

Nelson, J. R., Smith, D. J., Young, R. K., & Dodd, J. M. (1991). A review of self-management outcome research conducted with students who exhibit behavioral disorders. *Behavioral Disorders, 16,* 169–179.

Nelson, T. O., & Dunlosky, J. (1991). When people's judgments of learning (JOLs) are extremely accurate at predicting subsequent recall: The "delayed-JOL effect." *Psychological Science, 2,* 267–270.

Nemerowicz, G. M. (1979). *Children's perceptions of gender and work roles.* New York: Praeger.

Newby, T. J., Ertmer, P. A., & Stepich, D. A. (1994, April). *Instructional analogies and the learning of concepts.* Paper presented at the annual meeting of the American Educational Research Association, New Orleans, LA.

Newman, R. S., & Schwager, M. T. (1995). Students' help seeking during problem solving: Effects of grade, goal, and prior achievement. *American Educational Research Journal, 32,* 352–376.

Newmann, F. M. (1981). Reducing student alienation in high schools: Implications of theory. *Harvard Educational Review, 51,* 546–564.

Newmann, F. M., & Wehlage, G. G. (1993). Five standards of authentic instruction. *Educational Leadership, 50*(7), 8–12.

Nicholls, J. G. (1984). Conceptions of ability and achievement motivation. In R. Ames & C. Ames (Eds.), *Research on motivation in education: Vol. 1. Student motivation.* San Diego: Academic Press.

Nichols, M. L., & Ganschow, L. (1992). Has there been a paradigm shift in gifted education? In N. Coangelo, G. B. Assouline, & D. L. Ambroson (Eds.), *Talent development: Proceedings from the 1991 Henry B. and Jocelyn Wallace National Research Symposium on Talent Development.* New York: Trillium.

Nickerson, R. S. (1989). New directions in educational assessment. *Educational Researcher, 18*(9), 3–7.

Nielsen, L. (1993). Students from divorced and blended families. *Educational Psychology Review, 5,* 177–199.

Nieto, S. (1995). A history of the education of Puerto Rican students in U.S. mainland schools: "Losers," "outsiders," or "leaders"? In J. A. Banks & C. A. M. Banks (Eds.), *Handbook of research on multicultural education.* New York: Macmillan.

Nippold, M. A. (1988). The literate lexicon. In M. A. Nippold (Ed.), *Later language development: Ages nine through nineteen.* Boston: Little, Brown.

• Nisbett, R. E., & Bellows, N. (1977). Verbal reports about causal influences on social judgments: Private access versus public theories. *Journal of Personality and Social Psychology, 35,* 613–624.

Nist, S. L., Simpson, M. L., Olejnik, S., & Mealey, D. L. (1991). The relation between self-selected study processes and test performance. *American Educational Research Journal, 28,* 849–874.

Noddings, N. (1985). Small groups as a setting for research on mathematical problem solving. In E. A. Silver (Ed.), *Teaching and learning mathematical problem solving: Multiple research perspectives.* Hillsdale, NJ: Erlbaum.

Nolen, S. B. (1988). Reasons for studying: Motivational orientations and study strategies. *Cognition and Instruction, 5,* 269–287.

Norman, D. A. (1969). *Memory and attention: An introduction to human information processing.* New York: Wiley.

Nottelmann, E. D. (1987). Competence and self-esteem during transition from childhood to adolescence. *Developmental Psychology, 23,* 441–450.

Novak, J. D., & Gowin, D. B. (1984). *Learning how to learn.* Cambridge, UK: Cambridge University Press.

Novak, J. D., & Musonda, D. (1991). A twelve-year longitudinal study of science concept learning. *American Educational Research Journal, 28,* 117–153.

Nunnally, J. C. (1976). Vanishing individual differences: Just stick your head in the sand, and they will go away. *Journal of Instructional Psychology, 3,* 28–40.

Nunner-Winkler, G. (1984). Two moralities? A critical discussion of an ethic of care and responsibility versus an ethic of rights and justice. In W. M. Kurtines & J. L. Gewirtz (Eds.), *Morality, moral behavior, and moral development.* New York: Wiley.

Nussbaum, J. (1985). The earth as a cosmic body. In R. Driver (Ed.), *Children's ideas of science.* Philadelphia, PA: Open University Press.

• O'Donnell, A. M. (1996). Effects of explicit incentives on scripted and unscripted cooperation. *Journal of Educational Psychology, 88,* 74–86.

• O'Donnell, A. M., & O'Kelly, J. (1994). Learning from peers: Beyond the rhetoric of positive results. *Educational Psychology Review, 6,* 321–349.

• Ogbu, J. U. (1992). Understanding cultural diversity and learning. *Educational Researcher, 21*(8), 5–14, 24.

• Ogden, E. H., & Germinario, V. (1988). *The at-risk student: Answers for educators.* Lancaster, PA: Technomic.

O'Leary, K. D., Kaufman, K. F., Kass, R. E., & Drabman, R. S. (1970). The effects of loud and soft reprimands on the behavior of disruptive students. *Exceptional Children, 37,* 145–155.

O'Leary, K. D., & O'Leary, S. G. (Eds.). (1972). *Classroom management: The successful use of behavior modification.* New York: Pergamon Press.

O'Leary, S., & Schneider, M. (1977). Special class placement for conduct problem children. *Exceptional Children, 44,* 24–30.

• Olneck, M. R. (1995). Immigrants and education. In J. A. Banks & C. A. M. Banks (Eds.), *Handbook of research on multicultural education.* New York: Macmillan.

O'Malley, P. M., & Bachman, J. G. (1983). Self-esteem: Change and stability between ages 13 and 23. *Developmental Psychology, 19,* 257–268.

• O'Neil, J. (1990). Making sense of style. *Educational Leadership, 48*(2), 4–9.

Ormrod, J. E. (1985). Proofreading *The Cat in the Hat:* Evidence for different reading styles in good and poor spellers. *Psychological Reports, 57,* 863–867.

Ormrod, J. E. (1986). Differences between good and poor spellers in reading style and short-term memory. *Visible Language, 20,* 437–447.

Ormrod, J. E. (1995a). *Educational psychology: Principles and applications.* Upper Saddle River, NJ: Merrill/Prentice Hall.

Ormrod, J. E. (1995b). *Human learning: Theories, principles, and educational applications* (2nd ed.). Upper Saddle River, NJ: Merrill/Prentice Hall.

Ormrod, J. E., & Carter, K. R. (1985). Systematizing the Piagetian clinical interview for classroom use. *Teaching of Psychology, 12,* 216–219.

Ormrod, J. E., & Jenkins, L. (1989). Study strategies in spelling: Correlations with achievement and developmental changes. *Perceptual and Motor Skills, 68,* 643–650.

Ormrod, J. E., & Lewis, M. A. (1985). Comparison of memory skills in learning disabled, low-reading, and nondisabled adolescents. *Perceptual and Motor Skills, 61,* 191–195.

Ormrod, J. E., Ormrod, R. K., Wagner, E. D., & McCallin, R. C. (1988). Reconceptualizing map learning. *American Journal of Psychology, 101,* 425–433.

Ormrod, J. E., & Wagner, E. D. (1987, October). *Spelling conscience in undergraduate students: Ratings of spelling accuracy and dictionary use.* Paper presented at the annual meeting of the Northern Rocky Mountain Educational Research Association, Park City, UT.

Ormrod, R. K. (1974). *Adaptation in cultural ecosystems: Early 19th-century Jamaica.* Unpublished doctoral dissertation, Pennsylvania State University.

Osgood, C. E. (1949). The similarity paradox in human learning: A resolution. *Psychological Review, 56,* 132–143.

O'Sullivan, J. T., & Joy, R. M. (1990, April). *Children's theories about reading difficulty: A developmental study.* Paper presented at the annual meeting of the American Educational Research Association, Boston, MA.

• Otero, J., & Kintsch, W. (1992). Failures to detect contradictions in a text: What readers believe versus what they read. *Psychological Science, 3,* 229–235.

• Owens, R. E., Jr. (1992). *Language development.* New York: Merrill/Macmillan.

• Packard, V. (1983). *Our endangered children: Growing up in a changing world.* Boston: Little, Brown.

Paige, J. M., & Simon, H. A. (1966). Cognitive processes in solving algebra word problems. In B. Kleinmuntz (Ed.), *Problem solving.* New York: Wiley.

Paivio, A. (1971). *Imagery and verbal processes.* New York: Holt, Rinehart & Winston.

Paivio, A. (1986). *Mental representations: A dual-coding approach.* New York: Oxford University Press.

Palardy, J. M. (1969). What teachers believe—what children achieve. *Elementary School Journal, 69,* 370–374.

Palardy, J. M., & Mudrey, J. E. (1973). Discipline: Four approaches. *Elementary School Journal, 73,* 297–305.

Palincsar, A. S. (1986, April). *Interactive cognition to promote listening comprehension.* Paper presented at the annual meeting of the American Educational Research Association, San Francisco.

Palincsar, A. S., & Brown, A. L. (1984). Reciprocal teaching of comprehension-fostering and comprehension-monitoring activities. *Cognition and Instruction, 1,* 117–175.

Palincsar, A. S., & Brown, A. L. (1989). Classroom dialogues to promote self-regulated comprehension. In J. Brophy (Ed.), *Advances in research on teaching* (Vol 1). Greenwich, CT: JAI Press.

Palmer, E. L. (1965). Accelerating the child's cognitive attainments through the inducement of cognitive conflict: An interpretation of the Piagetian position. *Journal of Research in Science Teaching, 3,* 324.

• Pang, V. O. (1995). Asian Pacific American students: A diverse and complex population. In J. A. Banks & C. A. M. Banks (Eds.), *Handbook of research on multicultural education.* New York: Macmillan.

Paris, S. G. (1988). Models and metaphors of learning strategies. In C. E. Weinstein, E. T. Goetz, & P. A. Alexander (Eds.), *Learning and study strategies: Issues in assessment, instruction, and evaluation.* San Diego: Academic Press.

• Paris, S. G., & Ayres, L. R. (1994). *Becoming reflective students and teachers with portfolios and authentic assessment.* Washington, DC: American Psychological Association.

Paris, S. G., & Byrnes, J. P. (1989). The constructivist approach to self-regulation and learning in the classroom. In B. J. Zimmerman & D. H. Schunk (Eds.), *Self-regulated learning and academic achievement: Theory, research, and practice.* New York: Springer-Verlag.

Paris, S. G., Lawton, T. A., Turner, J. C., & Roth, J. L. (1991). A developmental perspective on standardized achievement testing. *Educational Researcher, 20*(5), 12–20, 40.

Paris, S. G., Newman, R. S., & McVey, K. A. (1982). Learning the functional significance of mnemonic actions: A microgenetic study of strategy acquisition. *Journal of Experimental Child Psychology, 34,* 490–509.

Paris, S. G., & Winograd, P. (1990). How metacognition can promote academic learning and instruction. In B. F. Jones & L. Idol (Eds.), *Dimensions of thinking and cognitive instruction.* Hillsdale, NJ: Erlbaum.

Parke, R. D. (1972). Some effects of punishment on children's behavior. In W. W. Hartup (Ed.), *The young child* (Vol. 2). Washington, DC: National Association for the Education of Young Children.

Parke, R. D. (1974). Rules, roles, and resistance to deviation: Explorations in punishment, discipline, and self-control. In A. Pick (Ed.), *Minnesota Symposia on Child Psychology* (Vol. 8). Minneapolis: University of Minnesota Press.

Parke, R. D. (1977). Some effects of punishment on children's behavior—revisited. In E. M. Hetherington & R. D. Parke (Eds.), *Contemporary readings in child psychology.* New York: McGraw-Hill.

• Parks, C. P. (1995). Gang behavior in the schools: Reality or myth? *Educational Psychology Review, 7,* 41–68.

Parnes, S. J. (1967). *Creative behavior guidebook.* New York: Scribner's.

Parsons, J. E., Adler, T. F., & Kaczala, C. M. (1982). Socialization of achievement attitudes and beliefs: Parental influences. *Child Development, 53,* 310–321.

Parsons, J. E., Kaczala, C. M., & Meece, J. L. (1982). Socialization of achievement attitudes and beliefs: Classroom influences. *Child Development, 53,* 322–339.

Patterson, G. R. (1981). Mothers: The unacknowledged victims. *Monographs of the Society for Research in Child Development, 45*(5, Serial No. 18b).

Patterson, G. R. (1982). *Coercive family processes.* Eugene, OR: Castilia Press.

Patterson, G. R., DeBaryshe, B. D., & Ramsey, E. (1989). A developmental perspective on antisocial behavior. *American Psychologist, 44,* 329–335.

Patterson, G. R., & Stouthamer-Loeber, M. (1984). The correlation of family management practices and delinquency. *Child Development, 55,* 1299–1307.

Patton, J. R., Beirne-Smith, M., & Payne, J. S. (1990). *Mental retardation* (3rd ed.). New York: Merrill/Macmillan.

Patton, J. R., Payne, J. S., Kauffman, J. M., Brown, G. B., & Payne, R. A. (1987). *Exceptional children in focus* (4th ed.). New York: Merrill/Prentice Hall.

• Paulson, F. L., Paulson, P. R., & Meyer, C. A. (1991). What makes a portfolio a portfolio? *Educational Leadership, 49*(5), 60–63.

Paulson, K., & Johnson, M. (1983). Sex-role attitudes and mathematical ability in fourth-, eighth-, and eleventh-grade students from a high socioeconomic area. *Developmental Psychology, 19,* 210–214.

Pavlov, I. P. (1927). *Conditioned reflexes* (G. V. Anrep, Trans.). London: Oxford University Press.

• Pawlas, G. E. (1994). Homeless students at the school door. *Educational Leadership, 51*(8), 79–82.

• Pea, R. D. (1993). Practices of distributed intelligence and designs for education. In G. Salomon (Ed.), *Distributed cognitions: Psychological and educational considerations.* Cambridge, UK: Cambridge University Press.

• Pellegrini, A. D., & Horvat, M. (1995). A developmental contextualist critique of attention deficit hyperactivity disorder. *Educational Researcher, 24*(1), 13–19.

Perera, K. (1986). Language acquisition and writing. In P. Fletcher & M. Garman (Eds.), *Language acquisition: Studies in first language development* (2nd ed.). Cambridge, UK: Cambridge University Press.

Perkins, D. N. (1990). The nature and nurture of creativity. In B. F. Jones & L. Idol (Eds.), *Dimensions of thinking and cognitive instruction.* Hillsdale, NJ: Erlbaum.

• Perkins, D. N. (1995). *Outsmarting IQ: The emerging science of learnable intelligence.* New York: Free Press.

Perkins, D. N., & Salomon, G. (1987). Transfer and teaching thinking. In D. N. Perkins, J. Lochhead, & J. Bishop (Eds.), *Thinking: The second international conference.* Hillsdale, NJ: Erlbaum.

Perkins, D. N., & Salomon, G. (1989). Are cognitive skills context-bound? *Educational Researcher, 18*(1), 16–25.

Perkins, D. N., & Simmons, R. (1988). Patterns of misunderstanding: An integrative model for science, math, and programming. *Review of Educational Research, 58,* 303–326.

Perlmutter, M. (1984). Continuities and discontinuities in early human memory paradigms, processes, and performances. In R. V. Kail, Jr. & N. R. Spear (Eds.), *Comparative perspectives on the development of memory.* Hillsdale, NJ: Erlbaum.

Perry, D. G., & Perry, L. C. (1983). Social learning, causal attribution, and moral internalization. In J. Bisanz, G. L. Bisanz, & R. Kail (Eds.), *Learning in children: Progress in cognitive development research.* New York: Springer-Verlag.

Petersen, G. A., Sudweeks, R. R., & Baird, J. H. (1990, April). *Test-wise responses of third-, fifth-, and sixth-grade students to clued and unclued multiple-choice science items.* Paper presented at the annual meeting of the American Educational Research Assocation, Boston, MA.

Peterson, C. (1990). Explanatory style in the classroom and on the playing field. In S. Graham & V. S. Folkes (Eds.), *Attribution theory: Applications to achievement, mental health, and interpersonal conflict.* Hillsdale, NJ: Erlbaum.

Peterson, C., & Barrett, L. C. (1987). Explanatory style and academic performance among university freshmen. *Journal of Personality and Social Psychology, 53,* 603–607.

Peterson, L. R., & Peterson, M. J. (1959). Short-term retention of individual items. *Journal of Experimental Psychology, 58,* 193–198.

Peterson, P. L. (1979). Direct instruction reconsidered. In P. L. Peterson & H. L. Walberg (Eds.), *Research on teaching: Concepts, findings, and implications.* Berkeley, CA: McCutchan.

Peterson, P. L. (1988). Teachers' and students' cognitional knowledge for classroom teaching and learning. *Educational Researcher, 17*(5), 5–14.

Peterson, P. L. (1992). Revising their thinking: Keisha Coleman and her third-grade mathematics class. In H. H. Marshall (Ed.), *Redefining student learning: Roots of educational change.* Norwood, NJ: Ablex.

Pettigrew, T. F., & Pajonas, P. J. (1973). The social psychology of heterogeneous schools. In C. S. Brembeck & W. H. Hill, *Cultural challenges to education: The influence of cultural factors in school learning.* Lexington, MA: Heath.

Pettito, A. L. (1985). Division of labor: Procedural learning in teacher-led small groups. *Cognition and Instruction, 2,* 233–270.

Pfiffner, L. J., & O'Leary, S. G. (1987). The efficacy of all-positive management as a function of the prior use of negative consequences. *Journal of Applied Behavior Analysis, 20,* 265–271.

Pfiffner, L. J., Rosen, L. A., & O'Leary, S. G. (1985). The efficacy of an all-positive approach to classroom management. *Journal of Applied Behavior Analysis, 18,* 257–261.

Phelan, P., Davidson, A. L., & Cao, H. T. (1991). Students' multiple worlds: Negotiating the boundaries of family, peer, and school cultures. *Anthropology and Education Quarterly, 22,* 224–250.

Phelan, P., Yu, H. C., & Davidson, A. L. (1994). Navigating the psychosocial pressures of adolescence: The voices and experiences of high school youth. *American Educational Research Journal, 31,* 415–447.

Phillips, B. N., Pitcher, G. D., Worsham, M. E., & Miller, S. C. (1980). Test anxiety and the school environment. In I. G. Sarason (Ed.), *Test anxiety: Theory, research, and applications.* Hillsdale, NJ: Erlbaum.

Phillips, E. L., Phillips, E. A., Fixsen, D. L., & Wolf, M. M. (1971). Achievement place: Modification of the behaviors of predelinquent boys within a token economy. *Journal of Applied Behavior Analysis, 4,* 45–59.

Phinney, J. (1989). Stages of ethnic identity development in minority group adolescents. *Journal of Early Adolescence, 9,* 34–39.

Phinney, J., & Alipuria, L. (1990). Ethnic identity in college students from four ethnic groups. *Journal of Adolescence, 13,* 171–183.

Piaget, J. (1928). *Judgment and reasoning in the child* (M. Warden, Trans.). New York: Harcourt, Brace.

Piaget, J. (1932). *The moral judgment of the child.* New York: Harcourt, Brace.

Piaget, J. (1952). *The origins of intelligence in children* (M. Cook, Trans.). New York: Norton.

Piaget, J. (1959). *The language and thought of the child* (3rd ed.; M. Gabain, Trans.). London: Routledge & Kegan Paul.

Piaget, J. (1970). Piaget's theory. In P. H. Mussen (Ed.), *Carmichael's manual of psychology.* New York: Wiley.

Piaget, J. (1972). *Science education and the psychology of the child.* New York: Viking.

Piaget, J. (1980). *Adaptation and intelligence: Organic selection and phenocopy* (S. Eames, Trans.). Chicago: University of Chicago Press.

Piaget, J., & Inhelder, B. (1967). *The child's conception of space.* New York: Norton.

Piaget, J., & Inhelder, B. (1969). *The psychology of the child* (H. Weaver, Trans.). New York: Basic Books.

Piersel, W. C. (1987). Basic skills education. In C. A. Maher & S. G. Forman (Eds.), *A behavioral approach to education of children and youth.* Hillsdale, NJ: Erlbaum.

Pigott, H. E., Fantuzzo, J. W., & Clement, P. W. (1986). The effects of reciprocal peer tutoring and group contingencies on the academic performance of elementary school children. *Journal of Applied Behavior Analysis, 19,* 93–98.

Piirto, J. (1994). *Talented children and adults: Their development and education.* New York: Merrill/Macmillan.

Pintrich, P. R., & Garcia, T. (1994). Regulating motivation and cognition in the classroom: The role of self-schemas and self-regulatory strategies. In D. Schunk & B. Zimmerman (Eds.), *Self-regulation of learning and performance: Issues and educational applications.* Hillsdale, NJ: Erlbaum.

Pintrich, P. R., Garcia, T., & De Groot, E. (1994, April). *Positive and negative self-schemas and self-regulated learning.* Paper presented at the annual meeting of the American Educational Research Association, New Orleans, LA.

Pintrich, P. R., Marx, R. W., & Boyle, R. A. (1993). Beyond cold conceptual change: The role of motivational beliefs and classroom contextual factors in the process of conceptual change. *Review of Educational Research, 63,* 167–199.

Piontkowski, D., & Calfee, R. (1979). Attention in the classroom. In G. A. Hale & M. Lewis (Eds.), *Attention and cognitive development.* New York: Plenum Press.

Plomin, R. (1989). Environment and genes: Determinants of behavior. *American Psychologist, 44,* 105–111.

Poche, C., Yoder, P., & Miltenberger, R. (1988). Teaching self-protection to children using television techniques. *Journal of Applied Behavior Analysis, 21,* 253–261.

Pollard, S. R., Kurtines, W. M., Carlo, G., Dancs, M., & Mayock, E. (1991). Moral education from the perspective of psychosocial theory. In W. M. Kurtines & J. L. Gewirtz (Eds.), *Moral behavior and development: Vol. 3. Application.* Hillsdale, NJ: Erlbaum.

Polloway, E. A., & Patton, J. R. (1993). *Strategies for teaching learners with special needs* (5th ed.). New York: Merrill/Macmillan.

• Poole, D. (1994). Routine testing practices and the linguistic construction of knowledge. *Cognition and Instruction, 12,* 125–150.

Popham, W. J. (1990). *Modern educational measurement: A practitioner's perspective* (2nd ed.). Upper Saddle River, NJ: Prentice Hall.

• Popham, W. J. (1995). *Classroom assessment: What teachers need to know.* Needham Heights, MA: Allyn & Bacon.

Porath, M. (1988, April). *Cognitive development of gifted children: A neo-Piagetian perspective.* Paper presented at the annual meeting of the American Educational Research Association, New Orleans, LA.

Porter, A. C. (1989). A curriculum out of balance: The case of elementary school mathematics. *Educational Researcher, 18*(5), 9–15.

• Posner, G., Strike, K., Hewson, P., & Gertzog, W. (1982). Accommodation of a scientific conception: Toward a theory of conceptual change. *Science Education, 66,* 211–227.

Posner, M. I. (1973). *Cognition: An introduction.* Glenview, IL: Scott, Foresman.

Postman, L., & Underwood, B. J. (1973). Critical issues in interference theory. *Memory and Cognition, 1,* 19–40.

Powell, B. M. (1990, April). *Children's perceptions of classroom goal orientation: Relationship to learning strategies and intrinsic motivation.* Paper presented at the annual meeting of the American Educational Research Association, Boston, MA.

Powers, S. I., Hauser, S. T., & Kilner, L. A. (1989). Adolescent mental health. *American Psychologist, 44,* 200–208.

Prawat, R. S. (1989). Promoting access to knowledge, strategy, and disposition in students: A research synthesis. *Review of Educational Research, 59,* 1–41.

Prawat, R. S. (1992). From individual differences to learning communities: Our changing focus. *Educational Leadership, 49*(7), 9–13.

• Prawat, R. S. (1993). The value of ideas: Problems versus possibilities in learning. *Educational Researcher, 22*(6), 5–16.

• Prawat, R. S., & Floden, R. E. (1994). Philosophical perspectives on constructivist views of learning. *Educational Psychologist, 29,* 37–48.

Premack, D. (1959). Toward empirical behavior laws: I. Positive reinforcement. *Psychological Review, 66,* 219–233.

Premack, D. (1963). Rate differential reinforcement in monkey manipulation. *Journal of Experimental Analysis of Behavior, 6,* 81–89.

• Presseisen, B. Z., & Beyer, F. S. (1994, April). *Facing history and ourselves: An instructional tool for constructivist theory.* Paper presented at the annual meeting of the American Educational Research Association, New Orleans, LA.

Pressley, M. (1982). Elaboration and memory development. *Child Development, 53,* 296–309.

Pressley, M., Borkowski, J. G., & Schneider, W. (1987). Cognitive strategies: Good strategy users coordinate metacognition and knowledge. In R. Vasta (Ed.), *Annals of child development* (Vol. 4). Greenwich, CT: JAI Press.

• Pressley, M., El-Dinary, P. B., Marks, M. B., Brown, R., & Stein, S. (1992). Good strategy instruction is motivating and interesting. In K. A. Renninger, S. Hidi, & A. Krapp (Eds.), *The role of interest in learning and development.* Hillsdale, NJ: Erlbaum.

Pressley, M., Harris, K. R., & Marks, M. B. (1992). But good strategy instructors are constructivists! *Educational Psychology Review, 4,* 3–31.

Pressley, M., Levin, J. R., & Delaney, H. D. (1982). The mnemonic keyword method. *Review of Educational Research, 52,* 61–91.

Pressley, M. (with McCormick, C. B.). (1995). *Advanced educational psychology for educators, researchers, and policymakers.* New York: HarperCollins.

Pressley, M., Snyder, B. L., & Cariglia-Bull, T. (1987). How can good strategy use be taught to children? Evaluation of six alternative approaches. In S. M. Cormier & J. D. Hagman (Eds.), *Transfer of learning: Contemporary research and applications.* San Diego: Academic Press.

Pressley, M., Woloshyn, V., Lysynchuk, L. M., Martin, V., Wood, E., & Willoughby, T. (1990). A primer of research on cognitive strategy instruction: The important issues and how to address them. *Educational Psychology Review, 2,* 1–58.

Pruitt, R. P. (1989). Fostering creativity: The innovative classroom environment. *Educational Horizons, 68* (1), 51–54.

• Pulos, S., & Linn, M. C. (1981). Generality of the controlling variables scheme in early adolescence. *Journal of Early Adolescence, 1,* 26–37.

Purdie, N., Hattie, J., & Douglas, G. (1996). Student conceptions of learning and their use of self-regulated learning strategies: A cross-cultural comparison. *Journal of Educational Psychology, 88,* 87–100.

Putnam, R. T. (1992). Thinking and authority in elementary-school mathematics tasks. In J. Brophy (Ed.), *Advances in research on teaching: Vol. 3. Planning and managing learning tasks and activities.* Greenwich, CT: JAI Press.

• Qin, Z., Johnson, D. W., & Johnson, R. T. (1995). Cooperative versus competitive efforts and problem solving. *Review of Educational Research, 65,* 129–143.

Raber, S. M. (1990, April). *A school system's look at its dropouts: Why they left school and what has happened to them.* Paper presented at the annual meeting of the American Educational Research Association, Boston, MA.

• Rabinowitz, M., & Glaser, R. (1985). Cognitive structure and process in highly competent performance. In F. D. Horowitz & M. O'Brien (Eds.), *The gifted and the talented: Developmental perspectives.* Washington, DC: American Psychological Association.

Rachlin, H. (1989). *Judgment, decision, and choice: A cognitive/behavioral synthesis.* New York: W. H. Freeman.

Rachlin, H. (1991). *Introduction to modern behaviorism* (3rd ed.). New York: W. H. Freeman.

Radke-Yarrow, M., Zahn-Waxler, C., & Chapman, M. (1983). Children's prosocial dispositions and behavior. In E. M. Hetherington (Ed.), *Handbook of child psychology: Vol. 4. Socialization, personality, and social development.* New York: Wiley.

Rakow, S. J. (1984). What's happening in elementary science: A national assessment. *Science and Children, 21*(4), 39–40.

Ramsey, P. G. (1987). *Teaching and learning in a diverse world: Multicultural education for young children.* New York: Teachers College Press.

Rapport, M. D., Murphy, H. A., & Bailey, J. S. (1982). Ritalin vs. response cost in the control of hyperactive children: A within-subject comparison. *Journal of Applied Behavior Analysis, 15,* 205–216.

Raudenbush, S. W. (1984). Magnitude of teacher expectancy effects on pupil IQ as a function of credibility induction: A synthesis of findings from 18 experiments. *Journal of Educational Psychology, 76,* 85–97.

Redfield, D. L., & Rousseau, E. W. (1981). A meta-analysis of experimental research on teacher questioning behavior. *Review of Educational Research, 51,* 237–245.

Reed, S. K., Ernst, G. W., & Banerji, R. (1974). The role of analogy in transfer between similar problem states. *Cognitive Psychology, 6,* 436–450.

Reich, P. A. (1986). *Language development.* Upper Saddle River, NJ: Prentice Hall.

Reif, F., & Heller, J. I. (1982). Knowledge structure and problem solving in physics. *Educational Psychologist, 17,* 102–127.

• Reimann, P., & Schult, T. J. (1996). Turning examples into cases: Acquiring knowledge structures for analogical problem solving. *Educational Psychologist, 31,* 123–132.

Reimer, J., Paolitto, D. P., & Hersh, R. H. (1983). *Promoting moral growth: From Piaget to Kohlberg* (2nd ed.). White Plains, NY: Longman.

Reis, S. M. (1989). Reflections on policy affecting the education of gifted and talented students: Past and future perspectives. *American Psychologist, 44,* 399–408.

• Reisberg, D., & Heuer, F. (1992). Remembering the details of emotional events. In E. Winograd & U. Neisser (Eds.), *Affect and accuracy in recall: Studies of "flashbulb" memories.* Cambridge, UK: Cambridge University Press.

Renzulli, J. S. (1978). What makes giftedness? Reexamining a definition. *Phi Delta Kappan, 60,* 180–184.

Rescorla, R. A. (1967). Pavlovian conditioning and its proper control procedures. *Psychological Review, 74,* 71–80.

Rescorla, R. A. (1988). Pavlovian conditioning: It's not what you think it is. *American Psychologist, 43,* 151–160.

Resnick, L. B. (1983). Mathematics and science learning: A new conception. *Science, 220,* 477–478.

Resnick, L. B. (1989). Developing mathematical knowledge. *American Psychologist, 44,* 162–169.

• Reusser, K. (1990, April). *Understanding word arithmetic problems: Linguistic and situational factors.* Paper presented at the annual meeting of the American Educational Research Association, Boston, MA.

Reynolds, M. C., & Birch, J. W. (1988). *Adaptive mainstreaming: A primer for teachers and principals* (3rd ed.). White Plains, NY: Longman.

Reynolds, R. E., & Shirey, L. L. (1988). The role of attention in studying and learning. In C. E. Weinstein, E. T. Goetz, & P. A. Alexander (Eds.), *Learning and study strategies: Issues in assessment, instruction, and evaluation.* San Diego: Academic Press.

Reynolds, R. E., Taylor, M. A., Steffensen, M. S., Shirey, L. L., & Anderson, R. C. (1982). Cultural schemata and reading comprehension. *Reading Research Quarterly, 17,* 353–366.

• Ricciuti, H. N. (1993). Nutrition and mental development. *Current Directions in Psychological Science, 2,* 43–46.

Riding, R. J., & Calvey, I. (1981). The assessment of verbal-imagery learning styles and their effect on the recall of concrete and abstract prose passages by 11-year-old children. *British Journal of Psychology, 72,* 59–64.

Rimm, D. C., & Masters, J. C. (1974). *Behavior therapy: Techniques and empirical findings.* San Diego: Academic Press.

Ripple, R. E. (1989). Ordinary creativity. *Contemporary Educational Psychology, 14,* 189–202.

• Ritts, V., Patterson, M. L., & Tubbs, M. E. (1992). Expectations, impressions, and judgments of physically attractive students: A review. *Review of Educational Research, 62,* 413–426.

• Roazzi, A., & Bryant, P. (1993). Social class, context, and cognitive development. In P. Light & G. Butterworth (Eds.), *Context and cognition: Ways of learning and knowing.* Hillsdale, NJ: Erlbaum.

• Roberge, J. J. (1970). A study of children's abilities to reason with basic principles of deductive reasoning. *American Educational Research Journal, 7,* 583–596.

Robinson, A. (1991). Cooperation or exploitation? The argument against cooperative learning for talented students. *Journal for the Education of the Gifted, 14,* 9–27.

Roblyer, M. D., Castine, W. H., & King, F. J. (1988). *Assessing the impact of computer-based instruction: A review of recent research.* New York: Haworth.

• Roderick, M. (1994). Grade retention and school dropout: Investigating the association. *American Educational Research Journal, 31,* 729–759.

Rogers, C. R. (1969). *Freedom to learn.* New York: Merrill/Macmillan.

Rogers, C. R. (1983). *Freedom to learn for the 80s.* New York: Merrill/Macmillan.

Rogoff, B. (1990). *Apprenticeship in thinking: Cognitive development in social context.* New York: Oxford University Press.

• Rogoff, B. (1994, April). *Developing understanding of the idea of communities of learners.* Paper presented at the annual meeting of the American Educational Research Association, New Orleans, LA.

Rogoff, B., & Morelli, G. (1989). Perspectives on children's development from cultural psychology. *American Psychologist, 44,* 343–348.

Rosch, E. H. (1973a). Natural categories. *Cognitive Psychology, 4,* 328–350.

Rosch, E. H. (1973b). On the internal structure of perceptual and semantic categories. In T. E. Moore (Ed.), *Cognitive development and the acquisition of language.* San Diego: Academic Press.

Rosch, E. H. (1977). Human categorization. In N. Warren (Ed.), *Advances in cross-cultural psychology* (Vol. 1). San Diego: Academic Press.

Rose, M. (1991, July 3). Education standards must be reclaimed for democratic ends. *Chronicle of Higher Education, 37*(42), A32.

Rose, S. C., & Thornburg, K. R. (1984). Mastery motivation and need for approval in young children: Effects of age, sex, and reinforcement condition. *Educational Research Quarterly, 9*(1), 34–42.

Rosenshine, B., & Meister, C. (1992). The use of scaffolds for teaching higher-level cognitive strategies. *Educational Leadership, 49*(7), 26–33.

• Rosenshine, B., & Meister, C. (1994). Reciprocal teaching: A review of the research. *Review of Educational Research, 64,* 479–530.

• Rosenthal, R. (1994). Interpersonal expectancy effects: A 30-year perspective. *Current Directions in Psychological Science, 3,* 176–179.

Rosenthal, R., & Rubin, D. B. (1982). Further meta-analytic procedures for assessing cognitive gender differences.

Journal of Educational Psychology, 74, 708–712.

Rosenthal, T. L., Alford, G. S., & Rasp, L. M. (1972). Concept attainment, generalization, and retention through observation and verbal coding. *Journal of Experimental Child Psychology, 13,* 183–194.

Rosenthal, T. L., & Bandura, A. (1978). Psychological modeling: Theory and practice. In S. L. Garfield & A. E. Begia (Eds.), *Handbook of psychotherapy and behavior change: An empirical analysis* (2nd ed.). New York: Wiley.

Rosenthal, T. L., & Zimmerman, B. J. (1978). *Social learning and cognition.* San Diego: Academic Press.

Ross, J. A. (1988). Controlling variables: A meta-analysis of training studies. *Review of Educational Research, 58,* 405–437.

• Rosser, R. (1994). *Cognitive development: Psychological and biological perspectives.* Needham Heights, MA: Allyn & Bacon.

Rosswork, S. G. (1977). Goal setting: The effects on an academic task with varying magnitudes of incentive. *Journal of Educational Psychology, 69,* 710–715.

Roth, K. J. (1990). Developing meaningful conceptual understanding in science. In B. F. Jones & L. Idol (Eds.), *Dimensions of thinking and cognitive instruction.* Hillsdale, NJ: Erlbaum.

Roth, K. J., & Anderson, C. (1988). Promoting conceptual change learning from science textbooks. In P. Ramsden (Ed.), *Improving learning: New perspectives.* London: Kogan Page.

Roughead, W. G., & Scandura, J. M. (1968). What is learned in mathematical discovery. *Journal of Educational Psychology, 59,* 283–289.

Rowe, M. B. (1974). Wait-time and rewards as instructional variables, their influence on language, logic, and fate control: Part One—wait time. *Journal of Research in Science Teaching, 11,* 81–94.

Rowe, M. B. (1978). *Teaching science as continuous inquiry.* New York: McGraw-Hill.

Rowe, M. B. (1983). Science education: A framework for decisionmakers. *Daedalus, 112,* 123–142.

Rowe, M. B. (1987). Wait-time: Slowing down may be a way of speeding up. *American Educator, 11,* 38–43, 47.

Ruble, D. N. (1980). A developmental perspective on theories of achievement motivation. In L. J. Fyans, Jr. (Ed.), *Achieve-ment motivation: Recent trends in theory and research.* New York: Plenum Press.

Ruble, D. N. (1988). Sex-role development. In M. H. Bornstein & M. E. Lamb (Eds.), *Developmental psychology: An advanced textbook* (2nd ed.). Hillsdale, NJ: Erlbaum.

Ruble, D. N., & Ruble, T. L. (1982). Sex stereotypes. In A. G. Miller (Ed.), *In the eye of the beholder.* New York: Praeger.

• Rudman, M. K. (1993). Multicultural children's literature: The search for universals. In M. K. Rudman (Ed.), *Children's literature: Resource for the classroom* (2nd ed.). Norwood, MA: Christopher-Gordon.

Ruebush, B. K. (1963). Anxiety. In H. W. Stevenson, J. Kagan, & C. Spiker (Eds.), *Child psychology: 62nd N.S.S.E. yearbook.* Chicago: University of Chicago Press.

Rueger, D. B., & Liberman, R. P. (1984). Behavioral family therapy for delinquent substance-abusing adolescents. *Journal of Drug Abuse, 14,* 403–418.

Rumelhart, D. E., & Ortony, A. (1977). The representation of knowledge in memory. In R. C. Anderson, R. J. Spiro, & W. E. Montague (Eds.), *Schooling and the acquisition of knowledge.* Hillsdale, NJ: Erlbaum.

Rushton, J. P. (1975). Generosity in children: Immediate and long-term effects of modeling, preaching, and moral judgment. *Journal of Personality and Social Psychology, 31,* 459–466.

Rushton, J. P. (1980). *Altruism, socialization, and society.* Upper Saddle River, NJ: Prentice Hall.

• Russell, D. L. (1994). *Literature for children* (2nd ed.). White Plains, NY: Longman.

• Ryan, R. M., Connell, J. P., & Grolnick, W. S. (1992). When achievement is *not* intrinsically motivated: A theory of internalization and self-regulation in school. In A. K. Boggiano & T. S. Pittman (Eds.), *Achievement and motivation: A social-developmental perspective.* Cambridge, UK: Cambridge University Press.

• Ryan, R. M., & Deci, E. L. (1996). When paradigms clash: Comments on Cameron and Pierce's claims that rewards do not undermine intrinsic motivation. *Review of Educational Research, 66,* 33–38.

• Ryan, R. M., Mims, V., & Koestner, R. (1983). Relation of reward contingency and in-terpersonal context to intrinsic motivation: A review and test using cognitive evaluation theory. *Journal of Personality and Social Psychology, 45,* 736–750.

Sabers, D. S., Cushing, K. S., & Berliner, D. C. (1991). Differences among teachers in a task characterized by simultaneity, multidimensionality, and immediacy. *American Educational Research Journal, 28,* 63–88.

Sadker, M. P., & Miller, D. (1982). *Sex equity handbook for schools.* White Plains, NY: Longman.

Sadker, M. P., & Sadker, D. (1985). Sexism in the schoolroom of the '80s. *Psychology Today, 19,* 54–57.

• Sadker, M. P., & Sadker, D. (1994). *Failing at fairness: How our schools cheat girls.* New York: Touchstone.

• Sadker, M. P., Sadker, D., & Klein, S. (1991). The issue of gender in elementary and secondary education. In G. Grant (Ed.), *Review of research in education.* Washington, DC: American Educational Research Association.

• Sadoski, M., Goetz, E. T., & Fritz, J. B. (1993). Impact of concreteness on comprehensibility, interest, and memory for text: Implications for dual coding theory and text design. *Journal of Educational Psychology, 85,* 291–304.

• Salend, S. J., & Taylor, L. (1993). Working with families: A cross-cultural perspective. *Remedial and Special Education, 14*(5), 25–32, 39.

• Saljo, R., & Wyndhamn, J. (1992). Solving everyday problems in the formal setting: An empirical study of the school as context for thought. In S. Chaiklin & J. Lave (Eds.), *Understanding practice.* New York: Cambridge University Press.

Salmon, P. (1979). The role of the peer group. In J. C. Coleman (Ed.), *The school years: Current issues in the socialization of young people.* New York: Methuen.

• Salomon, G. (Ed.). (1993). *Distributed cognitions: Psychological and educational considerations.* Cambridge, UK: Cambridge University Press.

Saltz, E. (1971). *The cognitive bases of human learning.* Homewood, IL: Dorsey.

Sanborn, M. P. (1979). Counseling and guidance needs of the gifted and talented. In A. H. Passow (Ed.), *The gifted and the talented: Their education and development. The 78th yearbook of the National Society for the Study of Educa-*

tion. Chicago: University of Chicago Press.

• Sanchez, F., & Anderson, M. L. (1990). Gang mediation: A process that works. *Principal, 69*(4), 54–56.

• Sanders, S. (1987). Cultural conflicts: An important factor in academic failures of American Indian students. *Journal of Multicultural Counseling and Development, 15*(2), 81–90.

Santiago, I. S. (1986). The education of Hispanics in the United States: Inadequacies of the American melting-pot theory. In D. Rothermund & J. Simon (Eds.), *Education and the integration of ethnic minorities.* New York: St. Martin's Press.

• Sarason, I. G. (1980). Introduction to the study of test anxiety. In I. G. Sarason (Ed.), *Test anxiety: Theory, research, and applications.* Hillsdale, NJ: Erlbaum.

Sarason, S. B. (1972). What research says about test anxiety in elementary school children. In A. R. Binter & S. H. Frey (Eds.), *The psychology of the elementary school child.* Chicago: Rand McNally.

Sattler, J. M. (1988). *Assessment of children* (3rd ed.). San Diego: Author.

Savin-Williams, R. C., & Demo, D. H. (1984). Developmental change and stability in adolescent self-concept. *Developmental Psychology, 20,* 1100–1110.

Sax, G. (1989). *Principles of educational and psychological measurement and evaluation* (3rd ed.). Belmont, CA: Wadsworth.

• Scarcella, R. (1990). *Teaching language-minority students in the multicultural classroom.* Upper Saddle River, NJ: Prentice Hall.

Scarr, S., & Weinberg, R. A. (1976). IQ test performance of black children adopted by white families. *American Psychologist, 31,* 726–739.

• Scevak, J. J., Moore, P. J., & Kirby, J. R. (1993). Training students to use maps to increase text recall. *Contemporary Educational Psychology, 18,* 401–413.

• Schank, R. C. (1979). Interestingness: Controlling inferences. *Artificial Intelligence, 12,* 273–297.

• Schell, T. L., Klein, S. B., & Babey, S. H. (1996). Testing a hierarchical model of self-knowledge. *Psychological Science, 7,* 170–173.

Schepis, M. M., Reid, D. H., & Fitzgerald, J. R. (1987). Group instruction with profoundly retarded persons: Acquisition, generalization, and maintenance of a remunerative work skill. *Journal of Applied Behavior Analysis, 20,* 97–105.

• Schiefele, U. (1991a). Interest, learning, and motivation. *Educational Psychologist, 26,* 299–323.

Schiefele, U. (1991b). Topic interest and levels of text comprehension. In A. K. Renninger, S. Hidi, & A. Krapp (Eds.), *"Interest" in development and learning.* Hillsdale, NJ: Erlbaum.

• Schiefele, U. (1992). Topic interest and levels of text comprehension. In K. A. Renninger, S. Hidi, & A. Krapp (Eds.), *The role of interest in learning and development.* Hillsdale, NJ: Erlbaum.

• Schiefele, U., Krapp, A., & Winteler, A. (1992). Interest as a predictor of academic achievement: A meta-analysis of research. In K. A. Renninger, S. Hidi, & A. Krapp (Eds.), *The role of interest in learning and development.* Hillsdale, NJ: Erlbaum.

• Schiffman, G., Tobin, D., & Buchanan, B. (1984). Microcomputer instruction for the learning disabled. *Annual Review of Learning Disabilities, 2,* 134–136.

Schlaefli, A., Rest, J. R., & Thoma, S. J. (1985). Does moral education improve moral judgment? A meta-analysis of intervention studies using the defining issues test. *Review of Educational Research, 55,* 319–352.

• Schliemann, A. D., & Carraher, D. W. (1993). Proportional reasoning in and out of school. In P. Light & G. Butterworth (Eds.), *Context and cognition: Ways of learning and knowing.* Hillsdale, NJ: Erlbaum.

• Schloss, P. J., & Smith, M. A. (1994). *Applied behavior analysis in the classroom.* Needham Heights, MA: Allyn & Bacon.

• Schmidt, R. A., & Bjork, R. A. (1992). New conceptualizations of practice: Common principles in three paradigms suggest new concepts for training. *Psychological Science, 3,* 207–217.

Schmidt, R. A., & Young, D. E. (1987). Transfer of movement control in motor skill learning. In S. M. Cormier & J. D. Hagman (Eds.), *Transfer of learning: Contemporary research and applications.* San Diego: Academic Press.

Schmuck, R. A., & Schmuck, P. A. (1974). *A humanistic psychology of education: Making the school everybody's house.* Palo Alto, CA: National Press.

• Schneider, W. (1993). Domain-specific knowledge and memory performance in children. *Educational Psychology Review, 5,* 257–273.

Schneider, W., & Shiffrin, R. M. (1977). Controlled and automatic human information processing: I. Detection, search, and attention. *Psychological Review, 84,* 1–66.

Schoenfeld, A. H. (1982). Measures of problem-solving performance and problem-solving instruction. *Journal for Research in Mathematics Education, 13,* 31–49.

Schoenfeld, A. H. (1985a). *Mathematical problem solving.* San Diego: Academic Press.

Schoenfeld, A. H. (1985b). Metacognitive and epistemological issues in mathematical understanding. In E. A. Silver (Ed.), *Teaching and learning mathematical problem solving: Multiple research perspectives.* Hillsdale, NJ: Erlbaum.

Schoenfeld, A. H., & Hermann, D. J. (1982). Problem perception and knowledge structure in expert and novice mathematical problem solvers. *Journal of Experimental Psychology: Learning, Memory, and Cognition, 8,* 484–494.

• Schofield, J. W. (1995). Improving intergroup relations among students. In J. A. Banks & C. A. M. Banks (Eds.), *Handbook of research on multicultural education.* New York: Macmillan.

Schommer, M. (1990). Effects of beliefs about the nature of knowledge on comprehension. *Journal of Educational Psychology, 82,* 498–504.

• Schommer, M. (1994a). An emerging conceptualization of epistemological beliefs and their role in learning. In R. Garner & P. A. Alexander (Eds.), *Beliefs about text and instruction with text.* Hillsdale, NJ: Erlbaum.

• Schommer, M. (1994b). Synthesizing epistemological belief research: Tentative understandings and provocative confusions. *Educational Psychology Review, 6,* 293–319.

• Schommer, M. (in press). The development of epistemological beliefs among secondary students: A longitudinal study. *Journal of Educational Psychology.*

• Schön, D. A. (1987). *The reflective practitioner: How professionals think in action.* New York: Basic Books.

• Schonert-Reichl, K. A. (1993). Empathy and social relationships in adolescents with behavioral disorders. *Behavioral Disorders, 18,* 189–204.

Schratz, M. (1978). A developmental investigation of sex differences in spatial (visual-analytic) and mathematical skills in three ethnic groups. *Developmental Psychology, 14,* 263–267.

• Schraw, G., & Bruning, R. (1995, April). *Reader beliefs and reading comprehension.* Paper presented at the annual meeting of the American Educational Research Association, San Francisco.

• Schraw, G., Potenza, M. T., & Nebelsick-Gullet, L. (1993). Constraints on the calibration of performance. *Contemporary Educational Psychology, 18,* 455–463.

Schraw, G., & Wade, S. (1991, April). *Selective learning strategies for relevant and important text information.* Paper presented at the annual meeting of the American Educational Research Association, Chicago.

Schubert, J. G. (1986). Gender equity in computer learning. *Theory into Practice, 25,* 267–275.

• Schultz, G. F., & Switzky, H. N. (1990). The development of intrinsic motivation in students with learning problems: Suggestions for more effective instructional practice. *Preventing School Failure, 34*(2), 14–20.

Schultz, K., & Lochhead, J. (1991). A view from physics. In M. U. Smith (Ed.), *Toward a unified theory of problem solving: Views from the content domains.* Hillsdale, NJ: Erlbaum.

• Schumaker, J. B., & Hazel, J. S. (1984). Social skill assessment and training for the learning disabled: Who's on first and what's on second? (Part 1). *Journal of Learning Disabilities, 17,* 422–431.

• Schunk, D. H. (1981). Modeling and attributional effects on children's achievement: A self-efficacy analysis. *Journal of Educational Psychology, 73,* 93–105.

Schunk, D. H. (1982). Effects of effort attributional feedback on children's perceived self-efficacy and achievement. *Journal of Educational Psychology, 74,* 548–556.

Schunk, D. H. (1983). Developing children's self-efficacy and skills: The roles of social comparative information and goal setting. *Contemporary Educational Psychology, 8,* 76–86.

Schunk, D. H. (1985). Participation in goal setting: Effects on self-efficacy and skills

of learning disabled children. *Journal of Special Education, 19,* 307–317.

Schunk, D. H. (1989a). Self-efficacy and achievement behaviors. *Educational Psychology Review, 1,* 173–208.

Schunk, D. H. (1989b). Self-efficacy and cognitive skill learning. In C. Ames & R. Ames (Eds.), *Research on motivation in education: Vol. 3. Goals and cognitions.* San Diego: Academic Press.

Schunk, D. H. (1989c). Social cognitive theory and self-regulated learning. In B. J. Zimmerman & D. H. Schunk (Eds.), *Self-regulated learning and academic achievement: Theory, research, and practice.* New York: Springer-Verlag.

Schunk, D. H. (1990, April). *Socialization and the development of self-regulated learning: The role of attributions.* Paper presented at the annual meeting of the American Educational Research Association, Boston, MA.

Schunk, D. H. (1991). *Learning theories: An educational perspective.* New York: Macmillan.

Schunk, D. H., & Hanson, A. R. (1985). Peer models: Influence on children's self-efficacy and achievement. *Journal of Educational Psychology, 77,* 313–322.

Schunk, D. H., Hanson, A. R., & Cox, P. D. (1987). Peer-model attributes and children's achievement behaviors. *Journal of Educational Psychology, 79,* 54–61.

Schwartz, B., & Reisberg, D. (1991). *Learning and memory.* New York: Norton.

Schwebel, A. I., & Cherlin, D. L. (1972). Physical and social distancing in teacher-pupil relationships. *Journal of Educational Psychology, 63,* 543–550.

Scott, J., & Bushell, D. (1974). The length of teacher contacts and students' off-task behavior. *Journal of Applied Behavior Analysis, 7,* 39–44.

Scott, R. C. (1989). *Physical geography.* St. Paul, MN: West.

Scott-Jones, D. (1984). Family influences on cognitive development and school achievement. In E. W. Gordon (Ed.), *Review of research in education* (Vol. 11). Washington, DC: American Educational Research Association.

Scruggs, T. E., & Mastropieri, M. A. (1989). Mnemonic instruction of learning disabled students: A field-based evaluation. *Learning Disabilities Quarterly, 12,* 119–125.

• Scruggs, T. E., & Mastropieri, M. A. (1992). Classroom applications of mnemonic

instruction: Acquisition, maintenance, and generalization. *Exceptional Children, 58,* 219–229.

• Scruggs, T. E., & Mastropieri, M. A. (1994). Successful mainstreaming in elementary science classes: A qualitative study of three reputational cases. *American Educational Research Journal, 31,* 785–811.

Seitz, V., Rosenbaum, L. K., & Apfel, N. H. (1985). Effects of family support intervention: A ten-year follow-up. *Child Development, 56,* 376–391.

• Seligman, M. E. P. (1975). *Helplessness: On depression, development, and death.* San Francisco: W. H. Freeman.

Seligman, M. E. P. (1991). *Learned optimism.* New York: Knopf.

Selman, R. L. (1980). *The growth of interpersonal understanding.* San Diego: Academic Press.

Selman, R. L., & Byrne, D. F. (1974). A structural-developmental analysis of levels of role taking in middle childhood. *Child Development, 45,* 803–806.

Seltzer, V. C. (1982). *Adolescent social development: Dynamic functional interaction.* Lexington, MA: Heath.

• Semb, G. B., & Ellis, J. A. (1994). Knowledge taught in school: What is remembered? *Review of Educational Research, 64,* 253–286.

Semb, G. B., Ellis, J. A., & Araujo, J. (1993). Long-term memory for knowledge learned in school. *Journal of Educational Psychology, 85,* 305–316.

Semmel, M. I., Gottlieb, J., & Robinson, N. M. (1979). Mainstreaming: Perspectives on educating handicapped children in the public school. In D. C. Berliner (Ed.), *Review of research in education* (Vol. 7). Washington, DC: American Educational Research Association.

• Shachar, H., & Sharan, S. (1994). Talking, relating, and achieving: Effects of cooperative learning and whole-class instruction. *Cognition and Instruction, 12,* 313–353.

Shade, B. J. (1983). Cognitive strategies as determinants of school achievement. *Psychology in the Schools, 20,* 488–493.

Shaffer, D. R. (1988). *Social and personality development* (2nd ed.). Pacific Grove, CA: Brooks/Cole.

Sharan, S., & Shachar, H. (1988). *Language and learning in the cooperative classroom.* New York: Springer-Verlag.

Shatz, M., & Gelman, R. (1973). The development of communication skills: Modifications in the speech of young children as a function of the listener. *Monographs of the Society for Research in Child Development, 38*(5, Serial No. 152).

Shavelson, R. J., & Baxter, G. P. (1992). What we've learned about assessing hands-on science. *Educational Leadership, 49*(8), 20–25.

Shavelson, R. J., Baxter, G. P., & Pine, J. (1992). Performance assessments: Political rhetoric and measurement reality. *Educational Researcher, 21*(4), 22–27.

Sheldon, A. (1974). The role of parallel function in the acquisition of relative clauses in English. *Journal of Verbal Learning and Verbal Behavior, 13*, 272–281.

• Shepard, R. N., & Metzler, J. (1971). Mental rotation of three-dimensional objects. *Science, 171*, 701–703.

Sherrill, D., Horowitz, B., Friedman, S. T., & Salisbury, J. L. (1970). Seating aggregation as an index of contagion. *Educational and Psychological Measurement, 30*, 663–668.

Shiffrin, R. M., & Schneider, W. (1977). Controlled and automatic human information processing: II. Perceptual learning, automatic attending, and a general theory. *Psychological Review, 84*, 127–190.

Shipman, S., & Shipman, V. C. (1985). Cognitive styles: Some conceptual, methodological, and applied issues. In E. W. Gordon (Ed.), *Review of research in education* (Vol. 12). Washington, DC: American Educational Research Association.

• Short, E. J., Schatschneider, C. W., & Friebert, S. E. (1993). Relationship between memory and metamemory performance: A comparison of specific and general strategy knowledge. *Journal of Educational Psychology, 85*, 412–423.

Short, P. M., & Noblit, G. W. (1985). Missing the mark in in-school suspension: An explanation and proposal. *NASSP Bulletin, 69*(484), 112–116.

Shrager, L., & Mayer, R. E. (1989). Notetaking fosters generative learning strategies in novices. *Journal of Educational Psychology, 81*, 263–264.

Shrigley, R. L. (1979). Strategies in classroom management. *NASSP Bulletin, 63*(428), 1–9.

• Shulman, L. S. (1986). Those who understand: Knowledge growth in teaching. *Educational Researcher, 15*, 4–14.

• Shulman, L. S. (1987). Knowledge and teaching: Foundations of the new re-

form. *Harvard Educational Review, 57*, 1–22.

Shultz, J., & Florio, S. (1979). Stop and freeze: The negotiation of social and physical space in a kindergarten/first grade classroom. *Anthropology and Education Quarterly, 10*, 166–181.

Shymansky, J. A., Hedges, L. V., & Woodworth, G. (1990). A reassessment of the effects of inquiry-based science curricula of the 60s on student performance. *Journal of Research in Science Teaching, 27*, 127–144.

Sieber, J. E., Kameya, L. I., & Paulson, F. L. (1970). Effect of memory support on the problem-solving ability of test-anxious children. *Journal of Educational Psychology, 61*, 159–168.

Siegel, L., & Hodkin, B. (1982). The garden path to the understanding of cognitive development: Has Piaget led us into the poison ivy? In S. Modgil & C. Modgil (Eds.), *Jean Piaget: Consensus and controversy.* New York: Praeger.

Siegler, R. S. (1986). *Children's thinking.* Upper Saddle River, NJ: Prentice Hall.

• Siegler, R. S. (1994). Cognitive variability: A key to understanding cognitive development. *Current Directions in Psychological Science, 3*, 1–5.

Siegler, R. S., & Richards, D. D. (1982). The development of intelligence. In R. J. Sternberg (Ed.), *Handbook of human intelligence.* Cambridge, UK: Cambridge University Press.

Silberman, M. L., & Wheelan, S. A. (1980). *How to discipline without feeling guilty: Assertive relationships with children.* Champaign, IL: Research Press.

Silver, E. A., Shapiro, L. J., & Deutsch, A. (1991, April). *Sense-making and the solution of division problems involving remainders: An examination of students' solution processes and their interpretations of solutions.* Paper presented at the annual meeting of the American Educational Research Association, Chicago.

• Simmons, R. G., & Blyth, D. A. (1987). *Moving into adolescence: The impact of pubertal change and school context.* New York: Aldine de Gruyter.

Simon, H. A. (1974). How big is a chunk? *Science, 183*, 482–488.

Simons, P. R. J. (1984). Instructing with analogies. *Journal of Educational Psychology, 76*, 513–527.

• Singley, M. K., & Anderson, J. R. (1989). *The transfer of cognitive skill.* Cambridge, MA: Harvard University Press.

Sisk, D. A. (1989). Identifying and nurturing talent among American Indians. In C. J. Maker & S. W. Schiever (Eds.), *Critical issues in gifted education: Vol. 2. Defensible programs for cultural and ethnic minorities.* Austin, TX: PRO-ED.

Skeels, H. M. (1966). Adult status of children with contrasting early life experience: A follow-up study. *Monographs of the Society for Research in Child Development, 31*(Serial No. 105).

• Skiba, R., & Raison, J. (1990). Relationship between the use of time-out and academic achievement. *Exceptional Children, 57*, 36–46.

Skinner, B. F. (1938). *The behavior of organisms: An experimental analysis.* Upper Saddle River, NJ: Prentice Hall.

Skinner, B. F. (1953). *Science and human behavior.* New York: Macmillan.

Skinner, B. F. (1954). The science of learning and the art of teaching. *Harvard Educational Review, 24*, 86–97.

Skinner, B. F. (1968). *The technology of teaching.* New York: Appleton-Century-Crofts.

Skinner, B. F. (1973). The free and happy student. *Phi Delta Kappan, 55*, 13–16.

Slavin, R. E. (1983a). *Cooperative learning.* White Plains, NY: Longman.

Slavin, R. E. (1983b). When does cooperative learning increase student achievement? *Psychological Bulletin, 94*, 429–445.

Slavin, R. E. (1987). Ability grouping and student achievement in elementary schools: A best-evidence synthesis. *Review of Educational Research, 57*, 293–336.

Slavin, R. E. (1989). Students at risk of school failure: The problem and its dimensions. In R. E. Slavin, N. L. Karweit, & N. A. Madden (Eds.), *Effective programs for students at risk.* Needham Heights, MA: Allyn & Bacon.

Slavin, R. E. (1990). *Cooperative learning: Theory, research, and practice.* Upper Saddle River, NJ: Prentice Hall.

Slavin, R. E., Karweit, N. L., & Madden, N. A. (Eds.). (1989). *Effective programs for students at risk.* Needham Heights, MA: Allyn & Bacon.

Slavin, R. E., Madden, N. A., & Karweit, N. L. (1989). Effective programs for students at risk: Conclusions for practice and policy. In R. E. Slavin, N. L. Karweit, & N. A. Madden (Eds.), *Effective programs for students at risk*. Needham Heights, MA: Allyn & Bacon.

• Sleeter, C. E., & Grant, C. A. (1994). *Making choices for multicultural education: Five approaches to race, class, and gender* (2nd ed.). New York: Merrill/Macmillan.

• Slusher, M. P., & Anderson, C. A. (1996). Using causal persuasive arguments to change beliefs and teach new information: The mediating role of explanation availability and evaluation bias in the acceptance of knowledge. *Journal of Educational Psychology, 88,* 110–122.

• Small, M. Y., Lovett, S. B., & Scher, M. S. (1993). Pictures facilitate children's recall of unillustrated expository prose. *Journal of Educational Psychology, 85,* 520–528.

• Small, R. V., & Grabowski, B. L. (1992). An exploratory study of information-seeking behaviors and learning with hypermedia information systems. *Journal of Educational Multimedia and Hypermedia, 1,* 445–464.

• Smetana, J. G. (1983). Social-cognitive development: Domain distinctions and coordinations. *Developmental Review, 3,* 131–147.

• Smith, D. C., & Neale, D. C. (1991). The construction of subject-matter knowledge in primary science teaching. In J. Brophy (Ed.), *Advances in research on teaching: Vol. 2. Teacher's knowledge of subject matter as it relates to their teaching practice*. Greenwich, CT: JAI Press.

• Smith, D. J., Young, K. R., West, R. P., Morgan, R. P., & Rhode, G. (1988). Reducing the disruptive behavior of junior high school students: A classroom self-management procedure. *Behavioral Disorders, 13,* 231–239.

• Smith, F. (1988). *Understanding reading* (4th ed.). Hillsdale, NJ: Erlbaum.

Smith, J., & Russell, G. (1984). Why do males and females differ? Children's beliefs about sex differences. *Sex Roles, 11,* 1111–1120.

• Smith, K., Johnson, D. W., & Johnson, R. T. (1981). Can conflict be constructive? Controversy versus concurrence seeking in learning groups. *Journal of Educational Psychology, 73,* 651–663.

• Smith, M. U. (1991). A view from biology. In M. U. Smith (Ed.), *Toward a unified theory of problem solving: Views from the content domains*. Hillsdale, NJ: Erlbaum.

• Smith, P. B., & Bond, M. H. (1994). *Social psychology across cultures: Analysis and perspectives*. Needham Heights, MA: Allyn & Bacon.

Sneider, C., & Pulos, S. (1983). Children's cosmographies: Understanding the earth's shape and gravity. *Science Education, 67,* 205–221.

Snow, C. E. (1990). Rationales for native language instruction: Evidence from research. In A. M. Padilla, H. H. Fairchild, & C. M. Valadez (Eds.), *Bilingual education: Issues and strategies*. Newbury Park, CA: Sage.

Snow, C. E., & Hoefnagel-Höhle, M. (1978). The critical period for language acquisition: Evidence from second language learning. *Child Development, 49,* 1114–1128.

• Snyder, M., & Swann, W. B. (1978). Behavioral confirmation in social interaction: From social perception to social reality. *Journal of Experimental Social Psychology, 14,* 148–162.

Solnick, J. V., Rincover, A., & Peterson, C. R. (1977). Some determinants of the reinforcing and punishing effects of time-out. *Journal of Applied Behavior Analysis, 10,* 415–424.

• Sosniak, L. A., & Stodolsky, S. S. (1994). Making connections: Social studies education in an urban fourth-grade classroom. In J. Brophy (Ed.), *Advances in research on teaching: Vol. 4. Case studies of teaching and learning in social studies*. Greenwich, CT: JAI Press.

Spaulding, C. L. (1992). *Motivation in the classroom*. New York: McGraw-Hill.

• Spencer, M. B., & Markstrom-Adams, C. (1990). Identity processes among racial and ethic minority children in America. *Child Development, 61,* 290–310.

Sperling, G. (1967). Successive approximations to a model for short-term memory. *Acta Psychologia, 27,* 285–292.

• Spicker, H. H. (1992). Identifying and enriching: Rural gifted children. *Educational Horizons, 7*(2), 60–65.

Spielberger, C. D. (1966). The effects of anxiety on complex learning in academic achievement. In C. D. Spielberger (Ed.), *Anxiety and behavior*. San Diego: Academic Press.

Spielberger, C. D., & DeNike, L. D. (1966). Descriptive behaviorism versus cognitive theory in verbal operant conditioning. *Psychological Review, 73,* 306–326.

Spires, H. A. (1990, April). *Learning from a lecture: Effects of comprehension monitoring*. Paper presented at the annual meeting of the American Educational Research Association, Boston, MA.

Spires, H. A., Donley, J., & Penrose, A. M. (1990, April). *Prior knowledge activation: Inducing text engagement in reading to learn*. Paper presented at the annual meeting of the American Educational Research Association, Boston, MA.

Sprafkin, C., Serbin, L. A., Denier, C., & Connor, J. M. (1983). Sex-differentiated play: Cognitive consequences and early interventions. In M. B. Liss (Ed.), *Social and cognitive skills: Sex roles and children's play*. San Diego: Academic Press.

Sroufe, L. A. (1983). Infant-caregiver attachment and patterns of adaptation in preschool: The roots of maladaptation. In M. Perlmutter (Ed.), *Minnesota Symposium on Child Psychology* (Vol. 16). Hillsdale, NJ: Erlbaum.

Stainback, S., & Stainback, W. (1990). Inclusive schooling. In W. Stainback & S. Stainback (Eds.), *Support networks for inclusive schooling: Interdependent integrated education*. Baltimore: Brooks.

• Stainback, S., & Stainback, W. (1992). Schools as inclusive communities. In W. Stainback & S. Stainback (Eds.), *Controversial issues confronting special education: Divergent perspectives*. Needham Heights, MA: Allyn & Bacon.

Stanley, J. C. (1980). On educating the gifted. *Educational Researcher, 9*(3), 8–12.

Steffensen, M. S., Joag-Dev, C., & Anderson, R. C. (1979). A cross-cultural perspective on reading comprehension. *Reading Research Quarterly, 15,* 10–29.

Stein, A. H. (1971). The effects of sex-role standards for achievement and sex-role preference on three determinants of achievement motivation. *Developmental Psychology, 4,* 219–231.

Stein, A. H., & Smithells, J. (1969). Age and sex differences in children's sex-role standards about achievement. *Developmental Psychology, 1,* 252–259.

Stein, B. S. (1989). Memory and creativity. In J. A. Glover, R. R. Ronning, & C. R. Reynolds (Eds.), *Handbook of creativity*. New York: Plenum Press.

Stein, B. S., & Bransford, J. D. (1979). Constraints on effective elaboration: Effects of precision and subject generation.

Journal of Verbal Learning and Verbal Behavior, 18, 769 777.

• Steinberg, E. R. (1989). Cognition and learner control: A literature review, 1977–1988. *Journal of Computer-Based Instruction, 16*(4), 117–121.

• Steinberg, L. (1993). *Adolescence* (3rd ed.). New York: McGraw-Hill.

Steinberg, L., Blinde, P. L., & Chan, K. S. (1984). Dropping out among language minority youth. *Review of Educational Research, 54,* 113–132.

• Steinberg, L., Elmen, J., & Mounts, N. (1989). Authoritative parenting, psychosocial maturity, and academic success among adolescents. *Child Development, 60,* 1424–1436.

Steinberg, L., Greenberger, E., Garduque, L., & McAuliffe, S. (1982). High school students in the labor force: Some costs and benefits to schooling and learning. *Educational Evaluation and Policy Analysis, 4,* 363–372.

Stephens, T. M., Blackhurst, A. E., & Magliocca, L. A. (1988). *Teaching mainstreamed students* (2nd ed.). Oxford, UK: Pergamon.

Stepich, D. A., & Newby, T. J. (1988). Analogical instruction within the information processing paradigm: Effective means to facilitate learning. *Instructional Science, 17,* 129–144.

Sternberg, R. J. (1984). Toward a triarchic theory of human intelligence. *Behavioral and Brain Sciences, 7,* 269–287.

Sternberg, R. J. (1985). *Beyond IQ: A triarchic theory of human intelligence.* Cambridge, UK: Cambridge University Press.

Sternberg, R. J., & Detterman, D. K. (Eds.). (1986). *What is intelligence? Contemporary views on its nature and definition.* Norwood, NJ: Ablex.

Sternberg, R. J., & Frensch, P. A. (1993). Mechanisms of transfer. In D. K. Detterman & R. J. Sternberg (Eds.), *Transfer on trial: Intelligence, cognition, and instruction.* Norwood, NJ: Ablex.

• Sternberg, R. J., & Wagner, R. K. (Eds.). (1994). *Mind in context: Interactionist perspectives on human intelligence.* Cambridge, UK: Cambridge University Press.

Steuer, F. B., Applefield, J. M., & Smith, R. (1971). Televised aggression and the interpersonal aggression of preschool children. *Journal of Experimental Child Psychology, 11,* 442–447.

• Stevens, R. J., & Slavin, R. E. (1995). The cooperative elementary school: Effects of students' achievement, attitudes, and social relations. *American Educational Research Journal, 32,* 321–351.

Stevenson, H. C., & Fantuzzo, J. W. (1986). The generality and social validity of a competency-based self-control training intervention for underachieving students. *Journal of Applied Behavior Analysis, 19,* 269–272.

• Stevenson, H. W., Chen, C., & Uttal, D. H. (1990). Beliefs and achievement: A study of black, white, and Hispanic children. *Child Development, 61,* 508–523.

Stiggins, R. J. (1994). *Student-centered classroom assessment.* Upper Saddle River, NJ: Merrill/Prentice Hall.

• Stiggins, R. J., & Conklin, N. F. (1992). *In teachers' hands: Investigating the practices of classroom assessment.* Albany: SUNY Press.

Stipek, D. J. (1981). Children's perceptions of their own and their classmates' ability. *Journal of Educational Psychology, 73,* 404–410.

Stipek, D. J. (1984). Sex differences in children's attributions for success and failure on math and spelling tests. *Sex Roles, 11,* 969–981.

Stipek, D. J. (1993). *Motivation to learn: From theory to practice* (2nd ed.). Needham Heights, MA: Allyn & Bacon.

Stipek, D. J., & Gralinski, H. (1990, April). *Gender differences in children's achievement-related beliefs and emotional responses to success and failure in math.* Paper presented at the annual meeting of the American Educational Research Association, Boston, MA.

Stodolsky, S. S., Salk, S., & Glaessner, B. (1991). Student views about learning math and social studies. *American Educational Research Journal, 28,* 89–116.

• Stokes, T. F., & Baer, D. M. (1977). An implicit technology of generalization. *Journal of Applied Behavior Analysis, 10,* 349–367.

• Suina, J. H., & Smolkin, L. B. (1994). From natal culture to school culture to dominant society culture: Supporting transitions for Pueblo Indian students. In P. M. Greenfield & R. R. Cocking (Eds.), *Cross-cultural roots of minority child development.* Hillsdale, NJ: Erlbaum.

Sullivan, J. S. (1989). Planning, implementing, and maintaining an effective in-school suspension program. *Clearing House, 62,* 409–410.

Sund, R. B. (1976). *Piaget for educators.* Columbus, OH: Merrill.

Sunshine, P. M., & Di Vesta, F. J. (1976). Effects of density and format on letter discrimination by beginning readers with different learning styles. *Journal of Educational Psychology, 68,* 15–19.

Swan, K., Mitrani, M., Guerrero, F., Cheung, M., & Schoener, J. (1990, April). *Perceived locus of control and computer-based instruction.* Paper presented at the annual meeting of the American Educational Research Association, Boston, MA.

Swann, W. B., Jr. (1992). Seeking "truth," finding despair: Some unhappy consequences of a negative self-concept. *Current Directions in Psychological Science, 1*(1), 15–18.

• Swanson, D. B., Norman, G. R., & Linn, R. L. (1995). Performance-based assessment: Lessons from the health professions. *Educational Researcher, 24*(5), 5–11, 35.

• Swanson, H. L. (1992). Generality and modifiability of working memory among skilled and less skilled readers. *Journal of Educational Psychology, 84,* 473–488.

• Swanson, H. L. (1993). An information processing analysis of learning disabled children's problem solving. *American Educational Research Journal, 30,* 861–893.

• Swanson, H. L., & Cooney, J. B. (1991). Learning disabilities and memory. In B. Y. L. Wong (Ed.), *Learning about learning disabilities.* San Diego: Academic Press.

• Swanson, H. L., O'Connor, J. E., & Cooney, J. B. (1990). An information processing analysis of expert and novice teachers' problem solving. *American Educational Research Journal, 27,* 533–556.

• Tamburrini, J. (1982). Some educational implications of Piaget's theory. In S. Modgil & C. Modgil (Eds.), *Jean Piaget: Consensus and controversy.* New York: Praeger.

Taylor, B. M. (1982). Text structure and children's comprehension and memory for expository material. *Journal of Educational Psychology, 74,* 323–340.

Taylor, I. A. (1976). A retrospective view of creativity investigation. In I. A. Taylor & J. W. Getzels (Eds.), *Perspectives in creativity.* Chicago: Aldine.

- Taylor, J. (1983). Influence of speech variety on teachers' evaluation of reading comprehension. *Journal of Educational Psychology, 75,* 662–667.
- Taylor, S. M. (1994, April). *Staying in school against the odds: Voices of minority adolescent girls.* Paper presented at the annual meeting of the American Educational Research Association, New Orleans, LA.
- Tennyson, C. L., Tennyson, R. D., & Rothen, W. (1980). Content structure and instructional control strategies as design variables in concept acquisition. *Journal of Educational Psychology, 72,* 499–505.
- Tennyson, R. D., & Cocchiarella, M. J. (1986). An empirically based instructional design theory for teaching concepts. *Review of Educational Research, 56,* 40–71.
- Tennyson, R. D., Youngers, J., & Suebsonthi, P. (1983). Concept learning by children using instructional presentation forms for prototype formation and classification-skill development. *Journal of Educational Psychology, 75,* 280–291.
- Terwilliger, J. S. (1989). Classroom standard setting and grading practices. *Educational Measurement: Issues and Practices, 8*(2), 15–19.
- Tharp, R. G. (1989). Psychocultural variables and constants: Effects on teaching and learning in schools. *American Psychologist, 44,* 349–359.
- Tharp, R. G. (1994). Intergroup differences among Native Americans in socialization and child cognition: An ethnogenetic analysis. In P. M. Greenfield & R. R. Cocking (Eds.), *Cross-cultural roots of minority child development.* Hillsdale, NJ: Erlbaum.
- Théberge, C. L. (1994, April). *Small-group vs. whole-class discussion: Gaining the floor in science lessons.* Paper presented at the annual meeting of the American Educational Research Association, New Orleans, LA.
- Thomas, A., & Chess, S. (1977). *Temperament and development.* New York: Brunner/Mazel.
- Thomas, J. R., & French, K. E. (1985). Gender differences across age in motor performance: A meta-analysis. *Psychological Bulletin, 98,* 260–282.
- Thomas, J. W. (1993). Expectations and effort: Course demands, students' study practices, and academic achievement. In T. M. Tomlinson (Ed.), *Motivating students to learn: Overcoming barriers to high achievement.* Berkeley, CA: McCutchan.
- Thomas, S. P., Groër, M., & Droppleman, P. (1993). Physical health of today's school children. *Educational Psychology Review, 5,* 5–33.
- Thomas, W. P., Collier, V. P., & Abbott, M. (1993). Academic achievement through Japanese, Spanish, or French: The first two years of partial immersion. *Modern Language Journal, 77,* 170–179.
- Thompson, A. G., & Thompson, P. W. (1989). Affect and problem solving in an elementary school mathematics classroom. In D. B. McLeod & V. M. Adams (Eds.), *Affect and mathematical problem solving: A new perspective.* New York: Springer-Verlag.
- Thorndike, E. L. (1924). Mental discipline in high school studies. *Journal of Educational Psychology, 15,* 1–22, 83–98.
- Threadgill-Sowder, J. (1985). Individual differences and mathematical problem solving. In E. A. Silver (Ed.), *Teaching and learning mathematical problem solving: Multiple research perspectives.* Hillsdale, NJ: Erlbaum.
- Thurstone, L. L., & Jeffrey, T. E. (1956). *FLAGS: A test of space thinking.* Chicago: Industrial Relations Center.
- Tirosh, D., & Graeber, A. O. (1988, April). Inconsistencies in preservice elementary teachers' beliefs about multiplication and division. In D. Tirosh (Chair), *The role of inconsistent ideas in learning mathematics.* Symposium conducted at the annual meeting of American Educational Research Association, New Orleans, LA.
- Tobias, S. (1977). A model for research on the effect of anxiety on instruction. In J. E. Sieber, H. F. O'Neil, Jr., & S. Tobias (Eds.), *Anxiety, learning, and instruction.* Hillsdale, NJ: Erlbaum.
- Tobias, S. (1980). Anxiety and instruction. In I. G. Sarason (Ed.), *Test anxiety: Theory, research, and applications.* Hillsdale, NJ: Erlbaum.
- Tobias, S. (1985). Test anxiety: Interference, defective skills, and cognitive capacity. *Educational Psychologist, 20,* 135–142.
- Tobias, S. (1994). Interest, prior knowledge, and learning. *Review of Educational Research, 64,* 37–54.
- Tobin, K. (1986). Student task involvement and achievement in process-oriented science activities. *Science Education, 70*(1), 61–72.
- Tobin, K. (1987). The role of wait time in higher cognitive level learning. *Review of Educational Research, 57,* 69–95.
- Tolman, E. C. (1932). *Purposive behavior in animals and men.* New York: Century.
- Tolman, E. C. (1938). The determiners of behavior at a choice point. *Psychological Review, 45,* 1–41.
- Tolman, E. C. (1959). Principles of purposive behavior. In S. Koch (Ed.), *Psychology: A study of a science* (Vol. 2). New York: McGraw-Hill.
- Tomlinson, T. M. (1993). Education reform: The ups and downs of good intentions. In T. M. Tomlinson (Ed.), *Motivating students to learn: Overcoming barriers to high achievement.* Berkeley, CA: McCutchan.
- Torgesen, J. K. (1977). Performance of learning disabled children: A theoretical assessment. *Journal of Learning Disabilities, 10,* 33–40.
- Torrance, E. P. (1970). *Encouraging creativity in the classroom.* Dubuque, IA: Wm. C. Brown.
- Torrance, E. P. (1976). Creativity research in education: Still alive. In I. A. Taylor & J. W. Getzels (Eds.), *Perspectives in creativity.* Chicago: Aldine.
- Torrance, E. P. (1989). A reaction to "Gifted black students: Curriculum and teaching strategies." In C. J. Maker & S. W. Schiever (Eds.), *Critical issues in gifted education: Vol. 2. Defensible programs for cultural and ethnic minorities.* Austin, TX: PRO-ED.
- Torrance, E. P., & Myers, R. E. (1970). *Creative learning and teaching.* New York: Dodd, Mead.
- Tourniaire, F., & Pulos, S. (1985). Proportional reasoning: A review of the literature. *Educational Studies in Mathematics, 16,* 181–204.
- Triandis, H. C. (1995). *Individualism and collectivism.* Boulder, CO: Westview Press.
- Trueba, H. T. (1988). Peer socialization among minority students: A high school dropout prevention program. In H. T. Trueba & C. Delgado-Gaitan (Eds.), *School and society: Learning content through culture.* New York: Praeger.
- Tryon, G. S. (1980). The measurement and treatment of anxiety. *Review of Educational Research, 50,* 343–372.

Tulving, E. (1962). Subjective organization in free recall of "unrelated" words. *Psychological Review, 69,* 344–354.

Tulving, E. (1983). *Elements of episodic memory.* Oxford, UK: Oxford University Press.

Tulving, E., & Thomson, D. M. (1973). Encoding specificity and retrieval processes in episodic memory. *Psychological Review, 80,* 352–373.

• Turiel, E. (1983). *The development of social knowledge: Morality and convention.* Cambridge, UK: Cambridge University Press.

• Turiel, E., Smetana, J. G., & Killen, M. (1991). Social contexts in social cognitive development. In W. M. Kurtines & J. L. Gewirtz (Eds.), *Moral behavior and development: Vol. 2. Research.* Hillsdale, NJ: Erlbaum.

• Turnbull, A. P., Turnbull, H. R., Shank, M., & Leal, D. (1995). *Exceptional lives: Special education in today's schools.* Upper Saddle River, NJ: Merrill/Prentice Hall.

• Turner, J. C. (1995). The influence of classroom contexts on young children's motivation for literacy. *Reading Research Quarterly, 30,* 410–441.

Tyler, B. (1958). Expectancy for eventual success as a factor in problem-solving behavior. *Journal of Educational Psychology, 49,* 166–172.

Udall, A. J. (1989). Curriculum for gifted Hispanic students. In C. J. Maker & S. W. Schiever (Eds.), *Critical issues in gifted education: Vol. 2. Defensible programs for cultural and ethnic minorities.* Austin, TX: PRO-ED.

• Ulichny, P. (1994, April). *Cultures in conflict.* Paper presented at the annual meeting of the American Educational Research Association, New Orleans, LA.

Underwood, B. J. (1948). "Spontaneous recovery" of verbal associations. *Journal of Experimental Psychology, 38,* 429–439.

Underwood, B. J. (1954). Studies of distributed practice: XII. Retention following varying degrees of original learning. *Journal of Experimental Psychology, 47,* 294–300.

Underwood, B. J. (1957). Interference and forgetting. *Psychological Review, 64,* 49–60.

• Valencia, S. W., Hiebert, E. H., & Afflerbach, P. P. (1994). Realizing the possibilities of authentic assessment: Current trends and future issues. In S. W. Valencia, E. H.

Hiebert, & P. P. Afflerbach (Eds.), *Authentic reading assessment: Practices and possibilities.* Newark, DE: International Reading Association.

• Van Houten, R., Nau, P., MacKenzie-Keating, S., Sameoto, D., & Colavecchia, B. (1982). An analysis of some variables influencing the effectiveness of reprimands. *Journal of Applied Behavior Analysis, 15,* 65–83.

Van Rossum, E. J., & Schenk, S. M. (1984). The relationship between learning conception, study strategy, and learning outcome. *British Journal of Educational Psychology, 54,* 73–83.

• VanSledright, B., & Brophy, J. (1992). Storytelling, imagination, and fanciful elaboration in children's historical reconstructions. *American Educational Research Journal, 29,* 837–859.

Vasquez, J. A. (1988). Contexts of learning for minority students. *Educational Forum, 6,* 243–253.

Vasquez, J. A. (1990). Teaching to the distinctive traits of minority students. *Clearing House, 63,* 299–304.

• Vaughn, S. (1991). Social skills enhancement in students with learning disabilities. In B. Y. L. Wong (Ed.), *Learning about learning disabilities.* San Diego: Academic Press.

Veenman, S. (1984). Perceived problems of beginning teachers. *Review of Educational Research, 54,* 143–178.

Vernon, M. D. (1969). *Human motivation.* Cambridge, UK: Cambridge University Press.

• Villegas, A. (1991). *Culturally responsive pedagogy for the 1990s and beyond.* Princeton, NJ: Educational Testing Service.

• Vorrath, H. (1985). *Positive peer culture.* New York: Aldine.

• Vosniadou, S. (1994). Universal and culture-specific properties of children's mental models of the earth. In L. A. Hirschfeld & S. A. Gelman (Eds.), *Mapping the mind: Domain specificity in cognition and culture.* Cambridge, UK: Cambridge University Press.

Vosniadou, S., & Brewer, W. F. (1987). Theories of knowledge restructuring in development. *Review of Educational Research, 57,* 51–67.

Voss, J. F. (1974). Acquisition and nonspecific transfer effects in prose learning as a function of question form. *Journal of Educational Psychology, 66,* 736–740.

Voss, J. F. (1987). Learning and transfer in subject-matter learning: A problem-solving model. *International Journal of Educational Research, 11,* 607–622.

Voss, J. F., Greene, T. R., Post, T. A., & Penner, B. D. (1983). Problem-solving skill in the social sciences. In G. H. Bower (Ed.), *The psychology of learning and motivation* (Vol. 17). San Diego: Academic Press.

• Voss, J. F., & Schauble, L. (1992). Is interest educationally interesting? An interest-related model of learning. In K. A. Renninger, S. Hidi, & A. Krapp (Eds.), *The role of interest in learning and development.* Hillsdale, NJ: Erlbaum.

Vygotsky, L. S. (1962). *Thought and language* (E. Haufmann & G. Vakar, Eds. and Trans.). Cambridge: MIT Press.

Vygotsky, L. S. (1978). *Mind in society: The development of higher psychological processes.* Cambridge, MA: Harvard University Press.

Vygotsky, L. S. (1981). The genesis of higher mental functions. In J. V. Wertsch (Ed.), *The concept of activity in Soviet psychology.* Armonk, NY: Sharpe.

• Vygotsky, L. S. (1987). *The collected works of L. S. Vygotsky, Vol. 3* (R. W. Rieber & A. S. Carton, Eds.). New York: Plenum.

• Wade, S. E. (1992). How interest affects learning from text. In K. A. Renninger, S. Hidi, & A. Krapp (Eds.), *The role of interest in learning and development.* Hillsdale, NJ: Erlbaum.

Wagner, A. R. (1976). Priming in STM: An information processing mechanism for self-generated or retrieval-generated depression in performance. In T. J. Tighe & R. N. Leaton (Eds.), *Habituation: Perspectives from child development and animal behavior.* Hillsdale, NJ: Erlbaum.

Wagner, A. R. (1978). Expectancies and the priming of STM. In S. H. Hulse, H. Fowler, & W. K. Honig (Eds.), *Cognitive processes in animal behavior.* Hillsdale, NJ: Erlbaum.

Wagner, A. R. (1979). Habituation and memory. In A. Dickenson & R. A. Boakes (Eds.), *Mechanisms of learning and motivation.* Hillsdale, NJ: Elrbaum.

Wagner, A. R. (1981). SOP: A model of automatic memory processing in animal behavior. In N. E. Spear & R. R. Miller (Eds.), *Information processing in animals: Memory mechanisms.* Hillsdale, NJ: Erlbaum.

Walberg, H. J., & Uguroglu, M. (1980). Motivation and educational productivity: Theories, results, and implications. In L. J. Fyans, Jr. (Ed.), *Achievement motivation: Recent trends in theory and research.* New York: Plenum Press.

Walker, L. J. (1984). Sex differences in the development of moral reasoning: A critical review. *Child Development, 55,* 677–691.

• Walker, L. J. (1991). Sex differences in moral reasoning. In W. M. Kurtines & J. L. Gewirtz (Eds.), *Moral behavior and development: Vol. 2. Research.* Hillsdale, NJ: Erlbaum.

Walters, G. C., & Grusec, J. E. (1977). *Punishment.* San Francisco: W. H. Freeman.

Walters, R. H., & Thomas, E. L. (1963). Enhancement of punitiveness by visual and audiovisual displays. *Canadian Journal of Psychology, 17,* 244–255.

Walters, R. H., Thomas, E. L., & Acker, W. (1962). Enhancement of punitive behavior by audiovisual displays. *Science, 136,* 872–873.

• Wang, M. C., & Stiles, B. (1976). An investigation of children's concept of self-responsibility for their school learning. *American Educational Research Journal, 13,* 159–179.

Ware, N. C., & Lee, V. E. (1988). Sex differences in choice of college science majors. *American Educational Research Journal, 25,* 593–614.

Warren, G. (1979). Essay versus multiple-choice tests. *Journal of Research in Science Teaching, 16*(6), 563–567.

Warren, R. L. (1988). Cooperation and conflict between parents and teachers: A comparative study of three elementary schools. In H. T. Trueba & C. Delgado-Gaitan (Eds.), *School and society: Learning content through culture.* New York: Praeger.

• Wasserman, E. A. (1993). Comparative cognition: Toward a general understanding of cognition in behavior. *Psychological Science, 4,* 156–161.

Waters, H. S. (1982). Memory development in adolescence: Relationships between metamemory, strategy use, and performance. *Journal of Experimental Child Psychology, 33,* 183–195.

Watkins, M. J., & Watkins, O. C. (1974). Processing of recency items for free-recall. *Journal of Experimental Psychology, 102,* 488–493.

Watson, J. B. (1914). *Behavior: An introduction to comparative psychology.* New York: Holt, Rinehart & Winston.

Watson, J. B. (1919). *Psychology from the standpoint of a behaviorist.* Philadelphia: J. B. Lippincott.

Watson, J. B. (1925). *Behaviorism.* New York: Norton.

Watts, G. H., & Anderson, R. C. (1971). Effects of three types of inserted questions on learning from prose. *Journal of Educational Psychology, 62,* 387–394.

• Webb, N. M., & Farivar, S. (1994). Promoting helping behavior in cooperative small groups in middle school mathematics. *American Educational Research Journal, 31,* 369–395.

• Webb, N. M., & Palincsar, A. S. (1996). Group processes in the classroom. In D. C. Berliner & R. C. Calfee (Eds.), *Handbook of educational psychology.* New York: Macmillan.

• Webber, J., Scheuermann, B., McCall, C., & Coleman, M. (1993). Research on self-monitoring as a behavior management technique in special education classrooms: A descriptive review. *Remedial and Special Education, 14*(2), 38–56.

Weiner, B. (1984). Principles for a theory of student motivation and their application within an attributional framework. In R. Ames & C. Ames (Eds.), *Research on motivation in education: Vol. 1. Student motivation.* San Diego: Academic Press.

Weiner, B. (1986). *An attributional theory of motivation and emotion.* New York: Springer-Verlag.

• Weiner, B. (1994). Ability versus effort revisited: The moral determinants of achievement evaluation and achievement as a moral system. *Educational Psychologist, 29,* 163–172.

Weiner, B., Russell, D., & Lerman, D. (1978). Affective consequences of causal ascriptions. In J. Harvey, W. Ickes, & R. Kidd (Eds.), *New directions in attribution research* (Vol. 2). Hillsdale, NJ: Erlbaum.

Weiner, B., Russell, D., & Lerman, D. (1979). The cognition-emotion process in achievement-related contexts. *Journal of Personality and Social Psychology, 37,* 1211–1220.

Weinstein, C. E. (1978). Elaboration skills as a learning strategy. In H. F. O'Neil, Jr. (Ed.), *Learning strategies.* San Diego: Academic Press.

Weinstein, C. E., Goetz, E. T., & Alexander, P. A. (Eds.). (1988). *Learning and study strategies: Issues in assessment, instruction, and evaluation.* San Diego: Academic Press.

Weinstein, C. E., Hagen, A. S., & Meyer, D. K. (1991, April). *Work smart . . . not hard: The effects of combining instruction in using strategies, goal using, and executive control on attributions and academic performance.* Paper presented at the annual meeting of the American Educational Research Association, Chicago.

Weinstein, C. S. (1979). The physical environment of the school: A review of the research. *Review of Educational Research, 49,* 577–610.

• Weinstein, R. S. (1993). Children's knowledge of differential treatment in school: Implications for motivation. In T. M. Tomlinson (Ed.), *Motivating students to learn: Overcoming barriers to high achievement.* Berkeley, CA: McCutchan.

• Weinstein, R. S., Madison, S. M., & Kuklinski, M. R. (1995). Raising expectations in schooling: Obstacles and opportunities for change. *American Educational Research Journal, 32,* 121–159.

Weiss, K. (1983). In-school suspension: Time to work, not socialize. *NASSP Bulletin, 67*(464), 132–133.

• Weissberg, R. P. (1985). Designing effective social problem-solving programs for the classroom. In B. H. Schneider, K. H. Rubin, & J. E. Ledingham (Eds.), *Children's peer relations: Issues in assessment and intervention.* New York: Springer-Verlag.

Welch, G. J. (1985). Contingency contracting with a delinquent and his family. *Journal of Behavior Therapy and Experimental Psychiatry, 16,* 253–259.

Wellman, H. M. (1985). The child's theory of mind: The development of conceptions of cognition. In S. R. Yussen (Ed.), *The growth of reflection in children.* San Diego: Academic Press.

• Wellman, H. M. (1988). The early development of memory strategies. In F. Weinert & M. Perlmutter (Eds.), *Memory development: Universal changes and individual differences.* Hillsdale, NJ: Erlbaum.

• Werner, E. E. (1995). Resilence in development. *Current Directions in Psychological Science, 4,* 81–85.

Wertsch, J. V. (1985). Adult-child interaction as a source of self-regulation in children. In S. R. Yussen (Ed.), *The growth of reflection in children*. San Diego: Academic Press.

West, C. K., Farmer, J. A., & Wolff, P. M. (1991). *Instructional design: Implications from cognitive science*. Upper Saddle River, NJ: Prentice Hall.

• White, A. G., & Bailey, J. S. (1990). Reducing disruptive behaviors of elementary physical education students with sit and watch. *Journal of Applied Behavior Analysis, 23,* 353–359.

• White, J. J., & Rumsey, S. (1994). Teaching for understanding in a third-grade geography lesson. In J. Brophy (Ed.), *Advances in research on teaching: Vol. 4. Case studies of teaching and learning in social studies*. Greenwich, CT: JAI Press.

• Wigfield, A. (1994). Expectancy-value theory of achievement motivation: A developmental perspective. *Educational Psychology Review, 6,* 49–78.

Wigfield, A., & Meece, J. L. (1988). Math anxiety in elementary and secondary school students. *Journal of Educational Psychology, 80,* 210–216.

Wiggins, G. (1989). The futility of trying to teach everything of importance. *Educational Leadership, 47*(3), 44–48, 57–59.

• Wiggins, G. (1992). Creating tests worth taking. *Educational Leadership, 49*(8), 26–33.

Wilkinson, L. D., & Frazer, L. H. (1990, April). *Fine-tuning dropout prediction through discriminant analysis: The ethnic factor*. Paper presented at the annual meeting of the American Educational Research Association, Boston, MA.

• Williams, B., & Newcombe, E. (1994). Building on the strengths of urban learners. *Educational Leadership, 51*(8), 75–78.

• Williams, J. P. (1991, November). *Comprehension of learning disabled and nondisabled students: Identification of narrative themes and idiosyncratic text representation*. Paper presented at the annual meeting of the National Reading Conference, Austin, TX.

Willig, A. C. (1985). A meta-analysis of selected studies on the effectiveness of bilingual education. *Review of Educational Research, 55,* 269–317.

Wilson, J. E. (1988). Implications of learning strategy research and training: What it has to say to the practitioner. In C. E. Weinstein, E. T. Goetz, & P. A. Alexander (Eds.), *Learning and study strategies: Issues in assessment, instruction, and evaluation*. San Diego: Academic Press.

Wilson, P. T., & Anderson, R. C. (1986). What they don't know will hurt them: The role of prior knowledge in comprehension. In J. Orasanu (Ed.), *Reading comprehension: From research to practice*. Hillsdale, NJ: Erlbaum.

• Wine, J. D. (1980). Cognitive-attentional theory of test anxiety. In I. G. Sarason (Ed.), *Test anxiety: Theory, research, and applications*. Hillsdale, NJ: Erlbaum.

• Wineburg, S. S., & Wilson, S. M. (1991). Subject-matter knowledge in the teaching of history. In J. Brophy (Ed.), *Advances in research on teaching: Vol. 2. Teachers' knowledge of subject matter as it relates to their teaching practice*. Greenwich, CT: JAI Press.

Wingfield, A., & Byrnes, D. L. (1981). *The psychology of human memory*. San Diego: Academic Press.

Winn, W. (1991). Learning from maps and diagrams. *Educational Psychology Review, 3,* 211–247.

• Winograd, P., & Jones, D. L. (1992). The use of portfolios in performance assessment. *New Directions for Education Reform, 1*(2), 37–50.

Winston, P. (1973). Learning to identify toy block structures. In R. L. Solso (Ed.), *Contemporary issues in cognitive psychology: The Loyola Symposium*. Washington, DC: V. H. Winston.

Witkin, H. A. (1969). *Embedded Figures Test*. Palo Alto, CA: Consulting Psychologists Press.

Witkin, H. A., & Goodenough, D. R. (1981). *Cognitive styles: Essence and origins—field dependence and field independence*. New York: International Universities Press.

Witkin, H. A., Moore, C. A., Goodenough, D. R., & Cox, P. W. (1977). Field-dependent and field-independent cognitive styles and their educational implications. *Review of Educational Research, 47,* 1–64.

• Wittmer, D. S., & Honig, A. S. (1994). Encouraging positive social development in young children. *Young Children, 49*(5), 4–12.

Wittrock, M. C. (1986). Learning science by generating new conceptions from old ideas. In L. H. T. West & A. L. Pines (Eds.), *Cognitive structure and conceptual change*. San Diego: Academic Press.

Wlodkowski, R. J. (1978). *Motivation and teaching: A practical guide*. Washington, DC: National Education Association.

Wolpe, J. (1958). *Psychotherapy by reciprocal inhibition*. Stanford, CA: Stanford University Press.

Wolpe, J. (1969). *The practice of behavior therapy*. Oxford: Pergamon Press.

• Wong, B. Y. L. (Ed.). (1991a). *Learning about learning disabilities*. San Diego: Academic Press.

• Wong, B. Y. L. (1991b). The relevance of metacognition to learning disabilities. In B. Y. L. Wong (Ed.), *Learning about learning disabilities*. San Diego: Academic Press.

• Wong-Fillmore, L. (1992). When learning a second language means losing the first. *Education, 6*(2), 4–11.

Wood, C. J., Schau, C., & Fiedler, M. L. (1990, April). *Attribution, motivation, and self-perception: A comparative study—elementary, middle, and high school students*. Paper presented at the annual meeting of the American Educational Research Association, Boston, MA.

Wood, D., Bruner, J. S., & Ross, G. (1976). The role of tutoring in problem solving. *Journal of Child Psychology and Psychiatry, 17,* 89–100.

• Wood, E., Willoughby, T., Reilley, S., Elliott, S., & DuCharme, M. (1994, April). *Evaluating students' acquisition of factual material when studying independently or with a partner*. Paper presented at the annual meeting of the American Educational Research Association, New Orleans, LA.

Wood, J. W. (1989). *Mainstreaming: A practical approach for teachers*. New York: Merrill/Macmillan.

• Wood, J. W., & Rosbe, M. (1985). Adapting the classroom lectures for the mainstreamed student in the secondary schools. *Clearing House, 58,* 354–358.

Woolfolk, A. E., & Brooks, D. M. (1985). The influence of teachers' nonverbal behaviors on students' perceptions and performances. *Elementary School Journal, 85,* 513–528.

Worthen, B. R., & Leopold, G. D. (1992). Impediments to implementing alternative assessment: Some emerging issues. *New Directions for Education Reform, 1*(2), 1–20.

Wozniak, R. H. (1987). Developmental method, zones of development, and theories of the environment. In L. S. Liben (Ed.), *Development and learning: Conflict or congruence?* Hillsdale, NJ: Erlbaum.

Wright, L. S. (1982). The use of logical consequences in counseling children. *School Counselor, 30,* 37–49.

• Wright, S., & Taylor, D. (1995). Identity and the language of the classroom: Investigating the impact of heritage versus second-language instruction on personal and collective self-esteem. *Journal of Educational Psychology, 87,* 241–252.

Wynne, E. A. (1990). Improving pupil discipline and character. In O. C. Moles (Ed.), *Student discipline strategies: Research and practice.* Albany: State University of New York Press.

Yarmey, A. D. (1973). I recognize your face but I can't remember your name: Further evidence on the tip-of-the-tongue phenomenon. *Memory and Cognition, 1,* 287–290.

Yee, A. H. (1992). Asians as stereotypes and students: Misperceptions that persist. *Educational Psychology Review, 4,* 95–132.

Yee, D. K., & Eccles, J. S. (1988). Parent perceptions and attributions for children's math achievement. *Sex Roles, 19,* 317–333.

• Yell, M. L. (1993). Cognitive behavior therapy. In T. J. Zirpoli & K. J. Melloy, *Behavior management: Applications for teachers and parents.* New York: Macmillan.

Yerkes, R. M., & Dodson, J. D. (1908). The relation of strength of stimulus to rapidity of habit-formation. *Journal of Comparative Neurology of Psychology, 18,* 459–482.

Ysseldyke, J. E., & Algozzine, B. (1984). *Introduction to special education.* Boston: Houghton Mifflin.

• Yu, S. L., Elder, A. D., & Urdan, T. C. (1995, April). *Motivation and cognitive strategies in students with a "good student" or "poor student" self-schema.* Paper presented at the annual meeting of the American Educational Research Association, San Francisco.

Yuker, H. E. (Ed.). (1988). *Attitudes toward persons with disabilities.* New York: Springer.

• Zeaman, D., & House, B. J. (1979). A review of attention theory. In N. R. Ellis (Ed.), *Handbook of mental deficiency: Psychological theory and research* (2nd ed.). Hillsdale, NJ: Erlbaum.

Zelniker, T., & Jeffrey, W. E. (1976). Reflective and impulsive children: Strategies of information processing underlying differences in problem solving. *Monographs of the Society for Research in Child Development, 41*(Serial No. 168).

Zelniker, T., & Jeffrey, W. E. (1979). Attention and cognitive style in children. In G. H. Hale & M. Lewis (Eds.), *Attention and cognitive development.* New York: Plenum Press.

Ziegler, S. G. (1987). Effects of stimulus cueing on the acquisition of ground-strokes by beginning tennis players. *Journal of Applied Behavior Analysis, 20,* 405–411.

Zigler, E. F., & Finn-Stevenson, M. (1987). *Children: Development and social issues.* Lexington, MA: Heath.

Zigler, E. F., & Seitz, V. (1982). Social policy and intelligence. In R. J. Sternberg (Ed.), *Handbook of human intelligence* (pp. 586–641). Cambridge, UK: Cambridge University Press.

• Zimmerman, B. J., & Bandura, A. (1994). Impact of self-regulatory influences on writing course attainment. *American Educational Research Journal, 31,* 845–862.

• Zimmerman, B. J., Bandura, A., & Martinez-Pons, M. (1992). Self-motivation for academic attainment: The role of self-efficacy beliefs and personal goal setting. *American Educational Research Journal, 29,* 663–676.

Zirin, G. (1974). How to make a boring thing more boring. *Child Development, 45,* 232–236.

• Zirpoli, T. J., & Melloy, K. J. (1993). *Behavior management: Applications for teachers and parents.* Upper Saddle River, NJ: Merrill/Prentice Hall.

Zook, K. B. (1991). Effects of analogical processes on learning and misrepresentation. *Educational Psychology Review, 3,* 41–72.

Zook, K. B., & Di Vesta, F. J. (1991). Instructional analogies and conceptual misrepresentations. *Journal of Educational Psychology, 83,* 246–252.

• Zuckerman, G. A. (1994). A pilot study of a ten-day course in cooperative learning for beginning Russian first graders. *Elementary School Journal, 94,* 405–420.

Name Index

Subject Index